Child Development
Early Stages Through Age 12

Student Textbook—Print or Online

The Student Edition of *Child Development: Early Stages Through Age 12* is available as a printed textbook or as an Online Textbook. The Student Edition offers a colorful design, easy-to-read typeface, and logical organization that supports reading, comprehension, application, and learning.

Workbook

The Workbook includes a wide variety of questions and activities to help students review and apply chapter concepts.

Online Student Center

The Online Student Center combines the Online Textbook and the Workbook in digital format. Pages from the Student Textbook and Workbook can be printed on demand. Students can complete workbook activities online using embedded form fields and print or e-mail the results for grading.

Companion Website

The easy-to-navigate Companion Website provides students with multiple opportunities to increase comprehension and retention of key concepts. The website includes printable graphic organizers, e-flash cards, interactive games, and quizzes.
www.g-wlearning.com/childdevelopment

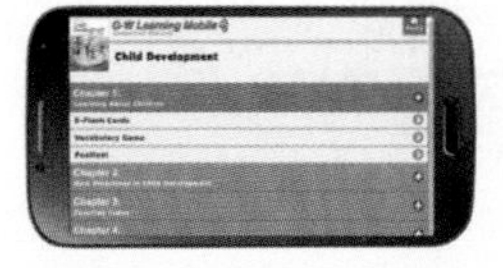

Mobile Site

Students are able to study on the go with the Mobile Site. E-flash cards and interactive games help students review vocabulary terms. Interactive quizzes help students review chapter materials, assess comprehension, and prepare for quizzes and tests.
www.m.g-wlearning.com/0384

The Essential Program Components

Instructor's Edition

The Instructor's Edition includes the Student Edition plus answer keys to the caption questions through the text, the *Review and Assessment* questions that appear at the end of each lesson, and some *Chapter Review and Assessment* activities.

Online Instructor Resources

The Online Instructor Resources subscription provides 1 year or 6 years of individual access to the classroom support materials used most often—all in one convenient location that can be accessed from anywhere. The Online Instructor Resources includes the Instructor's Resources, Instructor's Presentations for PowerPoint®, and ExamView® Assessment Suite.

Instructor's Resources

The Instructor's Resources include daily lesson plans, answer keys, teaching visuals, reproducible masters, and grading rubrics.

Instructor's Presentations for PowerPoint®

Includes colorful presentations for each chapter to reinforce main ideas and terms.

ExamView® Assessment Suite

Quickly and easily prepare and print tests with the ExamView® Assessment Suite. With hundreds of questions in the test bank, you can choose which questions to include in each test, create multiple versions of a single test, and automatically generate answer keys.

Instructor's Edition

Child Development

Early Stages Through Age 12

Eighth Edition

by

Dr. Celia A. Decker

Professor of Family and Consumer Sciences, retired
Castle Rock, Colorado

Publisher
The Goodheart-Willcox Company, Inc.
Tinley Park, Illinois
www.g-w.com

Manufactured in the United States of America.

ISBN 978-1-63126-044-5

1 2 3 4 5 6 7 8 9 – 16 – 20 19 18 17 16 15

Cover image: Rawpixel/Shutterstock.com

Contents

Introduction

Child Development: Early Stages Through Age 12 is a comprehensive text designed to help students understand children's physical, intellectual, and social-emotional development from the prenatal stage through the school-age years. The components of the teaching package contain a variety of features that can help you develop an effective child development program tailored to your students' unique needs. The package can also aid you in achieving a number of other educational objectives with your students, as described below.

Strategies for Successful Teaching

You can make the *Child Development: Early Stages Through Age 12* subject matter exciting and relevant for your students by using a variety of teaching strategies. Many suggestions for planning classroom activities are given in the teaching supplements that accompany this text. As you plan your lessons, you might also want to keep the following points in mind.

Helping Your Students Develop Critical Thinking Skills

As today's students leave their classrooms behind, they will face a world of complexity and change. They are likely to work in several career areas and hold many jobs. Young people must develop a base of knowledge and be prepared to solve complex problems, make difficult decisions, and assess ethical implications. In other words, students must be able to use critical thinking skills.

Critical thinking goes beyond memorizing or recalling information. It requires individuals to apply what they know about the subject matter. It also requires students to use their common sense and experience. It may even involve controversy.

Critical thinking requires *creative thinking* to construct all the reasonable alternatives, consequences, influencing factors, and supporting arguments. Unusual ideas are valued and perspectives outside the obvious are sought.

Finally, the teaching of critical thinking does not require exotic and highly unusual classroom approaches. Complex thought processes can be incorporated in the most ordinary and basic activities, such as reading, writing, and listening, when activities are carefully planned and skillfully executed.

Debate is an excellent way to explore opposite sides of an issue. You may want to divide the class into two groups, each taking an opposing side of the issue. You can also ask students to work in smaller groups and explore opposing sides of different issues. Each group can select students from the group to present the points for their side.

Problem-Solving and Decision-Making Skills

An important aspect in the development of critical thinking skills is learning how to solve problems and make decisions. Some very important decisions lie ahead for your students, particularly those related to their future education and career choices.

Simulation games and role-plays are activities that allow students to practice solving problems and making decisions under nonthreatening circumstances. In role-playing, students can examine others' feelings as well as their own. They can learn effective ways to react or cope when confronted with similar situations in real life.

Using Cooperative Learning

Because of the emphasis on collaboration in the workplace, the use of cooperative learning groups in your classroom will give students an opportunity to practice teamwork skills. During cooperative learning, students learn interpersonal and small-group skills that will allow them to function as part of a team. These skills include leadership, decision making, trust building, communication, and conflict management.

In cooperative learning groups, students learn to work together toward a group goal. Each member is dependent on others for the outcome. This interdependence is a basic component of any cooperative learning group. Students understand that one person cannot succeed unless everyone succeeds. The value of each group member is affirmed as learners work toward their goal.

The success of the group also depends on individual performance. Group members should be selected depending on the purpose of your grouping. As you differentiate your instruction, sometimes you may form groups based on interest. Other times, you may form diversified groups so a mix of abilities and talents are included. You might form groups with specific leveled learning tasks assigned to various groups. Within groups, individuals' roles can change so all students have opportunities to practice and develop different skills. In all situations, students can learn from working with one another.

As you monitor the effectiveness of group learning, you may need to intervene to provide task assistance or help with interpersonal or group skills. If you expect a group to carry out a particular skill on their own, you need to teach the skill to the large group first. Model the expected activity, assign various roles, and have students model the skills used in that role. Then, when you assign different tasks to groups, members will be able to move ahead on their own, utilizing the skills you taught.

Finally, you can evaluate each group's achievement of specific learning goals. Use rubrics to identify the extent to which the group reached the goal. In some scenarios, you may just give participation points to the group for completing their task. This is effective when you have differentiated the learning for the various groups and their tasks are not the same. In group settings, the learning that takes place is often in the discussion and processing of various ideas. In these cases, a summary of what students learned can be written in a journal or added to a portfolio.

Helping Students Recognize and Value Diversity

Your students will be entering a rapidly changing workplace—not only in the area of technology, but also in the diverse nature of the workforce. The majority of the new entrants into the workforce are women and people of varying ethnicities, all representing many different views and experiences. The workforce is aging, too, as the ranks of mature workers swell. Because of these trends, young workers must learn how to interact with a variety of people who are considerably unlike them.

Appreciating and understanding diversity is an ongoing process. The earlier and more frequently young people are exposed to diversity, the better able they will be to bridge cultural differences. If your students are exposed to different cultures within your classroom, the process of understanding cultural differences can begin. This is the best preparation for success in a diverse society. In addition, teachers have found the following strategies for teaching diversity helpful:

- Actively promote a spirit of openness, consideration, respect, and tolerance in the classroom.
- Use a variety of teaching styles and assessment strategies.
- Use cooperative learning activities whenever possible and make sure group roles are rotated so everyone has leadership opportunities.
- When grouping students, make sure the composition of each group is as diverse as possible with regard to gender, race, and nationality.

- Make sure one group's opinions do not dominate class discussions.
- If a student makes a sexist, racist, or other offensive comment, ask the student to rephrase the comment in a manner that will not offend other class members. Remind students that offensive statements and behaviors are inappropriate.
- If a difficult classroom situation arises involving a diversity issue, ask for a time-out and have everyone write down thoughts and opinions about the incident. This allows everyone to cool down and allows you to plan a response.
- Arrange for guest speakers who represent diversity in gender, age, and ethnicity.
- Have students change seats occasionally throughout the course and introduce themselves to their new "neighbors" so they become acquainted with all their classmates.
- Several times during the course, ask students to make anonymous, written evaluations of the class. Have them report any problems that may not be obvious.

Differentiating Instruction for Students with Varying Needs

In addition to having specific learning needs related to their abilities, students come to you with various backgrounds, interests, and learning styles. Differentiating instruction can help all students attain learning goals. The strategies you use to differentiate instruction in your classroom will depend on the specific learning needs of the students.

The table on pages T10 and T11 provides descriptions of several types of students you may find in your classes, followed by some strategies and techniques to keep in mind as you work with these students. You will be asked to meet the needs of all your students in the same classroom setting. It is a challenge to adapt daily lessons to meet the demands of all your students.

Assessment Techniques

Various assessment strategies are included throughout each lesson and chapter in this textbook. Some can be used to measure student progress in understanding the concepts (*formative assessment*), while others can be used to measure the extent to which they have mastered the concepts (*summative assessment*).

Formative assessment takes place often and is ongoing throughout a course. The many comprehension strategies used throughout the text can be used as formative assessment techniques. They measure students' grasp of the concepts as well as their abilities to internalize the skills and apply them to new situations. Many formative assessments can be completed as groups, because the main focus is on the learning that is taking place. Students can assess their team members and use a rubric to self-assess their own learning. The *Instructor's Resources* (including the *Instructor's Resource CD* and *Online Instructor Resources*) can be used to identify formative assessments for key knowledge, understandings, and skills being learned.

Tests in the ExamView® Assessment Suite have traditionally been used to evaluate performance. This method of evaluation is good to use when assessing knowledge and comprehension.

Performance Assessment

When assigning students some of the projects from the text that you plan to use as either formative or summative assessment, a rubric can be helpful for measuring student achievement. A *rubric* consists of a set of criteria that includes specific descriptors or standards that can be used to arrive at performance scores for students. A point value is given for each set of descriptors, leading to a range of possible points to be assigned, usually from 1 to 5. The criteria can also be weighted. This method of assessment reduces the guesswork involved in grading, leading to fair and consistent scoring. The standards clearly indicate to students the various levels of mastery of a task. Students are even able to assess their own achievement based on the criteria.

When using rubrics, students should see the criteria at the beginning of the assignment. Then they can focus their effort on what needs to be done to reach a certain level of performance or quality of project. They have a clear understanding of your expectations of achievement. Rubrics allow you to assess a student's performance and arrive at a performance score. Students can see what levels they have surpassed and what levels they can still strive to reach.

Portfolios

Another type of performance assessment that is frequently used by teachers today is the portfolio. A *portfolio* consists of a selection of materials that students choose to document their performance over a period of time. Therefore, it is a good tool for gathering formative assessment data. Students select their best work samples to showcase their achievement. These items might provide evidence of employability skills as well as academic skills. Some of the items students might include in portfolios are

- work samples that show mastery of specific skills, including photographs, video recordings, and assessments
- writing samples that show communication skills
- a résumé
- letters of recommendation that document specific career-related skills
- certificates of completion
- awards and recognition

The portfolio is completed at the culmination of a course to provide evidence of learning, and therefore can be used as a summative assessment tool. As students choose items to include in the final portfolio, they should include items that specifically show how they addressed the key questions for each chapter studied. A self-assessment summary report should be included that explains what has been accomplished, what has been learned, what strengths the student has gained, and any areas that need improvement. *College and Career Portfolio* activities are included at the end of every chapter in the student text.

Portfolios may be presented to the class by students, but they should remain the property of students when they leave the course. They may be used for interviews with potential employers.

Portfolio assessment is only one of several evaluation methods teachers can use, but it is a powerful tool for both students and teachers. It encourages self-reflection and self-assessment of a broader nature. Traditional evaluation methods of tests, quizzes, and papers have their place in measuring the achievement of some course objectives, but other assessment tools should also be used to fairly assess the achievement of all desired outcomes.

Integrating Academics

No matter what career path a student chooses, academic skills will be critical to his or her success. The following are core academic subjects in schools: English, reading, language arts, math, science, foreign languages, civics and government, economics, arts, history, and geography.

	Learning Disorders*	Cognitive Disabilities*	Behavioral and Emotional Disorders*
Description	Students with learning disorders (LD) have neurological disorders that interfere with their ability to store, process, or produce information, creating a "gap" between ability and academic performance. These students are generally of average or above average intelligence. They may have challenges in spoken or written language, math, or spatial orientation.	Students with cognitive disabilities (also known as intellectual disabilities) are a year or more delayed in their intellectual abilities when compared with others their age. They may have difficulty remembering, associating and classifying information, reasoning, problem solving, and making judgments. They may also have difficulties with such adaptive behavior as daily living activities and developing occupational skills.	Students with behavioral and emotional disorders exhibit undesirable behaviors or emotions that may, over time, adversely affect educational performance. The inability to learn cannot be explained by intellectual, social, or health factors. Such students may be inattentive, withdrawn, timid, restless, defiant, impatient, unhappy, fearful, unreflective, lack initiative, have negative feelings and actions, and blame others.
Teaching Strategies	• Assist students in getting organized. • Give short oral directions. • Use drill exercises. • Give prompt cues during student performance. • Provide computers with specialized software (that checks spelling and grammar and/or recognizes speech) to students with poor writing and reading skills. • Break assignments into small segments and assign only one segment at a time. • Demonstrate skills and have students model them. • Give prompt feedback. • Use continuous assessment to mark students' daily progress. • Prepare materials at varying levels of ability. • Shorten the number of items on exercises, tests, and quizzes. • Provide more hands-on activities.	• Use concrete examples to introduce concepts. • Make learning activities consistent. • Use repetition and drills spread over time. • Provide work folders for daily assignments. • Use behavior management techniques, such as behavior modification, in the area of adaptive behavior. • Encourage students to function independently. • Give students extra time to both ask and answer questions while giving hints to answers. • Give simple directions and read them over with students. • Use objective test items and hands-on activities because students generally have poor writing skills and difficulty with sentence structure and spelling.	• Call students' names or ask them questions when you see their attention wandering. • Call on students randomly rather than in a predictable sequence. • Move around the room frequently. • Improve students' self-esteem by giving them tasks they can perform well, increasing the number of successful achievement experiences. • Decrease the length of time for each activity. • Use hands-on activities instead of using words and abstract symbols. • Decrease the size of the group so each student can actively participate. • Make verbal instructions clear, short, and to the point.

	Academically Gifted	Limited English Proficiency	Physical Disabilities
Description	Students who are academically gifted are capable of high performance as a result of general intellectual ability, specific academic aptitude, and/or creative or productive thinking. Such students have a vast fund of general knowledge and high levels of vocabulary, memory, abstract word knowledge, and abstract reasoning.	These students have a limited proficiency in the English language. English is generally their second language. Such students may be academically quite capable, but lack the language skills needed to reason and comprehend abstract concepts.	Includes individuals who have physical, mobility, visual, speech, hearing (deaf, hard-of-hearing), or health (cystic fibrosis, epilepsy) impairments. Strategies will depend on the specific disability.
Teaching Strategies	• Provide ample opportunities for creative behavior. • Make assignments that call for original work, independent learning, critical thinking, problem solving, and experimentation. • Show appreciation for creative efforts. • Respect unusual questions, ideas, and solutions these students provide. • Encourage students to test their ideas. • Provide opportunities and give credit for self-initiated learning. • Avoid overly detailed supervision and too much reliance on prescribed curricula. • Allow time for reflection. • Resist immediate and constant evaluation. This causes students to be afraid to use their creativity. • Avoid comparisons with other students, which imply subtle pressure to conform.	• Use a slow but natural rate of speech; speak clearly; use shorter sentences; repeat concepts in several ways. • Act out questions using gestures with hands, arms, and the whole body. Use demonstrations and pantomime. Ask questions that can be answered by a physical movement, such as pointing, nodding, or manipulation of materials. • When possible, use pictures, photos, and charts. • Write key terms on the board. As they are used, point to them. • Corrections should be limited and appropriate. Do not correct grammar or usage errors in front of the class, causing embarrassment. • Give honest praise and positive feedback through your voice tones and visual articulation whenever possible. • Encourage students to use language to communicate, allowing them to use their native language to ask and answer questions when they are unable to do so in English. • Integrate students' cultural background into class discussions. • Use cooperative learning during which students have opportunities to practice expressing ideas without risking language errors in front of the entire class.	• Seat students with visual and hearing impairments near the front of the classroom. Speak clearly and say out loud what you are writing on the board. • To reduce the risk of injury in lab settings, ask students about any conditions that could affect their ability to learn or perform. • Rearrange lab equipment or the classroom and make necessary modifications to accommodate any disability. • Investigate and utilize assistive technology devices that can improve students' functional capabilities. • Discuss solutions or modifications with the student who has experience with overcoming his or her disability and may have suggestions you may not have considered. • Provide an opportunity for the student to test classroom modifications before utilizing them in class. • Ask advice from special education teachers, the school nurse, or physical therapist. • Plan barrier-free field trips that include all students.

*We appreciate the assistance of Dr. Debra O. Parker, North Carolina Central University, with this section.

The *Child Development: Early Stages Through Age 12* program supports student growth and achievement in key academic areas in several ways. The academic areas are highlighted where they are covered in the *Core Skills* end-of-chapter activities. Further connection to the academic areas of math, social studies, and science are provided in the *Focus on...* boxed features.

Math

To strengthen students' math skills, *Core Skills* activities involving math are found at the end of applicable chapters. *Focus on Financial Literacy* boxed features throughout the text apply these concepts to chapter content. Math activities may also appear in the *Student Workbook, Online Student Center,* and *Instructor's Resources* as chapter content dictates.

Science

Science plays an important role in the study of child development. Many *Investigate Special Topics* boxed features throughout the book cover brain development and research. *Focus on Science* boxed features are also found throughout the text. Science activities also appear in the *Core Skills* end-of-chapter activities and in the *Workbook, Online Student Center,* and *Instructor's Resources.*

Social Studies

Social studies and psychology are especially helpful in understanding child development. Appropriate activities are found at the end of each chapter under *Core Skills* and throughout the text in *Focus on Social Studies* boxed features. Additional activities appear in the *Workbook, Online Student Center,* and *Instructor's Resources.*

Reading, English, and Language Arts

The entire *Child Development: Early Stages Through Age 12* student text is designed to encourage reading and understanding. Each lesson begins with a *Reading and Writing Activity* to engage student interest. Key terms (terms essential to concepts covered in the lesson) are shown in bold and highlighted in the text copy to draw the reader's attention. Academic terms (terms defined for greater understanding) are shown in bold and blue. *Focus on Reading* and *Focus on Speech* boxed features also help students apply language arts skills to chapter content. Finally, end-of-chapter activities in the *Core Skills* section strengthen students' skills in reading, writing, and speaking. The *Workbook, Online Student Center,* and *Instructor's Resources* provide even more activities designed to help students develop skills in English and language arts.

Teaching Reading Across the Curriculum

All teachers need to be teachers of reading. In all content areas, teachers need to teach students how to use reading as a tool to enhance their learning. The following strategies will help you teach reading skills that help students create meaning and understand what they read.

- Use prereading activities to help students prepare for learning. A *Reading and Writing Activity* is included at the beginning of each lesson in the text to help students make the connection between what they already know and the new concepts to be learned. This connection is critical for students to be able to remember new information.

- Use strategies that help students comprehend what they read. Examples of comprehension strategies include having students question what they read, think about the concepts, talk about content with a partner or in small groups, summarize ideas, and organize ideas graphically. *Graphic Organizer* activities at the beginning of each lesson are included in the student text. The questions at the end of each lesson help students clarify their comprehension of key concepts. The various strategies for reteaching and reinforcing concepts in the *Instructor's Resources* are also designed to help students think about what they have read and gain understanding.
- Use strategies that help students incorporate the new knowledge they have acquired into their own system of thinking. Such internalization is needed for students to remember concepts and be able to apply them to daily living. The various chapter review and assessment activities listed under *Critical Thinking*, *Core Skills*, and *Observations* are designed to help students incorporate their new knowledge. Other strategies, such as journaling, allow students a time to connect new concepts to their personal situations. The *Investigate Special Topics* and *Focus on…* boxed features motivate students to seek further information related to chapter content. The *Instructor's Resources* also contain strategies for enriching and extending the text into real-life situations. As students extend and refine the new knowledge they have acquired, the learning takes on personal meaning.

It is important to model these three steps before, during, and after text reading. Explain to students why you are using various strategies. Continual practice of reading skills in all classes will help students develop these lifelong skills.

Planning Your Program

Pacing charts suggest ways to schedule the chapters of *Child Development: Early Stages Through Age 12* or different course calendars. Trimester, semester, and full-year course pacing charts are included on pages T14–T16. Chapters are grouped according to the suggested depth of coverage and duration of instruction time.

Correlation of National Standards with *Child Development: Early Stages Through Age 12*

By studying *Child Development: Early Stages Through Age 12*, students will be prepared to master the performance expectations for analyzing principles of human development. To help you see how this can be accomplished, a *Correlation of National Standards for Human Development with Child Development: Early Stages Through Age 12* is included on pages T17–T27, as well as in the *Instructor's Resources*. If you want to make sure you prepare students to meet the National Standards for Family and Consumer Sciences Education, this chart should be of interest to you.

Goodheart-Willcox Welcomes Your Comments

We welcome your comments or suggestions regarding *Child Development: Early Stages Through Age 12* and its supplements. Please send any comments you may have to the editor by visiting our website at www.g-w.com or writing to

Family & Consumer Sciences Editorial Department
Goodheart-Willcox Publisher
18604 West Creek Drive
Tinley Park, IL 60477-6243

Pacing Charts

Child Development: Early Stages Through Age 12 pacing charts are provided for trimester, semester, and full-year courses. Chapters are grouped according to the suggested depth of coverage and duration of instruction time.

Trimester Course
Two Grading Periods—Six Weeks Each

Week	Chapter Numbers and Names
First Grading Period	
1	**Unit 1 Children and Families in Today's World** 1 Learning About Children 2 New Directions in Learning 3 Families Today
2	4 Preparing for Parenting **Unit 2 Pregnancy and Childbirth** 5 Pregnancy
3	6 Special Circumstances of Pregnancy 7 Childbirth
4	**Unit 3 Infancy** 8 Physical Development in the First Year 9 Intellectual Development in the First Year 10 Social-Emotional Development in the First Year
5	**Unit 4 The Toddler Years** 11 Physical Development of Toddlers 12 Intellectual Development of Toddlers 13 Social-Emotional Development of Toddlers
6	**Unit 5 The Preschool Years** 14 Physical Development of Preschoolers 15 Intellectual Development of Preschoolers 16 Social-Emotional Development of Preschoolers
Second Grading Period	
7	**Unit 6 The School-Age Years** 17 Physical Development of School-Age Children 18 Intellectual Development of School-Age Children 19 Social-Emotional Development of School-Age Children
8	**Unit 7 Guiding and Caring for Children** 20 Encouraging Children's Play Experiences
9	21 Protecting Children's Physical Health and Safety
10	22 Handling Family-Life Challenges 23 Meeting Children's Special Needs
11	24 Providing Early Childhood Education in Group Settings
12	25 Preparing for a Child-Related Career

Semester Course
Two Grading Periods—Nine Weeks Each

Week	Chapter Numbers and Names
	First Grading Period
1	**Unit 1 Children and Families in Today's World** 1 Learning About Children
2	2 New Directions in Learning
3	3 Families Today 4 Preparing for Parenting
4	**Unit 2 Pregnancy and Childbirth** 5 Pregnancy
5	6 Special Circumstances of Pregnancy
6	7 Childbirth
7	**Unit 3 Infancy** 8 Physical Development in the First Year
8	9 Intellectual Development in the First Year 10 Social-Emotional Development in the First Year
	Second Grading Period
9, 10	**Unit 4 The Toddler Years** 11 Physical Development of Toddlers 12 Intellectual Development of Toddlers 13 Social-Emotional Development of Toddlers
11, 12	**Unit 5 The Preschool Years** 14 Physical Development of Preschoolers 15 Intellectual Development of Preschoolers 16 Social-Emotional Development of Preschoolers
13, 14	**Unit 6 The School-Age Years** 17 Physical Development of School-Age Children 18 Intellectual Development of School-Age Children 19 Social-Emotional Development of School-Age Children
15	**Unit 7 Guiding and Caring for Children** 20 Encouraging Children's Play Experiences 21 Protecting Children's Physical Health and Safety
16	22 Handling Family-Life Challenges 23 Meeting Children's Special Needs
17	24 Providing Early Childhood Education in Group Settings
18	25 Preparing for a Child-Related Career

Full-Year Course
Six Grading Periods—Six Weeks Each

First Grading Period

Unit 1 Children and Families in Today's World
1 Learning About Children
2 New Directions in Learning
3 Families Today
4 Preparing for Parenting

Unit 2 Pregnancy and Childbirth
5 Pregnancy

Second Grading Period

6 Special Circumstances of Pregnancy
7 Childbirth

Unit 3 Infancy
8 Physical Development in the First Year
9 Intellectual Development in the First Year
10 Social-Emotional Development in the First Year

Third Grading Period

Unit 4 The Toddler Years
11 Physical Development of Toddlers
12 Intellectual Development of Toddlers
13 Social-Emotional Development of Toddlers

Unit 5 The Preschool Years
14 Physical Development of Preschoolers

Fourth Grading Period

15 Intellectual Development of Preschoolers
16 Social-Emotional Development of Preschoolers

Unit 6 The School-Age Years
17 Physical Development of School-Age Children
18 Intellectual Development of School-Age Children
19 Social-Emotional Development of School-Age Children

Fifth Grading Period

Unit 7 Guiding and Caring for Children
20 Encouraging Children's Play Experiences
21 Protecting Children's Physical Health and Safety
22 Handling Family-Life Challenges

Sixth Grading Period

23 Meeting Children's Special Needs
24 Providing Early Childhood Education in Group Settings
25 Preparing for a Child-Related Career

Correlation of National Standards for Human Development with *Child Development: Early Stages Through Age 12*

The National Association of State Administrators of Family and Consumer Sciences (NASAFACS) established national standards for Human Development in partnership with the American Association of Family and Consumer Sciences. These standards provide the framework for national, state, and local family and consumer sciences education programs.

The following chart correlates these NASAFACS Standards with the content of the *Child Development: Early Stages Through Age 12* text. For each content standard, the chart lists explanatory competencies and the major text concepts that address each competency. Numbers indicate lessons in which the concepts appear. Additional resources may be required to cover these concepts as they pertain to individuals over 12 years of age.

Content Standard 12.1 **Analyze principles of human growth and development across the life span.**		
Competencies	**Text Concepts**	
12.1.1 Analyze physical, emotional, social, spiritual, and intellectual development.	1.1:	Understanding Child Development
	1.2:	Recognizing Principles and Theories of Growth and Development
	1.3:	Studying and Observing Children
	2.1:	Brain Studies
	2.2:	Acquiring Knowledge
	4.2:	Parenting Roles, Responsibilities, and Styles
	5.1:	A Baby's Beginning
	5.2:	Factors That Affect the Unborn Baby
	5.3:	Health Habits Prior to and During Pregnancy
	6.1:	Special Medical Concerns of Pregnancy
	6.2:	Teen Pregnancy
	7.1:	Decisions Concerning Childbirth
	7.2:	Time to Be Born
	7.3:	Newborn Medical Care and Tests
	7.4:	Postpartum Care
	8.1:	Growth and Development in the First Year
	8.2:	Meeting Nutritional Needs in the First Year
	8.3:	Meeting Other Physical Needs in the First Year
	9.1:	How Children Learn in the First Year
	9.2:	What Children Learn in the First Year
	9.3:	Meeting Children's Intellectual Needs in the First Year
	10.1:	The Social-Emotional World of Babies
	10.2:	Meeting Social-Emotional Needs in the First Year
	11.1:	Growth and Development of Toddlers
	11.2:	Meeting Nutritional Needs of Toddlers

Competencies	Text Concepts
12.1.1 *(Continued)*	11.3: Meeting Other Physical Needs of Toddlers 12.1: How Toddlers Learn 12.2: What Toddlers Learn 12.3: Meeting Toddlers' Intellectual Needs 13.1: The Social-Emotional World of Toddlers 13.2: Meeting Toddlers' Social-Emotional Needs 14.1: Growth and Development of Preschoolers 14.2: Meeting Nutritional Needs of Preschoolers 14.3: Meeting Other Physical Needs of Preschoolers 15.1: How Preschoolers Learn 15.2: What Preschoolers Learn 15.3: Meeting Preschoolers' Intellectual Needs 16.1: The Social-Emotional World of Preschoolers 16.2: Meeting Preschoolers' Social-Emotional Needs 17.1: Growth and Development of School-Age Children 17.2: Meeting Nutritional Needs of School-Age Children 17.3: Meeting Other Physical Needs of School-Age Children 18.1: How School-Age Children Learn 18.2: What School-Age Children Learn 18.3: Meeting School-Age Children's Intellectual Needs 19.1: The Social-Emotional World of School-Age Children 19.2: Meeting School-Age Children's Social-Emotional Needs 20.1: The Importance of Play 20.2: Play Activities for Children 21.1: Maintaining Children's Health 21.2: Ensuring Children's Safety 22.1: Helping Children Cope with Challenges 22.2: Protecting Children from Neglect and Abuse 23.1: Types of Special Needs 23.2: Help for Children with Special Needs
12.1.2 Analyze interrelationships among physical, emotional, social, and intellectual aspects of human growth and development.	1.1: Understanding Child Development 1.2: Recognizing Principles and Theories of Growth and Development 1.3: Studying and Observing Children 2.1: Brain Studies 2.2: Acquiring Knowledge 3.1: Healthy Family Development 3.2: Family Types 4.1: Deciding About Parenthood 4.2: Parenting Roles, Responsibilities, and Styles 5.2: Factors That Affect the Unborn Baby 5.3: Health Habits Prior to and During Pregnancy 6.1: Special Medical Concerns of Pregnancy 6.2: Teen Pregnancy 7.4: Postpartum Care

Competencies	Text Concepts
12.1.2 *(Continued)*	8.1: Growth and Development in the First Year 8.2: Meeting Nutritional Needs in the First Year 8.3: Meeting Other Physical Needs in the First Year 9.1: How Children Learn in the First Year 9.2: What Children Learn in the First Year 9.3: Meeting Children's Intellectual Needs in the First Year 10.1: The Social-Emotional World of Babies 10.2: Meeting Social-Emotional Needs in the First Year 11.1: Growth and Development of Toddlers 11.2: Meeting Nutritional Needs of Toddlers 11.3: Meeting Other Physical Needs of Toddlers 12.1: How Toddlers Learn 12.2: What Toddlers Learn 12.3: Meeting Toddlers' Intellectual Needs 13.1: The Social-Emotional World of Toddlers 13.2: Meeting Toddlers' Social-Emotional Needs 14.1: Growth and Development of Preschoolers 14.2: Meeting Nutritional Needs of Preschoolers 14.3: Meeting Other Physical Needs of Preschoolers 15.1: How Preschoolers Learn 15.2: What Preschoolers Learn 15.3: Meeting Preschoolers' Intellectual Needs 16.1: The Social-Emotional World of Preschoolers 16.2: Meeting Preschoolers' Social-Emotional Needs 17.1: Growth and Development of School-Age Children 17.2: Meeting Nutritional Needs of School-Age Children 17.3: Meeting Other Physical Needs of School-Age Children 18.1: How School-Age Children Learn 18.2: What School-Age Children Learn 18.3: Meeting School-Age Children's Intellectual Needs 19.1: The Social-Emotional World of School-Age Children 19.2: Meeting School-Age Children's Social-Emotional Needs 20.1: The Importance of Play 20.2: Play Activities for Children 21.1: Maintaining Children's Health 21.2: Ensuring Children's Safety 22.1: Helping Children Cope with Challenges 22.2: Protecting Children from Neglect and Abuse 23.1: Types of Special Needs 23.2: Help for Children with Special Needs
12.1.3 Analyze current and emerging research about human growth and development, including research on brain development.	1.1: Understanding Child Development 1.2: Recognizing Principles and Theories of Growth and Development 1.3: Studying and Observing Children 2.1: Brain Studies 2.2: Acquiring Knowledge

Competencies	Text Concepts
12.1.3 *(Continued)*	5.2: Factors That Affect the Unborn Baby 5.3: Health Habits Prior to and During Pregnancy 6.1: Special Medical Concerns of Pregnancy 7.1: Decisions Concerning Childbirth 7.3: Newborn Medical Care and Tests 9.1: How Children Learn in the First Year 9.2: What Children Learn in the First Year 9.3: Meeting Children's Intellectual Needs in the First Year 11.1: Growth and Development of Toddlers 12.1: How Toddlers Learn 12.2: What Toddlers Learn 14.1: Growth and Development of Preschoolers 15.2: What Preschoolers Learn 15.3: Meeting Preschoolers' Intellectual Needs 16.1: The Social-Emotional World of Preschoolers 18.1: How School-Age Children Learn 20.1: The Importance of Play 23.1: Types of Special Needs 23.2: Help for Children with Special Needs 25.2: Learning About Careers That Involve Children
Content Standard 12.2 **Analyze conditions that influence human growth and development.**	
12.2.1 Analyze the effect of heredity and environment on human growth and development.	1.1: Understanding Child Development 1.2: Recognizing Principles and Theories of Growth and Development 1.3: Studying and Observing Children 2.1: Brain Studies 2.2: Acquiring Knowledge 3.1: Healthy Family Development 3.2: Family Types 4.1: Deciding About Parenthood 4.2: Parenting Roles, Responsibilities, and Styles 5.1: A Baby's Beginning 5.2: Factors That Affect the Unborn Baby 5.3: Health Habits Prior to and During Pregnancy 6.1: Special Medical Concerns of Pregnancy 6.2: Teen Pregnancy 7.4: Postpartum Care 8.1: Growth and Development in the First Year 8.2: Meeting Nutritional Needs in the First Year 8.3: Meeting Other Physical Needs in the First Year 9.1: How Children Learn in the First Year 9.2: What Children Learn in the First Year 9.3: Meeting Children's Intellectual Needs in the First Year 10.1: The Social-Emotional World of Babies 10.2: Meeting Social-Emotional Needs in the First Year

Competencies	Text Concepts
12.2.1 *(Continued)*	11.2: Meeting Nutritional Needs of Toddlers 11.3: Meeting Other Physical Needs of Toddlers 12.1: How Toddlers Learn 12.2: What Toddlers Learn 12.3: Meeting Toddlers' Intellectual Needs 13.1: The Social-Emotional World of Toddlers 13.2: Meeting Toddlers' Social-Emotional Needs 14.1: Growth and Development of Preschoolers 14.2: Meeting Nutritional Needs of Preschoolers 14.3: Meeting Other Physical Needs of Preschoolers 15.1: How Preschoolers Learn 15.2: What Preschoolers Learn 15.3: Meeting Preschoolers' Intellectual Needs 16.1: The Social-Emotional World of Preschoolers 16.2: Meeting Preschoolers' Social-Emotional Needs 17.1: Growth and Development of School-Age Children 17.2: Meeting Nutritional Needs of School-Age Children 17.3: Meeting Other Physical Needs of School-Age Children 18.1: How School-Age Children Learn 18.2: What School-Age Children Learn 18.3: Meeting School-Age Children's Intellectual Needs 19.1: The Social-Emotional World of School-Age Children 19.2: Meeting School-Age Children's Social-Emotional Needs 20.1: The Importance of Play 20.2: Play Activities for Children 21.1: Maintaining Children's Health 21.2: Ensuring Children's Safety 22.1: Helping Children Cope with Challenges 22.2: Protecting Children from Neglect and Abuse 25.1: Making Career Decisions 25.2: Developing Skills for Career Success
12.2.2 Analyze the impact of social, economic, and technological forces on individual growth and development.	1.1: Understanding Child Development 1.2: Recognizing Principles and Theories of Growth and Development 1.3: Studying and Observing Children 2.2: Acquiring Knowledge 3.1: Healthy Family Development 3.2: Family Types 4.1: Deciding About Parenthood 4.2: Parenting Roles, Responsibilities, and Styles 6.1: Special Medical Concerns of Pregnancy 6.2: Teen Pregnancy 7.1: Decisions Concerning Childbirth 7.2: Time to Be Born 7.3: Newborn Medical Care and Tests 10.1: The Social-Emotional World of Babies

Competencies	Text Concepts
12.2.2 *(Continued)*	10.2: Meeting Children's Social-Emotional Needs in the First Year 12.3: Meeting Toddlers' Intellectual Needs 13.1: The Social-Emotional World of Toddlers 13.2: Meeting Toddlers' Social-Emotional Needs 15.3: Meeting Preschoolers' Intellectual Needs 16.1: The Social-Emotional World of Preschoolers 16.2: Meeting Preschoolers' Social-Emotional Needs 17.2: Meeting Nutritional Needs of School-Age Children 17.3: Meeting Other Physical Needs of School-Age Children 18.2: What School-Age Children Learn 18.3: Meeting School-Age Children's Intellectual Needs 19.1: The Social-Emotional World of School-Age Children 19.2: Meeting School-Age Children's Social-Emotional Needs 20.1: The Importance of Play 21.1: Maintaining Children's Health 21.2: Ensuring Children's Safety 22.1: Helping Children Cope with Challenges 22.2: Protecting Children from Neglect and Abuse 23.2: Help for Children with Special Needs 24.2: Choosing an Early Childhood Education Program
12.2.3 Analyze the effects of gender, ethnicity, and culture on individual development.	1.1: Understanding Child Development 1.2: Recognizing Principles and Theories of Growth and Development 1.3: Studying and Observing Children 2.2: Acquiring Knowledge 3.1: Healthy Family Development 3.2: Family Types 4.2: Parenting Roles, Responsibilities, and Styles 9.1: How Children Learn in the First Year 9.2: What Children Learn in the First Year 9.3: Meeting Children's Intellectual Needs in the First Year 12.1: How Toddlers Learn 12.2: What Toddlers Learn 13.1: The Social-Emotional World of Toddlers 13.2: Meeting Toddlers' Social-Emotional Needs 15.1: How Preschoolers Learn 15.3: Meeting Preschoolers' Intellectual Needs 16.1: The Social-Emotional World of Preschoolers 17.1: Growth and Development of School-Age Children 17.2: Meeting Nutritional Needs of School-Age Children 17.3: Meeting Other Physical Needs of School-Age Children 18.1: How School-Age Children Learn 18.2: What School-Age Children Learn 18.3: Meeting School-Age Children's Intellectual Needs 19.1: The Social-Emotional World of School-Age Children 19.2: Meeting School-Age Children's Social-Emotional Needs 20.1: The Importance of Play

Competencies	Text Concepts
12.2.3 *(Continued)*	22.1: Helping Children Cope with Challenges 22.2: Protecting Children from Neglect and Abuse 24.2: Choosing an Early Childhood Education Program 25.1: Making Career Decisions 25.3: Developing Skills for Career Success
12.2.4 Analyze the effects of life events on individuals' physical, intellectual, social, moral, and emotional development.	1.1: Understanding Child Development 1.2: Recognizing Principles and Theories of Growth and Development 1.3: Studying and Observing Children 2.1: Brain Studies 3.1: Healthy Family Development 3.2: Family Types 4.1: Deciding About Parenthood 5.2: Factors That Affect the Unborn Baby 5.3: Health Habits Prior to and During Pregnancy 6.1: Special Medical Concerns of Pregnancy 6.2: Teen Pregnancy 7.1: Decisions Concerning Childbirth 7.2: Time to Be Born 7.3: Newborn Medical Care and Tests 7.4: Postpartum Care 9.3: Meeting Children's Intellectual Needs in the First Year 10.1: The Social-Emotional World of Babies 10.2: Meeting Social-Emotional Needs in the First Year 13.1: The Social-Emotional World of Toddlers 13.2: Meeting Toddlers' Social-Emotional Needs 14.1: Growth and Development of Preschoolers 16.1: The Social-Emotional World of Preschoolers 16.2: Meeting Preschoolers' Social-Emotional Needs 18.3: Meeting School-Age Children's Intellectual Needs 19.1: The Social-Emotional World of School-Age Children 19.2: Meeting School-Age Children's Social-Emotional Needs 21.1: Maintaining Children's Health 21.2: Ensuring Children's Safety 22.1: Helping Children Cope with Challenges 22.2: Protecting Children from Neglect and Abuse 25.1: Making Career Decisions 25.2: Developing Skills for Career Success
12.2.5 Analyze geographic, political, and global influences on human growth and development.	1.1: Understanding Child Development 1.2: Recognizing Principles and Theories of Growth and Development 1.3: Studying and Observing Children 2.2: Acquiring Knowledge 3.1: Healthy Family Development 3.2: Family Types 9.2: What Children Learn in the First Year 15.3: Meeting Preschoolers' Intellectual Needs 16.1: The Social-Emotional World of Preschoolers

Competencies	Text Concepts
12.2.5 *(Continued)*	18.2: What School-Age Children Learn 18.3: Meeting School-Age Children's Intellectual Needs 19.1: The Social-Emotional World of School-Age Children 19.2: Meeting School-Age Children's Social-Emotional Needs 21.1: Maintaining Children's Health 21.2: Ensuring Children's Safety 22.1: Helping Children Cope with Challenges 22.2: Protecting Children from Neglect and Abuse 25.1: Making Career Decisions 25.2: Developing Skills for Career Success
Content Standard 12.3 **Analyze strategies that promote growth and development across the life span.**	
12.3.1 Analyze the role of nurturance on human growth and development.	1.1: Understanding Child Development 1.2: Recognizing Principles and Theories of Growth and Development 1.3: Studying and Observing Children 2.1: Brain Studies 2.2: Acquiring Knowledge 3.1: Healthy Family Development 3.2: Family Types 4.1: Deciding About Parenthood 4.2: Parenting Roles, Responsibilities, and Styles 5.2: Factors That Affect the Unborn Baby 5.3: Health Habits Prior to and During Pregnancy 6.2: Teen Pregnancy 7.4: Postpartum Care 8.1: Growth and Development in the First Year 8.2: Meeting Nutritional Needs in the First Year 8.3: Meeting Other Physical Needs in the First Year 9.1: How Children Learn in the First Year 9.2: What Children Learn in the First Year 9.3: Meeting Children's Intellectual Needs in the First Year 10.1: The Social-Emotional World of Babies 10.2: Meeting Social-Emotional Needs in the First Year 11.2: Meeting Nutritional Needs of Toddlers 11.3: Meeting Other Physical Needs of Toddlers 12.1: How Toddlers Learn 12.2: What Toddlers Learn 12.3: Meeting Toddlers' Intellectual Needs 13.1: The Social-Emotional World of Toddlers 13.2: Meeting Toddlers' Social-Emotional Needs 14.1: Growth and Development of Preschoolers 14.2: Meeting Nutritional Needs of Preschoolers 14.3: Meeting Other Physical Needs of Preschoolers 15.1: How Preschoolers Learn 15.2: What Preschoolers Learn

Competencies	Text Concepts
12.3.1 *(Continued)*	15.3: Meeting Preschoolers' Intellectual Needs 16.1: The Social-Emotional World of Preschoolers 16.2: Meeting Preschoolers' Social-Emotional Needs 17.1: Growth and Development of School-Age Children 17.2: Meeting Nutritional Needs of School-Age Children 17.3: Meeting Other Physical Needs of School-Age Children 18.1: How School-Age Children Learn 18.2: What School-Age Children Learn 18.3: Meeting School-Age Children's Intellectual Needs 19.1: The Social-Emotional World of School-Age Children 19.2: Meeting School-Age Children's Social-Emotional Needs 20.1: The Importance of Play 20.2: Play Activities for Children 21.1: Maintaining Children's Health 21.2: Ensuring Children's Safety 22.1: Helping Children Cope with Challenges 22.2: Protecting Children from Neglect and Abuse 23.2: Help for Children with Special Needs 25.1: Making Career Decisions 25.2: Developing Skills for Career Success
12.3.2 Analyze the role of communication on human growth and development.	1.1: Understanding Child Development 1.3: Studying and Observing Children 3.1: Healthy Family Development 4.1: Deciding About Parenthood 4.2: Parenting Roles, Responsibilities, and Styles 9.1: How Children Learn in the First Year 9.2: What Children Learn in the First Year 9.3: Meeting Children's Intellectual Needs in the First Year 10.2: Meeting Social-Emotional Needs in the First Year 12.2: What Toddlers Learn 12.3: Meeting Toddlers' Intellectual Needs 13.1: The Social-Emotional World of Toddlers 13.2: Meeting Toddlers' Social-Emotional Needs 14.2: Meeting Nutritional Needs of Preschoolers 15.1: How Preschoolers Learn 15.2: What Preschoolers Learn 15.3: Meeting Preschoolers' Intellectual Needs 16.1: The Social-Emotional World of Preschoolers 16.2: Meeting Preschoolers' Social-Emotional Needs 18.2: What School-Age Children Learn 18.3: Meeting School-Age Children's Intellectual Needs 19.1: The Social-Emotional World of School-Age Children 19.2: Meeting School-Age Children's Social-Emotional Needs 20.1: The Importance of Play 20.2: Play Activities for Children

Competencies	Text Concepts
12.3.2 *(Continued)*	22.1: Helping Children Cope with Challenges 22.2: Protecting Children from Neglect and Abuse 23.1: Types of Special Needs 23.2: Help for Children with Special Needs 24.2: Choosing an Early Childhood Education Program 25.1: Making Career Decisions 25.2: Learning About Careers That Involve Children 25.3: Developing Skills for Career Success
12.3.3 Analyze the role of family and social services support systems in meeting human growth and development needs.	1.1: Understanding Child Development 1.2: Recognizing Principles and Theories of Growth and Development 1.3: Studying and Observing Children 2.1: Brain Studies 3.1: Healthy Family Development 3.2: Family Types 4.1: Deciding About Parenthood 4.2: Parenting Roles, Responsibilities, and Styles 6.2: Teen Pregnancy 7.1: Decisions Concerning Childbirth 8.1: Growth and Development in the First Year 8.2: Meeting Nutritional Needs in the First Year 8.3: Meeting Other Physical Needs in the First Year 9.1: How Children Learn in the First Year 9.2: What Children Learn in the First Year 9.3: Meeting Children's Intellectual Needs in the First Year 10.1: The Social-Emotional World of Babies 10.2: Meeting Social-Emotional Needs in the First Year 11.2: Meeting Nutritional Needs of Toddlers 11.3: Meeting Other Physical Needs of Toddlers 12.1: How Toddlers Learn 12.2: What Toddlers Learn 12.3: Meeting Toddlers' Intellectual Needs 13.1: The Social-Emotional World of Toddlers 13.2: Meeting Toddlers' Social-Emotional Needs 14.1: Growth and Development of Preschoolers 14.2: Meeting Nutritional Needs of Preschoolers 14.3: Meeting Other Physical Needs of Preschoolers 15.1: How Preschoolers Learn 15.2: What Preschoolers Learn 15.3: Meeting Preschoolers' Intellectual Needs 16.1: The Social-Emotional World of Preschoolers 16.2: Meeting Preschoolers' Social-Emotional Needs 17.1: Growth and Development of School-Age Children 17.2: Meeting Nutritional Needs of School-Age Children 17.3: Meeting Other Physical Needs of School-Age Children 18.1: How School-Age Children Learn 18.2: What School-Age Children Learn

Competencies	Text Concepts
12.3.3 *(Continued)*	18.3: Meeting School-Age Children's Intellectual Needs 19.1: The Social-Emotional World of School-Age Children 19.2: Meeting School-Age Children's Social-Emotional Needs 20.1: The Importance of Play 20.2: Play Activities for Children 21.1: Maintaining Children's Health 21.2: Ensuring Children's Safety 22.1: Helping Children Cope with Challenges 22.2: Protecting Children from Neglect and Abuse 23.2: Help for Children with Special Needs 24.2: Choosing an Early Childhood Education Program 25.1: Making Career Decisions 25.2: Learning About Careers That Involve Children 25.3: Developing Skills for Career Success

Answer Key

The following pages contain answers for the caption questions, lesson reviews and assessments, and chapter reviews and assessments in the text. Unless otherwise noted, answers for caption questions and chapter review activities will vary.

Chapter 1
Learning About Children

Caption Questions

Figure 1.3 Mother and daughter have similar hair colors and facial structures.

Figure 1.6 Answers will vary. Principles of growth and development were developed through expert study and observation of children.

Figure 1.7 Answers will vary, but may include motor skills involved in lifting the head, crawling, creeping, and standing upright.

Figure 1.8 Answers will vary, but may include being eager to learn and active.

Figure 1.14 Direct observation done in an unnatural environment may lead to unnatural behavior in the child.

Lesson 1.1 Review and Assessment

1. *Child development* is the scientific study of children from conception to adolescence.
2. *Physical development* involves growth of the body and development of motor skills. *Intellectual development* includes how people learn, what people learn, and how they express what they know through language. *Social development* concerns interactions with people and social groups. *Emotional development* involves feelings and disposition.
3. prenatal (conception to birth), neonatal (birth through the first month), infancy (1 month through 12 months), toddler (12 months to 36 months), preschool (3 years to 6 years), school-age (6 years to 12 years)
4. heredity and environment
5. The *epigenome*, which means *above the genes*, can turn genes on and off.
6. Answers will vary.

Lesson 1.2 Review and Assessment

1. Growth and development tend to be constant, are gradual and continuous, progress in sequential steps, occur at different rates, and are interrelated.
2. First, new growth, knowledge, and skills are always built on those already acquired. Second, people often live in the same environment for years.
3. A *teachable moment* is a time when a person can learn a new task. (Examples will vary.)
4. *Developmental acceleration* occurs when a child performs like an older child. *Developmental delay* occurs when a child performs like a younger child.
5. A *theory* is a set of statements offered as possible explanations for a phenomenon.
6. (List three:) maturational, psychoanalytic, psychosocial, learning, cognitive-developmental, sociocultural, ecological systems
7. Answers will vary.

Lesson 1.3 Review and Assessment

1. to understand yourself, to be a responsible parent, to work with children, to protect children's rights
2. Basic needs include physical and psychological needs, and higher-level needs include self-actualization needs.
3. (List three:) ongoing nurturing relationships; physical protection, safety, and regulation; experiences tailored to individual differences; experiences that are developmentally appropriate; limit setting, structure, and expectations; stable communities and cultural continuity; protecting the future
4. CPS caseworkers make sure laws and policies are being carried out by families with minor children.
5. *Direct observation* involves watching children in their natural environments. *Indirect observation* is done by methods other than watching children, including asking other people questions about the children and observing the products children make.
6. Answers will vary.

Chapter 2
New Directions in Learning

Caption Questions

Figure 2.6 Yes, a neuron can connect with up to 250,000 other neurons.
Figure 2.9 Answers will vary. Overall nutrition can affect how well the body develops. The body, as well as the brain, needs certain nutrients to grow and function properly.
Figure 2.10 Answers will vary, but may include schools, family homes, or outdoor locations.
Figure 2.13 Answers will vary. Scientific knowledge is based on observation and principles of cause and effect.
Figure 2.16 Answers will vary, but should include interactions with people and objects in the environment.

Lesson 2.1 Review and Assessment

1. Brain scans allow researchers to see specific areas of the brain and note both growth and activity. These scans have resulted in information about brain development that earlier had to be inferred through observed behaviors in children, such as noting milestones.
2. *astrocytes*—nourish neurons, restrict certain substances from entering the brain, control chemical environment of brain; *microglia*—remove cellular waste; *ependymal*—protect spinal cord and brain; *oligodendrocytes*—help insulate axons with myelin
3. varies
4. A chemical and electrical signal (or *neurotransmitter*) jumps from the axon of one neuron to the dendrites of another neuron, across a space known as the *synapse*.
5. Pruning results from a lack of certain experiences or a lack of use. By eliminating connections that are not being used, the brain makes wiring more efficient.
6. Brain plasticity allows the brain to "catch up" on missed skills and to acquire new skills. It allows the brain to learn and reshape itself later in life and allows for recovery from brain damage.
7. *Critical periods* are windows of opportunity that are small and tend to shut. *Sensitive periods* are windows of opportunity that are large and tend to narrow, but not shut.
8. Answers will vary.

Lesson 2.2 Review and Assessment

1. stressors
2. The four types of knowledge are *explicit knowledge*, *implicit knowledge*, *scientific knowledge*, and *knowledge about experts*. Examples will vary.
3. Developmental tasks
4. physical maturation, social pressures, inner pressures

5. *working memory*—the ability to sort, organize, and manipulate information while working on a task; *cognitive flexibility*—the ability to adjust to changing demands; *inhibition*—the ability to filter thoughts and feelings and not act impulsively
6. The seven essential life skills are *focus and self-control*, *perspective taking*, *communicating*, *making connections*, *critical thinking*, *taking on challenges*, and *self-directed and engaged learning*. Examples will vary.
7. Answers will vary.

Chapter 2 Review and Assessment

16. **Math.** 60 months

Chapter 3
Families Today

Caption Questions

Figure 3.1 Marriage is the relationship into which many children are born, causing it to be foundational for family life.

Figure 3.2 Answers will vary. Both people seem interested in the conversation, judging from their use of gestures and posture of leaning in toward one another.

Figure 3.9 Some advantages might include a close relationship with the parent and increased involvement in family roles. Some disadvantages might include strain due to one individual shouldering the role of parenting, as well as financial strain.

Lesson 3.1 Review and Assessment

1. *Marriage* is a legal contract and, ideally, an emotional and social union between two partners. Marriage fulfills the emotional and social needs of both spouses and provides security and comfort for children; it is the foundational relationship of a family.
2. *Nonverbal communication* uses body language for sending and receiving messages through facial expressions, gestures, and other wordless means. *Verbal communication* uses words to send a message. Examples will vary.
3. A budget helps regulate spending and saving and thus lessens the stress that financial strain can place on a family. Money problems can spark conflict very easily in the family, and a reasonable budget can help prevent these conflicts.
4. beginning stage, childbearing stage, parenting stage, launching stage, mid-years stage, aging stage
5. Culture
6. Differing communication methods, cultural expectations, traditions, and family views can present challenges in multicultural families. Multicultural families may also experience unfavorable biases from others. Some benefits of multicultural families include increased diversity, strong self-respect, and increased strength in family relationships.
7. Before and during the Industrial Revolution in the U.S., children were viewed as a source of income and were valued for the work they could do and the money they could earn for the family. Today, children are not seen as sources of income, but rather as individuals to be nurtured.
8. Answers will vary.
9. Answers will vary.

Lesson 3.2 Review and Assessment

1. Disadvantages include a lack of contact with extended family and potential stress in the marriage relationship. Advantages include increased opportunities to share responsibilities and resources and increased opportunities for children to learn flexible role sharing.
2. child support order

3. Extended families may form when family members move in with each other for financial reasons, when grandparents move in for care and companionship, or when families share a cultural tradition that encourages them to live with one another.
4. (List three:) letting stepchildren set the pace of relationship building, showing verbal appreciation for stepchildren, explaining that a stepparent is another person there to love a stepchild, encouraging children to have time with biological parents, planning family activities, insisting on respect, avoiding showing favoritism, keeping family communication open
5. In a *closed adoption*, the identity of the birthparents and adopting family are not revealed. An *open adoption* involves some degree of communication between the birthparent(s) and adoptive family.
6. A *foster parent* temporarily looks after a child who has been removed from his or her birthparents. The foster parent does not have custody of the child, and the goal is that a child will eventually return to his or her birthparents. A *guardian* has legal custody and responsibility of a child in the case that his or her birthparents are deceased or unable to care for the child. A guardian may permanently care for a child.
7. Answers will vary. Possible reasons may include finances, a changing social landscape, or changing cultural expectations. Unique challenges may include the strain of shouldering the entire parenting role, the feeling of being "different," and the presence of only one source of parental guidance.
8. Answers will vary, but should reflect an understanding of Lesson 3.2.

Chapter 3 Review and Assessment

4. **Evaluate.** Answers will vary. Adrian wanting to please his parents and grandparents is not a healthy reason; he should not marry to please other people. His reason of wanting to be an "adult" reveals insecurity, and is thus also an unhealthy reason. Wanting to build a family, however, is a healthy reason.

Chapter 4
Preparing for Parenting

Caption Questions

Figure 4.1 Before 20 years of age, a woman's body is still developing and is not fully matured to conceive and carry a baby.

Figure 4.9 Answers will vary, but might include needs for quality experiences and quality time.

Figure 4.11 Answers will vary. Professionals suggest that induction is the best method of discipline for building character.

Lesson 4.1 Review and Assessment

1. (List three:) Wouldn't it be nice to have a cute little baby? Our parents want grandchildren. Our older child needs a brother or sister. A child can make us proud. A child will comfort us in our old age. A child will make us love each other (when marriage is failing).
2. *We want to share our love and time with a child.* All the other reasons have strings attached, such as to be of benefit to the parents, grandparents, or another child.
3. (List three:) We are not ready for a child. A baby costs a lot. A child will tie us down. A child will interfere with our careers. Our child could be sick or have a disability. Our marriage could fail, and I do not want to be a single parent.
4. (List three:) their knowledge about parenting; their maturity; how their relationships will affect children and how children will affect their relationships; their ability to manage resources—time and energy, home care, careers, finances, and other resources needed directly for children
5. Roles and concepts of parents develop (change) as their children grow and develop. According to Galinsky, parenting involves six stages of change that require many years of development on the part of parents.
6. A great deal of both physical and psychological energy is needed for parenting tasks. Careers and other activities deplete some of the parents' energy and to this depletion is added all the parenting tasks.

7. *Direct costs* are the expenses related to raising a child, such as clothing, food, housing, child care and education, and transportation. *Indirect costs* are the resources used to meet child-related costs that could have been used to meet other goals. Foregone income, foregone career opportunities, and time spent in child care are all examples of indirect costs.
8. Family planning affects how many children a couple will have and when they will have children.
9. *Birth control methods* are measures couples use to help prevent pregnancy.
10. Parenting is a challenging task under any circumstance. If a marriage is already weak, the extra challenges of parenting may further weaken the marriage because parenting affects the couple's relationship.

Lesson 4.2 Review and Assessment

1. Parents' roles and responsibilities mainly involve nurturance, socialization, and guidance and discipline.
2. providing all aspects of care for a child, which includes meeting physical, intellectual, and social-emotional needs
3. socialize
4. *Guidance* includes the words and actions parents use to influence their children's behavior. *Discipline* is the use of methods and techniques to teach children self-control. Discipline is part of guidance.
5. *Power assertion* occurs when parents use or threaten to use some form of physical punishment or deny privileges. In *love withdrawal*, parents threaten children with being unloved or suggest some form of parent/child separation. *Induction* happens when parents discipline children by reasoning and explaining to them why they should or should not use certain behaviors. (Answers will vary for effects.)
6. *authoritarian*—main objective is to make children completely obedient; *permissive*—parents give children almost no guidelines or rules; *overparenting*—parents desire to provide for and protect their children beyond what is in the best interest of children; *authoritative*—parents set some rules, but allow children some freedom
7. authoritative
8. Children can see the reasons for limits set by parents and choose to abide by them. This teaches children to reason independently and make good choices.

Chapter 4 Review and Assessment

8. **Make inferences.** Parents do not determine the characters of their children, but they can influence character with their parenting approach, decisions, and guidance.
9. **Determine.** Sheng's mother is using the discipline technique *love withdrawal*. Instead, she might use induction.

Chapter 5
Pregnancy

Caption Questions

Figure 5.1 Only one sperm penetrates the egg's surface and fertilizes the egg.

Figure 5.2 Sperm would travel up the vagina, through the cervix, into the uterus, and into the fallopian tubes.

Figure 5.3 The zygote, through rapid cell division, forms a *morula*, or a solid ball of cells. Then, a fluid-filled cavity forms in the morula, which is now called a *blastocyst*.

Figure 5.4 A baby might need protection from sudden jolts, impact, or infections.

Figure 5.5 Answers will vary, but may include beginning weight, body composition, size of the baby, or nutrition.

Figure 5.7 It means the two species are closely related and often bear genetic resemblances, such as similar physical, intellectual, and social-emotional traits.

Figure 5.8 female

Figure 5.12 They can make regular doctor appointments early in the pregnancy and attend follow-up appointments.

Figure 5.19 Answers will vary.

Figure 5.22 Mothers-to-be should avoid contact sports, activities that jolt the pelvic region, and activities that could result in falls.

Lesson 5.1 Review and Assessment

1. The ovum is released from one of the ovaries and swept into a fallopian tube. During intercourse, sperm leaves the male's penis and enters the female's vagina. Sperm swim through the female's reproductive organs toward the egg. Those sperm that survive surround the egg and try to enter. Only one sperm may penetrate the egg's surface and fertilize the egg. The zygote forms when the sperm reaches the center of the egg.
2. Female structures involved in conception include the ovaries, fallopian tubes, uterus, cervix, and vagina. Male structures include the testes and penis.
3. about nine months (three trimesters)
4. The zygote begins to divide until it becomes a blastocyst. The blastocyst enters the uterus, continues to divide rapidly, and then embeds itself in the uterus.
5. Almost all body systems are developing during the embryonic stage. This makes the embryo vulnerable to harmful substances.
6. heartbeat, movements, and the age of viability
7. *Quickening* is a baby's movements which can be felt by the mother. It generally occurs between 18 and 20 weeks in first-time mothers, and between 15 and 17 weeks in mothers who have already given birth.
8. From the embryonic stage onward, the developing baby is connected to the mother via a complex support system, through which nutrients and substances are passed from mother to child. Because of this, a mother's diet and other health habits affect her baby's development and health.

Lesson 5.2 Review and Assessment

1. The genome acts as a genetic blueprint that guides growth and development and gives cells instructions for family-like traits that will unfold throughout life. The epigenome can turn genes on and off, which can alter how the genes may function throughout life.
2. Mendel discovered the role of dominant and recessive genes in determining traits. His conclusions refuted the belief of his time that traits were sort of an "averaging" of the parents' traits.
3. A carrier of a *recessive trait* for a genetic defect can pass the trait on to the next generation. If both the male and the female are carriers, they are more likely to pass the defect to their children.
4. A *genetic disorder* is a defect caused by one or more abnormalities in the genome. A *chromosomal disorder* is a defect in the chromosome. Chromosomal defects are more serious because they involve so many genes.
5. parents' ages; the mother's physical health, including any illnesses, diseases, or infections and the substances or foods she consumes; and the mother's emotional health
6. A mother's stress hormones can cross the placenta to her baby, where prolonged exposure can lead to developmental problems and complications.
7. Paul and Emily's daughter can have blue eyes if Paul is a carrier of the recessive trait for blue eyes.
8. A woman can practice good health habits such as regular physical activity and good nutrition. She can avoid substances that are harmful to her health and her baby's health, and she can attend to her emotional health.

Lesson 5.3 Review and Assessment

1. Health habits before pregnancy can impact a woman's ability both to become pregnant and to carry that pregnancy to term. Healthy habits a woman forms before pregnancy will influence her health habits during pregnancy.
2. *Carbohydrates* supply energy to the body consistently and on short notice. *Proteins* build and maintain the body's cells and tissues. *Fats* supply energy to the body, cushion internal organs, and insulate the body. *Vitamins* regulate various body processes. *Minerals* promote normal growth and development. *Water* regulates body temperature, lubricates joints, protects sensitive tissues, and moves waste, nutrients, and oxygen through the body.
3. Answers will vary. Presumptive signs include nausea, tenderness and swelling of the breasts, amenorrhea, skin discoloration, internal changes, and increased frequency of urination. Positive signs include the presence of HCG; fetal heartbeat, movement, image, and shape; and uterine contractions.

4. The doctor will gather a woman's health and family history, answer questions about pregnancy, do a complete physical exam, advise the couple of health habits, and estimate a due date.
5. Blood tests check for chromosomal disorders and neural tube defects. An ultrasound produces an image of the baby with sound waves and can detect structural defects. Chorionic villus sampling (CVS) samples the chorion and can detect abnormalities early in the pregnancy. Amniocentesis samples the amniotic fluid and can detect over 100 congenital conditions.
6. The nutrients a woman consumes are passed to her baby. Low nutrition can lead to problems in the baby's weight, growth, physical performance, and intellectual capacity.
7. 25–35
8. Answers will vary. Margaret should sleep eight to nine hours each night, with a brief period of rest during the day. She can sleep later, spend less time at the gym, plan nutritious meals with the help of her husband, and make more time for her emotional health to counteract the stress at her job.

Chapter 5 Review and Assessment

6. **Draw conclusions.** Blood type O is possible if both parents are carriers for the recessive O blood type.
16. **Math.** 20–27% of her weight for a single baby, 31–35% of her weight for twins

Chapter 6
Special Circumstances of Pregnancy

Caption Questions

Figure 6.2 This ART method medically unites an ovum and sperm, circumventing problems that involve male and female gametes (such as low sperm count or irregular ovulation).

Figure 6.8 Sperm may fertilize more than one ovum, and one or more zygotes may split.

Figure 6.13 Answers will vary. Future plans determine what a person should or should not do now in order to reach those goals. Sexual decisions can have long-term consequences that affect future plans.

Figure 6.15 Prenatal care is vital to the health of both baby and mother. Lack of prenatal care can lead to serious pregnancy complications.

Figure 6.16 Answers will vary. People can offer emotional and financial support and can provide child care so that a teen has time to finish school.

Figure 6.17 Answers will vary, but may include lack of time for education, work, hobbies, and friends.

Lesson 6.1 Review and Assessment

1. *Infertility* is a couple's inability to conceive or carry a child within a year of trying. *Sterility* is a couple's permanent inability to conceive or carry children.
2. artificial insemination; in vitro fertilization (IVF); gamete intrafallopian transfer (GIFT)
3. Answers will vary. Drawbacks include emotional discomfort, loss of privacy, feelings of being damaged or guilty, no guarantee of success, expenses, and ethical issues.
4. *Fraternal births* occur when more than one ovum is fertilized. *Identical births* occur when a fertilized ovum splits. *Mixed-type births* occur when a woman carries both fraternal and identical multiple pregnancies.
5. (List two:) ectopic pregnancy, too much/too little amniotic fluid, bleeding in late pregnancy, placenta abruptio, placenta previa, pregnancy-induced hypertension
6. (List three:) cleft lip/palate, cystic fibrosis, diabetes, Down syndrome, Huntington's chorea, hydrocephalus, muscular dystrophy, phenylketonuria (PKU), sickle-cell anemia, spina bifida, Tay-Sachs disease
7. Twins of opposite genders must be fraternal because to be of different genders they obviously have a different pair of sex chromosomes (one XX and one XY). In order to be identical, the twins would have exactly the same genome, including identical pairs of sex chromosomes (both XX or both XY).

Lesson 6.2 Review and Assessment

1. abstinence
2. unwanted pregnancies; STIs; emotional scars if the relationship ends; conflicts with parents and other adults; conflicts with teens' consciences, goals, and values
3. Teen mothers may not think they are pregnant, feel their parents will be upset, be afraid the relationship with the baby's father will end, lack money for medical care or not know where to go for help, not be able to find transportation to medical facility, not know that medical care is necessary, or be afraid of medical procedures.
4. (List two:) may lack adequate child care, feel out of place in school settings, need a job to financially provide for child, have limited study time
5. Teen parents may encounter unhappy marriages; friction with parents; and feelings of isolation due to less time with friends. They also shoulder more responsibility and may experience depression.
6. Answers will vary. Resources may include medical facilities with low-cost prenatal care, school advising services, equal opportunity in school, school child care, TANF, SNAP, WIC, and child care assistance.
7. Answers will vary. Teen fathers may shoulder some of the responsibility for caring for a baby and may be required to pay child support. They may also face the stress of being a parent and the isolation of having little time for friends, as well as friction with their parents.

Chapter 6 Review and Assessment

5. **Analyze.** *Dizygotic* contains the prefix *di-*, which means *two*. This pregnancy stems from more than one zygote. *Monozygotic* contains the prefix *mono-*, which means *one*. This pregnancy stems from one zygote.
6. **Make inferences.** Answers will vary. Many multiple births are caused by ART methods, which increase the amount of ova available for fertilization. A lack of available ART methods may reduce the number of multiple pregnancies.

Chapter 7
Childbirth

Caption Questions

Figure 7.6 Breech birth position makes delivery more difficult and dangerous.
Figure 7.7 dilation of the cervix
Figure 7.8 to supply the baby oxygen and other nutrients
Figure 7.13 Newborns have immature livers, which cannot always handle bilirubin.
Figure 7.14 Sickle-cell anemia reduces the amount of oxygen that can be carried in red blood cells, leading to less oxygen circulation throughout the body.
Figure 7.21 Answers will vary, but may include support groups and child care programs.

Lesson 7.1 Review and Assessment

1. during the middle of pregnancy. Older children need to know by the time changes in the mother's body are noticeable.
2. Pregnancy Discrimination Act (PDA) and Family and Medical Leave Act (FMLA)
3. hospital, birthing room in a hospital, birth center, and home. Options may be limited by where the couple lives, who will deliver the baby, health conditions of the mother and baby, and extent of insurance coverage.
4. The three major methods are natural childbirth, Lamaze method, and delivery with the use of drugs. Choices may change if labor becomes too long, if pain becomes unbearable, or if complications occur.
5. Answers will vary. Fathers can provide emotional support and assist during labor. They can also take paternity leave and tend to the needs of the mother.

Lesson 7.2 Review and Assessment

1. a change in the baby's position, often to a position lower in the pelvis
2. irregular contractions that often occur before true labor
3. B, A, D, C
4. drug-assisted delivery, vaginal-assisted delivery, and cesarean section
5. (List two:) The mother's pelvis is small or not shaped for an easy birth. The baby or mother is at medical risk. The baby's head is large. Contractions are weak or absent. The baby is in an incorrect position for birth. The pregnancy is a multiple birth. The doctor feels that previous uterine scar(s) could rupture during labor.
6. The healthy baby is in a bassinet in the room with the mother. The medical care of the baby can be given in the mother's room, and nurses are still available to help the new mother. The father or a support person is provided with a bed.
7. (List three benefits to babies:) increased chance of survival; better weight gain; less crying, more smiles and laughter; fewer infections; possibly higher IQ; better language development (List three benefits to parents:) less incidence of child abuse, faster recovery from delivery, longer breast-feeding, more self-confidence as a parent, less incidence of depression after delivery
8. Answers will vary. Parents can hold, touch, or talk to the baby.

Lesson 7.3 Review and Assessment

1. neonate
2. heart rate, respiratory effort, muscle tone, reflex irritability, color
3. anemia, jaundice, developmental disorders
4. interacting with the environment, handling motor processes, controlling his or her physical state, responding to stress
5. routine medical visit in which the doctor examines a baby for signs of good health and proper growth
6. (List two:) Each baby (and family) is assigned one medical team. Except for emergencies, medical and nursing care coincides with the baby's sleep-wake cycles. Parents are encouraged to participate in their baby's care by feeding, rocking, and doing skin-to-skin holding. The NICU is decorated and parents have their own space around their baby's NICU bed. Soft lighting and low noise levels provide a soothing environment.
7. a heart rate of over 100 beats per minute; a good, strong cry; a well-flexed muscle tone; cries in response to stimuli; color is completely pink; is alert to the environment; is able to handle some motor processes; is able to control his or her physical state; has active reflexes in response to stress

Lesson 7.4 Review and Assessment

1. postpartum care (or postnatal care)
2. baby blues, postpartum depression (PPD), postpartum psychosis (PPP)
3. (List three:) age in the teen years or over 40 years old, family history of mood disorders, family history of thyroid problems, mood swings during the menstrual cycle, migraine headaches when taking hormones, fertility problems, severe family stress, lack of support from family and friends, previous postpartum mood disorder
4. paternal postpartum depression (PPPD)
5. If left untreated, postpartum mood disorders can have devastating effects on family life and can negatively affect a newborn.
6. (List four:) get enough rest, maintain a healthful diet, be physically active, stay organized, take care of legal matters, socialize with each other and with others
7. Fathers are likely getting up more during the night to tend to their babies because the mothers need their rest, too, especially now that they are also working. Also, the household tasks mothers were able to do while on maternity leave would now need to be done by both parents in nonwork hours. Both situations increase paternal stress. Men might have less financial stress after mothers return to work.

8. Answers will vary. Friends and family of someone suffering from a postpartum mood disorder can provide emotional support, socialize with the person, offer to bring food or provide child care, and encourage the person to seek treatment.

Chapter 8
Physical Development in the First Year

Caption Questions

Figure 8.7 two months

Figure 8.8 Answers will vary, but should reflect explanations in the text.

Figure 8.13 Answers will vary, but should reflect an understanding that weaning should be gradual.

Figure 8.15 Answers will vary, but may include ease of grip and chance of spill.

Figure 8.16 Answers will vary, but may include bite-sized pieces of bread or bagels, O-shaped oat cereal, cooked or diced vegetables, and small chunks of fruit.

Figure 8.17 Answers will vary. Garments that can be easily washed and have safety and growth features may be best for infants. Garments with difficult fasteners or safety hazards could be unsafe for infants.

Figure 8.20 Answers will vary. Parents might schedule infants' sleep times or set a timer.

Figure 8.21 Infants may play or lift their heads during tummy time, which is considered physical activity for infants.

Lesson 8.1 Review and Assessment

1. brain
2. An infant's head is one-fourth his or her length. Jaw and chin are tiny, the chin recedes, the trunk is long, and infants look "pot-bellied" with short legs. From birth until six months of age, the child's head is larger in circumference than the chest, but in most six-month-old children, the chest becomes larger. Most increases in length are due to the trunk growing; the legs do not grow much longer in the first year.
3. deciduous teeth
4. Answers will vary.
5. *Gross-motor skills* are the use and control of large muscles, such as the trunk, arms, and legs, which control mobility. *Fine-motor skills* are the use and control of small muscles, such as hands and fingers, which control grasping objects. Examples will vary.
6. Babies move slowly because they must think as they move. Babies' reactions develop from general (wiggling all over) to specific (reaching for objects and putting them in their mouths). Motor development occurs in two directions: head-to-foot and center-to-extremities. Head-to-foot direction means that the baby can lift the head and then the chest, the abdomen, and finally pull to a stand. Center-to-extremities development means the baby can control the trunk and then the arms, hands, and fingers.
7. (b) raises the head while on abdomen, (e) rolls over from front to back, (a) sits with support, (c) creeps, (f) stands without help, (d) walks
8. Infants' brains grow rapidly during the first year, increasing in weight and size. The head must also grow and remain large to accommodate the brain.

Lesson 8.2 Review and Assessment

1. Answers will vary, but should reflect an understanding of Figure 8.11.
2. *Weaning* is the gradual process of taking infants off the breast or bottle. Parents can gradually offer the new liquid as part of one feeding. Once the child consumes the new liquid for that feeding, the new liquid can be introduced into another feeding.
3. semiliquid, mushy foods, such as cereals, vegetables, and fruits

4. (List three:) Infants are not born with ability to swallow solids, do not have needed digestive enzymes, have an extrusion reflex until they are about 16 to 18 weeks old, do not need more nutrition than breast milk or formula until they reach 13 to 15 pounds, may have increased risk of developing chronic conditions from starting solids too soon.
5. Colic
6. (List two:) fussiness, rashes, upset stomachs, loose or watery stools
7. Answers will vary.
8. Infants push food out of their mouths because of the *extrusion reflex*, in which the tongue thrusts forward when touched. Infants are still developing the coordination of their muscles and do not voluntarily push food out of their mouths.

Lesson 8.3 Review and Assessment

1. Babies need clothing items that are comfortable, easy to put on and take off, suitable for weather and temperature, and safe.
2. length; weight; age (Note: length and weight can be in reverse order, but age must be the answer for the last blank.)
3. In a sponge bath, a child is not immersed in water. Rather, parents use a washcloth or sponge to wash the child's body.
4. gather materials, wash and dry hands, remove baby's clothing, place baby on changing pad, unfasten and dispose of soiled diaper, clean baby's genitals and buttocks, put on and fasten new diaper, redress baby, return the baby to a safe place, wash hands, wash and disinfect changing pad
5. 12 to 18
6. (List four:) Place the baby on his or her back on a firm surface to sleep. Do not use fluffy blankets, comforters, throws, stuffed toys, or pillows in the crib. Use a car seat for transport only. Make sure the baby does not get too warm while sleeping. Offer a pacifier for sleep. Avoid sharing a parent bed with a baby. Encourage adequate sleep. Attend regular well-baby checkups. Breast-feed the baby for at least seven months and preferably for one year. Keep the baby away from people who smoke and places where people smoke. Do not use breathing monitors and alarms or specialized products that claim to reduce the risk of SIDS unless recommended by a doctor.
7. tummy time
8. Answers will vary.

Chapter 9
Intellectual Development in the First Year

Caption Questions

Figure 9.1 Answers will vary. Surgeons can use localized symptoms (such as vision or hearing conditions) to predict where a brain injury has occurred.

Figure 9.6 Answers will vary. You would not know that objects stay the same. You might expect an object to change properties spontaneously.

Figure 9.8 Answers will vary. You might not understand why objects that have been thrown fall to the ground.

Figure 9.9 Answers will vary, but should reflect an understanding that infants learn cause and effect by observing events in their world.

Figure 9.11 The sounds that babies make train their brains to understand and produce language.

Figure 9.14 Answers will vary. The baby might be learning the physical properties of the toy or might throw the toy to witness cause and effect.

Figure 9.16 Answers will vary. Blocks are open-ended toys that can be used in many different activities. They can teach object constancy, spatial concepts, and even some number sense.

Figure 9.17 Answers will vary. The baby is learning that objects can fit inside larger objects.

Lesson 9.1 Review and Assessment

1. Babies come into the world using their sense organs. At birth they reflexively react to stimuli. The sense organs begin to mature. The brain begins to wire for sensory and motor experiences. Developing motor skills allows infants to engage in new sensory experiences. While taking in sensory and motor experiences, the brain begins wiring thinking and memory centers.
2. Stimuli
3. (List five:) acuity, contrast sensitivity, color sensitivity, eye movements and coordination, 3-D vision. Examples will vary.
4. Motor skills allow a baby to move toward interesting objects (and people) from which (or from whom) they will learn. Thinking skills involving space, weight, and depth mainly depend on motor experiences.
5. *Explicit memory* is conscious, intentional recollection. *Implicit memory* is unconscious awareness of past experiences.
6. making sense out of
7. Both Piaget and Vygotsky thought that the infant played a vital role in his or her own learning. The infant would seek out learning experiences, and it was the role of others to provide enriching environments for this learning. Piaget and Vygotsky differed in their beliefs in several ways. Piaget's theory focuses on children's *universal learning* (learning that occurs in all cultures, not specific to a culture) whereas Vygotsky's theory focuses on how children achieve *culture-specific understandings* (learn different skills and ideas in each culture). Piaget thought children should make their own discoveries in the enriched environment; Vygotsky believed that adults and older children should help infants and younger children make culture-specific discoveries (called *assisted learning*). Piaget's theory is developmental because it describes how children's abilities to learn change as they progress through the four stages; Vygotsky's theory is not stage-based, but is developmental in the sense that Vygotsky believed children's understandings changed over time.
8. Answers will vary. Students should see that babies exert great effort to make sense out of their world.

Lesson 9.2 Review and Assessment

1. Newborns can learn to remember an object for a short time, use different sucking techniques on the breast and pacifier, become aware of space around them, imitate the actions of others, differentiate between speech and other sounds, and exercise their reflexes.
2. (List three:) object constancy, object concept, object identity, object permanence, spatial concepts such as depth perception, number sense, object solidity, gravity
3. *Perceptual concepts* occur in the physical world because these concepts come through the senses. *Relationship concepts* occur in the mind. (We use thinking skills to both categorize and understand the cause-and-effect relationship between certain events.)
4. During the first six months, infants distinguish small differences in sounds. At 6 months of age, brain pruning begins, and infants only notice major differences in sounds. By 12 months of age, infants complete their auditory maps. Around 9 to 12 months of age, wiring in the brain's speech center also begins.
5. By listening to others talk to them, babies hear the *phonemes* (sounds) of the language(s) used; get the idea of "turn-taking" in conversations; note the boundaries of words; learn how to articulate sounds by not only listening to the sounds, but by also watching the mouths of speakers; hear inflections in language; and discover what words mean (passive vocabulary).
6. crying, cooing, marginal babbling, reduplication babbling, nonreduplicated babbling, protowords, real words
7. An eight-month-old begins to have goals and coordinate actions to achieve those goals. He or she repeats actions, babbles one-syllable sounds, understands about 36 words, and can follow one-step commands if adults also gesture.
8. Answers will vary.

Lesson 9.3 Review and Assessment

1. All infants, regardless of culture, are born with the internal drive (or are *preprogrammed*) to learn certain concepts and skills in holistic ways at approximately the same age. Examples of these concepts and skills include developing motor skills; learning language; understanding how objects work; seeking significant relationships for nurture, protection, and love; and learning ways to interact with others.
2. Learning in infancy is holistic; whereas, learning in older childhood happens in "bits and pieces."
3. (List five:) let babies try to solve problems on their own, let babies begin and expand most activities, watch for signs of babies' interests, repeat activities as much as possible, weave words and games into daily activities
4. newborns
5. Answers will vary.
6. (List four:) use complete short sentences, use nouns more than pronouns, use many adjectives, model language using gestures, expand single words, ask questions, describe baby's feelings, talk during daily routines
7. Answers will vary. Problem solving usually occurs during play, where children take learning in stride and continue to practice.

Chapter 10
Social-Emotional Development in the First Year

Caption Questions

Figure 10.3 Answers will vary, but should reflect an understanding of Galinsky's stages of parenting.

Figure 10.6 Babies' attachments to objects provide security and help them develop love for caregivers and other people.

Figure 10.7 At the time of departure, the transition between parent and caregiver should be as seamless and painless as possible. To soothe the baby, the caregiver can hold and rock the baby, speak in loving tones, assure the baby that the parent will return (if baby is old enough to understand somewhat), and once the baby is calm, engage him or her in an activity. The caregiver should never attempt to just distract a "grieving" baby right after the parent leaves. To the baby, this seems insensitive. Babies, like older people, need their "grief" acknowledged.

Figure 10.8 Infant rage is an instinctive response with no thought.

Figure 10.11 A caregiver can take some time to cool down or can pass a baby off to another caregiver until he or she no longer feels frustrated.

Figure 10.13 A caregiver should keep in mind that forming attachment takes time, but should also see a professional if he or she is seeing no progress.

Figure 10.14 Answers will vary. Parents can give babies toys and place them in spaces where they can observe the effects of their actions.

Lesson 10.1 Review and Assessment

1. disposition, social relations, emotions
2. Temperament
3. A *high-reactive infant* reacts to anything new with caution and can easily become physically agitated and distressed. A *low-reactive infant* tends to be sociable and bold (trying new challenges).
4. inadequate soothing, alarmist behavior, intrusive behavior
5. Parents send positive signals to the baby to encourage a response. Parents respond to a baby's signals of needs correctly and promptly. Examples will vary.
6. Attachment
7. (Examples will vary, but may include:) trying to stay close to the adult, following the adult, clinging to the adult, smiling at the adult, crying for the adult, calling to the adult, playing turn-taking games, showing preference for familiar caretakers, showing stranger anxiety

8. Love begins with attachment to caregivers and then to other children and objects. Fear arises from an infant's knowledge that he or she can be hurt. Anxiety usually stems from separation anxiety, the fear that a loved one will not return. Anger arises from a feeling caused by frustration that is directed or focused toward a certain person or object.
9. Very young infants have limited intellectual development. They have not yet become attached to certain people and may not know parents or caregivers are somewhere else.
10. Answers will vary. See Figure 10.9 in the textbook for a list of social-emotional developmental milestones children might achieve in the first year.
11. Answers will vary. Temperament accounts for many inherited aspects of personality.
12. Answers will vary. Brain development is essential to intellectual development in infants. Lack of attachment may stunt intellectual development by stunting brain growth.

Lesson 10.2 Review and Assessment

1. trust versus mistrust
2. Adults can show respect for a baby's temperament by adjusting their own behaviors to fit the baby's needs and interests rather than expecting the baby to fit their personality.
3. Co-regulating crying calms a baby and helps to teach the baby self-regulation. It also makes babies feel less alone or vulnerable.
4. Ignoring or rejecting a baby's signals leads to insecurity on the part of the baby. This can make a baby feel vulnerable or untrusting.
5. total number; strength
6. Adults can express unconditional love by meeting the baby's needs in a loving way. This is the most important asset in attachment. Adults can correctly, consistently, and promptly respond to a baby's signals of needs in a loving way. They can observe and learn to read a baby's signals, allow an infant to move and adjust proximity, minimize separation anxiety, and remember that attachment develops over time.
7. (List three:) hand regard, cause and effect, name recognition, recognition of body parts, mirror play, object possession
8. Answers will vary. Student should recognize that these tips encourage attachment, exhibit love, and respond to and learn to observe baby's signals of needs.

Chapter 11
Physical Development of Toddlers

Caption Questions

Figure 11.1 Answers will vary. Toddlers may become more independent upon learning to self-feed.

Figure 11.2 kidneys, ureters, urethra, bladder

Figure 11.4 Answers will vary. Adults hold their arms out while walking when they are having a hard time maintaining balance, such as while walking on a balance beam.

Figure 11.5 The number of contact points with a stable surface determines ease of balance. Thus, it is easier to balance oneself while standing on two feet (having two contact points) as opposed to standing on one foot. Unlike balancing while standing, climbing stairs means one foot is in the air during each step up or down. A person is literally balancing on one foot. A stair railing, baluster, or an adult's hand provides a second contact point while one foot is in the air; this greatly aids balance. These additional stable contact points also serve as handholds to prevent or recover from a near fall.

Figure 11.6 Answers will vary. Parents generally should not discourage their toddlers from throwing because throwing objects is part of toddlers' motor development.

Figure 11.11 Answers will vary. Most whole-grain foods are labeled as such in the grocery store. Nutrition Facts labels on food items provide a list of ingredients.

Figure 11.12 A proper balance of calories and physical activity is necessary to maintain a healthy weight. If a person consumes too many calories without getting enough physical activity, weight gain will result.

Figure 11.16 Answers will vary. Toddlers may climb on equipment, use slides, or use appropriate swings.

Lesson 11.1 Review and Assessment

1. myelin
2. heredity and other factors, such as physical activity level, health, and emotions
3. The toddler's head is about one-fifth of total height. A 24-month-old toddler's chest and abdomen measurements are about the same circumference, but by 30 months of age, the chest is larger than the abdomen. Body build becomes more apparent during the toddler years.
4. Ossification of bones continues, but is not complete; the hardness of bones varies throughout the body. The fontanels close. The spine changes from a C-shape to an S-shape, allowing the toddler to stand more upright. Between two and three years of age, toddlers will have all 20 deciduous teeth.
5. decrease
6. (List four:) walking, running, climbing, jumping, throwing, catching
7. Answers will vary. See Figure 11.8 in the text for a list of physical developmental milestones children might achieve during the toddler years.
8. A high synaptic density means that dendrites, axons, and neuron synapses are close together. The less space between neurons, the faster electrical signals can travel. As a result, learning occurs more quickly.

Lesson 11.2 Review and Assessment

1. table foods
2. One- to two-year-olds continue to be breast-fed or formula-fed. Complementary foods (solid foods) should constitute their diets more and more. During this time period, a child's diet is transitioning, and the toddler should be introduced to a variety of nutritious foods.
3. Two- to three-year-olds should begin eating according to MyPlate guidelines based on their age, height, weight, gender, and level of physical activity.
4. vegetables, fruits, grains, dairy, proteins
5. By eating small, healthy meals or snacks five or six times a day at regular intervals, toddlers can often learn to recognize when they are full or hungry.
6. food allergy
7. Answers will vary, but may include popcorn, hard candies, grapes, raisins, hot dogs sliced in rounds, or peanut butter.
8. Answers will vary.

Lesson 11.3 Review and Assessment

1. Self-dressing
2. Answers will vary. See Figure 11.14 in the textbook for a list of common clothing features.
3. Toddlers should wear shoes to protect their feet from cold, dampness, and harmful objects.
4. Answers will vary. See Figure 11.15 in the text for a list of water play learning experiences.
5. The timing of toilet learning varies from toddler to toddler. Many toddlers do not complete the toilet learning process quickly. Learning may take most of the toddler years and perhaps even longer to complete.
6. (List three:) eliminate or reduce time spent on all digital media to one hour or less daily; select play equipment designed for active movement, such as balls and pedal riding toys; plan a few movement activities, such as moving to music or navigating an obstacle course; take the toddler to a playground daily, if possible; plan activities, keeping in mind motor milestones; set an example of an active lifestyle and include toddlers in it
7. 12 to 14

8. Answers will vary. Toddlers who see other toddlers learning toileting may see toilet learning as more normal and may want to be like other toddlers and avoid embarrassment.

Chapter 11 Review and Assessment

9. **Evaluate.** Answers will vary. Habits that are formed during toddlerhood are likely to follow toddlers as they age. Sedentary behaviors during toddlerhood may lead to weight problems and a sedentary childhood. Lack of rest during the toddlers years can stunt physical development and may lead to sleeping problems later in life.

Chapter 12
Intellectual Development of Toddlers

Caption Questions

Figure 12.1 posture and coordination, binocular vision, vocabulary, attachment, control, coping with stress
Figure 12.3 Answers will vary. With imitation, children can begin learning behaviors even before they are fully able to understand them.
Figure 12.5 Toddler is observing color and size differences in toys.
Figure 12.6 Answers will vary. Caregivers can plan activities involving sound, movement, or visual changes.
Figure 12.7 Answers will vary. Toddlers may begin to learn what actions and features are associated with objects through observation or imitation.
Figure 12.10 Answers will vary. Adults tend to shape their language and vocabulary patterns depending on expectations they encounter.
Figure 12.11 Answers will vary, but may include visiting a new location or meeting new people.

Lesson 12.1 Review and Assessment

1. During toddlerhood, brain wiring is dense. Glial cells encourage myelination, which speeds up signal transmission and aids in learning. After toddlerhood, the brain will begin to prune connections, making toddlerhood a vital period for learning.
2. mental imagery
3. Younger toddlers solve problems through trial and error. Older toddlers solve problems by thinking through possible solutions.
4. working toward a goal, using imitation and pretense, and having a greater understanding of object permanence
5. Toddlers in substage 6 engage in thinking to achieve goals, thinking involved in imitation and pretense, and thinking involved in locating hidden objects.
6. *Collective symbolism* is Piaget's second level of pretense. At this level of pretense, a toddler uses one set of objects to represent another set of objects and pretends to do something that involves other people (parents) or objects (stuffed animals) in the play. Examples will vary.
7. Answers will vary.

Lesson 12.2 Review and Assessment

1. (List three:) distinguishing attributes of objects, noting cause and effect, using spatial relationships, solving problems, understanding quantity, using symbols. Examples will vary.
2. *Articulation* refers to a person's ability to pronounce words that can be understood by others.
3. Learning word meanings is difficult because children must link certain features with a name, and in many cases, objects with different names share some common features.
4. Vocabulary development is influenced by differences in environmental influence, bilingualism, word usage, and frequency of word usage.
5. Toddlers first use single words for the whole sentence. The meaning is carried in intonation, body language, or context. Older toddlers use two or more words for a sentence. Only main words are used at first, and the adult must mentally "fill in the gaps." Gradually the child will "fill in the gaps."

6. (List four:) hearing problems, lack of interest, low intellectual ability, male gender, minimal need for speech, nonstimulating environment, bilingualism, autism
7. A 17-month-old varies actions on objects to receive many results, notices attributes of objects, uses physical trial and error to solve problems, imitates others, looks for hidden objects in last place seen, points and vocalizes wants, points to named animals and objects in books, says 15 or more words, gestures when talking, and uses one-word "sentences."
8. Answers will vary. Scaffolding techniques, learning tools, and cultural environments will affect language development. The prevalence of bilingualism may also affect how quickly children learn language.

Lesson 12.3 Review and Assessment

1. Examples will vary.
2. (List four:) provide toddler with toys that have realistic purposes, initiate pretend play, play along when a toddler initiates the play and wants to include the adult, do not interrupt toddler, include play animals and objects during story time, encourage toddler to make representative sounds, encourage the toddler to "read" to an animal or object, initiate pretend play ideas
3. talking with toddlers, reading with toddlers, singing with toddlers
4. (List two:) talk with toddlers, name and describe objects and feelings, ask open-ended questions, add descriptive words, use clear and simple speech, make different sounds for toys, match sentences to child's level and pronounce words correctly
5. (List two:) how durable and washable the book is, how easy the pages are to turn, how colorful and simple the pictures are, how interesting the story line is to the toddler
6. Media content is vicarious, presents information in "bits and pieces," and tends to be passive. These qualities are not helpful for toddlers as they learn.
7. two
8. Answers will vary. Intonation communicates meaning and emotion and is used long after toddlerhood to clarify the meaning of a message.

Chapter 12 Review and Assessment

3. **Draw conclusions.** After a window of opportunity closes, learning is more difficult. A person can still learn, but it will be harder.
4. **Cause and effect.** The language of their world aids toddlers by refining and extending current knowledge, simplifying learning of difficult new concepts, and storing in memory what has been learned. Predictions will vary.
6. **Analyze.** Deferred imitation involves the ability to store a memory, later recall it, and then apply it to action.
7. **Evaluate**. Mikhail is exhibiting *collective symbolism*.

Chapter 13
Social-Emotional Development of Toddlers

Caption Questions

Figure 13.1 Answers will vary. Toddlers must see themselves as being separate from others (self-awareness) before they can have the desire for independence. No, because self-awareness only comes from seeing oneself as a separate person.

Figure 13.2 One aspect of self-awareness is *physical* self-awareness. How a person looks is a major aspect of physical self-awareness. (Later, children will learn more about other aspects of physical self-awareness, such as the efficiency of their motor skills.)

Figure 13.3 By imitating other children, toddlers learn how other children act and are able to conduct their own behavior accordingly.

Figure 13.5 Toddlers express love physically, by hugging, cuddling, or other displays of affection and by seeking to be near loved ones.

Figure 13.9 Answers will vary. Caregivers can explain to toddlers that they understand their emotions, but will not allow certain behaviors because of the consequences, such as by saying, "Biting hurts others." Caregivers can also confirm a similar feeling, such as by saying, "I'm hungry, too, but we must wait. We will all eat soon."

Figure 13.11 Answers will vary. Safe choices may include choices within parental limits (stated options) about what to eat, wear, or use for drawing or coloring.

Figure 13.12 Toddlers respond to what they can observe. If they cannot observe affection (if it is not directly expressed, such as working to provide for toddler needs), they are less likely to understand it.

Figure 13.14 Answers will vary. Plans can help reduce toddler stress and help the toddler know what to expect, such as limiting options (one bite-sized piece of candy) or forbidding something (not buying a toy) before the situation arises.

Lesson 13.1 Review and Assessment

1. Self-awareness during the toddler years involves seeing oneself as a unique person, recognizing oneself (as in a mirror), and developing early feelings of self-esteem. Adults can readily note toddlers' emerging self-awareness when toddlers express possession, identify their images as themselves, and are increasingly independent.
2. *autonomy versus shame and doubt*
3. As toddlers become more autonomous, parents transition from the *nurturing stage* of parenting to the *authority stage* of parenting. In the *authority stage* of parenting, the parenting role includes shaping a child's social behaviors.
4. In a secure attachment, a toddler sees a caregiver as a secure base from which to explore unfamiliar places and relationships. This leads to healthy development, including good mental health, throughout life. In an insecure attachment, a toddler does not have a trustworthy relationship with a caregiver; thus, the toddler feels confused or unworthy of care and feels vulnerable to trauma and outside influences, resulting in mental health vulnerabilities and lags in learning and exploration.
5. Insecure attachments are damaging to a child's self-esteem. If a child feels unworthy of protection or care and feels vulnerable, he or she is more likely to experience these feelings later in life.
6. Emotions become more intense—sometimes even overwhelming to toddlers, such as seen in tantrums. Due to the intensity of emotions and their increased motor skills, toddlers tend to express emotions physically more often than infants. On the other hand, toddlers' verbal skills enable them to express emotions verbally, too, if taught.
7. Answers will vary. See Figure 13.7 in the text for a list of social-emotional developmental milestones children might achieve during the toddler years.
8. Answers will vary.

Lesson 13.2 Review and Assessment

1. daily contact with his or her world
2. ensuring safety and encouraging efforts
3. Toddlers are learning to be independent and should be granted some freedoms. As they are learning autonomy, it is important that toddlers have self-assertion. At the same time, toddlers may take unsafe risks and also cannot self-regulate at all times; therefore, they need to be taught obedience by parents and caregivers.
4. premoral
5. Answers will vary.
6. Allow the tantrum to continue, because it is a form of release for the child. Stay nearby, but do not try to reason with the child. If a tantrum occurs in public, go to a quiet place, if possible, for the toddler to become calm.
7. (List three:) meeting toddlers' needs correctly, promptly, and consistently; helping the toddler feel nurtured and loved; aiding the toddler in control of emotions through co-regulation; helping older toddlers communicate needs and feelings by talking
8. Answers will vary.

Chapter 14
Physical Development of Preschoolers

Caption Questions

Figure 14.2 *Deciduous* is an adjective that means "falling off at a stage of development."

Figure 14.3 middle ear

Figure 14.4 Correct body rotation and weight shift provide most of the force needed to throw and thus lessens the need for force coming from the shoulder and arm. This frees the arm and hand to direct the object for accuracy of the throw and diminishes the risk of injury by using too much force from the shoulder and arm. (The core muscles of the trunk of the body are much stronger than the muscles of the shoulder and arm.)

Figure 14.9 Answers will vary. Siblings and adults can eat healthy foods and show that they enjoy those foods.

Figure 14.11 Answers will vary. Cutting foods into easy-to-eat and creative shapes can make mealtimes fun.

Figure 14.13 Answers will vary. Some features might include complicated lacing and zippers or buttons in the back. Also, fronts and backs of tee tops that look the same complicate dressing; that is, decorative features on the fronts make it easier to distinguish front from back of an outfit.

Figure 14.14 Answers will vary. Adults might create and post a schedule for their children somewhere, or compose a rhyme to help their children remember.

Lesson 14.1 Review and Assessment

1. functional specialization, greater myelination, pruning
2. The preschooler's heart rate slows and becomes steady and blood pressure increases. The preschooler uses adult-like chest breathing, but his or her air passages are small. The preschooler's stomach capacity is about one-half that of the adult, and the stomach is straight and upright, making it very easy to vomit. The preschooler's stomach lining is easily irritated by too much fiber or spices. The preschooler has more control over his or her bladder as compared with a toddler, but accidents still occur.
3. Preschoolers grow taller and gain weight, but their bodies become leaner because the fat-to-muscle ratio continues to decrease. Their body proportions begin to resemble those of an adult due to: growth in the lower face to accommodate the permanent teeth, which are replacing deciduous teeth; the lengthening of their trunks, causing their abdomens to protrude less; and the lengthening of the legs. Preschoolers' bones become harder and their muscles become larger and stronger.
4. Preschoolers develop *dynamic balance* (balance maintained while moving) and *static balance* (balance maintained while being still).
5. Answers will vary. Fine-motor skills include manipulation of objects with hands, using utensils, building block towers, drawing lines, doing buttons, cutting paper, combing hair, washing hands, lacing and tying shoes, and doing zippers.
6. Hand preference develops as children's brains specialize and myelination and pruning increase. Preschoolers' brains wire to designate tasks, including hand preference, to certain hemispheres of the brain. Usually, but not always, brain wiring for hand preference is on the opposite side of the brain from the preferred hand.
7. Answers will vary. See Figure 14.6 in the text for a list of physical developmental milestones children might achieve during the preschool years.
8. Answers will vary.

Lesson 14.2 Review and Assessment

1. nutrient-dense
2. Preschoolers need sufficient calories and nutrients to fuel their bodies' brain development, organ maturation, and skeletal growth. If preschoolers do not consume these needed nutrients, their growth may stall.
3. Forcing preschoolers to finish their meals may encourage children to eat even when they are not hungry. During this time, children are learning how to interpret their body's hunger signals, so this attitude is not helpful.

4. Answers will vary.
5. Answers will vary. Strategies include offering variety in foods, offering foods in a pleasant atmosphere, encouraging children to eat foods they like, not using food as a threat or reward, modeling healthy eating habits, and incorporating foods into celebrations.
6. Answers will vary. Strategies include considering the preschoolers' senses, aiming for visual appeal, keeping foods separate, serving foods at appropriate temperature, varying methods of preparation, offering new foods in small amounts, and preparing easy-to-eat foods.
7. Preschoolers' fine-motor skills are still developing. Handling eating utensils requires advanced fine-motor skills not yet possessed by the preschooler; thus, eating can be very messy still.
8. Answers will vary.

Lesson 14.3 Review and Assessment

1. personality
2. (List four:) large openings, especially for slipover garments; easy-to-recognize fronts and backs of garments, such as labels, threads, or tape sewn inside; front rather than back openings, such as front buttons and attached belts that hook in front; elastic in waistbands and sleeves (at wrist); easy-to-work fasteners, such as zippers with large pull tabs; shoes with self-adhesive straps
3. Answers will vary, but should reflect content in Lesson 14.3.
4. enuresis
5. (List four:) inherited problems, not being breast-fed for three or more months in infancy, urinary tract problems, deep sleeping; constipation causing pressure on the bladder, too much fluid in the evening hours, fear of getting up in the dark
6. twice
7. 11 to 13
8. Answers will vary.

Chapter 14 Review and Assessment

7. **Determine.** Haneul should try not to keep her son up and should make sure Hwan follows the same bedtime routine each night. A better time to talk with her son might be in the morning before school. If Haneul must wake Hwan up after work, she should wake him up at the same time on the same days each week.

Chapter 15
Intellectual Development of Preschoolers

Caption Questions

Figure 15.3 Answers will vary. Mental images can influence how people perceive objects and ideas even into the teen and adult years.

Figure 15.7 The child would say the quantity changes. The preschooler cannot reason that the quantity remains the same because no liquid was added or taken away. The needed logic for this thought does not usually develop until the very late preschool or school-age years.

Figure 15.8 Answers will vary. Preschoolers may not comprehend intermediate steps in physical changes they observe.

Figure 15.10 Preschoolers might focus on the apples, the comma, the banana, the scissors, the buttons, or the eraser.

Figure 15.11 Unless the child uses an object to justify dangerous actions, then no, a caregiver need not worry. Assigning actions to inanimate objects is a normal step in intellectual development.

Figure 15.12 Sorting is based on an object's attributes, whereas arranging shapes into a graphic collection is based on what looks best to the preschooler.

Figure 15.14 The preschooler will know where each piece of equipment is located even if not seen from the gate or other locations in the playground. He will also know the location of each play activity on the play structure and will take as direct of a route as the structure layout allows in moving to his favorite activity. Answers will vary for the second question.

Figure 15.18 Without an understanding of the one-to-one principle, numerals would be essentially meaningless. For example, if the child assigned two numerals to one object, then using numerals would not be useful for counting.

Figure 15.19 Adults can rely more on children's abilities to express the needs they want met.

Figure 15.28 The preschooler may learn that turning on the faucet will cause water to run, and that water running over his hands will wash off the soap.

Figure 15.30 masks; capes

Figure 15.32 Answers will vary. Adults can limit screen time and plan real-world activities.

Lesson 15.1 Review and Assessment

1. separate actions from events and separate thought from action
2. pretend play, mental images, drawing, language, memory
3. Answers will vary.
4. *Episodic memory* is the memory of personal experiences and events. Episodic memories include the emotion and the context of the event.
5. Children in the preconceptual substage begin to develop and understand some concepts. Many concepts, however, are still incomplete or illogical in the preschooler's mind. Children in the intuitive substage experience a brain growth spurt and are able to solve problems using intuition.
6. *egocentrism*—the belief that everyone sees the same as the child; *centration*—seeing one part instead of all parts; *problems with transformations and reversibility*—inability to note and reverse changes; *transductive reasoning*—the linking of events without logic; *problems with cause-and-effect reasoning*—inability to understand nonobservable and even some observable cause-and-effect relationships
7. pretend play props, language, imitation
8. Answers will vary.

Lesson 15.2 Review and Assessment

1. centration
2. animism, artificialism, finalism
3. Answers will vary.
4. egocentric speech
5. Achieving total mastery means that children can articulate sounds in different positions within words.
6. Three-year-olds understand some grammar rules, but apply these rules to all cases, including exceptions to some rules, which result in grammatical errors. They do not use correct word order for questions and make mistakes when using negatives, such as using double negatives. Four- and five-year-old children speak in longer, more complex sentences. They lengthen sentences by using clauses, conjunctions, and prepositions. They may still find word order confusing.
7. Answers will vary. See Figure 15.23 in the text for a list of intellectual developmental milestones children might achieve during the preschool years.
8. Answers will vary. Preschoolers comprehend observable concepts and ideas more easily than nonobservable concepts and ideas.

Lesson 15.3 Review and Assessment

1. physical movement
2. (List four:) help preschoolers understand stories and happenings before asking them to recall; use leading questions and prompting; ask the child to repeat the directions before starting on a task; use photos to remind a child about people, places, or events that are not regularly seen; use prompting photos to help a child recall specific events; reread stories as often as requested; frequently repeat safety rules and other concepts the child is learning

3. Answers will vary.
4. in pretend play and in art
5. (List three:) make language and literacy a part of all activities; read to children every day; after reading a book, talk about story plots with the preschooler by asking more comprehension questions; monitor television viewing; provide opportunities for preschoolers to observe adults reading and writing
6. *Reading readiness* is a belief that children should be formally taught reading and writing when developmentally ready for instruction. *Emergent literacy* is defined by theorists as the idea that all aspects of literacy, including reading and writing, are developmental and acquired in interactive ways, beginning in infancy as children learn to understand spoken words.
7. (List four:) screen time, effect, purpose, type, content, interactiveness, inclusiveness
8. Answers will vary. Fostering logical thinking during the preschool years will help prepare children for grasping these concepts later in life.

Chapter 16
Social-Emotional Development of Preschoolers

Caption Questions

Figure 16.6 Adults should reassure children of their love, even if they do not perform the task for the child. If the child needs help, they should offer help.

Figure 16.11 The preschooler is learning that mowing is a part of the male gender role.

Figure 16.12 The child's favorite foods are apples and potatoes. The child's favorite toy is the wolverine toy.

Figure 16.15 Within-context teaching is always more effective than teaching out of the context of use. Answers will vary for the second question.

Lesson 16.1 Review and Assessment

1. Children learn responsibility by taking part in the routines of their world in real and important ways. For example, preschoolers show responsibility by doing household tasks, such as cleaning and helping adults cook. They may also help with routine tasks in a child care or preschool center.
2. *Sex typing* is the process by which a person adopts the attitudes and behaviors considered culturally appropriate for his or her gender.
3. *Moral judgment and reasoning* is the ability to perceive an action as right or wrong. *Moral character* is acting in accordance with what is perceived as morally right. *Moral emotions* are a person's reactions to acceptable and unacceptable behaviors.
4. self-recognition, self-definition, self-esteem, self-correction
5. Taking initiative can lead to many failures, and if children are made to feel bad for failures, they may adopt a sense of guilt.
6. Preschool children have a rather self-centered view of friendships. They see friends as people who play with them, help them, and share their toys.
7. Answers will vary.
8. Answers will vary. See Figure 16.8 in the text for a list of social-emotional developmental milestones children might achieve during the preschool years.
9. Answers will vary. Developmental stress, and to some extent, environmental stress are both natural. Developmental stress is part of a child's growth and development. Environmental stress stems from the child's physical and social environments, such as storms or street violence. Tolerable, short-term stress is not necessarily negative for children.

Lesson 16.2 Review and Assessment

1. (List four:) decide which tasks are safe and within children's grasps; make physical conditions amenable; communicate plans and expectations clearly; do not expect perfection; incorporate tasks into games; respect children's priorities; reward children for tasks completed
2. *Shame* is egocentric and involves a loss or threat of a loss to a child's basic security. It crushes a young child's curiosity, exuberance, and desire for autonomy. Shaming does not model respect so it erodes the young child's self-esteem.
3. (List three:) expect preschoolers to exhibit never-ending curiosity, talk often and loudly, and move all the time; understand that preschoolers' initiatives can sometimes lead them to actions that are dangerous or beyond their abilities; give children some freedom to try; use positive statements to acknowledge children when they take initiative; set limits to help preschoolers develop appropriate initiative
4. (List four:) don't make children share any more than an adult would be expected to share; resolve conflicts for younger preschoolers; show older preschoolers how to resolve their own conflicts; teach children how to stand up for themselves without being aggressive; model concern for the hurt child instead of shaming the child who has done wrong; teach children to get adult help if needed
5. *Anger* is a feeling caused by frustration. *Aggression* is an attempt to hurt someone.
6. Answers will vary.
7. (List two:) identify the source of the stress; find positive ways to encourage and distract one's self; express emotions constructively; avoid angry or frustrated outbursts; seek professional help, if needed
8. Answers will vary, but should reflect an understanding that children learn to manage emotions and behaviors by watching and emulating adults.

Chapter 16 Review and Assessment

5. **Compare and contrast.** Children become less dependent on adults during the preschool years as compared with earlier years as they rely more on peers and friends. Adults should accept this change, but should still provide support and love for their children.
7. **Analyze.** Altruistic behaviors lay the groundwork for caring and compassion later in life. Adults can foster these behaviors by being a model of kindness, using supportive rather than punishing discipline to help the child develop moral reasoning skills, helping children "read" others' emotions, pointing out the consequences of negative actions, being supportive of the person who is harmed rather than giving attention to the aggressor, choosing children's media that is healthy and prosocial, allowing children to help with projects for those in need or to give some of their money to charity, and acknowledging children for their altruistic behaviors.
8. **Draw conclusions.** If they do not learn to label and discuss their feelings, children may repress their feelings, which can lead to more intense feelings and to psychological problems.

Chapter 17
Physical Development of School-Age Children

Caption Questions

Figure 17.3 Children's jaws lengthen as permanent teeth erupt. Children's waists and heads begin to look more in proportion to their bodies, their trunks grow longer and wider, and their arms and legs grow longer.

Figure 17.4 Permanent teeth are harder and less sharp than deciduous teeth and are intended to last a lifetime.

Figure 17.5 The development of fine-motor skills helps children do arts and crafts, build models, play musical instruments, dress themselves, use digital devices, and perform other tasks that require fine-motor precision.

Figure 17.6 Answers will vary.

Figure 17.8 Parents can increase the likelihood of their child eating his or her lunch by including the child in planning, shopping for, and preparing lunches.

Figure 17.9 Answers will vary. Ways to involve children in planning healthful meals may include reviewing the MyPlate daily food plans together, shopping for groceries with children, and involving children in food preparation.

Figure 17.11 Physical inactivity, family history of overweight or obesity, lack of sleep, and depression or other emotional issues are factors that may contribute to overweight and obesity in children.

Figure 17.13 Answers will vary. Some influences might be purpose of outfit (party, school, physical activities), color and fabric design, style, fit, and upkeep of garment.

Figure 17.14 Answers will vary. Adults can stress the importance of proper dental health, lead by example, and check to make sure children have completed their dental-care routines daily.

Figure 17.15 Answers will vary. Families can do activities such as running, swimming, cycling, and skiing.

Lesson 17.1 Review and Assessment

1. specialized
2. Puberty begins in the brain, where the hypothalamus releases GnRH, gonadotropin releasing hormone, into the endocrine system. GnRH causes the brain's pituitary gland to release two more hormones, follicle-stimulating hormone and luteinizing hormone. These hormones cause the ovaries in females and the testes in males to produce sex hormones (estrogen and testosterone, respectively), which are needed for puberty changes in girls and boys.
3. A *growth spurt* is a period of rapid growth that heralds pubescence. At 10 or 11 years of age, many girls have growth spurts, making them taller than boys until the early teen years. The age at which a child's growth spurt occurs will affect final adult height.
4. six-year molars
5. Children's muscles are trying to catch up with skeletal size.
6. *reaction time*—the time required to respond to a stimulus, such as a thrown ball; *precision*—the ability to perform motor skills accurately; *speed and strength*; *flexibility*—the ability to move, bend, and stretch easily
7. Answers will vary. See Figure 17.7 in the text for a list of physical developmental milestones children might achieve during the school-age years.
8. Answers will vary.

Lesson 17.2 Review and Assessment

1. When children are able to participate in planning and preparing their meals, they are more likely to eat them.
2. A healthful eating plan focuses on colorful fruits and vegetables, lean protein options, low-fat dairy products, and whole grains.
3. *Junk foods* are foods that are high in calories and low in nutrition. Junk foods diminish children's appetites for nourishing foods and provide calories, but not nutrients.
4. *Overnutrition* is the ongoing intake of more calories than is needed for good health. *Undernutrition* occurs when some food is being eaten, but is continuously lacking one or more nutrients required to meet the body's needs. *Malnutrition* describes diets that supply an excess, shortage, or imbalance of calories or one or more nutrients.
5. Overweight and obesity increase a person's risk for high blood pressure, type 2 diabetes, problems with weight-bearing joints (hips, knees, and ankles), and possibly some cancers. Obesity also results in serious social problems beginning as early as the school-age years. This, in turn, affects self-esteem and even academic performance.
6. (List three:) inadequate nutrition, heredity, altered bodily responses to foods (such as not absorbing certain nutrients), illness, long-term mental stress, eating disorders
7. (List five:) weight loss, skipped meals, baggy clothes, obsessive exercising, hoarding food, crankiness, difficulty concentrating
8. Answers will vary. Just because children receive many calories does not mean they are receiving needed nutrients for physical health.

Lesson 17.3 Review and Assessment

1. growth features, durability, some self-dressing features
2. Due to peer pressure, many school-age children choose clothes that will enable them to fit in with a peer group.
3. As children approach puberty, their bodies secrete pheromones through sweat. The pheromones in the sweat cause body odor through contact with bacteria. Bacteria are removed through body hygiene and clean clothing.
4. Adults can help children engage in competitive sports and can involve children in family physical activities.
5. 10 to 11
6. (List four:) inability to concentrate, which affects both learning ability and quality of work; impaired memory; weakened coping skills, behavioral problems, and low self-esteem; disruption in hormones affecting appetite and food choices; inability to use executive functions to achieve goals; increased chance of mental health problems, such as depression and anxiety
7. (List three:) setting a regular bedtime for each day of the week; getting out in the morning light for a few minutes each day; taking all digital devices out of a child's bedroom; planning a wind-down time of 30 to 60 minutes before bedtime; taking a child to be checked for sleep, respiratory, and emotional disorders if poor sleep habits persist
8. Answers will vary.

Chapter 18
Intellectual Development of School-Age Children

Caption Questions

Figure 18.1 The prefrontal cortex is involved in logical thinking, forming judgments, memory, weighing consequences, making decisions, and controlling impulses and emotions. Answers will vary for the second question.

Figure 18.2 Answers will vary, but may include reading, following a story, or creating artwork.

Figure 18.6 Answers will vary, but should reflect an understanding of reversals.

Figure 18.7 Adults can plan challenging activities while keeping in mind a child's development and ability to learn.

Figure 18.9 Answers will vary, but may include bodily/kinesthetic, naturalist, and visual/spatial intelligences.

Figure 18.10 Answers will vary. Other cognitive advances might include improvements in attention, memory, and fine-motor skills involved in playing a musical instrument.

Figure 18.11 Preschool children were able to understand only observable cause-and-effect relationships.

Figure 18.12 Answers will vary. Students progress as they build on the number and mathematical concepts they have already learned.

Figure 18.15 Treating a child with extra patience during this time will help the child adjust and feel confident about his or her abilities. The start of school is a poor time to add new lessons or tasks, such as music lessons or a new pet, to a child's life.

Figure 18.21 Answers will vary. Other activities might include dance classes, music lessons, team sports, or art classes.

Figure 18.22 Adults can save money by borrowing or renting expensive items.

Lesson 18.1 Review and Assessment

1. Wiring in the prefrontal cortex enables school-age children to think logically and engage in higher cognitive functions. However, the wiring will continue through the early adult years, so school-age children may still have trouble with making some decisions, forming judgments, and weighing consequences. Pruning makes for more efficient thinking, but most pruning in this area occurs after the school-age years. The entire prefrontal cortex is considered mature around 25 years of age.
2. rehearsing, organizing information, using visual and verbal aids

3. Children enter the concrete operational stage around seven years of age. In this stage, they gradually become less perceptual in their thinking and begin to think logically, but logic is based on their past experiences. In the formal operational stage, children are able to reason more abstractly, but this stage is not always achieved in the school-age years.
4. Answers will vary.
5. Vygotsky saw intellectual development as less dependent on brain development (*cognitive stage*) and more dependent on children's minds being stretched within their ZPDs. He also emphasized the importance of collaboration for learning.
6. Piaget felt that language *reflected* learning. On the other hand, Vygotsky saw language *as a way of* learning.
7. verbal/linguistic, logical/mathematical, bodily/kinesthetic, visual/spatial, musical/rhythmic, naturalist, interpersonal, intrapersonal, existential
8. Answers will vary.

Lesson 18.2 Review and Assessment

1. School-age children's sensory organs and brains have matured enough that they can process sensory stimuli very accurately and can understand how phenomena they did not act upon themselves can be affected by other phenomena, such as weather.
2. Answers will vary.
3. *Culture-specific knowledge* is culturally relevant knowledge that one learns by being told or shown. Culture-specific knowledge encompasses much of what children learn in school.
4. Around six or seven years of age, children's speech becomes more social. School-age children begin to see language as a way of communicating and want to talk with friends and adults.
5. When children *code-switch*, they change their usage of grammar and even vocabulary when communicating with different cultural and age groups.
6. The same area of the brain that is used for recognizing objects is also used to read. Young children begin to read by forming mental pictures (called *mental mapping*) of the words they see in their environments. They treat letters as three-dimensional objects. Children gradually change from mental mapping to seeing the relationships between letters and sounds because mental mapping would overtax the brain.
7. Answers will vary. See Figure 18.14 in the text for a list of intellectual developmental milestones children might achieve during the school-age years.
8. Answers will vary.

Lesson 18.3 Review and Assessment

1. (List three:) read and encourage children to read books about starting school; make transportation plans clear to children; help children view school attendance as a natural course of events; say good-byes at the bus stop, on the schoolyard, or at the classroom door; meet the bus or pick up children on time; show a strong interest in children's reports about their school days
2. (List two:) visit the school with the child beforehand; attend orientation meetings; purchase the correct supplies and uniforms; adjust home routines, such as bedtime, to work with the new school schedule; explain to the child that each teacher will have different expectations and classroom policies; encourage the child to attend clubs for making friends; have honest talks with the child about teasing and bullying behaviors; ask open-ended questions
3. reinforcing school tasks, strengthening executive functions, being a school advocate
4. Answers will vary. See Figure 18.20 in the text for examples of enrichment activities for each of the multiple intelligences.
5. (List four:) fit, schedule, cost, competition, safety
6. Adults can provide digital devices at appropriate times and protect children from media-related risks.
7. A *filtering program* is an application designed to prevent children from accessing inappropriate content. This type of program protects children when using electronic media.
8. Answers will vary.

Chapter 19
Social-Emotional Development of School-Age Children

Caption Questions

Figure 19.6 Answers will vary, but may include cleaning a room, washing dishes, organizing books, or gardening.

Figure 19.9 Examples will vary, but may include volunteering at food pantries, helping efforts to clean the environment, or fund-raising for social causes.

Figure 19.13 Examples will vary, but should reflect an understanding that the act involves selflessly doing for others without expecting anything in return.

Figure 19.14 Answers will vary. Love and support from a caregiver should be unconditional. On the other hand, acknowledgement from a teacher is conditional on some success.

Lesson 19.1 Review and Assessment

1. gender schools
2. *Conventional morality* is one of Kohlberg's levels of moral reasoning. School-age children are at this level. The level involves interpersonal conformity and maintenance of the social order. Many teens and adults remain at this level of moral reasoning.
3. Children are just coming to understand which domains of self-definition are deemed most important by their cultures.
4. Erikson's fourth stage of personality development is called *industry versus inferiority.* This stage involves a struggle between children's striving to become competent members of society and children's feelings of incompetence and low self-esteem.
5. Belonging to a peer group gives children feelings of sharing, loyalty, and security. Peer groups provide emotional support, reinforce self-esteem, help children learn how to get along with others, and teach children self-control.
6. home life, school life, peer relations, internal stress
7. Answers will vary. See Figure 19.11 in the text for a list of social-emotional developmental milestones children might achieve during the school-age years.
8. Answers will vary, but should reflect an understanding that the ways in which school-age children learn to express their emotions will likely affect their abilities to establish healthy relationships with others. An inability to express emotions in socially acceptable ways may lead to the development of serious emotional problems and have a negative effect on mental health.

Lesson 19.2 Review and Assessment

1. Chores help teach children skills and aid them in developing a work ethic.
2. (List four:) Adults can teach children to respect others; show responsibility; follow established limits; behave acceptably; express remorse for misdeeds; and think for themselves before acting on moral issues.
3. abilities; faults
4. (List two:) encourage children to participate in activities at school and in the community, plan family activities, suggest hobbies
5. keep family communication open; teach morals and values; balance dependence with independence
6. (List four:) modeling emotional control, normalizing emotions, respecting others, using loving discipline, suggesting indirect outlets, teaching skills
7. (List two:) watch and listen for signs of stress, give children constant love and support, provide a stable home environment, monitor children's habits, seek to understand causes of misbehaviors, avoid unrealistic expectations, keep communication open, talk with a mental health professional if necessary
8. Answers will vary. School-age children are learning independence and are more reliant on their peers. Encouraging these relationships will give children a sense of security and belonging.

Chapter 20
Encouraging Children's Play Experiences

Caption Questions

Figure 20.2 Young children may not be capable of grasping the concepts and skills needed to play at the older child's level.

Figure 20.4 Answers will vary, but may include hand puppets, stringing beads, playing games, or playing an instrument.

Figure 20.9 Answers will vary, but may include sand tables and beaches.

Figure 20.12 Answers will vary. Young children may be primarily manipulating the tools of art, rather than working in the representation stage. A child may not really be drawing an object or person that can be identified. Furthermore, children expect adults to know what they have drawn and may be hurt if an adult asks.

Figure 20.13 Answers will vary. Most preschool children have not found their singing voice. They mainly "sing" by talking in a sing-song way. Until children can accurately hear pitch and adjust their vocal cords to match the sound they hear, they cannot sing in unison. References to the high, sweet voices of children usually refer to children nine or ten years of age. For the most part, preschoolers are inept at singing in unison. Music teachers of preschoolers may jokingly say if you have 20 preschoolers singing together, you have 20 parts. Of course, some vocally gifted preschoolers may sing more like a much older child or even an adult.

Lesson 20.1 Review and Assessment

1. *practice play* (or *sensory motor play*)—corresponds to the sensorimotor stage; *symbolic play*—corresponds to the preoperational stage; *rule play*—corresponds to the concrete operational stage
2. *Associative play* occurs during the preschool and early school-age years. It involves two or more children playing at a common activity, but their activities are not organized in terms of goals and roles. *Cooperative play* occurs during the late school-age years. It involves two or more children sharing common goals and playing complementary roles.
3. *Active-physical play* is a type of play in which children use their gross-motor skills. It primarily affects physical development. Active-physical play also aids spatial and physical knowledge concepts.
4. Manipulative-constructive play
5. (List three:) planning, problem solving, decision making, leadership, creativity, memory, language, emotional expression
6. (List four:) language games (such as puns), chess, object puzzles, word problems, checkers
7. (List two:) allowing freedom for children to explore and play, modeling ideas or adding materials, playing along in a supportive role with children's pretend play, allowing the child to take the lead, explaining new concepts, displaying positive attitudes toward play, providing toys that children will like
8. Answers will vary. Research shows that the benefits of play are limitless and involve all domains of child development. Children play based on what they understand. If encouraged, they will go beyond their understanding to experiment and invent.

Lesson 20.2 Review and Assessment

1. (List five:) spatial concepts, classification, seriation, number concepts, shape concepts, physics concepts, social studies concepts, art concepts, language and literacy concepts
2. Adults set the stage for sand play by providing equipment and accessories. Adults can scaffold children's learning by asking questions, such as "What do you think would happen if you sprinkled more sand on top?" or "What shape are you making with that sand?" Finally, adults can show appreciation for children's sand play through photos, videos, drawings, and children's stories.
3. Adults help children more directly during cooking activities. They provide more guidance and supervision and ensure that cooking tasks are safe and developmentally appropriate.
4. representation stage

5. (List two:) introducing children to music activities suited to their interests, providing an environment that is rich in sound, modeling enthusiasm and enjoyment, listening to and praising children's musical attempts
6. Answers will vary, but may include block building, sand play, water play, or cooking activities. Answers should reflect an understanding that science can be taught in many ways.
7. Literature activities strengthen the adult-child relationship. They also help children better understand themselves.
8. No, water play does *not* teach scientific concepts to children who cannot yet think logically. The brain is not ready for logical concepts until the late preschool or early school-age years. Water play can, however, lay foundations for these concepts.

Chapter 21
Protecting Children's Physical Health and Safety

Caption Questions

Figure 21.2 Answers will vary. Parents' experience influences how easily parents identify health problems or concerns. It also influences how confident parents feel in meeting their children's needs.

Figure 21.5 No, casseroles need to be cooked to an internal temperature of 165° F.

Figure 21.12 Answers will vary. Bacteria on unwashed stuffed toys can cause infections. Loose parts, such as buttons or decorations, may present a choking hazard.

Figure 21.14 Answers will vary. Caregivers can encourage play and exploration activities while setting reasonable safety limits.

Figure 21.16 Young children may have difficulties chewing or swallowing medications. They may also have trouble drinking from a small cup or spoon.

Figure 21.18 Answers will vary. An adult might explain to the child that the bandage will help the cut heal. For older children, one might say that our skin protects our body from germs; when our skin is hurt, a bandage works like our skin to protect us. Using an attractive adhesive bandage that the child will like may also help the child keep the bandage on.

Figure 21.21 Professionals trained in administering emergency help will be the most qualified to handle an emergency. No matter how well you know emergency procedures, you should always call for emergency help so that professionals can take over.

Lesson 21.1 Review and Assessment

1. Wet hands with water and apply soap. Rub soap between hands, on backs of hands, between fingers, and under fingernails. Scrub lathered hands for at least 20 seconds. Rinse hands thoroughly. Dry hands with a clean towel or air dry.
2. to keep children well
3. (List two:) hearing, vision, certain special needs, some infections and diseases
4. *Immunization* is a process that protects children and adults from certain serious diseases. *Vaccines* are substances used to produce immunity. *Vaccination* is the process of administering vaccines through injections, oral medications, or sprays.
5. *Communicable diseases* are diseases that can be transmitted from an object to an individual or between individuals. *Noncommunicable diseases* are diseases that cannot be transmitted between an object and an individual or between individuals.
6. Keep the food preparation area clean to avoid the spread of harmful bacteria. Wash utensils, dishes, and preparation supplies thoroughly with soap and water to prevent cross-contamination. Ensure that all meats and egg dishes are cooked to the proper temperatures. Store foods safely before preparation and store leftovers safely after preparation. Keep foods at recommended temperatures. Return foods on recall and notify your physician if these foods were eaten prior to knowledge of recall.

7. Answers will vary. The cause of *type 1 diabetes* is mainly genetic, but other unknown factors may contribute as well. Causes of *type 2 diabetes* are genetic and lifestyle related. Genetic factors include a person's ethnicity and age. Lifestyle-related factors include poor diet and lack of physical activity. *Epilepsy*, which often begins in childhood, may be caused by defective genes or traced to accidents, diseases with high fevers, or medical trauma. An *allergy* is caused by a type of allergen, such as milk, an insect bite, or dust. Eighty-five percent of *asthma* cases are triggered by allergens. Asthma can be aggravated by a virus, secondhand smoke, cold or dry air, and exercise.
8. Answers will vary. In addition to what the child thinks of the person, parents need to assess prospective medical professionals. To do this, parents often ask themselves the following questions: Is the medical professional covered by their insurance? Does the medical professional answer questions clearly and calmly? Is he or she open to questions and emergency calls? Are office hours and location accessible?

Lesson 21.2 Review and Assessment

1. (List two from each stage shown in Figure 21.8 of the text.)
2. Childproofing
3. Answers will vary, but students may refer to Figure 21.9 and text examples in their answers.
4. Answers will vary, but students may refer to Figure 21.10 and text examples in their answers.
5. A *safety recall* is a notice by a product manufacturer stating a product has been found to be unsafe. Adults should pay attention because recalls indicate they must take action (take the item back or purchase extra parts) to ensure children's safety.
6. (List five:) size should be larger than the child's two fists; nonbreakable; no sharp edges or points; nontoxic; no long cords or strings; nonflammable, flame retardant, or flame resistant; washable and hygienic materials; no broken or uninflated balloons; no marbles or balls smaller than 1¾ inches in diameter; no small parts; no detachable clothing on dolls or stuffed animals; no springs or hinges; sounds at acceptable levels
7. (List three:) Be a model for children. Explain the boundaries of play. Couple warnings with reasons. Insist on obedience. Practice safety measures with children.
8. Answers will vary. Adequate supervision is not being preoccupied. It includes an adult devoting his or her full attention to the child. Adequate supervision also includes taking into account the child's development and anticipating possible hazards.

Lesson 21.3 Review and Assessment

1. (List four from Figure 21.15 in the text.)
2. Incorrect dosages may deliver too little medication and hinder infections from clearing up. Too much medication may poison the child.
3. *Shock* is a condition in which the heartbeat and breathing slow. If a child goes into shock while awaiting medical help, lay the child on his or her back and elevate the child's legs. Keep the child warm until medical help arrives.
4. (Choose one:) *First-degree burn:* Run cold water over affected area 15 to 20 minutes. Dry area and keep it clean. Cover the burn with a clean dressing. *Second-degree burn:* Run cold water over affected area 15 to 20 minutes. Dry area and keep it clean. Cover the burn with a clean dressing. If the second-degree burn is deep or large, seek emergency medical attention immediately. *Third-degree burn:* Seek emergency medical attention immediately. Do *not* try to clean a severe burn. Observe the child for signs of shock and respond accordingly. When treating a burn, it is *not* recommended that you use ointments or apply ice directly to the burn.
5. There is no way of knowing the severity of the injury without examination by a medical professional.
6. Adults should take immediate action and call a hospital or poison control center.
7. ARC and AHA
8. Answers will vary, but should reflect an understanding of content in Lesson 21.3.

Chapter 22
Handling Family-Life Challenges

Caption Questions

Figure 22.1 Yes, peer relations are more important for older children than for younger children. As children grow older, they interact more with other children and depend on others more for the formation of their self-concepts.

Figure 22.6 Answers will vary. Children become more expressive as they grow older and develop more interests. These interests can be reflected in their personal space.

Figure 22.12 Answers will vary. Repeated traumatic experiences put children at greater risk for toxic stress and some anxiety disorders. The risks from repeated experiences are considered exponential; that is, two experiences more than double the risks, and so on.

Figure 22.16 lags in attachment, self-regulation, affiliation, awareness, tolerance, and respect

Figure 22.18 Answers will vary, but may include a stable environment, ability to comfort children, and resources to meet children's needs.

Figure 22.19 Children need to be physically healthy to cope with the other aspects of their neglect or abuse. Physical health is a fundamental need according to Maslow's hierarchy of needs.

Lesson 22.1 Review and Assessment

1. (List two:) providing as much stability as possible, allowing the child to carry a favorite toy or photo, helping the child settle into new routines, providing books or stories that talk about moving, encouraging children to act out a move in play, helping children catch up in new classes (with workbooks or handouts), encouraging children to connect with new friends (through referral to tutoring or clubs)
2. Answers will vary, but students should refer to Figure 22.2 in their answers.
3. (List three:) limiting children's contact with those who have addictions, assuring children that the addiction is not their fault, protecting children from the hurtful words or actions of people who have addictions, ensuring that the person with the addiction is receiving help
4. (List two:) being understanding, not reacting harshly if children act out or express their emotions inappropriately, encouraging emotional expression, listening carefully, reducing other stressors, reminding children that adults love them, noting any especially severe or dangerous reactions that might require professional help
5. Children cannot understand these complex issues, and because they cannot help solve the problems of marriage, they should not be burdened with them. Instead, both parents should explain and repeat the message that the divorce is not the child's fault and that both parents still love the child.
6. shock and denial, anger, bargaining, depression, and acceptance
7. *Resilience* is the ability to recover from stressful situations. (List two inner qualities:) easy temperaments; affectionate and engaging personalities, vigorous, assertive, autonomous, healthy self-concept, able to distance themselves from their problems, believe they can beat the odds; communicate easily
8. Answers will vary.

Lesson 22.2 Review and Assessment

1. *Child neglect* is the failure of an adult to provide for a child's basic needs and supervision. *Child abuse* refers to an intentional act committed by an adult that harms or threatens to harm a child's well-being.
2. *physical neglect*—endangering a child's health or safety by failing to provide basic needs (such as food, clothing, and shelter) and supervision; *educational neglect*—failure to conform to state legal requirements regarding school attendance; *medical neglect*—harm or endangerment of a child caused by failure to seek treatment for health problems or accidents; *moral neglect*—failure to teach a child right from wrong in terms of general social expectations; *emotional neglect*—failure to meet a child's social-emotional needs at each stage of development; *physical abuse*—any intentional physical act that results in pain, injuries, or both, to a child; *sexual abuse—any* act of a sexual nature that involves an adult and a child; *emotional abuse*—the abuse of power through devaluing, undermining, and coercing a child; *verbal abuse*—the use of words to control and debase a child

3. (List two:) Neglectful and abusive parents come from all levels of income, intelligence, and education. Risk factors do exist for neglect and abuse. Experts cannot always predict from the risk factors which form the abuse will take. Abuse is a complex, interactive process.
4. attachment, self-regulation, affiliation, awareness (of how people are alike and different), tolerance, and respect
5. *Bullying* is the most common form of peer abuse. It involves inflicting physical, verbal, emotional, social, and sometimes sexual abuse of another person.
6. mandated reporters
7. Children may be returned to their parents with the requirement that the parents have therapy. Children may be put into the foster care system until the parents fulfill therapy and other requirements of the courts. Adults may be restricted from seeing the child or have their parental rights rescinded. Adults may be convicted of a crime or ordered to receive therapy.
8. Answers will vary.

Chapter 22 Review and Assessment

6. **Make inferences.** No, euphemisms are *not* a good way to explain illness and death to children. Children need clear, truthful explanations. They may feel lied to if adults give false or misleading information.

Chapter 23
Meeting Children's Special Needs

Caption Questions

Figure 23.1 Answers will vary, but should reflect an understanding that children have common physical, intellectual, and social-emotional needs (such as need for physical care and activity, quality learning experiences, responsive caregivers and teachers, and love).

Figure 23.4 Answers will vary, but may include vision therapy and certain types of surgery.

Figure 23.14 Answers will vary, but may include the Centers for Disease Control and Prevention or other authoritative organizations.

Figure 23.16 Answers will vary. Some print messages, such as signs, are important for community safety.

Figure 23.18 Answers will vary. Sessions should be regular so that mental health specialists can monitor children's improvements (and possible regression) and reinforce helpful coping mechanisms.

Figure 23.19 Hospitalization ensures that children receive appropriate medication and therapy and are safe.

Figure 23.21 IDEA guarantees education suited to the child's type of special need. Some children need more specialized instruction than other children. For example, a child with a physical disability may be placed in an accessible classroom. A child with an intellectual disability may be placed with a special education teacher.

Figure 23.22 Answers will vary. Parents may struggle emotionally with accepting (or may even deny) the possibility that their child has a special need. Parents also may not see the special need because they spend so much time with the child.

Lesson 23.1 Review and Assessment

1. (List two:) Special needs may occur in one or more areas of development. Special needs may develop due to acceleration or delay. Special needs are identified through observations and tests. Special needs vary in intensity. Special needs vary in duration and permanence. (Explanations will vary, but should reflect an understanding of explanations given in the text.)
2. A *physical disability* is a limitation of a person's body or its function. Possible causes include genetic disorders; congenital conditions; serious illnesses; and spinal cord, brain, or other bodily injuries.
3. (List three:) genetic disorders, congenital conditions, birth complications, injuries to or infections of the brain after birth, lack of basic experiences in the environment
4. *developmental dyslexia*—affects a child's ability to read, write, and spell; *developmental dyscalculia*—affects a child's mathematical abilities

5. An *anxiety disorder* a specific anxiety that interferes with a child's ability to achieve goals or enjoy life.
6. (List three:) lose their temper, even over small situations; argue with authority figures; actively defy or refuse to comply with adults' requests or rules; deliberately annoy others; blame others for personal mistakes or misbehaviors; are angry and resentful; are aggressively spiteful
7. communication, social, and behavioral
8. Answers will vary.

Lesson 23.2 Review and Assessment

1. The *Braille system* is a system of raised dots enabling people with vision conditions to read by touch.
2. Children with speech disorders need encouragement and sometimes therapy to communicate clearly.
3. Help for children with gifts and talents usually involves the placement of these children in groups of other children with gifts and talents.
4. Children with language disorders see a neurologist to help treat the underlying brain condition. Then they receive therapy to recover some language capabilities.
5. *Antidepressants* are medications that possibly correct the chemical imbalances in neurotransmitters in the brain and help children with depression get a mood boost. *Antipsychotics* are medications that reduce symptoms of psychosis and help children with schizophrenia.
6. (List four:) restricting stimuli; establishing and enforcing adherence to a routine; giving short, clear instructions; using acknowledgement and rewards; providing experiences that are challenging, but manageable; offering physical activities while curtailing overexcitement; ensuring the child has a healthful diet
7. *Individualized Family Service Plan (IFSP)*— guarantees that families can get the help they need under the terms of the law for qualifying children with special needs from birth to three years of age; *Individualized Education Plan (IEP)*— educational plan that is tailored to the specific educational needs of a child with special needs between 3 and 21 years of age; *Early Intervention Program for Infants and Toddlers with Disabilities*— program that provides intervention services for infants and toddlers with developmental delays or who have been diagnosed with physical and intellectual conditions that will likely cause developmental delays
8. Answers will vary. All children have the same basic needs. Help for children with special needs is based on the idea that, in addition to their basic needs, children with special needs have additional needs that require different care.

Chapter 23 Review and Assessment

4. **Cause and effect.** Answers will vary, but should reflect the following: *speech disorders* are usually caused by physical conditions (skills in talking, anatomy of vocal structures) and *language disorders* are caused by conditions in the brain (such as brain injury). As a result, children with speech disorders receive speech therapy from a speech pathologist, and children with language disorders may need the help of a neurologist followed by therapy from a speech-language pathologist.
5. **Draw conclusions.** Answers will vary, but should reflect that intellectual disabilities occur due to below-average intelligence, whereas children with learning disorders have average or above-average intelligence, but have other special needs due to neural misfirings in the brain that cause poor school performance.
7. **Determine.** Answers will vary, but should reflect that depression and schizophrenia, like other special needs, interfere with a child's daily functioning. These conditions create additional needs that need to met.
9. **Evaluate.** The infant who is legally blind is eligible for services provided by the Early Intervention Program for Infants and Toddlers with Disabilities and for child and family services outlined in an Individualized Family Service Plan (IFSP). The preschooler with gifts is not eligible for any services because gifts and talents are not qualifying special needs according to IDEA. The school-age child with ASD is eligible for appropriate educational services as outlined in his or her Individualized Education Plan (IEP).

Chapter 24
Providing Early Childhood Education in Group Settings

Caption Questions

Figure 24.4 Answers will vary, but might include group activities, outdoor play, stories, dramatic play, and block building.

Figure 24.6 According to Abraham Maslow, children need basic needs met before they can seek to meet additional needs, including learning.

Figure 24.7 Children learn many new concepts and ideas through their self-guided activities. Allowing children to learn at their own pace without direct input can help children enjoy learning concepts and build self-confidence in their abilities.

Figure 24.8 Answers will vary. Concepts learned through play are not as easily measured or observed by those not trained in child development and early childhood education as concepts learned through direct teaching.

Figure 24.9 Answers will vary, but may include scheduling or location challenges, limited income to meet costs, specific requirements for a child's care, and unfamiliarity with various types of early childhood education programs.

Figure 24.10 Early childhood education workers can research current standards at the Consumer Product Safety Commission.

Figure 24.15 Children come to know and appreciate different people and learn new concepts and skills from them. Parents and other adults feel like a part of their children's learning when they provide volunteer services.

Figure 24.16 content area, standard, learning objective, materials per child, procedure, assessment

Figure 24.17 Preschool children benefit from the holistic learning approach promoted by theme-based activity plans and from taking the lead in their own learning as opposed to a "bits and pieces" learning approach that is teacher-directed.

Lesson 24.1 Review and Assessment

1. *in-home child care*—care that takes place in the child's own home; *family child care*—care provided by a person for a small number of children in his or her own home; *center-based child care*—group child care provided in a center (not a home); *school-age child care*—child care for children between 5 and 14 years of age when school is not in session
2. Child development laboratories serve as both child care and education centers, child development research sites, and child care and education career training laboratories. As such, all of the activities in child development laboratories are directed or overseen by university-affiliated child development professionals.
3. (List one:) to provide educational, health, nutritional, social, and other services to children and their low-income families; to help parents progress toward their educational, literacy, and employment goals
4. *Preschool programs* refer to state-financed programs for three- and four-year-olds from low-income families, although a few states have universal preschool programs serving all children of specified ages. Most preschool programs are operated in public school settings or are affiliated with local Head Start programs. Most private center-based programs that call themselves *preschools* are in reality child care programs.
5. Montessori schools encourage young children to learn independently through the use of highly specialized materials rather than through direct input from teachers. Children are not separated by age, grade, or level. Rather, they are free to move about the classroom, work with other children, and use any materials they understand.
6. Froebel's kindergartens focused on play. Current kindergartens are more like first-grade classrooms with emphases on reading, writing, and arithmetic.
7. (List three:) growth in infant and toddler programs, growth in SACC programs, growth in work-related child care programs, growth in CCR&R agencies
8. Answers will vary.

Lesson 24.2 Review and Assessment

1. Regulations are minimum standards. Some regulations are easier to observe than others. Regulations are not always enforced.
2. whether the equipment meets children's needs
3. adult-child ratio
4. (List three:) Staff members work with parents as a team, convey the importance of parent participation in the program, know about each family they serve, and provide opportunities for parent communication and participation.
5. *DAPs* are practices that are based on knowledge about child development; the strengths, needs, and interests of each child within a group; and the social and cultural contexts in which children in a given program live. *DIPs* are practices that do *not* take into account child development, each child's strengths and needs, and the cultural context of the children's lives.
6. (List four:) Staff members affirm each child's identity; help children learn about people who are different from them; encourage children to see people as individuals, not groups; listen to and answer children's questions; help children learn that almost all human activities can be done in different ways; and respect diversity by making the program culturally rich.
7. *Hidden added costs* are costs that add to direct costs. *Hidden cost credits* are credits that lower direct costs of child care.
8. Answers will vary. Children may not always be able to clearly express program situations or people making them uncomfortable. Nevertheless, low-quality care can have damaging effects on children. Parents should investigate further to determine what is making a child uncomfortable.

Chapter 25
Preparing for a Child-Related Career

Caption Questions

Figure 25.14 More than ever before, the workplace relies on technology and employees' abilities to use technology efficiently.

Figure 25.15 Answers will vary. Having a positive attitude makes a person more approachable and easier to work with.

Figure 25.17 Most work tasks involve some degree of teamwork and thus require collaboration skills.

Figure 25.19 Answers will vary. Codes vary in content and comprehensiveness depending on the career area involved. The NAEYC's code is a shared framework of professional responsibility. It addresses professional relationships in these four areas: with children, with families, among colleagues, and with the community. The set of principles describes practices that are required, permitted, and prohibited. All of these principles stem from the principle with overall precedence—professionals will not participate in any practice that harms children. Examples of other principles based on the overall principle include the following: using relevant knowledge in all practices; taking needed actions on behalf of children and their families; making efforts to communicate with all others; maintaining appropriate confidentiality; sharing knowledge and resources, collaborating, and cooperating with families, colleagues, and staff members in other professional agencies in the community; avoiding any form of discrimination; and making no informal or formal reports based on hearsay.

Figure 25.23 Items that come first on a résumé are most likely to catch a reader's eye. Thus, the most important information should come before less important information.

Figure 25.25 It is common courtesy to ask a reference before giving out their contact information. References may miss the employer's or college's call or e-mail if they are not aware of the situation. When a reference knows in advance the nature of the job for which the person is applying, he or she can address the ability of the person to perform required tasks; otherwise, the reference may make statements that do not directly bear on the job which, in turn, makes the reference less important in the hiring process.

Figure 25.27 Showing your excitement will reinforce the positive impression you have made on your new employer.

Lesson 25.1 Review and Assessment

1. *Self-assessment* is the process of identifying your interests, aptitudes, and abilities. Completing a self-assessment helps you learn more about who you are as a person and which types of jobs might suit you well.
2. *Aptitudes* are talents with which people are born; they are natural and a part of heredity. *Abilities* are skills people learn or develop and acquire through effort and practice.
3. human services
4. *Professional organizations* are groups of professionals who meet to discuss their fields. They offer opportunities to meet people working in a particular career area; to become knowledgeable concerning industry-specific vocabulary, current research and issues related to the field, and career opportunities; and to work as a group to develop and promote certain policies (writing position statements and using their collective advocacy strength to promote certain ideas with those in influential positions, such as government officials).
5. co-op programs, apprenticeships, internships
6. Short-term goals help you break down long-term goals into manageable steps and focus on accomplishments you need to attain in the near future.
7. A *personal plan of study* is a plan that identifies the courses and other learning experiences a person needs to complete to meet his or her educational and career goals.
8. Answers will vary, but students should refer to Figure 25.4 for a list of education and training options.

Lesson 25.2 Review and Assessment

1. In *direct intervention*, adults work with children directly (for example, child care). In *indirect intervention*, adults work indirectly with children (for example, writing books for children).
2. (List three:) *child, family, and school social workers*—professionals who assist children and families in crisis, place foster children, arrange adoptions, and serve as a link between students' families and the schools; *child protective services social workers*—professionals who investigate reports of neglect and abuse and intervene, if necessary; *juvenile officers and family court judges*—professionals who make legal decisions about children and their families' rights and responsibilities; *licensing personnel*—professionals who check the quality of services for children; *medical and public health social workers*—professionals who help children and their families cope with chronic and terminal illnesses and help plan for the child's needs after hospital discharge; *mental health and substance abuse social workers*—professionals who provide individual and group therapy, crisis intervention, and other supportive interventions
3. People who work in design create products and design spaces that help meet children's developmental needs.
4. *Personal qualifications* are traits you possess that cannot be learned, but can be enhanced (such as through career training).
5. Children see adults and teens as leaders and imitate after the leadership models they see.
6. Child Development Associate (CDA) certification
7. NAEYC and ACEI
8. Answers will vary. Workers in child-related careers must always make decisions based on what is best for children.

Lesson 25.3 Review and Assessment

1. skills all employers seek in job candidates; includes interpersonal skills, collaboration skills, critical thinking and problem-solving skills, professionalism skills, strong executive function skills, and role-management skills
2. positive attitude, strong work ethic, good manners, excellent communication skills
3. (List three:) respect others' ideas, take responsibility for certain tasks, accept accountability for the team as well as for themselves, are adaptable and open to new ideas, share roles with team members, deal with personality clashes and manage conflicts, present an agenda, keep the team focused on goals, encourage every member to participate; analyze ideas presented, keep records of ideas and decisions

4. *Critical thinking skills* are the skills needed to analyze and evaluate situations to make reasonable judgments and decisions. *Problem-solving skills* are the skills used to analyze problems and formulate solutions.
5. codes of professional ethics
6. (List three:) focus on a stated goal, ask for help or get the information needed to achieve the goal, prioritize tasks and effectively manage time, organize workspace and thoughts, abandon ideas that are not working well and shift to alternative ways to reach a goal, outline major projects and create interim (in-between) deadlines, tackle one task at a time, tune out distractions, take regular breathers
7. For social-emotional and physical health, people must achieve a sense of balance among their roles. When roles do not balance well, *role strain* can occur, which can lead to role guilt. Role strain and role guilt can make people feel stressed, guilty, and unhappy. These problems can negatively affect their work performance and even lead to physical and mental health issues.
8. Answers will vary.

Lesson 25.4 Review and Assessment

1. *Networking* is making professional contacts with family, friends, and others for job information or referrals. Through networking, people can learn more about industry information, including potential job openings.
2. Many employers use applicant-tracking systems that perform *key word searches* based on the job description. These employers will view or not view your résumé depending on how many words it has in common with that description.
3. to highlight some of your job-related skills and qualifications and to capture the interest of the employer enough to arrange an interview with you
4. (List six:) your résumé and cover message; transcripts from your education and standardized test scores; samples of your best job- or school-related work, such as videos or writing samples; letters of recommendation documenting work-related skills; honors and awards; proof of membership in student or professional organizations; a personal statement describing your goals and how they came to be important to you; summaries of volunteer work; certifications or licenses; a list of references that can vouch for your character and qualifications
5. Asking these questions shows you have studied available information about this employer's workplace and are interested in the job and the employer.
6. Occupational Safety and Health Act
7. (List three:) Leave when the business is less busy, if possible. Avoid bragging about your new job. Show appreciation to your supervisor and coworkers for helping you to learn needed skills or for being positive role models. Consult the employee handbook or company policies to learn the correct procedure for terminating employment. Provide ample notice so the employer can find a suitable replacement. Complete a letter of resignation and any other termination forms, if required by the employer. Try to complete all current tasks.
8. Answers will vary. Sending a thank-you note shows that you are grateful for the opportunity to be considered for the job. It is an opportunity to remind the interviewer of your qualifications and express your enthusiasm.

Child Development

Early Stages Through Age 12

Eighth Edition

by

Dr. Celia A. Decker

Professor of Family and Consumer Sciences, retired
Castle Rock, Colorado

Publisher
The Goodheart-Willcox Company, Inc.
Tinley Park, Illinois
www.g-w.com

Manufactured in the United States of America.

ISBN: 978-1-63126-038-4

1 2 3 4 5 6 7 8 9 10 — 16 — 19 18 17 16 15

Cover image: Rawpixel/Shutterstock.com

About the Author

Celia A. Decker retired as a professor in the Department of Family and Consumer Sciences at Northwestern State University of Louisiana. She taught courses in early childhood education, child development, and family relations. Dr. Decker was coordinator of graduate studies in early childhood education. Before her position at Northwestern State University, she taught college courses at East Texas State University (now Texas A&M at Commerce) and at the University of Arkansas at Fayetteville. Dr. Decker also taught public school kindergarten in Kansas City, Kansas.

In addition to writing this text, Dr. Decker coauthors *Parents and Their Children* with Verdene Ryder. Dr. Decker has also published other books, numerous chapters in books, and articles. She presents papers at national and state annual meetings of professional associations, such as the National Association for the Education of Young Children, Southern Early Childhood Association, Association for Childhood Education International, National Association of Early Childhood Teacher Educators, and the Society for Research in Child Development. She does extensive consultant work for Head Start, Even Start, and local school systems.

During her years of teaching, Dr. Decker was named to Who's Who in Child Development Professionals, Who's Who in Personalities of the South, Who's Who in American Women, and the World's Who's Who in Education. In 1994, she was selected as the Outstanding Professor at Northwestern State University.

Reviewers

The author and publisher are grateful to the following reviewers who provided valuable input to this edition.

Sharon Allen
Family and Consumer Science Teacher
New Albany High School
New Albany, Indiana

Angelina Bencomo
Family and Consumer Sciences Teacher
Jefferson High School
El Paso, Texas

Mary Bond
Family and Consumer Sciences Teacher
Hononegah High School
Rockton, Illinois

Wendy Stewart Cox
Teacher
Oakmont High School
Roseville, California

DeLynn Fitzgerald
Child Development Teacher
Amarillo High School
Amarillo, Texas

Tracy Floeckher
Family and Consumer Science Instructor
Framingham High School
Framingham, Massachusetts

Jennifer L. Frye
Family and Consumer Sciences Teacher
Brookwood High School
Brookwood, Alabama

Lorie Boley Harper
Family and Consumer Sciences Teacher
Haynesville High School
Haynesville, Louisiana

Janice Imbrogno
Family and Consumer Science Teacher
Oceanside High School
Oceanside, New York

Linda Krause
Teacher
Franklin High School
Franklin, Wisconsin

Lois J. Lewis
Family and Consumer Sciences Teacher
Indus School
Birchdale, Minnesota

Mischel Luecke
Family and Consumer Sciences Teacher
Venture High School
Arlington, Texas

Renee Paulsin
Home Economics Department Chair
Hemet High School
Hemet, California

Cindy L. Sherwood
Family and Consumer Sciences Teacher
Coweta High School
Sharpsburg, Georgia

Laura Vaske
Family and Consumer Sciences Teacher
Linn-Mar High School
Marion, Iowa

Contents in Brief

Contents

Feature Contents

Case Study

Focus on Careers

Focus on Financial Literacy

Focus on Health

Focus on Reading

Focus on Science

Focus on Social Studies

Focus on Speech

Investigate Special Topics

Introduction

Child Development: Early Stages Through Age 12 will help you understand how to work with and care for children as they grow. It explains how children develop physically, intellectually, socially, and emotionally. *Child Development: Early Stages Through Age 12* will also help you apply what you have learned to meet children's needs in the best possible ways.

Children are different from adults. You need to know how children grow and develop to work with them effectively. This text begins by explaining the study of children. It helps you understand why studying child development is important—whether you become a parent, work in a child-related field, or just spend time with children. The text also discusses the choices and preparation involved in becoming a parent.

This text takes you from the prenatal stage through the child's school-age stage of development. The text presents the facts and theories about the child's development. Many examples are provided to help you apply this information when working with children of all ages.

Child Development: Early Stages Through Age 12 helps you explore how family situations affect children. It explores the special needs and concerns of children with special needs. You will also learn about ways to care for children, including play activities, ways to keep children healthy and safe, group programs, and child-related careers.

Unit 1 Children and Families in Today's World

CTSOs and Competitive Events

Career and Technical Student Organizations (CTSOs) are valuable assets to any educational program. These organizations support student learning and the application of skills learned in real-world situations. There is a variety of organizations from which to choose, depending on the goals of educational programs. Two that fit well with child development are *Family, Career and Community Leaders of America (FCCLA)* and *Future Educators of America (FEA)*. Participating in competitive events is a key aspect of membership in any CTSO. Participating in such competitions offers you an opportunity to expand your leadership skills and develop skills necessary for life and career. Scholarship opportunities also exist.

To learn more about competitive events, complete the following activities.

1. Talk with the local adviser or contact the organization before the next competition. This gives you time to review and decide which competitive events are best for you and your team.
2. Go to the organization website to find *specific* information for the competitive events. Visit the site often because information can change frequently.
3. Select one or two events of interest and print the event information. Competitive events may be written, oral, or a combination of both. Discuss the events with your instructor or adviser.
4. Read all event guidelines closely, including the rubrics against which you will be judged. To avoid disqualification from an event, strictly follow the rules and regulations.
5. Because communication plays an important role in competitive events, carefully research which communications skills are required in the event you select. Research and preparation are important factors in successful competition.

Chapter 1

Learning About Children

Essential Question

How can studying child development help you interact with children?

Lesson 1.1 **Understanding Child Development**

Lesson 1.2 **Recognizing Principles and Theories of Growth and Development**

Lesson 1.3 **Studying and Observing Children**

Case Study Is Aggression Caused by Heredity?

As a class, read the case study and discuss the questions that follow. After you finish studying the chapter, discuss this case study again. Have your opinions changed based on what you learned?

For years, Mrs. Lee had put up with her husband's bad temper. When events went wrong, he became angry and aggressive toward her and their 10-year-old son, but never really hurt them. All of the neighbors were aware of the couple's constant and loud fighting. The other day, her husband was involved in a road rage incident, but fortunately it never escalated beyond a word exchange. Today, Mrs. Lee received a call from her son's school principal saying that her son was involved in a bullying incident. By school policy, the son must now receive counseling with a local psychologist. The principal said the psychologist preferred to involve the whole family in the counseling sessions.

Mrs. Lee loves her husband and son and wants the aggressive acts to stop. When Mrs. Lee told her husband about the school incident and the principal's call, he emphatically stated that she can go to the counseling sessions with their son, but it would not help him and probably would be a waste of time for the son, too. She asked, "Why do you say this?" He replied that being aggressive is in the family genes, just like his eye color. He reminded her that his grandfather and father were aggressive, too. In fact, his father had spent some time in jail for assaulting another man during an argument.

Give It Some Thought

1. Do you think there is such a thing as genes for aggression? for a tendency toward aggression?
2. Is there another explanation for aggression across generations?
3. Why does the psychologist want to include the entire family in counseling sessions? How might the psychologist help this family?

While studying this chapter, look for the online resources icon  to:

- **Practice** terms with e-flash cards and interactive games
- **Assess** what you learn by completing self-assessment quizzes
- **Expand** knowledge with interactive activities and graphic organizers

Companion G-W Learning

www.g-wlearning.com/childdevelopment

Study on the go

Use a mobile device to practice terms and review with self-assessment quizzes.

www.m.g-wlearning.com/0384

Lesson 1.1 Understanding Child Development

Key Terms

child development
development
environment
epigenome
genes
genetics
heredity
individual life cycle
intellectual development
physical development
social-emotional development
stressors

Academic Terms

domains
growth
potential

Objectives

After studying this lesson, you will be able to

- define the term *child development*.
- describe the four domains of child development.
- summarize the six stages of the individual life cycle that involve children.
- explain how heredity and environment influence growth and development.

Reading and Writing Activity

Based on your own experiences and observations, list what you think the six stages of child development are called. Then write two or three characteristics of each stage. As you read this lesson, list the six stages of child development and characteristics of each stage as noted by the author. After you finish reading the lesson, compare the two lists. In what ways are they similar and different? Why do you think the six stages of child development are divided in this way? Write a paragraph to summarize your findings.

Graphic Organizer

In a chart like the one shown, write the four domains of child development. Then, as you read this lesson, categorize everything you learn about child development by domain.

Physical	Intellectual
Social	Emotional

Child development is one of the most fascinating subjects you can study. Children are constantly changing and discovering. They are also curious and creative. Who else would use a cardboard box for a house, a car, or a hiding place? If you spend any time with children, you know they can be lovable and challenging.

As you learn more about children, you will see that they go through many stages of growth and development. This book emphasizes the early years (before birth through the elementary school years) because these years are the most important in shaping children's lives.

What Is Child Development?

For many years, scientists and researchers have been studying children. The goal of these professionals is to learn more about how children grow and develop. **Development** is the gradual process through which babies become adults. Development begins at conception and continues until death. The process of development has many stages, such as before birth, infancy, childhood, adolescence, and adulthood.

Child development is the scientific study of children from conception to adolescence. Like lifespan development, child development is concerned with the whole child and the process or changes that occur in both growth and behavior. **Growth** is a change in size, such as height, or in quantity, such as vocabulary. Changes in behavior include any change in motor, thinking, and social skills.

By conducting research, experts in the fields of medicine, education, family and consumer sciences, and sociology help gather knowledge about children. People then use these facts to learn about children. Anyone who interacts with children can benefit from this knowledge. Child development teaches teens and adults how to care for children.

Domains of Child Development

Because the **domains** (areas) of child development are so highly related, child development experts must learn about all four of the domains (**Figure 1.1**). Experts usually discuss these domains separately. For the purposes of this text, however, social and emotional domains are frequently discussed together. Therefore, this text uses the following terms to describe the domains of child development:

- **physical development**—involves growth of the body and the development of both large and small motor skills.
- **intellectual development**—includes how people learn, what people learn, and how people express what they know through language.
- **social-emotional development**—concerns interactions with people and social groups, disposition, and emotions.

The domains of development constantly interact. For example, learning to walk (physical development) leads the more mobile child to explore and learn about objects (intellectual development). Showing caregivers what can be done with an object aids interactions with others (social development) and brings pleasure to the child (emotional development). These behaviors lead to changes in the brain (physical development).

Individual Life Cycle

The **individual life cycle** is a description of the stages of change people experience throughout life (from birth through old age). To help them study development over time, experts divide life into age-related stages. Each stage of life has unique opportunities, achievements, and challenges. Thus, each stage requires different ways of supporting growth and development.

Average ages are given for the stages to provide a basic idea of when stages may begin and end. The exact ages for a specific person, however, may vary. This book covers the first six stages, which are those

Figure 1.1 Child Development Domains

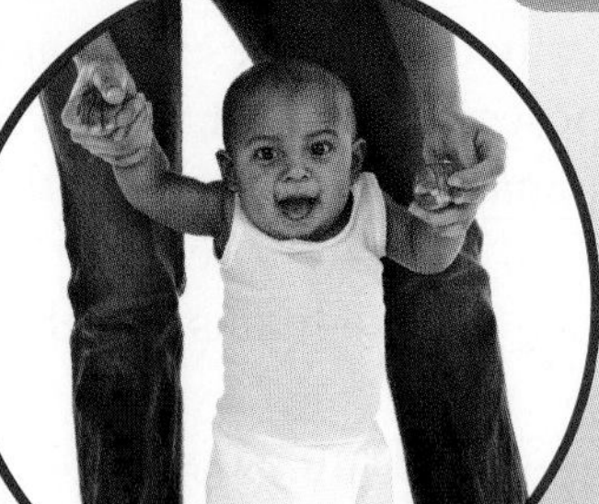

Physical growth and development

- How children's bodies grow and mature.
- How children's large and small muscles develop and aid movement.
- How children's motor skills aid perception and vice versa (called *perceptual-motor development*).

Intellectual development

- How children learn.
- What children learn.
- How language skills develop.

Social development

- How children develop and sustain relationships with others.
- How children develop a sense of self.
- How children become dependable.
- How children develop morals and character.

Emotional development

- How children identify and understand their feelings.
- How accurately children can read the emotional states of others.
- How children manage strong emotions and express their feelings in constructive ways (called *self-regulation*).

that involve children. These stages are described in **Figure 1.2**.

Factors That Influence Growth and Development

Why is each child different? Two main factors influence growth and development. First, each child has unique, inborn traits. **Heredity** includes all the traits that are passed to a child from blood relatives. Sometimes heredity is called *nature*. Second, a child's surroundings also play a large role. **Environment** includes all the conditions and situations that surround and affect a child. Sometimes environment is called *nurture*.

The way these two factors combine also makes children different from one another. Experts are studying how these two factors affect children's growth and development. They continue to learn, but unanswered questions remain.

Heredity

You have many traits in common with all the other members of your family. These traits pass to you in complex ways through your parents' genes at the moment of conception. Babies inherit about 23,000 genes from their parents. **Genes** are sections of the DNA molecule found in a person's cells that determine his or her individual traits. Genes carry the inborn instructions that help make you who you are. A person's genes are called the *structural genome* (JEE-nohm). Like computer hardware, this genome determines the boundaries of what is possible.

Child development researchers have long been interested in the effects of heredity. They noted

Figure 1.2 Child Development Stages

Prenatal

Begins at conception and ends about 9 months later at birth. The rate of growth at this stage is the fastest it will be in life. In this stage, a child grows from a single cell to a complete organism. Even before birth, babies can move, recognize the mother's voice patterns, and react to some strong stimuli.

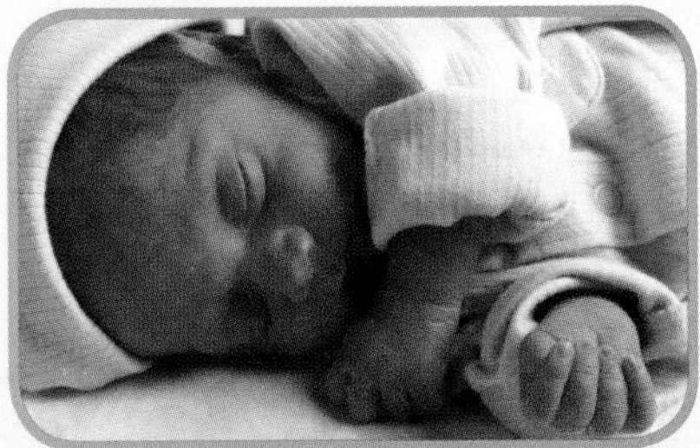

Neonatal

Extends from birth to 1 month. During this period, the baby physically adapts to life outside the mother's body.

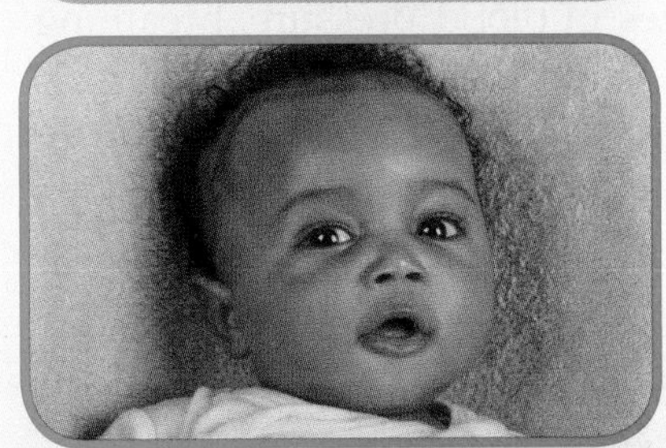

Infancy

Begins at 1 month and continues to 12 months. The infant develops the foundation for motor, thinking, language, and social skills.

Toddler

Begins at 12 months and ends at 36 months (the child's third birthday). In the toddler stage, the child makes great strides in motor, thinking, and language skills and begins to test his or her dependence on adults.

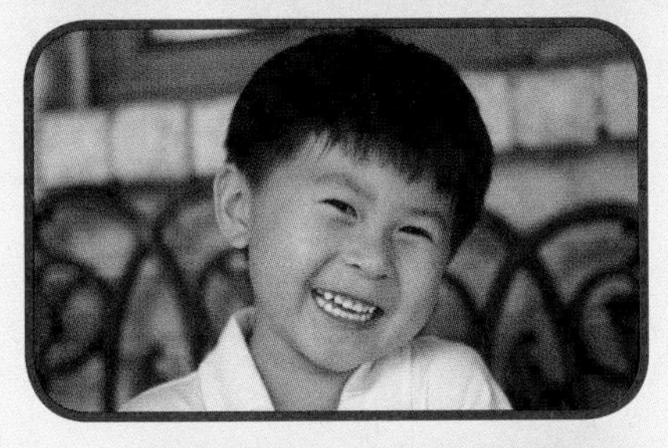

Preschool

Begins at 3 years and ends at 6 years. During this stage, the child becomes more self-sufficient, spends many hours in play exploring the physical and social world, and begins to develop knowledge of self.

School-age (middle childhood)

Begins at 6 years and ends at 12 years. This stage corresponds to the typical ages of children in the elementary school years. Achievement is the central goal of these years. School-age children master the basics of reading, writing, and arithmetic. They are exposed to many other learning opportunities, too. In school, children interact with peers more and learn by group instruction. This makes it important for them to learn self-control. Before the end of this stage, children have rather stable feelings about self and know how others feel about them.

that identical twins, who have the same structural genome, were more alike in physical traits and intellectual abilities than are brothers and sisters or other family members. The same similarities were found in identical twins reared apart.

Researchers also study the effects of heredity in virtual twins. *Virtual twins* are unrelated children of almost the exact same age raised by the same parents. Although the environment would be very similar for both children, virtual twins often are very different in most traits. Thus, heredity has a major impact in growth and development.

Today, most of the studies of heredity are conducted in a laboratory. **Genetics** (juh-NET-iks) is the study of the factors involved in the passing of traits in living beings from one generation to the next. In short, genetics is the study of heredity. *Geneticists* (biologists who study heredity) continue to make strides in learning which traits pass from parents to child. Almost every physical, intellectual, and social-emotional trait is affected by genes. Thus, genes influence your growth and development in many ways. The following points are known about heredity:

- Genes affect some parts of growth and development more than others. Genes determine body features, such as blood type, facial structure, and color of hair, eyes, and skin (**Figure 1.3**). Other traits, such as intellectual ability and social-emotional traits, are affected by both genes and the environment. Some genes determine whether a person will have a trait. For example, a person either is or is not an albino. (An *albino* is a person with white skin, almost white hair, and pink eyes.) This is determined by genes.
- Other genes affect the range of a trait. Traits such as height (very short to very tall) and athletic ability (almost no ability to greatness) come from these genes. These genes determine a trait's *potential*. (**Potential** is the greatest amount or level possible.) Whether a person will show or use that trait to its potential depends on the person's life. For instance, a healthful diet will help a child reach his or her height potential. The child cannot grow, however, beyond this potential. On the other hand, children with poor nutrition may not achieve their full potential.

Environment

All people live in both a physical and social environment. The unborn baby lives primarily in a physical environment that is almost totally dependent on the mother's physical condition. This environment may be beneficial due to proper prenatal care or harmful due to the lack of such care. After birth, physical conditions, such as food and rest, are part of the environment.

Beyond physical conditions, all other experiences are part of a person's social environment. To some degree, even unborn babies have a social environment. They can hear outside-the-womb sounds, especially the mother's voice that may be soothing or startling due to fear or anger. These sounds are reinforced by physical signals sent to the unborn by the mother—changes in blood pressure, breathing rate, and hormones. After birth, the social environment affects the way a child grows and develops in every developmental domain (**Figure 1.4**).

Figure 1.3 Because they share genes, parents and children often look alike. *What physical traits do this mother and daughter have in common?*

Figure 1.4 Environmental Impact on Growth and Development

How would the environmental impact be different in the home if parents...

- show unconditional love **versus** make "love" dependent on doing as "We, the parents, say"?
- are responsive **versus** nonresponsive to the child's needs?
- model the values and attitudes they expect **versus** saying one thing, but doing another?
- have clear and reasonable expectations **versus** unclear, unreasonable, or inconsistent expectations?
- set rules, give reasons, and apply appropriate consequences for misbehaviors **versus** commanding and punishing in anger for misdeeds?
- focus on the child's abilities **versus** the child's faults?
- keep communication open by listening to the child, making suggestions, giving alternatives, or problem-solving **versus** ignoring the child or commanding or threatening without listening?
- have a stable family life **versus** instability caused by situations, such as divorce, financial problems, or domestic violence?

How would the environmental impact be different in child care programs and schools if they...

- promote the cultural values of the community **versus** promote values not accepted by the community?
- are of high-quality **versus** low-quality?
- have expectations that are similar to those of parents **versus** have expectations that are dissimilar?
- encourage parents and teachers to work as a team **versus** compete with each other?
- employ teachers who have clear and reasonable expectations for each child **versus** those who have unclear and unreasonable expectations?
- ensure children will feel they can be successful **versus** promote children's realistic or unrealistic fear of failure?

How would the environmental impact be different in the community of peers if children...

- are accepted and liked **versus** ignored, teased, or bullied?
- engage in positive group behaviors **versus** behaviors that are high-risk, illegal, or in other ways less than positive?
- find group activities that are enjoyable and affordable for each child in the group **versus** activities that are not enjoyable or affordable for some children?
- resolve peer conflicts in constructive ways **versus** have conflicts that often result in anti-social behaviors?

How would the environmental impact be different in health care if staff members...

- provide services that fit parents' needs **versus** do not provide services that fit those needs, such as have inconvenient hours and/or locations, do not provide care needed by children with special needs or with certain chronic conditions, do not have staff members who speak the parents' language, or have charges that are not affordable to a family?
- give the needed time for each child and are pleasant **versus** seem to be hurried and are possibly curt?
- answer parent questions **versus** seem to be "put off" with questions or hesitant to answer?
- give clear instructions for treatment and follow-up **versus** not making instructions or follow-up very clear to parents?

How would the environmental impact be different in the community if agencies...

- provide a peaceful, safe environment for all **versus** cannot maintain community peace and safety?
- ensure that children have all they need for healthy development **versus** do not have child-centered agencies or have agencies that are targeted only at particular groups of children and their families?

(Continued)

Figure 1.4 *(Continued)*

How would the environmental impact be different in mass media if children...

- have needed and accessible materials to meet their developmental needs **versus** find needed materials scarce and/or not accessible?
- see content that is positive and safe for children **versus** negative and unsafe?

How would the environmental impact be different in the parents' workplace if the job...

- has secure employment **versus** less secure employment with many closures and layoffs?
- rewards work with wages or salaries that meet family needs and goals **versus** gives insufficient monetary rewards for work?
- has one worksite **versus** requires frequent mobility?
- is family-friendly (has reasonable work hours, grants parental leaves for new babies and severe family illnesses, has family benefits, such as child care services and family insurance policies) **versus** is not family-friendly?

Heredity and Environment Combined

For years, people argued about which affected growth and development more—heredity or environment. This argument was often called *nature versus nurture*. Of course, there is no way to study environment separate from heredity because the environment has to act upon the genes. Now, experts agree they work together. Following are a few examples of the interaction of heredity and environment:

- Genes control height potential, but a proper diet is needed to reach this height.
- Potential intelligence is inherited, but physical factors (nutrition and rest) and the quality of experiences determine whether the potential will be reached.
- Basic social-emotional traits are inherited, but greatly affected by experiences.

Heredity Affected by Environment

In recent years, geneticists have discovered genes are not fixed as once thought. The environment in which a person lives, both before and after birth, can alter genes through their epigenome. The **epigenome** (eh-pih-JEE-nohm), which means above the genes, consists of chemicals that can turn genes on and off. Thus, the epigenome is like the operating system of the computer. The epigenome explains why even identical twins who have the same structural genome are somewhat different before birth.

Mental Health Advisory

Toxic stress or prolonged and frequent tolerable stress can result in mental health problems throughout life.

How does the epigenome affect who people are? Although research is just beginning, the following is what is currently known:

- The epigenome is built through positive and negative factors from the environment. Positive factors cause the chemical compounds to turn on genetic potential—making the person all they can be. Negative environmental factors cause harm in all domains of growth and development.
- Positive environmental factors include health, quality learning experiences, and supportive and loving relationships. Negative factors include toxic substances, poor health practices, lack of quality experiences with objects and people, and some stressors. **Stressors** are situations that cause worry and anxiety.

Figure 1.5 Levels of Stress

Level	Definition	Examples	Results
Toxic	Strong and prolonged (over a long time) activation of the body's stress system	• Family and community violence • Multiple, repeated traumatic events	• Development of a smaller brain • Stress-related physical illness, such as heart disease, stroke, and possibly diabetes • Mental health problems, such as depression, anxiety disorders, and substance abuse
Tolerable	Not as long-lasting as toxic stress	• Death or serious illness of a loved one • Parental divorce	• Can be helped with loving and supporting relationships • Recovers with adult support • Becomes toxic without adult support
Positive	Moderate and short-lived stress	• Meeting new people • Attending a new child care and education program or a new school • Taking a test • Having a medical procedure	• Can become more serious if the setting is not warm or secure or if supportive adults are not available

- Stress can be both beneficial and harmful depending on the level of stress and how often and how long the body's stress system is turned on (**Figure 1.5**). Having loving and responsive people in a person's life reduces the effects of stress. Without these people, problems may occur even in later life.
- Although the epigenome can change throughout life, positive and negative experiences from conception to 12 months have the most lasting effects.
- The brain is the most susceptible to changes in the epigenome. Adverse experiences are not erased, but affect the person's overall well-being for the rest of his or her life.
- Changes in the epigenome— both positive and negative—can be passed down to the next generation if they occur in the unborn. Generally the chemical tags are erased, but about one percent of these tags are not erased and are passed on to the offspring due to changes in the egg and sperm. In these cases, nurture becomes nature.

Lesson 1.1 Review and Assessment 

1. Define the term *child development*.
2. List and describe the four domains of child development.
3. Name the six stages of the individual life cycle that involve children and give the average ages for each stage.
4. What are the two main factors that influence growth and development?
5. What does *epigenome* mean? What can the epigenome do?
6. **Critical thinking.** How have heredity and environment combined to affect your growth and development?

Lesson 1.2 Recognizing Principles and Theories of Growth and Development

Key Terms

age norm
developmental acceleration
developmental delay
principles of growth and development
sequenced steps
teachable moment
theory

Academic Terms

codified
confirm
constancy
disprove
interrelated
motivation

Objectives

After studying this lesson, you will be able to

- identify key principles of growth and development.
- assess how milestones aid people who are working with children.
- give examples of the major principles of growth and development.
- explain how child development research can become a theory.

Reading and Writing Activity

Skim through this lesson and list all of the headings you see. Leave one or two lines of space beneath each heading. Then, close your book and compose a "topic sentence" for each heading. Your topic sentence should summarize what information you think each section will include. After you read this lesson, return to your list and write a new topic sentence for each section, outlining the main points you learned.

Graphic Organizer

Write *Principles of Growth and Development* in the middle circle of a chart like the one shown. Then, as you read this lesson, write the major principles you learn in the surrounding circles. Beside each circle, write what interests you and what you have learned about each principle.

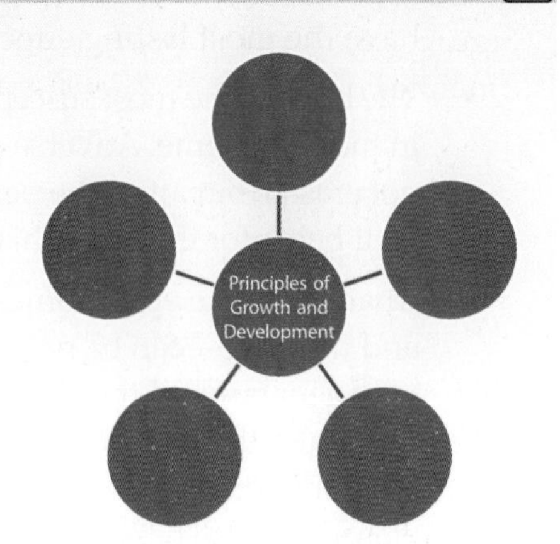

Every science works on certain *principles*—basic truths or assumptions. For example, in physics, one principle is: Every effect has a cause. Principles are generated through countless research studies over time. When the same results come up over and over again, a principle is noted.

In child development, you know that each child is unique. Yet, through research observations, you know there are basic patterns of growth and development called *principles*. These principles are *universal* (apply to all children throughout all times), *predictable* (will occur in future observations), and *orderly* (patterns are sequenced and will occur at approximate times).

Why are principles of development important? When you make any decision about a child, taking into account these principles will aid development, but ignoring the principles will likely hinder development. Researchers and theorists use their existing knowledge about principles of growth and development as they develop new theories.

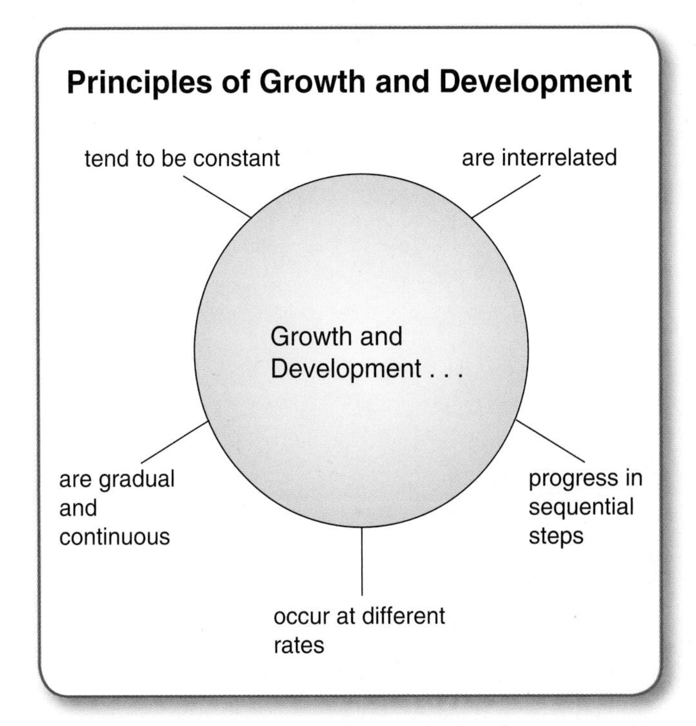

Figure 1.6 *How do you think these principles of growth and development were determined? Why?*

Principles of Growth and Development

Each person is unique, yet people are more alike than different. Experts study these likenesses to find patterns in the way people generally grow and develop. These patterns, or **principles of growth and development**, do not fit every person exactly. They are true enough to be used as a guide, however, when learning about children (**Figure 1.6**). The following sections describe key principles of growth and development.

Growth and Development Are Constant

Many aspects of a person's growth and development are unchanging. This is called **constancy**. Traits that children possess today are a good hint—but not proof—of traits that will be present in the future. For example, tall two-year-olds tend to be tall adults. Children who are good students in elementary school are likely to be good students in high school. Happy, secure children tend to be cheerful, confident adults.

Why is this so? There are two reasons for constancy in growth and development. First, new growth, knowledge, and skills are always built on those already acquired. One stage always prepares the way for the next, such as making sounds before speaking words. Second, people often live in the same environment for years. For major changes to take place in growth and development, major changes must take place in the environment.

Growth and Development Are Gradual and Continuous

Growth and development are, for the most part, gradual and continuous. A child does not grow or develop overnight. Consider a baby taking his or her first steps on a certain date. Each day before walking, the baby grew, the body matured, and the baby practiced motor skills, such as crawling and pulling to a stand. All these small changes lead to the baby's first steps (**Figure 1.7**).

Figure 1.7 Children must practice many motor skills before they take their first steps. *What are some of these motor skills?*

In a positive way, the principle suggests development does not reverse overnight. A few mistakes or stresses usually do not cause severe problems. As an example, a one-day junk food binge does not seriously harm a healthy person. The principle is also positive in that setbacks in development can be overcome with correct intervention and effort.

On the negative side, the principle can work to a person's disadvantage. It suggests that poor growth and development are not easily reversed. Consider a child with poor health due to a lifelong poor diet. It may take many months or years of eating a carefully planned diet to restore the child's health. In some cases, the body may never be able to overcome these obstacles. Consider, too, a child who lags in intellectual development due to the lack of quality experiences with adults and with toys and books. Once extremely behind in learning, it is difficult to overcome the learning gap between where the child is and where he or she should be.

Growth and Development Happen in Sequenced Steps

For growth and development to be continuous, change must build on what children have already learned. For instance, writing comes from making random marks. The steps in growth and development follow one another in a set order called **sequenced steps**. These sequenced steps are called *stages* or *milestones*. Researchers have **codified** (arranged in an orderly way) the milestones through many years of observations. The sequence should always lead to greater complexity of behaviors, such as scooting to skipping, thinking in prelogical to logical terms, and watching others play to interacting in team sports.

How do milestones aid those who are working with children? Milestones give adults ideas about teachable moments. A **teachable moment** is an optimal time when a person can learn a new task. Teachable moments occur when the body and mind are physically ready, when caregivers encourage and support the child, and when the child feels a strong desire to learn. If a child has not reached the teachable moment, he or she will feel stressed when trying to master a task or skill. Waiting too long after the teachable moment occurs may cause problems, too. For example, a child who is ready to ride a bicycle is not given the chance to learn. This child may then have trouble learning the skill as an adult.

Growth and Development Happen at Different Rates

Growth and development happen at different rates for different people. All people change with time. Some people enter a stage earlier and some later than the typical age. Researchers know the typical time when a developmental milestone occurs. The timing is called an **age norm** and can be expressed as an average age or age range. The age norm simply predicts when development will likely occur.

Developmental acceleration occurs when a child performs like an older child. For example, a 30-month-old child who speaks in long,

Focus on

Health

A Lesson on Safety

A *teachable moment* is any unplanned event that can be used as a learning opportunity. Teachable moments occur many times each day. By observing children, you can see these opportunities and teach to the moment. Children learn best when they show spontaneous interest and when learning is embedded in meaningful contexts.

Here is an example: A family is attending a barbecue at a friend's home. Their almost four-year-old daughter has never seen a grill and cannot be distracted from running up to the grill. Her mother explains a grill is just like their kitchen stove, but it is outside. Thus, it is very hot. She points out that the man cooking has special gloves and long-handled kitchen tools to protect him from the heat and fire. The mother positions her chair in view of the grill and has her daughter sit on her lap to watch the cooking. From time to time, the girl mentions the heat and the leaping flames.

Look at the first paragraph again. How did this example fit the criteria of a teachable moment?

complex sentences is developmentally accelerated in language. A **developmental delay** occurs when a child performs like a younger child. For example, a three-year-old who speaks in two-word sentences may have a developmental delay in language.

Why do the rates differ among people? The most common reasons include the following:

- The effects of genes and the epigenome differ in a given person. Even identical twins will vary in aspects of growth and development.
- Gender determines different growth rates. For example, girl's bones and organs are more mature than boy's at all ages.
- Environmental influences have a major impact on growth and development. Children need a supportive environment to grow at the best rate. A supportive environment includes much love and care and many ways to learn. If the environment is lacking, lags or delays in growth and development occur. On the other hand, an adult's attempts to hurry growth and development may cause a child harmful stress.
- **Motivation**, which is a child's desire to achieve, also makes growth and development rates vary (**Figure 1.8**). Some children are eager to achieve and others are more poorly motivated.

Rates of growth and development also vary within the individual. Some of the rate changes are expected. Biological maturation, especially of the brain, determines typical periods of fast and slow growth and development in all people. Beyond these expected differences in rates, other differences are mainly determined by a person's genetic makeup and environmental experiences. For example, a child may develop at a fast rate in motor skills and a slower rate in language usage. A child may be developmentally accelerated or delayed in one or more areas. It is even possible for a child to be delayed in one area and accelerated in another. A few children may be developmentally accelerated or delayed in most areas.

Growth and Development Are Interrelated

In this book, the physical, intellectual, and social-emotional aspects of growth and development are

Figure 1.8 Motivation is a person's desire to achieve or progress. *What are some qualities of a motivated person?*

often discussed in separate chapters. This is so you can better understand each aspect. In reality, however, all aspects are **interrelated**, or they interact in complex ways.

People who work with children must understand how areas of growth and development affect one another. For instance, a teacher's job is to improve children's intellectual growth. If children come to school hungry or sleepy, however, they will not do well in learning activities. Studies have shown that unless children have positive feelings about themselves (social-emotional domain), they cannot devote the attention and energy needed for learning. Understanding these interrelationships improves the way people work with children.

Theories of Growth and Development

Several researchers who studied children extensively have developed theories. A **theory** is a set of statements offered as a possible explanation for a phenomenon, such as child growth and development. Child development theories

- describe changes (may also be called *stages*) over time within one or more areas of development
- show changes among areas (domains) of development
- explain why the changes occur

No one theory has been adequate to describe the complexity of child development. Still, theories help to set goals and give direction to more research. Other research, done by the theorists or other researchers, may **confirm** (prove accurate) or **disprove** (show to be wrong or false) parts of the theory.

Theories of child development can be divided into categories. Some deal mainly with biology while others deal with the environment. Still others deal with combinations of biology and environment and the extent to which each affects development. Several major child development theory categories are described in **Figure 1.9**.

Why are there so many theories? Why cannot just one theory be validated by research? Theorists experience the following problems:

- Development is too broad and complex for one theorist to study all aspects of development.
- Research is not completely objective. Theorists begin with their personal knowledge, interests, and hunches. Their hunches determine what questions they ask and how they set up their research.
- New research has to begin with what is known based on theory.
- New research relies on available research tools. Most of the child development theorists were doing their work before the time of computers or even calculators.

Recording equipment was not available either, so all notes were handwritten. Technology, such as brain scans and computers, make a major difference in the ability to research child development. Even with the best of technology, however, research is a long and slow process.

- Theory development requires a knowledge network because answers come only when theories can be tested by others. Some child development theorists did work together, but most did not have easy access to the theories of others.

Lesson 1.2 Review and Assessment 

1. List the key principles of growth and development.
2. What are two reasons for constancy in growth and development?
3. What is a *teachable moment*? Give an example.
4. Differentiate between *developmental acceleration* and *developmental delay*.
5. What is a *theory*?
6. List three major child development theory categories.
7. **Critical thinking.** What are some examples of constancy in your growth and development?

Figure 1.9 Child Development Theory Categories

Theory	Description
Maturational	Arnold Gessell (1880–1961) believed that physical and intellectual development was determined by heredity and biological maturation. His theory established many of the age norms and ideas about "readiness."
Psychoanalytic	Sigmund Freud (1856–1939) believed personality (and mental health) was determined by how children coped with their physical drives. He examined how children regulate their desires and take on social norms. His theory was used primarily by psychiatrists.
Psychosocial	Erik Erikson (1902–1994) was concerned about conflicts that occur between a child's needs and social demands. He believed that people who can cope with each conflict develop a healthy personality and vice versa. His theory is used in preventing and treating mental health problems.
Learning	Several theorists, including B.F. Skinner (1904–1990) and Albert Bandura (1925–present), focused on how the environments affect observable behaviors, not internal changes, such as personality and how you learn. They studied how behaviors can be reinforced (made stronger) or extinguished (stopped). Learning theories are mainly used in behavior modification or in intervention methods for children having learning or behavioral problems.
Cognitive-Developmental	Jean Piaget (1896–1980) believed children think differently at different ages. He thought children constructed (built) their knowledge through experiences. As children learn new ideas, their minds adapt (change). His theory totally changed child development.
Sociocultural	Lev Vygotsky (1896–1934) disagreed with Piaget's theory that children totally construct their own knowledge. He believed that some knowledge was a personal construction, but much was a social construction (taught by people of one's culture). His idea of mentoring or tutoring learning is used in many schools today.
Ecological Systems	Urie Bronfenbrenner (1917–2005) noted that children's development is influenced by both heredity and their environment (family, friends, schools, and health services) as well as their indirect environment (parents' workplaces and general culture). He also believed that children affect their environment, such as how they treat friends may affect their friendships. His theory has made people more aware of how the many contexts (systems) affect child development.

Lesson 1.3 Studying and Observing Children

Key Terms

child-centered society
direct observation
indirect observation
self-actualization

Academic Terms

advocates
empathize
hierarchy
irreducible

Objectives

After studying this lesson, you will be able to

- recognize the benefits of studying children.
- assess Abraham Maslow's *hierarchy of human needs.*
- explain Brazelton and Greenspan's seven basic needs of all children.
- develop observation skills.

Reading and Writing Activity

In learning about children, you will also learn a great deal about yourself. As you read this lesson, consider what each concept you learn might teach you about yourself. Keep a list of these ideas, placing a star beside any concepts that especially interest you. After reading the lesson, pick two or three of these ideas and write a few paragraphs reflecting on how the content in this lesson helped or will help you understand yourself.

Graphic Organizer

As you read this lesson, use a tree diagram like the one shown to organize what you learn about observing children. Write *Observing Children* in the top circle and write major concepts and then smaller details in the circles below.

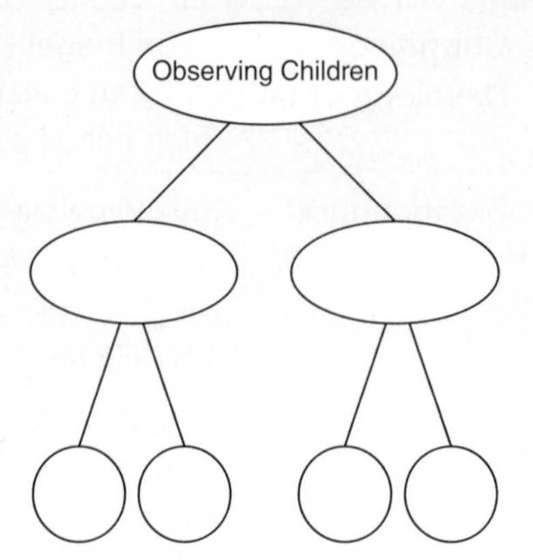

All sciences, including child development, are based on the idea that nature is orderly, and can be discovered through study and observation. People must have some understanding of children before they can understand their own "developmental roots" or be responsible for or take action on behalf of children. Much of a person's understanding can come from personal observations of children when these are combined with *informed knowledge* (knowledge from theory and research).

Benefits of Studying Children

How will studying children help you? Learning about children will help you to better understand yourself now and as you continue to develop. One of your future goals may be to become a responsible parent. You may even be interested in a career in a child-related field. All adults—regardless of parenthood or career—have responsibilities for protecting children.

Understand Yourself

Many times, adults are not fully aware that who they are today is a result of the children they once were. As you study children, you can gain insight into your own growth, development, and values. You can also understand how your values affect your feelings about, and reactions to, children. This knowledge can then help you to learn better ways in which to care for children.

Studying children can help you develop, too. It can help you appreciate all that goes into taking a first step or saying a first word. When you help a child overcome a fear or learn a skill, you feel good. Adults often enjoy just being with children. Children can share gifts that, sadly, adults often outgrow. Their awe of beauty, their frankness, and their world of magic please adults.

Be a Responsible Parent

Parenting is a mind-boggling task. How much adults know about children, however, can determine the kind of parents they become. Parents who are responsible meet all their children's needs. By studying children, parents know their children's needs at each stage of development. They also know the best ways to respond to those needs.

Maslow's Hierarchy of Needs

Abraham Maslow, a noted psychologist, was one of the first researchers to study human needs. Although his ideas were used to understand what motivates workers, his model was later extended to child development.

According to Maslow, people strive to fulfill their needs in a **hierarchy** (rank order). Maslow called this model *the hierarchy of human needs* (**Figure 1.10**). The first four levels are *basic needs* (inborn needs). The first level includes all *physical needs*. The other three levels are the *psychological needs* (related to feelings) of security, love and acceptance, and esteem. In addition to basic needs, Maslow also created a fifth level for higher-level needs, which he called *self-actualization needs*. **Self-actualization** means to grow and feel fulfilled as a person. Self-actualization needs include the drive to pursue talents and hobbies, gain skills, and learn more about the world. Education helps to meet a person's self-actualization needs. Complete self-actualization is a lifelong process that many people never attain.

If people's basic needs are not satisfied in order of level, they will no longer be concerned about pursuing higher-level needs. Therefore, parents and other adults must first help children meet their basic needs. For instance, adults can offer children nutritious foods. Once the basic need for food is met, adults can help children turn their attention from eating to meeting their psychological needs. These needs might include building relationships with friends and being respected by others. Higher-level skills help children reach their full potential as adults.

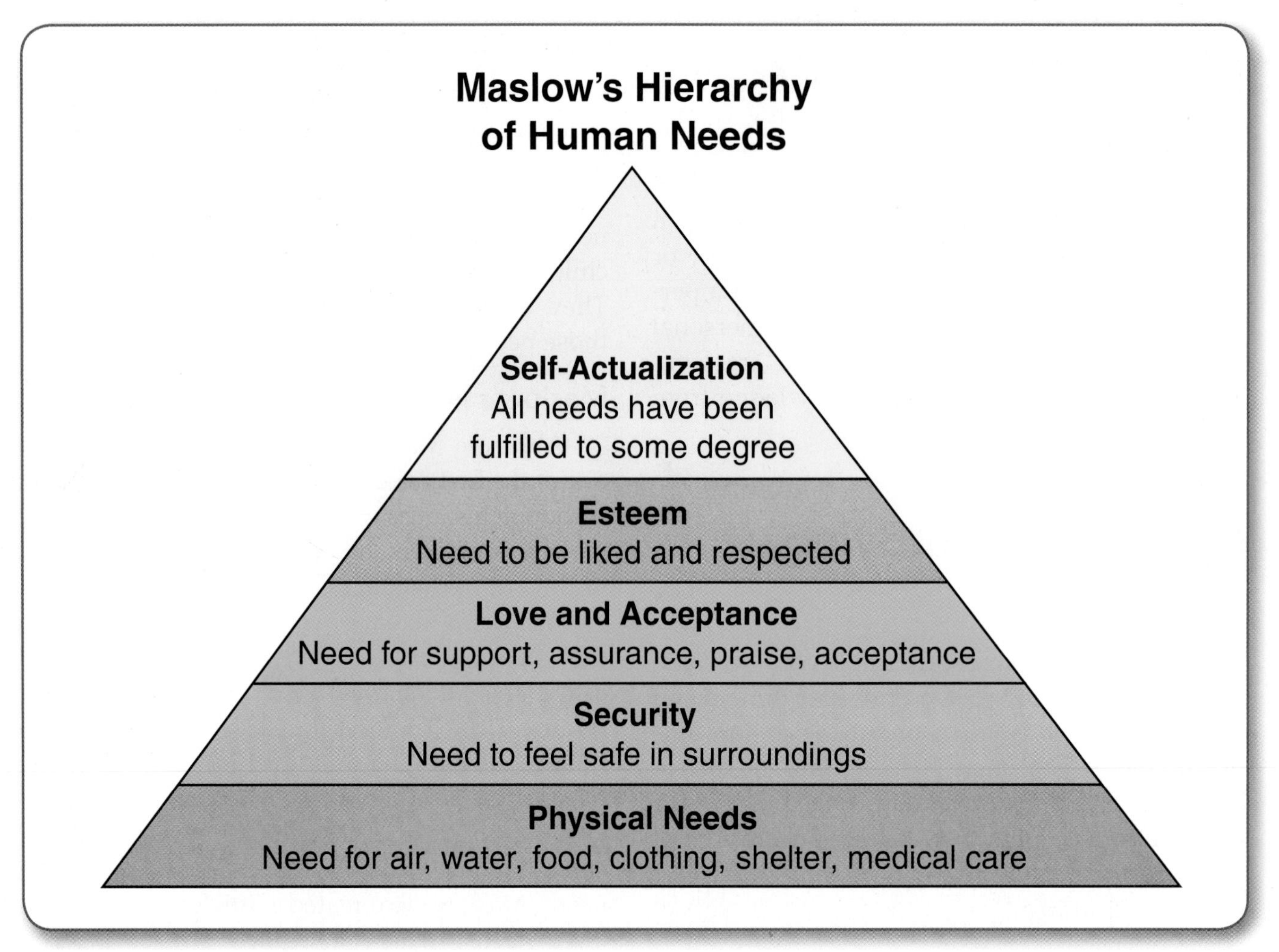

Figure 1.10 Maslow sees two kinds of needs in all humans—basic needs (physical and psychological needs) and higher-level needs (self-actualization needs). *Where would you place yourself on Maslow's hierarchy of needs? Which needs are met? Which needs are not met?*

Brazelton and Greenspan's Irreducible Needs

Currently, two noted researchers and physicians, T. Berry Brazelton and Stanley I. Greenspan, have researched the basic needs of all children. They identified seven needs children must meet to thrive and flourish for a lifetime, which they call the *irreducible needs of children*. (**Irreducible** means impossible to make smaller or simpler.) These needs include

- ***ongoing nurturing relationships.*** A nurturing relationship is critical for all development. Children from birth through the preschool years need nurturing interactions most of their waking hours. If this relationship is absent or interrupted, children are apt to develop disorders in their intellectual, social, and emotional development.
- ***physical protection, safety, and regulation.*** Children need an environment both before and after birth that protects them from physical and emotional harm. For example, this includes appropriate food, clothing, and shelter and protection from toxins, harm, and any form of abuse.
- ***experiences tailored to individual differences.*** Each child has a unique temperament and way of relating to the world of matter and people. Parents need to match the child's strengths and weaknesses with their experiences. In this way a child achieves his or her potential (**Figure 1.11**).

- ***experiences that are developmentally appropriate.*** Each child needs experiences tailored to his or her stage of development. Parents and those working in child-related careers need to know and apply "best practices" for each stage of development as the child matures.

Figure 1.11 Children achieve their potential through different experiences and rates of growth; it is important that parents recognize their children's strengths and weaknesses and nurture them accordingly. *Consider two children you know. What are their strengths and weaknesses? What experiences might encourage growth for each of them?*

- ***limit setting, structure, and expectations.*** Children need both structure and discipline in their lives. Parents and other adults need to **empathize** with children's feelings, or understand and relate to them, but set limits as well. In this way children can develop self-discipline and resolve conflicts in peaceful ways.
- ***stable communities and cultural continuity.*** Children need continuity of values in family, peer groups, and the broader community. Parents and others who work with children must work together, not compete. For example, when two adults have different ideas about what they think is best for children and are unwilling to work together, this would be considered competing.
- ***protecting the future.*** People live in an interdependent nation and world. Adults must meet the needs of all children. To protect the future for one child, people must protect it for all.

Work With Children

In the past, people thought all the knowledge and skills that adults need for child-related careers—including parenting—came naturally. Many felt just being raised in a family teaches adults all they need to know about children and child care skills.

Today, experts know that understanding children requires careful study. Changes continue to take place in society and in families. These changes require people to know more about children's growth and development than what they observe in their own families. Adults with child-related careers should study children. Some careers may seem to focus mainly on one aspect of children's development. The child is, however, a whole person. Anyone preparing for a child-related career should know some about all aspects of children's growth and development. Learning more about children enables workers in child-related careers to provide better care for children.

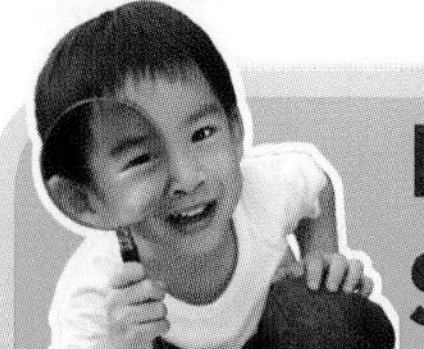

Investigate Special Topics: Children's Rights

Children are easily hurt because they are physically weaker than adults and cannot reason as adults. Society must protect them. By learning about children, lawmakers can pass laws that will keep children safe.

The Convention on the Rights of the Child (United Nations International Children's Education Fund) wrote 54 articles that set out the rights of every child in the world. These rights can be given under 11 major categories. The following categories explain children's rights to:

- ***an identity*** (government should protect children's names, family ties, and nationalities)
- ***a family*** (children should be able to live with their parents unless this is not in the children's best interest; parents have the responsibility for raising children with government support)
- ***express themselves and have access to information*** (children have the right to express their views; have freedom of thought, conscience, and religion; and obtain information)
- ***a safe and healthy life*** (children have the right to life; the government should do all it can to make sure children survive and develop; children should have access to medical services and a decent standard of living)
- ***special protection in times of war*** (children who are refugees are entitled to special protection; children who are under 15 should not take part in armed conflict)
- ***an education*** (primary education should be free and required of all children; secondary education should be accessible to all children)
- ***special care for the disabled*** (children with disabilities have the right to special care, education, and training)
- ***protection from discrimination*** (all rights apply to all children; children have the right to practice their own cultures, religions, and languages)
- ***protection from abuse*** (children shall be protected against abuse and neglect; government shall be involved with laws and programs concerned with abuse)
- ***protection from harmful work*** (children have the right to rest, leisure, play, and participation in cultural and artistic activities; children have the right to be protected from having to participate in work that threatens their health, education, and development)
- ***special treatment if arrested*** (children are entitled to assistance and treatment that respect their rights)

Discussion Activity

In small groups, list children's rights on the left side of a piece of paper. Then, brainstorm at least three practical situations in which each right can be applied. Use examples from everyday life and historical examples where needed. Choose one situation for each right and then share your group's examples with the rest of the class.

Protect Children's Rights

People live in a **child-centered society**—a society that sees children as important, cares about their well-being, and works to meet their needs. Some children also experience, however, a great deal of harm through abuse and neglect. Children need safe environments. They need homes, schools, and other places where they can develop to their full potential (**Figure 1.12**). All children should have the chance to grow in an environment that promotes their health and well-being. By studying children, you will learn how to provide these safe places.

Focus on

Careers

Child Care Worker

Child care workers work with young children who are not yet in school. They may also work with older children before or after school. Child care workers meet children's basic needs and provide activities to stimulate growth and development.

Career cluster: Education and training.

Education: Educational requirements vary greatly for each state. Requirements may include a Child Development Associate (CDA) credential or a bachelor's degree.

Job outlook: Future employment opportunities are expected to grow as fast as the average for all occupations.

To learn more about a career as a child care worker, visit the United States Department of Labor's *Occupational Outlook Handbook* website. You will also be able to compare the job responsibilities, educational requirements, job outlook, and average pay of child care workers with similar occupations.

Figure 1.12 Children need places where they can engage in fun and challenging activities that will encourage growth. *What activities do you think a child would consider fun and challenging?*

In the United States, parents have the rights of guardianship and determine their children's upbringing. For example, they control the children's level of financial support. They also control religious and moral teachings, as well as education and health care choices. The state can come between a parent and child only if the court feels the child needs more protection.

Each state makes laws and policies to protect children. The state can make laws to develop child welfare services. Each state has a department concerned with children's welfare and the obligations and responsibilities of parents. These state departments are usually called *Department of Human Services* (with offices pertaining to children within the larger department) or *Child Protective Services (CPS).* These offices are staffed with caseworkers who work to make sure laws and policies are being carried out by families with minor children. For example, laws exist regarding the quality of child care programs, school attendance, child labor, and illegal drug sales to help protect children and society. State laws also protect children from the results of their own lack of judgment. For example, young children are not responsible legally for their contracts. Children are treated differently from adults in court. The state can make laws to develop child welfare services.

Children have gained rights, too. Examples are the rights of due process and fair treatment in schools and juvenile and family courts. In some states, children may receive medical help without parental consent.

Investigate Special Topics: Child Protective Services

Because of deep concern for the welfare of children and their parents, each state has created an agency called *Child Protective Services (CPS)* or a child protection office under various titles within the state's *Department of Human Services*. The authority to provide certain services is vested in each agency through state laws and government policies.

The men and women who work in these agencies are caseworkers trained in social work. Besides their initial training, caseworkers can receive additional training specific to their jurisdictions through the National Resource Center for Child Protective Services (NRCCPS). This training is funded by the Children's Bureau, U.S. Department of Health and Human Services.

What are the basic responsibilities of caseworkers for CPS? Their roles include

- ***providing services to families in their homes.*** Caseworkers focus on family strengths and provide parents with assistance when needed to protect children within their home.
- ***investigating reports of child neglect and abuse.*** If the reports are *substantiated* (found true), they can decide whether to remove children immediately or provide the parents with assistance and continue follow-up visits.
- ***placing children in the state's foster care program.*** Caseworkers receive children who are abandoned, children they remove from homes, and children police remove from homes. They screen parents who have applied for the role of foster parents. Caseworkers also regularly visit foster homes after child placement.
- ***placing children in adoptive homes.*** In order to do this, parents either surrender their rights or caseworkers decide after a period of time that these children's parents will likely never be able to provide safe homes. They screen parents who have applied to be adoptive parents. (The courts make all final adoption decrees.)
- ***providing assistance to teens as they age-out of the foster care system and make a transition to independent living as adults.*** This assistance is primarily counseling in nature.

In many states, the work of the CPS is coordinated with agencies or *offices of child care assistance*. These agencies provide financial help to pay for child care so teenage and low-income parents can get an education or work. CPS is also coordinated with *child support enforcement*. (Enforces monetary decisions made by the courts on behalf of children when parents have never married, separated, or divorced.) Caseworkers with social work training do the needed investigations. After the investigations, enforcement of child support decisions are done by the courts.

Research Activity

Using online or print sources, conduct research to learn more about Child Protective Services in your community. Then, answer the following questions:

1. What services does Child Protective Services provide for your community?
2. What are the qualifications for becoming a CPS caseworker?
3. What should a person do if he or she is concerned for the welfare of a child?
4. How does CPS handle cases where a child's rights are being violated?

Focus on

Careers

Child Advocate

Child advocates represent the best interests of children who have been abused or neglected. They promote and protect the rights of children.

Career cluster: Law, public safety, corrections, and security.

Education: Educational requirements vary for each state. Training in laws regarding children in the state in which advocates practice is often required.

Job outlook: Future employment opportunities for child advocates are expected to grow much faster than the average for all occupations.

To learn more about a career as a child advocate, visit the United States Department of Labor's *Occupational Outlook Handbook* website. You will also be able to compare the job responsibilities, educational requirements, job outlook, and average pay of child advocates with similar occupations.

Laws can be enacted on the local level, too. An example is a curfew law. In addition, local citizen groups often become **advocates** (people who actively support a cause) of children's rights. These groups attempt to get needed laws passed and notify the appropriate people when it seems a child's rights have been violated. Men and women who are knowledgeable about child development make excellent advocates.

Observing Children

Observation is the oldest, most common, and best way to learn about human behavior, including the behavior of children. You have all the equipment you need for observing—your senses. Because the senses are the main tools you use, you might think observation skills come naturally. To some extent, they do. You see and hear what goes on around you every day. It takes training, however, to interpret what you see and hear into information you can use. For this reason, many observation skills must be learned. These skills come with knowledge and practice. As an example, when you look at an X-ray or sonogram, you probably just see shadows and lines. Why would your doctor see more? With his or her training and experience, your doctor can see meaning in these images you may not notice.

Why Observe Children?

By observing children, you can learn about their growth and development. To observe children, you must focus on a task—what you want to learn. For example, "Are boys in the block center more often than girls, and if so, why?" As you observe, you learn more about children when using your mind to "see" more. Child development researchers often work on specific problems for years—even a lifetime.

During your course in child development, you will receive assignments requiring observation of children. These assignments are an important part of your class for the following reasons:

- Observing children will help you understand what you read in this book and what you hear about children. At the same time, what you learn from your reading and class activities will help you see more when you observe, too (**Figure 1.13**). What you observe will depend on the purpose of observation. Because this book looks at the sequence of children's growth and development, you will consider these principles when you observe.
- You, too, will notice behaviors that are not part of your assigned work. You will want

Figure 1.13 Each time this student observes and takes notes, she learns to see more. *When was the last time you observed a child's behavior? What did you learn from that observation?*

to ask questions about what you see. This is how professional researchers learn.

- Like professional researchers, your assignment may cause you to want to learn more about a behavior. For example, you may hear three-year-olds reciting numbers from 1 to 10. Does this mean they can count objects to 10? To find out, you may need to observe behavior more closely.
- Observing children can help you better interact with the children in your care. You can learn this by observing how others work with children and how the children react to them. When you observe adults who work with children, you can learn to imitate their successful behaviors. For instance, if you observe a teacher sitting on the floor working with children, you might later try this, too. This can help you interact with children in a more positive way. Because many skills are learned through imitation, this type of observation is important.
- In some cases, you may be allowed to participate in the activities of children while observing. Extra "helping hands" are often needed and serve as a learning experience for you, too. In all cases, by watching carefully, you can respond quickly if dangers arise.

Ways to Observe

There are many ways to observe children. The best way is to observe children directly. Many observations, however, are done indirectly.

Direct Observations

A **direct observation** means watching children in their natural environments. These environments include home, play groups, child care programs, schools, and public places, such as shopping centers, parks, and restaurants (**Figure 1.14**). Most direct observations occur in these types of places.

Researchers often set up special laboratory settings where they can do direct observations of behaviors that do not occur in the natural environment. They may need to observe, for example, how a baby reacts when the mother leaves the room and a stranger enters. Researchers also use laboratory observations to speed up the observation process. Suppose researchers want to observe a child's balancing skills. If they go to a park with a balance beam, they may wait hours before they observe enough children to form a sample for their study. In a laboratory, however, children would arrive at the setting, walk the beam, and leave. Researchers also use laboratory settings when special equipment is needed.

Figure 1.14 Parks are one natural environment where direct observation may occur. *Why do you think direct observation must be done in a child's natural environment?*

Observations set in laboratories cannot answer all questions. For instance, it would be hard for researchers to know if children really like playing on a balance beam. Although some information in this book comes from research in the laboratory setting, this is not the way you will start observing. You will begin your observations in the natural setting, as do all researchers.

Indirect Observations

Although direct observation is the main way to learn about children, researchers also use other observation methods to study them. Sometimes they want to see something in more detail or check direct observations. One important method is **indirect observation**. This may include asking questions of parents, teachers, or children. Indirect observation also includes observing products children make, such as artwork or the stories children dictate or write. Studying test scores is an indirect observation. Generally speaking, a researcher can gather more data quickly through indirect observation than through direct observation.

Although you can learn a lot from indirect observations, such as children's artwork, you can learn even more when you observe children making these products. For example, by looking at a drawing, you can easily notice that a child has colored outside the lines. How can you tell if this is due to lack of motor control, a damaged crayon, or a rushed coloring job? Only direct observation will tell you.

Guidelines for Observing

Anyone observing children should follow certain guidelines (**Figure 1.15**). These guidelines are important for several reasons. First, they protect the rights of the subject and the observer. They also list proper behaviors you should follow when visiting a child care center. Finally, these guidelines will help you make meaningful and accurate observations.

Lesson 1.3 Review and Assessment 

1. List four benefits of studying children.
2. According to Maslow, what types of needs are included in a person's basic needs? higher-level needs?
3. List three of the seven irreducible needs of children as identified by Brazelton and Greenspan.
4. What is the primary responsibility of caseworkers for CPS?
5. Differentiate between *direct observation* and *indirect observation*.
6. **Critical thinking.** Why do you think direct observation is the main way to learn about children?

Figure 1.15 Guidelines for Observations

Guidelines	Details About Guidelines
Know your objectives.	Objectives tell you what age children to observe, what type of activity to observe, where to observe (in some cases), how much time to spend observing, what type of records to keep.
Obtain permission to observe.	In public places (a park or shopping center), you may observe children without permission. Parents or other adults are more cooperative, however, when they know what you are doing. To observe in private places (homes or child care programs), you will need prior approval from your teacher and permission from the adult at the home or program. Observe only on dates and times approved by your teacher.
Know what to do at the site.	Sites have different procedures. At some sites, you may observe in an observation room looking through a one-way mirror. At other sites, you may help with the children. In still other sites, you might sit away from the children. Find out in advance what you will be expected to do.
Ask questions at convenient times.	Never interrupt a staff member who is engaged with children or an adult.
Be sure observations do not distract children from regular activities.	Unless asked to help, do not get any closer to the children than necessary. If children come to you, answer them briefly, but encourage them to return to their activities. Also, avoid talking directly to children. Your objectives should never interfere with the program objectives.
Observe carefully and objectively.	Observe closely so you can remember the situation vividly. Many situations can affect objectivity, such as distractions, fatigue, or discomfort. Biases also affect objectivity, so observers should not study their own children or children of close friends or relatives.
Record accurately.	When recording information, avoid leaving out information that may help you understand the situation, recording behaviors that did not occur, and having notes out of sequence. Control this by writing the time in your notes every three to five minutes.
Protect the rights of all observed.	People have privacy rights observers must protect in the following ways: • Never discuss a child in front of that child or an adult except the child's teacher. • Use no name or the child's first name only during class discussions. • Respect parents' rights to refuse your request to observe. • Keep information confidential. • Destroy notes completely when they are no longer useful.

Chapter 1 Review and Assessment

Summary

The scientific study of children is called *child development*. The study of child development involves the physical, intellectual, social, and emotional development through six stages of the individual life cycle. Children's growth and development are affected by heredity and environment.

Most children follow similar patterns called *principles of growth and development*. Many researchers have formed theories about how children grow and develop. No one theory is adequate to describe the complexity of development. Theories, however, give direction for further study of children and provide information needed to work with children.

The study of children is important to understand yourself, be a responsible parent, work with children, and protect children's rights. Observing children is the best way to learn about their behavior. Child observations are done to answer questions, get new ideas, and look for causes that affect behavior.

College and Career Portfolio

Portfolio Foundations

When you apply for college admission, a job, or a community service position, you may need to tell others about your qualifications for the position. A *portfolio* is a selection of related materials you collect and organize. These materials show your qualifications, skills, talents, and interests. For instance, a certificate that shows you completed first aid and CPR training could help you get a summer job working with children through a park district program. An essay you wrote about protecting children from neglect may help you gain admission to the early childhood education college program you desire. A transcript of your school grades also shows your qualifications to a potential college.

There are two types of portfolios people commonly use: *print portfolios* and *electronic portfolios* (e-Portfolios). To learn more about portfolios, complete the following:

- Use the Internet to search for *print portfolios* and *e-Portfolio*. Read several articles about each type of portfolio. In your own words, briefly write a summary of each type.
- You will be creating a portfolio for this class. Based on your reading, which type of portfolio would you prefer to create? Why? Write a paragraph summarizing your thinking.

Chapter 1 Review and Assessment

Vocabulary Activities

1. In small groups, create categories for the following terms and classify as many of the terms as possible. Then, share your ideas with the rest of the class.

Key Terms

age norm (1.2)
child-centered society (1.3)
child development (1.1)
development (1.1)
developmental acceleration (1.2)
developmental delay (1.2)
direct observation (1.3)
environment (1.1)
epigenome (1.1)
genes (1.1)
genetics (1.1)
heredity (1.1)
indirect observation (1.3)
individual life cycle (1.1)
intellectual development (1.1)
physical development (1.1)
principles of growth and development (1.2)
self-actualization (1.3)
sequenced steps (1.2)
social-emotional development (1.1)
stressors (1.1)
teachable moment (1.2)
theory (1.2)

2. On a separate sheet of paper, list words that are related to each of the following terms. Then, working with a partner, explain how these words are related.

Academic Terms

advocates (1.3)
codified (1.2)
confirm (1.2)
constancy (1.2)
disprove (1.2)
domains (1.1)
empathize (1.3)
growth (1.1)
hierarchy (1.3)
interrelated (1.2)
irreducible (1.3)
motivation (1.2)
potential (1.1)

Critical Thinking

3. **Cause and effect.** Give an example of how learning a skill in one developmental domain affects other developmental domains.
4. **Draw conclusions.** What are the names of other stages in the life cycle that refer to teens and adults? What major developments or changes occur in these stages?
5. **Make inferences.** In what ways do you think you have developed from infancy until now?
6. **Determine.** Which of your traits were determined by genes that were passed to you by your parents?
7. **Identify.** Identify hereditary and environmental factors that make you unique.
8. **Cause and effect.** In small groups, discuss how developmental acceleration and developmental delay might affect a young child. Give examples of two developmental accelerations and two developmental delays and briefly summarize the impact they might have.
9. **Make inferences.** Trace the effects of a different problem, such as poor nutrition or lack of affection, on all areas of development. How are the areas of development interrelated?
10. **Compare and contrast.** Choose two theories of child development that are discussed in this chapter. Then, create a T-chart listing the components of each theory. Draw lines between components the theories have in common and highlight the differences between the theories. Discuss your charts in class.
11. **Assess.** Close your eyes and listen for sounds that could be used in an observation. What do you hear? How do you identify these sounds as ones being used in an observation?
12. **Draw conclusions.** What have you learned through observation?

Core Skills

13. **Writing.** Write phrases describing a child. The child could be one whom you know well, or one who is imaginary. How is the child creative? How is the child challenging? How do you think studying child development can help you interact with this child?
14. **Reading.** Read an autobiography or biography about the life of a famous person in any career. Look for examples of constancy in the person's growth and development. How did this constancy lead to fame in his or her career? Summarize, in your own words, the information presented in the text in simple, but accurate terms. Share your findings with the class.

15. **Listening, speaking, and writing.** Conduct an oral history interview with an older family member or with an older adult you know. Acquire permission to audio- or video-record the interview and to take any photos. Then do the following:
    - Share with the person what you have learned about developmental tasks.
    - Ask the person to describe developmental tasks he or she mastered that people seldom master today. Examples may include household tasks or chores, hobbies, games, and job duties of the past.
    - Listen carefully to encourage your interviewee. Use eye contact and nodding to give assurance you are listening.
    - Give a brief oral report to the class contrasting the accomplishment of developmental tasks in years past with those of today.
    - Use the interview as a foundation for creating a print or digital family history book. Add photos, written stories about family members, and memories to the history book. To take this project a step further, develop a self-directed FCCLA *Power of One* project on *Family Ties*. Use the *FCCLA Planning Process* to plan, carry out, and evaluate your project. Your FCCLA adviser can provide further information.
16. **Listening and speaking.** In small groups, discuss ways in which society is child-centered and ways in which society is adult-centered. Can a society resolve these dual interests? How can a new family find a balance for a happier family life? Build on one another's ideas and then express these ideas in a discussion with the rest of the class.
17. **Writing.** Write a one-page narrative on the history of child labor laws in the United States. How did the needs of children lead to the development of these laws?
18. **Listening and speaking.** Interview a person working with children in a child-related career, such as a child care teacher or child care provider. What characteristics does this person need to work with children? What are the job responsibilities? What are the educational and training requirements for the career? Give a one-minute oral presentation of your findings in class.
19. **Research and writing.** According to researchers from the *Center on the Developing Child* at Harvard University, "the foundations of lifelong health are built in early childhood." Research the core roots of health that support physical and mental well-being from early childhood through the lifespan. Read at least three articles on this topic and summarize your findings in writing. Begin your research at the Harvard University website. As you read, ask yourself:
    - Who are the researchers and why are they credible?
    - What foundations of health help nourish physical and mental well-being? Why are they important?
    - What do parents and caregivers need to do to build a foundation of health?
    - How do the articles support the information in this chapter?
20. **CTE Career Readiness Practice.** Everyone has a stake in protecting the environment. Taking steps as an individual to be more environmentally conscious is a behavior of responsible citizens. From a business standpoint, it may also help a company be more profitable. In what ways can child care workers in a day care save energy or other resources?

Observations

21. In small groups, list some specific observation topics, such as sharing toys, participating during group time, and performing certain physical skills. Discuss what behaviors you might expect to observe in each of these observations. Then, compare and discuss your lists and ideas in class.
22. In indirect observations, children are not directly performing an activity. Researchers observe artwork or interview caregivers for comments about children. In small groups, give examples of specific children's work/products that could be used in indirect observations. Discuss the types of information you can gather from using this observation method.
23. In small groups, observe a group of people in a public place such as a park or a shopping mall. List characteristics you see that are due to heredity and characteristics you see that are due to environment. Compare and discuss your lists in class.

Chapter 2 New Directions in Learning

Essential Question

How has recent brain research enlightened people's knowledge of child development?

Lesson 2.1 **Brain Studies**

Lesson 2.2 **Acquiring Knowledge**

Case Study Why Are Some Children So Disorganized?

As a class, read the case study and discuss the questions that follow. After you finish studying the chapter, discuss this case study again. Have your opinions changed based on what you learned?

As Jonathan approaches the end of the fourth grade, his teacher, Mrs. Truax, is considering retaining him rather than promoting him to the fifth grade. During a parent-teacher conference, Mrs. Truax talks with Jonathan's parents about his failing grades on homework assignments in all subjects. Mrs. Truax also points out that Jonathan dawdles during class and gives Jonathan's parents some examples of his behaviors. She then shows them his desk storage area where they find missing homework assignments and notes to go home, including a note about a school party. School supplies are also mixed with the crumpled papers. Mrs. Truax mentions that Jonathan is a polite child who always makes a promise "to do better." At the end of the conference, she schedules a follow-up conference next week with the parents and principal to finalize retention plans. She encourages the parents to express their ideas next week at the conference.

As they leave the school, Jonathan's father tells his wife that she is just too easy on Jonathan and spends way too much time helping him with homework, packing his backpack, et cetera. Jonathan's mother recognizes Jonathan's weaknesses, but sees him as an interesting and loving child. She does acknowledge that she spends more time helping Jonathan with his school preparations than most parents do and is frustrated by this.

Give It Some Thought

1. Do you think the teacher's idea of retention will help Jonathan? Why or why not?
2. Do you think the mother is babying Jonathan too much? Why or why not?
3. What do you think is Jonathan's problem? What could the parents do to help Jonathan be more organized? Explain your answer.
4. How might the teacher and parents approach Jonathan's problem?

While studying this chapter, look for the online resources icon  to:

- **Practice** terms with e-flash cards and interactive games
- **Assess** what you learn by completing self-assessment quizzes
- **Expand** knowledge with interactive activities and graphic organizers

Companion G-W Learning

www.g-wlearning.com/childdevelopment

Study on the go

Use a mobile device to practice terms and review with self-assessment quizzes.

www.m.g-wlearning.com/0384

Lesson 2.1 Brain Studies

Key Terms

axons
critical periods
dendrites
firing
glial cells
myelin
neurons
plasticity
pruning
sensitive periods
synapse
window of opportunity
wiring

Academic Terms

abundance
biochemistry
seldom
tentative

Objectives

After studying this lesson, you will be able to

- describe the two major goals of recent child development research.
- compare the basic differences between the functions of neurons and glial cells.
- illustrate the process by which neurons communicate with each other.
- give three reasons why brain plasticity is helpful.
- explain what is meant by using windows of opportunity to aid children's learning.
- identify two offenders of normal brain functioning.

Reading and Writing Activity

What do you already know about the brain? Copy the key terms from this lesson onto another piece of paper. Set a timer for three minutes and then write as many facts or predictions about the meanings of these key terms as you can. Once your three minutes are up, keep the paper and expand or correct your definitions while reading this lesson. Finally, after reading, write a summary paragraph of this lesson using all of the key terms.

Graphic Organizer

In a chart like the one shown, write the main headings of this lesson. As you read, take notes and organize them by heading. Draw a star beside any words or concepts you do not yet understand.

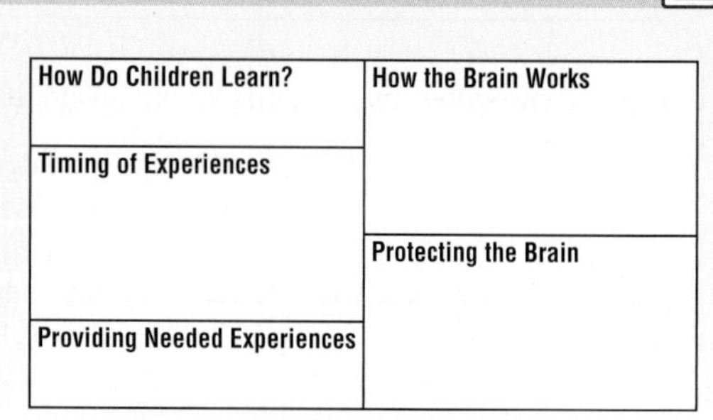

The study of children has changed over the years. The scientific study of children emerged from the field of psychology. First it was called *child study* and then *child development*.

As you may recall, one of the goals of scientists and researchers in child development is to learn more about children. The theorists had their own research interests, such as age norms or personality development. During the last half century, child development research has mainly focused on the cognitive theories (intellectual domain) of Piaget and Vygotsky. Although these theories are still being researched, the "new" research frontier of the 21st century is brain studies. Researchers have long been interested in the brain, but major technological advances allow for much more precise study. Because these studies are rather new, what findings come out today may be updated tomorrow.

How Do Children Learn?

In child development, people use the word *learning* in a broad sense. People might say *learning* is any permanent change in knowledge or behavior. The words *learning* and *development* are almost the same because both refer to changes in all domains. For example, a child

- learns motor skills (physical development)
- acquires knowledge of people, places, objects, and events, and even gains insight into how to learn (intellectual development)
- learns to understand, speak, read, and write words (intellectual development)
- learns how to interact with others (social development)
- learns to express emotions in a healthy way (emotional development)

All changes result from some type of experience, such as personal experiences in the environment, imitation, guided discovery, or direct instruction. Although the whole body is involved in learning, the command center of the body is the brain. The brain is responsible for controlling most body functions. These include operation of the body systems, movements, thinking, memory, and feelings.

How the Brain Works

Scientists and other people who study and work with children have long been curious about the brain's growth, developmental change, activity, and potential damage. Until recently, the brain was mostly a mystery although brain development was inferred through observed behaviors in children, especially through Piaget's research on intellectual milestones (stages). In recent years, however, scientists have learned much more about brain development. Much of this knowledge is gained from the use of high technology (brain scans) and advances in **biochemistry** (the chemistry of living organisms). **Figure 2.1** shows a *magnetic resonance image (MRI)*, which is a specific type of brain scan. An **abundance** (large amount) of brain research is now in progress. Although many questions have been answered, many more remain for scientists to unravel.

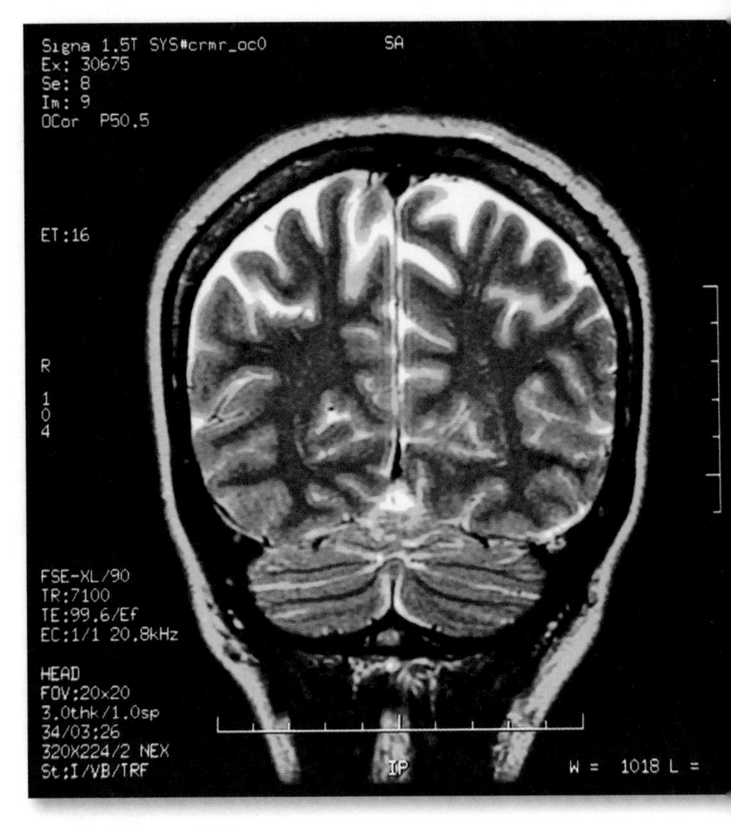

Figure 2.1 A magnetic resonance image (MRI) is a brain scan that can be used to diagnose diseases and disorders of the brain. These pictures of the brain have also helped scientists understand the brain at different stages of development. *Why do you think the ability to image the brain is so important to understanding it?*

Knowing Brain Biology

Brain development begins shortly after conception. Before birth, about 250,000 brain cells are formed each minute. Full-term babies have about 100 billion brain cells. The brain, however, is the least developed organ at birth. The brain is often compared to a computer, but unlike a computer, the brain is turned on long before it is completed.

A newborn's brain is only about 25 percent of the size of the adult brain. The newborn's brain develops rapidly in stages, which can be noted by

- increases in head circumference
- increases of 5 to 10 percent in brain weight during a stage (with only a 1-percent gain between each stage)
- changes in the cells

Brain growth happens when brain chemicals are released in waves. Brain growth occurs in a predictable, biological sequence that is the same for all people.

The stages of fastest growth after birth are shown in **Figure 2.2**. The time between each stage is used for practicing and gaining expertise and efficiency in the skills developed in previous stages. For example, between four and six years of age, motor and sensory skills combine to develop eye-hand coordination needed for activities, such as catching balls, drawing, writing, playing musical instruments, and eating with flatware.

The brain is made up of two types of cells—neurons and glial (GLEE-uhl) cells. **Neurons** (nerve cells) are brain cells that send and receive chemical and electrical impulses among each other to direct the various tasks of the brain. Their overall task is to receive, process, and transport information needed by the person to perform all tasks. (This is called *communication*.) There are three types of neurons, and each type has its own specific tasks and the following three parts (**Figure 2.3**):

- The *cell body* contains genetic information and proteins for cell maintenance.
- **Dendrites** (DEHN-drights), which means *trees*, are short, bushy cables that allow each neuron to receive signals sent by other neurons (the input function).
- **Axons**, which means *axis*, are long, thick cables with terminal buttons (small knobs at the end of the axons) that transmit all the signals from a neuron to other neurons (the output function).

Glial cells are brain cells that support neurons. Glial means *glue*. About 90 percent of the cells in the brain are glial cells. Four types of glial cells support the neurons (**Figure 2.4**). Unlike neurons, glial cells divide—especially during times of fastest brain growth. Perhaps because neurons need differing amounts of support, glial cells vary in density throughout the brain. Glial cells have a large cell body with legs extending out from the body.

Figure 2.2 Stages of Fastest Brain Growth After Birth

Age	Area Maturing
3–10 months	Activation (turning on) and control of motor actions.
2–4 years	Maturation of the senses. (The senses function near the adult level by the end of the stage.)
6–8 years	Emergence (beginning) of logical thinking about actual experiences. (Unlike the previous stages that are genetically programmed, logical thinking must be taught and practiced.)
10–12 years (females) and 12–14 years (males)	Beginning of generalized thinking beyond actual experiences—abstract reasoning. (This ability allows older children and teens to understand higher mathematics and science.)

Figure 2.3 Neurons

Types and functions of neurons

- ***Sensory neurons***—transfer information from the external environment to the central nervous system (CNS).
- ***Motor neurons***—transfer information from the CNS to the external environment.
- ***Interneurons (associative neurons)***—process information in the CNS and transfer information from one neuron to another within the CNS.

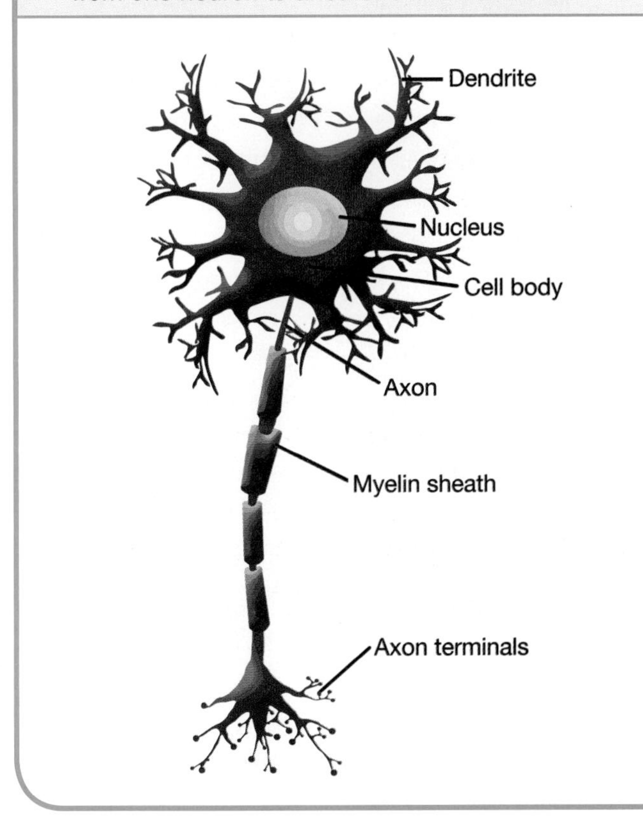

Making and Sorting Connections

Each area of the brain is highly specialized (**Figure 2.5**). Before birth, all cells must migrate to their special location. For example, neurons that migrate to the occipital (ahk-SIP-uh-tal) lobe become vision neurons during migration. Glial cells aid this migration by making fiber trails. Neurons use these trails to find the right location. While neurons are migrating, glial cells nourish them.

The Wiring Process

In the beginning, neurons that need to make connections (communicate) will be near each other. Later, neurons can grow very long axons to reach distant neurons. The network of fibers that carry brain signals between neurons is called **wiring**. Genes create the structure for wiring. Thus, wiring for each person is unique. Some neurons are permanently wired at birth. This wiring is needed to sustain life (breathing, heartbeat, blood pressure, reflexes, digestion, and excretion) and to begin learning through sensory input. All of the remaining wiring is **tentative** (not permanent; may change) due to experiences, which along with genes, makes each person unique.

The Sorting Process

As soon as sections of the brain are wired, connections must be sorted in a step-by-step process. The sorting process is called *learning*. Everything in the sorting process depends on physical well-being and quality, age-appropriate experiences.

With each experience (from simply looking at an object to working an equation), signals are sent from one neuron to others. One neuron can connect with as many as 250,000 other neurons at the same time. How does this happen? Neurons never touch each other. There is a tiny gap between neurons, which is called a **synapse** (SIH-naps). A chemical and electrical signal (called a *neurotransmitter*) leaves the axon of one neuron and jumps the synapse to travel to the dendrite of another neuron. This process is known as **firing** (**Figure 2.6**).

The Firing Process

Repeated and varied experiences trigger repeated firings in different parts of the brain. Repeated firings along the connections result in both strengthening the connections and forming even more synapses to enable more learning. Babies begin with about 1,000 trillion connections, which allows for very rapid learning during the early years.

Each sensory input (what you see, hear, feel, taste, or smell) goes to its own *primary sensory cortex*. Neurons in the primary sensory cortex receive only very basic information related to the five senses. For example, in the hearing area, the neurons receive pitch and volume. Unless sensory organs are damaged, everyone has these sensory inputs.

From here this information travels to neurons in the *sensory association area*, or the largest part of the

Figure 2.4 Glial Cells

Types	Functions
Astrocytes (AS-truh-sites)	• Help the neurons receive nourishment. • Control chemical environment of the brain. • Restrict certain substances from entering the brain.
Microglia (my-KRAWG-lee-uh)	• Remove cellular waste.
Ependymal (eh-PEN-duh-muhl)	• Form a protective covering around spinal cord and central brain cavities.
Oligodendrocytes (AW-lih-go-DEN-druh-sites)	• Help insulate the axons with myelin.

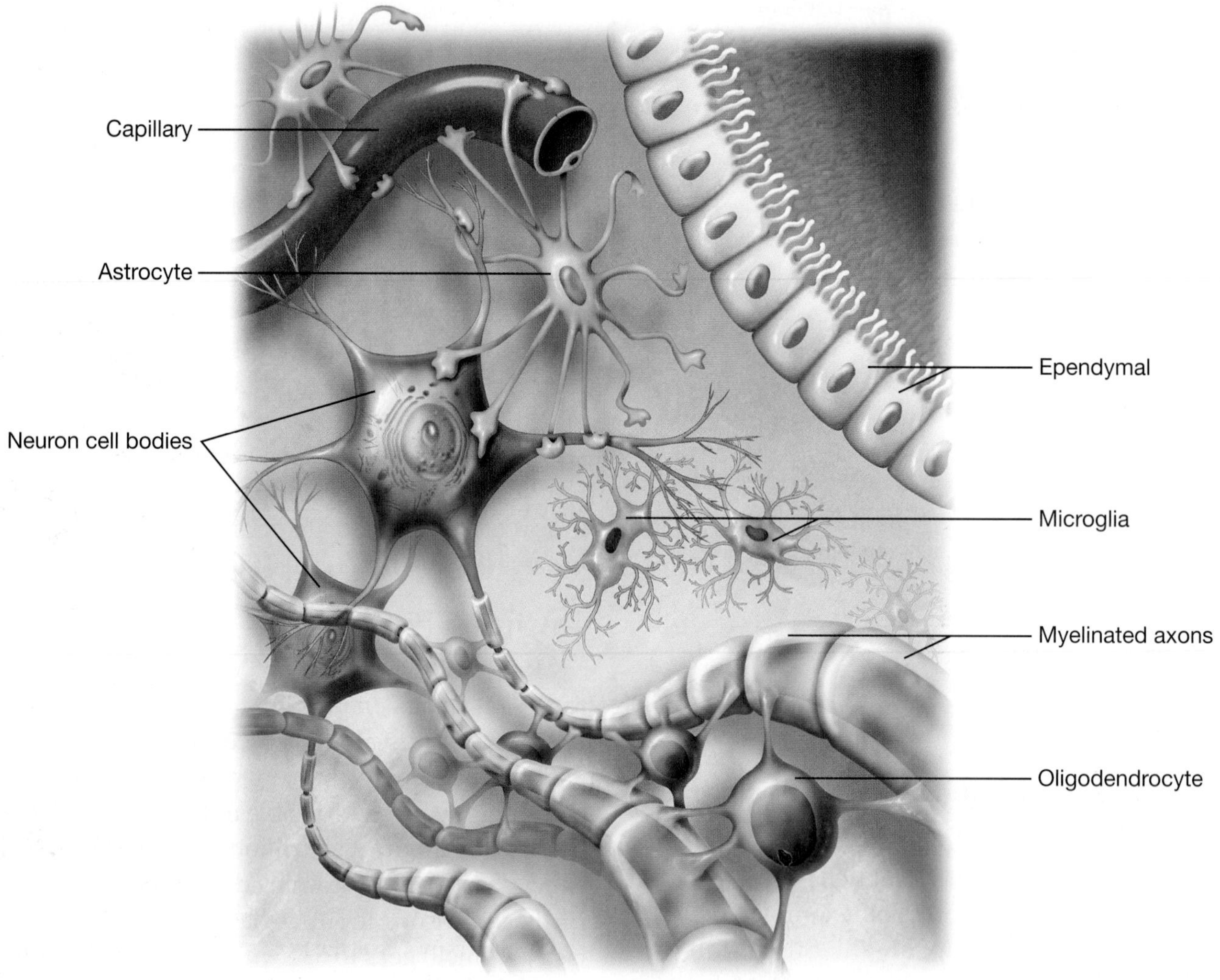

brain. Through many experiences, the brain makes sound associations, such as knowing the sound of an emergency vehicle siren, a bird call, or ice falling into a cup. Quality experiences determine the richness of associations and therefore learning.

Another area of the brain, the *multimodal area*, is used for combining two or more sensory association areas. For example, the brain can process motor movements used in talking and emotional overtones in what is said at the same time. The

Figure 2.5 Areas and Functions of the Brain

Areas	Functions
Temporal lobe	hearing, smell, memory, speech
Frontal lobe	memory, intelligence, behavior, emotions, motor function, smell
Parietal (puh-RYE-uh-tuhl) lobe	pain, touch, sensations of hot and cold, speech
Occipital lobe	vision, speech
Cerebellum (ser-uh-BELL-uhm)	body movements and balance
Brain stem	breathing, heart rate, blood pressure, reflexes, sleep

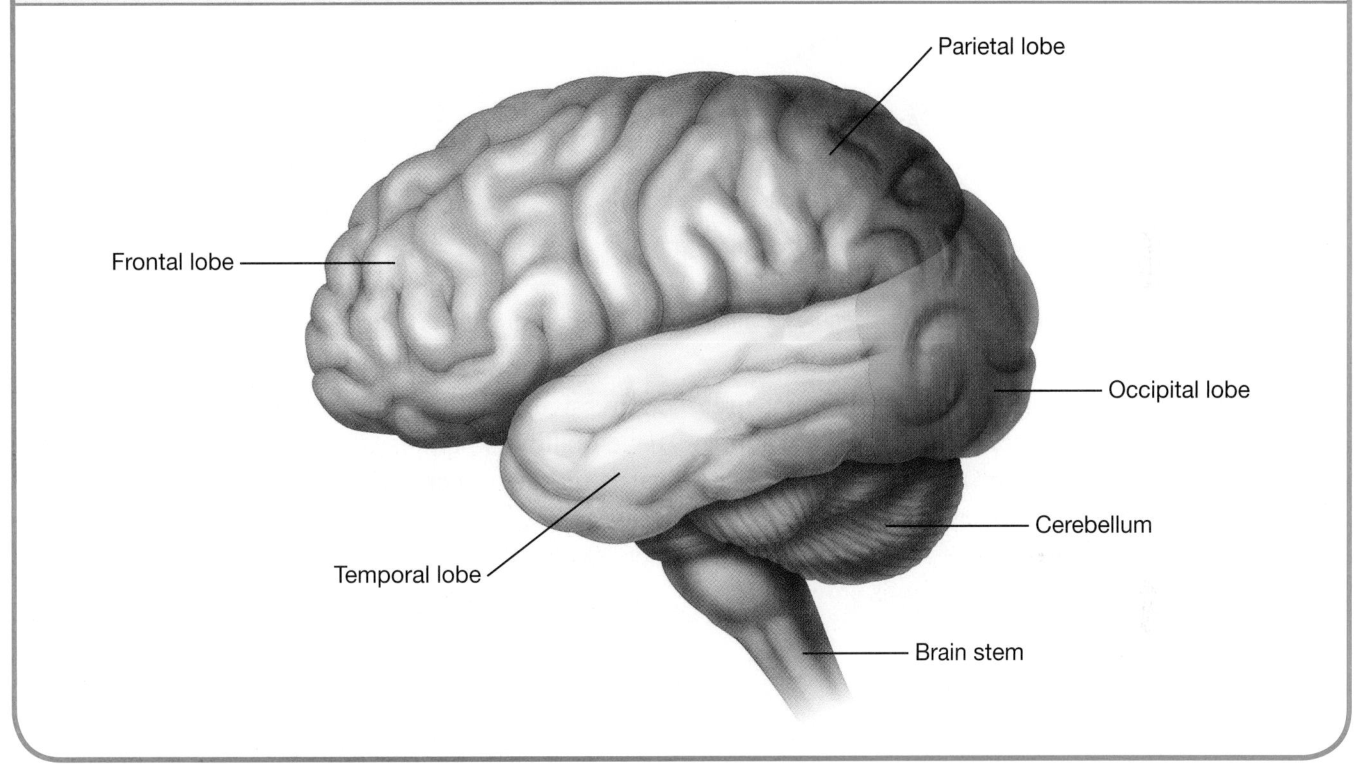

multimodal areas also process thinking that does not need sensory inputs, such as planning and decision making. **Figure 2.7** shows an overview of the firing process.

The brain can use a stronger connection more easily than a weak one. Over time, the brain continues to strengthen used pathways. Because some connections are used so much, they become automatic (or *hardwired*). For example, when you handwrite, you no longer think about forming letters. Hardwired connections are not forgotten. Riding a bicycle, playing a musical instrument, or playing a sport are other skills that become automatic once you learn them.

The Pruning Process

To make the brain more efficient, it cannot keep **seldom** (rarely) used or unused connections. The brain weeds out these connections in a process called **pruning**. Healthy pruning allows the remaining connections to become strong, which increases the speed and efficiency for often-used brain signals. Too much pruning means the person will find it most difficult to develop certain needed skills and abilities. Pruning begins in the very first years of a child's life and is almost completed by 10 years of age. For example, at birth, each neuron has 25,000 synapses. By three years of age, each neuron has pruned 10,000 tentative connections.

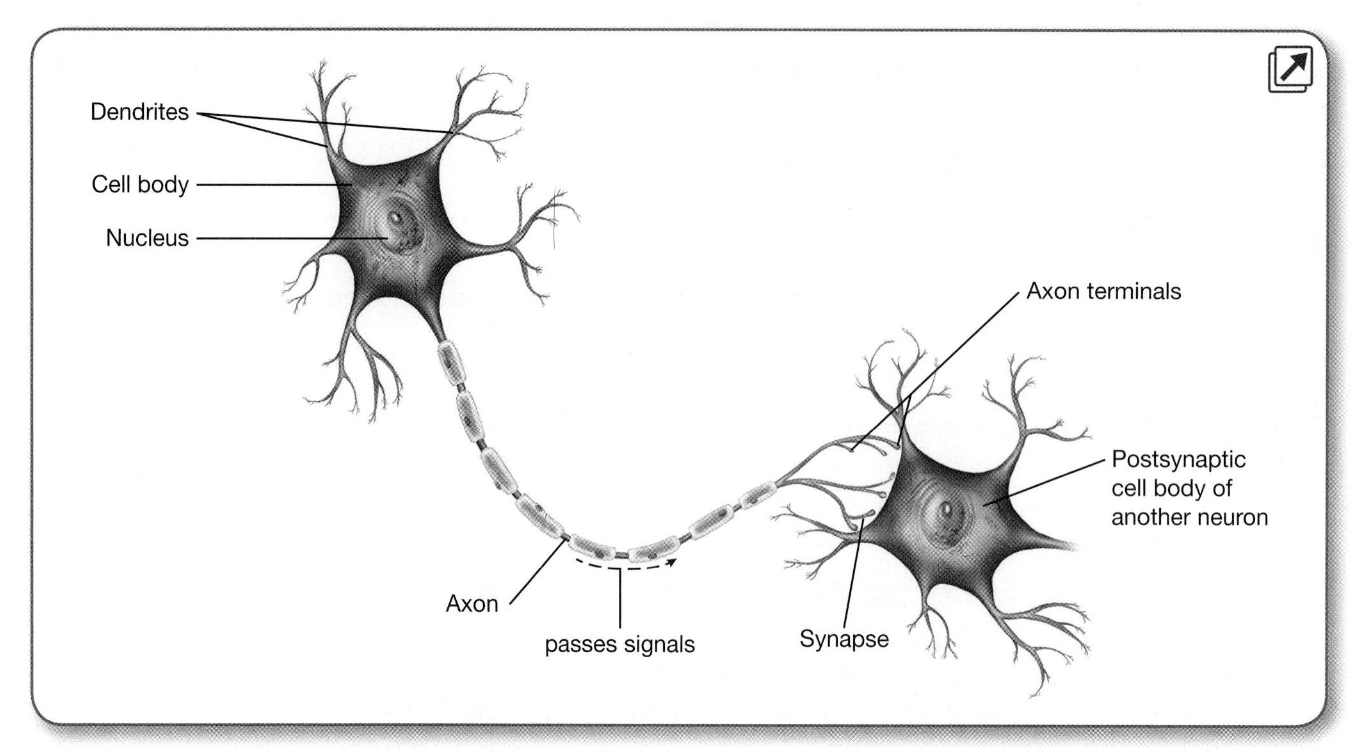

Figure 2.6 In the firing process, an electrical signal crosses the space or synapse between two neurons, jumping from one neuron's axon terminals to another neuron's dendrites. *Can one neuron communicate with multiple other neurons?*

For the brain to work well, signals must fire quickly. Similar to electrical tape wrapped around wires, **myelin** (MY-uh-luhn), a fatty substance formed by glial cells, wraps around longer axons and cushions the cell bodies of neurons. Without myelin, signals would travel 30 times slower.

Reshaping Connections: Brain Plasticity

As you have read, babies and children until 10 years of age create many new connections in their brains. After 10 years of age, pruning is rather aggressive. Does this mean the child who did not have quality experiences cannot learn and possibly catch up with peers? Can a person who suffers a brain injury recover? Can adults who need to learn new skills for their careers do so? Can older adults, who develop a new interest, gain new abilities? The answer to all of these questions is *yes* because the human brain is adaptable.

The brain has the ability to change or adapt to the environment. This ability to be shaped and reshaped is called **plasticity** (technically *brain plasticity*). For many years, scientists thought the brain was only plastic during the early years. Now

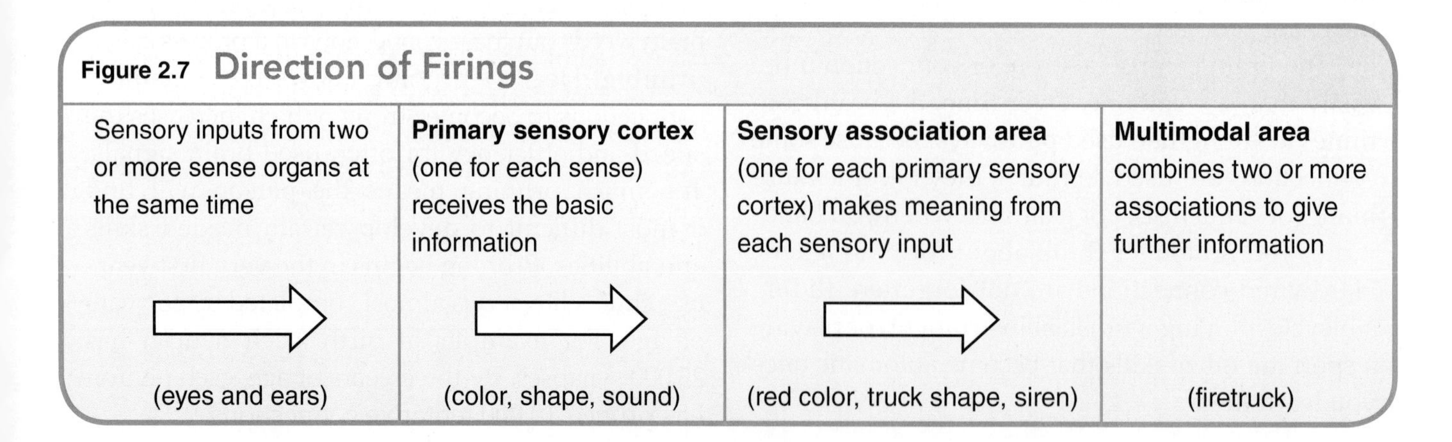

Figure 2.7 Direction of Firings

Sensory inputs from two or more sense organs at the same time →	**Primary sensory cortex** (one for each sense) receives the basic information →	**Sensory association area** (one for each primary sensory cortex) makes meaning from each sensory input →	**Multimodal area** combines two or more associations to give further information
(eyes and ears)	(color, shape, sound)	(red color, truck shape, siren)	(firetruck)

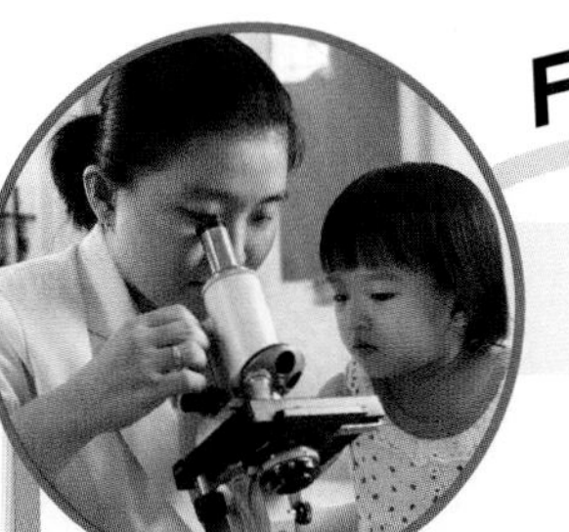

Focus on Science

Brain Development

Rich sensory experiences strengthen and refine the brain's wiring. A lack of stimulation can prevent some connections from forming and cause pruning to other connections. In fact, early experiences have such a dramatic effect on brain wiring that they can increase or decrease the final number of synapses by as much as 25 percent. The effects this has on future learning potential are life-long. What does this say about the importance of caring for babies and young children? What effects can effective caregiving have on the future of your community, country, and the world? What results might ineffective caregiving have?

they know that the brain is plastic each time a person learns something new. Glial cells aid plasticity by dividing as a person needs more memory cells. Because the brain is plastic, a person can make up for a lost function, too. For example, although damaged neurons cannot be replaced after an injury, nearby cells can change their functions to take on functions of the damaged cells. This is another example of plasticity.

Children's brains are more plastic than adults' brains for the following reasons:

- Children have more connections than they need to function. Adults have lost many of their connections. Rerouting communication among neurons is easier with more connections.
- Chemicals that aid making connections are far more active in the earlier years. The brain of a three-year-old is two and a half times more active than an adult's brain.
- Connections are more flexible in the early years and become more stabilized as people age.

Timing of Experiences

Although the brain is plastic, timing is an important concept when it comes to brain development. The entire brain is not wired at one time. Years ago, brain wiring was noted by observing the developmental skills in children. They called these periods the *stages of development*. Today, brain researchers use brain scans to note optimal times for making connections. They note two types of periods in wiring—*critical periods* and *sensitive periods*.

Critical periods are times when some part of the body is very vulnerable to lack of stimulation or to negative experiences. For example, if babies are born with cataracts and do not have them removed in the first few months, they will forever be blind. Vision neurons die without light stimulation. The brain is not plastic when it comes to most wiring completed during the first six months of pregnancy and for vision after birth.

Sensitive periods are times when the brain is best able to wire specific skills for all children. Although the brain is plastic, matching the right skills to the sensitive times means easier learning, a better foundation for later skills, and performance at a higher level than if learned later.

Why is this information useful? Knowing when the brain timing for various skills occurs helps parents and teachers offer the right kinds of experiences for a child at the best possible times. They will know which skills they should encourage most and which will likely come at a later time. This can help children's brains reach their full potential.

Offering the best experiences at the right times is called *using the windows of opportunity*. A **window of opportunity** is a prime period in a child's life for developing a particular skill. In this window, the child reaches a peak capacity to learn this skill if given the opportunity. At this time, a certain type of stimulation is more critical than others. Given the right stimulation at the right times is very positive for development. On the other hand, if a child does not receive the right stimulation within given time frames, these times could be called *windows of vulnerability*. During windows of vulnerability, development is likely to be impaired.

Each area has its own window of opportunity (**Figure 2.8**). Most windows are large, which means the favorable time for learning this skill is several years. Motor development is a good example. Some windows are small, which means the most favorable time for learning is a few months, such as the window for vision.

Often, the windows of opportunity for various tasks overlap. This means a child will likely be learning those skills at the same time if given the opportunity. Many of the overlapping skills are related, such as social attachments and emotional control.

Figure 2.8 Windows of Opportunity

	Skill Area	Sensitive Time
Motor	Posture and coordination	Birth–2 years
	Large muscle	Birth–5 years
	Small muscle	6 months–9 years
Vision	Sight	Birth–4 to 6 months
	Acuity	Birth–7 years
	Binocular	1–3 years
Language	Phonemes (FO-neems) in languages one will speak	Birth–7 to 11 months
	Idea of connections between words and objects	4 months–1 year
	Vocabulary	Birth–3 years
	Syntax	Birth–6 years
Social	Attachment	Birth–2 years
	Independence	1½ years–3 years
	Cooperation	2–4 years
Emotional	Trust	Birth–14 months
	Intelligence (read other's emotions)	Birth–4 years
	Control	Birth–3 years
	Cope with stress	Birth–2 years
Thinking skills (including math)	Prelogical (perceptual)	6 months–5 years
	Logical	5 or 6 years–puberty
Music	Absolute ("perfect") pitch	Birth–5 years
	Appreciation	Birth–9 years
	Learning	3–9 years

Providing Needed Experiences

Cutting-edge science on brain development confirms what many parents and caregivers have known for years. The earliest years are the most important for all areas of growth and development (physical, intellectual, and social-emotional). All experiences affect the brain's performance.

The best experiences for young children include interaction with loving adults engaged in daily tasks and family-type activities. (Even child care programs for children under three years of age should have

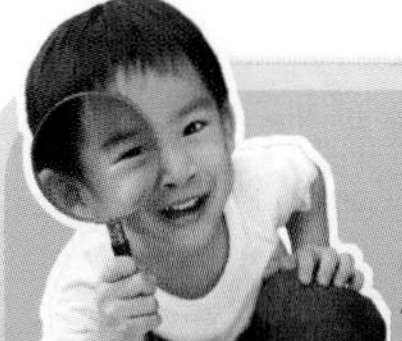

Investigate Special Topics: How Environmental Interactions Shape a Unique Brain

Think about this statement: The brain is the only body organ shaped by its interactions with the environment. A person's sensory organs receive information from the environment, but are not changed by how often or what they see, hear, feel, taste, or smell or by movements. (Sensory organs may be damaged by environmental factors, such as too much light or extremely loud sounds.) Sensory organs are simply essential conveyors of messages to the brain. Internal organs react to the environment only after getting brain signals. For example, the eyes see something dangerous. The brain sends a message to the heart and lungs to speed up, preparing the body to react. The brain monitors more sensory input and sends messages to "react more" or "all is well."

Because each person has different experiences, each brain is unique. Following are the major ways the environment shapes the brain:

- The brain is the most vulnerable organ to a person's overall health. Because the brain changes throughout life, proper nutrition, sleep, and physical activity are always critical.
- The brain only learns through quality experiences that are meaningful, relevant, and challenging. Because the sensory organs are the messengers to the brain, the brain learns through four *modalities*—seeing, hearing, moving, and touching. Although most people have a preferred modality for learning, the more ways a person can activate all modalities, the greater the learning.
- New learning must be linked to previous patterns of stored information, which is called *memory*. The brain is so organized that different types of memory (short-term, long-term—facts, experiences, and how to do things) are stored in different parts of the brain.
- The emotional aspects of all experiences are filtered by the "emotional brain." A little stress challenges a person to learn, but too much stress interferes with learning, including memory.

As you begin your study of child development, remember how a person's brain makes him or her unique. Not even the greatest theorist can put child development knowledge into a unique package to fit each child. Thus, children never come with a complete user's manual. Even if they did, the manual would change with each experience. Those who work with children must constantly respond to each child's manual based on their study of and experiences with children.

Writing Activity

A variety of factors—including life experiences, emotions, and physical health—can shape the brain and influence how a child or adult thinks or learns. Create a list of all the experiences, emotions, or physical states that you imagine may have influenced your brain. Then, write responses to the following questions: How did these factors shape your thinking patterns? How do you think your brain would work differently if you had been exposed to different conditions or experiences?

a home-like atmosphere.) Babies and very young children need not be taught in a formal way. These children learn by playing, especially with caring adults. Children need choices in what and how to learn. Closely observing children and following their lead in play activities is often "best practice." Children usually choose age-appropriate experiences that parallel the windows of opportunity. Children need time to practice and master skills. Repetition of experiences develops the brain.

Good books and a few quality toys that allow for different types of play (blocks, balls, art materials, sand, and water) are better than toys with limited play possibilities. Why is this true? There is a hierarchy of circuits in each area of the brain that mature at different times. Thus, the same environment will produce a different experience for a child at each stage of development. For example, in the vision area of the brain, seeing color, shape, and motion occurs before interpreting facial expression. Over a period of time, a child will learn something new from the same book.

Protecting the Brain

The brain is part of the human body. Nutrition, sleep, physical activity, and general health all affect a person's brain (**Figure 2.9**). For example, 60 percent of daily nutrients are used by the brain during the first year. The fat content in breast milk or formula for infants and whole milk for weaned toddlers is essential for myelin development. Do you know why tired people become fretful and say that their thinking is not clear? Without rest, the neurotransmitters become depleted. Rest restores the working of the brain.

Without quality early experiences, the brain connections can be pruned too much and the windows of opportunity are missed. Although it does not happen often, overstimulation can be harmful, too. It can make children tired, frustrated, and unable to focus. Overstimulation, such as loud music, can even cause hearing neurons to die.

The worst offenders of normal brain development are factors that can cause harm to the unborn child. After birth, the worst offenders are lack of positive give-and-take with parents or toxic stress due to neglect or abuse in the early years. When too much harm occurs, children often have less capacity to learn. Toxic and long-term stress leads to emotional and behavioral problems, too.

Figure 2.9 An infant or child's nutrition can dramatically affect his or her brain health and development. *Why do you think nutrition can have such an impact on the brain?*

Lesson 2.1 Review and Assessment 

1. Describe how technology has aided child development research.
2. List the four types of glial cells and their functions.
3. Neuron wiring _____ (varies/does not vary) according to a person's genes and experiences.
4. Explain and draw a diagram of the firing process.
5. Why does pruning occur?
6. Explain the concept of brain plasticity and why it is important.
7. What is the difference between *critical periods* and *sensitive periods*?
8. **Critical thinking.** Choose one window of opportunity and note the age range for that window. What are four age-appropriate experiences that could develop this particular skill?

Acquiring Knowledge

Lesson 2.2

Objectives

After studying this lesson, you will be able to

- differentiate between four types of knowledge.
- explain how knowledge of child development is used in education.
- identify and describe three executive functions.
- analyze Galinsky's seven life skills.
- assess the dangers of stress and trauma in children.

Key Terms

cognitive flexibility
developmental tasks
essential life skills
executive functions (EFs)
inhibition
lifelong learning
working memory

Academic Terms

explicit
implicit
manipulating
neuroscience
reinforcement

Reading and Writing Activity

Write the objectives for this lesson on a piece of paper and then, beneath each objective, rewrite it as a question. While reading this lesson, take notes about information relating to these objectives. After reading, refer to your notes and write two to three sentences answering each objective's question.

Graphic Organizer

Write *What Should Children Learn?* in the middle circle of a chart like the one shown. Then, as you read this lesson, write the major skills or types of information children should learn in the surrounding boxes. After you have filled in the boxes, consider how stress and environment might affect a child's ability to learn these types of information. Write or illustrate some of these factors around each box.

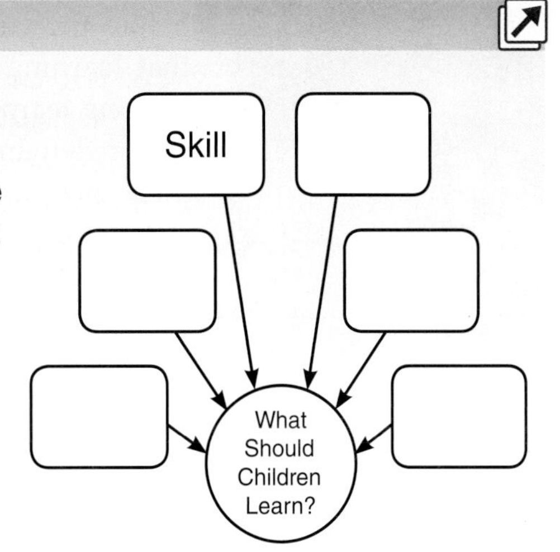

Child development involves the study of children and the adults in their lives. The first goal of child development research is to advance knowledge. The other goal is to apply knowledge. People who work with or for children, especially in education, not only use available research knowledge, but also create more knowledge. For example, child care and education programs are natural laboratories for the study of children (**Figure 2.10**). Schools for older children are also using child development research to guide curriculum decisions. Popular phrases in today's schools are words coming from brain studies, such as *windows of opportunity* and *brain-compatible learning*.

Professionals in health and protective services also contribute to the knowledge of child development. These experts try to prevent and treat mental health issues in children. They are returning to Erikson's theory and brain studies to provide more answers. It is becoming clear that the roots of mental health problems, for children and adults, are in the stressors of childhood. Although the scars of trauma and stress may be seen on the bodies of children and in their behaviors, the real scars may be within their brains.

Figure 2.10 Child care and education centers are natural, ideal environments in which to watch children interact and learn. *What other locations or situations would make an ideal environment for observing children?*

What Should Children Learn?

The last lesson posed the question, "How do children learn?" You learned that biology coupled with broad experiences determined how children learn. Because the brain is so plastic, people can learn almost anything. Thus, the *how* question does not answer *what* children should learn.

In every culture throughout history, adults have asked, "What should children learn?" The answer has always been, "Children need to know the values and practices of the culture and have the skills needed to thrive in their world." The answer to the question does not change, but the specifics do.

In this 21st century culture, the answer to the specifics of what children should learn rests in the educational system (the schools). Schools transmit the values of the culture and teach skills needed for the workforce. The responsibility of the schools, however, is no longer as simple as it was in the past.

Parents are looking to the schools to help educate their children at younger ages than in the past. By law children must receive 12 or 13 years of education. Today, however, many children enter the educational system during infancy or the preschool years and continue their education through college.

In this century, schools can no longer determine the exact skills needed for the workforce of the future. Because knowledge is expanding and changing so rapidly, the needed skills of today will change before the current workforce retires. This means that learning has to be ongoing, which is called **lifelong learning**. Workers must adapt to changing career demands or even to new careers. Furthermore, people in today's culture are part of a world community that requires broader knowledge, such as global economies and multicultural understandings. Schools today have a much broader responsibility for preparing students for today's world and also giving them the skills to adapt to a changing world.

Focus on

Careers

Elementary School Teacher

An elementary school teacher is responsible for creating lessons and teaching students appropriate grade-level materials. One teacher may be responsible for multiple subjects, including math, reading, language, science, and social studies. Teachers monitor educational development, assess student learning, and prepare students for the next grade level.

Career cluster: Education and training.

Education: Educational requirements vary by state, but a bachelor's degree in elementary education is the minimum. Other requirements may include an additional degree in a specific subject area, a teaching certificate, and a master's degree. Education requirements for private schools also vary. Continued education is also required.

Job outlook: Future employment opportunities for elementary school teachers are expected to grow as fast as the average for all occupations.

To learn more about a career as an elementary school teacher, visit the United States Department of Labor's *Occupational Outlook Handbook* website. You will also be able to compare the job responsibilities, educational requirements, job outlook, and average pay of elementary school teachers with similar occupations.

Types of Knowledge

Today, schools are teaching four types of knowledge needed now and in the future. The specifics of what children should know are embedded in each type of knowledge and are sequenced in state curriculum standards and college-degree programs. Your textbooks, other learning materials, and achievement tests closely follow these standards.

Explicit Knowledge

Explicit knowledge refers to knowledge about "facts." It is sometimes called *codified knowledge* because it is written. When young children learn to name colors, shapes, animals, and objects, they are acquiring codified knowledge (**Figure 2.11**). Schools require students to have a broad base of **explicit** (clearly described) knowledge. Because no one can learn more than a small amount of codified knowledge, education beyond high school focuses to a great extent on explicit knowledge in the specific area of study, such as computer technology, medicine, law, or child development.

Implicit Knowledge

Implicit knowledge (also called *experienced-based knowledge*) refers to skills-based knowledge. Think about the **implicit** (implied or understood without describing in detail) knowledge involved in specific

Figure 2.11 Children gain explicit knowledge by learning the names of colors, shapes, animals, and objects. *What is one way you use explicit knowledge in your typical day?*

tasks, such as teaching, managing a large corporation, or operating a complex machine. Often, this knowledge cannot be completely written. Young children begin acquiring implicit knowledge when they learn to ride a bike, swim, or balance blocks while building a structure (**Figure 2.12**). In school, implicit knowledge is needed to turn ideas into an essay or project or to become a leader in a student organization.

Scientific Knowledge

Scientific knowledge refers to the ability to create knowledge. This type of knowledge underlies new technological development, scientific discoveries, and process advances. Although the knowledge is often acquired in laboratories, it is used in many other careers. For example, as doctors learn about new drugs or procedures, they use them in their practices. Acquiring scientific knowledge begins when young children, even babies, try different actions with their toys (**Figure 2.13**). For example, their scientific questions might be, "How can I make the pans sound louder or the boat move faster?" Part of the curriculum in schools involves critical thinking and problem solving. Some teens take this form of knowledge to a high level as seen in science project competitions.

Figure 2.12 Implicit knowledge is skill-based and can be gained by learning to swim, ride a bike, interact with people, or balance blocks on a structure. *What are some ways you use implicit knowledge in your everyday life?*

Figure 2.13 Children gain scientific knowledge by experimenting with their toys and determining how their actions can affect objects in the physical world. *What do you think makes this type of knowledge scientific?*

Knowledge About Experts

Knowledge about experts (also called the *knowledge network*) involves knowing who has the other forms of knowledge. The knowledge network is used in all careers to get access to needed explicit, implicit, and scientific knowledge. Knowledge about experts is becoming more and more important. Again, even young children begin to acquire this knowledge. They quickly learn which parent, sibling, or friend has the knowledge or skills they desire. They even know whether or not this person gives them correct information.

Schools teach this type of knowledge when they require students to use valid and reliable sources of information. During this course, your teacher may ask you to interview someone or to give a group presentation. To do these activities will require you to choose someone who can share the information you need. Mastering this type of knowledge requires understanding what knowledge is needed, knowing who has this knowledge, and building a social relationship to get access to experts and their knowledge.

Linking Child Development Knowledge to Education

Until the 1950s, the schools were mainly concerned with preparing children to become productive workers for jobs in a slower-changing

Focus on Speech

Group Presentations

In small groups of six people, create a presentation on one of the following types of knowledge: explicit knowledge, implicit knowledge, scientific knowledge, or knowledge about experts. In your presentation, analyze how this type of knowledge is learned and practiced over each of the six stages of child development. (Review Figure 1.2 for the six stages of child development.)

Complete the following steps to prepare your presentation:

1. In your group, discuss examples of your chosen type of knowledge for each of the six stages of child development. Consider the question: How does this type of knowledge develop in each stage? Fill out a chart like the one shown to organize your discussion notes.
2. After discussing, divide the stages of child development among all group members. Each group member should be responsible for presenting on one stage of child development.
3. Make notes on index cards about important points to present. Before presenting, evaluate each other's notes and offer suggestions.
4. Deliver your presentation to the class. The person presenting on the first stage of child development should go first, the person presenting on the second stage second, and so on. Be prepared to answer any questions your classmates have, and ask questions about the other presentations in your class.

Stages of Child Development	How Does ____ Knowledge Develop in This Stage?
Prenatal	
Neonatal	
Infancy	
Toddler	
Preschool	
School-age	

world. Schools could teach the needed skills for a lifetime career, such as typing and shorthand to students wanting to be secretaries. These skills were not expected to change. *Rote memorization*, or memorization without full comprehension, was the way children learned many facts. Learning theories seemed to be the "best fit" for this type of education. Learning theories used **reinforcement** (rewards) for mastery of facts and skills. For example, children might be given a reward for learning multiplication tables. Rote learning did not work as well after the primary grades due to the complexity of many concepts and skills.

As the world changed, educators realized rote memorization was not best for learning needed skills. Robert Havighurst (1900–1991), a psychologist, began to develop educational theory based on child development concepts. His research led him to the concept of developmental tasks. **Developmental tasks** are skills that should be mastered at a certain stage in life. Havighurst coined the term *teachable moment* as the best time to teach a specific skill. He thought educators would be more effective if they used tasks for a particular level of development rather than using rote learning. Havighurst believed that the child's readiness for a developmental task came from the following three sources:

- ***physical maturation.*** A baby comes into the world as a helpless being. As his or her body matures, the child is able to learn many new skills, such as walking and reading.
- ***social pressures.*** Through rewards and penalties, society pressures the child to master important tasks. Developmental tasks differ from culture to culture because each group may value different skills. Tasks differ from region to region, too. Over time, tasks also change to reflect changes in society.
- ***inner pressures.*** The actual push to achieve comes from within children. In the end, the child is responsible for mastering each task. Children work harder to learn tasks they like (**Figure 2.14**).

The United States is no longer an industrial economy. Today, people live in a *knowledge-based economy* (knowledge and information along with technology drive the present production of goods and services and future economic growth). The schools now need to educate children for today's world and also to be adaptable and creative. Currently, the theories of Piaget and Vygotsky are being used to inform "best practices." Unlike Havighurst, Piaget and Vygotsky did not produce theories for education. Yet their theories give curriculum developers guidelines for knowing the best time for learning certain knowledge and skills (implies how to sequence the curriculum). These theories also give curriculum developers guidelines for knowing how children learn (implies how to teach or *methodology*).

Using Knowledge Effectively

For people to reach their full potential in school, in careers, and in their personal lives, they must not only acquire knowledge, but make good use of it. Everyone needs to know how to learn (study, recognize important information, remember, and make associations with other knowledge).

Figure 2.14 Developmental Tasks

Area: Motor task

Task for middle childhood: Learning physical skills needed for common games

Example of task: Learning skills needed to play ball

Tasks Arise from Three Sources

1. **Physical maturation.** Child needs bone and muscle growth. The child's eyes and hands must work smoothly together.
2. **Social pressures.** Other children reward skillful players (praise or accept them as friends) and punish failures (tease or reject them as friends). Parents and coaches may also expect children to master the skills.
3. **Inner pressures.** Child desires to be admired by other children, parents, and coaches.

Example of the Actual Push to Achieve

- **Child must see new possibilities for behavior.** Child sees older children playing ball.
- **Child must form new concept of self.** Child thinks, "I can be a player."
- **Child must cope with conflicting demands.** Child thinks, "I can get hit with a ball or be teased for striking out, but if I do not play, the other kids will make fun of me, and my parents and coaches will not consider me grown-up."
- **Child wants to achieve the next step in development enough to work for it.** Child now spends hours in practice.

People also need to know how to make plans, organize and prioritize tasks, keep track of information, and communicate effectively. Knowing how to stay focused on the task at hand, but being able to return to the primary task after being interrupted are also important skills to learn. Some people, however, are weak in these skills. Often, they cannot achieve as much as they should and have problems in working effectively with and for others. The good news is that these skills can be improved.

Executive Functions

Executive functions (EFs) are intellectual functions people use to manage themselves and their resources (knowledge, time) to achieve goals. (EFs are also called *managing functions.*) EFs are used in achieving all tasks. Some researchers believe EFs may predict a person's success more than intelligence. Not all researchers list the same EFs, but the following three functions are always listed:

- **working memory**—storing, organizing, and **manipulating** (moving or changing) information while working on a task. Some people refer to *working memory* as *short-term memory*, but *short-term memory* refers only to storing information while working on a task.
- **cognitive flexibility**—being able to adjust to changing demands.
- **inhibition**—filtering thoughts and feelings so as not to act impulsively (**Figure 2.15**).

EFs have their developmental roots in early childhood, are easily seen around nine years of age, and mature at 25 years of age. The lack of EFs is most often seen in children with learning and behavioral problems. Many other children, however, have weak EFs. EFs are fragile, and the lack of EFs can be seen for a short time in anyone who is sleep deprived or stressed. During these times, people cannot focus and distractions seem to rule behavior.

Figure 2.15 Symptoms and Aids for Weak Executive Functions

Working Memory	
Symptoms	**Examples of Aids**

• Has problems following multistep oral directions.
• Cannot tell or write story details in order of occurrence.
• Forgets a question or intended response while waiting.
• Cannot remember a phone number while placing a call or a thought while writing it.
• Forgets about assignments and projects.
• In sounding out letters, has problems remembering the first sounds by the end of the word, so cannot combine sounds to form one word.
• In reading a book section, has problems connecting concepts, so comprehension is weak.
• Cannot remember oral messages.
• In playing games, cannot keep track of moves (chess, checkers) or what has been played (dominoes, cards).
	• Sort many objects by one attribute (color, shape, size).
	• Play memory games, such as *concentration*.
	• Engage in dramatic play. (Child must remember the specifics of the role and keep track of sequence.)
	• Play games with rules.
	• Play games that require memory of moves or what has been played.
	• Break oral instructions into small chunks.
	• Use lists or drawings or repeat information to aid comprehension.
	• Establish routines.
	• Use calendars and assignment planners.
	• Organize materials and prioritize tasks:
	  • remove distracters
	  • make plans, follow plans, and discuss the activity at the end
	  • use memory aids such as acronyms

(Continued)

Figure 2.15 *(Continued)*

Cognitive Flexibility	
Symptoms	**Examples of Aids**
• Finds it difficult to change rules or directions, such as sort or classify by different attributes. • Has problems changing behaviors for different settings (inside/outside voices; behavior at ballgames versus behavior at a religious service; behaviors allowed at home versus school). • Cannot separate main ideas from supporting details. • Finds math word problems difficult due to the shift from words to equations. • Finds it difficult to see from another person's perspective.	• Sort or classify using the same materials, but changing attribute (use color then shape). • Do multiplicative classification, or recognize several possible categories for one object or person. • Engage in pretend play (changing roles and/or use the same prop, such as a block, to stand for different things). • Use words with multiple meanings, such as idioms, puns, and riddles. • Work jigsaw puzzles. • Take turns elaborating on a made-up story. • Learn more than one way to solve a problem. • Play "Turn It Around." (Say two things and have children reverse the order, such as "socks and shoes—shoes and socks.") • Ask about another person's perspective, such as "Why is Goldilocks afraid when the bears return?" (She's been in their house and knows they won't like it.)

Inhibition	
Symptoms	**Examples of Aids**
• Cannot pause and think before acting. (If bumped in a line, never evaluates that the bump might have been accidental. Just becomes angry and hits.) • Finds it easier to "give up" than to cope with a small set-back. • Has problems resisting temptations, such as watching TV when homework needs to be done or eating a piece of cake when trying to lose weight. • Becomes distracted when riding a bike or watching a program. • Has problems focusing on a conversation in a busy room. • Cannot hold a personal thought in order to not hurt someone else's feelings.	• Play "Simon Says" with new rules, such as do the action when Simon does not say it, or do the opposite of what Simon says, such as touch head when he says "toes." • Play a tapping game by doing the opposite of the adult. For example, if the adult taps twice, the child taps three times and vice versa. • Read color words written in the wrong color, such as RED written in green. • Delay gratification. (Get a bigger reward for waiting, such as saving money for a major purchase over several smaller purchases.) • Play games in which the child must wait for his or her turn.

The exact causes of weak EFs are not known. Adverse effects on EFs include a chaotic and stressful environment and child neglect and abuse. Treatments can only help, not cure, weak EFs.

Galinsky's Seven Essential Life Skills

Ellen Galinsky wanted to learn which skills had the greatest effects on children's development now and in the future. She spent eight years interviewing more than 75 of the leading researchers in child development and **neuroscience** (study of the brain) and filming aspects of their work.

Galinsky's study led her to identify seven basic skills, which she calls *essential life skills*. She defined **essential life skills** as the intellectual, social, and emotional skills that prepare children for the pressures of modern life. Following are Galinsky's *Seven Essential Life Skills*

- ***Focus and self-control.*** Focus and self-control allow children to achieve goals in a rushed world filled with distractions and information overload. This skill involves being oriented toward achieving a goal by being alert and paying attention to get more out of information. It also requires having cognitive flexibility, and exercising self-control by not going on "automatic pilot" and by delaying gratification.
- ***Perspective taking.*** Perspective taking is the skill of figuring out what others are thinking and feeling. Understanding and respecting other's intentions are needed in a complex world.
- ***Communicating.*** Communicating is more than just listening, speaking, and writing correctly, although these skills are highly important. This skill involves reflecting on the message. While doing this, one person must listen and understand another person's perspective and realize how his or her communication will be understood by others.
- ***Making connections.*** Making connections is a skill most similar to *intelligence* itself. This skill involves seeing how things are the same or different and determining how bits of knowledge relate to each other. People who can see unusual connections between concepts and facts are creative and make advances in their fields.
- ***Critical thinking.*** Critical thinking involves obtaining and using valid and reliable knowledge to guide a person's beliefs, decisions, and actions. Critical thinking requires scientific reasoning to determine "what causes what."
- ***Taking on challenges.*** Taking on challenges is the willingness for a person to "stretch" himself or herself rather than simply doing what is comfortable. The skill is based on an understanding that a person's abilities can grow.
- ***Self-directed and engaged learning.*** Self-directed and engaged learning is the willingness to continue learning for a lifetime. Everyone needs to find something they are passionate about and pursue the needed learning. This skill allows people to adapt to the changing world.

Essential life skills are closely related to EFs. For example, "perspective taking," one of Galinsky's seven skills, requires a person to remember all needed information about another person and to compare the current situation with similar situations (*working memory*). Perspective taking also requires the person to view the situation from both the other person's point of view and his or her point of view (*cognitive flexibility*). Finally, perspective taking requires the person to put his or her reactions aside while looking at another person's point of view (*inhibition*). For best results, these seven skills must be fostered beginning in early childhood.

How Can Adults Help Prevent Children's Stress?

Child development knowledge is being applied not only by educators, but also by those in health and protective services. The road from conception to the adult years is a long one. Children are not born with the ability to control the harm that may

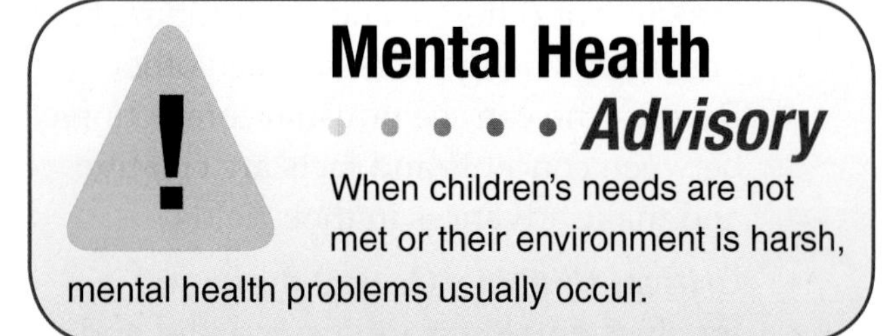

Mental Health Advisory

When children's needs are not met or their environment is harsh, mental health problems usually occur.

come to their developing bodies, including their brains. They are not born with any idea about the world into which they have entered. Only as they interact with people and objects in their environment do they come to realize how their world works (**Figure 2.16**).

Many children come into a world of loving parents, plentiful food and other necessities, and a supportive environment. Other children, however, are born into a world of less than responsive parents, scarcity of food and lack of other necessities, and a harsh environment—possibly even a violent one. What will be the difference in the life-paths these children will likely face? Most children in the first group will walk the path leading to a secure, happy, and fulfilling life. The children in the second group may be on the path of stress and trauma leading to an unhappy ending—mere survival at best or becoming self-destructive or a danger to others at the worst.

Figure 2.16 Children are not born knowing about their worlds. Rather, they learn through interactions with people and objects. *What interactions do you think first begin to teach children about their worlds?*

Can people keep children on the more positive life-path in this challenging world with its countless stressors? Can people guide those children already on the more dangerous life-path toward positive outcomes? The answers to both questions are *yes*. By nature children are survivors, but people must nurture and support each child. Applying what you know from child development research can have a powerful impact on all children.

As you read this book, you will learn when children are most vulnerable, what possible problems may occur, and how adults can help children thrive in childhood. Doing what is right for children is their best insurance for their future as adults and for the next generation of children.

Lesson 2.2 Review and Assessment 

1. According to professionals in child development, mental health problems find their roots in the _____ children experience during childhood.
2. Name the four types of knowledge, and give an example of a skill or activity that requires each type.
3. _____ are skills that should be mastered at a certain stage in life.
4. According to Havighurst, a child's readiness for developmental tasks stems from what three sources?
5. List and define the three executive functions (EFs).
6. Name the seven essential life skills identified by Galinsky, and give an example of an activity where each skill is required.
7. **Critical thinking.** How effectively do you think children can be sheltered from the stressful—or even violent—environments into which they are born? How can parents in these environments protect the health of their children?

Chapter 2 Review and Assessment

Summary

The study of children has changed over the years, and the new research frontier of the 21st century is brain studies. Brain growth occurs in waves, and the fastest growth is during the prenatal through early teen years. The brain is made up of neurons and glial cells. Neurons communicate with sensory organs and within the brain. Glial cells support neurons. Neurons are connected through *wiring*, which allows communications to travel from neuron to neuron in a specific order. People's experiences affect wiring, and wiring can change due to *brain plasticity*. Wiring that is seldom used is pruned. If needed, new wiring can also be made. Periods of fast brain growth signal *windows of opportunity* for learning certain skills. During these times, the brain is also more vulnerable and needs more protection.

Today's world requires children to adapt to many changes. Schools prepare children by teaching explicit knowledge, implicit knowledge, scientific knowledge, and knowledge about experts. To sequence content and determine the best ways to teach, schools often look to the theories of Piaget and Vygotsky. Schools also try to help children use knowledge effectively by strengthening EFs and life skills. Child development knowledge is being used by workers in health and protective services. Many children are vulnerable to countless stressors. Child development knowledge is being used to prevent and treat children's stress.

College and Career Portfolio

Portfolio Objective

Before you begin collecting information for your portfolio, you should write an objective for your portfolio. An objective is a complete sentence or two that states what you want to accomplish. The language should be clear and specific. The objective should contain enough details so that you can easily judge when it is accomplished. For instance, "I will create a portfolio for my future education" is too general. A better, more detailed objective might read: "I will work with my teacher and spend at least three hours per week creating, editing, and compiling items which will help me get into a college child care program." A clear objective is a good starting point for building a portfolio. As you think about building your portfolio, complete the following:

- Decide on the purpose of your portfolio—temporary or short-term employment, career, and/or college application.
- Use online or print resources to find articles about writing objectives. Also, look for articles containing sample objectives.
- Write an objective for your portfolio.

Chapter 2 Review and Assessment

Vocabulary Activities 

1. In teams, play *picture charades* to identify each of the following terms. Write the terms on separate slips of paper and put the slips into a basket. Choose a team member to be the *sketcher*. The sketcher pulls a term from the basket and creates quick drawings or graphics to represent the term until the team guesses the term. Rotate turns as sketcher until the team identifies all terms.

Key Terms

axons (2.1)	lifelong learning (2.2)
cognitive flexibility (2.2)	myelin (2.1)
critical periods (2.1)	neurons (2.1)
dendrites (2.1)	plasticity (2.1)
developmental tasks (2.2)	pruning (2.1)
essential life skills (2.2)	sensitive periods (2.1)
executive functions (2.2)	synapse (2.1)
firing (2.1)	window of opportunity (2.1)
glial cells (2.1)	wiring (2.1)
inhibition (2.2)	working memory (2.2)

2. Working in small groups, locate a small image online that visually describes or explains each of the following terms. To create flash cards, write each term on a note card and paste the image that describes or explains the term on the opposite side.

Academic Terms

abundance (2.1)	neuroscience (2.2)
biochemistry (2.1)	reinforcement (2.2)
explicit (2.2)	seldom (2.1)
implicit (2.2)	tentative (2.1)
manipulating (2.2)	

Critical Thinking

3. **Cause and effect.** Review Figure 2.2 and the stages of brain growth after birth. Working with a partner, discuss how brain growth and development might affect a child's everyday behavior. Give one concrete example for each age range listed.
4. **Compare and contrast.** In groups of three, research the three types of neurons and their functions. How are their structures and functions different? How are they similar? For each type of neuron, create a simple drawing that illustrates how the neuron works.
5. **Make inferences.** Two-year-old Tommy fell off a slide and is now having vision problems. His mother took him to the eye doctor, but Tommy's eyes are fine. The eye doctor recommended they see a neurologist. Why? What problems might the eye doctor suspect?
6. **Cause and effect.** Explain the effect of pruning on a person's ability to learn a skill.
7. **Analyze.** A disease that damages the myelin surrounding a neuron is known as a *demyelinating disease*. Based on what you know about neurons, what symptoms do you think this type of disease might exhibit? Explain your answer.
8. **Determine.** When is the best time to guide a child in reading others' emotions? What might happen if a child is pressured to learn these concepts too early? too late?
9. **Draw conclusions.** Based on what you have learned in this chapter, how would being deprived of loving attention and learning experiences impact the developing brain of a young child?
10. **Compare and contrast.** In what ways do you use explicit knowledge, implicit knowledge, scientific knowledge, and knowledge about experts in your everyday life? Compare answers with a partner and discuss your differences.
11. **Identify.** Identify examples of social pressures that motivate children to learn. From where do these pressures originate? Are these social pressures always positive, or can they have negative effects if applied excessively?
12. **Evaluate.** List Galinsky's seven essential life skills and assess your strength in each of these skills. Where are you strongest? Where are you weakest?

Core Skills

13. **Research and writing.** Using online or print resources, research historic theories regarding the roles of and expectations for children. Afterward, compare historic views of childhood with current views of childhood and write a short essay about how recent discoveries about the brain have impacted these views.

14. **Reading.** With a partner, make flash cards of all the key terms in this chapter. On the front of the card, write the term. On the back, write the phonetic spelling of the word. (You may use a dictionary to find the phonetic spelling.) Practice reading and defining the terms aloud, clarifying pronunciations where needed.
15. **Using technology.** Using a graphics editing software, create a line drawing of a neuron and label its parts. Print your image and then use it to explain to a partner how an electrical signal is passed from neuron to neuron.
16. **Math.** Review the windows of opportunity in Figure 2.8. At what age, in months, does the latest window of opportunity begin?
17. **Listening, writing, and speaking.** Interview a preschool, kindergarten, or elementary school teacher about how he or she incorporates the windows of opportunity into teaching. After the interview, create a brochure about the teacher's class, highlighting how the teacher's lessons take advantage of a child's natural windows of opportunities. Distribute your brochures to your class and persuade classmates why your teacher's class is the best.
18. **Speaking.** Divide into teams and have each team select one of the following topics:
    - the four types of knowledge
    - the three executive functions
    - Galinsky's seven essential life skills

    In your team, identify the components of your topic and brainstorm as many everyday examples as possible. Present your findings to the class, using props or demonstrations to illustrate each component.
19. **Listening.** As your classmates present their findings from the previous activity, listen closely to your classmates' examples. Take notes on anything you find particularly interesting, or write any questions you think of during their presentations. Once they are finished presenting, share with the class one thought or question you had regarding their presentation. Do this for all of the presentations in your class.
20. **CTE Career Readiness Practice.** Presume you are a teacher at a local preschool and kindergarten. The parents of your children are concerned that you are not teaching some topics and skills early enough, and you have scheduled a collective "parent-teacher conference" next week. In order to explain your teaching method, you decide to put together handouts about the following:
    - the windows of opportunity for children's learning
    - the four types of knowledge, the executive functions, and Galinksy's seven essential life skills—all of which you emphasize in your lessons

    Prepare these handouts and then write a short speech in which you acknowledge the parents' concerns while educating them about child development and your teaching method. Distribute your handouts and give your presentation to the class.

Observations

21. In small groups, set up a time with a local child care facility to observe young children. If you do not have access to a child care facility, you can ask to observe a family friend's children. During your observation, assess the child's or children's readiness for developmental tasks, including
    - physical maturation
    - social pressures
    - inner pressures

    Afterward, discuss your observations with your group. Do your group members agree with your assessment? Why or why not? If there are differences of opinion, consider how two people can observe a child and see two different things. As a group, present a short summary of your observations and discussion to the class.
22. If abandoned or isolated from a young age, some children may never learn language skills or other developmental tasks. These children are known as *feral children*. Watch a documentary about a feral child. Documentaries can be found at a local library or sometimes online. Be sure to note the title and citation information of the documentary you chose. As you watch the documentary, note any observations you have. Then, write a one-page essay about the documentary you watched and about what you learned. Include citations for the documentary in the APA and MLA formats. Share your essay with the rest of the class.

Chapter 3 Families Today

Essential Question

In what ways do family relationships affect children?

Lesson 3.1 Healthy Family Development

Lesson 3.2 Family Types

Case Study How Can Cultural Differences Be Merged for a Good Marriage?

As a class, read the case study and discuss the questions that follow. After you finish studying the chapter, discuss this case study again. Have your opinions changed based on what you learned?

Kate and Joel are looking for a place to live together after they get married next month. Joel sees a home for sale across the street from his parents' home. He is delighted at the find, especially since most of his siblings live nearby, too.

Kate finds Joel's family warm and welcoming, but is not sure that she wants to live so close to them. The interactions among Joel's family members are constant—similar to an extended family although each has their own home. Kate was raised in a nuclear family. Her family visited relatives mainly during holidays and vacation times, but otherwise her family lived as an independent family unit.

Kate understands that Joel's family means well, but she feels smothered when they want details about everything and are free with their advice. She mentions this to Joel, but he does not understand Kate's feelings. Kate does not know what to do and wonders whether this is just the beginning of problems due to differences in family culture.

Give It Some Thought

1. How can Kate explain her objections without hurting Joel's or his family's feelings?
2. Is there a compromise solution that would make both Kate and Joel happy?
3. If Kate accepts Joel's idea of buying the house next door, is it likely Joel would be willing to help Kate from feeling smothered by his family? For example, how will Joel feel if Kate does not want to include his family in all of their social activities? How will he feel if Kate wants to visit her family during some holidays?
4. Is Kate worrying needlessly, or can different family cultures make for long-term, serious marital problems?

While studying this chapter, look for the online resources icon  to:

- **Practice** terms with e-flash cards and interactive games
- **Assess** what you learn by completing self-assessment quizzes
- **Expand** knowledge with interactive activities and graphic organizers

Companion G-W Learning

www.g-wlearning.com/childdevelopment

Study on the go

Use a mobile device to practice terms and review with self-assessment quizzes.

www.m.g-wlearning.com/0384

Lesson 3.1 Healthy Family Development

Key Terms

active listening
body language
budget
communication
cultural diversity
culture
family life cycle
marriage
multicultural family
premarital counseling

Academic Terms

bias
comprise
discontentment
income
Industrial Revolution
inherent
norm

Objectives

After studying this lesson, you will be able to

- analyze factors couples should consider when preparing for marriage.
- assess changes that take place during the family life cycle.
- describe ways that culture influences the family.
- compare past and present societal influences on families.
- determine characteristics of healthy families.

Reading and Writing Activity

Skim this lesson, paying close attention to the photos included in each section. For each photo, write a one- to two-sentence prediction about how the photo illustrates a topic covered. Then, after reading, revisit your predictions and update or correct them to reflect what you learned. How well do the photos illustrate the concepts in this lesson? What other photo options might expand a student's understanding of a concept?

Graphic Organizer

The two main topics covered in this lesson are marriage and family. In a chart like the one shown, draw two circles, one labeled *Marriage* and the other labeled *Family*. As you read this lesson, write information you learn around the circle to which it most relates. If a piece of information relates to both marriage and family, write it between the circles.

Marriage

Family

The family is the oldest known social group. Couples begin to build the foundation for their family life together when they decide to get married. The start of this relationship together helps determine the stability of the family unit. Healthy families work on building healthy relationships. Families, just like individuals, change through the years, but continue to be the basic unit of society.

Figure 3.1 Marriage is the foundational relationship of the family, fulfilling spouses' and children's needs for love and security. *Why is marriage considered a foundational relationship?*

Building a Strong Foundation

The strength of a family's foundation depends on the strength of its **inherent** (basic) relationships. Building a strong foundation, whether in marriage or other key relationships, is essential to the satisfaction of family members, the stability of the family unit, and the health and development of any children. Many couples consider marriage before forming a family unit.

Considering Marriage

Marriages are the foundational relationships of families. **Marriage** is a legal contract and, ideally, an emotional and social union between two partners. In a healthy marriage, both partners desire to remain together and both partners feel satisfied, even if conflicts and periods of **discontentment** (unhappiness) occur. A happy marriage can be a source of love and security for two partners, as well as a source of stability and comfort for a couple's children (**Figure 3.1**).

When considering marriage, couples should evaluate their own desires, dreams, and goals for life. If marriage is a part of the life they want, there are still many factors for each partner to consider, such as the following:

- ***Why do I want to get married?*** Marriage is a serious commitment and each partner should assess why he or she is marrying. Some negative reasons might include loneliness, insecurity, or pressure from others. Positive reasons include the desire to grow together in mature love and build a family together.
- ***When do I want to get married?*** Marriage is not a decision anyone should feel pressured into. If a person decides to marry, he or she should be ready to love and commit to this partner for the rest of his or her life.
- ***What qualities would each partner bring to a marriage?*** Marriage involves love, trust, honesty, support, cooperation, caring, and kindness. Couples should determine their emotional stability and what each partner can contribute to the marriage to make it a success.
- ***Do we have similar life goals and values?*** Knowing personal desires is an important step in considering marriage. Couples should discuss what they want in their life together. Where do they want to live? What career goals do they have? Do they want children? If so, when? These are just a few questions that couples may want to discuss before they marry.

Communicating Effectively

Relationships can be either strengthened or hindered by people's communication skills. **Communication** is the exchange of messages and information between at least two people. Communication involves both sending and receiving messages. There are two types of communication: non-verbal communication and verbal communication.

Nonverbal Communication

Nonverbal communication is a way of sending and receiving messages without using words or in addition to using words. It includes **body language**, which is the sending of messages through body movements, such as facial expressions, eye contact, gestures, and posture. In relationships, it is important to assess what messages are being conveyed through nonverbal communication (**Figure 3.2**).

Verbal Communication

Verbal communication consists of the words used to deliver and receive messages. It includes not just what people say, but how they say it, and what specific words they use. When using verbal communication, people in healthy relationships choose words and word patterns that are constructive. For instance, when choosing what words to say, you might ask yourself, "What will saying this sentence achieve? What is my reason for saying it? Is the way I am phrasing this harmful or helpful to this relationship?"

Being a good listener is also an important part of verbal communication. **Active listening** occurs when the receiver of a message provides feedback to the speaker, indicating that the message is understood. Restating what the speaker says, nodding your head, maintaining eye contact, and asking questions are all ways of providing feedback.

Verbal communication is key to healthy relationships. Partners consider each other's feelings and talk about their problems. When challenges arise, couples in healthy relationships use problem-solving skills to address the issues (**Figure 3.3**).

Figure 3.2 Nonverbal communication includes facial expressions, eye contact, gestures, body movements, posture, and other elements of body language. All of these factors contribute to the message that is sent. *How are the two people in this photo communicating nonverbally? What messages are they sending?*

Managing Money Effectively

One significant challenge that couples face is effective money management. Poor money management can spark conflict in any relationship. Couples considering marriage must work together to decide how they will budget for their needs and wants. A **budget** is a financial plan for spending and saving money.

Maintaining a budget requires a balance of commitment, flexibility, and realistic planning. While buying decisions should be made based on the couple's budget, unforeseen expenses may still occur. Similarly, if a couple creates a budget they cannot meet, they will experience frustration. Money crises and conflicts can shake the foundation of any family. Effectively managing money, however, can help prevent financial crises and ensure the financial health of the family.

Preparing for Marriage

After two people decide to marry, they will most likely go through a period of engagement, in which they will prepare for life together. **Premarital counseling** is a type of therapy for couples who are preparing for marriage. During premarital counseling sessions, a licensed counselor will help both partners consider life goals and values and how they will handle the responsibilities of marriage. Discussing these aspects of life together can help the couple build a strong family foundation.

The Family Life Cycle

Many parents and their children go through similar stages called the **family life cycle**. The

Figure 3.3 Steps in Problem Solving

Step 1. Identify the problem

- What is the problem that is getting in the way of achieving a goal? Be specific.
- How is the problem affecting me? How is it affecting others?
- What is happening? When is it happening? What causes the problem?

Step 2. Look at alternative solutions

- Brainstorm as many solutions as possible.
- Do not discard any idea. Sometimes seemingly "bad ideas" can develop into "good solutions."

Step 3. Analyze the alternative solutions

- Write the good and bad points for each possible solution.
- Group alternative solutions, when possible.

Step 4. Select a possible solution

- Decide which solutions might have the most impact on the problem. Decide if the solution is realistic and manageable.
- As you consider possible solutions, think of the consequences of each. What is the extent of a risk involved in each possible solution?
- Do not hurry this step. Talk to others, including those affected by the problem.

Step 5. Implement a solution

- After choosing a solution, plan how and when you will implement it.
- Be specific on the steps to implement the plan.
- Communicate the implementation steps to all involved.

Step 6. Evaluate the results

- Evaluate the effectiveness of the solution. Is the solution achieving the desired goal? Did the solution have any unforeseen risks?
- If the problem has not been resolved, ask the following: Do I need to give it more time to work? Should I change the plan of action? Do I need to begin the entire process again?
- If the problem seems to be resolved, continue to monitor. Problems do not always stay solved.

family life cycle consists of six stages (**Figure 3.4**). In the *beginning stage*, the couple is a family of two. During this time, they get to know each other better. They also decide when they want to become parents and how many children they would like to have.

In the *childbearing stage*, parents give birth to one or more children and learn their roles in caring for and guiding children through their earliest years. As parents enter later stages, their roles continue to change.

During the *parenting stage*, parents focus on guiding and nurturing their children. They are preparing their children to become productive members of society. During these years, parents also realize other people will be teaching and guiding their children. Children begin to learn more from teachers and peers. During adolescence, parents begin treating their children as adults. They also know when to provide guidance and help.

The *launching stage* brings new feelings for parents. During this stage, children start to leave home to make their own lives. As each child leaves home, parents may feel lonelier. They may also feel their children no longer need them. In this stage, parents must acknowledge their children are adults and their relationships may be more equal. Parents may continue to be an important part of their children's lives.

Figure 3.4 The Family Life Cycle

Beginning Stage

A couple marries and determines when they want to become parents and how many children they would like to have.

Childbearing Stage

The couple starts having children. The stages of the family life cycle for parents of multiple children are overlapping.

Parenting Stage

The couple focuses on guiding their children through the school-age and teen years.

Launching Stage

The couple's children begin leaving home to live on their own.

Mid-years Stage

The couple focuses on their marriage, planning for their future, and becoming grandparents. This stage lasts until the couple retires.

Aging Stage

The couple retires and adjusts to this change in lifestyle. This stage lasts throughout the remainder of life as a couple.

Focus on Careers

Marriage and Family Therapist

Marriage and family therapists are professionals who work to improve the social and psychological functioning of children and their families and to maximize the family's well-being. They help families overcome stress, mental health issues, and behavioral problems.

Career cluster: Human services.

Education: Educational requirements often include a master's degree. All states have some licensure, certification, or registration requirement.

Job outlook: Future employment opportunities for marriage and family therapists are expected to grow much faster than the average for all occupations.

To learn more about a career as a marriage and family therapist, visit the United States Department of Labor's *Occupational Outlook Handbook* website. You will also be able to compare the job responsibilities, educational requirements, job outlook, and average pay of marriage and family therapists with similar occupations.

In some cases, economic troubles, divorce, or other situations may cause grown children to return to the family home. Families then return to the *parenting stage*, but parents may have to learn new ways to relate to their children. They may have adjusted to their children becoming adults and do not know how to treat them as adults when they all live in the same home. Open communication can help ensure that family members continue to get along.

In the *mid-years stage*, parents may find more time for themselves than they did when their children lived at home. They may devote more time to new interests or hobbies. Keeping in touch with their children is still important, and they may be involved with their grandchildren. The couple also begins to focus on retirement.

The final stage of the family life cycle is the *aging stage*. This stage lasts from retirement to the death of a partner. In this stage, the couple may pursue new hobbies and spend time with family and friends. They may have health conditions that cause them to need help from their children. The couple may face different challenges and have new concerns. During this stage, family members may need to make many adjustments.

Cultural Influences on Families

Families may go through similar stages and are alike in many ways, but they may differ in the cultural groups to which they belong. **Culture**, a way of life within a group of people that includes language, beliefs, attitudes, values, rituals, and skills, greatly affects a family's life (**Figure 3.5**). Because not every family belongs to the same culture, the effects of culture differ widely from one family to the next.

People of many cultural groups live in the United States. Families who once came from many parts of the world call the United States home. The United States is an example of a nation with great **cultural diversity**, which means it has more than one culture represented among its people.

How Cultures Vary

Families often identify their culture in terms of their origin or ancestors. People often reference a region of origin, specific country, or language to identify their culture because of the customs, traditions, values, and religions that **comprise**

Figure 3.5 Aspects of a Person's Culture

- History, folklore, heroes
- Language (written, verbal, slang, body language, and gestures)
- Humor
- Names (surname and given name)
- Holiday celebrations, traditions, and rituals
- Methods of greeting (such as eye contact, handshakes, hugs, kisses, and bowing)
- Preferences about personal space and touching
- Foods, eating methods, eating manners
- Dress and body decorations
- Home furnishings and decorations
- Arts and crafts
- Music

(make up) each culture. These components help describe a family's cultural identification.

Each culture's practices support its particular beliefs and customs. For example, goals for achievement vary from culture to culture. Some cultures stress academic achievement as a way to honor the family and achieve economic success that will help the entire family. These families view academic learning as the top priority for children. Other cultures stress achievement in social interactions. In these cultures, showing dignity and respect in interactions with others brings honor to the individual or family. These families emphasize play as well as academic skills. Because they have such different views, these two families differ in their parenting practices, modeling, praise, and criticism regarding the role of education.

Cultures differ in the way they view the concept of family. In some cultures, *family* includes only the immediate family. In other cultures, this term has a broader meaning that includes other relatives, close family friends, and neighbors.

The importance of the family also varies from culture to culture (**Figure 3.6**). In cultures with a group orientation, family is most important. Cultures with an individual orientation focus on each person as an individual more than on the family as a group.

Language and dialect can vary from one culture to the next, too. Families generally use their culture's native language and teach this language to their children. Using the language of their people can bring a sense of unity and belonging and contribute to their culture. Families may use language as a way to foster this involvement in the culture.

The use and meaning of body language can vary from group to group. This explains the well-known saying: *Not all people smile in the same*

Focus on

Social Studies

Cultural Diversity

Speaking different languages is not the only way communication differs across cultures. The role of language can differ, too. For instance, some cultures teach children to talk often, be open and direct, and be informal. These children might address people by their first names without asking and soon after meeting, use slang, and talk to strangers. Other cultures value silence—talking only when necessary. These cultures teach children to notice other body language clues (such as "reading the eyes") to help them understand without being told. These cultures prefer formal word choice and the use of courtesy titles when addressing elders or strangers. In these cultures, children are taught to address elders in a way that shows respect.

In what ways do you think your cultural background will influence the way you parent or care for children? How can children benefit from these influences?

Figure 3.6 Cultures See Families Differently

Group-Oriented Culture	Individual-Oriented Culture

• Family includes kin and perhaps others.	• Family includes parents and their children.
• Family members live in same house or near each other.	• Family members live in different houses and may live far away from one another.
• Status in the family (and possibly in the group) is achieved by age and/or gender.	• Status in the family is determined by achievement.
• Elders make decisions based on the welfare of the whole family (collective responsibility).	• The individual considers his or her own welfare when making decisions for himself or herself (individual responsibility).
• Members take pride in their family name, family history, and family honor.	• Members take pride in their own talents, achievements, and status.
• Family members conform to those in authority.	• Family members may challenge or question those in authority.
• Members cooperate in all tasks.	• Members may be competitive.
• Family harmony is emphasized.	• Individual happiness is emphasized.
• Early dependence on group is encouraged.	• Early independence is encouraged.
• Group members help each other, even at their own expense.	• Each person is expected to help himself or herself with little assistance from the family.
• Parent-child bond is stressed. Children are seen as extensions of parents (children bring honor to and help the family throughout life).	• Husband-wife bond is stressed. Children are seen as individuals who as adults take care of themselves.
• Parents ask, "What can we do to help each other?"	• Parents ask, "What can I do to help you?"
• Expression of emotion is more indirect (emotionally controlled; modest; formal toward elders to show respect).	• Expression of emotion is more direct (emotionally expressive; more "I-centered"; informal).

language. In some cultures, smiling expresses friendliness, pleasure, or understanding of humor. In other cultures, a smile is used to acknowledge a fault. Some cultures might use smiling to mask emotion (hurt or disagreement) or avoid conflict. In other cultures, people smile in response to a compliment if they feel verbal response would show a lack of modesty.

Multicultural Families

As the United States increases in cultural diversity, the number of *multicultural families* continues to grow. A **multicultural family** is a family with members from two or more cultural groups. Multicultural families are like other families in many ways. They have many of the same joys and challenges as other families. In some ways, however, multicultural families are unique. The diversity within their families can bring added joy as well as added challenges.

Everyone in a multicultural family needs to learn about the cultures of its members. Parents need to understand the roles and expectations of each of these cultures. This takes some time and effort, but it can help the family avoid misunderstandings and conflicts.

In some multicultural families, members do not know enough about the culture that is different from their own. Challenges in these families may occur because of

- verbal and nonverbal communication differences between cultures
- differing cultural expectations, roles, beliefs, and values
- differing traditions, including religious beliefs, rituals, and holidays
- differing views regarding family life
- expressions of **bias** (favoring; unequal treatment) or exclusion from others, especially family members

Most children raised in multicultural homes are happy and grow up to respect diversity and have a strong sense of self. The strongest multicultural families seem to have much in common (**Figure 3.7**).

Parents of multicultural families often explain to their children that people who express bias toward them may not know any better. The unkind words and actions of people who express bias may come from not knowing others who are different from them. Parents in strong multicultural families discourage their children from fighting in response to bias. They make it clear that it is not right to hurt people who are different or assume all people in a group behave the same way.

Figure 3.7 What Makes Multicultural Families Strong?

Studies have shown the strongest multicultural families often have the following in characteristics:

- Parents have strong cultural identities and feel good about their multicultural family.
- The family talks about cultural issues in the home.
- Parents and children develop creative ways to solve problems that show equal respect for both cultures.
- The family surrounds itself with supportive family and friends.
- Parents work with child care staff and teachers on behalf of their children.
- The family celebrates all cultures.
- Parents tolerate no biased remarks within their circle of family, friends, and peers.

Societal Influences on Families

Changes in society cause major changes in the family. In the past, before the **Industrial Revolution** (time in history in which society began to focus on industry and manufacturing), many families lived on farms and met most of their own needs. These families consisted of the immediate family (parents and their children) as well as grandparents and other family members. They often lived together or in nearby houses.

During the Industrial Revolution, many families left their farms and moved into the cities to work in factories, leaving behind relatives and friends. Away from other relatives, people began to turn to their immediate family members for companionship and emotional support. The immediate family became more important for love and security.

The societal views of children during this time were different from those of today. Children were considered an asset to the family because they helped the family earn money. When children reached four to seven years of age, they were expected to work long days in factories or on farms. Today, society values children and sees childhood as a special time. Labor laws changed the role children played in the economy while protecting them as individuals. Children now lead lives as *children*, not as a source of family **income** (money received for working).

Families continue to respond and adapt to societal changes, such as advancements in medicine and technology. Medical advances allow people to live longer. In the United States and elsewhere, the life expectancy rate has steadily increased in the past few decades. Technological advancements also change the **norm** (normal, socially acceptable pattern) of living. Electronic devices, such as home appliances, cell phones, tablets, televisions, and video consoles, affect how family members communicate with each other, use time for entertainment, and help complete tasks around the house. Technology also affects how people learn. Information is more readily available today than in the past.

Investigate Special Topics: Impact of Media and Technology on Families

Technology refers to the invention of useful items. Because technological inventions have been so useful, they have greatly impacted the family throughout history. Think about how the first crude tools helped the hunting and gathering families get more food. Being able to use fire kept early families warm, cooked their foods, and kept wild animals at a distance. The wheel made transportation over land much easier and was used in machines. From early civilization throughout all the intervening years, technology has been part of human life.

How is modern technology impacting family life—your life? Think about your morning. How many digital devices did you use before you got to school or work? Did you wake up to a beeping digital device? Did you use an electric toothbrush? What devices did you use in making breakfast? Did you watch TV, check for text messages or e-mails, or use other digital devices? Did you leave home in a car? What additional digital devices operate in the car?

Family members work, learn, and stay connected with others using digital devices. Some adults use their computers to send and receive needed work information and even videoconference with people from various parts of the world right from their homes. Children use digital devices to do homework and may be "homeschooled" using these devices. Some students are getting college degrees without ever seeing the college campus, if one even exists. Family members can quickly and easily communicate with one another by simply sending a text message.

Families watch TV programs, stream movies, play video games, and listen to music on digital devices for entertainment. Family health is monitored and treated using new technologies. With digital technology, some health information can even be sent from a person's home to a doctor's digital device.

Technology has improved the family's access to people, information, and goods from all over the world. Digital technology and media require people to become more globally aware. To keep up in an ever-changing world, people must forge new worldwide partnerships and operate in the international marketplace. Careers are quickly requiring global understandings. To be successful in a new world, people must not offend other people or exploit their cultures. This requires world citizens to have deep global awareness and respect.

Application Activity

On a piece of paper, draw three columns labeled *Morning*, *Afternoon*, and *Evening*. Then, take five minutes to brainstorm and write all the digital devices you use during each of these periods. Include devices you use to wake up, items you use during your morning routine, transportation methods, and any digital learning or social tools. Then, find a partner and share your findings. Finally, discuss how the devices you use impact your family life. What are some positive and negative effects? How might your life be different if you did not use these devices daily?

Characteristics of Healthy Families

There is no magic recipe to create a healthy family. Families can be very different and yet strong. Some characteristics are often seen in healthy families (**Figure 3.8**). The most common characteristic is that spouses enter marriage with shared values. They use these values to decide on goals throughout their marriage and guide them in parenting their children.

Closely tied to shared values is the belief that family members are individuals. Strong families accept that even people who share many values will be somewhat different. They also realize life itself can change the family's goals. Healthy families are willing to adjust as needed.

Healthy families share a mutual commitment to family life. In these families, parents want their own relationships to succeed. They want to be successful parents. Part of the commitment involves growth—becoming more loving, caring, and understanding. These family members also want to do many activities as a family unit.

In healthy families, members want to help each other rather than being self-centered. Members share responsibilities. Although each family may divide tasks differently, healthy families seem to happily follow their own choices about duties. Each member can depend on the others to keep promises, fulfill commitments, and be honest.

Lesson 3.1 Review and Assessment 

1. Define *marriage* and explain its functions and importance in family life.
2. Explain the difference between nonverbal and verbal communication, and give an example of both.
3. How is a budget important to a healthy marriage and family?
4. Name the six stages of the family life cycle.
5. _____ is a way of life within a group of people that includes language, beliefs, attitudes, values, rituals, and skills.
6. Describe some of the unique challenges and benefits of being part of a multicultural family.
7. How do societal views of children today differ from societal views of children before and during the Industrial Revolution?
8. **Critical thinking.** Write a one- to two-paragraph scenario in which two people are trying to resolve a conflict. Then, rewrite the scenario so that both people use active listening to reach an understanding.
9. **Critical thinking.** Review the characteristics of a healthy family and then consider the following: Why do these qualities signal health in a family? How is the family affected if one of these qualities is absent?

Figure 3.8 Characteristics of a Healthy Family

- Marriage built and directed by shared values
- Acceptance of family members' differences
- Expectation that family values and structure will change
- Willingness to adjust
- Mutual commitment to family life
- Others-centeredness, not self-centeredness
- Sharing of responsibilities
- Honesty and dependability

Family Types

Lesson 3.2

Objectives

After studying this lesson, you will be able to

- identify various types of family structures.
- analyze the main rewards of living in different types of families.
- evaluate the main challenges of living in different types of families.
- compare and contrast different types of adoptions.

Key Terms

adoption
adoption agency
child support order
closed adoption
custodial parent
extended family
foster family
guardian
illegal market adoption
independent adoption
joint custody
noncustodial parent
nuclear family
open adoption
single-parent family
stepfamily

Academic Terms

apt
circumstances
consenting
cope
recession
sever
vigor

Reading and Writing Activity

How would you describe your family? Before reading this lesson, write a one-page short story about a day in the life of your family. Try to include all of your family members in the story, and provide relevant information such as what they do for a living and what kinds of relationships you have with them. Keep your short story, and after reading this lesson, title it with the family type that best describes your family. Write one paragraph justifying this title and then share your short story with a classmate whose short story had a different title.

Graphic Organizer

Divide a piece of paper into eight columns and label each column with one of the types of families discussed in this lesson. As you read, write the pros of each type of family in the first row and write the cons in the second row.

Nuclear Families	Single-Parent Families	Extended Families	Stepfamilies	Families with Adopted Children	Foster Families	Families with Guardians	Families with Grandparents as Head of Household

There are many types of families that comprise the U.S. population. The *family type* describes which people live in the household and how these people are related. Children usually enter families through birth and live in these families throughout childhood. Some children, however, have families who form differently. In these cases, children can have more than one type of family. This lesson describes different family types and their effects on children.

Nuclear Families

A father, a mother, and their biological child or children who live together form a **nuclear family**. This type of family exists in most societies. In nuclear families, children often leave home when they become adults, especially when they marry and have their own families.

Compared to other family types, nuclear families can have some disadvantages. Family members, such as grandparents or aunts and uncles, do not live in the home and children may lose out on the skills these other people can teach them. The family may live too far from relatives to rely on them for support in times of stress. Parents who do not get along may expose children to stress. This is especially true if the relationship is abusive.

On the other hand, nuclear families have some advantages. Both the adults and the children may have their needs met more easily because family members can share responsibilities. Children may be **apt** (likely) to learn more flexible home and child care roles in the nuclear family. Adults often share these tasks, and children who see role sharing may be better prepared for the future than those who do not. Children also have the chance to see how spouses relate to each other in positive ways.

Single-Parent Families

A **single-parent family** is headed by one adult. At any given time in the United States, about a third of all families are headed by single parents. How do single-parent families form? In some cases, single parenting is caused by death of a spouse or separation and divorce. These **circumstances** (situations or conditions) change a nuclear family to a single-parent family (**Figure 3.9**). While some single-parent families form in this way, many also form by parents who never marry. Because these families start with just one parent, they may have somewhat different concerns than other single-parent families.

Challenges of Single-Parenting

Single-parent families face many of the same challenges as other families. Families with one parent, however, may experience some of these same challenges in different ways from other families. In addition, they may experience some challenges unique to their family structure.

Figure 3.9 Any number of circumstances can change a nuclear family to a single-parent family. *What are some advantages of single-parent families? some disadvantages?*

Focus on

Financial Literacy

Child Support

Calculating how much child support the noncustodial parent owes the custodial parent varies per state. In general, child support is determined by the number of children the couple has and the income of the noncustodial parent. If a parent has multiple children living in different households, the rates also vary. The following lists the average percentage of income owed to the custodial parent for child support per number of children:

- 1 child—20%
- 2 children—25%
- 3 children—30%
- 4 children—35%
- 5 or more children—40%

Suppose a noncustodial parent earns $60,000 per year and owes child support. Calculate the yearly amount owed to the custodial parent for each number of children listed above.

Financial Concerns

Financial concerns are often the greatest challenges single parents face. This is because the **custodial parent** (parent who heads the household and has legal responsibility for caregiving) is often the only parent who pays the children's expenses.

The **noncustodial parent** (parent who lives separately from his or her children) also has legal responsibility to contribute financially, but few noncustodial parents actually do. In some cases, the matter is never taken before the court, so a child support order is not issued. A **child support order** is a judgment of the court that states how much the noncustodial parent must pay toward the children's expenses. A child support order that is issued can be difficult to enforce if the parent does not willingly pay.

Emotional Concerns

Many single parents have strong emotional reactions to the circumstances that made them single parents. They may feel anger, resentment, depression, fear, or sadness at having to carry so much responsibility alone. In cases in which nuclear families lose a parent through death or divorce, family life is disrupted. Feelings of grief and confusion may also be present.

Single parents must learn to cope (handle challenges in a healthy manner) with their own feelings as well as help their children cope. Parents are the base from which children grow. When death or divorce ends a nuclear family, children feel the loss of a relationship and role model. In these families, children's daily routines change as one parent takes over the duties of two parents.

In never-married families, children may have other issues with which they must cope. If both parents are actively involved, these issues are lessened. When one parent is absent, however, children may wonder whether they caused the parent to abandon them. They may wonder why

Mental Health Advisory

Children living in single-parent families may face several challenges, such as their parent's emotional problems and financial concerns and their own emotional problems. These difficulties often affect the quality of the parent-child relationship and thus lead to mental health problems.

other children have two parents and they have only one. These children may feel a lasting sense of loss, especially if they have never known or no longer have contact with the second parent. They may feel angry toward this parent for not being involved. Some children blame the custodial parent for not staying with the other parent.

If only one parent participates in the child's life, there are other sources of support and help available. Other family members, friends, neighbors, or adults from an organization such as Big Brothers Big Sisters of America can serve as role models for the children. Some single parents find support groups or social groups, such as Parents Without Partners®, helpful. Social service agencies may offer emotional, practical, and financial help, too.

Rewards of Single-Parenting

Despite the challenges, single-parenting can also be very rewarding. Children in well-adjusted single-parent homes are often more stable than children in unhappy two-parent homes. The relationship between the children and their single parent is often very strong. Children in single-parent families may show independence at an earlier age than those in other family types. For example, these children may perform self-care tasks earlier and take responsibilities for the care of home and yard earlier than children in two-parent homes.

Living with a single parent does not always mean the other parent cannot take an active role in the children's lives. In fact, children are often happier when both parents are involved. When possible, parents can work together to raise the children even if they do not live in the same house. Some co-parents go to court to seek **joint custody**, which is the shared legal right to provide care for and make decisions about their children's lives. Joint custody avoids the issue of determining which parent will be the primary caregiver.

Extended Families

An **extended family** is a family that extends past the parent or parents and their children to include other adult relatives who interact within the same household. Extended families are very common in many countries around the world. In the United States, extended families may form as a single parent and his or her children temporarily move in with other family members to save money. Extended families may also form as aging family members who need short-term care move in with their adult children. When the economy is in **recession** (economic period with minimal or no growth), there are always more extended families. Other families choose this family structure due to cultural tradition.

Extended families experience certain challenges more often than members of other types of families. Sometimes children and even adults find they must deal with too many people. Also, decisions are often made for the good of the entire family rather than the needs of each person.

Extended families also have many advantages. Children learn to interact with people of all ages because younger and older members are in daily contact. Extended families are good at handing down family beliefs and *family history*, or stories of a family's past (**Figure 3.10**). Because there are so many members, extended families can perform more duties than small family groups. When stressful events, such as death, happen in extended families, many people are there to help children and adults.

Figure 3.10 Family history and beliefs can be passed down through conversations; through time spent together; through letters and heirlooms; or through scrapbooks, as shown in the picture above. *What family beliefs and history have been passed down to you?*

Stepfamilies

A **stepfamily** forms when a single parent marries another person. In many cases, two single parents marry each other. Families in which the children of both spouses live with the couple are sometimes called *blended families*.

The stepfamily is a fairly common family form. Many of today's children have two stepfamilies—that of the father and his new wife and that of the mother and her new husband. Often, children live with only one of these stepfamilies. Other times, children live with each stepfamily part of the year. Each situation is unique.

Although many stepfamilies have good relationships, adjustment challenges are common (**Figure 3.11**). When couples with children remarry, they have to mature into the marriage while helping the children adjust to a new family structure. Young children under 10 years of age often adjust more easily to the new situation than older children. Adjustments may be even more difficult if the new stepparent has children of his or her own who will join the household, too.

Some ways stepparents can help create a family bond include

- letting stepchildren set the pace for their relationships with stepparents
- showing verbal appreciation for stepchildren by telling them how much they are appreciated
- explaining to children that a stepparent is another person to love and support them
- encouraging stepchildren to have one-on-one time with both their biological parents
- planning activities with stepchildren, but avoiding attempts to try to "buy" their love
- insisting on respect, but letting biological parents remain primarily responsible for discipline until solid bonds are established
- avoiding showing favoritism among children by treating all children equally
- keeping family communication open and frequent

Figure 3.11 Adjustment Challenges of Stepfamilies

- Family members find themselves in instant relationships—stepparents must relate with stepchildren and stepchildren must relate with each other.
- Parents must adjust to their new roles as a married couple while dealing with children from the beginning of marriage.
- Both parents have to adjust from being heads of single households to sharing roles and discipline and guidance of children.
- Children usually maintain relationships with the family of their other parent, too. Many children must adjust to two sets of rules, which can be a major challenge for school-age children.
- Sibling rivalry is common in all families, but can be worse among stepsiblings.
- Housing space may be a concern.

Families with Adopted Children

Adoption occurs when a child of one pair of parents legally becomes the child of other parents (or parent). Adoption legally ends the rights and responsibilities between a child and the birthparents (biological parents). The adoptive parents are then granted these rights. Many of the children available for adoption are older, have special needs, are born outside the United States, or are living in foster families and group homes. People often want to adopt for the following reasons:

- The couple cannot give birth or can give birth only with great difficulty.
- The couple may want to add to their current family.
- The couple knows a child who needs a home.
- A single person wants to be a parent and provide a home for children.

Adoption Agencies and Independent Adoptions

Most parents who adopt children spend much effort finding them. Buying or selling a child for adoption, which is called an **illegal market adoption**, is illegal in all states. Legal adoptions are expensive because parents pay providers for their time and expenses. For example, some expenses may include maternal expenses, such as health care not covered by insurance, salary and transportation costs for social workers, legal fees, and office expenses. Paying expenses, however, is different from buying and selling children. There are two ways to adopt children legally—through an adoption agency and through an independent source.

An **adoption agency** is an agency licensed by the state to handle adoptions. The agency works out the details between the birthparents and the adoptive parents. State courts handle the final legal aspects of the adoption. Adoption agencies are either state-funded or private (managed by a religious or a service organization).

In an **independent adoption**, a person, such as a lawyer or physician, works out the details between the birthparents and adoptive parents. Independent adoptions are handled in state courts and thus follow state laws. Foreign adoptions can be handled through an adoption agency or an independent source. **Figure 3.12** compares the pros and cons of each type of adoption.

Adoption Options and Rights

The laws of each state govern adoption options and rights. Adoption rights protect those involved in an adoption. In most states, the birthfather has legal rights. State laws may permit the birthfather

Focus on

Careers

Social Worker—Adoption Coordinator

Social worker is a category of careers in which professionals help families meet their basic needs. Some social workers, called *adoption coordinators*, work with adoption agencies to help families going through the adoption process. Adoption coordinators facilitate the placement of children for adoption. They conduct home studies and monitor children throughout the adoption process. Adoption coordinators must also possess a working knowledge of state laws as they relate to adoption.

Career cluster: Human services.

Education: Educational requirements include a bachelor's or master's degree in social work.

Job outlook: Future employment opportunities for social workers are expected to grow much faster than the average for all occupations.

To learn more about a career as an adoption coordinator, visit the United States Department of Labor's *Occupational Outlook Handbook* website. You will also be able to compare the job responsibilities, educational requirements, job outlook, and average pay of adoption coordinators with similar occupations.

to deny *paternity* (fathering of a child), give all rights to the birthmother, and give permission along with the birthmother for the child to be adopted. In some states, if the father cannot be found, steps can be taken to end his rights to make decisions about the child.

Figure 3.12 Pros and Cons of Agency and Independent Adoptions

Type	Pros	Cons
Agency	• Agency handles the legal aspects to meet the needs of all involved. • Children are closely matched with adoptive families to ensure good placement. Emphasis is on meeting the child's needs. • Birthparents can request certain types of adoptive families. (They can choose or meet adoptive parents in an open adoption.) • Adoptive parent can choose a child of a certain gender, age, and family background. • Information is exchanged between birthparents and the adoptive family (non-identifying information only in a closed adoption). • Social workers counsel both sets of parents. • Adoptive families are supervised from the time children are placed until the time the adoption is final. • Cost may be lower for the adoptive parents. Agency may charge based on parents' ability to pay.	• Agency sets criteria for adoptive parents. Many suitable homes may be turned down in favor of "more qualified" homes. People who are newly married, remarried, single, or older may have a harder time using an agency. • Income, religious, and housing guidelines may also exclude some people wanting to adopt. • The study of people wanting to adopt is extremely detailed and goes into all aspects of personal and married life. • Fewer babies are available for adoption. Also, available children may not be of the same culture as the adoptive parents. • When fewer children are available for adoption, long waiting periods are common. • People wanting to adopt may wait a long time before a good match with a child is found.
Independent	• There are no stated qualifications for adoptive parents. Thus, many people who might not be chosen to adopt through an agency (people who are newly married, remarried, single, or older) can become adoptive parents. • If they wish, birthparents can arrange for someone they already know as adoptive parents. • It may be easier to adopt a baby or to adopt a child of the same culture as the adoptive parents.	• Less emphasis may be placed on the child's welfare. • Adoptive parents are screened less thoroughly. Placement occurs before a study is done, so child may be in an unsuitable home. • Adoptive parents may receive less information about the child's background and health history. • Adoptive parents need to hire lawyers to help with legal details. • May be less privacy for both sets of parents than in an agency adoption. • Counseling is not provided as part of the adoption. • Cost may be higher than with an agency. (Some adoptive parents unknowingly enter illegal market adoptions.)

Both agency and independent adoptions may be either closed or open adoptions. A **closed adoption** (also called *confidential adoption*) is an adoption in which the identity of the birthparents and adopting family are not revealed. An **open adoption** is a type of adoption that involves some degree of communication between the birthparent(s) and adoptive family. Birthparents and adoptive parents can choose the type they prefer. The two options differ in how much information is exchanged and how much contact occurs between the birthparents and the adoptive family (**Figure 3.13**).

For all adoptions, birthparents must sign papers **consenting** (giving permission) to the adoption. Adoption agencies will have a waiting period in which they determine "the fit" between the adoptive parents and the child. Then, the matter must be presented in court, and a judge must declare the adoption final. When the adoption is complete, the child's original birth certificate is placed under court seal. A new birth certificate is issued listing the adoptive parents as the child's parents.

Adoption Issues

Children who are adopted generally have stable, happy home lives because their adopted families want and love them very much. Some challenges, however, may exist. In most cases, adoptive parents do not have the nine months of pregnancy to make the transition to parenthood. Instead, they take on their new roles very quickly. People wanting to adopt may be on a waiting list for many years. Then one day the adoption agency may call and announce a child will be ready for them the next day.

Other challenges may arise related to the adopted child's birthparents, especially if the adoption is closed. Birthparents may want to see the child or become part of the child's life. Adoptive parents may not agree that this is best for the child.

Children who are adopted often ask questions about the adoption. They may want to know about or meet their birthparents. Older children who lived with their birthparents and are then adopted by a new family need time to adjust. These children may miss their birthparents or want to be with them. To help these children adjust, adoptive parents can

Figure 3.13 Differences in Closed and Open Adoptions

Closed Adoption	Open Adoption
• Certain identifying information, as determined by state law, is kept private. This information most often includes names, addresses, and other identifying information about the birthparents and adopting families. • Sometimes even adopted children as adults cannot obtain information about birthparents. • Adoption is handled through an adoption agency, attorney, or doctor and is finalized in the courts. • Birthparents can get information on the type of home in which their child is placed. • Adoptive parents receive medical and social backgrounds of the child. • Sometimes birthparents write a letter for the child to read when he or she is old enough to understand. (This letter is often signed with a non-identifying signature, such as *Your Birthmom*.)	• Birthparents often choose the adoptive parents from résumés and/or photographs sent to an agency or attorney. After the initial selection, identities of all parents are made known and birthparents may choose to meet the adoptive parents before making a final decision. • Information is exchanged between birthparents and adoptive families as an aid for parenting. • After the adoption, visitation and other forms of contact may continue between both families for as long as desired. • All adoption records are usually accessible to adopted children when they become adults. • Children benefit from knowing their adoptions are loving decisions that involve open communication between both sets of parents.

answer their children's questions about the adoption in direct and honest ways. Adoptive parents may also wish to seek counseling to help them guide the children and offer them the support they need to make the adjustment.

Adjustments to living in an adoptive family take time for all family members. Soon, however, families are likely to adapt. Many adoptive parents create a loving family life that helps adopted children overcome any stress they may feel.

Foster Families

A **foster family** is a family in which an adult provides a temporary home for a child who cannot live with his or her birthparents. Foster parents assume the parenting responsibilities for the children in their care. They fill these roles until children reunite with their birthparents, are adopted, or become adults. Some foster children live in institutions or group homes rather than in family settings.

Children often enter foster families because of problems in their birthfamilies. These problems often include abuse, neglect, or substance abuse by the birthparents or other family members. In these cases, the courts intervene to protect the children by placing them in a foster family and providing counseling, treatment, and other help for the birthparents. The goal is to reunite children with their birthparents if they are able to provide a safe, secure home for their children. In serious or prolonged cases of neglect or abuse, the court may **sever** (end or cut off) the rights of the birthparents. The children remain in foster care until they can be adopted and given a permanent home. Sometimes children can be adopted by their foster parents.

A foster family may have one or two parents, and may include other biological, adoptive, or foster children. A foster child may be placed with brothers and sisters or apart from them, depending on the situation. Foster families can offer a stable, secure home for children. Joining a foster family, however, is a major adjustment. In many cases, foster children need counseling for the problems they faced in their birthfamilies. They may also miss their birthparents and other family members. To ease separation stress, contact or visitation is sometimes granted. Other children may grieve if they know they will never return to live with their birthparents. Each situation is unique. Foster parents need to be flexible, supportive, and understanding of the children in their care.

Mental Health Advisory

Foster children have had the poorest quality of parenting from their birthparents. Thus, between 60 and 80 percent of foster children exhibit social-emotional competency problems. The National Institute of Mental Health reports almost half of these children have clinically significant mental health problems.

Families with Guardians

A **guardian** is a person who is legally appointed by the court to take responsibility for a child in the event of the birthparents' death or extended absence. The guardian is often chosen by a child's biological parents and is usually someone who has close ties to the family, such as a relative or friend. The guardian assumes parental responsibilities. Some guardians manage the child's inherited money, while others take full financial responsibility for childrearing costs. The court supervises the guardian and may even make some decisions for the child. A child remains with his or her guardian until the child becomes a legal adult or the court terminates the relationship.

Families with Grandparents as Head of Household

Over 10 percent of all children are living in households headed by grandparents and other relatives (**Figure 3.14**). These family heads often do not have legal guardianship, but assume the parenting responsibilities of a guardian. Not having legal rights as a guardian may present challenges for the children and the guardian.

Figure 3.14 Statistics on Raising Grandchildren

- Eighty percent of children who live with relations are with grandparents.
- Thirty-three percent of these households are without any parental help.
- Fifty percent of the children are younger than six years of age, which means many years of child-raising.
- Fifty percent of the children are raised by two grandparents, and fifty percent by grandmothers.
- Fifty percent of the households have two or more children.
- Twenty percent of the households are in poverty.
- Sixty-seven percent of grandparents are under 60 years of age.

Although grandparents are often the safety net for their grandchildren, parenting grandchildren is high-risk for grandparents. These risks include

- not being able to physically care for grandchildren until the children are grown. **Vigor** (strength and energy) and health decrease as grandparents age.
- having less income due to retirement or loss of a spouse. (About 20 percent of these grandparents live at the poverty level.)
- giving up plans for the retirement years, such as leisure, hobbies, or travel.
- grieving over their grandchildren's parents. Usually the need for grandparents to become the active parents is due to one of the *Four Ds*: drugs, divorce, desertion, or death. Because of the Four Ds, parenting the second time around is long-term.
- having anxiety about meeting the needs of grandchildren whose cultural experiences are often so different from their own.
- dealing with their grandchildren's special needs, such as addictions, malnourishment, disabilities, and disorders, often due to earlier parental neglect and abuse.

On the positive side, grandparents often do an excellent job in raising their grandchildren. Grandparents usually have good parenting skills and they love their grandchildren unconditionally. Grandchildren typically respond in positive ways to their grandparents.

Lesson 3.2 Review and Assessment 

1. List two disadvantages and two advantages of the nuclear family.
2. A(n) _____ is a judgment of the court that states how much a noncustodial parent must pay toward a child's expenses.
3. List three reasons people might choose to live in an extended family.
4. List three ways stepparents can help create a family bond.
5. Compare a *closed adoption* to an *open adoption*.
6. What is the difference between a *foster parent* and a *guardian*?
7. **Critical thinking.** The number of never-married single parents in the United States is on the rise. Why do you think this is? What unique challenges and strengths do you think these single parents and their children face?
8. **Critical thinking.** Based on the family life cycle, what challenges can you see for grandparents raising their grandchildren? Are there also challenges for grandchildren who are parented by their grandparents?

Chapter 3 Review and Assessment

Summary

The family is the basic unit of society. Several factors contribute to the health of a family. These include a mutual commitment to family life, others-centeredness, and good communication. The foundational relationship in nuclear families is marriage, and there are many factors to analyze when considering and preparing for marriage. Marriage and family relationships are nurtured by positive nonverbal and verbal communication skills as well as effective money management. Significant changes in these foundational relationships can disrupt families, but family bonds can be strengthened and renewed. Many changes affect families today. Some of these changes take place during the six stages of the family life cycle. From the beginning stage through the childbearing, parenting, launching, mid-years, and aging stages, the family grows and develops.

Culture, which is identified in different ways, influences how each family lives. Because the United States has such cultural diversity, the effects of culture vary widely. Multicultural families are becoming more common. These families may have more challenges, but they can be as happy and healthy as other families.

One major difference from years past is the variety in family types that occurs. Family types include nuclear, single-parent, stepfamilies, extended families, families with adopted children, foster families, families with guardians, and families with grandparents as the head of household. Each family type has unique challenges and strengths.

College and Career Portfolio

Portfolio Organization

As you collect items for your portfolio, you will need a method to keep the items clean, safe, and organized for assembly at the appropriate time. A large manila envelope works well to keep hard copies of your documents, photos, awards, and other items. For certificates that are framed or already in scrapbooks, you may want to include photocopies of these items. You may also choose to include photos of trophies and plaques for your portfolio. Three-ring binders with sleeves are another good way to store your information. A box large enough for full-size documents will also work. Plan to keep like items together and label the categories. Use notes clipped to the documents to identify each item and state why it is included in the portfolio. Before you begin collecting items for your portfolio, complete the following:

- Select a method for storing hard copy items you will be collecting for your portfolio. (You will decide where to keep electronic copies in a later activity.)
- Write a paragraph that describes your plan for storing and labeling the items. Refer to this plan each time you add items to the portfolio.

Chapter 3 Review and Assessment

Vocabulary Activities

1. On a separate sheet of paper, list words that relate to each of the following terms. Then, work with a partner to explain how these words are related.

Key Terms

active listening (3.1)
adoption (3.2)
adoption agency (3.2)
body language (3.1)
budget (3.1)
child support order (3.2)
closed adoption (3.2)
communication (3.1)
cultural diversity (3.1)
culture (3.1)
custodial parent (3.2)
extended family (3.2)
family life cycle (3.1)
foster family (3.2)
guardian (3.2)
illegal market adoption (3.2)
independent adoption (3.2)
joint custody (3.2)
marriage (3.1)
multicultural family (3.1)
noncustodial parent (3.2)
nuclear family (3.2)
open adoption (3.2)
premarital counseling (3.1)
single-parent family (3.2)
stepfamily (3.2)

2. With a partner, create a T-chart. Write each of the following academic terms in the left column. Write a *synonym* (a word that has the same or similar meaning) for each term in the right column. Discuss your synonyms with the class.

Academic Terms

apt (3.2)
bias (3.1)
circumstances (3.2)
comprise (3.1)
consenting (3.2)
cope (3.2)
discontentment (3.1)
income (3.1)
Industrial Revolution (3.1)
inherent (3.1)
norm (3.1)
recession (3.2)
sever (3.2)
vigor (3.2)

Critical Thinking

3. **Analyze.** What do you think it means that the strength of a family's foundation is dependent on the strength of its inherent relationships? Working with a partner, write two statements that capture this same idea. Analyze how this concept affects the way child development experts discuss families.
4. **Evaluate.** Adrian and Gem are in premarital counseling, and their counselor has asked Adrian to list his reasons for wanting to marry Gem. His reasons are as follows:
   - Adrian's parents and grandparents want him to get married.
   - Adrian feels like he will not really be an "adult" until he is married.
   - Adrian wants to build a family with Gem.

   Evaluate Adrian's reasons for wanting to marry. Are these positive reasons or negative reasons? If you were Adrian's counselor, what would you say to him?
5. **Make inferences.** Select one of the figures in this chapter and then write a short paragraph interpreting the body language in that image. Make inferences about what kind of situation is occurring.
6. **Cause and effect.** Identify two events that might cause a family to repeat stages of the family life cycle. For example, a grown child recently divorced and needs to move back into the parent's home. Then, describe how each event might affect the parents and their children.
7. **Draw conclusions.** Choose two current cultural events and choose two historical cultural events. Then, describe how each of these cultural events have impacted family life.
8. **Analyze.** Because family is the basic unit of society, culture plays a large role in impacting family life. Conversely, family types and behaviors influence culture. Analyze how family life influences cultural trends and behaviors. For example, how does a shift in family living affect society at large? Share your thoughts with the class.
9. **Compare and contrast.** Choose two of the types of families discussed in this chapter. For each type, make a T-chart listing the pros and cons of living in that family. Finally, write a one-page paper comparing and contrasting the benefits and challenges of these family types.
10. **Identify.** On a piece of paper, list your friends and acquaintances, whether current or from the past. Then, identify what type of family that person has. Is one type of family predominant over the others?
11. **Determine.** Consider some possible benefits and challenges of open adoption for each of the following: birthparents, adoptive family, and the adopted child. Whose benefit do you think should take priority, and why? What factors should each party consider when deciding between an open and closed adoption?

Core Skills

12. **Listening.** Ask a married adult what his or her reasons were for getting married. Demonstrate active listening by taking notes and being attentive. Ask if the adult has any advice for you about considering marriage. Share these pieces of advice with the class. Finally, as a class, discuss the most common reasons for marriage and assess the health of those reasons, as well as how adults' reasons related to their pieces of advice.
13. **Speaking.** In small groups, role-play the roles of family members in each stage of the family life cycle. In your role-plays, emphasize the changes that take place in each stage and how these changes impact relationships. After practicing, perform your role-plays for the class and ask the class to guess which stage of the family life cycle you are representing. Lead the class in a discussion about how roles changed during each stage.
14. **Research, social studies, and reading.** Choose a culture other than your own and then use a library or the Internet to locate a book about family living in that culture. Read a few chapters from the book and then write a short essay summarizing your findings.
15. **History and research.** Use Internet or print sources to research the Industrial Revolution time line. What invention started the Industrial Revolution? What other inventions contributed to the Industrial Revolution in the United States? How did the Industrial Revolution affect families? Share your findings with the class.
16. **Art and speaking.** Review the qualities of a healthy family listed in this chapter. Then, using this list, make a list of the qualities of an unhealthy family. Draw two pictures—one illustrating a healthy family and another illustrating an unhealthy family. Present and explain your drawings to the class.
17. **Math, technology, and speaking.** Visit the United States Census Bureau website and view the most current information about the marital statuses and living arrangements for adults of all races. Choose one marital status or living arrangement and note what percentage of the population it describes. Then, apply that percentage to the size of your class. Give a short presentation informing your class of how these statistics apply to them.
18. **Writing.** Write a fiction story entitled, "The Joys and Trials of Living in a _____ Family Type." Base the story on your own family type or describe what you think it would be like to live in a family type different from your own. Check your story for correct spelling, grammar, and punctuation.
19. **Listening.** Choose one family type you are not familiar with and interview a person living in that type of family. How did the person's family form? How long has the person been living in his or her type of family? In his or her opinion, what are the advantages and disadvantages of the family type? Take notes about the person's answers to these questions and then discuss with a partner.
20. **CTE Career Readiness Practice.** Presume you are a premarital counselor. Your interpersonal skills—your ability to listen, speak, and empathize—are a great asset in working with clients.

    You are currently counseling a woman named Deborah, who is months away from her wedding and is experiencing some doubts. She feels like her fiancé does not listen to her. When she talks to him, he seems distracted, and sometimes he gets angry when he misunderstands her. To give her fiancé a "taste of his own medicine," Deborah has started adopting the same behaviors. How would you counsel Deborah to resolve the conflict with her fiancé? What would you tell her about active listening and effective communication?

Observations

21. Choose a friend who has a different type of family from your own, and ask if you can come over for dinner one night. While at dinner, observe how the family interacts and consider how the family is similar to and different from yours. List these similarities and differences and write a short paragraph reflecting on how family types affect family living and behaviors.
22. Watch one or two episodes of a television show that features an entire family. Try to identify where the family is on the family life cycle and assess how healthy the family is based on how the members interact. Write a short report summarizing your thoughts and then present your assessment to the class.

Chapter 4 Preparing for Parenting

Essential Question

How are a couple's decisions about parenthood related to the way they fulfill their parenting roles and responsibilities?

Lesson 4.1 **Deciding About Parenthood**

Lesson 4.2 **Parenting Roles, Responsibilities, and Styles**

Case Study Are Some Forms of Discipline Better Than Others?

As a class, read the case study and discuss the questions that follow. After you finish studying the chapter, discuss this case study again. Have your opinions changed based on what you learned?

Andrea and Tyler Moore are polar opposites when it comes to disciplining their rather "headstrong" six-year-old son, Jayden. Andrea, who has taken a child development course, believes the best way to discipline is to give Jayden reasons for expected behaviors and use nonphysical punishment when need be. Tyler, who is a career military officer, believes his discipline methods will work with Jayden. Tyler says the only reason Jayden needs for following instructions and behaving in certain ways is "because I said so." He backs this statement up with the point that children must respect their parents and not question their judgments. He says, when Jayden disobeys, he needs a spanking. He tells Andrea that perhaps giving reasons for certain behaviors helps some children, but not Jayden because he's "headstrong."

Tyler says he was raised with spankings and is a well-adjusted and responsible adult. Andrea agrees with this statement. She also knows that Tyler has never physically hurt Jayden and is, in fact, calm when he spanks him. Andrea points out, however, that Jayden's behavior is not getting better even when he's spanked.

Give It Some Thought

1. Can children who are given reasons for certain behaviors develop respect for authority?
2. Do you think respect for authority is the same for "blind authority" (without reasons) and authority with reasons?
3. Do you think spankings are needed in the case of some children, such as those who are "headstrong"?
4. Do you think Jayden will respect the authority of teachers and other adults if he accepts his dad's authority? Why or why not?
5. As an adult, what type of employee or parent will Jayden likely be?

While studying this chapter, look for the online resources icon  to:

- **Practice** terms with e-flash cards and interactive games
- **Assess** what you learn by completing self-assessment quizzes
- **Expand** knowledge with interactive activities and graphic organizers

Companion G-W Learning

www.g-wlearning.com/childdevelopment

Study on the go

Use a mobile device to practice terms and review with self-assessment quizzes.

www.m.g-wlearning.com/0384

Lesson 4.1 Deciding About Parenthood

Key Terms

birth control methods
direct costs
family planning
foregone income
indirect costs
maturity

Academic Terms

ample
depleted
expenditures
procreation
socioeconomic
stifle

Objectives

After studying this lesson, you will be able to

- analyze motivations for choosing whether or not to become parents.
- describe aspects of parenting that couples may want to consider before having a child.
- explain how children affect couples' relationships and how couples' relationships affect children.
- summarize points couples may want to keep in mind as they plan families.

Reading and Writing Activity

Read the objectives for this lesson carefully and then write three paragraphs describing what you already know about these topics. Base your writing on personal experiences and observations of those around you. After reading this lesson, rewrite your three paragraphs to include relevant information you learned.

Graphic Organizer

In a mindmap like the one shown, organize your notes on the information covered in this chapter. Write *Deciding About Parenthood* in the middle circle and fill in the surrounding circles in a way that will help you study the chapter material.

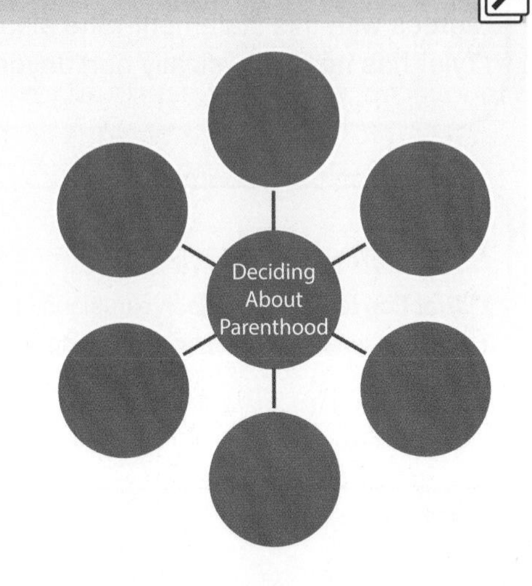

Couples have different motivations for choosing whether or not to become parents. Some of these are described in this lesson. Before deciding about parenthood, however, couples may want to consider all the aspects of parenting. After careful consideration, couples can agree on the decision and make their choice by respecting their partner's feelings and needs.

Choosing Whether or Not to Parent

The decision to parent is unlike many life decisions in two ways. First, the decision to parent is a *permanent* choice. Once a child is born, he or she is part of the parent's life forever. A person can choose to change careers, but having a child is different. Once a person is a parent, he or she will always be a parent.

Second, a decision not to parent is not permanent. Couples have some time to decide whether to become parents. Young couples have at least 15 safe childbearing years (**Figure 4.1**). The option of adopting a child may increase this time by a few years. Some couples may want to be parents, but might choose to wait until a more appropriate time. Other couples may not be sure about parenthood and will wait to decide. Even couples who decide they never want children can later change their minds.

Figure 4.1 The 15 safe childbearing years for couples are between 20 and 35 years of age. ***What complications might make childbearing less safe for women who are under 20 years of age?***

Reasons for Choosing Parenthood

Couples have various reasons for choosing parenthood. Although they may not always be able to explain why, they see children as part of their life. The following are reasons couples often give for wanting to become parents. Some are better reasons than others.

"We want to share our love and time with a child." This is perhaps the most important reason for wanting a child. A couple's desire to share their love and time with a child is the best reason for parenthood. Parents should want a child with no strings attached. If parents hope a child will fulfill other needs or goals, the parent-child relationship may not be healthy.

"Wouldn't it be nice to have a cute little baby?" When some couples see others with babies, they think it would be nice to have a cute little baby, too. It is good for couples to think positively about babies, but the problem is that babies are not always cute. All babies are sick, fussy, and cranky at times, and require round-the-clock care.

"Our parents want grandchildren." Some couples want to fulfill their parents' wishes to be grandparents. Grandparents can give a child much love, but the question is, "Who is responsible for the care of the child?" It is more important for the parents to want and love a child.

"Our older child needs a brother or sister." When a couple wants a playmate for an older child, the parents are fulfilling someone else's needs, not their own. Although a child might enjoy having a brother or sister, there are other ways to meet an only child's need for a playmate.

"A child can make us proud." Some couples see children as sources of pride. They want children to carry on the family name and customs, inherit the family business or money, or achieve certain goals. It is good for parents to be proud of their children and want them to achieve. They must be careful, however, not to let their hopes **stifle** (suppress) their children's goals. Parenthood is not a good choice if a child is wanted only to boost the parents' ego or meet their unfulfilled goals.

"A child will comfort us in our old age." Sometimes couples think of children as sources of help in their old age. It is natural for people to think about being helpless or lonely when they grow old. An aging parent, however, cannot count on a child's help.

"A child will make us love each other." Some couples hope that having a child will save a failing marriage. Children may enrich family life for stable couples. Unstable couples may find that having children makes their problems worse.

Reasons for Not Choosing Parenthood

Some couples plan to be childless permanently. Other couples decide to postpone parenthood—at least at the present time. Even couples who consider having children may want to think about how children can change their lives. Following are some reasons couples often give for not choosing parenthood.

"We're not ready for a child." When couples say they are not ready for children, they usually mean they need to mature. They may feel they need more time as a couple for their marriage to mature. They may want to devote more time to their education or job. Many people want to establish themselves in a career before becoming parents.

"A baby costs a lot." Babies are expensive. At one time, a large family was an economic asset because children helped with the work. Today, children cannot contribute a great deal, if anything, to family income. (Later in this lesson you will look more closely at the cost of having a child.)

"A child will tie us down." Unlike many other responsibilities, child care tasks cannot be put off until later. Parents are always called if children are hurt, ill, or need help. Even with the best babysitters in charge, parents cannot completely forget their roles.

"A child will interfere with our careers." When tending to both their career and children, parents face two common problems. First, it is difficult for parents to have enough time and energy for both parenting and succeeding at work (**Figure 4.2**). Second, it is difficult to find good child care services.

Some careers make parenting easier than others. School teachers have hours and vacation times similar to those of their older children. Other careers make parenting more difficult by requiring parents to work long hours or travel frequently. Highly stressful jobs are also difficult for parents. Couples who combine these types of jobs with parenting must plan carefully.

"Our child could be sick or have a disability." There is no guarantee that a child will be in perfect health when he or she is born. Babies can be born with disabilities or become seriously ill or injured. Good medical care before and after birth reduces—but does not eliminate—these risks. Children with disabilities or who are ill or injured, have special needs beyond those of other children. Many parents feel that raising children with disabilities, however, is highly rewarding.

Mental Health Advisory

A difficult parent-child relationship can result when couples decide to become parents for the wrong reasons or have an unplanned pregnancy after deciding not to have children. If the parent-child relationship remains difficult, the child is at high-risk for mental health problems.

Figure 4.2 The amount of time and energy both partners want to spend on their careers is an important consideration for couples thinking about having children. *What are some other reasons a couple might choose not to have children?*

"Our marriage could fail, and I don't want to be a single parent." Couples with marital problems may want to solve them before having children. Being a single parent is difficult. Single parents may lack money, help with household and child care tasks, and the support of a spouse. Without these resources, the single parent cannot always take part in adult activities, which can lead to feelings of isolation. Many single parents, however, can solve such problems.

Aspects of Parenting

Parenting is both a rewarding and challenging task (**Figure 4.3**). Many people invest more money, time, and emotions in their children than they do in any other investment in their lives. Most parents hope their children will inherit all their strengths and avoid their weaknesses. They also hope their children will have opportunities they did not have. Before having a child, a couple must seriously consider all aspects of parenting.

Knowledge About Parenting

Upon the birth or adoption of a child, a couple instantly becomes parents. Few, if any, other jobs give a beginner such responsibility without training. Many couples feel they need help in becoming good parents. Experienced family members or friends may help some new parents. Many places offer child care and parenting classes. Literature on parenting is plentiful, but sources may not always be reliable and accurate.

Maturity

Regardless of age, a person who may be biologically capable of conceiving a child may not have the *maturity* to become a parent. **Maturity** is having the intellectual and emotional capacity of a healthy, responsible adult. Maturity is different from age. People may be mature for their age, but there is a special type of maturity needed for parenting. Erikson's theory addresses this issue.

Erikson felt that teens and even young adults are not best suited for parenting. His theory states that teens need to explore their sense of independence and develop a sense of self. Young adults need time to find out what is important to them and what sort of person they want to be before entering into a truly committed relationship. To be successful in marriage, the primary focus should not be on self, but rather on each other as partners.

According to Erikson, at some point mature couples want to contribute to the next generation by "making their mark in life" and making the world a better place. Some adults do this through careers or volunteer work, but many do it through parenting. Parenting at a mature level involves more than **procreation** (the producing of children). True parenting is not a "self-centered" activity. It is a way of looking outside of yourself and giving back to society by the way you parent.

Relationships

Children are born into a network of people and relationships. They are parented within a couple's relationship and the relationships the couple have with family and friends. Children affect these relationships and these relationships affect children.

Figure 4.3 Challenges and Rewards of Parenting

Challenges
• Becoming parents means adjusting lifestyles. Lifestyles with children may be starkly different from lifestyles before children.
• Parents may feel they lack training and parenting skills. They can feel overwhelmed, especially as first-time parents. They may be unsure or unprepared for how to handle a situation.
• Roles change when a couple has children. Parents may disagree about parenting styles and how to handle certain situations. This may result in tension in the relationship.
• The parent-child relationship is often one-sided. For many years, parents are "givers" and children are the "takers." Parents must put their children's needs before their own needs.
• Parenting can be physically draining. Parents are often fatigued from a lack of sleep, especially during the early years.
• Parenting is a full-time, nonstop job. Parents have less time to spend alone or with friends.
• Parenthood may impact career choices. Some parents may forego career opportunities.
• Parenting is expensive. Meeting financial expenses is a major concern for most families.
• Parents may lack parenting support from their spouses. Similarly, relatives and close family friends may not have time or may live too far away to provide parenting support.
• Relatives, friends, and other parents may frequently offer parenting advice, even when not solicited.
• Parents may feel fear, frustration, and stress from parenting-related concerns.
Rewards
• Parents experience a new type of deep, unconditional love when they become parents.
• Building a family can positively add to the marriage dynamic when the marriage is healthy.
• Becoming parents can strengthen the couple's relationships with their own parents.
• Experiencing a child's first sounds, smiles, words, and steps can bring joy to parents' lives.
• Being called "Mom" or "Dad" can be rewarding.
• Parenting can be an adventure. Parents gain new experiences through their children's points of view and can explore the world with their children. Children may introduce activities or knowledge to parents' lives.
• Children can be funny and make ordinary situations comical.
• Parents feel a sense of satisfaction when they can successfully provide for their children and see their children happy.
• Parents also feel a sense of satisfaction and happiness when their children grow up to be happy, independent, successful adults.

Relationships are a two-way street. The couple may want to think about what changes parenthood will bring to their relationships.

Children Affect Relationships

To prepare for parenthood, couples need to know how children will change their lives. Unlike other relationships, parenting in the beginning is very one-sided. Babies are demanding of the parents' time and other resources. Babies have no idea that their parents are exhausted from round-the-clock care. Parents may even feel their needs go unnoticed by family friends when the focus is on the baby. Parenting during the first few months is quite challenging. Because parenting continues, parents must want more than to have a baby. They must want and be willing to change along with this baby

Developing Parenting Skills

Many couples feel they need help learning how to become good parents. Finding the following resources can help couples learn about child care and development:

- professionals and/or successful parents to give advice
- child development literature (books, journals, magazines) that is accurate, practical, and available
- child care and parenting classes (community colleges and local American Red Cross chapters may offer such classes)
- families with infants and young children (babysit and volunteer in schools and organizations to understand what it is like to care for children)

New parents should also realize there is not one right way to parent. Although some methods may be more respected than others, many factors influence parenting. The culture in which a child is raised affects how parents raise children. The personalities of parents and children also affect parenting. The ways couples have seen their parents or friends care for children influences how they care for their own. All these factors are important to think about when learning child care skills.

Research Activity

Choose one source of information couples could access for parenting advice or education. This might be a parenting book, an interview with someone who is a parent, an online article, or a brochure about parenting. Skim this resource and write three to four interesting pieces of advice the resource provides. Share your findings with the class. Then, choose a partner and discuss which pieces of advice you thought were most helpful.

over many years. In **Figure 4.4**, Ellen Galinsky, a psychologist, describes how parents develop.

Children usually do not strengthen a weak marriage. If a couple has good relationships both inside and outside their marriage, then having a child will likely enrich their lives. The couple may want to think about how committed they are to each other. They can also determine whether they have the time and energy to give to children. Do they want to share much of their time together with children? Are they doing in their daily lives what they want their children to do? (Children model parents' behavior.)

Relationships Affect Children

Couples can begin looking at their relationships by asking questions about their feelings for others. These kinds of questions relate directly to parenting. For starters, couples might ask themselves the questions in **Figure 4.5**.

Couples can also look at their present relationships with relatives and friends. Good relationships with others are positive for the couple and their possible children. Couples might want to ask themselves the questions in **Figure 4.6** about their relationships with others.

Couples also need to think about how their relationships with others can affect their children. There are at least three advantages to children's relationships with others. First, relatives and friends provide children with their first link to the outside world. Second, grandparents and older relatives can teach children about the past. Third, when many relatives and friends care for children, they feel more rooted to their family. Because each relative and friend is unique, children learn to understand that people are different. They also learn to accept people's unique traits. This interaction will help children get along well with others as they grow.

Figure 4.4 Galinsky's Parenting Stages

Stage	Timing of Stage (based on child's age/stage)	Parenting Tasks
Image-making	Before birth	• Prepare for changes in their lives. • Form images of what their child will be like and their roles as parents.
Nurturing	Birth–2 years	• Try to balance their baby's needs with their own needs. • Provide loving and consistent care to their baby. (This stems from emotional bonds.)
Authority	2 years–4 to 5 years	• Change their role as the family's authority figures (called *parenting style*). • Teach their child the "rules of behavior" through reasoning, rewards, and punishments.
Interpretive	4 to 5 years–12 to 13 years	• Share their knowledge about the world with their child. • Interpret other authority figures, such as teachers or coaches, by explaining what they expect. • Teach values and morals as the need arises. • Help their child accept social reality, such as "life may not always be fair."
Interdependent	Teen years	• Cope with their teen's changing needs for closeness and distance. • Monitor teen's behavior and give guidance as needed. • Begin to give more freedom with boundaries to their teen.
Departure	Teen or early adult years	• Evaluate themselves as parents. • Redefine their relationship with their child, such as allowing their child to make his or her own decisions. Provide guidance only when asked.

Figure 4.5 Questions Couples May Ask to Learn About Their Feelings for Others

- Are we loving and sensitive to others' needs?
- Are we careful not to judge people and their ideas?
- Can we recognize and respect others' rights?
- Are we self-disciplined?
- Do we relate well to others?
- Are we flexible enough to accept changes?
- Are we brave about challenges?
- Can we be honest about our feelings for others?

Management of Resources

Parenting involves management of time, energy, home care, careers, finances, and resources needed directly for children. The couple may want to consider all of these factors before having a child. Because these factors can change, couples may want to examine the factors each time before adding to their families.

Time and Energy

Time and energy are both *limited resources* and are **depleted** (used up) very quickly during parenting. Couples considering parenting may want to identify current and future demands on

Figure 4.6 Questions Couples May Ask to Learn About Their Relationships with Others

- Do our relatives and friends share our basic values?
- Can we tolerate differences in beliefs?
- Can we ask for advice and also use our own judgment?
- Can we tell others about our needs and accept the help they offer?
- Can we recognize others' needs and offer our help?
- Can we avoid abusing others' generosity, including time and money?
- Can we share fun times with others?

their time. To make time for parenting, couples may need to forego certain activities. Couples may also want to consider the availability of additional help if children take more parenting time than expected, such as with twins or triplets, or children with special needs.

Parenting is the most energy-depleting role a person will likely encounter. Without energy, parents cannot effectively take care of their children. A parent's energy is also depleted by other life activities, especially home care and career demands. Couples may want to consider their health, career demands, and current household tasks to determine if they have enough energy to effectively care for a child.

Home Care

Homes are resources for family life. Home is where people prepare meals and eat, sleep, groom, and store many personal possessions. Home is the center of the family's relationships and where extended family members and friends may gather (**Figure 4.7**). Because of their many uses, homes require a great deal of care. Home care responsibilities use much time and energy.

First, couples may want to consider how they currently share tasks and how they feel about this division of duties. Next, the couple may consider how children might affect how they share responsibilities. If they become parents, will there be major changes in the way they share responsibilities? Can they agree on how to divide home and child care tasks? How couples choose to divide tasks can depend on each person's needs. If couples plan carefully and try all ideas, they can divide tasks so both partners are satisfied.

Careers

Parenting is unlike other careers. Most jobs provide much more training than what new parents

Figure 4.7 Caring for the family's home is an important aspect of parenting, because homes are centers of teaching, care, and family resources. *How do you help in caring for your family's home?*

receive. Parents probably have studied and trained more for their careers than for their roles as parents. Their job skills may be better than their child care skills, for which they may have had little or no training. In addition to training differences, parenting is a 24/7 career that lasts for 18 or more years.

A family's major financial resources come from their careers. Couples may want to decide whether they will both work or whether one will care for children at home. The parents' workplaces also help determine the **socioeconomic** (social and economic) level of the family, where they live, possible mobility, the work hours/workdays, and possibly the parents' stress levels.

Finances

Couples must realize children cost a lot. **Expenditures** (expenses) on a child from birth through 17 years of age are over $245,000. Lower-income families spend 25 percent of their before-tax income on a child, while middle-income families spend 16 percent. Higher-income families spend 12 percent. Of course, the higher the income, the more actual dollars are spent on a child. The figures do not cover any expenses for children beyond high school, such as college expenses or financial help in starting a career.

The first year of childrearing is expensive, and expenses grow as the child grows. The **direct costs**, or expenses related to raising a child, include expenditures for clothing, food, housing, child care and education, and transportation. Other direct costs involve children's extra activities, such as toys, entertainment, and sports lessons. The first baby is often the most expensive. Additional children may use some of the firstborn's items. Each extra child increases the costs, and typically, a second child almost doubles the costs.

In addition to direct costs of having a child, there are indirect costs. **Indirect costs** are resources parents use to meet child-related costs that could have been used to meet other goals. Some indirect costs of having children include the following:

- *Foregone income.* **Foregone income** is the potential income given up by a parent who leaves the workforce and stays home to raise a child. Foregone income increases with the salary or wage level. Foregone income can be estimated.

Focus on Financial Literacy

Parenting Costs

Every family is unique in its needs and ability to meet those needs. Each family has many financial considerations, which vary according to factors such as number of people in the household, income earned, and individual needs. Some categories of expenditures, however, are predictable. For example, families in the United States spend a percentage of their incomes on average in the following categories:

- housing—34%
- transportation—17%
- food—13%
- life insurance and savings—10%
- health care—6%
- personal care (clothing, education, entertainment, physical care)—16%
- contributions—4%

Using the percentages above, calculate the amount spent in each category of expenditures for a family with a $75,000 income. Do you think the percentages spent in each category would be the same for a family that makes $30,000 per year compared to a family that makes $250,000 per year? What factors might affect how much income is spent on each category of expenditures?

Careers

Personal Financial Advisor

Personal financial advisors assess the financial needs of individuals. They use their knowledge of investments, tax laws, and insurance to recommend financial options to individuals. They help them to identify and plan to meet short-term and long-term financial goals.

Career cluster: Finance.

Education: Educational requirements include a bachelor's or master's degree in finance, business, accounting, mathematics, economics, or law. State licensure and certification may also be necessary.

Job outlook: Future employment opportunities for personal financial advisors are expected to grow much faster than the average for all occupations.

To learn more about a career as a personal financial advisor, visit the United States Department of Labor's *Occupational Outlook Handbook* website. You will also be able to compare the job responsibilities, educational requirements, job outlook, and average pay of personal financial advisors with similar occupations.

- ***Foregone career opportunities.*** A worker who is out of the workforce for several years may miss promotions and may even need to be retrained before working again. The cost of time out of the workforce is the most difficult indirect cost to calculate.
- ***Time spent in child care.*** Caring for children on a daily basis, driving them to activities, and using personal or sick days to care for a sick child are all indirect costs.

Couples think about many factors when they estimate the direct and indirect costs of parenting. Each family is different, and these differences show in the way families spend their money.

Carefully planning financial resources is important for everyone. In some ways, financial planning becomes more important when couples think about children. This is because children rely on their parents for financial support for many years. Parents also model for their children either good or poor consumer practices. Couples may want to ask themselves the following questions about finances before becoming parents:

- How do we currently earn and spend our money?
- Are we satisfied with our budget? Does the budget fit our needs and allow for a few luxuries?
- Do we have regular savings we could use to meet child-related expenses? If not, can we adjust our budget to meet such expenses?
- Can we expect more income or lower expenses during the next few years to help offset child-related costs?
- What type of savings goals do we need for a child?
- What is an estimate of child-related expenses for the first and next several years?

Other Resources

Couples may also want to consider other resources children need, such as child care and education programs, schools, park and recreation services, health and medical services, youth organizations, community programs, and religious groups. Parents often like to live near these services, which might require a change in housing location or even a change in a career.

Family Planning

Family planning involves decisions couples make about whether or not they want to have children and when to have them. Family planning is a couple's personal choice. There are some points couples may want to keep in mind as they plan families. Couples can consult with a doctor while planning for a family. Doctors may offer information and advice on the following:

- options in **birth control methods** (measures couples use to help prevent pregnancy). **Figure 4.8** shows some questions couples may want to ask their doctor to learn more about birth control methods.
- the impact their current health might have on a pregnancy.
- prepregnancy preparations, such as ideal weight, nutritious diet, prenatal vitamins, and lifestyle changes (no smoking or alcohol; less caffeine).
- spacing of pregnancies. As a general rule, doctors say a woman might want to wait 18 to 23 months after delivery to become pregnant again.

After consulting with a doctor, the couple may want to think about which birth control method they prefer. This might depend on their religious beliefs and their likes and dislikes of certain methods. Often couples change birth control methods due to side effects, needed changes after childbirth, or when their family is complete.

Although doctors can advise about the spacing of children or even whether to have another child, it is the couple's decision. Not all couples feel they can handle another child right away. These feelings depend on their finances, emotional and physical energy, career, age, and lifestyle. Couples should not feel guilty if they want only one child. The best reason for a couple to have another child is to share their love and time with this child, too.

For couples who want to add to their families, a spacing of about three years is advised for developmental reasons. **Ample** (a generous amount of) spacing gives parents time to work with each child alone before they need to divide their attention. In addition, less jealousy between children occurs when there is a three-year age difference.

Figure 4.8 Questions to Ask About Birth Control Methods

- How does the method work to prevent pregnancy? (For example, does the method block sperm's travel or provide hormones that prevent ovulation?)
- What is the time limit for the product's recommended use?
- How successful is the method at preventing pregnancy if properly used?
- What are the directions for using the method?
- What is the method's possible side effects and risks, including future fertility?
- What does the method cost?

Lesson 4.1 Review and Assessment 

1. List three poor reasons people give for wanting to become parents.
2. What is the most important reason for parenthood? Justify your answer.
3. List three reasons couples give for *not* choosing parenthood.
4. List three aspects of parenting couples might want to consider before having a child.
5. What does Galinsky say about parenthood?
6. Why is parenting an energy-depleting role?
7. Differentiate between the *direct costs* and *indirect costs* of raising a child.
8. How does family planning affect children?
9. What are *birth control methods*?
10. **Critical thinking.** Explain why parenthood is more apt to further weaken than strengthen an already weak marriage.

Parenting Roles, Responsibilities, and Styles

Lesson 4.2

Objectives

After studying this lesson, you will be able to

- explain parents' roles and responsibilities involving nurturance, socialization, and guidance and discipline.
- differentiate between the terms *guidance* and *discipline.*
- describe the three types of discipline and their effects on children.
- compare and contrast the following parenting styles: authoritarian, permissive, overparenting, and authoritative.

Key Terms

authoritarian
authoritative
character
discipline
guidance
induction
love withdrawal
nurturance
overparenting
permissive
power assertion
socialize

Academic Terms

aspects
conduct
endorse
entitlement
impart
incessantly
overindulgent
prone

Reading and Writing Activity

Read the key terms for this lesson and then write them on a separate piece of paper. Look up each of these terms in the glossary at the back of this textbook and then write the definition in your own words. Underneath each term and definition, write an example of the term's meaning in action. After reading this lesson, update your examples and share with a partner.

Graphic Organizer

In a chart like the one shown, write the parenting roles and responsibilities you learn in this lesson in the left column. Then, as you read this lesson's section on parenting styles, write each parenting style next to the parenting role or responsibility to which it most closely relates. If you think a parenting style relates strongly to more than one parenting role and responsibility, you may write the style twice. After reading this lesson, share your graphic organizer with a partner and compare notes.

Parenting Roles and Responsibilities	Parenting Styles

Couples who choose to become parents have many roles and responsibilities. Family culture determines the specifics of how the childrearing function will be fulfilled, which is what people call *parenting roles*. Perhaps the most widely identified parenting responsibilities involve *nurturing* (caring for) and *socialization* (social training), including guidance and discipline. The parenting role of socialization begins after infancy. As parents guide and discipline their toddlers, one of four parenting styles emerges and becomes very consistent by the preschool years.

Figure 4.9 Nurturance involves helping children meet their physical needs, as well as their intellectual and social-emotional needs. *What are some examples of children's intellectual and social-emotional needs? How can parents help children meet these needs?*

Parenting Roles and Responsibilities

Parents are responsible for the well-being of their children. Parents' roles and responsibilities mainly involve nurturance, socialization, and guidance and discipline. Children thrive in a nurturing environment. They learn to become responsible members of a community through socialization by their parents and other members of their family. Through their parents' guidance and discipline, children learn right from wrong.

Nurturance

Nurturance, in a narrow sense, includes the physical aspects of child care, such as feeding, dressing, and bathing children. In a broader sense, *nurturance* includes meeting intellectual needs, such as providing children with a stimulating environment. *Nurturance* also includes meeting social-emotional needs, such as helping children feel secure and loved (**Figure 4.9**). Physical care, love, and concern are important for children's healthy growth. Both mothers and fathers play an important role in nurturing their children.

Socialization

People are born into a community. From the beginning, people experience their world as one of relationships. Learning to form relationships is a key social need. Children need to form strong relationships with their parents. These relationships can help children feel secure and teach them how to respond and relate to other people.

Children also need a sense of belonging. To build this sense, parents **socialize** their children, or train them to live as part of the larger social group. Parents teach children about the way of life within the group. Each social group may have its own language, beliefs, attitudes, values, rituals, and skills that children learn through a process called *socialization*. Socialization is a major role of parents, for it allows children to fit into their social group.

Another name for a social group is *culture*. From birth onward, children grow up in a culture, or sometimes cultures, that mold their belonging to the group. Using the **aspects** (parts) of a person's culture to socialize is called *enculturation*. Parents, family members, schools, religious groups, and others influence children's enculturation.

Parents model, reward, and praise what their culture values. They criticize and correct that which does not fit with their cultural beliefs. In this socialization process, children learn most of their culture's values at home. These concepts are also taught indirectly by living within the culture.

Focus on

Reading

Culture

Read all or some of the chapters from Laura Ingalls Wilder's books, *Little House in the Big Woods* and *Farmer Boy*. As you are reading, look for specific examples of how the parents socialized their children. What skills, customs, and values did the parents hand down to the children in the stories? How are these teachings different from what your parents have passed down to you about your culture? Record your findings and share them with the class.

Some cultural concepts, such as history and heroes, are taught more directly. The reasons behind traditions of the culture are also often taught to children from an early age. Parents and other older family members may help **impart** (give or share) values to children through storytelling and answering children's questions about the culture or its practices.

Parents also teach their children how to respond in a culturally diverse society. Parents who value diversity point out the benefit of learning from people who are not like themselves. These parents teach their children to appreciate people of all cultures. They believe each group is different from, but equal to, other groups. Parents who do not value diversity often believe their group is better than others and that people of different groups should not interact with one another. Whatever their viewpoints, parents are passing these views to their children.

Guidance and Discipline

Child guidance and discipline are important responsibilities of parenthood. Parents guide their children in their daily interactions with them (**Figure 4.10**). **Guidance** includes the words and actions parents use to influence their children's behavior. For example, when parents face frustrations but react calmly, they guide their children to do the same. By showing children they are not upset when they do not get their way, parents are modeling good behavior. Guiding children in a positive way is an important parental role.

Discipline is part of guidance. **Discipline** is the use of methods and techniques to teach children self-control. Through discipline, children learn to act in ways that society finds acceptable. Punishment is not the same as discipline. *Punishment* is a consequence for a misdeed. For punishment to be effective, the negative consequences must fit the misdeed.

One major goal of guidance and discipline is to build character in children. **Character** is the

Figure 4.10 The teaching of children does not just happen in the classroom or child care center. Parents guide and teach their children through their daily interactions with them. *What have your caregivers taught you through their interactions with you?*

principles and beliefs that guide a person's **conduct** (actions and manners) and define his or her personality and behavior. Through love and guidance, parents help their children grow into self-directed adults (**Figure 4.11**).

Most parents would like to find the perfect method for handling their children's unpleasant or disruptive behaviors. Although there is no perfect method for use with every child, some forms of discipline are better than others. In choosing a method, parents need to remember that the goal is to teach children self-control, not just take care of the immediate misbehavior. This is important because parents will not always be able to guide children, especially as they become older. Studies report that parents use three types of discipline—power assertion, love withdrawal, and induction.

Power Assertion

Power assertion occurs when parents use or threaten to use some form of physical punishment (also called *corporal punishment*) or deny privileges. Although many parents use these methods, there are some negative long-term effects of power assertion. Certainly, many people can name children who were occasionally spanked and are now healthy, happy adults. Some adults even claim spankings were good for them. If this is true, why are most parenting experts against power-assertive techniques?

Figure 4.11 Parents administer discipline and guidance in order to shape their children's characters and steer them toward becoming healthy adults. *What kinds of discipline might encourage children to have character? What kinds might not?*

Following are the main reasons power-assertive techniques are not a healthy form of discipline:

- Power-assertive techniques are often used when parents are angry. If parents are **prone** (likely) to losing their tempers, their intended light physical punishment could become abusive when done in anger. For this reason, corporal punishment is illegal in child care programs and some other settings.
- Power-assertion is based on making a child fearful of the larger (and louder) adult. As the child grows physically, however, fear lessens and the technique no longer works.
- Power-assertion involves the fear of being caught and punished. Many power-assertive adults will threaten, "Don't let me catch you doing that again!" Thus, the child weighs the chances of being caught and the likely punishment. The child is not being guided by what is right or wrong.
- When a child is physically aggressive toward another child, such as hitting another child, corporal punishment seems like a double standard. The child may think, "You are hitting me; why can't I hit others?" This is a good example of the punishment not fitting the misdeed.
- Discipline techniques are imitated or modeled by children. Children disciplined through power assertiveness are more apt to use these methods in their own relationships. If they see their parents lose control, children may become violent during the teen years or abusive to their own spouses or children as adults.

Love Withdrawal

In a discipline technique called **love withdrawal**, parents threaten children with being unloved or suggest some form of parent/child separation. An example is parents telling children they do not want or love them. Some parents even tell their children they are going to give them away. Other forms of love withdrawal include ignoring the child or giving the child the "silent treatment." Experts consider love withdrawal to be emotional abuse. Love withdrawal creates stress and prevents the expression of feelings.

Induction

In the third technique, **induction**, parents discipline their children by reasoning and explaining to them why they should or should not use certain behaviors. The induction method involves several different techniques and is individualized to the child's age (**Figure 4.12**). Children disciplined by this technique tend to show better self-control, display more concern for others, and take responsibility for their own failures.

Parenting Styles

Most parents want to raise their children to become responsible, well-mannered adults. As children enter the toddler years, parents must begin using guidance and discipline. Within a year or two, parents develop a *parenting style* (an overall way of socializing children). The parents' own childhood experiences, beliefs, and temperament, as well as the temperament of the child influence parenting styles. Parenting styles are classified as *authoritarian*, *permissive*, *overparenting*, and *authoritative*. **Figure 4.13** shows results these parenting styles may have on children.

Figure 4.12 Some Induction Techniques and Examples

Induction Techniques	
Technique	**Tips**
Keep control as an adult.	• Stay calm. • Deal with issues quickly, but not impulsively. • Seek help if it becomes too difficult to remain calm.
Maintain realistic expectations in making decisions about what are and are not acceptable behaviors.	• Consider child's age/stage, temperament, and any special problems. • Try to prevent situations that lead to misbehaviors, such as child proofing and avoiding hunger, sleep deprivation, or overstimulation.
Be a positive model.	• Avoid doing or saying anything you would not want your child to model. • Avoid media that show aggressive acts. Choose books and media that have positive images.
Use positive words with children.	• Show respect when speaking to children. • Make the child's environment a "yes/yes/no" one rather than a "no/no/yes" one. (Using "no" mainly for safety reasons makes for a more positive environment.) • With older children, stick to one issue at a time rather than bringing up all issues. • Know that it is fine to say "I'm sorry" to a child.
Provide structure and consistency in the environment.	• Make the environment physically suitable for the child. (For example, children will try unsafe ways to reach items beyond their floor reach. Within-reach storage also allows children to keep their areas neat.) • Have a routine that lessens stress for both children and adults. • Explain any changes in routines and even rehearse new expectations.
Distract and redirect infants and young toddlers.	• Remove from an unsafe situation. • Involve child in a new activity.

(Continued)

Figure 4.12 *(Continued)*

Induction Techniques	
Technique	**Tips**
Set limits and reinforce them.	• State rules in positive words. • Make statements simple for young children. • Give options when possible.
Use problem-solving techniques with older children.	• Use the six steps in the problem-solving process. • Evaluate the effectiveness of the solution selected.

Use punishment with care.	• Help child see punishment as the result of his or her *willful* misbehavior.
	• Choose punishment that fits the misbehavior.
	  • For toddlers and preschoolers, a *time-out* (removing a child from an activity or the presence of others for less than five minutes) often works for a temper outburst or aggression toward others.
	  • *Natural consequences* (common results of misbehaviors, such as a broken toy caused by an action done in anger) teach children that actions have consequences.
	  • *Logical consequences* (adult-planned consequences to show a direct link between misbehavior and consequences, such as having to park a tricycle if riding limits are disobeyed) also teach children results of a specific misbehavior.

Encourage and support children's efforts.	• Use verbal encouragement rather than tangible (material) rewards. • Tell children what behavior was acceptable, such as "Your room looks nice when you put away your belongings." • Encourage younger children by helping them with a task, such as putting away toys. Ask older children if they can use a helping hand.

Authoritarian

Some parents use an **authoritarian** parenting style, in which the main objective is to make children completely obedient. These parents think obedience is the most important behavior their children should learn. They expect children to respect their authority with little or no explanation as to why children should obey. Authoritarian parents most often use power assertion as their discipline technique. Although these children often obey their parents, they do not understand why they should act as their parents wish. Beyond not developing self-control, power assertion can result in unhealthy long-term behaviors.

Mental Health Advisory

Of the three discipline methods, only induction aids children's self-control. When power-assertion or love withdrawal techniques become the primary forms of discipline, children often do not learn self-control—a mental health problem.

Permissive

Parents who use the **permissive** parenting style give children almost no guidelines or rules. They feel children should make their own decisions about right and wrong. They may think setting

Figure 4.13 Possible Results of Parenting Styles on Children

Parenting Style	Possible Results	
Authoritarian	• Moody • Unhappy • Aggressive, including violence, or *passive aggressiveness* (indirect expression of hostility, such as resentment or sullenness)	• Not friendly • Vulnerable to stress • Trouble getting along with those in authority
Permissive	• Not self-controlled • Not self-reliant • Impulsive	• Aggressive • Rebellious • Low achievement
Overparenting	• High perfectionist strivings, but are not willing to take risks • Lack leadership traits • Have unrealistic achievement goals • Lack emotional self-regulation and psychological resilience to handle typical problems on the road to adulthood	• Often do not achieve, but believe they are entitled to get what they want • May stay dependent on parents even as young adults (called the *Boomerang Generation*, some often move back in with their parents as adults—not for economic reasons, but for parental services)
Authoritative	• Self-reliant • Self-controlled • Curious	• Can handle stress • Engage in fewer risk-taking behaviors • Moral/good character

limits for their children will make the children feel unhappy or unloved. Some permissive parents become **overindulgent** (provide everything the child wants).

The truth is, without guidelines, these children may feel lost. Permissive parenting can also give children the impression that parents do not care enough to guide and teach them or that they are trying to buy their love. Permissiveness can result in unhealthy long-term behaviors.

Mental Health Advisory

Three parenting styles—authoritarian, permissive, and overparenting—produce children at risk for later mental health problems. Conversely, the authoritative parenting style is the only style that emphasizes self-control and handling stress.

Overparenting

Overparenting is a parenting style in which parents desire to provide for and protect their children beyond what is in the best interest of children. *Overparenting* can be defined as parenting by controlling every move of the child.

Overparenting often begins in infancy and becomes apparent from the toddler years through the teen and even young adult years. Some common characteristics of overparenting include

- hiring tutors beginning in the toddler or preschool years
- doing their children's projects
- resolving children's conflicts with adults and peers without allowing children to try resolving conflicts on their own
- discouraging their children from independent explorations by manufacturing almost every experience for their children

Focus on Speech

Parenting Styles

With a partner, role-play the parenting styles discussed in this lesson. Take turns being a parent and a young child. Choose a situation in which a child might behave poorly. You will role-play the following styles of parenting:

- authoritarian
- overparenting
- permissive
- authoritative

Before delivering your role-play, consider how you and your partner will present each situation. Write a script for each parenting style and take time to memorize your lines. Practice your portion of the role-play in front of a mirror until you feel comfortable speaking without your notes, and then make time outside of class to rehearse with your partner. Concentrate on speaking clearly and loudly so your classmates will be able to easily understand and hear you.

After the role-play, engage your class in a brief discussion about the following questions: Which response seems healthiest for the child, and why? Was each role-play representative of its parenting style? Take notes about your classmates' answers and be prepared to discuss and ask questions about your classmates' role-plays.

- contacting all adults who provide services for their children (teachers, coaches, youth directors) **incessantly** (constantly; without break) and supervising activities
- attending job interviews with their children and negotiating for them

Although many of these parents have good intentions, the results may not be positive for their children. These children may be more self-centered and have an exaggerated sense of **entitlement** (the right to particular privileges or benefits). They may also have more difficulty developing their own coping skills.

Authoritative

Many parents find a compromise between the authoritarian and permissive styles of parenting. They use an **authoritative** (also called *assertive-democratic*) style, in which parents set some rules, but allow children some freedom. Parents who typically use an authoritative parenting style also use the induction method of discipline. Their children learn self-discipline in a positive, encouraging setting. Parenting experts **endorse** (support) an authoritative parenting style as healthiest for children and families. The long-term results for children are most positive.

Lesson 4.2 Review and Assessment 

1. What do parents' roles and responsibilities mainly involve?
2. What does *nurturance* mean?
3. To build a sense of belonging, parents _____ their children, or train them to live as part of the larger social group.
4. Differentiate between *guidance* and *discipline*.
5. Describe three types of discipline and their effects on children.
6. List and describe four parenting styles.
7. Parents who typically use a(n) _____ parenting style also use the induction method of discipline.
8. **Critical thinking.** How does induction help a child develop self-control?

Chapter 4

Review and Assessment

Summary

Couples have different reasons for wanting or not wanting children. There are a number of factors couples must consider. Before having children, couples should determine whether their reasons for wanting to parent are good ones grounded in solid decision making and reality, or poor ones grounded in the expectations of others or a desire to solve marital problems.

Parenting is challenging because it involves a great deal of maturity. Parenting involves relationships, such as the parent-child relationship that changes over time due to the child's development and relationships with other family members, friends, and others. Finally, parenting involves management of critical family resources. Many couples today practice family planning. The use of birth control methods can make family planning more successful.

Parenting involves a number of roles and responsibilities including nurturance, the meeting of a child's needs; socialization, teaching children how to live in groups; and guidance and discipline. Parents can perform these roles and responsibilities through a number of parenting styles. These styles include authoritarian, permissive, overparenting, and authoritative. Parenting experts identify the authoritative parenting style as the healthiest for children and families.

College and Career Portfolio

Portfolio Electronic Organization

You will create both a print portfolio and an e-Portfolio in this class. You have already decided how to store hard copy items for your print portfolio. Now you will create a plan for storing and organizing your e-Portfolio. Ask your instructor where to save your documents. This could be on the school's network or a flash drive of your own. Think about how to organize related files into categories. For example, school transcripts and diplomas might be one category. Writing samples and statements of purpose might be another category, and so on. Next, consider how you will name the files. The names for folders and files should be descriptive, but not too long. You will decide in a later activity how to present your electronic files for viewers. To begin organizing your e-Portfolio, complete the following activities:

- Create a folder on the network drive or flash drive in which you will save your files.
- Write a few sentences to describe how you will name the subfolders and files for your portfolio.
- Create the subfolders to organize the files, using the naming system you created.

Chapter 4 Review and Assessment

Vocabulary Activities

1. Working in small groups, locate a small image online that visually describes or explains each of the following terms. To create flashcards, write each term on a note card and paste the image that describes or explains the term on the opposite side. After you finish creating your flashcards, find a partner and use the cards to quiz each other. Then, exchange flashcards with another pair and review those cards as well.

Key Terms

authoritarian (4.2)	indirect costs (4.1)
authoritative (4.2)	induction (4.2)
birth control methods (4.1)	love withdrawal (4.2)
character (4.2)	maturity (4.1)
direct costs (4.1)	nurturance (4.2)
discipline (4.2)	overparenting (4.2)
family planning (4.1)	permissive (4.2)
foregone income (4.1)	power assertion (4.2)
guidance (4.2)	socialize (4.2)

2. With a partner, create a T-chart. Write each of the following vocabulary terms in the left column. Write a *synonym* (a word that has the same or similar meaning) for each term in the right column. Discuss your synonyms with the class.

Academic Terms

ample (4.1)	impart (4.2)
aspects (4.2)	incessantly (4.2)
conduct (4.2)	overindulgent (4.2)
depleted (4.1)	procreation (4.1)
endorse (4.2)	prone (4.2)
entitlement (4.2)	socioeconomic (4.1)
expenditures (4.1)	stifle (4.1)

Critical Thinking

3. **Evaluate.** Felix and your friend, Aafia, have been married for six months and are considering having children. Aafia explains her reasons for wanting to be a parent and says the following:
   - Her parents and Felix's parents are getting old and want to have grandchildren before they die.
   - Aafia and Felix's marriage is strong and growing stronger, and they want to share their love with a potential child.

   Based on what she has said, evaluate your friend's reasons and how healthy they are. What, if any, follow-up questions would you ask Aafia?
4. **Make inferences.** If a married couple chooses not to have children or wants to wait several years before having a child, what can they say to their parents who want grandchildren? Why do older people often want grandchildren? Besides having grandchildren, what are some ways older people can fulfill their need to be with young children?
5. **Cause and effect.** List the aspects of parenting discussed in this chapter and then find a partner. Together, discuss how having children affects each of these aspects and why it is important that potential parents consider these effects. Take turns presenting the highlights of your discussion to the class.
6. **Identify.** Identify the decisions that are involved in *family planning*. Why is it important that potential parents consider these decisions? How does family planning differ from the decisions about whether or not to parent?
7. **Compare and contrast.** Parents' roles and responsibilities fall into four main categories: nurturance, socialization, guidance, and discipline. Define these four words, according to the glossary and according to a dictionary. Then, write a two- to three-page essay comparing and contrasting examples of behaviors that fall into these categories. Share your essays with the rest of the class by giving a one-minute oral presentation. Hold a question-answer session after your essay and be prepared to answer any questions your classmates may have.
8. **Make inferences.** This chapter states, "One major goal of guidance and discipline is to build character in children." Does this mean that parents can determine the characters of their children? Why or why not? Use evidence from this chapter to support your argument.
9. **Determine.** Sheng, a fourth-grader in your after-school program, seems sad and uninterested in playing one day. You ask him what is wrong, and he says that his mom will not talk to him since he failed his math test. You have a conference with Sheng's parents tomorrow. What kind of discipline is Sheng's mother using? What, if any, alternative types of discipline might you suggest during the conference?

10. **Draw conclusions.** Think of a time when you misbehaved as a young child and write a short paragraph describing the scenario. Then, use Figure 4.12 to imagine inductive techniques parents could use to respond to this scenario. Try to imagine how each inductive technique would play out in your scenario. Which technique do you think would work most effectively?
11. **Analyze.** Review the four parenting styles covered in this chapter. Then, in small groups consider the following questions:
    - What effects might each parenting style have on a child?
    - How likely do you think parents are to adopt the parenting style used by their parents?

    After you have answered these questions, share your thoughts with the class. As other groups share, support or challenge their conclusions. As a class, analyze the variety of answers represented.

Core Skills

12. **Listening and speaking.** Interview a couple who chose not to have children. What are their reasons? Present your findings to the class and discuss the most common reasons for choosing not to have children.
13. **Writing.** Compose a short paper giving your views on the kinds of maturity couples should have before becoming parents. How should couples exhibit this maturity? What are some signs of maturity? of immaturity? Check your paper for correct spelling, grammar, and punctuation.
14. **Art.** Children both affect and are affected by relationships. On a large piece of paper, draw the silhouette of a child. Then, as a class, draw arrows and illustrations pointing *in* to signify ways that children are affected by relationships. Draw arrows and illustrations pointing *out* to signify ways that children affect relationships. Then, review your class's final product and discuss the different factors you brought to each other's attention.
15. **Math.** Child care is an indirect cost of parenting when both parents work. Ask a local child care provider what rate is charged to provide child care for one infant full-time (nine hours a day, five days a week). Use this weekly rate to calculate the cost of child care during the first year of life (from age six weeks until the first birthday).
16. **Reading.** Search online or visit your local library to find and read a book about parenting. Create a bibliography that includes the title of the publication, name and address of the publisher, topics covered, ages of children discussed, and any information that you found particularly interesting. Share your findings with the rest of the class.
17. **Science and research.** In the case study for this chapter, Andrea was concerned about Tyler spanking their child. Using online or print resources, find and read a scientific study about spanking and child development. After reading the study, write a short essay assessing its reliability and summarizing its results. Read and discuss your essays in class.
18. **Writing and technology.** Choose one parenting style and, in groups, write a short script about a day in the life of a child whose parents use that parenting style. Include specific situations and reactions. Then, as a group, film a short movie that follows your script. Present your movie to the class and lead a discussion about which parenting style is being represented.
19. **CTE Career Readiness Practice.** As a journalist for a local newspaper, it has come to your attention that a high percentage of parents in your community yell at and physically punish their children. Your assignment is to write a full-page public service announcement that captures attention and educates parents on effective styles and methods of parenting. In your research, identify certain types of discipline that do not teach children and a number of possible alternatives. Present and discuss your public service announcement in class.

Observations

20. In an informal setting, observe parents who are having a difficult time with a child. What kind of parenting styles and methods are they using? What parenting skills might they need to help them with their children?
21. Visit your local library or bookstore and choose a book about parenting methods and preparing for parenting. Skim the chapters of the book and read three separate anecdotes about parenting. An *anecdote* is a brief account of a situation or story. Summarize each anecdote and analyze how it could be applied to the lives of parents and their children.

Unit 2 Pregnancy and Childbirth

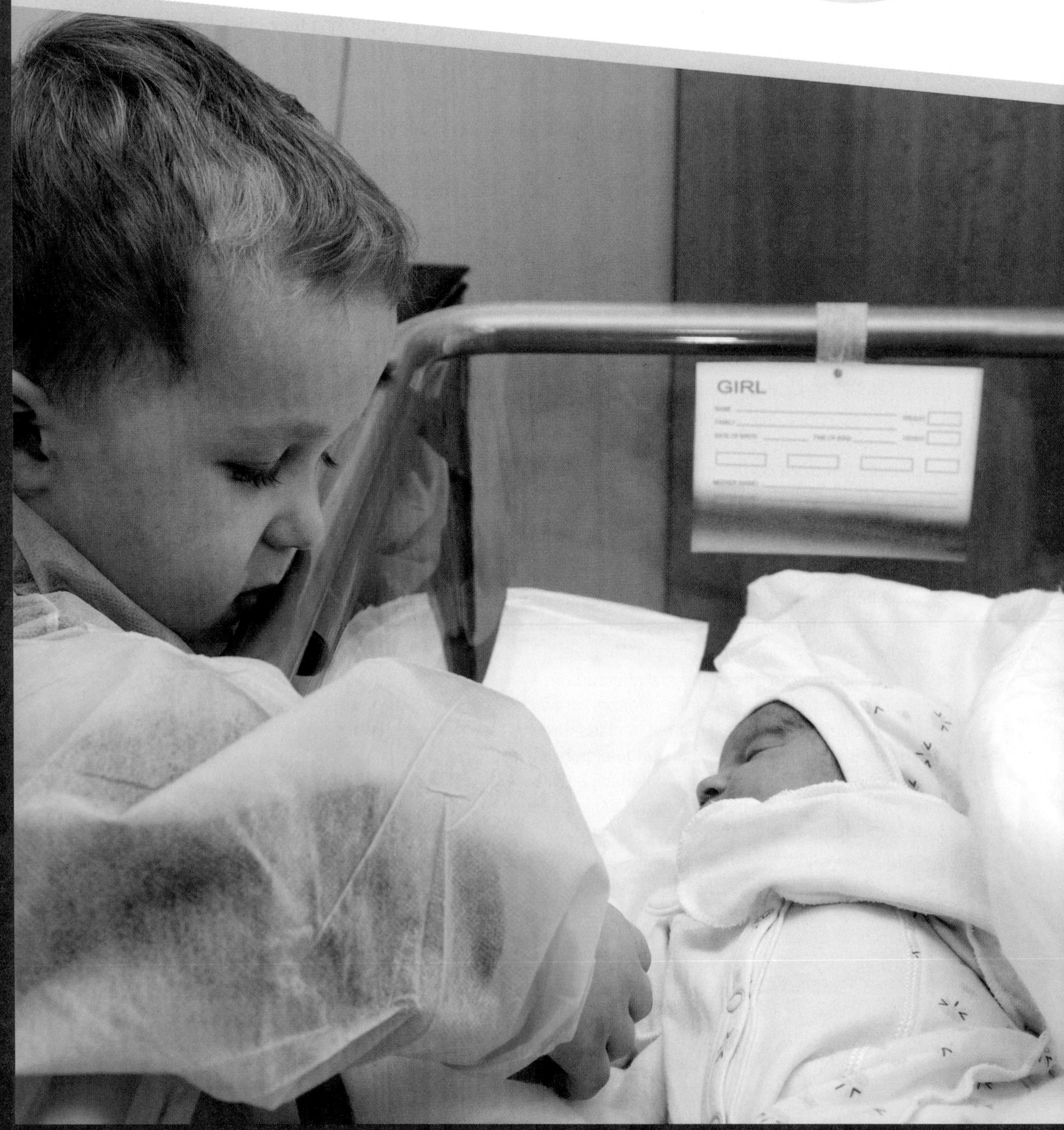

Chapter 5	Pregnancy
Chapter 6	Special Circumstances of Pregnancy
Chapter 7	Childbirth

Extemporaneous (Impromptu) Speaking

Extemporaneous or impromptu speaking is a competitive event you might enter with your CTSO. This type of event allows you to showcase your organizational and communication skills in making a presentation without prior preparation. At the competition, you will choose a topic in your content-related area. You will have a specific time limit in which to create and deliver your speech. During your presentation, judges evaluate your poise, self-confidence, and ability to logically organize material on your key points. The judges also evaluate your use of verbal and nonverbal skills as well as your ability to maintain a conversational tone and clear projection of your voice. To prepare for such an event, complete the following activities:

1. Ask your instructor for several topics, choose one, and then use a note card to jot down the ideas and points you want to cover. Remember, you only have a few minutes to prepare. Your ability to write down main ideas quickly helps you focus on what to actually say in the presentation.
2. Practice the presentation. Introduce yourself, the topic on which you are speaking, and your main point. Defend or give supporting evidence for your position on the topic, and conclude your speech with a summary.
3. At least once or twice per week leading up to your local, state, and possibly national competitions, ask your instructor for a topic and practice your speaking skills. You may want to ask your instructor and classmates to listen to your presentation and give feedback.
4. For the event, bring note cards and pencils to record your speech notes. Remember to follow the guidelines and regulations to avoid disqualification.

Chapter 5 Pregnancy

Essential Question

How does human life begin, and how can the unborn baby be protected?

Lesson 5.1	**A Baby's Beginning**
Lesson 5.2	**Factors That Affect the Unborn Baby**
Lesson 5.3	**Health Habits Prior to and During Pregnancy**

Case Study: Should Unborn Babies Have Health Protection Rights?

As a class, read the case study and discuss the questions that follow. After you finish studying the chapter, discuss this case study again. Have your opinions changed based on what you learned?

Susan and Don are attending a wedding reception with their close friends Jo and her husband. A few days ago, Jo excitedly told Susan and Don she was five weeks pregnant.

During the reception, Jo sips a glass of wine. Susan and Don cannot believe Jo is drinking alcohol while pregnant. Susan and Don attended classes before the birth of their child and know the dangers if mothers-to-be drink alcohol. Susan never touched alcohol while pregnant or breast-feeding, and Don supported her by also abstaining.

As they watch Jo finish her drink, Don whispers to Susan, "Shouldn't Jo be arrested for endangering her baby?" Susan thinks for some time, and responds, "Don't mothers-to-be have their own rights, too?"

Give It Some Thought

1. Don is not serious about having Jo arrested, but he is concerned and upset by Jo's behavior. Do you think his concern is justified over one drink? Why or why not? Do you think an arrest could be justified for a pregnant woman who is an alcoholic and is intoxicated in her own home? Explain your reasoning.
2. What do you think about Susan's response? Do you believe a doctor or the law should require a pregnant woman to give up some of her freedoms if they pose high risks for the unborn baby? Why or why not?
3. At what point in the pregnancy should concern for the well-being of the unborn baby supersede the pregnant woman's rights to live as she chooses? What types of legal sanctions (incentives, such as a warning, arrest, or hospitalization for addicts) do you think should be applied, if any?

While studying this chapter, look for the online resources icon  to:

- **Practice** terms with e-flash cards and interactive games
- **Assess** what you learn by completing self-assessment quizzes
- **Expand** knowledge with interactive activities and graphic organizers

Companion G-W Learning

www.g-wlearning.com/childdevelopment

Study on the go

Use a mobile device to practice terms and review with self-assessment quizzes.

www.m.g-wlearning.com/0384

Lesson 5.1 A Baby's Beginning

Key Terms

age of viability
amnion
cervix
chorion
conception
embryo
embryonic stage
fallopian tubes
fetal stage
fetus
germinal stage
ovaries
ovum
period of gestation
placenta
prenatal development
quickening
sperm
testes
umbilical cord
uterus
zygote

Academic Terms

cell
embed
formative
subsequent
trimester

Objectives

After studying this lesson, you will be able to

- summarize the female's role and the male's role in conception.
- identify the three stages of prenatal development.
- compare and contrast changes that occur within each stage of prenatal development.
- give examples of developmental changes that occur month-by-month during the period of gestation.

Reading and Writing Activity

Read the key terms for this lesson and look up any words you do not know in the dictionary. Then, using all of the key terms in this lesson, write two paragraphs summarizing what you already know about conception and prenatal development. If you do not know how a key term belongs to either of these concepts, write that key term below your paragraphs, and after reading, explain how it relates.

Graphic Organizer

Draw a comic strip and label it *Conception and Prenatal Development*. Then, as you are reading, illustrate each stage of conception and prenatal development in the comic strip squares. Use as many squares as you want.

Pregnancy is the process through which a new human prepares to enter the world. This process begins with conception when a baby is created inside the mother's body. Even before the mother knows she is pregnant, the baby affects her life. The mother's body changes to prepare for nine months of growth.

The prenatal period, from conception to birth, lasts about 280 days and is the shortest stage in the lifespan. This **formative** (shaping) stage is also the most critical time for a child's development. At no other time are two people closer than a mother and baby during the prenatal period.

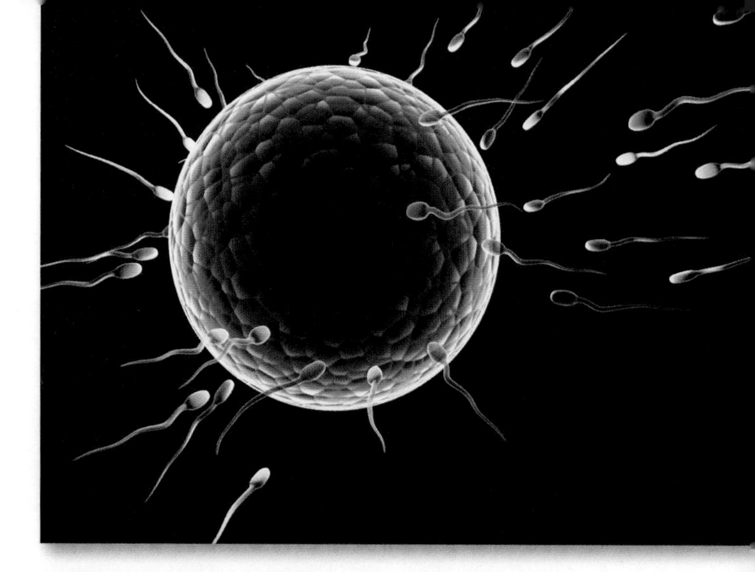

Figure 5.1 Conception occurs when the sperm and ovum unite to create a zygote. *How many sperm must successfully penetrate the egg's surface to fertilize the egg?*

Conception

A **cell** is the smallest unit of life that is able to reproduce itself. Human bodies have two types of cells. One type is *body cells*, the cells that make up the tissues and organs of the body. These cells reproduce themselves for growth and repair. The other type is called *germ cells* or *sex cells*, the cells involved in reproduction or the creation of a baby.

Life begins with the joining of two separate germ cells—one from the female and one from the male. The female germ cell is the **ovum** (often called *the egg*) and the male germ cell is the **sperm**. The joining of these two cells is called **conception** (**Figure 5.1**). At conception, ovum and sperm combine to form a single cell called a **zygote** (ZIGH-goht). Another name for the zygote is a *fertilized egg*.

The Female's Role

Before her own birth, the female produces and stores *ova* (eggs) in her **ovaries** (female reproductive glands). Inside the ovary, the ovum is stored in a small sac called a *follicle*. When the body becomes capable of reproduction, hormones cause some follicles to grow and fill with fluid each month. Around the middle of the menstrual cycle, one ovum is released from the follicle, and the other follicles that were growing become inactive. (Sometimes more than one ovum is released.) The release of the ovum from the ovary is called *ovulation*.

When the egg is released, it travels toward the fallopian tubes. The **fallopian tubes** are two hollow tubes that extend from the right and left sides of the uterus (**Figure 5.2**). The **uterus** is the organ in which the baby develops and is protected until birth. The **cervix** (SER-viks) is the lower, narrow portion of the uterus that connects the uterus to the vagina, or *birth canal*.

One end of each fallopian tube is connected to the uterus. The other end of each tube has finger-like projections. These projections lie near, but are not attached to, the ovary. The projections from the fallopian tube help gather the ovum as it emerges from the ovary. Once inside the fallopian tube, the ovum moves very slowly down the tube. Here, the ovum is ready and available to be joined by a sperm.

The Male's Role

Unlike a female who has all of her ova at birth, a male's **testes** (reproductive glands) do not produce sperm until the body is capable of reproduction. Sperm production continues throughout his lifetime. *Semen*, a liquid which contains over 300 million sperm, enters the female's body during intercourse. The sperm leaves the male's penis and enters the female's vagina. These sperm travel from the vagina to the cervix and through the uterus to reach the fallopian tube. The sperm's journey to the ovum lasts only minutes, and many sperm do not survive. Only 300 to 500 reach the fallopian tube.

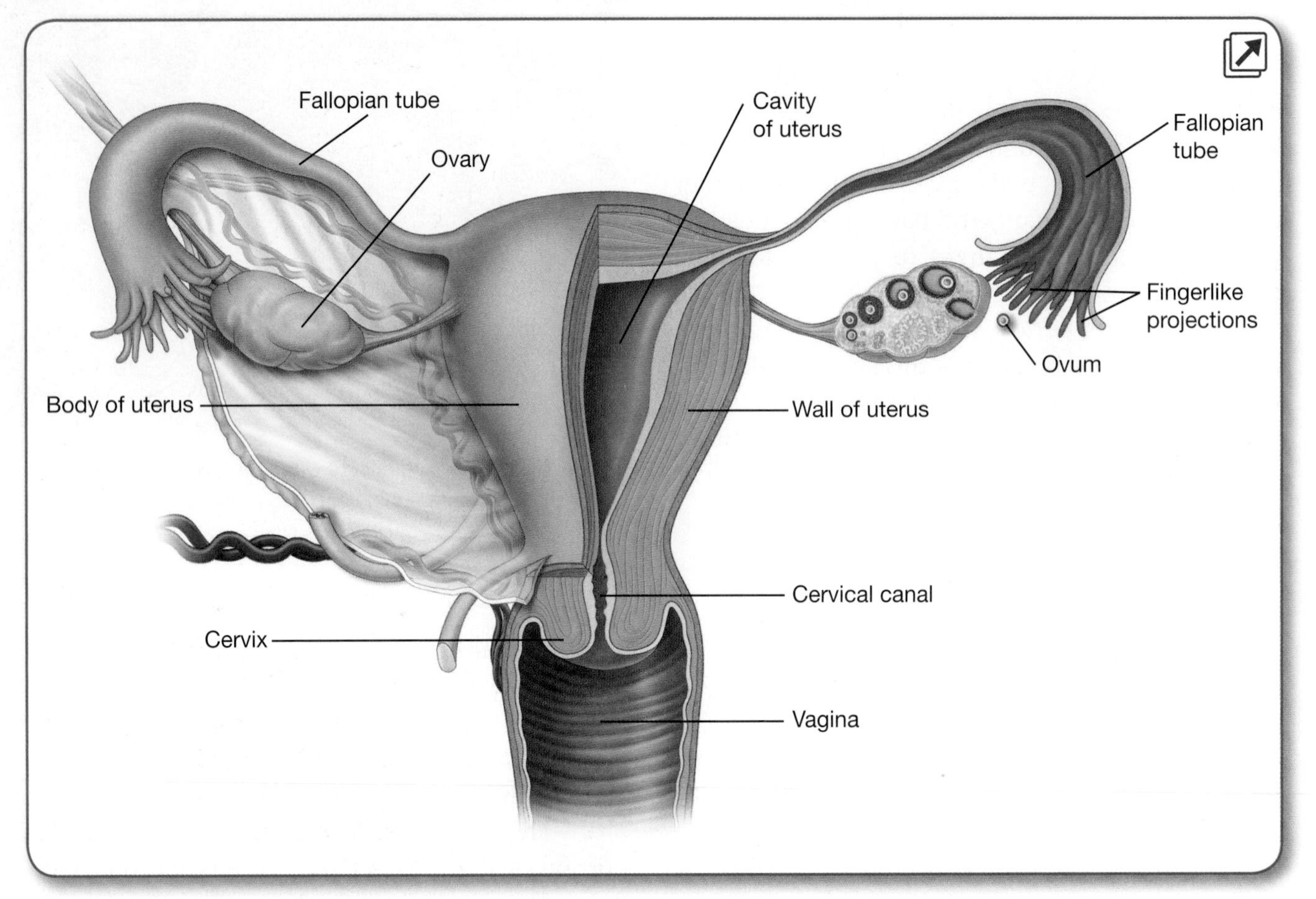

Figure 5.2 Eggs travel from the ovaries to the uterus via the fallopian tubes on either side of the uterus. *What route would sperm take to reach the fallopian tubes?*

Sperm may meet the ovum at any point. Conception usually occurs when the ovum is less than one-third of the way down the fallopian tube. After that point, conception is unlikely because the ovum has a short lifespan—only living about 24 hours after ovulation.

The sperm approach the ovum and try to break through its surface. Only one sperm successfully enters, or *fertilizes* the egg. Once one sperm is accepted, no other sperm can enter the ovum. Conception has occurred, and the zygote forms.

Stages of Prenatal Development

Many changes happen in the time between conception and birth, called the **period of gestation** (pregnancy). This period lasts approximately nine months, and is divided into three trimesters. A **trimester** is a period of three months. The baby's development that takes place during this time is called **prenatal development**. Prenatal development is divided into the germinal, embryonic, and fetal stages.

Germinal Stage

Conception marks the beginning of the first stage of prenatal development, the **germinal stage**. This stage covers the first two weeks of the pregnancy.

Once conception occurs, the fertilized egg (zygote) remains a single cell for about 30 hours before it starts to divide (**Figure 5.3**). On the third day, the zygote forms a solid ball of cells, which is called a *morula*. By the fourth day, a fluid-filled cavity forms within the ball of cells, which is now called a *blastocyst* (BLAS-toh-sist). The blastocyst enters the uterus, where cells continue to divide rapidly for about three more days. During this

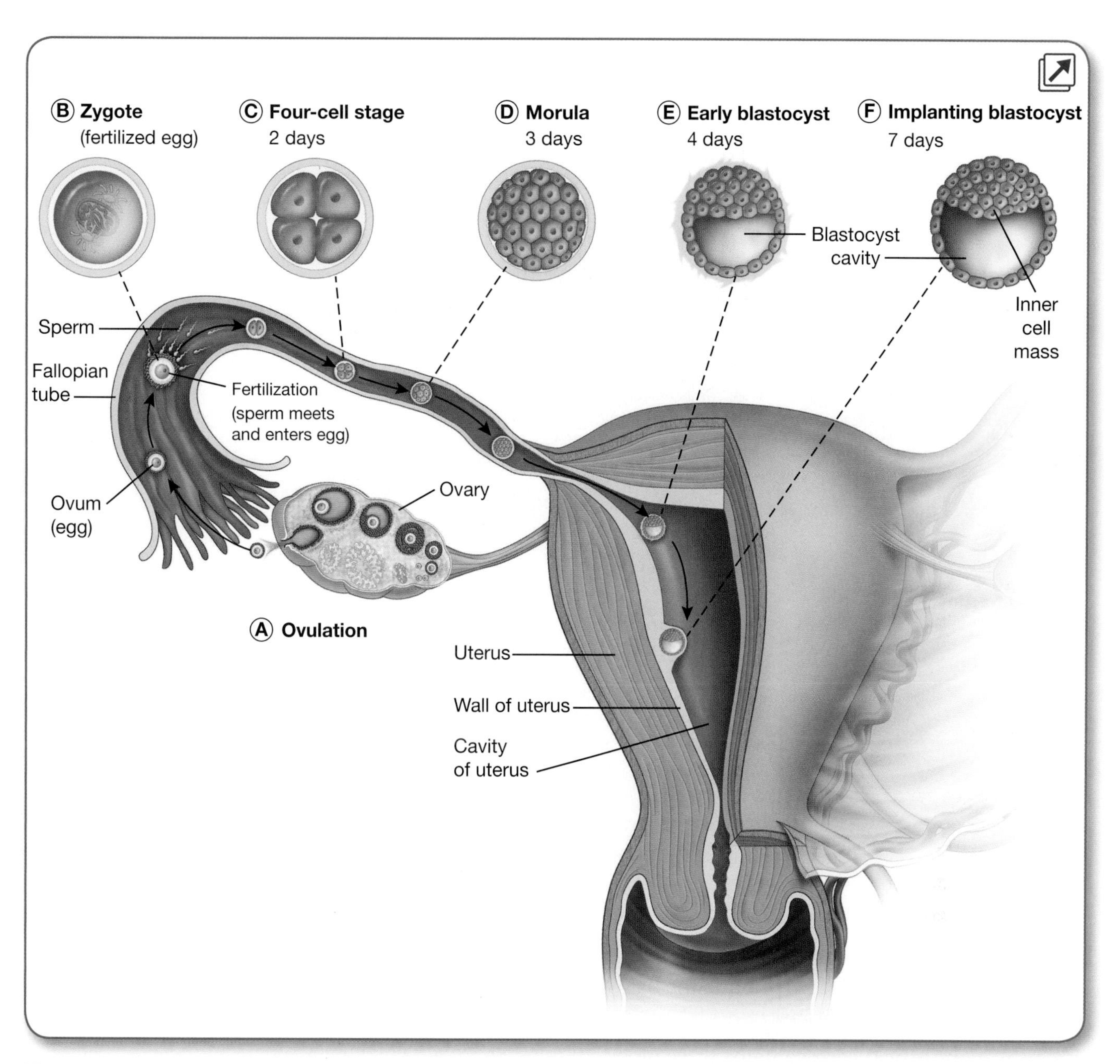

Figure 5.3 After 30 hours, the zygote divides rapidly, forming a *morula* and then a *blastocyst*. *What is the difference between a morula and a blastocyst?*

time, the blastocyst floats freely in the uterus. Then, the blastocyst begins to **embed** (attach) in the wall of the uterus where the cells continue to divide for several more days until implantation is complete. After implantation, the blastocyst will remain in the uterus until delivery.

Embryonic Stage

The second stage of prenatal development is the **embryonic stage**, which lasts six weeks. During this stage, the baby is called an **embryo**. The following support systems for the pregnancy develop during the embryonic stage:

- The **chorion** (CORE-ee-ahn), outermost membrane that surrounds the baby in the uterus, and **amnion** (a fluid-filled sac) begin to form. They surround the cells and protect the baby until birth (**Figure 5.4**).
- The **placenta** (pluh-SENT-uh), an organ filled with blood vessels, develops against the wall of the uterus. As the placenta develops, it will nourish the baby, remove

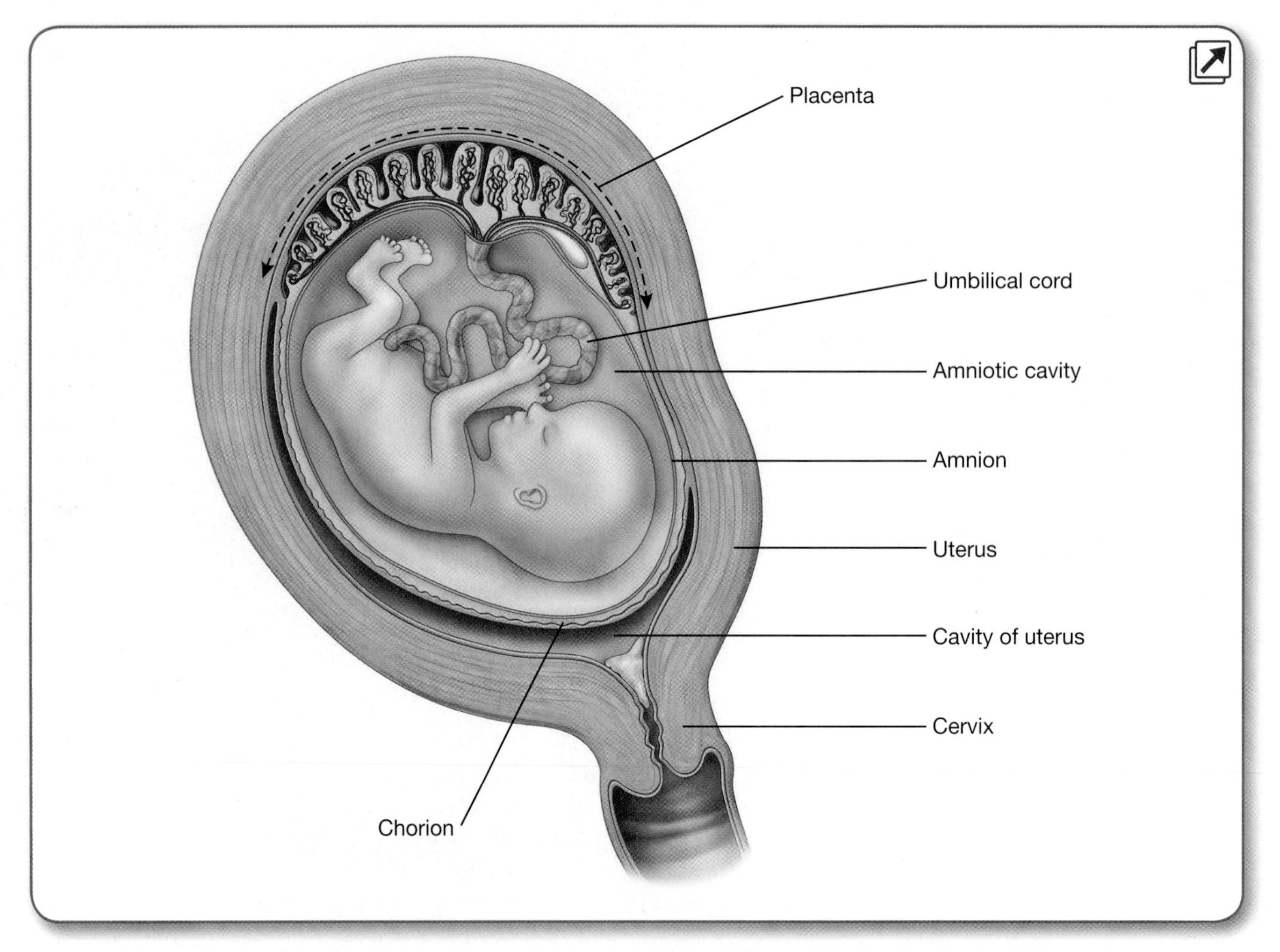

Figure 5.4 The chorion and amnion form to protect the developing baby. *What might the developing baby need protection from?*

the baby's wastes, exchange gases between mother and baby, and provide the baby with needed hormones.

- The **umbilical cord** contains three blood vessels that connect the baby to the placenta. The umbilical cord grows out from the developing child, at the site of the future navel, and connects with the placenta.

Experts say the embryonic stage is the most critical stage of prenatal development because almost all of the unborn baby's body systems develop during this time. The baby receives both good and harmful substances from the mother's placenta through the umbilical cord. Because the baby's body parts are developing so quickly, passing harmful substances to the child can affect him or her for life. Therefore, the mother's health habits are very important during this stage.

Fetal Stage

The **fetal stage** of prenatal development begins nine weeks after conception. From this point until birth, a baby is medically known as a **fetus**. During the fetal stage, all parts of the unborn baby's body mature, and overall size increases quickly. By the fourth month, the fetus has usually grown enough to give the mother's growing abdomen a pregnant look (**Figure 5.5**).

Following are several milestones that happen during the fetal stage:

- ***Heartbeat.*** The heartbeat of the unborn baby can be heard through the doctor's stethoscope (16 weeks).
- ***Movements.*** The baby's movements can be felt by the mother, called **quickening** (18–20 weeks for first-time mothers; 15–17 weeks for subsequent pregnancies).

- *Age of viability.* **Age of viability** is the time from when a baby can survive if born early. This time begins possibly as early as 23 weeks, chances improve for each **subsequent** (following) week of gestation.

Month-by-Month Development

Although describing prenatal development by stages is accurate—the germinal stage, the embryonic stage, and the fetal stage—these basic descriptions do not explain much about *how* the baby is developing. All developmental changes begin during the germinal and embryonic stages, which last most of the first trimester of pregnancy. The fetal stage lasts about 32 weeks beginning in the last one-fourth of the first trimester and continuing throughout the second and third trimesters of pregnancy. Due to the long time period of the fetal stage, it is difficult to easily describe how much a baby grows and changes.

It is most helpful to describe prenatal development in smaller segments. For instance, studying this development month-by-month makes it easier to describe how a baby grows and develops before birth. **Figure 5.6** shows details on this development.

Lesson 5.1 Review and Assessment 

1. Describe what happens during conception.
2. List the structures involved in conception in females and the structures involved in conception in males.
3. About how long is the human period of gestation?
4. Explain what happens during the germinal stage of prenatal development.
5. Why is the embryonic stage considered the most critical stage of prenatal development?
6. What three milestones occur during the fetal stage?
7. Define the term *quickening*. When does quickening occur?
8. **Critical thinking.** Explain why a mother's health habits are important to the development of her baby.

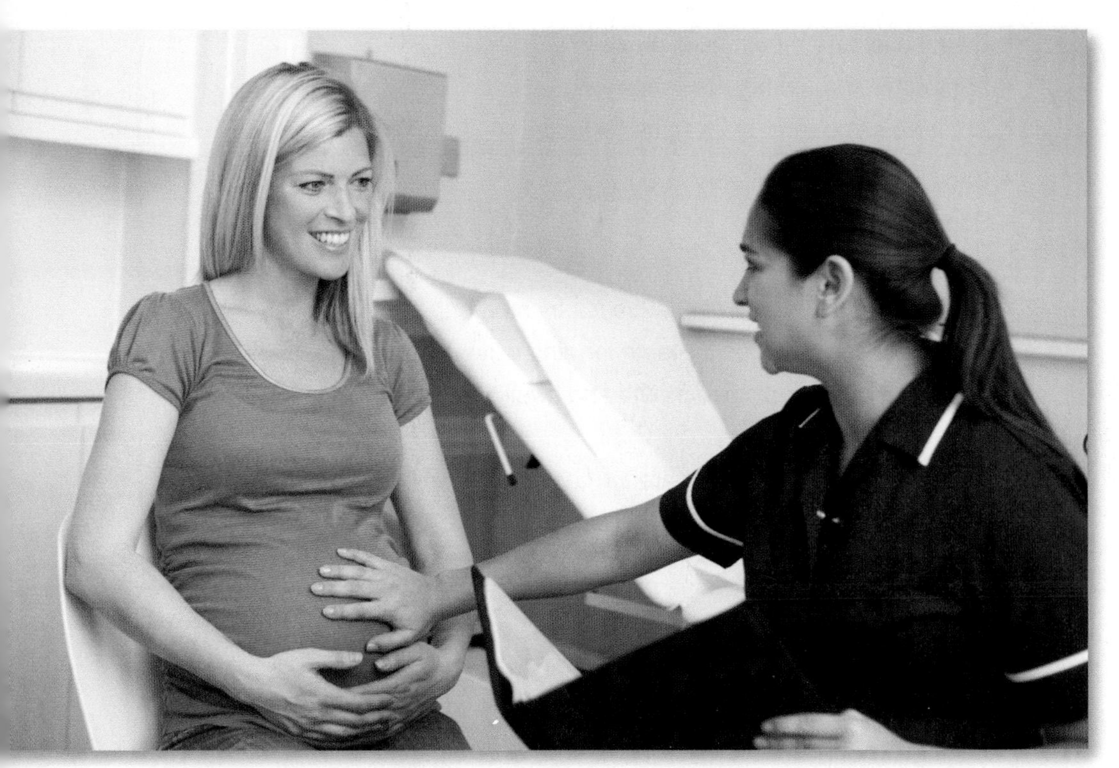

Figure 5.5 During pregnancy, the growing fetus gives the mother's abdomen a pregnant look. *What factors might affect how much a mother's abdomen grows during pregnancy?*

Figure 5.6 Prenatal Development

First Trimester	
First month 	• Baby begins as a *zygote*. It grows into a *blastocyst* and then into an *embryo*. • First signs of the baby's heart, lungs, face, arms, and legs show. • Heart begins beating and pumps blood through arteries. • Digestive system is forming. • Baby's brain and spinal cord develop from the neural tube. • Ears and eyes begin to form. • Tissue that will later form the baby's backbone, skull, ribs, and muscles can be seen on ultrasound. • By month's end, baby becomes an embryo and is ½ inch long. • By month's end, baby weighs much less than 1 ounce.
Second month 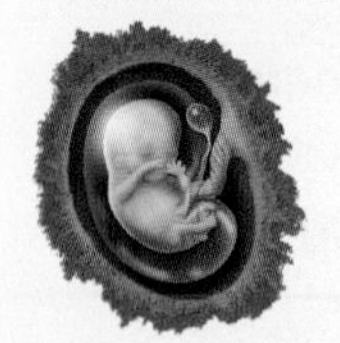	• Body organs and systems that began in the first month are continuing to develop. • Liver and stomach start to work. • Head makes up nearly half of the embryo. • Brain grows quickly and directs the baby's movements. • Arms and legs become longer and take shape. • Fingers and toes develop. • Distinct wrists, elbows, and hands are present. • Distinct knees and feet are present. • Eyes take on color. • Eyelids form, but are sealed shut. • Ears, nose, and mouth take shape. • At month's end, embryo is 1 inch long. • At month's end, embryo weighs ⅓ ounce.
Third month 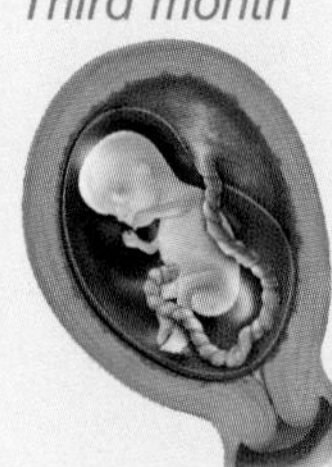	• Baby is now called a *fetus*. • Bones are growing. • Kidneys are working. • Fetus moves often, but cannot be felt by mother. • Tooth sockets and buds for teeth forming in jawbone. • Fetus can open and close mouth and swallow. • Fingerprints appear. • All parts of the baby's body are formed by the end of the month. • At month's end, baby is 4 inches long. • At month's end, baby weighs 1 ounce.

(Continued)

Figure 5.6 *(Continued)*

Second Trimester	
Fourth month 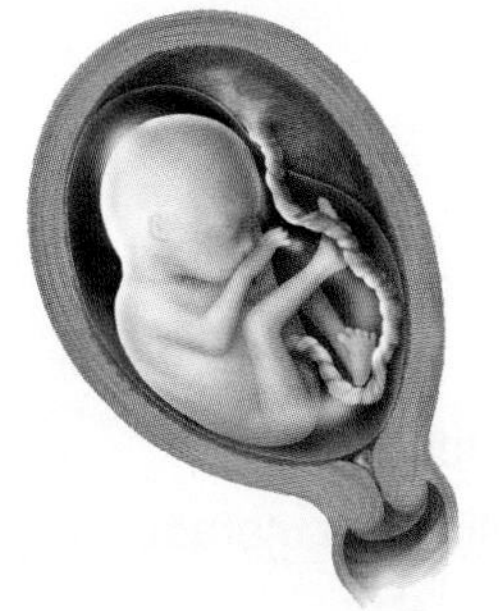	• Baby's heartbeat is strong. • Baby's airways develop, but are not in use. • Skin is transparent and thin. • Fingernails appear. • Baby sleeps and wakes. • Baby moves and kicks. • Toward the end of the month, the mother may feel the baby's movements. • Placenta is now formed. • Umbilical cord grows and thickens to carry enough blood and nourishment to baby. • By the end of the month, the baby is 6 to 7 inches long. • By the end of the month, the baby weighs about 5 ounces.
Fifth month 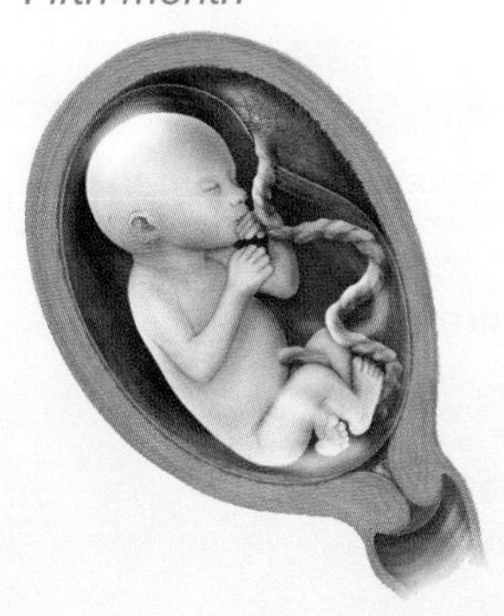	• Baby's internal organs continue to grow. • Blood supply to the lungs increases. • Eyelashes and eyebrows appear. • Scalp hair appears. • Silky body hair and a waxy coating protect baby's skin from its watery surroundings. • Baby sleeps and wakes in a pattern. • Baby turns from side to side. • Baby kicks and moves a lot. • By month's end, the baby is 12 inches long. • By month's end, the baby weighs about 1 pound.
Sixth month 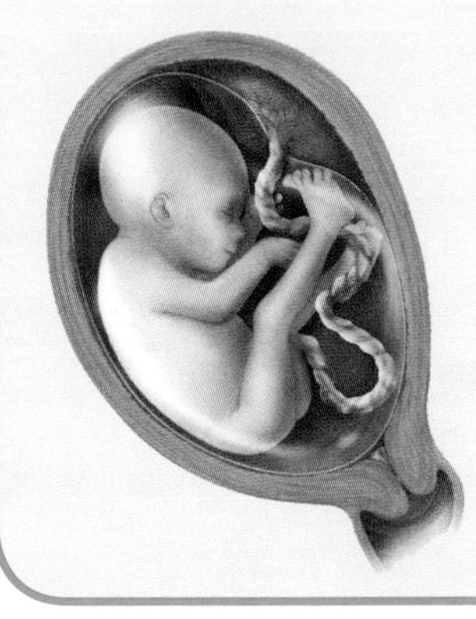	• Baby's growth speeds up. • Baby opens and closes its eyes. • Baby can hear sounds. • Skin is red, wrinkled, and oily. • Baby stretches and kicks. • Baby sucks its thumb. • At month's end, the baby is 12 to 14 inches long. • At month's end, the baby weighs about 1½ pounds.

(Continued)

Figure 5.6 *(Continued)*

Third Trimester

Seventh month

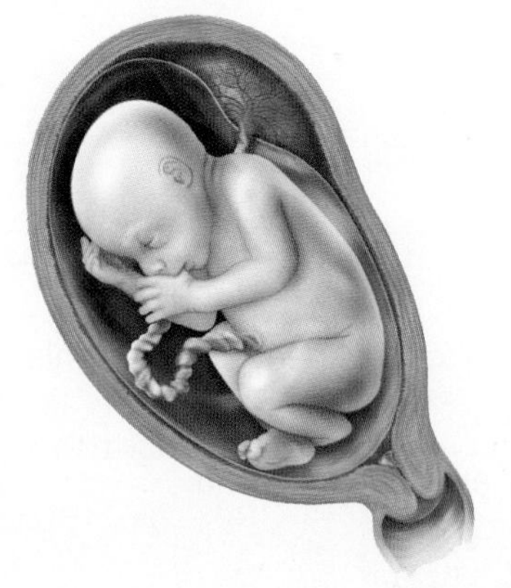

- Baby's brain, nervous system, and lungs have become much more mature.
- Bones are developed, but are soft and flexible. They are beginning to harden.
- Skin is wrinkled and covered with a thick, white protective coating called *vernix*.
- Fatty tissue begins developing under the surface of the skin.
- Lungs have matured and can support the baby outside the uterus.
- Baby kicks and stretches to exercise.
- The outline of the baby's fist, foot, or head may be seen outside the mother's body when the baby moves.
- At month's end, the baby is 15 inches long.
- At month's end, the baby weighs about 1½ pounds.

Eighth month

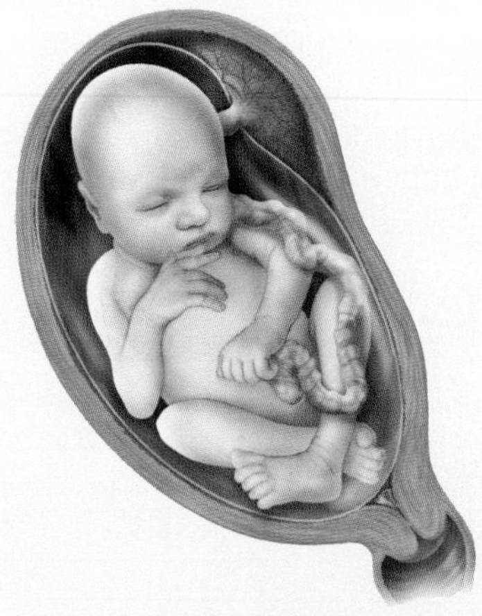

- Baby continues to grow in weight and length.
- Rapid brain growth continues.
- Skin is no longer wrinkled due to the layer of fatty tissue under the surface. The skin color is pink, not red.
- Baby has less room to move around, but kicks strongly.
- Baby may position itself head-down in the uterus.
- At month's end, the baby is about 18 inches long.
- At month's end, the baby weighs about 5 pounds.

Ninth month

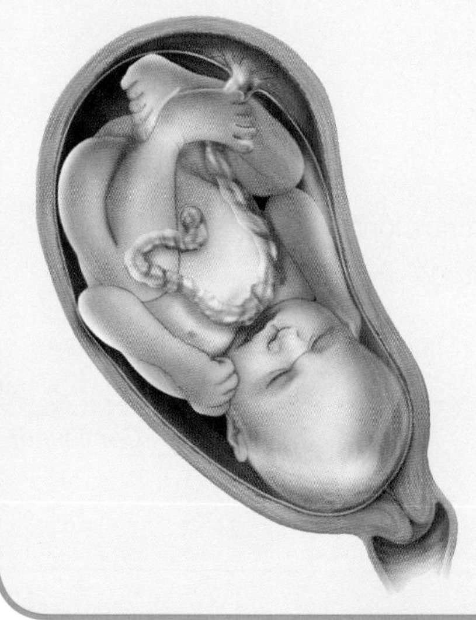

- Baby gains about ½ pound each week.
- Lungs continue to mature.
- Downy hair that covered the skin disappears.
- During the ninth month, the baby moves into final position—usually head down—and stays there until birth.
- At birth, babies are an average of 19 to 21 inches long.
- At birth, babies weigh an average of 6 to 9 pounds.

Factors That Affect the Unborn Baby

Lesson 5.2

Objectives

After studying this lesson, you will be able to

- summarize how genetic factors affect prenatal development.
- describe how a person inherits traits through genes.
- differentiate between dominant traits and recessive traits.
- explain the role of the environment on prenatal development and give examples of environmental factors that can harm the fetus.

Reading and Writing Activity

Imagine you are a doctor and one of your patients has just found out she is pregnant for the first time. What would you tell her about the factors that might affect her developing baby? Write a two-paragraph speech explaining these factors and then deliver your speech to a partner. After reading this lesson, discuss with your partner information you would add to your speech based on what you learned.

Graphic Organizer

As a class, draw a spectrum on a whiteboard. Label the two sides of the spectrum *Genetic Factors* and *Environmental Factors*. As you are reading and discussing, place key terms and factors where you think they fall on the spectrum.

			Environmental Factors
Genetic Factors			

Key Terms

AIDS
chromosomal disorders
chromosomes
diabetes
dominant traits
Down syndrome
environmental factors
fetal alcohol spectrum disorders (FASDs)
genetic disorder
genetic factors
HIV
pregnancy-induced hypertension (PIH)
recessive traits
Rh factor
rubella
sexually transmitted infections (STIs)

Academic Terms

abnormalities
botanist
exert
exponentially
vulnerable

At the moment the sperm enters the egg, the baby forms traits from both the mother and father. These inherited traits, including any disorders, are merged into a unique new person, and influence the child's growth and development throughout life. Development, however, is not determined solely by genetics. Immediately after conception, the environment also begins to **exert** (forcibly place) an influence on the unborn baby's traits.

Genetic Factors

Genetic factors are a person's inherited traits passed to him or her through the parents' genes at conception. Following certain rules, each parent's genes combine to make a blueprint for the unborn child's growth and development. During pregnancy, this blueprint, called a *genome*, guides growth and development. The *epigenome*, which can turn genes on and off, has a major impact on genes—altering how the genes may function throughout life.

Through the guidance of the genome and epigenome, the unborn baby changes from a zygote to a baby ready to be born. The child will come to look much like other members of the family. He or she will likely have abilities, interests, and personality traits similar to those of other family members, too.

During the prenatal period, the genetic blueprint also gives the cells instructions for family-like traits that will unfold throughout life. For example, during the prenatal period, a baby boy's cells receive instructions on hair loss later in life. These instructions determine whether he will be bald, what the pattern of hair loss will be, and when hair loss will occur. Some people's genes lead them to lose hair, while others have genes that promote keeping a full head of hair. Heredity causes each person to be different.

Heredity and Genetics

All people begin life as a single-celled zygote. The *nucleus*, or center, of this cell contains a set of instructions to build a living being. These directions are written in what scientists call a *genetic code*. The genetic code is stored in DNA, or deoxyribonucleic (dee-OXY-rye-bo-new-KLEE-ic) acid (**Figure 5.7**). DNA is a chemical compound found in threadlike structures called **chromosomes** (KRO-muh-zomes). The chromosomes carry genes in living cells.

Chromosomes and Genes

All living organisms have a certain number of chromosomes. Each human baby receives a total of 46 chromosomes—23 from each parent—that form 23 pairs in each of the body cells. Germ cells differ from body cells. The germ cells, or the sperm and egg, do not have 46 chromosomes. Just before the ova or sperm become mature, they go through a cell division process that leaves each egg or sperm with 23 single chromosomes. When the ovum and sperm meet in fertilization, the single zygote will have the 46 chromosomes. It is the final combination of these two sets of chromosomes during fertilization that make each person unique.

Each chromosome has about 20,000 genes with each gene having a specific location on the chromosome. When examining another cell and looking at the same chromosome, each gene is in the exact same location. The human genome has over three billion genes.

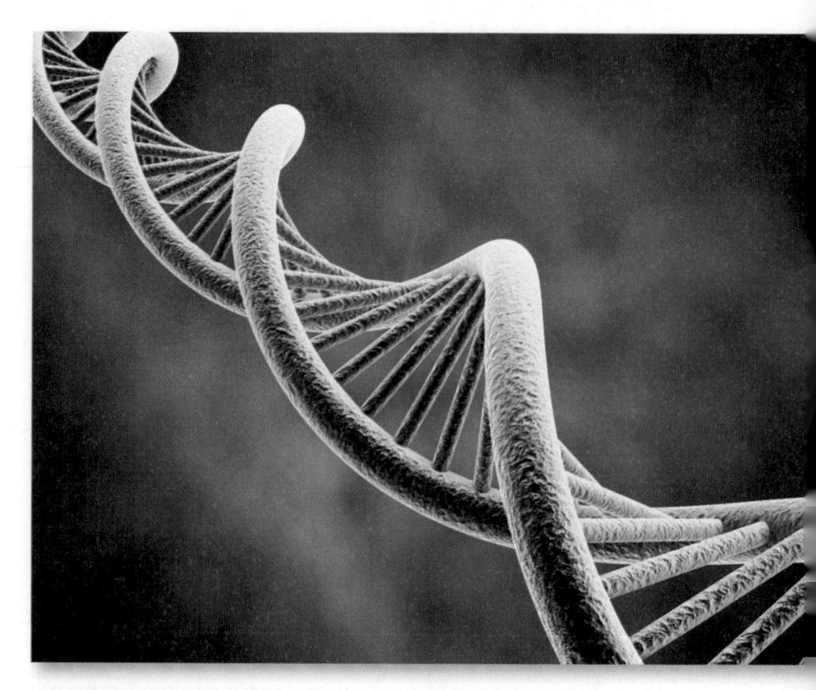

Figure 5.7 DNA contains the genetic instructions that guide the assembly of a living creature. *What does it mean if two species' DNAs are similar?*

These genes and the epigenome determine a person's individual traits. Sometimes one gene-pair determines a trait. Other times a group of gene-pairs decides a trait. In each gene-pair, one gene originates from the father, and the other gene is from the mother. The genes the child receives from each parent work together to determine the child's specific traits. In a few genes, only one gene (not a matched pair) determines certain traits for boys.

Dominant and Recessive Traits

The initial laws of heredity were discovered by Gregor Mendel (1822–1884), a **botanist** (person who studies plant life) from Austria. In the beginning, Mendel thought traits were handed down equally from both parents, such as a tall and short parent would produce an average height "child." (Mendel was actually studying peas.)

Mendel's conclusions, however, did not support the "averaging" idea. He soon discovered that the laws of heredity, which apply to all living beings, are based on dominant and recessive genes. For this reason, different traits come from each parent, and the child may express traits that both parents have, but are not expressed in either parent.

Dominant traits are always expressed in a person even if only one gene of the pair is inherited for that trait. **Recessive traits** are not typically expressed in a person unless both genes for the trait are inherited (one from each parent). A person who inherits only one recessive gene for a trait becomes a *carrier* of that trait. This makes it possible for the trait to be expressed in later generations.

People can have dominant, recessive, or both types of genes in their gene pair for blood type. For example, blood type A is a dominant gene, and blood type O is a recessive gene. A child with two blood type A genes or one blood type A gene and one blood type O gene will have blood type A. A child with two blood type O genes, one from each parent, will have blood type O.

Autosomes and Sex Chromosomes

Of the 23 pairs of chromosomes in each cell, 22 pairs (chromosomes 1–22) are *autosomes* (AW-tuh-zomes). The genes in these autosomes are always in

Dominant and Recessive Genes

At the time of conception, your parents together gave you gene pairs that have determined your unique traits. Your traits were randomly selected from among the traits of all generations of your blood relatives. Most traits, such as eye color, are the result of multiple gene pairs. Other traits, called *Mendelian inheritance*, are the result of one gene pair and follow the simple principle of being a dominant or recessive trait with no intermediate results. Remember for a dominant trait, only one dominant gene in the pair is needed, which can come from one or both parents. For a recessive trait, both genes in the pair must be for the recessive trait, which means both parents either have the recessive trait or are carriers. Thus, dominant traits are more common in the general population.

Some typical dominant traits include: dimples; cleft chin; ear lobe unattached from the head; right-handedness; freckles; blood types A, B, or AB (co-dominant); Rh+ blood factor; high blood pressure; nearsightedness; and baldness (in males). Recessive traits would be the opposites, such as no dimples, or another trait, such as blood type O.

From this listing, make a list of your dominant and recessive traits. Who else in your family shares each trait with you? Use the Internet to further research Mendelian inheritance traits and share your findings with the class.

matched pairs—one from the mother and one from the father—and are possessed equally by males and females. In these 22 pairs of chromosomes, all traits are based on the principles of dominant and recessive genes.

Unlike the autosomes, the 23rd chromosomes are called the *sex chromosomes* because they determine a person's gender (**Figure 5.8**). The gender of a child, however, is determined by the entirety of the chromosome pairs, unlike traits that are determined by only one or a few genes on each chromosome or the pair.

When viewing the chromosome pair for females and males under a microscope, the pair for each gender looks different in the following way:

- Females have the XX chromosome pair (because when viewing with a microscope, the pair looks somewhat like the letters *X* and *X*). When a female's chromosome pair splits to form germ cells (ova), all ova will be X because each chromosome pair is XX.
- Males have the XY chromosome pair (because when viewing with a microscope, the pair looks somewhat like the letters *X* and *Y*). When a male's chromosome pair splits to form germ cells (sperm), some will be X and some will be Y because each chromosome pair is XY.

All the mother's egg cells carry the X chromosome. If the egg is fertilized by a sperm carrying an X chromosome, the child will be female (XX). If the sperm cell carries the Y chromosome, the child will be male (XY). Because the father's sex chromosome is the one that varies (X or Y), the father's sperm always determines the gender of the child.

Although the whole chromosome pair determines gender, there are other traits determined by specific genes on the sex chromosomes. The laws of heredity are slightly different on this 23rd chromosome pair compared to the autosomes. To understand this, think of an X as having four legs and a Y as having three legs.

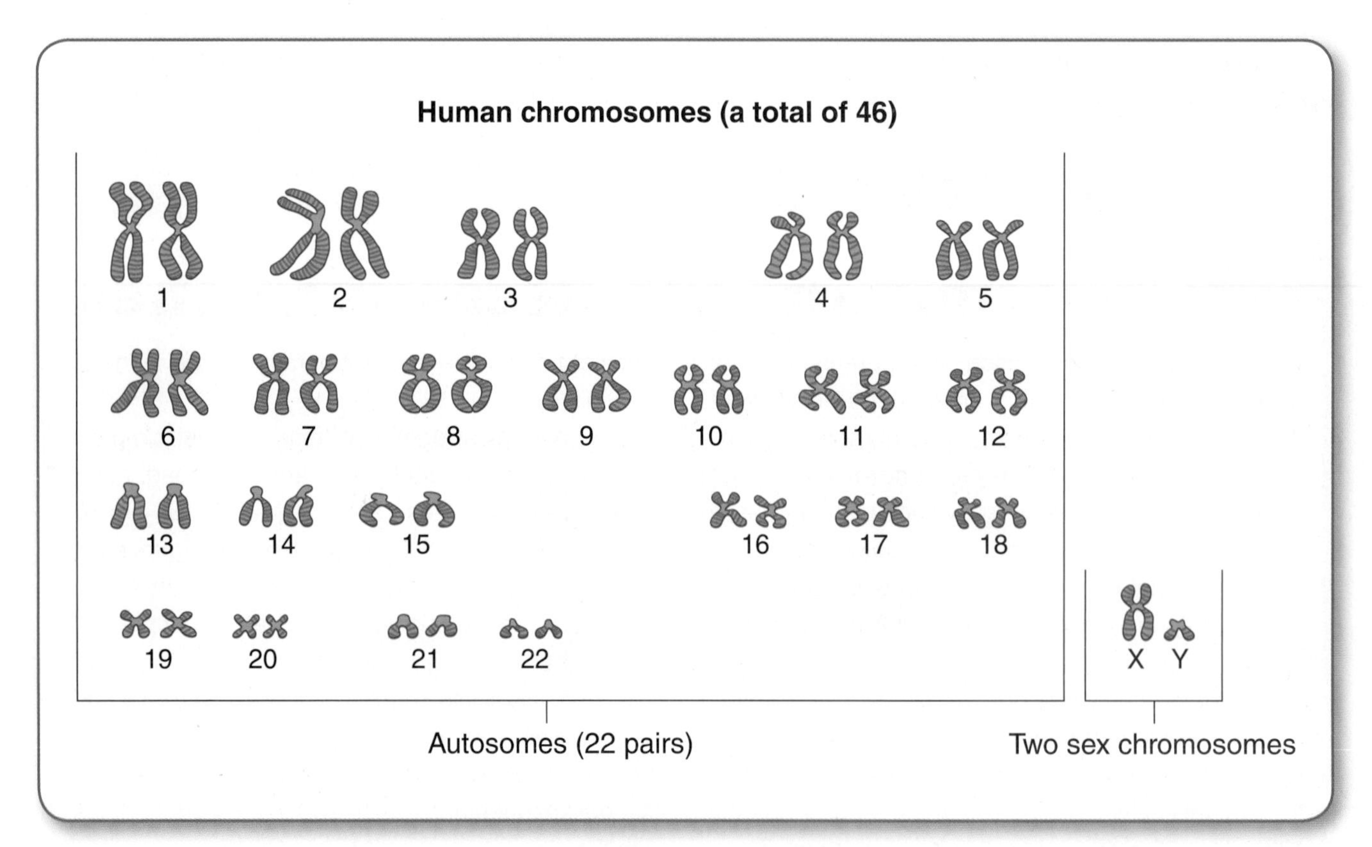

Figure 5.8 This example is male (XY). Females have two X chromosomes (XX). *If a male contributes an X chromosome to the genetic makeup of a baby, what gender will the baby be?*

A male's traits are determined by the pairing of dominant and recessive genes on the three matched legs of the X and Y, just as they are in the autosomes. There is no fourth leg of the Y, however, to follow the laws of dominant and recessive genes (**Figure 5.9**). (This is not the case for females whose sex chromosome pair is XX. All of females' genes will be in matched pairs.) For males, either the dominant or recessive genes on the unmatched fourth-leg of the X chromosome determine these traits, called the *sex-linked traits*. Some sex-linked traits include color blindness and *hemophilia* (HE-muh-FIL-lee-uh), a serious blood disorder. Females would only have these disorders if they received the recessive genes from both parents.

Figure 5.9 Sex Chromosomes

23rd Pair

X X

Genes on the female sex chromosomes are in matched pairs and follow the rules for dominant and recessive inheritance.

 Y

unmatched 4th leg — missing leg in males

Genes on the male sex chromosomes are in matched pairs, except for the missing section. All the genes in the matched sections follow the rules for dominant and recessive inheritance. In the missing section, males inherit the mother's traits whether dominant or recessive.

Genetic and Chromosomal Disorders

A **genetic disorder** is a defect caused by one or more **abnormalities** (flaws or irregularities) in the genome. Some disorders are inherited from parents as a dominant or recessive trait (**Figure 5.10**). Other defects are due to *mutations* (changes in the DNA). If the mutation is in the sex chromosome, it can be passed down to the next generation (**Figure 5.11**). Most genetic disorders are caused by a combination of small variations in genes and environmental factors.

Chromosomal disorders are defects in the chromosomes. These defects are often more serious than single-gene defects because they involve so many genes. Chromosome disorders are caused by changes in the number of chromosomes or by a structural abnormality, such as a deletion or duplication of part of the chromosome. Chromosomal

Figure 5.10 Genetic Alterations: Single Gene

Type of Alteration	Examples of Defects	Prevalence of Defects
Dominant gene (50% chance a child will inherit)	• ***Autosomal dominant polycystic kidney disease (ADPKD).*** Clusters of cysts (fluid-filled sacs) develop in the kidneys and sometimes in the liver. High blood pressure and kidney failure often occur.	1 in 1,250 births
	• ***Marfan syndrome.*** Damages connective tissues that support the skeleton and body structures. These connective tissues lose their elasticity and strength. Body structure looks much like that of Abraham Lincoln (tall and thin). If heart and blood vessels are affected, the syndrome is life threatening.	1 in 4,000 births
	• ***Huntington's disease.*** Disease injures the brain, which causes movement, cognitive, and psychiatric disorders. These disorders gradually worsen over time. Death occurs 10 to 30 years after disease onset. (If onset occurs in childhood, death often occurs within 10 years.)	1 in 10,000 births

(Continued)

Figure 5.10 *(Continued)*

Type of Alteration	Examples of Defects	Prevalence of Defects
Recessive gene (25% chance a child will have the disorder)	• ***Sickle-cell anemia.*** Disease that causes an abnormality in the red blood cells. The cells are rigid, sticky, shaped like sickles (crescent moons), and break easily. These sickle cells often block blood flow causing severe pain, damage to the retina, damage to the spleen resulting in infections, and swelling in the hands and feet. Sickle cells live only 20 days compared to a normal cell's lifespan of 120 days. Thus, victims do not have enough red blood cells to carry needed oxygen throughout the body. The disease is treated with blood transfusions, which are not without some risks.	1 in 625 births
	• ***Cystic fibrosis.*** Disease affects cells that produce mucous, sweat, and digestive juices. Secretions become thick and sticky and result in plugged passageways in the lungs and pancreas. Death often occurs in the 20s and 30s, but some victims live to middle age.	1 in 2,000 births
	• ***Tay-Sachs disease.*** A fatty substance in the child's brain builds up to toxic levels and affects neuron functioning. The disease leads to blindness, deafness, paralysis, and death. (In the infantile form, children die before the preschool years. In the juvenile form, death occurs in the mid-teen years.)	1 in 3,000 births
	• ***PKU or phenylketonuria*** (FEN-uhl-kee-tuh-NOOR-ia). Disease causes an amino acid, *phenylalanine*, to build up in the body due to the lack of an enzyme to break down the amino acid. Without dietary treatment, stunted growth, small head size, severe intellectual disabilities, and behavioral problems occur.	1 in 12,000 births
X-linked recessive (50% chance for boys being affected)	• ***Duchenne*** (doo-SHEN) ***muscular dystrophy.*** Muscle fibers are very susceptible to damage. Limbs contract making victims wheelchair-bound. Disease affects heart, lungs, and ability to swallow. Victims often die of respiratory failure before they reach 40 years of age.	1 in 7,000 births
	• ***Hemophilia.*** Disease is a disorder of the blood-clotting system. Disease causes severe bruising; internal bleeding; bleeding into the joints, urine, and stool; and extreme fatigue. Blood transfusions are used for treatment. Uncontrolled bleeding can lead to death.	1 in 10,000 births

defects usually occur due to an error in cell division. One example of a chromosomal condition is **Down syndrome**, which occurs when each body cell has three copies of chromosome 21 instead of two copies.

Most chromosome errors occur in the egg or in the sperm, so the defect is present in every body cell. In other cases, the defect occurs after conception, which means some cells carry the defect, but others do not. Parents' ages increase the risks of genetic and chromosomal disorders due to the aging of genetic materials in the germ cells.

Environmental Factors

Environmental factors are caused by a person's surroundings. The prenatal environment is the mother's body, which affects the baby. This means the substances a pregnant woman takes into her

Figure 5.11 Examples of Multiple Gene Alterations Combined with the Environment

- Asthma
- Autoimmune diseases, such as multiple sclerosis (MS), inflammatory bowel disease (IBD), and rheumatoid arthritis (RA)
- Cleft palate
- Diabetes
- Heart disease
- Mood disorders

body also affect the developing baby. Environmental substances include foods, beverages, drugs, and environmental pollutants, such as lead, chemicals, pesticides, and herbicides. Each of these substances can negatively impact the developing fetus.

An unborn baby depends on the mother for a healthy start. Women with good health habits and a healthy environment before pregnancy most often have healthy babies. Pregnant women with environmental factors that do not promote a healthy pregnancy are called *high-risk mothers-to-be*. Environmental factors that can affect the health of the pregnancy include the parents' ages and the mother's physical and emotional health.

Parents' Ages

In regard to health, the ideal time for a woman to have a baby is between 21 and 28 years of age. Teens and women over 35 years of age are high-risk mothers-to-be. Because pregnant teens are still growing themselves, their bodies cannot always meet the needs of their developing babies. Women who are over 35 years of age have a higher rate of babies with health problems, disabilities, and disorders. As mothers, they are also more prone to health problems.

For many years, geneticists have suspected that a father's age was involved in some genetic disorders. Mutations in the sperm occur as men age, and the number of mutations rise **exponentially** (rapidly). For example, at 36 years of age, men pass along twice as many new mutations as men at 20 years of age. By 70 years of age, this number has increased to eight times the number of new mutations seen in 20-year-olds. Most sperm mutations are harmless to children, but some result in disorders.

Focus on Careers

Genetic Counselor

Genetic counselors analyze the genetics of patients through DNA testing to identify possible syndromes or genetic disorders. Genetic information can be used to determine the likelihood of offspring developing a genetic disorder or syndrome.

Career cluster: Health care.

Education: Educational requirements include a minimum of a master's degree in genetic counseling or genetics. Some genetic counselors choose to further their education and earn a Ph.D. Most states also require certification and a license in genetic counseling.

Job outlook: Future employment opportunities for genetic counselors are expected to grow much faster than the average for all occupations.

To learn more about a career as a genetic counselor, visit the United States Department of Labor's *Occupational Outlook Handbook* website. You will also be able to compare the job responsibilities, educational requirements, job outlook, and average pay of genetic counselors with similar occupations.

Mother's Physical Health

Good health habits prior to and during pregnancy can promote a healthy pregnancy for both the mother and the baby. Good health habits include eating nutritious meals, maintaining a healthy weight, getting plenty of sleep and rest, and getting enough physical activity. When a pregnant woman does not practice good health habits, doctors become concerned. (You will learn more about health habits prior to and during pregnancy later in this chapter.) Other problems that are of concern to doctors include

- certain illnesses and diseases
- high-risk behaviors, such as drug or alcohol use
- emotional stress

Illnesses and Diseases in the Mother

Any health problems a woman has before and during pregnancy may play a role in the pregnancy and affect the baby's health. Women should ask their doctors (before pregnancy, if possible) how these problems might affect the pregnancy. In many cases, steps can be taken to protect the unborn baby. The doctor will want to monitor health problems more closely during pregnancy. Special testing might be done, and medications or treatments might need to be adjusted for the safety of the unborn baby.

Diabetes

Diabetes is a disorder caused by the body's inability to use sugar properly. In diabetes, the body inadequately produces or uses the hormone *insulin*. Some women might have diabetes before they become pregnant. If so, they should talk to their doctors about how to manage the disorder during pregnancy.

Another kind of diabetes, called *gestational diabetes*, can occur during pregnancy. Gestational diabetes appears in about 18 percent of women who did not have diabetes before pregnancy. Soon after pregnancy ends, gestational diabetes usually disappears. Women who experience gestational diabetes, however, have a 35 to 60 percent chance of contracting diabetes later in life. The chances of developing diabetes increase for their children, too.

Careful balance of diet, physical activity, and medication (if needed) can keep both types of diabetes under control. Pregnant women with either of these conditions should work closely with their doctors and dietitians to plan for a healthy pregnancy.

Pregnancy-Induced Hypertension (PIH)

Pregnancy-induced hypertension (PIH) is the name for high blood pressure caused by pregnancy (**Figure 5.12**). This dangerous condition can also be referred to as *preeclampsia* or *toxemia*. It includes a sudden increase in blood pressure, protein in the urine, and swelling. PIH appears late in pregnancy, but its cause is unknown. If untreated, PIH can lead to damage or death of the mother, baby, or

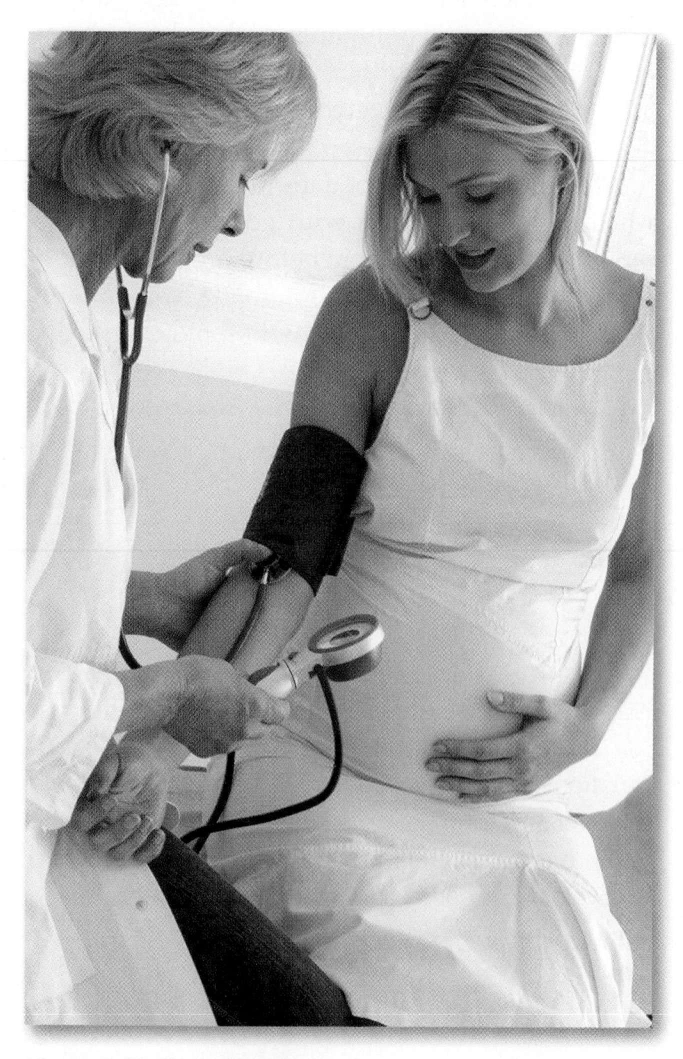

Figure 5.12 Early detection and treatment are important for women who have pregnancy-induced hypertension (PIH). *What can women do to reduce their risk of pregnancy complications remaining undetected?*

both. Early treatment, which may include bed rest, medicine, and perhaps early delivery of the baby, can help both mother and baby avoid serious health problems.

Rh Factor

The **Rh factor** is a protein substance found on the surface of red blood cells of about 85 percent of the population, mainly among Caucasians. People who have the substance are called *Rh positive (Rh+)*, and those who do not are called *Rh negative (Rh–)*.

The only time the Rh factor can cause the baby a problem is when the father is Rh+ and the mother is Rh–. If the baby inherits the Rh+ blood type from the father, the baby may develop Rh disease. *Rh disease* is a type of blood condition that destroys the baby's red blood cells.

Rh disease does not affect the first Rh+ unborn baby. During any pregnancy, however, some of the baby's Rh+ cells may enter the mother's bloodstream during birth. These cells are foreign to the mother's Rh– system. Her body fights these Rh+ cells by making antibodies, which then makes the mother immune to the blood cells of future Rh+ babies. In the next pregnancy, these antibodies cross the placenta. If the baby has Rh+ blood, the antibodies destroy the baby's red blood cells. A vaccine called *anti-Rh-immune globulin* greatly reduces the danger of Rh disease. (The vaccine is 99 percent effective.)

Sexually Transmitted Infections (STIs)

Sexually transmitted infections (STIs) are infectious illnesses contracted primarily through sexual intercourse. STIs are also known as *sexually transmitted diseases (STDs)*. The most dangerous STI is HIV/AIDS. **HIV** (human immunodeficiency virus) is the STI that causes the disease **AIDS** (acquired immunodeficiency syndrome). AIDS develops when HIV attacks the body's immune system until it is no longer able to fight illness.

HIV is spread through sexual relations or by contact with contaminated blood and bodily fluids. Among drug users, HIV can spread through the sharing of contaminated intravenous needles.

STIs can have serious effects on the unborn baby (**Figure 5.13**). A mother could be infected with an STI and not even realize it because she may not show any signs of infection. This could be extremely dangerous to her unborn baby. For example, some STIs can enter the bloodstream of the mother and cross the placenta to reach the fetus. Others infect the mother's reproductive tract and can pass to the baby during delivery. Still other STIs can be passed from mother to baby during breast-feeding. If a woman thinks there is a chance she was exposed to an STI, she should immediately communicate this to her doctor.

Rubella

Rubella (formerly called *German measles*) is a virus that can cross the placenta and affect the baby during the first three months of pregnancy. For the mother, this disease is mild. Infected babies, however, may be born blind, deaf, with an intellectual disability, and/or with heart problems. Mothers should have received an MMR (measles-mumps-rubella) vaccination for rubella during childhood. The MMR vaccine must be avoided during pregnancy, however, because the vaccine itself presents a risk to a fetus.

Radiation Exposure

During pregnancy, X-rays that are performed to help diagnose some physical conditions should be avoided if possible. This is because X-rays aimed toward the fetus increase the likelihood of childhood cancer. Some studies also link the use of X-rays in pregnancy to congenital disabilities in the fetus.

Pregnant women should inform their doctors or dentists of a possible or known pregnancy before X-rays are performed. Women should not work near X-ray or radiation treatment machines or stay in the room when an X-ray is being taken.

If an X-ray is necessary before delivery, it must be low in intensity, taken away from the fetus, and done only when the abdomen is shielded by a lead safety drape.

Drug and Alcohol Use

Harmful substances, such as nicotine, alcohol, medications, and drugs can enter the mother's body, pass through the placenta, and reach an unborn baby. Some of these substances can harm the baby in the early months of pregnancy, and many can harm the baby throughout pregnancy. Other drugs, such as aspirin, are most hazardous near delivery.

Figure 5.13 STIs and Their Effects on the Unborn/Newborn

STI	Transmission	Effects on Baby
Syphilis	Contracted by mother through sexual activity. Crosses the placenta beginning in the eighteenth week of pregnancy.	Effects prevented if treated before the sixteenth week. Untreated infection causes deafness, brain damage, skin lesions, bone and facial deformities, and fetal death.
Cytomegalovirus (CMV)	Transmitted by respiratory contact or sexual activity. CMV crosses the placenta.	Fatal for embryo or young fetus. In older fetuses, causes brain, liver, and blood problems. No treatment or means of prevention.
Herpes simplex (herpes)	Contracted primarily by sexual relations. Transmitted to baby at or shortly before delivery by baby's contact with infected secretions.	Newborns develop skin lesions and brain damage, and 50 percent die. May result in increased risk for mental health problems. No treatment available. C-sections may prevent contact with secretions.
Gonorrhea	Contracted by sexual relations. Transmitted to baby at or shortly before delivery by baby's contact with reproductive tract infection.	Blindness if untreated. Treatment includes placing silver nitrate in the infant's eyes and treating baby with antibiotics.
Chlamydia	Transmitted through sexual relations. (Twice as common as gonorrhea.) Women rarely experience symptoms. May lead to sterility.	Miscarriage, low birthweight, and death of infants due to lung disorders.
Pelvic inflammatory disease (PID)	Complication of some STIs due to sexual relations with an infected partner.	Damages reproductive organs, making it difficult to impossible to conceive. Often the cause of PID is gonorrhea or chlamydia. (See these effects on baby.)
Human papillomavirus (HPV)	Transmitted by all forms of sexual relations. Can cause genital warts and cancer. Vaccines are available to prevent HPV.	Warts may block the vaginal canal, requiring surgical delivery of the baby. Most babies overcome the virus without treatment. Babies may develop warts on the vocal cords (called *laryngeal papillomatosis*).
Acquired immunodeficiency syndrome (AIDS)	Acquired by mother through sexual relations or contact with infected blood or body fluids. Infected mothers transmit the virus in 25 percent of births. (Women who are pregnant usually have HIV only with full-blown AIDS following pregnancy.)	Illness and perhaps very early death of child. Treatment of symptoms. No cure.

Nicotine

When a pregnant woman smokes, her baby feels the effects. Because nicotine is a *stimulant*, it raises the mother's heart rate, blood pressure, and breathing rate. Nicotine also reduces the flow of blood. While a mother is smoking, the baby's oxygen is greatly reduced. Babies need oxygen as they grow, especially during the prenatal period. A parent or parents who smoke during pregnancy usually continue to smoke after pregnancy, too. Thus, the child continues to be affected by secondhand smoke (**Figure 5.14**).

Figure 5.14 Risks of Nicotine Use During Pregnancy

- Low birthweight or premature birth
- Congenital disorders
- Abnormal brain development, which can lead to learning problems, hyperactivity, and poor attention spans
- Ear infections and breathing problems
- Cleft lip or palate
- Delivery complications
- Possible miscarriage
- Newborn or infant death

Alcohol

Doctors advise women never to drink alcohol during pregnancy. Any alcoholic drink, whether beer, wine, or hard liquor, can harm an unborn baby. Alcohol is a type of *depressant*, which slows the central nervous system. A developing baby cannot process alcohol. Possibly taking even one drink may cause the baby to have birth defects.

Fetal alcohol spectrum disorders (FASDs) is a group of symptoms that occurs in babies whose mothers drank during pregnancy. FASDs are comprised of the following conditions:

- ***Fetal Alcohol Syndrome (FAS).*** FAS is at the severe end of the spectrum. These babies have abnormal facial features, growth problems, and brain disorders. They can have problems with learning, executive functions, vision, or hearing.
- ***Alcohol-Related Neurodevelopmental Disorder (ARND).*** These babies may have learning and behavioral problems (poor judgment and impulse control) often first noted near school-age.
- ***Alcohol-Related Birth Defects (ARBD).*** These babies often have problems with one or more of the following: heart, kidneys, bones, or hearing.

Medications

The effects of most medications on unborn babies are unknown. Therefore, a pregnant woman should not take any medication without consulting her doctor. This includes prescriptions prior to the pregnancy, over-the-counter medications, dietary supplements, and herbal products. Taking more than the prescribed amount of a medication can be dangerous, too.

Drugs

A growing number of babies are born to mothers using drugs, such as cocaine, crack, heroin, marijuana, ecstasy, and other hallucinogens. Some pregnant women may also be using powerful narcotics (pain-relieving or sleep-inducing drugs) with or without a prescription. Drugs can cross the placenta quickly and reach the baby. If a woman is addicted to drugs, chances are her baby is, too.

Some of the effects of drugs can be seen immediately in babies, such as

- early birth or death before birth
- *withdrawal symptoms* (high-pitched cry, shaking, twitching, vomiting, fever, trouble breathing, poor feeding, and rubbing the nose until the skin bleeds)
- damage to a baby's brain, eyes, heart, limbs, intestines, and urinary tract (with cocaine use)

Mental Health Advisory

Mothers who drink alcohol during pregnancy have a very high risk of having babies with ARND. These children show mental health problems by the school-age years.

Mental Health Advisory

Being exposed to illegal (recreational) drugs, such as cocaine, crack, or heroin, prenatally often results in mental health problems in the school-age and teen years.

How Early Exposures to Substances Affect the Prenatal Brain and the Child After Birth

Children's first environment is one of chemicals—substances. Some chemicals, such as quality nutrients from a pregnant woman's well-balanced diet, are essential to good health of the unborn and nursing baby. Some chemicals, however, are toxic and create devastating and lifelong impacts on children. Harmful substances are found in nicotine, alcohol, prescribed and over-the-counter medications, and in illegal recreational drugs. The effects of specific substances on the child are complex.

There are two ways in which substances taken by a mother-to-be alter a child's development. The first way is during the prenatal stage in which chemicals cross the placenta and enter the unborn baby's body. Many substances affect the neurotransmitters, which are also chemicals. Before neurotransmitters are involved in the brain's firing process, they are involved in the neurons' division, growth, migration, and *differentiation* (becoming specific types of neurons). Neurotransmitters are also involved in helping glial cells with myelination. Later in development, neurotransmitters make it possible for information to cross synapses between neurons, which allows for learning in all developmental domains.

If harmful substances occur during the germinal stage, death of the unborn is often the result. During the embryonic stage, harmful substances that reach the unborn baby's brain result in physical damage, such as a baby being born blind, deaf, without certain limbs, with heart problems, and with neural tube defects (defects related to the brain, spine, or spinal cord). If harmful substances affect the unborn during the fetal stage, neuron migration, firing, and myelination are all affected, causing intellectual and behavioral problems after birth.

The second period when substance abuse alters a child's development is in the neonatal period—often beginning 72 hours after delivery and lasting throughout the neonatal stage. The baby suffers harm from withdrawal symptoms called *neonatal withdrawal syndrome* or *neonatal discontinuation*. Substances taken by the mother-to-be in the last trimester often cause these problems: preterm delivery, poor feeding and diarrhea, irritability, tremors, convulsions, sleep disturbances, and respiratory problems. If the baby lives, the initial symptoms usually end within a month, but other effects, such as sensory-motor, intellectual, and behavioral problems, are seen throughout childhood and often beyond.

Thinking Activity

Many questions about the effects of toxicity remain unanswered. As a class, respond to the following questions.

1. What are the results of multiple substance exposures? How can harmful practices, such as not getting adequate nutrition and substance abuse, be separated when both often occur together?
2. Is there any way to overcome negative impacts on children due to their mother's substance abuse? How does substance abuse affect children's first social environments with their parents? (For example, how will parents react to a preterm baby undergoing withdrawal symptoms?)
3. What is the best way to reach mothers-to-be about the intake of substances under their control? How should substance abuse by pregnant women be handled in today's society?

By the school-age and teen years, children exposed to drugs during fetal development may show mood disorders and an inability to focus attention. In other words, the damage was done very early, but there was a "silent period" before the symptoms occurred.

Besides the direct effects of drugs, pregnant women who use drugs often neglect their own health. In many cases, these women eat poorly, smoke, or abuse alcohol. Some never see a doctor during pregnancy. For these reasons, babies whose mothers use drugs have a slim chance of living a healthy life.

Mother's Emotional Health

The mother's emotional health can also impact prenatal development. Positive thoughts and feelings are important for a woman to have a healthy baby. When a mother is happy and relaxed, her heartbeat and breathing are slow and her muscles are relaxed. Mothers who are relaxed have an easier pregnancy and delivery.

About one in eleven mothers experience depression and excessive stress during pregnancy, called *toxic stress*. These mothers are more likely to engage in unhealthy habits, refuse any treatment for depression and stress, and skip prenatal visits.

The mother's stress hormones cross the placenta to the baby. In the later stages of gestation, the baby can detect changes in the mother's heartbeat and breathing rates, too. The unborn baby can handle some stress, but if the stress is prolonged, severe, or frequent, it is dangerous to the unborn baby. Toxic stress may result in

- early birth and lower birthweight.
- lag in brain development.
- change in the epigenome, which "silences" the gene that controls overproduction of stress hormones. This causes the newborn to be most **vulnerable** (easily affected; sensitive) to the actions of others.
- fussy temperament and sleep problems.
- developmental delays and behavioral problems.

Mental Health Advisory

Your body has a gene that calms you after stress. The gene is "silenced" in unborn babies who receive excessive stress hormones from their mothers. After birth, these children cannot calm themselves, which can result in mental health problems.

Although some factors are uncontrollable during prenatal development, such as genetic factors, environmental factors are often controllable. A healthy pregnancy is possible with support from family and friends, a hazard-free environment, adequate sleep, and proper medical and nutritional care.

Lesson 5.2 Review and Assessment

1. What are the roles of the genome and epigenome in determining a person's genetic blueprint?
2. What was Mendel's contribution to developing the laws of heredity?
3. Explain why knowing one is a carrier of a recessive trait is important.
4. Explain the difference between a genetic and chromosomal disorder. Which is more serious and why?
5. List the environmental factors that have the potential to harm a fetus.
6. Describe how a mother's emotional health can affect her fetus.
7. **Critical thinking.** Paul has brown eyes, a dominant trait, and his wife Emily has blue eyes, a recessive trait. Paul and Emily's daughter has blue eyes. How is this possible?
8. **Critical thinking.** Based on the environmental risk factors described in this lesson, what can a mother do to protect her fetus from harm?

Lesson 5.3 Health Habits Prior to and During Pregnancy

Key Terms

amniocentesis
chorionic villus sampling (CVS)
congenital condition
folic acid
MyPlate
nutrients
obstetricians
premature birth
prenatal vitamin
ultrasound

Academic Terms

deflected
noninvasive
optimum
prompt
severity
synthetic

Objectives

After studying this lesson, you will be able to

- analyze the importance of good health habits prior to pregnancy.
- differentiate between presumptive and positive signs of pregnancy.
- explain the relationship between the health of the mother and the health of the baby.
- assess medical and nutritional needs during pregnancy.
- describe how health practices, such as physical activity, hygiene, and rest and sleep affect the mother and developing fetus.

Reading and Writing Activity

How much do a mother's daily habits affect her developing baby? Before reading this lesson, research this question using two to three online or print sources. Then, write a one-page essay summarizing your findings and identifying whether your sources are reliable. After reading this lesson, compare what you learned with your sources' information. How reliable were your sources?

Graphic Organizer

On a piece of paper, write the headings in this lesson, leaving space between them for your notes. Then as you are reading, write what you learn underneath or next to each heading. After reading, review your notes and highlight what you think are the most important points.

Health Habits Prior to Pregnancy	Health Habits During Pregnancy
medical exams = preventive care Getting plenty of physical activity	
Signs of Pregnancy	

The March of Dimes, an organization specializing in healthy pregnancies, urges mothers to "be good to your baby before it is born." Parents-to-be should take this message seriously. Because experts know more about pregnancy, childbirth, and infant care than ever before, parents-to-be can take many steps to keep mother and baby healthy and safe.

Optimum (the best) health care begins before conception. Why should women be concerned about their health in relation to pregnancy before they are pregnant? Good health habits throughout the younger years help prepare a woman for childbearing. It can take time to prepare the woman's body for a healthy pregnancy. Many doctors say that even for healthy women, prenatal care is a one-year event.

Health Habits Prior to Pregnancy

Health habits before pregnancy can impact a woman's ability both to become pregnant and to carry that pregnancy to term. Annual medical exams are a form of preventive care that can help women promote good overall health and well-being. By visiting the doctor regularly, diseases or disorders may be prevented or diagnosed early and treated. Annual exams will also establish a baseline against which a woman's health can be assessed while she is pregnant.

In addition to annual medical exams, women should also engage in other healthy habits to maintain good physical health prior to pregnancy. These healthy habits include

- getting plenty of physical activity
- making nutritious food choices
- maintaining a healthy weight
- minimizing stress
- getting plenty of sleep
- avoiding high-risk behaviors, such as smoking, drinking, or abusing drugs

MyPlate is a food guidance system developed by the U.S. Department of Agriculture (USDA) to help people two years of age and older make nutritious food choices. The MyPlate website provides the tools for people to develop their own daily food plans or to track the foods they eat each day. This interactive food guidance system enables people to make sure they are selecting foods that are rich in nutrients. **Nutrients** are substances that give the body what it needs to grow and function. There are six types of nutrients common in food. These nutrients are carbohydrates, proteins, fats, vitamins, minerals, and water (**Figure 5.15**).

A woman's healthy diet should also include taking 400 micrograms of folic acid every day before pregnancy. **Folic acid** is a B-vitamin that reduces the baby's risk for neural tube defects. Folic acid can be found in most enriched breads, pastas, rice, and cereals, as well as multivitamins.

Signs of Pregnancy

A woman cannot feel the sperm and egg unite. She cannot feel cells divide as the baby begins to develop. Typically, a woman will not even realize that she is possibly pregnant before a couple of weeks after conception. Nevertheless, her body immediately nourishes and protects the new life. Hormones trigger changes in some of the woman's organs. The signs of pregnancy help a woman recognize these changes.

The signs of pregnancy are divided into presumptive and positive signs (**Figure 5.16**). The *presumptive signs* could be signs of pregnancy or a medical condition. Doctors must determine their cause. Doctors identify *positive signs*, however, as definitely being caused by pregnancy.

Health Habits During Pregnancy

Good health habits are always important. Health habits for pregnant women are similar to good health habits for all people. When a woman is pregnant, however, health habits have an even greater effect on her health and her baby's health. Only a few health habits change during pregnancy. Because each pregnancy differs, the mother-to-be should ask her doctor for health guidelines to follow.

Figure 5.15 Types of Nutrients

Nutrient	What Does It Do?	Where Is It Found?
Carbohydrates	Supply energy to the body consistently and on short notice	Fruits, vegetables, grains, dairy products
Proteins	Build and maintain the body's cells and tissues	Meats, poultry, fish, eggs, dairy products, legumes, beans, nuts and seeds, grains
Fats	Supply energy to the body when food is unavailable, cushion internal organs, insulate body	Meat and dairy products, vegetable oils, nuts and seeds, and other plant-based products
Vitamins	Regulate various body processes such as blood clotting, the immune system, and maintaining healthy skin	Various foods depending on type of vitamin
Minerals	Promote normal growth and development	Various foods depending on type of mineral
Water	Helps regulate body temperature, lubricates joints, protects sensitive tissues, helps get rid of waste, and moves oxygen and nutrients throughout body	It is recommended that people drink 8 to 10 cups of water per day

Medical Care

Medical care is the best way to make childbearing safe and successful. If a woman believes she is pregnant, she should make an appointment with a doctor as soon as possible. This medical care is important, whether the pregnancy is a first, second, or later pregnancy. Starting good prenatal care early in pregnancy greatly reduces the risk of complications. Many pregnant women choose to visit **obstetricians**, or doctors who specialize in pregnancy and birth.

The First Appointment

Scheduling and attending the first medical appointment as soon as a woman discovers she is pregnant is critical. The first prenatal appointment sets a foundation for medical care throughout the pregnancy. It is a good idea for the couple to go to this visit together. They can share important information with the doctor and learn much about what to expect in the months ahead.

During the first appointment, the doctor will

- gather general information and health history.
- gather details on reproductive health, menstrual cycles, and any past pregnancies.
- answer questions about pregnancy.
- do a complete physical exam on the mother-to-be (**Figure 5.17**).
- advise the couple on health habits to follow. Both parents are encouraged to be supportive of each other in following the healthful habits as prescribed.
- give an estimate of the baby's *due date* (given as the expected week). This will be adjusted later in the pregnancy. The length of a healthy pregnancy varies by as much as 37 days. Only about 5 percent of women deliver on their doctor's estimated due date, but 70 percent deliver within 10 days of this date.

Follow-Up Appointments

Couples are advised about follow-up appointments. Usually the doctor sees a pregnant woman once a month during the first six months of pregnancy. Visits increase to twice a month during the seventh and eighth months. During the ninth month, visits increase to once a week or more.

Figure 5.16 Signs of Pregnancy

Presumptive Signs
• ***Amenorrhea*** (menstruation stops)—If the woman is usually regular in her menstrual cycle, a delay of 10 or more days is a sign.
• ***Nausea***—Nausea is present in about ½ to ⅔ of all pregnancies. Because it often occurs in the morning hours, it is called *morning sickness*. Nausea may happen at any time of the day. Nausea occurring at the same time daily from weeks 4 to 12 is a sign.
• ***Tiredness***—Many women feel tired during the first few months of pregnancy.
• ***Frequency of urination***—The growing uterus puts pressure on the bladder. Hormones may also cause more frequent urination.
• ***Swelling and tenderness of the breasts***—This is often the first sign women note.
• ***Skin discoloration***—Stretch marks may be seen as the breasts and abdomen enlarge. Darkening of skin may occur on the face and nipples.
• ***Internal changes***—Doctors often note softening of the cervix (Goodell's sign). There may also be a softening of the lower part of the uterus (Hegar's sign) and a bluish tinge to the vagina and cervix due to circulatory congestion (Chadwick's sign). The uterus is also enlarged with irregular areas of firmness and softness (Piskacek's sign).
• ***Other signs***—Other symptoms include backache, groin pains, dizziness, abdominal swelling, leg cramps, varicose veins, and indigestion.
Positive Signs
• ***HCG (Human Chorionic Gonadatrophin)***—HCG is a hormone found in the blood and urine of pregnant women. Lab tests done at home or in the doctor's office can detect the hormone's presence toward the end of the first week of pregnancy. Over-the-counter home pregnancy tests provide privacy and fast results, but may yield inaccurate results due to testing too early (before a missed period) or not following directions exactly. When HCG tests are done by doctors, the hormone can be detected sooner, more accurately, and can result in other findings, such as the week of the pregnancy and possible multiple children.
• ***Fetal heartbeat***—The baby's heartbeat can be heard through a special device at 12 weeks and through a stethoscope at 16 weeks.
• ***Fetal movement***—Spontaneous movement of the baby begins at 11 weeks, but is not felt until 16 to 18 weeks.
• ***Fetal image***—The baby's image may be seen with ultrasound scanning.
• ***Fetal shape***—The baby's shape may be felt through the abdominal wall.
• ***Uterine contractions***—A doctor may note these painless contractions.

Going to each of the follow-up appointments is important. Doctors continue to carefully monitor the pregnancy. Through regular appointments, the chance of delivering a healthy baby increases, the discomforts of pregnancy may be lessened, and the couple will likely gain confidence. Beyond the planned appointments, couples should call their health care providers if any alarming symptoms arise between visits.

Prenatal Testing

As a pregnancy progresses, doctors may also perform several types of prenatal tests, which help to monitor the health of the baby and the mother. These tests can help detect and, in some cases, correct abnormalities before they become too severe. They can also diagnose chromosomal disorders before birth and identify risk factors for the baby's development and delivery.

Figure 5.17 Physical Exam for Mothers-to-Be

- Weigh mother
- Record blood pressure, pulse, and respiration rates
- Check breasts
- Perform a pelvic exam, which may include a pelvic measurement
- Collect a blood sample to check for blood type; *anemia* (uh-NEE-me-uh), a condition caused by lack of iron; blood sugar level; and diseases that can harm a baby
- Do a urine test

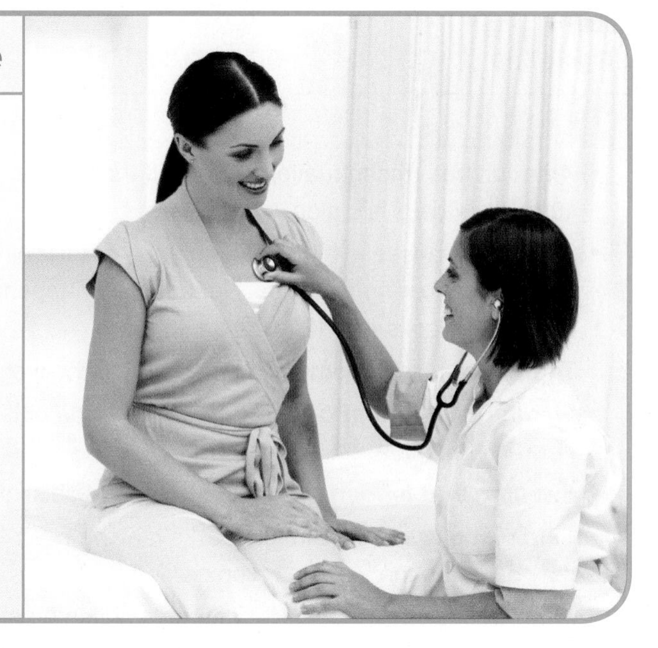

Blood Tests

There are three main blood tests that screen for major prenatal disorders (**Figure 5.18**). These tests are done by drawing blood from the mother. Because a blood test is **noninvasive** (not requiring insertion or cutting) for the fetus, it poses no risk to the unborn baby.

Other blood tests are used to check for conditions other than possible abnormalities in the fetus. Blood tests can screen for sexually transmitted infections at a mother's first medical visit. Another blood test, which is given at six or seven months, screens for gestational diabetes.

Ultrasound

An **ultrasound** is a test in which sound waves bounce off the fetus to produce an image of the fetus inside the womb. The picture of the fetus the ultrasound produces is called a *sonogram*. Sonograms are used to monitor the unborn baby.

Figure 5.18 Blood Tests that Screen for Major Prenatal Disorders

Test	Description
First Trimester Screen	Offered to all pregnant women between gestation weeks 11 to 14. It measures AFP (alpha-fetoprotein), HCG (human chorionic gonadotropin), and estriol (a protein found during pregnancy). The screening assesses the risk for three chromosomal disorders (Down syndrome, Edward's Syndrome, and Patau Syndrome) with 88 percent accuracy.
Cell-Free Fetal DNA Test (also called *Noninvasive Prenatal Diagnostic Testing*)	Given to women at high risk for certain chromosomal disorders. Women who are 35 years of age and older, who did not take the *First Trimester Screen*, or who had abnormal results on the *First Trimester Screen* can take this test at 10 weeks gestation or later. This test is 99 percent accurate.
Multiple Marker Screen	Given between 15 to 20 weeks gestation to women who did not take the *First Trimester Screen*, who are at high risk for chromosomal disorders, or who had *ultrasound* testing showing abnormalities. This test reveals the fetus's risk of having a chromosomal disorder or a neural tube defect, such as *spina bifida*.

Careers

Diagnostic Medical Sonographer

Diagnostic medical sonographers use equipment to collect reflected echoes to form an image that may be videotaped, transmitted, or photographed for interpretation and diagnosis by a physician. Obstetric and gynecologic diagnostic medical sonographers specialize in the imaging of the female reproductive system and the fetus of a pregnant woman to track the baby's growth and health.

Career cluster: Health science.

Education: Educational requirements include an associate's degree and special certification.

Job outlook: Future employment opportunities for diagnostic medical sonographers are expected to grow much faster than the average for all occupations.

To learn more about a career as a diagnostic medical sonographer, visit the United States Department of Labor's *Occupational Outlook Handbook* website. You will also be able to compare the job responsibilities, educational requirements, job outlook, and average pay of diagnostic medical sonographers with similar occupations.

To perform an ultrasound, a technician moves a *transducer* over the mother's abdomen for about 20 minutes. The sound waves the transducer emits are **deflected** (changing direction) or absorbed at different rates, depending on whether they hit bone, organ tissue, blood, or water. These differences are changed into electrical impulses, which produce a visual image of the fetus on a monitor. From this image, the doctor can see whether the baby seems to be developing correctly.

A 3-D ultrasound can help specialists look at the **severity** (seriousness) of structural defects. For example, these machines can detect the thickness of a fluid-filled area behind the unborn baby's neck (called *nuchal translucency*). This test can confirm Down syndrome early in the pregnancy and usually follows the *First Trimester Screen* if results of this test indicate abnormalities in the fetus.

Because ultrasounds are considered safe, they are used fairly routinely to check for abnormalities, size, gender, support systems (placenta, umbilical cord, amniotic fluid), multiple babies, and position prior to birth. Doctors discourage women from having ultrasounds made by retailers who simply make photos for parents.

Chorionic Villus Sampling

Chorionic villus sampling (CVS) is a procedure for finding abnormalities in the fetus. CVS is only done on women whose unborn children are at high-risk for abnormalities or whose *First Trimester Screen* revealed potential problems. This procedure is performed by testing a small sample taken from the chorion, which will later develop into the fetal part of the placenta. CVS is used between weeks 10 and 12 of pregnancy. This test can detect serious problems with the fetus early in the pregnancy.

CVS is completed by inserting a hollow tube through the vagina and cervix, into the uterus, and then guiding it to the chorion. (Another method is guiding a needle through the abdomen to the uterus.) *Chorionic villi* are fingerlike projections that branch out from the surface of the chorion and transport nutrients to, and wastes from, the unborn. A small section of the chorionic villi is painlessly suctioned off and analyzed for congenital problems. CVS has a slight risk (one percent) of infection, which can result in the loss of the baby.

Amniocentesis

Amniocentesis (AM-nee-oh-sen-TEE-sis) is a prenatal test used to check for the presence of over

100 congenital conditions. A **congenital condition** is a physical or biochemical problem in a baby that is present at birth and may be caused by genetic or environmental factors. An amniocentesis is given using the same criteria that is used for CVS. Usually it checks for conditions such as Down syndrome, Tay-Sachs disease, sickle-cell anemia, and cystic fibrosis.

To perform the test, a medical specialist inserts a needle through the abdominal wall into the uterus. An ultrasound is performed at the same time to position the needle. The specialist draws a small amount of fluid from the amniotic sac.

Amniotic fluid provides much information because cells cast off by the fetus float in the fluid. These cells are cultivated in a lab for three to five weeks and are then checked for congenital problems.

Amniocentesis cannot be done until the fetus is 15 to 18 weeks old. At this time, there is enough amniotic fluid for the test. Due to the lab time required, the woman will be 20 to 21 weeks pregnant when she learns the results. Amniocentesis is a safe procedure in 99.5 percent of cases, but it is not a routine procedure. This is because of the risks that may result, which include **premature birth** (born too soon) or even loss of the baby. Amniocentesis is used only when problems are suspected or the mother-to-be is older.

Nutrition

During the first week after conception, the baby is fed entirely on the contents of the ovum's yolk sac. After embedding, the fertilized egg feeds on mucous tissues that line the womb. By the twelfth week, the baby completely depends on the mother for food. There is a direct link between what a pregnant woman eats and the following factors:

- her weight gain
- the unborn baby's weight gain
- the baby's growth
- the baby's intellectual capacity
- the baby's physical performance

Focus on

Social Studies

The History of Ultrasound Technology

The science behind the ultrasound—in which sound waves are bounced off an area to create an image—was not discovered for the purpose of imaging fetuses and tracking their development. Rather, one of the earliest versions of ultrasound technology was what is now called SONAR (Sound Navigation and Ranging). Used by war ships during World War II, SONAR helped ships navigate unfamiliar and potentially dangerous seas by bouncing sound waves off the floor of the ocean and interpreting those sound waves to navigate and detect submarines. Because submarines were a common weapon during World War II, SONAR was an important and effective tactical tool.

In fact, it was not until the late 1940s that scientists began using ultrasound technology on the human body. Early ultrasound scans were conducted on patients who sat in water-filled gun turrets, and these scans looked similar to modern seismographs, which depict earthquake activity with a series of lines and spikes. Since then, science has come a long way to create the ultrasound technology doctors use to image mothers and their babies. Based on what ultrasound technology is used for now and on what it has been used for in the past, what other applications of this technology do you think science could explore? What else could be achieved through ultrasound technology? Find a partner and share your ideas.

Therefore, good nutrition during pregnancy is vital. Diets for pregnant and nursing mothers provide more calcium, iron, folic acid, and protein than diets for nonpregnant women. For example, pregnant women need 600 micrograms of **synthetic** (not natural) folic acid daily in addition to sources from their diet. Doctors often recommend pregnant women take a **prenatal vitamin** because it contains extra folic acid, iron, calcium, and other important vitamins and minerals.

Pregnant women should also have eight 8-ounce glasses of water daily. Caffeine intake should be limited during pregnancy. Daily intake of caffeine from all sources (including coffee, tea, soft drinks, and chocolate) should not exceed 300 milligrams.

Seafood is the best source of omega-3 fats. These fats provide benefits to both the pregnant woman and the baby she is carrying. Some types of seafood, however, are also sources of contaminants, such as mercury. Too much mercury can damage the fetus's developing brain and nervous system. For these reasons, pregnant women are encouraged to eat 8 to 12 ounces of seafood each week, but select varieties that are lower in mercury.

MyPlate provides guidelines to help women meet their nutritional needs during pregnancy (**Figure 5.19**). While this is a good basic guide, the need for some nutrients during pregnancy may be different for some women than for others. A pregnant woman's doctor or dietitian can advise her as to what specific diet changes she should make during pregnancy.

Weight Gain

Experts suggest women who maintain a healthy weight gain approximately 25 to 35 pounds during pregnancy. The exact amount depends on the woman's height and prepregnancy weight. Doctors also consider *body mass index (BMI)*, a calculation of weight and height that helps determine body fat. Women who enter pregnancy underweight may be advised to gain more. Overweight women may be advised to gain less than 25 to 30 pounds (**Figure 5.20**). More weight should be gained for multiples, such as 40 to 45 pounds for twins.

To meet the nutrient needs for themselves and their babies, pregnant women often need about 340 to 450 more calories per day in the second and third trimesters. More calories are added for multiple babies. Weight gain during pregnancy is not all stored as fat. Much of the weight gain goes to the growing baby and the supporting tissues (**Figure 5.21**).

Doctors carefully watch how much weight a pregnant woman gains. Gaining too much puts extra strain on the heart and makes the woman uncomfortable. Doctors also watch for sudden weight gain and unusual swelling. These conditions are serious and require **prompt** (immediate) medical attention. Gaining too little weight is not good for the developing baby, either. This can signal the baby is not growing properly or receiving enough nutrients.

A woman should steadily gain a healthy amount of weight throughout her pregnancy. Typically, a pregnant woman will gain about two to four pounds during the first trimester. During the second and third trimesters, a gain of about one pound per week is common. Sudden weight loss or gain during pregnancy may indicate a medical problem.

Physical Activity and Exercise

Unless advised by her doctor to limit physical activity, a pregnant woman can and should be active. Activity helps keep weight within normal limits, strengthens muscles used in delivery, increases energy, and relieves tension (**Figure 5.22**).

Many doctors advise mothers-to-be to avoid contact sports, activities that jolt the pelvic region, and activities that could result in falls. Doctors often advise women to walk during pregnancy. Some women take special exercise classes for pregnant women.

In childbirth classes, women may learn conditioning exercises to relieve back and leg strain that often occurs later in the pregnancy. They can also learn exercises that prepare the muscles for delivery.

Hygiene Practices

Women should continue their normal grooming and body care habits during pregnancy. Paying attention to her appearance may help the mother-to-be feel better during physical discomfort or emotional stress.

Daily Food Plan

For Moms

ChooseMyPlate.gov

	1st Trimester Apr – Jun Based on a 2200 calorie pattern*	2nd Trimester Jul – Sep Based on a 2400 calorie pattern*	3rd Trimester Oct – Dec Based on a 2600 calorie pattern*
GRAINS Make half your grains whole	**7 ounces a day** Aim for at least 3½ ounces of whole grains a day	**8 ounces a day** Aim for at least 4 ounces of whole grains a day	**9 ounces a day** Aim for at least 4½ ounces of whole grains a day
VEGETABLES Vary your veggies	**3 cups a day** Aim for this much weekly: Dark green veggies—2 cups Red and orange veggies—6 cups Beans & peas—2 cups Starchy veggies—6 cups Other veggies—5 cups	**3 cups a day** Aim for this much weekly: Dark green veggies—2 cups Red and orange veggies—6 cups Beans & peas—2 cups Starchy veggies—6 cups Other veggies—5 cups	**3½ cups a day** Aim for this much weekly: Dark green veggies—2½ cups Red and orange veggies—7 cups Beans & peas—2½ cups Starchy veggies—7 cups Other veggies—5½ cups
FRUITS Focus on fruits	**2 cups a day** Eat a variety of fruit Go easy on fruit juices	**2 cups a day** Eat a variety of fruit Go easy on fruit juices	**2 cups a day** Eat a variety of fruit Go easy on fruit juices
DAIRY Get your calcium-rich foods	**3 cups a day** Go low-fat or fat-free when you choose milk, yogurt, or cheese	**3 cups a day** Go low-fat or fat-free when you choose milk, yogurt, or cheese	**3 cups a day** Go low-fat or fat-free when you choose milk, yogurt, or cheese
PROTEIN FOODS Choose lean with protein	**6 ounces a day** Choose low-fat or lean meats and poultry. Vary your protein routine—choose more fish, beans, peas, nuts, and seeds.	**6½ ounces a day** Choose low-fat or lean meats and poultry. Vary your protein routine—choose more fish, beans, peas, nuts, and seeds.	**6½ ounces a day** Choose low-fat or lean meats and poultry. Vary your protein routine—choose more fish, beans, peas, nuts, and seeds.

* These are only estimates of your needs. Check with your health care provider to make sure you are gaining weight appropriately.

The calories and amounts of food you need change with each trimester of pregnancy. Your plan may show different amounts of food for different months, to meet your changing nutritional needs. Changing the amount of calories you eat each trimester also helps you gain weight at the correct rate.

Know your limits on fats and discretionary calories

	OILS	EXTRAS
	Aim for this much:	Limit extras (solid fats and sugars) to this much:
1st Trimester	6 teaspoons a day	266 calories a day
2nd Trimester	7 teaspoons a day	330 calories a day
3rd Trimester	8 teaspoons a day	362 calories a day

Figure 5.19 This sample diet is based on a moderately active 26-year-old woman who is 5'5" and who weighs 125 pounds before pregnancy. Nutritional needs differ slightly during pregnancy, so women should consult their doctors or dietitians about what to eat during pregnancy. *Based on this diet, what meals could this woman have for breakfast, lunch, and dinner?*

Figure 5.20 Typical Recommendations for Pregnancy Weight Gain

Weight Range	Average Recommended Weight Gain*
Underweight (below 18.5 BMI)	28–40 pounds
Healthy weight (18.5–24.9 BMI)	25–35 pounds
Overweight (25.0–29.9 BMI)	15–25 pounds
Obese (all classes: over 29.9 BMI)	11–20 pounds

*These weight gain recommendations by the Institute of Medicine are only typical for specific BMIs. The doctor will advise for each specific case.

Many doctors suggest pregnant women do the following:

- Have a dental checkup. Recent studies show a link between gum disease in pregnancy and early birth.
- Avoid very cold or very hot baths and hot tubs.
- Wear comfortable clothes with low-heeled or flat shoes.
- Replace baths with showers or sponge baths during the last four to six weeks of pregnancy. This practice helps to prevent internal infection. It also helps to prevent possible falls.

Rest and Sleep

A mother-to-be needs much rest and sleep. Many doctors advise eight to nine hours of sleep each night. In addition, pregnant women need at

Focus on Health

Reaching a Healthy Weight for Pregnancy

A woman's ability to reach a healthy weight for pregnancy is impacted by her weight before pregnancy. For this reason, women should work to maintain a healthy weight even before they become pregnant and should talk with their doctors to determine what a healthy pregnancy weight would be for them.

Women who start pregnancy at 15 percent or more under a healthy weight more often have low-birthweight babies when compared to women of healthy weight. Being underweight can also lead to other problems that endanger the health of both mother and baby.

Women who start pregnancy at 20 percent or above their healthy weight have more complications, too. They experience more fatigue, high blood pressure, heart strain, and blood sugar problems.

Each woman should know her healthy weight, which is based on body build and age. If unsure, doctors can provide this information. Reaching a healthy weight *before* becoming pregnant should be the goal.

A large or sudden weight change is not advised in pregnancy. Discuss in a small group why this might be.

Figure 5.21 Weight Gained During Pregnancy

Portion of Added Weight	Weight Gain in Pounds
Baby	7–8
Amniotic fluid	2
Placenta	1–2
Uterus growth	2
Extra blood volume	3–5
Breast tissue growth	1–2
Other body fluids	3–5
Fat stores and other body tissues	6–9
Total weight gain	**25–35 pounds**

least one 15- to 30-minute rest (with or without sleep) during the day. Many women feel the most tired during the first few months and last weeks of pregnancy. Exhaustion is never good, especially in pregnancy. A sleepless night, however, is not dangerous. If a woman has frequent sleep problems, she should talk with her doctor. She should never take drugs (even over-the-counter medications) unless prescribed by her doctor.

Lesson 5.3 Review and Assessment

1. How can a woman's health habits *prior to* pregnancy affect the health and development of her baby *during* pregnancy?
2. List the six types of nutrients and their functions.
3. What are some presumptive signs of pregnancy? What are some positive signs?
4. Describe a typical first prenatal appointment.
5. List the types of prenatal testing described in this lesson, as well as what each procedure tests for.
6. Why is a woman's nutrition important to her baby's development?
7. A woman should gain approximately _____ pounds during pregnancy.
8. **Critical thinking.** Margaret, a professional at a high-stress job, has just found out she is pregnant. Margaret sleeps about four hours every night and wakes up at five in the morning to go to the gym for two hours. By the time she gets home, she does not have time to cook dinner and so goes out with her husband instead. If you were Margaret's doctor, what changes would you suggest she make to her daily schedule? What would be your reasoning?

Figure 5.22 Physical activity has many benefits for pregnant women. *What types of physical activities should pregnant women avoid?*

Chapter 5

Review and Assessment

Summary

The nine-month pregnancy process begins with conception. At this moment, ovum and sperm unite and combine to form a single cell. In this one cell is all the genetic information the child will receive from each parent. Prenatal development is divided into three stages. In the germinal stage, the dividing cells of the zygote travel toward and then embed in the wall of the uterus. Almost all body systems develop during the embryonic stage. The fetal stage lasts from about nine weeks until birth. During this stage, the fetus grows and its body systems mature.

Children inherit an equal number of chromosomes from mother and father. A person's traits are determined through the pairing of dominant and recessive genes on the chromosomes. Genetic and chromosomal disorders can arise from genetic, environmental, or a combination of both factors. Prior to pregnancy, women should practice healthy habits such as good nutrition and regular exercise. Pregnant women should have frequent doctor appointments. During these appointments, doctors will monitor a pregnant woman's health and perform prenatal tests to track the baby's development and detect any possible complications. During pregnancy, a woman should maintain good nutrition, avoid harmful substances, and get plenty of exercise and sleep.

College and Career Portfolio

Portfolio Checklist

Now that you know the purpose of your portfolio and how you will organize your portfolio, consider what items you want to include. If your portfolio is for a college program, you might include transcripts, a statement of purpose, or samples of your work. As you progress through this book, you will be advised about additional items to include in your portfolio.

It is helpful to have a checklist of components that should be included in your portfolio. Your instructor may provide you with or guide you in creating a checklist. Make sure to create a checklist that works best for you and for the purpose of your portfolio. Complete the following steps to create your portfolio checklist:

- Compile a checklist of the items you want to include. If you need guidance, talk to your teacher or to a college or career counselor.
- Save your checklist to an easy-to-access location in your e-Portfolio. Also print a copy and place it somewhere you can easily reference it.

Chapter 5 Review and Assessment

Vocabulary Activities 

1. In teams, create categories for the following terms and classify as many of the terms as possible. Then, share your ideas with the remainder of the class.

Key Terms

age of viability (5.1)
AIDS (5.2)
amniocentesis (5.3)
amnion (5.1)
cervix (5.1)
chorion (5.1)
chorionic villus sampling (CVS) (5.3)
chromosomal disorders (5.2)
chromosomes (5.2)
conception (5.1)
congenital condition (5.3)
diabetes (5.2)
dominant traits (5.2)
Down syndrome (5.2)
embryo (5.1)
embryonic stage (5.1)
environmental factors (5.2)
fallopian tubes (5.1)
fetal alcohol spectrum disorders (FASDs) (5.2)
fetal stage (5.1)
fetus (5.1)
folic acid (5.3)
genetic disorder (5.2)
genetic factors (5.2)
germinal stage (5.1)
HIV (5.2)
MyPlate (5.3)
nutrients (5.3)
obstetricians (5.3)
ovaries (5.1)
ovum (5.1)
period of gestation (5.1)
placenta (5.1)
pregnancy-induced hypertension (PIH) (5.2)
premature birth (5.3)
prenatal development (5.1)
prenatal vitamin (5.3)
quickening (5.1)
recessive traits (5.2)
Rh factor (5.2)
rubella (5.2)
sexually transmitted infections (STIs) (5.2)
sperm (5.1)
testes (5.1)
ultrasound (5.3)
umbilical cord (5.1)
uterus (5.1)
zygote (5.1)

2. Read the text passages that contain each of the following terms. Then write the definitions of each term in your own words. Double-check your definitions by rereading the text and using the text glossary.

Academic Terms

abnormalities (5.2)
botanist (5.2)
cell (5.1)
deflected (5.3)
embed (5.1)
exert (5.2)
exponentially (5.2)
formative (5.1)
noninvasive (5.3)
optimum (5.3)
prompt (5.3)
severity (5.3)
subsequent (5.1)
synthetic (5.3)
trimester (5.1)
vulnerable (5.2)

Critical Thinking

3. **Make inferences.** How do the stages in prenatal development follow the principles of growth and development (that is, growth and development are constant, happen in sequenced steps, happen at different rates, and have interrelated parts)? Give specific examples as part of your explanation.
4. **Identify.** Create a checklist that contains all the prenatal changes described in this lesson. Make three copies of this checklist and label each checklist with one of the stages of prenatal development. Then, for each stage, check off the changes that have already occurred. Highlight the changes that are occurring. Have a partner check your checklists for accuracy.
5. **Compare and contrast.** On separate index cards, write three or more factors that might affect an unborn baby. Then, in small groups, pool your index cards and read them aloud. Through discussion, sort the index cards into genetic factors and environmental factors.
6. **Draw conclusions.** Two parents with blood types A and B want to have a child with blood type O. Is this possible? Under what, if any, circumstances could this couple have a child with blood type O?
7. **Cause and effect.** Divide a piece of paper into two columns—one labeled *negative effect* and the other labeled *positive effect*. Then, list at least twelve potential behaviors or habits of pregnant women, identifying what type of effect each behavior might have on the developing fetus.
8. **Analyze.** A young couple you know is trying to get pregnant, and recently they have splurged on junk food and stopped exercising, with the reasoning that they want to "have fun" before they become pregnant. Is this a good idea or a bad one? Analyze how, if at all, these actions might affect their planned pregnancy.

9. **Evaluate.** Imagine that you are a doctor, and a woman has just come to your office telling you she is pregnant. Her breasts feel tender, she has been having morning sickness, and she always feels tired. Evaluate these signs as either positive or presumptive. What other signs might you check for?
10. **Determine.** Your friend has just become pregnant, and she feels overwhelmed by all of the medical appointments and lifestyle changes suggested to her. To help her cope, create an organized list of all the medical appointments your friend should schedule, as well as any changes she should consider making to her lifestyle. Break these goals down into small tasks to help your friend feel less overwhelmed.

Core Skills

11. **Writing and speaking.** Imagine you are a school teacher, and your next unit in class is about conception. You must teach this concept to a class of sixth graders and a class of eighth graders. For each class, write a one-page explanation appropriate for that age group. Choose one explanation and give this speech to your class.
12. **Art, technology, and speaking.** Using material or electronic supplies, create a month-by-month illustration of a developing baby during gestation. (See Figure 5.6 for example.) Once you have finished these illustrations, compile them into a slideshow presentation describing the developmental changes that occur during the months of gestation. Deliver your presentation to the class.
13. **Writing.** Write a story about prenatal development from the unborn baby's point of view. Use your creativity to explore what life might be like for the baby as new developments occur before birth. Check your story for correct spelling, grammar, and punctuation.
14. **Health and technology.** Create an electronic presentation entitled "Eating for Two Requires Careful Planning." Include sample menus for a pregnant woman for one week. You might also include pictures or a list of some fattening, nonessential foods she should avoid. Share your presentations with the class.
15. **Reading, speaking, and listening.** Read at least three reliable articles concerning prenatal care. Write a brief essay describing the main points of each article. Include the title of each article and the author. Present your main points to the class. As you listen to other presentations, write three questions you have. Ask one of your questions and write the presenter's response.
16. **Math.** A newly pregnant woman has a healthy weight of 128 pounds. Based on the recommendations for pregnancy weight gain, what percentage of her own weight should she gain during her pregnancy? What percentage of her own weight should she gain if she is having twins?
17. **Research and advocacy.** Research organizations in your community that provide services for expectant parents. Do any of the organizations provide prenatal or childbirth classes? Are classes offered for parenting, providing daily care for infants, and first aid? Do any of the organizations use volunteers? Choose one organization to visit and learn more about its history and goals. Take it a step further and become a volunteer to help the organization.
18. **CTE Career Readiness Practice.** Complete an oral history by interviewing a relatively new mother about her pregnancy. If you are unable to interview someone, read one or more case studies about pregnancy from reliable Internet or library resources. How does the information you learned from the interview or reading compare to information presented by the author of your text? Write a detailed summary of your interview or reading, describing the experience of pregnancy.

Observations

19. Observe your physical features. Which features seem to come from your mother's family and which from your father's family? Which features do you share with other relatives? If you wish, you can observe another person and his or her family.
20. Either online or at a local art gallery, observe works of art that illustrate pregnancy. What aspects of pregnancy do they emphasize? Are there any aspects of pregnancy they avoid? How reflective do you think this art is of a woman's experience of pregnancy?

Chapter 6 Special Circumstances of Pregnancy

Essential Question

What are some medical and social circumstances that may affect a pregnancy?

Lesson 6.1 Special Medical Concerns of Pregnancy

Lesson 6.2 Teen Pregnancy

Case Study What Are the Consequences of Teen Parenthood?

As a class, read the case study and discuss the questions that follow. After you finish studying the chapter, discuss this case study again. Have your opinions changed based on what you learned?

Kelly, a high school junior, and Brantley, a high school senior, have been dating for a while. Kelly and Brantley had a magical evening together at prom and ended the night by having sex for the first time. Kelly thought that after having sex with Brantley, they would be even closer as a couple. Instead, they saw each other less and less. Then, to her dismay, Kelly discovered she was pregnant.

When Kelly told Brantley about the pregnancy, he angrily retorted, "Why weren't you using contraceptives? How do I even know the baby's mine? Maybe you should just get an abortion." Kelly tried to respond to Brantley, but he cut her off by saying, "I don't want anything to do with you or your baby."

Kelly was stunned and hurt by Brantley's reaction and didn't know what to do. She was afraid to talk to her parents because she knew they would be disappointed. They wanted her to go to college, and now she didn't even know if she would finish high school. She did not believe in abortion, but didn't know if she could raise a child on her own. Her parents could barely manage financially and she had no income herself. Kelly wondered whether she and the baby would be covered by her parents' insurance. If not, what then?

Give It Some Thought

1. Is Brantley being fair to Kelly? Is Kelly being fair to expect Brantley to be involved? What legal responsibilities or problems might Brantley face? Explain your answers.
2. What problems will Kelly likely face now and for many years to come? What other options might she have?
3. What plans do Kelly and her family need to make?

While studying this chapter, look for the online resources icon  to:

- **Practice** terms with e-flash cards and interactive games
- **Assess** what you learn by completing self-assessment quizzes
- **Expand** knowledge with interactive activities and graphic organizers

Companion G-W Learning

www.g-wlearning.com/childdevelopment

Study on the go

Use a mobile device to practice terms and review with self-assessment quizzes.

www.m.g-wlearning.com/0384

Lesson 6.1 Special Medical Concerns of Pregnancy

Key Terms

artificial insemination
assisted reproductive technologies (ARTs)
fertility counseling
fraternal births
gamete intrafallopian transfer (GIFT)
identical births
infertile
in vitro fertilization (IVF)
low-birthweight
miscarriage
mixed-type births
multiple pregnancy
preterm birth
sterile
stillbirth
surrogate mother

Academic Terms

defective
endeavors
expulsion
hamper

Objectives

After studying this lesson, you will be able to

- describe three of the most common ART procedures.
- recognize possible drawbacks of fertility treatments.
- compare and contrast the three different types of multiple pregnancies.
- explain two complications of pregnancy and three congenital conditions.

Reading and Writing Activity

Before reading, skim this lesson and write the caption questions on a separate piece of paper. Then, answer the questions based on what you already know. After reading, revisit the caption questions. Would you change any of your answers based on what you learned? For each correct answer, write a sentence explaining why your answer is still correct. For each incorrect answer, write a sentence explaining how you would correct your answer.

Graphic Organizer

Draw four columns and label each column with one of the lesson objectives. Then, as you are reading, write what you learn about each topic in the appropriate column. Share your responses with the class.

After studying this lesson, you will be able to			
describe three of the most common ART procedures.	recognize possible drawbacks of fertility treatments.	compare and contrast the three different types of multiple pregnancies.	explain two complications of pregnancy and three congenital conditions.

For many women trying to become pregnant, the course of events is to conceive a baby within a year. For some couples, however, fertility becomes an issue. The fertility rates in the United States are declining for two reasons. These reasons include trying to conceive after the optimal time for childbearing and having reproductive organ damage often caused by STIs and other high-risk behaviors, such as smoking and consuming alcohol, taking some harmful medications, and using illegal drugs. Thus, women and men wanting to conceive undergo fertility treatments.

Closely connected to fertility treatments is the rising occurrence of multiple pregnancies. When fertility treatments include hormones, the ovaries are stimulated to overproduce mature eggs resulting in multiple pregnancies. Similarly, just before the end of a woman's reproductive years, the ovaries may produce more hormones for a few months resulting in multiple pregnancies.

Infertility and Sterility

About 94 percent of all couples who try to conceive will do so within a year. Couples who try to conceive and are unable to do so within a year are known as **infertile**. If a woman loses pregnancies over and over, it is also called *infertility*. About 40 percent of infertile women do not want children. About two-thirds of infertile couples wanting children will conceive if treated for infertility. The remaining couples will not successfully conceive because one or both partners are sterile. Being **sterile** means the couple is permanently unable to conceive or the woman is unable to carry their biological child.

People often think that women account for almost all fertility problems. In one-third of the cases, infertility is due to the woman. In another one-third of the cases, it is due to the man. The remaining cases are caused by a combination of both partners or by unknown reasons. When both adults are infertile, they have a much lower chance to conceive than couples with only one infertile partner.

Reproductive diseases and problems with the reproductive organs are the main causes of infertility and sterility (**Figure 6.1**). Certain diseases, such as diabetes, and some prescription drugs, such as those for high blood pressure, may lessen fertility. Being exposed to drugs, chemicals, and radiation can **hamper** (interfere with) fertility. The same is true of sexually transmitted infections and smoking. Excessive physical activity, being overweight or underweight, and aging can also lead to fertility problems.

Treating Infertility

Infertile couples who want to pursue having biological children can seek fertility counseling. **Fertility counseling** is a medical evaluation that seeks to determine the reasons for fertility problems and explores available treatment options. Tests are given to determine the problem. If a problem is found, the doctor may suggest steps to restore fertility.

Assisted reproductive technologies (ARTs) are methods infertile couples may use to help them conceive. The most common treatments include using hormones or drugs to stimulate ovulation or balance hormone levels. Sometimes surgery is used to repair problems with the reproductive organs. If these treatments cannot correct the problem, then other methods may help infertile couples

Figure 6.1 Major Causes of Infertility and Sterility

Women	Men
Lack of ovulation	Low sperm count
Hormone deficiencies	Hormone deficiencies
Irregular ovulation	Inability of sperm to move (called *motility problems*)
Damage to reproductive organs	Damage to reproductive organs

conceive. Following are three of the most common ART procedures:

- **Artificial insemination** (also called *intrauterine insemination*) occurs when the sperm is introduced into the vagina or uterus by a medical procedure rather than by intercourse.
- **In vitro fertilization (IVF)** occurs when some of the mother's eggs are surgically removed and fertilized with sperm in a laboratory dish (**Figure 6.2**). After a few days, fertilized eggs are implanted in the mother's uterus.
- **Gamete intrafallopian transfer (GIFT)** occurs when a mixture of sperm and eggs is placed in the woman's fallopian tubes, where fertilization can occur. Because more than one egg is present, conception is more likely, but a *multiple pregnancy* can occur, too.

In some cases, problems exist with the sperm, eggs, or both the sperm and eggs of the couple. For example, one or both partners may be sterile. When these problems exist, couples may opt to use an ART with the germ cells (sperm, eggs, or sperm and eggs) donated by other people. These donor cells would be used to attempt conception usually through IVF or GIFT.

Figure 6.2 The in vitro fertilization process involves combining the egg and sperm in a petri dish and then implanting into the mother's uterus. *What fertility problems does this ART method seek to circumvent?*

If the wife cannot carry a baby, the couple might consider using a **surrogate mother**, or a woman who bears (sometimes both conceives and bears) a child for a couple. The surrogate would carry the baby in her uterus, give birth to the baby, and sign her parenting rights over to the couple. She could conceive using an ART with the wife's eggs or donate her own eggs if the wife's eggs cannot be used. **Figure 6.3** shows different ART methods and potential problems for each method.

Drawbacks of Fertility Treatments

There are many drawbacks to fertility treatments. Couples need to consider the following possible drawbacks:

- Fertility problems are emotionally painful for couples.
- Couples may also feel their privacy is violated during fertility testing and treatment.
- If only one partner has the fertility problem, he or she may feel damaged, **defective** (flawed; imperfect), or guilty.
- Only about 50 percent of couples having treatments succeed after just one treatment. Older couples often have the least chance of succeeding.
- Treatments are very expensive (**Figure 6.4**). Additional expense may be incurred traveling to major hospitals for treatment.
- For some couples, ethical issues are involved with the use of any ART. For many other couples, ethical, legal, and biological issues are involved when donor egg and sperm are used or if a surrogate mother bears the baby (**Figure 6.5**).

Because of these drawbacks, many couples choose not to pursue their options regarding ARTs. Others try, but find they cannot restore their fertility. Both types of couples may face or experience a crisis as they adjust to this reality. For some people who deeply desire children, there may be a lasting sense of being unfulfilled. Counseling may help them resolve these feelings. Many other couples become fulfilled parents through adoption or foster parenthood. Some childless couples find fulfillment in

Figure 6.3 ARTs Methods

Method	Used to...	Problems
Artificial insemination (also called *intrauterine insemination*)	Provide increased number of sperm for conception in biological mother. Impregnate surrogate mother.	Slight risk of infection If sperm is not husband's, moral issues and legal issues (legitimacy and biological father's rights)
Hormone therapy (fertility drugs)	Stimulate ovaries to function properly.	Multiple pregnancies Possible increased risk for female cancers
Microsurgery	Attempt to open the fallopian tubes.	Risks of surgery, such as anesthetic and infection risks
In vitro fertilization (IVF)	Allow a woman with permanently blocked fallopian tubes to have her eggs surgically removed and fertilized with her husband's sperm in a laboratory dish. After a few days, the fertilized eggs are implanted in the mother's uterus. Impregnate surrogate mother.	Risks of surgery Multiple births Moral and legal issues
Gamete Intrafallopian Transfer (GIFT)	Increase chances of conception if men have a low sperm count or women have problems ovulating. (A mixture of sperm and several eggs are surgically placed in the fallopian tubes.)	Risks of surgery Multiple births
Surrogate mother	Replace the infertile couple's role in bearing a child. Surrogate mother (a) may bear a child who is the infertile couple's biological child conceived by in vitro fertilization, (b) may bear a child with her egg and the husband's sperm—of the infertile couple—that were introduced to the surrogate mother through artificial insemination, or (c) may bear a child not biologically related to the infertile couple by using her own eggs and donor sperm introduced through artificial insemination.	Moral issues Legal issues

other **endeavors** (attempts to achieve plans and goals) involving families and children.

Multiple Pregnancies

Sometimes two or more babies develop in the same pregnancy (called a **multiple pregnancy**). Multiple pregnancies are far less common than single pregnancies (**Figure 6.6**). Notice twins are more common than triplets, and triplets are more common than quadruplets. As many as seven or eight babies can be conceived in the same pregnancy in very rare cases.

Doctors are often concerned about the health of multiple births with three or more babies. Most babies in these births are born early and have low-birthweights. A **low-birthweight** is a weight

Figure 6.4 Costs of ARTs

Treatment	Cost
Ovulation hormones	$20 per month
Microsurgery to open fallopian tubes	$90,000 to $100,000
Injectable hormones	$2,500 to $3,500 per month
Artificial insemination (intrauterine insemination)	$500 to $700 per try (but often combined with hormones or donor sperm)
In vitro fertilization	$13,000 to $14,000
In vitro fertilization with frozen embryo	$25,000 beyond IVF cost
Donor eggs	$24,000 to $25,000 per month
Donor sperm	$500 per vial
Surrogate mother	$80,000 to $100,000 through an agency; less expensive if using a relative or friend

under 5.5 pounds at birth for a single birth and under 3.3 pounds per baby in a multiple birth. This puts them at risk for severe vision, hearing, intellectual, and developmental disabilities. Twins are also almost 5 times (triplets almost 10 times) more likely to die in their first year than single-birth children.

Types of Multiple Pregnancies

Twin type or *multiple type* refers to the classifications of twins and larger sets of multiples. The most common way to describe multiples is by *zygosity* (zy-GAWS-uh-tee)—whether the multiples developed from one zygote or more. Types of multiple pregnancies include fraternal births, identical births, and higher-multiple births.

Fraternal Births

The most common multiple pregnancy is caused when multiple babies develop from two or more ova. Each ova is fertilized with a different sperm, which means each child has a different genetic makeup. These babies are as much alike and different as any other brothers and sisters. Children born in these multiple births are called **fraternal births** or *dizygotic* (DYE-zye-GAW-tik) *births*. (*Fraternal* comes from a Latin word meaning *brother*.)

Multiple ovulation, when more than one egg is released, makes fraternal multiples possible. Multiple ovulation is due to hormones that stimulate ovulation. The *Investigate Special Topics: Factors Affecting Fraternal Multiple Births* feature in this lesson explains this common factor. If you have a history of multiple births in your family, do you have a better chance of having multiple births? If *fraternal* multiples were born on your *mother's side* of the family, you have a better chance of having fraternal (not identical) births because the production of extra hormones is hereditary.

The most common type of fraternal births is fraternal twins. Fraternal twins represent about three-fourths of all twins. Fraternal children may or may not be the same gender. Of these fraternal twins, 25 percent are female pairs, 25 percent are male pairs, and 50 percent are female-male pairs. Fraternal twins can be as alike as or as different from any two single-born children in the same family. They often look different at birth and show greater differences as they mature.

Identical Births

In **identical births**, called *monozygotic* (MAWN-oh-zye-GAWT-ik) *births*, children develop from a single ovum fertilized by a single sperm. Before the zygote embeds in the uterine wall, the ovum splits to produce two or more children. Scientists

Figure 6.5 Issues Involving ARTs

Ethical issues	Ethical issues center on the artificial nature of conception. • Some couples do not approve of any ARTs, even when the procedure involves the couple's eggs and sperm. • More people believe ART is a moral issue when someone other than the couple is involved in the pregnancy by being an egg or sperm donor or serving as a surrogate mother. • For better outcomes for implanted embryos and the safety of the mother, most doctors today reduce the number of embryos to two or three before implantation in the IVF procedure. The age of the mother often determines how many are implanted (often three for older women). The "quality" of the embryos may determine which ones are selected for implantation. The moral issue centers on the destruction of the embryos that are not implanted.
Legal issues	Legal problems center on contracts and fees. **Contracts** • What if the donor of the egg or sperm wants parenting rights or changes her or his mind? • What happens if the surrogate decides she wants to keep the baby who may also be her child biologically? • What happens if the couple decides they do not want this child because they have conceived or adopted in the meantime or the child has a disability? **Fees** • Who pays if the surrogate mother's and/or the newborn's medical fees are much higher than the contract fee? • Who pays if the contract is broken by either party? How much? Who pays more for legal fees, time spent, or possible psychological issues?
Biological issues	Biological problems center on heredity issues involved in close relatives parenting. • Should egg and sperm donors be allowed to parent many offspring? (Some women have donated eggs several times, and some men have parented hundreds of children through donations to sperm banks. For banks, donors receive money for their donated egg and sperm cells.) • How can couples know for sure they are not marrying close relatives, even half brothers or sisters? How can they be protected from the higher risk of having children born with genetic defects?

do not know why the ovum splits. Heredity does not seem to contribute to monozygotic births. Identical twins occur in about one-third of multiple pregnancies. Thus, the chances of identical births are much less than the odds for fraternal births (**Figure 6.7**).

Babies from an identical birth have the same genome. Because identical children are very similar in appearance, people often confuse which child is which. Even family members may confuse them. Except for their genes, identical children are not exactly alike because their epigenome creates some

Figure 6.6 Chances of Having Spontaneous Multiples*

Twins	1 in 83 pregnancies
Triplets	1 in almost 7 thousand pregnancies
Quadruplets	1 in about 572 thousand pregnancies
Quintuplets	1 in about 47.5 million pregnancies
Sextuplets	1 in almost 4 billion pregnancies

*These numbers exclude pregnancies of women using ART.

Investigate Special Topics: Factors Affecting Fraternal Multiple Births

Although fraternal multiple pregnancies are not as common as single pregnancies, they have become more common. This is due to several factors.

Maternal age (Although it is more difficult for older women to conceive, those who do are more likely to have fraternal multiple births than younger women.)

- Rate doubles between 35 and 40 years of age.
- Rate decreases between 40 and 45 years of age.
- After 45 years of age, one in nine pregnancies are multiples.

Better nutrition

- Good nutrition aids hormones.
- Taller and heavier (not obese) women have more fraternal multiple births.

History of earlier pregnancies

- Compared to the first pregnancy, the rate increases four times for the fourth or fifth pregnancy.
- Rate is four times greater for women who have had multiples over those who have had singletons.

Fraternal multiple pregnancies on the maternal side of the family

- Production of extra hormones needed for multiple ovulation runs in families.
- Better nutrition from prenatal stage through childhood appears to run in families.

Use of ARTs

The hormones in fertility drugs stimulate ovulation. Thus, successful ARTs almost always produce fraternal multiple pregnancies. In the 1990s when ARTs were new, it was not uncommon for some of these women to have more than three babies. Higher-number multiples, however, are now on the decline due to improvements in ARTs.

Common factor in fraternal multiple births

Is there something common about these factors? Yes, they all increase the chances of multiple ovulation due to hormones.

Reading Activity

In small groups, write responses to the following questions. Then, pass your responses to the next group. Read the responses you receive and add any follow-up questions or comments.

1. What might be some benefits of having a multiple pregnancy?
2. What might be some challenges of having a multiple pregnancy?
3. How would having a multiple pregnancy change the way a mother prepares for childbirth and parenting?

differences. Their fingerprints, palm prints, and footprints are similar, but not exactly the same. Also, environment makes identical children different. For example, one child may be larger because of better nourishment, even before birth.

Some identical twins are *mirror twins*—they look the way you and your mirror image would appear. For instance, one may have a birthmark on the right shoulder and the other may have one on the left shoulder. One may be right-handed while the other is left-handed.

If the ovum does not completely split, the babies will be *conjoined twins*. The bodies of these twins are joined in one or more places. They may share external body parts, such as legs, or internal organs, such as the liver. Conjoined twins occur in about one in 250,000 live births.

Higher-Multiple Births

Higher-multiple births, three or more babies born to one woman from a single pregnancy, are sometimes called *supertwins*. In these higher-multiple

Figure 6.7 **Chances of Having Spontaneous Identical Multiples***

Twins	1 in 250 pregnancies
Triplets	1 in almost 62.5 thousand pregnancies
Quadruplets	1 in over 15.5 million pregnancies
Quintuplets	1 in almost 4 billion pregnancies

*These numbers exclude pregnancies of women using ART.

births, the children can be all identical, all fraternal, or mixed type. Of higher-multiple births, most are **mixed-type births** (two or more babies are identical and one or more are fraternal). If all the children are identical or fraternal, it is not a mixed-type birth.

In mixed types of pregnancies, separate sperm fertilize two or more eggs (fraternal). Then, one or more of the fertilized ova may split (identical). Triplets are often from a mixed-type pregnancy, with two children identical and one fraternal (**Figure 6.8**). Quadruplets are often from a mixed-type birth. With quadruplets, there could be several combinations of fraternal and identical children.

Testing for Multiple Pregnancy Type

Mixed-gender children are always fraternal. Same-gender children may be identical or fraternal. In higher multiples, both fraternal and identical are common. Sometimes it is impossible to tell zygosity by looking at children. The way children look is not the same as the genome.

At one time, doctors determined whether children were identical or fraternal by examining the amniotic sacs after delivery. Identical births share the same sac, but fraternal children each have their own sac. Today, ultrasound can be used to see the sac or sacs before birth. More accurate testing is done through blood specimens taken from newborns or their placentas. Cells can also be collected by swabbing the inside of babies' cheeks and sent to labs for valid DNA testing.

Why is testing important? Mainly, knowledge of DNA is helpful for medical reasons. Parents can also use this information to help them understand differences and similarities in their children's growth and development.

Pregnancy Complications

Any mother can have pregnancy complications. Some pregnancies, however, are considered "high risk" because of a great chance of complications. High-risk mothers include teen mothers, which is discussed in Lesson 6.2. Older mothers are also at greater risks for complications, and their babies are at an increased risk for abnormalities compared with those of younger women. Multiple births are high risk, especially higher-multiple births.

Figure 6.8 A combination of fraternal and identical multiples is called a *mixed-type pregnancy*. *How do mixed-type pregnancies occur?*

Finally, any mother-to-be not in optimal health before pregnancy has increased risks of pregnancy complications.

Pregnant women can greatly reduce the chance of complications in their pregnancies by receiving prenatal care, following their doctors' advice, and practicing good health habits. Complications can occur, however, in any pregnancy. **Figure 6.9** describes the major complications of pregnancy. Complications can damage the mother's health, and some can result in congenital conditions or the loss of the baby before birth. Prenatal care helps doctors note problems early, which allows for needed early treatment.

Congenital Conditions

Congenital conditions may be inherited, caused by environmental factors, or combined genetic and environmental factors. These disabilities and diseases occur with varying degrees of severity. **Figure 6.10** describes the most common congenital conditions.

Preterm Birth

Preterm birth is a delivery that occurs before 39 weeks of pregnancy. (Previously, a pregnancy of 37 weeks was considered term. Due to complications before 39 weeks, term is now considered at

Figure 6.9 Pregnancy Complications

Problem	Causes	Symptoms
Ectopic pregnancy (development of fetus outside of uterus)	Blocked fallopian tube	Spotting and cramping; uterus does not enlarge as it should; rupture of fallopian tube
Too much amniotic fluid	Uncontrolled diabetes; multiple pregnancy; incompatible blood types; congenital problems	Excessive pressure on mother's body; breathing problems; congenital problems in the newborn
Too little amniotic fluid	Congenital problems; growth problems; death of fetus	Fetal movement slows or stops
Bleeding in late pregnancy	Placenta abruptio; placenta previa; vaginal or cervical infection	Bleeding—often heavy
Placenta abruptio (placenta becomes detached from the uterine wall before it should)	Unknown Occurs more in women who smoke, have high blood pressure, have had previous children or a history of detached placentas, suffered injury to the abdomen, and are carrying multiples	Bleeding; cramping; abdominal tenderness
Placenta previa (placenta attaches itself to the uterus near or covering the cervix rather than in the upper half of the uterus)	Scarring of the uterine wall from a prior pregnancy; tumors of the uterus; surgery of the uterus; more common among women who smoke or use drugs, are older than 35, and are carrying multiples	Bright red bleeding without pain or tenderness of the abdomen
Pregnancy-induced hypertension (also called *preeclampsia* or *toxemia*)	Multiple fetuses; teen pregnancy or pregnancy of woman over 40 years of age; high blood pressure; kidney disease	Sudden swelling of hands and face; high blood pressure; headache; dizziness; fever; irritability; protein in urine; abdominal pain; blurred vision; seizures

Figure 6.10 Congenital Conditions

Condition	Symptoms	Causes	Treatment
Cleft lip/palate	Noticeable at birth. A cleft lip occurs when the two sides of the upper lip fail to grow together properly. A cleft palate occurs when an opening remains in the roof of the mouth. This creates problems in breathing, talking, hearing, and eating.	Variable; often caused by a number of factors working together; smoking and severe dieting may be factors	Corrective surgery and speech therapy
Cystic fibrosis	A chemical failure affects lungs and pancreas. Thick sticky mucus forms in the lungs, causing breathing problems. Reduced amounts of digestive juices cause poor digestion of food. An excess amount of salt is excreted in perspiration.	Recessive gene	No cure; physical therapy, synthetic digestive enzymes, salt tablets, and antibodies can lessen the effect of the symptoms; may have shorter-than-normal lifespan because of higher susceptibility to respiratory diseases
Diabetes	Metabolic disorders cause high blood sugar. The person feels thirsty, hungry, and weak and usually loses weight.	A number of factors working together	No cure; can be controlled by insulin injections, careful diet, and physical activity
Down syndrome	Distinct physical features are evident, such as slanting eyes; large, misshapen forehead; oversized tongue; single crease across palm of each hand; and varying degrees of intellectual disabilities are typical.	Chromosome abnormality; more likely to occur when mother is over age 35	Special educational needs; lifespan may be nearly normal
Huntington's chorea	The brain and central nervous system gradually deteriorate when the person is between 30 and 40 years old. This causes involuntary jerking, loss of mental abilities, insanity, depression, and finally death.	Dominant gene	None
Hydrocephalus	Extra fluid is trapped in the brain. The person's head is larger than normal.	A number of factors working together	Surgical removal of excess fluid; without treatment, children rarely survive
Muscular dystrophy	A group of disorders which damage muscles. They cause progressive weakness and finally death.	Often sex-linked	No cure; therapy and braces offer some relief

(Continued)

Figure 6.10 *(Continued)*

Condition	Symptoms	Causes	Treatment
Phenylketonuria (PKU)	An enzyme deficiency makes the person unable to digest a certain amino acid. The baby appears normal at birth, but slowly develops intellectual disabilities because the amino acid builds up in the body and causes brain damage.	Recessive gene	A carefully prescribed diet that balances the enzyme deficiency; the effects of the disease can usually be avoided if treatment begins within the first six weeks of birth
Sickle-cell anemia	Red blood cells are sickle shaped rather than round. They cannot carry oxygen efficiently throughout the body. People become pale, tired, and short of breath. They have occasional pains and low resistance to infection. Their lifespan in often shorter than normal.	Recessive gene often seen in people of Afro-American descent	No cure; various treatments relieve some symptoms; blood transfusions are needed occasionally
Spina bifida (also called *neural tube defect*)	A condition that causes partial paralysis and urinary and bowel incontinence due to an incompletely formed spinal cord. Learning disabilities are also common. Condition varies due to severity.	Heredity and environmental factors	Corrective surgery, physical therapy, and lifelong antibiotics; special educational needs
Tay-Sachs Disease	A lack of a specific chemical in the blood resulting in an inability to process and use fats. Leads to severe brain damage and death, often by age two or three years.	Recessive gene often seen in people of Eastern European Jewish descent	None

39 weeks.) Preterm births are higher for teen and older mothers and for multiple-birth pregnancies. Some common factors also linked to preterm births include having

- a family history of preterm babies
- a preterm baby in the past
- the spacing between deliveries of less than 18 months
- problems with the uterus or cervix
- poor health habits during pregnancy
- late or no prenatal care

Preterm delivery results in a high rate of death during the first month after birth. Preterm delivery can also result in a high incidence of brain disorders, cerebral palsy, chronic lung disease, and developmental delays. Preterm births take an emotional and financial toll on families, too.

When a woman goes into preterm labor, the doctor can try several treatments to prolong the pregnancy. Some treatments work to prevent early labor while others speed up the baby's lung development.

Loss of Baby Before Birth

A **miscarriage** is the **expulsion** (forcing out) of the baby from the mother's body before week 20 of pregnancy. The medical term for miscarriage is *spontaneous abortion*. About 50 to 75 percent of all miscarriages occur around the time of the woman's expected menstrual period. She is unaware of the pregnancy. About 10 to 25 percent of all *known* pregnancies end in the loss of the baby. Most of these miscarriages occur in the first 13 weeks of pregnancy. Although losses frequently occur for unknown reasons, some causes are known (**Figure 6.11**).

Often, the treatment for miscarriage occurring 10 to 12 weeks in the pregnancy is dilation and curettage (CURE-uh-tazh), which is usually called *D&C*. The purpose of a D&C is to remove small pieces of placenta not expelled during the miscarriage and to control heavy bleeding. The 10 to 15 minute outpatient or inpatient procedure involves anesthesia followed by dilating the cervix. The lining of the uterus and its contents are then scraped with a spoon-shaped instrument, called a *curette*, which prevents infections and excessive bleeding. Afterward, drugs to control bleeding and antibiotics are typically given.

Stillbirth is the loss of the fetus after 20 weeks of pregnancy. In a stillbirth, the baby is born dead. Stillbirth occurs in about 1 in 160 pregnancies. The main causes of stillbirth include birth defects, problems with the placenta, bacterial infections occurring between 24 and 27 weeks gestation, and the failure of the baby to grow. Several factors increase the mother's risk (**Figure 6.12**). A presumptive sign of stillbirth is when the mother no longer feels the baby's movements. Stillbirth is often confirmed by ultrasound. Babies who are stillborn are delivered by either *induction* (drugs that start labor) or when labor begins spontaneously. Doctors need to make this call.

Parents grieve after the loss of their unborn. Most parents cope with the support of family, close friends, religious groups, and/or professional groups.

Couples often seek answers about the cause of a miscarriage or stillbirth to help prevent this in a future pregnancy. Having a miscarriage or stillbirth does increase the risk of another. With good medical care, however, many couples can conceive again and deliver healthy babies after the loss of a baby.

Figure 6.11 Common Causes of Miscarriage

- Chromosomal abnormality (due to damaged egg or sperm or to incorrect cell division of the zygote)
- Mother's age (35 years old—15% chance; 36–45 years old—20% to 35% chance; over 45 years old—50% chance)
- Previous miscarriage
- Physical problems (hormones, infections, or other health problems)
- Lifestyle (exposure to health hazards)
- Maternal trauma (accident, extreme stress)

Figure 6.12 Factors That Increase Risk of Stillbirth

- Women 35 years and older
- Malnutrition
- Use of drugs
- Stress
- Genetic and chromosomal disorders of baby
- Separation of placenta from uterus (called *placental abruption*)
- Illness of the mother (diabetes, liver condition, or blood clotting problems)

Lesson 6.1 Review and Assessment 

1. Compare and contrast *infertility* and *sterility.*
2. List three of the most common ART procedures.
3. What are some drawbacks of fertility treatments?
4. List the three types of multiple pregnancies and explain how they occur.
5. Name two complications of pregnancy.
6. Give three examples of congenital conditions.
7. **Critical thinking.** If twins are opposite genders, why must the type of multiple birth be fraternal and not identical?

Lesson 6.2 Teen Pregnancy

Key Terms

abstinence
General Educational Development (GED) test
mortality rate

Academic Terms

adversely
friction
inconsolable
initiate
nonessential
practical

Objectives

After studying this lesson, you will be able to

- determine risks of a sexual relationship.
- describe the negative impacts of teen pregnancy.
- assess support systems available for teen parents.
- evaluate teen pregnancy prevention programs available to teens.

Reading and Writing Activity

Why do you think teen pregnancy is considered a *special circumstance of pregnancy*? Before reading, write a two- to three-paragraph essay explaining some of these reasons and comparing teen pregnancy to pregnancy in young adults. Then, after reading, consider what reasons you might add to your essay. Share your essay and any additional reasons with a partner.

Graphic Organizer

Draw a mindmap like the one shown and write *The Impact of Teen Pregnancy* in the middle circle. Then, as you are reading, write the different kinds of impact teen pregnancy can have on both mother and child.

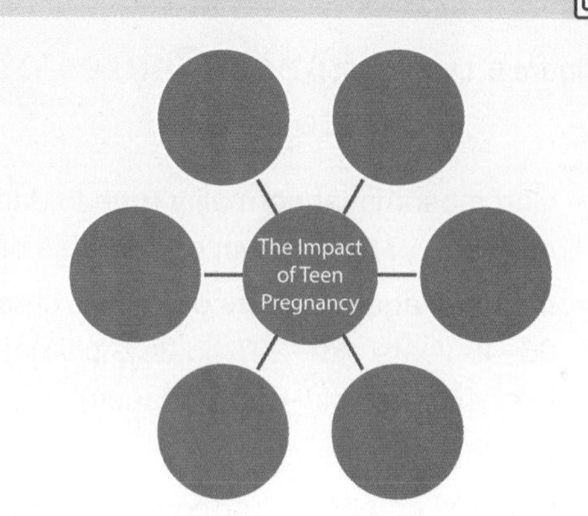

The developmental changes that occur in the teen years are often confusing for teens. Teens' developmental quests result in conflicting feelings. Teens have a quest for closeness in shared relationships. As teens become more physically mature, they experience their flourishing sexuality. Many teens experience romantic love for the first time and, due to their feelings, may seek sexual relationships. These feelings often interact with other quests, such as desiring more independence, learning skills that will allow for their eventual independence, and searching and finding their own identity (**Figure 6.13**).

Because of these quests, teens are not ready to be parents although they are physically capable of reproducing. Parenthood requires they turn their time, energy, and attention away from their own quests and focus on the helpless baby they have brought into the world. This lesson looks at the medical and social consequences of teen parenthood for the teens themselves and for their babies.

Risks of Sexual Relationships

Many teens (and even adults) ask the question: Why should I wait for marriage to have sex if I am in love? First, what many mistake as love is a passing feeling that does not last. Entering a sexual relationship can make a person feel emotionally tied to the other person. Imagine how painful this would make a breakup.

The results of a sexual relationship can be life-altering and permanent. Two of the most troubling risks are unplanned pregnancy and STIs, such as HIV/AIDS. Many birth control methods are available to help reduce the risk of unplanned pregnancy and STIs, but the idea of "completely safe sex" is a myth. The only guaranteed way to avoid unwanted pregnancies and STIs is **abstinence** (refusal to engage in a sexual relationship).

Other risks of sexual relationships teens may experience include

- emotional scars that may follow a broken relationship

Figure 6.13 Teens should consider their futures and plans when they make decisions about their sexuality. Some ways that teens can process these feelings and thoughts include talking with a trusted adult or journaling. *How do you think a person's future plans impact his or her sexual decisions?*

- conflicts with parents and other adults who care for them
- conflicts with their own consciences, goals, and values

Negative Impacts of Teen Pregnancy

Many teen girls become pregnant in the United States each year. One in ten new mothers is a teenager. The rates for teen pregnancies in the United States are higher than in many other developed countries.

Teen parenting is not a random sample of the teenage population. Many teen parents already live in poor circumstances and lack resources and support prior to pregnancy. For example, girls in rural areas of the country have nearly one-third more pregnancies than girls in cities and suburbs. Already being a parent is the greatest risk factor for a teen pregnancy. Eighty-five percent of all teen pregnancies are unplanned.

Teen parenting is a major risk. Becoming a parent in the teen years has no advantages over becoming a parent between 20 and 35 years of age. The risks of teen pregnancy and parenting affect many aspects of the teens' lives, and it is impossible to reverse most of the consequences (**Figure 6.14**). Many of these problems relate to health risks, educational impact, financial concerns, lifestyle changes, and stress and violence. Many teens who choose to parent their babies become single mothers. Being a single, never-married parent results in the highest risk for the child's overall well-being.

Health Risks

Teens' bodies are still growing and developing—only babies in the womb and infants develop more quickly. Because of all these physical changes, proper

Focus on Health

Food Assistance Programs

Many teen parents have an incredibly difficult road ahead for themselves and their children for many reasons. One major consequence of teen parenting is the reality of poverty. Any family living near, at, or below the poverty level will find meeting their basic necessities, such as having an adequate amount of nutritious foods, difficult to impossible unless they receive assistance.

The U.S. government has two food assistance programs that can aid qualifying pregnant teen mothers and teen parents and their children. One program is the *Supplemental Nutrition Assistance Program (SNAP)*. SNAP is an entitlement program provided to all eligible households who apply. The applicant must meet certain requirements pertaining to household size, income, certain expenses, and resources. The program allows recipients to buy almost all food items, but excludes other items sold in grocery stores, such as pet foods, toiletries, cleaning products, and drugs. SNAP also provides information on food purchasing and preparation.

Another program is the *Special Supplemental Nutrition Program for Women, Infants and Children (WIC)*. Like SNAP, WIC provides supplemental nutritious foods, nutrition education, and counseling. Unlike SNAP, WIC is a "discretionary" grant program, which means WIC programs, such as county WIC offices, must stay within their budgets in making eligibility and benefit decisions. WIC serves pregnant, postpartum, and nursing mothers, and infants and children up to their fifth birthdays. WIC applicants must qualify based on income and be considered a "nutrition risk" by a health care provider.

Figure 6.14 Consequences of Teen Parenting

For teen mothers	• Health risks are greater for younger teen mothers and for all teen mothers who do not receive quality prenatal and postnatal care.
	• Many teen mothers never complete high school.
	• Teen mothers lack entry-level skills for the job market. Their income is usually much below that of mothers who have their first child after the teen years.
	• Teen parents who marry are at high risk for divorce. The divorce rate increases between the first and sixth year after marriage.
	• Married teen mothers report major marital problems. These problems include the following:
	  • more sexual activity than they desire
	  • loneliness (Many times a teen husband maintains his social life while the wife assumes more child care responsibility. Also, most teen wives tend to lose touch with friends.)
	  • lack of support (Many times, older men who father many babies are not interested in marriage or parenting. The teen mother may not receive companionship, parenting support, or child support.)

For teen fathers	• Teen fathers have poor school performance and many times drop out of high school. • Teen fathers often lack education and training. For these reasons, they usually cannot earn adequate incomes to support their family. • Unmarried teen fathers report not being able to see their babies when they wish. Married teen fathers report problems with the child's maternal grandparents. • Teen fathers show less self-esteem than other teens because of less education and more financial problems.

For children of teen parents	• The mortality rate is high for babies of mothers who are age 15 years or younger. This death rate is twice as high as that for babies of mothers between ages 20 and 34 years.
	• Babies of teen parents are a greater risk for congenital problems.
	• Children of teens have lower achievement in school because of
	  • having birth defects
	  • being born too soon or too small
	  • having less family income
	• Children of teens are at a higher risk of being abused because of
	  • having birth defects
	  • being born too soon or too small
	  • having parents who do not know when a child is ready to do or learn a task
	  • crying when parents want to sleep, study, or socialize or when parents are depressed

For society	• Often extra child care tasks and the need for more income burdens the grandparents of the teen's child. • Teen parents lose productive income because of their lower-income jobs or unemployment. • Society pays the costs of assistance programs to teen parents. • Society pays for assistance to children and loss of productive income in the next generation if children do not overcome their problems. • Societies may be more violent if children are abused. • The numbers and problems faced by single-parent, divorced, and remarried families may increase.

nutrition is crucial for a teen. When a teen is pregnant, the baby depends on the mother for nutrition, which depletes the mother's body of nutrients. Poor nutrition before or during pregnancy puts both the mother and her baby at risk.

The lack of medical care is another health risk for teen mothers. All mothers-to-be need early and continuous prenatal care. They also need medical care for about two months after delivery. Although the rate of prenatal care has increased, some teens still do not receive care they need early in pregnancy. Approximately seven percent of teen mothers receive no prenatal care. Reasons for this risk are that teen mothers-to-be

- may think they are not pregnant
- feel their parents will be upset by the pregnancy
- are afraid the relationship with the baby's father will end once he learns about the pregnancy (**Figure 6.15**)
- lack money for medical care or do not know where to go for help
- cannot find transportation to a medical facility
- do not know that medical care is necessary
- are afraid of medical procedures

Both mother and baby are affected by these risks. Even with good health care, teen mothers experience other health risks. These include longer labors and thus a great many surgical deliveries. Compared to all mothers, teen mothers are at the highest risk of depression after pregnancy, too. Therefore, care after pregnancy is needed to protect both physical and mental health of the mother and her baby.

The **mortality rate** (rate of death) for the babies of teen mothers is high. Many of the babies who survive have low birthweights. These small babies have higher rates of slow growth throughout childhood. They may have more learning problems in school and more social problems with peers. Health risks increase even more for both mother and baby if the mother smokes, drinks alcohol, or has an untreated STI. Health risks also increase for both mother and baby if the teen mother is younger than 15 years of age or has had more than one pregnancy in the teen years. Many teens have a repeat pregnancy before 20 years of age. On a positive side, with good nutrition and prenatal care, teens are capable of having a healthy pregnancy and a healthy baby.

Figure 6.15 Many teen mothers do not receive prenatal care out of fear that the pregnancy will harm their relationships, either with their parents or with their boyfriends. *Why should a teen mother seek prenatal care even if she is afraid of the pregnancy's impact on her relationships?*

Educational Impact

Pregnancy is the leading factor in limiting a teen's education. Over two-thirds of teen mothers never graduate from high school. On average, teen mothers complete 11.9 years of education versus 13.9 years for teen girls who do not get pregnant.

Why is education often sacrificed? Teen parents find completing their education difficult or impossible for the following reasons:

- Adequate child care is unaffordable.
- Teen parents feel out of place in a traditional school setting because they are older than other students.

- The need for a job, even a low-paying one, may keep teen parents out of school.
- Teen parents' time to study is limited because of their parenting responsibilities.

Many teen-parent families live in poverty. Living in poverty causes problems that **adversely** (unfavorably) affect the lives of teen parents and their children.

Because schools are becoming more involved in educating teen parents, more teens are graduating. Teens who do not graduate can receive a state-issued certificate of high school equivalency if they pass a ***General Educational Development* (GED) test**. A few teen parents who graduate from high school or pass a GED test go to college. In fact, some teen parents are very motivated to get an education in order to better provide for their children. Teens with a high school diploma or a certificate of high school equivalency earn 44 percent more per year than teens not finishing high school or its equivalent (**Figure 6.16**).

Financial Concerns

Prenatal care and delivery are expensive. If teens are covered by their parents' insurance policies, the costs of pregnancy and childbirth may not be covered. Even if the teen mother is covered, the baby may not be covered.

Health problems add to the costs for mother and baby. The added expense of a baby is a real burden for teens, most of whom are financially strapped. Parents must pay for a baby's food, clothing, equipment, and perhaps child care. These costs increase as babies grow.

Sadly, these financial concerns can continue into adulthood. Studies show teens who become parents usually have financial problems all their lives.

Lifestyle Changes

When teens become parents, their lives change in dramatic ways. Those who marry because of a pregnancy may find themselves in unhappy

Figure 6.16 Between the responsibilities of caring for a child and the financial need for a job, it can be difficult for teen parents to study and continue their education. Graduating from high school or earning a GED is important for teen parents because this education can help them obtain higher-paying jobs in the future. *How can the people around a teen parent encourage him or her to pursue an education?*

marriages. They may encounter problems living with their baby in their parents' home. Besides financial pressures, many also socialize less often with friends because they have more responsibility. Teen parents usually lead stressful lives.

Life with Mom and Dad

Teen parents who continue to live with their own parents report additional **friction** (conflict; tension) at home. A teen's parents may have a difficult time adjusting to their teen's early parenthood. They may be disappointed and concerned. They may insist the baby's other parent stay out of the baby's life. Grandparents of the baby often feel the most stress because they are juggling child care, work, and other family obligations. There are often conflicts about childrearing between the teen mother and her parents. Conflicts may concern the general parenting style or possibly specific issues, such as taking responsibility for the child.

Social Life Changes

Before pregnancy, a teen's life focuses on school, social activities, and family. Once a teen becomes a parent, life changes (**Figure 6.17**). Now the teen focuses on the medical aspects of pregnancy, the costs of a baby, and ways to meet the baby's needs. Teen parents have little time to study or spend with friends because baby care takes too much time. Baby expenses leave little or no money to spend on **nonessential** (not vital) items.

Many teen mothers say they feel isolated. Although friends usually stand by teen mothers, they may not maintain the same social contact. This often happens during the pregnancy and after the baby is born, which can lead to depression and frustration for the teen parent.

Figure 6.17 Having a baby changes a person's life, and teen parents often find that their lives are consumed with the responsibilities of caring and providing for a child. This leaves little time for teens to spend time with friends. *What are some other life changes that might come with having a baby?*

Stress and Violence

Teen stress and frustrations may **initiate** (start) family violence. Spouse abuse may occur in unhappy marriages. Children of teens are at high risk for child neglect and abuse. Why does this happen? The major reasons include:

- Teens' needs, such as resolving their own identity, work, study, and socialization do not mesh well with their children's needs.
- Teen parents rarely have enough support in parenting tasks.
- Teens seldom know about child development and may expect their children to reach unreasonable goals. The parents' frustration with a child's "lack of progress" or the **inconsolable** (unable to be soothed) crying baby often leads to child neglect and abuse.

Support Systems for Teen Parents

Although teen parents face challenges, many overcome them and have positive experiences as young parents. Teen parents are individuals, so they differ some in their need for support. Every successful teen parent, however, has a strong support system. Teen mothers with the most support believe their opportunities are not limited. They realize their success only comes from taking responsibility for the pregnancy and having the drive, dedication, and commitment to succeed.

What resources do teen mothers need? As soon as they know they are pregnant, they need to make plans. They need to decide where they are going to live. Teens need to explore other resources quickly because some take time to negotiate (**Figure 6.18**). Teen parents also need people they can turn to for help. Joining support groups may be very helpful for both **practical** (useable; applicable) and emotional support.

Teen Pregnancy Prevention

Teens who have not yet become pregnant need support for pregnancy prevention. Basically, these teens need knowledge about the consequences of teen parenting and pregnancy prevention before they make decisions about sexual activity. Thus, support needs to include the following:

- knowing how to cope with peer sexual pressures, such as an understanding that the majority of teens do not engage in sexual relationships during high school and ways to say "no"

Figure 6.18 Possible Resources for Teen Mothers

Health Care
• Health departments or university clinics offer free or low-cost prenatal care and have patient confidentiality policies. • Schools may have health care services or can advise the teen mother.
Education

• If you are pregnant or parenting, Title IX states that you may go to your school (do *not* have to go to an alternative school), participate in extracurricular activities, access the same quality of classes as other students, and will receive an excused absence from school during childbirth, recovery, and when your child is ill. (*Note*: All schools have a Title IX coordinator.)
• Some schools are dedicated to serving teen mothers and
  • have health care and child care services
  • provide academic support
  • provide group and individual counseling
  • teach parenting skills
  • collaborate with other community organizations
(*Note*: Often a school social worker coordinates the services.)

Financial Support
• *Temporary Assistance for Needy Families (TANF).* Assistance can be provided to low-income teen parents who are in school and meet other qualifications. • *Supplemental Nutrition Assistance Program (SNAP).* Teen mother qualifies if her parents qualify or if married and living with a husband and is financially needy. • *Women, Infants, and Children (WIC).* Provides food and health assistance, such as nutrition education for teen mothers. • Child care assistance. Often local human resource departments issue a child care voucher for a discounted rate. Some states offer child care if the teen stays in school. Check with the local Child Care Resource and Referral Agency (CCRR).

Focus on

Careers

Social and Human Service Assistant

Social and human service assistants work with people in need to determine what type of benefits and community services are available to help them. They determine eligibility for services, such as food assistance or child care programs, and then help the clients complete the necessary paperwork to receive benefits. Social and human service assistants also check in with clients to make sure the services are meeting their needs. They may work under the direct supervision of social workers or other professionals who have more experience.

Career cluster: Human services.

Education: Educational requirements may include an associate's degree or certificate and on-the-job training.

Job outlook: Future employment opportunities for social and human service assistants are expected to grow much faster than the average for all occupations.

To learn more about a career as a social and human service assistant, visit the United States Department of Labor's *Occupational Outlook Handbook* website. You will also be able to compare the job responsibilities, educational requirements, job outlook, and average pay of social and human service assistants with similar occupations.

- knowing how to prevent pregnancy (abstinence or correct and consistent use of effective contraceptive methods) and recognizing myths about pregnancy prevention, such as douching after intercourse
- understanding that most contraceptives do not prevent STIs and no contraceptive can prevent or mend a broken heart
- being aware of the medical and social consequences of pregnancy (and STIs)

Many pregnancy prevention programs are available to teens through their schools, youth organizations, and religious organizations. Two national programs are the *National Campaign to Prevent Teen Pregnancy* and the *President's Teen Pregnancy Prevention Initiative (TPPI)*. Most importantly, parents must guide their teens during their turbulent years by promoting responsible values and behaviors by both men and women.

Lesson 6.2 Review and Assessment 

1. The only guaranteed way to avoid unwanted pregnancies and STIs is _____.
2. What are some risks of sexual relationships?
3. Why might teen mothers-to-be *not* receive necessary prenatal care?
4. List two reasons teen parents find completing their education difficult or impossible.
5. What lifestyle changes accompany teen pregnancy and parenting?
6. List some resources that are available for teen mothers.
7. **Critical thinking.** Discussions about teen pregnancy often center on the challenges and responsibilities of teen mothers, but teen fathers are also affected. What are some ways teen pregnancy impacts teen fathers?

Chapter 6

Review and Assessment

Summary

Many special circumstances can influence the existence or progression of a pregnancy. Some couples may be *infertile*, meaning they cannot conceive children, and some couples may be *sterile*, or permanently unable to conceive children. For infertile couples, there are a variety of ARTs (assisted reproductive technologies), including artificial insemination, in vitro fertilization (IVF), and gamete intrafallopian transfer (GIFT). Couples should consider the drawbacks of these treatments when deciding whether to pursue them.

Multiple pregnancies occur when one or more eggs are fertilized by one or more sperm. Two types of multiple births are fraternal and identical. While fraternal twins differ genetically, identical twins share the same genetic makeup. Higher-multiple births often include combinations of fraternal and identical children. DNA testing can confirm the type of multiple births. Pregnancy complications and congenital conditions can also affect pregnancy and may be damaging to the mother's and the baby's health.

Another special circumstance is teen pregnancy. The only sure way to prevent unwanted pregnancies is abstinence, and there are many risks involved in teen sexual relationships. Teen mothers are at higher risk than older mothers and many do not receive prenatal care. Teen pregnancy can affect teens' educations, finances, and lifestyles, and can also cause stress and lead to child abuse or neglect. Teens should seek support and take advantage of resources to reduce their risks of teen pregnancy.

College and Career Portfolio

Portfolio Resources

Some components of your portfolio may require the help of an outside professional. Before you compile items for your portfolio, identify *where* you will acquire these items, *how* you will acquire them, and *what resources* you will need.

Locate your portfolio checklist and review the items you plan to include. Then, identify any items which you will need outside help to acquire. Identifying these items early will enable you to compile these items in a timely and organized manner.

As you review the items you plan to include in your portfolio, complete the following activities:

- Research how you will acquire these items and then make note of where you need to go or whom you need to talk to, in order to include this item in your portfolio.
- Note the contact information of any people or resources that have been of particular help to you so far in constructing your portfolio.

Chapter 6 Review and Assessment

Vocabulary Activities

1. Review the following terms and identify any terms that can be divided into smaller parts, having *roots* and *suffixes* or *prefixes*. Write these terms on a sheet of paper. Beside each term, list the root word and prefix or suffix. How do root words help you understand meaning? suffixes and prefixes?

Key Terms

abstinence (6.2)
artificial insemination (6.1)
assisted reproductive technologies (ARTs) (6.1)
fertility counseling (6.1)
fraternal births (6.1)
gamete intrafallopian transfer (GIFT) (6.1)
General Educational Development (GED) test (6.2)
identical births (6.1)
infertile (6.1)
in vitro fertilization (IVF) (6.1)
low-birthweight (6.1)
miscarriage (6.1)
mixed-type births (6.1)
mortality rate (6.2)
multiple pregnancy (6.1)
preterm birth (6.1)
sterile (6.1)
stillbirth (6.1)
surrogate mother (6.1)

2. Work in pairs to write a *simile* for each of the following terms. Remember that a simile is a direct comparison of two items or factors that are *not* generally alike. When creating a simile, the comparisons are generally introduced by the words *like*, *as*, *seem*, or *appear*.

Academic Terms

adversely (6.2)
defective (6.1)
endeavors (6.1)
expulsion (6.1)
friction (6.2)
hamper (6.1)
inconsolable (6.2)
initiate (6.2)
nonessential (6.2)
practical (6.2)

Critical Thinking

3. **Cause and effect.** In small groups, use reliable online or print resources to research reproductive diseases that can cause infertility or sterility. Choose three reproductive diseases and summarize their symptoms, causes, and treatments. How do these diseases cause infertility or sterility?
4. **Identify.** ART methods are expertly designed to treat specific fertility problems; therefore, the method of ART chosen depends on a couple's problem. Working with a partner, use Figure 6.3 to match each ART method to one or more major causes of infertility.
5. **Analyze.** Fraternal multiple births are known as *dizygotic*, and identical multiple births are known as *monozygotic*. With a partner, analyze these words and what they mean. How can they help you distinguish between fraternal and identical births?
6. **Make inferences.** Why do statistics for multiple births vary in different parts of the world? Discuss in terms of technology, medical practices, and methods of assisting infertile couples. Is there a connection between infertility treatments and multiple births? Explain.
7. **Compare and contrast.** Choose three congenital conditions discussed in this chapter and identify the causes of the conditions and the types and severities of the disabilities they may cause. Compare and contrast your findings for all three conditions.
8. **Evaluate.** Imagine that your friend has been dating someone at school for six months, and that one day he or she approaches you for advice. His or her dating partner wants to have sex, but your friend is not sure if that is a good idea. With a partner, role-play this conversation and guide your friend through the process of evaluating the situation and measuring the pros and cons of each decision.
9. **Draw conclusions.** Write a short essay drawing conclusions about why mortality rates for teen mothers are higher than they are for mothers of other ages. In your essay, cite examples from this textbook and from reliable scientific sources. Read and discuss your essays in class.
10. **Cause and effect.** Sit in a circle with your classmates and have a round-table discussion about the effects of teen pregnancy on teen lives. Go around the circle clockwise three times. During the first round, name effects on the teen mother. During the second round, name effects on the teen father. During the third round, name effects on families and society.

11. **Determine.** In some cases, teen parents' stress and frustration can lead to family violence. This can be devastating to both teens and their children. What are some ways your community can support teen parents and prevent family violence? Write a letter to your teacher with some recommendations.

Core Skills

12. **Research, speaking, listening, and writing.** As a class, choose an ART method and debate the medical effectiveness (drawbacks versus advantages) and ethics for that method. Divide into two teams. Each team should gather information in support of the method or in opposition to the method. Use your textbook as well as outside sources for support. Compose a presentation arguing for your stance and then deliver it to the other team. As the other team delivers its presentation, listen carefully to their arguments. Take notes on important points and write any questions that occur to you. Ask questions to obtain clarification or additional information, and, if possible, counter their information with information of your own.
13. **Reading.** Read about some court cases involving surrogate mothers. What were the outcomes when the surrogate mother changed her mind about giving her child to the couple as agreed? How might these problems impact the child involved? Write a short account of the court case as well as a summary of your thoughts.
14. **Writing and speaking.** Pick 5–10 key terms from this chapter and write a brief scene in which those 5–10 terms are used as you imagine them being used by medical professionals in a real-life context. Then, rewrite the dialogue using simpler sentences and transitions, as though an adult were describing the same scene to elementary or middle-school students. Read both scenes to the class and ask for feedback.
15. **Research and writing.** In small groups, choose one of the pregnancy complications discussed in this chapter. Identify reliable online or print resources and research how the complication is treated, as well as the chances of survival for both mother and baby. Compose a presentation on the complication and its treatments, and deliver your presentation to the class. Include MLA citations for your sources in the presentation.
16. **Math.** Browse the job listings in your community until you find a job that does not require a high-school education. Note the salary for that job and calculate that employee's total revenue working maximum hours for a year. Compare that number with the current average cost of caring for a child for one year.
17. **Research, technology, and speaking.** Using online or print resources, research teen pregnancy prevention programs available in your community. Then, create a brochure cataloging these resources and giving a brief explanation. Finally, give a short presentation introducing your brochure. If possible, make your brochure available somewhere in your community.
18. **CTE Career Readiness Practice.** The ability to read and interpret information is an important workplace skill. Presume you work for a company that administers ART methods to infertile couples. The company is considering adding gamete intrafallopian transfer (GIFT) to its procedures, but wants you to evaluate and interpret some research on the method. You will need to locate three reliable sources of the latest information and research on GIFT. Read and interpret the information. Then write a report summarizing your findings.

Observations

19. Outside of ARTs, there are many alleged infertility treatments available to the general public. In small groups, research infertility treatments not covered in this chapter. If possible, read accounts of people who tried these treatments. Discuss how one can decide if an infertility treatment is reliable and safe.
20. Observe fraternal or identical siblings and take notes about how similar or different they are. If possible, observe how these siblings' upbringings might differ from the upbringings of single children. Based on these observations, form a hypothesis on why multiple pregnancies are considered a special circumstance.
21. Talk to another teen whom you know has said *no* to sexual activity within his or her dating relationship. How did this teen handle pressures to be sexually active? What were his or her reasons for choosing abstinence? How does he or she feel about that choice?

Chapter 7 Childbirth

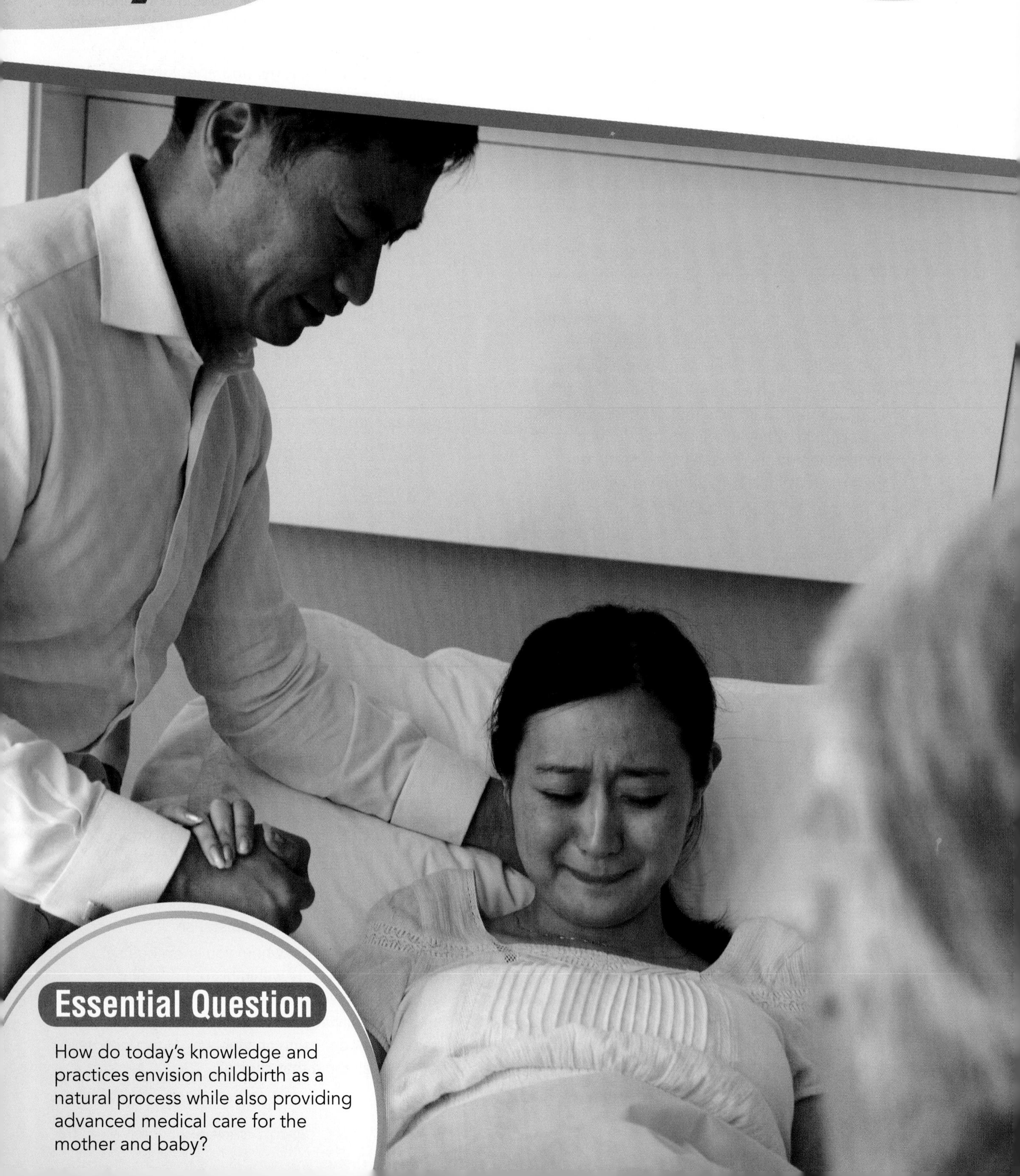

Essential Question

How do today's knowledge and practices envision childbirth as a natural process while also providing advanced medical care for the mother and baby?

Lesson 7.1	Decisions Concerning Childbirth
Lesson 7.2	Time to Be Born
Lesson 7.3	Newborn Medical Care and Tests
Lesson 7.4	Postpartum Care

Case Study How Can Parents Best Cope with a Preterm Birth Crisis?

As a class, read the case study and discuss the questions that follow. After you finish studying the chapter, discuss this case study again. Have your opinions changed based on what you learned?

Some babies are born prematurely and no one knows the cause. So it was with Christy and Matt's baby girl who was born at 25 weeks. The baby was rushed from the delivery room to the neonatal intensive care unit (NICU). The neonatologist told Christy and Matt the baby had a very small chance of surviving, but everything possible would be done for her.

Matt tearfully said to Christy, "I'm not visiting her in the NICU. Did you see how pathetic our baby looked? If I go and become attached to her and she dies, I think I would die, too. If I don't visit and she dies, it will be easier. If she survives and comes home, I'll love her then."

Although Christy knew Matt faced devastating deaths in his childhood, she is unable to understand why he will not see their baby and try to contribute to her survival chances. She would never think of staying home, especially when this could be their only chance with the baby. Christy tries to convince Matt to change his mind. She insists they are both the baby's parents, and the baby needs them both.

Give It Some Thought

1. Matt mentioned how pathetic their baby looked. How does a 25-week baby look?
2. If the baby dies, do you think staying away would help Matt avoid possible pain or increase his pain in the future? Explain your answers.
3. If the baby survives, do you think Matt will feel guilty for not helping during the long hospital stay?
4. How might Christy deal with her husband's reluctance to help?
5. If you were the neonatologist, would you intervene? Explain your answer.

While studying this chapter, look for the online resources icon  to:

- **Practice** terms with e-flash cards and interactive games
- **Assess** what you learn by completing self-assessment quizzes
- **Expand** knowledge with interactive activities and graphic organizers

Companion G-W Learning

www.g-wlearning.com/childdevelopment

Study on the go

Use a mobile device to practice terms and review with self-assessment quizzes.

www.m.g-wlearning.com/0384

Lesson 7.1 Decisions Concerning Childbirth

Key Terms

certified nurse-midwife (CNM)
Family and Medical Leave Act (FMLA)
labor
Lamaze method
maternity leave
natural childbirth
paternity leave
Pregnancy Discrimination Act (PDA)
pregnancy leave

Academic Terms

exclusively
hectic
reassure

Objectives

After studying this lesson, you will be able to

- assess ways family members can be involved during pregnancy.
- describe the *Pregnancy Discrimination Act* and the *Family and Medical Leave Act* and explain how each law affects families during the birth or adoption of a child.
- differentiate among options for a birthplace.
- compare and contrast three methods of delivery.

Reading and Writing Activity

Write a short dialogue in which a couple addresses all the decisions you think need to be made before childbirth. Then, as you are reading, take note of any decisions the couple in your dialogue did not make. Finally, after reading, write a short paragraph detailing what might happen if the couple made only the decisions you wrote about in your dialogue.

Graphic Organizer

In a diagram like the one shown, draw a pregnant couple in the middle circle. Then, as you are reading, write in the outer circles all the decisions and considerations the couple should discuss before childbirth.

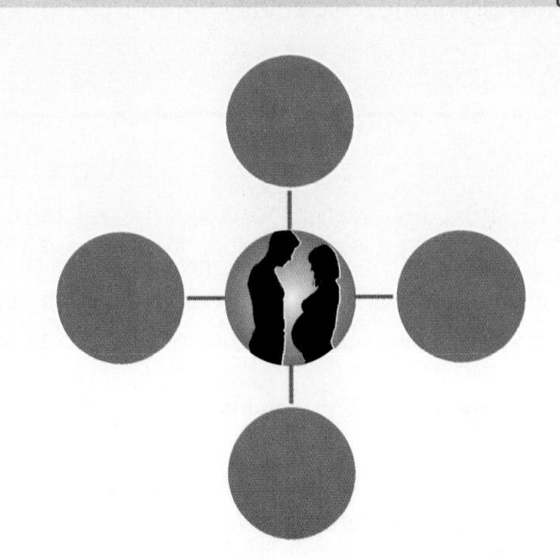

During pregnancy, family members can be involved in the excitement as they offer support to the mother and help prepare for the baby's arrival. The middle part of pregnancy is often the most pleasant for the entire family. Mothers-to-be usually feel their best. Husbands and family members are more aware of the baby because they can see the mother's abdomen grow and feel the baby move. Couples and their children may decorate a nursery and gather items needed for the baby. Couples also take time to plan for the many aspects surrounding childbirth, such as scheduling time away from work, choosing a birthplace, and selecting a method of delivery.

Family Considerations

Parents have many decisions to make before the baby is born. Because these are important decisions, couples need to research each topic before making a decision. **Figure 7.1** shows decisions families may make during the prenatal period. At times, unexpected events may cause couples to change their decisions.

One major decision parents make is to inform other children about the pregnancy. Parents often decide to tell young children about the new baby during the middle of the pregnancy. To some degree, the timing depends on the age of the child. Older children need to know by the time changes in the mother's body are noticeable. In many cases, explanations occur over time, such as when the child asks questions and when preparations are being made.

Parents' explanations may be along the following lines:

- Explain about changes in the body of the mother-to-be or how a baby is born, if asked.
- Familiarize an older child with newborns. Explain how newborns look and act (**Figure 7.2**).
- Assure an older child about what factors will remain the same, such as lots of love, certain activities, and specific housing arrangements.
- Explain and make any changes in housing arrangements or routines before the baby arrives. For example, if the older child is moving to a toddler bed, explain the reason for the new bed is because he or she is growing up. Then wait a while before putting the crib in the area for the new baby.

Figure 7.1 Decisions Facing Parents-to-Be

- Health care provider for prenatal care and delivery
- Birthplace (often tied to the choice of the health care provider)
- Health care provider for the baby
- Mother's support person for delivery
- Name(s) for the baby (babies)
- Breast-feeding or formula-feeding
- Housing arrangements for the baby
- Clothing and equipment for use with the baby
- Support people to help after the baby is born, possibly including child care and education program
- Work and leave options

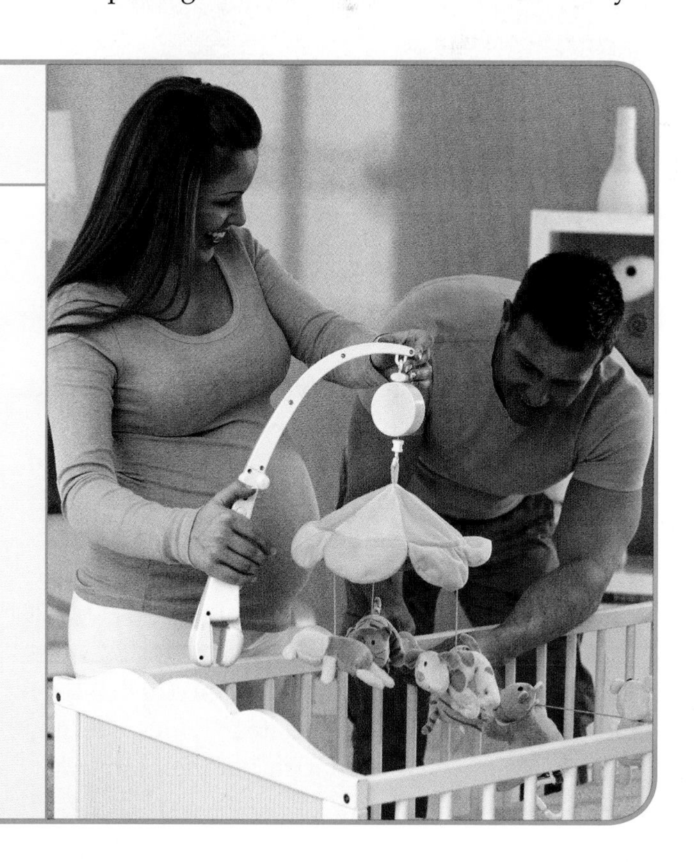

Figure 7.2 **Ways Parents Can Help Young Children Learn About Newborns**

- Explain what "new" babies can and cannot do. For example, parents might say, "Crying is a baby's way of talking."
- Visit with (or babysit for) a friend with a newborn or young infant. Encourage the older child to observe and talk about the baby.
- Show the older child his or her baby book and photos.
- Read children's books about families with newborns.

- Engage the older child as a "special helper" to prepare the house for the new arrival.
- When receiving gifts before or after the baby's arrival, plan a small gift or something special for the older child, too.
- When the baby arrives, ask the older child to "introduce" the new baby to family members and friends. Give the older child a photo of the new baby to take to his or her child care program or school for "show-and-tell."

Children have both sad and happy emotions about a new baby. Parents need to **reassure** (encourage; remove doubts and fears) older children they are loved and appreciated. Older children need to feel they are a vital part of their family.

Employment Considerations

During pregnancy, parents decide how much time off from work they want to take when the baby is born. The amount of time parents schedule often depends on their employer's leave policies, the mother's and baby's health during pregnancy, and the family's financial considerations.

Many pregnant women work until just before their babies are born. Mothers-to-be may require a **pregnancy leave** if they cannot work for part or all of the pregnancy due to health reasons. About two-thirds of U.S. working women are covered by the **Pregnancy Discrimination Act (PDA)**, a law that protects the rights of pregnant women who work (**Figure 7.3**).

Employers may grant maternity and paternity leaves to new parents. **Maternity leave**, the time a woman takes off from work for the birth or adoption of a child, is more common than pregnancy leave. Maternity leave allows the new mother time to recover from childbirth, regain her strength, and get to know her newborn. Life with a newborn is usually **hectic** (very busy) and exhausting for the first few weeks. The mother needs time to rest and adjust to her new role and bond with the baby.

Some employers grant **paternity leave** to fathers, which is time off (usually unpaid) for a set period after a child's birth or adoption. Paternity leave gives the new father time to care for his family and bond with the child. Men may face challenges in taking paternity leave, such as economic hardship, if the leave is unpaid.

The **Family and Medical Leave Act (FMLA)** is a law that protects the rights of qualified employees to take unpaid leave for various family-related reasons, such as maternity or paternity leave (**Figure 7.4**). About half of U.S. working women and men are covered by FMLA. Companies not covered by FMLA may have their own maternity (and possibly paternity) leave policies.

The length of maternity leave varies from company to company. Six weeks is often the minimum length offered and 12 weeks if covered by FMLA. Maternity leave may be paid, partially paid, or unpaid. Companies may grant benefits and a

Figure 7.3 Pregnancy Discrimination Act (PDA)

Who qualifies?

- Pregnant women working for companies employing 15 or more people.
- Both married and single women.
- Women who work in companies that provide job security and benefits for other medical conditions.

What is guaranteed under the law?

- Employer cannot fire a woman due to pregnancy or force her to take a maternity leave.
- A pregnant woman is guaranteed the same health, disability, and sickness-leave benefits as other employees with medical conditions.
- A pregnant woman may work as long as she can perform her job duties.
- Depending on company policy, pregnant women may be given modified tasks, alternate assignments, disability leave, or leave without pay upon request.
- Job security is guaranteed during a leave.
- A pregnant woman continues to accrue seniority and remains eligible for pay increases or benefits during a leave.

Figure 7.4 Family and Medical Leave Act (FMLA)

Who qualifies?

- Employees who have worked at least 12 months for a covered employer.
- Employees who provide employers 30 days notice of the need to take leave when the need is foreseeable. Employees must provide evidence of the need for the leave.
- Workers in the following circumstances:
  - Worker or worker's spouse has just given birth to or adopted a child.
  - Worker must provide care for a seriously ill family member.
  - Worker has a serious health condition of his or her own.

What is guaranteed under the law?

- Qualified employees have up to 12 weeks of leave; time does not have to be taken in one block.
- Leave is unpaid. Employer can pay salary or wages during some or all of the leave time. Employer may require workers to use any accrued paid leave while taking FMLA leave.
- Employer guarantees an employee can have his or her job (or an equal job) upon return to work.
- Employee maintains all health care benefits during the leave time.

percentage of salary during maternity leave. Other companies might grant a longer unpaid leave, such as several months or a year.

Delivery Considerations

Perhaps the most pressing decisions parents make during pregnancy involve choosing a birthplace and method of labor and delivery. **Labor** is the process that moves the baby out of the mother's body. When making these decisions, factors parents may want to consider include

- the type of care the mother-to-be might require during childbirth
- whether the delivery will involve the use of drugs

Choosing a Birthplace

Parents have several options to consider before deciding where they want their baby to be born. Options may be limited by where the couple lives, who will deliver the baby, health conditions of the mother and baby, and extent of insurance coverage. A family's choice of birthplace may include the following:

- ***Hospitals.*** Hospital deliveries are the most common. In a hospital, mothers labor in a maternity room and are taken to a delivery room shortly before the baby's birth. Mothers who require surgical delivery of their babies use a surgical room. The delivery or surgical room in a hospital is the best place for high-risk deliveries. After the birth, mothers spend time in a recovery room before returning to their maternity room. Newborns stay in the hospital nursery.
- ***Birthing room in a hospital.*** Many hospitals offer parents the option of a homelike room in the hospital for low-risk deliveries. The birthing room is furnished like a bedroom, but has all the needed hospital equipment. A nurse stays with the parents during labor. The doctor and delivery nurses are present for delivery or if problems arise. The baby remains with the parents in the birthing room until the mother is discharged.
- ***Birth center.*** Mothers-to-be who have low-risk pregnancies may opt for a birth center that provides health care before labor as well as delivery services. Birth centers are often located near hospitals, and employ certified nurse-midwives. A **certified nurse-midwife (CNM)** is a nurse who has special training in delivering babies during low-risk pregnancies. Many CNMs work with hospitals where they can call for help if an emergency arises. One drawback of birth centers is that mothers are often released within hours after giving birth.
- ***Home.*** Mothers may choose to give birth in their own homes. Home births can be risky, especially when emergency services are not nearby. Parents may lessen the risks of home births by having a CNM present for the delivery. The newborn death rate for home births, however, is higher than for hospital births.

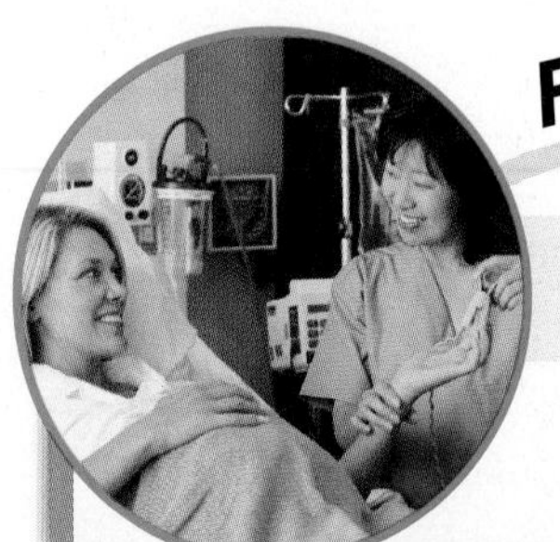

Focus on Careers

Nurse-Midwife

Nurse-midwives provide primary care to women, including gynecological exams, family planning advice, prenatal care, assistance in labor and delivery, and neonatal care.

Career cluster: Health science.

Education: Educational requirements include a master's degree and classroom and clinical experience. Programs may also require candidates to become a registered nurse (RN) before pursuing higher education.

Job outlook: Future employment opportunities for nurse-midwives are expected to grow much faster than the average for all occupations.

To learn more about a career as a nurse-midwife, visit the United States Department of Labor's *Occupational Outlook Handbook* website. You will also be able to compare the job responsibilities, educational requirements, job outlook, and average pay of nurse-midwives with similar occupations.

Choosing a Method of Delivery

Before choosing a method of delivery, parents discuss their options with the health care provider. All methods of delivery try to make labor and delivery safer and more comfortable for both the mother and baby. When choosing a method of delivery, parents may want to keep the following points in mind:

- The length of labor is unknown, but tends to be longer for a woman's first delivery.
- The amount of pain is unknown. Labor is difficult and requires the use of many muscles. Pain is a part of labor, but if muscles are tense, the mother has even more pain. Any complications will also increase the pain.
- Unforeseen complications may cause the method of delivery to change during labor.

Natural Childbirth

Natural childbirth is a delivery method in which the pregnant woman learns about the birth process and uses breathing and relaxation techniques to reduce fear and pain during labor. Women who choose natural childbirth do not use any pain-relieving drugs during labor or delivery. The most common approach to natural childbirth is the Bradley® method, which is both a prenatal care and delivery method.

Focus on Health

Labor and Delivery Positions and Movements

Until rather recently, women who chose hospital births would typically use the *back childbirth position* for labor and delivery. During labor, women would lie flat on their backs and their feet would be in stirrups for exams and delivery. The back childbirth position is a good position for the health provider to monitor and assist with childbirth. On the other hand, the back childbirth position does not use gravity to aid the descent of the baby, which results in an ineffective labor and delivery position. The back childbirth position also compresses blood vessels, which can impede blood flow to the baby.

Today, except for high-risk conditions, doctors encourage women to vary their positions and move during childbirth. Many obstetricians believe that lessening stress during childbirth also reduces fetal complications. Varying labor positions from which women can choose include

- lying on their side
- standing and walking, especially in early labor
- rocking or swaying back and forth
- squatting with support
- getting on all fours to reduce back pressure (pain)

Two aids for changing position and movement are popular. The first aid is the *birthing ball* or *birth ball*. A birthing ball is a large physical therapy ball that comes in slightly different sizes for different height women. During labor, women can use the birthing ball to aid their movements, such as sitting, rocking, squatting, and leaning on or over the ball. The second aid is the *water tub* or *pool*. The buoyancy of water enables women to change positions and move more easily. Warm (not hot) water is relaxing, improves blood flow, and reduces vaginal tearing. Women may use the water tub during labor or during both labor and delivery, which is a *water birth*.

Women discuss labor and delivery positions and movements with their health care providers well in advance of childbirth. For example, not all hospitals have birthing balls or water tubs. Like all other delivery plans, changes may be necessary if delivery conditions warrant.

In natural childbirth, the father usually plays an active role in prenatal study and support of the mother-to-be through the delivery process. Parents may use a *doula* (DOO-luh), a female helper, who reassures and guides the mother through labor. Doulas, however, cannot deliver babies. Parents also use CNMs or nurses to aid the mother.

Doctors may use the natural childbirth method of delivery in hospitals. At birth centers, CNMs use this delivery method **exclusively** (not shared; the only one). Unless attended by a doctor, natural childbirth is used for home deliveries.

Lamaze Method

Another delivery method is the *Lamaze (luh-MAHZ) method*, named for Dr. Ferdinand Lamaze, the French doctor who made the approach popular. In the **Lamaze method** of delivery, the pregnant woman is trained to use breathing patterns to keep her mind off the pain. The idea behind the Lamaze method is that women may already be conditioned to fear childbirth. In Lamaze training, the mother learns to focus on something other than pain.

The following features describe the Lamaze method:

- Childbirth training classes occur weekly for eight to 12 weeks before the delivery date. These classes teach mental and physical exercises and breathing patterns needed for delivery.
- The woman's coach, usually the father, learns the breathing patterns and helps the mother-to-be through labor.
- The woman receives medication when necessary during labor. Not all women can deliver without drugs, even when they are informed about childbirth.

Delivery with the Use of Drugs

Newer drugs and the way they are given make their use safer for the mother and baby and may make labor shorter. Thus, many women opt for a more pain-free labor and delivery. Drugs are also used when complications of delivery arise. Women must be in the hospital (including a birthing room) to receive most drugs.

Drugs for labor and delivery can be grouped in three ways. *Sedatives* reduce anxiety and are used in the early stages of labor. *Analgesics* (ANN-uhl-GEE-siks) reduce pain, but they do not take it away. *Anesthesia* (ANN-uh-STEE-shuh), also called *anesthetics*, blocks pain. Drugs may be used separately or in combination. All drugs can have side effects, but general anesthesia has the most side effects.

Figure 7.5 describes options for using drugs for pain relief during labor and delivery. To make sure the drug is safe for both mother and baby, the doctor must know the mother's health history. The doctor must also know the mother's current health status and any food or drink intake during the last several hours.

Fathers as Helpers

Regardless of which method of delivery couples choose, mothers need emotional support, especially during delivery. Many fathers act as helpers and provide support and assistance during labor. Helpers tend to calm mothers and reduce their feelings of anxiety. Anxiety can be a problem in labor because it causes changes in the mother's blood chemistry. These changes decrease the flow of blood to the baby, which can harm the baby, and slow contractions, resulting in a longer labor.

Another benefit of fathers as labor and delivery helpers is family closeness. Fathers who participate in labor and delivery are there to help the mother welcome their new son or daughter into the world.

Lesson 7.1 Review and Assessment

1. When do parents often decide to tell young children about a new baby?
2. What two laws protect the employment rights of pregnant couples as they prepare for childbirth?
3. List four options families might consider when choosing a birthplace. In what ways are parents' options of a birthplace limited?
4. What are the three major methods of delivery? Why might parents' choices for method of delivery change?
5. **Critical thinking.** Identify ways fathers might take an active role during pregnancy and childbirth.

Figure 7.5 Commonly Used Drugs for Labor and Delivery

Drug	Comment
Sedative	Drug given by injection or intravenously (IV) to help reduce pain and ease anxiety.
Local anesthesia	Drug injected to numb the vaginal area when birth is near, an incision will be made, or sutures (stitches) are needed.
Regional anesthesia	Drug injected to numb one area (region) of the body.
Epidural (eh-pih-DURE-uhl)	Drug given through a tiny tube (catheter) placed in the small of the back, just outside the spinal canal. Mothers feel touch and pressure, but not pain.
Spinal	Drug administered into spinal canal. Side effects are similar to those of epidural, but may be more dangerous. Epidural has almost replaced the spinal.
Combined spinal epidural (CSE anesthesia); also called *walking epidural*	A low dose is injected below the spinal cord into the spinal fluid. A combined diluted analgesic and anesthesia are given as an epidural. The low dose allows the mother to move and walk as desired.
General anesthesia	Drug given intravenously (by IV) or by breathing a gas that puts the mother to sleep. General anesthesia is reserved for when complications arise, such as when an emergency C-section must be done. General anesthesia has more side effects for both mother and baby than other types of anesthesia.

Cord-Blood Banking

In addition to choosing a birthplace and delivery option, expectant parents also make decisions about cord-blood banking. *Cord blood* is blood drawn from the umbilical cord after the baby is born. When parents choose cord-blood banking, the blood is taken to a blood bank where stem cells are removed and stored for possible future use. Research is finding ways to transplant these stem cells into children with certain life-threatening illnesses. For example, some cancers (especially leukemia), blood disorders (various types of anemia), and immune deficiencies are being treated with cord blood. New studies are being conducted on the use of cord blood for treating sickle-cell anemia, cerebral palsy, type 1 diabetes, heart defects, and brain injuries.

Cord blood may be stored in a private bank or in a public bank. Cord blood stored in a private bank enables a child to use his or her own stem cells if necessary, which eliminates the need for doctors to find a match. The cord blood may also be used to help a parent or sibling. The American Academy of Pediatrics (AAP) suggests that parents use a private bank only if certain illnesses are common in their family because of the high cost associated with banking cells.

Donating the cord blood to a free, public bank is also an option parents may consider. Stem cells donated to a public bank are used to help other children or to aid research. Parents decide about cord-blood banking well before the baby's due date.

Speaking Activity

Take three to five minutes to consider the pros and cons of donating to a cord-blood bank. What legal, ethical, and personal issues might influence a parent's decision? With a partner, discuss your thoughts.

Lesson 7.2 Time to Be Born

Key Terms

bonding
breech birth position
cesarean section
contraction
dilation
episiotomy
forceps
hysterectomy
lightening
vacuum extraction

Academic Terms

dislodged
elastic
incision
intervals
involuntary
irregular
sequential

Objectives

After studying this lesson, you will be able to

- identify and describe the signs of labor.
- explain important events that occur during each of the three stages of labor.
- differentiate among the most common procedures used for complications of childbirth.
- compare and contrast a mother's and baby's stay in a hospital room with a stay in a birthing room.

Reading and Writing Activity

Using online or print resources, find an article that explains the stages of childbirth and possible complications. Take notes about the article, and then compare your notes about the article with this lesson. How does the article differ from this lesson? Do the article and this lesson contain different information or use different writing styles? Write a short essay comparing the article and this lesson and assessing how and why they are different.

Graphic Organizer

Draw four squares and label each square with one of the main headings in this lesson. As you read, write your notes in the appropriate squares.

Signs of Labor	Stages of Labor
Complications of Childbirth	The Hospital Stay

The months of waiting and excitement during pregnancy come to an end sooner than expected as labor takes most parents by surprise. Labor may begin any time and any place—even in the middle of sleep. The first signs of labor let parents know the time for delivery is near. Once begun, labor and delivery are completed within hours. Many deliveries happen without complications, but even in low-risk pregnancies problems may still occur during or after childbirth.

Signs of Labor

Birth occurs about 266 days after conception (or about 280 days from the mother's last menstrual cycle). During the last few weeks of pregnancy, especially for a first pregnancy, the mother experiences **lightening**, or a change in the baby's position. When lightening occurs, the uterus settles downward and forward, and the baby descends lower into the pelvis. In most cases, the baby's body rotates so the head is toward the birth canal. In about five percent of the cases, however, the baby moves into a **breech birth position** in which the baby's feet, legs, or buttocks emerge first (**Figure 7.6**). When lightening happens, the mother can breathe easier. Leg cramps may result, however, and frequent urination is often common due to the increased pressure of the baby on the mother's bladder.

Because the mother's body is preparing for labor during lightening, she may have a few **irregular** (occurring at different times; unusual) contractions. A **contraction** is the tightening or shortening of a muscle. Irregular contractions are known as *false labor*. These contractions are real, but true labor has not begun. Parents-to-be may go to the hospital only to find the contractions are false labor. Carefully timing the **intervals** or periods of time in between contractions can help parents know whether the mother is really in labor.

Labor begins when a series of contractions in the uterine (YOO-teh-rhine) muscles move the baby out of the mother's body. These contractions are **involuntary** (not by choice), the mother cannot make these contractions happen. Natural signals from the mother's body control the onset, duration, and strength of the contractions. Contractions occur at rather regular intervals that allow the mother's muscles to relax. As labor progresses, contractions increase in both duration and strength. The intervals of relaxation between contractions decrease. Parents who are in doubt about the type of contractions should call the health provider and go to the planned birthplace.

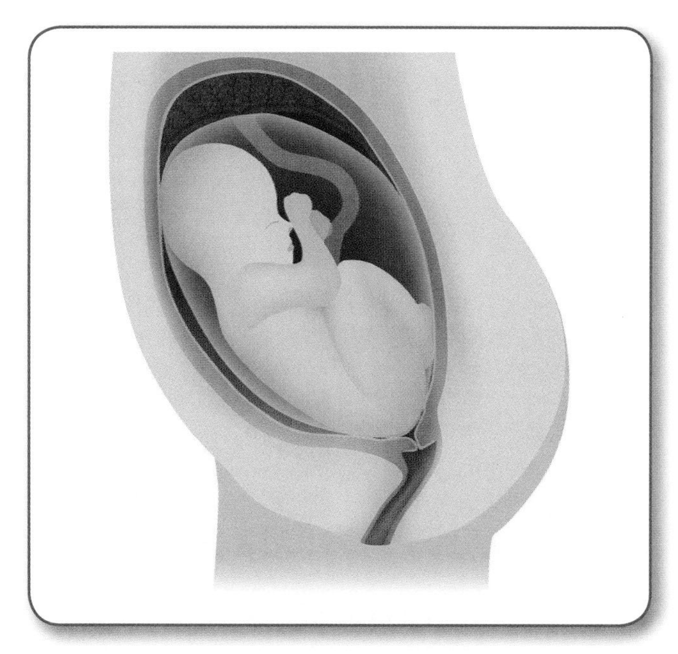

Figure 7.6 In a breech birth, the baby is not in a head-first position. *How does breech birth position affect labor and delivery?*

Besides regular contractions, there are several other signs of labor. One sign the mother may feel is a burst of energy due to increased adrenaline. Another sign of labor is the loosening of the mucous plug in the cervix. The small amount of blood in the mucous is called *the show*, which means labor should start within 24 hours. Another sign of labor may occur when part of the amniotic sac breaks before labor begins. (Often the sac breaks after labor begins.) If the mucous plug becomes **dislodged** (forcefully removed) or the amniotic sac breaks, the mother should notify her health care provider.

Stages of Labor

In medical terms, labor is divided into three stages: (1) **dilation**, or opening, of the cervix; (2) delivery of the baby; and (3) delivery of the placenta (**Figure 7.7**).

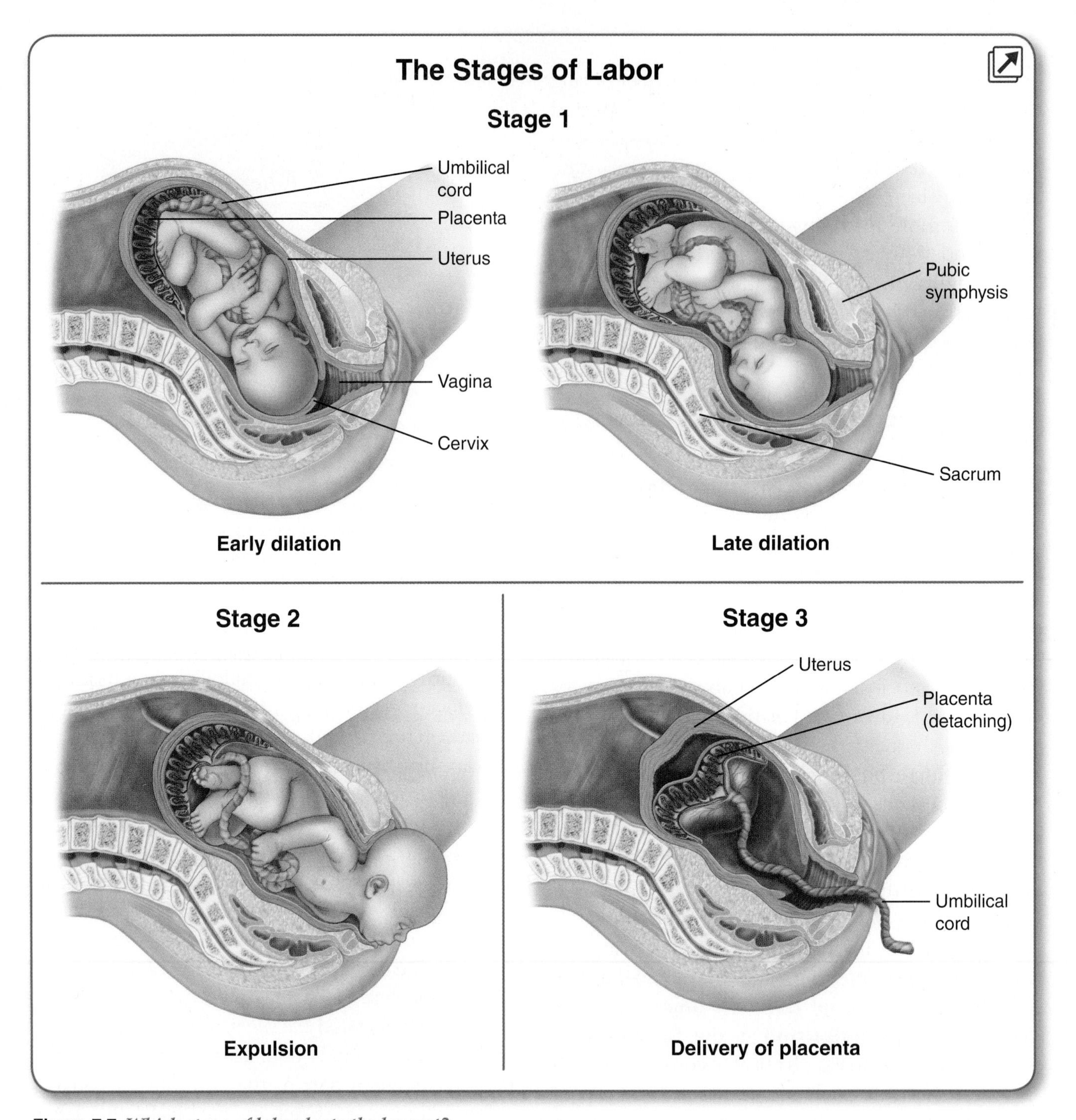

Figure 7.7 *Which stage of labor lasts the longest?*

Dilation of the Cervix

In the early part of labor, contractions come every 15–20 minutes and last about 30 seconds. In the middle part of the first stage of labor, contractions may last 45–60 seconds and are 2–4 minutes apart. The most difficult labor occurs in the later part of the stage, or the *transition*. Contractions last for 90 seconds and are so close apart they often feel continuous. Contractions cause the uterus to narrow, which straightens the baby's body and presses the baby's head (or buttocks) against the cervix. As the baby pushes against the cervix, the cervix flattens and opens (dilates).

If the amniotic sac has not broken, the doctor will break it when the cervix is fully dilated. Full dilation of the cervix measures about 4 inches (10 centimeters) in width, which is the size of a small grapefruit. The first stage of labor ends when the cervix is completely open. The length of time for this stage varies a great deal, but the average length is eight hours for a first pregnancy (less for later pregnancies).

Delivery of the Baby

After the transition phase of the first stage of labor, the second stage of labor begins with the lessening of contractions for about an hour. This allows mothers to rest before the very active delivery phase begins. During the delivery stage, the baby's head enters the birth canal and the mother's muscles push to move the baby down. The walls of the upper part of the birth canal are **elastic** (stretchable). The arrangement of muscles in the lower part of the canal, however, causes resistance and pain.

The doctor may have the mother use natural techniques, such as breathing, to reduce pain. Sometimes an **incision** (cut), called an **episiotomy** (ih-pea-zee-AW-tuh-mee), is made to widen the birth canal and prevent tearing. Another practice is to lubricate the birth canal to ease the baby out. After delivery, the doctor *sutures* (stitches) any incision.

The baby changes position during birth and faces downward as the widest part of the baby's head becomes visible (called *crowning*). Soon, the face appears from forehead to chin. The doctor usually suctions fluid from the mouth and nose and checks that the umbilical cord is not wrapped around the baby's neck. The baby's head turns to the side as the shoulders rotate inside the pelvis. This position allows one shoulder and then the other shoulder to emerge. Finally, the baby's entire body comes out, often with the help of the doctor. The remaining fluid from the amniotic sac is expelled. Instruments are used to suction fluid from the baby's air passages, which helps the baby take his or her first breath.

The second stage ends when the baby is free of the mother's body. The time of birth is noted. The second stage usually lasts between two and three hours with the longer time required for first-time mothers. The doctor (or sometimes the father) clips the umbilical cord before the third stage begins (**Figure 7.8**).

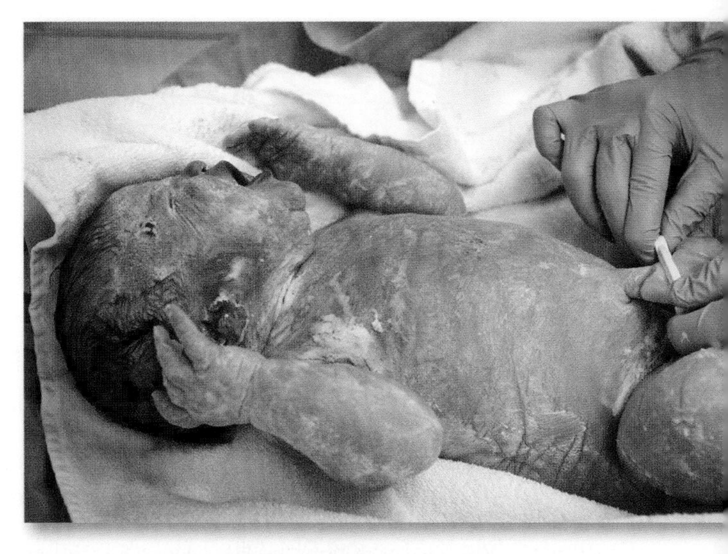

Figure 7.8 Before the third stage of labor, a doctor or the baby's father clips the umbilical cord. *What was the function of the umbilical cord before birth?*

Delivery of the Placenta

In about 5–10 minutes and up to 30 minutes after birth, the mother has a few irregular contractions. These cause the placenta to completely detach from the uterus and descend. The placenta and fetal membrane expelled following the birth of a baby are called the *afterbirth*. The drug *pitocin* is often used to help the uterus contract, which stops the main flow of blood. Nurses also massage the lower abdomen to aid contraction. As the third stage ends, mothers feel a little cold and tired. They also feel relief and joy.

Complications of Childbirth

Complications may occur in childbirth that can put both mother and baby at risk (**Figure 7.9**). When complications arise, special medical care involving the use of delivery-aid techniques protects the health of the mother and baby. Which technique is used depends on the nature of the problem. Each technique poses risks, but has important advantages. Before delivery, a woman's doctor explains to her any technique, risks, and advantages. The woman can then decide whether to have the procedure. The most common procedures used for complications

Figure 7.9 Complications of Childbirth

Complication	Explanation
Premature delivery	Baby may not be mature enough to survive. Baby is often not in the correct position for delivery.
Premature rupture of membranes (PROM)	Amniotic sac breaks, but labor does not begin. Infection is a danger. Baby who is mature will be delivered. With an immature baby, drugs are given to prevent infection until delivery.
Prolonged delivery	Both mother and baby are at risk for other complications.
Abnormal position for delivery	Baby may be injured and uterus may rupture. Sometimes the position may be corrected; if not, the baby must be surgically removed.
Cephalopelvic (SEF-a-low-PEL-vik) **disproportion**	Baby's head is too large to pass through mother's pelvic bones. Baby is often surgically removed.
Umbilical cord problems	*Compression*—hollow cord is wrapped around the baby's body *Prolapsed*—cord slips into the birth canal and is trapped between the baby and canal The umbilical cord supplies oxygen. A baby who is deprived of oxygen may be born with cerebral palsy, visual problems, and brain damage, or may even die. If the cord cannot be returned to the proper position, the baby is surgically removed.
Asphyxia (as-FIX-eeuh)	Oxygen supply is cut off due to problems with the placenta or umbilical cord, which can cause brain damage or death. After birth, breathing problems may result if lungs contain fluid or waste materials. Chest massage, drugs, and respirators can be used to stimulate breathing.
Meconium (mih-KO-nee-uhm) **aspiration**	If the baby passes a stool before birth, the meconium in the amniotic fluid may be swallowed or aspirated (breathing it in), and the baby may be covered in meconium. Swallowing sterile meconium is not a problem. Aspirating it will cause the baby to have mild to severe breathing problems, which can last for years. Doctors attempt to suction meconium from the baby's nose and mouth before the first breath.
Postpartum bleeding	The uterus should contract and squeeze the blood vessels shut that supplied the uterus during pregnancy. Massage and hormones are given to help the uterus return to its original size. In rare cases, surgery may be needed to close the blood vessels and stop bleeding.

of childbirth are drug-assisted deliveries, vaginal-assisted deliveries, and surgical removal of the baby.

Drug-Assisted Deliveries

Complications of childbirth increase pain. If complications occur, doctors administer or increase the amount of drugs, such as anesthesia and sedation. Other drugs are used if an episiotomy is needed, and still other drugs are used for excessive bleeding during the third stage of labor. (Refer to Figure 7.5 to review different options for using drugs for pain relief during labor and delivery.)

Vaginal-Assisted Deliveries

About five percent of all deliveries in the United States are vaginal-assisted deliveries. Doctors may offer the following two types of assistance:

- ***Manual assistance.*** Doctors often use *version*, or manually rotating the unborn baby into the correct position for delivery. If the baby's shoulder is caught after the head is free of the birth canal, manual assistance is one of several options to free the shoulder.
- ***Operative vaginal delivery.*** The doctor may choose to use **forceps**, a curved instrument that fits around the sides of a baby's head. Forceps aid in easing the baby down the birth canal during a contraction. Forceps can also be used safely with premature babies and can be used to aid version. Forceps may cause more trauma for the mother than the baby. The other option is **vacuum extraction**, in which suction is used to attach a cuplike device around the top of the baby's head. Vacuum extraction allows the doctor to gently pull the baby down the birth canal. Vacuum extraction may cause more trauma for the baby than the mother. The option usually depends on the nature of the complication.

Cesarean Births

Many delivery complications are handled through the cesarean (sih-ZARE-ee-uhn) section (or C-section) method. In the **cesarean section**, the mother's abdomen and uterus are surgically opened and the baby is removed. The incisions are then closed as with any other surgery. **Figure 7.10** lists medical reasons doctors might use C-section deliveries.

C-sections have the same risks as other major surgeries. Recovery after childbirth is longer than for vaginal deliveries. Also, **sequential** (following in an order) C-sections raise risk factors for future complications. With each C-section, the risk of needing a **hysterectomy** (HIS-ter-ECK-toh-mee), a surgical removal of the uterus, increases. More than one C-section also slightly increases the risk factor for a miscarriage or stillbirth with the next pregnancy or a uterine rupture during a vaginal birth after cesarean (VBAC).

The Hospital Stay

For parents who choose hospital births, both mother and baby can expect to remain in the hospital for 24–60 hours after delivery. The stay will be longer for a complicated or C-section delivery. Babies who are born at-risk are placed in special nurseries, which you will learn more about in the next lesson. These babies are often kept beyond the normal hospital stay for mothers. Parents visit their babies in these special nurseries.

During the hospital stay, medical care is given to ensure the health and safety of both mother and baby. The mother is closely watched to ensure her body is recovering from the exhausting delivery.

Figure 7.10 Medical Reasons for C-section Deliveries

- The mother's pelvis is small or not shaped for an easy birth.
- The baby or mother is at medical risk.
- The baby's head is large.
- Contractions are weak or absent.
- The baby is in an incorrect position for birth.
- The pregnancy is a multiple birth, although some multiple births are vaginal or vaginal-assisted deliveries.
- The doctor feels that previous uterine scar(s) could rupture during labor, although one cesarean birth does not mean all later births must be C-sections, too.

The baby must be monitored for health conditions and adjustments to life outside the mother's body.

Most hospitals have nurseries for a healthy baby's care. Nurses are on duty in the nursery at all times. Except for times when the mother is breast-feeding her baby, much of the baby's stay will be in the nursery. Visitors may see the baby through the nursery window during certain times. Young brothers and sisters may or may not be allowed to visit the hospital.

Hospitals that have birthing rooms encourage a *rooming-in arrangement*. If the baby is healthy, he or she is in a bassinet in the room with the mother. The medical care of the baby can be given in the mother's room, and nurses are still available to help the new mother. The father or a support person is provided with a bed.

A rooming-in arrangement enables the parents to begin **bonding**, developing a feeling of affection, with their baby immediately. Bonding helps parents and their baby (**Figure 7.11**). The first hour after birth is perhaps the most sensitive bonding time for both parents and their babies. The baby will watch, hear, and respond to the body movements, voice, and touch of the mother and father. Bonding continues during the next few weeks as parents become more and more attached to their babies.

Lesson 7.2 Review and Assessment 

1. What is *lightening*?
2. What is meant by *false labor*?
3. Place the following events of labor in proper order:
   (A) delivery of the baby;
   (B) dilation of the cervix;
   (C) delivery of the placenta;
   (D) cutting of the umbilical cord.
4. List the three most common procedures used for complications of childbirth.
5. List two medical reasons for C-section deliveries.
6. Describe a *rooming-in arrangement* in a hospital.
7. List three benefits of bonding to babies and three benefits to parents.
8. **Critical thinking.** What activities can new parents do to bond with their babies while still in the hospital?

Figure 7.11 Benefits of Bonding

To Babies
• Increased chance of survival • Better weight gain • Less crying, more smiles and laughter • Fewer infections • Possibly higher IQ • Better language development
To Parents
• Less incidence of child abuse • Faster recovery from delivery • Longer breast-feeding • More self-confidence as a parent • Less incidence of depression after delivery

Newborn Medical Care and Tests

Lesson 7.3

Objectives

After studying this lesson, you will be able to

- describe the first medical care babies receive at birth.
- differentiate between the Apgar test and the Brazelton scale.
- give examples of newborn screening tests often performed within 24 to 48 hours of birth.
- evaluate the types of care and treatment needed at birth for premature and other high-risk babies compared to healthy babies.

Key Terms

anemia
Apgar test
Brazelton scale
jaundice
neonatal intensive care unit (NICU)
neonate
neonatology
pediatrician
well-baby checkup

Academic Terms

metabolize
resuscitate

Reading and Writing Activity

List the key terms for this lesson on a piece of paper and then look them up in the glossary, defining each term in your own words. Revise your definitions as needed while reading and then write two to three summary paragraphs using the key terms in this lesson.

Graphic Organizer

Divide a piece of paper into two columns. Label one column *Care* and label the other column *Conditions*. As you read, write medical care and tests under the *Care* column and medical conditions under the *Conditions* column. Draw lines between items or notes in the two columns if you think a type of care and a condition are related.

Care	Conditions
Apgar test *Blood tests* →	*Anemia*

At birth, babies enter a more exciting world. They are exposed to light and noise. The newborn's life support system—the placenta and umbilical cord—stops functioning minutes after birth. The newborn's air passage is drained of water. The lungs expand as the baby takes his or her first breath.

Newborns can show physical signs that might worry parents. They cough and sneeze to clear mucus from their air passages and lungs. They breathe unevenly, about 46 times per minute, from the diaphragm in the abdominal area. (Adults breathe about 18 times per minute, usually from the chest.) Newborns' heart rates are often between 120 and 150 beats per minute. (Adults' heart rates are 70 or fewer beats per minute.) To ensure newborns are healthy, doctors perform a series of medical tests on the day of birth and in the following weeks thereafter. Babies who are born premature or born with other medical conditions receive special care.

First Medical Care of the Baby

From birth to one month of age, a baby is medically known as a **neonate**. (Neonate is from the Latin words *neo*, meaning new, and *natus*, meaning born.) Generally, in hospital births, a pediatrician often comes to the delivery or birthing room just as the baby is born. A **pediatrician** is a doctor who cares for infants, children, and teens until adulthood when growth is complete. If the mother is using an obstetrician, this doctor continues to complete the delivery process. Family doctors might do both jobs, but, as you can imagine, this becomes almost impossible if either the mother and/or the baby need extra assistance.

After delivery, the baby is often held head downward and the doctor suctions fluid from the nostrils and mouth. The mother may hold the baby on her abdomen until the cord is clipped. The nurse then takes the baby to a special table with a heater and dries the newborn with warm towels. Pediatricians oversee the medical testing and care of the new baby.

The Apgar Test

Pediatricians measure the newborn's chance of survival using the **Apgar test**. The Apgar test checks the baby's pulse, breathing, muscle tone, responsiveness, and skin color. The baby's heart rate and breathing are most important. Skin color, which is a sign of circulation, is least important. The test is given one minute and five minutes after delivery. The baby scores a 0, 1, or 2 in each of the five areas (**Figure 7.12**). The best total score possible is a 10. For the first scoring, the umbilical cord is often still working, but usually has been clipped for the second check. The score at five minutes should be higher.

Healthy babies often score 6 or 7 at one minute and 8 to 10 at five minutes. If a baby scores 7 or less at five minutes, he or she is tested again at ten minutes after birth. A low score means the baby needs special

Figure 7.12 Apgar Test

Sign	Scores		
	0	1	2
Heart rate	Absent	Slow; fewer than 100 beats per minute	More than 100 beats per minute
Respiratory effort	Absent	Weak cry; hyperventilation	Good; strong cry
Muscle tone	Limp	Some flexing and bending of extremities	Well flexed
Reflex irritability	No response	Some motion	Cry
Color	Blue; pale	Body pink; extremities blue	Completely pink

medical care. If the vital signs are not good, the pediatrician will attempt to **resuscitate** (bring to an active state; revitalize) and stabilize the newborn. If there are still problems or if the baby is a preterm birth, the pediatrician orders care by other means (as you will read later in this lesson).

Immediate Care

For healthy newborns, the nurses begin health care after the Apgar tests. Antibiotic drops are put into the newborn's eyes. Because a newborn's temperature is not very stable, a thermometer is attached to the chest, and the baby wears a snug cap. Newborns typically receive a vitamin K injection to help their blood clot. An injection of penicillin may be necessary for newborns fighting a possible strep infection. Nurses take a sample of cord blood to determine the newborn's blood type and antibody status. Before the newborn is taken from the delivery room, footprints are made and name bands are placed around the newborn's wrists and/or ankles for identification purposes. The pediatrician looks over the records and checks the newborn again.

Newborn Screening Tests

Before the mother and the newborn leave the hospital, the pediatrician will order other tests to determine the newborn's health status. Screening tests are performed within 24 to 48 hours of birth and are repeated in two weeks. Any tests with out-of-range results require further testing. These tests can make the difference between wellness and permanent disorders or death.

Blood Tests

Doctors conduct blood tests on newborns by collecting a few drops of blood from a heel prick. Screening can check for anemia, jaundice, and developmental disorders. **Anemia** is a condition that occurs when the level of healthy red blood cells, which carry oxygen to all parts of the body, becomes too low. Mild anemia often does not require any treatment, but a blood transfusion may be necessary to treat more severe anemia.

Jaundice is a liver condition that can make the skin, tissues, and body fluids look yellow. A buildup in the blood of *bilirubin* (bih-lih-ROO-buhn), a yellow pigment, causes jaundice. Newborns, especially premature babies, have problems handling bilirubin due to their immature livers. Doctors treat jaundice by using *light treatment* or *phototherapy* to help reduce the skin's yellow color (**Figure 7.13**). Hospitals may also treat newborn jaundice with *fibreoptic phototherapy* in which a flexible light pad is wrapped around the baby. More research needs to be done on this newer method,

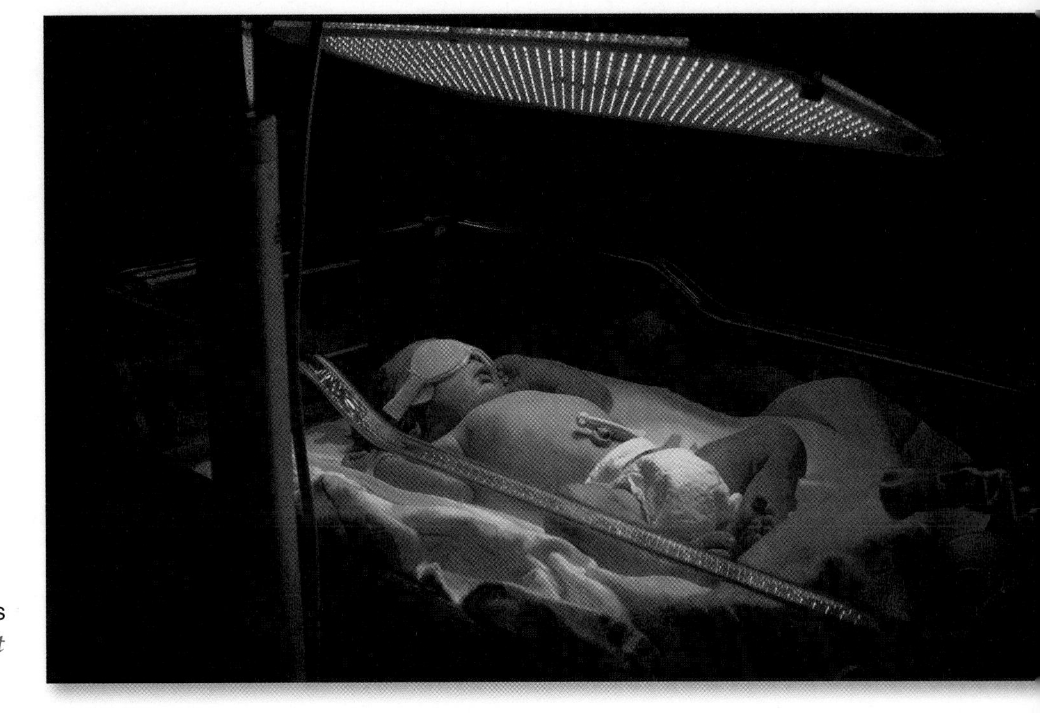

Figure 7.13 In light treatment or phototherapy, the newborn is placed in a cot under special lights. A mask protects the baby's eyes from the lights. ***Why might newborns develop jaundice?***

but current studies show it to be less effective than conventional methods for full-term babies, but equally effective in treating preterm babies.

Doctors also screen newborns for developmental disorders. The number of disorders a doctor will check varies depending on each state's screening program. Most states require tests to check for the following conditions:

- *Phenylketonuria (PKU)*—condition in which the body is unable to **metabolize** (break down in the digestive system) an amino acid, *phenylalanine* (FEN-uhl-AL-eh-neen). PKU is treated by diet. Untreated PKU can lead to seizures and impaired intellectual abilities. (All states check for this condition.)
- *Hypothyroidism*—thyroid hormone deficiency that can lead to slow growth and abnormal brain development if left untreated.
- *Galactosemia*—condition in which the body is unable to digest the sugar in milk. Blindness, impaired intellectual abilities, and death may result if left untreated.
- *Sickle-cell anemia*—disease in which the body makes sickle-shaped red blood cells (**Figure 7.14**). The cells become blocked in the blood vessels causing pain and body damage and increasing the risk of infection and possibly death. Blood specialists provide regular medical care for this disorder.

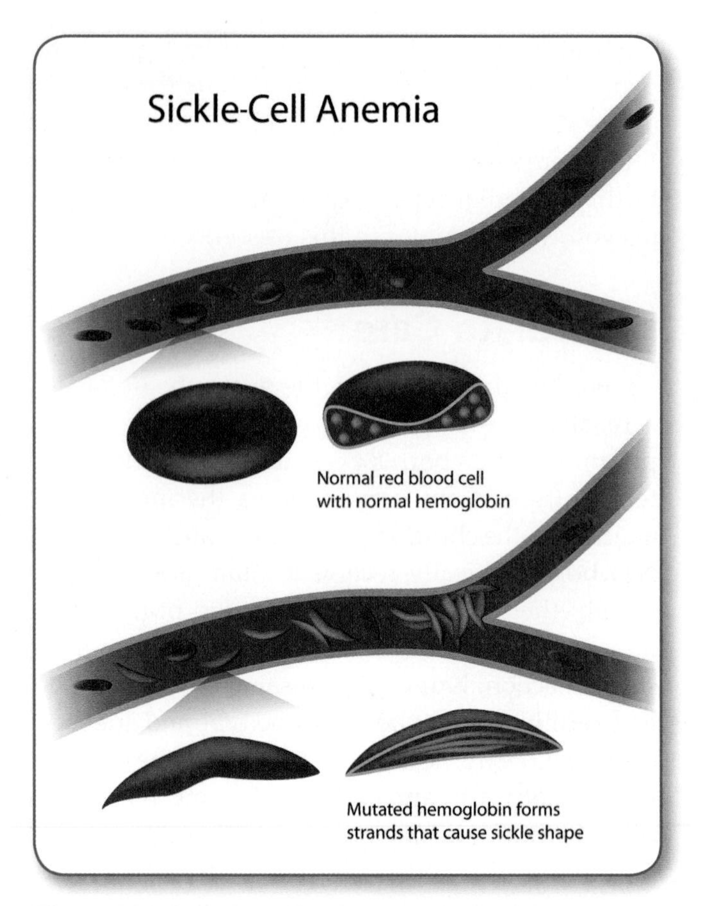

Figure 7.14 A newborn blood test checks for sickle-cell anemia, a condition in which the red blood cells are irregularly shaped. ***Explain how sickle-cell anemia might damage the body.***

Hearing Test

Doctors often conduct hearing tests on newborns. To get accurate results, doctors first drain any fluids in the middle ear. The fluid is usually squeezed out during a vaginal delivery, but babies born via C-section should wait about 48 hours after delivery before being given a hearing test. A loss of hearing can delay language and concept development.

Heart Test

Life-threatening heart defects may affect the way babies' hearts function or the way their hearts are shaped. Heart defects may not be apparent at birth, but become evident or critical soon after birth. A group of severe heart defects is medically referred to as *critical congenital heart disease (CCHD)*. Doctors conduct newborn screening for CCHD by using *pulse oximetry* (AWK-sim-uh-tree), a noninvasive test that determines how much oxygen is in the newborn's blood.

Neonatal Behavioral Assessment Scale

The Neonatal Behavioral Assessment Scale, or the **Brazelton scale**, is a test doctors use to test newborns and babies up to two months of age. The Brazelton scale determines whether a baby has problems

- ***interacting with the environment.*** Checks alertness; attention to sound, light, and other factors; and tendency to cuddle.
- ***handling motor processes.*** Assesses general activity level and reflex behaviors.

- *controlling his or her physical state.* Looks at self-quieting behaviors and levels of excitement and irritability.
- *responding to stress.* Checks startle reactions and trembling.

Male Circumcision

In the United States, parents have a choice of whether they do or do not want their newborn boy to be circumcised. *Circumcision* is a surgical procedure that involves removing the skin from the end of the penis (called *foreskin*). Parents choose circumcision primarily for religious or cultural and health reasons. The procedure is often performed one or two days after birth. Circumcision for religious reasons often occurs soon after discharge from the hospital. Circumcision carries benefits and risks, and parents may wish to seek advice from their doctor or religious leader before making their decision.

Well-Baby Checkup

Before the newborn leaves the hospital, the pediatrician will ask the parents to make an appointment for a well-baby checkup within three to five days. A **well-baby checkup** is a routine medical visit in which the doctor examines a baby for signs of good health and proper growth.

During this checkup, the nurse weighs the newborn and measures the length, head, and chest. The pediatrician reviews the family's health history, examines the newborn, answers parents' questions, and makes recommendations. Parents then schedule their baby's next checkup.

Care for High-Risk Newborns

High-risk newborns are babies who are born premature, have a low-birthweight, or have another high-risk condition, such as a congenital condition. In the United States, about 12 percent of newborns are born premature every year and about 8 percent have low-birthweights. Congenital conditions can affect the baby's heart, digestive tract, spine, or brain.

High-risk newborns are admitted into a **neonatal intensive care unit (NICU)**, also called

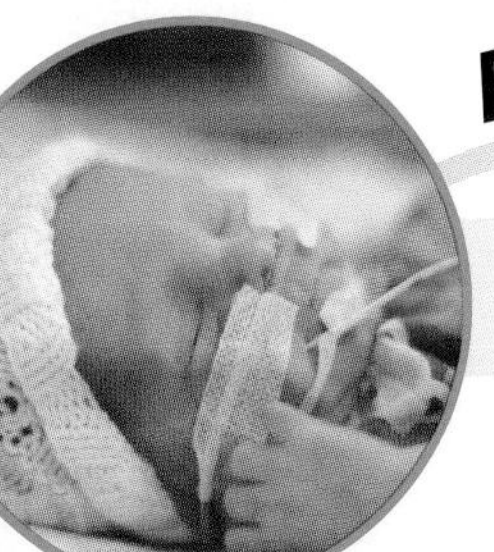

Focus on Careers

Physician—Neonatologist

Physician is a category of health careers in which health professionals provide physical care to patients. *Neonatologists* are physicians who specialize in the care of premature and ill newborns in a neonatal intensive care unit. Neonatologists diagnose and treat a variety of ailments specific to newborns.

Career cluster: Health science.

Education: Educational requirements include an advanced degree, four years of medical school, and three to eight additional years of internship and residency. Licensure is also required.

Job outlook: Future employment opportunities for neonatologists are expected to grow faster than the average for all occupations.

To learn more about a career as a neonatologist, visit the United States Department of Labor's *Occupational Outlook Handbook* website. You will also be able to compare the job responsibilities, educational requirements, job outlook, and average pay of neonatologists with similar occupations.

Mental Health Advisory

Without a developmentally supportive environment in the NICU, including parents who regularly help with their babies' care, preterm babies often become depressed and die. For the babies' mental health, a supportive environment must be continued after babies are discharged, too.

an *intensive care nursery (ICN)*, where they receive immediate, specialized, round-the-clock care and treatment. NICUs are rated by level—1 to 4. Higher numbers are used for the treatment of high-risk newborns who are the smallest and most ill. The doctors and nurses who work in NICUs have special training in neonatology. **Neonatology** (NEE-oh-nay-TAW-lo-gee) is a branch of medicine concerned with the care, development, and diseases of newborns.

More lives are saved in NICUs now than in the past—due in part to medical and technological advances. A change in policy, however, also contributes to more newborns surviving. Today, NICUs throughout the United States implement *family-centered care policies,* which encourage parental presence in the NICU as well as parental involvement in the newborn's care and treatment. Parents are encouraged to visit the NICU and feed, touch, talk, and sing to their newborns. Hospitals even employ surrogate nonfamily members in the NICU to hold and rock babies. Family-centered care policies promote a developmentally supportive environment, which provides newborns with the love, attention, and support they need for healthy growth and development (**Figure 7.15**).

Lesson 7.3 Review and Assessment 

1. From birth to one month of age, a baby is medically known as a(n) _____.
2. List the five signs the Apgar test checks to measure a newborn's chance of survival.
3. Doctors conduct blood tests on newborns to check for _____, _____, and _____.
4. List the four areas that are tested in the Brazelton scale.
5. Define the term *well-baby checkup.*
6. Give two examples of ways in which family-centered care policies promote a developmentally supportive environment in the NICU.
7. **Critical thinking.** Based on the Apgar test and Brazelton scale, explain what qualities are present in a healthy newborn.

Figure 7.15 NICU Developmentally Supportive Environment

- Each baby (and family) is assigned one medical team.
- Except for emergencies, medical and nursing care coincides with the baby's sleep-wake cycles.
- Parents are encouraged to participate in their baby's care by feeding, rocking, and doing skin-to-skin holding.
- The NICU is decorated and parents have their own space around their baby's NICU bed.
- Soft lighting and low noise levels provide a soothing environment.

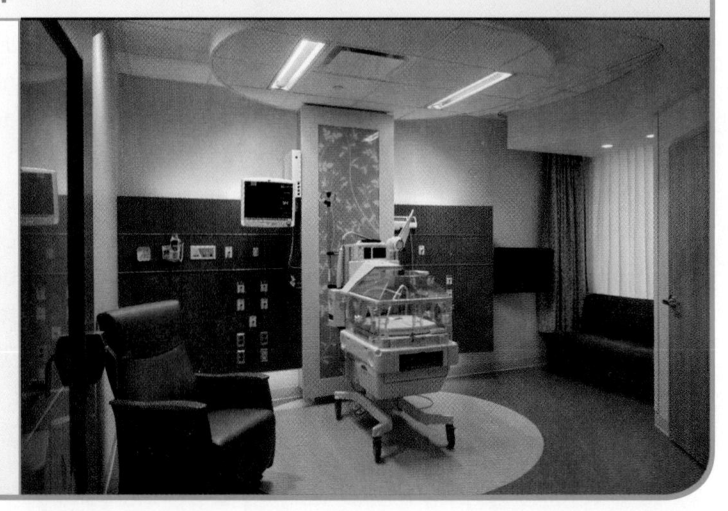

Postpartum Care

Lesson 7.4

Objectives

After studying this lesson, you will be able to

- describe physical care the mother receives during the postpartum period.
- compare and contrast mood disorders that mothers may experience in the postpartum period.
- identify common symptoms of paternal postpartum depression (PPPD).
- give examples of ways parents can meet their own needs while caring for their newborn.

Key Terms

baby blues
paternal postpartum depression (PPPD)
perinatal depression
postpartum care
postpartum depression (PPD)
postpartum mood disorder (PPMD)
postpartum psychosis (PPP)

Academic Terms

coincides
competent
subside

Reading and Writing Activity

Skim the photos and tables in this lesson. For each photo or table, write a one- to two-sentence prediction about how the photo or table illustrates a topic covered. Then, after reading, revisit your predictions and update or correct them to reflect what you learned.

Graphic Organizer

Using a colored pen or pencil, write the key terms for this lesson on a piece of paper, leaving space around them for your notes. Then as you are reading, write your notes around the key term to which they most relate, until you have created a cloud of notes for each term.

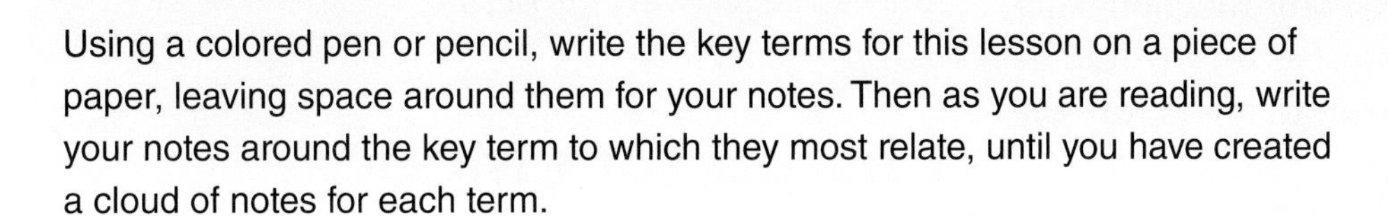

Just as a mother's body undergoes changes beginning at conception and continuing throughout pregnancy, new changes once again occur after childbirth. Most of these changes help the mother's body recover from pregnancy and childbirth. Physical and psychological changes during the postnatal period are normal for new mothers. Abnormal side effects of pregnancy and labor may occur, however, and are warning signs needing immediate medical attention.

Postnatal care for the mother is important not only for maternal health, but also for the well-being of the baby. Poor maternal health impedes and delays the mother's ability to meet the baby's care needs. Studies show that poor maternal physical health negatively affects a baby's development in all domains through the infant and toddler years. Maternal depressive symptoms have an even greater impact on children than poor maternal physical health. Maternal mood disorders adversely affect children's intellectual and emotional development for as long as 14 years.

Figure 7.16 Typical Side Effects of Delivery

- Mild cramping
- *Lochia* (LO-kia), or vaginal bleeding caused by the shedding of the uterine lining
- Some loss or thinning of hair
- Facial blemishes or acne
- Night sweats
- Frequent urination to eliminate excess body fluid
- Urinating "accidents" due to the weakening of bladder muscles (called *stress incontinence*)
- Sore nipples and engorgement of breasts if breast-feeding
- Extra soreness due to any delivery complication

Physical Care of the Mother

Postpartum care, or *postnatal care*, is the care the mother receives during the 6 to 8 weeks following the birth of her baby. Women who had cesarean births may need 12 weeks of recovery time. Mothers may experience typical side effects of delivery during this postpartum period (**Figure 7.16**).

The first hour after birth is a critical time for restoring the mother's body stability. Vital signs (pulse, respiration, and other body functions) are measured every few minutes just as they would be following surgery. Doctors want to make sure the uterus contracts properly.

To regain their strength and avoid health concerns, women do not remain in bed for long after childbirth. After a few days, the doctor might allow a new mother to perform certain exercises that will help tone the abdominal muscles. These exercises are done slowly and gradually for safety.

During the postpartum period, mothers usually want to lose the extra weight from pregnancy. On average, a woman loses 11 pounds during birth and another 7 pounds within a few weeks after birth. If mothers do not nurse their babies, they can return to their prepregnancy healthful eating patterns. Nursing mothers, however, require more nutrients to create the breast milk that sustains their babies. A doctor or dietitian can help women determine their nutritional and activity needs after pregnancy.

Doctors often want mothers to schedule a postpartum checkup about six weeks after delivery. At this appointment, doctors check to see how well the mother is recovering. If the mother must return to work before the end of the postpartum period, nurses and doctors can provide special guidance. The key to complete recovery, whether the mother is at home or on the job, is to get plenty of rest and to go slow with activity. Too much activity may hinder the recovery process.

Postpartum Mood Disorders

Parents often think the time after the birth of their baby will be happy and exciting. Sometimes, however, both men and women may experience a **postpartum mood disorder (PPMD)**, mental health condition, characterized by feelings of sadness, guilt, or depression after the birth of their baby. PPMDs are made worse by other stressors, such as financial challenges, social isolation without parenting support, family conflicts, health concerns, increased work schedules, mood disorder in the partner, and a fussy baby.

Maternal Mood Disorders

Approximately 20 percent of mothers suffer from depression during or after pregnancy. Women who are depressed during pregnancy are also often depressed during the postpartum period and even afterward. For these women, the most vulnerable time is between 12 and 24 months post-delivery. Because of the timing before and long after delivery, **perinatal** (per-ih-NAY-tuhl) **depression** is the newer term used.

Mood disorders mothers may experience in the postpartum period range from mild to severe (**Figure 7.17**). Each PPMD has its own symptoms. **Baby blues**, the most common mood disorder, is a mild postpartum mood disorder that goes away on its own. Baby blues usually begin 4 or 5 days after childbirth and disappear in 10 days. **Figure 7.18** lists suggestions for coping with baby blues. **Postpartum depression (PPD)** is a serious form of depression that occurs less frequently than baby blues. **Postpartum psychosis (PPP)** is a rare and extremely severe mental illness. (*Psychosis* means *mental illness*.)

Generally, PPD and PPP occur a little later than baby blues and do not **subside** (lessen in severity) without treatment. In these cases, negative thoughts and feelings go beyond common negative thoughts, such as "I look awful," or "My baby is so fussy." Mothers with serious mood disorders may think about harming themselves, their babies, and even older children. Some actually do cause harm.

Although the exact causes of postpartum mood disorders are unknown, scientists believe causes may be due to a variety of factors, including genetics, chemical changes, and stress. All women in the postpartum period are at risk of developing a PPMD, but some women have higher risk factors.

Figure 7.17 Maternal Postpartum Mood Disorders

Name	Rate of Incidence	Symptoms	Appearance and Duration
Baby blues	40–85% of all deliveries	Irritability; anxious spells; sleep and appetite problems; weeping; feeling tired	Peaks between 3 and 5 days postpartum. Often resolves itself within a few days.
Postpartum depression (PPD)	10–15% of all deliveries (26–32% of teen deliveries)	Restlessness; exhaustion; inability to concentrate; memory loss; uncontrollable crying; trouble making decisions; lack of interest in pleasurable activities; appetite and sleep problems; overconcern or lack of interest in baby; fear of harming self or baby; guilt	Occurs within first 6 weeks postpartum. If untreated, may last a year or longer. Often happens again in future deliveries.
Postpartum psychosis (PPP)	0.1% of all deliveries (1 in 1,000)	Severe mental illness; includes delusions that often focus on the infant dying; sees the infant as either perfect or defective; desires to kill self or infant	Occurs between 1 and 3 months postpartum with a second peak at 18 to 24 months postpartum. Continues until treated.

Figure 7.18 Coping with Baby Blues

- Remember the feelings are temporary. The "blues" are due to a drop in the hormones estrogen (ES-truh-jehn) and progesterone (pro-JES-teh-rohn); recovery from pregnancy, labor, and delivery; and stress caused by the new maternal role.
- Make grooming a regular and relaxing time. Keep hair styles simple for easy care. Consider outfits that can be adjusted to fit as weight loss occurs.
- Use physical activity as a way to increase *endomorphins* (feel-good hormones). A 30-minute walk alone, with a family member or friend, or with the baby in a stroller is most helpful to the new mother's physical and psychological well-being.
- Make sure to get some sunshine.
- Sleep, nap, or relax whenever possible.
- Snack on nutritious foods.
- Take a few minutes daily to do something beyond baby care, such as chat with friends or family, or run an errand.
- Ask for child care help.
- Lower expectations concerning household responsibilities.
- Keep visitors to a minimum.
- Cry, if need be, but avoid indulging in "self-pity parties." Doctors can help if crying is too frequent or uncontrollable.
- Do not expect to be completely comfortable in the new "maternal shoes." Forget ideas of perfect parent and perfect baby. Within an instant, a person becomes a parent, but the parenting role evolves over many years.

Women with the following characteristics have an increased risk factor for developing a PPMD:

- age in the teen years or over 40 years of age
- family history of mood disorders
- family history of thyroid problems
- mood swings during the menstrual cycle—often called *PMS*
- migraine headaches when taking hormones (including birth control pills)
- fertility problems
- severe family stress
- lack of support from family and friends
- previous postpartum mood disorder

Paternal Mood Disorders

About 10 percent of men show signs of depression during their wife's pregnancy through six months after delivery. The percentage spikes to approximately 26 percent from three to six months after delivery. This timing **coincides** (happens together) with the timing of when many mothers return to work. Also, half of depressed fathers have wives who are depressed, too.

Mood disorders that appear in men are often called **paternal postpartum depression (PPPD)**. Fathers experience similar problems as their wives, such as a change in hormones and additional stressors. Certain PPPD symptoms are common (**Figure 7.19**).

Figure 7.19 Symptoms of Paternal Postpartum Depression (PPPD)

- Appear sad and quiet or irritable and agitated.
- May experience heart palpitations and shortness of breath.
- May experience panic attacks.
- Lose interests in hobbies and socializing.
- Feel worthless.
- Lose appetite and become sleep deprived.
- Work excessively (60+ hours per week).
- May engage in risky behaviors (substance abuse, gambling).

Treatment for Mood Disorders

Mood disorders are just as common and real as physical disorders. If untreated, like other problems, they can have devastating effects on the entire family. Yet only about 15 percent of women receive treatment and likely far fewer men. Treatment is critical because mood disorders not only cause problems for the parents, but can be devastating for the newborn.

Treatments for mood disorders vary due to the severity of the condition. Examples may include medication for PPD and PPPD and behavior therapy to replace drug treatment for nursing mothers. Training in parent-child interactions, participating in support groups, and receiving help with child-rearing are other examples of treatment options.

Meeting the Parents' Needs

Once the newborn is at home with parents, roles and responsibilities change. The first few weeks with the newborn are especially difficult. Parents find every waking moment dedicated to their newborn and family, and may soon feel overwhelmed. As parents care for their newborn during the postpartum period, they also need to care for themselves. Parents can learn to meet their own needs while being wonderful parents to their newborn by

- ***getting enough rest.*** Being tired can lead to illness, irritability, and depression. Therefore, resting whenever possible is especially important for parents. Sleeping or resting while babies sleep and taking turns getting up with the baby at night can help parents get the rest they need.
- ***maintaining a healthful diet.*** Eating nutritious, simple meals helps parents have the energy needed for parenting (**Figure 7.20**). Healthful snacks packed with nutrients, such as fruits and vegetables, are helpful for getting through the day.
- ***being physically active.*** Being physically active for 30 minutes each day helps keep parents alert. Putting the baby in a stroller and going for a walk outside can be excellent for a parent's physical health and mood.

Figure 7.20 Preparing meals ahead of time and freezing them for a later date can be an easy and efficient way of planning ahead for postpartum nutritional needs. *What healthy freezer meals could a couple prepare?*

- ***staying organized.*** Parents can avoid wasting time looking for misplaced household and baby items by keeping them organized and easily accessible. A bulletin board in a convenient location may be useful for posting doctors' recommendations, appointments, bills, shopping lists, and other reminders.
- ***taking care of legal matters.*** While in the hospital, parents can apply for their baby's birth certificate and Social Security number. (Social Security numbers are needed for tax forms, bank accounts, savings bonds, and medical coverage.) Parents may also enroll their baby in a family health care policy and add the baby as a beneficiary to life insurance policies, investment accounts, and their will.
- ***socializing.*** Spending time with other new parents provides socialization opportunities for the parents and their newborns. Hiring a **competent** (knowledgeable) babysitter can also help parents have outings without babies (**Figure 7.21**).

The healthy development of newborns depends on the parent-child relationship. With their own needs met, parents are better able to meet their newborn's needs. Babies whose needs are met by loving parents are off to a good start.

Lesson 7.4 Review and Assessment 

1. Care the mother receives during the six to eight weeks following the birth of her baby is called _____.
2. Identify the three maternal postpartum mood disorders from least to most serious.
3. List three characteristics that might signal an increased risk factor for maternal postpartum mood disorders.
4. Postpartum mood disorders in men are known as _____.
5. Explain the importance of seeking and receiving treatment for postpartum mood disorders.
6. List four ways parents can meet their own needs while caring for a newborn.
7. **Critical thinking.** Why does PPPD spike when mothers return to work? What paternal stress might be relieved when mothers go back to work?
8. **Critical thinking.** How can friends and family help a parent who is suffering from a postpartum mood disorder?

Figure 7.21 Parents need to spend time together away from the home and with other adults to restore their physical and mental energy. *What types of socialization opportunities might be available for parents and their newborns?*

Chapter 7

Review and Assessment

Summary

Pregnancy is a family affair. Fathers-to-be and children should be involved. Family decisions to be made before birth include where the baby will be born and which method of delivery will be used.

When delivery nears, the mother-to-be will go into labor. If complications occur during or after childbirth, special medical attention will be needed, such as drug-assisted deliveries or vaginal-assisted deliveries. When a vaginal birth is not safe for mother, baby, or both, the doctor may perform a C-section.

Soon after birth, newborns undergo tests to assess their health. Among these are the Apgar test, various blood screening tests, hearing tests, heart tests, and the Brazelton scale. Premature babies must be cared for in a neonatal intensive care unit (NICU), where the touch and attention of parents is vital to the newborn's survival. After delivery, bonding is important for parents and the baby. Bonding will continue for many weeks.

During the postpartum period, the mother's body returns to normal. She will need to rest, get physical activity, and eat nutritious meals. Postpartum mood disorders are common. These disorders are mainly due to hormonal changes in the body. Fathers may also have mood disorders due to the major changes in their lives. Treatment is critical in moderate and severe cases. Untreated depression can be devastating for the entire family, including the newborn. In addition to meeting their baby's needs, parents must take time to respond to their own needs.

College and Career Portfolio

Portfolio Prioritization

Identifying priorities is an essential part of any project, and is especially important for a self-guided project like compiling a portfolio. Before you begin compiling your portfolio, identify which items are most important. Your priorities will depend on the purpose of your portfolio and on where your strengths lie.

When prioritizing, consider which items best showcase your work and talents. Also consider where you can compensate for any weaknesses. To identify your priorities as you compile a portfolio, complete the following activities:

- Consider which items will best highlight your strengths and which items are most important to your objective.
- Highlight the most important items in your portfolio. These will be your top priorities.

Chapter 7 Review and Assessment

Vocabulary Activities

1. Work with a partner to write the definitions of the following terms. Then pair up with another team to discuss your definitions and any discrepancies. Discuss the definitions with the class and ask your instructor for correction or clarification.

Key Terms

anemia (7.3)
Apgar test (7.3)
baby blues (7.4)
bonding (7.2)
Brazelton scale (7.3)
breech birth position (7.2)
certified nurse-midwife (CNM) (7.1)
cesarean section (7.2)
contraction (7.2)
dilation (7.2)
episiotomy (7.2)
Family and Medical Leave Act (FMLA) (7.1)
forceps (7.2)
hysterectomy (7.2)
jaundice (7.3)
labor (7.1)
Lamaze method (7.1)
lightening (7.2)
maternity leave (7.1)
natural childbirth (7.1)
neonatal intensive care unit (NICU) (7.3)
neonate (7.3)
neonatology (7.3)
paternal postpartum depression (PPPD) (7.4)
paternity leave (7.1)
pediatrician (7.3)
perinatal depression (7.4)
postpartum care (7.4)
postpartum depression (PPD) (7.4)
postpartum mood disorder (PPMD) (7.4)
postpartum psychosis (PPP) (7.4)
Pregnancy Discrimination Act (PDA) (7.1)
pregnancy leave (7.1)
vacuum extraction (7.2)
well-baby checkup (7.3)

2. For each of the following terms, draw a cartoon bubble to express the meaning of each term as it relates to the chapter.

Academic Terms

coincides (7.4)
competent (7.4)
dislodged (7.2)
elastic (7.2)
exclusively (7.1)
hectic (7.1)
incision (7.2)
intervals (7.2)
involuntary (7.2)
irregular (7.2)
metabolize (7.3)
reassure (7.1)
resuscitate (7.3)
sequential (7.2)
subside (7.4)

Critical Thinking

3. **Identify.** At one time, pregnancy and childbirth were considered a "woman's affair." Now this event is thought of as a family affair. What changes in society have led to pregnancy and childbirth being a family affair? Are there ways in which society still considers pregnancy and childbirth a "woman's affair"? Identify ways family members can be involved.
4. **Determine.** Imagine you are a doctor and your patient, Anna, is nearing her due date. She expresses concern that her four-year-old son might be upset about the new baby. Even though she has explained to her son that the baby is coming, he seems anxious and has been misbehaving at the child care program. With a partner, role-play this scenario, and determine what advice you would give Anna.
5. **Compare and contrast.** Compare and contrast the birthplaces and methods of delivery available to pregnant mothers. Create a resource for pregnant women, listing these options and identifying three pros and three cons for each.
6. **Evaluate.** What are the advantages and disadvantage of rooming-in arrangements in a hospital birthing room? If you were a new parent, would you choose this method if it were available to you? Why or why not?
7. **Draw conclusions.** Why is it best for the baby to be in a specific position for childbirth? Review the information in this chapter about lightening, childbirth, and breech birth position. Draw conclusions about why the ideal position for childbirth is ideal. What are the disadvantages if a baby is in the wrong position?
8. **Analyze.** Review the Apgar test and Brazelton scale and consider: how exactly do these measurements determine the health of a newborn? Why would a low score indicate that a newborn needs special medical attention? Why would a high score indicate a healthy baby?
9. **Make inferences.** Imagine a couple with a premature baby who will likely remain hospitalized for several weeks. What challenges might the couple face in terms of bonding? What can family and friends do to help?
10. **Cause and effect.** Imagine you are a counselor, and you are talking with a couple suffering from PPD and PPPD. How would you explain the causes of these conditions? How would you respond to the couple's feelings that something is "wrong" with them?

Core Skills

11. **Research and writing.** Maternity, paternity, and family leave policies vary by company and by country. Research the legal requirements for leave policies in the United States and in at least two other countries. How are the legal requirements similar? How are they different? Based on your research, how, if at all, would you change leave policies in the United States? Write a two- to four-page essay summarizing your research and proposing any changes.
12. **Art and writing.** Imagine you are teaching the stages of labor to a group of students who learn best when they create models and replicate processes with their hands. In small groups, devise a hands-on activity that simulates and teaches the process of childbirth, using classroom materials or materials from home. The activity should be school appropriate. Write a two-page proposal describing your activity and its educational merit.
13. **Speaking and listening.** Once your activity idea for #12 has been approved, acquire all the materials you will need for your class to participate in this hands-on activity. Create and pass out a sheet of instructions. Then, as a group, lead your class through the hands-on activity you devised. Be prepared to clarify any steps and to answer questions from your classmates. Participate fully and ask questions during all the activities devised for your class.
14. **Reading and writing.** Locate a book written for pregnant woman and read the chapters on childbirth. Consider the language and tone. How does the book's coverage of childbirth differ from this textbook's coverage? Write a short essay identifying the audience of the book you read and analyzing why the author might have chosen the tone and language he or she did.
15. **Technology and speaking.** Review the Apgar test, Brazelton scale, and newborn screening tests covered in this chapter. Then, using digital resources, create a newborn "report card." Your report card should be an easy-to-use, easy-to-read log where parents can record their newborn's test results and easily reference them. Present your "report card" to the class and explain your rationale for the design.
16. **Listening and speaking.** In small groups, discuss with your classmates your knowledge about childbirth and postpartum care. Conduct this discussion as though you had never read the chapter. Take notes on the observations expressed. Then review the points discussed, factoring in your new knowledge about childbirth. Develop a summary of what you have learned and present it to the class, using the terms you have learned in this chapter.
17. **Math.** Review the rates of incidence for maternal postpartum mood disorders in Figure 7.17. Research the total number of births in the United States in the current year, and using that number, calculate how many new mothers should statistically have experienced the baby blues, PPD, and PPP.
18. **CTE Career Readiness Practice.** Historically, childbirth has claimed the lives of many mothers and children. Medical advances have reduced the number of fatalities due to childbirth, but in some areas of the world, childbirth can still be a hazardous affair. Using online or print resources, identify areas where childbirth fatalities are still high. What are the reasons for these fatalities? What are the social and economic impacts? What steps can these areas and the world take toward reducing the number of fatalities due to childbirth? Write a report of your findings to share with the class.

Observations

19. As a class, organize a trip to a local hospital or birthing center, and tour the facility. Observe how the facility is organized, what amenities are available, and what kind of environment is created by the decorations and staff. Discuss why the facility chose to arrange and decorate as it did and how other facilities might differ depending on their purposes and locations.
20. Interview two women in your family or in a friend's family who gave birth two or three generations apart. Ask each to describe her childbirth experience. Where did she give birth, and who was allowed to be with her? What rules did she have to follow in pregnancy and childbirth? How much technology was involved in the birth? Summarize your interviews in a written report.

Unit 3 Infancy

Chapter 8	Physical Development in the First Year
Chapter 9	Intellectual Development in the First Year
Chapter 10	Social-Emotional Development in the First Year

Community Service Project

An entire CTSO chapter typically carries out a community service project, which often takes several months to a year to complete. There may be several parts to this type of event—written and oral. The event may also involve preparation of a display or portfolio. The CTSO chapter designates several members to represent the team at the competitive event.

To prepare for a community service project, complete the following activities:

1. Read and analyze the event rules and guidelines.
2. Select a theme for your chapter's community service project as a team.
3. Identify the target audience of the community service project. Your project may include businesses, schools, and community groups.
4. Decide on which roles the team needs to carry out the plan, such as a team captain, secretary, or treasurer.
5. Use a decision-making planning process to create a project rationale that identifies the project goals and needs. What is the desired end result of this project? What are the benefits of supporting and completing the project? Identify goals, tasks, and ways to execute the plan.
6. Have group members report on progress during regular chapter meetings. Create a draft report based on guidelines from your CTSO organization. Update and refine your group's written report, creating necessary visuals or a portfolio until the project is complete. Include an analysis of the success of your project as part of the presentation.
7. Practice the presentation for the competitive event. Chapter members and the instructor can serve as judges during practice. Incorporate suggestions for refinement.

Chapter 8 Physical Development in the First Year

Essential Question

How do babies grow and make great advances in motor skills, and how do parents and other caregivers provide everything babies physically need?

Lesson 8.1	Growth and Development in the First Year
Lesson 8.2	Meeting Nutritional Needs in the First Year
Lesson 8.3	Meeting Other Physical Needs in the First Year

Case Study Why Do Some Newborns Fail to Thrive?

As a class, read the case study and discuss the questions that follow. After you finish studying the chapter, discuss this case study again. Have your opinions changed based on what you learned?

Before leaving the birthing center with her baby boy, the certified nurse-midwife reminded Sharon to nurse every three hours. At the end of the first week, Sharon took her baby for his first well-baby checkup. Although the doctor mentioned the baby's weight loss, all seemed to be well. At the baby's second checkup a week later, the doctor frowned and said, "I thought he would at least be at birth-weight by now." Because the baby had gained only a very small amount, the doctor wanted to weigh the baby again in three days. After examining the baby for the third time, the doctor wrote on the baby's chart, "failure to thrive." He lectured Sharon about nursing him more often—every two hours—so he would gain weight.

Those words, "failure to thrive," shook Sharon's confidence. Sharon believed she was doing everything right. She thought, "How could the doctor use such horrible words? What kind of mother doesn't feed her baby and take care of him? I have kept him clean, warm, dry, and content. He has been a dreamy baby, so easy to lull into extended periods of sleep. What's wrong with my baby?"

Give It Some Thought

1. Why do you think the doctor waited until the third appointment before mentioning more frequent nursing to Sharon? Explain your answer.
2. Why might the doctor suspect inadequate nutrition as the cause of the "failure to thrive"? Besides loss of weight, what other signs might the newborn have shown?
3. Should a caring mother be embarrassed by the words, "failure to thrive"? Why or why not?
4. If the baby had inadequate nutrition, hypothesize why he did not cry and become more distressed. Why did he sleep for extended hours?

While studying this chapter, look for the online resources icon  to:

- **Practice** terms with e-flash cards and interactive games
- **Assess** what you learn by completing self-assessment quizzes
- **Expand** knowledge with interactive activities and graphic organizers

Companion G-W Learning

www.g-wlearning.com/childdevelopment

Study on the go

Use a mobile device to practice terms and review with self-assessment quizzes.

www.m.g-wlearning.com/0384

Lesson 8.1 Growth and Development in the First Year

Key Terms

body proportions
cephalocaudal development
crawl
creep
cruising
deciduous teeth
developmental milestones
failure to thrive
fine-motor skills
gross-motor skills
infancy
motor development
ossification
proximodistal development
reflexes
skeletal system
voluntary grasping

Academic Terms

cartilage
circumference
innate
onset
protrudes
stamina

Objectives

After studying this lesson, you will be able to

- describe a child's physical growth in the first year, including specific examples of organ maturation and skeletal growth.
- compare and contrast different types of reflexes.
- differentiate between gross-motor skills and fine-motor skills.
- explain the order in which a child's motor skills develop in the first year.
- give examples of physical developmental milestones children might achieve in the first year.

Reading and Writing Activity

Arrange a group study session to read this lesson aloud. Before each main heading, stop to discuss the main points and to note any unfamiliar words you and your partner encounter. Write a summary of the lesson and list and define the words you or your partner did not know. Share your summary and notes with the class.

Graphic Organizer

Write each of the five objectives for this lesson on index cards and arrange these cards near you as you read. On each index card, take notes about the appropriate objective. Then, trade your index cards with a partner. Discuss how your notes are similar or different.

describe a child's physical growth in the first year, including specific examples of organ maturation and skeletal growth.

Physical growth and development during the first year of life are exciting because children grow and develop new skills each day. Of all the changes that occur during infancy, physical growth is the most noticeable. Parents and others often remark, "Look how he (or she) has grown!" Growth occurs both outward, such as height and weight, and inward, such as tissue and organ growth. A person's physical growth may continue until the early years of adulthood. This growth period is longer than that of any other living creature.

From birth, infants make great physiological adaptations (change from being helpless newborns to being "up and about" infants) in their new world outside the womb. These adaptations occur due to their impressive advances in motor skills. Development proceeds in two directions—from head downward and from the center of the body to the *extremities* (fingers and toes). Through biological maturation and experiences in the first year of life, the infant's world becomes most accessible.

Physical Growth in the First Year

As you may recall, from birth to one month of age a baby is medically known as a *neonate* or *newborn*. Between one month and one year after birth, a baby is commonly called an *infant*. The stage of development during this first year of life is known as **infancy**.

Much physical growth and development occur during infancy. At birth, a newborn looks much different from the plump, beautiful infants you see in the media who are usually several months old (**Figure 8.1**). Besides changes in physical traits during the first year, changes also occur in organ maturation and skeletal growth.

Figure 8.1 Changes in Appearance Between Birth and Six Months of Age

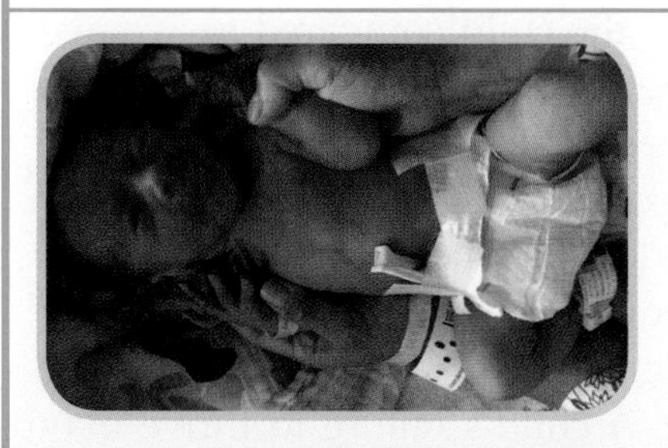

Newborn (one day after birth)

- Eyes are dull-gray blue
- Stomach protrudes; pelvis and hips are narrow
- Legs drawn up
- Skin is blotchy; some blood vessels are visible
- Have a protective, cheese-like covering called *vernix caseosa*

Three months

- Eyes are able to produce tears
- Round and chubby
- Body and limbs begin to stretch out
- Head is large compared to body

Six months

- Eyes begin to work together
- Eye color develops
- Rapid increases in length of body
- Chest becomes larger in circumference than the head

Maturation of Organs

The brain grows faster than any other tissue or organ in the child's body during the first year. Most neurons develop during the prenatal period, but "fine tuning" occurs during infancy. The neurons increase in size, more glial cells form, more dendrites develop, and myelination continues to speed up connections. The brain weighs one pound at birth and two pounds at one year of age. You will learn about specific areas of brain growth as you read about intellectual development in the first year.

Newborns are born with a complete set of immature muscles. During infancy, muscles increase in size through physical activity and hormones. The infant's strength and **stamina** (ability to continually do something) increase with muscle development.

After birth, the child's digestion is aided by "friendly" intestinal bacteria, increased stomach size, and salivation. During the first year, the digestive system remains immature. Caregivers see evidence of this through frequent spitting up and partially digested foods in the child's stools.

As a child's lung capacity increases and the lungs mature, the child's breathing rate decreases. This decreased breathing rate does not negatively affect oxygen transfer to the bloodstream. Like newborns, infants still breathe from the diaphragm in the abdominal area rather than from the chest like adults. Infants' lung tissue is highly vulnerable to viruses, bacteria, and pollution (including second-hand smoke).

Newborns' hearts are immature, but improve in strength throughout infancy. The pumping of the blood becomes better regulated, which lowers blood pressure. During this first year, the heart becomes stronger, giving children more stamina.

Skeletal Growth

The **skeletal system** is the framework of the body that consists of cartilage, bones, and teeth. Skeletal growth refers to the changes in a child's length and weight, body proportions, and bones and teeth.

Length and Weight

A child's length and weight change quickly during the first year. (The term *length* is used for the first year because the child does not stand. Once the child can stand, the term *height* is used.) Changes happen so quickly that even people who see the child daily are amazed at how fast he or she grows.

All children grow at individual rates, but the average length of a newborn is 20 to 21 inches. Many children increase their birth lengths by about 30 percent in the first five months. They often grow about 9 to 10 inches and almost triple their weight during the first year (**Figure 8.2**). Usually, males are slightly longer and heavier than females (by about ¾ of an inch and 1½ pounds) by one year of age.

Around nine months of age, an infant is rather chubby because of an increase in fat tissues under the skin. After this time, fat tissues begin to decrease. Even at this early age, males have more muscle length and thickness while females have more fat.

A child's *rate of growth* is more important than his or her actual length and weight. The pediatrician uses a growth chart to record the child's growth at each checkup. This growth chart shows several measurements for the child compared to average growth rates. The pediatrician will compare the child's actual measurements to the growth rates. As long as growth continues at a constant rate, the pediatrician will not likely be concerned.

Sometimes, however, children may experience a **failure to thrive**, which means they fail to grow at a healthy rate. A child's failure to thrive may indicate a health condition exists. In this case, the

Figure 8.2 Average Length and Weight During the First Year

Age in Months	Length in Inches	Weight in Pounds
Birth	20	7½
3	23¾	12½
6	26	16¾
9	28	20
12	29½	22¼

growth chart would show a steady growth rate and then a decline. Possible causes of failure to thrive include the following:

- diseases that prevent all or some nutrients from being absorbed or that cause nutrients to be quickly expelled from the body
- insufficient nutrients in the baby's food—diluted formula or poor quality or insufficient amount of breast milk caused by the mother's malnutrition (called *marasmus*)
- infrequent or short feeding times
- abuse or neglect—the baby is not held, touched, or talked to enough

With the proper care and attention, the child's health can often be restored. How long this will take depends on the **onset** (beginning) and severity of the problem.

Body Proportions

A child's **body proportions** (relative size of body parts) differ from those of an adult during the first year. For example, an infant's head is about one-fourth his or her total length, while an adult's head is one-eighth of his or her total height (**Figure 8.3**). An infant also has a tiny jaw and chin, a long trunk, a "pot-bellied" abdomen, and short legs.

More than half of the total growth of a child's head occurs during the first year of life. The head **circumference** (linear distance around the edge of a closed curved or circular object) grows from an average of 13.5 to 18.5 inches in the first year. From birth until six months of age, the child's head is larger than the chest, but in many six-month-old children, the chest becomes larger. The difference in the distance around the chest as compared to the distance around the head continues to increase with age.

A child's gain in length during the first year is because the trunk grows. The legs do not grow much longer at this time. The abdomen **protrudes** (sticks out) because the internal organs are large for the child's small body. Because the center of gravity is high on the child's body, the result is poor balance.

Figure 8.3 An infant's head is about one-fourth of his or her length; whereas, an adult's head is about one-eighth of his or her height. *Do these proportions match what you typically see in everyday life?*

Bones and Teeth

At birth, newborns have *fontanels* (FAHN-ta-NEHLS), or *soft spots*, where the skull is not closed. Fontanels enable the baby's skull to compress while passing through the birth canal. Fontanels also allow the skull and brain to grow. The fontanels fill with bone as the skull grows. The skull completely closes in about two years.

A baby's skeleton is mainly made of **cartilage** (firm, but flexible connective tissue found in parts of the body). Some of a baby's bones are made entirely of cartilage while others are partly made of cartilage. There are large spaces between the baby's "bones" to help the joints bend easily without breaking. Young babies can suck their toes with no trouble, but sitting and standing are impossible because their skeletons are not sturdy.

Due to their softness, a newborn's or infant's bones can easily become misshapen. For example, the soft bones of a newborn's skull may be molded into an egg shape to make birth easier. The molded shape of the head will disappear in a couple weeks. A misshapen skull can also result from lying in one position all the time, causing an infant's head to flatten in one place. This has become more common in recent years with the need for babies to sleep on their backs for safety reasons, which you will learn more about later in this chapter. Severe head flattening can be prevented by methods shown in **Figure 8.4**.

Figure 8.4 Prevent Head Flattening

- Change the position of the sleeping baby's head from day to day, but do not take the baby off his or her back.
- Take an alert baby out of the crib.
- Use baby seats, bouncers, and swings for only a little while at a time.
- Remove a sleeping child from a car seat when not traveling.
- Use "tummy time," or time spent on the stomach, several times a day when babies are awake.
- Move objects of interest to encourage the baby to look from side to side when on his or her back.
- Encourage the infant to sit with support around three or four months. (Hold your hand a short distance behind his or her head to provide head support if needed.)

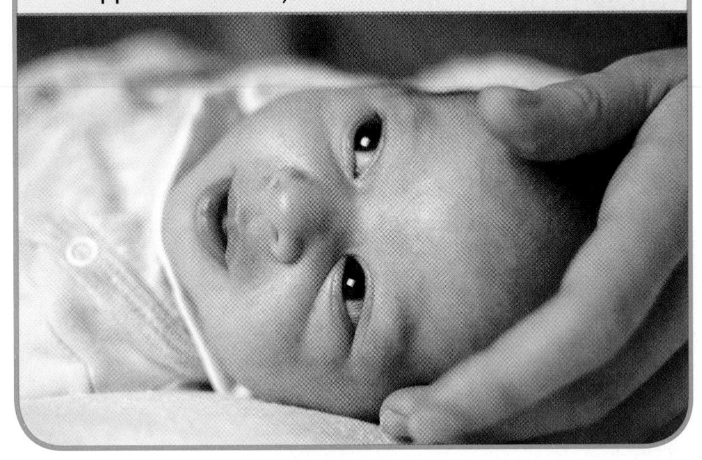

During the first year, three changes occur in a child's bones. First, the length of the bones increases. Second, **ossification** (AWS-sih-fih-CAY-shun), the hardening of bones caused by the depositing of the minerals *calcium* and *phosphorus*, begins. Ossification helps the skeletal frame become sturdy, which in turn helps the infant to sit and eventually walk. Third, the number of bones changes. For example, a baby's body has about 300 bones at birth. These eventually fuse (grow together) to form the 206 bones that adults have. Some of a baby's bones are made entirely of cartilage while others are partly made of cartilage. During childhood, the cartilage grows and is slowly replaced by bone, with help from calcium.

Teeth, a part of the skeletal system, begin forming in the sixth week of prenatal life. By birth, all 20 **deciduous** (deh-SID-joo-uhs) **teeth** (also called *nonpermanent teeth* or *baby teeth*) and a few permanent teeth are developing deep in the jaw. Deciduous teeth are the first set of teeth, which will later be replaced by permanent teeth. The deciduous teeth may begin appearing during the second half of the first year (**Figure 8.5**). The sequence (order) of teething is easier to predict than when teeth will appear (timing). In fact, some newborns are born with one or more teeth. Other children are more than a year old when their first teeth appear.

Reflexes

Newborns enter the world with some **innate** (inborn; natural) **reflexes** (automatic, unlearned movements in response to stimuli) needed for

Figure 8.5 Deciduous Teeth Emergence

Upper Teeth	Approximate Time of Teeth Emergence
Central incisor	8 to 12 months
Lateral incisor	9 to 13 months
Canine (cuspid)	16 to 22 months
First molar	13 to 19 months
Second molar	25 to 33 months
Lower Teeth	**Approximate Time of Teeth Emergence**
Central incisor	6 to 10 months
Lateral incisor	10 to 16 months
Canine (cuspid)	17 to 23 months
First molar	14 to 18 months
Second molar	22 to 31 months

Central incisor
Lateral incisor
Canine (cuspid)
First molar
Second molar

Deciduous teeth

survival. For example, the *rooting reflex* helps newborns search for food by turning their heads and moving their mouths in response to a touch on the cheeks or mouth. After finding objects with their mouths, newborns begin to suck. Newborns also come into the world with the *palmar (grasping) reflex*, which enables them to automatically grasp objects placed in their hands. **Figure 8.6** illustrates some major reflexes that help newborns and infants survive and learn.

Some reflexes, like the rooting reflex, disappear within a few months, while other reflexes remain the same throughout life, such as your knee jerking when tapped with a mallet. Still other reflexes lead to learned, voluntary behaviors essential for development. For example, when infants are about four months old, the grasping reflex is replaced by **voluntary grasping** (the intentional grasping of objects). Babies' first grasps are crude, but with practice, infants refine their skills as they learn to grab and hold many objects.

Reflexes are a clue to the health and maturity of the nervous system. The absence or weakness of a reflex may result from premature birth or a congenital condition. For example, pricking the soles of newborns' feet causes them to jerk or withdraw their legs (called the *withdrawal reflex*). The withdrawal reflex continues throughout life, and its absence may be a sign of brain damage. Reflexes that should disappear in time, but do not disappear, may also signal a problem.

Motor Development

Motor development is the use and control of muscles that direct body movements. Children develop **gross-motor skills** as they learn to use and control large muscles—the trunk, arms, and legs—to roll over, sit, crawl, stand, and walk. Being able to control the small muscles, such as those in the fingers and hands, leads children to develop **fine-motor skills**. Having control over the body is a sign of children's growth and development.

A child's motor skills develop in three main patterns that build on the order of brain development. The following list shows the patterns of motor development:

1. Until brain firings are hardwired, babies move slowly because they must think as they move.
2. Babies' reactions develop from general to specific. For example, if young infants see something they want, they wiggle all over. Older infants smile and reach for the object.
3. Motor development occurs in two directions—from head to foot and from the center of the body to the extremities (from the spine area of the trunk to the hands and feet).

Head-to-Foot Development

Head-to-foot development, **cephalocaudal** (sef-uh-lo-KAW-dahl) **development**, describes the progression of development beginning with the head and moving down to the feet. Cephalocaudal

Figure 8.6

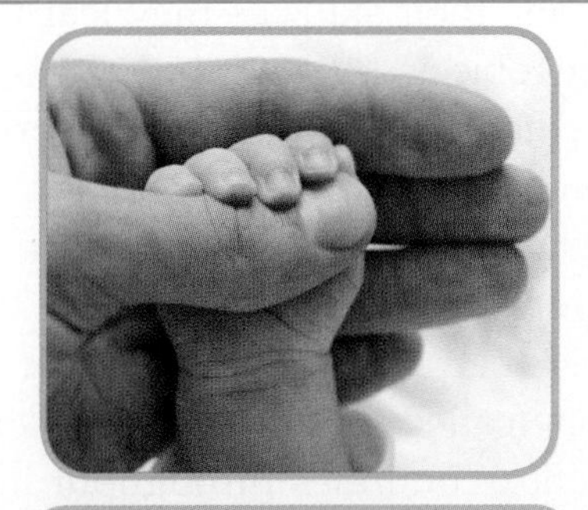 Palmar (grasping) reflex	 Plantar (grasping) reflex	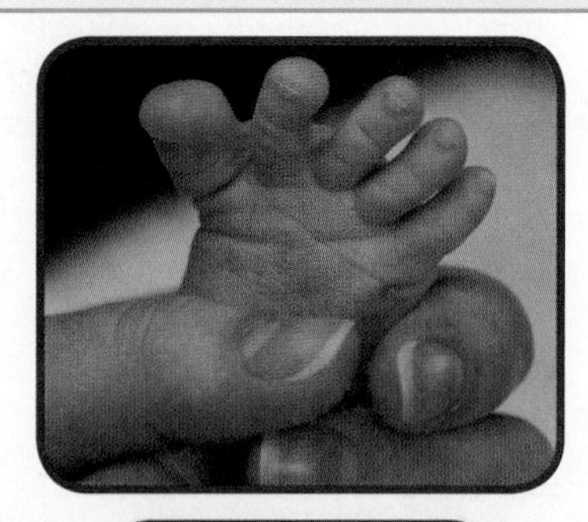 Babinski reflex
Newborns' fingers tighten around any object placed in the palm. Grasp is strong enough to lift them into a sitting position.	Newborns' toes tighten around any object when the ball of the foot is stroked. This reflex disappears between eight and 15 months of age.	Newborns' toes fan out if the outside of the sole is stroked from heel to toe. Reflex ends at about one year of age.

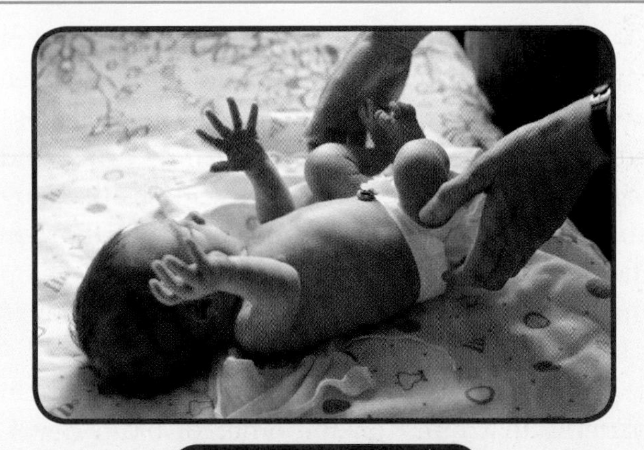 Moro (startle) reflex	 Walking reflex
The reflex consists of two movements: (a) newborns fling arms and legs out and (b) pull them back again when they are startled.	When babies' feet touch a solid surface, alternating steps are taken as in walking. This reflex disappears in three or four months.

development begins before birth. The fetuses head develops, then arm buds, and then leg buds. At birth, newborns have well-developed facial muscles, but less well-developed leg muscles. During infancy, children develop head and neck control more quickly than trunk and leg control.

Head and Neck Control

Newborns need to have their heads continually supported because their muscles are not strong enough to hold their heads steady themselves (**Figure 8.7**). Some newborns can raise their unsteady heads briefly, however, when lying on their stomachs during supervised tummy times. By two months of age, many infants spend a great deal of time with their heads raised. Between three and four months of age, infants can hold their heads and chests up with arm support. Head control is almost complete when infants are about six months old. By this time, infants can raise their heads briefly while lying on their backs. They can also hold their heads steady while sitting in a high chair.

Trunk Control

Control of the trunk develops more slowly than control of the head. Infants placed on their

Focus on

Health

Tummy Time

Child development experts recommend that newborns and infants sleep on their backs, mostly for safety reasons. Lying on their backs, however, does not strengthen babies' neck muscles and upper bodies. Professionals recommend "tummy time" as an activity parents can do with their babies to promote motor skills, such as rolling over, reaching, and crawling. During tummy time, infants and newborns are lying on their bellies to play. Tummy time may begin with a few minutes several times a day. Additional minutes can be added to tummy time as infants develop more head and neck control.

Tummy time should occur only when both parent and baby are alert. Parents should always supervise the baby's movements and awareness and end tummy time before a baby gets drowsy. Parents might read to their babies during tummy time or they might provide toys that encourage babies to lift their heads and reach. These exercises and challenges promote motor development, aid in bone growth, and stimulate babies' brains.

stomachs can lift their heads before they can lift both their heads and chests. Trunk control enables infants to develop motor skills, such as rolling over and sitting.

Infants often learn to roll over between two and five months of age. Usually, they first learn to roll over from stomach to back. Then, about a month later, they learn to roll over from back to stomach. Infants have an easier time lifting their heads and trunks while lying on their abdomens than while lying on their backs.

Figure 8.7 Because newborns are not strong enough to hold their heads steady, their large heads must be supported at all times. *By what age are infants usually able to spend a great deal of time with their heads raised?*

Learning to sit takes several months. Infants must first gain strength in their necks and backs and be able to control their heads. Infants can sit briefly with support (being held or with pillows placed at their backs) at three or four months of age. By seven months of age, infants can often sit for a short time without support. For longer periods of sitting, infants lean forward and support themselves with their arms and legs, but may topple over if distracted. Progress becomes rapid during the next few months, and by nine months of age, many infants can sit unaided.

Leg Control

Leg control is the last phase of head-to-foot development. As infants gain leg control, they usually go through the stages of crawling, creeping, standing, and walking.

- ***Crawling.*** Around five or six months of age, infants learn to **crawl** by pulling with their arms, but not lifting their abdomens from the floor. The common term for this is *belly-crawling*.

- *Creeping.* Between 6 and 8 months of age, infants learn to **creep** by lifting their abdomens off the floor and using their hands and knees or hands and feet to move. The common term for creeping is *knee-crawling*. (**Figure 8.8** illustrates the movements of crawling and creeping.)
- *Standing.* Around 6 months of age, infants enjoy standing as they push with their feet and bounce while parents provide support under their arms. A few months later, infants can pull themselves into a standing position and then hold onto something for support. Many children first learn to stand alone between 12 and 14 months of age.

Figure 8.8 When crawling, infants pull themselves along by their arms, not lifting their abdomens off the floor. When creeping, infants do lift their abdomens and move along the floor using their hands and knees. *How would you explain the difference between crawling and creeping to a new mother or father?*

- *Walking.* After infants learn to stand alone, they usually begin **cruising** (walking by holding onto something for support). As leg control develops, infants can stand further away from objects and hold on with only one of their hands to maintain balance. Infants also take a few cautious steps between objects and people. Around 15 months of age, many children are able to walk alone.

Center-to-Extremities Development

The direction of development from the center of the body to the extremities is called **proximodistal** (prahk-sum-oh-DIS-tahl) **development**, or center-to-extremities development. In center-to-extremities development, control begins with the trunk, then arms, hands, and fingers. This control extends to the hips, then legs, feet, and toes.

Center-to-extremities development aids infants' abilities to move about. For example, infants use their arms and hands to crawl and creep and as a balancing aid for standing and walking. For the most part, however, center-to-extremities development aids in the performance of fine-motor skills. These skills begin with the palmar reflex and are soon followed by voluntary swiping at objects. With time and experience, babies soon begin to grasp objects and even their own feet with their palms and fingers, but not with their thumbs. Near the second half of the first year, babies begin using the thumb and fingers with greater and greater skill until they can hold small objects between the tips of the thumb and the index finger. Grasping skills aid hand manipulation as shown in **Figure 8.9**.

Physical Developmental Milestones

Developmental milestones are physical, intellectual, and social-emotional tasks many children learn to accomplish by a certain age. Developmental milestones identify age approximations for when children, on the average, can demonstrate certain growth and development tasks. Each child, however, develops at his or her own rate. The rate is affected by

Figure 8.9 Stages of Hand Manipulation

Age	Type of Hand Manipulation
Two months	***Rotation:*** Twists the wrists to look at an object from different angles.
Three months	***Translation:*** Moves objects closer to and further away from face.
Four months	***Vibration:*** Shakes and waves objects.
Five months	***Two-handed hold:*** Holds an object with both hands. ***Bilateral hold:*** Uses both hands to explore objects.
Six months	***Hand-to-hand transfer:*** Passes object from one hand to the other. ***Coordinated action holding an object:*** Holds an object with one hand; uses the other hand to finger or pull an object apart.
Eight months	***Coordination action with two objects:*** Holds two objects (one in each hand); coordinates actions (banging objects together; stacking). ***Deformation:*** Uses hands to crush, tear, or flatten a malleable object.
Nine months	***Sequential actions:*** Uses both hands to perform a sequential action, such as one hand raises an object, and then the other hand pulls out the object below.

heredity, nutrition, illnesses, and activity. Whether a child is praised and encouraged (environment) can also make a difference.

Some infants develop more quickly than the age norm while others lag behind. A particular infant may also develop quickly in one area, but more slowly in another. For example, learning to creep is a developmental milestone of a seven-month-old infant. Some infants, however, will learn to creep later.

Physical developmental milestones concern the development of gross-motor skills and fine-motor skills. Many researchers classify these skills as *postural*, *locomotor*, and *grasping* skills. *Postural skills* have to do with aligning the body in an erect position and maintaining the position through balance. Postural skills include holding the head erect, sitting erect, and standing erect without leaning or support. *Locomotor skills* involve the ability to move from place to place using the arms, legs, and feet. Locomotion includes rolling over, crawling, creeping, and walking. *Grasping skills* have to do with small movements of the hands, wrists, and fingers and often require the use of the eyes to coordinate movements. Examples of grasping skills are picking up, carrying, and manipulating small objects. **Figure 8.10** lists physical developmental milestones of newborns and infants.

Lesson 8.1 Review and Assessment 

1. The _____ grows faster than any other tissue or organ in the infant's body during the first year.
2. Describe an infant's body proportions and physical development in terms of: (a) head, (b) jaw and chin, (c) head compared to chest circumference, (d) abdomen, and (e) legs.
3. Nonpermanent teeth, sometimes called *baby teeth*, are technically called _____.
4. Give two examples of reflexes and explain how they are important for survival.
5. What is the difference between gross-motor skills and fine-motor skills? List some examples for each type of skill.
6. Explain the *three patterns* and *two directions* involved in motor development.
7. List the following motor skills in order of occurrence: (a) sits with support, (b) raises the head while on abdomen, (c) creeps, (d) walks, (e) rolls over from front to back, and (f) stands without help.
8. **Critical thinking.** Why are infants' heads so large during the first year of life?

Figure 8.10 Newborn and Infant Physical Milestones

One month

- Has reflexive movements.
- Has Moro reflex.
- Roots for breast.
- Turns head or eyes in the direction of sounds.
- Stares at objects, but does not try to grasp.
- Attempts to lift head when on tummy.

Two months

- Has more voluntary actions.
- Cycles arms and legs.
- Holds head up when on stomach at 45-degree angle above surface.
- Uses a reflexive grasp. Holds objects placed in hands for a few seconds.

Three months

- Leans on elbows and holds chest up and head erect for 10 seconds.
- Moves arm and leg on each side of the body in unison.
- Holds hands open.
- May swipe at dangling objects.
- Explores face with hands.
- Grasps what is seen.

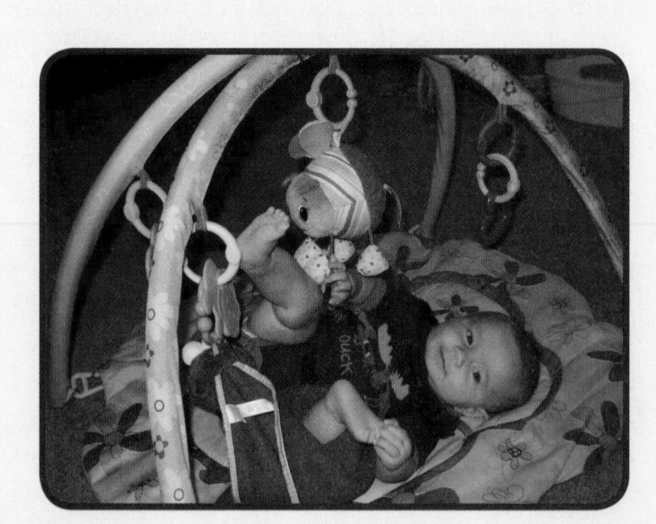

Four months

- Rolls from stomach to side.
- Holds head steady for a short time; turns head in all directions.
- Splashes and kicks in bath.
- Sits with support of cushions for a short time.
- Touches objects close to hand and may bat objects.
- Pulls objects placed in hand toward mouth.

Five months

- Rolls from stomach to back.
- Holds head erect when supported in a sitting position.
- Kicks while on back and may move by pushing feet against the wall or footboard of a crib.
- Grasps a dangling, large ring.
- Shakes rattle placed in hand.
- Plays with toes.

Six months

- Rolls from back to stomach.
- Bounces when held in standing position.
- Makes crawling motions with arms and legs.
- Opens hands wider for larger objects than for smaller objects.
- Examines objects with eyes and hands; explores objects.
- Grasps small objects with palm.

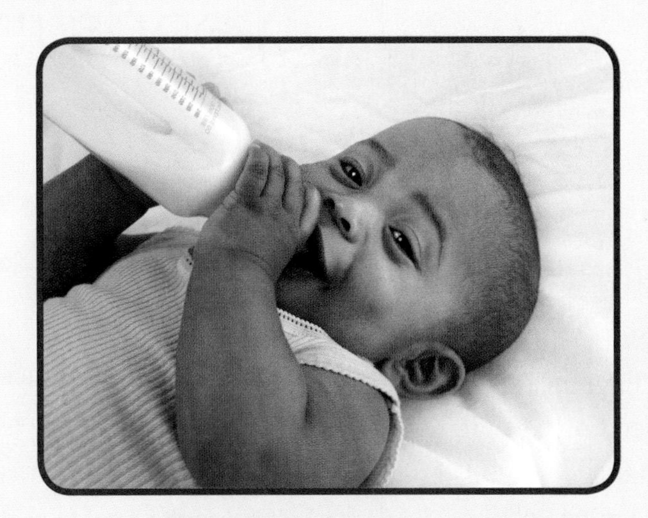

Seven months

- Sits without support for a few minutes.
- Creeps.
- Holds objects in both hands; bangs objects together.
- Brings fingers to mouth.

Eight months

- Pushes up on knees and rocks back and forth on knees.
- Stands if helped.
- Puts feet in mouth.
- Transfers toys from hand to hand.

Nine months

- Pulls self up using people or furniture for support.
- Stands holding with one hand while leaning on something.
- Claps and waves hands.
- Tastes everything.
- Pokes at objects with forefinger.

Ten months

- Rocks and bounces to music when held.
- Sits without support indefinitely.
- Has superior palm grasp.
- Carries three objects in one hand.

Eleven months

- Walks when led.
- Turns around while creeping.
- May stand a few seconds without support.
- Lowers body from standing position without falling or sitting hard.
- Puts objects into containers.
- Eats finger foods; brings spoon to mouth.

Lesson 8.2 Meeting Nutritional Needs in the First Year

Key Terms

colic
intolerance
lactation consultant
solids
weaning

Academic Terms

abrupt
adverse
alleviates
dilute
satiety

Objectives

After studying this lesson, you will be able to

- describe how to meet nutritional needs from birth to six months of age.
- identify advantages of breast-feeding for babies, mothers, and families.
- explain the process of weaning babies from breast milk and formula.
- describe how to meet nutritional needs from six months to one year of age.
- give examples of finger foods that are safe for infants to eat.

Reading and Writing Activity

Read the lesson title and tell a classmate what you have experienced or already know about meeting nutritional needs in the first year. Write a paragraph describing what you would like to learn about the topic. After reading this lesson, share two concepts you have learned with your classmate.

Graphic Organizer

Draw a time line illustrating the first year of an infant's life. Then, as you are reading, take notes about nutritional needs in the first year and how they are met at each point on your time line.

0 months	6 months	12 months

A healthful diet provides the essential nutrients a child needs to grow, explore, and develop in the first year. Meeting a baby's food and nutrition needs quickly **alleviates** (relieves) hunger. Responding promptly to the baby's need for food teaches the baby his or her needs will be met. Erikson calls this learning a sense of *basic trust*.

Babies go through different stages of the feeding process. For the first six months of life, newborns and infants are completely dependent on breast milk or formula. After six months, infants may begin eating solid foods from a spoon. By the end of the first year, infants are beginning to self-feed using their fingers. As infants are developing new feeding skills, mealtimes can be frustrating and messy. Remaining calm can help make mealtimes pleasant for infants and their parents.

In all situations, parents and other caregivers need to make a priority of meeting their infants' nutritional needs. Nutrition during the first year of life can affect development in all areas later in life. The American Academy of Pediatrics (AAP) has made recommendations for meeting infants' nutritional needs.

Breast-Feeding and Formula-Feeding

Because babies grow quickly throughout the first year, their nutritional needs are especially important. Parents can meet these needs by either breast-feeding or formula-feeding. Both methods provide opportunities for parents to bond with their babies as they hold and cuddle them during feeding times.

Breast-Feeding

In the first six months, breast milk best meets the baby's nutritional needs. The AAP recommends breast-feeding continue for at least the first 12 months of life. Breast-feeding has advantages for baby, mother, and the family (**Figure 8.11**).

Figure 8.11 Advantages of Breast-Feeding

For Babies	For Mothers and Families
• Breast milk contains the right proportions of proteins, carbohydrates, fats, vitamins, minerals, and water. This makes it easier to digest than formula. The baby is exposed to different flavors according to the mother's diet. • Mother's immunities to certain diseases are passed to the baby. • Breast milk is sterile (unless put in a bottle) and is ready immediately. • Breast-fed babies are usually a healthy weight because the milk content is perfect for the baby's needs and the mother does not overfeed the baby. • Vigorous sucking required for breast-feeding satisfies the need for sucking and promotes good development of facial structures and healthier, straighter teeth. • Babies rarely choke because they can control the flow of milk.	• Breast-feeding has health benefits for the mother, such as causing the uterus to contract to original size and helping bones regain minerals. • Breast-feeding can save the family money on formula, bottles, and nipples, and can save time in formula and bottle preparation. • Breast-feeding is environmentally green. • Food is available during emergencies. • Breast-feeding women can offer their babies the most nutritional food, even while returning to their careers. (Mothers who work can pump the milk several times during the day and refrigerate or freeze it. The baby takes this milk in a bottle while the mother is away.) • Mother and baby develop a warm relationship because of touch and eye contact. Thus, breast-feeding helps with bonding. (When the mother pumps breast milk, other family members also have opportunities to bond with the baby.)

Mothers who breast-feed their babies have higher nutritional needs for some vitamins and minerals. Nursing mothers can help meet their nutritional needs by choosing foods high in vitamins and minerals from each of the food groups—fruits, vegetables, dairy, grains, and proteins. In addition to a healthful diet, doctors may recommend some nursing mothers take a vitamin and mineral supplement to help meet their nutritional needs.

Fluid needs also increase while breast-feeding. Mothers need to drink plenty of water to meet these needs and satisfy their thirst. One way nursing mothers can help meet their fluid needs is to drink a glass of water each time they are breast-feeding or pumping their breast milk for use in a bottle. Drinks that contain caffeine or added sugars, such as soft drinks or fruit drinks, should be limited or avoided. These substances can affect the mother's milk and the baby.

Any over-the-counter drugs mothers take could also pass from the mother's breast milk to the baby. Therefore, nursing mothers should check with a doctor before taking any drugs. For breast-feeding advice, mothers may wish to consult with a doctor, nurse, or **lactation consultant** (breast-feeding expert).

Formula-Feeding

Many mothers choose breast-feeding, but some cannot breast-feed. Even when mothers can breast-feed, sometimes they choose not to do so. Parents who choose formula-feeding may want to consult with a doctor about the type and amount of formula to use. Most formulas are based on cow's milk, but soy formulas are often used for babies who have problems digesting milk-based formulas.

When formula-feeding, parents should only use commercially prepared (store bought) formulas, regulated by the Food and Drug Administration (FDA), and not homemade formulas or whole cow's milk. Commercially prepared formulas contain specially

Focus on Health

Formula-Feeding

For caregivers using formula to meet the infant's nutritional needs, it is important to follow certain safety and sanitation procedures. The following guidelines are precautions caregivers should follow while preparing formula and bottle-feeding the baby.

- Keep mixed and ready-to-use formula refrigerated to prevent the growth of bacteria.
- Boil any water added (including bottled water) to powdered or liquid concentrate formulas for one to two minutes and then cool.
- Keep utensils, bottles, and nipples completely clean.
- Check the quality of bottle nipples. Large or clogged holes cause feeding problems. Torn or worn nipples could cause the baby to choke. Buy special nipples for premature and sick infants so they can nurse successfully.
- Do not prop the bottle. Babies can choke while feeding. (If a baby chokes, parents should turn the baby on his or her side or abdomen, and then pat on the back.)
- Report any digestive upsets or rash to the baby's doctor. These problems might indicate the baby is reacting to the ingredients in the formula.
- Throw away all formula the baby does not finish. The baby's saliva causes bacteria to grow.

Why are these safety precautions necessary when preparing a bottle of formula? What signs can caregivers watch for that might indicate a negative reaction to the formula?

processed milk products that provide the needed nutrients for the baby. These formulas are processed in a way to make it easier for the baby to digest. Commercially prepared formulas are available in powdered, liquid concentrate, or ready-to-feed forms.

Burping the Baby

Whether breast-fed or formula-fed, babies must be burped. Burping rids the body of the air swallowed while sucking or crying. To burp a baby, complete the following steps:

- Place the baby in a sitting position on your lap with a hand on the collarbone and under the chin. You may also lay the baby down on his or her stomach across your lap with baby's face toward your knees. (You may burp a newborn on your shoulder, but this position is easier when the baby is larger.)
- Lightly pat the baby's back once he or she is in position. Pat the baby below the ribs for two or three minutes unless the baby burps sooner.
- Burp a baby before, midway, and/or after feeding.

The Feeding Schedule

Daily feeding schedules depend on babies' unique needs. Doctors suggest newborns feed on demand and mothers watch for clues of hunger (newborns are alert, mouthing, and rooting). Newborns nurse about every 2 hours, or 8 to 12 times in 24 hours. They breast-feed until **satiety** (being full), which takes at least 15 minutes per breast. Doctors suggest arousing a sleeping newborn every 3 or 4 hours for feedings. **Figure 8.12** shows a typical daily feeding schedule for the first six months.

Many babies will establish eating patterns as they get older. Some infants prefer smaller, more frequent meals while others prefer to eat more food less often. Even with established eating patterns, infants will be hungrier some days more than others. Feeding on demand will help parents address infants' hunger needs. How much food infants need depends on their size and how fast they are growing. Infants' health, heredity, and level of activity also affect their needs. As infants' growth rates slow toward the end of the first year, their appetites decrease, too.

Weaning

Weaning is the gradual process of taking infants off the breast or bottle. Weaning from the breast cannot be **abrupt** (sudden; unanticipated) for infants or mothers. Abrupt weaning for infants is stressful because they need time to learn a new way to drink. For mothers, abrupt weaning can cause blockage of the milk ducts and possible depression. When weaning occurs gradually, both infants and mothers have time to adapt to this change.

When to begin weaning depends on the infant's age and whether the infant is fed breast milk or formula. If weaning from breast milk before one year of age, the AAP recommends giving babies iron-fortified formula for the remainder of the first year. At one year of age, doctors suggest switching from iron-fortified formula to whole cow's milk. For formula-fed babies, weaning from a bottle to a cup may begin as early as the child can use the cup and shows interest in doing so (**Figure 8.13**). Although this may be as early as 9 months of age,

Figure 8.12 Daily Feeding Schedule for the First Six Months

Months	Hours Between Feedings
Less than one	2 to 3
One to five*	3 to 4
Six	6**

*Often sleeps through the night in about three months. Infants are given a late evening feeding (about 11 p.m.). They sleep until early morning (5:30 or 6:00 a.m.).

**Nutritious snacks of regular baby food (cereals, vegetables, fruits, etc.) or breast milk or formula and water should be offered about halfway between feedings (2½ to 3 hours after each feeding) if the infant is awake. Until a sufficient quantity of solids is given, breast milk or formula must be part of the snack.

Figure 8.13 A child's cup has two handles and is weighted to prevent tipping. Some cups also offer features that make liquid less likely to spill. *How could a parent determine when his or her child is ready to use a cup?*

the recommended age to start weaning from the bottle to a cup is 12 months. At this time, whole cow's milk can be given instead of formula.

To begin weaning, parents may gradually offer the new liquid (formula or whole milk, depending on age) as part of one feeding. Increase the amount of the new liquid at this feeding until the baby takes an entire feeding by bottle or cup for several days. Wait at least three days before replacing another feeding with the bottle or cup. Then, apply the same steps to other feeding times. Children are often completely weaned by 18 to 24 months of age.

Starting Solid Foods

Around six months of age, while continuing on breast milk or formula, infants may be ready to start eating solid foods from a spoon. **Solids** for infant feedings are semiliquid, mushy foods, such as cereals, vegetables, and fruits. Solid foods include commercially prepared baby foods and homemade mashed, pureed, or strained table foods. Doctors often recommend a commercially prepared single grain, iron-fortified cereal as the first solid food. Pureed vegetables should be the next food offered around six months of age. To encourage eating vegetables, they should be the first food offered to infants at mealtime. Avoid feeding infants hard, round foods and sticky, hard-to-swallow foods because they may cause choking (**Figure 8.14**).

The AAP advises parents to wait until infants are around six months old before starting solids for the following reasons:

- Babies are not born with the ability to swallow solids. Their jaw and throat muscles must develop before swallowing is easy and safe.
- Infants do not have the needed *enzymes* (special proteins that aid digestion) or saliva for digesting solid foods before six months of age.
- Until infants are 16 to 18 weeks old, they have an *extrusion reflex* (the tongue thrusts forward when touched by an object) that causes them to push foods out of their mouths.

Figure 8.14 Foods Choking Hazards for Infants

- Rounded, small foods, such as carrots, berries, grapes, and raisins
- Thick-skinned fruits, such as raw apples (unless peeled)
- Stringy foods, such as celery or spaghetti
- Hard candy
- Nuts and peanut butter
- Cherries with pits
- Hot dogs sliced in rounds
- Meat with bones
- Pretzels
- Whole kernel cooked corn and popcorn
- Soft, sticky foods, such as large marshmallows, jelly, gummy candies, peanut butter, and other nut butters

- Infants do not need more nutrition than breast milk or formula until they reach 13 to 15 pounds, which is near five to six months of age.
- Infants may have an increased risk of developing chronic conditions, such as high blood pressure or obesity, later in life from starting solids too soon.

Spoon-Feeding

Like many other skills, eating from a spoon is a developmental milestone that many parents are excited to see their infants achieve. For the first spoon-feedings, parents often **dilute** (mix with liquid to reduce strength) about one teaspoon of single grain, iron-fortified cereal with two tablespoons of breast milk or formula. Using breast milk or formula rather than water to dilute infants' cereal provides more nutrients and offers a familiar taste.

To feed an infant with a spoon, parents may place a small amount of the diluted food on the tip of the spoon. A few bites of cereal about halfway through breast-feeding or formula-feeding times are often enough for the first spoon-feedings. Very gradually, parents can make the cereal thicker at each spoon-feeding as infants learn to use their tongues and tolerate the texture.

Using a small spoon with a long handle may make spoon-feeding easier. Also, a plastic-coated baby spoon is better for the infant's sensitive gums than a metal spoon (**Figure 8.15**). During spoon-feedings, parents hold the infant in their lap in an almost upright position. Later, infants can sit in an infant seat or high chair for spoon-feedings.

Once infants turn their heads or close their mouths during spoon-feeding times, parents may stop feeding the solids and give babies a sip or two of water. Then, breast-feeding or bottle-feeding can resume so babies' meals begin and end with the familiar taste of breast milk or formula.

Introducing New Solids

Many doctors recommend offering infants new solids early in the day and no later than early afternoon. They advise this because infants are more apt to have *colic* in the evening hours. **Colic** is a condition in which a baby has intense abdominal pain and cries inconsolably. Also, an allergic reaction following a night feeding would occur in the wee hours of the morning rather than during the early evening. As cereal and other solids are introduced, infants will need water for proper kidney action. A pediatrician can advise parents how much water to offer each day.

When feeding new solids to infants, parents may want to introduce one food at a time in small amounts, such as a bite or two. To see whether foods have any **adverse** (harmful) effects on infants, wait at least five days before introducing another new

Figure 8.15 Long, plastic-coated spoons are ideal for feeding infants because they are less likely to cause a spill and do not irritate an infant's sensitive gums. *What other qualities might make a type of spoon ideal for feeding infants?*

food. If infants exhibit negative effects after eating a new food, they may have an intolerance to that food. **Intolerance** is a negative physical reaction that eating a certain food can cause. For example, intolerance to foods may result in infants becoming fussy, developing rashes, or having upset stomachs. If infant's stools are loose, watery, or contain mucous, parents should inform the infant's pediatrician.

Food intolerance among infants often shows one to four days after trying a new food. Many pediatricians suggest waiting until after the infant's first birthday before retrying an offending food. If too many foods cause a negative reaction, doctors can test the infant and prescribe a special diet.

Self-Feeding

Near the end of the first year, infants often develop the skill of self-feeding finger foods around the same time they develop the pincer grasp. Finger foods aid the infant's growing independence as well as grasping and chewing skills (**Figure 8.16**).

Examples of foods infants can eat using their fingers include

- bite-sized pieces of toasted bread or bagels
- O-shaped toasted oat cereal
- cooked and diced vegetables, such as carrots or sweet potatoes
- small chunks of fruit, such as bananas, peaches, or pears

As infants begin self-feeding, parents may want to choose from the foods they know their infants already tolerate. Eating finger foods is fun, but can also be hazardous because infants may choke or gag at the new textures. For this reason, infants need supervision when they are eating.

Around eight or nine months of age, infants often let their parents know they are ready to self-feed. For example, infants may want to help their parents by grabbing the spoon during a feeding. They may also try to grab food off their parents' plates. Giving infants a spoon to hold or letting infants use the spoon on the last few bites is good practice for later self-feeding.

Figure 8.16 Fine-motor skill development is evident when infants self-feed and can grasp finger foods, such as bite-sized pieces of bagel or bread. ***What are some other examples of safe finger foods for infants?***

Lesson 8.2 Review and Assessment 

1. Describe three advantages of breast-feeding for babies, mothers, and families.
2. Define *weaning* and describe the methods parents can use to help in the process.
3. What kinds of solids can six-month-old infants consume?
4. Give three reasons the AAP recommends parents wait until infants are around six months old before starting solids.
5. _____ is a condition in which an infant has intense abdominal pain and cries inconsolably.
6. List two symptoms of food intolerance in infants.
7. List three finger foods that are safe for infants to eat.
8. **Critical thinking.** Explain why pushing the food out of the mouth is not an infant's way of showing a dislike for the food or being stubborn.

Meeting Other Physical Needs in the First Year

Lesson 8.3

Objectives

After studying this lesson, you will be able to

- describe types of clothing that are suitable for babies during infancy.
- demonstrate how to give sponge baths to newborns and tub baths to infants.
- demonstrate how to diaper a baby.
- give examples of positive steps parents can take to protect their babies from SIDS.
- identify ways parents can encourage physical activity during infancy.

Key Terms

bassinet
playyard
sponge bath
sudden infant death syndrome (SIDS)

Academic Terms

eco-friendly
flame-resistant
immerse

Reading and Writing Activity

Before reading this lesson, write a one- to two-page essay answering the question: Why is it important to appropriately meet babies' physical needs during infancy? In answering this question, use your notes from previous chapters as well as your personal experiences and knowledge from other sources.

Graphic Organizer

As you are reading, arrange your notes into a list of considerations for parents of newborns and infants. Your list should include all of the major points covered in this lesson. Also, include annotations briefly describing why each consideration is important.

Considerations for Parents of Infants	
Infant clothes should not have drawstrings.	*Drawstrings are a strangulation hazard for infants.*

Babies need others to meet all their physical needs. When physical needs are not met, it affects other areas of development. Babies who are hungry, tired, or sick suffer in physical, intellectual, social, and emotional ways. For example, a baby who is fed late may not want to play and explore. The baby may also be fussy.

As you may recall, Maslow noted that physical needs are the most basic needs of humans. These needs must be met before other needs can be met. In Lesson 8.2, you learned about meeting nutritional needs in the first year. In this lesson, you will learn about meeting other physical needs during infancy, such as clothing and dressing and bathing and diapering babies. You will also learn about meeting babies' needs for rest and sleep and physical activity.

Clothing and Dressing Babies

One basic human need is for clothing. During the first year, babies need clothing items that are comfortable, easy to put on and take off, suitable for weather and temperature, and safe. Soft, loose-fitting clothes are easy for infants to move around in and are comfortable. Uncomfortable clothes include those with too much fabric, skin irritants (flat seams and fasteners), and fuzzy trims that tickle. Because the AAP recommends no blankets in the first year, clothing that can keep infants warm is a good choice. Layering clothing is a good way to keep babies warm. Parents need to be careful, however, not to overdress babies.

Clothes for infants must also be safe. Clothes that have ties, buttons, bows, or hooks can be choking hazards for infants. Clothing items that are loosely knitted may also pose a safety hazard because they can trap babies' fingers or toes. Clothes with drawstrings are a strangulation hazard. To protect infants from burns, sleepwear must be made of **flame-resistant** (resist burning) fabric or must fit snugly.

Shopping For Clothing

Babies grow quickly and outgrow their clothing several times in the first year. Because of their rapid growth, babies, especially newborns, do

Focus on Careers

Retail Sales Worker

Retail sales workers sell merchandise, such as clothing, to consumers. Retail sales workers who sell children's clothing must have some knowledge of sizing and clothing features to help customers find and select items based on their needs and wants. Retail sales workers must be able to answer customers' questions, total purchases, and take payments. Finally, retail sales workers need to have the abilities and experience to effectively sell quality products. For this reason, interpersonal skills are important for retail sales workers.

Career cluster: Business management and administration.

Education: Educational requirements typically include a high school diploma or equivalent and on-the-job training.

Job outlook: Future employment opportunities for retail sales workers are projected to grow about as fast as the average for all occupations.

To learn more about a career as a retail sales worker, visit the United States Department of Labor's *Occupational Outlook Handbook* website. You will also be able to compare the job responsibilities, educational requirements, job outlook, and average pay of retail sales workers with similar occupations.

not need too many clothes. During the first year, length and weight are better indicators of clothing size than age. Baby clothes in stores, however, are usually based on age. Companies use different sizes, so reading hangtags carefully before buying is necessary to select the right size for the baby.

When purchasing baby clothes, parents may want to look for clothes with built-in growth features that can help clothes last longer, such as a double row of snaps or buttons at the waistline. Knit garments and clothes with stretch waists and stretch leg and arm openings are also good choices. Clothes that must be hand-washed, dry-cleaned, or ironed are not practical.

Purchasing clothing in outfits has advantages and disadvantages. Two-piece outfits (tops and bottoms) can often be worn longer because they do not get as tight in the crotch as one-piece outfits. Two-piece outfits make changing the diaper easy, too. One-piece outfits, such as jumpsuits and overalls, look neater on crawlers because they do not separate. These outfits are also warmer.

Parents may consider buying baby shoes, but shoes are not needed until infants walk outdoors. Shoes protect and cushion the feet from outside dangers. Indoors, infants should walk without shoes to prevent flat-footed walking. Most shoes that infants wear in the first year are for decoration. These shoes have soft, cloth soles. Babies need to wear socks or footed clothing in cool weather to keep their feet warm.

Because baby clothes are so cute, parents can easily make unwise financial choices. Parents can stay within their clothing budget by watching for sales and borrowing baby clothes. Choosing clothes suitable for either boys or girls (and storing for the next child) is also cost-effective. Another cost-effective idea is for parents to buy or make clothes the baby can grow into.

Dressing Babies

Newborns are easier to dress than older infants because they do not squirm as much. To make dressing babies easy and safe, parents can have the baby's clothes ready and undo any buttons or snaps before getting the baby. Remembering to support the baby's head while lifting him or her is also important to avoid unnecessary jostling. Because newborns cannot push, parents need to pull babies' arms and legs through garment openings (**Figure 8.17**). If babies become fretful, parents can cuddle them before continuing to dress them. Finally, parents can use dressing times to talk with their babies and even tell them what they are doing. ("I'm snapping your shirt. Snap...snap...snap.")

Caring for Baby Clothes

Many parents store baby clothes for future children or as keepsakes. Before storing, clothes need to be clean. Soiled spots change over time, and then stains cannot be removed. When clothes are clean and dry, they are ready to be stored. Parents can care for baby clothes properly by following these practices:

- Read labels and tags before cleaning clothes. Follow the directions.
- Pretreat stains before washing clothes to prevent the stains from setting. Also, mend tears before washing to prevent them from getting larger.
- Rinse babies' and children's clothing more often than other clothes. Extra rinses help remove detergent from clothes. Babies' skin is more sensitive than adults' skin, and detergent residue may cause skin rashes. Parents might also want to choose a gentle detergent designed for baby clothes.

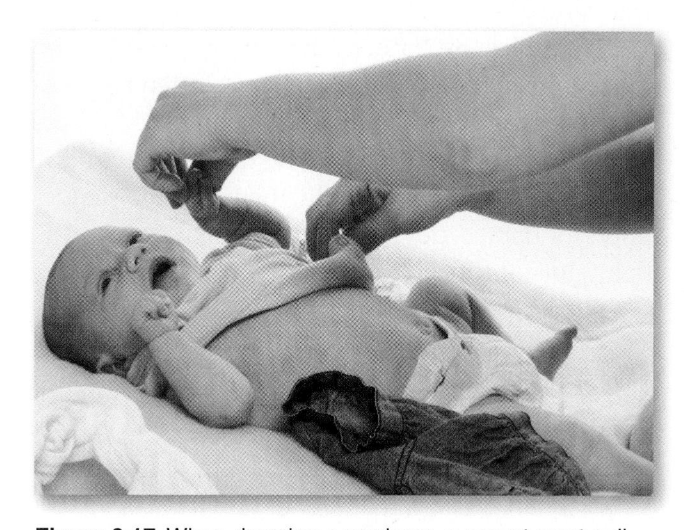

Figure 8.17 When dressing a newborn, a parent must pull the newborn's arms and legs through the garments. *What types of garments would be easy for dressing a newborn? What types of garments would be more difficult?*

- Avoid using fabric softener when washing sleepwear. The chemicals in fabric softeners can reduce the flame-resistant qualities of the clothing.

Bathing

Newborns do not need baths every day because they do not get too dirty except for their faces, necks, and diaper areas. Parents keep these areas clean as they burp and diaper their babies. Parents can bathe their newborns several times a week by giving sponge baths. In a **sponge bath**, parents do not **immerse** (cover in liquid) the baby in water, but instead use a washcloth or sponge to wash the baby's body. Doctors recommend sponge baths for newborns until the navel heals completely—up to three weeks after birth. (Keep the cord stump dry and never pull on it even when it starts coming loose. The doctor will tell parents any other procedure in cord care.)

Tub bathing can begin as soon as the newborn's navel and circumcision have healed. The preparation steps for tub bathing are the same as those for sponge bathing. The only difference is that a small tub is filled with about three inches of comfortably warm water. Tub baths should be given carefully and quickly for the baby's comfort and safety. Whenever giving babies sponge baths or tub baths, parents should *never* leave their babies unattended—even for a second.

As babies are bathed, they enjoy parents who talk, sing, cuddle, and smile. Babies often respond well because warm water is relaxing. As infants grow, they enjoy kicking and splashing in the water as their parents hold them. Water play is good for babies' developing motor skills as well as being lots of fun.

Diapering

Babies require frequent diaper changes throughout the first year. Parents can use either disposable or cloth diapers for babies. Both disposable and cloth diapers have advantages and disadvantages. When deciding which type of diapers to use, parents often consider cost and convenience.

Disposable diapers are often costly, but can be easy and convenient for parents. There are many different brands and sizes of disposable diapers available from which parents can choose. Newborn disposable diapers have a cut-out in front so the baby's cord stump does not get wet. Disposable diapers have waterproof outer layers. For child care, disposable diapers are often required.

Cloth diapers can be less expensive than disposable diapers, but can also be less convenient because parents have to spend time washing them. Babies who wear cloth diapers also need to wear waterproof cloth diaper covers to protect from leaks. Some parents prefer to use cloth diapers because they are **eco-friendly** (not harmful to the environment). In some places, parents have the option of using a diaper service that picks up soiled diapers and delivers sterilized cloth ones.

Once the type of diaper is selected, parents are ready to change the baby's diaper (**Figure 8.18**). Older infants wiggle more and may protest when diapered, which makes the task harder for adults. To keep the infant's interest, parents may talk, sing, and play with the infant during diaper changes. Parents and other caregivers should wash their hands (and the baby's hands and any toys the baby is holding) after each diaper change.

Diaper rashes may develop from the constant use of the waterproof diaper covers or from the outer layer of disposable diapers. In a diaper rash, bacteria grow rapidly on the warm, moist, and air-free skin. Most babies develop diaper rash at one time or another. The most common treatment is to wash the area with soap and water after each change, expose the area to air, and use petroleum jelly or a rash ointment before diapering. If the rash persists following several days of treatment, parents should consult a pediatrician.

To prevent the spread of germs, diaper-changing areas need to be clean. When cleaning a diaper-changing table, first dispose of any paper on the table. Next, clean any visible soil with a detergent and water mixture and rinse with water. Then, spray the entire changing surface with a sanitizing solution, such as one teaspoon of household bleach per one cup of water. Finally, leave the solution in contact with the surface for two minutes and allow to air-dry or wipe-dry with a clean cloth.

Figure 8.18 How to Diaper a Baby

1. Gather diapering materials before you get the baby. You will need the following:
   - changing pad for baby to lie on (if not using a changing table)
   - clean diaper (if using cloth diapers, have diaper folded and ready for use)
   - clean cloth, such as a burp cloth
   - fasteners for prefold cloth diapers
   - baby wipes
   - lotion or diaper rash ointment may be recommended by doctor
2. Wash and dry your hands and then remove the baby's clothing.

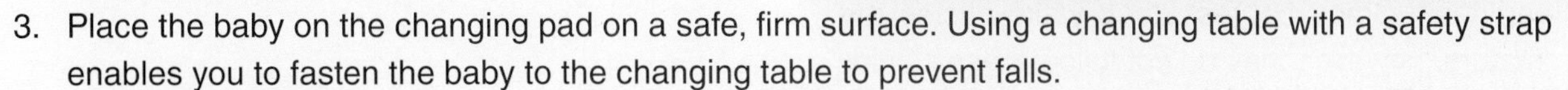

3. Place the baby on the changing pad on a safe, firm surface. Using a changing table with a safety strap enables you to fasten the baby to the changing table to prevent falls.
4. Unfasten, remove, and dispose of the soiled diaper. If diapering a male baby, place a clean cloth over the penis to prevent spraying.
5. Use baby wipes to clean the baby's genitals and buttocks from front to back. Be sure to also clean between skin folds.
6. With one hand, grasp the baby's ankles and slide a fresh diaper under the baby's bottom. Apply any necessary lotion or diaper rash ointment. Then, pull the front of the diaper up between the baby's legs.
7. Fasten the diaper. When using disposable diapers, the tape fastens from the back to the front. Some cloth diapers use Velcro or snaps as fasteners while other cloth diapers use diaper safety pins as fasteners. Place two fingers in the top front of the fastened diaper to make sure it is not too loose or too tight.
8. Redress the baby and return him or her to a safe place.
9. Wash your hands thoroughly.
10. Do not forget to clean and disinfect the changing table or wash the changing pad.

Resting and Sleeping

Babies vary in the amount of rest and sleep they need. Because newborns are growing so rapidly, their tiny bodies need lots of rest. On average, newborns need about 12 to 18 hours of sleep per day. (Some sleep as few as 11 hours daily, while others, especially preterm babies, sleep as many as 22 or 23 hours per day.) Newborns do not sleep quietly between feedings. They usually take seven or eight naps in which they suck, wheeze, and gurgle. This pattern of light sleep continues for the first half year.

Between 6 and 12 months of age, infants typically need 14 to 15 hours of sleep. By 6 months of age, many infants sleep through the night and often take morning and afternoon naps. As infants near their first birthday, nap times often become fewer and many infants drop the morning nap.

Sudden Infant Death Syndrome

Sudden infant death syndrome (SIDS) is a condition in which a sleeping baby dies without warning and for medically unexplained reasons. SIDS is the leading cause of death in babies during their first year of life. SIDS is especially common between two and four months of age. In many cases, seemingly healthy babies simply stop breathing in their sleep. Although the cause of SIDS is unknown, some risk factors are known (**Figure 8.19**).

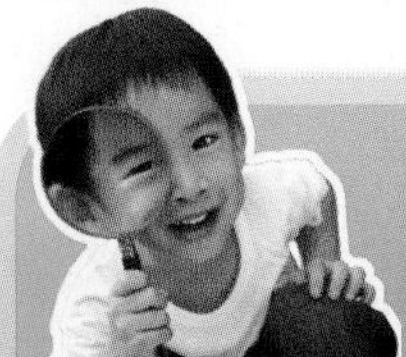

Investigate Special Topics: Circadian Rhythms and Routines

Babies, especially newborns, are well-known for not sleeping through the night. This is because babies are still developing circadian rhythms. The *circadian* (sir-CAY-dee-uhn) *rhythm*, also known as the *sleep-wake cycle*, is an internal system that regulates feelings of sleepiness and alertness. Circadian rhythms are regulated by hormone (serotonin) production in the brain. Lightness and darkness in the environment also guide circadian rhythms. Light triggers feelings of alertness, and darkness triggers feelings of sleepiness. Since babies' sleep-wake cycles are immature, however, they do not follow these signals in the environment for sleep and wake time.

Establishing routines is important to help babies develop and maintain regular sleep habits. Routines also help babies develop a basic sense of trust. Babies feel secure because they know what to expect. To make sure routines fit babies' and adults' needs, parents can develop a nighttime ritual (routine) for putting a baby to bed. This needs to be a quiet time. Some parents bathe their infants before bedtime. Reading a story or listening to some quiet music may also be part of nighttime rituals. Babies need to be soothed until they are drowsy. Crying babies need parents to help them calm down and feel comfortable. Parents may darken a room to induce feelings of sleepiness.

Routines need to be flexible and change as infants mature. For example, the many short daytime and nighttime naps are gradually replaced by fewer, but longer, daytime naps and longer periods of sleep at night. If the infant does not sleep well at night, parents may try to rearrange the schedule. Waking infants after four hours of daytime sleep may help infants sleep longer at night. Eventually, circadian rhythms stabilize between three and six months of age and infants sleep through the night.

Reading Activity

Managing infants' sleep-wake cycles is a major topic for new parents, many of whom grow tired from waking up to soothe their infants. In small groups, research books or articles that give advice to new parents about managing their infants' sleeping schedules. As a group, discuss the following questions:

1. How authoritative are the sources your group chose? How do you know?
2. How do the stated pieces of advice help new parents manage their infants' sleeping schedules?

Until the cause and prevention of SIDS is found, parents can take the following positive steps to protect their babies:

- Avoid as many of the risk factors as possible both before and after the baby is born.
- Place the baby on his or her back to sleep during naps and at night. Remember the saying, "Back to sleep." Placing the baby on his or her stomach increases the chance of SIDS. Stomach-sleeping may put pressure on the baby's jaw and narrow the airway. It also increases the risk of the baby rebreathing exhaled air (which contains carbon dioxide rather than oxygen). Caregivers should never place babies on their sides to sleep because babies can roll from their sides to their stomachs.
- Place the baby on a firm surface to sleep. Cribs should meet current safety standards with no broken or missing parts or drop-side rails. Babies should not sleep on chairs, sofas, cushions, sheepskins, beanbag chairs, or waterbeds.

Figure 8.19 Risk Factors for Sudden Infant Death Syndrome (SIDS)

- Teen pregnancy
- Insufficient prenatal care
- Exposure to tobacco, alcohol, or illegal drugs (especially cocaine) before birth
- Premature birth (especially for infants born more than two weeks before due date)
- Low-birthweight (less than 5½ pounds)
- Multiple birth (especially if weighing less than 3.3 pounds)
- Exposure to cigarette smoke after birth
- Occurrence of an older sibling who died of SIDS
- Babies who are male and have other risk factors listed above
- Infants between two and four months of age
- Sleep-deprived infants

- Do not use fluffy blankets, comforters, throws, stuffed toys, or pillows in the crib or **playyard** (an enclosed play space for babies; formerly called a *playpen*). Soft items and loose bedding in these areas can increase the risk of suffocation or strangulation.
- Use a car seat for transport only. A baby's position in a car seat reduces his or her breathing capacity. Babies sleeping in car seats, swings, and baby seats are more prone to SIDS.
- Make sure the baby does not get too warm while sleeping. The temperature of a baby's room should be comfortable. Babies who become very warm may go into a deeper sleep and find it more difficult to wake up. Because of this, it is best not to overdress the baby for sleep.
- Offer a pacifier for sleep from birth and continue its use for sleep even after the baby no longer uses a pacifier while awake.
- Avoid sharing a parent bed with a baby (called *co-sleeping* or *co-bedding*). Young babies are safest in their own crib in their parent's room. Babies should not sleep with older children either.
- Encourage adequate sleep (**Figure 8.20**).
- Schedule and attend regular well-baby checkups.
- Breast-feed the baby for at least seven months and preferably for one year.
- Keep the baby away from people who smoke and places where people smoke.
- Do not use breathing monitors and alarms or specialized products that claim to reduce the risk of SIDS unless recommended by a doctor.

Bedding Safety

A bed is one of the most essential pieces of furniture a baby needs. During the first few weeks after birth, parents may prefer their newborns sleep

Figure 8.20 Sleep deficits of even two hours on a given day are associated with SIDS. *What can parents do to make sure they are giving their infants enough sleep time?*

in a cradle or small **bassinet** (basketlike bed). As babies grow, they will need a crib. Some parents are purchasing *convertible furniture*, or furniture that easily becomes useful for other purposes. Convertible furniture can grow with the child. For example, some cribs can be converted to youth or even adult beds.

Safety in the baby's bedding and supplies is essential. A baby bed should be high and stable enough to prevent young children or pets from tipping it over. If the cradle or bed has slats, distance between the slats must be 2⅜ inches or less. This prevents infants from wiggling feet first through the slats until their heads are caught, which could cause serious injury or death. The mattress on the bed should be snug-fitting and any sheets should be firm-fitting, not loose-fitting. Loose fabric can tangle around the baby and smother or strangle him or her. Also, drop-side cribs and bumper pads should not be used.

Figure 8.21 Tummy time both provides physical activity for infants and aids in their motor development. *Why do you think tummy time is considered physical activity for infants?*

Encouraging Physical Activity

Movement is a large part of life—before and after birth. Watch the constant movement of newborns lying awake on their backs. Physical activity is important for muscle development, coordination, and even relaxation. Helping babies move their muscles will not cause them to crawl or walk sooner, but may help the general development of the muscles.

To help babies with physical activity, parents often engage their babies in tummy time several times each day (**Figure 8.21**). Playyards also provide a safe place for infants to play. Parents should limit total time spent in a playyard, however, to no more than two hours per day. Infants need to be able to move and explore freely in order to develop crawling, creeping, and walking skills.

Physical activity, if started early in life, may become a daily, lifelong habit. Daily physical activity is also a way to have fun with babies and develop a warm relationship. Many families find that doing physical activities together is great family fun.

Lesson 8.3 Review and Assessment

1. Describe the features needed for infant clothing.
2. During the first year, _____ and _____ are better indicators of clothing size than _____.
3. What is a sponge bath?
4. Explain the steps involved in diapering a baby.
5. On average, newborns need about _____ hours of sleep per day.
6. List four recommendations for reducing the chance of SIDS.
7. To help babies with physical activity, parents often engage their babies in _____ several times each day.
8. **Critical thinking.** Where could a new parent go to get the most up-to-date information on infant safety and care procedures?

Chapter 8

Review and Assessment

Summary

An infant's physical development is rapid during the first year. The brain grows faster than any other organ. The muscles and organs will continue to mature. Skeletal growth is rapid. Length and weight increase quickly. The infant's body proportions soon change. Motor development is the ability to control the large and small muscles that direct body movements. Until brain firings hardwire connections, infants must think about their movements, which cause these movements to be slow. Infants' reactions to what they see and hear are general and then become more specific. Control of the body begins from head to foot and also goes from the trunk outward. Because body development is directional, there is a sequence to infants' motor development. Babies reach postural, locomotor, and grasping milestones.

Only breast milk or formula is recommended for the first six months. After that, adults can introduce solid foods one at a time along with the breast milk or formula. Learning to drink from a cup, eat finger foods, and use a spoon takes time. These tasks require the child to use throat and tongue muscles and develop coordination.

Infants' clothing should be comfortable, safe, and easy to put on and take off. Using disposable or cloth diapers is a decision that parents make based on expense and convenience. All clothing, bedding, and equipment must be safe. Other needs include bathing, sleeping, and having places to sleep and play. When giving a tub or sponge bath, take appropriate safety precautions. To lessen the chance of SIDS, keep the infant's bed free of soft, fluffy products, and put all infants on their backs to sleep. All play spaces for infants should be safe, yet provide stimulating play and physical activity.

College and Career Portfolio

Portfolio Transcripts

One of the most important elements of a portfolio—whether for college or for a first job—is a transcript. Transcripts take time to request and receive.

Procedures for requesting a transcript vary depending on your school and the purpose of the transcript. If you need to request a transcript, it is best to do so well in advance, since they take time to generate. To include a transcript in your portfolio, complete the following steps:

- Research how to request a transcript from your school. If you need help, ask your teacher or consult a career counselor. In a college or university, student's transcripts are available in the Office of the Registrar.
- Follow the procedure to request your transcript in advance. Seek help if necessary.

Chapter 8 Review and Assessment

Vocabulary Activities 

1. Work with a partner to write the definitions of the following terms based on your current understanding of the chapter. Then, pair up with another pair to discuss your definitions and any discrepancies. Finally, discuss the definitions with the class and ask your instructor for necessary correction or clarification.

Key Terms

bassinet (8.3)	intolerance (8.2)
body proportions (8.1)	lactation consultant (8.2)
cephalocaudal development (8.1)	motor development (8.1)
colic (8.2)	ossification (8.1)
crawl (8.1)	playyard (8.3)
creep (8.1)	proximodistal development (8.1)
cruising (8.1)	reflexes (8.1)
deciduous teeth (8.1)	skeletal system (8.1)
developmental milestones (8.1)	solids (8.2)
failure to thrive (8.1)	sponge bath (8.3)
fine-motor skills (8.1)	sudden infant death syndrome (SIDS) (8.3)
gross-motor skills (8.1)	voluntary grasping (8.1)
infancy (8.1)	weaning (8.2)

2. Working in pairs, locate a small image online that visually describes each of the following terms. Create flashcards by writing each term on a note card. Then, paste the image that describes or explains the term on the opposite side. After creating your flashcards, exchange them in small groups. Discuss the images your group members selected.

Academic Terms

abrupt (8.2)	flame-resistant (8.3)
adverse (8.2)	immerse (8.3)
alleviates (8.2)	innate (8.1)
cartilage (8.1)	onset (8.1)
circumference (8.1)	protrudes (8.1)
dilute (8.2)	satiety (8.2)
eco-friendly (8.3)	stamina (8.1)

Critical Thinking

3. **Compare and contrast.** Using a life-size doll, demonstrate each reflex and identify what stimulus causes each response. Then, as a class, compare and contrast reflexes during infancy.
4. **Cause and effect.** Identify the two directions of a baby's physical development in the first year. Then, imagine you are trying to explain these directions to a student you are tutoring. Use visual methods to explain the two directions of development and to assess how they affect a child's development.
5. **Draw conclusions.** Using Figure 8.10, describe a baby of an age you choose using the developmental milestones listed. Then, close your book and find a partner. Give your partner a brief description of the milestones the baby you chose has achieved. Then, ask your partner what age he or she thinks the baby is. Switch roles and listen to your partner's description. Then, discuss your answers with your partner.
6. **Analyze.** After discussing your answers to the #5 activity, find a different partner. As a pair, consider the following questions:
   - How easy was it to identify a baby's age based on milestones?
   - How difficult do you think it is to do this in real life?
7. **Determine.** Many parents track their baby's physical and motor development, and may worry if their child does not mature or achieve milestones as they think he or she should. In small groups, consider under what circumstances a parent might worry about his or her baby's lack of development. What should a parent then do to resolve these concerns?
8. **Evaluate.** Child development experts often advise parents to follow the baby's lead. Brainstorm with classmates how you can follow a baby's lead in meeting his or her needs. Are there times when newborns should follow their parents' leads? Why or why not?
9. **Identify.** Imagine that one of your friends is a new mother and is nervous about the processes of breast-feeding, weaning, and introducing solid foods. She is insecure in her ability to wean her child and is embarrassed about asking. With a partner, role-play this conversation, and identify methods of weaning and introducing solid foods for your friend. Encourage her to seek advice from her doctor as well.

Core Skills

10. **Math.** Interview at least six parents whose children were full-term or almost full-term. Ask each parent what the child's weight and height were at birth, six months, and one year. Record these figures in a master list. Showing your work, figure the average weight and height for this group of babies at each age.
11. **Speaking.** Find a quality infant toy that would encourage an infant to develop gross- and fine-motor skills. Determine the children's ages for which the toy would be safe. Make an oral presentation to the class showing how your selected toy promotes both types of skills, and explaining what age range should use the toy and why.
12. **Writing.** Write a paragraph from the perspective of a baby during the first year of life, describing what the baby can and cannot do, how he or she feels, and what he or she is learning to do.
13. **Technology, writing, and speaking.** As a group or class project, create a one- or two-page brochure that explains both the skeletal and organ maturation that occurs during infancy and the milestones parents can expect babies to meet. Your goal is to create a brochure that will help parents keep track of what changes they should see in their babies during the first year of life. List all of the milestones and significant physical changes described in this chapter, and then choose the ones you think parents will most easily recognize and most worry about. Then, organize the information and discuss how you will lay out your brochure. Finally, arrange the information in a logical and easy-to-understand way. Use pictures to accent the information described in your brochure. Finally, present your brochure to the class and explain why you chose certain changes and milestones.
14. **Listening and speaking.** Organize a debate about breast-feeding versus formula-feeding. Divide into two teams—one to argue in favor of breast-feeding and the other to argue in favor of formula-feeding. For each method, emphasize the physical, social, emotional, and intellectual aspects; parental bonding issues; adaptations for working parents; and costs. During the debate, deliver persuasive opening statements, arguments, and closing statements. Afterward, discuss the issues raised as a class.
15. **Reading.** Locate a book or collection of recipes for infants up to one year of age and then read at least five recipes. Take notes on the types of foods described and consider how safe and healthy the recipes are based on what you learned in this chapter. Then, choose two recipes and evaluate them in terms of nutrition, safety, and age-appropriateness. Present your findings to the class.
16. **Health safety.** Use a life-size infant doll to demonstrate the following skills needed for infant care: feeding, sponge and tub bathing, diapering, putting a baby to bed, and dressing. Treat the doll as you would a newborn, being gentle with the baby and supporting its head. Which skills were easiest for you, and which will take much more practice? In what ways might these tasks be different with a real infant than with a doll?
17. **CTE Career Readiness Practice.** The director of the child care center where you work overheard you explaining to parents the precautions they can take against SIDS. Your center has recently hired a new employee, and your director asks you to train this new employee on methods of preventing SIDS and on educating parents about these methods. In preparation for training, develop materials for the new employee, including
    - authoritative information about SIDS and what resources provide accurate information about it
    - the precautions your child care center takes against SIDS
    - a script in which you train the employee to talk with parents about SIDS

Observations

18. Observe two infants who are the same age. How do they differ in their physical maturity? How do they differ in their motor skills? Does one infant have an acceleration or delay in maturity or skills?
19. Many parents keep a "baby book," a small book that contains pictures of the baby at each month for the first year, as well as some descriptions of when the baby achieved certain milestones. Read your own baby book or a classmate's baby book, and write observations about changes in size, shape, and motor skills.

Chapter 9 Intellectual Development in the First Year

Essential Question

How do infants come to make sense of their world, and how can parents and other caregivers support the baby's agenda for learning?

Lesson 9.1 **How Children Learn in the First Year**

Lesson 9.2 **What Children Learn in the First Year**

Lesson 9.3 **Meeting Children's Intellectual Needs in the First Year**

Case Study: Can Baby Signing Delay Learning to Talk?

As a class, read the case study and discuss the questions that follow. After you finish studying the chapter, discuss this case study again. Have your opinions changed based on what you learned?

Joan and Ted began to teach their daughter, Ashley, *Baby Signs* at 6 months of age. By 8 months, Ashley was signing back and learned new "words" quickly. Joan's friend, Drew, began teaching her son, Kylan, *Baby Signs* when he was 6 months of age, too. Kylan also learned and used many signs in just a few months, and by 12 months, Kylan was beginning to say a few of the words he could sign.

At Ashley's 12-month-old well-baby checkup, Joan and Ted told the pediatrician that Ashley was not talking yet. The pediatrician replied, "Oh, I'm sure she will soon." As the months passed, Ashley continued to smile, gesture, and use *Baby Signs*, but didn't talk. Ashley's grandmother said that *Baby Signs* had probably kept Ashley from talking because "babies don't talk unless they need to talk."

Joan was becoming concerned that something might be wrong with Ashley. She began thinking that maybe they should take Ashley to see a child development expert.

Give It Some Thought

1. Ashley's grandmother said that *Baby Signs* had probably kept Ashley from talking because "babies don't talk unless they need to talk." Do you think the grandmother made a good point? Why or why not?
2. Do you think the lack of spoken vocabulary words at 12 months of age should concern the pediatrician? Why or why not?
3. Do you think Ashley needs to see a child development expert? Why or why not?
4. What might be some disadvantages of baby signing? in settings in which people do not know signing? during the stage in which infants naturally focus on the speaker's mouth? in the joint adult-child interactions required in gazing and pointing?

While studying this chapter, look for the online resources icon  to:

- **Practice** terms with e-flash cards and interactive games
- **Assess** what you learn by completing self-assessment quizzes
- **Expand** knowledge with interactive activities and graphic organizers

Companion G-W Learning

www.g-wlearning.com/childdevelopment

Study on the go

Use a mobile device to practice terms and review with self-assessment quizzes.

www.m.g-wlearning.com/0384

Lesson 9.1

How Children Learn in the First Year

Key Terms

binocular vision
cognition
explicit memory
implicit memory
perception
perceptual learning
scaffolding
sensorimotor stage
stimuli
zone of proximal development (ZPD)

Academic Terms

imitating
sociocultural
subtle
wane

Objectives

After studying this lesson, you will be able to

- describe how brain development supports learning.
- give examples of ways in which a baby's vision matures during the first six months.
- explain the difference between sensory stimuli and perceptual learning.
- compare and contrast Piaget's and Vygotsky's cognitive development theories.

Reading and Writing Activity

Skim through this lesson and list all the headings you see. Leave one or two lines of space beneath each heading. Then, close your book and compose a "topic sentence" for each heading. Your topic sentence should summarize what information you think each section will include. After you read this lesson, return to your list and write a new topic sentence for each section, outlining the main points you learned.

Graphic Organizer

Draw an outline of the human brain like the one shown. Then, organize your notes according to regions of the brain and their functions. If a piece of information does not relate to a particular region of the brain, then create a category for it beneath the brain and continue your notes there.

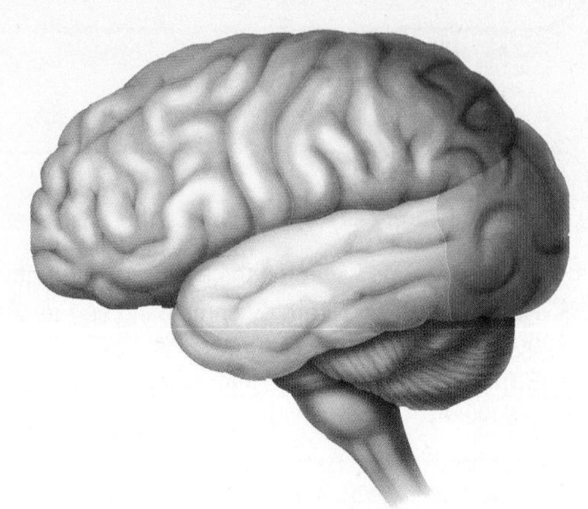

As you may recall, *intellectual development* is how and what people learn and how they express what they know through language. Intellectual development is also called *cognitive development*. During the baby's first year, intellectual development happens as quickly as physical development. The learning process begins right after birth. In fact, the brain and some of the senses are active before birth. Learning, however, involves more than physical growth and development. Many researchers in child development believe babies *want* to learn. Each month babies exert more and more effort to explore their world. Because learning begins so early, parents are a child's first teachers.

Brain Development Supports Learning

Newborns come into the world using all their sense organs (eyes, ears, nose, tongue, and skin), which are rapidly maturing. Environmental **stimuli** (light, sound, heat, texture) are agents that affect the sensory organs causing a person to react. Early reactions are mainly reflexive. For example, when babies see a bright light (stimulus), they close their eyes (reaction). As their senses develop, babies use stimuli to learn. For example, when handed an object (stimulus), infants will look at it (reaction) and mouth it (reaction).

Brain research has noted much activity in the vision and motor centers of the baby's brain during the first year. As motor skills develop, infants are able to move toward many sights, sounds, and other stimuli. While taking in sensory and motor experiences, the brain is wiring the thinking and memory centers. **Figure 9.1** shows the functions of the brain.

Vision Center

The vision center of the brain allows babies to process the sights of their world into information. The brain makes some connections from the sensory receptors before birth, but wiring increases dramatically after birth. Vision dominates how babies interpret their world early in life. For this reason, the vision center is very active in early infancy. The window of opportunity for sight is from birth to four to six months of age. During this time, a baby's vision matures rapidly in the following areas:

- *Acuity*—the ability to see clearly in each eye. To see clearly, muscles must contract and relax the lens of each eye so an image is projected clearly on the retina. (**Figure 9.2** shows the internal structures of the eye.) Because babies do not have good control of the lens muscles, their

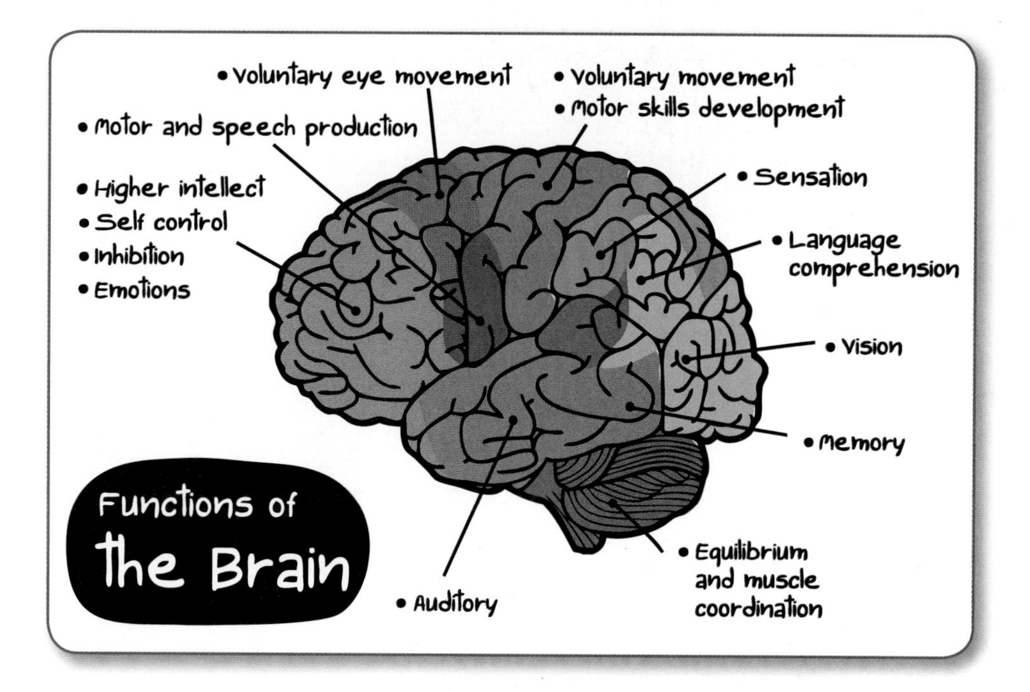

Figure 9.1 Different sections of the brain are responsible for different functions. *How do you think the divided responsibilities within the brain affect how surgeons diagnose localized brain injuries?*

Figure 9.2 The Internal Structures of the Eye

Structure	Description
Cornea	Transparent covering that protects the eye.
Aqueous (AY-kwee-us) **humor**	Liquid that fills the cavity between the cornea and pupil of the eye; maintains the eye's shape.
Pupil	Opening through which light passes into the interior of the eye.
Iris	Structure that widens or narrows the size of the pupil, controlling how much light enters the eye; gives the eye its color.
Lens	Transparent, curved structure that changes shape to clearly focus on objects at various distances.
Vitreous (VIT-ree-us) **humor**	Liquid that fills the cavern of the eye behind the lens; maintains the eye's shape.
Retina	Innermost layer of the eye, which contains light-sensitive nerve endings.
Choroid (KOR-oyd) **layer**	Middle layer of the eye, which contains blood vessels that nourish the eye.
Optic nerve	Nerve that transmits electrical impulses from the eye to the brain.

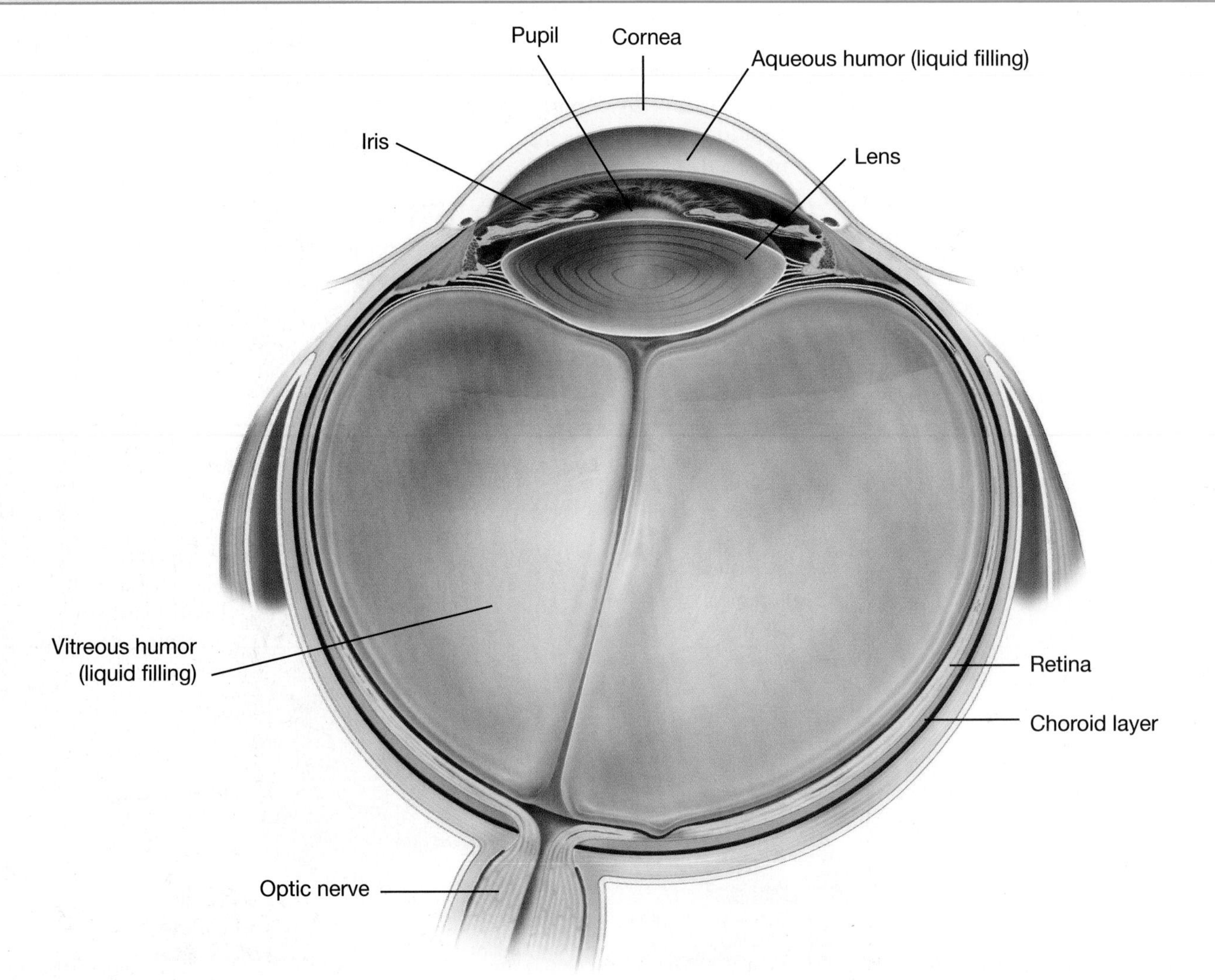

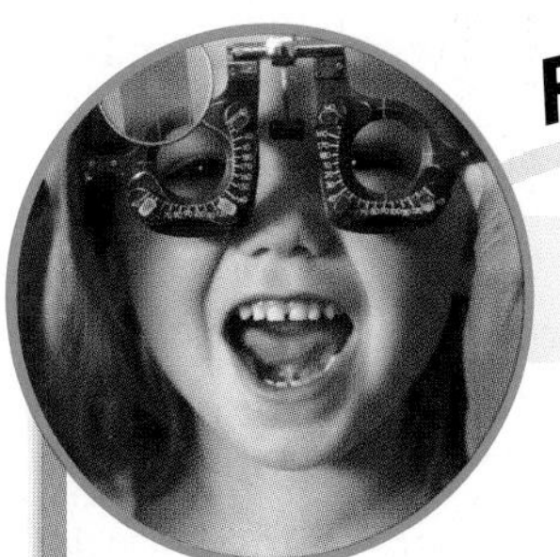

Focus on Careers

Physician—Pediatric Ophthalmologist

Many physicians work in medical specialties and even subspecialties. For example, an *ophthalmologist* is a highly trained medical doctor who is an eye specialist. A *pediatric ophthalmologist* further specializes in working with children. Pediatric ophthalmologists examine children's eyes and treat eye conditions, diseases, and illnesses. They can perform eye surgery, if necessary. Babies should have a six-month appointment with a pediatric ophthalmologist or at least an ophthalmologist.

Career cluster: Health science

Education: Educational requirements include an advanced degree, four years of medical school, and three to eight additional years of internship and residency. Licensure is also required.

Job outlook: Future employment opportunities for pediatric ophthalmologists are expected to grow faster than the average for all occupations.

To learn more about a career as a pediatric ophthalmologist, visit the United States Department of Labor's *Occupational Outlook Handbook* website. You will also be able to compare the job responsibilities, educational requirements, job outlook, and average pay of pediatric ophthalmologists with similar occupations.

focus is often not correct for distance. They may focus in front of or behind the object. Acuity is also dependent on the maturity of the retina and the brain. Early blurry vision does not last long. The newborn's acuity is about 20/120 (top letter on an eye chart). By four months of age, acuity is about 20/60. By eight months of age, acuity is about 20/30 (normal adult acuity is 20/20). Going from 20/30 acuity to 20/20 acuity takes years. The window of opportunity for acuity is from birth to seven years of age.

- ***Contrast sensitivity***—the ability to see objects with varying degrees of contrast from their background. Objects and their backgrounds have differing degrees of contrast. The contrast between an object and its background is given as a percentage. Higher percentages mean greater contrasts while lower percentages mean little contrast. For example, a light gray object on a white background has low contrast, making the object more difficult to detect. An example of high contrast would be a white object on a black background. Newborns can only see objects that have high contrast, such as black and white, which is a 100 percent contrast. By nine weeks of age, an infant's contrast sensitivity is near the adult level. They can see objects on backgrounds with as low as a 0.2 percent contrast (almost the same color intensity).
- ***Color sensitivity***—the ability to see color. When matched for contrast, two-week-old newborns can distinguish red from green objects. Color receptors are not yet mature, so newborns may not be able to distinguish between **subtle** (not obvious) color differences (blue versus aqua) or among very light pastel colors.

- *Eye movements and coordination*—the ability to move both eyes perfectly together so a person sees the world as a fused picture. Between one and three months of age, infants begin to look at objects with both eyes. Watching a young infant, the adult may notice his or her eyes do not seem to work together. Often, one of the baby's eyes will drift off focus. At first, the baby's brain "sees" two slightly separated images of the same object. Around three months of age, the infant's brain can fuse the images together. To fuse an image requires the eyes to stay focused together on the object. Fusing images typically happens naturally unless the baby has weak eye muscles. Once the infant can use both eyes in unison, equally, and accurately to fuse in the brain the two images into one image, he or she has **binocular vision**. The window of opportunity for binocular vision is from one year to three years of age.
- *3-D vision*—the ability to see the world in three dimensions. The focus on the eye's retina is always two-dimensional (flat). Seeing in three dimensions requires the brain to interpret the image from each eye. Each eye sees an image somewhat differently because of the space between a person's eyes. The image must also be fused through binocular vision. Infants develop 3-D vision between three and six months of age.

Motor Center

As reflexes **wane** (diminish) during infancy, much activity occurs in the motor center of the baby's brain. Fast brain wiring in the motor center often starts around two months of age. At this time, infants begin the multiyear process of learning voluntary gross-motor movements. Wiring for fine-motor movements begins around two or three months of age when infants make their first attempts to grasp objects.

During infancy, babies depend on their motor skills as they react to environmental stimuli. These motor experiences within their environment enable infants to learn about important ideas, such as space, weight, and depth. For example, when an infant sees something interesting, he or she moves toward the object. As the infant reaches for the object, using 3-D vision, he or she must assess the space between his or her hand and the object to know how far to reach for the object. Young infants look back and forth between hand and object, which slows the movement. After many experiences, infants have an understanding of space and can grasp objects with just a quick glance.

Thinking Center

Thinking requires more than the physical ability of the sensory organs to receive input from stimuli. Thinking also requires the ability to interpret sensory information the brain receives. A sensory association area of the brain inputs the basic sensory information received, such as shape, color, pitch, and location, and processes it into recognizable objects, such as dogs, trees, and faces. Recognizing a parent takes thousands of neurons firing in the brain. Repeat experiences help infants make these sensory associations.

Just as babies need good nutrition for physical growth, they also need quality experiences for intellectual development. Interesting things to see, hear, and touch are "food for thought." Because the world is new to babies, common objects and experiences in their environment provide quality learning opportunities. The adult's face, a cardboard box, some pans and spoons, or a trip to the yard can provide good learning experiences. **Figure 9.3** shows how babies change their seeing, hearing, and touching preferences for experiences as they try to learn about their new world.

Memory Centers

Thinking and learning require memory, and memory abilities begin very early in life. There are two main categories of memory. **Explicit memory** is the conscious, intentional recalling of experiences and facts, or the "knowing what" memory. For example, explicit memory involves remembering a person's name, a pet's name, or even landmarks

Figure 9.3 Babies' Preferences for Sensory Experiences

Approximate Age	Sensory Experience (S) = Seeing, (H) = Hearing, (T) = Touching
Birth to 3 months	• Prefers patterns to solids. (S)
3 to 6 months	• Prefers red and blue to green and yellow. (S) • Enjoys mirrors, but does not know his or her image until after 1 year of age. (S) • Likes small objects. (S)
6 to 9 months	• Takes pleasure in hearing singing and tries to sing along. (H) • Prefers toys with moving parts such as dials and wheels. (T)
9 to 12 months	• Shows less interest in faces except to quickly identify the familiar face and the strange face. (S) • Watches dropped objects with interest to see whether they roll, break, or bounce. (S) • Likes hiding games, such as hide and seek. (S) • Takes pleasure in hearing own name. (H) • Enjoys self-feeding. (T) • Likes dropping objects into pails and boxes. (T) • Enjoys stacking blocks and knocking them down. (T) • Shows interest in nesting (putting smaller into larger) objects. (S and T)

on the way to a park. **Implicit memory** is the unconscious awareness of past experiences to perform tasks, or the "knowing how" memory. Examples of implicit memory include rolling over, walking, or playing a familiar game.

Although infants' memories are much more fragile than adults' memories, infants (and people of all ages) remember better when

- directly engaged in an experience rather than just watching
- experiences are meaningful
- experiences happen over and over (reinforced)
- cues (or reminders) are used, such as showing an object or picture or seeing a landmark

Memories are important even to babies because the brain draws on past learning experiences to build new learning experiences. Think about how difficult it would be to start learning from "scratch" every day.

Perceptual Learning

Perceptual learning, which is the process of making sense out of sensory stimuli, is highly important in infancy. Perceptual learning happens because the sense organs mature, the brain develops, and preferences for certain stimuli change. To learn, infants must choose from among stimuli. Researchers believe babies have inborn abilities to choose the stimuli that will most help them learn. **Figure 9.4** shows how babies' preferences, or choices, for certain objects change during infancy.

The outcome of perceptual learning is called **perception**. Perception involves

- ***organizing information that comes through the senses.*** This is a major step in learning. People perceive by noting how objects are alike and different in size, color, shape, and texture. Perceptions about form, space, weight, and numbers come through the senses, too.

Figure 9.4 How Babies' Preferences for Certain Objects Change

- **Preferences change from parts of objects to complete objects.**
  At first, babies react to, or study, parts of objects. Later, they pay more attention to the entire object. For instance, two-month-old babies smile at eyes drawn on a blank background. At three months of age, they study a picture that has eyes and a nose. By five months of age, they smile only at the picture of the full face. At this point, infants prefer the complete objects rather than parts of objects.
- **Preferences change from simple to complex objects.**
  Until babies are almost two months old, they do not prefer one object to another. After that, infants prefer more complex objects. For example, infants prefer 3-D objects over 2-D pictures. They prefer patterned or textured cards over plain white or solid-colored cards. Infants also prefer a drawn human face over any other drawn pattern or solid-colored card. Other preferences include slow-moving objects over nonmoving objects and curved lines over straight lines. They may show little or no reaction to complex stimuli because they cannot understand them.
- **Preferences change from familiar to new objects.**
  After two months of age, infants begin to explore objects that are new to them. They ignore objects that are too different because they may not understand them.

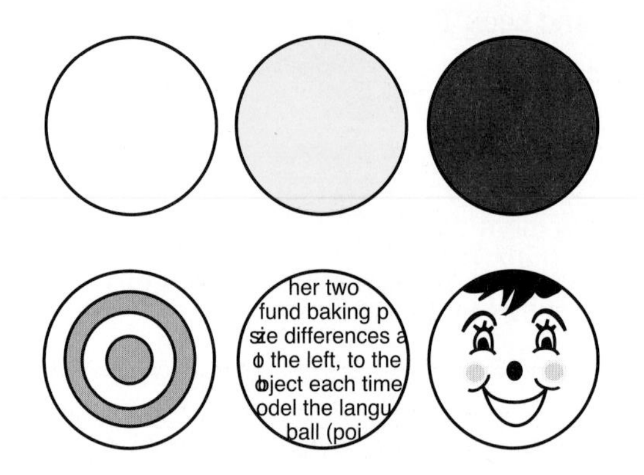

When shown each of these figures, babies' preferences from least to most liked were—white circle, yellow circle, red circle, concentric circles, circle with words, circle with face. (Frantz's study.)

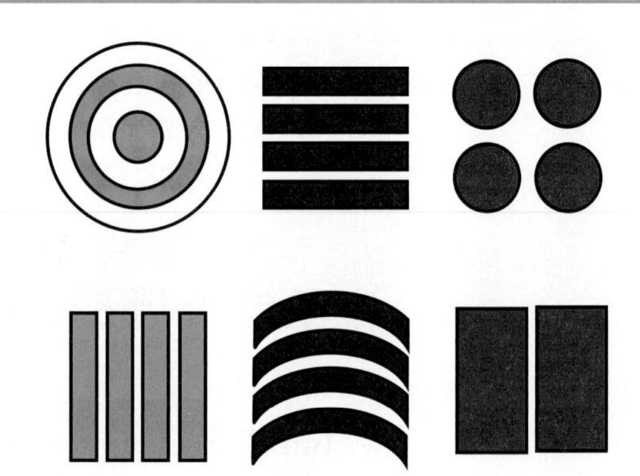

When shown each of these pairs of lines, infants liked the curved lines more than the straight lines. (Frantz's study.)

- ***how fast the brain organizes information.*** For example, a mature reader can tell the difference between the letters *b* and *d* faster than a beginning reader.
- ***the way a person reacts to different sensory experiences.*** For example, a child in a room crowded with strangers may run to his or her mother and play with a toy while sitting on the mother's lap. If the child is alone with the mother, however, he or she may play with a toy on the floor rather than on the mother's lap.

Cognitive Development Theories

Cognition is the act or process of knowing or understanding. Cognition gives meaning to perceptions. The baby's brain begins to piece together perceptions to form a picture in the mind.

Two highly recognized cognitive psychologists who described how children learn are Jean Piaget and Lev Vygotsky. Both men agreed that children construct their knowledge from their experiences. They believed learning attempts must be respected by allowing the child to take the lead. Their ideas influence education even today.

Piaget's Cognitive-Developmental Theory

Piaget thought children learn through their environment by making their own discoveries. He felt that the role of the adult was to provide a stimulating environment. Piaget's research led him to believe that children go through four stages of cognitive development. His theory is known as the *cognitive-developmental theory* (**Figure 9.5**).

Because babies explore with their senses and motor actions, Piaget called the first stage of cognitive development the **sensorimotor stage**. This stage begins at birth, and most children complete it in two years. During this stage, children use their senses and motor skills to learn and communicate. Piaget described learning experiences of the sensorimotor stage through six substages. As you can see by looking at Figure 9.5, babies work through four of the six substages during their first year. (You will learn about the last two substages later in this text.) Learning during the sensorimotor stage is particularly important because this stage is the basis for all future intellectual development.

In the beginning of the sensorimotor stage, connections babies make between themselves and

Figure 9.5 Piaget's Cognitive-Developmental Theory

Stages and Substages	Characteristics
Stage 1: Sensorimotor stage (birth to 2 years)	Children learn through the senses and physical actions in six substages.
Substages 1 and 2 involve the baby's own body.	
Substage 1: Practicing reflexes (birth to 1 month)	• Find stimulation through inborn reflexes, such as sucking and looking. • Practice these reflexes making them strong and more efficient.
Substage 2: Primary circular reactions (1 to 4 months)	• Use voluntary actions that came from the reflexes, such as sucking at will. • Adapt these basic actions, such as sucking with more force for nourishment and with less force for pleasure (pacifier or hand).
Substages 3 and 4 involve people and objects.	
Substage 3: Secondary circular reactions (4 to 8 months)	• Notice some responses to their actions such as crying brings a nearby parent and kicking makes the mobile bounce (cause and effect). Practice their action-response sequences. • Can imitate some actions of others.
Substage 4: Coordination of secondary circular reactions (8 to 12 months)	• Begin to have goals, such as wanting a toy. • Problem-solve by combining two or more actions, such as *crawling* toward a toy and then *grasping* it. • Use a few tools to attain goals, such as using an object's string to pull it within reach.
Substages 5 and 6 involve creative actions and thinking before acting. (12 to 24 months)	
Stage 2: Preoperational stage (2 to 7 years)	Children learn through symbols, but with logical limitations.
Stage 3: Concrete operational stage (7 to 11 years)	Children begin to think logically, but base their logic on past experiences.
Stage 4: Formal operational stage (11 years of age and older)	Older children, teens, and adults reason abstractly.

the environment are accidental. Later, infants note the repeated connections between what they do (action) and what happens (response). This is the beginning of seeing cause and effect. Infants repeat their actions many times (called *circular*) to verify the results and bring pleasure.

During the third and fourth substages, infants learn by **imitating**, or copying another person's actions. Imitation is an important way to learn. Between 8 and 12 months, infants have goals, such as wanting a toy, that direct their actions. They can now combine several actions to achieve their goals or *problem solve*.

Vygotsky's Sociocultural Theory

Like Piaget, Vygotsky believed children's thinking changes as they develop. Although he knew children learned some skills through their own discoveries, he felt children learned mainly through interactions with others within their culture. Vygotsky believed the culture and social environment (family, school, community) in which a child is reared determine how a child will think and the skills he or she will develop. His theory is known as the *sociocultural theory of development*.

Vygotsky's **sociocultural** (relating to social and cultural factors) theory emphasizes how more knowledgeable adults and even other children guide younger children's discoveries (called *assisted discoveries*).Vygotsky saw teaching children as the basic sociocultural activity of humans. He believed teaching occurs through modeling, instructing, and working together on tasks or projects. The varying levels of instructional support given to help children learn a new concept or skill is called **scaffolding**.

To be effective as a "teacher" (or anyone who helps a child learn), Vygotsky thought it was most important to provide instructional supports at the right moments. For each concept or skill, teachers must first find the level in which a child can learn with help. This level is called the **zone of proximal development (ZPD)**. The match is correct when the child can be challenged to learn new concepts or skills, but will not be overwhelmed. Working within a child's ZPD shows respect for what the child is learning and for his or her interests, which is called *following the child's lead*.

Once in the child's ZPD, teachers provide much scaffolding at first. After many experiences, some scaffolding or help is reduced. Once all the scaffolding is removed for a given learning experience, a new ZPD appears and the child becomes ready for a higher level of learning. The gradual withdrawal of help makes the child more self-confident, too.

During infancy, parents can best scaffold through emotional communication. In the very early months, parents try to interpret their baby's cries or sucking behaviors. Around four months of age, infants' signals become clearer as they use body language. For example, infants may kick when they want out of a high chair or turn their head away when bored. Babies become calm when parents scaffold correctly. If parents read the cues and respond, the foundation for learning begins.

Lesson 9.1 Review and Assessment 

1. How does the brain support infant learning?
2. _____ are agents that affect the sensory organs, causing a person to react.
3. List five areas in which vision must mature. Give an example of a task that requires each area.
4. How do motor skills aid intellectual development?
5. Explain the difference between *explicit memory* and *implicit memory*.
6. Perceptual learning is the process of _____ sensory stimuli.
7. What are some similarities between Piaget's and Vygotsky's cognitive development theories? What are some differences?
8. **Critical thinking.** Early psychologist William James once described the infant's world as a "blooming, buzzing mass of confusion." Based on what you have learned in this chapter, do you agree? How would you describe the infant's world?

What Children Learn in the First Year

Lesson 9.2

Objectives

After studying this lesson, you will be able to

- give examples of what newborns can learn through their senses and reflexes.
- explain the concepts infants develop.
- differentiate between perceptual concepts and relationship concepts.
- describe examples of brain wiring for language and social interactions for language.
- summarize communication development during infancy.
- identify intellectual developmental milestones children might achieve in the first year.

Key Terms

active vocabulary
babbling
concept
coo
depth perception
object concept
object constancy
object identity
object permanence
parentese
passive vocabulary

Academic Terms

articulate
auditory
categorization
conversely
habituated
inflections
intricate
monotone
penetrate
proficiency
spatial

Reading and Writing Activity

Before reading, use reliable online or print resources to research opinions about what children should learn in the first year. Create a list of ten concepts children should learn and then write a few sentences for each concept, explaining why you agree or disagree with your sources' assessments. While reading this lesson, look for any references to the concepts you listed. After reading, write two to three paragraphs reflecting on your list in light of what you learned in this lesson.

Graphic Organizer

Write the key terms for this lesson on a separate sheet of paper. As you are reading, organize your notes around the key terms, writing each note next to the key term it most relates to.

active vocabulary *versus passive*

babbling

concept

coo

How babies learn is related to what babies learn. As motor skills and the brain continue to develop, babies are better able to make sense of their surroundings. Babies develop many ideas about their environment during infancy. They learn about objects and people in their environments, and relationships between objects and themselves.

Babies also learn about language and communication. At birth, the main sound newborns make is crying. By the end of the first year, infants recognize many words, and some can even say a few words. Babies also know the tones of a language and may recognize the meaning of body language, such as shaking the head or smiling. Some babies, if taught, also learn sign language.

What Newborns Can Learn

As you read in the previous lesson, newborns learn through their senses and reflexes and show they are learning by their behavior. When newborns are learning, their eyes are more alert, they become quiet, and their heart and breathing rates increase. During infancy, newborns can learn to

- remember an object for a short time (beginning of memory)
- use a different sucking technique on the breast and the pacifier
- become aware of the space around them
- imitate the actions of another person, such as facial expressions and hand gestures
- differentiate between speech and other sounds and recognize parents' voices
- exercise their reflexes (firings in the brain will lead to voluntary motor skills)

Concept Learning

As babies explore their world, they learn many concepts. A **concept** is an idea formed by combining what is known about a person, object, place, quality, or event. Thinking is organized through concepts. For example, if you see an animal you believe is a cat, you immediately think of all you know about cats. Then you note how this animal is like or unlike the cats you recall.

Concepts change throughout a person's life as he or she learns more. For example, you likely know more about children now than you did when you began studying child development. Your concepts have developed (changed). Concepts change by shifting from

- concrete to abstract
- subclass to class (Sometimes children use a *class name*, such as "money," before they use the *subclass names*, such as penny or nickel. This is only due to the names used by parents or caregivers.)
- simple to complex
- incorrect to correct

Concepts are different for each person, because no two people have exactly the same experiences. Also, many concepts involve emotions. For example, the concept of school may be pleasant for one person, but unpleasant for another. During the first year, babies form many concepts. These concepts help children make sense of their world and further their intellectual development.

Perceptual Concepts

Babies form perceptual concepts by making sense out of what they see, hear, smell, taste, and touch and mentally organizing this information. Infants are able to develop perceptual concepts through many experiences in their world. The following sections describe major perceptual concepts children learn in the first year.

Object Constancy or Sameness

Object constancy refers to knowing that objects remain the same even if they appear different. For example, a child may see a large airplane with bright colors take off and then look small and gray in the distance. Children learn that, although the airplane may look different in size, shape, or color, it is still the same plane. Object constancy begins during the first year, but is not fully developed until the second or third year.

Object Concept

Object concept is the understanding that objects, people, and events are separate from a person's interactions with them. Object concept has two parts—object identity and object permanence. **Object identity** is knowledge that an object stays the same from one time to the next (**Figure 9.6**). For example, each time a child sees a toy bear, the bear is the same. **Object permanence** is knowledge that people, objects, and places still exist even when they are no longer seen, felt, or heard. For example, an infant may know his or her mother is still present in the house, even though she is not in the same room.

Like other concepts, object permanence develops with many experiences over time. The concept begins to develop as early as one to two months of age and often involves the baby's own hands that come in and out of view. At this time, infants will stare for a second at the place where an object or person was just seen, but has disappeared. A few months later, infants will gleefully recover an object partially hidden. Toward the end of infancy, infants will watch adults completely hide objects and will then search for them.

Spatial Concepts

Infants learn about **spatial** (pertaining to space) concepts in many ways. Some examples include visually *tracking* (following with one's eyes) the movements of people and objects or fitting objects into openings, such as placing shapes into shape sorters. Squeezing their bodies into tight spaces, hiding behind furniture, and looking at objects from different perspectives are other examples of ways infants learn about space.

One important spatial concept infants form, after they develop binocular vision, is **depth perception** (the ability to tell how far away something is). Accurate depth perception enables infants to judge how far to reach for an object. Using binocular vision, the eyes guide the hand in knowing how far the arm must extend before the hand can grasp the object (**Figure 9.7**). As children learn to walk, depth perception is necessary to keep them from stepping off an object far from the ground and falling. The eyes guide the feet in knowing how far up, down, or away the next step will be. Infants often develop depth perception by seven to nine months of age. Even with some depth perception concepts, babies are not safe from falls.

Number Sense

Infants' brains appear to be wired for understanding numbers. Brain scans show that both infant and adult brains light up in the same area when processing numerical information.

Research suggests babies can detect changes in quantities (numbers) of items. When babies were repeatedly shown the same number of objects on a screen, although the arrangement of the objects changed, they became **habituated** (familiarized) and

Figure 9.6 Object identity, the knowledge that an object stays the same from one time to the next, can be learned through something as simple as repeatedly touching a teddy bear or other object. *What would your perception be like if you had no grasp of object identity?*

Figure 9.7 Depth perception involves learning how far one has to reach to touch an object. *How do you use your depth perception in your daily life?*

bored. When the numbers changed, they became interested again. The amount of change in quantity needed for babies to detect difference depended on the babies' ages. (Under six months required a 1:3 ratio change—4 to 12 dots; six-month-olds needed a 1:2 ratio change—6 to 12 dots; and nine-month-olds only needed a 1:1.5 ratio change—8 to 12 dots). Babies can also detect these same changes in quantities when they are presented as distinct sounds (taps on a drum).

Infants can also keep track of an added object. Researchers noted that five-month-old infants would watch while a single toy was placed on a table. Then a screen was placed in front of the toy. Next a hand placed, or seemed to place, a second toy behind the screen. The screen was removed to reveal one or two toys. If only one toy was behind the screen, the baby would stare longer than if two toys were shown. The longer stare is the baby's way of saying, "This was unexpected. I should see more toys."

Infants can also recognize exact amounts. Researchers showed six-month-olds three pictures—one with one dot, one with two dots, and one with three dots. After the researcher tapped on a drum one to three times, the baby's eyes would focus on the corresponding picture.

Physical Concepts

Infants understand two physical concepts, object solidity and gravity, very early. *Object solidity* means one solid object cannot move through another solid object and *gravity* involves objects falling to the floor or ground (**Figure 9.8**).

When experiments are done that have unexpected results, infants stare longer. For example, in experiments on object solidity, infants were shown a glass with dyed blue water and another glass with blue solid matter. The experimenter moved a straw in and out of the water. The infants stared longer when the straw would not **penetrate** (enter) the blue solid matter, which looked like the glass with water. Conversely, when the experimenter first showed how a straw could not penetrate the blue solid matter, the infant stared longer when the straw was easily moved in and out of the glass with the dyed water. In experiments on gravity, when helium-filled balloons were released, the infants saw the floating balloons as unexpected and stared longer because they are familiar with objects falling. These experiments show that infants are learning about their physical world in a perceptual way, or based on expectations.

Figure 9.8 Gravity can be understood by observing an object falling after it is thrown into the air. An experience as simple as playing in leaves can teach this concept. *What would your perception be like if you had no understanding of gravity?*

Relationship Concepts

Relationship concepts differ from perceptual concepts. Whereas perceptual concepts occur in the physical world, relationship concepts occur in the mind. Infants are aware of relationships between objects in their physical world.

One relationship concept is called **categorization**, or grouping similar objects or events into a group. For example, red objects, letters, or foods may be grouped together because they are the same color. Categorization reduces the amount of new information people have to learn. By three months of age, infants can recognize same shapes, colors, and sizes. With quality experiences, six-month-old infants can form other categories, such as foods, toys, animals, and vehicles. By one year of age, infants note subtle differences in the features of objects, such as differences between butterflies and birds.

Because infants do not sort objects into groups, how do researchers test these abilities? Researchers show infants several objects, one at a time, within a category, such as animals, until the infants are habituated. Then, researchers bring out two more objects at the same time—one in the original category (another animal) and one in a new category (a car, for example). Infants ignore the object from the old category (animals) and focus on the object from the new category (vehicles).

Infants are also interested in cause and effect (**Figure 9.9**). Infants see cause and effect as they smile at or cry for a nearby parent and get a response. They also learn cause and effect by making things happen while playing with their toys. For example, kicking their feet (cause) makes their mobile shake (effect) or knocking over a block tower (cause) makes a loud noise (effect).

Figure 9.9 Infants can learn cause and effect by making things happen, such as pressing a piano key in order to hear a sound. *What other activities can help infants learn cause and effect?*

Language Learning

Language is a complex system of sounds, words, grammar, letters or symbols, and social knowledge. To a great extent, language is a unique human endeavor. Although animals communicate, they cannot master the complex language systems of people. Language learning begins early. Two processes—brain wiring and social interactions involving language—interact in helping infants learn language.

Brain Wiring for Language

Brain development research shows language wiring begins at birth, if not before. The first wiring has to do with the sounds of language, which are needed to understand speech and to speak.

Brain wiring follows a sequence. During the first 6 months, infants distinguish small differences in sounds. They are prepared to learn any language. At 6 months of age, brain pruning begins because there are so many connections. Infants come to notice only major differences in sounds in the languages they hear from caring adults. By 12 months of age, infants complete the **auditory** (relating to hearing) maps needed for their primary language(s). Learning to speak another language without an accent becomes much more difficult as the wiring for the sounds of other languages begins to be pruned away. Around 9 to 12 months of age, wiring in the brain's speech center also begins.

The windows of opportunity for language are early in life. For example, studies of babies who are born deaf show waiting until two years of age to restore hearing through surgery results in language lags. If surgery occurs after four years of age, language delays are profound and lifelong. Other studies of immigrants show that as the age of immigration increases, **proficiency** (mastery of a skill) in the second language decreases. This is because a language different from their primary language is being learned outside the windows of opportunity for language development.

Social Interactions Involving Language

Many language development experts believe language development occurs due to the interaction between brain wiring and social interactions involving language. The following types of social language interactions seem to be the most important for encouraging language development:

- ***Turn-taking.*** Parents and other caregivers need to respond to babies' sounds from birth. As babies listen to spoken language, they make more sounds. Infants' pre-talk includes many language sounds. By 8 to 10 months of age, infants' "talk" reflects the sounds and pitch patterns of the language or languages heard. Infants also learn turn-taking in conversations if adults respond after a baby finishes a sound sequence.
- ***Parentese.*** Parents and other caregivers often use **parentese**, an infant-directed, sing-song, and high-pitched speech, when speaking to babies (**Figure 9.10**). Parentese helps babies clearly hear the sounds of language, learn facial expressions, and note *boundaries of words* (where words start and stop).

Focus on

Speech

The Greatest Language Achievements Occur in Infancy

Language development is somewhat of a mystery. During the first six months, babies cry, coo, and babble with or without social interactions. Language development changes around the second half of the first year. At this point, social interactions are necessary for continued language development. Otherwise, development is arrested. Language development is now something infants and their parents or caregivers do together. The following two critical achievements occur:

- Babies develop a desire to communicate so they can achieve the goals of their agenda. Because they are still in the pre-speech stage, they use gestures, especially gazing, and vocalizations to send their messages. Parents and caregivers know what infants mean and also know hollering will soon start if they do not respond.
- Babies discover people and things have "sound names." Their brains are wired to catch and remember these arbitrary symbols necessary for communication, and their vocal apparatus is quickly becoming ready to make these sounds.

Without these two achievements, oral language would not exist. Language development of infants is perhaps the best example of how all developmental domains work together—the physical, intellectual, and social-emotional. Exactly how it works remains a mystery debated by linguists. Yet, the same language milestones occur across cultures at nearly the same ages. How do you think language development occurs?

Figure 9.10 Characteristics of Parentese

- Vocal range—two-octave, rather than the typical one-octave, speaking range
- Sing-song sound
- Slow with clear pronunciation of sounds
- Short phrases and sentences
- Exaggerated facial expressions—joy, surprise, and concern and comfort
- Face often close to the child's face

- ***Connecting objects with words.*** Because sounds have *referential meaning* (refer to something), parents and caregivers must help infants make associations. When babies see connections, they are *mapping words*. To do this, the adult simply looks at or points to the object or the person they are talking about. Even 3- to 4-month-old infants gaze in the same general direction adults are looking. By 10 to 12 months of age, infants realize the purpose of the adult's gaze—to talk about an object or person. Infants begin to point around eight months of age. Joint attention by gazing and pointing contributes greatly to word mapping.
- ***"Face time."*** Parents and caregivers need to provide quality "face time" to help babies **articulate** (clearly vocalize) sounds (**Figure 9.11**). When talking to infants, 4-month-olds gaze mostly at the eyes of the adult. By 6 months of age, infants spend equal amounts of time looking at the eyes and the mouth. The 8- to 10-month-old mainly looks at the mouth. By 12 months of age, infants once again look at the eyes more in "face time" talk. If a second language is introduced to 1-year-old infants, they will once again "lip read."
- ***Language-rich environment.*** Parents and caregivers need to be talkative. Children do not learn language by watching television, DVDs, or online videos. Children from talkative families with good vocabularies learn many more words than children from less talkative families.
- ***Imitation.*** Spoken language is mainly learned through imitation. By participating in a language-filled world, babies learn the sounds, vocabulary, facial expressions, and turn-taking aspects of language.

Communicating

From the time babies are born, they are communicating. Through the sounds they make, others learn to understand their language.

Stages in Communication

Before the baby's first birthday, he or she has made impressive gains in speaking and understanding language. From birth, babies listen to language and make speech-like sounds. Within a few months, they recognize facial expressions that accompany language, know what some words mean, and understand the idea of turn-taking in conversations. During the latter part of the first year, they may say their first words.

Figure 9.11 Long before they learn to speak, infants make speech-like sounds. *How does making speech-like sounds prepare babies to eventually speak?*

Crying and Cooing

Newborns do not have control over the sounds they make. They make many noises while eating and sleeping. They swallow, smack, burp, yawn, and sigh. During the first two months, babies mainly cry. Parents can quickly learn what their baby's cries mean.

Between the sixth and eighth week, infants often begin to **coo**—a vowel-like sound (*ah-ah-ah; oh-oh; ooh-ooh*) made in the back of the throat. Coos are light, happy sounds. The coo sounds are often made at different pitches. Along with cooing, infants will smile, blow bubbles, gurgle, and squeal. Infants coo more when others talk to, smile at, and touch them. Because turn-taking in conversations is so new to infants, they seldom coo on cue. Infants are more likely to respond to parentese by smiling and wiggling all over.

Babbling

Cooing is slowly replaced by **babbling** (using the tongue and the front of the mouth to make a consonant-vowel sound, such as *ba*). Babbling is an important pre-talking skill. When babbling begins, infants practice all the sounds of most of the world's languages. Babies are ready to learn any language or languages they hear. Around one year of age, infants make only the sounds needed to speak the languages they hear. This is because the brain has pruned away the connections needed to make sounds from other languages. Infants who are deaf, however, babble very little after six months of age and do not learn the sounds of their culture's language.

Babbling is not **monotone** (single pitch without variation). Infants babble with **inflections** (changes of pitch) to express happiness, requests, commands, and questions. An infant often babbles with so much feeling you can almost guess what he or she is saying. Language experts refer to three types of babbling (**Figure 9.12**).

First Words

Infants may begin talking as early as nine months of age, but many start talking later. Before talking, infants must do the following:

- understand object permanence
- understand that people, objects, places, and events have names
- remember words that go with people, objects, places, and events
- have the ability to make the sounds
- realize talking is important

Many experts believe a sound counts as a word only when the same sound is used each time to refer to a specific person, object, place, or event. Most first words are *protowords* (*proto* means *first*), which are not words listed in a dictionary. Protowords are also different from babbling, and are usually only one or two syllables. Each protoword consistently refers to something concrete. These made-up words for family members, food, a special toy, or a pacifier are important ways for infants to communicate. Parents and caregivers learn what the child means. Sometimes protowords are sounds similar to a word, such as *baba* for *bottle*. Most frequently, the protoword is completely unique to

Figure 9.12 Types of Babbling

Type	Description
Marginal babbling	Between 4 and 6 months of age, the infant combines consonant-vowel single sounds (*baaa*) or vowel-consonant single sounds (*uuum*). Marginal babbling is mixed with squeals and coos.
Reduplication babbling	Between 6 and 10 months of age, infants repeat the same syllable over and over, such as *da-da-da-da*. During this stage, infants do a great deal of *reciprocal* (turn-taking) babbling.
Nonreduplicated babbling	Between 9 and 12 months of age, varied babbling sounds begin to sound more like words, such as *gima*. Infants have excellent inflectional changes in this stage. For example, their babbling sounds as if they are asking questions, exclaiming, or making statements.

the baby, such as *gaga* for *ice*. Infants will soon begin to say their first "real words," but protowords may long remain part of the child's store of words.

Passive Versus Active Vocabulary

A person's vocabulary consists of the words he or she understands and uses. Although infants can say only a few words, they understand many more. The words people understand, but do not speak or write are called their **passive vocabulary**. In contrast, **active vocabulary** includes the words used in speaking or writing.

Infants' passive vocabulary far exceeds their active vocabulary. For example, infants know their own names around 16 weeks of age. They recognize the words "mommy" and "daddy" around six months of age. At eight months of age, infants know about 36 words, and at ten months they know about 67 words. **Conversely** (versus; on the other hand), infants' active vocabularies are about 3 words by their first birthday.

Once infants get the idea that objects in their world have names, they learn these names quickly. They even understand phrases and sentences that refer to part of their daily routines such as, "Time for breakfast." Soon their favorite spoken word may be *whaddat* (What is that?) as they begin to learn language.

Baby Signing

With their limited active vocabularies, babies cannot tell others what they want or need, but they may make up signs for certain objects. Based on this information, Linda Acredolo and Susan Goodwin, professors in California universities, developed *Baby Signs*, a formal sign language for hearing infants. The gestures come from American Sign Language (or ASL, the sign language for people who are deaf) and from infant-friendly modifications of ASL gestures.

Infants can use their hands before using the more **intricate** (complex) throat, tongue, and mouth muscles needed for many words. Research shows that when parents begin signing to six- or seven-month-old infants, the infants will often begin signing about two months later. Although some research studies point to positive outcomes for infants, there have been very few studies on baby signing. Thus, more studies are needed before advantages and disadvantages of baby signing can be determined.

Intellectual Developmental Milestones

As you can see, babies learn many new concepts and abilities during infancy. **Figure 9.13** outlines intellectual developmental milestones from birth through 11 months of age. These milestones are simply a guide because infants will develop at their own rate. Also, many factors will influence infants' rates of intellectual development. Understanding intellectual milestones, however, can help parents and caregivers plan appropriate activities to help meet infants' intellectual needs.

Lesson 9.2 Review and Assessment

1. Using their senses and reflexes, what can newborns learn?
2. List three major perceptual concepts that infants learn in the first year.
3. Explain the difference between perceptual concepts and relationship concepts.
4. Describe the brain-wiring sequence for language.
5. Why is it important to talk with babies before they can talk?
6. List the following skills in the order of their occurrence: protowords, cooing, marginal babbling, crying, reduplication babbling, nonreduplicated babbling, and real words.
7. Based on the intellectual milestones that children might achieve in the first year, describe the intellectual level of a typical eight-month-old.
8. **Critical thinking.** Give an example of each of the following concepts: object constancy, object concept, spatial concepts, number sense, physical concepts, and relationship concepts.

Figure 9.13 Newborn and Infant Intellectual Milestones

One month

- Remembers objects if they reappear in a couple of seconds.
- Recognizes mother's voice and smell.
- Cries for assistance.
- Is alert for more time than at birth.

Two months

- "Sees" connections within his or her own body (uses mouth and thumb to suck).
- Looks for a few seconds where object or person was last seen (beginning of object permanence).
- Follows slow movement of objects with eyes (called *tracking*).
- Discriminates among voices, people, tastes, and objects.
- Attends and responds to voices.
- Cries and coos some.

Three months

- Studies own hands.
- Seeks sources of sound by turning head and neck.
- Cries less.
- Gurgles and coos.

Four months

- Notices response of an object to his or her action; repeats action to get same response.
- Remembers object for 5 to 7 seconds.
- Likes detail in objects.
- Recognizes specific characteristics of some things in the environment (bottle, family pet, a toy).
- Makes new sounds.
- Vocalizes to social stimulation.

Five months

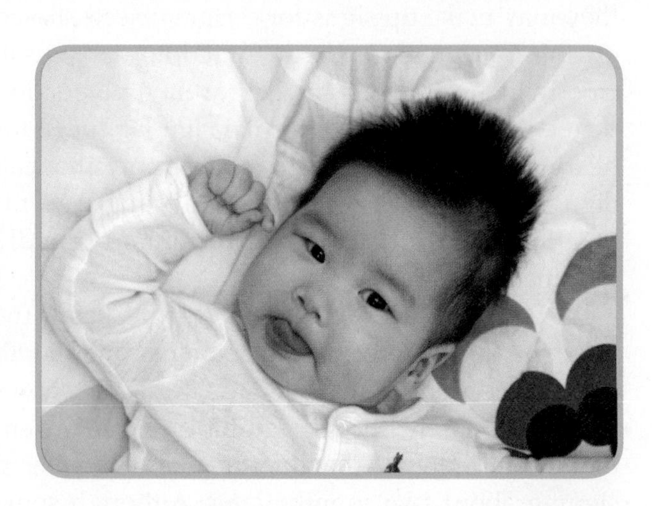

- Learns new actions to repeat.
- Looks around when in new places.
- Wants to explore objects.
- Utters a few consonants.
- Babbles one syllable repeatedly, such as *baa* (called *marginal babbling*).
- Imitates sounds and gestures with model present.

Six months

- Inspects objects for a long time.
- Looks at objects upside down to create a new perspective.
- Compares two objects.
- Connects own actions to environmental response (shaking rattle causes the sound).
- Utters more and more consonants.

Seven months

- Discriminates between familiar and unfamiliar adults.
- Searches for an object partially hidden (object permanence is well underway).
- Picks out his or her name in a conversation.
- Makes more consonant-vowel combinations.
- Babbles two syllables by repeating the first syllable (*ma ma*).

Eight months

- Begins to have goals and combines actions to achieve goals (pushes a pillow away to reach a block).
- Imitates somewhat new actions and makes some effort to improve imitation.
- Babbles by repeating one syllable many times close together, such as *da-da-da-da* (called *reduplication babbling*); may use inflections while babbling.
- Understands about 36 words.
- Follows a one-step command if adult also gestures.

Nine months

- Actively tries to recover a totally hidden toy where last seen (object permanence is mature).
- Remembers games played on previous day.
- Understands and uses gestures (shaking head and waving).
- Responds to the word *no*.
- Babbles nonreduplicated syllables.
- Follows a one-step command without adult gestures.

Ten months

- Tries to fit things together.
- Responds to commands.
- Understands idea of verbal labeling (people and things have names).
- Understands about 67 words.

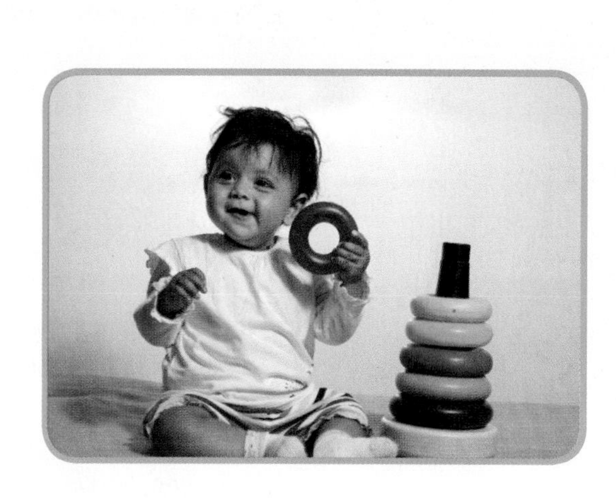

Eleven months

- Imitates inflections and speech rhythms.
- Begins to understand more and more labels (words) for people and things.
- Says first words, which may be protowords.
- May make sounds of some animals.

Lesson 9.3

Meeting Children's Intellectual Needs in the First Year

Key Terms

baby agenda
coordination
enriched environment
sensory stimulation

Academic Terms

consolidate
holistic

Objectives

After studying this lesson, you will be able to

- explain how learning during infancy is different from learning during later childhood.
- describe guidelines for helping babies learn and reinforce concepts.
- develop a stimulating activity that could aid babies' intellectual development for each of the following areas: sensory, motor, memory, and problem-solving.
- identify four ways to talk to babies.

Reading and Writing Activity

As you read this lesson, consider what questions you would ask if you wanted to assess whether a student has read and understood the information. Write a ten-question quiz by recording these questions on a separate sheet of paper. Then, create an answer key for your questions on the back of the paper. After reading, exchange quizzes with a partner. Assess each other's understandings of the lesson.

Graphic Organizer

Stimulating activities for babies can be classified into several categories: *sensory activities*, *motor activities*, *memory activities*, *problem-solving activities*, and *language activities*. Organize your notes for this lesson by category in a graph like the one shown.

Motor activities
Language activities
Memory activities
Sensory activities
Problem-solving activities

Just as parents need to meet babies' physical needs, they also need to meet intellectual needs. Babies need an environment that offers them chances to learn (called an **enriched environment**). Adults can provide learning experiences for babies soon after birth. In fact, the sooner adults provide activities, the more babies want to learn. There are many activities that can help babies improve their sensory, motor, memory, language, and problem-solving skills (**Figure 9.14**). These activities help form the baby's enriched environment.

Remember, however, that babies learn at different rates. The rate of learning cannot be increased with lots of activities and toys. Babies can only take in so much. Too many activities and toys can overstimulate the baby causing the baby to become overwhelmed or to tune out stimuli for self-protection.

Figure 9.14 Playing with toys and spending time with caregivers can provide babies with opportunities to learn problem-solving, motor, sensory, memory, and language skills. *What skills is this baby learning by playing with his toy?*

The Baby Agenda for Learning

How babies learn is very different from how older children learn. Babies have a **baby agenda** that is not culture specific, but is universal to all babies due to genetic brain wiring. This means that learning certain concepts and skills happens around the same time for most babies, regardless of culture. Baby agenda has been the same for all periods of time and in all cultures. According to Ronald Lally, a noted psychologist, the main aspects of a baby's agenda include the following:

- developing motor skills
- learning language
- understanding how objects work
- seeking significant relationships for nurture, protection, and love
- learning ways to interact with others

The type of learning during infancy differs from learning during later childhood. Learning during infancy is more **holistic** (whole; complete) as opposed to the "bits and pieces" learning of older children. For example, when playing with balls, infants may learn about the colors of balls, how they roll, words associated with balls, and play approval from the adult all in one experience. Older children, however, may learn about naming the colors of the balls or sorting the balls by color.

Because a baby also has his or her own learning agenda, adults who try to "teach" something may slow the learning process and frustrate the baby. For example, an adult might hope a baby would use a color sorter to put all the red discs on one peg, but the baby's agenda might be to mouth them or mix discs of all colors over the pegs. Parents and caregivers need to trust a baby's own agenda for learning as best for babies.

Types of Stimulating Activities

A skillful parent or teacher uses activities to meet intellectual needs during infancy. The following are some guidelines for helping babies learn and reinforce concepts:

- Let babies try activities on their own to help them learn to solve problems. Piaget thought this was crucial for learning.
- Let the baby begin most activities and then expand them. For example, an infant may be patting a high chair tray. Expand the activity by patting a different sounding object or by patting the tray harder, softer, faster, or slower than the infant.
- Watch for signs of the baby's interest in certain experiences. To check for interest, show the baby how to use a toy, and then give him or her a turn. Repeat several times. If there is little or no interest, the toy or game is probably too advanced for the baby. Try again in a few days or weeks. Parents who match a toy or game with their child's abilities and interests are working in the child's zone of proximal development (ZPD).
- Repeat games many times. Using games over many months helps the baby retain the skills he or she learns by playing each game.
- Weave words, songs, and games into daily routines, such as feeding, bathing, and diapering. Adults do not need to have a set schedule of daily games. The number and types of games are not as important as the warmth and caring adults show for babies.

Activities for Newborns

Most of the stimulation for newborns comes from being near parents and other caregivers. Newborns are fascinated at seeing faces, hearing sounds, and feeling warm and loved when cuddled. Warm and expressive talk stimulates newborns. Newborns love to hear singing and other soothing sounds, such as a wind chime, music box, or soft music.

Newborns enjoy looking at objects with certain features (**Figure 9.15**). Because their distance vision is limited, newborns often cannot see mobiles hung above their beds. Newborns can see, however, objects attached near to or in the corners of their beds as they tilt their heads back or turn their heads left and right. Changing objects frequently or rotating them prevents newborns from getting bored. (Well into infancy, babies see rotated objects as "new.") Since grasping objects during the newborn stage is a reflex action, objects should be securely fastened, nontoxic, and too large to swallow.

Sensory Activities

Sensory stimulation involves using the senses to learn about the environment. According to Piaget, babies use their senses as a major way of learning. Babies use their senses to explore objects and to discover how objects operate.

For the baby to develop fully, all five senses (sight, hearing, touch, taste, and smell) must be stimulated. One example of a sensory stimulation activity is to let the baby touch a number of safe objects around the room or outdoors. For example, letting the baby touch the bark of a tree helps improve sensory development. Placing a mobile on the baby's crib or playyard also provides sensory stimulation.

Motor Activities

Movement is important for babies. As babies explore, motor activity helps their coordination and intellectual development. **Coordination** is the working together of muscles to form movements, such as walking. Although motor nerves are not fully developed for four or five years, coordination improves quickly after birth.

If babies are free to move, they engage in many motor activities on their own. Babies do, however, need some encouragement from caregivers. Infants use their large muscles as they perform gross-motor skills, such as rolling over, sitting, crawling, standing, and walking. An example of an activity that encourages gross-motor skills is crawling in and out of boxes or cartons. Coordination in the small muscles, especially those in the fingers and hands,

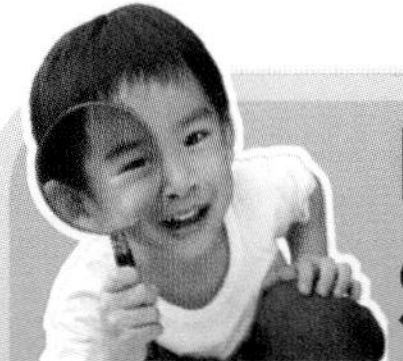

Investigate Special Topics — Tune In to Infants' Cues for Stimulation

The message is out that infant experiences set the foundation for all later learning. The commercial world has responded to this knowledge through an explosion of media and "must-have" products aimed at enhancing infant development.

Babies need an enriched environment, but there are no "must-have" products. Babies need many sensory experiences naturally available in most homes and yards. A few toys that react to a baby's actions are desirable, such as an activity gym, squeeze toys, colorful ball, rattle, two or three soft blocks, an unbreakable mirror, and a few baby books. A warm social environment is most important. Babies are stimulated by the vocalizations and talk of people, their movements, smiles, and the baby games (gentle touching and peekaboo) they initiate.

Beyond the basic environment, parents need to tune in to infant cues for stimulation. Following are some hints:

- Stimulation is most effective during alert times. Alertness differs in babies. Newborns tend to sleep more than older infants, but even babies of the same age differ in their hours of being alert.
- Babies differ in their desire for stimulation. Some seem to be always eager to explore and master while others show less interest and energy.
- Babies differ in their abilities to prevent overstimulation. Some babies cannot sleep after much play and seem frustrated about missing out on anything. Other babies give very exact cues about the need to tune out and may even fall asleep on a pile of toys.

How do parents or caregivers handle these differences? Babies who are alert and interested, but also tune out on their own, get the right amount of stimulation without much adult help. Babies who are on-the-go and cannot tune out on their own are in danger of possible overstimulation. Parents can help by reducing the amount of stimuli at one time (rotating toys) and having only quiet interactions before naps and bedtime. For the least alert babies, the danger is understimulation. Parents need to try to increase periods of alert time and keep the baby engaged while alert.

The bad news about stimulation is that adult actions can also lead to both over- and understimulation. Parents who decide that if a little is good, more is better, may provide too many toys. Because these babies are often so overstimulated, they may tune out normal stimuli and attend only to intense stimuli. On the other hand, through neglect or abuse adults may deprive babies of almost all stimuli. The tragic results of severe understimulation are long-term developmental delays and depression. The good news is that most babies have a normal amount of stimuli in their environments, and they can and do match the amount of stimulation to fit their own needs.

Research Activity

In small groups, choose two baby products that are advertised as "must-haves." Using reliable online or print resources, answer the following questions.

1. On what basis do the manufacturers claim that these products are "must-haves"? What intellectual value do these products have?
2. What experiences or activities could replicate what these products provide?
3. How do these products contribute to over- or understimulation?

Figure 9.15 Visual Preferences of Newborns

Designs and Patterns

Newborns like bold, black-and-white patterns. They prefer horizontal and diagonal designs to vertical ones. Babies like spiral patterns and concentric circles more than solid-colored circles. Newborns like fabrics that have simple designs in high contrast with the background.

Objects that Move

Newborns like objects that flutter with the breeze or move with the crib's, stroller's, or car seat's movement.

Circular-Shaped Objects

Newborns enjoy balls, rings, and hoops.

Faces

Newborns' favorite visual preference is the face. Newborns enjoy seeing people, especially their parents, and even their own reflections in a baby mirror. They also like to see dolls or toy animals with painted or embroidered faces.

is evident in the use of fine-motor skills. Playing with blocks is a fine-motor skill that requires coordination of the small muscles (**Figure 9.16**).

Memory Activities

As you read earlier, babies' explicit and implicit memories are rapidly developing. Even a newborn recognizes his or her mother's voice. The following are suggestions for how parents can aid their baby's memory:

- Have consistent routines so babies remember and anticipate activities.
- Keep toys in the same place because babies watch as parents get them. Once their motor skills are advanced, infants will seek the toys and pull them from shelves or out of containers.
- Sing songs, say rhymes, and read books many times the same way with the same actions.

Figure 9.16 A baby can learn fine-motor skills by using blocks in different ways, such as stacking them, hitting them together, or placing them in a line. *Why do you think blocks are such a popular toy for babies? What other skills can blocks help babies learn?*

- Use the baby's name when speaking and referring to his or her toys and other items. Also, use family names consistently. For example, do not change from "Momma" to "Mommy" or vice versa.
- Engage in turn-taking conversations to help the baby remember the back and forth patterns of conversations.
- Make associations between words and objects and between short phrases and sentences with actions. Use gazing and pointing gestures to connect words with people and objects and some safe and appropriate actions to give meaning to action words.
- Create a photo album of the baby's activities and show it often. (Children will not recognize themselves until the toddler years, but they will recognize their toys.)
- Give the baby a toy, such as a rattle or pull-apart toy. Once he or she learns the skill, take the toy away for a couple days and then reintroduce the toy. Note whether the skill is learned more quickly the second time. Repeat the sequence.
- Make sure the baby gets enough sleep to **consolidate** (combine together) and retain memories.

Problem-Solving Activities

As babies use their senses to observe their world, they try to make sense of what they see, hear, smell, touch, and taste. In an enriched environment, babies learn how their world works as they explore.

Because babies learn in a holistic way, they make connections with objects in their environment and larger concepts. Babies will often problem-solve during play, but this problem-solving usually goes unnoticed by adults (**Figure 9.17**). The following are some examples of "hidden" problem-solving by infants:

- putting an object on a shelf or trying to crawl behind a couch (spatial relationships)
- placing a toy in front, behind, to the side, and on top of another object or container (spatial relationships)

Figure 9.17 Babies can learn problem-solving skills that relate to spatial relationships by placing objects inside other objects. *What is this baby learning about spatial relationships?*

- knocking over a block tower and throwing toys while sitting in a high chair, crib, or playyard (physical knowledge of gravity)
- putting like-items together, such as farm animals, cars, or certain blocks, in a container (categorization)
- dropping an object (physical knowledge of gravity; cause and effect—what happened to the object on impact, including the sound)
- looking at an object on the floor from different perspectives (object constancy)
- playing peekaboo (object permanence)

Language Activities

Babies learn language by hearing people talk. Adults can talk about the foods, toys, people, and routines that are part of the baby's world. Exact words are not as important to the baby as hearing language. How should adults talk to babies? Some ideas are given in **Figure 9.18**. Although it does not matter exactly which words parents use, words should be pronounced correctly. Changing pitch or singing also varies the sound and adds interest. Adults can encourage infants to talk, too, such as by asking a question and then pausing before continuing to talk to the baby. Often, the infant will babble in response.

Reading to infants daily exposes babies to new words and ideas. Even babies who cannot comprehend the words benefit from having books, magazines, and newspapers read to them. Time spent reading and hearing words is important at all ages.

Language games can be worked into daily routines, and can provide a special time of sharing for babies and adults. Perhaps one of the earliest language action games infants enjoy is pat-a-cake.

Lesson 9.3 Review and Assessment 

1. What is meant by infants having a "baby agenda" for learning?
2. Summarize how learning in infancy differs from learning in older childhood.
3. List five guidelines for helping babies learn and reinforce concepts.
4. Most of the stimulation for _____ comes from being near parents and other caregivers.
5. Give two examples for each of the following types of activities: sensory, motor, memory, and problem-solving.
6. List four ways to talk to babies.
7. **Critical thinking.** Why might babies' problem-solving activities often be "hidden" to adults?

Figure 9.18 Talking to Babies

- Use complete short sentences. Remember that the last word is the one the infant will most note, such as "See the ball."
- Use nouns more than pronouns. For example, refer to yourself by name rather than *I*.
- Use lots of adjectives to describe nouns (*red* ball).
- Model language by using gestures to give meaning to words, such as pointing to the object being named or described.
- Expand single words an infant uses. For example, if the infant says, "Daddy," respond by saying, "Yes, Daddy has come home."
- Ask questions although the baby cannot respond at first.
- Describe the baby's feelings although the baby will not yet understand, such as "Kelly fell. Kelly is crying because falling hurts."
- Talk during routine care. For example, while dressing a baby, the parent could say "Mommy is putting on Jack's green shirt. Does Jack like green?"

Chapter 9

Review and Assessment

Summary

Intellectual development includes how babies learn, what they learn, and how they communicate. Brain development and wiring supports learning, and affects the sensory, motor, thinking, and memory centers of the brain. Quality experiences aid this fast-paced wiring. Organizing sensory stimuli, or *perceptual learning*, is a major step in infant learning. Cognition develops as babies piece together and give meaning to their perceptions. Piaget believed that children learn when newborn reflexes give way to voluntary movement and sensory perceptions. He found that children go through substages before they discover new ways to solve problems. Vygotsky saw children's development determined by culture and adult guidance.

Infants learn a great deal in their first year. Their perceptual concepts include object constancy, object concept, spatial concepts, number sense, and physical concepts. They also develop relationship concepts. Language development involves major brain wiring changes—both making new connections and pruning. Social interactions involving language are crucial to language development. The stages in language development include crying, cooing, babbling, and first words. To develop intellectually, children need an enriched environment, but the best learning agenda for infants is the "baby's agenda," not an "adult's agenda." Babies need activities that stimulate all the senses. For language development to take place, it is important to talk to children and encourage them to make sounds and words.

College and Career Portfolio

Portfolio Letters of Recommendation

Whether for a college or job application, most schools and employers require applicants to provide letters of recommendation or references. Letters of recommendation and references can take time to acquire.

Consider which teachers, employers, or other adults can best speak about your skills and work. Then, decide on two to three individuals you want to ask to be your references, and complete the following activities.

- Ask the individuals you chose if they would be willing to be your reference. Make sure to be polite and grateful and give them time to respond.
- If the purpose of your portfolio requires a letter or recommendation, ask the individuals you chose to write a letter of recommendation for you. Be courteous, and make sure to communicate the deadline for your application.

Chapter 9 Review and Assessment

Vocabulary Activities 

1. Write each of the following terms on a separate sheet of paper. For each term, quickly write a word you think relates. In small groups, exchange papers. Have each person in the group explain a term on the list.

Key Terms

active vocabulary (9.2)
babbling (9.2)
baby agenda (9.3)
binocular vision (9.1)
cognition (9.1)
concept (9.2)
coo (9.2)
coordination (9.3)
depth perception (9.2)
enriched environment (9.3)
explicit memory (9.1)
implicit memory (9.1)
object concept (9.2)
object constancy (9.2)
object identity (9.2)
object permanence (9.2)
parentese (9.2)
passive vocabulary (9.2)
perception (9.1)
perceptual learning (9.1)
scaffolding (9.1)
sensorimotor stage (9.1)
sensory stimulation (9.3)
stimuli (9.1)
zone of proximal development (ZPD) (9.1)

2. Read the text passages that contain each of the following terms. Then write the definitions of each term in your own words. Compare your definitions to those of your classmates. How were the definitions similar? How were they different? Also compare your definitions to definitions in a dictionary.

Academic Terms

articulate (9.2)
auditory (9.2)
categorization (9.2)
consolidate (9.3)
conversely (9.2)
habituated (9.2)
holistic (9.3)
imitating (9.1)
inflections (9.2)
intricate (9.2)
monotone (9.2)
penetrate (9.2)
proficiency (9.2)
sociocultural (9.1)
spatial (9.2)
subtle (9.1)
wane (9.1)

Critical Thinking

3. **Analyze.** New, quality experiences are vital to development of the infant's thinking center. In small groups, visit a new location, and note everything about the location that is "new" to you. Then, compare lists and analyze how this new experience fosters learning.
4. **Identify.** Identify three examples of perceptual learning that you experience daily. In what situations do you have to sort through sensory stimuli? Choose one example and explain how it results in the three outcomes of perceptual learning.
5. **Make inferences.** Why is it important to "follow the child's lead" when teaching new concepts and activities in a child's zone of proximal development? Why does this approach differ from learning approaches used with older children?
6. **Evaluate.** For each of the four directions of concept development (concrete to abstract, class to subclass, simple to complex, and incorrect to correct), write a short paragraph illustrating the direction. Then, trade papers with a partner. Evaluate your partner's illustrations and identify which directions each paragraph describes. Discuss your answers with your partner.
7. **Compare and contrast.** In small groups, compare and contrast active vocabulary and passive vocabulary. List at least ten examples of each and deliver a presentation summarizing your discussion to the class.
8. **Determine.** Few studies have been conducted on the advantages and disadvantages of baby signing. As a class, debate the possible advantages and disadvantages of baby signing. Research the topic beforehand and come to class with a stance on the technique.
9. **Analyze.** In small groups, analyze the idea that babies have a baby agenda for learning that is not culture specific. What does this mean for babies around the world? How does the baby agenda differ from learning (such as school learning) later in life?
10. **Draw conclusions.** Bring an infant toy to class with you and trade toys with another student. Then, handle the toy and describe what an infant might perceive about the object, including its size, shape, color, texture, weight, and number. Write two to three paragraphs summarizing your observations.

Core Skills

11. **Science and technology.** Use the Internet to research brain development in the first year. Choose a specific research topic that interests you, such as "How is brain development affected by nutrition?" or "Which influences brain development more: genes or the environment?" Then, use word processing software to write a report of your findings. Check your paper for correct spelling, grammar, and punctuation. Adhere to all copyright laws and cite any sources you may use for the report.
12. **Technology and speaking.** Imagine you are a schoolteacher who is teaching Piaget's and Vygotsky's theories to a class of elementary school students. Choose a grade level for your students and then create an age-appropriate lesson plan and electronic presentation that will help you teach and reinforce the information. Present a three-minute sample of your lesson to the class. For each presentation, provide feedback for the presenter, and take notes on the feedback you receive.
13. **Math.** Within the first year, children develop "number sense," or the ability to detect changes in numbers and recognize amounts. Imagine you are a child care worker who needs to develop an activity to reinforce babies' number senses. Outline an age-appropriate activity to help babies recognize number changes and number amounts. Conduct your activity within your class and then explain how the activity reinforces number sense.
14. **Art and speaking.** In small groups, review the intellectual milestones children achieve within the first year of life. Then, using art supplies or electronic resources, collaborate to create an easy-to-follow visual representation of the milestones an infant achieves during each of the first twelve months. Your illustration should include drawings or pictures of infants achieving milestones during each month, and should be an effective study tool and synthesis of the information you learned in this chapter. After completing your illustration, present it to the class and make it available for other students to reference while studying.
15. **Reading and writing.** Using online or print resources, find a nonfiction book that describes stimulating activities for babies. Read at least two chapters of the book, noting where the book overlaps with your textbook and where it might differ. Finally, write a report comparing the activities covered in the book you chose with the activities covered in your textbook. Incorporate quotations from both books and cite these quotations using MLA style.
16. **Writing.** Review the ways that caregivers can talk to babies, even when babies cannot yet talk back. Then, write short scenarios for at least three of the ways suggested in your textbook. For each scenario, explain how talking to the baby is helping the baby learn language.
17. **Research and listening.** Interview a *child development professional* (person with a college degree in child development, child and family studies, or early childhood education) regarding ways parents and caregivers can stimulate brain development in infants. What types of stimulation appear to be best for babies? What is the professional's opinion regarding the use of "brain development aids," such as flash cards, videos, and kits marketed to "boost a baby's brain power"? If the professional does not recommend these techniques, what techniques does he or she recommend?
18. **CTE Career Readiness Practice.** Use Internet or print resources, or the help of a science teacher, to examine how brain wiring changes in the first year of life. Prepare a storyboard with diagrams that illustrate what happens as babies learn new concepts and develop language skills. Explain how quality experiences and the baby agenda influence the wiring process.

Observations

19. For one week, observe an infant exploring his or her world for 30 minutes per day. Record what the baby does during this time. What senses were used? What concepts and skills might the baby have been learning?
20. As a class, assign groups to record or find recordings of sounds made by two- to twelve-month-old babies. In your group, listen to the recording you created or found. Distinguish between the sounds babies make and identify sounds such as cooing and babbling. Play your recording for the class and deliver a presentation identifying these sounds.

Chapter 10 Social-Emotional Development in the First Year

Essential Question

What is taking place in the first social and intensely emotional baby-adult interactions, and how can parents lay the "best" foundations for this relationship?

Lesson 10.1 **The Social-Emotional World of Babies**

Lesson 10.2 **Meeting Social-Emotional Needs in the First Year**

Case Study Can an Infant's Parents Be *Too* Cautious?

As a class, read the case study and discuss the questions that follow. After you finish studying the chapter, discuss this case study again. Have your opinions changed based on what you learned?

The Millers have been very protective of their daughter since birth. Once she started crawling, everything in the house seemed dangerous even though a professional had childproofed their home. The Millers purchased pillows, cushions, and mats to protect their daughter from germs on the floor and from bumping into furniture. They even bought her a helmet and special pants with kneepads.

During the last few well-baby checkups, the pediatrician noted how the Millers constantly said *no* to their daughter if she reached for items in his examination room because these "had germs." Seeing the helmet, however, triggered the pediatrician to remark to the Millers that the baby needs a balance between natural risk taking and their safety precautions.

Stunned by this comment, the Millers sat in silence. What does the pediatrician mean? Wasn't it their job to keep their daughter healthy, safe, and happy? Shouldn't they always be protective?

Give It Some Thought

1. What does the pediatrician mean by finding a balance between the baby's natural risk taking and the parent's safety practices? Do you think there is just one balance point or could there be more than one? Explain your answer.
2. How might allowing some risk taking keep children safer in the long run?
3. What beliefs and negative emotions might the Miller's be possibly instilling in their daughter?
4. In some medical circles, there is a belief called the "hygiene hypothesis." This hypothesis suggests infant exposure to some bacteria and viruses builds a strong immune system and protects children from allergies, asthma, and autoimmune diseases during adulthood. Exposure during infancy may also promote less body inflammation associated with other diseases, such as heart disease. What do you think about the "hygiene hypothesis"?

While studying this chapter, look for the online resources icon  to:

- **Practice** terms with e-flash cards and interactive games
- **Assess** what you learn by completing self-assessment quizzes
- **Expand** knowledge with interactive activities and graphic organizers

Companion G-W Learning

www.g-wlearning.com/childdevelopment

Study on the go

Use a mobile device to practice terms and review with self-assessment quizzes.

www.m.g-wlearning.com/0384

Lesson 10.1 The Social-Emotional World of Babies

Key Terms

age-appropriate behaviors
anxiety
attachment
attachment behaviors
disposition
emotions
high-reactive infants
low-reactive infants
separation anxiety
temperament

Academic Terms

intrusive
precedes
siblings

Objectives

After studying this lesson, you will be able to

- identify the three main aspects of social-emotional development.
- differentiate between *high-reactive infants* and *low-reactive infants* and then identify three parenting behaviors (environmental factors) that influence high-reactive children's temperaments.
- explain the meaning of "serve and return" in infant-adult relationships and give an example of a positive and a negative interaction.
- describe how babies develop *focused attachment*.
- explain the roots of four emotions—love, fear, anxiety, and anger.
- give examples of social-emotional developmental milestones children might achieve in the first year.

Reading and Writing Activity

Skim this lesson, paying close attention to the figures included in each section. For each figure, write a one- to two-sentence prediction about how the figure illustrates a topic covered. Then, after reading, revisit your predictions and update or correct them to reflect what you learned. How well do the figures illustrate the concepts in this lesson? What other figure options might expand your understanding of the concepts?

Graphic Organizer

Organize your notes for this lesson according to the three aspects of social-emotional development. In the middle circle of a chart like the one shown, write *Aspects of Social-Emotional Development*. Then, draw three outer circles labeled *disposition*, *social relations*, and *emotions*. For each note you take, place it next to the circle to which it most closely relates.

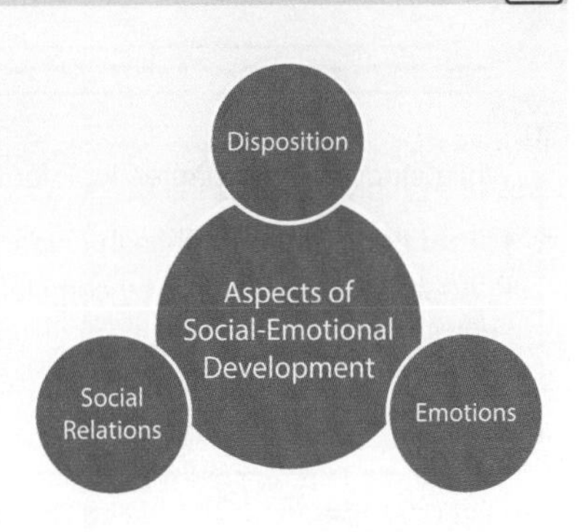

Social-emotional development is an important type of development that happens as quickly during the first year as physical and intellectual development. A baby enters the world with unique traits, which are the roots of the child's later personality. By the end of the first year, personality traits are even more evident. As a baby's social-emotional world expands, he or she forms ideas about him- or herself and whether the world is a friendly place. The baby begins to express feelings with different emotions.

Aspects of Social-Emotional Development

Social-emotional development involves a person's concepts about him- or herself as well as concepts about others. There are three main aspects or parts of social-emotional development.

1. **Disposition** or general mood of a person. Some people have a more cheerful disposition, and others are more moody.
2. Social relations, such as interactions with people and social groups. These interactions may include family members, friends, schools, and clubs (**Figure 10.1**).
3. Ways people express feelings through **emotions** (thoughts that lead to feelings, such as joy, fear, and anger, and cause changes in the body). For example, if you are upset at someone or something (a thought), you may become angry (a feeling), which may increase your heart rate (a change in the body). Even babies have emotions, which they display through their interactions with others.

Temperamental Differences in Babies

Temperament is the inherited tendency to react in a certain way, such as being cheerful or grumpy. Sometimes the word *disposition* also defines the ways people react consistently in different settings and over a long period of time.

Jerome Kagan, a well-known psychologist and researcher, has extensively studied personality, including temperament, in children. He theorizes that temperament is inherited and very noticeable by three months of age. Some children inherit genes that cause them to become overexcited and have problems calming down whereas other babies are rather easy-going.

Kagan believes temperament does not determine behavior, but does push a child to react in a certain way. In his research, Kagan compared infants who are *high reactive* and *low reactive*, and then studied

Figure 10.1 Social relations, one of the three aspects of social-emotional development, involves interactions with family members, friends, and other people. *What are the most important social relations in your life? With whom do you interact the most?*

the same children as teens. **High-reactive infants** react to anything new with caution and can easily become physically agitated and distressed. **Low-reactive infants** tend to be sociable and bold (trying new challenges).

High-reactive (formerly called *difficult*) infants are irregular in their habits. They may withdraw or protest—even scream—when facing new situations. High-reactive infants often have a rough start, which may cause parents increased feelings of anxiety. Low-reactive (formerly called *easy*) infants are cheerful, have regular habits, such as eating and sleeping, and respond quickly to a new situation. Low-reactive infants usually get off to a good start with their parents.

Through his studies, Kagan found the following parenting behaviors (environmental factors) negatively influence high-reactive children's temperaments:

- ***Inadequate soothing.*** High-reactive children need parents who help them calm down and regulate their emotions. Without help, these children become more reactive.
- ***Alarmist behavior.*** Parents who are alarmist see dangers everywhere. Infants can sense parents' feelings of anxiety and become anxious themselves.
- ***Intrusive behavior.*** Parents who are intrusive (controlling) become overprotective. These children may have difficulty developing their own coping skills.

Kagan's research showed that no high-reactive child later became a low-reactive child. Parents can effect a compromise, however, by working on their high-reactive child's temperament. Good, consistent care of high-reactive babies may make them happier (**Figure 10.2**). Easing these children into new situations and alerting them to upcoming changes are also helpful. As children get older, parents can even rehearse certain expectations with them.

Figure 10.2 Supportive care of high-reactive babies includes extra holding, cuddling, and soothing. *Were you a low-reactive or high-reactive baby? Explain.*

Social Relations

Social refers to a relationship between two or more people. Social development in the first year is shaped by how other people affect the baby and how the baby affects other people. By the end of the first year, social development is well underway. This section will focus on social relations in the first year that involve interacting with others and showing attachment.

Interacting with Others

Human relationships are the building blocks of healthy development. Babies are born with tools for social development. At birth, newborns can turn their heads in the direction of the human voice. They move their arms in rhythm of human speech. They like to look at people's faces.

Positive interactions between babies and their caregivers are sometimes called "serve and return," like the game of tennis. Babies understand social messages by the way others talk to, look at, or hold them. Babies send signals to others through their cries, coos, and smiles. These "serve and return" signals change in the following ways throughout the first year:

- Signals begin as early as two weeks after birth. Smiles with expressive eyes often occur around the fifth or sixth week.
- From three to six months, infants become even better at understanding and sending social signals. They also begin to distinguish between those who care for them and strangers.
- Once infants have better arm and hand control and can easily creep, they initiate social contact. For example, infants may follow other family members around the house. Infants will also reach with their arms to signal they want to be held.

Interacting with Adults

Babies thrive most when they are held, talked to, cuddled, and comforted. They are often happier babies, crying less than those who receive little attention. Parents and caregivers help their baby's intellectual development, as well as social development, by providing lots of loving care. At this stage, parents are in Galinsky's nurturing stage of parenting (**Figure 10.3**).

Grandparents, friends, babysitters, and others are helpful to a baby's total development. When these people care for and show an interest in them, babies learn to understand and trust others, which helps expand their social environment.

If the baby's first relationships are negative due to parental depression, conflicts in the home, or other crises, social connections in the baby's brain do not form properly. This is because "serve and return" relationships are faulty. In these faulty relationships, the adult does not "serve," or when the child "serves," the adult either does not return or returns without sensitivity.

Interacting with Other Children

Infants enjoy being around **siblings** (brothers and sisters) and other children, and tend to watch and follow them. Infants learn from older children and like to play with older children's toys. Older children can learn lessons in loving and caring for others from infants, too. All children benefit in these relationships.

Showing Attachment

Attachment is closeness between people that remains over time. As you may recall, *bonding* (developing a feeling of affection) is a special

Figure 10.3 Galinsky's *nurturance* parenting tasks include balancing a baby's needs with personal needs and providing loving and consistent care to a baby. *How do you think parenting tasks change as a child ages?*

type of attachment between parents and their children. Bonding begins at birth and continues throughout infancy. Bonding happens through closeness, feeding times, bathing, and playtime. This connection lays the foundation for forming an attachment (**Figure 10.4**).

Babies are motivated to form attachments. They need a parent's love and care to survive and desire to feel secure. Thus, babies develop an attachment to those who care for them. They show this attachment through **attachment behaviors**, or actions one person demonstrates to another person to show closeness to that person. Attachment behaviors change from birth through the school-age years. Attachment is developmental, which means attachment behaviors often occur in a set order. The attachment behavior in infancy is called *focused attachment* (**Figure 10.5**).

Attachment is closely related to positive interactions with parents and with future health and well-being. Attachment is positive in the following ways:

- Everyone needs to love and to be loved. For healthy social-emotional development, attachment is critical. Establishing healthy attachments helps babies feel loved.
- Attachment helps intellectual development. Attached infants tend to explore their world through play more than infants who are not attached to others.
- Healthy brain development depends on attachment. Overcoming stress throughout life is easier for infants who formed strong attachments early in infancy. For example, through attachment, the toddler and young preschooler learn to deal with the fear of strangers and the fear of being left alone in the care of other adults.

Figure 10.4 Bonding and Attachment

Relationship	Term Used
Parents come to love their babies soon after birth. Parents → Baby	Bonding
Babies whose needs are met come to love their parents. Infants realize this tie after six months of age. Baby → Parents	Attachment

Figure 10.5 Development of Focused Attachment Behaviors

Approximate Age	Focused Attachment Behaviors
1 month	• Newborn recognizes familiar and unfamiliar voices. • Newborn turns toward familiar voices.
2 weeks to 2 months	• Baby smiles.
3 months	• Infant responds by giving joyful sounds (coos and gurgles) and movements (kicks). • Infant may laugh.
4 to 6 months	• Infant engages in more turn-taking games, such as peekaboo. • Infant begins to show a preference for familiar people. • Infant becomes still and breathing becomes shallow when unknown people are close.
7 to 12 months	• Infant shows a strong preference for primary caregivers. • Infant cries when a stranger is nearby—fear of strangers. • Infant cries when left alone in an effort to bring a caregiver back into his or her presence. (Object permanence allows infant to know caregiver exists even when not present.)

Some infants have attachment problems. The main causes of attachment problems are: loss of the primary caregiver, inconsistent or angry care by the primary caregiver, abuse, and changes in other caregivers (turnover of staff in child care). Poor attachment can cause social and emotional problems throughout life.

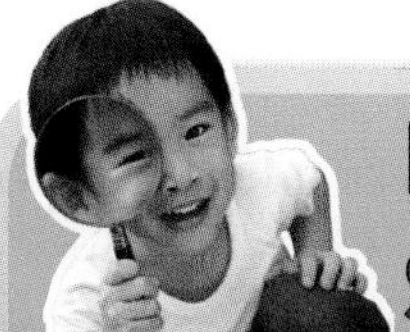

Investigate Special Topics: Attachment Theorists

Most, but not all, of the child development theorists primarily focused their research on the child's development with little emphasis on family life. For about the last 75 years, other researchers have directly focused on the effects of early significant social interactions of infants and children under three years of age. *Attachment studies*, as they are known, began with a focus on the mother-child relationship, but now encompass bonding, infant care, stranger fear, separation anxiety, and the effects of the relationship between the baby and all caregivers. Four major theorists have shaped current knowledge of attachment.

John Bowlby, the father of attachment theory, found WWII in Great Britain had ruptured many family bonds. Specifically, Bowlby found the lack of maternal care, distortions of maternal care (neglect and abuse), and discontinuity in maternal care (maternal separations and multiple mothering figures) all resulted in lifelong mental health problems. Bowlby advocated early intervention for the country's youngest citizens and worked to change government policies for families.

Mary Ainsworth, born in the U.S., served as Bowlby's research assistant for three years. Her lifelong, cross-cultural studies led her to develop listings of baby indicators of attachment, such as an infant crying when the mother leaves the room, showing excitement when the mother returns, and staying close to the mother if a stranger is nearby. As a fastidious researcher, she came up with the well-known method of testing infant attachment called the *Strange Situation*. From these experiments, she developed lists of variables for secure and insecure attachments, which will be explained later in the text.

John Kennell and **Marshall Klaus** had a 40-year research collaboration. Their studies led to understandings about parent-newborn bonding. From their studies, they called for changes in the inflexible hospital practices that isolated babies from their parents. Their works led to the hospital birthing room, use of the doula during childbirth, parental holding in the NICU, and hospital classes on baby care. They also researched family problems (grief, depression, marital problems) that prevented optimal bonding.

T. Berry Brazelton focused on assuring parents about attachment. He promoted the idea of attachment as a gradual process. His *Touchpoints* helped prepare parents for the infant's developmental changes. He believed in a close partnership between parents and child care providers and researched the infant's ability to form multiple attachments. Through his writings and mass media appearances, he provided know-how and encouragement to all families—single parents, working families, adoptive parents, and parents with ill newborns—to bond with their babies as a foundation for children's mental health.

Research Activity

In small groups, choose one of the theorists described above. Then, using online or print resources, find a reliable article describing the theorist's life and work. Read the article individually and then discuss as a group what facts were especially interesting to you. Present the highlights of your discussion to the class.

Expressing Emotions

After disposition and social relations, the third aspect of social-emotional development involves expressing feelings. Long before babies express feelings, the emotion center of the brain becomes active. Because feelings are complex and tied to thinking, memory, and even language, wiring for emotions takes four years to complete.

Brain development research shows that by two months of age, infants begin constructing emotions. Infants first get visual cues of emotions in others at this age. During the first three or four months, infants have two basic responses to their world. The first is distress, shown by crying and muscle tension. The second is excitement, shown by smiling, cooing, and wiggling the body. By the end of the first year, infants can express love, fear, anxiety, anger, jealousy, joy, and sadness. Infants who express a range of emotions, from happy to unhappy, show healthy development.

Love

As parents care for their babies and meet their needs, babies become attached to them and begin to feel and show love and affection. Babies show love not only to important adults, but also to children who keep them company.

Besides people, babies also become attached to objects, such as pacifiers, stuffed toys, or blankets (**Figure 10.6**). Babies seem to need these objects even more when they are upset or afraid, or when routines change. Sometimes adults worry about children's love for these objects. Such attachments, however, tend to give babies security and are important to them. Children give up these objects in time.

Fear

The true emotion of fear is not present at birth. Instead, newborns react with the startle reflex when they hear loud sounds or do not have support for their bodies. The stimulus of a loud sound or bodily

Figure 10.6 Babies may express love by becoming attached to objects, such as pacifiers or blankets. *How do you think babies' attachments to objects encourage the development of love?*

displacement causes the reflex. For example, by four or five months of age, infants may show some wariness of adult strangers, called *stranger fear*. They may even see adults they know who have new hairstyles, hats, sunglasses, or other such changes, as unfamiliar. Infants do not seem to have the same reaction to adults seen from back view or to young children they do not know.

Fear, as an emotion, occurs around six months of age. To experience true fear, infants must know they can be hurt. Three kinds of fear include the following:

- ***Fear of the unknown.*** Infants fear adult strangers, a new bed, or a sudden movement. They also fear different sounds, such as thunder or a siren.
- ***Fear learned from direct experiences.*** Infants may fear getting soap in their eyes, being in a doctor's office, or seeing a snapping dog because of a negative past experience.
- ***Fear learned from adult influence.*** What adults say and how they act affect babies' fears. Adults who act or look fearful in a storm, for example, will cause children to be fearful. Adults who tell babies that many situations can hurt them teach children to fear.

Of course, some fear is good. Too much fear, however, is not healthy. Fear affects motor and intellectual development because fearful babies often will not welcome new experiences.

Anxiety

Anxiety is fear of a possible future event. Sometimes the words *worry* and *concern* are used to describe anxiety. The first anxiety of an infant is called **separation anxiety**, which is the fear that loved ones who leave them with other caregivers will not return. Separation anxiety is seen around 8 months of age and peaks between 10 and 18 months (**Figure 10.7**). The reason very young infants show little separation anxiety is because of their limited intellectual development. Young babies have not yet become attached to certain people. They do not know parents or main caregivers are somewhere else when out of sight or how long they will be gone. These young babies are accepting of all who care for them. There are some indications of anxiety, however, between 4 and 6 months of age. (Review Figure 10.5.)

Around 8 months of age, infants develop the idea about their loved ones being somewhere else when out of sight. They also begin to anticipate future events. During this time, infants become

Figure 10.7 *Separation anxiety* is a baby's fear that a loved one who leaves him or her with other caregivers will not return. *What are some ways caregivers can soothe babies with separation anxiety?*

anxious when the adults they love must leave them for a time. This is common when a parent goes to work or leaves the house to run an errand.

The anxiety begins when the infant sees clues of the upcoming separation, such as a parent picking up car keys or telling the infant good-bye. Separation anxiety is more intense when strangers, such as new babysitters, are near. Infants cannot anticipate a reunion with their loved ones. Thus, during separations, they cry as though their heart will break. When this occurs, infants are most difficult to console.

Reactions to anxiety normally fade when infants are around two years of age, which may be due to the following:

- Children younger than two years of age cannot understand why parents must leave whereas two-year-olds have some understanding about why their parents must leave them with others.
- Unlike two-year-olds who remember their parents have returned after each separation, infants do not have the memory of past events.
- Infants are dependent on others to fulfill their needs whereas two-year-olds are more independent.
- Two-year-olds can express their needs better than infants who cannot express their needs to others well, especially to adults they do not know. Infants' inability to express themselves can lead to anxiety.

Anger

Just as the startle reflex **precedes** (comes before something) true fear, *infant rage* precedes true anger. Infant rage occurs when babies are distressed. When infants feel distressed, they may swing their arms and legs excitedly, turn red, and cry loudly (**Figure 10.8**). Infant rage is not true anger, because

Figure 10.8 Infant rage precedes true anger, which typically does not develop until around 8 to 10 months of age. *How would you describe infant rage to a new parent who is frustrated with his or her baby?*

infant rage is an instinctive response with no thought. *True anger* is a feeling caused by frustration that is directed or focused toward a certain person or object.

By 8 to 10 months of age, infants develop true anger, which is often expressed in physical ways, such as kicking or hitting a person or object. Infants often show anger if

- they are being held, diapered, or dressed when they do not want to be. Being in a confined space (crib, high chair) when they do not want to be may make them angry, too.
- they cannot reach a toy they want or if toys are taken from them.
- their needs are not being met and caregivers are trying to distract them. For example, showing a crying, hungry infant a toy may cause the infant to cry louder and push the toy away.

Infants express their anger in physical ways because they lack language skills. Infants with calm dispositions may seem to show little anger during the first year. Infants whose dispositions tend to be negative may show much more anger. Meeting the infant's needs quickly often prevents anger. Staying calm by talking in a quiet voice and not looking upset are ways to show children how to control their anger. Parents might reduce an infant's anger by holding him or her close for a short time.

Social-Emotional Developmental Milestones

Sometimes adults say, "Children should act their age." This means that as people mature, the way they respond to their feelings changes. When people act their age, they use **age-appropriate behaviors** (proper or expected ways to express emotions at certain ages). For example, two-month-old infants will soothe themselves by sucking, which is an appropriate behavioral response for infants. This same response, however, may not be appropriate for school-age children.

Infants display many age-appropriate behaviors, which are also developmental milestones. **Figure 10.9** lists social-emotional developmental milestones during infancy. Understanding social-emotional milestones can help parents and caregivers plan appropriate activities to meet babies' social-emotional needs.

Lesson 10.1 Review and Assessment 

1. Name the three aspects of social-emotional development.
2. _____ is the inherited tendency to react in a certain way, such as being cheerful or grumpy.
3. Contrast the temperaments of a *high-reactive infant* and a *low-reactive infant*.
4. What three parenting behaviors negatively influence high-reactive children's temperaments?
5. What is the meaning of "serve and return" in infant-adult relationships? Give an example of a positive and a negative interaction.
6. _____ is closeness between people that remains over time.
7. Give two examples of focused attachment behaviors.
8. What are the roots of the four emotions—love, fear, anxiety, and anger—in infants?
9. Why do very young infants show little separation anxiety?
10. Describe three social-emotional developmental milestones children might achieve in the first year.
11. **Critical thinking.** What is meant by the saying, "Temperament is the forerunner of personality"?
12. **Critical thinking.** Attachment is important to healthy brain development in infants. Based on what you know about the intellectual development of infants, how important is healthy brain development for intellectual growth? What could be the result if a child does not form attachments?

Figure 10.9 Newborn and Infant Social-Emotional Milestones

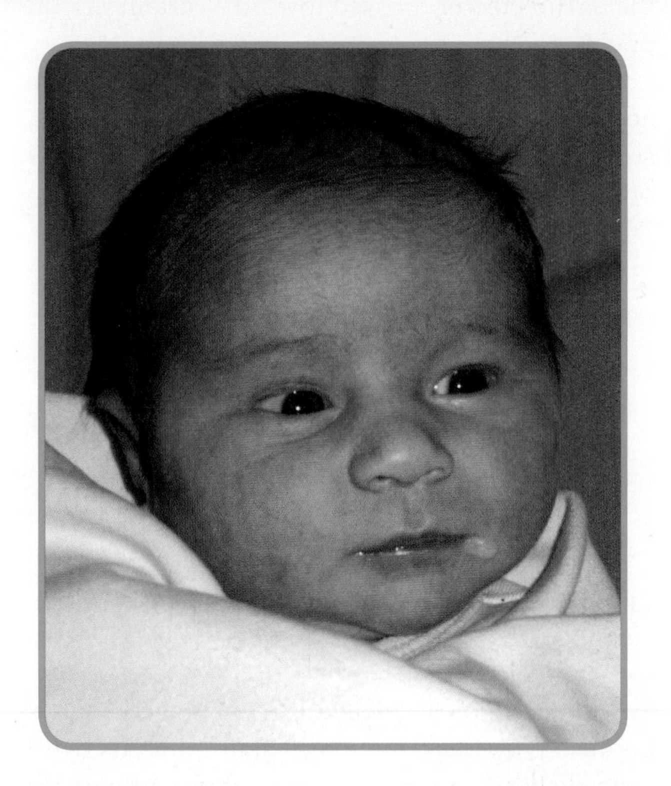

One month

- Is quiet and still when looking at a face within 12 inches.
- "Molds" to adult's body when held.
- Responds to human voices by moving.

Two months

- Can be soothed by being held or rocked.
- Soothes self by sucking.

Three months

- Shows excitement when people are nearby.
- Smiles when stimulated by a face.
- Tries to attract people's attention.
- Shows delight and distress.

Four months

- Smiles broadly and laughs.
- Vocalizes to initiate socializing.
- Cries if play is disrupted.
- Becomes easily excited or upset.

Five months

- Imitates facial expressions.
- Distinguishes strangers from family members.
- Recognizes voices of family members.
- Responds to his or her name.

Six months

- Turns when name is said.
- Becomes disturbed by the presence of strangers.
- Reacts to differences in tones of voices.
- Vocalizes pleasure and displeasure.
- Protests if toys are taken.

Seven months

- Pats mirror image.
- Wants to be included in group.
- Understands *no* by tone of adult voice.
- Shows humor.

Eight months

- Pats, smiles, and kisses mirror image.
- Shouts for attention.
- Pushes away unwanted objects.
- Becomes "angry" during confinement.
- Shows some separation anxiety.

Nine months

- Performs for others.
- Shows "focused attachment" to parents.
- Initiates play.
- Shows intense stranger anxiety.

Ten months

- Seeks social approval.
- Enjoys games, such as peekaboo.
- Displays affection and anger.

Eleven months

- Shows or offers toys to others.
- Is sometimes uncooperative during daily routines.
- Becomes angry when enjoyable play is stopped.
- Shows intense separation anxiety.

Lesson 10.2 Meeting Social-Emotional Needs in the First Year

Key Terms

co-regulation
self-awareness
trust versus mistrust
unconditional love

Academic Terms

inadvertently
overtures
predictor
proximity
psychosocial

Objectives

After studying this lesson, you will be able to

- describe the conflict infants must resolve in the first stage of Erikson's psychosocial theory.
- explain and give an example of how parents can respect an infant's temperament.
- explain newborn's social-emotional needs for interacting with caring parents and co-regulating their crying.
- identify ways a caregiver might soothe a baby.
- describe how parents can aid infant-adult interactions through "serving and responding."
- list the requirements for infant attachment and explain the importance of attachment.
- give examples of ways infants develop self-awareness.
- identify helpful tips for reducing a baby's stress.

Reading and Writing Activity

Write the objectives for this lesson on a piece of paper and then, beneath each objective, rewrite it as a question. While reading this lesson, take notes about information relating to these objectives. After reading, refer to your notes and write two to three sentences answering each objective's question.

Graphic Organizer

In a chart like the one shown, write the main headings of this lesson. As you read, take notes and organize them by heading. Draw a star beside any words or concepts you do not yet understand.

Erikson's Psychosocial Theory	Helping Infants Develop Self-Awareness
Aiding Baby-Adult Interactions	**Handling Stress and Special Problems in Infancy**

Babies have needs that must be met for healthy social-emotional development. Each baby is an individual. Some babies are more active, some like to be cuddled, some cry a lot, and others seem happy. This individuality influences the parents' responses to the baby, just like a person's personality affects the way others respond to him or her.

During the first year, social-emotional development seems to center on baby-adult interactions, the baby's developing self-awareness, and adults' ways of handling special problems. Social-emotional development affects the baby's mental health both now and in the future.

Erikson's Psychosocial Theory

Psychologist Erik Erikson was concerned about conflicts that occur between a child's needs and social demands. He theorized that people go through eight stages of personality development in their lifespan. His theory is known as *psychosocial theory*. Each stage of Erikson's **psychosocial** (relating to psychological and social aspects) theory of development presents a specific developmental task for each age group (**Figure 10.10**).

Erikson believed that each task can have either a positive or negative outcome. Depending on the outcome of each stage, a person's personality could develop in healthy or unhealthy ways. If the person successfully resolves the conflict, he or she will feel a sense of achievement, resulting in healthy personality development. If the person is unsuccessful in resolving the conflict, he or she is more likely to feel inadequate, causing his or her personality to be more vulnerable during other stages. Erikson believed a person can overcome failures in resolving past conflicts, but positive changes later in life are more difficult. He saw the family and other factors as major influences on personality.

Infants are in the first stage of Erikson's psychosocial theory, called **trust versus mistrust**. In this stage, infants are tasked with learning whether to trust or mistrust others. Trust is a key part of social development. How much a person trusts or does not trust other people affects how he or she interacts with them.

Erikson stated that two key factors are essential in whether infants learn to trust. First, infants need a consistent environment, which includes sameness in routines, caregivers, and surroundings. Second, infants learn to trust by having their basic needs met promptly each time. According to Erikson, if a baby's basic needs are consistently met, then babies feel the world is a good and happy place. This helps them learn to trust others and adapt to their world. If basic needs go unmet or partly met and the surroundings are unstable, then babies feel helpless and confused and develop mistrust.

Aiding Baby-Adult Interactions

Interacting with the baby is the baby's means to social contact. In an earlier chapter, you read about a baby's learning agenda. Part of a baby's agenda is seeking significant relationships and learning to interact with people. Just as parents aid their baby's motor, sensory, concept, and language development, they must also aid social-emotional development through interactions with their baby. Parents can develop positive interactions with their baby by respecting the baby's temperament, interacting with newborns when alert, soothing infants when discomforted, serving and responding, and encouraging attachment.

Respecting the Baby's Temperament

One of the most important aspects of baby-adult interaction involves respecting the baby's temperament. Each baby comes into the world with a unique temperament. Adults respond positively or negatively toward the newborn's temperament and convey their feelings mainly through the way they hold, touch, and look at the baby. The newborn reacts to adults' feelings and actions (**Figure 10.11**). For example, if adults are tense or the newborn's needs are unmet, then he or she

Figure 10.10 Erikson's Psychosocial Theory

Approximate Age	Stage
Infancy (Birth to 1 year)	***Trust versus mistrust.*** Newborns and infants need consistency in having their needs met and sameness in environment to develop a feeling the world is reliable—a sense of basic trust. If the world is not seen as a reliable place, the baby develops a sense of basic mistrust.
Toddler years (1 to 3 years)	***Autonomy versus shame and doubt.*** Toddlers seek some autonomy so they can use their new skills and knowledge. They seek control over whether to rely on others as they see fit. Autonomy learned in this stage leads to pride. Failure to achieve autonomy leads to feelings of shame in front of others and self-doubt.
Preschool years (3 through 5 years)	***Initiative versus guilt.*** Preschool children have growing abilities, much energy, and desire to engage in activities. They begin trying things on their own initiative. The sense of initiative learned at this stage leads to ambition and purpose. Too many failures and too many negative responses from adults lead to guilt and fear of trying new activities.
School-age years (6 through 12 years)	***Industry versus inferiority.*** Middle childhood is the time for developing the tools of society in preparation for adult work. If children are encouraged to use these tools, they develop a sense of industry. If too little is expected or if children are criticized for their efforts, a sense of inferiority develops. Inferiority results in poor work habits, avoidance of competition, and the inability to cope with later tasks.
Adolescence (13 through 18 years or older)	***Identity versus role confusion.*** Teens confront the question, "Who am I?" Role identity occurs when teens become certain about who they are in terms of career focus, important attitudes, and values. Role confusion results when others cannot confirm that teens are who they think they are and where they are headed.
Young adulthood (19 through 39 years)	***Intimacy versus isolation.*** Intimacy results when a young adult can "lose and find him- or herself in another." Intimacy occurs when the young adult trusts he or she can surrender self (identity) to another person or relationship. Isolation occurs if the adult feels others cannot be trusted in an intimate way.
Middle adulthood (40 through 65 years)	***Generativity versus stagnation.*** Generativity or productivity may be in the forming of a family, in achieving in one's career, and/or in providing significant services to others. This is the adult's way(s) of contributing to the next generation. Stagnation or self-absorption occurs when a person becomes concerned only with self.
Older adulthood (66 years and older)	***Integrity versus despair.*** If older adults see their lives as unique and meaningful, they see a picture of a life well-spent. In this way integrity or the state of feeling complete has been achieved. Despair comes with feelings of regret about the way one's life was lived and causes anxiety about the end of life.

becomes fussy and difficult. On the other hand, when adults are relaxed and the newborn's needs are promptly met, he or she is more often quiet and cooperative.

Sometimes there is a *goodness of fit* between a parent's personality and a child's temperament. This means that the child's temperament matches the parent's ideal. Sometimes the fit is not so good. Adults who have good relationships with babies seem to respect their temperaments regardless of fit.

Two nationally-known infant educators, Alice Sterling Honig and Magda Gerber, have taught the need to respect each baby's individual temperament and interests. For example, active babies often get into places they do not belong. They require more watching than less active children. These parents need to adjust their own behaviors to provide this extra level of care.

Figure 10.11 Newborns are attuned to their caregivers' feelings and behaviors and may react to expressions of love and expressions of frustration or stress. *How can a caregiver avoid upsetting his or her baby when frustrated?*

Focus on

Health

Optimal Infant Care Practices

Knowledge of optimal infant care practices has grown out of attachment studies. Two major researchers and teachers of infant care practices were Magda Gerber and Alice S. Honig.

Gerber advised parents to slow down, avoid exhaustion, and get to know the baby. She encouraged parents to provide a safe, challenging, and nurturing environment. Within this environment babies become independent by being active participants in routine care, exploring their environments, and having time to play alone. Gerber believed parents should give babies their full attention part of the time rather than half-attention all of the time. Her major point was for parents to live with babies in the moment—"to try less and enjoy it more."

Honig called for close observation of infants in order to provide needed nurturing. Her ideas included

- sending emotional signals (admiring eyes, crooning baby's name, loving tone of voice) so babies know they are cherished
- watching for signs of stress and providing nurturance through holding, staying nearby, and talking quietly
- creating loving, leisurely rituals for care
- knowing milestones and windows of opportunity and then "dancing up and down the developmental ladder" to provide the ability-activity match for babies
- helping babies rejoice in their mastery of skills

Honig emphasized these loving actions would become part of "body-memory" and nurture a baby's life journey toward positive relationships. Based on these guidelines, how do you think parents and caregivers can balance maintaining their own health with optimizing the health of their infant? What strategies would you suggest to a parent who is struggling with his or her health and is thus unable to promote an infant's health?

Interacting with Newborns

Newborns need social interaction for development, too. Not only do babies seem to learn best when they are alert and inactive (not fussy), they also develop warm relationships with others in this state. Newborns differ in alertness because of their individuality. For example, premature babies are often not as alert as full-term babies. Also, babies differ in the length of time they are alert. There seems to be a general pattern in the development of alertness.

Unless affected by drugs used in delivery, newborns are usually alert for a while after birth. Then, newborns tend to sleep a lot during the next few days. With each passing week, newborns spend more time in the alert-inactive stage. They total about 11 hours alert in the first week and 22 hours alert in the fourth week.

Parents work to establish a good relationship early in the newborn's life, even if the baby is sleepy or fussy most of the time. Parents communicate their feelings through facial expressions and vocalizations when engaging babies. Emotional wiring begins in newborns and young infants during times of parent-child interactions (feeding, other physical care tasks, comforting, and holding). Babies learn through the filter of feelings. If parents are harsh or nonresponsive because they are depressed, babies are likely to develop learning delays and social-emotional issues.

Parents need to cuddle and play with their babies in the alert state. They can try to soothe fussy newborns and enjoy them during their alert times. If parents are experiencing depression or having other issues, they should seek treatment and support.

Mental Health Advisory

Emotional wiring is based on early parent-child relationships. Parents who are depressed and harsh or nonresponsive to their babies run a major risk of damaging the mental health of their babies. Treatment and support for depressed parents are needed for the sake of the entire family.

Soothing a Fussy Newborn

All newborns cry, and some babies cry up to ¼ of each day, even when nothing is wrong. Parents who meet their newborns' needs should understand this crying is not related to their parenting abilities. Some babies just cry more and are harder to soothe than others.

Newborns cry for almost any reason because crying is the way they "talk." They may cry because they are tired, hungry, lonely, or uncomfortable. Newborns also cry to relax from tension. *Colic* (a condition in which the baby has intense abdominal pain) is one major reason babies cry, especially during the first three months. There are many causes of colic, such as allergies, tension, swallowing air when sucking or crying, and hunger. Soothing a baby who has colic often works, but in severe cases of colic, a pediatrician may prescribe medication to treat the condition.

Parents will not spoil newborns by answering their cries and soothing them. Major stress relievers for newborns are hearing familiar voices talking quietly, breast-feeding, and regulating temperature through contact with the parent's warm body.

Adults can *self-regulate* (calm down without help), but because this is a learned skill, newborns need help through co-regulation. **Co-regulation** is soothing the baby to aid him or her to calm down. A caregiver who soothes the newborn is called a *co-regulator*. Newborns who do not receive help in calming down feel vulnerable and often have difficulties with self-regulation later in life. Soothing not only helps babies feel less alone in a big world, but also teaches self-regulation. Newborns may show the beginnings of self-regulation. For example, when startled or overstimulated, they may turn their heads, close their eyes, or suck their hands or fingers.

To soothe a newborn, a caregiver tries to interpret the baby's cry and then responds. **Figure 10.12** describes three distinct cries and how a person might respond to them. Following are some ways a caregiver might soothe a baby:

- Rock the baby in a vertical (over the shoulder) position. Place one hand behind the baby's head and rock quickly.
- Carry the baby around the house or yard.

Figure 10.12 The Meanings of Cries

Cause	Sounds of Cry	Ways to Respond
Pain	Cycle begins with shrill scream, followed by silence, and ends with short gasps. Cycle is repeated.	Respond immediately. Ease pain if possible. Cuddle baby to calm.
Hunger or boredom	Slow cries that become louder and rhythmic.	Feed if near feeding time. OR Entertain by giving baby a tour of the house or yard.
Upset	Fussy, rather quiet cry. Cry sounds a bit forced.	Cuddle or entertain.

- Sing and play music. Babies like the quiet tones of lullabies or even a steady tone, such as the hum of a ceiling fan or the bubbling sound from an aquarium.
- Take the baby for a car ride or a ride in a stroller.
- Stroke the baby to relieve tension.

A newborn's constant cries cause tension in parents. Relief from tension is good for family relationships. Using a babysitter for an hour or even an entire afternoon may help parents reduce their tension.

Serving and Responding

Babies need parents who serve and respond. Physical and vocal signals and responses shape the feelings between parents and their newborns. Babies feel love through physical contact with the adult. The quality of the relationship is influenced less by the total number of messages than by the quality of these messages. Even the most loving parents may miss a few opportunities to serve or respond because they are hurried or tense. In a healthy relationship, the balance must be on the positive side.

Child-adult relationships are mostly one-sided for many years. Infants may give some smiles and hugs, but adults do most of the giving. This giving is important, because the feelings adults show for babies help to shape the picture children form of themselves. Fostering good feelings in babies seems to increase the joy and love between children and their caregivers.

Encouraging Attachment

The most important asset a child can have is the knowledge that someone has **unconditional love** (deep affection without limitations) for him or her and will always be supportive. A child becomes attached to this person. The quality of this attachment is a powerful **predictor** (something that is useful in making a prediction) of social-emotional outcome (**Figure 10.13**).

Many years will pass before children can verbally identify those who unconditionally love and support them. How do infants sense this love and support and develop attachments? Babies have needs and can signal these needs. Infants attach to caregivers who bring warmth, care, and security and make them feel loved, worthy of care, and safe. Through the nurturing relationship, positive connections are made in the brain. Depriving a child of the nurturing relationship leads to negative brain effects.

To encourage attachment, parents and other caregivers need to understand and practice the following:

- Realize the most important adult behavior in forming attachment is correctly, consistently, and promptly responding to the baby's signals of needs in a loving way.

Figure 10.13 A baby's attachment is a powerful influence on his or her social-emotional development. Without strong, positive attachment, babies may experience social-emotional developmental delays. *If a caregiver is worried that his or her baby is not forming attachment, what should he or she do?*

- Observe and learn to read the baby's signals and consider his or her preferences for meeting needs. Babies prefer to be soothed in different ways.
- Allow the mobile infant to seek **proximity** (nearness) and maintain contact. For example, most infants prefer to play within a few feet of their parents—not in a far-off playroom or nursery. Ignoring or rejecting an infant's **overtures** (cues for positive relationship building) leads to insecurity for the infant.
- Minimize separation anxiety by leaving the infant for a short period of time, if possible, and with a familiar caregiver who will soothe him or her once the parent leaves. Infants can develop multiple attachments, which also depend on how other caregivers respond to the infant's needs.
- Realize attachment develops over time. No parent can be 100 percent correct and responsive in meeting each and every need of a baby. Because babies develop so rapidly, even the best adult observers can miss a cue. Like all other interactions, the balance of correct readings and consistent responses needs to be on the positive side.

Helping Infants Develop Self-Awareness

Through infant-adult interactions, parents and caregivers can help infants learn more about themselves. In the first year, an infant begins to develop **self-awareness** or an understanding of him- or herself as a unique person. As infants develop self-awareness, they form a mental picture of themselves and an idea of who they are and what they can do. Infants develop self-awareness in the following ways:

- ***Hand regard.*** Infants gaze at their hands for hours, making slight movements (called *hand regard*). As their brains process the sight and sensation of the moving hands, infants learn their hands are a part of their bodies.
- ***Cause and effect.*** Infants learn how their movements can affect other objects (**Figure 10.14**). For example, an infant might move a hand, bat a toy on an activity gym, and make the toy turn. This discovery teaches the infant which objects are part of him- or herself (the hand) and which are not (the toy and the activity gym). When an infant crawls to get a toy, the infant learns his or her actions can make things happen.

Figure 10.14 Infants develop self-awareness by learning cause and effect and by witnessing how their movement and actions affect the environment around them. *How can parents encourage their babies to learn about cause and effect?*

- ***Name recognition.*** By four months of age, infants recognize their names if used often. Calling the infant by name during happy times gives the infant positive feelings about his or her name. Happy times include reunions between the adult and infant, such as after a nap or when the adult returns from work. Parents can also call the infant by name when talking to him or her during child care tasks or games.
- ***Recognition of body parts.*** During the second half of the first year, infants can learn to touch body parts (nose, ears, mouth, and hair) upon request and find these same body parts in other people and stuffed animals.
- ***Mirror play.*** Looking in mirrors also increases self-awareness. Infants enjoy seeing themselves in mirrors even before they know the images they see are their own. Calling the infant's image by name is helpful. Infants like trying to identify body parts in their mirror image. Adults may place infants in front of mirrors so they can watch themselves eat, dress, and move. Infants also enjoy having nonbreakable play mirrors as toys.
- ***Object possession.*** Toward the end of the first year, infants become possessive about some objects. This should be encouraged, because infants' understanding that some objects belong to them is part of self-awareness. Also, infants must possess things before they can learn to share in a few years. Adults can help teach possession by making statements or asking questions, such as "Here's Adora's dress," or "Where are Will's blocks?"

Handling Stress and Special Problems in Infancy

When parents and other caregivers meet babies' needs, babies have surges of positive hormones. These babies signal, play, learn, and show affection. All babies, however, have some problems or causes of stress. These may include feeding and sleeping problems, fear of strangers, or excessive crying.

Sometimes, parents and caregivers may **inadvertently** (unintentionally) cause stress in a baby's environment. Main stressors include not meeting a baby's physical needs, limiting a baby's body contact with a parent, and not being a co-regulator when the baby is stressed. Not providing the baby with "serve and return" signals or providing harsh signals can also cause stress for the infant.

When the baby's environment is neglectful or chaotic, the baby has to adapt either by showing little response to the environment or by over-responding (being hypersensitive) to it. In both cases, these babies have surges of negative hormones, especially *cortisol*. Chronic elevation of cortisol increases blood pressure, pulse, and blood sugar level and interrupts digestive and *excretory* (kidney and bowel) functions. It also destroys brain cells, weakens attachment to parents, and is related to later depression.

Infants need constant emotional support. Parents and other caregivers can provide this support by responding to the baby's needs, holding the baby to a parent's body, talking in a soothing voice, and being a co-regulator when the baby is distressed. Parents may also breast-feed to soothe the baby. (Compared with formula-feeding, breast-feeding reduces stress hormones.) Monitoring the baby's environment, such as keeping noise levels down, can also be helpful for reducing stress.

When problems arise, the following additional tips may help:

- ***Decide if the problem is temporary.*** If the baby seems ill, seek prompt medical attention. If the baby does not seem ill, wait a few days. Babies do have mood

Mental Health Advisory

The lack of correct and prompt care, consistency in the baby's environment, and/or quality social interactions between a baby and his or her caregiver(s) are often the roots of many mental health problems.

changes. Also, the problem may be because of a hurried or tense caregiver. In these cases, the problem will likely end as soon as the adult slows down or relaxes.

- *Get help when needed.* For example, parents who have a fussy baby may need to ask loving babysitters to give them time to rest or leave home for a few hours. Parents who need help coping with stressful situations may seek treatment from a mental health counselor.
- *Give in to an infant's demands sometimes, if the results are not serious.* Even infants have wills of their own, and letting them have their way sometimes is not going to spoil or harm them. For example, if an infant refuses to eat peas, try other vegetables with similar nutrients.
- *If the problem continues, talk to an expert.* A pediatrician or family doctor can determine if there are any underlying health issues.
- *Remain calm.* This helps the baby and the adult.

Experienced caregivers tend to almost ignore many common, not-too-serious problems. Experience teaches that all babies are different and many minor problems solve themselves in time.

Lesson 10.2 Review and Assessment

1. What conflict must infants resolve in the first stage of Erikson's psychosocial theory?
2. How can parents show respect for their baby's temperament?
3. Explain the importance of co-regulating crying in infant-adult relationships.
4. Why is it important to soothe a fussy or crying newborn?
5. The quality of an infant-adult relationship is influenced by the _____ of messages and by the _____ of the messages.
6. What can adults do to encourage infant attachment?
7. Name three ways infants develop self-awareness.
8. **Critical thinking.** How do each of the tips for reducing a baby's stress align with the guidelines for infant attachment and respecting temperament earlier in this lesson?

Focus on Careers

Mental Health Counselor

Mental health counselors encourage clients to discuss their social-emotional problems. They work with their clients to develop skills that will help them cope with difficult situations. Mental health counselors help people understand and deal with their feelings. They also diagnose and treat mental health disorders, such as depression.

Career cluster: Human services.

Education: Educational requirements include a master's degree in a mental health field, such as social work, psychology, or counseling. Licensure is also required.

Job outlook: Future employment opportunities for mental health counselors are expected to grow much faster than the average for all occupations.

To learn more about a career as a mental health counselor, visit the United States Department of Labor's *Occupational Outlook Handbook* website. You will also be able to compare the job responsibilities, educational requirements, job outlook, and average pay of mental health counselors with similar occupations.

Chapter 10 Review and Assessment

Summary

Social-emotional development involves a person's basic disposition, social relations, and emotions. Babies vary in their temperaments. High-reactive infants are the most vulnerable to stress and its effects, especially when parenting expectations are unrealistic.

An infant's social development is affected by interacting with others and showing attachment. Babies interact with others through a "serve and return" relationship. Without positive serve and return, social connections in the baby's brain do not form correctly. In the first year, babies begin to develop attachment for their parents and others who are close to them (called *focused attachment*). The results of poor attachments are similar to the results of negative interactions with adults.

Emotional wiring of the brain begins at birth and is completed in the preschool years. Emotions of love, fear, anxiety, and anger arise in all children. These emotions consist of thoughts that lead to feelings and, in turn, cause changes in the body. It is healthy for babies to express a wide range of emotions.

According to Erikson's psychosocial theory, babies must resolve the conflict of *trust versus mistrust*. Babies learn trust by having their basic needs met. Positive baby-adult interactions must be encouraged for healthy development. Interactions should focus on respecting the baby's temperament and on correctly, consistently, and promptly responding to baby's signals of needs in a loving way. The beginnings of self-awareness become obvious during the first year and should be encouraged.

College and Career Portfolio

Portfolio Standardized Test Scores

For college portfolios and for some career portfolios, you may be asked to provide your standardized test scores. *Standardized tests* are national tests that assess your education level in general subjects, such as math, science, reading, and writing. Standardized tests vary by state and region, but include the ACT, PSAT, and SAT. To obtain your test scores, complete the following activities.

- Determine which, if any, standardized test scores you need to include in your portfolio. If you are unsure, ask your teacher or a guidance counselor.
- Research the steps for requesting your standardized test scores and submit the request or set a date to submit it based on the deadline for your portfolio. Request your scores well in advance of when they are needed.

Chapter 10 Review and Assessment

Vocabulary Activities 

1. In teams, play *picture charades* to identify each of the following terms. Write the terms on separate slips of paper and put the slips into a basket. Choose a team member to be the *sketcher*. The sketcher pulls a term from the basket and creates quick drawings or graphics to represent the term until the team guesses the term. Rotate turns as sketcher until the team identifies all terms.

Key Terms

age-appropriate behaviors (10.1)
anxiety (10.1)
attachment (10.1)
attachment behaviors (10.1)
co-regulation (10.2)
disposition (10.1)
emotions (10.1)
high-reactive infants (10.1)
low-reactive infants (10.1)
self-awareness (10.2)
separation anxiety (10.1)
temperament (10.1)
trust versus mistrust (10.2)
unconditional love (10.2)

2. Work with a partner to write the definitions of the following terms based on your current understanding before reading the chapter. Then pair up with another team to discuss your definitions and any discrepancies. Finally, discuss the definitions with the class and ask your instructor for necessary correction or clarification.

Academic Terms

inadvertently (10.2)
intrusive (10.1)
overtures (10.2)
precedes (10.1)
predictor (10.2)
proximity (10.2)
psychosocial (10.2)
siblings (10.1)

Critical Thinking

3. **Compare and contrast.** Review the three aspects of social-emotional development described in this text. Then, working with a partner, compare and contrast these three aspects. How are they alike? How are they different? Give concrete examples of each aspect.
4. **Evaluate.** Babies' temperaments often shape their personalities. How would you describe your temperament? Have you had these characteristics for a long time? Do others in your family have the same temperament?
5. **Draw conclusions.** Write four infant-adult scenarios that illustrate each of the four emotions infants develop in the first year. Then, trade papers with a partner. Draw conclusions about what emotions are being depicted in your partner's scenarios. After you have finished, discuss your answers.
6. **Cause and effect.** Feelings of mistrust and vulnerability in infancy can affect a child over the course of his or her life. How do you think feelings of mistrust surface in adults?
7. **Analyze.** Working with a partner, take turns explaining why interactions with caregivers are so important for infants' social-emotional development. Cite evidence from your textbook and create a compelling argument.
8. **Determine.** Some parents believe babies can be spoiled if people hold or soothe them when they do not have physical needs. Based on what you have read in this chapter, do you agree with this assessment? Explain why or why not.
9. **Make inferences.** Why do you think infant-adult interactions are described in terms of "serving and responding"? If you were to create your own catchphrase to describe the dynamic of positive infant-adult relationships, what would it be?
10. **Compare and contrast.** Create a list of ten parental behaviors that inhibit attachment and ten parental behaviors that encourage attachment. Then, compare and contrast these behaviors. Write a short essay explaining what makes these parental behaviors positive or negative.
11. **Identify.** List ten attachment behaviors, both positive and negative. Then, trade papers with a partner and identify the behaviors your partner listed as indicative of weak or strong attachment.

Core Skills

12. **Technology.** In small groups, create a video tutorial on handling and interacting with high-reactive babies. Write a three-minute screenplay about two new parents caring for a high-reactive baby. In your video tutorial, demonstrate proper techniques for holding infants and for soothing fussy or crying infants. Also, include a section about what parents should *not* do, and demonstrate those behaviors. After you have composed your screenplay, practice and then film your video tutorial. Present your tutorial to the class.

13. **Technology and science.** Use Internet sources to search for information about how brain development affects social-emotional development in the first year. Create an electronic presentation of your findings to share with the class. Adhere to all copyright laws and cite any sources you may use for the presentation.
14. **Research and writing.** Using reliable online or print resources, research how social-emotional development during infancy affects a person as a child, as an adolescent, and as an adult. As you conduct your research, assess the reliability of your sources, and compile a bibliography with citations in APA style. Take notes about facts or concepts that interest you and then compare notes with a partner. After discussing your findings, write a collaborative four- to five-page essay detailing your findings and comparing them to the information in your textbook. Include a cumulative bibliography with your essay.
15. **Art and speaking.** In small groups, review the social-emotional milestones children achieve within the first year of life. Then, using art supplies or electronic resources, collaborate to create an easy-to-follow visual representation of the milestones a baby achieves during each month in infancy. Your illustration should include drawings or pictures of children achieving milestones during each month, and should be an effective study tool and synthesis of the information you learned in this chapter. After completing your illustration, present it to the class and make it available for other students to reference while studying.
16. **Writing.** Write a one- or two-page brochure about the importance of trust in the infant's life. Incorporate Erikson's psychosocial theory and explain how adults can promote trust in the infant. Check your brochure for correct spelling, grammar, and punctuation.
17. **Reading and writing.** Using online or print resources, find personal accounts of new parents caring for an infant who is twelve months old or younger. Read three of these accounts and take notes about the infants' social-emotional development and the interactions between the caregivers and infants described. Then, using what you have learned in this chapter, write a short essay relating these stories to infants' social-emotional development and evaluating whether the infant-adult interactions are positive or negative.
18. **Listening and speaking.** Interview two parents about the expanding social worlds of their babies. Prepare your list of interview questions in advance. Some questions might include: Besides parents, who are other important people in your baby's life? How did your baby react to siblings and other children? Did your baby become attached to an object? After the interview, consider what the parents' responses tell you about the differences in the social-emotional development of their babies. Report your findings to the class in an oral report.
19. **CTE Career Readiness Practice.** Suppose you work in an infant day care center where ensuring the health and safety of the children in your charge is of utmost importance. One day, you notice one of your coworkers becoming frustrated with a fussy infant and responding harshly to the infant's crying. In response, the infant cries more loudly, and, fearing that your coworker may shake the infant, you offer to hold the infant for a while. You finish the day without saying anything about the incident to anyone, but that night, you start to wonder if you should mention the incident to your supervisor. You begin to ask yourself, "Did I act responsibly by not talking to my boss about my coworker's behavior? Could I be legally liable, if abuse occurred, and I didn't report it?" In small groups, discuss this scenario. What is the responsible thing to do in this situation? Role-play a conversation in which you respond to the dilemma in an appropriate way.

Observations

20. In small groups, listen to recordings or videos of infants crying. If possible, listen to videos where caregivers respond to infants' cries. Then, individually, try to determine what each infant cry is communicating. Is the infant crying angrily? Is the infant afraid? Observe how the caregiver responds to the cry and assess how accurate your interpretations were. Afterward, reflect as a group on how caregivers learn to understand and respond to infants' cries.
21. Observe an infant with a parent or regular caregiver. How does the baby demonstrate attachment? How does the adult encourage attachment? Write a short report answering these questions, and then present your report to the class.

Unit 4 The Toddler Years

Chapter 11	Physical Development of Toddlers
Chapter 12	Intellectual Development of Toddlers
Chapter 13	Social-Emotional Development of Toddlers

Teamwork

Some CTSO competitive events have a performance section of the event. For a team event, the team making the presentation needs to prepare together to operate as a cohesive unit.

To prepare for team events, complete the following activities:

1. Read and follow the guidelines and regulations for team performances your organization provides.
2. Practice performing as a team by completing the team activities throughout this text.
3. Locate the rubric or scoring sheet for the event on your organization's website. Analyzing the scoring process offers insight into the criteria that judges use to assess your team.
4. Review the rules and regulations to confirm whether the judges will ask questions of the team or whether the team will need to defend a case or situation.
5. Make notes about important points and have team members evaluate one another's notes. You may also be able to use these notes during the event.
6. Assign each team member a role for the presentation and practice performing as a team. Have each team member introduce him- or herself, review the case or point of the presentation, make suggestions, and conclude with a summary.
7. Ask your instructor to serve in the role of competition judge as your team practices its presentation. When your team finishes the presentation, ask your instructor for feedback on the performance. In addition, you may also consider having a student audience listen and give feedback.
8. Keep practicing. Use the feedback and evaluation requirements as a guide to polishing the presentation.

Chapter 11 Physical Development of Toddlers

Essential Question

How do toddlers physically grow and develop, and how can parents meet their toddler's physical needs while coping with the toddler's indomitable will?

Lesson 11.1	**Growth and Development of Toddlers**
Lesson 11.2	**Meeting Nutritional Needs of Toddlers**
Lesson 11.3	**Meeting Other Physical Needs of Toddlers**

Case Study: Should Parents Push Motor Skills?

As a class, read the case study and discuss the questions that follow. After you finish studying the chapter, discuss this case study again. Have your opinions changed based on what you learned?

Jeff is a sweet and playful 30-month-old toddler. He didn't walk until 17 months of age and is still behind in his motor skills. In fact, he seems to have little interest in most gross-motor activities. Jeff's parents are concerned, especially because they are both athletic and sports are an important value to them. Jeff's parents have even been planning to enroll Jeff in a T-ball program that Jeff's dad has coached for several years.

Six months before the time to enroll Jeff in T-ball, Jeff is still awkward in his movements. Jeff's parents want to enroll Jeff in a gymnastics program to help develop his gross-motor skills. They also want Jeff to practice throwing and catching balls. Before enrolling Jeff in the gymnastics program, they took him to a well-known doctor who treats children who have muscular-skeletal conditions. The doctor could not find anything wrong with Jeff. After Jeff's parents explain their plans to the doctor, he says, "I don't think it's best to overdo it."

Give It Some Thought

1. Do you think having athletic parents gives Jeff a better chance of being athletic compared with other children whose parents do not have these abilities? Why or why not?
2. Do you think the parents' plan will be helpful for Jeff? Why or why not? Explain your answer.
3. According to Galinsky, all parents go through an imaging stage of parenting. How long should parents pursue their dreams for their children? Should parents encourage a child to follow parental interests or should parents follow the child's lead? Explain your answer.
4. What did the doctor mean by not "overdoing it"? What do you think are the doctor's concerns? Do you think Jeff's parents are apt to "overdo it"? Explain your answers.

While studying this chapter, look for the online resources icon  to:

- **Practice** terms with e-flash cards and interactive games
- **Assess** what you learn by completing self-assessment quizzes
- **Expand** knowledge with interactive activities and graphic organizers

Companion G-W Learning

www.g-wlearning.com/childdevelopment

Study on the go

Use a mobile device to practice terms and review with self-assessment quizzes.

www.m.g-wlearning.com/0384

Lesson 11.1 Growth and Development of Toddlers

Key Terms

dexterity
eye-hand coordination
large-muscle development
muscle development
small-muscle development

Academic Terms

constrict
deformation
dilate
rigid
stature
timid

Objectives

After studying this lesson, you will be able to

- describe a child's organ maturation in the toddler years, specifically focusing on changes in the brain.
- explain body growth and development in the toddler years in terms of changes in height and weight, body proportions, bones and teeth, and fat and muscles.
- distinguish between *large-muscle development* and *small-muscle development* and give examples of major gross- and fine-motor skills children develop during the toddler years.
- give examples of physical developmental milestones children might achieve in the toddler years.

Reading and Writing Activity

Before reading, skim this lesson and write the caption questions on a separate piece of paper. Then, answer these questions based on what you already know and what experiences you have already had. After reading, revisit the caption questions. Would you change any of your answers after what you have learned? For each of your answers, write a sentence explaining why your answer is still correct or a sentence explaining how you would correct your answer.

Graphic Organizer

Draw four columns and label each column with one of the lesson objectives. Then, as you are reading, write what you learn about each topic in the appropriate column.

After studying this lesson, you will be able to			
describe a child's organ maturation in the toddler years, specifically focusing on changes in the brain.	explain body growth and development in the toddler years in terms of changes in height and weight, body proportions, bones and teeth, and fat and muscles.	distinguish between *large-muscle* and *small-muscle development* and give examples of major gross- and fine-motor skills children develop during the toddler years.	give examples of physical developmental milestones children might achieve in the toddler years.

Children between one and three years of age are called *toddlers*. This name fits them because toddlers toddle during almost all their waking minutes as they explore the world around them. As toddlers develop physically, their bodies mature, which helps them handle more complex tasks. Although toddlers do not grow as quickly as infants, they go through many important physical changes.

Toddlers' organs are maturing. By the end of the second year, the brain is four-fifths of its adult weight and closer to maturity than any other organ. The other body organs continue to mature, but they do so at a slower rate than the brain. (This is an example of the *head-to-foot* or *cephalocaudal principle*—developmental sequence from the brain down the spine.)

Newborns do not have much control over their muscles when they are born. By the end of their first year, infants are just learning to control voluntary muscle movements. These movements continue to improve during toddlerhood. In fact, both the gross- and fine-motor skills of toddlers improve so much that, by the end of their second year, toddlers can run, jump, throw, and feed themselves (**Figure 11.1**).

Maturation of Organs

From birth to one year of age, a child's brain doubles in size. Brain growth is particularly rapid in the areas that allow for the development of vision and other sensory organs, motor skills, memory, perception, and the sounds of language.

The brain continues to mature in the toddler years. By three years of age, the brain reaches 80 percent of adult volume. Synaptic density also increases during toddlerhood. This means there are more dendrites, and they are closer together. Synaptic density permits additional connections and enables much faster learning. By two years of age, toddlers have as many synapses as the adult brain. By three years, the synapses are two times the density of the adult brain. These waves of brain growth—branching dendrites and connections—will not occur again at this rate until the teen years. The density in the toddler's brain aids coordination of sight with body movement, memory, comprehension, cognitive flexibility, the explosion of language, and self-awareness.

Myelination, the process by which myelin wraps around longer axons and cushions the cell bodies of neurons, aids the speed of neuron transmissions. Now toddlers can perform complex tasks and

Figure 11.1 By the end of the second year, toddlers are able to feed themselves. *How do you think a toddler's ability to self-feed impacts the toddler-caregiver relationship?*

store memories through language, which supports learning. Myelination also aids the toddler's ability to be more aware of him- or herself and his or her emotions.

Brain growth is directly impacted by genes and the environment. During the toddler years, environmental experiences significantly affect the brain. Although connections allow for firings, experiences determine actual firings. Once the toddler period ends, serious pruning of connections begins. As the connections are pruned, the windows of opportunity begin to close. Researchers also believe that brain development during the toddler years plays a major role in mental health.

In addition to brain maturation, toddlers' other organs are maturing, too. The heart and lungs become more efficient. Between 12 and 24 months of age, the digestive system improves making toddlers better able to digest fibrous foods. Between 18 and 24 months, toddlers can regulate their body temperature. Blood cells in the skin's surface **constrict** (become smaller; more closed) to conserve heat when the body is cold. These blood cells can also **dilate** (become larger; more open) to release heat when the body is hot. Toward the end of the toddler years, the *excretory system*, which is responsible for removing waste products from the body, matures enough for toilet learning to begin (**Figure 11.2**).

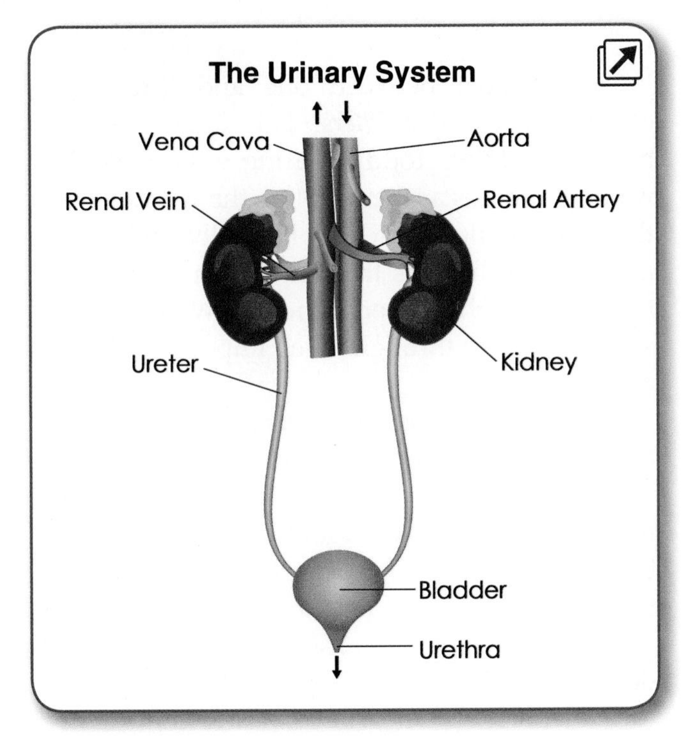

Figure 11.2 The excretory system organs include the urinary system, lungs, skin, large intestine (colon), and liver. *What are the primary organs that make up the urinary system?*

Skeletal Growth

Toddlers grow at different rates due to heredity and environment. Because of these factors, toddlers sometimes grow at different rates than norms predict for their ages. In this section, you will learn about changes that occur in the toddler's height and weight, body proportions, bones and teeth, and fat and muscle.

Height and Weight

Heredity affects a toddler's height and how fast the toddler grows in height. Because genes determine height, they also influence weight. (A person who is tall in **stature**—a person's height—usually weighs more than a person who is short in stature.) Other factors can also significantly affect his or her weight and even height, depending on nutrition. Some of the factors include a person's physical activity level, health, and even emotions. Because of heredity and other factors, the height and weight of toddlers can vary.

After a child's first birthday, body growth slows. For example, toddlers grow about half as much in height during the second year as compared with the first year. Children often triple their birthweight during the first year, then gain only one-fourth of that amount during the second year. Some toddlers grow a little faster than these norms in their second year. (They may be "catching up" to norms after a premature birth or first-year illness.) Girls often reach half their adult height by 20 months of age while boys achieve half their adult height by 27 months. Many factors can affect growth rates.

After 24 months of age, children grow at a slower, but steadier, rate. They tend to gain 2 to 3 inches and about 6 pounds per year throughout childhood. (This rate of growth continues until about 11 years for girls and 13 years for boys.) **Figure 11.3** shows the height and weight norms for children from 12 to 36 months of age.

Figure 11.3 Average Height and Weight from 12 to 36 Months

Age in Months	Height in Inches	Weight in Pounds
12	30	21
18	32	24.5
24	34	27
30	36	30
36	38	32

Body Proportions

The body proportions of a two-year-old are not the same as those of an adult. At 24 months of age, the toddler's head is a little more than one-fifth of his or her total height. An adult's head is one-eighth of his or her height. A 24-month-old toddler's chest and abdomen measurements are about the same circumference, but by 30 months, the chest is larger than the abdomen. As the child matures, the difference between chest and abdomen size becomes even greater. The child's body-build type becomes apparent during the toddler years, too.

Bones and Teeth

As toddlers grow, their bones continue to become harder, though the degree of ossification is not the same throughout the body. Due to the cartilage, the toddler's bones are more flexible and less likely to break than an adult's bones. The softer bones, however, are more prone to disease or **deformation** (abnormal or unusual formation). The toddlers' *fontanels* (gaps between the skull bones, also called *soft spots*) are closed or almost closed. The toddler's spine changes from the infants' C-shaped spine to the S-shaped spine of adults. The S-shape, called the *lumbar curve*, allows the posture to become straighter and more upright, making standing and walking easier.

Shortly after two years, a child has the full set of deciduous teeth, or *baby teeth*. (Refer to Figure 8.5 to review the emergence of deciduous teeth during infancy and toddlerhood.) The early care of teeth is critical for lifelong dental health. A pediatric dentist needs to regularly examine a toddler's teeth. Parents must follow the dentist's suggestions for dental hygiene.

Fat and Muscle

Fat deposits under the skin decrease rapidly between 9 and 30 months, and the chubby baby becomes a slender child. The "baby fat" that is noticeable during infancy is decreasing and muscle is increasing as children grow and develop. Children who are still chubby at the end of the toddler years might not be at a healthy weight, and parents may wish to consult with a pediatrician or registered dietitian.

Forming healthy habits during the toddler years, such as eating nutritious meals and snacks and getting plenty of physical activity, can help shape children's eating habits throughout life. Following a nutritious diet, being physically active, and getting adequate rest and sleep can also help build muscles. **Muscle development** (the lengthening and thickening of muscles) is slow during the toddler stage.

Motor Development

As children grow and develop, their motor skills also develop. Toddlers improve the motor skills they developed as infants, and they learn many new skills. As toddlers practice these new skills, motor development improves even more.

Large-Muscle Development

Large-muscle development refers to the development of the trunk and arm and leg muscles. Movements, such as walking, jumping, and running, mainly depend on the large muscles. (These movements are examples of *gross-motor skills*.) During the first year, babies may develop these muscles at least to the point of standing and walking with support. After one year, children master walking and begin learning other motor skills. Toddlers love to run, jump, and use other large muscles. When children this age are held in one place too long, they often begin squirming, as if to say, "I want down!"

Walking and Running

Children learn to walk at different ages. Typically, children begin to walk without support within two to three months before or after their first birthday. Some children may take even longer to make walking attempts. Children learn to walk in their own time and in their own way—each child is unique. As children try to take their first steps, they need warm adult support, a positive reaction to walking attempts, and a safe area.

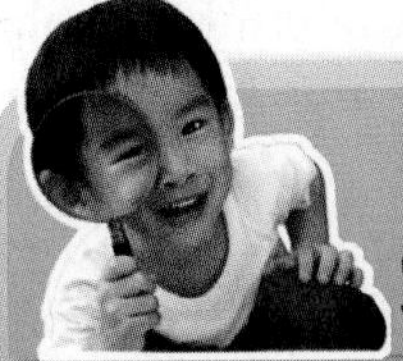

Investigate Special Topics: The Muscular System

Muscles are soft tissues, which have blood vessels, *tendons* (fibrous tissue attaching muscle to bone), and nerves. The cells of the muscles do not increase in number after the prenatal and very early postnatal period. Muscle growth is seen in the increase of diameter and length of muscle fiber, but not in new muscles. Muscles make up half a person's weight, which is three times the weight of bones. Muscles give the body shape, hold the skeleton together, and are responsible for both internal and external movement and strength.

Muscles can be classified into the following three groups:

- ***Visceral (also called smooth muscles).*** Seen only through a microscope, visceral muscles are in sheets or layers with one layer behind another. These muscles line the walls of blood vessels and most organs, such as the digestive tract, liver, kidneys, and uterus. Controlled in the unconscious part of the brain, they relax and contract allowing food to be digested, waste products to be excreted and retained, the baby to be pushed out at birth, and the eyes to focus.
- ***Myocardium (also called the cardiac muscle).*** This muscle allows the heart to contract and relax (beat), which moves the blood. The myocardium is a *striated muscle* (striped with light and dark muscle fibers as seen through a microscope). Like the visceral muscles, the myocardium is unconsciously stimulated by hormones and signals from the brain, making the heart a natural pacemaker.
- ***Striated muscles (also called skeletal muscles).*** About 700 skeletal muscles cover the entire skeleton of the body. These striated muscles are usually attached to two bones through tendons. Controlled consciously, one bone is pulled closer to another bone across a joint to another bone that remains stationary. This allows for movement. Skeletal muscles keep a person's body upright, allow for voluntary movements, control the tongue in eating and talking, permit facial movements, and give overall power and strength to the body. Most of these highly specialized muscles are named based on their location, size and direction, or function.

Throughout life, muscles need to grow in size, strengthen, and repair their microscopic cellular tears due to activity. Muscle growth, strength, and repair in children come from eating a variety of nutritious foods, doing lots of physical activities, and getting enough sleep. It does not come from eating a special diet and "working out."

Research Activity

In small groups, choose one muscle in the body—a muscle that you think is especially important. Use reliable online or print resources to research whether that muscle is *visceral* or *striated* as well as how the muscle achieves movement in the body. Give a short presentation about the muscle to your class.

Regardless of age, beginning walkers often share some common traits, which include the following:

- Feet are wide apart, giving children a wider base of support.
- Feet are turned outward and knees are slightly flexed.
- First steps often seem like staggers. Children may also step backward or to the side, take irregular steps, lurch forward, and weave.
- Tiptoe walking may be common because children have not learned to lower their heels. (By two years of age, tiptoe walking is a developmental lag.)
- Arms are often held up or out for balance and do not swing alternately with foot movement (**Figure 11.4**).
- Posture may be slightly tilted forward when walking because the spine is not fully developed. (The development of the lumbar curve enables children to walk more upright and steadily.)
- Falls are likely due to poor balance caused by body proportions, such as large head size. Also, beginning walkers rarely go around small obstacles on the floor, such as a toy or book. They simply walk over these objects, which increases their chances of falling. (Toddlers must watch their foot placement while walking until almost three years of age.)

As children's walking abilities improve, their walk may look more like a run, but it is not a run. In fact, toddlers take about 170 steps per minute and their stride is half the length of an adult's stride. Can you imagine doubling your steps, taking 170 steps per minute, and having someone hold onto your hand above your head? Yet, this is how many toddlers walk with adults.

True running (not just a hurried walk) often begins around two years of age. Two-year-olds are not skillful runners because their movements are still rather awkward. For example, toddlers tend to hold their arms up or out as they run and cannot start or stop quickly. With much practice, these skills improve.

Figure 11.4 When toddlers walk, they often hold their arms out for balance. *Are there situations in which adults hold their arms out for balance? Explain.*

Climbing and Jumping

Children may begin to climb as soon as they can crawl or creep. Between 15 and 18 months, toddlers will climb onto furniture. They will walk up and down stairs by holding onto the stair railing or balusters and the adult's hand. They may also turn to the side and hold the railing or balusters with both hands (**Figure 11.5**). For toddlers, going up stairs is easier than coming down stairs. Toddlers do not alternate feet while climbing until after their second birthday.

There is not a set time for when climbing begins. Climbing ability relates to the kinds of stairs and other objects near the toddler. Toddlers can more easily climb if stairs are enclosed and not too steep. Climbing also relates to courage. A courageous toddler is likely to try climbing sooner than a physically **timid** (shy) one.

Stepping off low objects at about 18 months is the way children learn to jump. Before two years of age, children may step off a low object and remain suspended in air for a brief moment. Around two years of age, children can jump off low objects

Figure 11.5 When toddlers walk up or down stairs, they often hold the railings or balusters with both hands. ***How does holding onto railings or balusters help stabilize toddlers as they learn to climb up and down stairs?***

with both feet. They move their arms backward, however, instead of helping the jump by swinging their arms forward.

Throwing and Catching

Around one year of age, children may begin throwing on purpose, usually from a sitting position, such as from the high chair (**Figure 11.6**). After toddlers feel secure standing or walking, they throw from standing positions. Children less than three years of age are not very skillful throwers. These children typically use a **rigid** (stiff; restricted) throw and do not shift their weight. In fact, when throwing with one hand, they often step with the same-side foot. They also cannot release the ball at the right time, which sends the ball in almost any direction.

Children first learn to "catch" by squatting and picking up an object. Around two years of age, children will bend at the waist to pick up the thrown object. Two- and three-year-olds may try to catch by standing in one position with arms extended and elbows stiff. For the child to catch a ball, it must be exactly on target, because the child does not move toward the ball. In fact, many children close their eyes as the ball comes toward them.

Small-Muscle Development

Small-muscle development refers to the development of small muscles, especially those in the hands and fingers. The movements that depend on these muscles are *fine-motor skills*. Fine-motor skills depend on a child's level of **eye-hand coordination**, which is the ability to coordinate sight with movement of the hands. Eye-hand coordination matures because of brain development. As small muscles develop and eye-hand coordination improve, toddlers can better handle complex fine-motor skills. With time and experience, clumsy and difficult movements become smoother and require less effort, which is called **dexterity**.

By 12 months of age, children begin to develop the pincer grasp, which helps them learn many new fine-motor skills. One of the major changes in fine-motor skills in the toddler years is the ability to grasp writing tools (**Figure 11.7**). Toddlers use

Figure 11.6 One-year-old toddlers throw objects from a sitting position. ***Should parents discourage their toddlers from throwing objects? Explain.***

Figure 11.7 Toddlers' Ability to Grasp Writing Tools

About 18 to 24 months

Toddlers hold a crayon or pencil with the thumb on one side and fingers on the other side.

About 24 to 26 months

Toddlers hold a crayon or pencil with the thumb and fingers in an adult-like grasp.

both hands to some extent and often switch hands. A definite hand preference for right or left hand, however, usually does not occur until the preschool years.

Between 12 and 18 months, toddlers can hold spoons in their fists, feed themselves, and drink from cups. They can also fill and empty containers, insert rather large objects into holes, and build a tower of two or three soft blocks.

Throughout the toddler years, children's fine-motor skills continue to improve. With practice and better eye-hand coordination, toddlers become better at feeding themselves. Between 18 and 24 months of age, children are able to turn door knobs, hit pegs with a hammer, and string large beads on cords. After 24 months, toddlers can draw or copy vertical lines and build a straighter tower with blocks.

Physical Developmental Milestones

The refinement of brain wiring, greater muscle control, and a positive environment enable toddlers to develop their physical capabilities rapidly. **Figure 11.8** lists physical developmental milestones throughout the toddler years. Parents and caregivers study these charts to better meet toddlers' physical needs.

Lesson 11.1 Review and Assessment 

1. What substance aids the speed of neuron transmissions, enabling toddlers to perform more complex tasks?
2. Name two factors that impact a person's weight and increase in height.
3. Describe the body proportions of toddlers.
4. Describe development of the bones and teeth in toddlers.
5. Fat deposits under the skin _____ (increase/decrease) during the toddler years.
6. List four movements that depend mainly on the large muscles.
7. Name seven physical developmental milestones that toddlers achieve between one and three years of age.
8. **Critical thinking.** How does synaptic density lend itself to faster learning?

Figure 11.8 Toddler Physical Milestones

12 to 18 months

- Takes a step or two without support (12 months).
- Walks without assistance (13 to 14 months).
- Walks sideways (16 months) and backward (17 months).
- Creeps up and down stairs (14 months) and walks up and down stairs with help (16 months).
- Squats or stoops without losing balance.
- Throws ball while sitting.
- Pushes, pulls, and dumps objects while sitting.
- Uses cup and holds spoon in palm and attempts to feed self (messy).
- Fills and empties containers.
- Picks up small objects with thumb and index finger.
- Makes a few marks on paper.
- Places pegs in a pegboard.
- Turns two or three book pages at one time.
- Builds a crooked tower of two or three blocks.

18 to 24 months

- Pushes and pulls objects while walking.
- Does a hurried walk that resembles a run (both feet do not leave surface as they do in running).
- Steps off low objects (first stage in jumping).
- Stands on one foot unsteadily.
- Climbs on furniture.
- Walks stairs without adult help, but needs hand railing or baluster; does not alternate feet.
- Throws ball while standing.
- Squats or bends to "catch" a ball.
- Turns pages in a book one at a time.

18 to 24 months *(Continued)*

- Builds a crooked tower of three or four one-inch cube blocks.
- Strings one to three large beads on a cord.
- Imitates horizontal and vertical lines drawn on paper.
- Tries to fold a piece of paper in half (edges will not meet).
- Holds crayons or pencils with the thumb on one side and fingers on the other side.
- Helps wash hands.
- Scribbles.

24 to 36 months

- Carries a large toy or several smaller ones while walking.
- Stands on tiptoes.
- Runs awkwardly, but cannot stop or change directions easily.
- Jumps down with both feet (24 months); jumps up with both feet (28 months).
- Bends over easily without falling.
- Kicks ball with legs straight and little body involvement.
- Climbs on play equipment.
- Rides push and pedal toys and starts to pedal a tricycle, but finds it difficult.
- "Catches" a ball by bending at the waist to pick it up or by responding to an aerial ball with delayed arm action.
- Strings four beads on a cord.
- Holds pencil or crayon with the thumb and fingers in an adult-like grasp.
- Drinks from a straw; feeds self with a spoon (less messy).
- Uses a fork (awkwardly) to pierce food.
- Builds a somewhat straighter tower of several blocks.
- Unscrews lids from jars.
- Cuts snips in paper.
- Rotates handle (like on a jack-in-the-box toy).
- Is ready to start potty training due to the ability to manage pull-down clothing.

Lesson 11.2 Meeting Nutritional Needs of Toddlers

Key Terms

complementary foods
food allergy
oils
table foods

Academic Terms

erratic
merits

Objectives

After studying this lesson, you will be able to

- explain how a child's eating experience changes during the toddler years.
- describe the nutritional needs of one- to two-year-old toddlers.
- develop a meal plan that meets the nutritional needs of two- to three-year-old toddlers and prepare healthy meals and snacks based on these guidelines.
- identify common feeding problems that might occur during the toddler years and give examples of possible ways to solve these problems.

Reading and Writing Activity

Arrange a study session to read this lesson aloud. Before each main heading, stop to discuss the main points and to note any unfamiliar words. Write a summary of the lesson and list and define the words you or your partner did not know. Share your summary and notes with the class.

Graphic Organizer

Draw a time line illustrating the toddler years of a child's life. Then, as you are reading, take notes about toddlers' nutritional needs and how they are met at each point on your time line.

1 year	2 years	3 years

Eating experiences change in the toddler years. Toddlers make a transition from breast- or formula-feeding to eating a variety of table foods with their new tastes and textures. Parents often overestimate their toddler's appetite. Toddlers' growth slows after infancy, but toddlers are much more active than infants. Pound for pound, toddlers have lower caloric needs than infants. The importance of good nutrition through a balanced diet is not diminished, however. In fact, a diminished appetite means every bite needs to count.

Getting any toddler to eat a balanced diet every day is quite a challenge. Many toddlers do not achieve this goal. If consistently offered a balanced diet through tasty foods, however, most toddlers eat well. Parents should talk with a registered dietitian or a doctor if concerned.

Parents often make two mistakes due to their concerns. First, turning mealtimes into sparring matches seldom works and often makes toddlers less likely to comply. Parents need to offer the right foods, serve as a good-eating model, and not provide "junk foods" to meet the balance of toddlers' caloric needs. Second, when self-feeding begins, some parents start emphasizing table manners. Due to their lack of eye-hand coordination, toddlers' eating styles define the term "mess hall." Eventually, eating behaviors become more civilized and then table manners can be introduced.

The Toddler's Eating Experience

During the toddler years, the eating experience changes. Children graduate from drinking breast milk or formula and eating baby foods to eating **table foods** (foods prepared for the entire family). In preparing table foods for toddlers, parents can use the helpful hints shown in **Figure 11.9**.

Figure 11.9 Preparing Table Foods for Toddlers

- Avoid adding salt or sugar to the food served to toddlers. (Parents can separate the toddler's serving from the dish before adding these for other family members.)
- Cook and refrigerate all foods properly.
- Continue to introduce new foods at five-day intervals to check for allergies and intolerances.
- Mash foods or cut them into bite-sized pieces for toddlers.
- Offer toddlers six offerings of food (meals and snacks) per day. Use a toddler-sized plate to avoid overwhelming the toddler with too much food.

Toddlers' appetites decrease as their physical rate of growth slows. Instead of parents feeding them every few hours, toddlers are feeding themselves and joining the family for meals. Toddlers' self-feeding skills improve as they learn to use a cup and spoon instead of their fingers. Because their fine-motor skills are not mature, toddlers can still be messy eaters.

Toddlers are often picky eaters, developing definite food likes and dislikes. In fact, toddlers frequently get on "food kicks" in which the same foods are preferred for days or even weeks and perhaps rejected later. Being assertive about foods and eating is part of what it means to be a toddler.

Because toddlers have so much energy, they often prefer nibbling foods while on-the-go rather than sitting to eat a full meal. Skipping a meal or two and then eating as though they are starved a few hours later is also common. Parents often worry that these **erratic** (unusual; inconsistent) eating habits may cause the child harm. Feeding toddlers a variety of healthy, nutritious meals and snacks, however, can help meet their nutritional needs during these active years.

Healthful Food Choices

Meeting nutritional needs in the toddler years is a top priority because children need a variety of nutritious foods for bodily growth and repair. During toddlerhood, the nutritional needs of one- to two-year-olds are different from the nutritional needs of two- to three-year-olds. Some children have special nutritional needs.

Nutritional Needs of One- to Two-Year-Olds

Solid foods that provide the nutrients infants and toddlers need in addition to their breast milk, formula, or whole cow's milk are called **complementary foods**. Having nutritional needs met in this way for infants and toddlers, 6 to 24 months of age, is called *complementary feeding*. Complementary feeding is a transitional diet that bridges exclusive breast- or formula-feeding to family foods.

Two changes occur in the complementary feeding of toddlers from 12 to 24 months. First, with each passing month, toddlers' nutritional needs are met more and more through complementary foods. Second, children who are breast-fed or formula-fed at 12 months of age are then changed to whole cow's milk. (Toddler formulas should not be used unless medically advised, and reduced-fat cow's milk is not usually recommended before two years of age.) Pediatricians may advise a later change to whole cow's milk for toddlers who were premature infants or who have certain illnesses.

Toddlers eat smaller amounts of food than infants or adults, and their daily caloric intakes vary depending on age, size, and activity level. To meet their nutritional needs, toddlers should eat a variety of nutritious foods each day, such as vegetables, fruits, whole-grain breads or cereals, lean meats, and beans. Toddlers also need about two cups of whole milk each day (**Figure 11.10**). Juices should not be served in place of milk because these drinks do not provide the calcium and other minerals toddlers need for proper bone growth and ossification.

Parents may have difficulty determining their child's varying food needs during the first year of toddlerhood. Following the toddler's cues for fullness and hunger is especially important. Typically, toddlers eat three small meals and two or three snacks each day. Parents should let toddlers eat a variety of nutritious foods until they are full. The exception to this recommendation would be if a toddler has a health concern that **merits** (deserves; warrants) a special nutritional plan.

Figure 11.10 In addition to milk, calcium-rich foods, such as yogurt, cheese, and cottage cheese can be offered as part of toddlers' meals and snacks. ***Besides milk, what calcium-rich foods do you consume on a daily basis?***

Nutritional Needs of Two- to Three-Year-Olds

Parents of two- and three-year-old toddlers can refer to the MyPlate food guidance system to help them determine their child's nutritional needs. The United States Department of Agriculture (USDA) designed this system to help people two years of age and older make more healthful food and physical activity choices. MyPlate has five major food groups, excluding oils. The following groups are included in the MyPlate plan:

- ***Vegetables.*** The vegetable group includes a variety of colorful foods, such as lettuce, tomatoes, corn, carrots, potatoes, and squash. Vegetables provide vitamins, folate, minerals, and fiber. Based on the MyPlate food guidance system, half of a person's plate should be filled with fruits and vegetables.
- ***Fruits.*** Examples of foods in the fruit group include apples, pears, oranges, bananas, peaches, kiwis, and strawberries. Fruits and 100% fruit juices provide needed amounts of potassium and vitamins A and C. Limit fruit juices with added sugars because they contain fewer nutrients and are likely to cause tooth decay.

- *Grains.* This group includes breads, cereals, rice, and pasta. Grains provide carbohydrates (starches), which are a good source of energy and fiber. They also provide many needed vitamins and minerals. As shown on MyPlate, half the grains a person consumes should be whole grains (**Figure 11.11**). Examples of whole grains include oatmeal and whole-wheat crackers, breads, and pastas.
- *Dairy.* Milk, yogurt, and cheese are examples of dairy products. Foods in the dairy group provide calcium, protein, vitamins, and minerals. Consuming dairy products is highly important during childhood to promote bone growth. Two- to three-year-olds should have about two cups of reduced-fat dairy each day.
- *Proteins.* This group includes meat, poultry, fish, dry beans, eggs, and nuts. (Nuts are a choking hazard, however, and are not recommended for this age group.) Foods in this group provide protein, B vitamins, minerals, iron, and zinc. In following the USDA's recommendations for MyPlate, a person should eat lean meats and choose from a variety of seafood at least twice a week. Young children should be offered seafood that is lower in mercury, such as salmon, shrimp, tilapia, and cod.

Although oils are not a food group, oils are essential to a healthy diet. **Oils** are fats that are liquid at room temperature, like the vegetable oils used in cooking. Foods that are mainly oil include mayonnaise, certain salad dressings, and soft (tub or squeeze) margarine. Because oils contain essential fatty acids, there is a limited allowance for oils in the food guide.

The USDA recommends offering smaller portion sizes to two- and three-year-olds. By preparing small, healthy meals or snacks five or six times a day at regular intervals, toddlers can often learn to recognize when they are full or hungry. The MyPlate website offers food plans for people according to age, weight, height, gender, and level of physical activity. These food plans show a person's daily recommended amount from each food group. **Figure 11.12** shows a daily food plan for a two-year-old toddler whose results are based on a 1,000 calorie pattern.

Special Nutritional Needs

Food intolerances and allergies require a special diet. A **food allergy** is an abnormal response to a food triggered by the body's immune system. Allergic reactions can be very severe, sometimes causing serious illness or even death. The most common foods that are responsible for a large percentage of food allergies include milk, eggs, peanuts, fish, shellfish, wheat, soy, and tree nuts. All food labels are required to list the presence of these eight ingredients.

A physician or registered dietitian nutritionist can develop a meal plan for children who have food intolerances and allergies. These professionals may

Figure 11.11 Whole-grain foods (bottom row) contain the entire grain kernel; whereas, refined grains (top row) have been processed for a finer texture and increased shelf life. Whole grains are a more nutritious source of carbohydrates. *How could you identify whole-grain foods in a grocery store?*

also make special food recommendations for the following reasons:

- height and weight are significantly out of the norms
- family history of weight gain
- physical activity level
- anemia and other illnesses
- disorders present at birth, such as PKU and galactosemia

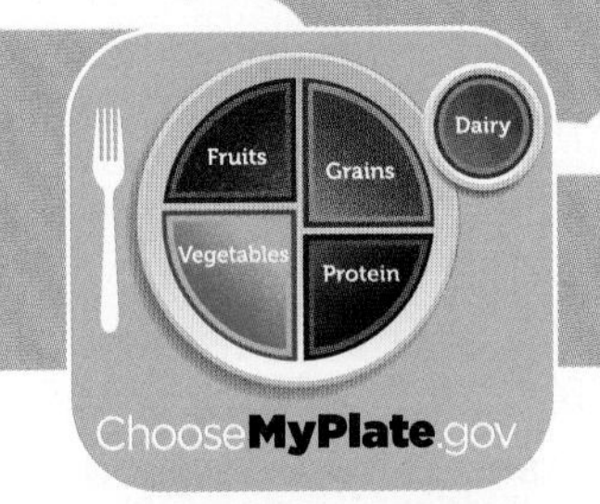

Daily Food Plan

Based on the information you provided, this is your daily recommended amount from each food group.

GRAINS 3 ounces	VEGETABLES 1 cup	FRUITS 1 cup	DAIRY 2 cups	PROTEIN FOODS 2 ounces
Make half your grains whole Aim for at least **1½ ounces** of whole grains a day	**Vary your veggies** Aim for these amounts **each week**: **Dark green veggies** = ½ cup **Red and orange veggies** = 2½ cups **Beans & peas** = ½ cup **Starchy veggies** = 2 cups **Other veggies** = 1½ cups	**Focus on fruits** Eat a variety of fruit Go easy on fruit juices	**Get your calcium-rich foods** Go low-fat or fat-free when you choose milk, yogurt, or cheese	**Go lean with protein** Choose low-fat or lean meats and poultry Vary your protein choices with more beans, peas, nuts, and seeds Choose seafood twice a week

Find your balance between food and physical activity	Know your limits on fats, sugars, and sodium
Children two to five years of age should play actively every day.	Your allowance for oils is **3 teaspoons a day**. Limit extras—solid fats and sugars—to **140 calories a day**. Reduce sodium intake to less than **2300 mg a day**.

Your results are based on a 1000 calorie pattern **Name:** ____________

This calorie level is only an estimate of your needs. Monitor your body weight to see if you need to adjust your calorie intake.

Figure 11.12 For good health, a two-year-old needs physical activity as well as these recommended amounts from each food group of MyPlate every day. *Why is it so important to find the balance between food and physical activity?*

Preventing Feeding Problems

Just like infants, toddlers need to be carefully watched while eating because they can easily choke on foods. Toddlers who are crawling, creeping, walking, or running while eating are more likely to choke than those who are sitting or standing still while eating. Foods that are choking hazards during infancy remain choking hazards during toddlerhood. Examples of foods to avoid include popcorn, hard candies, grapes, raisins, hot dogs sliced in rounds, and peanut butter. Softer raw foods may be safer in larger pieces than in finely chopped pieces because they are easier for the older toddler to hold.

Sometimes toddlers develop feeding problems, such as refusing to eat a meal or new foods, taking only a few bites, or showing a lack of self-feeding skills. Many of these problems stem from the toddler's stage of development—the slowing growth, improving motor and learning skills, and changing social needs. Toddlers work out most feeding problems in time with the help of patient adults.

Lesson 11.2 Review and Assessment 

1. Toddlers gradually graduate from consuming breast milk or formula to consuming ______.
2. Describe the nutritional needs of one- to two-year-olds.
3. Describe the nutritional needs of two- to three-year-olds.
4. List the five food groups included in the MyPlate plan.
5. Why does the USDA recommend offering smaller portion sizes to two- to three-year-olds?
6. A(n) _____ is an abnormal response to a food triggered by the body's immune system.
7. Give two examples of foods that may be choking hazards for toddlers.
8. **Critical thinking.** Compose a short dialogue in which you explain to a toddler that he or she cannot eat a certain food because of a food allergy. How would you explain the food allergy? How would you encourage the toddler to take precautions?

Focus on

Careers

Registered Dietitian

A registered dietitian (RD), also called a *registered dietitian nutritionist (RDN)*, has special training in food and nutrition. Registered dietitians assess group or individual nutrition needs, plan food and nutrition programs, and evaluate the effectiveness of a dietary plan. They prevent and treat illnesses by promoting healthy eating habits and recommending dietary modifications.

Career cluster: Health science.

Education: Educational requirements typically include a bachelor's degree in dietetics, foods and nutrition, or a related area and an internship. Many dietitians have advanced degrees. Licensure and certification requirements vary by state.

Job outlook: Future employment opportunities for RDs or RDNs are projected to grow faster than the average for all occupations.

To learn more about a career as a registered dietitian nutritionist, visit the United States Department of Labor's *Occupational Outlook Handbook* website. You will also be able to compare the job responsibilities, educational requirements, job outlook, and average pay of registered dietitians with similar occupations.

Lesson 11.3

Meeting Other Physical Needs of Toddlers

Key Terms

regression
toilet learning
training pants

Academic Terms

indomitable
lenient
sedentary

Objectives

After studying this lesson, you will be able to

- give examples of features to consider when choosing garments for toddlers.
- describe water play learning experiences during the toddler years.
- explain the process of toilet learning and identify factors involved.
- identify children's needs for physical activity, rest, and sleep during the toddler years.

Reading and Writing Activity

In learning about children, you learn a great deal about yourself. As you read this lesson, consider what each concept might teach you about yourself. Keep a list of these ideas, placing a star beside any concepts that especially interest you. After reading the lesson, pick two or three of these ideas and write a few paragraphs reflecting on how the content in this lesson helped or will help you understand yourself.

Graphic Organizer

Write *Physical Needs of Toddlers* in the middle circle of a chart like the one shown. Then, as you read this lesson, write the physical needs of toddlers in the surrounding boxes. After you fill in the outer boxes, consider how these physical needs can be met. Write or illustrate ways to meet these needs around each box.

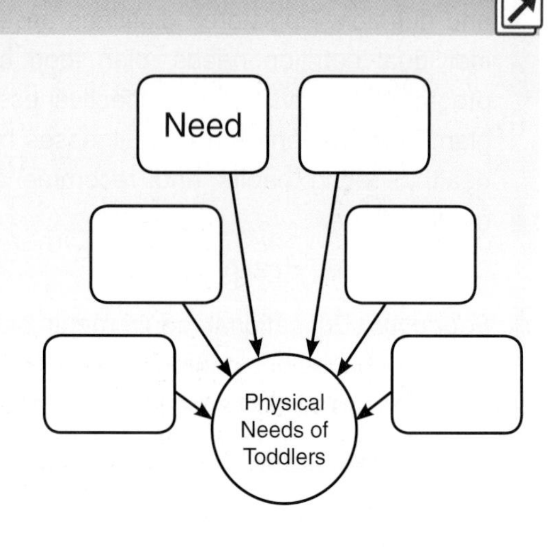

During the toddler years, children still depend on adults to provide for their needs and to keep them healthy and safe. To meet toddlers' physical needs, adults make sure toddlers are fed, clothed, cleaned, and rested. Adults also guide toddlers' self-care skills, such as dressing themselves, bathing, and toileting. As toddlers learn self-care skills, they can begin to meet their physical needs.

As you read in the opening of Lesson 11.2, meeting a toddler's nutritional needs can be challenging due to the toddler's growing will. In like manner, the **indomitable** (incapable of being subdued; stubborn-like) will of the toddler also affects meeting other physical needs. For example, toddlers often take issue with wearing clothing appropriate for the weather or activity. They may also refuse to cooperate with or learn skills needed for grooming or toileting. Success occurs only with adult patience and some creative methods of getting the toddler to comply.

Clothing

Choosing the right clothes and shoes for toddlers is important. Proper clothing helps toddlers stay active, comfortable, and safe. Clothing also stands the strain of constant movement and messy play.

Choosing Garments

Although toddlers grow more slowly than infants, they still outgrow their clothes quickly. The way clothing fits is important for the toddler. Clothes that are too tight can bind and restrict movement while clothes that are too loose can be uncomfortable and unsafe.

To ensure proper fit, parents often have toddlers try on garments rather than rely on garment sizing, which can be confusing. For example, some companies use descriptive terms, such as *small*, *medium*, and *large* as their sizes. Other companies set sizes by age, such as *18 mo. (1T)*, *24 mo. (2T)*, *3T*, and *4T*. The most accurate sizing method for toddlers' garments is the weight range or weight and height ranges. A few companies provide more than one type of sizing on their labels for easy comparison. Sizes vary from one company to the next, but an example is provided in **Figure 11.13**.

During the toddler years, children are learning how to undress and dress themselves. Undressing is always easier than dressing. For example, it is

Figure 11.13 Toddler Clothing Sizes

Size	Height in Inches	Weight in Pounds
18 mo./1T	30¾ to 32	22 to 24
24 mo./2T	32½ to 35½	24½ to 28
3T	36 to 38½	28½ to 32
4T	39 to 41	32½ to 36
5T	41½ to 43	36½ to 41

easier to pop open snaps than match both sides of snaps and press them together. Toddlers can often push down their clothes for toileting, but may find it difficult to get both under- and outer-garments up and straight when dressing. Because of this, parents often consider self-dressing features when choosing clothing for toddlers.

Self-dressing features in toddlers' clothes make dressing and undressing without help easier. Some self-dressing features are critical when toddlers begin toilet learning because they must be able to remove clothing very quickly to avoid toileting accidents. For example, teachers of toddlers in group settings often request toddlers wear elastic-waist pants or shorts instead of jumpsuits or overalls. Belts and difficult clothing fasteners, such as small buttons, are also a problem.

In addition to self-dressing features, parents consider other features when choosing garments for toddlers. These features may include safety, comfort, growth features, quality construction, and easy care. **Figure 11.14** shows some examples of each of these features.

Fitting Shoes

Toddlers need shoes to protect their feet from cold, dampness, and harmful objects. Shoes that fit properly have ½ inch of space between the large toe and shoe when the toddler stands. They also have a flexible sole and snug-fitting heel. New

Figure 11.14 Important Features in Toddler Clothes

Safety	
• Flame-resistant (will burn, but smolders slowly rather than flaming when on fire) • No drawstrings or loose buttons, fasteners, or trim	• Belts, ties, and sashes fastened to the garment securely to prevent tripping, choking, or strangling • Bright-colored clothing (increases ability to see toddlers)
Comfort	
• Made of lightweight and absorbent fabrics • Made of stretch fabrics • Elastic encased or nonbinding • Fullness in pant legs to permit knee bending and stooping with ease	• Collars and sleeves that do not rub or bind • Coats, sweaters, and jackets that can fit over clothes without binding • Underwear that is not binding • Neck openings large enough for ease of dressing
Growth Features	
• Made of stretch fabrics • Dresses without definite waistlines • Pants and skirts with elastic or adjustable waistbands	• Adjustable shoulder straps • Clothes with deep hems, large seams, and pleats or tucks that can be easily let out • Two-piece outfits
Quality Construction	
• Reinforcement at points of strain such as seams, knees, pockets, and pocket edges • Stitches that are even and not too long • Seams that are flat, smooth, and finished	• Securely attached fasteners and trims • Built-in growth features, such as deep hems • Patterns are matched at seams
Easy Care	
• Washable (especially machine washable with other colors)	• Little or no ironing needed • Easy to mend

shoes are recommended over hand-me-downs, except for rain or snow boots worn over shoes. Each foot is shaped differently. With even a little wear, shoes conform to a person's foot.

Because the bones and muscles of the foot are developing, shoe fit is very important for toddlers' proper growth and comfort. Shoes that fit improperly can cause permanent damage to the child's feet. Toddlers often outgrow their shoes before they wear them out. The average rate of foot growth for toddlers is one shoe size every three to four months.

During the toddler years, children have flat feet because their arches are relaxed. For many children, this flat-footed look disappears around three years of age. Going barefooted or wearing socks without shoes is good for the development of the arch. Shoes, even high-top shoes, do not provide support.

Bathing

Although toddlers may want to try to bathe themselves, they are not yet able to do so. Toddlers still need close supervision and are not safe to be left alone. Parents and other caregivers should never leave toddlers unattended or unsupervised while they are in or near water—not even for a minute.

Regular bathtubs are quite spacious for toddlers. Young toddlers may feel more secure bathing in a child's tub placed inside the regular bathtub. Other parents find their toddlers enjoy special bathtub seats designed specifically for toddlers.

Toddlers have fun during bath time splashing water and trying to hold slippery soap. Bath time for toddlers is a good opportunity to engage in water play. Children can learn many concepts from playing in the tub (**Figure 11.15**). Special bath toys are available for toddler water play, but toys can also be made easily from household objects. Unsafe items for toddler floor play should not be used in tub play.

Toilet Learning

Toilet learning is one of the most discussed aspects of the toddler years. **Toilet learning** is the process by which adults help children control their excretory systems, namely bowel movements and urination. Experts have found two things are certain in toilet learning. First, the timing of learning varies from toddler to toddler. Some children may be ready to begin toilet learning around 18 to 24 months of age while others are not ready until much later. Second, many toddlers do not complete the learning

Figure 11.15 Water Play Learning Experiences

- Some toys float and some sink.
- Water power, such as moving water with your hands or feet, can push floating toys.
- Water can be held for a brief time in the cupped hand or in a toy with "holes."
- Water makes all things wet.
- Water can splash, squirt, and drip.
- The bottom of the tub can be seen through clear water. Bubbles make it harder to see the bottom.
- Soap makes bubbles that pop and disappear.
- Solid objects can be pushed down through the water.
- Play can be described by naming objects (boat, cup, bubbles) and actions (push, pop or burst, splash, squirt, drip, float or sink).

process quickly. Learning may take most of the toddler years and perhaps even longer to complete.

Readiness for Toilet Learning

Before toddlers can begin toilet learning, they must be developmentally ready. Toddlers vary in age of complete control, or ability to wait until they are at the toilet to release bodily waste. The average age for complete day control is 28 months of age, but the normal range varies greatly. Usually, a child must be able to stay dry for two or more hours before he or she can begin to learn.

Three years of age is often a difficult time to begin toilet learning. This is because three-year-old toddlers experience a brief, but intense stage of *regression* in their desire to be independent. **Regression** means going back to an earlier stage of development. A toddler should not begin toilet learning during regression or periods of family or child stress.

Even before toddlers are ready for toilet learning, adults can help them see what is expected. If an adult notes the child is eliminating, he or she can say something to make the child aware of it. Adults can also show the child the potty he or she will use. Special equipment available for toilet learning may include a child-sized toilet, a potty chair, or a potty seat that fits on many standard-sized toilet seats. When standard toilets are used (with or without toddler seats), toddlers often need a sturdy stool near the toilet to climb onto and turn around before sitting. Some toddlers want to sit on the potty first with their clothes on to check it out.

Focus on

Health

Physical and Emotional Factors of Toilet Learning

Toilet learning involves factors like physical development, motor skills, and emotional readiness. The physical and motor skills include the ability to

- feel a full bowel and bladder. Until about 15 months of age, children have bowel movements and pass urine without knowing in advance or realizing they have done so. Many disposable diapers and disposable pull-up pants do not help with the feeling of wetness because they are designed to keep the skin drier.
- know what the sensation of needing to eliminate means in time to get to the potty.
- control muscles used for holding in or letting go. These muscles, which are low in the body, are among the last to develop. (This is a good example of the cephalocaudal development principle.) Nerves can control these muscles around 18 months of age. Children tend to learn to control bowel movements before they learn to control their bladders.
- walk (or often run) to the potty.
- remove or push down clothes.
- redress and wash hands with help.

For toilet learning to work, emotional readiness must occur at the same time the child is physically developed. Toddlers must see the need to use the potty. Busy toddlers often do not want to sit on the potty for the needed amount of time. Saying *no* to using the toilet is part of the self-will toddlers want to express. Toddlers may also need to master fears of falling in, the flushing water, and even fear of bowel movements.

Starting Toilet Learning

Once toilet learning begins, adults need to provide a supportive learning environment for the toddler and accept success and failure in a matter-of-fact way. Toddlers need some encouragement, but too much adds pressure.

No matter how much care is taken, accidents will happen. Being prepared, however, helps prevent accidents from causing too much stress for toddlers or adults. **Training pants** (pants made of disposable diaper material, pants with a multi-layered cotton fabric crotch, or specially designed pants for wading or swimming use) help lessen the mess of accidents. Using diapers during sleep times, when traveling, or when away from home for long periods makes learning less stressful, too. Caregivers should stop the learning routine during an illness or if a child shows signs of stress.

If the toddler is in a group program, toilet learning must be a team effort—child, family, and caregivers. Toilet learning is something adults do *with* a child. A constant exchange of information between the home and the program is needed. Child care programs are often good places for toilet learning. This is due to the experience of the staff, child-sized bathrooms, and the program focus on helping children develop competence in self-care. Toddlers in child care programs often learn rapidly because they see their friends learning toileting skills.

Physical Activity

Physical activity is important for toddlers because it increases the strength and endurance of the cardiac and skeletal muscles and improves motor skills. Physical activity encourages attention during quiet learning times because it prevents restlessness. Physical activity also lessens the chance of some problems and diseases, such as obesity, heart problems, type 2 diabetes, and mental health problems.

Because most toddlers are so active, they usually get all the exercise they need. A few toddlers, however, are too sedentary (characterized by little physical activity). Sedentary toddlers spend up to 75 percent of their waking day in non-active ways. Most research suggests toddlers spend at least 50 percent of each day in active play. How can parents and other caregivers encourage sedentary toddlers to be more active? The following ideas can encourage an active lifestyle:

- Eliminate or reduce time spent on all digital media to one hour or less daily.
- Select play equipment designed for active movement, such as balls and pedal riding toys.
- Plan a few movement activities, such as moving to music or navigating an obstacle course.
- Take the toddler to a playground daily, if possible (**Figure 11.16**).
- Plan activities keeping in mind motor milestones.
- Set an example of an active lifestyle and include toddlers in it.

Rest and Sleep

Toddlers often sleep fewer hours and take fewer naps than infants. Between one and three years of age, children typically need 12 to 14 hours of sleep. Around 18 months, toddlers often reduce naps to once daily for about one to three hours. Between 31 and 36 months, naps begin to disappear.

Toddlers, even when tired, are more likely than babies to resist rest and sleep. Bedtime problems stem partly from the toddlers' struggle for independence. Often, parents become physically tired from coping with toddlers who resist sleep. They may even feel stress if bedtime becomes a battle of wills. The following tips may help parents handle naptime and bedtime problems:

- Avoid scheduling naptime too close to bedtime.
- Maintain a consistent sleep schedule. Have the toddler go to bed at the same time every night. If the schedule must be adjusted, shift the toddler's bedtime gradually.

Figure 11.16 Taking toddlers to the playground is an effective way of encouraging physical activity in their lives. *What kinds of physical activities can toddlers participate in at playgrounds?*

- Notify the toddler about 20 minutes before naptime or bedtime. Use a neutral sign, such as a clock (not a person), to signal the hour.
- Set a bedtime ritual or routine that includes only restful activities, such as a warm bath, drink of water, story, song, and hug. Naptime rituals can be developed, too.
- Tell a toddler who resists sleep that he or she does not have to sleep, but does need to stay in bed. (Parents can purchase an alarm device that has a night-light that comes on after a set period of time. Children are taught to stay in bed until they see the light.) Refer to daytime naps as "rest" and provide the toddler with books.
- Comfort a fearful toddler or a toddler who wakes during the night with nightmares. Provide a night-light in the toddler's room to ease fears or encourage the use of a security object, such as a stuffed animal or blanket.
- Return the toddler to bed if he or she gets up during naptime or bedtime. Meet any real needs, but calmly refuse nonessential requests.

Parents' actions determine toddlers' behavior. From parents' responses and actions, toddlers may learn to stay in bed during rest time. If parents are usually **lenient** (easy-going; not strict), however, toddlers may instead learn tricks to get what they want. Learning to stay in bed helps toddlers get their needed rest. Parents also need this time to meet their own needs.

Lesson 11.3 Review and Assessment 

1. _____ features in toddlers' clothes make dressing and undressing without help easier.
2. Choose one type of feature for toddlers' clothing and explain how this feature benefits the toddler and benefits the parent.
3. Describe why toddlers should wear shoes.
4. Name four water play learning experiences.
5. What two principles have experts found to be certain in toilet learning?
6. Name three ways caregivers can encourage toddlers to lead active lifestyles.
7. Between one and three years of age, children typically need _____ hours of sleep.
8. **Critical thinking.** Why do you think seeing other children learn toileting skills helps a toddler learn the skills him- or herself?

Chapter 11

Review and Assessment

Summary

During the toddler years, a child's brain continues to mature. Brain volume, synaptic density, and myelination increase rapidly. Toddlers grow more slowly than infants and grow at different rates due to heredity and environment. Toddlers' bones harden, and fat deposits under the skin decrease, making the toddler more slender. Toddlers refine gross-motor skills, such as walking, climbing, and throwing. They also learn to run, jump, and catch objects. Fine-motor skills, including the toddler's ability to grasp writing tools, depend on the child's eye-hand coordination.

Toddlers eat table foods and can feed themselves. One- to two-year-olds engage in a diet called *complementary feeding*, which is a transition diet that includes breast milk, formula, or whole cow's milk and solids. Two- to three-year-olds should eat according to the MyPlate food guidance system's recommendations. A number of feeding problems can arise because of toddlers' slowing growth rates and growing independence. In some cases, toddlers will have special nutritional needs due to food allergies or other factors.

Clothing and shoes that fit and allow for growth are important. Other clothing features for toddlers include safety, comfort, growth features, quality construction, and easy care. Before children can begin toilet learning, their bodies must be physically ready. Children should not be shamed or punished when they have accidents. When successful, they need encouragement. Toddlers should be encouraged to engage in physical activity so they can form these habits early in life. Sleep and rest requirements for toddlers have changed since infancy. Bedtime problems can develop, but adults can establish quiet nighttime rituals and try other tips to lessen sleep problems.

College and Career Portfolio

Portfolio Samples

Portfolios for college or job applications often include *samples of work*. A sample of work might be an especially well-written paper, a persuasive presentation, or a hypothetical lesson plan. To identify your portfolio samples, complete the following activities.

- Review samples of your work of which you are most proud. These samples might be from your schoolwork, from your participation in an extracurricular activity, or from personal projects you have completed.
- Consult with your teacher or with a college and career counselor about which samples of work would be most appropriate for your portfolio. Create a list of samples you want to use.

Vocabulary Activities

1. With a partner, choose two words from the following list to compare. Create a Venn diagram to compare your words and identify differences. Write one term under the left circle and the other term under the right. Where the circles overlap, write three characteristics the terms have in common. For each term, write a characteristic unique to that term in its respective outer circle.

Key Terms

complementary foods (11.2)
dexterity (11.1)
eye-hand coordination (11.1)
food allergy (11.2)
large-muscle development (11.1)
muscle development (11.1)
oils (11.2)
regression (11.3)
small-muscle development (11.1)
table foods (11.2)
toilet learning (11.3)
training pants (11.3)

2. Draw a cartoon for one of the following terms. Use the cartoon to express the meaning of the term. Share your cartoon with the class.

Academic Terms

constrict (11.1)
deformation (11.1)
dilate (11.1)
erratic (11.2)
indomitable (11.3)
lenient (11.3)
merits (11.2)
rigid (11.1)
sedentary (11.3)
timid (11.1)

Critical Thinking

3. **Identify.** Identify ways in which the brain develops and other organs maturate during the toddler years that enable toddlers to engage in more activities and learn through new experiences. How important is biological maturation to toddler growth? Explain your answer.
4. **Make inferences.** Based on your own experiences and learning, which factor do you think affects height and weight more: heredity or environment? In teams, debate this topic and explain the reasoning behind your answer.
5. **Draw conclusions.** The text indicates that toddlers walk at a rate of about 170 steps per minute. Walk quickly, counting your own steps for one minute as a partner times you. How do your results compare with the average rate for toddlers? What conclusions can you draw from this experiment?
6. **Analyze.** One- to two-year-olds have a different eating experience than two- to three-year-olds. Analyze how these eating experiences differ, and imagine what it would be like to transition from eating during infancy to eating during late toddlerhood. Write two to three paragraphs reflecting on how a child's experience of eating might change.
7. **Compare and contrast.** Compare the MyPlate recommendations for toddlers with those for you—especially in terms of daily amounts for the food groups. What does this comparison indicate in terms of planning family meals?
8. **Determine.** Review the water play learning experiences described in Figure 11.15. Why are these learning experiences important? Determine how each learning experience prepares toddlers to learn more about themselves and their environments outside of the tub.
9. **Evaluate.** Evaluate ways in which toddlers' habits of physical activity and rest might affect them later in life. How might being sedentary during toddlerhood affect a child's physical activity in the future? How might not getting enough sleep as a toddler impact a young child's sleeping pattern?
10. **Cause and effect.** Review the tips for handling toddler bedtime problems, and then determine how each tip achieves its intended effect. Why does each tip succeed in encouraging rest and sleep? Based on the reasons for the tips covered in this chapter, write your own list of tips for toddlers' caregivers.

Core Skills

11. **Writing.** As a group or class project, write a one- or two-page brochure explaining the progression of toddlers' motor skills. Include information on the order (and approximate age) when toddlers learn motor skills. Also, explain the motor actions used when walking, running, climbing, jumping, throwing, and catching. Include illustrations for these actions. Have your teacher check your brochure, then make copies. Give copies to parents and adults at a program that serves toddlers, such as a child care program or preschool.

12. **Art and speaking.** As a class, divide into three groups, and assign each group one of the age ranges covered in this chapter's table of physical developmental milestones (Figure 11.8). Then, create an art project that involves drawing based on a model, coloring within lines, or assembling art supplies. Assign your art project to one of the other groups in the class, and then review the project you have been assigned. In your group, attempt to complete the art project with only the motor skills your age range of toddlers can perform. For example, using your assigned toddler age range and keeping in mind the milestones these toddlers have achieved and have yet to achieve, you must hold any art supplies or utensils and draw and color as these toddlers would likely perform. After completing your art projects, grade them as a class and discuss what you learned about toddlers' motor skills.
13. **Technology and speaking.** In child care centers, meeting the special nutritional needs of toddlers with food allergies can be challenging. Imagine you are a teacher at a child care center and several of your toddlers have food allergies. The parents have inquired as to how you will protect their children against food allergens. Create a slide show presentation outlining how you will keep the toddlers who have food allergies safe while still providing for their nutritional needs. Deliver your presentation to the class.
14. **Research, technology, and listening.** Using reliable online or print resources, research toddlers' feeding problems. Working with a partner, use a doll to role-play one feeding problem and employ some recommended methods for solving the problem. Film your role-play and play it for the class. Ask your classmates for any feedback they would give to the caregivers in the role-play. Listen closely to your classmates' role-plays so you can offer helpful feedback.
15. **Reading and writing.** Many products for toddlers are constructed with dressing ease in mind. Using online or print resources, find an advertisement for one of these products and then print it or make a copy. Read the advertisement and identify how the product makes dressing and undressing toddlers easier. Then consider: Would this product be effective? Is there anything that could be added to or changed about the product to make it even more effective? Write a two-page report detailing your findings and assessing the product.
16. **Research and writing.** In small groups, research toilet learning strategies currently popular among parents and caregivers. You may find these strategies in parenting magazines, online, or in published parenting books. Choose three toilet learning strategies that especially interest you and then write a short article marketing these strategies. In your article, explain the benefits of your chosen strategies and argue for their effectiveness based on the information covered in this chapter.
17. **CTE Career Readiness Practice.** As a new employee at a child care center, you are taking on the challenge of making your center a healthy environment for young children. Part of your job includes taking initiative to serve healthy meals and snacks. Use the menu planner on the MyPlate website to plan healthful meals, compare food choices to recommendations for meeting nutrient needs, and identify ways to improve physical activities. Plan a one-week menu (meals and snacks) for the two- to three-year-old toddlers at your center. Your menu should satisfy all of the daily values these toddlers should consume. Print your menu and bring it to class. Working with a partner, exchange menus and discuss the various options chosen.

Observations

18. Compare a picture of yourself as a baby to a picture of yourself as a toddler. If you do not have these pictures of yourself, then find two pictures of the same child—one from infancy and one from toddlerhood. Observe how height and weight, body proportions, bones and teeth, and fat and muscles change over time. Write a two- to three-page essay analyzing the changes that took place and relating them to what you learned in this chapter.
19. In small groups, visit a home with a toddler or a child care center and observe how the toddler walks. If you are unable to arrange a visit, watch a video of a toddler online. Which of the common walking traits described in this chapter does the toddler exhibit? Is the toddler in a safe and supportive environment for walking? Discuss each group member's observations. Finally, compile your findings into a digital presentation and share with the class.

Chapter 12 Intellectual Development of Toddlers

Essential Question

How do toddlers make a transition to learning through mental rather than physical actions, and how can parents and other caregivers encourage toddlers' curiosity and active exploration?

Lesson 12.1 **How Toddlers Learn**

Lesson 12.2 **What Toddlers Learn**

Lesson 12.3 **Meeting Toddlers' Intellectual Needs**

Case Study Which Language Should Be the Language of Instruction?

As a class, read the case study and discuss the questions that follow. After you finish studying the chapter, discuss this case study again. Have your opinions changed based on what you learned?

A new toddler-preschool program will serve children of Spanish-speaking families in a mostly English-speaking town. The teachers and director are deciding which language (Spanish or English) to use as the language of instruction in the center by considering the following factors:

- The optimal time for learning a second language is before 10 years of age.
- When a second language is introduced to young children, the best technique is immersion in the language. Immersion, however, often results in children becoming less fluent in their first language.
- The language of the home is not always a good model of that language.
- Many people who are bilingual are not equally fluent in both languages. They have a dominant or preferred language.
- Because English is the dominant language in the schools and community, the children may see English as the more valued language by the school-age years.

Give It Some Thought

1. Which language would you vote for to be the language of instruction in this center? Why?
2. How do you think these children's feelings of competence could be affected if English were chosen as the language of instruction? if Spanish were chosen?
3. When schools have more than two primary languages represented, which language should become the language of instruction?
4. Who should make decisions about the language of instruction? the parents? the local schools? the state government? the federal government? Why?

While studying this chapter, look for the online resources icon  to:

- **Practice** terms with e-flash cards and interactive games
- **Assess** what you learn by completing self-assessment quizzes
- **Expand** knowledge with interactive activities and graphic organizers

Companion G-W Learning

www.g-wlearning.com/childdevelopment

Study on the go

Use a mobile device to practice terms and review with self-assessment quizzes.

www.m.g-wlearning.com/0384

Lesson 12.1

How Toddlers Learn

Key Terms

collective symbolism
deferred imitation
mental imagery
pretense
solitary symbolic play

Academic Terms

actuality
deferred
havoc
repertoire
tertiary

Objectives

After studying this lesson, you will be able to:

- summarize brain development during the toddler years.
- describe three characteristics of the toddler's learning in substage 5 of the sensorimotor stage.
- summarize three characteristics of the toddler's learning in substage 6 of the sensorimotor stage.
- explain how culture is involved in scaffolding for toddlers.

Reading and Writing Activity

As you read the lesson, record any questions that come to mind. Indicate where the answer to each question can be found: within the text, by asking your teacher, in another book, on the Internet, or by reflecting on your knowledge and experiences. Pursue the answers to your questions.

Graphic Organizer

Two of the main topics covered in this lesson are Piaget's *Cognitive-Developmental Theory* and Vygotsky's *Sociocultural Theory*. In a chart like the one shown, draw two circles, one labeled *Piaget* and the other labeled *Vygotsky*. As you read, write information you learn around the circle to which it most relates. If a piece of information relates to both theories, write it between the circles.

Toddlers are eager to learn and curious about everyone and everything. When learning about and working at a task they choose, toddlers stay with the task until they are satisfied with the results. Because toddlers have their own agenda, however, they may not always be interested in learning what adults want them to learn.

During the toddler years, children truly begin to understand their environment. They remain holistic learners. Toddlers younger than two years old learn about objects and what happens when they manipulate these objects. They must meet their goals through physical trial-and-error. Because older toddlers learn to think before acting, they plan new ways to achieve goals. Toddlers also become able communicators as they learn new words and speak in short sentences.

Figure 12.1 Experiences dictate which brain connections are strengthened, and the lack of certain experiences determine which are pruned. These experiences are vital to learning within windows of opportunity. For instance, picking out clothes is giving this toddler experience in *independence*, a skill for which the window of opportunity ends in the toddler years. *What other windows of opportunity end in the toddler years? (Review Figure 2.8 for the windows of opportunity.)*

Toddlerhood: A Biologically-Primed Time for Learning

As you read in the chapter on toddler's physical development, the brain undergoes a growth spurt during toddlerhood. The toddler's brain becomes super dense in synapses and has a high concentration of neurotransmitters. Glial cells responsible for myelination are also very active. All of these happenings are genetically preprogrammed and should occur except in cases of brain abnormalities or trauma.

The dense wiring allows for new learning, and myelination increases speed of connections. A competition among these wirings will occur, however. Used wirings remain and become stronger, but unused wirings will be pruned soon after toddlerhood. This competition among the wirings is experience dependent (**Figure 12.1**).

The toddler's brain continues to develop in the sensory and motor areas. Toddlers can make fine sensory discriminations, such as seeing various shades of a given color or hearing small differences in sounds. These sensory discriminations lead to rather accurate perceptual concepts, but not to logical understandings. Furthermore, gross- and fine-motor skills are becoming very coordinated, and motor activities, such as assembling take-apart objects, will enhance learning.

Brain development in toddlerhood allows for the great intellectual advance called **mental imagery** (seeing in the "mind's eye" or hearing in the "mind's ear" in the absence of a stimulus). Mental imagery will eventually lead to abstract thinking and creativity. Unlike infants who simply adjust their actions to the properties of objects (moving after a rolling ball; hitting metal objects to make loud sounds), toddlers begin to impose their mental ideas on objects as seen in pretend play. Soon a block is not just for stacking, but can be a chair or a shaker for a spice.

Development in the language and memory areas of the brain aids toddlers' thinking. The language of their world aids toddlers by

- refining and extending current knowledge. Verbalization of adults helps toddlers see important criteria in their problem-solving activities. For example, the parent might say, "Because you kept your blocks *straight*, your tower will not fall so easily." Now the toddler sees one important criterion, alignment, for physical stability in block building.

- simplifying learning of difficult new concepts. Language clues help people think by focusing their attention on specific things. For example, in an experiment toddlers were asked to match patterned blocks. Toddlers simply told to match the blocks had a more difficult time with the task than toddlers given some verbal clues about the different patterns—those with *stripes* and those with *dots*. Even mature listeners and readers get constant clues from language through words, such as *similar to*, *for example*, *in contrast*, *on the other hand*, *essential question*, in *three* ways, and *to summarize*.
- storing in memory what has been learned. Verbalization greatly aids remembering. For example, toddlers who tell about their trip to the zoo or who retell a story about the zoo by looking at the pictures in the book will retain more information than toddlers who do not verbalize their experiences. Frequent retelling makes the memory even stronger.

Brain development leads to many windows of opportunity for toddlers. On the other hand, toddlerhood is a period of vulnerability if environmental conditions are not optimal. Optimal conditions include nutrition adequate to support the fast growing brain, general physical health, a rich play environment surrounded by quality language exposure, and an emotionally supportive, stress-free world.

Piaget's Cognitive-Developmental Theory

Piaget uses stages to describe children's cognitive development. In the first stage, called the *sensorimotor stage*, children from birth to two years of age learn through their senses and motor actions. The sensorimotor stage includes six substages. During infancy, babies work through the first four substages. During the toddler years, Piaget believed children complete the last two substages (**Figure 12.2**).

In substage 5 (called *tertiary circular reactions*), younger toddlers, around 12 to 18 months of age, learn by discovering new ways to solve problems through physical trial and error. In substage 6 (called *mental imagery or representation*), older toddlers, around 18 to 24 months of age, begin to think about how to solve a problem without using physical actions. By the end of the toddler years, a few children may enter Piaget's second stage of cognitive development, called the *preoperational stage*. (You will learn about the preoperational stage later in this text.)

Substage 5

Piaget called children in substage 5 "little scientists" because they are so busy exploring and discovering the possibilities in their world. In the previous substage, infants practiced the same actions of exploring and experimenting. In substage 5, however, toddlers take another intellectual step as they further their curiosity and show lots of interest in new actions. After discovering one way to use an object, toddlers are interested in discovering what else they can do with the same object. Children in this substage vary their actions to see why different actions get different results.

As you read, Piaget called substage 5 *tertiary circular reactions*. He used the term **tertiary** (third in a sequence), because it is the third major change in intellectual development. (The first two changes happened during infancy.) He used the term *circular*, because toddlers enjoy repeating their actions. Repeating actions helps toddlers verify their observations, which is similar to how scientific findings are verified through additional research and experiments. In substage 5, children's learning is characterized by working toward a goal, using imitation and pretense, and having a greater understanding of object permanence.

Working Toward a Goal

In this substage, toddler's actions involve reaching a goal. Toddlers experiment by using physical trial and error methods to solve problems. They first try what worked in the past. If this is not successful, they change their behaviors. As toddlers are exploring, experimenting, and discovering ways to reach their goals, they get into everything and can cause **havoc** (chaos) in their environment.

Figure 12.2 Piaget's Cognitive-Developmental Theory

Stages and Substages	Characteristics
Stage 1: Sensorimotor stage (birth to 2 years)	Children learn through the senses and physical actions in six substages.
Substages 1 and 2 involve the baby's own body.	
Substages 3 and 4 involve people and objects.	
Substages 5 and 6 involve creative actions and thinking before acting. (12 to 24 months)	
Substage 5: Tertiary circular reactions (12 to 18 months)	*Sometimes called the substage of "little scientists."* • Experiment with objects to receive various results. • Notice some attributes of objects (sometimes color, sometimes size). • Use physical trial and error to solve problems. • Imitate behaviors they have never done before; imitate only in the presence of the model. • Look for hidden objects in the last place seen.
Substage 6: Mental imagery or representation (18 to 24 months)	• Can think about different ways to solve problems without using physical actions in a trial and error way. • Can think through the sequence of a few steps to solve a problem. • Begin to do some deferred imitation. • Know all objects and people are someplace. Hunt for objects in every possible place (completion of object permanence).
Stage 2: Preoperational stage (2 to 7 years)	Children learn through symbols, but with logical limitations.
Stage 3: Concrete operational stage (7 to 11 years)	Children begin to think logically, but base their logic on past experiences.
Stage 4: Formal operational stage (11 years of age and older)	Older children, teens, and adults reason abstractly.

To an adult, the toddler's goal may be obvious. For example, a toddler might try to take a lid off a container to see what's inside. Sometimes, the toddler's goal may not be so obvious to the adult. The child may seem to be only playing with or throwing objects. In **actuality** (reality; fact), the child is trying to figure out how these objects work. Young toddlers want to know what happens to objects when they roll, shake, throw, or move them in other ways. Repeating actions with minor changes helps toddlers learn the best way to reach their goals. These experiments are signs of developing intellectual skills.

Using Imitation and Pretense

A toddler's imitation with the model present is quick and accurate. For example, toddlers can watch others make facial expressions and gestures (nod, wave) and listen to others' sounds and words and quickly imitate these (**Figure 12.3**). Imitation is a major way of learning.

Pretense, symbolic actions seen in play that mimic real situations, also begins. There are different levels of pretense. Piaget referred to the first level of pretense as **solitary symbolic play**. Young toddlers pretend using either real objects or realistic toys; they cannot use objects to represent something entirely different. At this level, the toddler

Figure 12.3 Toddlers are likely to imitate their caregivers, adults other than caregivers, and other children. *What lessons have you learned through imitation? Why is imitation a valuable learning tool?*

pretends to do something that has to do with him- or herself. For example, the toddler might pretend to eat. The pretense does not involve dolls, stuffed animals, or other people, although the young toddler might try to get others to watch the play. The second level of pretense, called *collective symbolism*, occurs in substage 6.

Having Greater Understanding of Object Permanence

Toddlers develop a greater understanding of object permanence in substage 5. Before this stage, infants would look for a missing object where it was *first seen or found*. Infants cannot conceive that an object might be where they last saw it. Unlike infants, young toddlers will look for a completely hidden object where it was *last seen or found*. They cannot, however, imagine the object might be hidden in some other place. Therefore, understanding of object permanence is *almost* complete in substage 5.

Substage 6

Younger toddlers do not have very developed thought processes. They learn through trial and error methods. Around 18 to 24 months, toddlers' intellectual abilities change again as they enter substage 6. Older toddlers, 18 to 36 months of age, now think about what they do before they do it. The three main characteristics that describe substage 6 are identified by thinking. Toddlers think to achieve goals, imitate and engage in pretense, and locate hidden objects.

When you see toddlers pause in mid-action, they are probably thinking. They will "figure things out" intellectually instead of testing them physically. For example, the two-year-old realizes a large object will not fit through a small opening in a container. He or she mentally visualizes trying to put the object through the opening before concluding the object is too big to fit. A one-year-old, however, would try to push the large object through the small opening and then realize the object does not fit.

Older toddlers will mainly think in terms of actions. They even identify objects in terms of actions. For example, a 30-month-old toddler may answer the question, "What is a ball?" with the reply, "To play with," or "To roll."

Thinking to Achieve Goals

Thinking shows in the older toddler's way of reaching goals. For example, the toddler's goal may be to reach a toy on a high playroom shelf. The toddler thinks about the stepstool he or she uses in the bathroom to reach the sink. The toddler then gets the stool to reach the object on the playroom shelf. If the toddler cannot bring the stool into the playroom, he or she may use another object as a stool to reach the toy on the shelf. The toddler has thought through how to reach the goal.

Thinking Involved in Imitation and Pretense

Young toddlers can only imitate a person's actions when the model is present. Older toddlers, however, can imitate a person's actions without the model present. The ability to recall and later imitate someone's behavior is called **deferred imitation**. (Deferred means delayed or postponed). Children use deferred imitation in both pretend play and language.

Symbolic play moves to another level, too. The older toddler extends pretend play beyond him- or herself in two ways. First, pretend play now includes others (**Figure 12.4**). Second, the toddler begins to use actions that are not part of his or her own personal repertoire (reh-pur-TWAHR), or skill set. For example, a toddler might use deferred imitation of his father shaving and pretend to shave.

Older toddlers also enter Piaget's second level of pretense called **collective symbolism**. By two years of age, toddlers can use one set of objects to represent another set of objects. For example, blocks can be cars and trucks or leaves can be dishes. Pretense now extends beyond the toddler him- or herself and involves other people (parents) and objects (stuffed animals) as part of the play. At this age, a few toddlers can also combine actions, such as feeding a doll, "reading" the doll a story, and putting the doll to bed, but most toddlers just do one action at a time.

Thinking Involved in Locating Hidden Objects

During substage 6, children's understanding of object permanence is complete. Older toddlers may demonstrate this understanding by searching for hidden objects. For example, an adult might pretend to hide a toy in one place, but really hides it in another. The toddler knows the toy still exists (object permanence) and thinks about where the toy might be hidden. To find a hidden object, the toddler must also think in terms of spatial concepts. For example, the toddler considers which objects would be large enough to conceal the hidden toy.

Vygotsky's Sociocultural Theory

Vygotsky felt teaching children is a basic sociocultural activity. He believed "teachers" (anyone guiding a child in the learning process) should scaffold (help the child learn) within his or her zone of proximal development (ZPD). In most cultures, if not all, scaffolding begins during the toddler years. In a group-oriented culture, scaffolding is

Figure 12.4 Pretend play in toddlers includes other people and objects. *What types of pretend play did you engage in as a young child?*

often done by parents, extended family members, and siblings. In an individual-oriented culture, parents are the primary teachers.

Scaffolding strategies used in teaching children are also affected by the culture and social environment in which a child is reared. Some families prefer to use direct methods of instruction to support children's learning. For example, some families direct the child's attention, model and instruct, help the child perform, and provide feedback. Others prefer less hands-on methods. These families might model, but may not directly engage the child by getting his or her attention first and explaining exactly how to do a task.

What is taught to children involves cultural values of families, too. For example, some cultures like to show affection more than other cultures. In "teaching" pretend play, families in group-oriented cultures will show more affection (hugs and kisses) to dolls than families in individual-oriented cultures. (Review Figure 3.6 to see other ways in which group-oriented and individual-oriented cultures see families differently.)

Lesson 12.1 Review and Assessment 

1. Explain why toddlerhood is a biologically-primed time for learning.
2. What intellectual advance is responsible for toddlers engaging in pretend play and eventually developing creativity?
3. According to Piaget's developmental stages, contrast how problem solving is achieved by younger and older toddlers.
4. In substage 5, what are the three characteristics of toddlers' learning?
5. Describe the three characteristics of thinking used during substage 6.
6. Define and give an example of *collective symbolism*.
7. **Critical thinking.** Brainstorm scaffolding techniques that are used to help toddlers learn in your culture.

Investigate Special Topics: Successfully Scaffold Toddlers' Learning

To successfully scaffold the toddler's learning, "teachers" need to first recognize the child's ZPD. Ways to recognize a toddler's ZPD include

- noting the toddler's explorations and interests
- observing the toddler's goals
- watching the toddler's body language and vocal cues for signs of pleasure or frustration during play
- recognizing the toddler's learning style, such as a preference for visual things

Once the ZPD is determined, the adult is ready to scaffold the toddler's learning. Some possible ways to support learning within the child's ZPD include

- watching and showing interest in toddler's play through eye contact, smiles, and a few words
- changing the level of toy difficulty as needed
- showing pride in a toddler's new skill
- introducing novelty into an activity if the toddler appears uninvolved
- demonstrating the use of a toy, but not interrupting a toddler's use of a toy in a different way than usual, as long as it is safe
- offering help when the toddler is struggling to solve a problem, such as sorting toys
- showing pride in a toddler's new skill
- reacting with patience to a toddler's frustration

Application Activity

In groups, imagine you are teachers at a local child care center. The toddlers in your center vary widely in skill level and ZPD. Brainstorm ways your group can scaffold learning for the multiple skill levels and ZPDs in your center. Share your ideas with the class.

What Toddlers Learn

Lesson 12.2

Objectives

After studying this lesson, you will be able to:

- identify the major areas of concept learning for toddlers and describe one skill a toddler might learn in each area.
- give examples of two common types of articulation errors heard in toddler speech.
- identify two factors that influence vocabulary development.
- explain the sequence of grammar development in toddlers.
- describe three factors affecting the language development of toddlers.
- identify intellectual developmental milestones toddlers might achieve.

Key Terms

articulation
bilingual
grammar
monolingual

Academic Terms

attributes
intrinsic
phonics
refined
trajectories

Reading and Writing Activity

After reading each section, stop and write a three- to four-sentence summary of what you just read. Be sure to paraphrase and use your own words. Once you have finished reading this lesson, compare your summaries with a partner's summaries. Compare how they are similar and how they are different.

Graphic Organizer

As you read this lesson, use a tree diagram like the one shown to organize what toddlers should learn. Write *What Toddlers Should Learn* in the top circle and write major categories and then specific concepts and notes in the circles below.

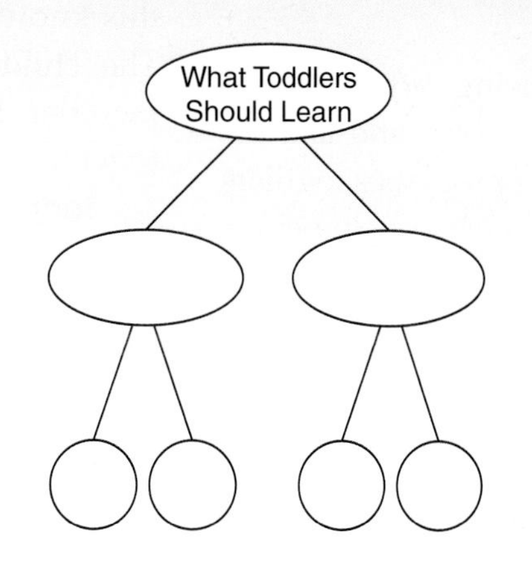

During the toddler years, concepts become more complex and abstract, as seen through pretense and language. These concepts pave the way for what toddlers learn. Younger toddlers (12 to 18 months of age) work toward a goal, imitate others, and develop their understanding of object permanence. As ways of thinking about objects and people in the environment mature, older toddlers (18 to 36 months of age) further their comprehension of physics and the world around them. They learn to identify details of objects and solve problems. They begin to understand symbols and the language system and successfully communicate with others.

Figure 12.5 Young toddlers begin to distinguish between size and color differences in objects. *What size and color differences is this toddler observing?*

Concept Learning

Concepts infants start learning during infancy, such as object permanence, spatial relationships, and cause and effect, mature and become more **refined** (sophisticated; fine-tuned) during toddlerhood. It will be many more years, however, before these concepts are fully mature. The major areas of concept learning for toddlers include the following:

- distinguishing **attributes** (properties) of objects
- noting cause and effect
- using spatial relationships
- solving problems
- understanding quantity
- using symbols

Distinguishing Attributes of Objects

For young toddlers, noticing attributes of objects, such as their shape, size, color, and texture, is just beginning. Usually the first properties toddlers notice are major color and size differences in objects (**Figure 12.5**). Attributes become more important for creating mental images, especially as thought processes begin to form in older toddlers. For example, a toddler might often refer to attributes when talking about objects, such as a *red* ball or a *big* dog.

Toddlers often know the attributes of new objects based on prior experiences. They then use this knowledge in play. For example, suppose a child has already been exposed to the loud noise made by hitting metal objects and the lack of noise made by dropping soft objects. He or she will use this knowledge when given new objects for play. The child might immediately bang metal pans together, but would not bang two balls of yarn together. This is a very valuable thinking skill.

Toddlers also begin to perceive differences in attributes. Noting these differences is a thinking skill because it requires comparison. This skill is needed to identify objects. For example, toddlers can distinguish between similar animals, such as ducks and geese, and between closely-related colors, such as red and pink. Toddlers mentally compare differences before they know the terms for objects. Although toddlers sometimes use the wrong word for an attribute, they do note the differences among objects. Seeing differences enables toddlers to sort information by attributes and to later classify objects.

Noting Cause and Effect

Young toddlers learn by throwing, rolling, shaking, or moving objects. Toddlers learn that round objects roll and flat objects slide. They also learn that hard objects will make a loud noise when hit together, but soft objects will not. For the most part, young toddlers are learning physical knowledge concepts rather than the more advanced logical thinking skill—cause and effect.

Older toddlers, however, test their actions by repeating and varying them. For example, they may throw objects in different ways and note their **trajectories** (paths objects take). They hear the noise when the object lands and see what happens to the object upon landing (rolls, breaks). They can use different objects to hit pots and pans. While doing this, they may note different sounds caused by where the pan is hit, the type of object used to hit the pan, or the strength of the hit. Once older toddlers see the relationship between an action and the observable results, they are noting cause and effect (**Figure 12.6**).

Using Spatial Relationships

Toddlers learn about spatial relationships as they play. For example, toddlers learn how objects fit together as they nest containers and fit pieces into a puzzle board or shapes into a shape sorter. Toddlers also learn about spatial relationships as they move through spaces. For example, toddlers may crawl under or jump over objects in a simple obstacle course.

To test toddlers' abilities to mentally map space, an experimenter set up a small room with one piece of furniture on each wall. A toddler was brought into the room and given commands to walk to different pieces of furniture. Once the toddler was familiar with the setup, the toddler was taken out of the room. The furniture was rotated 90 degrees, but kept in the same angular relationships. The toddler was then blindfolded and brought back into the room. Commands were once again given. Toddlers who were tested remembered the relationship of each piece of furniture to another. They had created a mental spatial map, which enabled them to walk through the room with ease.

Solving Problems

Toddlers solve their problems the best way they know how, which is by trial and error or by thinking through what solution will work. To problem-solve, toddlers combine actions and even use objects as tools to reach a goal. Because their understanding of cause and effect is somewhat limited, they do not think about the consequences of their actions. For example, to reach a piece of fruit on the kitchen table, a toddler may pull on the tablecloth until the fruit falls (along with other items on the table).

Understanding Quantity

By the toddler years, number words are a major part of language. Toddlers pick up on these words and use them, but often incorrectly. For example, "two" may mean any quantity greater than "one." Older toddlers often count by rote (memory), but

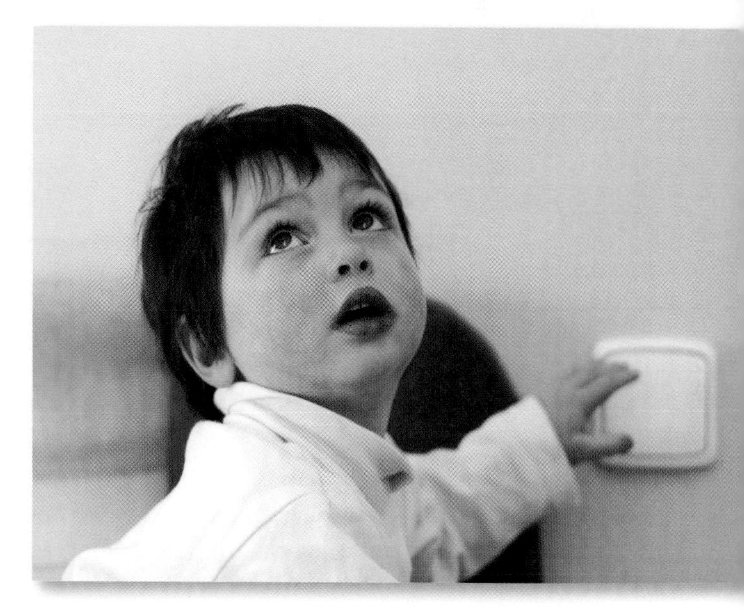

Figure 12.6 Toddlers who can associate their actions with results begin to comprehend cause and effect. *What are some activities caregivers can do with toddlers to demonstrate cause and effect?*

many toddlers do not understand the quantity associated with each number.

Quantity concepts are much more difficult to grasp than noting the attributes of objects. Color, for example, is often **intrinsic** (naturally occurring trait) in a specific object. Numbers, however, are not inherent in an object. The number two, for example, only exists when combining a second object with a previous one. The combining of numbers is an intellectual act. What happens when a toddler counts two objects in reverse order? (The object called "two" is now "one" and vice versa.)

Using Symbols

Through pretend play, toddlers begin to use symbols (**Figure 12.7**). For infants and very young toddlers, a doll is an object. The doll is shaken, sucked on, thrown, dropped, and carried by its arm or leg or even by its hair. With the beginning of pretend play, however, toddlers think of the doll as a baby needing to be fed, rocked, and put to bed—and never treated as an object. Pretend play that begins in the toddler years is usually done alone.

Figure 12.7 Pretend play involves the use of *symbols*, usually objects that can be associated with actions or features. *How do you think toddlers begin to learn what actions and features are associated with certain objects?*

Besides using objects in pretense and seeing pictures in books and drawings as symbols (not the real things), toddlers also begin to understand the complex system of letters, words, and numbers as symbols. These symbols are used as labels for people, objects, and ideas. Unlike other symbol systems, words do not sound or look like the people or objects they represent. Thus, *language* is the most abstract symbol system used by toddlers.

To learn language, children use two thinking skills. First, they must associate the word with the person or object to which it refers. Second, children must recall the word and its meaning when they hear the word or want to say it. Language requires high-level thinking skills.

Communicating

Spoken language develops at a faster rate between one and three years of age than at any other time in a person's life. Learning to talk takes time and effort, however, because speaking involves learning the sounds and meanings of words.

Learning to Articulate

Articulation refers to a person's ability to pronounce words that can be understood by others. If a child is to be **bilingual** (fluent in two languages), infancy is the best time to learn the **phonics** (sounds of letters and syllables) of both languages. Learning to control the tongue, lip muscles, and vocal chords to articulate the words of any language, however, takes practice. Toddlers do not pronounce sounds accurately each time. In fact, most toddlers have some problems making all the sounds in their spoken language.

Toddlers who cannot make one sound often substitute another. For example, they may use a *d* sound for a *th* sound, such as *dat* for *that*. Sometimes children can articulate the correct sound in one

Focus on

Careers

Speech-Language Pathologist

Speech-language pathologists assess, diagnose, and treat disorders related to speech, language, cognitive-communication, voice, swallowing, and fluency. Many work with children who cannot produce speech sounds or cannot produce them clearly; those with speech rhythm and fluency problems, such as stuttering; and those with voice disorders.

Career cluster: Health science.

Education: Educational requirements include a master's degree and clinical experience. Licensure is also required.

Job outlook: Future employment opportunities for speech-language pathologists are expected to grow faster than the average for all occupations.

To learn more about a career as a speech-language pathologist, visit the United States Department of Labor's *Occupational Outlook Handbook* website. You will also be able to compare the job responsibilities, educational requirements, job outlook, and average pay of speech-language pathologists with similar occupations.

place in a word, but not in another. For example, a toddler may pronounce the *m* sound correctly at the beginning of a word, such as *milk*. The same toddler may have trouble, however, making the *m* sound in the middle of a word, such as *hammer*, or at the end of a word, such as *broom*.

Toddlers may also change the sound order of a word, such as saying *perslip* to mean *slipper*. They may even change an entire word, such as saying *book* to mean *bird*. Sometimes toddlers will drop a sound they cannot pronounce. For example, they may say *seepy* instead of *sleepy*.

Few children articulate sounds correctly from the beginning, but tend to correct themselves over time. Pronouncing words correctly, even if the toddler's way of saying words sounds cute, sets a good example for children to follow. In time, children will learn from listening. Having children repeat a word again and again is not a recommended way to correct pronunciation because it may cause the child stress.

Learning Word Meanings

Learning the meanings of words is difficult. To do so, children must link certain features with a name. Older toddlers learn meanings better if parents show or point to what is being talked about or taught. Still, learning meanings is difficult because many objects with different names share some common features. For example, both dogs and ponies have four legs and run outside. Sometimes children confuse the meanings of words they hear. They may use a wrong name for an object, such as call a cow, *moo*, or a stove, *hot*. Without meanings attached to spoken sounds, there would be no language. These meanings give children two new tools—communication and a new way to think.

Communication is the skill needed to understand others and be understood by them. Already, toddlers can understand many words and sentences. When they begin to talk, they want to be understood. Toddlers often use their communication for three reasons (**Figure 12.8**). All children communicate to achieve goals. Some toddlers primarily communicate to learn names that refer to people, places, and objects (nouns), explain actions (verbs), and describe nouns and verbs (adjectives and adverbs) to talk about their world. These toddlers' speech is referred to as *referential*. On the other hand, other toddlers primarily communicate with affective words (hug, kiss) to create social bonds with others.

Figure 12.8 Communication as a Tool

Reasons to Communicate	Examples of Communication
To achieve a goal	"Want cookie." (I want a cookie.) "Go bye-bye." (I want to ride in the car.) "No!" (I don't want _____.)
To identify an object	"See doggie." (I see a dog.) "Big!" (That is big.) "What dat?" (What is that?)
To create a bond with another person	"Mommy?" (Where are you mommy? I want you.) "Kiss." (I love you.) "Hurt." (Please help me.)

These toddlers' speech is referred to as *expressive*. Although all toddlers use both types of vocabulary, most toddlers tend to use either more referential or expressive words in their spoken vocabulary.

Language is part of the thinking process. In other words, people learn to think in words. As children learn to talk, words go with actions. For example, toddlers will learn to say *goodbye* while waving. Later, children talk aloud to themselves as they play or lie in bed. They then often whisper words. Finally, they can just think with words, but without saying them aloud.

As children learn language, they develop both vocabulary and grammar. They attach meanings to words and to the order of words. This process, however, is gradual.

Vocabulary

Most children's vocabularies grow slowly until they are 18 to 24 months of age. The fastest growth occurs around 30 months of age. Toddlers vary in the number of words their vocabularies include at different ages. Variances in vocabulary occur for the following reasons:

- ***Differences in environmental influences.*** How many words a child understands or speaks is related to the quality of interactions the toddler has with parents and caregivers. Parents who are talkative and use higher levels of vocabulary and sentence structure are providing quality learning experiences for their toddlers. Studies show that by 20 months of age, toddlers of talkative caregivers know more words than toddlers of less talkative caregivers. By 24 months of age, the gap doubles in favor of toddlers with talkative caregivers.
- ***Bilingualism.*** Bilingual toddlers divide their vocabulary evenly across two languages. For each language, their vocabulary is about half as large as the **monolingual** (speakers of one language) child's vocabulary. This difference disappears by the preschool years and is not considered a developmental delay.
- ***Word usage.*** Vocabulary count can also depend on whether all spoken words are counted or only those used correctly are counted as part of the vocabulary.
- ***Frequency of word usage.*** Toddlers may use words for a while, drop them, and pick them up again months later.

The size of the vocabulary is easier to measure in children three years of age and older than in younger children. Vocabulary by three years has a major impact on school achievement.

Toddlers use words that represent the actions they see and the people and objects they know (**Figure 12.9**). Thus, toddlers learn different types of words in a certain order. First words are usually

Figure 12.9 Toddlers learn words that represent the objects and actions they witness each day. A toddler who plays with her dog might learn the word *dog* sooner than she learns the word *cat*. *What were your first words? How, if at all, do you think they are representative of the objects and actions you witnessed as a young child?*

nouns and simple action verbs. Nouns may include words such as *mama*, *daddy*, and *kitty*. Action verbs may include *run* and *fly*. Next, toddlers learn descriptive words (adjectives and adverbs), such as *big*, *hot*, *pretty*, *loud*, *quickly*, and *slowly*. Young children quickly learn words for human interactions, such as *hi* and *bye*, and words for love and affection, too, such as *hug*.

Cultural differences also affect the words children learn. Toddlers learn the words from their parents' career area and interests or hobbies. Toddlers from individual-oriented cultures tend to have vocabularies with more referential than expressive words. On the other hand, toddlers raised in group-oriented cultures have vocabularies with more expressive than referential words.

Grammar

Grammar is the study of word usage and order in a given language. Each language has grammar rules. Children begin to learn these rules during toddlerhood. This learning process begins with single-word "sentences" and often progresses to simple sentences of a few words during the toddler years. Within six months of saying their first words, toddlers usually begin to put words together. Combining words is an advanced skill because word order affects the meanings of sentences.

By listening to adults and having good books read to them, toddlers learn the basic rules for the language they hear (**Figure 12.10**). They then apply these rules to their own phrases and sentences. If children are going to be bilingual, toddlerhood is the best time for learning the grammar of both languages.

Grammar knowledge develops in stages. First, toddlers learn single-word sentences. From 12 to 18 months of age, toddlers use sentences of only one word. This single word is often used by the toddler to mean different ideas at different times. For example, a child may say *bye-bye* both to identify a moving object (a car) and to make a request ("Let's go!"). To understand these meanings, the caregiver must note how the child says the word, what gestures he or she uses, and what is happening at the time.

After 19 months, many children begin combining two or more words to form multi-word sentences. At the early stage of combining words, toddlers use only the most necessary words. By 24 to 30 months, many toddlers begin using three or more words in their sentences. When the child begins to use these multi-word sentences, the added words fill in the gaps of former simple sentences. For example, "Gone milk" becomes "Milk is gone." By the time the child uses three-word sentences, word order

Figure 12.10 Toddlers learn grammar by listening to others' speech and by being read to from books. Hearing correct grammar will encourage a toddler to use correct grammar. *To what extent do you think adults' communication is affected by what they read and hear?*

is often used correctly. The child may say, "Bird is flying," instead of saying, "Fly bird."

Different Rates of Learning to Talk

The rate at which toddlers learn to talk can vary by several months. Many adults worry about a slow talker, only to see the toddler become a non-stop talker a few months later. These toddlers are hearing sounds and learning meanings all along. When they begin to talk, they progress quickly.

A number of factors can affect language development. Learning to talk depends on the following factors:

- ***Hearing.*** A child must hear human speech clearly to learn to talk without special training. Even ear infections can delay speech in toddlers.
- ***Interest.*** Some active toddlers are more interested in motor skills than in talking. Within a few months, they often catch up to earlier talkers.
- ***Intellectual abilities.*** Because language is so closely related to thinking, a child with an intellectual disability is often slower to talk. On the other hand, the ability to talk early does not mean that a child has above average intellectual abilities. Children of average and even below average intellectual abilities may talk at a young age simply by repeating what they hear.
- ***Gender.*** From the first year of life, girls tend to excel in verbal skills more than boys. Researchers do not know whether this is due to heredity or the environment. (For example, adults may talk more often to girls than to boys.)
- ***Need for speech.*** Some children get what they need without saying anything. For example, if a toddler receives milk by pointing, holding a cup, or crying, there is no need for the child to learn to say, "I want milk."
- ***Stimulating environment.*** Just as adults have more to say when they have new experiences, so do toddlers (**Figure 12.11**).
- ***Bilingualism.*** Bilingual toddlers spread their learning of language across two languages. Unless other factors are involved, bilingual toddlers appear delayed, but are not.
- ***Autism.*** *Autism* (a developmental disorder) affects language. Language delays or losses are often early signs of autism. (Autism is discussed in more detail later in this text.)

Figure 12.11 Stimulating, new experiences encourage toddlers to learn and use new words. *What do you think are some stimulating experiences that might improve a toddler's vocabulary?*

In some cases, the rate of language development may lag far behind the norms. In these situations, children need professional help. Each child needs the best opportunity to develop language because language is essential to healthy intellectual and social-emotional development.

Intellectual Developmental Milestones

As toddlers explore and learn, they continue to achieve intellectual milestones. Pinpointing when toddlers learn a certain concept, however, becomes more difficult as the age of reaching milestones begins to vary among children. Because the exact timing of achievements varies, intellectual developmental milestones in toddlerhood are grouped by months (**Figure 12.12**). Being aware of these developmental tasks and age groups can help parents and caregivers create a stimulating environment for toddlers to help meet their intellectual needs.

Lesson 12.2 Review and Assessment

1. List three major areas of concept learning for toddlers and give an example of a skill in each.
2. Describe what the term *articulation* means.
3. Explain why learning word meanings is difficult for toddlers.
4. Summarize the four factors that influence vocabulary development.
5. Describe the sequence of grammar development in toddlers.
6. What are four reasons children may be late talkers?
7. Based on the intellectual milestones that children might achieve in the first year, describe the intellectual level of a typical 17-month-old.
8. **Critical thinking.** How might cultural factors delay or speed up language development in toddlers?

Figure 12.12 Toddler Intellectual Milestones

12 to 18 months

- Varies actions on objects to receive many results.
- Notices attributes of objects.
- Uses physical trial and error to solve problems.
- Imitates others—coughing, sneezing, and making animal sounds.
- Looks for hidden objects in last place seen (almost mature object permanence).
- Points and vocalizes wants.
- Points to named objects and animals in books.
- Says 3 words (12 months) to 15 or more words (17 months).
- Gestures when talking.
- Uses one-word "sentences."

18 to 24 months

- Thinks how to solve some problems without using physical actions.
- Solves simple problems requiring two or three steps.
- Begins deferred imitation.
- Hunts objects in all possible places (mature object permanence).
- Pictures objects mentally.
- Realizes words have referential meaning.
- Says about 200 words.
- Uses two- and three-word sentences.
- Enjoys "singing" a few songs.
- Understands questions, such as "Can you show me your eyes?"
- Names pictures in a book.
- Repeats actions of others (20 to 21 months).

24 to 36 months

- Involves others in play activities.
- Begins to use a few symbols in pretend play, such as a doll for a baby.
- Has many jumbled ideas (preconcepts).
- Says up to 500 words.
- Uses three- or more-word sentences.
- Laughs at silly labels ("Cow goes quack, quack").
- Enjoys some books over and over.
- Repeats a few rhymes.
- Asks for information ("Why?" "What's dat?").

Meeting Toddlers' Intellectual Needs

Lesson 12.3

Objectives

After studying this lesson, you will be able to:

- plan activities and toys for stimulating motor, sensory, and basic concept comprehension for toddlers.
- explain how to stimulate symbolic learning in the toddler.
- list and describe three ways to help toddlers develop emerging language skills.
- evaluate electronic media activities currently available for older toddlers to determine their educational value.

Key Terms

closed-ended questions
intonation
open-ended questions

Academic Terms

onomatopoeic
vicarious

Reading and Writing Activity

While reading this lesson, place sticky notes next to sections that interest you or next to sections where you have questions. Write your questions or comments on the sticky notes. After reading, find a partner and share your questions and comments. If there are any questions that the two of you cannot answer together, then ask your teacher.

Graphic Organizer

In a chart like the one shown, write the main headings present in this lesson. As you read, take notes and organize them by heading. Draw a star beside any words or concepts you do not yet understand.

Motor Activities	Symbolic Learning Activities
Sensory Stimulation Activities	Language Activities
Basic Concept Activities	Electronic Media Activities

Adults can use everyday activities to help meet toddlers' intellectual needs. For example, bathing and dressing provide the means for encouraging perceptual learning, good hygiene practices, and language and motor development. Helping with household tasks allows toddlers to develop spatial concepts as they put items in drawers or laundry in a basket. Vocabulary increases as toddlers learn the names of common objects found in the home and yard. Science becomes a part of everyday life as toddlers see how the vacuum cleaner picks up dirt, how air dries clothes, and how heat makes dough change into cookies.

Toddlers learn as they play in a safe environment with many objects to explore. Play enables toddlers to check and recheck concepts. Adults may play with toddlers sometimes. For the most part, however, adults should allow toddlers to play by themselves, and step in only when toddlers need help (Vygotsky's principle) or show a desire for adult participation. For example, a parent or caregiver may show the toddler how to put a piece in a puzzle or introduce new play ideas to enrich toddlers' learning experiences.

Motor Activities

During the toddler years, children develop both gross- and fine-motor skills quickly. Because toddlers are often on-the-go, they need few planned motor activities. As children run, climb, jump, and crawl, they are developing their gross-motor skills. Any activities that require the use of the small muscles help children develop their fine-motor skills.

Many fine-motor activities children perform aid other areas of learning. For example, drawing a picture, which requires the ability to grasp a writing tool, also aids symbol making and creativity. Building block towers, playing with shape sorters and puzzles, and stacking and nesting objects teach toddlers spatial concepts and physical

Focus on

Science

Using the Senses to Make Observations

Through the use of their senses, toddlers can learn about the world around them. They learn to distinguish sounds, identify smells, recognize sights, and remember the texture of an object. These lessons occur at a critical time of brain development. During the toddler years, a child's brain grows rapidly, and once the toddler years end, pruning of seldom used or unused brain connections increases. While toddlers learn many lessons through their own encounters with their environment, sensory stimulation activities can enrich what toddlers learn.

By providing opportunities for toddlers to use their senses, adults can encourage sensory learning. As toddlers play games, adults can teach them about their senses by talking through activities. For example, when a caregiver notices a toddler hears a sound, the caregiver might stop briefly and listen. Then, the caregiver can point in the direction of the sound and say, "I hear a _____. Do you hear it, too?" This helps stimulate the toddler's sense of hearing. As another activity, caregivers can sniff loudly and tell toddlers what they smell. Later, they can ask the toddler, "What's cooking? What smells so good?" Caregivers can talk about a variety of odors. Flowers, an outdoor barbecue, and the rain all have distinct smells.

In small groups, brainstorm sensory stimulation activities for each of the major senses. Review the information you have already learned about toddlers' brain development and then discuss why sensory stimulation is vital to children during the toddler years.

knowledge. **Figure 12.13** lists common gross- and fine-motor activities that can help toddlers improve their skills.

Sensory Stimulation Activities

Through the senses, toddlers can learn about the qualities (also called *properties* or *attributes*) of objects. Through sight, for example, toddlers can learn about an object's color and size. Touch teaches toddlers whether objects are rough, smooth, hard, or soft. Through listening, toddlers learn the sounds of language. Taste teaches about different flavors, such as sweet, sour, salty, and bitter. Scent lets toddlers recognize familiar aromas in foods. Using the senses helps toddlers form concepts about objects.

When with toddlers, adults can name attributes of nearby objects, such as color and shape names, to help toddlers learn. Toddlers can do some sorting

Figure 12.13 Gross- and Fine-Motor Activities

Gross-motor activities

- Walk in different directions (sideways, backward)
- Spin around and whirl
- Roll and toss objects (beanbags and soft balls)
- Use push and pull toys
- Climb using low steps and couch cushions
- Jump on mats or pillows with adult guidance
- Build with large, hollow blocks
- Crawl through tunnels
- Play with sand and water
- Slide down a child-size slide
- Use push and pedal riding toys
- Run outdoors

Fine-motor activities

- Assemble and take apart items, such as pop beads and Legos®
- Poke holes in soft objects
- Use a hammer and peg set or beat a drum
- Use Play-Doh® and finger paints
- Build a tower with blocks
- Use a shape sorter
- Complete a simple jigsaw puzzle
- Stack and nest objects
- Turn pages in books
- Cut paper with child safety scissors
- Draw with thick crayons
- Play with felt and stickers

by attributes, such as putting all the farm animals in a picture-labeled basket or on a picture-labeled shelf. Toddlers enjoy matching socks by color or matching flatware in a drawer. Commercial materials are also available for sorting by color, shape, and size. Self-guided, hands-on play activities are excellent for sensory learning.

Basic Concept Activities

Basic concept activities encourage toddlers to try out their ideas (**Figure 12.14**). During the toddler years, many concept activities involve gross- and fine-motor skills. This is because toddlers, especially young toddlers, are still learning through physical trial and error. Therefore, toys for toddlers need to be simple to use. For example, simple puzzles for young toddlers often include only a few pieces, and each piece shows an entire picture of an object. A knob on each puzzle piece aids fine-motor control. As older toddlers begin to think through problems, puzzles with a few more pieces may be more appropriate.

Symbolic Learning Activities

Toddlers 12 to 18 months of age use toys in the ways they are intended, such as using blocks for stacking and balls for throwing. Around 18 months, however, toddlers may engage in some symbolic play. By two years of age, more extended pretend play begins, which leads to the rich imaginary play seen in the preschool years.

Following are some suggestions for ways adults can encourage toddlers' symbolic play:

- Provide the toddler with toys that have a realistic purpose, such as a doll to represent a baby, when the toddler first begins symbolic play. Toy cars, trucks, planes, trains, animal figures, and stuffed animals are also good choices.
- Initiate pretend play, when the toddler is ready to include others, by asking to taste the "soup" or the "taco" or to "kiss" the stuffed toy or doll.

Figure 12.14 Basic Concept Activities

- ***Opening lids.*** Place a small object in a container with a snap-on lid and then show the toddler how to open and close the lid. Then, let the toddler try to open and close the lid. When the toddler masters one type of lid, try another type, such as a screw-on lid. Do *not* use containers with safety caps.
- ***Nesting and stacking.*** Give the toddler two or three objects for nesting and stacking or rings for sequencing. Add other objects or rings as the toddler masters the game. If there is very little difference in the size of the objects, the task becomes much more difficult and may be more appropriate for children who are a little older.
- ***Where Am I?*** Hide from a toddler who is involved in another activity. Call the toddler's name and have him or her look for you. Praise the toddler for finding you. Of course, do not hide behind locked doors or other places where the toddler cannot look for you.
- ***Rolling cars.*** Place toy cars on a flat board on the floor. (You may use chair cushions, sturdy cardboard lids, or trays as a board.) Point out to the toddler that the cars are not moving. Then, raise one end of the board and say, "Look at the cars go." After the toddler plays with the cars in this way many times, ask, "Can you make the cars go down the board fast (slow)?" See if the toddler increases (decreases) the slope of the board.
- ***Through the tunnel.*** Show the toddler how to roll objects through a cardboard tube so the toddler learns how objects can go in one open end and come out the other end. After much play, some toddlers may learn to vary the slope of the tube to control the speed of the object's roll.

- Play along when the toddler initiates ideas to include others in the pretend play. Allow the child to take the lead, but extend the play if it seems appropriate. For example, if the toddler stirs a pot for a long time, suggest pouring the "soup" into the bowls.
- Do not interrupt a toddler who is talking aloud while playing. At this point, the toddler is in his or her own world of play and language.
- Include play animals and objects during story time. Finger puppets are also good in creating an imaginary world.
- Encourage the toddler to make sounds to represent animals and machines in his or her world. Read books with **onomatopoeic** (ahn-uh-mat-uh-PEE-ik) words, or words that imitate sounds, such as *pop*, *fizz*, and *buzz*, and ask the toddler to make these sounds.
- Encourage the toddler to "read" a book he or she enjoys to a favorite doll or teddy bear.
- Initiate a couple of pretend ideas when the toddler enters the second level of pretense and is ready to use one object to represent another object (*collective symbolism*). For example, ideas may include using a block for a car, a series of blocks for a train, a large box for a house, or a small container for a hat. Once the possibility is seen, toddlers come up with their own ideas (**Figure 12.15**).

Language Activities

The toddler's active world needs a background of language. Talking with the toddler during games and daily routines and describing the actions being performed can enhance the toddler's use of language and conceptual development. Reading books and singing songs can promote language learning, too.

Talking with Toddlers

Adults can begin talking with the toddler in a conversational manner even before the child can respond verbally. For example, while preparing lunch, the adult might say, "Aren't you hungry?"

Figure 12.15 Using boxes to represent cars, houses, or other objects can encourage pretend play in toddlers. *What are some stimulating pretend play activities that can be done with boxes?*

and then pause briefly as though the child will answer. Then, the adult might respond to the child's imagined *yes* answer by saying, "Surely you are. Lunch smells good, doesn't it?"

Some general suggestions for talking experiences with toddlers include the following:

- Talk *with* not *at* the toddler and respond to the toddler's vocalizations.
- Name and describe objects, experiences, and the child's feelings.
- Discuss past experiences in rich and interesting detail with an older toddler, which help to create better memories in the toddler.
- Ask **open-ended questions** (questions that require a descriptive response for an answer) to aid conversation. Questions that only require a one- or two-word response, **closed-ended questions**, can limit conversation. For example, saying, "Did you like the zoo?" is a closed-ended question. Asking "What did you see at the zoo?" is more open-ended.
- Add descriptive words and sentences to the toddler's "talk." For example, if the toddler says, "ball," the adult might say, "Yes, the ball rolls and bounces."
- Use clear and simple speech and all types of sentences when talking with the toddler. Using statements, questions, and exclamations helps the toddler hear **intonation**, or the rise and fall of a person's voice while speaking.
- Make different sounds that go with toys, such as *rrr* for a siren, to help the toddler learn to make sounds.
- Match sentences to the child's level and pronounce words correctly. Explain new words using words the child already knows. Slightly challenging children helps their development. (This is Vygotsky's principle of using the child's ZPD.)

Adults are language models for toddlers. Children learn and repeat words they hear others say, including words or phrases that adults do not want children to use. If a toddler repeats unsuitable words, adults might correct the child by saying, "These are not words we use here (at home, at school)." By modeling correct language, adults can teach toddlers new words and correct toddlers' language errors. In each of the modeling examples in **Figure 12.16**, the adult does not point out the child's language error, but rather guides by expanding the toddler's sentence. Toddlers (and even older children) often feel defeated when adults only correct errors.

Reading with Toddlers

Reading books and saying poems and rhymes are activities adults can do with toddlers to help them develop language and literacy skills. Typically, toddlers will not sit still and look at books for a

Figure 12.16 Examples of Ways to Model Language to Toddlers

Purpose for Modeling Language	Example
To correct pronunciation	Toddler—"My wed (red) sooes (shoes)." Adult—"Yes, these are your pretty red shoes."
To correct grammar	Toddler—"I singed a song." Adult—"You sang a song about a rainy day."
To introduce a new word	Toddler—"See the plane go." Adult—"The plane flies fast."
To correct the meaning of a word	Toddler—"See the smoke." Adult—"It does look like smoke." Sniff loudly. "It doesn't smell like smoke though. We see fog. Fog is a cloud near the ground. Can you say *fog*?"

long time. Young toddlers may enjoy glancing at a page and turning it. Using the motor skill of turning the page is often more fun for the toddler than looking at the pictures. Later, toddlers spend more time looking at the pictures, but they still may not want to hear the story. When choosing books for toddlers, look for books that

- are made of cloth, vinyl, and heavy cardboard with a plastic coating. These books are durable, sturdy, and washable.
- have pages that are easy for the toddler to turn and keep open.
- include colorful and simple pictures.
- contain story lines that focus on the toddler's favorite subjects, which may include animals, toys, fun places to visit, cars and trucks, or home and family. Whenever possible, link the book to events that occur in the toddler's real world. For example, if the toddler goes to the zoo, read a book about a zoo shortly thereafter. Talk with the toddler about the similarities between the book and the toddler's trip to the zoo.

To engage young toddlers in reading books, the adult can name and point to one object on the page. Then, the adult can ask the toddler to point to the object. As language develops, toddlers can name objects in the pictures and even make some sounds of animals or other objects. By two years of age, toddlers often enjoy hearing a whole story that contains only a short sentence or two for each picture page (**Figure 12.17**).

Many older toddlers (and even preschool children) insist on hearing the same story over and over. They often request the same story at bedtime. Routines, including favorite, repeated stories, help the toddler feel secure. The child knows what will happen in the story's beginning, middle, and end. Sometimes children will insist that not even a word be changed. The loving adult who reads daily to a child is likely to make the child feel more secure than the story itself.

Singing with Toddlers

Singing songs in which toddlers act out the meanings of words is a good way to help toddlers learn language. An example of an action song is

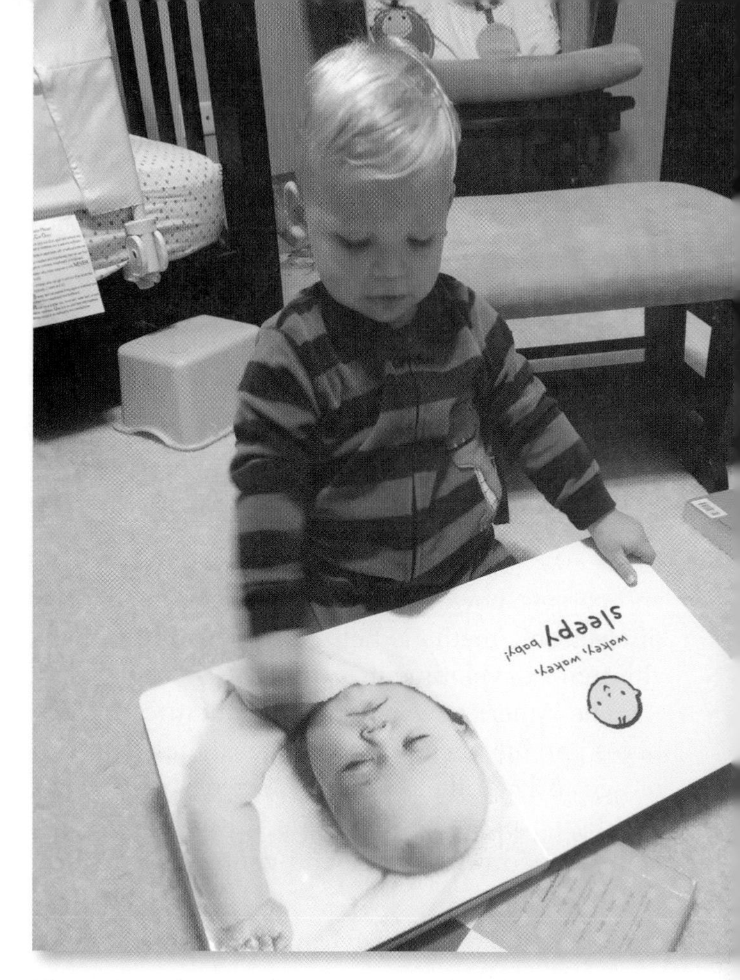

Figure 12.17 Young children's books are called *picture books* because pictures, rather than words, carry the story. Some picture books do not even have words. *What children's books did you enjoy as a child? Why?*

"Here We Go 'Round the Mulberry Bush." While singing this song, toddlers get to act out lines such as, "This is the way we eat our soup," and "This is the way we wash our hands." Toddlers can sing and act out many other verses, too. Adults and children can even make up new lyrics to fit almost any activity by using this so-called mileage tune. Other common mileage tunes children enjoy are "Do You Know the Muffin Man?"; "Twinkle, Twinkle Little Star"; and "London Bridge Is Falling Down." (**Figure 12.18** shows other language games that are fun and encourage children to use language.)

Electronic Media Activities

In today's world, children live in a media-rich environment. Companies specifically design television programs, videos, and interactive games for young children. Many child development experts

Figure 12.18 Language Games for Toddlers

- ***Show Me.*** Young toddlers enjoy running around and pointing to objects. When an adult names objects for the toddler to touch, the toddler's language skills improve. Make statements such as, "Show me the door." As the toddler touches the door, praise him or her with a statement such as, "You're right. That's the door."
- ***Follow Directions.*** Give the toddler simple directions using familiar objects. For example, say, "Bring me the ball." Praise the toddler for following directions promptly. You may also play the game, "Follow the Leader." Give simple directions such as, "clap your hands" or "pat your head."
- ***Telephones.*** Listening to voices on a phone and talking into a phone can help language develop. Toddlers enjoy play phones. Talking on a real phone with adult supervision is also a good language practice.

and parents, however, question whether the impact of electronic media is helpful or harmful to their children's development.

The American Academy of Pediatrics (AAP) urges parents of children younger than two years of age to keep their children "screen-free." Why are digital mediums not good learning tools for children two years of age and younger? Consider the following:

- Media content is **vicarious** (experienced through another person or object). This means the toddler watches images instead of experiencing objects in real life. Because toddlers are still learning about objects, they may not be able to make the connection from images on the screen to objects in real life.
- Toddlers are still holistic learners, but the majority of children's media content is "bits and pieces learning," such as drills on shapes, colors, and letters. Young toddlers are not yet at this stage of learning.
- Around 30 months, toddlers' brains are laying the foundation for many skills requiring effort. Media tends to be a very passive way to learn. Children who watch television as toddlers have more learning problems in school.

For children between two and three years of age, child development experts recommend limiting screen time to no more than two hours per day. When choosing electronic media activities for older toddlers, consider the educational value of the materials. Carefully selected television programs, videos, and interactive games can be interesting and may have a positive impact on children's learning. Through content-rich media interactions, older toddlers can begin to learn socially acceptable behaviors, and math, language, and science concepts. Electronic media usage is best with adult supervision and when an adult describes a program's activities with the toddler.

Lesson 12.3 Review and Assessment 

1. Give an example of a motor activity, a sensory stimulation activity, and a basic concept activity for toddlers.
2. Summarize four ways that caregivers can encourage symbolic learning in toddlers.
3. Describe three ways that caregivers can help toddlers develop language skills.
4. What are two ways caregivers can enhance talking experiences with toddlers?
5. List two considerations caregivers should take into account when choosing books for toddlers.
6. Explain why the AAP urges parents of children younger than two years of age to keep their children "screen-free."
7. For children between two and three years of age, child development experts recommend limiting screen time to no more than _____ hours per day.
8. **Critical thinking.** How does intonation aid in language development? How does it aid in comprehension of language after toddlerhood?

Chapter 12 Review and Assessment

Summary

During the toddler years, brain wiring is dense, making the toddler's brain ripe for learning. After the toddler years, the brain will begin pruning seldom used or unused connections. Toddlers develop mental imagery, which encourages pretend play. Piaget categorizes toddler learning into two stages: substage 5 and substage 6. During substage 5, young toddlers learn using trial and error. Once they reach substage 6, older toddlers can think through actions. Teaching by scaffolding also begins in the toddler years. Vygotsky's theory shows how cultural differences affect scaffolding.

Concepts that children start learning during infancy mature during toddlerhood. The major areas of concept learning for toddlers are distinguishing attributes, noting cause and effect, using spatial relationships, solving problems, understanding quantities, and using symbols. Toddlers learn language by learning to articulate and learning word meanings. Toddlers need experiences in hearing language. Toddlers first use single words before joining words to form sentences. A number of conditions—including hearing problems, interest in talking, intellectual abilities, gender, need for speech, environment, bilingualism, and autism—can affect and cause delays in language development.

Toddlers learn through various play activities, such as motor activities, sensory stimulation activities, basic concept activities, symbolic learning activities, language activities, and electronic media activities. Adults can enrich toddlers' learning environment by providing helpful materials and planning appropriate activities for the toddler.

College and Career Portfolio

Portfolio Sample Editing

Portfolio samples are examples of your best work, so it is important to read and edit them. Correct spelling and grammar are important in school and in the workplace, and your best work should display your grasp of language. To make sure you are providing the best samples in your portfolio, complete the following activities:

- Proofread the samples for your portfolio. Check for spelling using a print or online dictionary. Check for grammar by reading aloud and researching grammar rules.
- Trade samples with a trusted classmate and proofread your classmate's samples for him or her. Afterward, review and incorporate corrections your classmate made to your samples.

Chapter 12 Review and Assessment

Vocabulary Activities

1. In teams, play *picture charades* to identify each of the following terms. Write the terms on separate slips of paper and put the slips into a basket. Choose a team member to be the *sketcher*. The sketcher pulls a term from the basket and creates quick drawings or graphics to represent the term until the team guesses the term. Rotate turns as sketcher until the team identifies all terms.

Key Terms

articulation (12.2)
bilingual (12.2)
closed-ended questions (12.3)
collective symbolism (12.1)
deferred imitation (12.1)
grammar (12.2)
intonation (12.3)
mental imagery (12.1)
monolingual (12.2)
open-ended questions (12.3)
pretense (12.1)
solitary symbolic play (12.1)

2. With a partner, create a T-chart. Write each of the following terms in the left column. Write a *synonym* (a word that has the same or similar meaning) for each term in the right column. Discuss your synonyms with the class.

Academic Terms

actuality (12.1)
attributes (12.2)
deferred (12.1)
havoc (12.1)
intrinsic (12.2)
onomatopoeic (12.3)
phonics (12.2)
refined (12.2)
repertoire (12.1)
tertiary (12.1)
trajectories (12.2)
vicarious (12.3)

Critical Thinking

3. **Draw conclusions.** After the toddler years, the brain begins pruning connections; this makes toddlerhood the ideal period for learning skills and concepts. What do you think would happen if learning did not occur during the toddler years? Can a child learn a skill after this period closes?
4. **Cause and effect.** How does the development of language aid toddlers' thinking skills? Predict how a toddler's thinking would be affected if language development were delayed.
5. **Compare and contrast.** Review the discussion of *Piaget's Cognitive-Developmental Theory* in Lesson 12.1. Then, compare and contrast substages 5 and 6. Write a three- to four-paragraph essay explaining how the substages are similar and how they are different.
6. **Analyze.** Why is deferred imitation a more advanced intellectual ability than imitating while seeing an action performed?
7. **Evaluate.** Mikhail is 24 months old. In the past, when his parents have bought a stuffed animal of his favorite superhero, Mikhail has chewed on the stuffed animal and thrown it around the room. This year, however, Mikhail has started reading to his stuffed animal and taking it on walks. Evaluate the situation. How would Piaget describe what Mikhail has learned?
8. **Determine.** Concept learning that begins in infancy advances during toddlerhood. Review the major concept areas of toddler learning, and if needed, review Chapter 9, *Intellectual Development in the First Year*. For each concept area, write a paragraph describing how the foundations of this concept are laid during infancy and determining how the concept lesson is refined during toddlerhood.

Core Skills

9. **Research and speaking.** Advances in neuroscience have helped experts understand childhood windows of opportunity and ideal periods for learning. Using reliable online or print resources, research how brain development affects when and how toddlers learn. Try to understand the anatomy that allows for learning and take notes on any facts or concepts that you find interesting. Finally, present your research to the class. Include a bibliography and be prepared to defend the reliability of the sources you used.
10. **Listening and speaking.** Imagine you are a third-grade teacher at a local elementary school and your curriculum requires you teach Piaget's *Cognitive-Developmental Theory* and Vygotsky's *Sociocultural Theory*, as they relate to toddlers. Review this chapter's information about the two theories and then draft an age-appropriate lesson plan to teach and then assess this knowledge in your students. Prepare two to three activities to reinforce these concepts and deliver your lesson in a small group.

11. **Math.** Conduct a survey asking caregivers how many words they would estimate their toddler knows. Try to survey at least 10 caregivers and make note of the toddlers' ages. Enter data into a spreadsheet. After compiling your results, calculate the average number of words a toddler knows. Show your work and turn in your spreadsheet and calculation to your teacher.
12. **Writing and speaking.** Review the table of intellectual milestones for toddlers (Figure 12.12), and in small groups, choose one of the three age ranges covered. Discuss in your group how a toddler changes when he or she crosses into your chosen age range, and then create a brochure for parents and caregivers titled "What to Expect When Your Toddler Is _____ Months Old." In your brochure, detail the major changes a toddler undergoes and a parent or caregiver might observe. Make your brochure visually appealing and informative. Finally, distribute the brochure to the class and deliver a presentation about its contents.
13. **Reading.** With a partner, search online or visit a local library to find parenting books that advise caregivers how to improve their toddlers' language development and grammar. Read one of these books and take notes about strategies the book suggests. Assess these strategies against what you learned in this chapter and research additional sources to verify each strategy's effectiveness. Finally, write a two- to three-page book review evaluating the book's accuracy and helpfulness.
14. **Writing and art.** Reading with toddlers encourages visual imagery, language development, and fine-motor skills (involved in turning a book page). Review the considerations for choosing children's books and then identify a topic you think would be interesting to a toddler. Write a short children's book based on that topic and be sure to illustrate it with large, colorful pictures. Finally, bring your children's book to school and read it to the class. After reading, ask your class for feedback and take notes about what they would change.
15. **Research and technology.** Many electronic products claim to be effective teaching tools for toddlers. It is up to individual caregivers, however, to evaluate whether these tools are as helpful as they say. In small groups, choose an electronic product (such as a television program, video, or interactive game) that is marketed as being educational for toddlers. Conduct an investigation about how helpful the product actually is. This investigation might involve reading reviews or articles about the product or applying information about toddlers that you learned in this chapter. Once you have reached a consensus, create a poster that markets the product accurately and realistically.
16. **CTE Career Readiness Practice.** Imagine you are a new teacher at a local child care center. Your employer values your creativity and fresh take on planning activities for children, so she asks you to renovate the activities program for toddlers. She asks you to plan two weeks of activities for the toddlers' growth and development and to include a motor activity, sensory stimulation activity, basic concept activity, symbolic learning activity, language activity, and electronic media activity for each day. She also asks you to incorporate math, science, physical movement, outdoor play, art, and music into these activities. Create a two-week program of activities for toddlers at the child care center, including activity details, instructions, and time estimates. Once you have created your program, present it to the class and ask for feedback on how well you completed your employer's assignment.

Observations

17. In small groups, search online or at a local library for recordings or videos of toddlers and then analyze any articulation errors present in the toddlers' speech. Take notes about these errors and then play the recording or video for your class. Ask the students in your class to list the articulation errors they note and then lead a group discussion about your analysis and your classmates' responses.
18. As a class, visit a local child care center and observe several toddlers. For each toddler, note goals you witness the toddler striving to achieve. Record the actions the toddler uses and the outcomes of these actions. Note especially how thinking is evident. What concepts are the toddlers learning? What intellectual activities might be appropriate for them? Discuss your findings as a class.

Chapter 13 Social-Emotional Development of Toddlers

Essential Question

What interrelated toddler developments serve as preparation for the emergence of a social child, and how can adults gradually and effectively begin to socialize their toddlers?

Lesson 13.1 **The Social-Emotional World of Toddlers**

Lesson 13.2 **Meeting Toddlers' Social-Emotional Needs**

Case Study How Can Toddlers' Separation Anxiety Be Handled?

As a class, read the case study and discuss the questions that follow. After you finish studying the chapter, discuss this case study again. Have your opinions changed based on what you learned?

Mariam, an attorney at a prestigious law firm, is going back to work after 13 months of maternity leave. Mariam does not want to leave her daughter, Avra, but she has to work to help support the family. While Mariam and her husband, Seth, are working, Avra will attend a toddler program.

To prepare Avra for the program, Mariam and Seth played "bye-bye" with Avra in the house by waving and going into another room. The family enjoyed the game. On Avra's first day at the center, however, she began crying when she realized "bye-bye" meant her mother was gone. The next day, Avra began crying inconsolably as soon as she saw the doors of the toddler center.

Mariam was upset about her daughter's distress. Avra had stayed with unfamiliar caregivers before without crying. As the caregiver approached, Mariam asked, "Did something go wrong yesterday? Avra has never cried like this before. Maybe you don't know how to handle her." The caregiver was offended and replied, "If you don't want Avra to cry, then don't leave her with us."

The director, who overheard the exchange and noticed that Mariam was becoming even more upset, stepped in to diffuse the situation.

Give It Some Thought

1. Why was Avra crying? What does this behavior show about Avra's relationship with her mother? Why do you think Avra had not cried during earlier child care situations?
2. Why was Mariam so upset on the second day? What other ways do parents react to their children's cries? Why?
3. Do you think the caregiver should have handled the situation differently? Explain your answer.

While studying this chapter, look for the online resources icon  to:

- **Practice** terms with e-flash cards and interactive games
- **Assess** what you learn by completing self-assessment quizzes
- **Expand** knowledge with interactive activities and graphic organizers

www.g-wlearning.com/childdevelopment

Study on the go

Use a mobile device to practice terms and review with self-assessment quizzes.

www.m.g-wlearning.com/0384

Lesson 13.1 The Social-Emotional World of Toddlers

Key Terms

autonomy versus shame and doubt
gender identity
self-esteem
temper tantrum

Academic Terms

assimilate
autonomy
cognizant
competence
control
feats
worth

Objectives

After studying this lesson, you will be able to

- describe how self-awareness develops in toddlers.
- identify the conflict toddlers must resolve in the second stage of Erikson's psychosocial theory.
- explain how the parent-child relationship changes from infancy to the toddler years.
- describe secure attachments in toddlers and explain why insecure attachments lead to negative social-emotional outcomes.
- summarize how children express their emotions in the toddler years.
- give examples of social-emotional developmental milestones toddlers might achieve.

Reading and Writing Activity

Before you read the lesson, interview a child care worker. Ask the person why it is important to know about the social-emotional development of toddlers and how this topic affects the child care center. Take notes during the interview. As you read the lesson, highlight the items from your notes that are discussed in the lesson.

Graphic Organizer

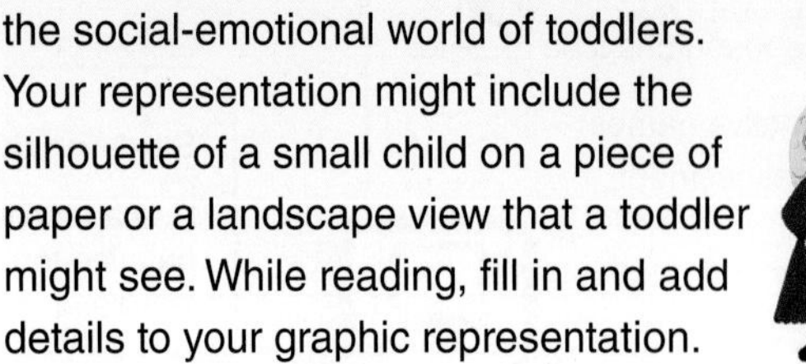

Create a graphic representation of the social-emotional world of toddlers. Your representation might include the silhouette of a small child on a piece of paper or a landscape view that a toddler might see. While reading, fill in and add details to your graphic representation. Use this representation as notes for reviewing the lesson.

Most babies begin life surrounded by people who meet all their needs. Babies' needs are usually simple, so caregivers can meet most of them promptly. When their needs are met and their environments are consistent, babies develop focused attachment to their caregivers and, in turn, learn to trust their world.

As babies become toddlers, three changes happen. First, toddlers find out more about themselves as individuals and about their world. Second, toddlers realize the world is not solely devoted to meeting their needs. Third, toddlers' emotions become more elaborate, specific to events, and intense (strong). Toddlers also directly sense the expressions of other people's emotions. Thus, during the toddler years, children develop self-awareness, achieve *autonomy*, and reach out to form social relations with others. They also begin to show attachments and express emotions. These three interrelated developments serve as a preparation for the emergence of a truly social being.

Figure 13.1 As toddlers become more self-aware, they also become more independent and more conscious of what they possess. *Why do you think self-awareness is a key component for independence? Could someone be independent without being self-aware?*

Developing Self-Awareness

Self-awareness (the understanding a person has of him- or herself) begins to develop at birth and continues to build throughout life. A good sense of self-awareness is essential to a person's well-being. Without a sense of self, children cannot develop close relationships and adults cannot share intimacy.

Self-awareness in the toddler years involves seeing oneself as a unique person, recognizing oneself (as in a mirror), and developing early feelings of self-esteem. Adults can readily note a toddler's emerging self-awareness when toddlers express possession (concerned about *me* and *mine*), identify their images as themselves, and are increasingly independent (**Figure 13.1**).

Seeing Oneself as a Unique Person

Around two years of age, toddlers begin to see themselves as separate from other people and objects. Toddlers demonstrate their understanding of being a unique person in the following ways:

- ***Body awareness.*** Toddlers become more aware of their bodies and what their bodies can do. By 24 months of age, children know and can name at least seven of their body parts. They can also distinguish their body parts from those of others, such as "my nose," "mommy's nose," and the "kitty's nose."
- ***Sense awareness.*** Toddlers know they can see, hear, touch, taste, and smell. They may not know, however, which body part controls each sense.
- ***Gender identity.*** Toddlers develop **gender identity**, the ability to label self and others as male or female (also called *gender labeling*). These labels are often based on physical differences, such as length of hair. Toddlers become upset if someone mislabels them.

- ***Object possession.*** Toddlers define themselves by what belongs to them, and will tell you so by saying, "Mine."
- ***Family names.*** Toddlers can state their own names and the names of family members.
- ***Assimilate their culture.*** Toddlers begin to notice the physical traits of their ethnic group and the behaviors and values of their cultural group. They do not fully **assimilate** (fully understand and use knowledge of) their ethnicity and culture, however, for many years. For example, some verbal comparisons with other groups (expressions of self-awareness) are most often heard beginning in the preschool years.

Although toddlers are becoming **cognizant** (aware) of themselves, their understanding of self is still incomplete. For example, toddlers feel pain, but do not always know where the pain is located. Unless they can see a cut, scrape, or burn, they cannot tell someone where it hurts. More advanced body concepts develop later.

Recognizing Oneself

Toddlers can recognize themselves in mirrors between 15 and 18 months of age. Between 18 and 24 months, they can point to their reflection in the mirror, say their own names, and point to themselves in recent photos.

To study toddlers' ability to recognize themselves, researchers have conducted *mark and mirror* experiments. In one mark and mirror experiment, toddlers first looked at themselves in a mirror. While pretending to wipe the children's faces, the experimenter put dots of red lipstick on their noses. Once again the toddlers looked at themselves in a mirror. Toddlers who recognized themselves in the mirror wiped at their noses. Those who did not recognize themselves would wipe at the nose on the face in the mirror.

Once toddlers recognize themselves in mirrors, they enjoy looking at themselves, and begin to distinguish their physical features (**Figure 13.2**). Some child care and education programs use large, unbreakable mirrors near the floor to help toddlers develop self-awareness. Toddlers and older children enjoy seeing how they look while playing.

Focus on Careers

Survey Researcher

Survey researchers plan and develop surveys for scientific research in a variety of fields, such as child development. Survey researchers also determine the type of survey method, use statistics, analyze the survey data, and summarize the data using tables, graphs, and charts. Many survey researchers work in colleges, universities, research firms, and government organizations.

Career cluster: Science, technology, engineering, and mathematics.

Education: Educational requirements include a master's degree or Ph.D. Certification is available, but often not mandatory.

Job outlook: Future employment opportunities for survey researchers are expected to grow faster than the average for all occupations.

To learn more about a career as a survey researcher, visit the United States Department of Labor's *Occupational Outlook Handbook* website. You will also be able to compare the job responsibilities, educational requirements, job outlook, and average pay of survey researchers with similar occupations.

Figure 13.2 Mirrors help toddlers recognize themselves and develop self-awareness. In mirrors, toddlers can learn to distinguish their physical features and recognize those features as their own. *How does self-recognition contribute to self-awareness?*

Developing Early Feelings of Self-Esteem

A portion of **self-esteem** involves feelings of **worth** (usefulness; importance). Infants sense how others feel about them from the way they are spoken to and held. Toddlers can also sense how others feel about them. Toddlers must feel loved, even when they are difficult or make mistakes. If adults scold toddlers each time they do something wrong, toddlers will feel they are beyond being loved. With the help of caring adults, children develop good feelings of self-worth.

The confidence a person has in his or her own abilities (**competence**) is part of self-esteem. As toddlers achieve goals, their competence increases. Toddlers gain another aspect of self-esteem, **control** (influence over one's environment of people, things, and events), by figuring out what works and what does not. Adults who do not rescue toddlers from small frustrations too quickly are aiding a growing sense of control over outcomes and events. As toddlers make mistakes, try again, and practice what works, they will achieve autonomy as explained in the next section.

As toddlers develop good feelings of self-worth, confidence in their own abilities, and gain control in their environment, they are developing self-esteem. When toddlers feel good about themselves, they seem to admire themselves and their growing control over their bodies. They are confident and like to show off their physical **feats** (accomplishments) for others. They will often clap for themselves and laugh with delight at their new skills.

Achieving Autonomy

According to Erikson, social-emotional development begins in infancy when babies learn to trust or mistrust. Babies whose needs are met and who have a consistent environment develop a sense of trust. This sense of trust helps them as they enter Erikson's second stage of personality development, called **autonomy versus shame and doubt**. In this stage, toddlers are tasked with achieving **autonomy** (a form of self-governance in which a toddler seeks to do his or her will). For most children, this stage begins sometime between 12 and 18 months of age and is completed at about 36 months.

Autonomy builds on the toddler's expanding motor and intellectual skills. Toddlers are proud of their new skills and want to use them. They have the energy to carry out their goals. Because toddlers have much more "know how" than infants, they feel very independent. The independent feeling comes from toddlers' increasing self-awareness of their abilities. Erikson explained *autonomy* as the toddler's feeling of being able to do some tasks without help from others. He felt that caregivers should recognize toddlers' desire to be more independent and allow them to do what they can at their own pace.

Erikson believed damage occurs, however, when impatient caregivers complete tasks that toddlers are capable of doing themselves. Consistently criticizing or overprotecting toddlers leads them to feel they cannot control themselves and their world. Erikson called this feeling *a sense of shame and doubt*.

Extending Social Relations

As children get older, their growing motor and intellectual abilities help them interact more with adults and other children. These early social interactions teach children new skills and attitudes, which help them get along with other people. This process of interacting with others socializes children.

Focus on

Health

Promoting Self-Esteem

Self-esteem tremendously impacts a person's well-being. Healthy self-esteem leads to joy. Low self-esteem causes anxiety and feelings of inadequacy. Because self-esteem can fluctuate, handling life's challenges is part of self-esteem.

Toddlers' feelings of self-esteem differ from those of adults. Adults' self-esteem is compartmentalized, but toddlers tend to see themselves as a whole. Self-esteem fluctuates only slightly in adults, but toddlers can go from a high (comparing themselves to superheroes) one minute and to low (inconsolable because something does not work) the next.

Parents can foster self-esteem in toddlers in the following ways:

- ***Worth.*** The roots of worth are unconditional love. More than cuddling, this love requires giving undivided attention at times throughout each day. Toddlers need their words and feelings understood and validated ("I know you are sad about _____"). Feelings of worth also come from having behavioral limits that are reasonable, clearly stated, and consistently enforced.
- ***Competence.*** Offering toddlers a couple of toddler-friendly options says to the toddler, "I have faith in your decisions." Adults also build competence by acknowledging progress and supporting struggles in toddlers. Specific acknowledgement works, but general praise can erode toddlers' competence by making toddlers feel they are perfect or should be perfect, which is impossible.
- ***Control.*** Toddlers need to pursue their own interests/goals. Adults should allow the child to take safe risks, make mistakes without saying, "I told you so," and recover from mistakes. Adults also aid toddlers' success by providing the appropriate books/toys, tools for self-help, and activities.

All three aspects of self-esteem work together. Over time, feelings of self-esteem should become stronger.

Interacting with Adults

The parent-child relationship begun in infancy serves as the foundation for future social connections. Social relations with parents, caregivers, and other adults, such as grandparents and family friends, become well established in the toddler years. Although toddlers know more people now, they need a great deal of guidance from parents and other caregivers to establish relationships with adults and other children.

Toddlers who have formed healthy attachments to caregivers have a safe base from which to meet people. Although toddlers continue to look to their main caregivers for social interaction, they now spend more time with adults other than their caregivers. These adults include babysitters, relatives, and neighbors. Having more than one caregiver often helps toddlers adjust to others and expect differences among people. When children have positive experiences with several adults, they develop trusting relationships with them. Having many caregivers, however, is not in the best interest of toddlers who need to develop secure attachments (as described later in the next section).

Interacting with Other Children

During the second year, toddlers tend to interact more with other children, although their first interactions are usually brief. For example, they often imitate each other's actions with a toy without talking to each other (**Figure 13.3**). Later, they talk as they play. Toward the end of the toddler years, a couple of toddlers may play together. For example, they may help each other fill a dump truck with sand.

Toddlers are possessive of their toys and belongings when they play. Toddlers have not yet learned about ownership and, therefore, are not quite ready to share with other children. When toys are involved, they often grab, hit, or even bite. As they play, toddlers also explore other children in much the same way as they explore objects. They often feel that "overcoming" another child is positive. Harvey Karp, a popular writer of parenting books, jokingly says that toddlers have some "caveman-like qualities" when they play with other children.

Figure 13.3 While children do not interact much during the toddler years, they do imitate one another before talking. *How does imitation lay a foundation for social interactions with other children?*

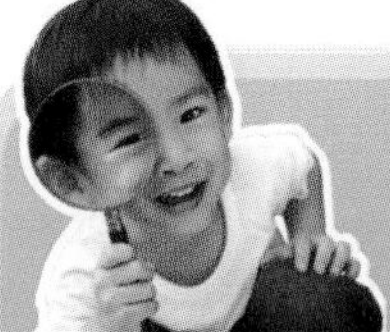

Investigate Special Topics: Establishing a Parenting Style in the *Authority Stage* of Parenting

The parent-child relationship changes in toddlerhood. In the first year of toddlerhood, parents are still in Galinsky's *nurturing stage* of parenting in which they try to read children's signals of need and then respond correctly, promptly, and consistently. As toddlers become more mobile, curious, and assertive, parents enter the *authority stage* of parenting.

In the *authority stage* of parenting, the parenting role includes shaping a child's social behaviors. Parents teach children to be *compliant* (agreeable) to parents' and other adult's wishes and to get along with other children.

The *authority stage* of parenting can be difficult to enter. The newly developed assertiveness of toddlers puts a strain on parent-child relationships. Toddlers seem to misbehave much of the time, partially because they explore everything. They frequently ignore parents' commands because they want to see whether their parents really mean what they say. Toddlers may laugh and continue to repeat their misbehavior.

As they respond to toddlers' assertiveness and start to shape and teach their children, parents begin to establish a parenting style. As you have already learned, there are four types of parenting styles, which are permissive, authoritarian, overparenting, and authoritative. Use of the permissive, authoritarian, and overparenting styles often results in toddlers who are noncompliant and aggressive. Parents who try to see issues from the toddlers' perspectives and use the authoritative style, however, usually have more compliant and nonaggressive toddlers.

Critical Thinking Activity

Review the information about parenting styles in Lesson 4.2 and take notes about the behaviors associated with each parenting style. Then, in small groups, discuss what actions and responses shape parents' parenting styles. Consider how the way parents respond to children's assertiveness during toddlerhood affects which parenting style they use from that point onward.

With appropriate adult guidance, toddlers can learn to interact with other children in positive ways. For example, they can sometimes share, return a snatched toy, and show concern for someone who is hurt. When children are better able to communicate, getting along with playmates becomes much easier.

Insecure attachments damage a child's self-esteem and make him or her more vulnerable to the impact of trauma. These factors can affect the child's mental health throughout life.

Showing Attachments

A child's attachment to a caregiver begins in infancy and is completed between 12 and 18 months of age. Attachment has its biological roots in survival, but is learned by the child through correct, prompt, and consistent caregiving. A child shows attachment to his or her caregiver through attachment behaviors, which are seen when the infant or toddler feels stress or anxiety. For example, the crying that occurs with separation anxiety is an attachment behavior. In these cases, the child seeks proximity with the caregiver to whom he or she is attached. The child views this adult as the person best able to cope with the world. Children are often attached to several people. Each attachment a child has is a positive force in his or her life.

When a toddler seeks out and tries to maintain proximity with a special caregiver, the toddler has a *secure attachment*. The child uses this caregiver as a secure base from which to explore an unfamiliar setting or approach an unfamiliar person. The child also seeks this caregiver's protection and comfort if a situation is perceived as dangerous or distressing. Secure family attachments often encourage out-of-family attachments.

After 18 months of age, if attachments are secure, toddlers are more apt to cooperate even when adult-child goals differ. When children who have secure attachments become adults, they will be able to

- calm themselves
- be confident in their abilities
- form lasting and positive relationships with others
- be overall well-adjusted

Toddlers who get inconsistent care, regardless of the reason, develop *insecure attachments*. Because of a lack of consistent care, toddlers are confused or feel they are not worthy of care or protection. A lack of adult support leads to toddlers who are vulnerable to the impact of trauma from any source. Because of trying so hard to get their basic needs met, they often lag behind secure toddlers in learning, too.

Insecure attachments are most damaging to a person's self-esteem and thus to his or her mental health. **Figure 13.4** lists several types of insecure attachments, their causes, and outcomes for children during later stages of life. People who have insecure attachments, however, can overcome them and learn new relationship skills.

Expressing Emotions

During the toddler years, children's developing abilities alter how they experience and express emotions. Due to their increasing intellect, toddlers' emotions become more elaborate. They react to more stimuli than infants. They know more people to love and fear, experience more events, and can even imagine unreal things. Toddlers can better sense emotions in others, too. Also, emotions become more specific. For example, they may fear a neighbor's dog, but love their dog. In addition, emotions become more intense—sometimes even overwhelming to toddlers.

Due to the intensity of emotions and their increased motor skills, toddlers tend to express emotions physically more often than infants. On the other hand, toddlers' verbal skills enable them to express emotions verbally, too, if taught. Because of these new and improved abilities, children's expressions of love and affection, fear, anxiety, and anger change during the toddler years.

Love and Affection

Toddlers are still attached to their caregivers and express love and affection by wanting to be near them. They seek caregivers when faced with a strange situation. This attachment seems to help other aspects of social-emotional development because the love a toddler feels for caregivers also extends to other adults, children, and pets (**Figure 13.5**).

Fear

Many fears that begin during infancy are evident after the first birthday. Fears increase quickly after two years of age because toddlers know about

Figure 13.4 Insecure Attachments

Anxious-Ambivalent Attachment (also called *resistant*)	
Description	Toddlers show distress when unfamiliar people are nearby even when parents are present. Toddlers stay close to their mothers, and react with great distress during separation. Once mothers return, toddlers resist their mothers' offers of comfort. Toddlers' reactions upon reunions are ambivalent and resistant.
Parents' behaviors*	• Parents do not read their infants' and toddlers' signals of needs correctly. They respond in ways that do not fit, such as offering play activities when toddlers are hungry or tired. • Parents respond to infants' and toddlers' needs inconsistently. • Parents respond in different degrees to the same needs. For example, if the child falls, the parent may ignore the child one time and overly comfort the child the next time.
Long-term child results*	• As toddlers, they are very clingy. • As toddlers and older children, separation anxiety is longer than average. • As school-age children, they want attention and are overemotional. They do not like to work on their own. • As young adults, they are scared of entering into a close relationship with others. If they do, they are controlling in these relationships. • Throughout life, they are easily frustrated.
Anxious-Avoidant Attachment	
Description	Toddlers explore toys and show no preference for mother versus stranger. During separations, toddlers show no distress. Once mothers return, toddlers ignore and avoid their mothers.
Parents' behaviors*	• Parents respond to children's physical needs, but not promptly. • Parents do not often respond to emotional needs, such as fear, by comforting. Infants and toddlers are left alone to deal with these nonphysical needs. • Parents ignore delight or excitement shown by their infants and toddlers.
Long-term child results*	• As infants and toddlers, they see no need to communicate needs. • As toddlers, they appear "mature" during separations because anxiety is not exposed. • As preschool and school-age children, they seem too independent. Even when frustrated, they do not ask for help. They also tend to be aggressive in play. • As school-age children and teens, they show impulsive behaviors, including bullying. • As adults, they prefer to be alone. They value their independence. They rarely admit to having positive feelings for others.

(Continued)

Figure 13.4 *(Continued)*

Disorganized Attachment	
Description	Toddlers are inconsistent in attachment behaviors. For example, they may act as though they want to be picked up, but they stiffen once held. They make poor eye contact with parents and other adults.
Parents' behaviors*	• Parents rarely respond to the needs of their infants or toddlers. • If parents respond, the responses do not fit the needs. • Parents often neglect or abuse. • Parents are often depressed or are on drugs. • Parents are absent and children have multiple foster home placements.
Long-term child results*	• As toddlers, they often freeze in their footsteps for no apparent reason. • As preschool and school-age children, they are often hard to understand because of exceptionally fast speech. They have a difficult time understanding other people's feelings. Their pretend play may be violent. • As adults, they do not form lasting intimate relationships and are anxious and depressed. • Throughout life, their behaviors seem different from day to day.

*The way parents have responded to the child determines the type of attachment the child has for the parent and the long-term child results. Attachment is very critical to a child's mental health.

more things to fear. They know of more objects and situations that can hurt them. Survival fears (such as fears of crossing the street, falling from heights, guns, and poisons), however, are not well-developed. Safety remains in the hands of caregivers.

Figure 13.5 Toddlers show affection to personal possessions or objects, including toys. *What are some ways toddlers express love?*

Toddlers also cannot distinguish real from unreal. They imagine many unreal things, such as monsters. Toddlers may also fear animals, darkness, nightmares, "bad people," injury, gestures, and startling noises.

Toddlers tend to act out their fears during play. For example, a 30-month-old who fears dogs may be seen barking and growling in play. Toddlers may imitate bad people seen on television or in books. Adults should handle these fears in a matter-of-fact way, and never tease toddlers about their fears or push them into scary situations.

Anxiety

Toddlers may begin to experience nightmares around two years of age as a way of dealing with anxiety. These nightmares can stem from fears of being left alone, getting hurt, or angering adults. The details of the nightmares are unreal, often including unknown lands and monsters. If toddlers are content during the day, their nightmares do not reveal a problem. For most children, nightmares decrease in time. A trip to the library or bookstore may result in some humorous books to help the child deal with nightmares.

Another form of anxiety is displayed through separation anxiety. Older toddlers between 30 and 35 months of age show less separation anxiety than younger children. Some separation anxiety continues into the toddler stage and sometimes beyond. Many toddlers overcome some of their separation anxiety if they feel a caregiver's love and know the caregiver will return. Increased language skills help toddlers understand why parents sometimes leave. Parents must make sure their toddler receives good and loving care during separations. Children with insecure attachments may show separation anxiety even well beyond the toddler years.

Anger

Toddlers desire more independence and have a strong will. When defeated in their goal-seeking behaviors, toddlers react with anger. A sudden emotional outburst of anger, called a **temper tantrum**, often appears during the second year of life. A temper tantrum averages about five minutes in length. The child goes through five stages during the tantrum (**Figure 13.6**).

Tantrums tend to happen when something does not go a toddler's way. Because this is often the case, temper tantrums are common for toddlers. Temper tantrums are meant to attract attention, but often are not directed at anyone. (In the next lesson, you will learn about ideas for handling toddlers' temper tantrums.)

Social-Emotional Developmental Milestones

Children achieve a number of social-emotional developmental milestones during the toddler years. Due to changes in brain development, motor skills, and intellectual/language abilities, toddlers' social-emotional worlds begin to mature, which lays the foundation for development beyond the toddler years. **Figure 13.7** lists some developmental milestones of social-emotional development during the toddler years.

Figure 13.6 Stages of Temper Tantrums

1. Experiences anger, shown by throwing self on the floor, kicking, and screaming.
2. Experiences anger and sadness, manifested by crying, whining, and whimpering.
3. Feels anger level drop.
4. Desires cuddling.
5. Forgets about tantrum and engages in other activities.

Lesson 13.1 Review and Assessment 

1. Explain how toddlers develop self-awareness.
2. The central conflict of the second stage in Erikson's psychosocial theory is called _____.
3. What changes in the parent-child relationship occur when infants become toddlers?
4. Summarize the difference between secure and insecure attachments, including results on toddlers.
5. Why do insecure attachments lead to negative social-emotional outcomes?
6. How do the ways children *express* emotions change in the toddler years?
7. Identify three social-emotional developmental milestones as well as the ages at which these milestones occur.
8. **Critical thinking.** What are some ways caregivers can scold or correct toddlers without making them feel unloved?

Figure 13.7 Toddler Social-Emotional Milestones

12 to 18 months

- Seeks attention.
- Shows affection.
- Protests when frustrated.
- Shows intense separation anxiety.
- Resists napping and bedtime even when tired and sleepy.
- Plays alone on floor with toys for a few minutes.
- Looks at the person who is talking to him or her.

18 to 24 months

- Directs another's attention to an object.
- Says *hi*, *bye*, and *please* (if reminded).
- Shows some separation anxiety.
- Is shy around strangers.
- Wants things now.
- Becomes more independent and defiant when challenged; may be aggressive when frustrated.
- Often responds with *no*.
- Uses possessive words (*me*, *mine*).
- Shows attachment to a toy or blanket.
- Responds to simple requests.

24 to 36 months

- Verbalizes feelings.
- Shows love to non-caregiving adults, children, and pets.
- Begins to interact more with children, especially by chasing after others.
- Is possessive about toys.
- Fears more real and imaginary things.
- Begins having nightmares.
- Is persistent and demanding.
- Has tantrums.
- Is curious about self (wants to know names of body parts).
- Shows empathy.
- Takes turns, especially on slides.
- Knows much about what is and is not acceptable to parents and regular caregivers, but will test limits.

Meeting Toddlers' Social-Emotional Needs

Lesson 13.2

Objectives

After studying this lesson, you will be able to

- plan activities and toys for stimulating self-awareness in toddlers.
- explain how parents and caregivers can help toddlers achieve autonomy.
- describe how parents and caregivers can foster self-assertion and teach obedience in the toddler years.
- give examples of ways parents and caregivers can help toddlers co-regulate their emotions.
- demonstrate how to handle a toddler's temper tantrum.
- identify ways parents can help prevent stress in the toddler years.

Key Terms

delay gratification
obedience
premoral
self-assertion
self-restraint
social referencing

Academic Terms

bewilders
contrariness
empathy

Reading and Writing Activity

Find the list of terms at the beginning of the lesson and write what you think each term means. You can use your previous knowledge and experiences to define these terms. After reading the lesson, look up the terms in the textbook glossary or in a dictionary and write a new definition based on what you have learned.

Graphic Organizer

Using a colored pen or pencil, write the key terms for this lesson on a piece of paper, leaving space around them for your notes. Then as you are reading, write your notes around the key term to which they most relate, until you have created a cloud of notes for each term.

delay gratification **self-assertion**

self-restraint

set limits
provide guidance **obedience** *be consistent*
show love and respect

premoral

Meeting social-emotional needs in the toddler years differs from meeting needs during infancy. Infants are totally dependent on their parents and other caregivers to help meet their needs. Toddlers, however, are no longer completely dependent on adults due to their advancing physical, intellectual, and social-emotional skills. As toddlers learn they can do things on their own, they desire more independence (autonomy).

For toddlers to grow and develop and have self-esteem, parents must allow toddlers to do the things they are able to do. Toddlers, however, are far from being ready to be independent. They still need adult help in achieving goals. Adults are also needed to set limits (exercise authority). Thus, Galinsky noted that parents are still nurturing, but soon will be in the *authority stage* of parenting. The *authority stage* of parenting requires parents to find their parenting style often through much trial and error. In sum, the overall adult goal is to find a healthy, overall stress-free balance between toddlers' goals and expressions of emotions and adult control.

Supporting the Toddler's Self-Awareness

Self-awareness grows mainly out of the toddler's daily contact with his or her world. Parents and caregivers can enhance the toddler's self-awareness and acknowledge the child as a unique person in the following ways:

- Pay attention when a toddler wants to talk. Ask yourself this question, "How would you feel if you wanted to talk and were ignored?" Acknowledge a toddler's feelings with descriptors, such as "You look happy" or "You look so sad." Sit together and talk about how the toddler has grown and how loved he or she is.
- Provide a place for the toddler's possessions, especially toys, and encourage him or her to take responsibility for them. Also, let the toddler decide about sharing these possessions.
- Encourage the toddler to self-feed and help with his or her hygiene. Let the toddler help around the house, too. Comment on his or her skills and how they help you.
- Plan a few specific activities to enhance the toddler's self-awareness (**Figure 13.8**).

Self-awareness is well underway by the end of the toddler years, but continues to grow throughout life. A happy, secure toddler will develop positive feelings about him- or herself.

Helping Toddlers Achieve Autonomy

Autonomy is a very important part of the developing toddler's life. Parents and caregivers can help toddlers on this journey toward achieving autonomy by ensuring their safety and encouraging toddlers' efforts.

Ensuring Safety

Parents and caregivers can help toddlers achieve autonomy by keeping them from harm. Caregivers can make sure toddlers' indoor and outdoor environments are safe. This will decrease the number of times caregivers have to warn a toddler. They can give a toddler safe choices so he or she can build feelings of independence and use his or her skills. Parents and caregivers should redirect toddlers before they engage in a forbidden or unsafe action. This is more helpful than waiting to intervene after a toddler is already performing the action. It is also more helpful than simply reacting to the consequences.

When ensuring safety, parents and caregivers need to recognize that toddlers will sometimes misjudge their skills and need help. Toddlers do not understand possible results of some of their actions. Sometimes, toddlers find limits to their actions through failed attempts. This is frustrating for toddlers. If the goal is unsafe, parents and caregivers need to set limits for a toddler while understanding the child's perspective.

Figure 13.8 Self-Awareness Activities

- ***Name the parts of the face.*** Place the toddler's hands on your face. Name aloud each part of your face as the child feels it. Ask the child to name the parts.
- ***Mirrors.*** With the toddler on your lap, hold a mirror to reflect the toddler's face. Ask, "Who is that?" If the toddler does not answer, say, "That is you." Say the toddler's name.
- ***Dressing up.*** Toddlers enjoy dressing up in adults' old hats, clothes, accessories, and shoes. To help the toddler play while dressing up, show the child one object. For example, show the toddler a hat and say, "Look at this pretty hat. I'm going to wear it." Place the hat on your head and talk about how pretty it is. Then say, "Do you want to wear a hat?" Place a hat on the toddler's head, saying how nice it looks. If the toddler enjoys this, try other items.
- ***Pretend.*** Have a pretend tea party with a toddler. Talk about the pretend foods in much the same way you would talk about real food. If the toddler looks confused, say, "How funny! We can pretend to have a party!"
- ***A book about me.*** Take pictures of the toddler's daily activities. Place the pictures in a photo album. (Toddlers often take these albums to child care programs to reduce separation anxiety. Be sure to include photos of parents, siblings, and other loved ones.)
- ***Photo gallery.*** Keep a family photo album or place photos of the toddler in various spots around the house (at the toddler's eye level). Toddlers like photos capturing their experiences.
- ***Measuring chart.*** Measure the toddler's height on a growth chart and keep a running tally of the growth changes.

Encouraging Efforts

In addition to ensuring safety, parents and caregivers can encourage toddlers' efforts at achieving autonomy. Caregivers can avoid excessive criticism or correction of toddlers by letting them make mistakes without scolding and by not making demands that are too rigid for toddlers to follow. Parents and caregivers can encourage a toddler to make choices by offering suggestions on how to complete a task instead of doing the task for the child.

Parents and caregivers can acknowledge toddlers' efforts to become more autonomous and avoid mixing encouragement with criticism. They can celebrate and help toddlers remember personal achievements by taking photos or videos.

Balancing Self-Assertion and Obedience

Because of toddlers' newfound skills, they become willful and curioua. Toddlers find it most difficult to **delay gratification** (wait until later to get what is wanted) and inhibit intense emotions (**Figure 13.9**). Problems occur when the personalities and needs of parents and other adults conflict with the needs of toddlers.

Toddlers need both attachments for protection and comfort as well as for their growing autonomy. They will go back and forth between wanting to be totally independent and wanting to be totally dependent. For parents and other caregivers, getting

Figure 13.9 Toddlers find it difficult to control intense, new emotions, and may act on these intense emotions around adults and other children. *What can caregivers do to acknowledge toddlers' emotions while still teaching obedience?*

the balance between allowing autonomy and dependency in toddlers is critical.

These changes in toddlers' wills confuse adults. Most adults find they have to give toddlers freedom at times and be firm at other times. Their actions depend on toddlers' needs.

Fostering Self-Assertion

Toddlers need some freedom, and adults need to guide toddlers' **self-assertion** (doing as one chooses rather than what others want). Giving toddlers choices allows them to express their preferences. For example, parents can let a toddler choose between two sets of clothing to wear that day. A toddler may also choose between self-control and adult-control. The adult may say, "You may color on the paper, or I'll have to put the crayons away." Toddlers seem more willing to accept a firm *no* when given choices at other times. Through choices, toddlers develop *autonomy* and avoid feelings of *shame* for their mistakes and *doubt* about their abilities.

Figure 13.10 By setting limits, caregivers teach toddlers to behave in socially acceptable ways and to stay safe. *What limits did you have a hard time learning as a young child? Why?*

Teaching Obedience

Toddlers do not have **self-restraint**, or the ability to control themselves. They also do not know all the rules of acceptable behavior. Adults not only foster self-assertion, but they also teach **obedience** (acting within the limits set by others) to help toddlers understand what is socially acceptable behavior. The best way to teach obedience is to meet toddlers' needs and not punish what they do wrong. There are positive ways to help toddlers learn obedience.

Setting Limits

Parents can help toddlers learn socially acceptable behaviors by setting limits for toddlers. Limits keep toddlers safe and show them how to become more socially acceptable (**Figure 13.10**). Setting limits is part of Galinsky's *authority stage* of parenting. Adults need to decide which limits are necessary ("choose your battles") and whether the limits are appropriate for the toddler. (Am I expecting my toddler to wait too long? Am I always saying *no*?)

When setting limits, parents and other adults need to remember toddlers are **premoral** (not self-guided by internal values). Toddlers are guided by outside rules, and they need help learning these rules. Ways in which adults may help toddlers learn rules include

- modeling what is being taught, such as helpfulness, kindness in words, and sharing.
- making simple rules as needs arise. Simple rules may include "Be kind to others," "Always ask for help," "Say *please* and *thank you*," and "Do not hit, bite, or scratch others."
- getting on eye level with the toddler and matching tone of voice to concern. (For example, adults should express by tone of voice more concern about biting than forgetting to say *please*.) Do not yell when talking to the toddler.

- encouraging the toddler to use **social referencing** (evaluating how to respond to a situation by getting a social cue from a more experienced person). When a toddler looks at an adult, he or she is asking, "May I do this?" Adults should send the cue. Toddlers can even pick up on subtle cues. Social referencing aids the child in learning what is and is not acceptable without direct experience.
- telling the toddler when his or her behaviors are acceptable.

Providing Guidance

By 18 months of age, many toddlers show definite signs of **contrariness** (tendency to oppose almost everything others do or say). They tend to oppose adults and even other toddlers. They replace *yes* with *no*, even when *yes* is what they really mean. *Me want* is replaced with *No want*.

Adults may find it difficult to help toddlers achieve autonomy while keeping them safe and preventing conflicts. Erikson felt adults should firmly reassure the toddler. Adults do not need to give in to the child's will all the time. When they confront a child, however, parents should stay calm and assure the child they still love him or her. This protects children from harm without making them feel ashamed or guilty. Oftentimes, adults can prevent the battle of wills. The following ideas may reduce conflicts:

- ***Let the toddler choose.*** Providing the toddler with choices promotes autonomy as well as helps avoid conflicts (**Figure 13.11**). The simplest way to avoid conflict is to let the toddler make some choices. As long as results are not harmful, allowing toddlers some freedom makes obeying easier.
- ***Tell the toddler in advance.*** Telling the toddler about upcoming events in advance helps reduce contrariness. This lead-time allows the toddler to prepare emotionally for the change of activities. If the toddler resists the change, use calming actions, such as picking up the toddler.
- ***Word commands in positive ways.*** Wording a command in a playful way can often prevent struggles with the toddler. For example, to let a child know about an upcoming car ride, a parent might say, "Pilot to copilot—it's time to go."
- ***Use pretend games.*** Playing a pretend game of obedience is another way to reduce contrariness. For example, to get the toddler to wash his or her hands before meals, the adult might say, "I'm going to wash my hands before you do." (Of course, after much scrubbing, the toddler wins.) Sometimes pretend games of obedience become rituals, such as a chase to the bedroom at naptime.

Figure 13.11 Letting a toddler choose between options in some situations, such as going swimming or playing in the park, promotes autonomy and reduces the chance that the toddler will insist on choosing later. *What are safe choices toddlers can be allowed to make?*

Toddlers will make frequent mistakes. Even then, adults need to remain positive. When toddlers are always made to feel they are "bad," they may grow to dislike themselves. Adults should label incorrect behavior as a mistake, and not call the child *bad*, *selfish*, *naughty*, or *mean*. Harsh punishment may cause toddlers to feel they are bad, too.

Being Consistent

Consistency helps people feel secure. When there is a conflict between toddler goals and adult expectations, children will test limits. Toddlers are checking adult reactions because they want to know whether these are *real* limits. Consistency in rules and follow-up is the teacher.

From time to time, people need flexible rules. Toddlers may need flexible rules when they are ill or when other problems occur. Once the situation is back to normal, rules can become consistent again. Of course, as children grow, discipline changes and children are often allowed more freedom.

Showing Love and Respect

Toddlers are worthy of the same respect other people receive. Adults should not respond to toddlers' mistakes with hurtful teasing or anger. Respecting toddlers helps them like themselves. It also serves as the model for the growing child's relationships with others.

More than anything else, toddlers need to feel loved by caring adults. They seem to sense love that is shown to them physically and directly (**Figure 13.12**). Toddlers do not seem to sense love shown in indirect ways, such as having cooked meals or clean clothes (although these are important). Toddlers have good days and problem days, just like adults. When limits are set and discipline is firm, yet kind, the toddler will begin to have good days more often. Good days are a sign that toddlers are getting better at balancing self-assertion and the need to obey. Balancing the two is a skill they will need throughout life.

Figure 13.12 Most toddlers respond to cuddling, loving words, and special times each day when attention is focused on them. *Why do you think toddlers respond best when love is shown in direct ways?*

Guiding the Toddler's Emotions

Toddlers show a variety of emotions, ranging from very positive to negative. Toddlers have a broader range of negative emotions because of their increased intellectual abilities, lack of inhibition, and immature language skills needed to express needs and resolve conflicts. They need parents and other caregivers to help them co-regulate their emotions.

The goal of co-regulation of emotional expression is to help a child develop a rather high-level of self-regulating abilities by four or five years of age, which is when the *authority stage* of parenting ends. A child's temperament is involved in co-regulation to some degree, but parent or caregiver behaviors play the central role in the development of children's self-regulation. These behaviors must be guided by a child's developmental level. In infancy and early toddlerhood, co-regulation involves soothing. Between 18 and 30 months, toddlers' emerging intellectual and language abilities increase dramatically and likely contribute to what works best in co-regulation.

Once a toddler develops language skills, *adult explanation* is considered the best method of co-regulation. An adult explanation might include

- the cause of the problem ("____ wanted to play with your toy")
- the child's emotional feeling ("You are angry and that is all right because you were playing with ____")
- a response strategy ("Hitting hurts! So just tell ____ that we have another ____. Let's get it. Then you can both play with ____")

Reasoning should be at the child's zone of proximal development (ZPD) to help a toddler learn more sophisticated strategies for coping. Toddlers must grow in their understandings and responses to develop a cache of strategies needed for self-regulation.

Another co-regulation method that works with older toddlers who need to delay gratification is *distraction*, which refocuses the toddler's attention. For example, car toys and books or a family game often serve as a distraction for a whining, tired toddler on a long drive.

Love and Empathy

Toddlers who have formed secure attachments know they are loved and protected. In turn, they love their parents and other caregivers. Toddlers show their love by cuddling and snuggling, sharing joy in new experiences and skills, and showing delight when parents return after separation.

Toddlers also show love to friends and their "loveys" (attachment items). "Loveys" help toddlers make it through separations. In a way, these attachment items represent family and security and are similar to the beloved stuffed animals of older children or photographs displayed at the workplace of adults.

Toddlers also begin to learn about empathy. The capacity for **empathy**, the ability to recognize and identify with the emotions of others, is inborn. Developing empathy skills, however, requires learning. Before empathy can develop, toddlers must begin to see the goals and emotions of others (called *taking another's perspective*), which require understanding of self- versus other-awareness. Then, toddlers need to see examples of empathy in their environment.

Toddlers with secure attachments recognize that their parents and other caregivers have understood and accepted their needs. These adults have modeled empathy. Toddlers develop empathy by using social referencing as adults model repeated, sincere actions of empathy. Although infants can mimic empathy, two-year-olds can initiate empathy. **Figure 13.13** shows some tips for developing this complex skill.

Figure 13.13 Tips for Developing Empathy

- Verbally reflect on how children are feeling rather than immediately saying, "Everything is (or will be) all right."
- Have children practice "reading" feelings in expressive photographs and drawings.
- Ask older toddlers how specific characters in stories feel in certain situations.
- Read stories about feelings.
- Encourage empathy in pretend play, such as asking, "Does (*doll's name*) need a nap?"
- Teach words about feelings—*happy*, *mad* (or *angry*), and *sad*.

Anger and Temper Tantrums

As you read earlier, toddlers express anger through aggressive acts and temper tantrums. Anger is a very strong emotion that **bewilders** (confuses) toddlers. The lack of mature language skills is a major challenge in resolving conflicts. Since toddlers cannot articulate their angry feelings, they express anger through aggression.

Many two-year-olds have temper tantrums, but some do not. Toddlers who are lively, under stress (even the stress of being hungry), and cannot yet talk are prone to tantrums.

Parents and other caregivers can learn to handle tantrums by understanding the cause of the child's tantrums. Parents can avoid tantrums in some cases by seeing the situation from the toddler's perspective. The following actions may help prevent temper tantrums:

- Meet the toddler's needs before involving the toddler in adult activities. For example, a toddler may need a nutritious snack or a nap before accompanying the adult on errands.
- Avoid making demands when a toddler is tired, hungry, or ill.
- Remove toys or play equipment that seems to frustrate the toddler.
- Have enough toys to prevent boredom or duplicate toys to share with a friend.

- Give in on small demands, such as staying up a few minutes later when cousins are visiting or spending a few more minutes in the park because it was hard to get a turn on the slide.
- Offer help before the toddler becomes too frustrated.
- Find fun ways to gain toddler compliance.
- Acknowledge signs of control.

If a tantrum occurs because the toddler is making demands of his or her own, tantrums may need to be handled in a different way. Caregivers can tell the toddler beforehand what he or she can or cannot have or do. They can plan something for the toddler to do in the setting, such as carry a box to the check-out lane in the store (**Figure 13.14**). Most importantly, parents and caregivers cannot give in, even if the tantrum becomes full blown. (Giving in teaches the child that tantrums work.)

Figure 13.14 Making plans for a toddler to follow, such as telling a toddler he or she can pick out a book from the library, can help reduce temper tantrums. *Why do you think having a plan to follow reduces temper tantrums?*

Once a temper tantrum is underway, allow the tantrum to continue. It is a form of release for the child. Stay nearby, but do not try to reason with the child. If a tantrum occurs in public, go to a quiet place, if possible, for the toddler to become calm. Do not act embarrassed if others watch.

Avoid using spankings to punish tantrums. If the adult expresses displeasure (or even anger) in a physical way, he or she is modeling that behavior for the toddler. Tantrums, when handled calmly, often decrease during the preschool years. Also, adult calmness serves as a model for children as the best way to deal with anger.

Once the child is calm, adults should acknowledge the feelings of toddlers and show comfort. The adult may say, "I know you really wanted to stay outside. I'm sorry you are so upset about coming in the house." After the tantrum, hugs are often helpful. When adults hold back this comfort, toddlers may feel unlovable.

Fears and Anxieties

For toddlers to overcome fears and anxieties, they need to see and talk about their fears in safe ways. Telling toddlers other children have the same fear may comfort them. Gradual exposure to a feared subject may also help. For example, if the toddler is afraid of dogs, the adult may talk about dogs. Later, the adult may read a story about playful dogs or give a cute toy dog to the child. After some time, the toddler may stand near a friendly puppy or small dog that is safely behind a fence. This method is better for the toddler than suddenly exposing the child to fearful situations.

Giving toddlers security also reduces fear. Night-lights, toys (especially "loveys") in bed, and familiar caregivers add security (**Figure 13.15**). In many cases, adults can avoid situations that cause much fear or anxiety. Some situations, however, such as going to the doctor, cannot be avoided. These situations can be explained to the toddler in a simple, honest way. As they are explained,

Figure 13.15 Toys and familiar caregivers give children a sense of security, which reduces fear. *What familiar objects or experiences reduce fear for you?*

adults should address only fears the toddler has already shown.

Adults can acknowledge toddlers for their small steps toward overcoming fears. For example, toddlers can receive encouragement for only crying a little or for not running from the puppy behind the fence. Most of the toddler's fears and anxieties will disappear with age. If parents handle fear and anxieties in understanding ways, toddlers will be better able to cope with present and future fears and anxieties.

Based on the Harvard Growth Studies, research is leaning toward the belief that some children are genetically vulnerable to stress. These children may be more fearful or anxious throughout life than others. More sensitive and responsive caregiving is needed for these vulnerable children.

Focus on

Health

Maternal Depression: A Major Child Development Concern

Depression, a sad mood that continues, affects a person's energy level, social functioning, and body functions (eating and sleeping problems, headaches). Even mild forms (*dysthymia*, pronounced dis-THY-me-uh) affect mothers and their families. In fact, depression affects at least 12- to 25-percent of all mothers. Common factors causing depression are genetic predisposition, perinatal physical changes, and trauma (violence, abuse), and thus cannot be helped by mothers.

- ***Toddler risks.*** Toddler care requires much energy, ingenuity, and calmness. Feeling overwhelmed, depressed mothers often withdraw from care tasks (neglect). Others provide controlling, but inconsistent care. They show less affection for, talk and play less with, and seldom encourage their toddlers. The worst problem, however, comes in the maternal parenting style—being too critical of their toddlers' behaviors and reacting with anger, hostility, and even abuse.
- ***Toddler outcomes.*** When mothers withdraw from care, toddler accidents are three times more frequent. Maternal hostility results in toddlers' intellectual (delays, learning disorders) and behavioral (severe tantrums, biting, conduct disorders) problems, which continue throughout childhood or longer. These toddlers are also prone to depression before adulthood.
- ***Maternal support.*** Almost all depression can be successfully treated. The first task is identification of symptoms. The second task is providing needed treatment, such as antidepressant medications, "talking therapies," and parenting education and support. Depressed mothers need to develop routines, have some respite from child care, and take time for themselves. When mothers feel a sense of self-control, parenting becomes easier and the toddler outlook is brighter.

Handling Stress in the Toddler Years

One of the best ways to deal with stress is through prevention. Parents can help prevent stress in the toddler years by

- meeting toddlers' needs correctly, promptly, and consistently (which encourages secure attachments)
- helping the toddler feel nurtured and loved even when the toddler's actions might be considered unlovable
- aiding the toddler in the control of his or her emotions through co-regulation
- helping older toddlers communicate needs and feelings by talking

Parents might also ask themselves questions, such as: Am I making different child care arrangements too frequently? Is our family life peaceful? Am I allowing my toddler to watch adult-oriented media content, such as scary movies? Am I helping my toddler by being his or her *security-base* (being the important person in his or her life)?

Sometimes stress cannot be prevented. Parents and caregivers can, however, respond to the stress and identify stressors. Major stressors that can affect toddlers include parent-toddler conflicts, insecure attachments, concerns and traumatic events in the family, and maternal depression in the toddler's second and third years.

Maternal depression puts the mental health of the toddler at risk because the toddler's brain systems that generate depression are developing at this time. In the toddler period, the personality and emotional reaction area of the brain is being established. Calm, responsive parenting behaviors are needed to handle the needs of toddlers. Depressed mothers are often not responsive, or normal toddler behaviors evoke an irritable, even a hostile, response. In turn, cortisol spikes in the toddler's developing brain, including the areas that generate depression. Thus, maternal depression begins a chain of events that puts the mental health of the toddler at risk. For many mothers, depression is an unavoidable illness, but successful treatments are available.

Caregivers can recognize stress in toddlers by paying attention to signs, such as frequent nightmares, unusually intense fears, and aggressive behaviors. Coping with a toddler's stress involves being patient and supportive. Listening for clues about the source of the stress is important. All toddlers need consistency in their lives. If the symptoms of stress continue or worsen, seek professional help.

Mental Health Advisory

The toddler's brain system can generate depression. Stress caused by strong and continuous parent-child conflicts, insecure attachments, traumatic events, and/or maternal depression is very damaging to mental health throughout life.

Lesson 13.2 Review and Assessment

1. Self-awareness grows mainly out of the toddler's _____.
2. Describe two ways that parents and caregivers can help toddlers achieve autonomy.
3. Explain why it is important for parents and caregivers to both foster self-assertion and teach obedience.
4. Toddlers are _____, which means they are not self-guided by internal values.
5. Choose one emotion discussed in this lesson and explain how parents and caregivers can help toddlers co-regulate that emotion.
6. How should a temper tantrum be handled once it is underway?
7. Summarize three ways that parents and caregivers can help prevent stress in the toddler years.
8. **Critical thinking.** In small groups, brainstorm age-appropriate toys that might help toddlers develop self-awareness. How might these toys help? Justify your answers.

Chapter 13 Review and Assessment

Summary

During the toddler years, children begin to develop *self-awareness*. Besides seeing themselves as unique people and recognizing themselves, toddlers' self-awareness involves early feelings of self-esteem. Toddlers are in Erikson's second stage of personality development, known as *autonomy versus shame and doubt*. During the toddler years, social relations are extended. The parent-child relationship, which was solely nurturing during infancy, changes to include socialization and authority. Toddlers spend more time with adults other than parents. Interactions with other children are brief, though children often imitate each other. Developing secure attachments is critical for social-emotional outcomes throughout life.

Toddlers experience a wider range of emotions than infants. They are still attached to caregivers, but also begin to show affection for others. Fears tend to intensify during this period, and being separated from parents continues to make toddlers anxious. Anger occurs when events do not go how the toddler wants, often resulting in temper tantrums.

Toddlers are still dependent on adults to meet their social-emotional needs. Adults can help toddlers develop self-awareness, and parents who use the right types of support aid toddlers' feelings of autonomy. Parents must help their toddlers find a balance between self-assertion and obedience. To do this, toddlers need to know what is and is not acceptable. Parents and other caregivers must guide and co-regulate toddlers' positive and negative emotions. Stress is common in the toddler years. Most stress is short-lived, but stress associated with insecure attachments or trauma in toddlers, including depressed mothers, is serious and requires professional treatment.

College and Career Portfolio

Portfolio Sample Rationale

Portfolio samples are chosen to exhibit your best work in one way or another. Because portfolios can be made up of a variety of pieces, you should be prepared to explain why you chose the portfolio samples you did and how they portray your best work. To determine rationale for your portfolio samples, complete the following activities.

- For each portfolio sample, consider what you like about the sample and what it illustrates about you.
- Write a two- to three-sentence justification for the choice of each sample. Include your explanations in your portfolio or be prepared to repeat them in an interview.

Chapter 13 Review and Assessment

Vocabulary Activities 

1. Find online images or videos that visually express the meaning of each key term. In small groups, take turns describing the visual meanings for each term.

Key Terms

autonomy versus shame and doubt (13.1)
delay gratification (13.2)
gender identity (13.1)
obedience (13.2)
premoral (13.2)
self-assertion (13.2)
self-esteem (13.1)
self-restraint (13.2)
social referencing (13.2)
temper tantrum (13.1)

2. Work in pairs to write a *simile* for each of the following terms. Remember that a simile is a direct comparison of two items or factors that are *not* generally alike. When creating a simile, the comparisons are generally introduced by the words *like*, *as*, *seem*, or *appear*.

Academic Terms

assimilate (13.1)
autonomy (13.1)
bewilders (13.2)
cognizant (13.1)
competence (13.1)
contrariness (13.2)
control (13.1)
empathy (13.2)
feats (13.1)
worth (13.1)

Critical Thinking

3. **Identify.** Use the dictionary to find the definitions of the terms *autonomy*, *shame*, and *doubt*. List common situations that toddlers might experience, and identify whether each experience promotes autonomy or shame and doubt. Compare your list to that of a classmate.
4. **Make inferences.** What do you think would be the most challenging part about a toddler's desire for independence? What do you think would be the most gratifying aspect of this for caregivers?
5. **Compare and contrast.** In small groups, compare and contrast behaviors that indicate secure and insecure attachments in toddlers. Create a list of three to five guidelines that caregivers can reference to assess how secure a toddler's attachment is.
6. **Analyze.** Why is it important for parents and caregivers to control their emotions when dealing with toddlers? Analyze what emotional control or loss of control communicates to toddlers and what habits this might teach them.
7. **Draw conclusions.** Draw conclusions about what might happen if a parent or caregiver is permissive and gives in to a toddler's desires all the time.
8. **Cause and effect.** What do you think is the effect on the toddler if an adult fails to respect him or her? List ways that adults frequently fail to respect toddlers and imagine how this lack of respect would affect other relationships in the adult's life, such as a marriage or friendship. How might adults better respect toddlers to prevent a similar outcome?
9. **Evaluate.** Work with a partner to role-play a situation in which a toddler fears the dark and monsters in the closet. Take turns playing the toddler and the parent coping with the toddler's fears. Present your role-play to the class and evaluate how well the parent copes with the toddler's fears in each role-play you see.
10. **Determine.** How do you think toddlers' temper tantrums and other displays of emotion relate to their central conflict of autonomy versus shame and doubt? Explain your answer.

Core Skills

11. **Math.** Draw a thermometer to illustrate your self-esteem, with 100 being maximum self-esteem and zero being the minimum. Draw a line at the number 50; this will be your baseline self-esteem at the beginning of the day. As you go through your day, make note of any compliments or positive remarks that are made to you. Also note any insults, criticisms, or names you are called. For each positive comment made to you, add one to your self-esteem thermometer. Subtract one for each negative comment made to you. At the end of the day, calculate your self-esteem. What did this exercise teach you about self-esteem? What did it teach you about environment and about how caregivers should conduct themselves around young children?
12. **Listening and speaking.** In small groups, find a children's television show or book that is intended for children as young as toddlers. View or read the show or book and take notes about how young children's struggles for autonomy are referenced or depicted. Do any of the characters in the story yearn for independence? Do any of them end up in dangerous situations as a result? Afterward,

discuss the story with your group and compare notes. Together, present an analysis of the story to your class and explain how it speaks to young children's struggles for autonomy.

13. **Research and writing.** When children become toddlers, the parent-child relationship changes as parents enter the *authority stage* of parenting. Using reliable online or print resources, research changes in the parent-child relationship during the toddler years. How do other experts and sources explain this transition? Do they have a different perspective than the one covered in this chapter? Read and write summary statements for at least three sources. Finally, write an essay comparing and contrasting these sources and evaluating the information you found. Include a complete bibliography with your essay.
14. **Listening and speaking.** As a class, write all of the social-emotional developmental milestones for toddlers on index cards or other pieces of paper. Then, shuffle the cards around the room. Without speaking, try to group yourselves according to the appropriate age range. You can communicate what milestone you are by acting, using hand gestures, or writing words that are not included in your milestone's description. After grouping yourselves, check your accuracy by reading off your milestones.
15. **Technology and speaking.** Imagine you are a child development expert who has been asked to give a presentation to first-time parents about fostering self-assertion while teaching obedience to toddlers. In small groups, review this chapter's information about self-assertion and obedience and then research and brainstorm practical ways that parents and caregivers can encourage self-assertion while communicating to a toddler that he or she must obey. Film a three- to five-minute video demonstrating effective techniques for achieving this balance. Your video should include role-plays of realistic situations involving caregivers and their toddlers. Play your video for the class and answer any questions your classmates have.
16. **Writing.** During the toddler years, children feel emotions they do not understand and do not know how to express and control. For this reason, parents and caregivers should help toddlers co-regulate their emotions. Review this chapter's information about co-regulation and toddlers' emotions and then write three short stories—one about love, empathy, or affection; one about fear or anxiety; and one about anger. Your short stories should be written from a toddler's perspective. These stories should describe how the toddler is feeling and how the caregiver co-regulates the emotion being expressed.
17. **Art.** The toddler years can be difficult for parents and caregivers, and stress in caregivers can easily lead to stress in toddlers. Working with a partner, create a colorful, motivational poster with tips to help parents and caregivers manage the stress of the toddler years and help their toddlers cope with any stress they may experience. Your poster should be informative, encouraging, and visually appealing. Display it somewhere for your classmates to see.
18. **CTE Career Readiness Practice.** As a child care worker at a center for toddlers, it has come to your attention that the local newspaper will soon be interviewing you about what you are doing to teach toddlers self-awareness. You think your lessons for self-awareness are strong and well-researched, but you want to make sure you present the information clearly to the journalist. Describe your plan for teaching toddlers self-awareness—including activities for each day of the week and toys for 10 children—and as preparation for the interview, write and practice a short speech. As further preparation, consider questions the journalist might ask, and write and practice two to three planned answers. (Writing information organizes a person's thinking, and orally practicing written materials aids fluency, especially if nervous.)

Observations

19. Find a film, online video, or article with pictures that illustrates a caregiver coping with a toddler's temper tantrum. Watch the video or read the article and then assess how well the caregiver handled the tantrum based on what you have learned in this chapter. Write a summary of your assessment, and if the caregiver did not handle the temper tantrum well, explain what he or she could have done differently.
20. Observe several toddlers playing together at a local child care center. Are the toddlers possessive about toys? How do they reclaim a special toy from another child? How do they react when a toy is taken from them? How do adults settle toddlers' disputes?

Unit 5 The Preschool Years

Chapter 14	Physical Development of Preschoolers
Chapter 15	Intellectual Development of Preschoolers
Chapter 16	Social-Emotional Development of Preschoolers

Public Speaking

Public speaking is a competitive event or part of a competitive event you might enter with your CTSO. This allows you to showcase your organizational skills along with nonverbal and verbal communication in making an oral presentation. Public speaking is generally a timed event. You will have time to research, prepare, and practice before attending the competition.

To prepare for a public-speaking event, complete the following activities:

1. Read the rules and guidelines your organization provides. Note the topics from which you may choose to make a speech.
2. Locate the rubric or scoring sheet for this event on your organization's website.
3. Confirm whether you can use props or visuals as part of your presentation. Determine how much setup time the guidelines permit.
4. Analyze the rules to confirm whether the judges will ask questions of you or whether you will need to defend a case or situation as part of your speech.
5. Make notes on index cards about important points to remember and use them to study. You may be able to use your notes during the presentation, depending on the guidelines for your event.
6. Practice your presentation. Introduce yourself and the topic of your presentation, defend your position on the topic with supporting evidence, and conclude with a summary.
7. Ask your instructor to serve as competition judge when you practice your speech. You might also have a student audience listen and give feedback.
8. Keep practicing until you are comfortable and can give your speech without flaw.

Chapter 14

Physical Development of Preschoolers

Essential Question

How do growth and developmental changes in preschoolers support a vast expansion of motor skills, and how can parents ensure optimal physical development?

Lesson 14.1	Growth and Development of Preschoolers
Lesson 14.2	Meeting Nutritional Needs of Preschoolers
Lesson 14.3	Meeting Other Physical Needs of Preschoolers

Case Study Should Preschoolers Be Taught Handwriting?

As a class, read the case study and discuss the questions that follow. After you finish studying the chapter, discuss this case study again. Have your opinions changed based on what you learned?

Hector, a preschool teacher, took his four-year-old son, Diego, to the public school kindergarten for entrance testing. Afterward, he told a coworker, "Diego was tested on writing letters, but we don't teach our preschoolers how to write letters." During the staff meeting that afternoon, Hector brought up handwriting for preschoolers.

"I think we need to teach how to write letters," said Hector. "Not having this skill is not fair to preschoolers when they start kindergarten."

Lei, a former first-grade teacher, said, "I agree. We could teach straight line capital letters (E, F, H, I, K, L, and T) to our three-year-old preschoolers. The four-year-old class could learn the remaining letters."

Zahra, the program director, asked, "What about the three-year-olds who still switch hands while drawing?"

"All the better," said Lei. "We can teach them how to write right-handed."

"Wait," said Zahra. "I was forced to write with my right hand for years before switching to my left hand. I was so uncomfortable."

This jogged Hector's memory of an article he had seen. "I once read that forcing children to go against their hand preferences can lead to stress and other problems."

Zahra said, "Before we make any decisions, I'll talk to the curriculum director of the public schools to see what they really expect of children entering kindergarten."

Give It Some Thought

1. Do you think preschoolers should be taught how to write letters? Should they be taught to write only with their right hands? Explain your answers.
2. Do you think preschool programs should teach all of the content included on kindergarten entrance tests? Why or why not?
3. If the preschool staff members decide not to teach writing letters, are there other activities that would help prepare the children for learning to write letters? Describe these activities.

While studying this chapter, look for the online resources icon  to:

- **Practice** terms with e-flash cards and interactive games
- **Assess** what you learn by completing self-assessment quizzes
- **Expand** knowledge with interactive activities and graphic organizers

Companion G-W Learning

www.g-wlearning.com/childdevelopment

Study on the go

Use a mobile device to practice terms and review with self-assessment quizzes.

www.m.g-wlearning.com/0384

Lesson 14.1 Growth and Development of Preschoolers

Key Terms

ambidextrous
body rotation
dynamic balance
functional specialization
hand preference
internal organs
manipulate
reaction time
static balance
weight shift

Academic Terms

dehydration
elongates

Objectives

After studying this lesson, you will be able to

- describe the major changes in brain development during the preschool years.
- list the major changes in the heart, airways, stomach, and bladder.
- describe changes in the skeletal system.
- summarize major changes in gross- and fine-motor development during the preschool years.
- explain how hand preference develops.
- give examples of physical developmental milestones children might achieve in the preschool years.

Reading and Writing Activity

Arrange a study session to read the lesson with a classmate. After you read each section independently, stop and tell each other what you think the main points are in the section. Continue with each section until you finish the lesson.

Graphic Organizer

Draw a comic strip and label it *Growth and Development of Preschoolers*. Then, as you are reading, illustrate preschoolers' growth and development at three, four, and five years of age in the comic strip squares. Use as many squares as you want.

Preschoolers, children between three and five years of age, are looking more grown up. If you were to compare a child at the end of toddlerhood with a child nearing school-age, you would note dramatic physical changes. The maturation of all organs slows, but stabilizes during the preschool years. Growth rates during the preschool years are slower than they have been at any other time in the child's life. As the bodies of preschoolers continue to mature, proportionately they begin to look more like adults and less like younger children.

By the beginning of the preschool years, mastery of basic gross-motor movements (walking, bending, stretching) set off an explosion in preschoolers' abilities to control body movements as they develop more and more gross-motor skills. Preschoolers improve their skills of walking and running and learn jumping, hopping, catching and throwing, and balancing skills. Similarly, they are developing an expansive repertoire of fine-motor skills aided by establishing hand preference. The combined gross- and fine-motor skills allow preschoolers to control body movements to achieve complex goals in both play and self-help tasks.

Maturation of Organs

During the preschool years, the brain is still the fastest growing organ. Because of its rapid growth, the brain uses 30 percent of the body's energy, which makes good nutrition a must for healthy development. By five years of age, preschoolers' brains are 90 percent of adult weight. Boys have larger head circumferences than girls.

The following three major developments occur in a preschooler's brain:

1. **Functional specialization**, the development of special abilities in different regions (areas) of the brain, occurs. For example, different areas of the brain will store long-term memories and use memory to tell or retell stories or events. Functional specialization of the brain enables people to develop *executive functions* (working memory, cognitive flexibility, and inhibitions), control negative emotions, handle *expressive* (speaking, writing) as well as *receptive* (listening, reading) language, and allow for more logical concept development.
2. Greater myelination improves visual-motor coordination and intellectual development.
3. Pruning occurs in unused connections and thus begins to "close" many windows of opportunity.

Besides the brain, other organs are also maturing. As the heart matures, heart rate slows and becomes steady. Blood pressure increases. By three years of age, children use adult-like chest breathing. Children's air passages, however, are small. They have large tonsils and *adenoids* (lymphoid tissues).

By four years of age, the stomach capacity of a preschooler is about one-half of the adult stomach. Preschoolers' stomachs are straight and upright, making it very easy to vomit. The stomach lining is easily irritated by too much fiber or spices. Digestive upsets are also caused by viruses and bacteria. **Dehydration** (condition in which the body is lacking fluids) is common in the preschool years. The preschooler's bladder is also maturing. Because preschoolers have better control over their bathroom needs, there are fewer trips to the bathroom and fewer "accidents."

Skeletal Growth

Preschoolers grow more slowly than toddlers. The growth rate slows down for most children at an approximately equal rate. This means children who are larger than their peers at three years of age are likely to be larger at five years, too. In addition to changes in height and weight, changes also occur in preschoolers' body proportions, bones and teeth, and fat and muscle.

Height and Weight

Although growth slows during the preschool years as compared to the first three years of life, preschoolers are not finished growing. In the preschool years, height increases about 7 inches, and weight increases by about 13 pounds (approximately 3 to 5 pounds per year). Seventy-five percent of preschoolers' weight gain is due to muscle development. **Figure 14.1** shows the height and weight norms for children from three to five years of age.

Focus on

Science

The Digestion Process

Digestion is the process of breaking down foods into *nutrients* (molecules of proteins, carbohydrates, fats, vitamins, minerals), which the body uses for energy, growth, and cell repair. Every morsel of food has to be broken down before nutrients are absorbed by the blood and transported throughout the body.

The digestive system, called the *gastrointestinal (GI) tract*, is mainly comprised of three hollow organs (mouth, stomach, rectum) connected by almost 30 feet of tubes (esophagus and small and large intestines). Two solid organs (pancreas and liver) are part of the digestive system. Besides these organs and tubes, nerve and hormone cells and "good bacteria" (microbiome) help with digestion.

The digestive process begins in the mouth in which chewing and saliva break down some carbohydrates. Swallowing pushes food into the esophagus. From this point on, involuntary muscles, which contract and relax, propel foods through the GI tract (called *peristalsis*). The esophagus empties its contents into the stomach, which mixes foods with stomach enzymes (stomach acids), producing a mixture called *chyme*. Chyme is released into the small intestine where it is mixed with more digestive juices from the pancreas and liver. The molecules are then absorbed into the blood stream. Undigested foods, liquids, and salts move to the large intestine, which creates the stool and stores it in the rectum. During a bowel movement, the stool is pushed through the anus. This completes the digestive process.

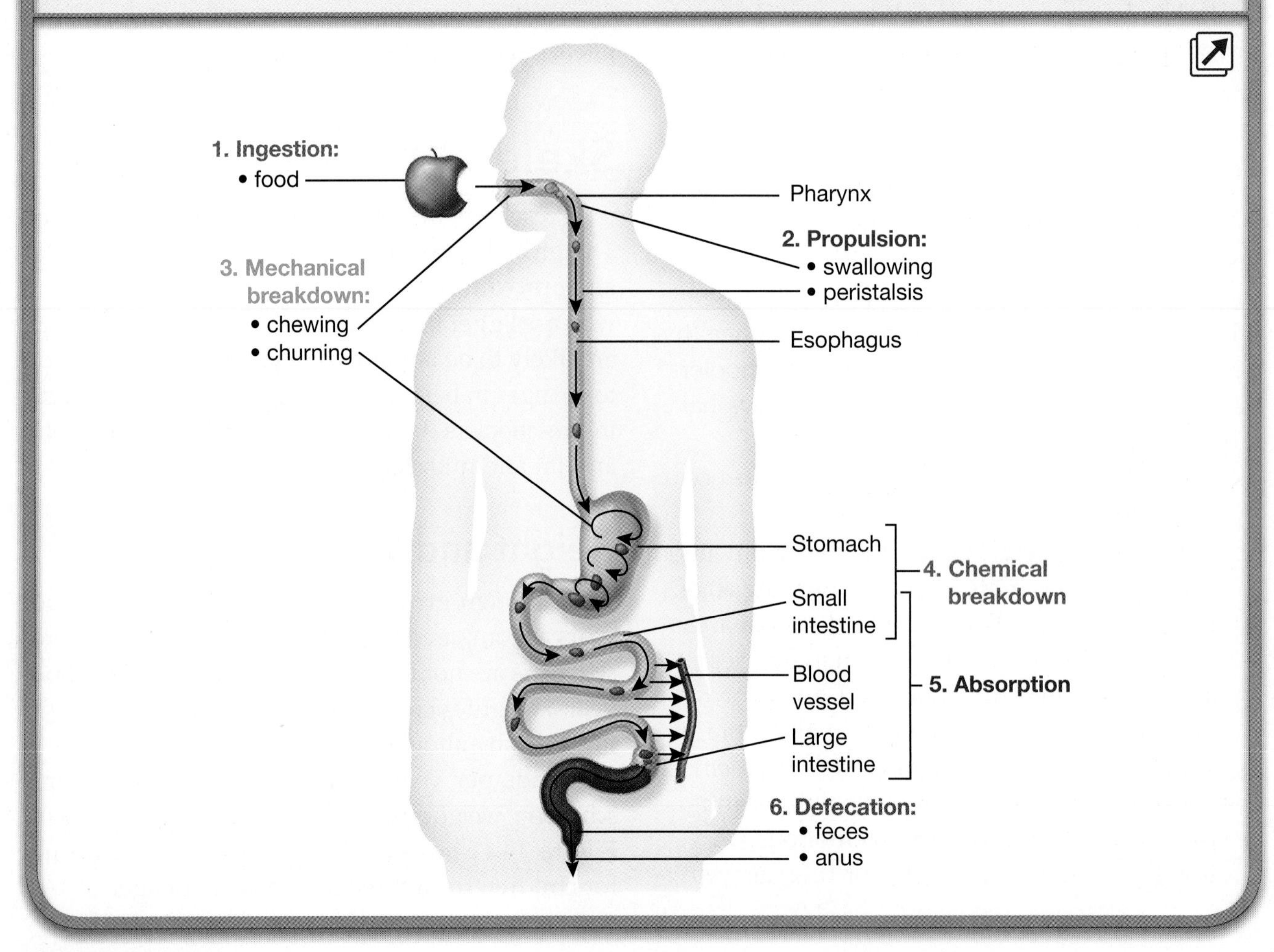

Figure 14.1 Average Height and Weight From Three to Five Years

Age in Years	Height in Inches		Weight in Pounds	
	Boys	Girls	Boys	Girls
3	38	37¼	32¼	31¾
3½	39¼	39¼	34¼	34
4	40¾	40½	36½	36¼
4½	42	42	38½	38½
5	43¼	43	41½	41
5½	45	44½	45½	44

Body Proportions

As toddler features begin to disappear, the preschooler's body becomes taller and leaner and body proportions begin to look more like those of an adult. The lower face grows more rapidly than the head, resulting in the preschooler's face looking more like an adult's. Until 30 months of age, a child's waist, hips, and chest measure almost the same. By five years of age, the waist is smaller than the shoulders and hips.

The preschooler's trunk and legs also grow to resemble adult proportions. The trunk grows to allow more space for the **internal organs** (heart, lungs, liver, and others). As the preschooler's trunk grows, the abdomen protrudes less. The legs grow rapidly, too. By five and one-half years, most children's legs are about half the length of the body—the same as an adult's leg-to-body proportions.

Bones and Teeth

Preschoolers' bones continue to ossify and grow larger and longer. Deciduous (baby) teeth begin to fall out between four and five years of age (**Figure 14.2**). Although permanent teeth may not erupt until the early school-age years, they are growing under the gums. The jaw **elongates** (lengthens) to accommodate these teeth. Tooth decay is also very common during the preschool years. Proper care of teeth is extremely important for lifelong dental health.

During the preschool years, bone and teeth development can be harmed by malnutrition and other health problems. Bones, muscles, and joints are more prone to injury in preschoolers than in older children. There are two main reasons for injury. First, the *ligaments* (the elastic-like bands that hold bones together) are loose and bones are not fully formed (thinner and less hard than teen bones), which causes injuries, such as some bones are prone to slip out of place. Second, certain diseases, such as *osteomyelitis* (infection of a bone), childhood diabetes, Down syndrome, obesity, and sickle-cell anemia can all lead to bone and joint deformities and increase the severity of injuries.

Figure 14.2 Between four and five years of age, children's deciduous teeth begin to fall out. *What does the term* **deciduous** *mean?*

Fat and Muscle

The ratio of fat to muscle tissue continues to decrease slowly during the preschool years. Boys lose baby fat more quickly than girls. With good nutrition and physical activity, most of the baby fat disappears by the first day of kindergarten. At five and one-half years, a child's fat deposits are less than half as thick as they were at one year of age. Girls will have more fat than boys.

As preschoolers' *skeletal muscles* (muscles attached to the bones) and bones are made stronger by ossification, their bodies are strengthened. Muscle fiber, which consists mainly of water, is now being replaced with more protein.

Preschoolers' activity levels also affect muscle development. Besides protein content changes in muscle tissue, the fiber size of muscles responds to physical activity. Thus, a three-year-old's skeletal muscles develop rapidly because children are more active at this age than at any other age in the lifespan. Boys have more muscle and bone growth than girls. Because boys have greater muscle development during the preschool years, they are, on average, a pound heavier than girls their age.

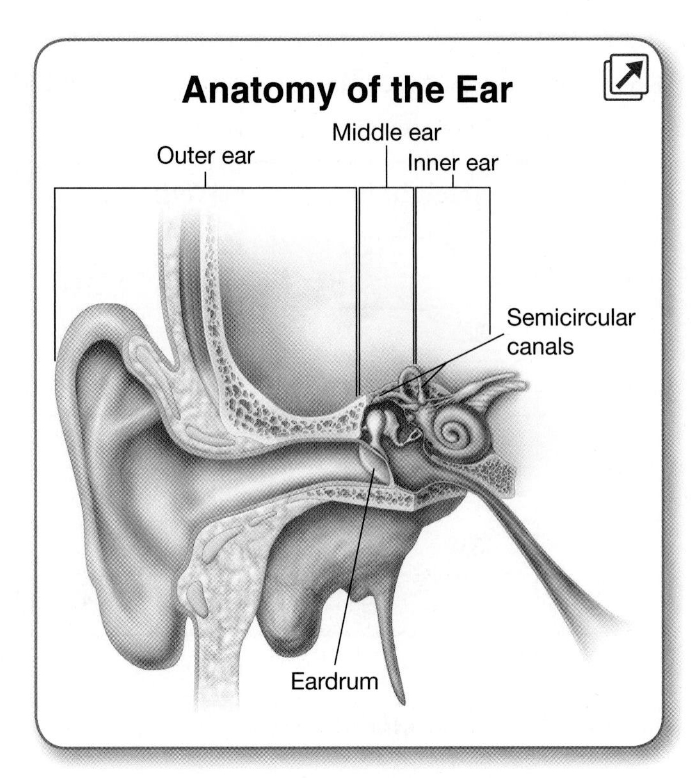

Figure 14.3 The movements of fluids in the ear's semicircular canals help the body maintain balance. *Which part of the ear are the semicircular canals in—the inner, middle, or outer ear?*

Motor Development

Preschoolers' motor development improves due to physical activity and increasing body growth and development. Preschoolers have an increase in muscle development and develop better balancing skills. Their eye-hand coordination becomes more refined. Their **reaction time** (time required to respond to a sight, sound, or other stimuli) becomes shorter. Preschoolers are able to perform many physical activities. Through play, their gross- and fine-motor skills develop quickly.

Large-Muscle Development

As preschoolers' large muscles develop, balance develops, too. This complex skill requires coordinating signals from the eyes and the movement of fluids in the semicircular canals of the inner ears (**Figure 14.3**). These signals are sent to the brain and then transmitted to the muscles of the body. Based on these signals, the muscles make constant adjustments to maintain balance, which keeps a person upright and affects many gross-motor activities. A person's ability to maintain balance is also a measure of eye, ear, and brain health.

During the preschool years, children differ widely in their balancing skills. Through regular physical activities, children develop two types of balance. **Dynamic balance**, balance maintained while moving, develops when preschoolers walk in a line or on a balance beam. **Static balance**, balance maintained while being still, develops when preschoolers stand on one foot with arms outstretched or folded across their chests. Dynamic balance is easier to develop than static balance. You may realize this if you have ridden a bicycle or watched or participated in dance or gymnastics.

Through muscle development and balancing skills, preschoolers become stronger and more coordinated. Preschoolers walk more smoothly than toddlers, and like to try more challenging ways to move. They run faster, and their arms and legs alternate in rhythm. Four-year-olds use a forward arm action to jump higher. With increased courage and better balance, climbing becomes easier. They can catch balls better when they are bounced to them rather than thrown to them. Three-year-olds begin hopping, but older preschoolers can hop and skip faster and for longer distances than younger preschoolers. Older preschoolers' actions become more advanced in all areas.

Two new actions, body rotation and weight shift, help the preschooler's throwing ability. **Body rotation** is the action of turning the hips (pelvis) and then the shoulders backward while the throwing arm comes forward. **Weight shift** is the change of weight from the back leg to the forward leg, which is done by shifting the hips forward. Body rotation and weight shift may begin during the third year, but both become much more pronounced by the end of the preschool years (**Figure 14.4**). Refinement of these skills continues for many years with athletes able to do both actions at the same time. This creates a 20 to 30 percent increase in the force of their throw while allowing the arm and hand mainly to direct the throw.

Figure 14.4 Body rotation and weight shift improve the force behind and thus the speed of the thrown object. *How does body rotation and weight shift improve the accuracy of throwing and protect the throwing arm from injury?*

Small-Muscle Development

Preschoolers' ability to **manipulate**, work with an object by using the hands, is still awkward. As preschoolers play with small objects, however, their small muscles develop and eye-hand coordination improves, which strengthens fine-motor skills. Preschoolers' fine-motor skills change and develop over time.

Three Years

At three years of age, children can usually feed themselves using a spoon and fork, but they are still rather messy. They can build towers from small blocks although the towers may be crooked. Three-year-olds can also draw straight lines and roughly copy circles. They can unbutton buttons and pull large zippers.

Four Years

By four years of age, preschoolers' movements are steadier. In addition to using forks and spoons, four-year-olds may try to use knives designed for children when they feed themselves. They are able to build straight towers and place blocks with steady hands. Four-year-olds begin to cut along lines with rounded-tip scissors. They can also comb their hair, wash their hands, and begin to lace, but probably will not tie their shoes.

Five Years

At five years of age, eye-hand coordination is greatly improved. Five-year-olds use a spoon, fork, and knife to feed themselves. They can build towers and play with other small toys with skill. They can make simple drawings freehand. Five-year-olds can also fasten large buttons, work large zippers, and may even be able to tie their shoelaces.

Hand Preference

During the preschool years, and sometimes during late toddlerhood, children begin to show hand preference. **Hand preference** is the tendency to use one hand more skillfully than the other hand for most tasks, making this hand the dominant hand (**Figure 14.5**). Hand preference is also called *handiness* and *hand dominance*. Most people think of hand preferences in categories—right, left, and **ambidextrous** (am-bih-DECK-struhs), ability to use the right or left hand, as the preferred hand, almost equally well for many tasks. Today, many researchers see handedness on a continuum with preferences in varying degrees.

Generally, hand preference is not firmly established until the end of the preschool years. During this stage, the brain specializes and myelination allows for better connections between brain areas. This is needed for hand preference. Child development experts believe that other factors, such as genetics, birth trauma, and social pressures, also affect hand preference.

Because researchers believe hand preference is determined by brain wiring, they feel each child should determine his or her own preference.

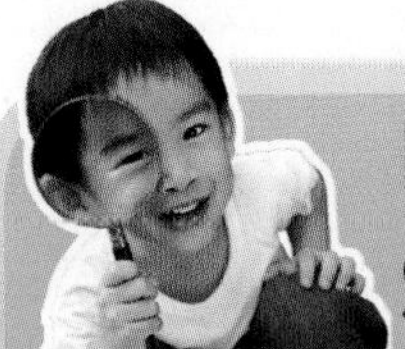

Investigate Special Topics: Hand Preference and the Brain

Hand preference and brain specialization occur at the same time. The brain is divided into two halves called the *right* and *left cerebral hemispheres*. *Brain lateralization* means these halves are not exactly alike. Different skills, called *specializations*, are associated with either the right or left sides. The left side is typically wired for language and logical thinking skills. The right side is typically wired for spatial abilities, visual images, and music. To a great extent, brain dominance is *contralateral* to the body, which means that the right side of the brain controls the left side of the body and vice versa. Thus, the left side of the brain is dominant for right-handed people, who comprise about 95 percent of the population.

Researchers originally thought that brain specialization for hand preference always occurred opposite from brain specialization for language (largely because the brain typically has a left-side language specialization). This, however, is not true for about 60 to 70 percent of left-handed people who have language *and* hand-preference specialization in the left hemisphere. Because left-handed people comprise less than 10 percent of the population, this represents very few people. The brain link between hand preference and language specialization is high, but not perfect.

In some cases, left-handed people have been pressured to switch their hand preference because left-handedness was seen as negative. In fact, the Latin term for left-handedness is *sinistra*, derived from the English term, *sinister* (meaning *evil*). Other people have switched their hand preference due to accident or illness affecting the preferred hand. Switching can happen because the brain is plastic and can be rewired with effort.

Research Activity

Using reliable online or print resources, research how left-handedness was viewed in a historical period and location of your choosing. Choose a specific date range, such as 1940–1950, and choose one country in particular to research. After conducting your research, write a two- to three-page summary of how left-handed people were viewed and treated in your chosen country during your chosen time. Include a bibliography with citations in APA format.

Figure 14.5 Children who have developed hand preference tend to use one hand more effectively than the other for tasks such as throwing a ball, drawing a picture, or writing. *What is your hand preference? Do you know when you developed this preference?*

Adults can help very young children develop hand preference by placing or holding objects at a child's *midline* (center of body) rather than to the right or left of the child. This gives the child an easier choice in hand use. Adults can also encourage activities that require the use of both hands for doing different actions, such as bead stringing. Preschoolers need ample time for brain wiring to determine their hand preference. Adults should never force a change in preference.

Physical Developmental Milestones

Physical capabilities greatly expand during the preschool years. Children are better able to explore and interact with the world around them. **Figure 14.6** describes the physical developmental milestones of preschool children.

Preschoolers need support as they grow and develop physically. Parents and caregivers can support a child's growth and development through proper nutrition and a healthy diet.

Lesson 14.1 Review and Assessment 

1. What three major developments occur in the preschooler's brain?
2. Summarize how preschoolers' hearts, airways, stomachs, and bladders mature.
3. Describe how skeletal growth changes the appearances of children during the preschool years.
4. Name and define the two types of balance that preschool children develop through regular physical activities.
5. List four fine-motor skills that children develop during the preschool years.
6. Explain the process by which hand preference develops during the preschool years.
7. Name three physical developmental milestones for children three, four, and five years of age.
8. **Critical thinking.** Why do you think left-handedness in children has been discouraged or frowned upon in the past?

Figure 14.6 Preschooler Physical Milestones

Three years

- Walks with arms swinging alternately and runs with some arm movement.
- Walks a straight line heel-to-toe.
- Walks on tiptoes.
- Walks upstairs by alternating feet.
- Hops one to three steps on preferred foot (three and one-half years).
- Turns body slightly when throwing a ball.
- Catches a ball by trapping ball in arms.
- Kicks a ball.
- Pedals a tricycle.
- Puts on shoes (cannot tie laces).
- Opens and closes twistable lids.
- Grasps marker with thumb and pad of index finger.

Four years

- Walks downstairs by alternating feet.
- Walks in a line around the periphery of a circle heel-to-toe.
- Walks a balance beam.
- Runs with ability to start, stop, and turn as needed.
- Hops four to six steps on preferred foot.
- Jumps with forward arm motion.
- Pedals and steers tricycle skillfully.
- Throws ball with a slight weight shift from back to front foot when thrown.
- Catches a bounced ball with stiff, outstretched hands (four years) and with arms to the side (four and one-half years).

Four years *(Continued)*

- Colors between two parallel lines without crossing either line more than twice.
- Copies a few capital letters (T, E, F, H).
- Draws human figure by adding arms and legs extending from face.
- Cuts a straight line with rounded-tip scissors.
- Builds a straight block tower.
- Works a 40-piece jigsaw puzzle.
- Dresses and undresses with assistance needed for tying shoes and working difficult fasteners.

Five years

- Runs with good speed.
- Skips and jumps rope.
- Ascends and descends slide ladders and play structures by alternating feet.
- Hops eight to 10 steps on preferred foot.
- Throws ball with definite weight shift.
- Rides bicycle with training wheels.
- Copies most letters and writes first name from memory.
- Colors within lines.
- Draws human figure with neck, torso, arms and legs extending from torso, and details on face.
- Cuts and pastes simple shapes.
- Builds with smaller interlocking blocks.
- Builds taller towers and other structures (bridges, buildings) with blocks.
- Works a 50-piece jigsaw puzzle.
- Strings small beads and laces lacing cards.
- Dresses and undresses without much assistance, including tying shoes.
- Handles keyboard and mouse in digital devices.

Lesson 14.2 Meeting Nutritional Needs of Preschoolers

Key Terms

empty calories
nutrient-dense foods
solid fats

Academic Terms

acrid
susceptible
uniform

Objectives

After studying this lesson, you will be able to

- summarize the importance of meeting preschoolers' nutritional needs.
- develop healthful eating plans for preschoolers.
- identify unhealthful food choices and eating habits.
- assess foods for their appeal to preschoolers.

Reading and Writing Activity

Before reading, review this textbook's information about meeting the nutritional needs of toddlers. Collect your notes from that topic and then take notes while reading this lesson. After reading, write a two- to three-page summary of how meeting children's nutritional needs changes between the toddler and preschool years.

Graphic Organizer

On a piece of paper, write the headings in this lesson, leaving space between them for your notes. Then as you are reading, write what you learn underneath or next to each heading. After reading, review your notes and highlight what you think are the most important points.

You Are What You Eat *food affects development*
children need nutrient-dense foods

Healthy Eating Plans

Unhealthy Food Choices

To meet the preschooler's nutritional needs, adults provide a variety of healthful foods at regularly scheduled meal and snack times. Parents need to be flexible, however, and listen to their preschooler's indications of fullness or hunger. Children grow at different rates and their energy output can vary from month to month. Preschoolers become more interested in foods prepared in different ways. Eating *junk foods* (foods low in nutritional value) may become more of a problem in the preschool years.

You Are What You Eat

Have you ever heard someone say, "You are what you eat"? This statement is correct. What people eat affects their growth and development, overall health, general alertness, and emotions.

A preschooler's diet must supply the nutrients needed to support brain growth and other developing body systems. Children (as well as adults) need **nutrient-dense foods**, those that are high in lean protein, complex carbohydrates, healthy fats, vitamins, and minerals and contain relatively few calories. Fruits and vegetables are examples of nutrient-dense foods.

When nutritional needs are not met, children's growth will stall. Children will also be more **susceptible** (prone) to diseases, and when they become ill, their recovery time is slower.

Healthful Eating Plans

To meet the needs of their growing bodies, preschoolers should be offered nutritious foods at meal and snack times. The MyPlate website is a tool parents and caregivers can use to find individualized, healthful eating plans for preschoolers as well as sample menus and tips for healthy eating. These plans show how much food a preschooler needs from each food group. At this age, children often get hungry between meals. One or two healthful snacks per day may be planned between meals to satisfy hunger pangs (**Figure 14.7**). Snacks, however, should not be so large or so close to mealtime that the preschooler has no appetite for the meal.

To help children learn to choose healthful amounts of food, parents and caregivers often let them eat only as much as they want. When children are old enough, they can serve themselves appropriate amounts of foods. To teach children how to determine healthful portion sizes, parents and caregivers may suggest children take small portions at first. Children can then come back for more if they are still hungry. Rather than forcing children to finish all their food, parents and caregivers should allow them to stop eating once they feel full. A child who learns to pay attention to what his or her body is signaling is more likely to maintain a healthy weight. When a child needs a special diet for health reasons, adults should consult a doctor or registered dietitian nutritionist.

Unhealthy Food Choices

When planning meals and snacks, foods that contain empty calories should be limited or avoided. **Empty calories** supply the body with energy, but few or no nutrients. Added sugars and solid fats are sources of empty calories in foods. **Solid fats** are fats found mainly in animal-based foods, such as butter and beef fat. These fats are solid at room temperature. Foods such as cookies, hot dogs, or sugar-sweetened cereals contain some nutrients, but many empty calories. Other foods such as sodas or candy provide only empty calories and are considered *empty-calorie foods*.

Eating too many empty calories may cause a child to gain too much weight now or in the future. When children are eating empty-calorie foods instead of nutrient-dense foods, their bodies are not receiving the nutrients needed for proper growth and development.

Experts say children, as well as adults, should reduce their intake of sugar, salt, and solid fats. Eating excessive amounts of sugar can lead to tooth decay, obesity, and other health concerns that often last for years. A majority of overweight preschoolers, for example, are still overweight at 12 years of age. Consuming too much fat and salt early in life may increase chances of high blood pressure in later years. Chances are compounded if high blood pressure exists in the family's health history. Snack foods that are high in sugar, salt, and solid fats should be avoided (**Figure 14.8**).

Meal and Snack Pattern A

These patterns show one way a **1200 calorie MyPlate Plan** can be divided into meals and snacks for a preschooler. Sample food choices are shown for each meal or snack.

Breakfast	Breakfast Ideas		
1 ounce Grains ½ cup Fruit ½ cup Dairy*	Cereal and Banana *1 cup crispy rice cereal* *½ cup sliced banana* ½ cup milk*	Yogurt and Strawberries *½ cup plain yogurt** *4 sliced strawberries* 1 slice whole-wheat toast	Applesauce Topped Pancake *1 small pancake* *¼ cup applesauce* ¼ cup blueberries ½ cup milk*

Morning Snack	Morning Snack Ideas		
1 ounce Grains ½ cup Fruit	1 slice cinnamon bread ½ large orange	1 cup toasted oat cereal ½ cup diced pineapple	Frozen Graham Cracker Sandwich *2 graham crackers (4 squares)* *½ cup mashed banana*

Lunch	Lunch Ideas		
1 ounce Grains ½ cup Vegetables ½ cup Dairy* 1 ounce Protein Foods	Open-Faced Chicken Sandwich and Salad *1 slice whole-wheat bread* *1 slice American cheese** *1 ounce sliced chicken* ½ cup baby spinach (raw) ¼ cup grated carrots	Soft Taco (meat or veggie) *1 small tortilla* *½ cup salad greens* *¼ cup chopped tomatoes* *3 Tbsp shredded cheese** *1 ounce cooked ground beef or ¼ cup refried beans*	Bagel Snack *1 mini whole-grain bagel* *¼ cup sliced cherry tomatoes* *¼ cup diced celery* *1 ounce tuna* ½ cup milk*

Afternoon Snack	Afternoon Snack Ideas		
½ cup Vegetables ½ cup Dairy*	½ cup sugar snap peas ½ cup yogurt*	½ cup veggie "matchsticks" (carrot, celery, zucchini) ½ cup milk*	½ cup tomato juice 1 string cheese*

Dinner	Dinner Ideas		
1 ounce Grains ½ cup Vegetables ½ cup Dairy* 2 ounces Protein Foods	Chicken & Potatoes *2 ounces chicken breast* *¼ cup mashed potato* ¼ cup green peas 1 small whole-wheat roll 1 cup milk*	Spaghetti & Meatballs *½ cup cooked pasta* *¼ cup tomato sauce* *2 meatballs (2 ounces)* ½ small ear corn on the cob 1 cup milk*	Rice & Beans with Sausage *½ cup cooked brown rice* *¼ cup black beans* *¼ cup bell pepper* *1 ounce turkey sausage* ¼ cup broccoli 1 cup milk*

*Offer your child fat-free or low-fat milk, yogurt, and cheese.

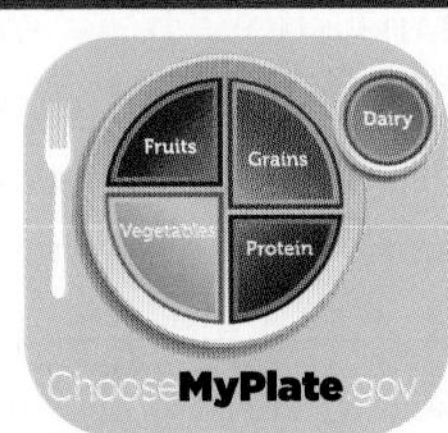

Figure 14.7 For good health, a four-year-old needs physical activity as well as these recommended amounts from each food group of MyPlate every day. *What do you think are the most appealing food items on this plan?*

Figure 14.8 Reducing Added Sugars

Instead of:	Offer:
Flavored milk	Unflavored fat-free or low-fat milk
Sweetened yogurt	Fat-free or low-fat plain yogurt topped with fruit
Ice cream or frozen yogurt	Frozen fruits with no sugar added, or frozen 100% fruit bars
Sweetened breakfast cereals	Cereals with little or no added sugars, whole-grain cereals, or oatmeal with fruit
Cookies	Whole-grain crackers, graham crackers, or plain animal crackers
Canned fruit in syrup or sweetened applesauce	Fruit canned in water or 100% fruit juice; unsweetened applesauce
Doughnuts, pies, or cakes for dessert	Fruits (fresh, frozen, or canned in water or 100% juice), fruit salads, or baked fruits (like baked apples or pears)
Jam or jelly	100% fruit spread
Soda, fruit-flavored drinks, fruit cocktails, or fruit punch	Water, fruit-infused water, fat-free or low-fat milk, or 100% fruit juice (no more than one ½-cup serving per day)

teamnutrition.usda.gov/library

Forming Healthful Food Attitudes

The food attitudes preschoolers learn may last a lifetime. Offering a variety of foods in a pleasant atmosphere helps preschoolers form healthful food attitudes.

For the most part, people like variety in their lives. This includes variety in the foods they eat. Some children may go through phases during which they want the same food(s) day after day. Others eat or drink a few of the same foods daily, but vary other foods.

Many healthful options are available within each food group. Children should be able to eat foods they like and still meet their nutritional needs. Forcing children to eat foods they do not like can cause them to have negative feelings toward healthful foods. Using food to reward or punish can also have a bad effect. Children who are rewarded and punished with food may learn to eat as a way of bribery. For example, some parents reward with food by saying, "If you pick up your toys, you can have an ice cream cone." It would be better to say, "We'll go to the park and play catch as soon as you pick up your toys."

Some parents may punish their picky eaters by threatening to withhold food. A parent might say, "You can't have dessert until you eat your peas." This teaches the child that the dessert is the desirable food and peas are only the means to obtaining the dessert. If access to a food is restricted, it may encourage overeating of that food when it is available.

Preschoolers observe the behavior of those around them. They often copy the actions of the role models in their lives, such as parents, older siblings, and caregivers. If a role model makes negative comments about a food, the preschooler is likely to adopt a negative attitude also. Role models can encourage positive food attitudes in preschoolers by setting a good example (**Figure 14.9**).

Providing an attractive room and table setting for eating can contribute to a healthful food attitude. Dishes and flatware suited to the child's hands make mealtime easier and also lessen the chance of accidents. Children may want to help make the

Figure 14.9 If a child sees an older family member enjoying vegetables or drinking milk, the child is more likely to develop a positive attitude about these foods. *In what ways can family members model healthy eating habits to preschoolers?*

table attractive by choosing the napkins, picking a flower from the garden for the table, or helping set the table.

Food becomes a part of many celebrations. Preschoolers may look forward to helping prepare a special holiday dish or choosing their birthday menu. Trying different eating styles is fun, too. A restaurant, cafeteria, picnic, or cookout provides children with more food experiences.

Foods with Preschooler Appeal

Meal and snack time success is more likely when foods are offered that are appropriate for the age group. The tips in this section address some of the unique considerations when serving food to preschool-age children.

Consider the Preschooler's Senses

Children and adults have different senses of taste and smell. For example, many children are "bitter sensitive" to some foods, such as spinach, broccoli, and cabbage. There is an acid in spinach (oxalic acid) that leaves a bitter aftertaste in the mouths of children, but not adults.

Children often prefer mild flavors and aromas over stronger, **acrid** (bitter and unpleasant) flavors and scents. They also tend to dislike foods that are too spicy. Children are influenced by other food tastes and qualities as well. Often by the preschool years, children begin to like their family's favorite cultural dishes. Keeping these differences in mind when offering foods to preschoolers may contribute to a successful meal.

Aim for Visual Appeal

How food looks may influence whether children think they will like it. Children like attractive-looking foods. Foods of different sizes, shapes, colors, textures, and temperatures look better than foods that are **uniform** (look the same). Plates should have some empty space. A plate that appears too full can seem overwhelming before the child has even taken one bite. Instead, serve less food on the plate and offer the child a second helping if he or she is still hungry. Children also enjoy foods prepared especially for them. Special dishes, napkins, or centerpieces may make eating a meal or snack even more special.

Keep Foods Separate

Children often prefer to eat foods separately rather than eat foods that are combined (**Figure 14.10**). If children see or taste one food they do not like in a casserole, soup, or salad, they may reject the entire dish. They are more likely to accept mixtures of fruits than mixtures of vegetables. Children may eat self-made mixtures more readily than adult-prepared mixtures. For example, children may prefer to mix their own salads from several bowls of precut vegetables.

Serve Foods at Acceptable Temperatures

Preschoolers do not like foods that are served at extreme temperatures. In fact, they can easily burn their mouths on foods that are too hot. Some of these foods (such as hot drinks) can simply be avoided because many children do not like them anyway. Soups are good for children, but young children cannot manage a steamy bowl or cup of soup. One easy solution is to drop a few ice cubes into hot soup just as the child begins to eat. As the ice melts, the temperature of the soup will drop to an acceptable level.

Very cold foods present a problem, too. Children eat these foods very slowly, because eating large bites can cause a sharp headache. Thus, there may be more ice cream on the outside of a preschooler than on the inside. Parents can start offering suggestions for managing hot and cold foods during the late preschool years.

Vary Methods of Preparation

Children show likes and dislikes for ways foods are prepared. A child who turns down cooked carrots may eat a crisp, raw carrot. A salad dressing or dip that is mild in flavor may make almost any vegetable or fruit easy to eat. Dressings made from yogurt and cheese can help meet the calcium needs of young children, too.

Offer New Foods in Small Amounts

Children will often taste one bite or a small amount of a food just to see whether they like it. Give children new foods in small amounts (one slice or a tablespoon). Serve new foods with ample portions of foods children like to eat. The new food may be rejected, but do not give up. Foods may need to be offered many times before children accept them.

Figure 14.10 Children prefer foods that are separated over foods that are combined. *What are some combined foods adults might separate out for their children?*

Prepare Easy-to-Eat Foods

Foods should be easy for preschoolers to eat (**Figure 14.11**). Bite-sized and finger foods are preferred over foods that are harder to eat. Most children at this age cannot cut food. They may not hold spoons and forks correctly. These problems make eating messier for preschoolers than for older children and adults.

Making Meals Fun

By helping to prepare food, children have fun while they learn about colors, shapes, tastes, aromas, textures, and appliance names (*blender*, *oven*). They learn food preparation terms (*cut*, *boil*, *poach*, *bake*) and food names. Cooking teaches math concepts (*measurement*, *numbers*, *temperature*, *time*, *shapes*) and science as they see changes in foods (*rising*, *baking*, *freezing*, *boiling*). As an added bonus, children often eat what they help prepare.

Children enjoy eating with others. Meals can be a time to relax, share, and have fun. Enough time should be given for the meal itself, because eating with children takes time.

Setting an example by taking turns talking and demonstrating other table manners allows children to learn at mealtimes. Have realistic expectations for behavior at mealtime. Preschoolers are often messy eaters because their fine-motor skills are still developing. This behavior is normal. Rather than scolding, include the child in cleanup and praise his or her efforts.

Lesson 14.2 Review and Assessment 

1. Children (as well as adults) need _____ foods, or foods that are high in vitamins and minerals and contain relatively few calories.
2. Explain how nutrition is vital to preschoolers' growth and development.
3. Why should adults *not* force preschool children to finish their meals?
4. List three examples of empty-calorie foods and foods that contain solid fats.
5. Summarize three ways that adults can help preschoolers form healthful food attitudes.
6. What are three ways adults can make foods appealing for preschoolers?
7. Why are preschoolers often messy eaters?
8. **Critical thinking.** How could an adult explain to a preschooler why junk foods are unhealthy?

Figure 14.11 Preschooler foods should be fun and easy to eat. ***What are some creative ways adults can make foods easier and more fun for their children?***

Meeting Other Physical Needs of Preschoolers

Lesson 14.3

Objectives

After studying this lesson, you will be able to

- give examples of features to consider when choosing garments for preschoolers.
- describe toileting problems and dental care guidelines for preschoolers.
- summarize physical activity guidelines for preschoolers.
- explain preschoolers' need for rest and sleep.

Key Terms

enuresis
plaque

Academic Terms

agile
cavities

Reading and Writing Activity

Imagine you are a psychologist and one of your clients is feeling overwhelmed by the pressure to meet the physical needs of his preschool daughter. What would you tell this father about what his daughter needs from him right now? Write a two-paragraph speech explaining these needs and then deliver your speech to a partner. After reading this lesson, find your partner again and discuss what you would add to your speech based on what you have learned.

Graphic Organizer

In small groups, collect photos or other illustrations that depict the physical needs discussed in this lesson. Arrange your photos into a collage and write a two- to three-sentence summary about what each photo represents. Share your collage with another group.

Preschoolers' physical, intellectual, and social-emotional skills develop at rapid rates. These improved skills help children meet their own needs. Preschoolers want to do tasks for themselves and others. For example, they like to use their motor skills to feed and dress themselves and help parents with everyday tasks. Because their abilities quickly develop, preschoolers need a great deal of support from and time with caring adults.

Although preschoolers are able to do many tasks on their own, they still need adult help and guidance. Just as in infancy and toddlerhood, parents and caregivers still need to meet preschoolers' physical needs for clothing, good hygiene practices, sleep, and physical activity.

Figure 14.12 During the preschool years, children begin to express their unique personalities through clothing. *What sorts of clothes did you wear as a young child? How did these clothes express your personality?*

Clothing

Besides protecting a child's body from harsh weather conditions, cuts, and scrapes, clothing also becomes important to a child's growing self-concept during the preschool years. Clothing can also aid the learning of self-help skills as preschoolers learn to dress themselves.

Choosing Garments

Allowing preschoolers to make some choices about their clothes is one way children can express their personality (**Figure 14.12**). Perhaps preschoolers can choose the color they want from similar outfits. Not only will children enjoy clothes they have chosen, but they also learn to make decisions.

When selecting clothes for preschoolers, fit is an important feature to consider. Sizes for preschoolers' clothes are often given as *4* through *6X* or *7*. Hangtags and charts on children's sizes often give measurements for chest, waist, hips, inseam, and other features. Boys and girls often have similar measurements. Therefore, measurements for a given size may be the same for both males and females. Some clothes are also sold in more specialized sizes to fit slender and heavier children. The clothing chosen should give the active child freedom to move and thus should never be too tight in any measurement.

Preschoolers' clothes have most of the same quality fabric and construction features as toddlers' clothes. Preschoolers grow mainly in the length of the arms and legs and the width of the shoulders. For these reasons, their clothes should have features that allow parents to let out the hems as children grow. Adjustable shoulder straps and waistbands also allow room for growth.

Because preschoolers explore indoor and outdoor areas, their clothes need to have certain safety features. Outdoor clothing worn after dark should be light-colored or have a trim of reflective tape that will reflect the light from cars or other vehicles. Hoods attached to coats and rainwear should easily detach if caught on large objects.

Some clothing features may present a safety hazard for children and should be avoided. For example, large, loose headwear can prevent children from seeing traffic or other hazards. Loose or wide pant legs and long shoelaces can cause tripping. Other loose clothing, such as long or wide sleeves, drawstring ties, long sashes and scarves, and extra large clothes can also present safety concerns.

Self-Dressing Features

By the end of the preschool years, many children can dress themselves with only a little help from adults. Adults should always be near, however, to help the child and check the child's attempts. The following features aid self-dressing:

- large openings, especially for slipover garments
- easy-to-recognize fronts and backs of garments, such as labels, threads, or tape sewn inside
- front rather than back openings, such as front buttons and attached belts that hook in front (**Figure 14.13**)
- elastic in waistbands and sleeves (at wrist)
- easy-to-work fasteners, such as zippers with large pull tabs
- shoes with self-adhesive straps

In addition to self-dressing features in garments, special toys are available to help children learn to button, snap, zip, and manipulate other closings. These give children extra dressing practice.

Fitting Shoes

Many preschoolers grow one shoe size every four months. Along with size, caregivers should check for the following fitting features in each shoe style:

- ***Activity shoes.*** Look for flexible soles that are ¼- to ⅜-inch thick to absorb the pounding of walking, running, and jumping.
- ***Sneakers and athletic shoes.*** Make sure arch support is in correct position. Check fit with the socks to be worn with the shoes. Socks are often bulky, requiring larger shoes.
- ***Sandals.*** Consider adjustable straps and buckles that do not press into the foot.
- ***Dress shoes.*** Make sure the sole is as flexible as possible. (Thin soles of dress shoes do not absorb pounding. For this reason, dress shoes should only be worn for short periods.)

Figure 14.13 Self-dressing features, such as buttons at the front of a shirt, make it easier for preschoolers to dress and undress themselves. *What are some clothing features that would make it difficult for preschoolers to dress or undress?*

Hygiene

By the preschool stage, children have begun to learn and establish hygiene practices (**Figure 14.14**). They still need help and supervision in completing hygiene tasks, however, including using the bathroom and brushing their teeth.

Toileting Accidents

Toileting accidents occur once in a while with preschoolers. Daytime accidents are most often a result of children waiting too long to go to the bathroom. Children may need reminders to go to the bathroom after they wake up in the morning or from naps, before going outside, before and after meals, and before leaving the house.

Figure 14.14 Preschool children often have hygiene practices, such as bathing, already in place. *What are some ways adults can remind preschoolers about their hygiene routines?*

Time seems to be the major cure for preschoolers' bedtime toileting accidents. Most children are not night-trained in toilet learning until at least three years of age. For a child over three years of age, involuntary urination two or more times a week for at least three months is called **enuresis** (en-yoo-REE-sis). Sometimes, people use the term to apply to bed-wetting when the child no longer has daytime accidents. There may be many causes of bedtime accidents in the late preschool years (and even in the school-age years). Possible causes include

- inherited problems
- not being breastfed for three or more months in infancy
- urinary tract problems
- deep sleeping
- constipation causing pressure on the bladder
- too much fluid in the evening hours
- fear of getting up in the dark

Children often outgrow these problems within a few years. For children who are afraid to get up in the middle of the night, a night-light near the child's bed and in the bathroom may help reduce fears. Dim hallway lights or a dimly lit path to the bathroom may also help. If toilet accidents still occur, medical help may be needed.

Dental Care

Preschoolers are prone to **cavities** (areas of decay in teeth). **Plaque**, a sticky, mineral deposit coating the teeth while it colonizes bacteria on food particles left in the mouth, can cause cavities and lead to gum disease. To help prevent tooth decay and gum disease, adults should make sure preschoolers brush their teeth twice a day with a fluoride toothpaste.

To ensure proper brushing, adults should also monitor preschoolers as they brush their teeth. Just as in toilet learning, preschoolers may need reminders or help in the process. For example, preschoolers may need help from an adult to squeeze a pea-sized amount of toothpaste onto their toothbrush. Once children have two or more teeth that are touching, parents or caregivers should also floss a preschooler's teeth once a day. To make sure teeth are clean, healthy, and properly growing, dentists recommend preschoolers have two dental checkups per year.

Physical Activity

As preschoolers' gross-motor skills and eye-hand coordination improve, they become more **agile** (able to move quickly and easily). Because of these improved skills and children's high energy level, preschoolers usually get ample physical activity in their daily routines. These activities might be planned or unplanned. Common physical activities include throwing and catching balls, riding tricycles, or playing tag. Playground activities, such as climbing equipment, swinging on the swings, and running around the playground, are also popular physical activities. **Figure 14.15** shows motor physical activities preschoolers commonly enjoy.

Focus on

Careers

Dental Hygienist

Dental hygienists check teeth and gums and take X-rays to check for non-visible problems with the teeth, and they clean and polish patients' teeth. They assist the dentist as necessary. Dental hygienists also teach people about proper dental care, such as brushing and flossing.

Career cluster: Health science.

Education: Educational requirements include an associate's degree in dental hygiene and state licensure.

Job outlook: Future employment opportunities for dental hygienists are expected to grow much faster than the average for all occupations.

To learn more about a career as a dental hygienist, visit the United States Department of Labor's *Occupational Outlook Handbook* website. You will also be able to compare the job responsibilities, educational requirements, job outlook, and average pay of dental hygienists with similar occupations.

Parents can encourage physical activity and help preschoolers avoid a sedentary lifestyle. The American Academy of Pediatrics recommends limiting screen time to less than two hours per day. Limiting screen time encourages a physically active lifestyle. Parents can encourage activity by enrolling their children in classes and programs, such as swim or gymnastics classes. Adults can also structure indoor activities for preschoolers when outdoor play is not an option.

Rest and Sleep

Preschoolers need about 11 to 13 hours of sleep daily. Sleep needs are somewhat individual, but younger preschoolers often need more sleep than older preschoolers. Most children give up daytime naps during the preschool years.

Preschoolers still want (and need) a bedtime ritual. If bedtime rules have been enforced in the toddler years, most children accept them during the preschool years. Fears of the dark and monsters still exist, but many preschoolers develop their own routines to help ease such stress. Locking windows or sleeping with a doll or stuffed animal may comfort the child.

Lesson 14.3 Review and Assessment

1. Choosing their clothes is one way preschoolers can express their _____.
2. Name four self-dressing features for preschoolers' clothing.
3. Choose one type of preschooler shoe and describe the fitting features adults should check for.
4. For a child over three years of age, involuntary urination two or more times a week for at least three months is called _____.
5. List four possible causes of regular toileting accidents during the preschool years.
6. To help prevent tooth decay, adults should make sure preschoolers brush their teeth _____ a day.
7. Preschoolers need about _____ hours of sleep daily.
8. **Critical thinking.** What types of physical activities did you enjoy as a very young child? How do you think the types of activities preschoolers enjoy have changed since you were that age?

Figure 14.15 Motor Skill Activities

Gross-Motor Activities

- Walk backward, sideways, heel-to-toe on a drawn line, or on tiptoes and heels.
- March to music.
- Run to a given point (tree), run around it, and run back.
- Jump off a low, sturdy object.
- Jump over two drawn lines or two ropes placed parallel on the floor.
- Hop on one or both feet, in different directions (backward or sideways), or as far as possible. Add music or a rhythmic beat to help the child skip with the beat.
- Roll or pass a ball back and forth (while counting).
- Throw and catch balls.
- Bounce balloons up from the hand or toss balloons to different distances.
- Ride tricycles and scooters.
- Push strollers and pull wagons.
- Climb, slide, and swing on playground equipment.
- Crawl through straight and curved tunnels or a tunnel on a hill.
- Walk forward and backward on a balance beam. Use specific arm movements, such as a bird flapping its wings while on the balance beam.
- Dance freestyle or to songs with movements ("I'm a Little Teapot").
- Use pretend movements to music (plane, animals).
- Play "Red Light/Green Light" or circle games.
- Sing and use movements to "Head, Shoulders, Knees, and Toes" or the "Hokey Pokey."
- Play a modified version of hopscotch.

Fine-Motor Activities

- Engage in sand play, cooking activities, and art activities, and play with a toy carpenter bench.
- Learn finger plays, such as "The Itsy Bitsy Spider."
- Use "manipulative toys," such as stringing beads, lacing cards, small blocks and tinker toys, and cube block designs.
- Use finger puppets with stories, songs, poems, and finger plays.
- Trace with templates or cookie cutters for eye-hand coordination.
- Clip clothespins to the rims of containers or to the edges of cardboard. Punch holes with a single-hole punch to strengthen fingers.

Chapter 14

Review and Assessment

Summary

During the preschool years, three major brain developments occur: functional specialization, greater myelination, and pruning. The heart, airways, stomach, and bladder also mature. Preschoolers gain in height and weight. Their faces begin to look more like those of adults, and their waists become smaller than their shoulders and hips. Bones grow harder, larger, and longer, and deciduous teeth begin to fall out. Fat deposits decrease, and muscle tissue increases in size and strength. Balance and other gross-motor skills develop through preschoolers' physical activities, and their fine-motor skills improve as they manipulate small objects.

Hand preference also develops during the preschool years and is associated with functional specialization, genetics, birth trauma, and social pressures. Each child should determine his or her own hand preference.

Preschool children need to eat nutritious meals and snacks. They learn attitudes about food from others. Preschool children like foods that look good, are separated, are served at acceptable temperatures, are prepared in different ways, are served in small amounts, and are easy to eat.

Clothing for preschool children must be appealing and fit properly. When selecting clothing for children, adults should look for safety and self-dressing features. Preschool children generally have control over their bladders, but some toileting accidents may occur. Adults should help preschool children maintain basic hygiene, such as using the bathroom and dental care. Physical activity is vital for preschool children's health and motor skill development. Preschoolers should get 11 to 13 hours of sleep per night.

College and Career Portfolio

Portfolio Résumé

Whether your portfolio is for a school or for a job, you will need to include a résumé. A *résumé* is an outline of your education and relevant experience. It should be concise, detailed, and attractive, and should advertise why your chosen school or company needs *you*. To create your résumé, complete the following activities.

- Visit your school's career center, writing center, or a local library to learn more about résumés. For more information about résumé writing, you can also read Chapter 25, *Preparing for a Child-Related Career*, in this textbook or view sample résumés online.
- Write a draft of your résumé and have it reviewed by a teacher. Then, edit your résumé accordingly.

Chapter 14 Review and Assessment

Vocabulary Activities 

1. Before reading the chapter, work with a partner to write the definitions of the following terms based on your current understanding. Then team up with another pair to discuss your definitions and any discrepancies. Finally, discuss the definitions with the class and ask your instructor for necessary correction or clarification.

Key Terms

ambidextrous (14.1)
body rotation (14.1)
dynamic balance (14.1)
empty calories (14.2)
enuresis (14.3)
functional specialization (14.1)
hand preference (14.1)
internal organs (14.1)
manipulate (14.1)
nutrient-dense foods (14.2)
plaque (14.3)
reaction time (14.1)
solid fats (14.2)
static balance (14.1)
weight shift (14.1)

2. With a partner, create a T-chart. Write each of the following terms in the left column. Write a *synonym* (a word that has the same or similar meaning) for each term in the right column. Discuss your synonyms with the class.

Academic Terms

acrid (14.2)
agile (14.3)
cavities (14.3)
dehydration (14.1)
elongates (14.1)
susceptible (14.2)
uniform (14.2)

Critical Thinking

3. **Compare and contrast.** Obtain two pictures of a child—one as a baby and one at four or five years of age. Compare and contrast the child's physical appearance in these pictures. What physical differences are evident? What physical features have remained the same?
4. **Cause and effect.** The author states that food attitudes learned in the preschool years may last a lifetime. What is meant by a *food attitude*? What food attitudes do you have that you think may have been impacted by your experiences as a young child?
5. **Identify.** Search the Internet for creative foods for young children. Choose four food ideas you find especially creative and then identify what makes them so appealing. Also, identify the nutritional content of the food and assess how healthful it would be for a growing preschooler.
6. **Evaluate.** Find a magazine that contains pictures and descriptions of gifts (such as toys and clothes) for preschool children. As you read the magazine, choose three gifts and evaluate their usefulness and appeal based on preschoolers' physical abilities and preferences. Which gifts would preschoolers most like? Which gifts would be too easy or too advanced for preschool children?
7. **Determine.** When Haneul's son, Hwan, started preschool, Haneul took advantage of the opportunity to start taking late-afternoon shifts at her job. Unfortunately, some of these shifts would run until 8:00 p.m. on weeknights. While Hwan's babysitter had already put him to bed by this time, Haneul wanted to hear about her son's day some nights and woke him up to talk with her. Hwan has had trouble sleeping the past few months and always seems tired. How can Haneul help her son get sufficient sleep? How can she balance her desire to spend time with Hwan and also help him meet his physical needs?

Core Skills

8. **Writing.** Review this chapter's information on the organ maturation and skeletal growth of preschoolers. Then, imagine you have been hired to write a creative and engaging book for parents of preschoolers, with the goal of teaching them what they should expect as their children grow. Write a short, entertaining book chapter covering preschool organ maturation and skeletal growth. Keep your audience in mind and write using a conversational tone.
9. **Reading.** Imagine you are a teacher at a preschool center. Your director has asked you to help preschoolers develop their fine-motor skills through a series of entertaining crafts. In preparation for these activities, search a local library or the Internet for fun and simple craft ideas that would help children develop fine-motor skills. Craft a lesson plan based on these activities, including what materials you will need, what additional support you will have to give the children, and how each activity will aid fine-motor development.

10. **Technology and speaking.** In groups of three, review the physical developmental milestones children achieve at three, four, and five years of age. Have each group member select one age, and then, using art supplies or electronic resources, create an easy-to-follow visual representation of the milestones children achieve during these years. Your project should include drawings or pictures of children achieving various milestones during each year, and should be an effective study tool and synthesis of the information you learned in this chapter. After completing your project, make a group presentation to the class.
11. **Listening and speaking.** Using MyPlate and the nutritional information covered in this chapter, plan a week's worth of healthful snacks and meals for a preschool child (three meals and two snacks per day). Plan meals that satisfy MyPlate's recommendations in each food group and choose online or print recipes for each food you include.
12. **Technology and art.** Clothing becomes more important to children during the preschool years. Preschool children are developing unique personalities and want to express these personalities in their clothing. Adults, however, still need to ensure that clothing contains appropriate safety and self-dressing features. In small groups, use software or sketch paper to design a preschooler's outfit. First, describe the personality of the preschooler you want to design for and then work together to create a quality outfit that contains some of the safety and self-dressing features covered in this chapter. After completing your design, present it to the class and describe how it meets the preschool child's needs.
13. **Research and speaking.** Lack of dental care in early childhood can lead to serious tooth decay in the teen and even adult years. For children in underserved areas, this can be a complicated problem because dental care is inaccessible or unaffordable. In small groups, research the effects of children's lack of dental care. Document the possible consequences of this problem and identify three organizations that are working to provide dental care to these underserved children. Finally, deliver a five minute group presentation detailing how lack of dental care affects children and what organizations are doing to remedy the problem.
14. **CTE Career Readiness Practice.** Imagine you are the director of a preschool center, and that recently, one parent complained that her child was not getting enough physical activity. Upon further investigation, you find that children spend more time playing with digital devices than they do playing outside. You gather your three-person team to talk about the problem, but you're afraid of being too harsh with them. In preparation for your team meeting, complete the following steps:
    - **Identify the problem.** Write a two- to three-sentence summary of the problem. Choose words that will challenge your team, but will not discourage them.
    - **Create a plan to fix the problem.** Outline a weekly routine that will provide the children with more physical activity.
    - **Delegate the parts of the plan.** Decide who will fulfill each part of the plan (person one, person two, or person three) and document how you will describe each person's job responsibility.

    After making these preparations, rehearse the meeting in groups of four. Give each other feedback.

Observations

15. As a class, observe preschoolers in a child care program eating lunch or a snack. What foods are they provided? Do the children seem to like some foods and reject others? Why do you think certain foods are rejected? How did adults at the child care center respond to children rejecting the foods? After the observation, have a class discussion concerning how to improve the eating experiences of the preschoolers in this child care program.
16. Interview a teacher at a local preschool center about how the children in his or her center have physically changed between three and five years of age. Before the interview, identify some questions you want answered. Some possible questions might be: How do children's growing bodies affect their motor development? How do you see hand preference develop? What are some signs that a preschooler's balance is improving? Take notes about your interview and then discuss your findings in small groups.

Chapter 15 Intellectual Development of Preschoolers

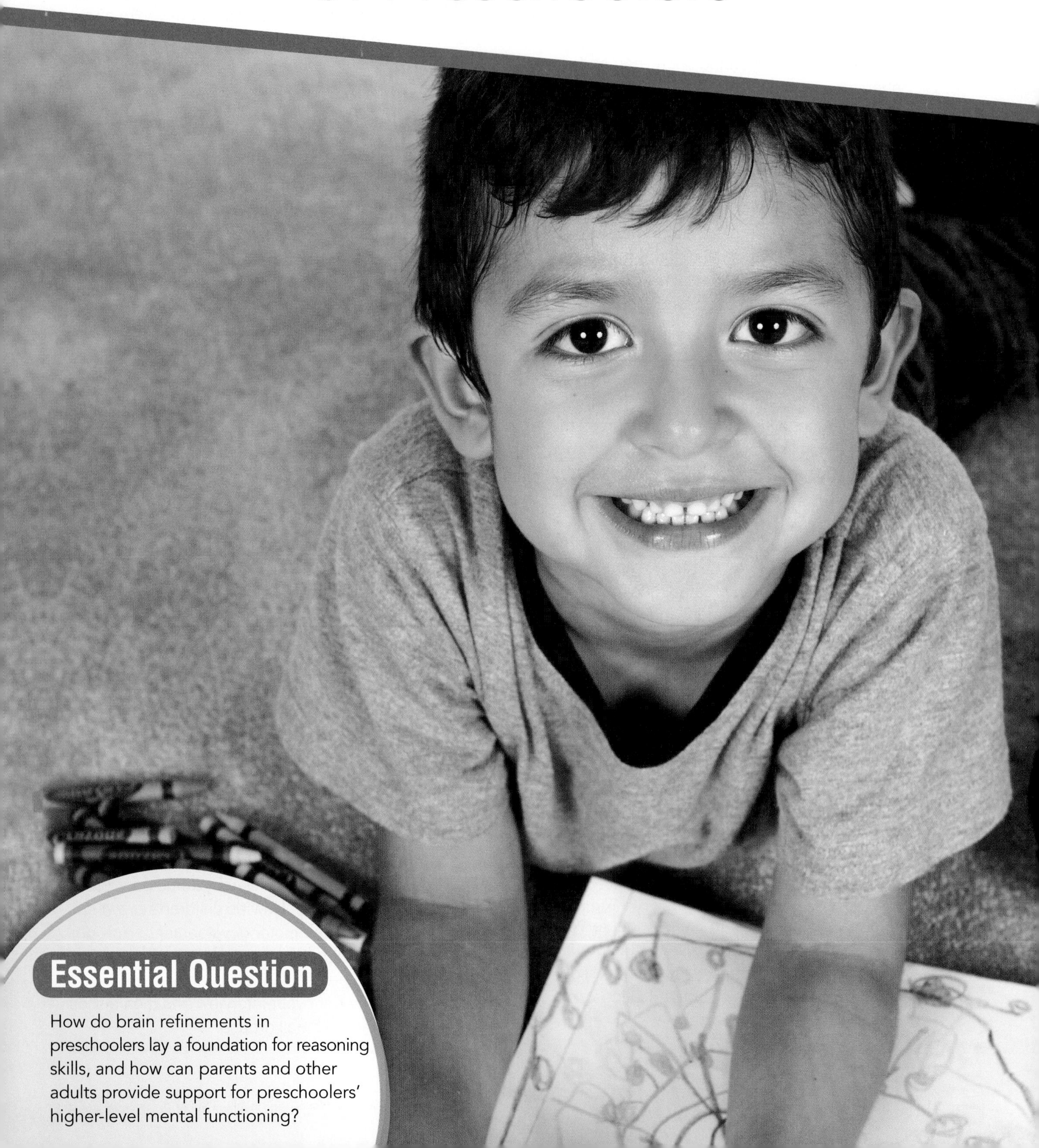

Essential Question

How do brain refinements in preschoolers lay a foundation for reasoning skills, and how can parents and other adults provide support for preschoolers' higher-level mental functioning?

Lesson 15.1 **How Preschoolers Learn**

Lesson 15.2 **What Preschoolers Learn**

Lesson 15.3 **Meeting Preschoolers' Intellectual Needs**

Case Study Can Imaginative Preschoolers Confuse Reality and Fantasy?

As a class, read the case study and answer the questions that follow. After you finish studying the chapter, discuss this case study again. Have your opinions changed based on what you learned?

Amber's parents took her to Disney World to celebrate her fourth birthday before her preschool program resumed for the fall. Amber liked books about princesses, and at Disney World, she had a day as a "princess," complete with a beautiful dress, makeup, a tiara, and photos. When the day ended, it was difficult for Amber's parents to convince her to remove the princess trappings.

After that day, Amber insisted she was Cinderella and expected everyone to call her by that name. Her preschool teachers chuckled and decided to play along. Almost every day, Amber would wear a formal dress from the preschool's dress-up box and play the role of Cinderella. She expected her friends to be her stepsisters. When her friends no longer wanted to play the role of her stepsisters, Amber could not understand why.

Amber no longer played in all of the program centers as she once did. She would not cook dinner, but would attend tea parties in the housekeeping center. Amber wouldn't even play outside if she couldn't wear her formal dress. She would only engage in activities for a princess. By this point, some of the teachers and Amber's parents were becoming concerned that Amber was taking this role too far.

Give It Some Thought

1. Do you think Amber believes she's really Cinderella? Explain your answer.
2. Do you think Amber's dedication to her fantasy role suggests a developmental problem? Explain.
3. Do you think Amber's parents and the teachers at the preschool program were right in "playing along" with Amber, or should they have insisted that the role could only be played a few minutes each day? Explain your thinking.

While studying this chapter, look for the online resources icon  to:

- **Practice** terms with e-flash cards and interactive games
- **Assess** what you learn by completing self-assessment quizzes
- **Expand** knowledge with interactive activities and graphic organizers

Companion G-W Learning

www.g-wlearning.com/childdevelopment

Study on the go

Use a mobile device to practice terms and review with self-assessment quizzes.

www.m.g-wlearning.com/0384

Lesson 15.1 How Preschoolers Learn

Key Terms

centration
egocentrism
episodic memory
intuitive substage
memory capacity
mental images
preconceptual substage
preoperational stage
symbolic thought
transductive reasoning
transformations

Academic Terms

conceptualize
crystallized
intuition
overgeneralization
transposition

Objectives

After studying this lesson, you will be able to

- relate how brain development and symbolic thought aid the emergence of new thinking skills in preschool children.
- summarize the changes in pretend play, mental images, drawing, language, and memory that occur during the preschool years.
- explain the major changes that occur between the preconceptual and intuitive substages of the preoperational stage.
- describe the five major obstacles to preschoolers' logical thinking.
- explain the three major origins of abstract thought in preschoolers, as identified by Vygotsky.

Reading and Writing Activity

In learning about children, you learn a great deal about yourself. As you read this lesson, consider what each concept you learn might teach you about yourself. Keep a list of these ideas, placing a star beside any concepts that especially interest you. After reading the lesson, pick two or three of these ideas and write an essay reflecting on how the content in this lesson helped, or will help, you understand yourself.

Graphic Organizer

Two of the main topics covered in this lesson are Piaget's Cognitive-Developmental Theory and Vygotsky's ideas about preschool learning. On a separate sheet of paper, draw two circles, one labeled *Piaget* and the other labeled *Vygotsky*. As you read, write information you learn around the circle to which it most relates. If a piece of information relates to both theorists, write it between the circles.

Preschool children build on what they have learned as infants and toddlers. Because preschoolers have better motor skills, their world broadens. Preschoolers can interact with more objects and people and participate in more events. This enables them to observe more and develop more advanced ideas about the physical attributes of their world.

Preschoolers' intellectual development also broadens their world. Thinking skills are well underway in the preschool years, as brain development allows fast learning. Preschoolers can **conceptualize** (form a concept of) objects and actions. Cognitive changes in pretend play, mental images, drawing, language, and memory help them use their skills more effectively. Preschoolers are in the *preoperational stage*, a developmental stage in which they solve problems first by using only their present perceptions, which can lead to many faulty concepts, and later through intuition by which their rich mental imagery and memory improve their problem-solving abilities. Scaffolding is less hands-on during the preschool years, and preschoolers' maturing brains make this stage vital to learning.

Brain Development and Cognitive Changes

Brain development is still rapid during the preschool years. Brain specialization allows for many new abilities, myelination speeds connections between areas, and pruning makes the remaining connections more efficient.

By three years of age, preschoolers use thinking to solve problems even better than before. They do not always have to use trial and error. Their problem-solving skills are affected by past sensory and motor experiences.

Beginning between three and four years of age, one of the most important cognitive advances is *symbolic thought*. **Symbolic thought** is the ability to use symbols to represent objects, actions, or events from a person's world of experiences. Children learn symbolic thought through pretend play, also known as *symbolic play*, where they make associations between their real worlds and the symbols they use (**Figure 15.1**). Because of symbolic thought, children can separate actions from events. For example, a preschooler can understand that a car does not just "go," but is used as a means of going to some place. Symbolic thought also enables children to separate thought from action. For example, a child can think about some actions without actually doing them. Symbolic thought affects a number of abilities—pretend play, mental images, drawing, language, and memory.

Pretend Play

During late toddlerhood, pretend play begins with the development of deferred imitation. *Deferred imitation* is a child's ability to imitate the actions of a model who is no longer present. Pretend play develops and changes in the following areas during the preschool years:

- ***Symbol realism.*** Children engaging in early pretend play prefer realistic symbols that closely represent the intended object. Later, children change their pretend play to include objects that may stand for anything they want.

Figure 15.1 In pretend play, preschoolers associate symbols with real-world objects and events. *What types of pretend play did you engage in as a young child? What symbols did you use while playing?*

- *Context.* Children's early pretend play takes place within the context of real experience. As pretend play develops, children might choose less realistic contexts.
- *Roles.* Early pretend play involves children role-playing themselves or those similar to them. Later, children begin to take on a greater variety of roles, such as role-playing adults or even animals.
- *Number of actions.* Early pretend play experiences often involve one action, such as combing hair. Later, children may pretend play a sequence of actions, such as several grooming tasks.
- *Involvement of others.* Early pretend play is usually done alone, but as pretend play develops, children play pretend games with other children and sometimes with adults.

Figure 15.2 Mental images exist within a person's mind; they may become observable through drawings. Children's drawings tend to mirror their mental images. *What mental images do you have when you hear the following words:* **cat, thunderstorm,** *and* **flower?**

Mental Images

Mental images are symbols of objects and past experiences that are stored in the mind. These images function as a form of mental representation. The imagery is experienced through all sensory modes, such as the appearance, feel, sound, odor, or flavor of anything. Therefore, mental images resemble a perceptual experience, but occur in the absence of that experience. Mental images are not exact copies of real objects and experiences, but they do relate to the real world (**Figure 15.2**). Mental images are triggered by words, new experiences, memories, and even "What if…." thoughts.

Mental images function in preschoolers' and even adults' thinking in the following ways:

- Memories are often stored as mental images. Through memory a person recalls the past. As you read, *learning* is defined as an adaptation of a past understanding. You modify your current thinking based on recall (memory) and then store the new learning in memory. Thus, learning and memory are interactive processes.
- Imagery is crucial to *language meanings* (semantics). Preschool children store the meanings of concrete words (*cat*, *apple*, *building*) as mental images although this does not work for more abstract words, such as *hope* or *joy*. As people of all ages hear or read words, they link the sounds or graphics to meanings through their mental images. Descriptive writers of both prose and poetry rely on their readers to create mental images from their words.
- Imagery is involved in spatial reasoning as a person "sees" how something would look if rotated, turned over, or *synthesized* (putting together shapes to form new shapes). Playing with jigsaw puzzles or block building aid mental imagery of young children. This early spatial imagery will allow adults to draw images from any perspective. Frank Lloyd Wright, the great American architect, said he used his mental images from childhood block building to create his designs (**Figure 15.3**).
- Mental imagery plays a crucial role in inventive or creative thinking. Creative preschoolers use mental imagery in their pretend play, artistic creations, and language. They imagine new "what if" configurations for a marble shoot or a building and refine their physical knowledge concepts. Adult inventors, including Einstein and Tesla, used mental imagery because it allowed them to modify their ideas quickly.

In short, mental imagery plays a crucial role in *all* thought processes.

Drawing

Unlike younger children, preschoolers no longer scribble. Instead, they attempt to draw objects and depict their world through drawings. Preschoolers intend their drawings to be realistic. They draw what they think or know about a person, not what is visually accurate. For example, a side view of a goldfish in a drawing may show both eyes and even a smiling mouth. Drawing mixes the skills involved in pretend play and mental images. Preschool children draw first and then decide what their pictures represent. In contrast, older children decide what to draw, form a mental image of the object, and then draw it.

Language

Spoken and written words are symbols used to represent ideas or actions. Compared with child-created symbols seen in pretense and drawing, language symbols are more abstract and thus more difficult for the child to understand. Unlike symbols used in pretense or in drawing, children do not *decide* on language symbols. Language symbols *already exist* in a culture and must be learned. Therefore, words are more abstract compared with most other symbols. For example, the word *car* does not look, sound, or move like a car.

Figure 15.3 Taliesin West, Frank Lloyd Wright's winter home and architectural school, is an example of his great skill at designing attractive and creative buildings and structures. *How much do you think the mental images formed in childhood affect a person's perceptions later in life?*

Memory

Memory is a complex mental process involved in most, if not all, aspects of thinking and learning. Memory begins at birth when the newborn remembers the rhythm and intonation of the mother's voice heard in the prenatal period. Infants have amazing, although rather short-term, memories. Toddlers remember better and for much longer periods of time, and preschoolers remember even more.

A major change in memory occurs during the preschool years due to brain development and experiences. Preschoolers remember more and retain memories longer than younger children. Preschoolers remember not only images, but also language components. Preschoolers often replay their memories by talking about events or rehearsing what they have learned in a song or a story. **Memory capacity**, or what a person does with his or her memory (not how *much* is remembered), increases during the preschool years. Memory capacity increases in both working and long-term memories (**Figure 15.4**).

Working Memory

Working memory (also called *short-term memory*) is critical for executive functioning and is closely related to Galinsky's essential life skills. Working memory improves a great deal in the preschool years. These improvements allow preschoolers to follow directions, connect events in stories, stay true to the pretend roles they play, play games with several rules, and follow new sequences of rules.

Long-Term Memory

Explicit and implicit memories (also called *long-term memories*) continue to develop in the preschool years. Preschoolers' explicit memory develops as they learn more facts, concepts, and words associated with these facts and concepts. Implicit memories, especially motor skills, also dramatically increase as preschoolers play and learn self-help tasks.

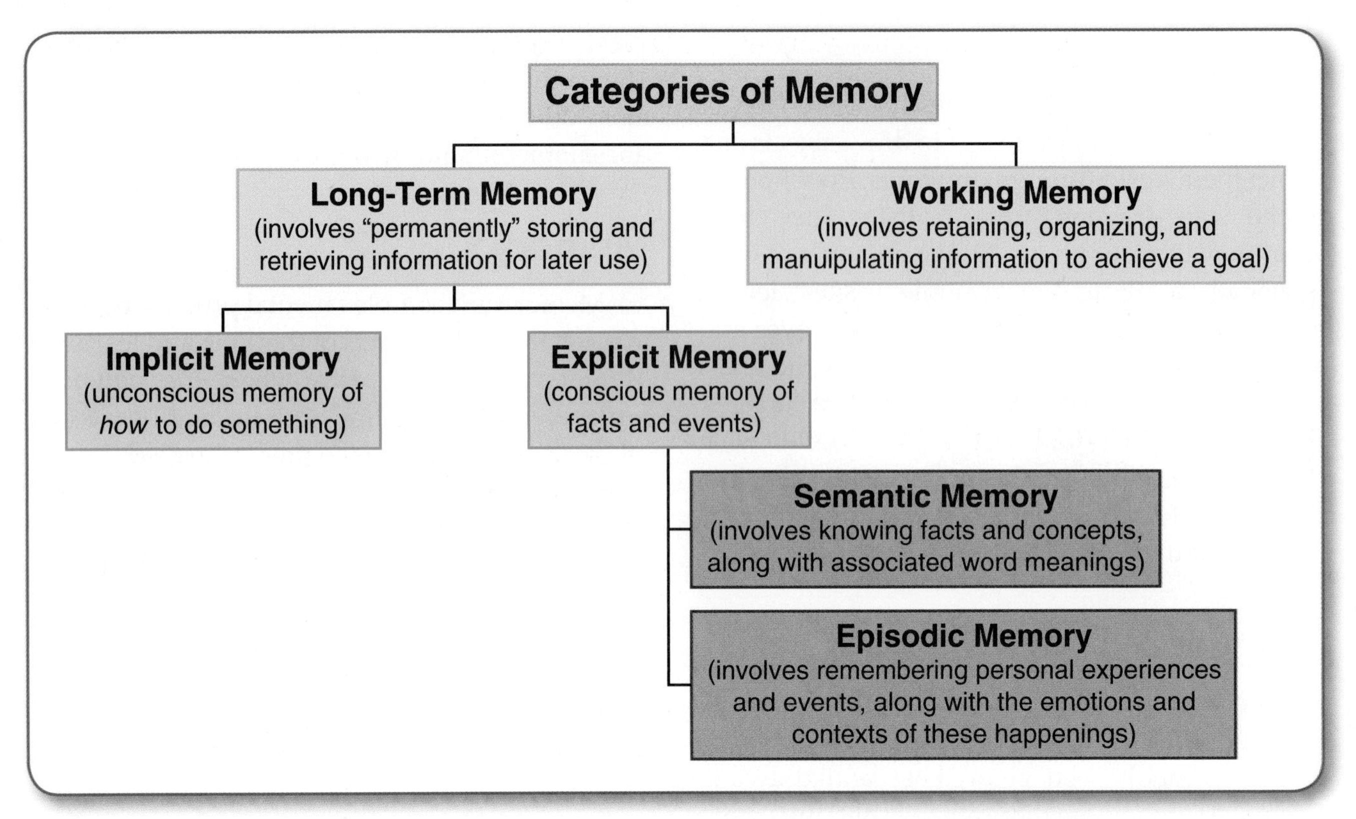

Figure 15.4 Memory can be divided into two categories: long-term memory and working memory. Long-term memory can be further divided into implicit and explicit memory, which includes semantic and episodic memory. ***What are some examples of memories that fall into each of these categories?***

Preschoolers develop what is called *episodic memory*. **Episodic memory**, which is a type of explicit memory, is the memory of personal experiences and events. Episodic memories include the emotion and the context of the event. People usually see themselves as "actors" in these memories. Episodic memories begin between preschoolers' third and fourth birthdays. Even then, children may forget these early memories. Episodic memories are not **crystallized** (KRIS-tuh-lyzd), or clear and fully formed in the mind, until 10 years of age. The inability to remember events before 3 or 4 years of age or the forgetting of recalled events in the preschool and early school years is called *infantile amnesia*. Although more research is needed, the following is known about children's early episodic memories.

- Infants and toddlers do not have the thinking or language skills necessary to store memories of personal events.
- For life experiences to feel real to children, children must have a sense of self and personal identity.
- Cultural differences influence early memories. Individual-oriented cultures stress self-awareness more than group-oriented cultures. Group-oriented cultures talk more about events within the context of the group. Although there are wide variations among children within any culture, the earliest personal memories of children from group-oriented cultures occur a year or more later than for children from individual-oriented cultures.
- All memories, including most episodic memories, fade with time or are replaced.

Episodic memories are valuable. They make experiences and understandings more vivid. For example, seeing the Rocky Mountains, as compared with reading some facts about them, would be far more meaningful and lasting in memory. Episodic memories also allow for a special type of cultural communication. Episodic memories of events and experiences bind people with these experiences closer together (**Figure 15.5**). Episodic memories may help in planning or decision making if future events bear similarity to a remembered event. In this case, a child can remember what helped the situation and what did not.

Piaget's Cognitive-Developmental Theory

Both Piaget and Vygotsky note that children gain new intellectual abilities by developing abstract meanings separate from their real world. Piaget focuses on the limitations of these abilities. Both theories shape understanding of the preschooler's intellectual world.

The Preoperational Stage

Piaget describes the second stage of cognitive development as the **preoperational stage**. This is the stage children reach before they acquire logical thinking skills, which Piaget calls *operations*. These logical thinking skills require the mind to think through problems and act accordingly. Examples of logical thinking skills include combining ideas or objects, placing them in order, and engaging in "if-then" (cause and effect) thinking. Preschool children have not entered the logical thinking stage yet. Just as toddlers who are walking are prone to missteps, preschool children who are thinking are prone to logical thinking errors.

Figure 15.5 Episodic memories bind people and cultures together. *What episodic memories bind your family together? What types of memorable experiences have made you feel closer to them?*

The preoperational stage spans six years of childhood, beginning in the last year of toddlerhood, extending through the preschool years, and ending after the first two school years. The preoperational stage is divided into two substages: the *preconceptual substage* and the *intuitive substage* (**Figure 15.6**).

The Preconceptual Substage

The **preconceptual substage** (also known as the *symbolic substage*) is a substage in which children two to four years of age begin to develop and understand some concepts. These children are able to form mental images of what they see around them. Many concepts, however, are still incomplete or illogical in the preschooler's mind. Some examples of these incomplete concepts include

- the identification of an object by one part or attribute rather than by several parts or attributes. For example, a preschooler may identify a dog as any animal that plays with a ball.
- the belief that if an attribute of an object changes or is not present, then that object becomes a different object. For example, a preschooler might believe that an unripe orange is a "ball."
- the inability to distinguish between *similar* and *same*. If two objects share a similar attribute, a preschooler may see them as the same. For example, all collies are *Lassies*, and all hot objects are *stoves*.
- difficulty differentiating between people or objects and their symbols. For example, young preschoolers may see themselves and their photos as the same and may believe that anyone who wears a fire hat is a fireman. Because of this incomplete concept, pretend play and reality are not truly separated for preschoolers.

Figure 15.6 Piaget's Cognitive-Developmental Theory

Stages and Substages	Characteristics
Stage 1: Sensorimotor stage (birth to 2 years)	Children learn through the senses and physical actions in six substages.
Substages 1 and 2 involve the baby's own body.	
Substages 3 and 4 involve people and objects.	
Substages 5 and 6 involve creative actions and thinking before acting. (12 to 24 months)	
Stage 2: Preoperational stage (2 to 7 years)	Learning through symbols, such as pretend play, mental images, drawing, language, and memory, but with logical limitations. The word *preoperational* means before (*pre*) logical mental actions (*operations*).
Substage 1: Preconceptual or symbolic (2 to 4 years)	• Begins to develop concepts. • Has rapid development of language. • Does not think logically.
Substage 2: Intuitive (4 to 7 years)	• Figures things out through perception more than through logic; that is, cannot explain "Why." • Shows improvement, especially in classifying, ordering, and numerical skills.
Stage 3: Concrete operational stage (7 to 11 years)	Children begin to think logically, but base their logic on past experiences.
Stage 4: Formal operational stage (11 years of age and older)	Older children, teens, and adults reason abstractly.

The Intuitive Substage

Growth spurts in the brain always lead to leaps in the thinking processes, which are referred to as substages and stages in intellectual development. A growth spurt in the brain helps preschoolers make a transition from the *preconceptual* to the *intuitive* substage. At this time, brain pruning refines the sensory and motor skills developed earlier. Memory and problem-solving functions increase. Functional specialization and lateralization of the brain begin toward the end of the *intuitive* substage.

In the **intuitive substage**, children are sometimes able to grasp a problem's solution by relying on their mental imagery rather than using logical reasoning. By using their **intuition** (the natural ability to know something without evidence), they "feel their way through" problems instead of thinking logically about them. In the intuitive substage, children can

- imagine new roles for themselves. For example, they can imagine themselves as fathers, mothers, and firemen. They can also imagine relationships between objects—one doll might be a "mother" and the other her "baby."
- understand how one factor affects another. For example, preschoolers can understand that a cart's being full of blocks makes it harder to push.
- use intuition to solve problems. Older preschoolers may or may not solve problems correctly. For example, a preschooler may keep track of an object by envisioning it in his or her "mind's eye," instead of by logically thinking through where the object should be.

Focus on

Science

Using Intuition to Solve Problems

During the preschool years, children are more able to solve problems. Problem solving, however, does not rely on logic at this stage. Rather, preschoolers solve problems using their intuition.

One example of a child using intuition to solve a problem is a preschooler keeping track of several balls in an *opaque* (nontransparent) tube. A preschooler can be shown three balls—a blue ball, yellow ball, and a red ball on top—all in a vertical, opaque tube. If the preschooler is tasked with finding the red ball once the tube is rotated, he or she will watch as the tube is turned and keep track of the red ball in his or her "mind's eye." The preschooler will not use logic—such as knowledge about complete and half turns—to find the red ball.

In situations like the one described, preschoolers' reliance on intuition does not make much difference. Many times, however, preschoolers develop incorrect ideas because their intuition misleads them. For example, a preschooler standing on a ladder may say to his or her parent, "I am taller than you," because he or she can see over the parent's head.

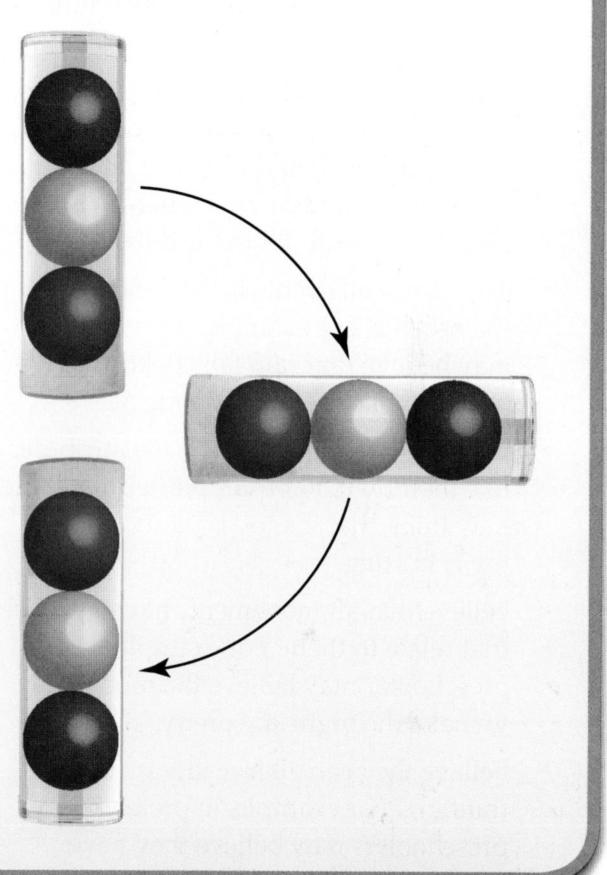

Obstacles to Logical Thought

While preoperational children in the intuitive substage have many correct ideas due to the accuracy of their intuition, they are not logical in their thinking. Logical thinkers, unlike intuitive thinkers, construct "rules" to guide their thinking. For example, in the experiment with the three balls (in the *Focus on Science* feature), the "rule" is that one turn keeps the balls in the same order, but a half turn reverses the order. The intuitive thinker does not use the "rule," but simply forms a mental image of the balls as the tube is turned. The child may track accurately for a few turns, but likely loses track after more turns.

Why are these preschool children intuitive rather than logical? In his work, Piaget notes several obstacles to logical thinking in preoperational children.

Egocentrism

Piaget describes **egocentrism** (ee-goh-SEN-trism) as the preschooler's belief that everyone thinks in the same way and has the same ideas as he or she does. Egocentrism does not mean children are selfish or too concerned with themselves, but rather that they view the world in relation to themselves. Egocentrism can cause preschoolers to

- believe that others like what they like. For example, preschoolers may offer others candy from their mouths because they are enjoying the candy and think others will, too.
- think others see objects the way they do. For example, if a preschooler thinks a slide is tall, he or she will think adults find it tall, too.
- believe others understand what they are thinking. For example, preschoolers may leave out facts in telling about an event and become exasperated when an adult asks questions to fill in the details.
- experience all events in reference to themselves. For example, a preschooler may believe that rain falls to keep him or her from playing in the sand.
- believe inanimate objects have attributes like their own. For example, a preschooler may think that if a toy is damaged, that toy is hurting.
- believe that all movements have purposes that relate to them. For example, a preschooler may believe the moon rises to make the night sky pretty.
- believe they can alter reality by their thinking. For example, in pretend play, preschoolers may believe they have become the person they are role-playing.

Centration

Because preschoolers try to solve problems through perception, they may center their attention on only one part of an object or event instead of seeing all parts at the same time. This is known as **centration** (sen-TRAY-shun). For example, preschool children know that the amount of liquid in two equal-sized glasses is the same. When the liquid of one container is poured into a tall beaker or a wide bowl, however, preschool children incorrectly think the amount of liquid has changed even though it is still the same (**Figure 15.7**).

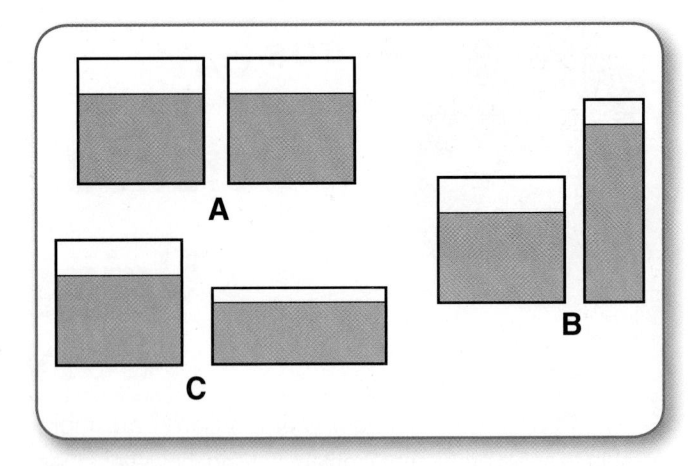

Figure 15.7 Children usually think that *wide* means *more* liquid (B) and that the *lower* height means *less* liquid in the bowl than in the glass (C). *If an adult pours the liquid back and forth from the original-sized glass to the beaker or bowl, do you think a preschooler would say the quantity changes or remains the same with each pour?*

Problems with Transformations and Reversibility

Centration makes it difficult for preschoolers to see **transformations**, which are sequences of changes. Preschool children tend to focus on single steps, stages, or events, and may have difficulty following transformations. Piaget describes preschoolers as focusing on each frame of a film rather than seeing a running story. If shown an object that stands upright and then falls, preoperational children will draw only the first state, in which the object is upright, or the last state, in which the object lies horizontal (**Figure 15.8**).

Because they have difficulty following transformations, preoperational children also struggle to trace actions in reverse, or reverse the transformations. Preschoolers cannot follow a line of reasoning back to where it starts, which is called a *lack of reversibility*. For example, preschoolers cannot reverse or "undo" addition. If they know that adding two and three equals five, they will not be able to infer that subtracting two from five equals three. (You will learn more about transformations and reversals later in the text.)

Transductive Reasoning

Preschoolers also use **transductive reasoning**, which is mentally linking events without using logic. Preschoolers often link one particular event

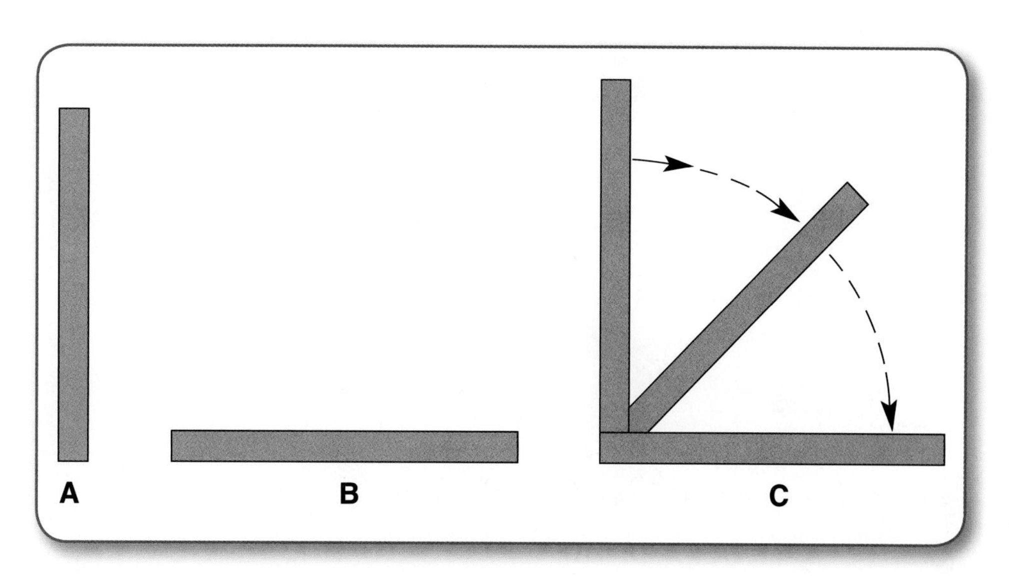

Figure 15.8 When preschool children are asked to watch as a rod is dropped and then draw what they have seen, they draw only the first state (A) or the last state (B). They do not draw any of the in-between states (C). *How do you think preschoolers' difficulty comprehending transformations limits their perceptions of the real world?*

or object with another, without any reference to the general big picture. Reasoning this way causes flaws in logic, such as overgeneralization. **Overgeneralization** is the assumption that because something is true for one event or object, it is true for all similar events or objects. An example of overgeneralization might be concluding that all dogs are friendly because the child's own dog is friendly.

Problems with Cause-and-Effect Reasoning

Logic is required for understanding cause and effect. Because of this, preschoolers' lack of logic causes many problems with cause-and-effect reasoning. Some of these problems include the

- belief that any observable attribute of an object can cause an effect (outcome) they have noted. In one recorded interview, Piaget asked the child, "The sun does not fall from the sky. Why?" The child responded, "Because it is hot." In this case, the child is saying the heat of the sun (observable attribute) can affect the outcome (keep the sun from falling). Instead of saying, "Because it is *hot*," he or she could have just as easily said, "Because it is *round*, *yellow*, or *far away*."
- **transposition** (changing of the order) of cause and effect. For example, a preschooler might say, "Because I'm wearing my raincoat, it is raining," instead of recognizing that wearing a raincoat is an effect of the rain.
- mistaken linking of events occurring close in time. If a mother makes coffee just before a father comes home from work each day, a preschooler may conclude that the coffee brings the father home.
- belief that any event or cause must be recreated in precisely the same way to get the same effect (**Figure 15.9**). For example, if a preschooler experiences many nighttime storms with lightning and thunder, he or she may conclude that it must be night before lightning causes thunder.

Vygotsky's Sociocultural Theory

Both Piaget and Vygotsky studied symbolic representation in children, but came to different conclusions. Piaget believed imitation, pretense, and language were indicators of the child's current level of thinking. Conversely, Vygotsky saw these preschool abilities as laying the foundation for more abstract thinking. In fact, Vygotsky identified these abilities as the three important origins of abstract thought in the preschool years.

- ***Pretend play props.*** Objects used in children's pretend play serve as foundations for imaginative thinking and abstract concepts. During pretend play, children first use realistic props and then they begin to use more abstract ones.

Figure 15.9 Preschoolers believe that an event must be reconstructed in precisely the same way each time to achieve the same effect. *How might this belief hinder a preschooler's understanding of an everyday event?*

- ***Language.*** For preschoolers, language becomes more than a means to express knowledge or communicate with others. At this time, language becomes a tool for thinking. Language aids thought and vice versa. Children actually talk to themselves as they perform tasks, which is a way of thinking about their actions and thus staying on track. Over time, this kind of speech will diminish, but even adults sometimes whisper or talk quietly to themselves while working on challenging tasks. By using language as part of the thinking process, children's language skills increase. Children want to learn more words and varying ways of using them to express their ever-growing knowledge. In this way, language and thinking impact each other.
- ***Imitation.*** For preschoolers, imitative acts used in pretend play are a means of learning new skills. Lessons learned by imitation vary among cultures. For example, people in different cultures prepare different foods and may use different tools in the process.

Scaffolding techniques also change during the preschool years. Studies of scaffolding for preschoolers note that scaffolding is not as "hands-on" as it is in the toddler years. Generally, scaffolding during the preschool years involves a mentor directing the child's attention to a problem to be solved, suggesting possible strategies, monitoring the preschooler's attempts with less directive feedback, and then continuing to direct the child through encouragement.

Lesson 15.1 Review and Assessment 

1. What are preschoolers able to do as a result of symbolic thought?
2. Name five abilities in which preschoolers express symbolic thinking.
3. Choose one of the five abilities in which preschoolers express symbolic thinking and summarize the changes in this ability that occur during the preschool years.
4. Explain what is meant by *episodic memory.*
5. Summarize the changes that occur between the preconceptual and intuitive substages of the preoperational stage.
6. Name and describe Piaget's five obstacles to preschoolers' logical thought.
7. What are the three major origins of abstract thought, as identified by Vygotsky?
8. **Critical thinking.** Do you think children and adults continue to use intuition to solve problems, even after the preschool years? Why or why not?

What Preschoolers Learn

Lesson 15.2

Objectives

After studying this lesson, you will be able to

- describe the major areas of concept learning during the preschool years.
- summarize preschoolers' efforts to understand logical thinking concepts, such as sorting and classifying, ordering by attributes, seeing cause and effect, understanding spatial concepts, understanding number concepts, and noting time concepts.
- chart preschoolers' progress in learning word meanings and communicating more effectively.
- identify intellectual developmental milestones preschoolers might achieve.

Key Terms

classifying
collective monologue
egocentric speech
logical thinking concepts
mental maps
monologue
physical knowledge
seriation
tag questions

Academic Terms

animism
coherently
numerosity
physical attributes
rote memorization

Reading and Writing Activity

Read the key terms for this lesson and look up any words you do not know in the dictionary. Then, using all of the key terms in this lesson, write two paragraphs summarizing what you already know about what preschoolers learn. If you do not know how a key term relates, write that key term below your paragraphs, and after reading, explain how it relates.

Graphic Organizer

Write each of the four objectives for this lesson on index cards and arrange these cards near you as you read. On each index card, take notes about the appropriate objective. Then, trade your index cards with a partner. Discuss how your notes are similar or different.

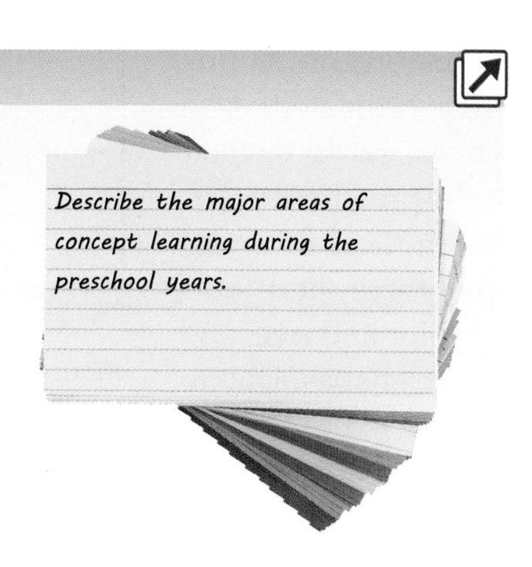

During the preschool years, brain development and cognitive changes in pretend play, mental images, drawing, language, and memory lead to better comprehension of complex concepts. While preoperational children do not use logic to solve problems, they are capable of symbolic thought and use their perceptions and intuition to reach solutions. Toward the end of the preschool years, children make advances in several areas of concept learning and begin to lay the foundation for understanding and using logical concepts. They also learn new word meanings and develop more complex grammar skills.

Concept Learning

In addition to the development of existing concepts, many new concepts emerge during the preschool years. The major areas of beginning concept learning for preschoolers include the following:

- noting physical attributes
- understanding physical knowledge
- using logical thinking concepts, such as sorting and classifying, ordering by attributes, seeing cause and effect, understanding spatial concepts, understanding number concepts, and noting time concepts

Noting Physical Attributes

From the moment they are born, children use their senses to develop concepts about size, shape, color, texture, and other **physical attributes** (concrete qualities that can be sensed) of objects. During the preschool years, children's sensory organs mature, and their senses become more coordinated. As a result, children's abilities to make sense of their environments improve during the preschool years.

Preschoolers focus on some physical attributes more than others. For example, three- and four-year-olds may pay attention to color and size, and five-year-olds may primarily note shapes. Due to centration, preschoolers are limited in the abilities to comprehend a variety of physical attributes at the same time. Therefore, they *center* (focus) on the attribute that stands out to them.

Preschoolers who are learning to note physical attributes may make mistakes. While preschoolers may note many features about an object, they may not note the object's most important features. For example, a preschooler may notice a zebra's ears, but not notice the zebra's stripes, which are most important in distinguishing the zebra from a horse. Because preschoolers tend to focus on individual attributes of an object, they do not always mentally "see" the whole object. When preschoolers are shown drawings such as those in **Figure 15.10**, they tend to recognize the parts, but not the whole.

Figure 15.10 Most preschoolers will see only parts of these drawings, not the whole. ***What individual parts of these drawings might distract preschoolers from seeing the faces these parts make up?***

Understanding Physical Knowledge

Starting at four months of age, infants begin learning what happens when objects are acted upon by people or other objects. Piaget calls these types of lessons *physical knowledge*. **Physical knowledge** is knowledge acquired through observations of the physical world, such as attributes of objects (color, shape) and observable phenomenon (how gravity works and the comparative speed of balls rolled on flat surfaces and inclines).

Many physical knowledge concepts, including natural events like evaporation and thunder, are too complex for children to understand. Preschoolers lack the logic needed to understand these concepts, so instead they settle on their own ideas about how the physical world works. Some of these illogical ideas include the following:

- ***Animism.*** **Animism** (AN-ih-mism) is the attribution of living qualities to inanimate objects. Preschoolers may assign human qualities to nonhuman objects, such as plants, animals, and possessions. For example, a preschooler who falls off a bike may say, "The bike was mad at me and made me fall." Sometimes, preschoolers use animism to avoid being punished or having to do something they do not want to do (**Figure 15.11**).
- ***Artificialism.*** Preschoolers may believe that everything is made by a real or imaginary person. For example, a preschooler may say that the sun was rolled into a ball by giants.
- ***Finalism.*** Preschoolers may see everything as having an identifiable and understandable purpose. For example, a preschooler may say, "The ball rolled away so I would have to chase it."

Teaching physical knowledge concepts by telling preschoolers about the world around them is difficult and usually ineffective. Preschool children best learn physical knowledge concepts through experimentation. Therefore, preschoolers need to be given opportunities to experiment with objects and events they can observe.

Figure 15.11 In an effort to avoid punishment, preschoolers may blame inanimate objects that they believe have lifelike qualities. For instance, a preschooler may say, "My teddy bear left my toys outside." *Should caregivers be worried if preschoolers blame objects for their actions?*

Using Logical Thinking Concepts

From an early age, children participate in problem solving. *Problem solving* is a broad term that most often includes noting a problem, observing and questioning what is observed, and solving the problem. By the preschool years, children use both physical (trial and error) and intellectual (intuition) problem-solving skills.

Intellectual problem solving depends on children's understanding of *logical thinking concepts*. **Logical thinking concepts** are those not directly experienced through the senses, but are developed through thought, such as noting similarities and differences in objects and coordinating simple relationships (classifying, ordering by attribute, counting). While these concepts cannot be physically observed, they can be "seen" in the mind. As the name suggests, these concepts will not fully develop until children are able to think logically. As a result, preschoolers' abilities to use logical thinking concepts are immature. Logical thinking concepts that begin to develop during the preschool years include sorting and classifying objects, ordering by attributes, seeing cause and effect, understanding spatial concepts, understanding number concepts, and noting time concepts.

Sorting and Classifying Objects

During the preschool years, children's abilities to sort objects improve. Preschoolers' sorting techniques differ from adults' techniques. For example, a preschooler might sort a boat, a paper plate, and artificial flowers into one group because these objects were involved in a recent picnic. If sorting by shape, young preschoolers often make a *graphic* (picture-like) collection of shapes (**Figure 15.12**).

Around four years of age, preschoolers develop the executive functions needed to change sorting criteria. *Cognitive flexibility* allows preschoolers to change sorting rules, such as sorting by circles and then by squares. *Working memory* helps preschoolers remember sorting rules. *Inhibitory control* keeps preschoolers focused on the sorting criteria, even if they would like to sort another way. Many older preschoolers sort by attributes, such as color, shape, size, material, patterns, and functions.

Figure 15.12 Preschoolers tend to sort shapes into graphic collections. For example, they may be sorting rectangles and see circles as wheels that they can put below the rectangle like a wagon. *How does sorting differ from creating graphic collections of shapes?*

Preschoolers also learn how to *classify*. **Classifying** involves choosing an attribute, selecting all objects that contain the given attribute (called the *class*), and then recognizing items that do not contain the attribute (called the *class complement*). Classifying is a more difficult skill than sorting. This is because sorting involves paying attention to a variety of attributes whereas classifying involves focusing on one chosen attribute while considering all others as not belonging to the class. Classifying is not usually mastered until children are school-age.

Ordering by Attributes

During the preschool years, children also begin to learn how to seriate. **Seriation** (seer-ee-AY-shun) is arranging objects in order by the increasing or decreasing magnitude of one of the object's attributes, such as length, shade of a color, texture, or pitch. Preschool children can easily identify extremes in most attributes, such as the largest and smallest square. Because noting extremes is an easy skill, young preschoolers often just alternate between large and small objects rather than truly seriating objects.

Seriating three or more objects is more difficult than finding two extremes in an attribute because it requires a two-way, simultaneous mental-comparison of an object's attribute (size, length) to the same attribute in other objects. For example, when a person is ordering on a decreasing (also called *descending*) magnitude, the object placed next must be less in that magnitude than all of the preceding objects and more in that magnitude than all of the other objects. As you look at **Figure 15.13**, suppose you are trying to place the fourth rod of the ten rods in descending order of length. The fourth rod must be shorter than the third rod, but longer than the remaining rods. If ordering in increasing (also called *ascending*) magnitude, the reverse would be true requiring the fourth rod to be longer than the third rod, but shorter than all other rods.

Toward the end of the preschool years, children's seriating skills improve. Many older preschoolers

Figure 15.13 To seriate these number rods, the child must compare each rod in turn with the rod placed on the table just before it (first relationship) and with the remaining rods (second relationship). Thus, seriating is always a two-way comparison. *What other attributes could be used for seriating activities?*

are successful because they use their perceptions and also physically manipulate the objects. For example, these preschoolers can arrange dowel rods and sticks in order of their lengths, but to do this, they must physically lay the rods beside one another and align all of the bottom ends evenly. To seriate other attributes, they must physically place the objects next to each other often arranging and rearranging them. In contrast, older children can seriate by just pointing to the order without actually moving the objects.

Seeing Cause and Effect

Because preschool children are not logical thinkers, they have difficulty seeing cause and effect, especially when the cause-effect relationship is not directly observable. As a result, preschoolers tend to create their own explanations of events.

While preschoolers have difficulty with unobservable cause-effect relationships, studies show that preschoolers can understand many visual displays of cause and effect. Preschoolers may still have problems with the complex sentence structure of cause-effect language, however, and may reverse cause and effect when speaking. Unobservable and difficult cause-effect relationships are often misunderstood until the teen years.

Understanding Spatial Concepts

While preschoolers understand the words that indicate spatial relationships, they still have trouble comprehending spatial concepts. Preschoolers think about spatial relationships in reference to themselves. While they understand what is on their right and left, knowing right and left from another person's perspective or in a spatial relationship to an object is much more difficult. Preschoolers tend to draw what they think about a space, rather than what they actually see.

As early as toddlerhood, children have some spatial memory, usually in the form of *mental maps*. **Mental maps** are remembered mental constructions (seen in the "mind's eye") that organize spatial relationships from an individual's perspective. A mental map enables a person to navigate his or her own house or other familiar places without thinking and to envision these places without being physically present (**Figure 15.14**). While these mental maps are far from perfect in the preschool years, preschool children exhibit some understanding of mental mapping, especially if mapping in a three-dimensional form. For example, mapping in three-dimensional form means making a mental image of spatial arrangements after seeing a furniture arrangement in three-dimensions in a real house or a three-dimensional model of a house (doll house). Conversely, two-dimensional mapping, which preschoolers cannot typically do, means forming mental maps using two-dimensional images, such as maps or floor plans, and being able to envision these spatial arrangements when not looking at the images.

Understanding Number Concepts

From a young age, children have a basic comprehension of quantity. Many older toddlers and young preschoolers show counting-like behaviors or can say counting words. Such counting, however, does not show they understand numbers. For example, a preschool child may be able to count to five by saying the numbers (called *rote counting*), but may have trouble when asked to find five apples in a basket.

During the preschool years, children's comprehension of number concepts increases dramatically due to brain development. The left parietal lobe is being wired for understanding numbers and their functions. Also, synaptic "communication" across many parts of the brain is needed for math success.

Figure 15.14 Three-dimensional mental mapping enables preschoolers to remember spatial arrangements in their world. *How might this preschooler show his mental mapping of the playground and the complex play structure? What mental maps do you use on a daily basis?*

For example, memory areas are needed for remembering rules and recognizing patterns; language areas are used for understanding vocabulary and rules; and visual-spatial processing is essential for recognizing math symbols.

Number concepts require several complex understandings (**Figure 15.15**). Even before the preschool stage, many children understand the concept of *more*. Young preschoolers can imitate the counting-like behaviors of adults. Adults are often misled about preschoolers' understanding of counting, however. Although many preschoolers can rote count, young preschoolers seldom understand the one-to-one relationship that takes place when counting objects (called *rational counting*). Even when watching older children or adults count while touching objects, they often do not understand that one (and only one) number can be assigned to each object and that all objects must be touched once (and only once). Although they go through the counting motions, they will often miss some objects and/or count other objects twice. The approximate benchmarks for preschoolers' learning to count are shown in **Figure 15.16**.

Figure 15.15 Number Concept Understandings

- All discrete living or nonliving objects, whether alike or different, can be counted.
- An amount does not change unless another amount is added to or subtracted from it; that is, the size of objects and the way objects are arranged do not affect amount. If the elements of two sets can be paired so that each element is linked with exactly one element from the other set, there is *one-to-one correspondence* (equivalence) between the two sets.
- Counting involves assigning one and only one number to each item (called the *one-on-one principle*). Each item must be "counted" only once; no item can be missed; and the order of counting is irrelevant.
- "How many" (called *numerosity* or *cardinal principle*) is the last number assigned to the last item counted. Verbal or written number names, called *numerals*, are symbols for "how many."
- Items can be added to or subtracted from a given amount (called *numerical operations*). Numerical operations change "how many."

Figure 15.16 Benchmarks for Preschool Counting

Age	Forward Counting	Backward Counting
3 years	Children can count from 1 to 2 or 3.	Children cannot count backward.
4 years	Children can count from 1 to 10.	Children can count back from 5.
5 years	Children can count from 1 to 20.	Children can count back from 10.

Number Concepts at Three Years of Age

Three-year-old preschoolers can handle one-to-one correspondence for groups up to three. When shown two rows of four or more objects in physical one-to-one correspondence, they can identify that they are the "same." However, if one row is slightly spread out or compressed or even if another object is added to a compressed row, these perception-bound children use the end points to determine which row has "more" (**Figure 15.17**).

Number Concepts at Four and Five Years of Age

Around four years of age, children's comprehension of number concepts leaps forward. Math understandings are logical concepts, not physical concepts. Four-year-olds who can count will use counting to determine equivalence or nonequivalence of two rows and can use the one-to-one principle (**Figure 15.18**).

Until about five years of age, **numerosity** (noo-mer-AHS-ih-tee), numerousness, is difficult for preschoolers to comprehend. Numerosity is difficult for preschoolers because, unlike names, which refer to one object, a number does not refer just to the last object named, but also to the entire group of objects. Thus, a child must mentally "see" that the number one is in two and that two is in three.

By five years of age, many preschoolers can add and subtract concrete objects. If they know the number sequence, five-year-olds can make mental comparisons, such as "four is more than three." Older preschoolers can plot numerals on a number line, but the spaces between the consecutive numbers will not be kept equal. In effect, forward counting by ones is *adding* increments of one, and backward counting by ones is *subtracting* increments of one.

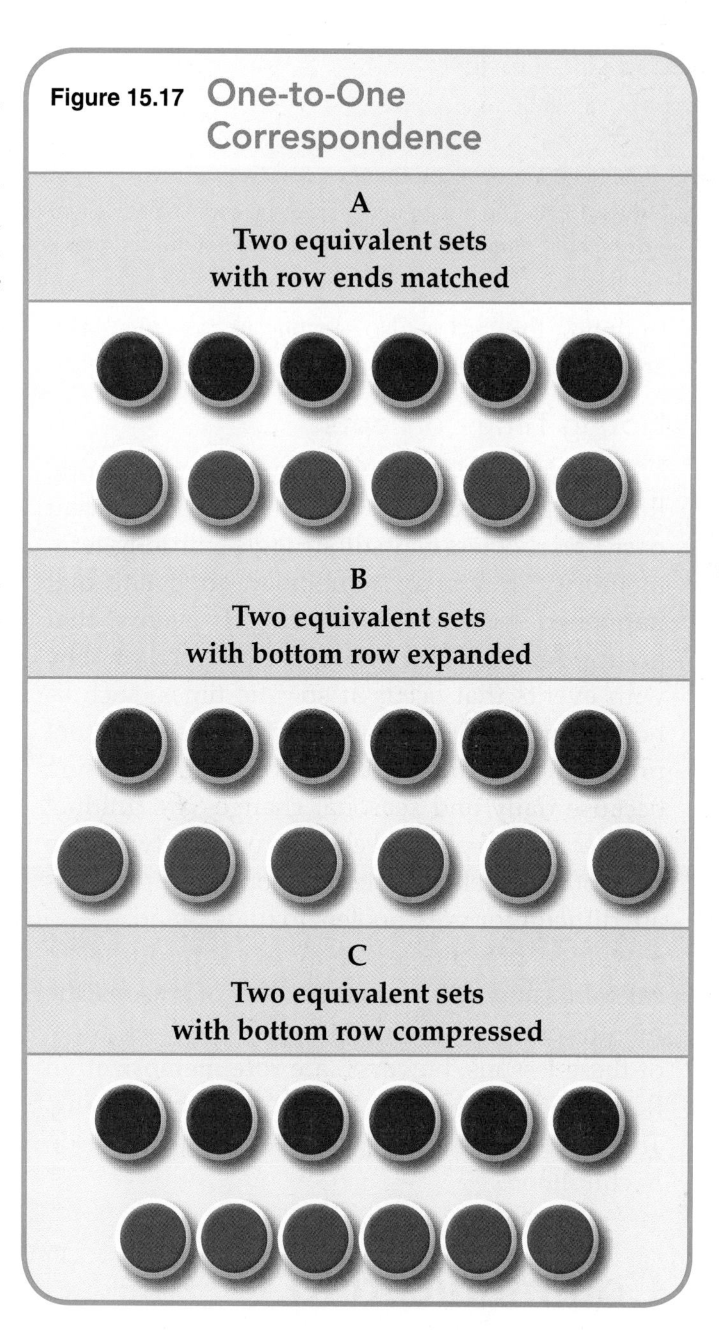

Figure 15.17 Preschoolers may have difficulty understanding that the rows shown in A, B, and C contain the same number of discs. *How would you go about determining whether the rows were equivalent?*

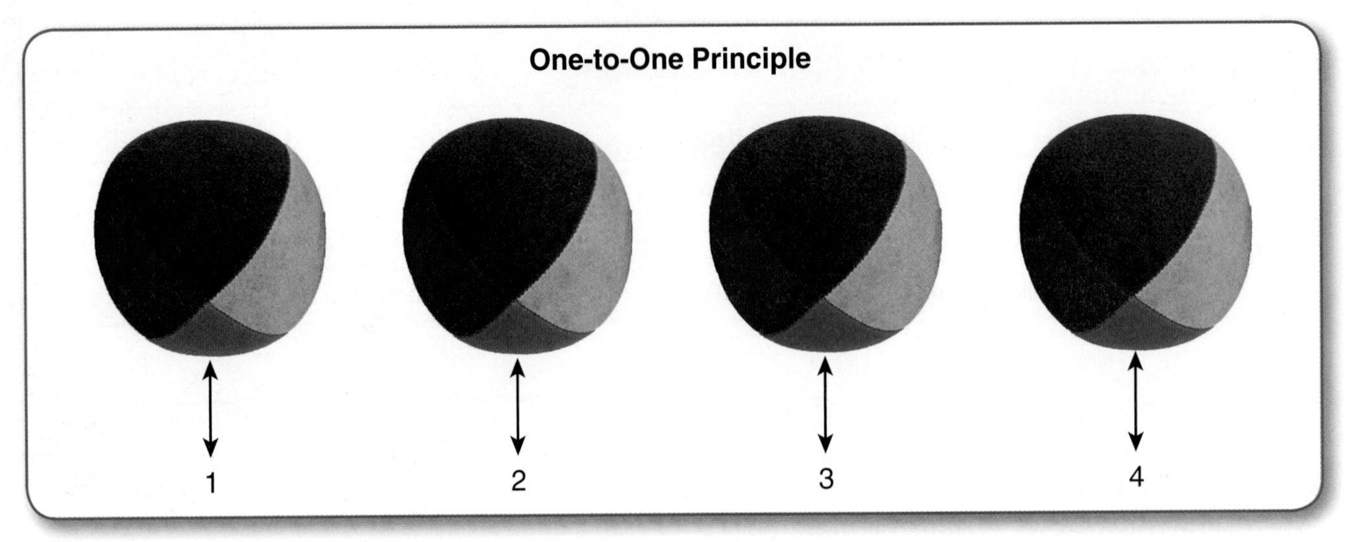

Figure 15.18 The one-to-one principle in counting holds that one number, and only one number, is assigned to each object. ***Why would numerals be difficult to understand without a thorough understanding of the one-to-one principle?***

Counting forward is also *seriating in ascending order*, and counting backward is *seriating in descending order*.

Noting Time Concepts

Improvements in working memory during the preschool years help children recall the recent past. Preschoolers may still struggle with long-term memory. They may remember an event that happened yesterday, but forget events that occurred a week or a year ago. Children link time with events that occur at specific times, such as home routines or regular activities in a preschool program's schedule. They do not see time passing because daily and seasonal changes are gradual and because no physical changes occur between the days of the week. For these reasons, time concepts are difficult for preschoolers to understand.

Older preschoolers may be introduced to calendars and may learn the names of seasons, the months of the year, and the days of the week. Most of these lessons, however, are **rote memorization** (learning by repetition) without much meaning. Time concepts are among the last concepts to develop in childhood.

Communicating

During the preschool years, language and communication abilities continue to improve. Preschoolers are better able to articulate and are rapidly learning the vocabulary and grammar they will need to communicate their needs and feelings effectively (**Figure 15.19**).

Preschoolers' egocentrism impacts their speaking in that their language often reflects their exact thinking. Preschoolers use **egocentric speech**, which means preschoolers talk as though the listener will understand what they are trying to communicate in the same way as they do. Thus, they often do not communicate all the needed information. Examples of preschoolers' egocentric speech include telling a story from the middle instead of the beginning and using pronouns without naming the pronoun's object.

Egocentric speech also includes repeating words without speaking to anyone. Sometimes children speak in **monologue** by talking to themselves as though thinking aloud. Other times, they engage in **collective monologue** by talking to another person, but not listening to what the other person is saying. All children go through this stage of language development.

Toward the end of the preschool years, egocentric speech gradually disappears, which makes communication easier. Communication also becomes easier as preschoolers are learning articulation, expanding their vocabularies, and learning grammar.

Learning Articulation

In the English language, children are able to articulate words fluently and **coherently** (clearly

Figure 15.19 Having made strides in language development, preschoolers are better able to communicate their needs and feelings. *How do advances in communication impact how adults should meet preschoolers' needs?*

and understandably) between three and eight years of age. Although the timing in which preschoolers master the sounds of language varies, the order in which they master these sounds is about the same for most children. Children achieve *total mastery* when they can articulate sounds in different positions within words. **Figure 15.20** shows the typical order and ages for preschoolers' articulation mastery.

Expanding Vocabularies

Children continue to expand their vocabularies as they learn words and their meanings during the preschool years. At three years of age, children know about 900 words in the English language. By four years of age, children know about 1,500 words and at five years of age they know about 2,000 words.

Preschoolers tend to learn the words and names for *concrete items*, such as objects and people, before they learn those that symbolize *abstract ideas*, such as emotions. Preschool children also often assign their own meanings to words. The window of opportunity for vocabulary growth never closes, so vocabulary continues to grow and develop far beyond the preschool years.

Figure 15.20 Articulation Mastery of Preschool Children

Age	Sound	Word Examples
3 years	m	monkey, hammer, broom
	n	nails, penny, lion
	p	pig, happy, cup
	h	hand, doghouse
	w	window, bowl
4 years	b	boat, baby, tub
	k	cat, chicken, book
	g	girl, wagon, pig
	f	fork, telephone, knife
5 years	y	yellow, onion
	ng	fingers, ring
	d	dog, ladder, bed

Learning Grammar

Brain development research shows that the window of opportunity for learning grammar through listening closes at five or six years of age. Because of this, grammar development is critical during the preschool years and becomes more difficult once children are school-age. During the preschool years, children begin to use more complex sentence structures and comprehend correct word order. Children's grammar matures dramatically between three and five years of age.

Grammar at Three Years of Age

Three-year-olds can begin to understand some grammar rules (**Figure 15.21**). Once they learn these rules, they tend to apply them to sentences and words, including those that are exceptions to the rules. Three-year-old preschoolers may know that *-ed* indicates past tense, but once they know this rule, they may apply it to all verb forms. Over time, preschoolers will learn the exceptions to these rules.

Young preschoolers do not always comprehend word order. They will use incorrect word order at times and correct word order at other times. Preschoolers may also have a difficult time with questions because of how word order is switched. Three-year-olds may use question words, such as *when* and *why*, but have not mastered the switched order of the noun and verb used for questions. (The typical noun- then verb-order for a declarative sentence is switched in an interrogative sentence to a verb- then noun-order.)

Negative words are also very difficult for young preschoolers. Once preschoolers know about negatives other than *no*, they may use double or multiple negatives in sentences. For example, sentences such as "I don't never want no more spinach" are common at this age.

Grammar at Four and Five Years of Age

Four- and five-year-old children speak in longer, more complex sentences. They lengthen sentences by using clauses, conjunctions, and prepositions.

Figure 15.21 Grammar Rules that Three-Year-Olds Begin to Use

Rules of Grammar	Examples
Add *–ing* to the end of a regular verb for present continuous tense.	roll ⟶ rolling fall ⟶ falling
Add *–ed* to the end of a regular verb for past tense.	roll ⟶ rolled walk ⟶ walked
Change some irregular verbs from simple present tense to simple past tense.	sink ⟶ sank eat ⟶ ate
Use a linking verb (*is*, *am*) to link noun to adjective.	The truck *is* red. I *am* good.
Add *–s* to make a plural.	car ⟶ cars doll ⟶ dolls
Add an *'s* to form possessive.	*Bob's* book *Daddy's* car
Use an article (*a*, *the*) to precede or modify a noun.	*a* toy *the* library
Use a preposition referring to space (*on*, *in*).	*on* the table *in* the room

Instead of saying, "We play games. I had fun," an older preschool child may say, "I had fun because we played games" (**Figure 15.22**).

Four-year-old children may still find word order in questions confusing. They may form questions by moving the question word to the beginning of the statement, such as "What the dog is eating?" Five-year-old children begin using **tag questions**, which are formed by making a statement and then adding *yes* or *no* to ask the question. An example of a tag question is, "The baby is small, yes?" By five years of age, however, children are able to identify and use correct word order more consistently.

Grammar Problems

Although older preschool children consistently use correct word order and have made large advances in grammar comprehension, they continue to have two problems with grammar. One problem is using the correct case for pronouns. Older preschoolers often use objective case pronouns where they should use the subjective case. For example, an older preschooler may say, "Him and me went to town," instead of "He and I went to town."

The second problem older preschoolers have with grammar is that they continue to apply some grammar rules too widely. They may say *eated* instead of *ate*. Once they learn irregular forms, they may even say *ated*. A five-year-old may learn to use the plural form *feet* and ask, "May I go barefeeted?" The many irregular forms in the English language will trouble some children for years, even if they hear and make strides in using correct grammar.

Intellectual Developmental Milestones

Concepts and abilities that develop during the infant and toddler years continue to mature in the preschool years. Although preschoolers are not yet capable of logical thinking, they use both their perceptions and intuition for solving problems that, in turn, lay the foundation for logical thinking. The preschool years are critical times for learning vocabulary and especially grammar. **Figure 15.23** lists some intellectual developmental milestones for preschool children.

Figure 15.22 As four- and five-year-old preschoolers discover new parts of speech, they become more animated when talking to others. ***What characteristics would you use to describe preschoolers' speech?***

Lesson 15.2 Review and Assessment 

1. Due to _____, preschoolers are limited in their abilities to comprehend (mentally "take in") a variety of physical attributes at the same time.
2. Name three illogical ideas that preschoolers have about the physical world.
3. Choose one logical thinking concept and explain why it is difficult for preschoolers.
4. Preschoolers use _____, which means they talk as though the listener will understand their words just as they do.
5. What does it mean for children to achieve *total mastery* of sounds?
6. Explain how children's grammar matures between three and five years of age.
7. Give three examples of milestones a preschooler typically achieves at three, four, and five years of age.
8. **Critical thinking.** Why do you think preschool children comprehend words for concrete items easier than they comprehend words for abstract ideas?

Figure 15.23 Preschool Intellectual Milestones

Three years

- Expresses thinking through pretend play, drawings, and language.
- Gives illogical "reasons" for events.
- Matches attributes of objects and sorts by shape and color.
- Rationally counts two to three objects.
- Knows about 900 words.
- Knows his or her name and the names of family members and friends.
- Knows the names of common objects, some colors, and three basic shapes.
- Articulates sounds with others understanding them about 75 percent of the time.
- Uses four- to five-word sentences.
- Knows some grammar rules (*s* sound for plurals; *ed* sound for past tense), but overgeneralizes rules to include irregular forms (says *singed* instead of *sang*).
- Understands a few prepositions (*on*, *in*, *under*) and a few time words (*now*, *soon*, *later*).
- Tells a simple story often with some incorrect facts.

Four years

- Enjoys pretending and has a vivid imagination.
- Solves some problems correctly through intuition (not logic).
- Sorts by shape, color, and size.
- Begins classifying by one attribute (but often changes attributes while classifying).
- Rationally counts 7 to 10 objects and recognizes a few numerals.
- Arranges by size with the help of a base line.

Four years *(Continued)*

- Knows about 1500 words.
- Knows most basic colors by name and knows some opposites, math words, and prepositions.
- Has some sense of time (but says *yesterday* for the past and *tomorrow* for the future).
- Uses five- to six-word sentences.
- Has trouble with the word order of questions and the use of negatives.
- Recognizes a few written words (name, STOP sign, and EXIT sign).
- Follows a three-part command.
- Recalls parts of a story and can play a role in a simple story.

Five years

- Likes to pretend play with themes and uses props.
- Has better problem-solving skills, but still uses intuition.
- Knows own right and left, but finds recognizing right and left from other perspectives is difficult.
- Draws pictures that represent real objects or people (called *representational art*).
- Names basic colors and knows names of some additional colors (*pink*, *grey*, *white*).
- Rationally counts 10 or more objects.
- Extends or makes patterns with beads or blocks.
- Knows 2000 to 2200 words.
- Articulates most sounds that are understood about 90 to 95 percent of the time.
- Uses complex sentences.
- Speaks using present, past, and future tense.
- Recognizes several words in books.

Lesson 15.3 Meeting Preschoolers' Intellectual Needs

Key Terms

emergent literacy
interactive media
maturational theory of child development
noninteractive media
reading readiness

Academic Terms

inclusive
pique
stipulation
ubiquitous

Objectives

After studying this lesson, you will be able to

- describe activities to foster the preschooler's memory capacity.
- summarize activities that aid in preschoolers' comprehension of logical thinking concepts.
- explain how to stimulate symbolic learning in the preschooler.
- describe language activities that help preschoolers develop language skills.
- evaluate electronic media activities currently available for preschoolers to determine their educational value.

Reading and Writing Activity

Skim this lesson, paying close attention to the photos included in each section. For each photo, write a one- to two-sentence prediction about how the photo illustrates a topic covered. Then, after reading, revisit your predictions and update or correct them to reflect what you have learned. What other photo options might expand your understanding of a concept?

Graphic Organizer

Stimulating activities for preschoolers can be classified into several categories: motor activities, memory activities, concept learning activities, symbolic learning activities, language activities, and electronic media activities. Organize your notes for this lesson by category in a graph like the one shown.

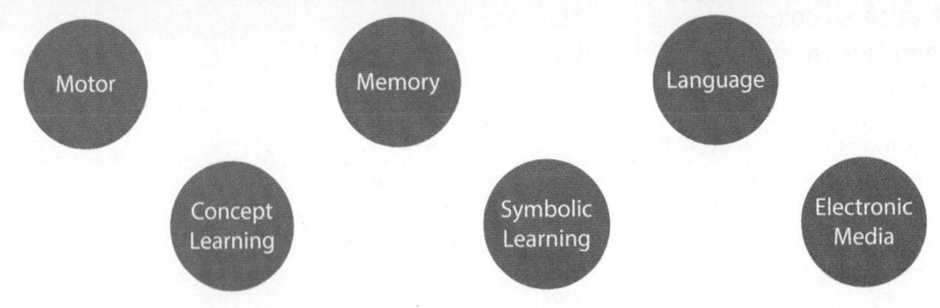

During the preschool years, adults continue to help preschool children meet their intellectual needs. As they did during the toddler years, adults direct children's attention to activities and to problems that must be solved. For preschoolers, the home, child care and education programs, and neighborhood play groups are the most important places for learning.

Preschool children are still holistic learners. Their intellectual abilities can and do develop at many times and in many places. Think about how much a child can learn from a simple shopping trip (**Figure 15.24**).

Motor Activities

Preschool children are "on the go." Their motor skills usually improve in conjunction with other lessons they are learning. For example, preschoolers use their gross-motor skills when they engage in pretend play and their fine-motor skills when they sort and draw. To help preschoolers hone their motor skills, caregivers can plan activities that, among other skills, involve physical movement.

Preschoolers need lots of opportunities for physical play. Not only are physical activities vital to building motor skills, they are also needed for physical health. (See Figure 14.14 to review motor skill activities parents and caregivers can plan for their preschoolers.)

Memory Activities

Memory develops rapidly during the preschool years, as brain development makes way for preschoolers' frequent use of working and episodic memory. Memory is vital to all domains of development, and it is important that caregivers and teachers plan numerous activities to help preschoolers develop and practice their memory skills.

Many memory games are commercially available for preschool learning, but these games do little for children in comparison to everyday activities that caregivers and other adults can plan. Parents and other adults can help preschoolers develop and practice their memory skills in the following ways:

- Help preschoolers understand stories and happenings before asking them to recall. Children have a difficult time recalling what they do not understand.

Figure 15.24 While shopping, a child can observe attributes of items, such as color, size, shape, and texture; sort and classify items; learn number skills; and learn language skills in naming and describing items. *What other daily activities can help children learn sorting and classifying?*

- Use leading questions and prompting to **pique** (stir up interest in) the child's memory. Instead of asking, "What did you do yesterday?" a caregiver or other adult might ask, "What game did you play with your uncle yesterday?"
- When giving directions, ask the child to repeat the directions before starting on the task. This aids the child's working memory.
- Use photos to remind a child about people, places, or events not regularly seen.
- Use prompting photos to help a child recall specific events from his or her past.
- Reread stories as often as requested (**Figure 15.25**). When rereading stories or repeating songs and rhymes, change something in the story or song and see whether the child notices.
- Frequently repeat safety rules and other concepts the child is learning. Repeat lessons after a lapse of time to help children remember and easily recall.

Concept Learning Activities

During the preschool years, children are learning a variety of concepts. They learn to note physical attributes, understand physical knowledge, and begin to comprehend logical thinking concepts using their perceptions and intuition. For each area of concept learning during the preschool years, parents and caregivers can aid intellectual development by planning helpful activities.

Noting Physical Attributes

Preschool children learn to note physical attributes through observation and through their senses of sight, hearing, touch, smell, and taste. During the preschool years, children learn to compare and contrast the attributes of various physical objects.

Adults can help children learn and distinguish between physical attributes by inviting preschoolers to analyze physical attributes with them. When interacting with preschoolers, adults can call attention to physical attributes and then describe or ask the child to describe a sight, sound, texture,

Figure 15.25 Rereading books can help children practice their memory skills. In rereading, children can be prompted to identify whether they have heard a story before. *When you reread a book, how easy is it for you to recall what you previously read?*

odor, or taste. Adults can emphasize the names of attributes and can help preschoolers compare and contrast physical objects. Noting attributes shown in books and other media can also help preschool children process and remember physical attributes. There are many games and activities adults can plan to foster these skills (**Figure 15.26**).

Figure 15.26 Attribute Games and Activities

Using the Senses	
Seeing	• Give a child a magnifying glass. Help the child look at a leaf, penny, fingernail, piece of food, or other small object. Use a pencil to point to details you want the child to see. Later, ask the child to describe the objects he or she saw. • Go on an "I Spy" walk or ride. Have the child identify a given attribute, such as a color or shape.
Hearing	• Encourage the child to identify sounds in the environment and use these sounds in pretend play. • As you read stories, ask the child to make the sounds of animals and machines. • Depict emotions through your voice as you read stories.
Touching	• Ask the child to describe textures in the environment and in books in which texture is applied to the photos or drawings. • Ask the child to describe texture before feeling an object. • Ask the child to add texture to Play Doh® creations. • Ask the child to seriate texture from roughest to smoothest or vice versa.
Smelling	• Ask the child to go on "sniffing walks" and describe odors. • Ask the child to sniff and describe spices or identify foods by odor. • Read "scratch and sniff" books.
Tasting	• Ask the child to describe how foods taste. • Ask the child to identify texture of foods by tasting.
Comparing and Contrasting Attributes	
Alike and different	• Gather pairs of objects or pictures that are exactly alike. Mix up the objects and have the child sort into like pairs. • Have the child explain how some items are similar and different.
Shape sorting	• Have the child fit various shapes through the holes of a shape sorter. As children master simple shape sorters, more advanced ones can be used. • Ask older children to name shapes and explain how they recognized each shape.
Varieties of liquids	• Show the child varieties of liquids, such as water, milk, fruit juice, molasses, cooking oil, tempera paint (in one or more thicknesses), and dish detergent. Have the child describe similarities and differences in the liquids in the following experiments: (A) rub a drop of each liquid between the thumb and forefinger; (B) place a drop of each liquid on wax paper and blow at the drops through a straw. • Have the child watch the pouring of three liquids differing in *viscosities* (thicknesses). Ask the child which liquid pours the fastest and the slowest.

Understanding Physical Knowledge

Preschoolers are fascinated by natural events and ask many *why* questions, even though they do not yet have the logical capabilities to understand the answers. As a result, they come up with illogical thoughts of their own. When preschoolers communicate illogical explanations for events they cannot understand, parents and caregivers can correct them, but should not expect the preschooler to comprehend the correct explanation. Caregivers can keep these explanations simple and remember that children have many more years to learn all of these facts.

Physical knowledge lessons are closely tied to children's perceptions of cause and effect. Because cause and effect is a logical thinking concept, it is difficult for preschoolers.

Figure 15.27 When asking preschoolers to pick up all of their toys or clothes, a caregiver might suggest the child pick up all the blue or yellow blocks. ***What other chores might caregivers be able to turn into intellectual activities?***

Using Logical Thinking Concepts

Because preschoolers do not think logically, their use of logical thinking concepts does not fully mature during the preschool years. Nevertheless, there are activities that caregivers can plan to help children begin to understand these essential concepts. Preschoolers can benefit from activities that encourage sorting and classifying, ordering by attributes, seeing cause and effect, understanding spatial concepts, understanding number concepts, and noting time concepts.

Sorting and Classifying

To help children practice sorting, parents and caregivers can use commercial sorting materials, such as shape sorters for three-dimensional geometric shapes. Common household items, such as clothing, toys, flatware, or groceries, can also be used to teach sorting lessons (**Figure 15.27**). For example, to turn a grocery shopping trip into a sorting lesson, an adult might say, "Let's put all the foods that are in boxes together and then put all the canned foods together."

Parents and caregivers can also begin to teach preschoolers classifying techniques. For example, after showing a child small blocks that may be classified by color or shape, an adult may ask, "Are any of these alike in some way?" When the child singles out a common attribute, such as some of the blocks are *round*, the adult might say, "Can you find all the round pieces and put them in this box? Then we will put all the other blocks that are not round in the other box."

Ordering by Attributes

While preschool children have trouble putting items in order by a magnitude of an attribute, many activities can help children understand how to practice this concept. Parents and caregivers can plan activities that involve observable differences in height, weight, pitch, or appearance. For example, a caregiver might ask a child to arrange objects from shortest to tallest or to order the keys of a piano by pitch from high to low. Children can see and hear these differences, which helps them comprehend the arrangement.

When helping preschoolers with seriating activities, caregivers need to keep the difficulty level of the task in mind and make the task appropriate for the child. Following are several factors that can make seriating tasks less difficult:

- having fewer numbers of objects to arrange
- using objects with equal differences in increments, such as shown in Figure 15.13 versus trying to seriate people's heights
- using objects that differ in only one attribute, such as different sizes of squares rather than different sizes of mixed shapes
- having greater differences between increments of magnitude, such as 3-, 6-, and 10-inch rods as compared with 3-, 4-, and 5-inch rods

It is difficult to find household items suitable for seriating, especially due to the problem of finding objects that differ in only one attribute. Because of this **stipulation** (specified condition), commercial seriating materials are often better than adult-collected items. Some commercial materials include cylinder blocks, baric tablets, color tablets, nesting objects, unit blocks, and Cuisenaire® rods.

Seeing Cause and Effect

For preschool children, observable cause-effect relationships are easier to understand than non-observable relationships. Parents and caregivers can help preschoolers comprehend cause and effect in the following ways:

- Ask children to predict regular household happenings (**Figure 15.28**). Ask, "What will happen when water is turned on above your glass?" or "What will happen when I open the drain in the bathtub?"
- When reading picture books, read the title, show children the cover, and then ask children to predict what each story is about or who the main characters are. Continue to ask for predictions throughout the story. Choose picture books that involve cause-effect relationships, such as those by Laura Numeroff.
- When speaking with children, make cause-effect statements, such as, "The room is sunny because the sun is shining through the windows" or "Your cup is empty because you drank your milk."

Figure 15.28 Asking children to predict household happenings can help them understand cause and effect. ***What cause-and-effect relationship might this preschooler learn to grasp if asked to predict what will happen?***

- Encourage children to experiment with cause and effect using physical movements. For example, a caregiver could help preschool children build ramps with blocks and then let balls roll down the ramps. Ask, "What makes the ball go *down* the ramp? Which ramp makes the ball go the fastest? the slowest? Why?"

Understanding Spatial Concepts

As preschool children's understanding of spatial concepts deepens, several activities can be used to enhance their learning. The first spatial concepts should pertain to the self. Caregivers can use spatial words in everyday conversation. They can say, "Put your hat *on* your head" or "Put your clothes *in* the closet." They can also use these words in games like "I Spy." Caregivers can encourage children to act out the directional words they hear and can read stories while emphasizing directional actions.

Activities that teach preschool children spatial concepts in relation to themselves are also helpful. Caregivers can play games that require children to position their bodies (**Figure 15.29**). They can tell them to "jump *forward* two jumps" or "put the shoe *under* your chin." "Simon Says" and "Hokey Pokey" are also fun games that require positioning. As preschool children grow older, they can learn more difficult spatial words, such as *away from*, *toward*, *right*, *left*, *center*, and *corner*.

Hands-on projects can help older preschoolers understand spatial concepts that pertain to other objects. Caregivers can help preschoolers grasp spatial concepts by assigning them simple spatial tasks, such as setting the table. Caregivers can help children build simple bridge-type structures and ask children to place blocks *on*, *under*, *behind*, or *in front of* the bridge. They can ask preschoolers to place objects in different positions on magnetic or flannel boards and can ask children to name the positions of given objects in relation to other objects.

Understanding Number Concepts

Preschoolers learn counting concepts rapidly. Once they can count both forward and backward, they can name numbers that come before or after any given number. Parents and caregivers can help preschoolers learn counting by arranging sets of objects in straight rows or columns and gradually increasing the size of sets children are expected to count. Other ways parents can help preschoolers learn counting may include asking children to touch each item while counting and exposing children to counting picture books, rhymes, and finger plays.

Figure 15.29 Activities that prompt children to move their bodies in various directions can help preschoolers understand spatial concepts. ***What specific games might prompt children to move their bodies in various directions?***

To teach numerals, parents and caregivers can explain that *numerals* are names for "how many." Some activities for learning numerals include matching numerals with sets of objects, identifying numerals in a game, completing a puzzle with numerals, making a "number line," and playing "I Spy" with numerals. Numeral concepts should be taught through activities involved in everyday life. At this stage, numeral concepts presented in workbooks are meaningless and not fun.

Preschoolers may encounter challenges with the language surrounding number concepts. They may equate indefinite terms, such as *less*, *few*, *many*, and *some*, with numbers. When helping preschoolers learn number concepts, caregivers should avoid these indefinite terms and be as clear as possible.

Noting Time Concepts

Time concepts will be difficult for preschoolers, whether caregivers plan activities to encourage these concepts or not. While children will not fully comprehend time concepts until the school-age years, caregivers can use "time words" as they talk with preschoolers. Some time words include: *before*, *after*, *then*, *yesterday*, *tomorrow*, *soon*, *morning*, and *night*. To help preschool children understand the passing of time, caregivers and teachers can use picture schedules of children's daily activities. In these schedules, children can "read" what will happen at each time.

Symbolic Learning Activities

Children's understanding of symbols continues to mature during the preschool years, as preschoolers develop symbolic thought and are able to imagine scenarios and symbols outside their realms of experience. Parents and caregivers can plan a variety of activities to help preschoolers grasp these concepts.

Using Symbols in Pretend Play

Children use symbols in pretend play by using props and by taking on the representation of another person or object (**Figure 15.30**). To understand these forms of symbolism, preschoolers need many opportunities to play and pretend they are other people and objects. They also need objects that they can pretend represent other things.

Figure 15.30 By using symbols, preschoolers take on the representation of another person or object. *What symbols help these children pretend to be superheroes?*

For the most part, children need only a little help in pretending. Their imaginations allow them to pretend they are other people with minimal props and encouragement. If an adult suggests a preschooler pretend to be an underwater diver, the preschooler might pretend to be putting on a deep-sea fishing outfit and then "dive" after lost treasures while being careful not to be attacked by sharks.

Using Symbols in Art

Children also use symbols when they paint, color, or create other forms of art. Younger children tend to create art products first and then decide what they represent. As children mature, however, their ideas about what a piece of art represents tend to precede the actual creation of the product. As is true of all symbolic representations, children decide what objects and art pieces represent, not adults.

Investigate Special Topics: Using Symbols in Written Communication

Written word and math symbols are society-determined and the most abstract of all symbols, which makes preschoolers' learning of these symbols difficult. Learning these symbols usually requires direct instruction, which is a practice that is widely debated among early childhood education experts. Why? Experts debate teaching written symbols for the following reasons:

- Young children learn best when they create their own symbols. Unlike society-determined symbols, preschoolers' symbols are products of their own symbolic thought. Society-determined symbols generally must be taught to children through rote memorization. Without having rich meanings for these symbols, the child may become what is called a "word caller" (reader without a high level of comprehension).
- Preschool children learn best by solving real-world problems. In many cases, the same concepts taught through drill-type lessons and workbooks can be learned in meaningful ways. Preschoolers can see written words while adults read them stories or written signs in their environment. Soon they will be saying, "What does this say?" just as they once questioned the names for objects by asking, "What dat?" They will notice that the "C" in their name appears in other words, too. In setting the table, a child will see the need for counting forks. Concrete counting makes numerals meaningful. Thus, instead of using lessons or workbooks to teach preschool children symbols, parents and caregivers can present preschool children with practical applications for their learning as the foundation for using abstract symbols.
- Problem-solving skills are best learned through *divergent thinking* (the act of coming up with different possible ideas). Divergent thinking is more often developed through rich, everyday experiences than through formal learning tasks. Formal learning tasks are more likely to encourage *convergent thinking* (the act of coming up with only one right answer or way to do a task). Workbooks and worksheets call for convergent thinking so that the child's responses match the "answer key." Because convergent thinking is used in teaching written symbols, the child may come to believe that all of life's problems have only one right answer. In short, creativity is stunted.
- Using "bits and pieces learning," such as learning initial consonant sounds and rhyming words, seldom make sense to preschoolers. Drill techniques are rarely fun either. Thus, many of these young children become frustrated. This frustration may sour a child's attitude toward learning and formal education.

Learning symbols, like so many other skills, is developmental. For these reasons, children need many experiences with real objects first. Next, the child should begin symbolic thinking by using symbols of his or her own choosing or making as seen in pretense and drawing. Spoken words are vital at both of these stages. These growing skills will prepare children for reading and writing words and math symbols with comprehension and joy.

Speaking Activity

Imagine you are a child development expert speaking to an audience of caregivers and teachers. You have just delivered a presentation about how preschoolers use symbols in pretend play and art, and one of the teachers asks you whether she should encourage preschoolers to use symbols in written communication. In small groups, practice delivering a concise, but well-supported answer using the information covered in this feature.

Preschoolers may use a variety of objects, such as crayons, paints, building blocks, or clay, to represent who or what they want. Even if children's art products do not resemble the real-life objects or people they represent, these art products symbolize the real world for the child.

Language Activities

Preschool children learn language by paying attention to what they hear, including how other people articulate sounds, use vocabulary, and use grammar. Through the observation of adults in their lives, preschoolers also learn about the process of reading and writing. For this reason, adults must be the best language and literacy models they can be and should make efforts to talk and read with preschoolers.

Preschool Language Supports

Preschool children need many daily chances to talk with adults and older children and see them engaged in the literacy tasks of reading and writing. When preschool children play only with peers or younger children, they do not learn as quickly as they do by talking with adults. Following are a few suggestions for ways in which adults and older children can support language and literacy development of preschoolers:

- Make language and literacy a part of all activities. Use important words in daily tasks and games.
- Read to children every day. In addition to exposing children to the real world and expanding concepts, reading books to preschoolers helps children understand language and grammar. Preschoolers who are exposed to reading and writing more often are likely to learn these concepts faster and better. What's more, story concepts can be stretched to involve pretend play and other activities.
- After reading a book, talk about story plots with the preschooler by asking more comprehension questions, such as, "Why do you think this happened?" or "Why did the character do what she did?"
- Monitor television viewing, including types of programs and total length of viewing time. While some programs can be helpful, holding actual conversations with adults and other children is a much better learning experience.
- Provide opportunities for preschoolers to observe adults reading and writing, both for work and for pleasure. Use correct grammar and articulation. Children imitate what they see and need to observe how literacy functions in their parents' and caregivers' lives.

Reading Readiness Versus Emergent Literacy

Beyond the need for talking and reading with preschoolers, some parents and teachers in preschool programs are beginning to teach "actual" reading and writing before the school years. This early instruction has become an issue among early childhood educators and has resulted in differing approaches (reading readiness and emergent literacy) to fostering early literacy skills.

Reading readiness is a belief that children should be formally taught reading and writing when developmentally ready for instruction. The concept of reading readiness is based on the principles of the *maturational theory of child development*. The **maturational theory of child development** holds to the belief that children mature on a genetic timetable (upon which the environment has little impact) and that skills and concepts should only be taught when children are biologically ready to learn them. These theorists believed that children were biologically mature enough to learn reading and writing at six years of age. Gradually, schools started teaching reading and writing at five years of age and then in some pre-kindergarten programs. The purpose of reading readiness programs is to prepare children for formal reading instruction.

By contrast, many of today's theorists believe in *emergent literacy*. **Emergent literacy** is defined by theorists as all aspects of literacy, including reading and writing, are developmental and learned in interactive ways, beginning in infancy as children learn to understand spoken words. Emergent literacy is based on the theories of Piaget and Vygotsky. Research shows that, beginning in the late toddler or early preschool years, young children pass through several stages in the learning of literacy.

Differences between reading readiness and emergent literacy are shown in **Figure 15.31**. Although preschool and kindergarten programs are divided in the way they approach teaching reading and writing skills prior to first grade, research evidence seems to support emergent literacy as the more effective method of teaching reading and writing.

Electronic Media Activities

Technology devices are **ubiquitous** (yoo-BIH-kwuh-tuhs), found everywhere, and even preschoolers experience technology as a major part of the context of their lives. Technological devices can be classified as either *interactive media* or *non-interactive media*. **Interactive media** refer to media systems, such as computers, that respond to the user's actions. **Noninteractive media** (also called *passive media*) refer to media systems, such as television programs, over which the user has only a limited amount of control. Interactive media systems are used for communication, collaboration, learning, entertainment, and daily life management. Culture demands that people develop digital literacy, even from an early age.

The *National Association for the Education of Young Children*, in conjunction with the *Fred Rogers Center for Early Learning and Children's Media*, has developed a joint statement concerning media integration in learning environments for young children. This statement holds that media integration needs to

Figure 15.31 Reading Readiness Versus Emergent Literacy Concepts

Reading Readiness	Emergent Literacy
Basic concept: At some point between three and five years of age, a child should be introduced to reading readiness. Reading readiness programs teach three basic skills: • *phonemic awareness* (being able to distinguish sounds in words). For example, although *bat* and *light* have a different number of letters, they each have three phonemes or sounds—b/a/t/ and l/igh/t/. Early instruction focuses on hearing initial sounds of words and rhyming sounds at the ends of words. • *letter recognition* (being able to see differences in letter shapes and knowing letter names). Children are taught to recognize letters individually and in words and to write in manuscript (often called *printing*) all the letters in uppercase and lowercase. • *phonics* (the relationship between letters and sounds), such as the letter *b* stands for the sound /b/ heard at the beginning of *bat*. Once children see the relationship between a letter and its sound, they can sound out and read words. Most reading readiness programs use workbooks, worksheets, and audio or digital programs that introduce and review each skill in more or less the same way.	**Basic concept:** At two or three years of age, children *spontaneously* (without instruction) begin to notice print in their environment and can identify some signs and logos. They also begin scribbling marks characteristic of the writing they see. For example, older preschoolers' scribbling style will be different depending on whether they see Chinese or English writing. All aspects of literacy are emerging at the same time. Children do not develop these skills in a hard and fast sequence—listen, speak, read, and write. In fact, most children try writing before reading. The knowledge of one aspect of literacy adds to the knowledge of other aspects. In short, the end goal is not to be literate, but to use literacy to achieve other goals. Parents and adults support emergent literacy in these ways: • being a speaking, reading, and writing model. • reading daily to their child. Hearing parents read motivates the child to be a reader. • having books, digital devices, and traditional writing materials available for the child to use as literacy emerges.

be assessed against what is already known about children's development. With this criterion (kry-TIR-ee-uhn) in mind, parents and caregivers can discern what types of media are appropriate for preschoolers. Parents and caregivers can follow some basic principles suggested by experts. Some of these principles include the following:

- ***Screen time.*** Total screen time for all devices in all settings must be monitored and limited by caregivers. Recommendations by different authorities for total daily screen time vary from 30 minutes to two hours. Within this time frame, screen time can increase for older preschoolers. Total screen time should be broken into short segments of time.
- ***Effect.*** Parents and caregivers should assess media systems to determine what effect they may have on preschool children (**Figure 15.32**).
- ***Purpose.*** Media should always be used for learning, never just for technology's sake. Media should support and enhance learning, not drive it.
- ***Type.*** Interactive media should be used rather than noninteractive media. Media should be chosen for its ability to foster active and creative use by the child and for its likelihood to encourage social interactions.
- ***Content.*** Electronic media should be developmentally appropriate for the child. The content of media systems matters much more than the format.

Figure 15.32 Media experiences should never interfere with social interactions, communications, physical activity, real-life exploration, or pretend play. *How can adults encourage children not to let media distract them from their real worlds?*

Focus on

Careers

Children's Media Developer

Children's media developers are responsible for creating children's computer programs, applications, and other digital media products. They are also responsible for programming products and ensuring easy and accurate operation.

Career cluster: Information technology.

Education: Education requirements vary, but children's media developers must be adept at computer programming. As a result, many obtain bachelor's degrees in computer science.

Job outlook: Future employment opportunities for children's media developers are expected to grow much faster than the average for all occupations.

To learn more about a career as a children's media developer, visit the United States Department of Labor's *Occupational Outlook Handbook* website. You will also be able to compare the job responsibilities, educational requirements, job outlook, and average pay of children's media developers with similar occupations.

- ***Interactiveness.*** Use of media should emphasize co-participation between adults and children and among children.
- ***Inclusiveness.*** Media use in child care and education programs should be **inclusive** (accessible to a variety of people). Caregivers and teachers should realize that children differ in their home access to digital devices and software just as they do to print media (books).

Parents, caregivers, and teachers should keep in mind that there is conflicting evidence about the value of technology in preschool children's development. Experts have identified some possible negative outcomes, including behavioral issues, problems focusing on tasks, irregular sleep patterns, and negative effects on socialization and language skills. These problems may result from too much screen time, poor-quality software, or incorrect use of technology. Electronic media activities can be beneficial for preschool learning, but parents, caregivers, and teachers should always assess research findings on technology in the lives of young children.

Lesson 15.3 Review and Assessment 

1. To help preschoolers hone their motor skills, caregivers can plan activities that, among other skills, involve _____.
2. Name four ways that caregivers can foster preschoolers' memories.
3. Choose one logical thinking concept and describe how caregivers can foster this concept during the preschool years.
4. In what two areas do preschoolers most easily grasp symbolic learning?
5. Summarize three ways that caregivers can support language development in preschoolers.
6. Explain the difference between *reading readiness* and *emergent literacy.*
7. List four principles that caregivers should consider when choosing electronic media for preschoolers.
8. **Critical thinking.** Why is it worthwhile for caregivers to plan logical thinking activities, even though preschoolers are not yet logical thinkers?

Chapter 15 Review and Assessment

Summary

Preschoolers begin to think rather than depend on trial and error. Through their brain development and new cognitive abilities, they are better able to solve problems and communicate. According to Piaget, preschool children are in the *preoperational stage* and do not yet think logically. In the preconceptual substage, they learn by developing some concepts using trial and error and their perceptions. In the intuitive substage, they solve problems using intuition. There are a number of barriers that prevent them from thinking logically. Vygotsky identified several origins of abstract thinking in preschoolers.

Preschoolers develop concepts about physical attributes and understand some physical knowledge concepts. Older preschoolers begin to learn logical thinking concepts, such as sorting and classifying, ordering by attributes, seeing cause and effect, understanding spatial concepts, understanding number concepts, and noting time concepts. Preschool is an important time in language development, which is now linked to thinking. Communication is easier because preschoolers can articulate better and their vocabularies have increased. Sentence structure and grammar rules tend to be difficult.

Preschoolers still learn through motor activities, though usually in conjunction with other activities. Learning by creating their own symbols is critical for preschoolers because it prepares them for handling more abstract, society-determined symbols. Adults should foster preschoolers' growing memory capacities and provide opportunities for concept learning. During the preschool years, children will learn most basic physical attributes and enjoy activities involving physical knowledge. Although preschoolers do not master logical thinking skills, they do begin laying a foundation for later logical reasoning. Language skills improve through modeling and using language as a part of daily activities. Many preschoolers learn using interactive media, too. Even when using interactive media, screen time should be limited and media content carefully chosen.

College and Career Portfolio

Portfolio Cover Message

Many school and job applications require a cover message to accompany a portfolio or résumé. A *cover message* is an outline and explanation of your experiences. It should explain *why* and *how* your experiences have made you uniquely qualified for your desired school or job.

- Write a cover message explaining how your experiences have prepared you for your desired role.
- Ask a career counselor or teacher to review your cover message. Edit your message according to his or her feedback.
- Carefully proof your cover message.

Chapter 15 Review and Assessment

Vocabulary Activities 

1. On a separate sheet of paper, list at least two other words that relate to each of the following terms. Then, work with a partner to explain how these words are related. As a team, decide which of the words you selected best relates to each term. Share your results with the rest of the class.

Key Terms

centration (15.1)
classifying (15.2)
collective monologue (15.2)
egocentric speech (15.2)
egocentrism (15.1)
emergent literacy (15.3)
episodic memory (15.1)
interactive media (15.3)
intuitive substage (15.1)
logical thinking concepts (15.2)
maturational theory of child development (15.3)
memory capacity (15.1)
mental images (15.1)
mental maps (15.2)
monologue (15.2)
noninteractive media (15.3)
physical knowledge (15.2)
preconceptual substage (15.1)
preoperational stage (15.1)
reading readiness (15.3)
seriation (15.2)
symbolic thought (15.1)
tag questions (15.2)
transductive reasoning (15.1)
transformations (15.1)

2. Read the text passages that contain each of the following terms. Then, write the definition of each term in your own words. Double-check your definitions by rereading the text and using the text glossary. Finally, in small groups, compare your definitions. Discuss why you wrote your definitions the way you did.

Academic Terms

animism (15.2)
coherently (15.2)
conceptualize (15.1)
crystallized (15.1)
inclusive (15.3)
intuition (15.1)
numerosity (15.2)
overgeneralization (15.1)
physical attributes (15.2)
pique (15.3)
rote memorization (15.2)
stipulation (15.3)
transposition (15.1)
ubiquitous (15.3)

Critical Thinking

3. **Draw conclusions.** Preschool children solve problems using intuition and tend to have difficulty following nonobservable cause-and-effect relationships. In small groups, compile a list of nonobservable cause-and-effect relationships that you acknowledge and use each day. Draw conclusions about how your perceptions would be changed if you did not understand these relationships.
4. **Analyze.** In small groups, pick out children's books that illustrate cause and effect. Read one book aloud in your group and then analyze what the book would teach preschool children about cause-effect relationships. Write a two-page book report containing your analysis.
5. **Identify.** In small groups, assemble a collection of colored shapes or blocks in various shapes, sizes, and colors. Then, identify all the ways the objects can be *sorted* and all the ways they can be *classified*. Demonstrate to the class one sorting and one classifying activity telling fellow students the criterion being used for each.
6. **Cause and effect.** How do your patterns of speech and grammar reflect the language used by your parents or caregivers? How do you think the language models children are exposed to early in life impact their use of grammar?
7. **Compare and contrast.** Compare and contrast how language development in preschool children relates to language learning in older children and adults. Will learners of a second language have the same obstacles when it comes to language learning? Will they have different obstacles?
8. **Determine.** Anuj, a teacher at a local preschool, has been criticized for the amounts of dramatic play, art, and literature or language activities he incorporates into lessons. Anuj, however, feels these activities are not "just play," but are vital to intellectual development. Determine ways that Anuj can explain this to the parents of his students. Write a short script he can follow.
9. **Evaluate.** Watch a movie or television show for preschool children. While watching, take notes on what preschool children might learn or where an adult could ask a question that prompts learning. Afterward, evaluate the program and rate it on a scale from 1 to 10, with 1 being least educational and 10 being most educational.

Core Skills

10. **Research and writing.** Preschool learning is enabled by brain development leading to changes in cognition. Using reliable online or print resources, research how the brain changes and develops between three and five years of age. Also, research symbolic thought and how it fosters new abilities in preschoolers. Finally, write a three- to five-page report detailing how preschoolers' brains are uniquely prepared to learn and develop skills that are typically understood at this age.
11. **Technology and writing.** With a partner, review this chapter's information about preschoolers' comprehension of logical thinking concepts and appropriate activities caregivers can use to foster these concepts. Then, create a comprehensive brochure that explains this information to parents and caregivers. Your brochure should both describe reasonable expectations for preschooler logic and advocate for activities that encourage the development of these concepts. Afterward, display your brochure in class.
12. **Art.** In understanding spatial relationships, preschoolers learn mental mapping, which enables them to envision spaces they do not presently see. Using a pencil and paper or a graphics editing software, draw a spatial map of your home from memory. You must be in a location other than your home when you do this activity. After completing your map, compare it to the actual space of your home. How accurately did your mental map resemble the physical space?
13. **Math.** Using reliable print or online resources, research the typical size of an adult's vocabulary. Then, review the sizes of children's vocabularies at three, four, and five years of age. What percentage of their adult vocabularies do children know at each of these ages?
14. **Technology and speaking.** Review the table of intellectual milestones for preschoolers (Figure 15.23), and in small groups, choose one of the three ages covered. Create a checklist for parents and caregivers titled "What My Preschooler Should Understand at Age _____." In your brochure, detail the major milestones a preschooler should achieve and that a parent or caregiver might observe during this time. Make your brochure visually appealing and informative. Finally, distribute the brochure to the class and deliver a presentation about its contents.
15. **Reading.** Research at least three schedules for preschool centers in your area. These schedules should include activities done each day as well as snack and nap times. Read each schedule carefully and note each activity that involves a gross- or fine-motor skill. Are most of these activities primarily structured as motor activities, or are the motor activities secondary to the intent of the lesson?
16. **Listening and speaking.** As a class, divide into two teams—one team advocating reading readiness and one team advocating emergent literacy. In your teams, interview supporters of your theory and note their arguments. Verify the information given using reliable print or online resources. Finally, compose an opening statement and debate your theory with the opposing team. Be prepared to defend your theory with relevant facts and to create a closing statement based on the discussion that takes place.
17. **CTE Career Readiness Practice.** Presume you are the director of a new preschool center. Recently, parents have been asking you and your staff to explain certain terminology, such as *Piaget's preoperational stage*, *the preconceptual substage*, and *the intuitive substage*. You have planned a staff meeting to ensure that all of your employees know how to respond to the parents' questions. In preparation for this meeting, prepare fact sheets that outline what the staff must know and communicate about the preoperational stage and its substages.

Observations

18. In small groups, make or find an audio recording of preschool children speaking while playing. Listen to the recording in your group and then answer the following questions: What articulation errors did you hear? Did you hear complex sentences—both statements and questions? What incorrect grammar did you hear? Afterward, play your recording and share your findings with the class.
19. In small groups, visit a local child care center and observe preschoolers speaking. Observe any instances of monologue or collective monologue and take notes about the contexts in which these speaking patterns occur. When do preschoolers most often use monologue and collective monologue? For what purpose do they use them? Discuss your findings in class.

Chapter 16 Social-Emotional Development of Preschoolers

Essential Question

How do preschoolers piece together their unique self-portraits while assimilating family and societal expectations, and how do adults, especially parents, serve as mirrors for the child's self-awareness and function as socializing agents?

Lesson 16.1 The Social-Emotional World of Preschoolers

Lesson 16.2 Meeting Preschoolers' Social-Emotional Needs

Case Study How Should Teachers Address Parents' Beliefs About Gender Roles?

As a class, read the case study and discuss the questions that follow. After you finish studying the chapter, discuss this case study again. Have your opinions changed based on what you learned?

Three-year-old Sylvan lives with his mechanic father and stay-at-home mother in small-town southern Louisiana, where he attends preschool with many boys and girls. One day, Sylvan asked his parents for a doll so he could play in the preschool's housekeeping center.

Sylvan's father, Mr. Fontenot, was not happy when he heard his son's request, and he called Sylvan's preschool teacher, Shenequa, right away. "If Sylvan plays in the housekeeping center, he won't grow up to be *masculine*," Mr. Fontenot told Shenequa. "He will learn to be *girly*, and he might never grow out of it. *I* never played with dolls when *I* was a kid."

Shenequa replied, "I'm not sure that's what this is, Mr. Fontenot. Sylvan plays in the housekeeping center because he's better friends with some of the girls."

Mr. Fontenot asked, "Does my son ever dress up like a girl?"

Shenequa pondered how to answer this and said, "Truth be told, Mr. Fontenot, many of the boys play in the housekeeping center, and several dress in women's clothing and pretend to be mothers. Playing multiple gender roles is good for young children."

After this explanation, Mr. Fontenot seemed calm, but Shenequa worried that Mr. Fontenot might complain to the school.

Give It Some Thought

1. Why do you think Mr. Fontenot was concerned about his son's desire for a doll? Why does this contradict his script about masculinity?
2. If Mr. Fontenot complains to the school and scolds his son about playing with dolls, how might the experience affect Sylvan and his feelings about his gender and gender roles?
3. Shenequa asserts that there's value in children playing in ways that are traditionally associated with the opposite gender. Do you agree or disagree with Shenequa?

While studying this chapter, look for the online resources icon  to:

- **Practice** terms with e-flash cards and interactive games
- **Assess** what you learn by completing self-assessment quizzes
- **Expand** knowledge with interactive activities and graphic organizers

Companion G-W Learning

www.g-wlearning.com/childdevelopment

Study on the go

Use a mobile device to practice terms and review with self-assessment quizzes.

www.m.g-wlearning.com/0384

Lesson 16.1

The Social-Emotional World of Preschoolers

Key Terms

emotional dependency
fear-conditioning
gender constancy
gender-role learning
gender stability
initiative versus guilt
moral character
moral development
moral emotions
moral judgment and reasoning
repressed jealousy
self-concept
sex typing
sexual stereotyping

Academic Terms

constitute
cumulative
derived
initiative

Objectives

After studying this lesson, you will be able to

- explain how preschoolers learn even more about themselves as they show responsibility, learn gender roles, begin moral development, and expand their self-concept.
- analyze the problems preschoolers face as they develop initiative.
- describe preschoolers' interactions with adults, siblings, and peers, and discuss the role of imaginary friends in some preschoolers' lives.
- assess how feelings and emotions change during the preschool years.
- evaluate how to recognize developmental and environmental stress during the preschool years.
- give examples of social-emotional developmental milestones preschoolers might achieve.

Reading and Writing Activity

Arrange a study session to read this lesson aloud with a classmate. Take turns reading each section. Stop at the end of each section to discuss what you think are the section's main points. Take notes indicating what your study group learned about child development to share with the class.

Graphic Organizer

Draw two columns for taking notes. As you read, write main ideas in the left column and subtopics and detailed information in the right column. After reading this lesson, use your notes as a study guide. Cover the right column and use the left column to quiz yourself about the content in this lesson.

Main Topics	Subtopics and Detailed Information
Preschoolers' self-awareness expands	*Preschoolers show more responsibility (such as by doing household tasks)*

Due to their expanding self-awareness, children's personalities blossom and become more stable during the preschool years. Preschoolers learn more about themselves, including how to answer questions, such as "Who am I?" and "What can I do on my own?" Preschoolers test their skills through a series of successes and mistakes. As they show responsibility, learn gender roles, begin moral development, and expand their self-concept, they make strides toward taking initiative in life.

During the preschool years, children's social worlds expand to include many new adults, friends, peers, and perhaps younger siblings. Preschoolers engage in more friendships, and imaginary friends may become an important part of preschoolers' lives. Preschoolers' emotions also become more complex as they develop a greater understanding of their world. As preschool children grow, they must learn how to control and express emotions. Preschoolers experience stress due to their illogical ideas, lack of language skills, and fearful temperaments, including memories of fearful events that are all typical during this developmental stage. Preschoolers' ever-widening social environments also create more possibilities for stressful situations.

Expanding Self-Awareness

Toddlers begin to develop self-awareness and self-esteem based on how parents and other caregivers react to them. During the preschool years, children learn even more about themselves as they show responsibility, learn gender roles, begin moral development, and expand their self-concept. The feedback children receive during these experiences helps shape the image they have of themselves and determines whether the image is positive or negative.

Showing Responsibility

During the preschool years, children take their first steps toward becoming dependable people. They begin to show *responsibility*, which is a sense of accountability and a sign of trustworthiness. Learning to show responsibility takes time and calls for experience.

Adults can help children learn to show responsibility by setting examples and giving children tasks they can do based on their abilities. Parents and caregivers may need to show children how to do a task first and then give children time to perform the task (**Figure 16.1**). At home, parents may ask children to help with household tasks, such as setting the table, cleaning the kitchen, or folding laundry. In preschool programs, caregivers may ask children to put away toys, distribute snacks, and care for plants and animals. According to Erikson, children can learn responsibility by taking part in the routines of their world in real and important ways.

Figure 16.1 Preschoolers learn to show responsibility when adults teach and then assign them tasks. *What household tasks were you assigned as a child? How did they help you learn responsibility?*

As preschoolers learn to show responsibility, they will have many successes and failures. Adults and caregivers should acknowledge preschoolers' successes and offer support after failures. Children who learn responsibility become more considerate of others and more dependable, which are important qualities as they continue to learn and grow.

Learning Gender Roles

A major part of self-awareness is *gender-role learning*. **Gender-role learning**, which involves knowing what behaviors are expected of males and females within one's society, aids children in their social relations and in their development of self-awareness. Through gender-role learning, children learn what is expected of them as a result of their genders.

Before preschoolers can understand gender roles, they must grasp the following basic concepts about gender:

- ***Gender identity.*** *Gender identity* is the ability to label one's self and others as male or female. Children develop gender identity around two years of age.
- ***Gender stability.*** Between three and four years of age, children begin to grasp **gender stability**, which is the understanding that a person who is born either male or female will remain so throughout life. Confusion about gender stability may persist until the early school-age years.
- ***Gender constancy.*** Older preschoolers begin to comprehend **gender constancy**, which is the understanding that clothing, hairstyles, and actions do not change a person's gender. As with gender stability, confusion about gender constancy may persist into the early school-age years.

Once preschoolers understand these basic concepts about gender, they begin to learn gender roles through *sex typing*. **Sex typing** is the process by which a person adopts the attitudes and behaviors considered culturally appropriate for his or her gender. Families and even child care programs "teach" sex typing based on how they interpret varying cultural expectations. In the United States, some adults still follow traditional gender roles while other adults stress similarities between male

Focus on

Social Studies

Gender Roles in the United States

For much of the history of the United States, men and women have adhered to a pattern of gender roles known as *traditional gender roles*. In traditional gender roles, males are typically the economic heads of their families and are seen as having more assertive traits. Females typically stay home to care for the house and children and are seen as having more nurturing traits. These gender-role norms led to a societal system that encouraged males and females to embrace their respective roles.

Traditional gender roles in the United States, however, are on the decline as men and women adapt their roles to new lifestyles and expectations. This change began in the 1960s when women entered the workforce. In the workforce, both men and women show assertive traits (such as sharing opinions) on the job. With their wives working, more men shared household and child care duties. Both men and women showed loving, gentle, and nurturing traits toward their children.

Today, different cultures and groups in the United States hold varying beliefs about gender roles. Some groups support more traditional gender roles while others follow less traditional roles. Families' gender-role beliefs influence how their children perceive gender during the early years. By the teen and young adult years, however, people's opinions on gender roles may change just as other attitudes and behaviors change.

and female roles. The toys and clothing given to a child, how a child's emotional expressions are received, and a child's observations of others filling male and female roles impact sex typing.

Children learn sex typing by observing how others treat them and how others express male or female roles. Preschoolers begin to sense that boys and girls act differently in many situations, and they will often identify with and model themselves after same-gender family members and friends. They may also model themselves after teachers and characters from television, movies, and storybooks.

In the United States, children who are taught traditional gender roles may learn them at an earlier age compared to children who are taught similarities between male and female roles. Traditional gender-role learning, however, may also lead to sexual stereotyping. **Sexual stereotyping** is stating or even hinting that men and women always behave in certain ways or should always do particular tasks. Examples of sexual stereotyping may be apparent in various books, television programs, movies, and even in some people's conversations. Due to changing social expectations, children who learn sexual stereotyping will likely find it more difficult to adjust to mainstream U.S. society with its less clearly defined roles. Regardless of whether children are taught traditional gender roles or similar roles, the gender roles they learn will affect other roles, such as career roles and roles in friendships, dating, and family life.

Learning to Be Moral

During the preschool years, children begin a process known as **moral development**, the process by which children develop proper attitudes toward others (based on sociocultural, familial, school, peer, religious, and societal expectations). Moral development affects children's moral judgment and reasoning, moral character, and moral emotions.

Moral Judgment and Reasoning

Moral judgment and reasoning is the ability to perceive an action as right or wrong. The development of judgment and reasoning coincides with children's development of thinking skills. Jean Piaget and Lawrence Kohlberg researched moral judgment and reasoning.

Piaget exposed children to a number of moral dilemmas and published his findings as part of his *Social Theory of Development*. He called his theory *social*, rather than *intellectual*, because he noted moral judgments involved not only intellectual reasoning, but also adult limits and peer-group cooperation. Lawrence Kohlberg expanded on Piaget's research by studying children of different ethnic, religious, and social groups. Kohlberg's methods mirrored Piaget's, and his findings were similar.

During the preschool years, both Piaget and Kohlberg noted that children's decisions were regulated by adult limits, not by personal convictions. In **Figure 16.2**, you can see that preschoolers are in Piaget's *heterogeneous* (HEH-tuh-ruh-JEE-nee-us) stage of morality, which spans from four to seven years of age. In Lawrence Kohlberg's theory, preschoolers occupy the *obedience-punishment orientation* and *individualism and exchange* stages of moral reasoning. Both of these stages are in Kohlberg's first level called *preconventional morality* (level in which people make moral decisions based on how these decisions will impact them as individuals). During these stages, young children see rules as fixed and see punishments as inhibitors to unacceptable behaviors. Older preschoolers tend to believe that "being good" merits some type of reward. (During the school-age years, children enter the next stages of moral judgment and reasoning, which you will learn about later in this text.)

Moral Character

All studies show that **moral character**, acting in accordance with what is perceived as morally right, never bears a one-to-one correspondence with judgment and reasoning. Character requires having the strength and independence to act in accordance with what is perceived as morally right.

Preschoolers may fail to exhibit moral character because they do not always understand the reasoning behind certain limits. Their natural curiosity leads them beyond adult authority. Because punishment is perceived as a controlling factor, young preschoolers often weigh their

Figure 16.2 **Piaget's and Kohlberg's Stages of Moral Judgment and Reasoning During the Preschool Years**

Jean Piaget	
Stage	**Characteristics of Stage**
Heterogeneous morality* (also called *moral realism*)	Children are regulated by others (parents and teachers), not by personal conviction. Children's beliefs include • Rules are fixed and inflexible. • Consequences of actions, not intentions, determine the "badness" of actions. • Punishment is automatic. • Not only do adults punish, but objects, such as trees, rocks, and toys, can also punish. This physically implausible connection between objects and punishment is called *immanent justice*.

**Heterogeneous* means "from without."

Lawrence Kohlberg's Preconventional Stages of Moral Reasoning	
Stage	**Characteristics of Stage**
Obedience-punishment orientation	• Children obey rules as taught by authority figures. • Children determine how good or bad an action is by its consequences. • Children fear punishment for wrongdoing.
Individualism and exchange	• Children note people have different viewpoints about right and wrong. • Children obey rules if they benefit them, but expect something in return for obedience. • Children exact justice in an eye-for-eye manner because they see this type of justice as fair.

chances of being caught and how severe the punishment might be. Older preschoolers often follow adult limits because they understand the reasons for certain behaviors and feel they will be rewarded. Some older preschoolers may even try to bargain with adults.

Moral Emotions

Moral emotions, which are a person's reactions to acceptable and unacceptable behaviors, emerge first in children who are other-oriented. Other-oriented people behave acceptably out of respect for others and feel remorse when they behave unacceptably. This remorse becomes a person's *inner voice of conscience*. Over time, conscience will take the place of authority figures as a moral guide. Young preschoolers may develop some remorse for wrongdoings, especially when adults emphasize the reasons for acceptable behaviors and how unacceptable behaviors damage others.

Developing a Self-Concept

During the preschool years, children expand their *self-concepts*. **Self-concept** is the picture a person has of him- or herself. Self-concept is always **cumulative** (KYOO-muh-luh-tihv), meaning it is composed of accumulated parts. A person's experiences can positively and negatively affect his or her self-concept.

Several factors **constitute** (make up) self-concept (**Figure 16.3**), including the following:

- ***Self-recognition.*** In the toddler years, self-recognition begins when toddlers identify, but do not mentally separate, themselves and their mirror images or photos of themselves. During the preschool years, children can distinguish the "real me" from symbols of themselves.
- ***Self-definition.*** Preschoolers begin to develop *self-definition*, which is the describing of one's self. In the preschool years, self-definition is based on one's physical features, gender, physical skills, possessions, and activities. Even though the descriptors change, people continue to practice self-definition throughout their lives.
- ***Self-esteem.*** As toddlers, children begin to develop feelings of *self-esteem*, or self-worth. In preschoolers, healthy self-esteem is **derived** (sourced) from being unconditionally loved and accepted, having secure attachments, and receiving positive discipline and guidance. Opposite adult behaviors will damage a child's self-esteem.

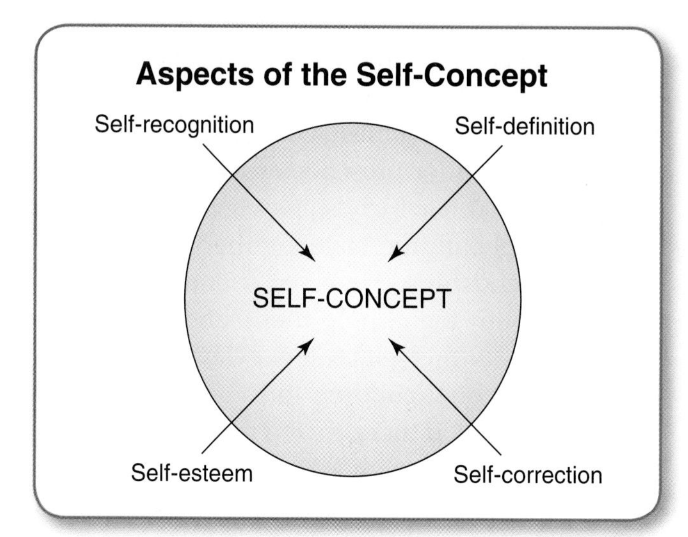

Figure 16.3 Although self-concept evolves and is cumulative for a lifetime, its four aspects begin to emerge during the preschool years. *In your own words, how would you define each of the four aspects of self-concept?*

Preschool children who have unhealthy self-esteem often show aggression and other antisocial behaviors, which can lead to mental health issues in the school-age and teen years.

- ***Self-correction.*** Preschoolers begin to exhibit *self-correction*, the belief that one can do better and the ability to act on that belief. Preschoolers often self-correct drawings or tasks by starting over and correcting their methods.

As preschoolers develop self-concept, they will choose to imitate certain individuals and will willingly participate in some experiences. They will begin to describe themselves with sayings, such as "I'm good (or bad)" or "I can (or cannot) draw that."

Taking Initiative

Between three and six years of age, children grow in independence. Because of their improved abilities and limitless energy, they have a strong desire to learn, explore, and act. These children yearn for many experiences.

Children at this age are in Erikson's third stage of personality development, which is called **initiative versus guilt**. During this stage, children's **initiative** (the ability to think or act without being urged) encourages them to try new activities. At the same time, initiative can lead to failures, and failures may lead to *guilt* (the blaming of one's self for something done wrong) and a fear of trying new things.

When preschool children make mistakes, they may feel badly about themselves, and if they feel too guilty, their desires to be obedient become so important they are afraid to try new things. Fear and guilt stifle initiative, and to prevent guilty feelings, children must know it is okay to make mistakes.

Extending Social Relations

Preschool children not only improve their motor skills and knowledge through social activities, but they also learn many social lessons, such as

- the social skills needed to form friendships
- the ability to recognize and respond to social cues from others
- the ability to cooperate with and show empathy for others (**Figure 16.4**)
- conflict-resolution skills
- the ability to regulate emotions

Figure 16.4 As preschoolers cooperate with others, they begin to develop close relationships with other children. *Who were your first friends? When did you become friends?*

Children learn these lessons through their interactions with adults, other children, and even imaginary friends.

Interacting with Adults

Preschoolers continue to depend on parents and other adults to meet many of their needs. As authority figures, parents must impose limits on certain behaviors of their children as well as explain the reasons for the limits. In addition to being caregivers and authority figures, adults also serve as social models for preschoolers. By their examples, adults teach children about responsibility, gender roles, relationships, morals, self-control, manners, and much more. Preschoolers with secure attachments to their parents, caregivers, and teachers are more successful at learning tasks and are more self-confident.

Interacting with Other Children

Siblings and peers are more important to preschool children than to toddlers. Among young preschoolers, reactions to siblings and peers differ. Some preschoolers enjoy playing with other children while others do not. It is not until the late preschool years that children form their first real friendships.

A child's ease of making friends depends on the child's friendliness, ability to follow group rules, and lack of dependence on adults. Preschool children tend to prefer making friends with children of the same gender, although within-gender friendships strengthen in the school-age years. While these friendships may last, conflicts can end them just as easily. Older preschoolers do not have the social skills to sustain friendships when conflicts arise.

Preschool children have a rather self-centered view of friendships. They see friends as people who play with them, help them, and share their toys. Because of this self-centered view, usually two or three preschool children form a close circle of friends. After all, if there are too many friends, one child may not get enough attention from a friend. To protect their interests, preschool children will often call out, "You can't play with us." When a friend does not do as a child desires, feelings quickly change. A child takes a new best friend—at least for the moment.

Preschool children learn many social skills while playing with other children, such as taking turns, giving to others, and receiving from others. They also learn to see from other children's perspectives and to manage their own impulses. Friendships are important for preschoolers, and children with limited peer involvement may experience negative developmental consequences.

Investigate Special Topics: Sibling Interactions

In many families, children grow up with at least one sibling. In some families, children have several brothers and sisters. Siblings influence each other's lives in many ways. Siblings can play many roles with each other. They can be teachers and learners, protectors, and even rivals.

Sibling interactions influence both intellectual and social-emotional development as children play roles of teachers and learners. Older children often act like teachers while younger siblings will play the part of eager learners. As teachers, siblings explain, define, describe, show, and offer examples. Older siblings also model social skills, so younger children learn the difference between acceptable and unacceptable social behaviors. From a child's point of view, a sibling shows acceptable social behavior if he or she plays nicely, helps with chores, and does not tattle.

If you have ever seen an older child run to a younger sibling's defense, you know that siblings protect each other. Much as they may compete, siblings often have a sense of *family togetherness* and a desire to protect and look after their siblings (especially younger siblings or siblings with special needs). Siblings are more likely to protect each other if they have an age gap of three or more years, come from large families, are in unsupervised places, or if one sibling is attacked physically or verbally by his or her peers.

Even if siblings teach and protect each other, they may think of each other as *rivals*. Siblings will often compete with one another in both physical and verbal ways for the love and attention of adults and friends. This competition can develop for several reasons. Children may be jealous of siblings who seem more capable than they are. They also may not be able to see a situation from other points of view. Children who have siblings with special needs may become jealous of the amount of time parents need to spend meeting these special needs. To young children, *fair* means *equal*, so some children may feel they are being treated unfairly if their siblings are given different treatment, privileges, or responsibilities from those given to them.

Adults cannot prevent rivalry among siblings. As children develop distinct identities and self-concepts, they will unavoidably compare themselves to their siblings and peers. Adults can lessen rivalry, however, by giving each child lots of love and positive feedback. Adults should take care not to compare one child with another. Children are different, and comparing them usually makes one child resent the other and feel angry toward the adult. Rather, adults should stress the importance of family togetherness and support and should plan some activities everyone enjoys. Adults should teach children to take pleasure in another's good fortune and should explain that family members love one another although they sometimes get angry at each other. Above all, parents should encourage loving behaviors between a child and his or her siblings.

Writing Activity

Read a story or watch a film or television show in which two young siblings interact. Take notes about the siblings' relationship, including how they teach each other, protect and support each other, and compete with each other. Write a two- to three-page analysis of the relationship identifying these behaviors and discussing how this portrayal of a sibling relationship is or is not realistic.

Interacting with Imaginary Friends

During the preschool years, children may also begin to interact with imaginary friends. About two-thirds of children from two to seven years of age have imaginary friends. These "friendships" can last long past seven years of age and sometimes even into adulthood. For example, fiction writers talk about their book characters taking on a life of their own. Although these are not "real friendships," imaginary friends can be very important for preschoolers and can occupy much of their time and energy. Often, these friendships involve the entire family. A preschooler may also try to get other adults and children to acknowledge the imaginary friend.

In the past, researchers have thought that imaginary friends are created to fill a void in the lives of some children. Recent research, however, does not support this idea and instead has led to many other discoveries (**Figure 16.5**).

Expressing Emotions

During the preschool years, children experience many emotions and express them in intense ways. While preschool children feel many positive emotions, such as love and dependency, they also experience negative emotions when faced with the following types of stressors:

- ***Common childlike stressors.*** These include short separations from caring adults and fear of monsters.
- ***Short-term stressors and "bad days."*** These occur when preschoolers' initiative requires more "no" responses from parents and caregivers. These also occur when preschoolers' emotions seem out of control.
- ***Long-lasting and serious stressors.*** These may include illness, moving, death, adult quarrels, and divorce.

Figure 16.5 Imaginary Friends

Which children are most likely to have imaginary friends?	• Children who create imaginary friends are outgoing and have many real friends. • Oldest children, only children, and children who do not watch television are most likely to have imaginary friends. These children's unstructured time (not loneliness) enables them to invent friends. • Children who have imaginary friends are not shy or maladjusted.
What are the characteristics of imaginary friends?	• Imaginary friends, estimated to be over 16 million in number, are a diverse group. Researchers cannot categorize these friends. • Imaginary friends can be one friend or a group of friends. For example, one child's imaginary friends were a herd of cattle. Imaginary friends may be as small as a mouse or as large as a dinosaur. • Imaginary friends are rarely younger children. • Imaginary friends often possess the skills that a child desires. • Children can describe imaginary friends in the same detail as they can their real friends.
Which types of relationships do children have with imaginary friends?	• Very few preschoolers insist imaginary friends are real. In fact, over 75 percent voluntarily disclose this information during an interview. • Children with imaginary friends have a very involved form of pretend play. These children expect others to play along. • Unlike play with stuffed animals and dolls, play with imaginary friends treats the imaginary friend as an equal. • Imaginary friends are seldom scapegoats for preschoolers' misbehaviors. In reality, imaginary friends are often role models.

Mental Health Advisory

When children repress the feelings underlying their negative emotions, they can become emotionally troubled. Adults should help a child admit his or her negative feelings, but should not encourage the child to let these feelings override control of his or her actions.

As preschoolers, children are expected to control many of their intense feelings. Controlling outward signs of emotions, such as crying, screaming, or hitting, helps children become socially acceptable. Children need to express their feelings. Statements such as "I am angry," or "I am afraid" are healthy. During the preschool years, children learn how to control and express a variety of emotions, including love and dependency, fear and anxiety, anger, and jealousy.

Love and Dependency

Preschoolers feel love for their parents, other family members, teachers, friends, and pets. Preschool children tend to be less defiant than toddlers and express affection with hugs, kisses, and snuggling.

Preschool children often experience conflict between their needs for dependence and independence. Preschoolers show fewer attachment behaviors than do toddlers, but attachment has not disappeared. In times of stress, preschool children may try to recapture the early attachment feelings. These children may cry, cling, show signs of emotional dependence, and have toileting accidents. **Emotional dependency** is the act of seeking attention, approval, comfort, and contact. In emotional dependency, a child is usually dependent on only one or two people. Unlike toddlers, preschoolers are apt to accept comfort from strangers, but still prefer to be comforted by a loved adult or peer.

Around five years of age, children begin to seek help in achieving a goal more often than they seek contact or approval (**Figure 16.6**). In most cases, older preschool children really do need help. From time to time, however, preschoolers may ask for

Figure 16.6 Older preschool children may ask an adult to tie their shoes or reach toys on a high shelf, even if the preschooler is capable of performing the task. *How should adults respond when preschoolers make these requests?*

help that is not needed. Usually, preschool children do this to gain reassurance of the adult's love or concern. Thus, older preschoolers still express emotional dependency in asking for help—this emotional dependency is just better disguised.

Fear and Anxiety

Preschoolers' fears often stem from a lack of understanding, the inability to separate reality from fantasy, or a preschooler's own experience of being hurt. Some fears keep preschoolers safe, but preschoolers may also exhibit unhealthy fears.

Many of the fears experienced in the toddler years disappear by the preschool years, and new fears replace the ones that fade. While boys tend to experience a greater variety of fears, girls tend to experience less fears, but will have more intense reactions to these fears. Most preschoolers share common fears, such as fear of the unknown or imagined, fear of physical injury, or fear of pain.

As with fears, preschoolers' anxieties change with their growing minds. Preschoolers understand many new concepts, but their understandings may still be limited. This lack of understanding often creates new fears and anxieties. Children's specific fears may become general anxieties. For example, fear of a tornado may spread to general anxiety during a thunderstorm or even a strong wind.

During the preschool years, separation anxiety often disappears. Preschool children are able to handle separations better, especially when they see where their parents work and what they do. Visiting parents' or caregivers' workplaces helps preschoolers develop mental images of the parents at work and understand why the parent must go to work. In turn, this causes the preschooler to be less anxious about the separation.

Anger and Aggression

Feelings of anger begin around 10 months of age and peak with displays of temper in the toddler years, sometimes continuing into the preschool years. Anger often stems from stress, fatigue, frustration, and rejection. At times, anger leads to aggression in children. Aggression is associated with the child's temperament, the child's ability to distinguish between accidental and intentional aggression from other children, adult models of aggression, power-assertive discipline techniques, and real and fantasy violence.

Expressions of anger and aggression change in the preschool years. While preschool children tend to hit or bite less than toddlers, they threaten and yell more. This is due to preschoolers' increasing language skills and sometimes due to gender (**Figure 16.7**). Preschoolers' anger and aggression tend to be directed more at siblings and close friends than at casual peers. By the time children reach the preschool years, they appear to have learned that aggression toward adults, especially physical aggression, is not acceptable.

Jealousy

During the preschool years, children commonly experience jealousy. Jealousy begins when children realize they must share love, attention, possessions, and time with others. Preschoolers are trying to figure out who they are as individuals, and to do this, they compare themselves with others. These comparisons often lead to jealousy. Jealousy may also emerge when there are changes in a family, such as a new sibling. Having to share parents' love and attention may make a preschooler feel jealous and less loved. Preschoolers may even experience jealousy over material objects, such as other children's toys.

Some preschool children may experience **repressed jealousy**, which is jealousy that is not directly expressed and may even be denied. Children who repress jealousy may experience the emotion through nightmares or physical problems, such as upset stomachs, headaches, fevers, and changes in appetite.

Recognizing Preschoolers' Stress

Stress and trauma occurring before six years of age have the most powerful negative effects on the developing child. In the United States, there is a growing awareness of children's emotional and behavioral problems and how these problems affect their classroom conduct, abilities to learn, and their friendships with other children. Stress

Figure 16.7 Boys tend to express anger physically more often than girls, whereas girls tend to express anger verbally. ***In your opinion, are gender differences in expression primarily based in biology or in societal expectations?***

and mental health problems often stem from preschoolers' developmental stage and social environments, including the home, preschool center, and neighborhood.

Developmental Stress

Developmental stress during the preschool years involves factors related to preschoolers' developmental stage and personal development. These factors include the following:

- ***Way of thinking.*** Preschoolers do not always have a firm grasp of reality. Their fears can be worsened by their skewed perspectives of cause and effect and their tendencies to overgeneralize. They also may not understand that the loss of a loved person, pet, or object may be permanent.
- ***Lack of language skills.*** Preschoolers have few language skills required to explain how they feel or ask for help when they need it. Thus, preschoolers' responses to emotional experiences differ from those of older children and adults. Preschoolers are just beginning to learn how to think about emotions and what triggers them.

Mental Health Advisory

Toxic stress without adult buffers has powerful, lifelong negative effects on children, especially those younger than six years of age. Negative effects include impaired brain development, severe learning and social problems, and mental health issues. Often, clues to stress can be detected in preschoolers' behaviors. Preschoolers who experience toxic stress need to be seen by mental health specialists.

Focus on Health

Clues to Stress in the Preschool Years

Preschoolers respond to stress in several recognizable ways. Some of these behaviors are normal if they last only a short time and are not too intense. Often, the more clues the adult sees, the greater the stress.

- The reliving of a trauma over and over, whether by talking about the event, depicting it through drawings, or acting it out in pretend play. While reliving trauma for a short period of time may relieve stress and help children understand the event, reliving the trauma too many times reinforces it in children's memories and heightens stress.
- Heightened arousal, such as disturbed sleep or being "jumpy."
- Heightened separation anxieties and clinging to adults.
- Regression to toddler-like behaviors.
- Physical complaints, such as tummy aches.
- Changes in appetite.
- Development of new fears not related to the trauma.
- Behavioral changes, such as *defiance* (talking back to adults, temper tantrums, refusing to cooperate), *aggression* (being cruel, destroying toys and other property, fighting peers), and *regression in social competence* (sharing less often, not wanting to play with friends, being more impulsive).

- *Fearful temperament.* Some preschoolers have fearful temperaments that lead to anxiety and depression. Preschoolers are vulnerable to **fear-conditioning** (associating a fearful stimulus with a neutral stimulus). For example, if a loud clap of thunder occurs (fearful stimulus) while a preschooler is playing alone in his or her room (neutral stimulus), the child may then be fearful of playing alone in his or her room (fear-conditioning). Because of fear-conditioning, preschoolers may experience strong stress responses to the stimuli they associate with fear. As a result, a wide range of conditions can trigger anxiety. Fear-conditioning underlies many anxiety disorders.
- *Episodic memories.* As preschoolers' episodic memories improve, they are able to relive stressful, fearful experiences. Recall strengthens stress and makes it more difficult to forget. These stressful memories may impair new memory functions, such as learning.
- *Delays or illnesses.* Some preschoolers may experience developmental delays or illnesses. Being delayed or ill is stressful in itself, and stress can make the delay or illness worse.

Environmental Stress

Social environments, such as the preschooler's home, preschool center, and neighborhood, can play a large part in contributing to preschoolers' stress. Preschoolers are much less vulnerable to stress if their parents or caregivers are not experiencing stress or mental health issues. When parents face trauma and stress, they have less time to devote to parenting and are less able to provide the predictable and stable home environment needed by a preschooler. Parents' and caregivers' problems can spill over into their children's lives. Changes in family life, such as a new baby or a parent's new career, can also be stressful for a preschooler.

Besides adults' stressors that affect preschoolers, other environmental stressors may come from factors associated with low-quality preschool programs (too many children, inappropriate activities, not enough toys), peer aggression, and stressful situations in the neighborhood (violence, poverty).

Social-Emotional Developmental Milestones

As preschool children's worlds expand, they develop self-awareness and learn to take initiative. They also learn new ways to interact with others and express and control their maturing and expanding emotions. Children achieve a number of social-emotional developmental milestones during the preschool years. Some of these milestones are shown in **Figure 16.8**.

Lesson 16.1 Review and Assessment 

1. Explain the ways that preschoolers can show responsibility.
2. What is *sex typing*?
3. Define *moral judgment and reasoning*, *moral character*, and *moral emotions*.
4. Name the factors that constitute preschoolers' self-concepts.
5. Why do preschoolers' struggles for initiative sometimes result in guilt?
6. Describe preschoolers' view of friendships.
7. Choose one emotion covered in this lesson and explain how it changes during the preschool years.
8. Choose one age range in the preschool years and name the milestones a child that age has most likely achieved.
9. **Critical thinking.** Compare and contrast developmental and environmental stress. Is one natural and one not? Is either type of stress avoidable?

Figure 16.8 Preschool Social-Emotional Milestones

Three years

- Shows interest in trying new things.
- Seeks attention and approval of adults.
- Shows affection for special friends; comforts hurt children.
- Enjoys helping parents with household tasks.
- Takes turns; shares toys at times.
- Expresses a wide range of emotions.
- Fears the unknown, the imagined, pain, and the dark.
- Displays less physical aggression when angry.
- Realizes some actions are wrong and acts "sorry" for some actions.

Four years

- Seeks attention from friends more than from adults.
- Plays "team roles" in pretend play.
- Takes turns, shares, and cooperates (as long as things go his or her way).
- Resents adult directions and limits and challenges authority.
- Is boastful at times.
- Fears monsters.
- Tattles, uses "shock" words, and lies to protect him- or herself.
- Expresses anger by yelling; sometimes regresses to physical expressions of anger.

Five years

- Often agrees to limits, but also seeks to be more independent.
- Plays with two or three best friends and excludes others.
- Is sensitive to the feelings of other children.
- Protects younger children.
- Begins to follow rules and plays fairly.
- Distinguishes right from wrong (but does not recognize intent).
- Begins to distinguish fantasy from reality.
- Argues, but can negotiate solutions to conflicts.
- Has a gender-role concept.

Lesson 16.2

Meeting Preschoolers' Social-Emotional Needs

Key Terms

altruistic behaviors
assertive
self-reward
shame
tattling behaviors

Academic Terms

altruism
ambiguous
amenable
cooperation
egalitarian
elicits
placate
prosocial

Objectives

After studying this lesson, you will be able to

- plan activities for supporting self-awareness in preschoolers.
- give examples of two ways to foster preschoolers' altruistic behaviors.
- describe what to teach preschoolers about avoiding conflicts during play with other children.
- identify two ways to reduce preschoolers' fears and anxieties.
- assess why punitive discipline is an inappropriate discipline choice for controlling preschoolers' aggression.
- explain how preschoolers' jealousy may be lessened.
- describe how to help preschoolers cope with stress.

Reading and Writing Activity

As you read this lesson, record any questions that come to mind. Indicate where the answer to each question can be found: within the text, from your teacher, in another book, on the Internet, or through your own knowledge and experience. Pursue the answers to your questions.

Graphic Organizer

As you read this lesson, use a tree diagram, like the one shown, to organize information about meeting preschoolers' social-emotional needs. Write *Meeting Preschoolers' Social-Emotional Needs* in the top circle and then record major categories and specific activities and notes in the circles below.

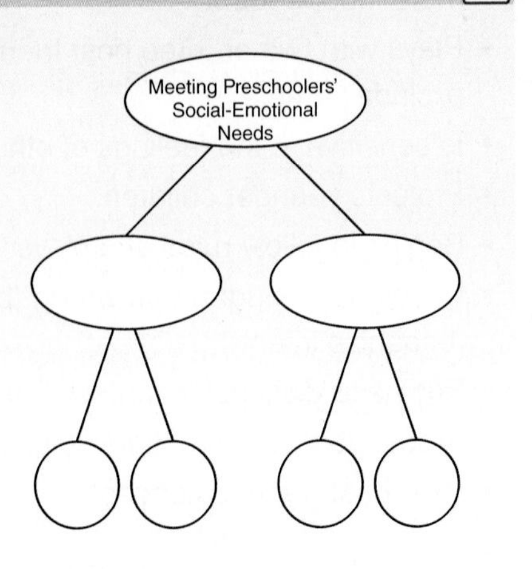

Because the preschool years are a time for socialization into the family and other groups, preschoolers have many social-emotional needs. Adults, as the socializing agents, are responsible for teaching children "rules" about how to handle those needs. Due to their growing self-awareness, preschoolers become more and more independent. As they become more independent, one critical source of their self-awareness comes from the reflected appraisals of parents and other adults. Children come to see and value themselves in keeping with the positive and negative reactions of others. Preschoolers need gentle guidance to prevent damaging their self-esteem. Preschoolers are eager to master many things to be part of the group—the family, the preschool, and the neighborhood. Adults need to help preschoolers take the initiative and react calmly when exuberant efforts lead to less than desirable results. Adults must often explain to preschoolers the reasons for limits or requirements and repeat this information frequently in a firm, but fair, way.

Parents and other adults should support preschoolers as they attempt to develop positive social relationships with both adults and children. Learning cooperative behaviors takes many lessons. Preschoolers learn best when adults notice and show approval for their positive behaviors and explain specifically the effects of these behaviors on others.

Unlike younger children whose emotions are more general, such as crying when tired, preschoolers' emotions are situation-specific. For example, preschoolers may express excitement over plans to go to the park or fear of storms. Adults can help preschoolers learn to seek out situations associated with positive feelings and avoid situations that lead to negative emotions. Adults can also teach preschoolers when and how it is appropriate to display certain emotions. Preschoolers need to learn how to interpret the emotional expressions of others. Because children are especially vulnerable to stress in the preschool years, adults should provide supportive environments and model positive ways of coping with stress.

Supporting the Preschooler's Self-Awareness

As early as the toddler years, children begin to develop self-awareness and exert some autonomy. This discovery of self-awareness continues into the preschool years, at which time children begin to understand their own uniqueness, including their physical traits and some skills (**Figure 16.9**). To develop self-awareness, children need to live in environments that promote healthy personal development. Parents, caregivers, and teachers can encourage children to show responsibility, understand gender roles, begin moral development, and develop a healthy self-concept.

Sharing Responsibility

To teach children how to show responsibility, parents, caregivers, and teachers can *share* responsibility. Preschool children view tasks as a way of

Figure 16.9 As preschoolers discover their own unique traits and abilities, they develop self-awareness. *What unique traits have you observed in preschool children?*

learning new skills, pleasing others and having fun, and taking the initiative. Adults can help children become more dependable and responsible by sharing responsibilities with them.

Parents, caregivers, and teachers must strike a careful balance to share the right amount of responsibilities with preschool children. Some adults offer few, if any, opportunities for children to help. These adults may see preschool children as unwilling to help or as unable to do certain tasks. Conversely, some adults may place too many demands on children and expect them to perform at adult standards. In a healthy environment, adults hold that family life and school life are made better when both adults and children help each other. This environment can be created if adults and children adhere to a set of realistic guidelines, such as the following:

- Children may suggest tasks, but adults must decide which tasks are safe and within children's grasps.
- Physical conditions should be **amenable** (uh-MEH-nuh-buhl), receptive to, to children performing a task, such as having a sturdy stool to help the child reach a cabinet (**Figure 16.10**).
- Plans and expectations should be communicated clearly by the adult. Adults can talk about tasks planned for the day and can tell children what they are to do.
- Adults should not expect perfection. If a finished task is not satisfactory, the task should be explained again for the child to do over. When adults redo tasks for children, children feel a sense of failure.
- Tasks can be made fun by incorporating games. For example, if an adult asks a child to pick up his or her blocks, the adult can ask the child to haul the blocks to the "lumberyard" (the shelf).
- At times, adults should respect children's priorities. There may be no harm in letting a child do a job 10 minutes later. It is healthy for children to decide on some priorities.
- Children should be rewarded for tasks completed. Adults can reward children either with love only or with pay (money or a want fulfilled). Whether adults pay or do not pay, they should thank children and acknowledge their skills.

Figure 16.10 If an adult asks a child to help put away laundry, he or she should make sure the laundry basket and clothes are within the child's reach. *What chores are typically accessible to young children? What chores are typically not accessible?*

Helping Children Learn Gender Roles

Preschoolers' learning about gender roles will affect the way they act as children and as adults. As is true with all personal values, parents, caregivers, and teachers should be informed about the issues and make decisions about what gender roles they want to teach children.

Adults express their feelings about gender roles to children in many ways. The roles they allow or encourage children to try and the day-to-day attitudes they convey affect how children perceive gender. For example, parents who model traditional roles in the home may express these roles by the father not doing housework and by his daughter being discouraged from doing heavy outdoor work. On the other hand, parents who believe in and practice more **ambiguous** (am-BIH-gyuh-wuhs), less-defined, gender roles might not model these divisions of labor and may allow children to choose activities according to their own interests and skills. Preschool children will rapidly learn gender roles by observing adults of the same gender (**Figure 16.11**). Toys, media, and books may also affect how children perceive gender roles.

Figure 16.11 Preschoolers may learn gender roles as they help their mothers or fathers with household tasks and errands. *What is this preschooler learning about gender roles while helping his grandfather mow?*

Encouraging Moral Development

During the preschool years, children look primarily to adults as their guides for moral development. As children begin to learn what is right and wrong and develop conscience, adults can aid them in a number of ways, including the following:

- ***Explain the reasoning behind acceptable and unacceptable behaviors.*** This will help children understand moral judgment and reasoning and begin to develop personal convictions of their own.
- ***Model acceptable behaviors to encourage moral character.*** Morality grows out of a child's love for parents and teachers. In their parenting styles, adults should model mutual respect and inductive discipline techniques with their children.
- ***Explain how unacceptable behaviors damage others.*** An explanation given in context of love, respect, and explicit guidance will help children develop moral emotions.
- ***Avoid shaming children.*** **Shame** is focused on self and involves a loss or threat of a loss to a child's basic security. Examples of shaming include name-calling and negative reactions to a child's wants, feelings, or needs. Corporal punishment also shames because it never feels loving. Shame does not aid character development. Rather, it crushes a young child's curiosity, exuberance, and desire for being independent. Shaming does not model respect so it erodes the young child's self-esteem.

Promoting a Healthy Self-Concept

During the preschool years, a child's self-concept is closely tied to his or her awareness of physical characteristics and abilities. While forming their self-concepts, children need nurturance, affection, guidance, encouragement, and affirmation. Parents, caregivers, and teachers can plan many activities that encourage children to view their physical characteristics in positive ways. Some examples of these activities include setting up a full-length mirror so the child can see him- or herself at play or having a child draw a self-portrait. Adults can celebrate preschoolers' physical accomplishments by marking a height and weight chart at regular intervals.

Adults can also plan activities that encourage children to view their skills, interests, and abilities in positive ways. Some of these activities include having a child make a collage of favorite things and keeping a scrapbook album of a child's activities. Parents, caregivers, and teachers can also have children create a "Me Box," in which a child can collect some of his or her favorite things, or a "Me Book," in which a child can display his or her handprint and pictures of favorite foods and activities (**Figure 16.12**). Some picture books and other resources can also help children develop healthy self-concepts.

Helping Preschoolers Take Initiative

As preschool children discover motivation to perform new tasks and struggle against a sense of guilt, the adults in their lives can play an important role. Parents, caregivers, and teachers can help their preschoolers take initiative, thereby reducing the chances of guilt in a number of ways. Some of these ways are as follows:

- Expect preschoolers to exhibit never-ending curiosity, talk often and loudly, and move all the time. Parents and caregivers need to encourage these qualities in children. Children develop initiative when they ask questions, experiment, and explore.
- Understand that preschoolers' initiatives can sometimes lead them to actions that are dangerous or beyond their abilities. Sometimes preschoolers may use inappropriate initiative, such as aggression, to control others.
- Give children some freedom to try, especially in play activities. Children learn more by their own attempts than by having adults perform actions for them or tell them what to do. Adults should model how to do certain tasks and give ample time for children to practice.
- Use positive statements to acknowledge children when they take initiative. For example, parents can say, "It was *nice* of you to be so *loving* toward your baby sister." Parents might also say, "You were showing *kindness* when you shared your toys. *Kindness* makes people want to be your friend." In every case, caregivers should use adjectives to refer to a specific case. It is best not to overgeneralize, such as saying, "You are *always* nice, loving, and kind." Case descriptions refine preschool children's self-images and promote feelings of self-esteem.
- Set limits to help preschoolers develop appropriate initiative. During the preschool years, parents and caregivers are in Galinsky's *authority stage* of parenting. Too much or too little guidance will weaken preschoolers' abilities to discover and foster appropriate initiative.

Balancing Initiative with Limits

While preschool children want to take initiative and explore, parents and caregivers need to set limits to help children develop initiative and keep them safe (**Figure 16.13**). Preschool children define themselves in terms of what they can do, and to find out what they can do, children try many activities.

Figure 16.12 A "Me Book," such as the one shown, can encourage children's skills, interests, and hobbies. *Judging from this "Me Book," what are the skills and interests of this child?*

Figure 16.13 Limits, such as rules for swimming or other activities, keep children safe. *What other limits are important for children's safety?*

Because preschoolers lack inhibitory control, they do many things on impulse without thinking about the results of their actions. Preschool children may often go beyond their abilities and make mistakes. Because preschool children see almost everything as within their control, they often see these mistakes as a defeat. Too many mistakes may bring on guilt.

Although preschoolers can learn from both successes and mistakes, some mistakes are not safe or acceptable behaviors. Preschoolers need limits for safety purposes and to prepare them for the real world. Part of growing up is testing adult limits, and adults must accept that children will try some activities even when adults say "no." Some preschool children may decide the pleasure of doing something is worth the punishment received. Other children may dream up new activities not presently covered by the rules.

Preschool children should be given reasonable, spelled-out limits, and failure to obey should result in loving, yet firm, discipline. Parents and other adults need to communicate honestly when guiding and disciplining children. Being honest helps children build trusting relationships. It also helps children realize they should be truthful.

Children need to know that adults, too, make mistakes. Children learn this when they hear adults say, "Oops!" or "I'm sorry." In these situations, children begin to understand that all people make mistakes and that making mistakes does not make them bad.

Helping Preschoolers Develop Social Relations

During the preschool years, children's social worlds extend beyond their parents or caregivers to include other family members and many other adults, such as teachers, friends' parents, and their caregivers' friends. Parents and caregivers can begin to teach preschool children how to interact with others and how to behave in socially acceptable ways. Parents and caregivers can help preschool children extend their social relations by making time for friendships, fostering altruistic behaviors, reducing conflicts, and teaching manners.

Investigate Special Topics — Helping Children Who Are Shy and Introverted

Some preschoolers may have difficulty making friends due to shyness or introversion. Shyness and introversion are different. Children who are *shy* desire to join groups of children, but are not sure how to do so. These children may avoid other people's gazes and appear both physically and verbally hesitant to join conversations and activities. Shyness is caused by temperamental differences among children, lessons a child has learned from his or her cultural background or family environment, and new and overwhelming social encounters.

Unlike children who are shy, children who are *introverted* are content on their own or with just one or two friends. These children do not have social anxiety. They often have excellent social skills, but may feel drained emotionally after prolonged contact with people.

Children who are shy can be helped to overcome their shyness, although they are unlikely to become intensely social. On the other hand, introversion is a personality trait inherent in some children. Trying to change a child's introversion may cause stress and lowered self-esteem. Constant stress and low self-worth can eventually lead to mental health issues. Instead, adults can teach introverts coping strategies for social encounters.

Following are some suggestions for helping preschoolers who are shy and introverted:

Shy

- Have realistic expectations for the child. A shy child rarely becomes the leader of a group.
- Gradually expose the child to new people and novel situations.
- Invite two or three children for play. If only one child is invited, the shy child may feel forced to interact with this child.
- Help the child prepare for new situations by explaining to the child who will be there and what will happen. Role-playing social skills and staying close to the child may also help.
- Allow autonomy.
- Build self-esteem by affirming the child's strengths.

Introverted

- Set aside quiet time before going to a highly social activity and leave early if possible.
- Allow the child to watch from the sidelines and get used to activity and noise.
- Do not overschedule the child.
- Do not allow extroverts to take over conversations and exclude the introvert or supply answers for the introvert.
- Do not allow siblings or peers to make an introverted child a scapegoat for their unacceptable behaviors.
- Find private spaces for the introvert to re-energize.
- Invite just one other child for play.

Research Activity

Strategies for engaging shy and introverted children are widely discussed in childhood education circles. Talking with and including these children can be a challenge for many teachers. In small groups, research strategies for engaging shy and introverted children and "getting them to talk." Choose four or five of these strategies and then deliver a short presentation explaining them and assessing whether they are effective or not.

Making Time for Friendships

Friendships become very important to most preschoolers and are a way for children to learn from others. Unlike adults, friends and sometimes siblings treat children as equals. A preschool child's friends will not always give him or her special favors like a caregiver or other adults would. For example, a child will not always be given the first turn when playing with friends.

Living in a social world involves preschoolers' balancing of *self-assertion* (doing as one chooses rather than what others want) and **cooperation** (the action of helping or working with someone). Friendships with peers help preschool children see the differences in people, and friction, which almost always occurs in play groups, shows children how others see issues differently.

Preschoolers want and need friends. To preschoolers, friends are resources for social play. The preschool period is often called "the play years."

Friendships differ from family relationships in that friendships are formed due to mutual choice. Unlike adult-child relationships, peers interact on an **egalitarian** (belief that all people are equal) basis; that is, children have the same status and authority in the friendship. Because children's friends are often age-mates, too, they are similar developmentally.

Adults can foster preschoolers' friendships in certain ways. Adults can help preschoolers form friendships by giving them both opportunity and time to play with peers. These peers may be neighborhood playmates, children from a preschooler's child care and education program, children in a special interest group (such as swimming or dance classes), or children in a house of worship. Sometimes, peers are introduced through the friendships of parents.

Although adults cannot make friends for their preschoolers, they need to teach preschoolers that to have friends, they must be friends. To do this, adults must teach friendship skills—cooperating, sharing, and turn-taking. Adults must explain why trying to gain power by aggression never works. With adult guidance over time, preschoolers move beyond self-focus, become more social, and develop feelings of belonging to a group of friends.

Fostering Altruistic Behaviors

In peer groups, children also witness actions that show concern for others, or **altruistic behaviors**. **Altruism** (ALL-troo-ih-zuhm), a desire to help others, develops as young children sense the needs and wants of others. While helping behaviors may be carried out for some type of reward (concrete or social), altruism is carried out without any expectation of a reward except possibly **self-reward** (a person's good feelings about his or her actions). Adults can increase the likelihood of a preschooler using altruistic behaviors by

- being a model of kindness
- using supportive rather than punishing discipline to help the child develop moral reasoning skills
- helping children "read" others' emotions
- pointing out the consequences of negative actions
- being supportive of the person who is harmed rather than giving attention to the aggressor
- choosing children's media that is healthy and **prosocial** (encouraging of kind behaviors)
- allowing children to help with projects for those in need or to give some of their money to charity
- acknowledging children for their altruistic behaviors

Reducing Conflicts

Most preschool children's conflicts are disputes about toys or an area of play. Adults should allow children to interact with each other and should not interfere with minor conflicts (except for safety reasons). Adults can reduce conflicts between preschoolers in the following ways:

- Do not make children share any more than an adult would be expected to share. Sometimes adults expect children to share all of their toys, even with casual friends. Adults are not expected to share all of their belongings, even with close friends.

- Resolve conflicts for younger preschoolers (**Figure 16.14**). To do this, explain the feelings of both children. Often, this will diffuse the conflict.
- Show older preschoolers how to resolve their own conflicts. Adults can teach children conflict-resolution skills, such as asking another child to return a toy, playing with another toy, or asking to take turns with a toy.
- Teach children how to stand up for themselves without being aggressive. Teach children to communicate clearly with statements such as, "Stop hitting me!" or "I do not want to do that."
- Model concern for the hurt child instead of shaming the child who has done wrong. Children learn more when adults show real concern for the hurt or wronged child while ignoring the child who was in the wrong. Aggressors see that care is given to children who are harmed.
- Teach children to get adult help if needed.

As preschoolers' social worlds extend, they may also start engaging in **tattling behaviors** (behaviors that seek to get another child in trouble by telling adults or other children about something a child has done). To deter tattling behaviors, adults can explain to children when it is appropriate to tell an adult, such as when fighting occurs or someone is hurt. In other cases, when a child tattles, the adult might say to the tattler, "I will worry about that. This is not your job." Then, the adult can deal with the situation when the tattler is not listening; otherwise, tattling will likely be reinforced.

Teaching Manners

Older preschoolers can begin to learn that everyone likes being treated with good manners. They can also learn appropriate manners for their culture. To teach children manners, adults can make sure to always live by the manners they want to instill. They can explain that manners are a way to be nice to other people and give reasons for using any specific manners they decide to teach. Examples of basic manners adults teach preschoolers include saying "please," "thank you," and "you're welcome"; not interrupting others who are talking; chewing with their mouths closed; and not grabbing food (**Figure 16.15**).

Adults can also explain to preschoolers what good manners are *not*. They can explain that rude

Figure 16.14 In helping children resolve conflicts, adults can explain situations, such as by saying, "Maria needs to play with the shapes for a little while but, when she's ready to give them up, she will let you know." *What are other ways adults can explain conflicts about sharing?*

Figure 16.15 Teaching table manners, while at the table, is often effective. *Why is this a good place for teaching table manners? What other places are good for teaching manners?*

remarks and name-calling are always inappropriate. This may be difficult for young children to understand because some rude comments might be true and children are taught that lies are wrong. For example, a child might make a comment about someone who has a disability. In this situation, the adult can apologize for the child and then explain to the preschooler in private why the comment was hurtful.

Guiding Preschoolers' Emotions

Emotions are intense in the preschool years. The growing minds of preschool children not only broaden their emotions, but also help children control how they express their emotions. While preschool children and even adults cannot control their feelings, they can learn to control how they *express* these feelings. When preschoolers express intense emotions, adults should affirm their emotions and address their concerns. For example, a parent or caregiver might say, "I understand why you are angry. I am so sorry your daddy and I could not work out our problems. I can tell you that we will always love you and make sure you are cared for and loved."Adults can also help preschoolers control how they express emotions in the following ways:

- ***Expose children to positive examples.*** Children imitate how adults do or do not control their emotions. They also imitate the emotional expressions of other children and people seen in television programs or movies.
- ***Help children label their emotions.*** As preschoolers' language abilities expand, they are more able to name and verbally express their emotions. When emotions are labeled, preschool children can name their emotions to others and often solve or prevent conflicts with peers.
- ***Explain that feeling emotions is all right.*** Children need to know that it is okay to feel sad, angry, hurt, or happy. They need to know that adults feel and express these emotions, too.
- ***Tell children it is okay to express some emotions.*** Repressing emotions is unhealthy for children and adults. Children need to know that it is all right to cry when sad or laugh when happy.
- ***Insist that aggression is not an acceptable way to handle anger.*** Children need to learn that people must not hurt others, even when they are wronged. Adults can explain this to children by naming the consequences of aggression, such as by saying that hitting hurts people or name-calling makes others feel sad.
- ***Talk about how all people have to work to control their feelings.*** Children need to know they are not alone in trying to control their feelings. Adults can talk about times they have to control their feelings and can help preschoolers read books about feelings. There are many good preschool books on this topic (**Figure 16.16**).

Love and Dependency

When preschoolers express love and dependency, knowing when and how to help them can be difficult. Some children will seek help from adults even when they do not need it. Other children are unable to handle some tasks on their own, but do not want the help adults offer. Adults can help preschoolers by finding a balance between helping and not helping preschoolers with tasks.

Figure 16.16 Preschool Books on Emotions

Albee, S. *Sesame Street All About Feelings—My First Manners* 2006

Bloom, S. *What About Bear?* 2010

Bowman, C. *Little David and His Best Friend* 2010

Cain, J. *The Way I Feel* 2008

Curtis, J. L. *Today I Feel Silly & Other Moods That Make My Day* 2007

Finn, C. *Manners on the Playground* 2007

Graham, B. *"Let's Get a Pup," Said Kate* 2001

Keats, E. J. *The Snowy Day* 1963

Mayer, M. *I Was So Mad* 2000

Offill, J. *17 Things I'm Not Allowed to Do Anymore* 2006

Shuman, C. *Jenny Is Scared: When Something Happens in the World* 2003

vanHout, M. *Happy* 2012

Viorst, J. *Alexander and the Terrible, Horrible, No Good, Very Bad Day* 1987

Wilhelm, H. *I'll Always Love You* 1988

Adults can help preschoolers by loving and respecting them. This gives children a secure base from which to try tasks on their own. When children ask for help, adults should be willing to help, but adults should also judge how much help children need. Physically arranging the house in helpful ways can make tasks more manageable for children, and adults should plan tasks for preschoolers that are within their abilities. Children need encouragement when they try tasks on their own. This positive reinforcement will acknowledge children's attempts and help them take pride in their achievements.

Fear and Anxiety

Some fears and anxieties help protect children and urge them to stay safe. Too many fears and anxieties, however, may be harmful. Adults can help preschoolers keep fear and anxiety in check by accepting the expressed fears and anxieties of children and never making fun of them. They can help children feel secure by assuring children they will be kept safe and never threatening them, even in a playful way. Adults can help children face fear by modeling courage and handling a child's fears one at a time. Adults can remind children of the reasons they need not be afraid and can urge children to take small steps in dealing with fears, such as watching from a safe location or drawing one's fear. Lastly, adults should consult a doctor if children's fears seem too prolonged or intense. Sometimes, intense fears can indicate emotional or behavioral problems in children and professional help may be needed.

Anger and Aggression

Handling preschoolers' anger and aggression is not only draining, but often stirs up angry feelings in adults. Adults should note the difference between *anger* (a feeling caused by frustration) and *aggression* (an attempt to hurt someone). While it is natural that children feel anger, adults need to help children manage anger in ways other than aggression. One of the first steps in handling preschoolers' anger is to look for reasons the preschooler feels angry. Does he or she want attention? Is he or she frustrated in reaching a goal? Is he or she looking for revenge? Understanding motives makes finding ways to manage anger easier (**Figure 16.17**).

Children are more likely to act aggressively when they see aggression modeled by adults, peers, or people and characters in television programs, films, or other types of media. Even letting a child hit a pillow or kick a tree trunk communicates that aggression is acceptable. Instead, adults should teach children it is all right to feel angry, but that acts of anger must be controlled.

Society tries to teach that, instead of being aggressive, people should be **assertive** (able to speak out, stand up for one's rights, and defend one's self). Finding the line between assertiveness and aggression can be difficult for preschool children, and even for adults, at times. Because of this, preschoolers may act in an aggressive way when they are trying to be assertive.

When children do need to be corrected for aggressive acts, adults should use nonphysical methods of discipline. Studies show that punishment by aggression, such as spanking, increases

Figure 16.17 Ways to Help Preschoolers Manage Anger

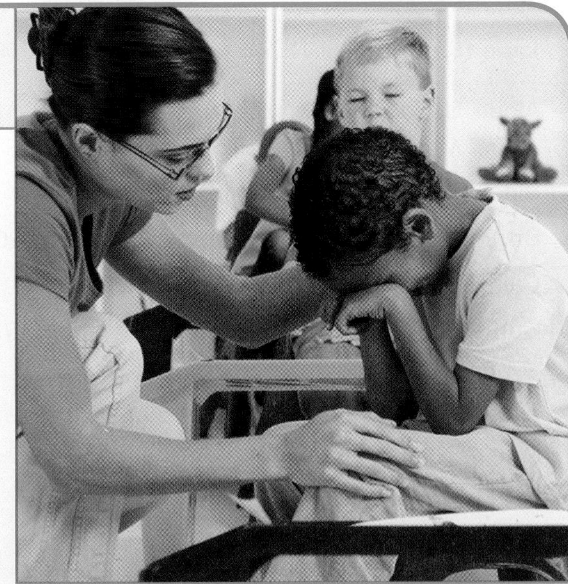

- ***Direct preschoolers' energy levels appropriately.*** When preschoolers spend too much time in quiet activities, they begin to squirm with pent-up energy. Physical play can release some of this energy in more constructive ways than possibly aggravating another child. Conversely, when preschoolers are *overexuberant* (wound-up), they tend to engage in rowdy, physical play that can easily cross-the-line into anger and aggressive acts. Except for resting and sleeping times, make certain preschoolers are not sedentary for more than 60 minutes at a time. When sedentary, preschoolers can engage their brains through reading or fine-motor activities. Excited preschoolers should have a 30-minute wind-down time.
- ***Reduce competitive situations between peers.*** Competition can be reduced by supplying plenty of toys so that children do not have to wait too long for a turn. If games become aggressive, adults should step in to de-escalate the situation.
- ***Watch peer play groups closely.*** Often, adults can stop aggression before it occurs by providing a calming touch or encouraging the child to release negative energy in other ways, such as deep breathing or singing.
- ***Reinforce acceptable responses to anger.*** Acknowledging children for not using aggression will encourage them to express anger in other ways in the future.

aggression in preschool children, especially if these punishments are given in response to a child's aggressive acts. Spanking increases children's feelings of anger and **elicits** (calls forth) a negative, aggressive response from the child. Instead of physical punishments, parents and caregivers can discipline children with time-outs or losses of privileges.

Jealousy

Jealousy is common among preschoolers and often leads to anger. In fact, most preschoolers label *jealousy* as being "mad." Learning to tame jealousy is a lifelong process, but the preschool years are the best time to begin helping children control this powerful emotion. Two common sources of jealousy over the preschool years are siblings and friends. Adults can help children control jealousy in both of these contexts.

Jealousy over Siblings

Preschoolers may be jealous over the attention given to a new baby or other sibling. These feelings occur because preschoolers may think parents love these siblings more than them. Adults can help preschoolers accept their siblings in the following ways:

- Describe what care the sibling requires in a realistic way, including the work involved and other facts. Unlike toddlers, preschool children are better able to understand their parents' explanations.
- Spend time alone with the preschooler. This is the best way to say, "I love you."
- Allow the preschooler to help with the new baby or younger sibling (**Figure 16.18**). Then sincerely thank the preschooler for his or her help. Preschoolers can feel important by helping with a sibling.

Focus on

Careers

Developmental-Behavioral Pediatrician

Developmental-behavioral pediatricians are doctors who specialize in children's developmental and behavioral problems. They diagnose, counsel, and treat children and their families. Developmental-behavioral pediatricians work with children who have a variety of behavioral problems, such as learning disorders, ADHD, behavioral disorders, developmental disabilities, and delayed development.

Career cluster: Health science.

Education: Educational requirements include four years of medical school, three years of residency pediatric training, and additional specialty training in developmental-behavioral pediatrics.

Job outlook: Future employment opportunities for developmental-behavioral pediatricians are expected to grow faster than the average for all occupations.

To learn more about a career as a developmental-behavioral pediatrician, visit the United States Department of Labor's *Occupational Outlook Handbook* website as well as the American Academy of Pediatrics. You will also be able to compare the job responsibilities, educational requirements, job outlook, and average pay of developmental-behavioral pediatricians with similar occupations.

- Expect a preschooler to show some regressive behaviors. It is natural for preschoolers to wish for the attention given to another sibling. Preschoolers enjoy being told or shown with photos how they were once cared for in the same ways.

Jealousy Among Friends

Because preschoolers learn about themselves by comparing themselves with friends, even minor inequalities among friends can seem like a big deal. Love, attention, and material goods are all coveted by preschoolers.

To help preschoolers cope with jealousy among friends, parents and caregivers can talk with their children to explain acceptable ways of expressing jealousy. Jealousy may still bubble up and cause the child to be sullen or aggressive. In these situations, adults should validate children's jealous feelings, but should not **placate** (calm; soothe) children by giving in to jealous wishes. Instead, adults can give preschoolers plenty of love and attention and lessen the insecurity that often breeds jealousy.

Repressed Jealousy

Even preschoolers who do not act jealous may be experiencing *repressed jealousy*. Parents, caregivers, and teachers should note any symptoms

Figure 16.18 Allowing preschoolers to help with younger siblings can reduce feelings of jealousy. ***What are some ways preschoolers can help with their younger siblings?***

of repressed jealousy and keep in mind that the continued repression of jealousy can have negative side effects on preschoolers' social-emotional health. When a preschooler has repressed jealousy, adults should find ways to make the child feel special, whether by spending time alone with the preschooler or bringing the preschooler a thoughtful gift.

Helping Preschoolers Cope with Stress

As with all behaviors, preschoolers learn to handle stress by witnessing others' examples. Parents and other adults should take care to model healthy ways of coping with stress (**Figure 16.19**). Adults experiencing overwhelming stress or mental health issues should seek professional help for themselves and their children.

To reduce preschoolers' stress, adults can provide an environment of consistency and predictability and can make sure to give preschoolers personal space and some "alone time." However, overparenting, by overprotecting, is not a good way to reduce stress because the child never learns coping skills.

Adults can alleviate stress in preschoolers by expressing unconditional love and maintaining a supportive relationship. A supportive relationship is the most protective aspect of development. Without it, children are vulnerable to stress for a lifetime.

Figure 16.19 Modeling Healthy Ways to Cope with Stress

- ***Identify the source of the stress.*** Once stress can be pinpointed, it can be reduced. Encourage children to use language in identifying stressors. When stressed, tell the child, "I am stressed because I have a test tomorrow."
- ***Find positive ways to encourage and distract one's self.*** Some of these ways might be going for a walk, exercising, talking with a friend, or reading a good book. Adults can invite children to do some of these activities with them.
- ***Express emotions constructively.*** Adults should express their emotions, but not let their emotions get out-of-control. When children see adults talking or writing in a journal about their emotions, they are more likely to adopt these techniques later in life.
- ***Avoid angry or frustrated outbursts.*** Children who see these outbursts will learn that outbursts are an acceptable way of dealing with stress.
- ***Seek professional help, if needed.*** Adults should never feel ashamed in seeking help for stress or other emotional problems. If they feel overwhelmed or out of control, adults should get help and explain to children that it is never bad to ask for help.

Lesson 16.2 Review and Assessment 

1. Describe four guidelines adults should follow when sharing responsibility with children.
2. Define *shame* and explain why it is not a healthy way of encouraging moral development.
3. Summarize three ways adults can encourage children to take initiative while reducing the chance of guilt.
4. Name four ways that adults can reduce conflicts between preschoolers and their peers.
5. Explain the difference between *anger* and *aggression*.
6. Choose one type of jealousy and explain how adults can help preschoolers express and control it.
7. Name two ways that adults can model healthy methods of coping with stress.
8. **Critical thinking.** Based on what you learned in this lesson, explain why physical punishment is or is not a healthy form of discipline.

Chapter 16 Review and Assessment

Summary

Preschool children develop more self-awareness as they learn to show responsibility, learn basic concepts about gender roles, develop morally, and expand their self-concept. Preschoolers' expanding self-awareness involves taking initiative and doing new activities. If preschoolers have too many failures or limits from adults, they may feel guilty and fear trying new things on their own. While preschool children are still dependent on adults, siblings and friends become more important to them. Creative, outgoing preschoolers often develop imaginary friends.

Preschoolers' emotions are becoming more complex. Most preschoolers show love and are still dependent on adults, especially for emotional support. Some fears and anxieties have disappeared, but others have surfaced. Preschoolers feel anger, but must learn not to express it through aggression. Preschoolers also experience jealousy. Preschoolers are vulnerable to both developmental and environmental stress.

Adults can help children expand self-awareness by sharing responsibility, aiding gender roles, encouraging moral development, and promoting a healthy self-concept. Adults should also help preschoolers expand their social worlds, especially friendships. This often involves making time for preschoolers' friendships, fostering altruistic behaviors, reducing conflicts, and teaching manners.

Preschoolers' emotions are intense, and they must move toward self-regulation. Adults must help preschoolers find a balance between dependency and greater independence. When children have fears and anxieties, adults should never make fun of them. Modeling courage and handling one fear at a time is helpful. Adults should teach children how to express their feelings without hurting others. When acts of aggression occur, adults should always use nonaggressive means to end these acts. When preschoolers feel jealousy, adults can help by giving them plenty of love and attention. Because most preschoolers experience some stress, adults need to provide a supportive environment to reduce stress and help them learn coping skills.

College and Career Portfolio

Portfolio Personal Statement

Many portfolios require a *personal statement*, or a short essay describing why one wants to pursue a degree or job and what experiences have honed that vision. Whereas a cover message focuses primarily on experience, a personal statement includes one's personal drive and interest in a career area.

- Write a personal statement for your intended college or career.
- Seek feedback from a career counselor, teacher, or staff member in the school writing center. Apply the feedback given and proofread your personal statement carefully.

Chapter 16 Review and Assessment

Vocabulary Activities 

1. In teams, play *picture charades* to identify each of the following terms. Write the terms on separate slips of paper and put the slips into a basket. Choose a team member to be the *sketcher*. The sketcher pulls a term from the basket and creates quick drawings or graphics to represent the term until the team guesses the term. Rotate turns as sketcher until the team identifies all terms.

Key Terms

altruistic behaviors (16.2)
assertive (16.2)
emotional dependency (16.1)
fear-conditioning (16.1)
gender constancy (16.1)
gender-role learning (16.1)
gender stability (16.1)
initiative versus guilt (16.1)
moral character (16.1)
moral development (16.1)
moral emotions (16.1)
moral judgment and reasoning (16.1)
repressed jealousy (16.1)
self-concept (16.1)
self-reward (16.2)
sex typing (16.1)
sexual stereotyping (16.1)
shame (16.2)
tattling behaviors (16.2)

2. In teams, create categories for the following terms and classify as many of the terms as possible. Then, share your ideas with the remainder of the class.

Academic Terms

altruism (16.2)
ambiguous (16.2)
amenable (16.2)
constitute (16.1)
cooperation (16.2)
cumulative (16.1)
derived (16.1)
egalitarian (16.2)
elicits (16.2)
initiative (16.1)
placate (16.2)
prosocial (16.2)

Critical Thinking

3. **Identify.** In small groups, identify examples of sexual stereotyping in children's movies or television. What are the most common forms of sexual stereotyping? How should caregivers protect children from this influence? Discuss your group's thoughts and ideas with the rest of the class.
4. **Make inferences.** Based on preschoolers' stage of moral development, how moral can adults expect preschool children to be? How do children's conceptions of morality influence how they should be treated by adults?
5. **Compare and contrast.** Compare and contrast children's interactions with adults in the preschool years and in the infant and toddler years. How do these interactions change when children enter the preschool years? How should adults interpret these changes?
6. **Cause and effect.** Research has shown that imaginary friends do not signal psychological problems in children. Rather, they are beneficial as children learn to interact with their worlds. How do you think interactions with imaginary friends affect children's interactions with adults and other children? How important are imaginary friends for social development?
7. **Analyze.** Analyze the importance of altruistic behaviors in children's lives and futures. How important is it that adults teach children these behaviors? What are the most effective ways adults teach them?
8. **Draw conclusions.** Why is it important to encourage a child to label and discuss his or her feelings? What could be the effects if a child was never taught to do this?
9. **Determine.** Consider the fears and anxieties you had as a child. What caused these fears and anxieties? How did the adults in your life help you express and cope with fear or anxiety? If you met a child who had the same fear or anxiety, describe two ways you would encourage or help that child.
10. **Evaluate.** In small groups, list five ways that you have seen adults try to teach preschool children manners. The adults' methods should vary in effectiveness. Discuss these methods and evaluate which are healthy and which are not. Finally, present these methods to the class and ask them to evaluate the methods' effectiveness.

Core Skills

11. **Art.** Review the aspects of self-concept discussed in the first lesson of this chapter. Then, using art supplies or a graphics editing software, create visual representations for each of these aspects. Present your illustrations to the class and be prepared to explain your creative decisions.

12. **Research and speaking.** With a partner, research the history of gender roles in the United States and in one other country. While researching, take notes about what roles people filled and how those gender roles were taught to children. Discuss current gender roles in both countries and how those ideas are transmitted to children. Finally, deliver a presentation summarizing your research and discussing how children learn gender roles.
13. **Writing.** Interview a teacher of preschool children and ask this person to give examples of ways in which the preschool's indoor and outdoor spaces, equipment, and materials aid social-emotional development. How do these factors encourage children to take initiative and show responsibility without experiencing guilt? After the interview, write a two- to three-page report reflecting on the teacher's answers. Check your report for correct spelling, grammar, and punctuation.
14. **Math.** In small groups, make a list of 10 behaviors that you would classify as *angry* and 10 behaviors that you would classify as *aggressive*. Discuss these behaviors with your teacher to ensure accuracy and then conduct a survey asking classmates and other people to identify the angry and aggressive behaviors. Calculate what percentage of people classified the behaviors correctly. Discuss your findings with your group, including how society's views of anger and aggression affect what children learn.
15. **Art.** Review Figure 16.8, which lists the social-emotional developmental milestones for preschoolers. Then, create a visual representation of each age range, including as many milestones as you can. Once you are done, place your visual representations on separate desks or on the walls. As a class, walk around the room and identify which age range each visual representation is illustrating. Afterward, share your answers as a class.
16. **Reading and writing.** Find a children's book that discusses a preschool child taking initiative. Read the book, taking notes about ways in which the child expresses initiative and how love and dependency factor into the child's decisions. Finally, rewrite the story from an adult's perspective observing the child. How does the adult interpret the child's initiative? How should the adult balance initiative with limits?
17. **Listening and speaking.** In small groups, interview a parent of a preschooler and ask the parent to describe a time when his or her preschooler was stressed, as well as how the parent handled the situation. Then, as a group, discuss the scenario the parent described and identify two other ways the situation could have been handled—one more healthy way and one less healthy way. Role-play and film each of these scenarios and then play them for the class. Ask the class to identify which scenario is the least healthy, the most healthy, and the real scenario described.
18. **CTE Career Readiness Practice.** Imagine you are a child care worker and that you are holding an open house for parents of your preschoolers. During the open house, one of the preschoolers throws a handful of crayons, and his parents respond in loud voices, threatening to spank him. You are concerned because this is a shaming technique (a negative public reaction and a threat of corporal punishment), but you know that there are cultural differences that inform these parents' behaviors. You have parent-teacher conferences next week, so you begin to plan what you will say about discipline. In preparation, write a script for yourself and include answers to questions the parents might ask. Then, role-play the conversation with a classmate until you feel prepared.

Observations

19. Visit a preschool center and observe the children playing. Take note especially of any conflicts that occur between friends. When taking notes, try to identify the source of the conflict and then observe how a child care worker does or does not intervene to reduce the conflict. If the child care worker did intervene, what strategies did he or she use? If not, why not?
20. Interview a parent or teacher about situations in which preschool children act out of jealousy. During the interview, ask for two to three specific examples and take notes about them. Write a narrative describing one of the examples and then exchange narratives with a classmate. Read the narrative you received and make observations about the type of jealousy the child experienced and how the jealousy was handled.

Unit 6 The School-Age Years

Chapter 17 Physical Development of School-Age Children

Chapter 18 Intellectual Development of School-Age Children

Chapter 19 Social-Emotional Development of School-Age Children

Role-Play or Interview

Some competitive events for CTSOs require entrants to complete a role-play or interview. Participants will receive information about a situation or topic and time to practice the event. A judge or panel of judges will review the presentations or conduct the interviews.

To prepare for the role-play or interview event, complete the following activities:

1. Read and analyze the guidelines your organization provides for this event.
2. Visit the organization's website to look for previous role-play and interview events to use in practicing for future competitions. (Many times, organizations also post online videos of top performers in their competitive events.) In addition, locate the evaluation criteria or rubric for this event to help you determine what the judges will look for in your presentation.
3. Practice speaking in front of a mirror. Are you comfortable speaking without directly reading your notes? Do your eye contact, facial expressions, and gestures convey the same message as your words?
4. Ask a friend to practice your role-play or interview with you as your instructor takes the role of competition judge. Give special attention to your posture and how you present yourself. Concentrate on your tone of voice—it should be pleasant and loud enough to hear without shouting. Make eye contact with the listener to engage the person's attention.
5. After making the presentation, ask for constructive feedback from your instructor. Implement any necessary changes and keep practicing.

Chapter 17 Physical Development of School-Age Children

Essential Question

Why do prepubescent school-age children appear to be marking time in terms of their physical growth and development, and how can parents ensure optimal development?

Lesson 17.1 **Growth and Development of School-Age Children**

Lesson 17.2 **Meeting Nutritional Needs of School-Age Children**

Lesson 17.3 **Meeting Other Physical Needs of School-Age Children**

Case Study How Might Parents Approach the Topic of Precocious Puberty with Their Child?

As a class, read the case study and discuss the questions that follow. After you finish studying the chapter, discuss this case study again. Have your opinions changed based on what you learned?

When Valencia took her second-grade daughter swimsuit shopping, she was shocked to see that Antonia was developing breasts and dark hair under her arms. Valencia noticed that Antonia was shooting up in height lately, but had attributed this to a growth spurt. Now, she wasn't so sure.

Valencia made an appointment with Antonia's pediatrician, who ran some tests and said that Antonia has a type of precocious puberty and should see a pediatric endocrinologist. The specialist diagnosed Antonia with *central precocious puberty* (CPP) and prescribed monthly injections of medication in hopes of delaying further development until Antonia reaches a normal age for puberty to begin. The pediatric endocrinologist also told Valencia that, as a result of the CPP, her daughter may be shorter than average as an adult, but the drug may help with this and other problems.

This news upset Valencia. She had never discussed puberty with Antonia because she thought her daughter was too young, and her daughter's school did not cover this topic until fourth or fifth grade. Now, she would have to discuss puberty and the CPP diagnosis with Antonia. Valencia was concerned about her daughter feeling like the "odd one out." She didn't want Antonia to grow up too quickly.

Give It Some Thought

1. How do you think Valencia should explain puberty and CPP to Antonia? What might be Antonia's reactions now and in the future?
2. What are some ways in which Antonia's family can help her remain a little girl for several more years?
3. Should Antonia's parents and other parents encourage the school to give lessons on puberty at the second-grade level or even before? Why or why not?

While studying this chapter, look for the online resources icon  to:

- **Practice** terms with e-flash cards and interactive games
- **Assess** what you learn by completing self-assessment quizzes
- **Expand** knowledge with interactive activities and graphic organizers

Companion G-W Learning

www.g-wlearning.com/childdevelopment

Study on the go

Use a mobile device to practice terms and review with self-assessment quizzes.

www.m.g-wlearning.com/0384

Lesson 17.1 Growth and Development of School-Age Children

Key Terms

flexibility
growth pains
growth spurt
permanent teeth
precision
puberty
six-year molars

Academic Terms

heralds
menarche
pubescent
spermarche
surpass

Objectives

After studying this lesson, you will be able to

- describe brain development and other organ maturation during the school-age years.
- explain the process of puberty and describe physical changes that occur in pubescent children.
- describe changes in the skeletal system during the school-age years.
- summarize major changes in motor development during the school-age years.
- give examples of physical developmental milestones children might achieve in the school-age years.

Reading and Writing Activity

Before reading, use reliable online or print resources to research information about how children develop physically during the school-age years. Create a list of ten facts you learn. While reading this lesson, look for any mentions of the facts you listed. After reading, write two to three paragraphs reflecting on your list in light of what you learned in this lesson.

Graphic Organizer

Draw a time line illustrating the school-age years. Then, as you are reading, take notes about children's physical development at each point on your time line.

6 years	8 years	12 years

School-age children, children between 6 and 12 years of age, are in a period of development known as *middle childhood*. Many physical changes occur during this period because all of a child's body systems are maturing. The growth rate is rather obscure due to slow and consistent growth and changes in the body proportions. Between 6 and 11 years of age, however, children grow about one-foot in height and double their weight. Girls, who grow a little faster than boys, reach about 90 percent of their adult height by age 10 or 11 years; boys achieve about 80 percent of their adult height by 11 years of age. Overall, until the last two years of middle childhood, this is a period of physical calm. Averages, however, obscure the wide individual differences in height, weight, and body proportions. If you look at children in the fifth or sixth grades, some children still look like children while others are beginning to look more like teens.

Due to increases in muscle growth and strength and increased myelination in the central nervous system, both children's gross- and fine-motor skills improve to a marked degree. This improvement is often referred to as the "hallmark" of middle childhood. Unless hampered by inadequate nutrition and lack of activity, most school-age children excel in gross-motor skills. Their movements show an ease and grace due to strength and coordination. School-age children become skillful at fine-motor skills, too, such as model building and other crafts, playing musical instruments, and handwriting. Some of these changes may seem awkward to children as they occur, but all changes help school-age children become more coordinated.

Maturation of Organs

With the coming of the school-age years, brain growth slows dramatically. After the preschool years, head circumference only increases one-half inch every five years until maturity. The brain, which reached 90 percent of its adult weight during the preschool years, grows to reach 95 percent of its adult weight by 10 years of age. Instead of growing rapidly, the brain becomes more specialized during the school-age years. Specific areas of the brain coordinate specific tasks. By this time, the brain has established a visual center for processing visual stimuli, a speech center for comprehending speech, and so on. From the school-age years onward, rewiring in the brain is difficult, if not impossible. Brain connections will continue to be made at a rapid pace until about eight years of age. These connections, as well as increased myelination, allow for better memory capacity, language and literacy development, focus and motivation, problem-solving skills, and emotional control.

Besides the brain, other organs continue to mature in school-age children. The heart grows slowly, and while it does become more efficient at pumping blood, it is small in relationship to the rest of the body. Too much strain on the heart during this period is dangerous. Blood pressure increases in school-age children and is about the same for boys and girls.

Children's lungs continue to grow until eight years of age, and breathing becomes less abdominal and more efficient. School-age children's *respiratory rate* (number of breaths per minute) decreases, and children lose less oxygen to exhalation.

As the gastrointestinal system matures, school-age children have fewer stomach upsets, steadier blood sugar levels, and greater stomach capacities than in the preschool years. Bowel and bladder control are usually firmly established.

Children's senses also improve during the school-age years. As the eyes mature, binocular vision is established by 6 years of age and acuity established between 9 and 11 years of age. Auditory (hearing) sensitivity improves until 10 years of age and then declines to adult levels. Maximum hearing sensitivity is established first for mid-range, second for high-range, and last for low-range tones.

During the later school-age years, children begin to enter puberty. **Puberty** is the process by which the body becomes capable of reproduction. Puberty begins in the brain, where the *hypothalamus* (section of the brain responsible for hormone production as well as other functions) releases *GnRH*, gonadotropin (GOH-nad-oh-TROH-puhn) releasing hormone, into the endocrine system. GnRH causes the brain's *pituitary gland* to release

Focus on

Science

Circulatory System

The heart, a striated muscle, is about the size of a clenched fist. It is located between the lungs in the chest cavity.

Parts of the Heart

The heart has four *chambers*. The two top chambers are called *atria* (RA, right atrium, and LA, left atrium). The two chambers on the bottom are called *ventricles* (RV and LV). The atria pump blood to the ventricles, which then push blood out of the heart. This is felt as pulse.

Each chamber has door-like valves that keep blood flowing forward and prevent backflow. Between the RA and RV is the *tricuspid valve*, and between the LA and the LV is the *mitral valve*. The *pulmonary valve* on the right side and the *aortic valve* on the left side of the heart shut blood out of the heart. As the valves close, a *lub-dub* sound is heard through a stethoscope.

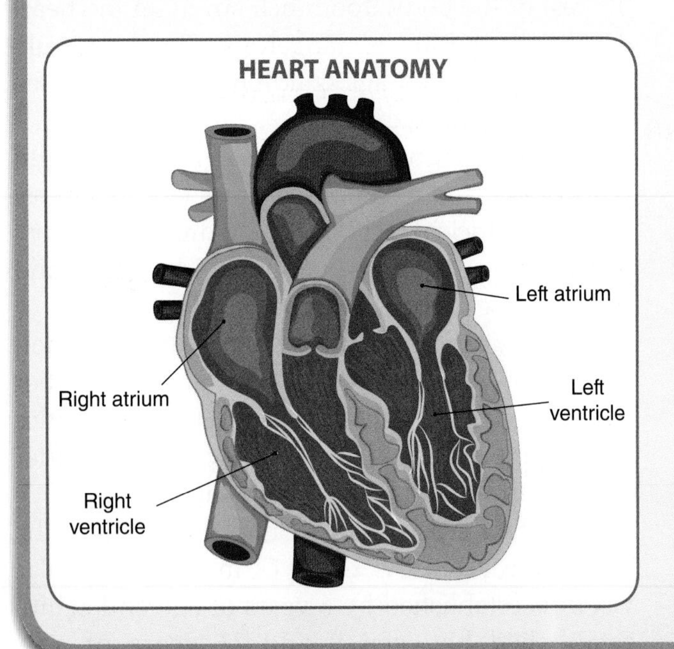

How the Heart Functions

The heart's function is to circulate blood. Blood delivers oxygen to the cells and brings back carbon dioxide and other waste products to the heart. To do this, the blood follows a particular path in and out of the heart. Deoxygenated blood enters the RA and is pumped to the RV, where it is then pumped to the lungs. The lungs remove waste products when exhaling and intake fresh oxygen when inhaling. Oxygen-rich blood flows into the LA and is pumped into the LV and then out of the heart to the body. The blood flow through the heart is coordinated; so when the ventricles contract, the atria refill.

two more hormones, *follicle-stimulating hormone* and *luteinizing* (LOO-tee-uh-NY-zing) *hormone*. These hormones cause the ovaries in females and the testicles in males to produce *sex hormones* (estrogen and testosterone, respectively), which are needed for puberty changes in girls and boys. Physical changes in **pubescent** (being in puberty) children occur over a period of years (**Figure 17.1**). *Sexual maturity* occurs when females ovulate and when males produce enough sperm for reproduction. The arrival of sexual maturity is signaled by the **menarche** (men-AR-kee), the first menstrual cycle, in girls and by **spermarche** (SPERM-ar-kee), the first ejaculation, in boys. After these events, reproductive organs must continue to mature another 12 to 18 months before reproduction can occur.

Skeletal Growth

Children continue to grow slowly and steadily during the early school-age years. In the late school-age years, some children—mainly girls—begin a **growth spurt**, a period of rapid growth that **heralds** (signals the beginning of something) pubescence. During these years, body proportions in children

Figure 17.1 Puberty Changes

Change	Years of Age	
	Girls	Boys
Hypothalamus triggers surge of hormones.	8	11
Growth spurt begins.	10½	12½
Growth spurt peaks.	12	14
Growth spurt ends.	16	18
Secondary sex characteristics (visible body changes that distinguish males and females; not directly related to reproduction) develop.	8–14	10–15
Primary sex characteristics (body changes directly related to reproduction) develop.	9–16 average 12½	11–17 average 13½

change. Children's teeth and jaws grow, and additional changes occur in fat and muscles.

Height and Weight

School-age children's height increases more steadily than their weight. This is because, for the most part, genes determine height. Unlike weight, height is not easily affected by the environment, unless by long-term conditions, such as *malnutrition* or certain illnesses.

Weight increases somewhat parallel to height. Taller children tend to weigh more, and shorter children tend to weigh less. Children's environments also influence their weight because of factors such as nutrition, illness, activity level, and stress.

Generally, boys are taller and heavier than girls until 10 or 11 years of age (**Figure 17.2**). At this time, most females experience a growth spurt and become taller than boys. School-age children are often sensitive to these size differences, especially if they are becoming interested in the opposite gender. In reality, the average size difference between school-age boys and girls is only about one inch at 12 years of age. Most boys catch up in size during the early teen years.

Body Proportions

During middle childhood, children's body proportions become more similar to adult proportions. Children's waists and heads begin to look more in proportion to their bodies. The arms and legs grow longer, which gives children a lower center of gravity and better balance. The trunk grows until it is two times as long and two times as wide as it was at birth. Children's abdomens protrude even less than in the preschool years because of their longer trunks (**Figure 17.3**).

Bones and Teeth

The skeletal system continues to mature during the school-age years. Bones ossify and grow larger

Figure 17.2 Average Height and Weight from 6 to 12 Years of Age

Years of Age	Height in Inches		Weight in Pounds	
	Boys	Girls	Boys	Girls
6	45¾	45	45½	43
7	48	47½	50¼	48½
8	50	49¾	55¾	54¾
9	52	53	62	62¾
10	54¼	54½	69¼	71¾
11	55¾	57	77¾	81¼
12	59	60	90	92¼

Precocious Puberty

Typical puberty occurs over a span of years, usually beginning in the late school-age or early teen years. Some children, however, may experience *precocious puberty*. Precocious puberty is the *precocious* (early) onset of puberty and is usually defined by breast development before eight years of age in girls and by testicle development before nine years of age in boys.

There are two types of precocious puberty. The first type, *central precocious puberty (CPP)*, begins, as typical puberty does, with the release of hormones in the brain and stimulation of sex hormones. This process is the same as the one described in Figure 17.1, but occurs much earlier than the norm. The second type, *peripheral precocious puberty (PPP)* is less common and is not always triggered in the brain. PPP occurs when sex hormones are released into the body earlier than the typical age, possibly due to problems with the ovaries, testicles, or adrenal glands. Unlike CPP, PPP affects only one or two puberty changes, such as breast or testicle development, but seldom menarche or spermarche.

Causes of Precocious Puberty

The causes of CPP and PPP are numerous. In about 90 percent of girls and 50 percent of boys, early puberty is considered *idiopathic* (having no known cause). In about 1 percent of girls and 5 percent of boys, precocious puberty is inherited. Some other risk factors for early puberty include the following:

- infections, head injuries, tumors, and other known medical problems
- high-fat diets
- obesity
- inactivity
- family breakups
- endocrine disruptors, such as fire retardants, plasticizers, pesticides, lead, mercury, nanomaterials, radon, and soy infant formulas
- exposure to estrogen or testosterone creams, ointments, sprays, or oral medications
- radiation treatments for cancers

Effects of Precocious Puberty

Because precocious puberty causes a child to enter the adolescent growth spurt early, he or she misses several years of regular skeletal growth. Soon after puberty, bone plates fuse. Thus, the child does not reach his or her genetic potential for height. Precocious puberty increases the risk for estrogen-dependent cancers of the breast and ovaries and can also lead to higher rates of type 2 diabetes, heart problems, and asthma. Social-emotional problems, including poor body image, depression, moodiness, aggression, sexual feelings and behaviors without emotional maturity, and a higher incidence of substance abuse, may also result from early puberty.

Treatments for Precocious Puberty

Pediatricians send suspected cases of early puberty to *pediatric endocrinologists* (doctors who specialize in treating hormone-related conditions in children) for diagnosis and treatment. Generally, only CPP is treated with a drug regimen. These drugs tell the pituitary to ignore GnRH signals, and within a year, stop the puberty process. Physical conditions seen in PPP are usually found and treated in other ways, such as the surgical removal of cysts or tumors.

Research Activity

In small groups, research stories about children who experience precocious puberty. How does precocious puberty affect their social-emotional lives? What are some ways that schools and educational programs are supporting families whose children are experiencing precocious puberty?

Figure 17.3 As children grow, their body proportions develop and change to be more adult-like. *In what ways do children's body proportions become more adult-like during middle childhood?*

and longer. The most significant growth occurs in the teeth and jaw, leading to children having a more mature-looking face. School-age children are losing deciduous teeth. They are growing **permanent teeth** (teeth that are intended to last a lifetime; are harder and less sharp than deciduous teeth). Girls often lose their deciduous teeth and grow permanent teeth before boys do.

The first two deciduous teeth, often the bottom front teeth, fall out during the late preschool years, and the last of the 20 deciduous teeth (the cuspids) fall out around 12 years of age. The first permanent teeth to come in are **six-year molars** (large teeth near the back of the jaw that come in around 6 years of age and are used for grinding food). Six-year molars do not replace any lost teeth; rather, they grow behind the second set of deciduous molars (**Figure 17.4**). Subsequent permanent teeth replace lost deciduous teeth. The growth of these permanent teeth changes the look of the lower part of the face in school-age children.

Fat and Muscle

Fat accounts for about 15 percent of an average school-age child's total body weight. Girls have more fat than boys at six years of age, but girls and boys accumulate fat at the same rate until puberty. Starting in puberty, girls again accumulate fat at a higher rate than boys.

Muscles increase in size and strength during middle childhood. Muscle strength doubles during these years, but children's strength is still immature compared to muscle strength in teens. Muscles also

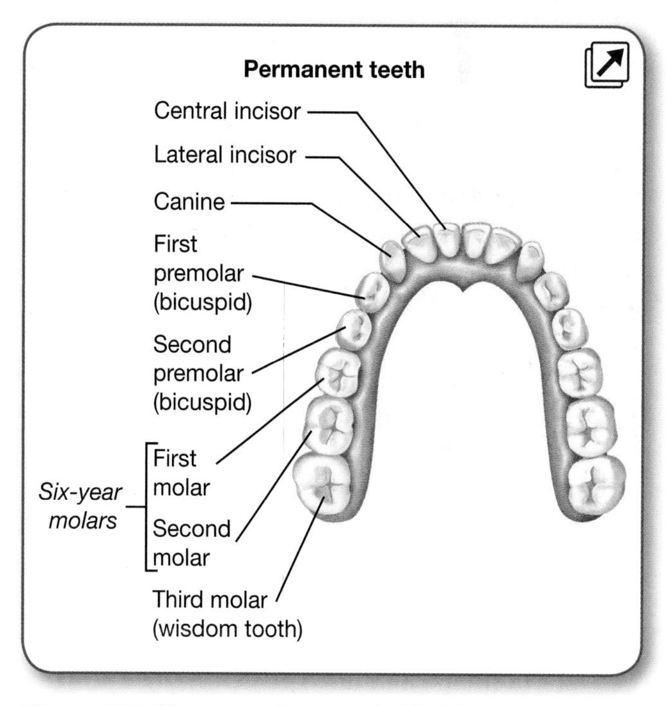

Figure 17.4 Six-year molars grow behind the second set of deciduous molars. *How are permanent teeth different from deciduous teeth?*

become more firmly attached to bones. Because the skeleton grows more quickly than the muscles, school-age children may have a loose-jointed, somewhat awkward look. Children of this age cannot completely keep their muscles from moving. This makes sitting completely still almost impossible.

School-age children may complain of aches and pains. These muscle aches are called **growth pains**, which are caused by muscles trying to catch up with skeletal size.

Motor Development

The maturation of children's bodies during the school-age years leads to refined motor development. School-age children often have a surplus of energy, which they use in practicing motor activities. Between 6 and 8 years of age, children generally enjoy active games that use their gross-motor skills. This is because children's large muscle coordination is more developed than their small muscle coordination. Children in this age range enjoy running, jumping, climbing, and playing simple games, such as tag and catch. Children between 9 and 12 years of age develop interests in more structured gross-motor activities, such as organized sports, skating, or bicycling. This is due to children's increased mental abilities as well as improved large-muscle coordination.

Older school-age children have highly developed fine-motor skills. Advances in fine-motor development help children do arts and crafts, build models, play musical instruments, dress themselves, use digital devices, write, and handle other tasks that require fine-motor precision (**Figure 17.5**). These skills seem to increase steadily during the school years.

In the early part of middle childhood, boys generally perform better than girls in tasks requiring power, force, and speed. After girls begin their growth spurt, however, they often equal or **surpass** (do better than) boys of the same age in these tasks. School-age girls tend to perform better than boys in tasks requiring flexibility or rhythm. Experts do not know whether these motor differences between genders are due to genes or environment. Children who are highly skilled in one motor activity tend to also excel in others.

Figure 17.5 Fine-motor skills increase each year, as seen in writing samples. ***What other skills improve as fine-motor skills develop?***

Motor skills improve during middle childhood due to the following *physiological factors* (changes in physical attributes) (**Figure 17.6**):

- ***Reaction time.*** School-age children have faster *reaction time* (the time required to respond to a stimulus, such as a thrown ball).
- ***Precision.*** School-age children have improved **precision** (the ability to perform motor skills accurately). Precision is used in skills such as balancing, steadiness, and aim.
- ***Speed and strength.*** Children have greater speed and improved strength during the school-age years.

Figure 17.6 Better reaction time and flexibility enable children to participate in more complex and competitive physical activities. *What are some examples of physical activities that require reaction time or flexibility?*

- *Flexibility.* School-age children have a great deal of **flexibility** (ability to move, bend, and stretch easily).

Physical Developmental Milestones

During the school-age years, children grow to look more like adults. Some children begin experiencing puberty changes, as their reproductive organs mature. Children grow in height and weight, grow permanent teeth, and develop stronger muscles. Their gross- and fine-motor skills improve, and they are better able to perform structured and unstructured motor skills. **Figure 17.7** lists some physical developmental milestones for school-age children.

Lesson 17.1 Review and Assessment 

1. Instead of growing rapidly, the brain becomes more _____ during the school-age years.
2. Explain the process of puberty, including how the body signals pubescent changes.
3. Define *growth spurt* and describe how growth spurts affect height and weight differences between school-age boys and girls.
4. The first permanent teeth to erupt are _____.
5. Why do school-age children sometimes experience growth pains?
6. Name and describe four physiological factors that improve during middle childhood and thus aid motor skills.
7. Choose one age during the school-age years and describe at least three physical developmental milestones a child that age might achieve.
8. **Critical thinking.** How much information do prepubescent children need to know about the physical changes that occur with puberty? Explain.

Figure 17.7 School-Age Physical Milestones

Six to seven years

- Is constantly active.
- May fidget.
- Can skate and jump rope with ease.
- Has a better sense of balance and timing.
- Copies or draws complex shapes.
- Ties own shoelaces.
- Uses self-care tools, such as combs, brushes, toothbrushes, and flatware.
- Has improved eye-hand coordination.
- Has established hand preference.
- Writes in manuscript style (commonly called *printing*).
- Colors within lines and cuts on lines.
- Draws pictures.

Eight to nine years

- Is in constant motion—jumps, climbs, and chases.
- Kicks, throws, catches, and hits balls with growing skill.
- Has smooth and quick large-motor skills.
- Enjoys organized games.
- Dresses self completely.
- Is skillful with hands; uses tools, does handicrafts, plays musical instruments, writes and draws with control.
- Is almost as coordinated as an adult.

Ten to twelve years

- Shows greater strength and endurance.
- Engages in sports and games.
- Applies gross-motor skills to sports and games.
- May feel awkward during growth spurt.
- Has excellent fine-motor coordination.

Meeting Nutritional Needs of School-Age Children

Lesson 17.2

Objectives

After studying this lesson, you will be able to

- summarize strategies that encourage healthful eating in school-age children.
- plan healthful lunches and snacks for school-age children.
- differentiate among *overnutrition*, *undernutrition*, and *malnutrition*.
- recognize common causes and risks of overweight and underweight.
- recall indications that a child may be developing an eating disorder.

Key Terms

eating disorder
food-insecure households
heavily processed foods
junk foods
malnutrition
overnutrition
undernutrition

Academic Terms

binge
pivotal

Reading and Writing Activity

Read the lesson title and tell a classmate what you have experienced or already know about the topic. Write a paragraph describing what you would like to learn about the topic. After reading the lesson, share two things you have learned with your classmate.

Graphic Organizer

Draw a school-age child in the middle of a piece of paper. Then, as you are reading, write all the considerations adults should take into account when meeting the nutritional needs of school-age children.

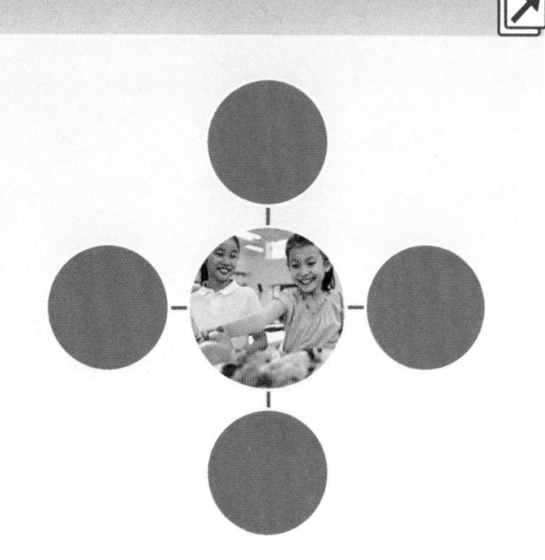

Although most school-age children are able to feed themselves, they still rely on adults to meet their nutritional needs. As children begin to think for themselves and as peers become more important, meeting these needs becomes more complex. School-age children may express strong preferences in foods, and their food preferences may be heavily influenced by the food choices of their peers. To a school-age child, having a meal similar to a peer's meal may be more important than eating a meal that is nutritious.

Eating nutritious foods is vital to a school-age child's growth, development, and increased energy demands. School-age children also need to store some nutrients for the rapid growth that occurs in puberty. Eating plans focused on healthful foods also help school-age children resist infections and avoid nutrition-related risks.

Healthful Eating in the School-Age Years

During the school-age years, children have more control over the foods they eat. School-age children are more likely to be eating meals away from home with less direct supervision than when they were younger. Meeting the nutritional needs of children this age, however, is no less important than when they were preschoolers. It is important for adults to work with school-age children, as a team, toward a common goal of healthful eating.

For school-age children, lunch is a **pivotal** (crucial or key) meal for a number of reasons. Children who skip lunch have more trouble concentrating in class, have less energy for sports, and are more likely to **binge** (overeat) on unhealthy snacks after school. Furthermore, when children start school, adults are no longer in control of what their children eat at lunchtime (**Figure 17.8**).

Adults and schools can use several strategies to improve the chances of children selecting and eating a nutritious lunch. For instance, some schools publish their weekly menus to help parents plan their children's meals and snacks for the day. However, children may not always eat what they are served at school. Even children who carry their lunches to school may give or throw away some of their food. To increase the likelihood of lunches being eaten, parents can include children in planning their meals eaten away from home. For example, the parent and child can review

Figure 17.8 At an age when a nutritious meal has such impact, an adult must rely on his or her child to consume it. *How can parents increase the likelihood of their child eating his or her lunch?*

the school menu together and discuss healthful choices among the child's preferred foods. If lunches are brought from home, the child can be involved in shopping for and preparing his or her lunch. When children are able to participate in planning and preparing their meals, they are more likely to eat them. School staff can also urge children to make nutritious food choices while away from home.

Healthful Eating Plans

During the school-age years, children begin to learn about healthful eating plans. A healthful eating plan focuses on colorful fruits and vegetables, lean protein options, low-fat dairy products, and whole grains. **Heavily processed foods** containing hidden sources of solid fats, sodium, and added sugars should be limited or avoided. Examples of heavily processed foods include many ready-to-eat foods, such as cereals, typical snack foods, lunchmeats, and boxed and frozen meals. Too much of a good thing is not always good, however, and even healthful foods must be consumed in appropriate amounts.

Adults can determine the amounts and types of food that are appropriate for their children by creating daily food plans to meet their children's specific needs. Adults can do this on the ChooseMyPlate website. Daily food plans list the recommended amount of foods from each food group based on the average height and weight for children's ages and genders and on how much time the child spends in physical activity on most days. For children nine years of age and older, a daily food plan is calculated using the child's own height and weight, not an average (**Figure 17.9**). For children who are at nutritional risk due to a condition or illness, adults should consult with the child's doctor or a registered dietitian nutritionist. Adults can use daily food plans to prepare healthful lunches and healthful snacks for their children.

Healthful Lunches

Whether purchased at school or brought from home, lunches should include some protein, a grain (preferably whole grain), fruit, vegetable, dairy, and a small treat. To make lunch selection easier, consider creating a master chart of foods the child likes for each food group. For instance, the protein foods list might include cheese cubes, sunflower seeds, thin-sliced turkey breast, or nut butter. The list for the grains group might include whole-wheat pita bread, whole-grain crackers, or a mini bagel. When it is time to assemble lunch, the parent and child can refer to the chart, and select one or more items from each list as called for in the daily food plan.

It is important that, in addition to meeting the child's nutritional needs, the lunch is also safe. Reusable lunch bags or boxes should be cleaned with warm, soapy water each day. Before assembling the lunch, the kitchen counter should be cleaned and hands washed. Fruits and vegetables should be washed before packing. Perishable foods must be kept at safe temperatures. Ice packs can be used with insulated lunch bags, and beverages can be frozen ahead of time.

Healthful Snacks

For school-age children, snacking is often unsupervised. Many children buy snacks, including **junk foods** (foods that are high in calories and low in nutrition), with their spending money. National Cancer Institute research shows that school-age children get up to one-fifth of their calories from sugar. Other studies show that school-age children who participate in sports, such as soccer, burn about 150 calories per game. Often, adults provide these children with postgame, nutrient-poor snacks containing between 300 and 500 calories. Children who eat too much junk food can lose their appetite for nourishing food. These children may receive adequate calories, but they do not receive enough of the nutrients their bodies need for growth. Junk foods also contribute to other health risks, such as obesity and tooth decay.

Adults can promote healthy snacking by keeping nutritious, ready-to-eat snacks readily available (**Figure 17.10**). Adults can also urge children to prepare their own nutritious snacks. Because school-age children like to eat, they often enjoy cooking. Many good cookbooks are written for this age group. Simple recipes allow children to prepare foods on their own or with a little help.

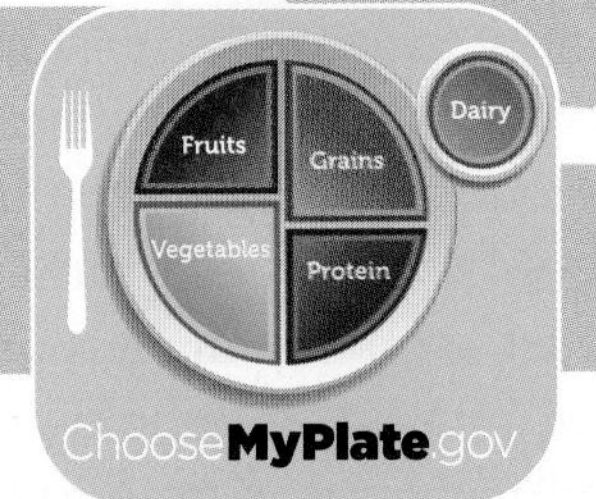

Daily Food Plan

Based on the information you provided, this is your daily recommended amount from each food group.

GRAINS 6 ounces	VEGETABLES 2½ cups	FRUITS 1½ cups	DAIRY 3 cups	PROTEIN FOODS 5 ounces
Make half your grains whole Aim for at least **3 ounces** of whole grains a day	**Vary your veggies** Aim for these amounts **each week**: **Dark green veggies** = 1½ cups **Red and orange veggies** = 5½ cups **Beans & peas** = 1½ cups **Starchy veggies** = 5 cups **Other veggies** = 4 cups	**Focus on fruits** Eat a variety of fruit Go easy on fruit juices	**Get your calcium-rich foods** Go low-fat or fat-free when you choose milk, yogurt, or cheese	**Go lean with protein** Choose low-fat or lean meats and poultry Vary your protein routine–choose more beans, peas, nuts, and seeds Choose seafood twice a week

Find your balance between food and physical activity	Know your limits on fats, sugars, and sodium
Be physically active for at least **60 minutes** every day, or most days.	Your allowance for oils is **5 teaspoons a day**. Limit extras—solid fats and sugars—to **160 calories a day**. Reduce sodium intake to less than **2300 mg a day**.

Your results are based on a 1800 calorie pattern **Name:** ______________________

This calorie level is only an estimate of your needs. Monitor your body weight to see if you need to adjust your calorie intake.

Figure 17.9 School-age children need a nutritious diet to meet their growth and energy needs. The recommended amounts shown in this sample are for a nine-year-old boy who is active 30–60 minutes daily. *What are some ways to involve children in planning and preparing healthful meals?*

Nutrition-Related Risks

Healthful eating every day should be the goal for school-age children. For most children, the occasional poor food choice causes little or no harm, but when poor food choices are the norm, children are at greater nutrition-related risk.

There are risks associated with both over- and undernutrition. **Overnutrition** is the ongoing intake of more calories than is needed for good health.

Figure 17.10 Healthful Snack Ideas for School-Age Children

- Pita chips with hummus dip
- Whole-grain pretzels with mustard
- Low-fat pudding topped with graham-cracker crumbles
- Yogurt parfait (layers of low-fat plain yogurt, granola, and berries)
- Whole-grain waffles topped with cinnamon applesauce (no sugar added)
- Fruit smoothie (blend low-fat plain yogurt, frozen berries, and 100% fruit juice)
- *Custom trail mix (combine dried fruits, unsalted nuts, and oat cereal)
- Whole-grain English muffin pizza (top-toasted muffin with pizza sauce, chopped vegetables, and low-fat mozzarella cheese; melt in microwave or toaster oven)
- Hard-cooked egg
- Baked tortilla chips with fat-free refried beans
- Baby whole carrots and cherry tomatoes with low-fat ranch dressing
- Toasted whole-grain mini bagel topped with flavored Greek yogurt
- Apple slices dipped in peanut butter
- Whole-grain macaroni floating in a cup of tomato soup
- Whole-wheat English muffin spread with ricotta cheese, sprinkled with lemon pepper, and lightly browned in toaster oven

*For older children

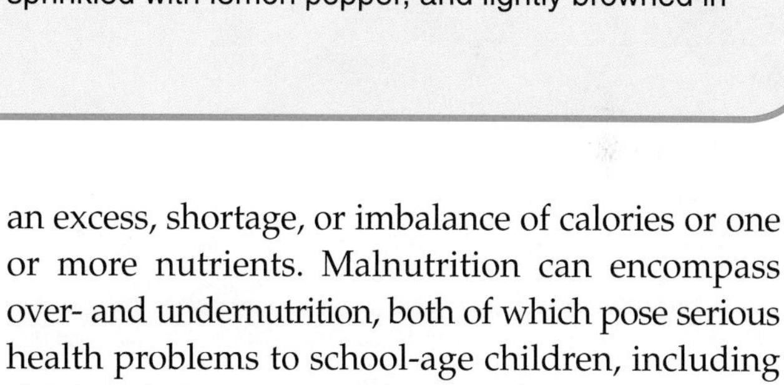

This condition is common in the United States today. It is seen in both children and adults, and increases people's risks for a number of chronic diseases. **Undernutrition** occurs when some food is being eaten, but is continuously lacking one or more nutrients required to meet the body's needs. In the United States, undernutrition is rare and usually due to illness or extreme poverty.

Another nutrition-related risk involves children living in *food-insecure households*. Children in **food-insecure households** (households that are regularly unable to supply healthful meals) do not have enough food available or may have diets that supply adequate calories, but are lacking in one or more nutrients. These children may be normal weight or even overweight, but are not receiving the nutrients necessary for proper growth and development. These children are experiencing *malnutrition*. **Malnutrition** describes diets that supply an excess, shortage, or imbalance of calories or one or more nutrients. Malnutrition can encompass over- and undernutrition, both of which pose serious health problems to school-age children, including children being overweight or underweight.

Being Overweight

Today, overnutrition combined with other factors has contributed to nearly one in three school-age children being either overweight or obese. Children who are obese may have up to three times the amount of fat tissue as children of normal weight. School-age children no longer have what is commonly referred to as "baby fat," which they will "grow out of." Rather, children who are overweight or obese are far more likely to become teens and adults who are overweight or obese. Overnutrition in children is often caused by the consumption of fast foods, snacking on junk foods, and eating take-out or heavily processed foods (**Figure 17.11**). Overweight and obesity in children can be caused by a number of factors, such as

- consumption of more calories than are used by the body
- easy access to high-calorie, processed foods
- physical inactivity
- family history of overweight or obesity
- lack of sleep
- depression or other emotional issues

Overweight and obesity increase a person's risk for high blood pressure, type 2 diabetes, problems with weight-bearing joints (hips, knees, and ankles), and possibly some cancers. These health conditions, which have traditionally been diagnosed in adults, are being observed more frequently in children. Obesity also results in serious social problems beginning as early as the school-age years. Obese children are often teased and rejected by their peers. This, in turn, affects self-esteem and even academic performance.

Figure 17.11 Overnutrition in children can be avoided by making healthful choices, like choosing more nutritious meals when eating out. *What other factors contribute to overweight and obesity in children?*

Being Underweight

Underweight in school-age children may be the result of inadequate nutrition, heredity, altered bodily responses to foods (such as not absorbing certain nutrients), illness, long-term mental stress, or eating disorders. In the United States, underweight is more often due to health concerns than to insufficient food. Incidence of underweight in children has decreased significantly in recent decades. Roughly 3.5 percent of children in the United States are classified as underweight.

Children who are underweight due to illness or abnormal eating patterns should be seen by a doctor. If underweight is a family trait, however, health risks due to underweight are unlikely.

Eating Disorders in School-Age Children

More and more, school-age children are facing pressure from peers and the media to look "good." Unfortunately, "good" often translates to "thin." School-age children who are overweight or a healthy weight often want to lose weight. This intense focus on appearance can contribute to the development of *eating disorders*. An **eating disorder** is an illness

Mental Health Advisory

Many school-age children develop eating disorders. Parents often think this "dieting" is just being a picky eater. Besides being a physical health risk, an eating disorder is a serious mental health issue involving body image. Thus, an eating disorder requires professional dietetic and mental health diagnosis and treatment.

characterized by distorted behaviors and emotions about food and weight. If untreated, an eating disorder can threaten a child's health and even life.

Eating disorders, such as *anorexia, bulimia nervosa,* and *binge-eating*, often develop in the school-age years and are observed in boys, but far more often in girls (**Figure 17.12**). In recent decades, hospitalizations for eating disorders of children under 12 years of age accounted for the largest increase of any age category. An eating disorder is both a physical and mental health issue.

Indications that a child is developing an eating disorder might include

- weight loss
- skipped meals
- baggy clothes
- obsessive exercising
- hoarding food
- crankiness
- difficulty concentrating

Eating disorders can cause malnutrition, imbalance in body chemicals, and death due to heart failure. Puberty, with its growth spurt and other changes, requires adequate nutrition. Children who exhibit warning signs for an eating disorder should be assessed by a physician. Treatment for these disorders often requires a team of health professionals.

Lesson 17.2 Review and Assessment 

1. What is the advantage of including children in the process of planning their meals?
2. Name the types of foods included in a healthful eating plan.
3. Define *junk foods* and explain why they are not healthful snacks for children.
4. Explain the difference among *overnutrition*, *undernutrition*, and *malnutrition*.
5. Describe the risks associated with children being overweight or obese.
6. Name three common causes of children being underweight.
7. List five indications that a child might have an eating disorder.
8. **Critical thinking.** How is it possible that some children who consume large amounts of calories still experience malnutrition?

Figure 17.12 Eating Disorders

Cause	Types
The Academy of Eating Disorders states that the eating disorders of middle childhood stem from a child's, especially a girl's, preoccupation with weight and body shape. Because the child does not have a good understanding of body weight and shape, the eating disorders often lead to growth and health problems and even to death.	• *Childhood-onset anorexia nervosa*. To lose weight, these children have an inadequate intake of food and engage in excessive exercise. Regardless of their hunger, they work hard to achieve their weight and body shape goals. • *Binge eating disorder*. Binge eating consists of eating excessive quantities of food at one time. Binge eaters may consume up to four times the amount of food that would constitute a normal meal. • *Childhood-onset bulimia nervosa*. These children may try a very restrictive diet, but end up bingeing on foods. Out of guilt, they purge themselves of the foods they have just ingested by vomiting. Alternately, they use laxatives to control their weight. Sometimes they lose weight, but their weight may also be normal or high.

Lesson 17.3

Meeting Other Physical Needs of School-Age Children

Key Terms

orthopedic problems
peer pressure
pheromones
sleep-deprived

Academic Terms

antiperspirants
cursory
deodorants
innocuous
sufficient

Objectives

After studying this lesson, you will be able to

- name some features of clothing that school-age children need and want.
- explain how peer pressure can affect school-age children's clothing preferences.
- describe hygiene needs during the school-age years.
- give examples of ways parents can encourage their children to get enough physical activity during the school-age years.
- identify problems caused by sleep deprivation and describe how parents can help their school-age children get enough rest and sleep.

Reading and Writing Activity

List the key terms for this lesson on a piece of paper and then look them up in the glossary, defining each term in your own words. Revise your definitions as needed while reading and then write two to three summary paragraphs using all of the key terms in this lesson.

Graphic Organizer

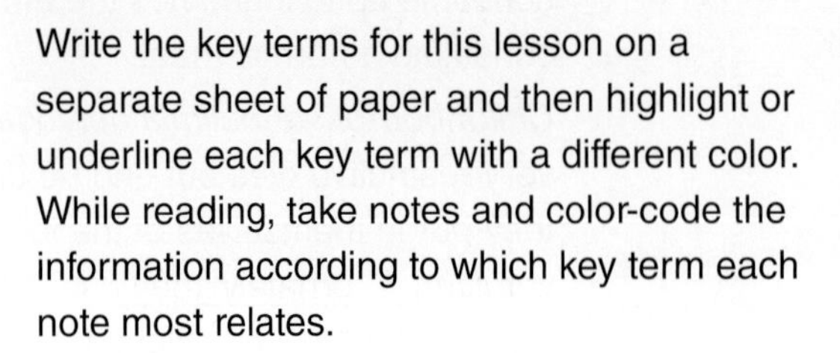

Write the key terms for this lesson on a separate sheet of paper and then highlight or underline each key term with a different color. While reading, take notes and color-code the information according to which key term each note most relates.

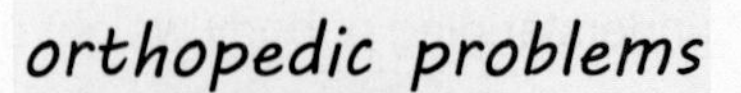

peer pressure

pheromones

sleep-deprived

Although children in the school-age years are learning to meet their own needs, they still rely on parents to provide them with basic physical necessities, such as clothing and toiletries, and to guide their clothing choices and health practices, such as hygiene, physical activity, and rest and sleep. Although school-age children want more independence and do have less direct adult supervision, parents and other significant adults can shape children's choices and behaviors. They can have a positive, moderating effect that overcomes negative external forces, such as unacceptable marketing approaches and peer practices.

Because children's understandings and attitudes develop rapidly at this time, middle childhood offers an unprecedented time for children to develop lifelong habits of tasteful dress and health behaviors. During this interpretive stage of parenting, children need to see how even seemingly **innocuous** (not harmful) issues can have a harmful impact. For example, suggestive clothing can negatively affect adult approval and positive peer relationships. Poor hygiene can damage the body and cause a loss of self-esteem due to peer comments. Inadequate rest and sleep affect learning and mood. Lack of regular physical activity endangers health and makes a person feel less physically confident. In addition, because school-age children will be spending the night with each other and going on outings with their youth groups, they will need to know how to meet their own needs, especially hygiene.

Clothing

During the school-age years, children have more say in the types of clothes they wear. They are able to choose clothing and dress themselves and may express opinions about what clothes they want.

Fit and Construction Features

Like children of all ages, school-age children need clothing that fits and is well constructed. School-age children are still growing, and especially when they hit their growth spurt, they may need garments that have growth features. Because school-age children are active, clothing should be able to withstand stress and strain. Most school-age children are able to dress themselves, though they may still have trouble with hard-to-reach buttons or a specially tied bow. Younger school-age children may still need to have clothes with some self-dressing features. Shoe and sock sizes change on the average of every six months for children between 6 and 12 years of age.

Clothing Preferences

School-age children begin to develop their own preferences for clothing, such as colors and styles (**Figure 17.13**). During the school-age years, children begin to experience **peer pressure** (the desire to be like their peers). Many school-age children choose clothes that will enable them to fit in with a peer group. If clothing and shoes are too different from what others wear, children may feel rejected.

Child development experts advise parents to take a close look at how clothing items for school-age children are marketed. Some clothes may have inappropriate logos or be constructed in styles that

Figure 17.13 Many school-age children express an interest in picking out their own clothes. *What factors besides peer pressure might influence the clothes a child chooses to wear?*

are more suitable for teens or young adults than for young school-age children. Parents should assess clothing options and provide guidance to help their children make appropriate choices. Parents should also listen to why a child wants a particular outfit. If a child says, "All my friends are wearing this," a parent might ask *why* the child's friends like it. This helps the child become a critic and express his or her own views. Parents can help their children make appropriate choices by offering options within set limits and explaining their reasons for saying "no" to specific outfits.

Due to school-age children's emphasis on clothing, many school systems institute school uniforms. This is usually an effort to improve school performance and reduce negative behaviors. Uniforms seem to improve children's focus on learning and decrease distractions about clothing choices. Uniforms are also often cheaper for parents who may not be able to afford an individual school wardrobe. Opponents to school uniforms claim that uniforms do not reduce behavioral problems or create a sense of socioeconomic equality among students. They also claim that uniforms limit the ability of students to express themselves and their cultures. Furthermore, opponents say that one style does not fit all tastes. For example, a typical uniform for girls may be a skirt or jumper, but some girls prefer pants. Finally, some parents point out that buying uniforms for children at the beginning of the school term is hard on the family budget. Parents must also buy clothes for nonschool hours in addition to the uniforms.

Hygiene

Adults should continue stressing the importance of hygiene skills and teaching these skills, if deemed necessary, during the school-age years. Dental hygiene problems often begin in middle childhood. Permanent teeth replace deciduous teeth at a rate of about four per year, yet many children do not receive regular check-ups. Adults often quit brushing their children's teeth in middle childhood. Problems may arise because many school-age children regularly snack on sugary foods and drinks, wear dental braces, or use a quick, **cursory** (nonthorough) approach to dental hygiene. By the end of the school years, the majority of children have more than four decayed or filled teeth. Dental hygienists and adults should stress the importance of dental hygiene and the "how to" of keeping teeth clean (**Figure 17.14**).

Body hygiene (also called *personal hygiene*) is a common problem for school-age children. Body odor becomes a problem as children approach puberty. Body chemicals called **pheromones** (FER-uh-mohns) are produced and secreted through sweat. Without regular baths or showers, clean clothing, and **deodorants** (substances that hide body odor) or **antiperspirants** (substances that dry up sweat), these pheromones will produce body odor due to contact with bacteria. Because young children often play in the water while their parents bathe them, they may not know the importance of or the "how to" of bathing, showering, and shampooing. Once a child has mastered tub baths and is comfortable with water on the head and streaming into the face, he or she is ready for learning showering techniques. As the child becomes proficient at getting his or her body clean, shampooing techniques can gradually be introduced.

Physical Activity

School-age children spend many hours during the day attending school and using digital devices. As a result, children may become inactive during these years. Studies show that aerobic exercise in children and adults not only aids physical fitness,

Figure 17.14 It is important for children to develop good dental hygiene habits to avoid dental problems later in life. Adults should stress the importance of proper dental care. *How can adults encourage children to clean their teeth properly?*

but also aids the brain and other parts of the body. Physical activity is known to increase children's levels of concentration. Eye physicians recommend that 10 to 14 hours of outside play per week may reduce nearsightedness in children.

Many school-age children are physically active due to participating in competitive sports. Adults should help their children select appropriate sports and coaches and should caution their children about injuries due to sports and "daring feats." Sports injuries often occur because of bone fractures and muscle pulls. Although physical activities help strengthen muscles, **orthopedic problems** (those relating to the bones and muscles) are the most common physical problems at this age.

In addition to sports taught in schools or youth programs, the family plays an important role in children's physical activity. A good plan is for the family to take up vigorous physical activities parents and children can enjoy together. These activities, unlike some sports, should be potential lifelong activities, such as running, swimming, cycling, hiking, and skiing (**Figure 17.15**). These should not be done for competition, but for purposes of family physical fitness and fun. For many children, these physical activity patterns will last a lifetime.

Figure 17.15 Parents can encourage physical exercise by planning fun family activities, such as hiking. These activities encourage children to be physically active and may become lifelong habits. *What are some other activities families can do to stay physically active?*

Rest and Sleep

Research shows that school-age children need 10 to 11 hours of sleep nightly. Younger school-age children tend to need more sleep than those who are older. While school-age children are more likely to want control over their bedtimes, adults should still ensure that their children get enough sleep each night.

Focus on Careers

Coach

Coaches teach children the skills they need to perform a particular sport, such as soccer, swimming, or volleyball. They supervise practice sessions, develop game strategies, instruct and motivate athletes, and keep track of the team's performance. Coaches typically work in schools and recreation industries. They must often work irregular hours, such as evenings and weekends, for practices and games. Travel to sporting events is also required.

Career cluster: Education and training.

Education: Educational requirements include a bachelor's degree and knowledge of a sport.

Job outlook: Future employment opportunities for coaches are expected to grow faster than the average for all occupations.

To learn more about a career as a coach, visit the United States Department of Labor's *Occupational Outlook Handbook* website. You will also be able to compare the job responsibilities, educational requirements, job outlook, and average pay of coaches with similar occupations.

Mental Health Advisory

School-age children who are depressed or anxious often experience sleep deprivation problems. Conversely, sleep deprivation caused by other factors, such as using digital devices during time for sleep, can result in mental health problems. Sleep deprivation should be professionally diagnosed and treated.

Sleep Deprivation

During the school-age years, children may become **sleep-deprived** (having less than the recommended amount of sleep) due to other demands on their lives, such as homework, extra-curricular activities, social activities, interest in digital devices, and consumption of caffeine. Sleep deprivation can lead to a number of problems, including

- inability to concentrate, which affects both learning ability and quality of work
- impaired memory
- weakened coping skills, behavioral problems, and low self-esteem
- disruption in hormones affecting appetite and food choices
- inability to use executive functions to achieve goals
- increased chance of mental health problems, such as depression and anxiety

Mental Health Advisory

Sleep deprivation can have a negative impact on school-age children's academic performance. One study showed that children deprived of one hour of sleep nightly performed more than two years below expectations on academic tasks.

Helping School-Age Children Get Rest and Sleep

While sleep deprivation is more likely to become a problem in children's lives during the school-age years, adults can use many strategies to help children get **sufficient** (adequate) amounts of rest and sleep. Some of these strategies include

- setting a regular bedtime for each day of the week. Varying bedtimes on weekends is not in the child's best interest.
- getting out in the morning light for a few minutes each day.
- taking all digital devices out of a child's bedroom. If digital devices are in a child's bedroom, the child is likely to use that device instead of sleeping.
- planning a wind-down time of 30 to 60 minutes before bedtime. During this time, digital devices should be put away and the television turned off.
- taking a child to be checked for sleep, respiratory, and emotional disorders if poor sleep habits persist.

Lesson 17.3 Review and Assessment

1. Name clothing features that are important for children in the school-age years.
2. How does peer pressure affect school-age children's clothing preferences?
3. Explain why body hygiene can be a problem for school-age children.
4. Describe two ways that adults can encourage physical activity in school-age children.
5. Research shows that school-age children need _____ hours of sleep nightly.
6. Name four potential consequences of sleep deprivation in school-age children.
7. Summarize three ways that adults can help school-age children get adequate amounts of sleep.
8. **Critical thinking.** In small groups, discuss the pros and cons of school uniforms.

Chapter 17 Review and Assessment

Summary

School-age children's physical development continues slowly and steadily. Brain development slows as the brain focuses on specialization. Heart development lags behind the maturation of the other organs as the lungs, gastrointestinal system, eyes, and hearing all improve to almost adult levels. Puberty changes begin, and some children complete this process during the school-age years. School-age children's skeletal systems are maturing. Bones grow and harden, and body proportions become more adult-like. Permanent teeth erupt and change the look of the face. Children's large motor skills become impressive due to improved reaction time, precision, speed and strength, and flexibility. Their fine-motor skills become highly developed.

During the school-age years, children have more say about the foods they eat. At school, they may trade foods or not consume foods that are packed for them. Adults should take this opportunity to teach children healthful attitudes about eating. Adults should also pack children healthful lunches and provide healthful snacks for their children. School-age children are prone to some nutrition-related risks, including overweight, obesity, underweight, and eating disorders.

School-age children still depend on adults to meet many of their physical needs. Children often want to choose their own clothes to fit in with their peers; however, adults still need to help children choose appropriate features and styles. Adults also need to encourage good health habits, such as dental and body hygiene. School-age children should get plenty of physical activity and sleep. Sleep deprivation can have harmful effects on children's health and development.

College and Career Portfolio

Portfolio Design

Using technology effectively in your portfolio gives you an opportunity to demonstrate your skills while making your portfolio look more professional and polished. To create your portfolio design, you can use publishing and design software. To determine the software you would like to use, complete the following activities:

- Research available publishing and design software. View samples of products the software has created. (Keep in mind that your portfolio should look professional and design elements should highlight accomplishments, not take away from them.) After reviewing the samples, choose two types of software you want to use.
- Download a free trial or use a library or school computer to modify one of your portfolio samples in the software. Evaluate if the software makes your sample look more professional.

Chapter 17 Review and Assessment

Vocabulary Activities

1. In small groups, locate an image online that visually describes or explains each of the following terms. To create flashcards, write each term on a note card and paste the image that describes or explains the term on the opposite side. After your group finishes creating the flashcards, trade flashcards with another group. Using the new flashcards, quiz one another to determine how well you know the vocabulary terms in this chapter.

Key Terms

eating disorder (17.2)
flexibility (17.1)
food-insecure households (17.2)
growth pains (17.1)
growth spurt (17.1)
heavily processed foods (17.2)
junk foods (17.2)
malnutrition (17.2)
orthopedic problems (17.3)
overnutrition (17.2)
peer pressure (17.3)
permanent teeth (17.1)
pheromones (17.3)
precision (17.1)
puberty (17.1)
six-year molars (17.1)
sleep-deprived (17.3)
undernutrition (17.2)

2. With a partner, create a T-chart. Write each of the following terms in the left column. Write a *synonym* (a word that has the same or similar meaning) for each term in the right column. Discuss your synonyms with the class.

Academic Terms

antiperspirants (17.3)
binge (17.2)
cursory (17.3)
deodorants (17.3)
heralds (17.1)
innocuous (17.3)
menarche (17.1)
pivotal (17.2)
pubescent (17.1)
spermarche (17.1)
sufficient (17.3)
surpass (17.1)

Critical Thinking

3. **Make inferences.** When did your growth spurt occur? Describe some of the feelings and changes associated with your growth spurt. How can adults help school-age children manage some of these feelings?
4. **Evaluate.** Watch a group of school-age children playing outside and try to determine the children's ages. Then, evaluate the children's motor skills for evidence of reaction time, precision, speed and strength, and flexibility. Cite your evidence. What skills need further improvement?
5. **Cause and effect.** Working with a partner, review this chapter and brainstorm ways that adults can encourage school-age children's healthful eating. How do adults' and schools' attitudes toward eating affect school-age children's food choices? Share some highlights from your conversation with the class.
6. **Analyze.** Research the lunch menu at a local primary or middle school in your community. What lunch options are available for the children? Are children encouraged to bring lunches or eat lunches made at the school? Write a few paragraphs analyzing how healthful the schools' lunch menu is and how lunch arrangements might affect children's food choices.
7. **Draw conclusions.** In small groups, discuss why many school-age children worry about their appearance more than the warmth and comfort of their clothing. How can adults and caregivers respect children's clothing preferences while emphasizing appropriate clothing choices?
8. **Identify.** As school-age children approach puberty, they are likely to experience body odor. In small groups, search online or at local stores for deodorants and antiperspirants that are geared toward school-age children. Identify products that you think would appeal to school-age children and discuss how an adult could introduce the concept of body odor to a child.
9. **Determine.** Research local primary and middle schools' start and end times. In small groups, determine what times children would have to wake up to get to school on time. What times, then, should the children go to bed? How could a typical evening be structured for a school-aged child to get sufficient sleep?

Core Skills

10. **Research and writing.** Once children reach the school-age years, their brains begin to specialize rather than rapidly wire new connections. Using reliable online or print resources, research how brain development changes during the school-age years. How do 12-year-olds' brains differ from 6-year-olds' brains? Write a short essay summarizing how the brain changes between 6 and 12 years of age.

11. **Reading and writing.** In small groups, research programs and materials for explaining puberty to school-age children. Choose two programs or materials and read them carefully, paying attention to how the physical changes of puberty are presented. Then, develop your own set of materials for teachers who need to introduce puberty to their students. Be sure to tailor the language to the developmental level of the children and consider how parents, teachers, and school nurses will respond to your materials.
12. **Technology.** Obtain photos of yourself from each year between 6 and 12 years of age. If possible, choose photos that include your whole body. Then, arrange the photos into a slideshow presentation showing how you grew over time. Include annotations in the presentation noting years in which your body proportions significantly changed. Present your slideshow to the class and narrate your growth during the school-age years.
13. **Technology and speaking.** In groups of seven, review the physical developmental milestones children achieve during the school-age years (Figure 17.7). Have each group member select one age, and then create an easy-to-follow visual representation of the milestones children achieve during these years. Your project should include drawings or pictures of children achieving various milestones during each year, and should be an effective study tool and synthesis of the information you learned in this chapter.
14. **Research and speaking.** Overweight and obesity in children can be caused by many factors, including genetics, overeating, and some illnesses. In small groups, research the most current information about factors that contribute to overweight and obesity. What do experts say about the most significant causes of overweight and obesity? What measures can adults take to prevent these conditions in children? What national or local programs are available to educate children about overweight and obesity? Compile your findings into a speech and create a bibliography listing your sources. Present the information to the class. Be prepared to answer any questions your classmates might have.
15. **Technology and speaking.** School-age children develop eating disorders for a number of reasons, including societal pressure to be "thin." In small groups, identify one type of media that school-age children regularly view. Then analyze examples used in this medium and identify pictures, words, or attitudes that might contribute to school-age children's desires to change their bodies. Finally, compile three examples into an electronic presentation and share with the class. Lead a group discussion analyzing the examples and brainstorming ways to combat negative messages about children's bodies.
16. **Listening and speaking.** Interview a dental hygienist or dentist about common problems in dental hygiene during the school-age years. What factors contribute to childhood tooth decay? What methods or activities can be used to teach children proper brushing and flossing techniques? After the interview, compile your notes and share your findings with the class.
17. **Math.** Survey three families with school-age children and ask about the schedules those children follow. If possible, ask the families to account for each hour of time during the day. After the survey, calculate what percentage of the children's time is spent doing physical activities. Also, calculate the average number of hours the children spend being physically active. Identify any hours in the families' schedules that could include more physical activities.
18. **CTE Career Readiness Practice.** Imagine you are a health teacher at a primary school. The principal has asked you to send out a sample weekly lunch plan for adults trying to pack healthful lunches for their nine-year-olds. In preparation, check the MyPlate recommendations for a nine-year-old child of average height and weight. Then, craft a newsletter outlining one week's worth of healthful lunches. Make your newsletter visually appealing with pictures of the foods included.

Observations

19. Visit a local primary or middle school and observe children of a certain age in art and physical education classes. During the observation, take notes about what fine- and gross-motor skills the children exhibit. What motor skills do they possess? What motor skills are they still developing?
20. Observe a primary- or middle-school cafeteria at lunchtime and watch for children who trade lunches or foods with their peers. What foods are children most likely to trade or discard? What foods are they most likely to consume? What role do teachers and other adults play in encouraging children to eat the foods they have been given?

Chapter 18 Intellectual Development of School-Age Children

Essential Question

How do children in middle childhood develop more logical and systematic reasoning abilities, and how do parents and teachers challenge children's intellectual progress in ways not before possible?

Lesson 18.1	**How School-Age Children Learn**
Lesson 18.2	**What School-Age Children Learn**
Lesson 18.3	**Meeting School-Age Children's Intellectual Needs**

Case Study: At What Age Should Children Have Their Own Cell Phones?

As a class, read the case study and discuss the questions that follow. After you finish studying the chapter, discuss this case study again. Have your opinions changed based on what you learned?

As Abden's eleventh birthday approached, he told his parents he wanted a smartphone. When his parents were less than eager about the idea, Abden explained that getting a smartphone would help him do his homework, that he needed a smartphone to call his friends, and lastly, that all his friends had a smartphone.

Abden's mother, Mona, felt frustrated with her son's persistent asking. After Abden went to bed that night, Mona talked with her husband about their son's request. "I don't think it's true that *all* of Abden's friends have smartphones," Mona said.

Abden's father went on to say, "I really don't think Abden is ready for a smartphone. Also, we need to read up on how to protect Abden once he's old enough to have a smartphone. Maybe we could get him a phone that allows him to call and text only until he is 13 or so."

Mona agreed, but still worried that her son might resent them for not getting him a smartphone. She wanted to talk with some other parents about how they were handling this issue.

Give It Some Thought

1. Do you think it is true that *all* of Abden's friends have smartphones? What do you think he means when he says that?
2. What do you think Abden's father is talking about when he says he and Mona need to read up on how to protect Abden if he gets a smartphone? What types of dangers might school-age children who have personal smartphones or computers face?
3. What do parents need to do before giving smartphones or other digital devices to their children for the first time? What skills and lessons do children need to learn before having their own digital devices?

While studying this chapter, look for the online resources icon  to:

- **Practice** terms with e-flash cards and interactive games
- **Assess** what you learn by completing self-assessment quizzes
- **Expand** knowledge with interactive activities and graphic organizers

Companion G-W Learning

www.g-wlearning.com/childdevelopment

Study on the go

Use a mobile device to practice terms and review with self-assessment quizzes.

www.m.g-wlearning.com/0384

Lesson 18.1 How School-Age Children Learn

Key Terms

concrete operational stage
conservation
deductive reasoning
formal operational stage
inductive reasoning
multiple intelligences
nucleus accumbens
prefrontal cortex

Academic Terms

metacognition
simultaneously

Objectives

After studying this lesson, you will be able to

- explain brain development and cognitive changes that affect children's learning in the school-age years.
- list several major gains in school-age children's thinking skills based on Piaget's theory.
- name the two ways Vygotsky believed that children learn.
- contrast Piaget's and Vygotsky's beliefs about the role of language during the school-age years.
- summarize the types of intelligences Gardner proposed in his theory of multiple intelligences.

Reading and Writing Activity

Before reading this lesson, review this text's lessons about how infants, toddlers, and preschoolers learn. Summarize how children learn at each stage and then read this lesson. Afterward, summarize how school-age children learn as compared to how they learned earlier in their development.

Graphic Organizer

Draw five columns and label each column with one of the lesson objectives. Then, as you are reading, write what you learn about each topic in the appropriate column.

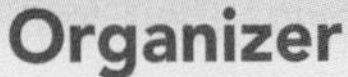

After studying this lesson, you will be able to				
explain brain development and cognitive changes that affect children's learning in the school-age years.	list several major gains in school-age children's thinking skills based on Piaget's theory.	name the two ways Vygotsky believed that children learn.	contrast Piaget's and Vygotsky's beliefs about the role of language during the school-age years.	summarize the types of intelligences Gardner proposed in his theory of multiple intelligences.

Children make dramatic gains in intellectual development during the school-age years. Advances in brain development and cognitive changes make them more capable of logical thought. As their brains mature, school-age children enter into Piaget's last two stages of intellectual development in which they rely less on perception and think more logically. Vygotsky theorized that children's intellectual development is also dependent on the environment for learning. The environment includes the learning opportunities provided and supported by peers and adults.

As you have read throughout the text, the intellectual changes from stage to stage have focused on the common features of children's thinking abilities and limitations. Yet, there are wide differences in intellectual abilities of children of the same age and stage, which is commonly called *differences in intelligence*. Gardner's theory of multiple intelligences represents one of the more recent theories concerning these differences.

Brain Development and Cognitive Changes

During the school-age years, children become capable of logical thought as a result of several advances in brain development and cognitive changes. Brain development and cognitive advances work together to create the "logical brain."

The Making of the "Logical" Brain

From the preschool years until 7 or 8 years of age, few structural changes occur in the brain. Still, this is an important period in brain development because early experiences determine how well or how poorly the brain functions in later stages. Around 8 years of age, when children are completing the third grade, the following two major changes in the brain begin to occur, and will continue until 11 years of age:

- ***Wiring in the prefrontal cortex.*** During the school-age years, wiring in the *prefrontal cortex* allows for higher cognitive functions.

  The **prefrontal cortex** is a section near the front of the brain that is involved in logical thinking, forming judgments, memory, weighing consequences, decision making, and controlling impulses and emotions (**Figure 18.1**). As the prefrontal cortex develops, children are better able to engage in these behaviors.
- ***Pruning.*** Pruning makes for faster and more efficient thinking. Pruning occurs after brain wiring, and begins in the back of the brain (where the first connections were made) before moving toward the front of the brain. The prefrontal cortex is last to be pruned and myelinated; it does not fully mature until the young adult years.

When puberty begins, the brain starts a reorganization process. The exact timing of this process is influenced not only by age, but also by memory, problem-solving skills, and **metacognition** (the awareness of one's own knowledge and thinking). As the brain reorganizes, connections between association areas and language areas allow for richness in communication. Executive functions begin to mature and pruning fosters more efficient thinking and allows for more abstract and hypothetical reasoning. While decision-making skills do not fully mature until pruning is complete in the prefrontal cortex, the ***nucleus accumbens*** (NOO-klee-us uh-KUM-buhnz), the pleasure and reward system of the brain, is overly developed. As a result, older school-age children and even young adults may make poor decisions in anticipation of pleasure or reward. (Figure 18.1 shows the location of the *nucleus accumbens* in the brain.)

In the school-age years, children's brains become less plastic than they were in earlier stages (infancy through the preschool years). As a result of this lessening plasticity, many older school-age children and teens begin to narrow their interests and focus less on areas of weakness. Many researchers feel it is too soon for such decisions and hope parents and other adults will encourage children and teens to maintain broad interests. Traumatic brain injuries (TBIs), which are rather common among school-age children and teens, may also lead to lessening plasticity.

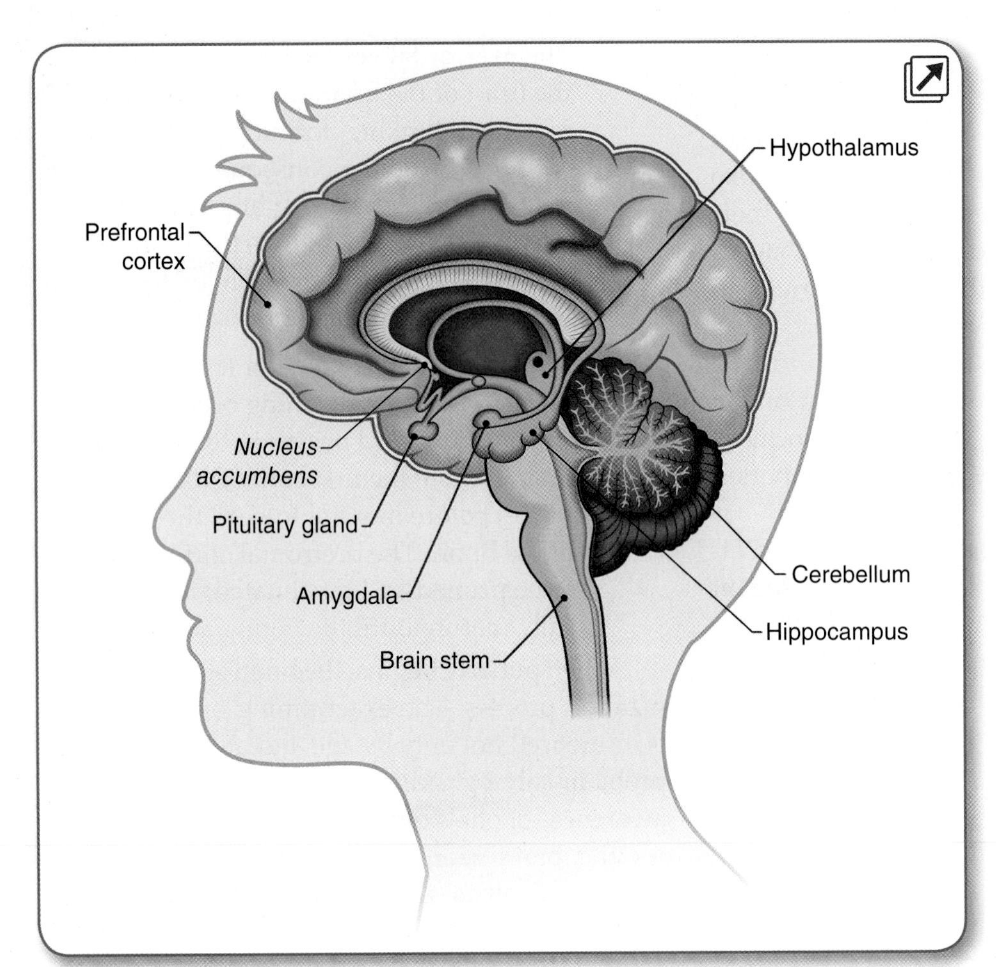

Figure 18.1 The prefrontal cortex is located near the front of the brain and allows for higher cognitive functioning in school-age children. *What are some activities in which the prefrontal cortex is involved? How do school-age children engage in these activities with more ease than when they were younger?*

Cognitive Advances in the School-Age Years

Brain development during the school-age years leads to a number of cognitive changes, all of which make logical thinking more possible. To develop concepts and solve problems, children must acquire and process knowledge. To do this, theorists believe that children must attend to relevant information, store it in their memories, and retrieve the information and apply it (**Figure 18.2**). Children's abilities to do these tasks are dependent on cognitive changes in attention and memory.

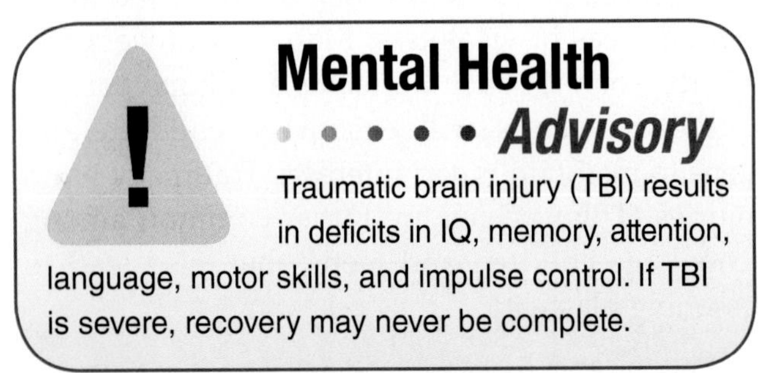

Mental Health Advisory

Traumatic brain injury (TBI) results in deficits in IQ, memory, attention, language, motor skills, and impulse control. If TBI is severe, recovery may never be complete.

Attention

To be able to think logically and solve problems, children must be able to pay attention and focus on relevant aspects of the environment and disregard irrelevant aspects. Preschool and young school-age children often focus on what "stands out" and thus may miss what is relevant. For example, in learning the letters *p*, *q*, *b*, and *d*, they may focus on the line and loop and miss what is important, which is the position (*up* or *down*) of the line and the orientation (*left* or *right*) of the loop. Older school-age children learn what is important in solving a task and focus attention on this aspect. During the late school-age years and even into adulthood, however, children and adults are vulnerable to noticing what "stands out," not necessarily what is relevant.

Memory

Memory is vital to logical thinking and problem solving. Children and adults alike draw on what they already know to solve current problems and acquire new information.

Figure 18.2 Due to cognitive changes during the school-age years, these children are able to store information about geography and then recall that information to locate countries on the globe. *What are some other activities in which children must recall stored information and apply it?*

Working memory (also known as *short-term memory*) does not increase much after the early school-age years. Explicit and implicit memories (also known as *long-term memories*), however, grow significantly during the school-age years. Throughout this time, children develop the following specific skills to help them access their explicit and implicit memories:

- ***Rehearsing.*** School-age children learn how to *rehearse* (repeat information until it is learned). While a young school-age child might rehearse by repeating one word over and over and then doing the same with the next word, an older school-age child might repeat the first and second words, then the first, second, and third words, and so on (**Figure 18.3**).
- ***Organizing information.*** School-age children learn to organize information for long-term memory storage. They often do this by categorizing items or events.
- ***Using visual and verbal aids.*** During the school-age years, children learn how to use visual aids, such as charts and outlines, and verbal aids, such as acronyms and sayings, to help them recall information.

Besides an increased ability to remember, school-age children have better understandings about how their memories work. These understandings aid school-age children in both selecting the right memory strategies and knowing when information is truly memorized.

Piaget's Cognitive-Developmental Theory

Young school-age children learn in much the same way that older preschoolers do. Around seven or eight years of age, however, changes in thinking begin to occur, and children enter Piaget's third stage of intellectual development.

The Concrete Operational Stage

Piaget noted that between 7 and 11 years of age, school-age children's thinking skills are no

Figure 18.3 School-age children are able to learn stories and facts by rehearsing them, either on their own or in a group. *What songs and stories can you think of that include word sequences that can be rehearsed?*

longer dominated by perception. Children gradually learn to use logical thinking concepts to manipulate information, and their thinking becomes more flexible and organized as compared to younger children. Piaget called this third stage of intellectual development the **concrete operational stage**. The concrete operational stage is *concrete* because logic is based on the child's past experiences.

The transition between the preoperational stage and the concrete operational stage is very gradual. Young school-age children do not automatically apply logical thinking to all tasks. Rather, with each advancing year, children become more logical and less dependent on their perceptions. Some children, and even adults, remain in the concrete operational stage for much of their thinking.

The Formal Operational Stage

Piaget's last stage of intellectual development is called the **formal operational stage**. In this last stage, children and adults are able to reason more abstractly. Some child development experts place the beginning of the formal operational stage at 12 to 14 years of age, but the age at which the stage begins varies from person to person. For most day-to-day activities, even adults reason in the concrete operational stage. People who use formal operations regularly in their occupations are mathematicians, engineers, scientists, and network architects.

The difference between the concrete and formal operational stages can be seen in how a child plays a game of checkers or chess. In the concrete operational stage, the child can play checkers or chess by the rules. He or she makes each move based on which pieces are on the board at that time, but does not think in terms of the next three to five moves. A child in the formal operational stage, however, can think ahead and plan strategies for winning the game. **Figure 18.4** shows the differences in the ways children think in the concrete and formal operational stages.

Overcoming Obstacles to Logical Thought

As children enter the concrete and formal operational stages, they begin to overcome many of the obstacles to logical thought they experienced during the preschool years. School-age children entering these stages overcome egocentrism by learning to see from the viewpoints of others. They overcome centration by learning to focus on more than one aspect at a time. They also learn to note transformations, understand reversals, and learn to use deductive and inductive reasoning rather than transductive reasoning.

Seeing from the Viewpoints of Others

While preschoolers and younger children are primarily *egocentric* (focused on self), school-age children begin to understand that other people have ideas that differ from their own. They learn to recognize others' points of views and notice how these views compare or contrast with their own ideas. Realizing that others have different ideas leads children to question their previous thoughts and search to find right answers. School-age children use logic to prove or deny these answers.

During the school-age years, children who try to solve difficult tasks may still exhibit some traces of egocentrism. When a school-age child forms a hypothesis about how or why an object or situation works, the child may force contradictory facts into his or her hypothesis rather than changing the hypothesis to fit the facts. This is because school-age children want to be right. These traces of egocentrism often disappear during the teen years.

Focusing on More Than One Part

During the school-age years, children begin to overcome their perceptions of *centration* (exclusive focus on one part of an object). School-age children learn to focus on more than one part of an object or situation at a time and are able to see more than one change at a time. For instance, if you refer again to Figure 15.7, notice that preschoolers were unable to see changes in length and width **simultaneously** (at the same time). In the school-age years, however, children are able to focus on the different-sized glasses and see that the greater width in the first glass makes up for the greater height in the other glass. Because they can note these changes simultaneously, school-age children are able to understand how the same amount of liquid looks taller in a thinner glass.

Figure 18.4 Piaget's Cognitive-Developmental Theory

Stages and Substages	Characteristics
Stage 1: Sensorimotor stage (birth to 2 years)	Children learn through the senses and physical actions in six substages.
Substages 1 and 2 involve the baby's own body.	
Substages 3 and 4 involve people and objects.	
Substages 5 and 6 involve creative actions and thinking before acting. (12 to 24 months)	
Stage 2: Preoperational stage (2 to 7 years)	Children learn through symbols, but with logical limitations.
Substage 1 involves the development of concepts.	
Substage 2 involves the use of perception.	
Stage 3: Concrete operational stage (7 to 11 years)	Children begin to think logically, but base their logic on past experiences. • Can see things from various perspectives. • Focus on more than one aspect of something at the same time. • Gradually note transformations (conserve). Number—5 to 7 years of age Continuous quantities (liquid)—6 to 8 years of age Mass (like clay)—6 to 8 years of age Length—6 to 8 years of age Area—7 to 9 years of age Weight—8 to 10 years of age Volume—10 to 14 years of age • Invert a sequence of steps (reversibility). • Use better reasoning skills.
Stage 4: Formal operational stage (11 years of age and older)	Older children, teens, and adults reason abstractly. • Can hypothesize. • Do scientific and mathematical abstract reasoning.

Focusing on more than one aspect allows school-age children to use *conservation*. **Conservation** is the concept that changing an object's shape, direction, or position does not alter the quantity of the object. Children must be able to understand the principles of conservation before they can form accurate concepts related to number, *continuous quantities* (liquids), mass, length, area, weight, or volume (**Figure 18.5**).

Noting Transformations

Perceptions of centration made noting transformations difficult for children during the preschool years. However, as school-age children learn to note more than one aspect of an object at a time, they are better able to watch and understand certain *transformations* (sequences of changes). School-age children can mentally arrange events to see a series of changes in objects. For example, school-age children can note that a caterpillar transforms into a butterfly or heat transforms ice into water. As shown in Figure 18.5, children understand certain transformations earlier than others.

Understanding Reversibility

School-age children are better able to understand reversals. *Reversibility*, the ability to follow a line of reasoning back to where it started, enables children to carry out a task in reverse order. Reversibility depends on the understanding that if an object is changed and then returned to its original shape or form, it will be the same. For example, the school-age child who flattens a ball of clay understands that the flattened clay can be restored to the original ball.

Figure 18.5 Piagetian Conservation Tasks

Type of Conservation	Initial Presentation *Note:* During the initial presentation, the experimenter will ask a *basic question* (*Q*) to establish equivalence.	Transformation Presentation *Note:* The transformation presentation is always done with the child watching, but without any comment from the experimenter.
Number (5 to 7 years of age)	Two identical rows of objects are aligned. 	One row is lengthened. 
	Q: Are there the same number of _____ (name of objects) in each row, or does one row have more _____? **A:** A *preconserving* child says the longer row has more _____. A *conserving* child says both have the same number.	
Continuous quantities—liquid (6 to 8 years of age)	Two identical glasses contain the same amount of colored water. 	One glass remains the same; water from the other glass is poured into a third glass with a smaller (or larger) diameter. 
	Q: Is there the same amount of water in both glasses, or does one glass have more water than the other? **A:** A *preconserving* child will say, "No." Usually, the child points to the glass with the water coming up higher as having more water. A *conserving* child will say, "Both are the same."	
Mass or matter—clay (6 to 8 years of age)	Two identical balls are formed out of clay. 	One ball is kept the same; the other ball is elongated.
	Q: Do the two balls have the same amount of clay, or does one ball of clay have more than the other? **A:** A *preconserving* child will say, "No." Usually, the child points to the elongated piece as having more clay. A *conserving* child will say, "Both are the same."	
Length (6 to 8 years of age)	Two rods are aligned. 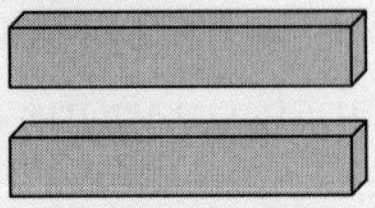	One rod is moved to the right. 
	Q: Are the rods the same length, or is one rod longer than the other? **A:** A *preconserving* child will say, "This one is longer because it sticks out." A *conserving* child will say, "Both are the same."	

(Continued)

Figure 18.5 *(Continued)*

Type of Conservation	Initial Presentation	Transformation Presentation
Area (7 to 9 years of age)	Two identical sheets of cardboard or wood have one-inch cube blocks. 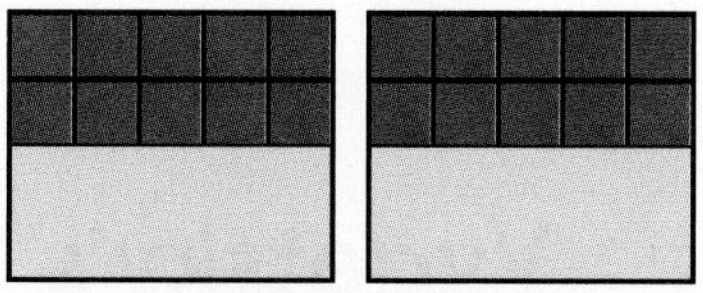	One board of blocks remains the same; the other board has the blocks scattered. 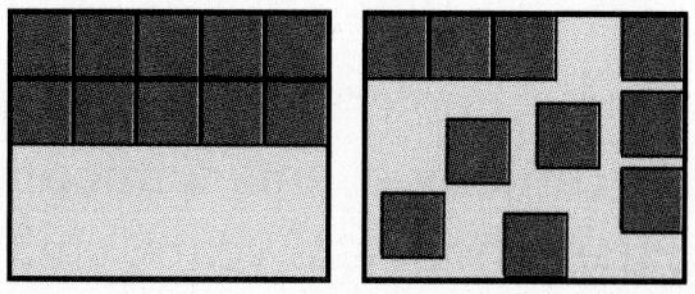
	Q: Do both boards have the same amount of open space, or does one board have more open space than the other? **A:** A *preconserving* child will say, "This one has more space." Usually, the child points to the board on which the blocks remain clustered. A *conserving* child will say, "Both have the same amount of open space."	
Weight (8 to 10 years of age)	Two sets of three blocks are placed in horizontally aligned rows. 	One set of blocks remains in horizontal position; the other set is stacked vertically. 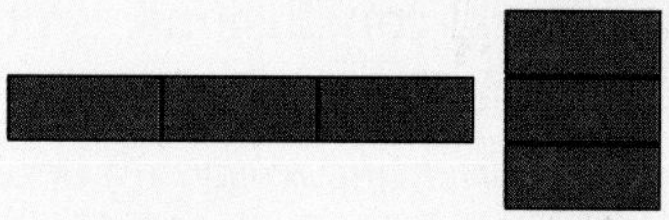
	Q: Do the sets of blocks weigh the same, or does one set of blocks weigh more? **A:** A *preconserving* child will say, "This one weighs more." Usually, the child points to the vertical arrangement. A *conserving* child will say, "Both weigh the same."	
Volume (10 to 14 years of age)	Two identical glasses are filled with the same amount of water. Two identical balls of clay are dropped into the glasses. 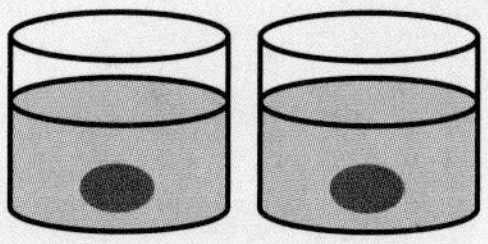	One glass with clay remains untouched; the clay in the other glass is removed, flattened, and laid by the second glass. 
	Q: Will the two pieces of clay displace the same amount of water, or will one displace more water? **A:** A *preconserving* child will say, "One will displace more water." Usually, the child points to the flattened clay. A *conserving* child will say, "The water displacement will be the same."	

Note: Piaget indicated the age in which 75 percent of children in his experiments could conserve and justify their answers. An age range is now given by more recent researchers. Justification of conservation can be done in one of three ways: (1) *Identity*—nothing is added or taken away; therefore, it is identical. (2) *Reversibility*—the alignment or shape of objects can be restored. (3) *Compensation*—one dimension of an object makes up (compensates) for another dimension (longer on one end, but shorter on the other; clay spreads out when flat, but is thinner than the ball).

Reversibility also means knowing that one change, such as in height, can lead to another change, such as in width. Consider the example of the clay. The school-age child knows that the flattened clay will most likely have a larger diameter than the round ball of clay.

To help children understand intellectual reversals, adults can first expose them to physical reversals, which can be observed and experienced

(**Figure 18.6**). After physical reversals are "mastered," adults can ask children to form a mental image of what happens during reversibility. Finally, children should understand the principle. (The principle can be stated in one of three ways as shown in the "Note" at the bottom of Figure 18.5.)

Using Deductive and Inductive Reasoning

As preschoolers, children use *transductive reasoning* (linking events without using logic), but during the school-age years, children graduate to using *deductive reasoning* and then *inductive reasoning*. **Deductive reasoning** is reasoning from the general to the specific. For example, if a child is presented with the general statement that all fish live in water, and if the child knows that guppies are fish, then the child can use deductive reasoning to conclude that guppies live in water.

Inductive reasoning, reasoning from specific facts to general conclusions, is often used by children 11 years of age and older. Inductive reasoning is also called *scientific reasoning* because it is the form of logic commonly used by scientists. Children who use inductive reasoning can weigh several ideas, test them, and then draw a conclusion. For example, a child who knows that water turns to ice when exposed to cold temperatures might use inductive reasoning to conclude that cold temperatures will also transform other liquids. To test this hypothesis, the child might put water and other fluids, such as juice, milk, and soft drinks, into the freezer. After weighing and testing several ideas, the child concludes that exposure to cold temperatures changes liquids into solids.

Vygotsky's Sociocultural Theory

While Piaget concluded that children's intellectual development was primarily due to brain development (*cognitive stage*), Vygotsky saw intellectual development as less dependent on the brain and more dependent on a child's *ZPD* (*zone of proximal development*). Vygotsky argued that children always learn best when their minds are "stretched" within their ZPDs (**Figure 18.7**). A child has different ZPDs depending on the intellectual (academic) area, such as math, language, and the arts.

Vygotsky also believed that collaboration among peers and between adults and children had a

Figure 18.6 An example of a physical reversal might be letting a child pour water or sand from one container into a different container and back again. *What are some other physical reversals that a child can perform?*

major impact on learning. Like Piaget, Vygotsky believed that children learn by doing, but he also thought that children learn by talking and working with others. He felt it was important for children to persist at tasks until they could perform them.

Piaget felt that language *reflected* learning. On the other hand, Vygotsky saw language *as a way of* learning. For example, children understand the process of learning through verbal interactions, such as explaining what they know and questioning others to clarify. During interactions, children also learn the needed tools and most effective ways to perform tasks. Vygotsky felt that after learning how to do a task, using silent words was important to performing the task independently.

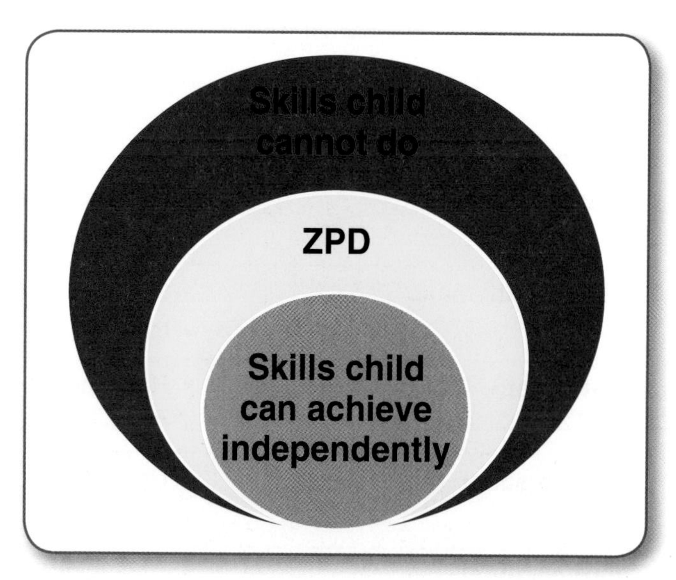

Figure 18.7 The ZPD is the difference between what a child can do independently and what he or she can do with guidance. *How can adults plan activities that "stretch" children's minds without going beyond their ZPDs?*

Gardner's Theory of Multiple Intelligences

As children approach middle childhood, it becomes very evident that they vary in their abilities to reason and learn new concepts. A person's intellectual competence is usually called *intelligence*. For many years, researchers thought of intelligence as a general capacity or trait and called the measurement of this trait a person's *intelligence quotient* (IQ). These researchers believed that if a person had a high level of intellectual competence (measured as a high IQ), then his or her cognitive behaviors would be outstanding in all areas. In like manner, people with a low level of competence would not achieve to a high extent in most areas of intellectual performance.

The cognitive theories of Piaget and Vygotsky, as well as other research findings, show that the intellect reflects the diverse and complex skills children develop through their interactions within their natural and social worlds. Thus, more recently, psychologists have come to believe that intelligence consists of separate abilities not a general overall trait. Harold Gardner goes a step further and sees the intellect as separate, distinct "intelligences."

The many ways that children learn are reflected in Harold Gardner's *theory of multiple intelligences*. **Multiple intelligences** are intellectual abilities that contribute to overall intelligence. The types of intelligences Gardner proposed are listed in **Figure 18.8**. All children use all of these intelligences to learn, but use some to a greater extent than others.

Figure 18.8 Gardner's Multiple Intelligences

Type of Multiple Intelligence	Ability to...
Verbal/Linguistic	• Understand communication • Communicate
Logical/Mathematical	• Understand principles of cause and effect • Understand math principles
Bodily/Kinesthetic	• Control and coordinate one's body to achieve goals • Demonstrate both gross- and fine-motor control and coordination

(Continued)

Figure 18.8 *(Continued)*

Type of Multiple Intelligence	Ability to...
Visual/Spatial	• "See" space in one's mind • Convey visual and spatial ideas through the visual arts
Musical/Rhythmic	• Recognize and appreciate tones and rhythmic patterns • Convey tone and rhythm in performing and composing
Naturalist	• Recognize and categorize living and nonliving things in nature • Show sensitivity to features of the natural world
Interpersonal	• Understand motivations and intentions of others and act with empathy • Lead or work with others to achieve goals on behalf of others
Intrapersonal	• Understand one's self, especially one's motivations and emotions • Recognize one's strengths and abilities to accomplish goals
Existential	• Pose questions about beliefs and values • Cause people to think about ethical issues

School learning usually reinforces verbal/linguistic and logical/mathematical intelligences. As a result, school-age children may not have the opportunities to exercise other intelligences. As much as possible, adults should ensure that school-age children learn using the intelligences in which they excel, as well as the intelligences in which they feel challenged (**Figure 18.9**).

Figure 18.9 It is important for school-age children to practice all of their intelligences, not just the intelligences that are measured and encouraged in school. *What types of intelligence are involved in children playing outside?*

Lesson 18.1 Review and Assessment

1. Explain how wiring and pruning in the prefrontal cortex affect school-age children's thinking and decision-making skills.
2. List three specific skills that help school-age children access their explicit and implicit memories.
3. Explain how children progress from the concrete operational stage to the formal operational stage.
4. Choose one obstacle to logical thought and describe how children overcome this obstacle during the school-age years.
5. Summarize Vygotsky's ideas about school-age children's learning.
6. Describe the difference between Piaget's and Vygotsky's ideas about the role of language in learning.
7. List the different intelligences that make up Gardner's theory of multiple intelligences.
8. **Critical thinking.** Why would overdevelopment in the brain's *nucleus accumbens* lead to poor decision-making skills? Write your answer as if you were explaining to an older school-age child.

What School-Age Children Learn

Lesson 18.2

Objectives

After studying this lesson, you will be able to

- explain the differences among *physical knowledge concepts, logical thinking concepts*, and *culture-specific knowledge* and name one example of each.
- summarize school-age children's abilities to use logical thinking concepts, such as classifying; ordering by attributes; understanding cause and effect; applying spatial concepts; using number concepts; and noting distance, time, and speed.
- chart school-age children's progress in learning articulation, expanding vocabularies, and learning grammar.
- describe children's reading abilities during the school-age years.
- identify intellectual developmental milestones school-age children might achieve.

Key Terms

code-switch
culture-specific knowledge
hierarchical classification

Academic Terms

alphabetize
extraneous
subdivided
syntax

Reading and Writing Activity

Review the headings in this lesson and use them to create an outline for taking notes during reading and class discussion. Under each heading, list any key or academic terms. Finally, write two questions you expect to be answered from reading this lesson.

Graphic Organizer

Using the chart you created for the reading and writing activity, organize your notes by the headings in this lesson. Draw a star beside any words or concepts you do not yet understand.

Concept Learning
Understanding Physical Knowledge
Understanding Logical Thinking Concepts ★

School-age children's logical brains enable them to develop and understand many more advanced concepts than those learned in the preschool years. During the school-age years, children understand physical knowledge, use logical thinking concepts, and acquire culture-specific knowledge. School-age children's communication skills improve as they articulate more clearly, expand their vocabularies, and use correct grammar. Their reading skills also improve. During the school-age years, children achieve a number of significant intellectual developmental milestones.

Concept Learning

As their brains mature and school-age children become more capable of logical thought, they develop and understand many new concepts. The major areas of concept learning for school-age children include understanding physical knowledge, using logical thinking concepts, and acquiring culture-specific knowledge.

Understanding Physical Knowledge

Physical knowledge involves learning about attributes of objects and what happens to objects when they are acted upon. Young children acquire physical knowledge by acting upon objects and observing what happens. By the school-age years, children begin to understand what scientists have observed, such as gravity, force of wind, and weather. In short, *physical knowledge* is any knowledge of the physical world that is gained through experimentation with objects and includes the academic subjects of chemistry, physics, and astronomy.

During the school-age years, physical knowledge concepts mature as children do more in-depth exploring of their worlds. For example, by nine years of age, children use their eyes or fingertips to trace outlines of objects instead of just glancing at them quickly. This more thorough examination helps children note details in objects.

As they examine objects, children learn what information to act upon and what information to ignore. For example, if a school-age child is tasked with identifying geometric shapes, he or she will ignore the colors of the shapes. Children also learn to correctly pair visual and auditory stimuli, such as letters with their sounds (**Figure 18.10**). Improved memories help children pay attention to important attributes and recall the names of attributes.

Using Logical Thinking Concepts

During the preschool years, children began to grasp *logical thinking concepts*, which are concepts that are not experienced through the senses, but are understood intellectually. These concepts were immature in preschool children due to their reliance on physical observation. Due to the development of their logical brains, however, school-age children better understand a number of logical thinking concepts. These concepts include classifying objects; ordering by attributes; understanding cause and effect; applying spatial concepts; using number concepts; and noting distance, time, and speed.

Classifying Objects

Classifying is part of the reasoning process, and is a mentally economical way of thinking. Once a new phenomenon is catalogued as part of a particular class about which a person has some

Figure 18.10 Another way children can learn to correctly pair visual and auditory stimuli is by associating written music notes with their pitches. ***What other cognitive advances might make school-age children better able to read sheet music?***

knowledge, the new phenomenon can be dealt with quickly. For example, suppose your biology teacher said, "Today, we are going to talk about a mallard duck." Although you may not have seen a mallard, once the word *duck* is said, you already know lots of information about a mallard.

Classification is the grouping of objects into a class and its complement. While preschool children struggled to classify by one stable attribute, such as color or shape, school-age children classify accurately. For example, a school-age child can focus on one attribute and include all objects that contain the attribute for that class. By middle childhood, children fully understand the class and the complement.

School-age children also learn a new classification, called *hierarchical* (HY-uh-RAHR-kuh-kul) *classification*. **Hierarchical classification** is a type of classification in which select classes may contain other classes, or *subclasses*. For example, a large class of *animals* can be divided into subclasses, such as *birds* and *fish*. Groups of *birds* and *fish* can be **subdivided** (divided into smaller parts) as well. School-age children also understand the reverse; that is, subclasses can be combined to form larger classes.

Ordering by Attributes

As preschoolers, children learned to *seriate* (arrange objects in order by the increasing or decreasing magnitude of one of the object's attributes). By the school-age years, children are able to illustrate relationships among objects by putting them in order according to a variety of attributes. Ordering attributes might include those that can be seen (color, shape, size), heard (pitch, loudness), or felt (texture and temperature). Other attributes involve time or the order of events. School-age children can order objects by even the smallest differences and use ordering in their daily lives, such as learning to read calendars, write lists, and **alphabetize** (put in alphabetical order).

Understanding Cause and Effect

School-age children begin to comprehend and resolve many of the cause-effect relationships that they could not grasp during the preschool years (**Figure 18.11**). As children become less egocentric, they understand that humans do not always cause natural happenings and begin to adopt a more scientific approach to their thinking.

Figure 18.11 School-age children's knowledge of cause and effect enables them to understand more about their world, including the environment and natural events. *Which, if any, cause-and-effect relationships were children able to understand during the preschool years?*

The preschool belief that nonliving objects have lifelike qualities (called *animism*) is surrendered in favor of scientific answers. Some school-age children may still assign lifelike qualities to especially powerful aspects of nature (the sun and stars, oceans, mountains), but most school-age children understand that inanimate objects are not living. School-age children's understandings of cause and effect help them learn facts about the natural world.

Applying Spatial Concepts

School-age children have many correct ideas about spatial relationships. They can identify whether objects are *open* or *closed* and *far* or *near*. They also understand relationships between two or more objects. School-age children can note and apply spatial concepts, such as *close to*, *connected*, *behind*, *in front of*, *above*, *below*, *left*, or *right*. School-age children know that objects, such as flying jets, do not get smaller even though they appear so as they move farther away.

Using Number Concepts

During the late preschool and early school-age years, children learn basic concepts about numbers. They start to comprehend number concepts, such as *greater than*, *less than*, *equal to*, and others. As they begin to learn math in school, children use the number concepts they learned during the late preschool years and early middle childhood (**Figure 18.12**). School-age children learn that groups are changed in number if more objects are brought into the group (*added*). They also learn that groups change in number if objects are taken away from the group (*subtracted*). Before the end of middle childhood, children can multiply and divide; understand the concept of measurement; begin to understand the relationships among fractions, decimals, and percentages; develop the ability to work word problems; and can estimate quantities.

Noting Distance, Time, and Speed

Children younger than eight years of age typically have difficulty grasping distance, time, and speed concepts, especially pertaining to the ways these concepts relate. Time and distance are often confused during the school-age years. For example, a young school-age child might say that walking some place is *far*, but that running makes it *near*. Except for understanding more complex topics regarding time and distance, such as different time zones and very great distances (solar system distances), many older school-age children develop rather accurate concepts of time and distance.

School-age children generally learn clock time and calendar time in the first or second grade. They do not note calendar time well, however, until 10 or 11 years of age. The timing of historical events can be difficult for children to grasp even into the teen years. Stories written for children often reflect childlike understandings of time. As children grow older, their stories graduate from starting with "once upon a time" to giving hints about seasons or years. By the late school-age and teen years, stories mention exact time periods.

Figure 18.12 School-age children can apply the number concepts they learned during the late preschool years to simple math equations like addition and subtraction. *How do math problems progress in difficulty throughout the school-age years?*

Acquiring Culture-Specific Knowledge

As children interact within their physical world, they develop physical knowledge concepts and logical knowledge concepts. These concepts are universal. For example, facts about gravity and three plus two equals five are the same in all cultures. One other type of knowledge is not universal, but culture-specific. **Culture-specific knowledge** is culturally relevant knowledge that one learns by being told or shown. A person does not learn culture-specific knowledge by experimenting within his or her physical world. Piaget referred to culture-specific knowledge as *social knowledge*. Language and literacy lessons, including vocabulary, articulation, and grammar, are generally culture-specific knowledge. History concepts, literature, and the arts are also considered culture-specific knowledge.

A culture's educational system often determines what culture-specific knowledge children must learn. Often, this knowledge changes as cultural needs change. For example, lessons in cursive writing have been replaced by keyboarding lessons in some schools. In like manner, many schools have replaced lessons about telling time using analog clocks with digital clocks.

Focus on

Social Studies

The Impact of Culture-Specific Knowledge

Culture is a way of life within a group. With culture comes a collection of culture-specific knowledge that children gain over many years. Through this knowledge, children develop a *cultural lens*, which is a perspective through which they view the world. One example of culture-specific knowledge is history. As children learn their culture's history in school, they learn a distinct outlook on their culture, on other cultures, and on the world. Culture-specific knowledge also affects children's understanding of other subject areas and events. Some of these affected areas include

- ***Reasoning.*** Culture-specific knowledge affects which types of reasoning children value. Many European cultures believe that information acquired through scientific reasoning is most valid. Other cultures, such as some African cultures, prefer *affective* (feeling-based) ways of knowing.
- ***Communication.*** Culture-specific knowledge also affects which types of communication children prefer. Some cultures (especially German- and English-speaking cultures) use explicit and specific communication. Other cultures teach knowledge that will help children "read between the lines."
- ***Relationships.*** Children's approaches to relationships are also affected by the culture-specific knowledge they learn. Some cultures prefer establishing relationships before performing tasks while other cultures develop relationships as they work. Culture-specific knowledge will typically teach American children to handle conflicts directly. Other cultures will promote quiet and indirect ways of resolving conflict.

In small groups, discuss what subject areas of knowledge affect these habits and behaviors. Are there any school subject areas that are not culture-specific? Explain why or why not.

Communicating

Around six or seven years of age, children's speech becomes more social. School-age children begin to see language as a way of communicating and want to talk with friends and adults. They make great strides in learning articulation, expanding vocabularies, and learning grammar. By the beginning of the school-age years, children learn the basic concepts involved in learning how to read, such as associating letters with sounds. By the fourth grade, children have mastered many concepts about learning how to read. They begin to read to learn about social studies concepts, science concepts, and literature.

Learning Articulation

By eight years of age, most children have mastered the articulation of all sounds in their spoken language. Children who begin learning a second language as toddlers are often proficient in both languages by the school-age years. Children with articulation problems at the end of the preschool years, however, often continue to have speech problems in the school-age years. These speech problems are commonly related to reading problems because children need to articulate sounds to decode the sounds of letters, a skill that is needed for reading and spelling.

Focus on

Speech

Bilingualism

Older school-age children trying to learn a second language may have more difficulty articulating the sounds of the new language than younger children learning the same language. Learning language during early childhood allows the child to use a natural approach to language learning. The child will listen to and understand the language, speak it, and then become symbol-literate in interactive ways (such as through reading and writing). After about seven years of age, most children learn a new language through a more direct-instruction approach instead of a natural approach to language learning.

Before seven years of age, two or more languages may use the same location in the brain. After seven years of age, new locations are needed for each language. The window of opportunity for language learning begins in infancy and starts to close in the late school-age years (around 10 years of age). The sensitive periods for language learning close in this order: articulation, grammar, and then vocabulary. Despite this, the window of opportunity for language learning never completely closes. Many adults may also achieve almost total mastery of new languages.

Expanding Vocabularies

Children's active vocabularies continue to expand in middle childhood. School-age children give more exact definitions than younger children do. If asked to define the word *orange*, a preschool child may say, "You eat it." A school-age child would give a more precise definition, such as, "It is a color or a fruit." Tests in school often ask school-age children to define words. Reading, spelling, and writing all help school-age children's vocabularies grow.

Middle childhood is also an age when children have fun with words. School-age children enjoy using the words they know to perform word rhymes, raps, and chants (**Figure 18.13**). They also have fun telling jokes, riddles, and simple puns. As their vocabularies continue to expand, children often engage in more complex word play, such as doing crossword puzzles or word jumbles. They also enjoy board games involving words, such as Scrabble®.

Learning Grammar

School-age children refine their understandings of **syntax** (sentence structure). Until nine years of age, children are often confused by **extraneous** (ek-STRAY-nee-us), nonessential, information in a sentence. For example, in the sentence "The sun, which is almost 93 million miles from Earth, contains gases that are converted into energy for heat and

Figure 18.13 School-age children often engage in clapping word games with friends. *What word or rhyme games did you like to play at this age?*

light on Earth," the distance between the sun and the Earth might be considered extraneous information. Sentences in the passive voice are also difficult for children younger than nine or 10 years of age. A sentence in the passive voice might read, "Pete was seen by Bill at the mall." If rewritten into the active voice, the same sentence would read, "Bill saw Pete at the mall."

Although school-age children understand the grammar of different cultural groups who speak their basic language, they often use their own set of grammar rules to make plurals, use pronouns, and show tense. These rules may or may not be those of standard grammar. School-age children speak and write the grammar they hear, and some children may **code-switch** (change their usage of grammar and even vocabulary when communicating with different cultural and age groups). If children have not learned standard grammar by the school-age years, using standard grammar after this age will require breaking incorrect grammar habits and relearning standard grammar.

Reading in the School-Age Years

Human brains do not have a specialized location for reading. Rather, the same area of the brain that is used for recognizing objects is also used to read. Young children begin to read by forming mental pictures of the words they see in their environments. They treat letters as three-dimensional objects, so school-age children often see letters, such as *b, d, g,* and *p*, as the same.

Because there are too many words for children to mentally map, children will begin to associate letters with sounds; called *grapheme-phoneme* (graf-EEM FOH-neem) *associations*. This may become difficult when the letter-to-sound relationships are not consistent, such as in the words *rain* and *rein*. Beginning readers must see each letter and then think the sound. Experienced readers begin to process several letters at once. During the school-age years, children become more adept at this and are better able to read quickly and accurately.

Intellectual Developmental Milestones

School-age children are better able to grasp concepts and communication. Their logical brains can now use logical thinking concepts, and they begin to perceive language as a social tool. While school-age children are more capable of reasoning, their prefrontal cortexes are still wiring, which may lead to poor decision-making skills. **Figure 18.14** lists some intellectual developmental milestones for school-age children.

Lesson 18.2 Review and Assessment 

1. Explain why school-age children are able to understand physical knowledge more accurately than earlier in their development.
2. Choose one logical thinking concept and explain how learning of this concept matures during the school-age years.
3. What is *culture-specific knowledge* and how does it become important during the school-age years?
4. Summarize how communicating becomes more important for children during the school-age years.
5. What does it mean for children to *code-switch*?
6. Describe the role of mental mapping in children learning to read.
7. Choose one age during the school-age years and give three examples of intellectual developmental milestones a typical child of this age might achieve.
8. **Critical thinking.** Choose one logical thinking concept and make inferences about how a school-age child's learning of this concept changes the way the child sees the world.

Figure 18.14 School-Age Intellectual Milestones

Six to seven years

- Sits and pays attention for about 15-20 minutes at a time.
- Is eager to learn.
- Begins to rely on reason, rather than perception, in problem solving.
- Tells and retells stories in logical order.
- Sees others' points of view.
- Begins to note several aspects of a situation at one time.
- Begins to note transformations; to understand reversibility; and to conserve numbers, continuous quantities, liquid, mass, and length.
- Wants detailed explanations for some complex "why" and "how" questions.
- Begins to read, write (with phonetic spellings, such as *kat* for *cat*), and do some arithmetic.
- Knows day segments and reads clock and calendar time.
- Uses descriptive phrases in talking.
- Expresses needs by "begging."
- Is confused by extraneous information, complex sentence construction (including passive voice), and implied word meanings.
- Appreciates humor in language.
- Locates letters, numbers, and special keys on the computer keyboard; begins learning a word processing program; uses subject-specific software programs to reinforce school subjects.

Eight to nine years

- Sits and pays attention for about 45 minutes at a time.
- Remembers large amounts of information.
- Uses oral language to inform, persuade, and entertain.
- Likes intellectual competition.
- Knows the days of the week, months of the year, and day's date.

Eight to nine years *(Continued)*

- Conserves area.
- Draws three-dimensional figures.
- Knows left and right.
- Describes objects in detail.
- Has a vocabulary over 5,000 words.
- Is a more proficient reader; enjoys recreational reading.
- Uses meaning clues in reading (titles, pictures).
- Knows key elements of stories (characters, plots, main ideas).
- Writes legibly and organizes writing.
- Becomes more advanced in keyboarding and using word processing programs; uses computer peripherals (printers and scanners); uses more sophisticated creativity programs to make slide shows and animations; uses search engines on the Internet to locate information for school assignments; uses skills to do school assignments.

Ten to twelve years

- Likes cooperative (group) learning projects in school and youth groups.
- Applies math and science concepts to daily activities.
- Conserves weight and volume.
- Expresses needs and verbally tries to justify needs.
- Has a vocabulary of 7,200 words.
- Reads for information and recreation.
- Can keep informational details straight.
- Writes notes and letters.
- Links information across curriculums.
- Understands that words can have multiple meanings.
- Paraphrases and summarizes content.
- Compares and contrasts stories.
- Has executive functions.
- Searches for needed information (in books and on the Internet).
- Develops plans to meet goals.
- Writes in different genres (factual essays, creative stories, poems).
- Edits writing for grammar, mechanics, and spelling.
- Learns computer-use ethics; uses digital cameras; begins to use spreadsheets and database software; learns basics of multimedia software programs; uses computers for school assignments, hobbies, and socializing; uses other types of digital equipment.

Lesson 18.3 Meeting School-Age Children's Intellectual Needs

Key Terms

after-school programs
enrichment activities
filtering program
flipped classroom
middle school
primary school
special lessons and activities

Academic Terms

belabor
grapple
mitigate
underutilized
upheaval

Objectives

After studying this lesson, you will be able to

- explain how parents can prepare their children for both primary and middle schools.
- describe three ways adults can support their children in school.
- give examples of ways in which parents can provide enrichment activities for school-age children.
- determine criteria adults and children can consider when making decisions about participating in special lessons and activities.
- assess how adults can guide children's electronic media use during the school-age years.

Reading and Writing Activity

Read this lesson's title and tell a classmate what you have experienced or already know about meeting school-age children's intellectual needs. Are intellectual needs during the school-age years met in the same way they were earlier in children's development? Why or why not? Write a paragraph describing what you would like to know about this topic. After reading, write two facts you learned from the lesson.

Graphic Organizer

Draw two columns, one labeled *Meeting Children's Intellectual Needs in School* and the other labeled *Meeting Children's Intellectual Needs Outside of School*. As you read, classify your notes into one of these two categories. If any notes do not fall into a category, write them below your chart.

Meeting Children's Intellectual Needs in School	Meeting Children's Intellectual Needs Outside of School

As school-age children mature and their brains become more able to grasp intellectual concepts and activities, it is important that their intellectual needs are met. The majority of a child's intellectual needs will be met *in school* once this stage begins. The meeting of intellectual needs in schools, however, does not **mitigate** (lessen) the importance of parents' efforts to meet their children's needs. In fact, children only spend about 20 percent of their total hours each day in school. Thus, the home is also an important learning environment.

During the school-age years, parents can meet children's intellectual needs by preparing their children for school, supporting them in school, planning activities for children to learn outside of school, and guiding children's media use. Parents' interests in what their children learn affect children's achievement.

Preparing Children for School

After completing preschool, school-age children are not automatically prepared to enter school and learn in this new, structured environment. The start of school may be exciting for some children and scary for others. No matter a child's feelings toward school or the grade a child is starting, entering school is a new developmental task for children. School-age children must interact with new people—both children and adults. They must process new concepts and skills and adjust to a different and maybe uncomfortable daily structure (**Figure 18.15**). Parents can help meet school-age children's intellectual needs by

- helping children make the transition from home to school
- making the new structures of school as enjoyable as possible

How a parent helps his or her child prepare for school may depend on what level of schooling the child is entering. School-age children experience the most **upheaval** (potentially upsetting change) when they enter primary school and when they enter middle school.

Figure 18.15 When children start school, stress may accompany the new hours and routines. ***How can parents and caregivers help a child adjust to the start of school?***

Preparing Children for Primary School

After the preschool years, young school-age children enter **primary school** (also called *elementary school*), which usually includes the elementary grades first through fifth or sixth and sometimes kindergarten. (The primary school should not be confused with what early childhood educators call the *primary grades*, kindergarten or first grade through third grades.) Many young school-age children express stress and anxiety about school. Unlike preschool relationships, school relationships are more teacher directed. Children sit, line up, work, eat, and share with other children per their teacher's instructions. School means getting along with other children for many hours.

Children who are adaptable and have had many interactions with other children usually find it easier to adjust. **Figure 18.16** lists ways that adults can help young school-age children transition to primary school. If the first days go well, children look forward to school. Negative experiences, however, may lead to children wanting to avoid school and stay home.

Preparing Children for Middle School

Toward the end of the school-age years, children often enter *middle school*. **Middle school** is school

Figure 18.16 Helping Children Transition to Primary School

- Read and encourage children to read books about starting school. If possible, visit the school and meet the teacher prior to the first day.
- Make transportation plans clear to children. Younger children who walk or take a bus need instructions and practice. Adults or older children should be nearby, and children should be reminded not to talk to or go with strangers. Children should know their full names, as well as parents' names, addresses, and phone numbers.
- Help children view school attendance as a natural course of events. Tell children that "everyone goes to school." Adults can plan a normal routine for the first few days of school. Taking too many photos, sounding anxious, getting children ready too early or too late, or serving a special breakfast may make children even more anxious.
- Say good-byes at the bus stop, on the schoolyard, or at the classroom door. These good-byes should be warm, but not clingy. Teary-eyed children often regain control soon after parents are out of sight.
- Meet the bus or pick up children on time. Being late adds stress to a new beginning.
- Show a strong interest in children's reports about their school days.

for children approaching the teen years and often includes children in the fifth or sixth through eighth or ninth grades. Middle school age and grade ranges depend on the school's location and population. Upon entering middle school, children transition from being the most advanced children in their primary school to being the least advanced children in their middle school. Unlike primary schools, middle schools are often large; and children may have six or more teachers and have to walk between classes in crowded halls. Children's friends from primary school may not be in the same classes, and children are more likely to be bullied at this age. **Figure 18.17** lists ways adults can help older school-age children make smooth transitions to middle school.

Supporting Children in School

School-age children need daily encouragement and help. Adults can meet children's intellectual needs by working with and helping them with their schoolwork. Help is not effective if given only after the teacher shares negative reports with parents. Parents should take active roles in supporting their children at school and work as a team with

Figure 18.17 Helping Children Transition to Middle School

- Visit the school with the child beforehand so the child will know his or her way around the campus.
- Attend orientation meetings.
- Purchase the correct supplies and uniforms. If possible, purchase school-spirit items to make the child feel more a part of the school.
- Adjust home routines, such as bedtime, to work with the new school schedule.
- Explain to the child that each teacher will have different expectations and classroom policies. The child will need a planner for writing assignments and testing dates.
- Encourage the child to attend clubs for making friends.
- Have honest talks with the child about teasing and bullying behaviors. Tell the child what he or she should do if bullied.
- If the child has problems adjusting, ask open-ended questions. Suggest options, but try to help the child make decisions about handling these problems.

teachers to give their children the best possible education. Parents can support their children in school by reinforcing school tasks, strengthening executive functions, and being a school advocate.

Reinforcing School Tasks

Parents can help meet children's intellectual needs by reinforcing the tasks their children learn in school. To do this, parents can ensure that children complete any activities or homework assignments the school sends home with them. Parents should supervise school-age children's homework. In primary school, homework is most often assigned to reinforce skills learned in the classroom. Some classrooms use a **flipped classroom** mode of teaching in which children learn concepts and facts by reading their textbooks and watching videos at home, and then do homework-type assignments while at school.

While adults can help children with their homework, they should not do it for them. Doing children's homework, whether in a traditional or a flipped classroom, causes children to rely on adults to solve their tasks and problems. It also prevents children from getting needed practice and taking responsibility for learning. If the homework assigned seems too difficult, parents may want to talk to their children's teachers. Some positive ways parents can help children with their homework are shown in **Figure 18.18**. Children who are younger or who have weak executive functions will need more supervision. By the teen years, parents typically do not have to supervise homework on a day-by-day basis.

Figure 18.18 Supervising School-Age Children's Homework

- Set up a quiet work area without distractions. Supplies should be available at the work area.
- Meet any of the child's needs, such as a nutritious snack, before beginning work.
- Use the child's planner to go through daily assignments. Consult the calendar for progress made on long-term assignments. Help the child prioritize before beginning work on the assignments. The child needs to learn to do more difficult tasks first.
- Monitor the child's work.
- Help the child with any content needing practice, such as learning spelling words, memorizing, and reviewing for tests.
- Explain and provide strategies for problem-solving assignments or projects. Teach the child how to locate resources for papers.
- Help the child check for the completion of the assignment.
- Do not correct assignments, but encourage the child to check and self-correct. Have the child pack the assignment in a binder or backpack.

Strengthening Executive Functions

By nine years of age, children should be able to use executive functions. *Executive functions (EFs)* are skills that people use to manage themselves and their resources to achieve goals. The executive functions are necessary for success in life and school. The most commonly identified executive functions are working memory (also called *short-term memory*), cognitive flexibility (the ability to adjust to changing demands), and inhibition (the ability to filter thoughts and feelings). Weak executive functions, especially in older school-age children, often indicate learning problems or behavioral disorders.

School-age children with weak executive functions are easy to identify. These children tend to be disorganized and take a very long time to do simple tasks. They often fail to record assignments, lose papers and notes, procrastinate, and **belabor** (drag out for too long) the decision-making process in writing a paper or doing a project. Other signs of weak executive functions include a lack of focus and problems managing frustrations.

Parents of children with weak executive functions need to do more to help a child through home routines and school assignments. **Figure 18.19** lists ways that parents can help these children. In addition to these suggestions, parents should seek professional help for their children through consultation with a pediatrician or school counselor.

Being a School Advocate

When parents become involved in their children's schools and think of themselves as teammates to the school's administrators and teachers, children do better in almost every way. Parents who are school advocates

- make an effort to attend orientation meetings and parent-teacher conferences
- respond to teacher communications
- approach teachers or counselors with any concerns
- participate in follow-up communication if needed
- volunteer in schools
- attend school events when their children are involved

Adult involvements in these activities help children feel more at-home during school and feel more protected. Knowing their parents are involved in the primary meeting of their intellectual needs often increases the achievement of students.

Meeting Intellectual Needs Outside of School

Children's intellectual needs are primarily met through schools during the school-age years. Adults can plan many activities to help school-age children learn in their school environments, but the home is also an important place for meeting school-age children's intellectual needs. Parents can meet children's needs in the home by providing enrichment activities and special lessons and activities.

Focus on Careers

School Counselor

School counselors work with students to help them set academic and career goals and develop a plan to meet these goals. They counsel students individually and in groups depending on their needs. They also provide guidance to help students deal with social and behavioral problems. School counselors work jointly with other teachers and parents to help students succeed.

Career cluster: Education and training.

Education: Educational requirements include a master's degree and state-issued credential.

Job outlook: Future employment opportunities for school counselors are expected to grow as fast as the average for all occupations.

To learn more about a career as a school counselor, visit the United States Department of Labor's *Occupational Outlook Handbook* website. You will also be able to compare the job responsibilities, educational requirements, job outlook, and average pay of school counselors with similar occupations.

Figure 18.19 Guiding School-Age Children with Weak Executive Functions

Home routines

- Develop consistent rituals and routines.
- Never try multitasking. Focus on one task at a time.
- Reduce distractions.
- Make checklists with pictures or words. Include each step for morning and evening routines, household tasks, and homework.
- Reduce steps in the morning routine by doing some tasks at night, such as laying out clothes and packing a backpack for the next day.

Homework routines

- Organize work space with supplies. Some children need separate work areas for different activities. Minimize clutter and clean and organize space regularly.
- Make a general checklist for different types of assignments, such as "get pencil and paper," "put name on paper," and so on.
- Use a planner to look over all assignments.
- Prioritize assignments and make a schedule. Break long assignments into "chunks" with time frames for each "chunk."
- Scan directions for each assignment and repeat directions before beginning the task.
- Help children learn how to study.
  - Show children how to use text features, such as headings, words in bold, and figures.
  - Sequence tasks, such as alphabetizing words before finding meanings in a glossary or dictionary.
  - Explain that for multiple-choice tests one must study details, but for essay tests one must "tell the story."
  - Explain that in social studies one looks for main ideas, but in math one works sample problems.
- Help children remember by giving other examples of a concept, summarizing, or applying lessons.
- Explain the rationale for learning a concept or skill. Children with weak executive functions spend lots of time weighing the worth of a lesson versus the effort to learn it.
- Use a pocket folder for storing and transporting school materials.

Providing Enrichment Activities

Intellectual development includes more than the academic subjects taught in schools. It also includes children's reasoning, hobbies, and the multiple intelligences outlined in Gardner's theory of multiple intelligences. Schools tend to emphasize verbal/linguistic and logical/mathematical intelligences. It is important, however, that children practice their strongest intelligences and engage in all intelligences to some degree. Adults can help their children develop these intelligences by planning **enrichment activities** (any activities beyond academic subjects that help children develop intellectually). Through enrichment activities, school-age children often tap underutilized (underused) intelligences, increase their self-concepts, and importantly, have fun. **Figure 18.20** lists enrichment activities for each type of intelligence. Enrichment activities can occur both in after-school programs and in the actual home.

In After-School Programs

Working parents often cannot bring their children home immediately after the school day. As a result, many school-age children attend **after-school programs**, which are programs that supervise, care for, and teach children after school until parents or caregivers finish the workday. When choosing after-school programs for their children, parents can note the enrichment activities that programs provide. Enrichment activities might include

Figure 18.20 Enrichment Activities for the Multiple Intelligences

Type of Multiple Intelligence	Enrichment Activities
Verbal/Linguistic	• Reading activities • Storytelling • Word puzzles (such as crosswords) • Writing
Logical/Mathematical	• Math • Logical problems • Science experiments • Strategy games
Bodily/Kinesthetic	• Dramatic play • Dancing • Science experiments • Arts and crafts
Visual/Spatial	• Visual art • Puzzles • Mazes
Musical/Rhythmic	• Activities involving hearing • Music • Dancing
Naturalistic	• Outdoor activities • Hands-on activities • Field trips • Journaling
Interpersonal	• Group discussions • Group activities
Intrapersonal	• Reflective activities • Journaling
Existential	• Activities comparing points of view • Develop rubrics for self-evaluation of learning performance-based tasks

helping children with their hobbies and interests and helping children with homework and general academic skills.

In the Home

Parents can also plan enrichment activities for the hours their children are home. Some examples of these activities include

- visiting museums, aquariums, zoos, and other places of interest
- enrolling and supporting children in youth groups, such as scouting, 4-H, religious groups, or local sports teams
- involving children in volunteer work
- attending special community programs, such as plays, concerts, dance performances, and sporting events
- engaging in physical activities, such as walking, going to neighborhood parks, playing ball, and using media for physical fitness routines
- engaging in crafts and hobbies
- playing board games and working puzzles
- enjoying books
- going on outings and vacations
- sharing household responsibilities, such as cooking dinner

Parents can also encourage intellectual development in the home by modeling their interests in their own activities. Adults whose skills and satisfactions grow over long periods of time are children's best models.

Providing Special Lessons and Activities

Very closely related to enrichment activities are **special lessons and activities**, classes or clubs where children can discover their own interests and talents (**Figure 18.21**). Many of these lessons and activities involve a team aspect, and as school-age children grow older, wider varieties of activities will be available to them. Many school-age children want to sign up for every activity they hear their friends are doing. The best way for children to

Figure 18.21 Special lessons and activities, such as karate classes or other clubs, offer a way for children to explore their talents and abilities. *What are some other lessons or activities children can participate in to explore their talents?*

discover their interests and talents is to have a wide range of experiences. If children stretch themselves too thin, however, they may not excel in the activities they choose. Decisions about participating in these lessons and activities should be made by parents and children cooperatively. When deciding among activities, parents and children can consider the following criteria:

- ***Fit.*** Do the activities fit well with the child's interests and strengths? If the child wants to quit an activity in which he or she is talented, parents may try to negotiate with the child. Some children just need a short break from an activity. If after a waiting period, the child still finds no joy in the activity, he or she can try another one.
- ***Schedule.*** How will the activities fit into the child's daily schedule? Children need time to do homework and chores, eat, sleep, play, and relax. The combined schedules of all family members may also affect the child's ability to participate in certain activities.
- ***Cost.*** Do the lessons and activities involve extra costs, such as prices for instruments and music, sports gear, and dance costumes (**Figure 18.22**)? Some adults borrow or rent expensive items until they know their children are committed to an activity.
- ***Competition.*** Will the activities be too demanding or competitive for the child's age? Activities for children should be fun and age appropriate. Coaches and other adults who are overly demanding or competitive may put too much pressure on children.

Figure 18.22 Equipment or clothing for activities, such as costumes for ballet, can become costly. *What are some ways parents can save money on these items?*

- *Safety.* Are the activities safe for the child's age and health? Is proper safety equipment provided? Leaders of activities should always consider the safety of all participants.

A lack of a supportive environment during the newborn through the school-age years can result in feelings of insecurity, neglect, and unworthiness. Children whose caregivers are frequently distracted by digital devices often develop serious mental health issues.

Guiding Electronic Media Use

During the school-age years, children become more skilled at using electronic media. By nine years of age, they are more independent in their media choices and activities and know how to use electronic media without adult supervision. Adults and caregivers may feel anxious about their children using media, but electronic media activities have many benefits for school-age children. For example, quality media can be used to support school lessons and enhance problem solving, decision making, creativity, concepts, language lessons, and even social skills. With good software and access to the Internet, children can

- retrieve information
- communicate (send and receive e-mails, "talk" with experts, and compose stories and poems)
- publish their works
- visit interactive sites

To meet children's intellectual needs and ensure their safety when using electronic media, adults should guide their school-age children's media use. This guidance may mean providing digital devices at appropriate times and protecting children from media-related risks.

Providing Digital Devices at Appropriate Times

Adults often ask, "When is the right time for my child to have his or her own digital devices, especially mobile devices?" When considering this question, a child's age is typically not as important as a child's developmental maturity. As adults **grapple** (struggle) with this question, they can ask themselves a number of questions, including the following:

- ***How have I modeled the use of digital devices to my child?*** Adults are models for their children's digital device use. Some studies show that children whose parents are frequently distracted by digital devices may grow up feeling insecure, neglected, and unworthy.
- ***Why does my child need a digital device?*** By the middle-school years, children are often more independent and may stay home alone or attend activities on their own. These children may benefit from digital devices that help them keep in contact with caregivers.
- ***What security controls should I implement?*** Adults should consider what security controls they want to put in place for their children and then talk with their children about these controls.
- ***What usage rules should I set and will my child respect these rules?*** Adults should set rules for their school-age children's media use and ensure that their children follow these rules. A good indicator of willingness to follow rules may be how well the child followed rules for family-shared devices.
- ***How will I supervise my child's use of digital devices?*** School-age children need guidance in using media devices. Adults should plan how they will supervise their children's media use and discuss this with their children.

Protecting Children from Media-Related Risks

As positive as media use can be for children, there are also risks involved with children's media use. For example, on the Internet, children can be exposed to inappropriate or even illegal content, either on purpose or by accident. They can connect online to strangers who have harmful intentions.

One of the best ways adults can protect their children in a digital age is to establish use guidelines for media and digital devices, set and enforce rules, and supervise use of all Internet-enabled devices. Some examples of guidelines might be using safe search engines that forbid inappropriate content, teaching children to use the Internet for specific purposes, explaining the difference between private and public information, teaching children about passwords and location systems, and setting safety rules for use of media and digital devices (**Figure 18.23**).

In addition to teaching safety guidelines, parents should establish barriers and modes of supervision for their children's media use. Some adults use *filtering programs*. A **filtering program** is an application designed to prevent children from accessing inappropriate content. Filtering programs

- provide information concerning children's specific activities on their digital devices and are able to block access to websites with adult content

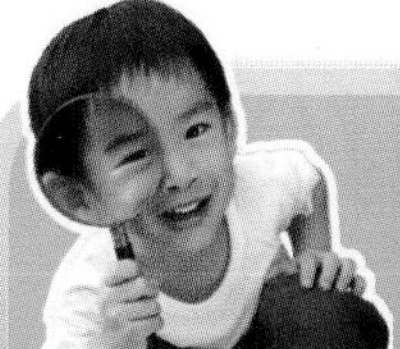

Investigate Special Topics — Assessing Children's Digital Media

With each passing year, school-age children spend more time *using* technology as a means of learning rather than *experimenting* with the tools. School-age children enjoy media programs that make learning fun.

The International Society for Technology in Education (ISTE) has developed six areas of student standards that should be integrated into media use within the school curriculum. The technology areas include

- creativity and innovation
- communication and collaboration
- research and information fluency
- critical thinking
- digital citizenship
- technology operations and concepts

Using these standards parents can assess the electronic media software, including websites, apps, and computer programs their children will use both in and outside of school. Teachers may also be able to provide parents with a list of suitable software that children use in their classrooms. Based on this information, parents can choose appropriate media hardware.

Knowing how children use digital media to do homework and projects will enable parents to closely supervise their children's media use. If parents are uncomfortable with their children's media use, there are many resources they can access. Much literature on children's media use is available through parenting magazines, children's magazines, newspapers, the Internet, and in professional books and articles.

Application Activity

In small groups, choose three electronic media devices, software, websites, or apps that school-age children access regularly. Research how these products can be used and test them in your group. Then, evaluate the three products according to the criteria in this lesson. Present your findings to the class.

Figure 18.23 Media and Digital Device Safety Rules for Children

- Use media and digital devices only at times approved by adults. (Some parents collect all mobile devices and laptops during red-light times to lessen temptations.)
- Limit website visits and IMs to an adult-approved list.
- Do not use chat rooms, bulletin boards, and social networking sites unless approved by adults.
- Demonstrate responsibility in caring for media and digital devices by protecting them from damage, breakage, loss, or theft.
- Do not give out any personal information or send any photos. (Children should use a pen name when on the Internet.) Insist children always come to the adult and ask about giving out any information.
- Tell adults about any uncomfortable images, information, or message, and never respond to such messages. (One out of five children have received unwanted sexual solicitations online. About 75 percent did not tell a parent. About 80 percent of children seven years of age and older receive some form of an inappropriate message on a daily basis.)
- Do not meet in person with anyone with whom you have communicated with only online without a parent with you. Explain the Internet is not a place to make friends.
- Never open an e-mail message from someone you do not know.
- Use ethical behavior at all times.
- Do not try to override technological barriers or erase browser history. Accept the fact adults will supervise media and digital device use.

- limit access to the Internet during set hours
- create a log of visited sites
- track Internet discussions in chat rooms
- monitor software downloaded to a personal digital device

Most companies that provide filtering programs also provide parental intelligence systems. These systems allow adults to note the calls and texts their children are making, what apps they are using, when they are surfing, and shut-down times. Providers can tailor parental alerts for child's media devices, such as voice minutes, text messages, data usage, and app downloads (including purchases).

Most basic service providers have parental controls. Even with these barriers in place, however, adult supervision and rule enforcement is still needed. Guiding children's use of digital and media devices involves both safeguards and close supervision. Finally, as with all aspects of life, adults must set a good example for their children when using digital devices.

Lesson 18.3 Review and Assessment 

1. Describe three ways adults can help children prepare for primary school.
2. Explain two ways adults can help children prepare for middle school.
3. Identify three ways adults can support their children in school.
4. Give two examples of enrichment activities for each of the multiple intelligences.
5. List four criteria adults and children can consider when choosing special lessons and activities for children.
6. Summarize two ways adults can guide school-age children's media use.
7. What is a *filtering program* and how does it help children?
8. **Critical thinking.** Brainstorm enrichment activities in the home for school-age children. What enrichment activities did you enjoy as a child? Why?

Chapter 18 Review and Assessment

Summary

Wiring and pruning in the brain's prefrontal cortex during the school-age years enables children to think logically. Cognitive advances, including attention and memory, also aid intellectual development. During the school-age years, children enter Piaget's concrete operational stage. They think logically though logic is based on past experiences. Upon entering the formal operational stage, children reason more abstractly. According to Vygotsky, school-age children learn as a result of brain development, of being stretched in their ZPDs, and through collaboration. Piaget and Vygotsky differed about the role of language in intellectual development. Harold Gardner's theory of multiple intelligences also outlines many ways in which children learn.

School-age children's understanding of physical knowledge expands. Logical thinking concepts of classification; ordering by attributes; cause and effect; space; number; and distance, time, and speed improve. Children learn culture-specific knowledge through school and home teachings. By middle childhood, children have mastered most of the rules of language, including articulation and grammar. Their vocabularies continue to broaden. Children learn to read by making letter-sound associations and later in middle childhood use reading as a way of learning other subject matter. They also achieve a number of intellectual developmental milestones.

School-age children's intellectual needs are primarily met through school. Parents can help children learn in school by preparing them for school experiences and supporting their endeavors by reinforcing school tasks, strengthening executive functions, and being a school advocate. Outside of school, parents can provide enrichment activities and special lessons and activities. In addition to providing these activities, parents can guide their children's media use by providing digital devices at appropriate times and protecting children from media-related risks.

College and Career Portfolio

Portfolio Enhancement

A strong portfolio uses technology to enhance its contents. Ways to use technology in your portfolio might include adding a video to your portfolio samples or an audio recording narration to a presentation.

- Choose one portfolio sample you can improve using technology.
- Use technology to enhance your portfolio sample and then present that sample to the class.

Chapter 18 Review and Assessment

Vocabulary Activities

1. For each of the following terms, identify a word or group of words describing a quality of the term—an *attribute*. Pair up with a classmate and discuss your list of attributes.

Key Terms

after-school programs (18.3)
code-switch (18.2)
concrete operational stage (18.1)
conservation (18.1)
culture-specific knowledge (18.2)
deductive reasoning (18.1)
enrichment activities (18.3)
filtering program (18.3)
flipped classroom (18.3)
formal operational stage (18.1)
hierarchical classification (18.2)
inductive reasoning (18.1)
middle school (18.3)
multiple intelligences (18.1)
nucleus accumbens (18.1)
prefrontal cortex (18.1)
primary school (18.3)
special lessons and activities (18.3)

2. Work with a partner to write the definitions of the following terms based on your current understanding of the chapter. Then team up with another group to discuss your definitions and any discrepancies.

Academic Terms

alphabetize (18.2)
belabor (18.3)
extraneous (18.2)
grapple (18.3)
metacognition (18.1)
mitigate (18.3)
simultaneously (18.1)
subdivided (18.2)
syntax (18.2)
underutilized (18.3)
upheaval (18.3)

Critical Thinking

3. **Analyze.** In small groups, analyze why attention and memory are crucial to a child's ability to process and learn information. Why would learning be difficult without these skills?
4. **Compare and contrast.** Brainstorm examples of transductive, deductive, and inductive reasoning. For each type of reasoning, write a short scenario in which a child reasons accordingly. Then, working with a partner, compare and contrast the three types of reasoning.
5. **Make inferences.** During the school-age years, children gain an understanding of time. Working with a partner, make inferences about why children learn time concepts better once they begin school. Could time concepts that are taught in school be effectively taught in a preschool?
6. **Draw conclusions.** Children's articulation, vocabulary, grammar, and reading skills are interrelated. Draw conclusions about how these aspects of communication relate. Write a brief description for each aspect-pairing.
7. **Determine.** Recall your experience starting primary school or middle school. What would you have liked to know before starting school? How could the adults in your life have better prepared you? Based on your experience, determine ways adults could prepare children for primary or middle school.
8. **Cause and effect.** Executive functions are critical to a person's motivation and ability to do work. Review the executive functions discussed in this chapter, and in small groups, discuss the long-term effects of weak executive functions in children. Also discuss the long-term effects of strong executive functions.
9. **Identify.** Visit a local library or community center and identify special lessons or activities that are available for children. List at least five activities and explain how they would benefit a school-age child.
10. **Evaluate.** In small groups, research filtering programs and other software that protect children from inappropriate content. Choose two programs and then evaluate them based on customer reviews and the information available. How effective would this program be in protecting children? What other safeguards should adults put into place alongside each program?

Core Skills

11. **Research and writing.** During puberty, the brain reorganizes as the prefrontal cortex continues to mature. Using reliable online or print resources, research brain development in older school-age children. How does the brain begin to reorganize during these years? How do these changes affect children's perceptions and thinking skills? After compiling your research, write a short report based on your findings. Include a bibliography with citations in APA style.

12. **Speaking.** In groups of three, research Piaget's, Vygotsky's, and Gardner's theories about how school-age children learn. During your research, take notes about areas of agreement and disagreement. Then, assign each group member one theorist to portray. In a class presentation, role-play a "conversation" between these three theorists. Each group member should present his or her theorist's theory and then dialogue with the other theorists. After the conversation, take questions from the class and respond in character.
13. **Reading.** Starting in the school-age years, children understand the logical thinking concepts they had difficulty grasping as preschoolers. In small groups, review this chapter's information about logical thinking concepts and obstacles to logical thought. Also review this text's information about logical thinking during the preschool years. Then, create an informative and visually appealing poster charting children's progress in understanding logical thinking concepts and in overcoming obstacles to logical thought. Include pictures and use your poster as a studying tool for your group.
14. **Math and writing.** In small groups, research math problems for school-age children. Try to find math problems for school-age children in various grades. Then, write a brief essay explaining how children learn more complex number concepts with each school grade. Include examples of math problems and relate these problems to how school-age children develop and learn to think logically.
15. **Reading and speaking.** In small groups, use Internet or print resources to find articles on language development geared toward school-age children. Choose two articles and read the information examining vocabulary and articulation. After reading, present a group report assessing each article's effectiveness and relating the content to the information about vocabulary and articulation covered in this chapter.
16. **Speaking.** Review the intellectual developmental milestones for children in the school-age years (Figure 18.14) and then pick one topic you think school-age children should learn. This topic might be a hobby of yours or a piece of information you find interesting. Then, write a short speech as if you were presenting this topic to one age group of school-age children. While writing the speech, keep in mind the attention spans and interests of children that age. Consider what milestones those children have achieved. Practice your speech and then deliver it to the class as though speaking to your intended audience.
17. **Listening and technology.** Interview a parent of a school-age child about how he or she helps the child with homework. Ask which helping strategies have been most effective. How has help with homework changed as the child grows older? After the interview, work in small groups to film a tutorial about effectively helping school-age children with their homework. Include a list of "do's and don'ts" in your video.
18. **Listening and technology.** Interview three school-age children about the role of electronic media in their lives. What digital devices do the children have? How old were they when they received their first digital device? What do the children like about the role of electronic media in their lives? What do they dislike? Working with a partner, compare findings and create a digital presentation explaining what you discovered about school-age children's electronic media use. Deliver your presentation to the class.
19. **CTE Career Readiness Practice.** Presume you are the principal of a middle school. Many of the new middle-school students do not get help with their homework and seem to have weak executive functions. Their parents and guardians do not seem interested in partnering with the school. After a discussion with your staff, you decide to send a letter home to parents and guardians, explaining the importance of supporting children in school. Draft this letter, taking care to be respectful and informative. Have a partner read your letter and give you feedback.

Observations

20. As a class, visit a local primary school and observe children playing at recess or in the classroom. Make observations about the way children play and about how they use logic when interacting with others. Then, discuss how the development of logical thinking concepts alters children's approach to play.
21. Visit a class of school-age children or watch a documentary in which school-age children speak to one another and to teachers. While listening to the children, make observations about how the children use grammar and whether they code-switch during or between conversations. Write a short reflection about your observations.

Chapter 19 Social-Emotional Development of School-Age Children

Essential Question

How does a child's expanding social world present new challenges during middle childhood, and what types of social support are needed to help school-age children?

Lesson 19.1 The Social-Emotional World of School-Age Children

Lesson 19.2 Meeting School-Age Children's Social-Emotional Needs

Case Study Are Friendship Rejections Serious?

As a class, read the case study and discuss the questions that follow. After you finish studying the chapter, discuss this case study again. Have your opinions changed based on what you learned?

Meiling and Ailin had been friends since preschool, where they met while finger painting. They proceeded to share activities, sleepovers, family outings, secrets, and laughter. Meiling thought she and Ailin would be friends forever and was excited as they both prepared to enter middle school.

At the end of the fifth grade, Meiling and Ailin tried out for the basketball team. Ailin made the team, but Meiling could not even get a spot as a "bench-warmer." Meiling was happy for Ailin and looked forward to watching her play. Little did Meiling know that their friendship was about to change.

Ailin loved being on the basketball team and quickly became friends with her teammates. Now, Ailin rarely had time to spend with Meiling because she was always practicing or hanging out with her new friends. Even when Meiling and Ailin did spend time together, all Ailin talked about was the basketball team.

Later that school year, Ailin asked Meiling if she wanted to play some basketball with her. Meiling jumped at the chance to spend time with her friend. Ailin scored repeatedly, but Meiling struggled and often lost track of the ball. Ailin became frustrated and left early. After Ailin left, Meiling went to her room and cried, feeling sad and alone. That night, Meiling told her mother what happened. Meiling's mother wondered how she might comfort her daughter.

Give It Some Thought

1. Was it reasonable for Meiling to expect that she and Ailin would always be best friends? Why or why not?
2. Should Meiling's mother view her daughter's fading friendship as a serious or just a passing problem? Explain your answer.
3. What could Meiling's mother say to comfort her daughter? What might be some ways she can help her daughter?

While studying this chapter, look for the online resources icon  to:

- **Practice** terms with e-flash cards and interactive games
- **Assess** what you learn by completing self-assessment quizzes
- **Expand** knowledge with interactive activities and graphic organizers

Companion G-W Learning

www.g-wlearning.com/childdevelopment

Study on the go

Use a mobile device to practice terms and review with self-assessment quizzes.

www.m.g-wlearning.com/0384

Lesson 19.1 The Social-Emotional World of School-Age Children

Key Terms

domains of self-definition
gender schools
goal-corrected partnership
guilt
industry versus inferiority
psychological security
scapegoating
shortcomings
work ethic

Academic Terms

deemed
deviate
drastically
industry
inferiority
infringe
instilling
prodigious

Objectives

After studying this lesson, you will be able to

- explain how school-age children's self-awareness grows as they show responsibility, learn gender roles, establish a moral conscience, and expand self-concept.
- analyze how school-age children develop a sense of industry despite the risk of inferiority.
- describe how school-age children's interactions with adults and children (including friendships and peer groups) change.
- summarize how school-age children learn to express emotions in socially acceptable ways.
- name the four sources of children's stress during the school-age years.
- give examples of social-emotional developmental milestones school-age children might achieve.

Reading and Writing Activity

In groups of three, review social-emotional development during infancy, the toddler years, and the preschool years. Assign each group member one of these stages to review and summarize in two to three paragraphs. Then, discuss each summary with the group. After reading this lesson, draw connections between the social-emotional development that occurs during the school-age years and in earlier stages.

Graphic Organizer

Draw a comic strip and label it *Social-Emotional Development of Children*. Before reading this lesson, use your notes from this lesson's reading and writing activity to illustrate the social-emotional development of infants, toddlers, and preschoolers in the comic strip squares. Then, as you are reading, illustrate the social-emotional world of school-age children. Use as many comic strip squares as you want.

A whole new social experience begins in middle childhood, and children must make many new adjustments. During the school-age years, children have to strive to become competent members of society. The schools prepare children to become independent and productive citizens. Similarly, parents often give their school-age children chores that help develop responsibility and work ethic. Children's learning of gender roles is influenced by parents, peers, the school environment, and media. Moral development that began in the preschool years continues in the school-age years. By the end of the school years, children establish a moral conscience and their self-concepts are well-developed.

In many ways, social development becomes the most important aspect of development in middle childhood. While parents are still vital in providing security and helping children become more independent, children's peer groups grow in importance. Relationships with peers affect all aspects of development, and school-age children often compare themselves with their peers. As school-age children interact more with other adults and children, they must learn new ways to express their emotions, which are closely connected to their personalities. Because of their increased interactions with others, children often experience more stress during the school-age years. School-age children make great strides in social-emotional development and achieve a number of developmental milestones.

Figure 19.1 School-age children take pride in their achievements and acknowledgements. *What achievements and acknowledgements shaped your self-concept as a school-age child?*

Expanding Self-Awareness

During middle childhood, children show greater awareness of their responsibilities and roles in society. They try to learn what is expected of them, and their self-concepts often depend on their sense of achievement and the acknowledgement of others (**Figure 19.1**). School-age children's self-awareness grows as they show responsibility, learn gender roles, establish a moral conscience, and expand their self-concepts.

Showing Responsibility

Doing chores in the home and at school encourages school-age children to show responsibility. Keeping their rooms clean, doing the dishes, doing homework, and mowing the lawn are just a few ways children demonstrate responsibility during the school-age years. If adults serve as good role models, doing chores will help school-age children develop a healthy *work ethic*. A **work ethic** is a person's sense of responsibility and diligence toward work tasks. By eight years of age, children can do moderately demanding jobs well, though adults are still involved in planning, demonstrating, and supervising chores.

Learning Gender Roles

School-age children's gender roles continue to develop and are influenced by a number of sources, including family, peers, the school environment, and media. These influences play a **prodigious** (pruh-DIH-jus), tremendous, role in children's learning of gender roles. School-age children may get uniform or mixed signals from these influences.

Family

Parents' actions and examples continue to influence children's learning of gender roles during the school-age years. Some children are learning traditional gender roles while other children are learning similarities between male and female roles. As children observe their parents and other caregivers, they often adopt these people's behaviors as their own. Even children's perceptions of career options are influenced by their parents' and caregivers' career attitudes.

Figure 19.2 In *gender schools,* boys and girls learn behavioral norms (including clothing choices and appearance) from their same-sex peers. *Do gender schools exist even beyond the school-age years? Explain.*

Peers

School-age children prefer to be friends with peers of the same sex. This preference becomes stronger throughout the school-age years. Thus, groups of same-sex peers become **gender schools** (peer groups that teach members what it means to be masculine or feminine). In gender schools boys teach other boys male behavioral norms, and girls teach other girls female behavioral norms. Some of the behavioral norms that children learn may include preferences in personal appearance, clothing choices, and activities (**Figure 19.2**).

While gender schools teach children masculinity and femininity, children who **deviate** (depart; stray) from acceptable behavioral norms may be faced with sexual stereotyping pressure. These children need positive adult role models to reassure them and promote their self-concepts.

School Environment

In schools children are exposed to other adults and children who have varying gender-role ideas. This affects children's gender-role learning. Historically, schools have treated boys and girls differently, often encouraging children to take different, gender-specific classes. Currently, however, gender-role attitudes in the school environment are **drastically** (greatly) different. Now, care is often taken to ensure that boys and girls are treated equally and not discouraged from taking certain classes.

Even today, though, with changes in educational and career opportunities, some cultures and families still teach their children sexual stereotyping. Because schools must serve all children, regardless of the child's family's beliefs, school-age children may still be exposed to sexual stereotyping in the school environment.

Although schools cannot **infringe** (restrict) on students' personal beliefs about gender roles, they can encourage gender equity and give all children fair opportunities. Some ways that schools can encourage gender equity include

- making curriculum and teaching unbiased
- requiring respect between male and female students
- supporting students who make nontraditional choices

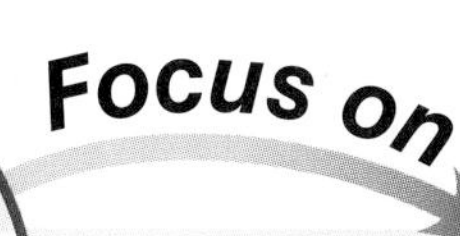

Social Studies

Gender-Role Attitudes in Schools

In past decades, school curriculums were constructed to mirror the traditional gender roles of men and women in the home and at work. As a result, boys and girls were often encouraged to take different classes. For example, boys were often expected to take math and science classes while girls were not. As a result, boys had somewhat higher achievement in math and science than girls for many years. In many cases, girls simply did not enroll in math and science classes beyond those required. Schools justified this difference in achievement by claiming that men and women had different "biological tendencies." Research has shown, however, that these achievement differences were not due to natural differences in *capabilities* (aptitudes).

Since then, schools have worked toward gender equity to boost girls' self-esteem and achievement and prevent gender bias. One positive result of schools' efforts to boost girls' self-esteem and achievements is that the gender gap in math and science classes has almost closed. Gender gaps in other areas, such as physics and technology, still exist, however. This is because males, more than females, are encouraged to enter these areas. Today, schools are still making strides to provide more gender equity and prevent achievement gaps.

Media

School-age children are often more exposed to electronic and print media. Television shows, movies, magazines, and books represent gender roles in many different ways. Children often identify with and model themselves after the characters they see and read about. Therefore, the media messages children view greatly influence their learning of gender roles. As expected, the more stereotyped media children view, the more stereotyped their beliefs become.

Establishing a Moral Conscience

Although moral development begins in the preschool years, **instilling** (gradually establishing) a conscience for acting acceptably continues in the school-age years. School-age children's moral development is influenced by authority figures and peers. Helping children establish a moral conscience becomes the responsibility of all social institutions and groups entrusted with raising children. Some examples of these groups include families, schools, youth organizations, and religious groups. The family, however, still has the central role in children's moral development during the school-age years. Moral development continues to affect school-age children's moral judgment and reasoning, moral character, and moral emotions.

Moral Judgment and Reasoning

During the school-age years children's *moral judgment and reasoning,* ability to perceive an action as right or wrong, begins to change from an *egocentric* (self-interested) concern to a consideration for the needs of the social group. School-age children have entered into Piaget's *autonomous reality* stage of morality and Kohlberg's level of moral reasoning known as *conventional morality* (**Figure 19.3**). During these stages children see rules as changeable and set by mutual consent. Younger school-age children see rules as important for working and living together in families, classrooms, and youth groups. Older school-age children see laws needed by larger social groups, such as different levels of government.

Figure 19.3 Piaget's and Kohlberg's Stages of Moral Judgment and Reasoning During the School-Age Years

Jean Piaget	
Stage	**Characteristics of Stage**
Autonomous reality	Children are regulated by rules set with mutual consent and for reasons of fairness and equity. Children's beliefs include the following: • Rules are not "set in stone," but are arbitrary. • Consequences of actions are determined by intention, not physical damage. • Punishment is based on intent and ability to see rules from the perspectives of others.
Lawrence Kohlberg's Conventional Stages of Moral Reasoning	
Stage	**Characteristics of Stage**
Interpersonal conformity	• Children do what a social group (family, school) says is right or wrong. • Children believe certain behaviors are acceptable because they are good for the social group. • Children want approval by others and want to be considered "good" or "nice" if they live by the code.
Maintaining the social order	• Children believe they must live by the rules of the larger society in which they live. • Children feel compelled to do their duty for society and show respect for authority.

Moral Character

Parents and caregivers are children's first teachers of character. Unlike in the preschool years, school-age children can comprehend the reasoning behind certain limits. Therefore, they are better able to act in accordance with that which is perceived as morally right. As school-age children develop character, they see themselves as socially valued people. (A feeling of worth is an important aspect of a person's self-esteem.)

School-age children are greatly influenced—for good or for bad—by the people around them. Parents and caregivers, however, have the best chance of wielding that influence as compared to others. Showing children love and being a positive role model can make an enormous difference in building children's character.

Moral Emotions

School-age children who are others-oriented begin to develop a conscience from their feelings of *guilt* after misdeeds. **Guilt** is a feeling of remorse that comes from the inner voice of conscience when a person has behaved unacceptably. Guilt is based in *empathy* (concern for the injured person) and remorse for the misdeed. Generally, guilt is emotionally healthy because it leads a person to compensate for a misdeed and avoid the mistake in the future.

Instead of feeling guilt for misdeeds, some children feel *shame*. These children have often experienced shaming by those closest to them—parents, other adults, or peers—in the preschool and school-age years. As a result, their remorse for wrongdoings is focused inward and based on how

Investigate Special Topics: Moral Development in Teens and Adults

According to Kohlberg's theory of moral development, many teens and adults remain at the level of moral reasoning known as *conventional morality*. Conventional morality, which includes interpersonal conformity and maintenance of the social order, guides a person's decisions and views for most of his or her life. About 10 to 15 percent of people, however, do *not* remain at the conventional level of morality. Rather, they reason in the level of morality known as *postconventional morality*, which includes the stages described in the following chart.

At the postconventional level, morality is viewed more abstractly and concerns what constitutes *universal morality* (morality that goes beyond specific laws). Postconventional morality is similar to Piaget's discussions about "ideal reciprocity," the positive treatment of others because ideally one would also want to be treated well. Moral reasoning has usually matured in an individual by 35 years of age. At this time, the person's level of moral reasoning is unlikely to change or graduate to another level.

Lawrence Kohlberg's Postconventional Stages of Moral Reasoning

Stage	Characteristics of Stage
Social contract and individual rights	• Teens and adults believe acceptable behaviors are determined by socially agreed-upon standards, which vary among cultures and subgroups within a culture. • Teens and adults believe that the chosen code of conduct is based on the greatest good for the greatest number, even if the code works against the interests of some individuals.
Universal and ethical principles	• Teens and adults believe that all acceptable behaviors are based on justice, human dignity, and equality. • Teens and adults believe they should defend personal principles over laws that are deemed as *aberrant* (diverging) from acceptable principles.

Research Activity

In small groups, review the stages of postconventional morality and discuss the required reasoning skills for this level of moral reasoning. Develop a list of questions that would assess the moral level at which a teen or adult is reasoning. Then, survey at least 10 teens and adults using these questions. Evaluate the survey responses and determine the level of morality at which each person is reasoning. Share your group's findings with the rest of the class.

others perceive them rather than on how their actions have affected others.

Shaming does not build character because respect is not the core of these adult-child and peer relationships. The child is not learning how to behave acceptably or respond appropriately to misdeeds. Instead, the child becomes more and more concerned with self and his or her failure to please adults. Once shame becomes a self-conscious emotion, it erodes self-esteem and leads to many mental health problems that may affect the person throughout his or her life (**Figure 19.4**).

Expanding Self-Concept

Preschool children begin to develop self-concept and describe themselves (called *self-definition*). They may say comments such as, "I'm good (or bad)." By seven or eight years of age, a child begins to perceive his or her self-definition in terms of multiple **domains of self-definition** (categories in which children can describe themselves). School-age children are typically able to describe their abilities in each domain shown in **Figure 19.5**. How school-age children evaluate their own abilities (called *self-evaluation*) in each domain can positively or negatively affect self-concept.

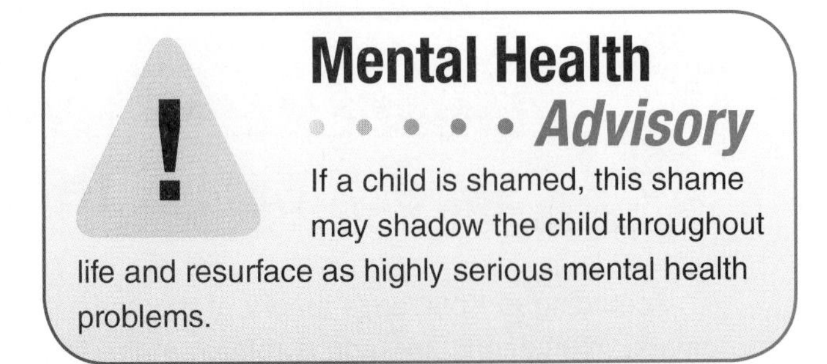

Figure 19.4 Results of Shaming

- Creates a perfectionist attitude, an unrealistic goal, which results in more erosion of self-esteem when perfection cannot be achieved.
- Promotes overwork or compulsive-type habits (overeating and constant viewing of media) if repressed shame later resurfaces.
- Influences a withdrawal from social relationships due to fear of any form of embarrassment.
- Inhibits emotions except for anger, which may appear in a rage-anger cycle.
- Generates the substitute emotions of depression and anxiety.
- Triggers the rise of *defense mechanisms* (blaming others, being supercritical of others, taking revenge, showing exaggerated pride).
- Induces conduct disorders (as discussed later in the text).
- Inhibits moral conscience.
- Leads to a replaying of parents' and others' shame-scripts and using these shame-scripts on the next generation of children.

Self-evaluation can be complex during the school-age years because children are just coming to understand which domains are **deemed** (considered to be) most important by their cultures. Conflicts between families and peers about the importance of each domain often occur. Until the teen or young adult years, people rarely make decisions about each domain's importance for themselves.

As school-age children evaluate themselves in each domain, they assess how they compare with their peers in terms of abilities. Peers can judge harshly, especially in school environments, and adults can often not change how peers judge each other. These peer comparisons cause children to become keenly aware of their **shortcomings** (areas in which they want or need to improve) and failures, which can affect how children define themselves. Unconditional love and acceptance and acknowledgement of achievements by parents and other adults can help build school-age children's self-esteem during these formative years.

Developing a Sense of Industry

School-age children begin to feel more like members of society. They want to excel alongside their peers and tend to fear rejection or incompetence. School-age children enter Erikson's fourth stage of personality development, which is called **industry versus inferiority**. This stage involves a

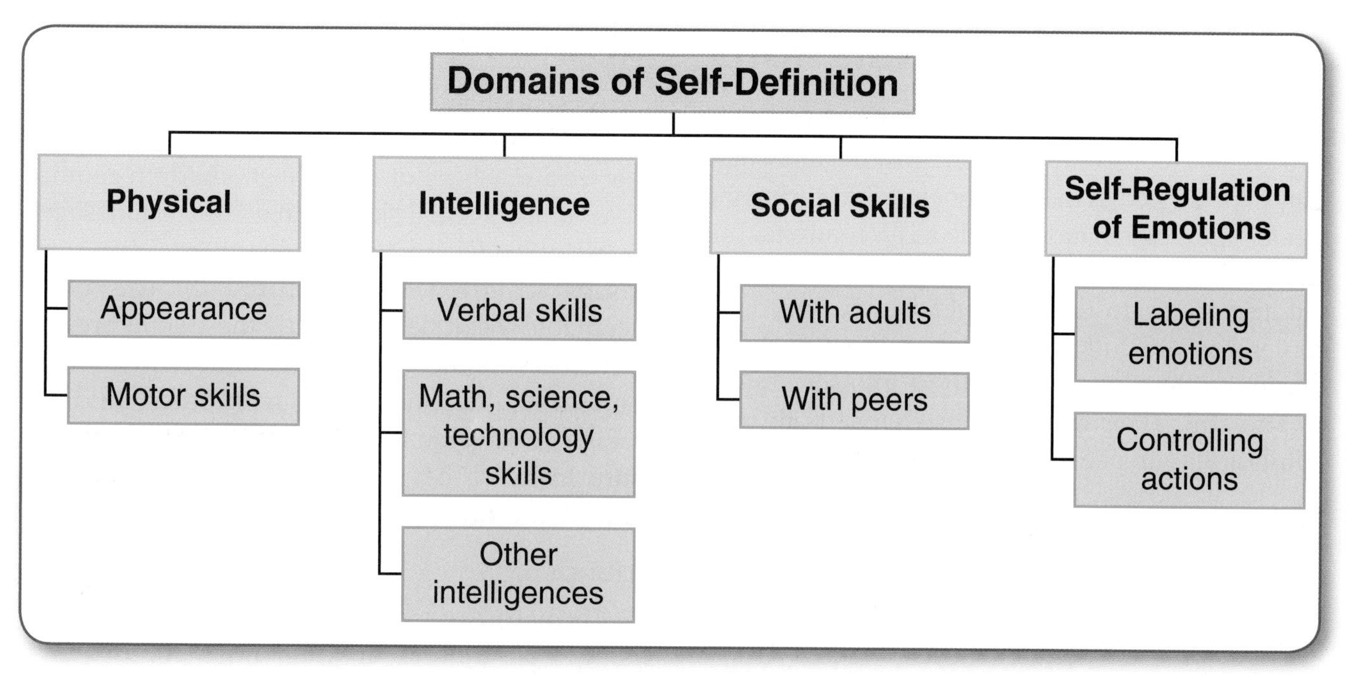

Figure 19.5 The school-age child's perceived importance for each domain depends on his or her cultural experiences and family values. *Which three domains of self-definition are most important to you?*

struggle between children's **industry** (desire to join others in striving to become a competent member of society) and **inferiority** (feeling of incompetence and low value as a member of society).

Industry builds off *initiative*, a sense of motivation children form during the preschool years. Like initiative, industry involves doing and making things. Industry differs from initiative, however. Industry involves the drive to accomplish school tasks and other projects, whereas initiative involves learning tasks that will reduce the need for adult help. Industry also involves joining others and working as a team member, whereas initiative is more personal. Lastly, industry focuses on recognition from peers and important adults, whereas initiative focuses on pleasing self and parents.

If school-age children embrace industry and are successful in this stage, they feel confident and productive. Being industrious increases children's feelings of self-esteem and responsibility. Children will see that what they do makes a difference. If children's efforts and work are demeaned or ignored, the outcome may be a lasting sense of inferiority.

During the school-age years, children learn a lifelong attitude toward work. Though play is still important for school-age children, the play of earlier years is often replaced with more meaningful work (at least by adult standards). School-age children with a sense of industry see work as a route to learning new ideas and skills and to performing in worthwhile ways. They also see work as a way to win approval from parents and caregivers, teachers, and peers. School-age children enjoy doing activities with and for others (**Figure 19.6**). They enjoy learning and practicing cooperation as they interact in their expanding and changing social worlds.

Figure 19.6 As they develop a sense of industry, school-age children enjoy doing tasks that bring joy to others, such as watering a garden. *What are common tasks that school-age children can do for others?*

Changing Social Relations

School-age children's social relationships grow and become more complicated than the relationships they experienced in the preschool years. During the school-age years children still rely on adults, but want to be more independent. School-age children are also trying to develop friendships, which are sometimes difficult. School-age children find that mastering the skills needed to fit into society can be stressful. Their relationships change both with adults and with peers.

Interacting with Adults

At the beginning of the school-age years, children enter into a **goal-corrected partnership**, a relationship in which children and parents, or caregivers are willing to compromise to reach a common goal. The goal between children and their parents is for the relationship to be a loving one. Attachments are no longer based on physical proximity, but instead are based on *availability*, which can be both physical and emotional in nature. An adult's physical presence does not mean he or she is psychologically available. Even the self-reliant child still needs loving adults for guidance and security.

By eight or nine years of age, children and their parents and caregivers move toward a *partner relationship* method of co-regulation as long as the child acts responsibly. In this relationship, parents and caregivers provide a balance between letting go and holding on in the school years. Parents allow their school-age child some freedom, but maintain communication and supervision of the child. This enables children to think of their parents as *home base*. They think of home as a safe place where they can go and their needs for food, clothing, shelter, and *psychological security* will be met. **Psychological security** is a feeling that someone cares and will help when needed.

In some cases, school-age children do not make the transition to a partner relationship method of co-regulation because their earlier attachments were not secure. A partnership relationship requires trust on the part of both parent and child.

Interacting with Other Children

As school-age children spend more time with peers, they depend less on adults for company. The peer relationships of school-age children require more complex social skills than earlier relationships. To maintain friendships and status within peer groups, children must continually use peer-acceptable social skills. Because these skills are just being learned, most school-age children will have some difficulties interacting with other children. In **Figure 19.7**, you will see that some children are more likely to have negative social experiences with friends and peer groups than others.

Friendships

The nature of school-age children's friendships changes as children mature. Boys choose boys for friends, and girls choose girls; and both boys and girls generally show dislike for the opposite gender. Around 11 years of age, however, girls may experience puberty and begin to show interest in boys.

During the school-age years children often see a friend as someone who helps them. School-age children seldom think in terms of how they can help their friend. The concept of *give and take* is familiar to school-age children, but it often serves the child rather than the mutual interests of his or her friends. Between 9 and 11 years of age, more close friendships form. Similar interests and tastes

Figure 19.7 Children at Risk for Negative Peer Relations

- Children who are aggressive and have disruptive behaviors are often rejected by others. Many rejected children become bullies, which diminishes their chances for friendships.
- Children who are introverted or shy are often ignored by their peers. Shy children are especially lonely.
- Children who are very different from their peers may be ignored.
- Children who are immature in their social skills are often ignored or teased.
- Children with bad reputations may be rejected as early as nine years of age.

often determine these friendships rather than physical nearness. The nature of these friendships becomes one of cooperation and helping each other to achieve group goals.

If a friendship ends, the loss of the friend can be devastating to the school-age child. There are many causes for losing a friendship, such as moving away or attending a different school. Friendship loss hurts the most when a child feels his or her trust has been broken. Children often see friendship as a place for self-disclosure. When this is violated, the child is hurt and the friendship ends.

Peer Groups

Peer groups are important for school-age children. Belonging to a peer group gives children feelings of sharing and loyalty. Children feel a sense of security when working or playing with others in their group. Peer groups provide emotional support, too. Adults cannot provide the comfort that children feel when they realize others their age share similar feelings. Peer groups also reinforce self-esteem. School-age children are highly concerned about how they appear to others. In peer groups, children tag others with labels, such as *captain of the team* or *the last one chosen*. These labels make children aware of how others feel about them. Once they absorb these peer attitudes, children react to themselves as others have reacted to them.

Through peer groups children learn how to deal with rules and get along with others. Children learn that social relationships involve rules and that rules help groups work as teams. Children must use self-control to follow these rules. Peer groups also help school-age children depend less on adults. Peer groups serve as sifters for thinking through adult-taught values. Peer groups often share information with each other and peers help children decide which values to keep and which to adjust.

School-age peer groups are smaller, especially for girls, as compared with those of the preschool years. Children may feel hurt if one of their friends chooses another child or group for friendship. This often happens when one child enters puberty far ahead of his or her friend or matures in other ways.

Focus on **Health**

Helping Children Overcome Rejection

Because peer groups are so important during middle childhood, many school-age children experience intense fears of rejection. Every child, at one time or another, feels rejected by peers. A school-age child might say, "Nobody likes me," or "I can never do anything right." If a school-age child struggles with rejection, an adult can help by

- trying to discover the problem behind the rejection (such as physical appearance or a lack of certain skills)
- giving the child direct help overcoming the problem behind the rejection (encouraging better grooming skills, teaching new activities)
- planning games and activities in which there is not much pressure
- reassuring the child that he or she is accepted by others and that rejection by a person or group does not alter the child's value as a person or how much the child is loved

If school-age children continue to feel rejected, adults can speak with school counselors or seek professional help for children. If left unaddressed, long-term rejection can lead to mental health problems, such as anxiety and depression.

Expressing Emotions

By the time they enter school, children have fairly well-established patterns of emotional behavior. Personality traits continue to emerge and stabilize. The emotions felt by school-age children affect their behaviors which, in turn, influence their personalities. As school-age children interact more with adults and other children, they are expected to express their emotions in new, socially acceptable ways. School-age children learn to express emotions such as love, fear and anxiety, and anger and aggression.

Love

All school-age children need to feel and express love. They show love to adults and peers who care about them and accept them as they are. School-age children do not seek relationships in which they must give too much in return. They tend to care for others who share common interests (**Figure 19.8**).

School-age children's need for love is expressed in their great desire to be accepted by others—both adults and peers. Most children, however, do not express love as openly (with hugs and kisses) as younger children. School-age children may be embarrassed about being openly affectionate with family members. Instead, they may express love for adults by showing kindness and doing activities with them. Children may show affection for peers by wanting to be with them; by sharing secrets; by communicating through phone calls, messages, or notes; and by giving small presents.

Figure 19.8 School-age children's friendships tend to be grounded in common interests and experiences. *Who were your first friends? What did you have in common?*

Mental Health Advisory

Children who do not feel like they are loved unconditionally tend to develop severe emotional problems and may act in antisocial ways.

School-age children who do not feel loved have a narrowed emotional range, causing them to experience little or no joy, grief, or guilt. Thinking abilities are hindered because unloved children have trouble concentrating. These children often turn to antisocial behaviors, such as hostile acts, and may seek acceptance from peers and circles of friends who are poor role models.

Fear and Anxiety

During the school-age years, many fears and worries from a child's early years become less threatening. Children better understand the separation of fantasy and reality. Fear of the dark disappears after seven years of age, and fears of the supernatural decline by 9 or 10 years of age. Fears of physical harm (disease, injury, or death) continue into the school-age years. School-age children's fears and anxieties tend to center on the future, embarrassment, and people and their actions. The fears and anxieties of middle childhood often do not disappear with age. Sometimes, school-age children's fears and anxieties persist into the adult years.

Anger and Aggression

Expressions of anger and aggression change once children enter the school-age years. School-age children do not display anger as physically as younger children do. Older children are better able to control their bodies and express themselves verbally. By this time they know what is and is not acceptable. Therefore, children in middle childhood tend to express their anger indirectly. For example, anger may be expressed in the forms of disrespect, sulkiness, or **scapegoating** (blaming others for one's own mistakes). School-age children also show anger by gossiping, plotting, and even imagining the downfall of their enemies. Withdrawal from a situation, such as quitting or using less ability, may be another sign of anger. Some older school-age children may be physically aggressive, and these acts can have devastating outcomes.

As children grow older, they become angry about different things. Like preschool children, school-age children are angered when their wants are denied or their possessions are threatened. Unlike preschool children, however, school-age children are also angered by what they see as wrongs to others. In later years, anger at social wrongs may fuel positive social action (**Figure 19.9**).

Jealousy

The feelings of jealousy that children began to experience during the preschool years continue, and sometimes intensify, during the school-age years. School-age children have more social relationships and must interact with other adults and children on a regular basis at school and during activities outside of school. The increase in social interactions makes school-age children more likely to compare themselves with their peers.

School-age children may also experience intense jealousy due to competitive school environments and school relationships. In the classroom, children are assessed based on a variety of abilities. As they watch their peers being assessed and even acknowledged, school-age children may feel jealous of peers' accomplishments.

Recognizing School-Age Children's Stress

As the school-age child's world expands to include new relationships and responsibilities, stress can originate from many new and different sources. For this reason, stress often increases in the school-age years. Some new sources of stress for school-age children include the following:

- ***Home life.*** Stress may come from a lack of family routines and from overscheduling activities. Adults who have unclear or unreasonable expectations (such as being intolerant of anything less than excellence) may cause stress in their children. Stress can also come from changes in the family situation, such as divorce, deaths, financial problems, and domestic and community violence.

Figure 19.9 School-age children are sometimes angered by wrongs done to others. This type of anger can be healthy, and if directed appropriately, can even fuel positive social action. *What are some examples of ways school-age children can take positive social action?*

- *School life.* School life brings major changes for school-age children. Play evolves into competitive sports, and curiosity and fun learning activities become a struggle to excel. The most stress occurs when the classroom environment is unstructured, when teachers have unclear or unreasonable expectations, and when children realistically or unrealistically fear failure, especially on major tests.
- *Peer relations.* Children may experience stress due to peer rejection, dealing with bullies, and dealing with "unknown peers" due to changing schools.
- *Internal stress.* Stress can occur due to poor nutrition, sleep deprivation, or illnesses. Stress hormones increase during puberty changes. Mental health disorders are also likely to cause stress in children.

Due to added stressors during the school-age years, it can sometimes be difficult for adults to distinguish between typical adjustment behaviors and true stress-related problems. School-age children often communicate less with adults because they want to be independent, and adults have less supervision of their children during the school-age years. Nevertheless, some changes may indicate stress-related problems in children. **Figure 19.10** lists some of these warning signs.

Figure 19.10 Warning Signs of Stress in School-Age Children

- Eating disorders
- Sleep difficulty or nightmares
- Overreactions to minor problems
- Trouble concentrating or completing schoolwork
- Drop in grades
- Withdrawal from family and friends
- Hyperactive behavior
- Increased aggression
- Unexplained headaches or stomachaches
- Negativism and lying
- Regressive behaviors
- Experimentation with alcohol and other drugs

Social-Emotional Developmental Milestones

Children's social-emotional worlds transform when they enter school. Self-awareness expands as they learn to take responsibility, understand gender roles, and develop their self-concept. School-age children learn to be industrious and are exposed to numerous new social relations and situations in which they must express their emotions carefully. **Figure 19.11** lists social-emotional developmental milestones that children achieve during the school-age years.

Lesson 19.1 Review and Assessment 

1. In _____ boys teach other boys male behavioral norms, and girls teach other girls female behavioral norms.
2. Define *conventional morality* and describe its associated behaviors.
3. Why is self-evaluation complex during the school-age years?
4. Name and define Erikson's fourth stage of personality development.
5. Explain why peer groups are important for school-age children.
6. List four new sources of children's stress during the school-age years.
7. Choose one age range during the school-age years and describe at least three social-emotional developmental milestones of that age.
8. **Critical thinking.** Why is it especially important for school-age children to express their emotions in socially acceptable ways?

Figure 19.11 School-Age Social-Emotional Milestones

Six to seven years

- Defines *self* in terms of appearance, possessions, and activities.
- Has friendships based on play interest.
- Becomes "unfriendly" toward the opposite gender.
- Has unstable friendships due to taking a rigid position in conflicts.
- Wants to be independent, but shows anxiety in some cases.
- May be afraid of monsters and the dark and may have nightmares.
- Tattles to check sense of right and wrong.
- May be moody.
- Wants approval from adults and peers.

Eight to nine years

- Is sensitive to what others think.
- Wants to look and act like peers.
- Shows embarrassment if parents are around when with friends.
- Likes friendship groups and enjoys group activities.
- Is more self-critical and worries a great deal.
- Wants more independence from parents.
- Has preference for certain friends.
- Is anxious about school failure.

Ten to twelve years

- Defines *self* in terms of physical attributes, intellectual abilities, social skills, and regulation of emotions.
- Shows growing independence.
- Builds self-image as a worker and can take some responsibilities.
- Is friend-focused, shares secrets with friends, and constantly talks about friends.
- Conforms to peer groups.
- Is self-conscious.
- Has reality-based fears.
- Gets feelings easily hurt.

Lesson 19.2

Meeting School-Age Children's Social-Emotional Needs

Key Terms

interpretive stage
society of children

Academic Terms

bolster
diligent
solidarity

Objectives

After studying this lesson, you will be able to

- plan activities for promoting self-awareness in school-age children.
- explain how adults and caregivers can help children be industrious.
- describe ways adults can aid school-age children's friendships and expand their other social horizons.
- summarize how caregivers in Galinsky's *interpretive stage* of parenting can guide and model school-age children's behaviors and help them manage their conflicts.
- list four ways adults can help school-age children control their emotions.
- discuss how adults can help reduce children's stress during the school-age years.

Reading and Writing Activity

Before you read this lesson, view all of the tables and photos. Read all of the photo captions and take notes about what material the captions and tables cover. What do you know about the material covered in this lesson just from viewing the figures and captions? Write two to three paragraphs predicting what this lesson will be about.

Graphic Organizer

Create a KWL chart to organize what you already *know* (K), what you *want* (W) to know, and what you *learn* (L) as you read this lesson.

K What you already **K**now	W What you **W**ant to know	L What you **L**earn

Although the peer group becomes an important part of school-age children's social lives, adults still play a significant role in meeting school-age children's social-emotional needs. As children's self-awareness expands during the school years, adults can encourage children's successes, support them through their failures, and appreciate them as unique children. Parents can serve as the physical and psychological home base while providing time for friendships. Parents should also realize that school-age children have mood swings and emotional difficulties from time to time, which are normal. Lack of emotional control, however, often signals the need for professional help.

Promoting Self-Awareness

By the school-age years, children are very self-aware. Their self-awareness is influenced by how they believe others (parents and caregivers, teachers, and peers) think of them. Because their self-concepts are fragile, they need support and encouragement. Adults can promote their children's self-awareness by giving children responsibility, guiding their gender roles, instilling morality, and building a healthy self-concept.

Giving Responsibility

As school-age children learn to take responsibility for their schoolwork and other tasks, adults can support them by *giving* them responsibilities. Adults should supervise school and household tasks, but may give children more responsibility and freedom as children prove themselves to be **diligent** (hardworking).

While adults cannot assign children too many tasks, they can give responsibility by asking children to do chores. Chores help teach children skills and aid them in developing a work ethic. Some chores are best seen as "labors of love," even if parents want to pay the child for some extra work. Teaching responsibility and the value of work requires effort on the part of parents and other adults. **Figure 19.12** lists some other ways parents and caregivers can give responsibility to school-age children.

Figure 19.12 Giving Responsibility to School-Age Children

- As a parent or caregiver, be a model of good work ethic in the home.
- Explain to the child that chores come before recreational activities and that some chores have to be done at specific times to prevent harm.
- Compile a list of chores that the child is able to do or learn to do.
- Allow the child some choices among chores and rotate tasks from time to time.
- Teach the child the needed skills to complete a task.
- If the child completes a task poorly, find out why. Reteach needed skills, or have the child repeat the chore if the results were a matter of not trying.
- Allow flexibility in completing chores if another responsibility takes priority, but encourage the child to plan ahead next time.
- Show appreciation for what the child does. For example, say "thank you" for a job well done or provide a special treat for doing all chores for a week.
- If a child earns money for going beyond the chore list, then parents and caregivers need to help the child learn about saving, giving, and spending earnings.

Guiding Gender Roles

School-age children's perceptions of gender roles are under constant influence from families, peers, the school environment, and media. As societal views change and children develop narrower areas of interest, it is important for parents and caregivers to guide their children's learning of gender roles and help children understand the influence of the sources they encounter.

For the most part, school-age children learn gender roles through adult models. Mothers and other female adults close to school-age girls affect those girls' perceptions of feminine gender roles. These perceptions can impact a girl's goals in the world of work and at home. Fathers and other male adults close to school-age boys affect boys' perceptions of masculine gender roles. Conversely, fathers and other adult males who model warmth and sureness in their masculine roles affect femininity in girls. In addition, mothers and other female adults who model warmth and sureness in their feminine roles affect masculinity in boys.

Instilling Morality

Children learn morality through the examples of the adults in their lives. Even as school-age children begin to develop their own moral consciences, adults are responsible for instilling morality and encouraging the growth of that conscience. Parents and other adults can aid school-age children's moral development by teaching them to

- *respect others.* Respect is always a two-way street between an adult and a child or among peers.
- *show responsibility.* Giving children responsibilities in the family and other social groups helps them become *altruistic* (selflessly concerned for the welfare of others) and act on these feelings as a universal moral principle (**Figure 19.13**).
- *follow established limits.* School-age children and even adults accept limits if they believe the imposed limits are for their welfare.

Figure 19.13 Showing compassion for others is one way school-age children may act altruistically. *What is an example of an altruistic act that you or someone you know has performed?*

- *behave acceptably.* Children need to understand why certain behaviors are unacceptable. For example, children need to know that bullying hurts, lying destroys trust, and stealing violates the owner of the property. (This is part of Galinsky's *interpretive stage* of parenting.)
- *express remorse for misdeeds.* Children need to take appropriate actions to restore their **solidarity** (sense of belonging) within their social groups, such as returning stolen property with an apology for the misdeed.
- *think for themselves before acting on moral issues.* Children need to put themselves in another person's shoes, such as by asking, "How would I feel if _____?" They also need to ask themselves, "What will the consequences be?"

Building a Healthy Self-Concept

Children's feelings about themselves are influenced by how those who are important in their lives treat them. School-age children need to know they are important to their families. As school-age children seek parental affection and approval, parents need to communicate their love and acceptance to their children. Parents, caregivers, and other adults who provide love, appreciation, and encouragement form the foundation for a child's positive self-concept.

Every child has special talents and abilities. Parents can help build healthy self-concepts in their children by acknowledging and encouraging these traits. They can also offer positive feedback for tasks children did well. "You did a good job," is an important message for children to hear. Helping children believe in their own abilities can help school-age children build their confidence. With much love and support, adults can help school-age children in their struggle for a healthy self-concept (**Figure 19.14**).

When children need to be disciplined, parents should take care to discipline their children in ways that express caring and love. Research shows that the authoritative parenting style produces better self-concepts in children than the authoritarian, permissive, or overparenting styles. Adults should discipline children privately, not in front of their peers or others. If criticism must be given, the act should be criticized and not the child. If done this way, criticism can teach school-age children that their actions were wrong, but they can still be trusted and loved as a person.

Helping Children Be Industrious

In middle childhood, children develop a sense of industry, which begins to prepare them for adult work. To help children develop positive feelings about work, adults can lead children to focus on their abilities rather than on their faults. Adults should set reasonable standards. When standards are too high, children feel they cannot reach them and will not try. If standards are set too low, children may not work at their potential. Even small successes help children feel positive about their work, which increases their self-esteem.

Adults can also help children be industrious by encouraging them to succeed in school. Children do better in school when they have loving, caring adults who want them to do well than when they have adults who show little or no concern.

Supporting Social Relations

Despite children's growing reliance on peer groups, the parent-child relationship is still the most important influence in a child's life. School-age

Figure 19.14 School-age children need love and support to help them establish healthy self-concepts. *How do love and support from a caregiver differ from the acknowledgement of a teacher?*

children whose parents have high expectations, but who are also responsive to the child's growing independence, have children who thrive. In most families, the parent-child relationship is well established by the school-age years. Unlike the parent-child relationship, friendships are just being developed and are thus not well established until the later school-age years. Parents and caregivers can support school-age children's relationships by making time for friendships, expanding children's horizons, guiding and modeling behaviors, and managing conflicts.

Making Time for Friendships

School-age children spend more and more time with peers. Parents and other caregivers should encourage children to form friendships and relationships with other children. Children need time to be with friends. If parents and caregivers have many other plans for children, then children do not always have a chance to form friendships.

The peer groups children form, called a **society of children** by sociologists, prepare children for independence from parents when children grow up. Parents should understand that children will like their best friends almost as much as their families and will want to include their friends in family outings. Making friends welcome in the home and encouraging peer activities will help children establish these relationships.

Expanding Horizons

During the school-age years, children's social worlds expand, and parents and caregivers can help children form relationships by expanding their children's horizons. One way parents can help is to encourage their children to participate in activities with their peers at school and in the community. Parents can support children in their endeavors by helping them organize their activity schedules, ensuring that needed equipment is ready, and then driving children to and from activities.

Another way to help children form relationships is to plan family activities that can extend the skills children learn in school-age peer groups. Family activities can **bolster** (lend support to) children's physical, intellectual, and social skills. Suggesting hobbies in which their children can succeed is another good way for parents to help children expand their horizons. Children enjoy the tasks involved in their hobbies and like to display their new abilities and knowledge in their peer groups.

Focus on Careers

Sociologist

Sociologists study their own societies and other societies around the world. They examine social behaviors and traditions by studying individuals, cultures, groups, institutions, and human development. They typically work at colleges or universities, in research organizations, or as consultants.

Career cluster: Human services.

Education: Educational requirements include a master's degree or Ph.D.

Job outlook: Future employment opportunities for sociologists are expected to grow faster than the average for all occupations. There are not as many jobs available in this field, however, so there will be much competition for positions.

To learn more about a career as a sociologist, visit the United States Department of Labor's *Occupational Outlook Handbook* website. You will also be able to compare the job responsibilities, educational requirements, job outlook, and average pay of sociologists with similar occupations.

Guiding and Modeling Behaviors

During the school-age years, parents enter Galinsky's **interpretive stage** of parenting. Parents in this stage are tasked with modeling their values and attitudes about almost all aspects of life. School-age children watch and listen to important adults in their lives. They pattern many of their thoughts and actions after these adults. Parents should provide guidance and continue to support the parent-child relationship. Some ways that parents and caregivers can support this relationship include the following:

- ***Keep family communication open.*** It is important for parents and children to talk about and express their feelings openly. By 9 or 10 years of age, children begin to see parents' mistakes, which may strain family communication. As a result, parents and their children need to keep the lines of communication open (**Figure 19.15**). If good communication patterns are established during middle childhood, the parent-child relationship during the teen years will be much better.
- ***Teach morals and values.*** School-age children face moral decisions daily. At school they may be exposed to cheating, lying, stealing, and other negative activities. Parents and caregivers can help children build an internal moral system by providing love, respect, and mutual trust; by modeling

Figure 19.15 How to Keep Parent-Child Communication Open

Type of Problem	Parent-Child Communication Skills
Parent has a concern, such as a child coming home late.	• Parent can take a few moments to calm down. • Parent and child can communicate clearly and effectively using I-statements, such as "I became worried when I didn't know where you were after school." I-statements allow children to have points of view whether or not they are right. Avoid you-statements, such as "You should have at least called me." • Child can present his or her point of view. Parent can ask the child, "How can we solve this problem?"
Child makes a general accusation, such as "You always pick on me."	• Parent can listen until the child finishes talking. If the child is angry, the parent can say, "We will talk about this later," and then follow up. • Child can explain feelings and parent can paraphrase the child's feelings to ensure understanding. • Parent can ask, "Can you give me an example?" Avoid interrupting the child. • Parent and child can ask, "How can we both work on this problem so we do not have negative feelings?"
Child comes to parent with a problem.	• Child can come to parent and clearly explain feelings and problem. • Parent can focus on the child and his or her message, show interest, and clarify anything not understood. • Parent can say, "I can see that this is important to you," and ask, "What would you like to do about it? Do you have any ideas?" Parent can offer some suggestions if the child seems willing. • If the problem is severe and beyond what the child can handle, the parent can explain how he or she will handle it. • Parent can confirm interest and concern for the child by saying, "Let me know how this works out. Thanks for telling me."

what they expect; and by setting rules, giving reasons for rules, and applying logical consequences when the child misbehaves.

- ***Balance dependence with independence.*** School-age children often question caregivers' guidance. They need parents and caregivers to listen to them and, at times, to advise and set limits. Parents must learn the balance between letting go and being there for children, which is not easy. Parents do not always know whether they should protect children from problems with friends or let them cope on their own. Parents may be torn between trying to enforce their teachings and allowing children to make some of their own decisions. Parents should communicate with children about how to strike this balance and be responsive to their children's needs and concerns.

Managing Conflicts

For the most part, children are reluctant to tell adults about what goes on in their world of peers. This becomes especially true during the late school-age years. When children experience conflicts and friendship difficulties, adults should be ready to encourage and support them. Ways that adults can help school-age children manage conflicts and difficulties include the following:

- Give direct assistance to children who experience rejection. Some children may need counseling for aggression or shyness.
- Realize that children often need help when they lose their best friends, whether because of conflicts, new interests, moves, or death (**Figure 19.16**). School-age children can suffer great pain, even depression, from ended friendships. Depression can cause eating and sleeping problems, as well as indifference toward working or playing. Adults can help children who are depressed by talking about emotions, staying neutral if the ended friendship was caused by a conflict, and by preparing children for friendship losses.
- Set firm limits on risky or inappropriate behaviors. Adults should not allow children to attend parties or events in which the activities make them uncomfortable as a parent or caregiver. Parents can also tell children that they can always say, "My parent will not let me," if they feel an activity or situation is inappropriate. Many children are relieved by this option.

Figure 19.16 School-age children may struggle with the sadness of losing a friend. Talking with a parent may help these children process the loss. *Think of a time when you lost a friend as a child. How did you feel at the time? How did you express your feelings?*

- Watch for inappropriate friendships and talk about inappropriate behaviors (such as bullying, using alcohol or drugs, and shoplifting) of peer groups. Adults can explain to children why these behaviors are wrong and outline the consequences. Adults can also offer guidance on what children might do if such a situation arises.

Helping Children Control Their Emotions

During the school-age years, children continue working toward self-regulation. Older school-age children can often self-regulate emotions consistently and analyze the causes of their feelings and the consequences of certain behaviors. They are capable of thinking before they act. At times, however, school-age children may still experience some mood swings and outbursts and need adults to help them control their emotions.

Some ways adults continue to guide children's emotions during the school-age years include the following:

- ***Modeling emotional control.*** Children need to observe parents modeling control of their own emotions. Children learn by watching adults handle frustration and anger.
- ***Normalizing emotions.*** Children need to know that all people have strong feelings. School-age children may be helped by reading about the struggles of other children and adults to control feelings. Adults may want to talk about their own struggles, too, such as controlling their tempers or managing jealousy.
- ***Respecting others.*** Children need to be told that control of emotions is done out of respect for others.
- ***Using loving discipline.*** Parents and caregivers can model acceptable ways of guiding and disciplining their children. Physical punishment can show a loss of control by the adult.
- ***Suggesting indirect outlets.*** Children need indirect ways to control emotions, such as physical activity and creative tasks (**Figure 19.17**).
- ***Teaching skills.*** Caregivers and other adults can teach skills that help children overcome fears and anxieties, as well as other strong emotions.

Figure 19.17 Engaging in physical activity can help school-age children control their emotions. *What indirect outlets help you control emotions?*

Mental Health Advisory

School-age children who cannot control their sadness may sink into depression and be unable to experience the joys of life. Deep depression can lead to self-harming behaviors. Depressed children who cannot appraise ambiguous situations or control their anger may develop mental health problems that lead to disastrous results, such as violence.

In some cases, school-age children need professional help if their behavior goes beyond the boundaries (in intensity and length of time) of what most children do. Two common problems that require professional help are sad and withdrawn behaviors and aggressive and defiant behaviors.

Sad and withdrawn behaviors often suggest depression. Children cannot just "get over" depression. Aggressive and defiant behaviors, especially in children who cannot appraise ambiguous situations, may signal poor anger management. These children may interpret many actions as hostile and immediately react with anger. The risk factors for this problem are an irritable temperament and exposure to models of poor anger management. Often these problems occur together. Professionals have to train children how to appraise situations and how to be assertive rather than aggressive.

Helping School-Age Children Cope with Stress

Parents and teachers can work together to try and prevent chronic and toxic stress in school-age children. One way to do this is by watching for signs of stress, which can appear as both physical and psychological symptoms. Some of these symptoms may be prolonged or severe. Listening for signs of stress is also important. Most children will not say, "I'm stressed," but they may say, "I'm angry" or "I'm worried." Stressed children are more likely to say negative things about themselves, about others, or about the world around them.

Mental Health Advisory

Children who feel overburdened with chronic stress or experience toxic stress are likely to develop mental health problems. Mental health problems also lead to stress.

At home, parents and caregivers can reduce stress by giving children constant love and support. They can provide a stable home environment and monitor children's eating and sleeping habits. Parents can also seek to understand the causes of misbehaviors rather than just punishing children. Avoiding unrealistic expectations is important, too. Parents can let children know they can help them with their problems through open communication and possible suggestions. Lastly, working with a licensed mental health professional may be necessary if stress seems to overwhelm the child.

Lesson 19.2 Review and Assessment 

1. Explain how chores help school-age children show responsibility.
2. List four ways adults can aid school-age children's moral development.
3. To help children develop positive feelings about work, adults can lead children to focus on their ______ rather than on their ______.
4. Summarize two ways adults can expand school-age children's horizons.
5. Name three ways parents and caregivers can provide guidance to support the parent-child relationship.
6. List four ways adults continue to guide children's emotions during the school-age years.
7. What are two ways parents and caregivers can reduce stress in school-age children?
8. **Critical thinking.** Explain why it is important for adults to make time for and encourage school-age children's friendships.

Chapter 19 Review and Assessment

Summary

School-age children's self-awareness expands as they take on and show new responsibilities. Children also learn more about gender roles and begin to establish a moral conscience during the school-age years. Their self-concepts are affected by comparisons with other peers. School-age children are in Erikson's fourth stage of personality development, called *industry versus inferiority*. School-age children learn to be industrious both in schoolwork and with home responsibilities. They struggle, however, with feelings of inferiority. During the school-age years, children enter into a *goal-corrected partnership* with their caregivers. Peers and friends, however, become much more important in children's lives as compared with their importance during the preschool years. School-age children are learning to control their emotions and express love, fear and anxiety, anger and aggression, and jealousy in socially acceptable ways. As school-age children adjust to their new responsibilities and relationships, adults should watch for signs of stress.

In meeting school-age children's social-emotional needs, caregivers can plan activities to encourage self-awareness. They can give children responsibilities (such as chores) and can guide gender roles. They can instill morality and help children build a healthy self-concept. Caregivers should encourage their children to be industrious and try to reduce feelings of inferiority. In guiding school-age children's social relationships, parents and other adults can make time for children's friendships, expand children's horizons, guide and model important behaviors, and help manage conflicts. For the most part, school-age children are able to regulate their emotions. Adults, however, can guide school-age children's emotions through modeling and providing outlets for the control of emotions. Finally, if adults notice stress in school-age children, they should take steps to help children cope.

College and Career Portfolio

Portfolio Website

Making your portfolio available electronically can make it easier for colleges and employers to review the portfolio's contents. Some professionals make their portfolios available through a website.

- Research platforms for making your portfolio available online.
- Use one platform to create a sample portfolio. Then, evaluate whether the platform is right for your portfolio.

Chapter 19 Review and Assessment

Vocabulary Activities

1. Read the text passages that contain each of the following terms. Then write the definitions of each term in your own words. Double-check your definitions by rereading the text and using the text glossary.

Key Terms

domains of self-definition (19.1)
gender schools (19.1)
goal-corrected partnership (19.1)
guilt (19.1)
industry versus inferiority (19.1)
interpretive stage (19.2)
psychological security (19.1)
scapegoating (19.1)
shortcomings (19.1)
society of children (19.2)
work ethic (19.1)

2. With a partner, create a T-chart. Write each of the following terms in the left column. Write a *synonym* (a word that has the same or similar meaning) for each term in the right column. Discuss your synonyms with the class.

Academic Terms

bolster (19.2)
deemed (19.1)
deviate (19.1)
diligent (19.2)
drastically (19.1)
industry (19.1)
inferiority (19.1)
infringe (19.1)
instilling (19.1)
prodigious (19.1)
solidarity (19.2)

Critical Thinking

3. **Evaluate.** Choose one media depiction of a school-age child. Then, evaluate how this school-age child shows responsibility. What tasks does he or she perform to demonstrate responsibility? How might the child show *more* responsibility? Share your thoughts with the rest of the class.
4. **Draw conclusions.** As children develop a sense of industry, play can take a different role in their lives. In small groups, discuss how the importance of play changes during the school-age years. Should play take a "backseat" to industrious activities? Why or why not?
5. **Analyze.** During the school-age years, peers become increasingly important to children. Children may rely more on friendships than they do on their parents and caregivers. Analyze why peer relationships become so important during this stage of development. What factors contribute to this importance? How does this importance affect the way school-age children behave?
6. **Make inferences.** Children in the school-age years compare themselves with one another and tend to judge harshly. Why do you think this is? What developmental changes contribute to these behaviors? What societal factors influence peers' judgments?
7. **Determine.** Choose one emotion discussed in this chapter and determine concrete ways parents and caregivers can help school-age children control this emotion. How well were you able to control this emotion as a school-age child?
8. **Cause and effect.** Forming a self-concept becomes more complex for children during the school-age years. In small groups, identify and summarize reasons for this complexity. Then, analyze how these reasons affect school-age children's self-esteem. Finally, discuss ways adults can help children build healthy self-concepts.
9. **Compare and contrast.** Review the ways adults and caregivers can help school-age children manage conflicts. Choose two of these ways to compare and contrast. How do the two ways help manage a conflict? How effective are the two ways? Is one way more effective than the other?
10. **Identify.** Many school-age children experience difficulties adjusting to relationships with peers. Some of these children may benefit from outside help whether in the form of a social group or counselor. In small groups identify helpful community resources for children who have difficulties with peer relationships. Create an easy-to-follow list of these resources and their objectives.

Core Skills

11. **Research, listening, and speaking.** Using reliable online or print resources, research how gender roles develop during the school-age years. Where do children learn about gender roles? How do they express them? Take notes about your findings and compile a short bibliography.

Then interview a school counselor (at a primary or middle school) and discuss your research. Does the school counselor agree with your research findings? What, if anything, would the school counselor add or change? After the interview, deliver an oral presentation summarizing your research and interview.

12. **Listening, speaking, and writing.** Interview a primary or middle school teacher about school-age children's morality. According to the teacher, what kind of morality do school-age children possess? How do they act on that morality? During the second half of your interview, discuss Kohlberg's theory of moral reasoning with the teacher. Draw connections between Kohlberg's theory and the teacher's real-life experience. After the interview, write a short reflection about what you learned from the discussion.
13. **Writing.** Review this chapter's information about the school-age child's struggle between *industry* and *inferiority*. Then, write a short story for school-age children exploring this struggle and encouraging children to keep striving for industry and to protect themselves from feelings of inferiority. Include a summary for your short story explaining how it will help children in their struggle.
14. **Technology and speaking.** In small groups, arrange to visit a primary or middle school. Interview 5 to 10 school-age children of various ages about their friendships and experiences with peers. Ask questions about how important the children's friendships are, what makes a good friend, and whether the children feel that their peers are judging them. If possible, obtain permission to film the children's responses to these questions and compile the responses into a video. Play your video for the class and then discuss what your video reveals about school-age children's social worlds.
15. **Listening and speaking.** As a class, write a different social-emotional developmental milestone for school-age children (Figure 19.11) on index cards or other pieces of paper. Then, shuffle the cards around the room. Without speaking, try to group yourselves according to the appropriate age range. You can communicate which milestone you are depicting by acting, using hand gestures, or writing words that are not included in your milestone's description. After grouping yourselves, check for accuracy by reading off your milestones.
16. **Listening and math.** Interview a parent and his or her school-age child. During the interview, ask the parent and child to identify behaviors they have in common and behaviors they do not have in common. Which behaviors does the parent think the child learned from him or her? Which behaviors of the parent does the child reject? After the interview, tally the number of behaviors in common and the number of behaviors not in common. What percentage of the child's behaviors were guided or modeled by the parent?
17. **Reading.** Using a local library or the Internet, search for and locate two scholarly articles about stress in school-age children. Read these articles and take notes about what causes stress, how stress impacts children, and how adults can help alleviate stress. Afterward, write a comprehensive summary for each article. Print your summaries and place them on the walls of the classroom. As a class, walk around the room and read about articles your classmates found.
18. **CTE Career Readiness Practice.** Presume you are a social counselor at a middle school and your principal has asked you to deliver a presentation at sixth-grade orientation about children's emotional control. Your presentation will be for parents and caregivers and should highlight how children are learning to control emotions and ways in which adults can help them. Write a script for your presentation and memorize it. Practice until you feel confident. Finally, deliver your presentation to the class.

Observations

19. As a class, visit a local primary or middle school. Sit near the outside of the school's lunchroom and observe how school-age children interact in their peer groups. How much are the children trying to impress one another? Do you see signs of peers judging one another? of peers comparing abilities and skills? Discuss your observations as a class.
20. Visit a local library or search online to locate a documentary about school-age children's stress and the social-emotional risks school-age children face. Watch the documentary in a small group and take notes about what you learn. Then, discuss how your group members have witnessed these social-emotional risks, either personally or at their former schools.

Unit 7 Guiding and Caring for Children

Job Interview

Job interviewing is an event you might enter with your CTSO organization. By participating in the job interview, you will showcase your presentation skills, communication techniques, and ability to actively listen to the interviewer's questions. Written expectations for this event often include the creation of a cover message, résumé, portfolio, and completion of a job application.

To prepare for a job interview event, complete the following activities:

1. Use Internet and print resources to research the job-application process and interview techniques.
2. Write your cover message, résumé, and complete the job application (if provided for the event).
3. Prepare your portfolio. Include a table of contents, cover message, résumé, job application, and relevant samples of your work. Check the rules and regulations for your CTSO event for any other items to include in your portfolio and for presentation format (print or digital). *(Note: Your organization may require that you submit these materials prior to the event or at the event.)*
4. Make certain each piece of communication is complete and free of errors.
5. Solicit feedback regarding your written materials from peers, instructors, and family members.
6. Ask a peer to take the role of interviewer as you practice answering interview questions. Your instructor or classmates may serve as competition judges during your practice sessions. Incorporate suggestions for improvement in your responses.

Chapter 20 Encouraging Children's Play Experiences

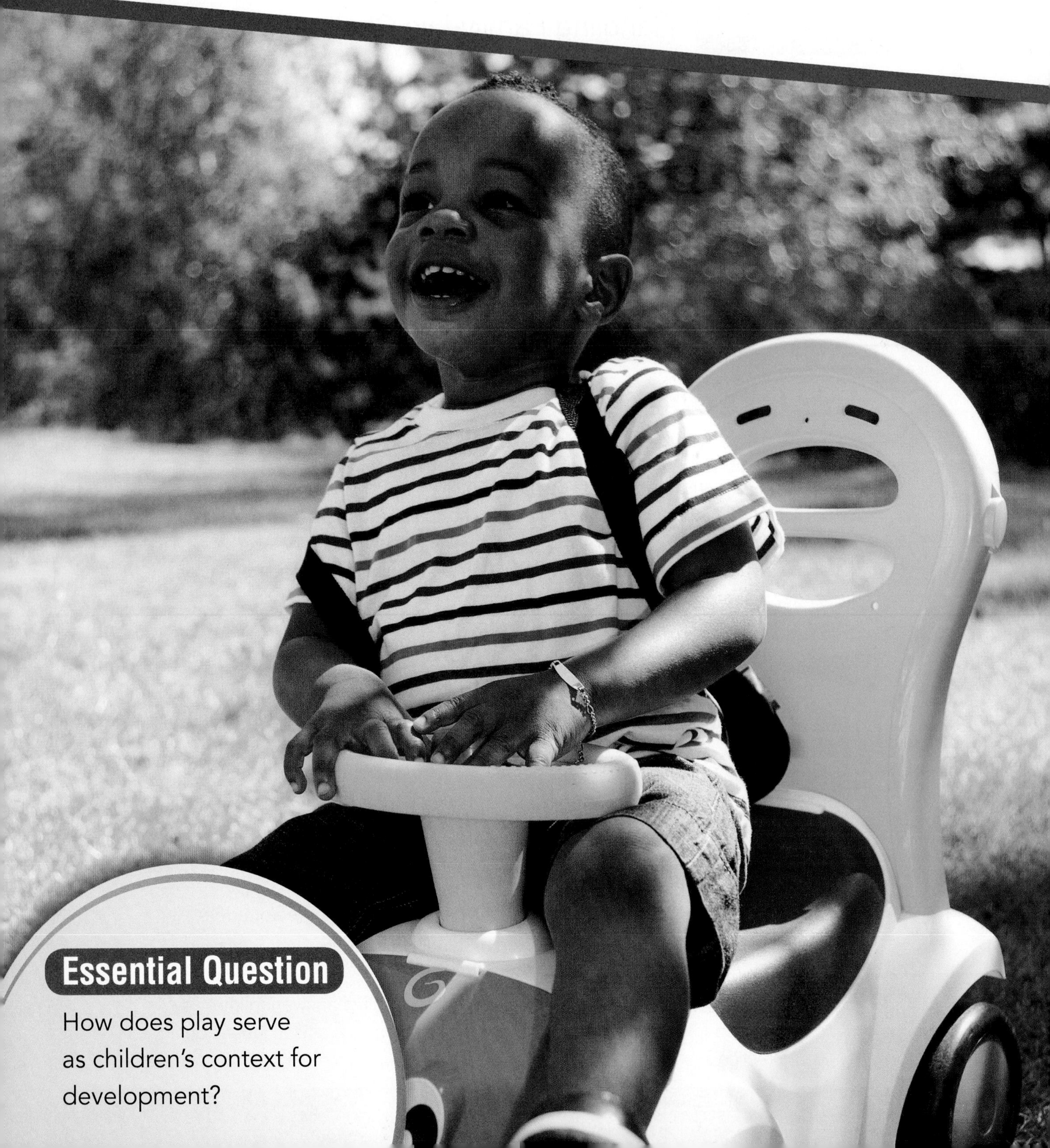

Essential Question

How does play serve as children's context for development?

Lesson 20.1 **The Importance of Play**

Lesson 20.2 **Play Activities for Children**

Case Study How Do Children Learn Through Art?

As a class, read the case study and discuss the questions that follow. After you finish studying the chapter, discuss this case study again. Have your opinions changed based on what you learned?

After completing his degree in early childhood education, Hiroto was excited to land a job teaching preschoolers. From the moment he received the job offer, Hiroto started planning creative art activities that would promote holistic learning. Hiroto excelled at his job and received only praise from his director for the first few months.

One Friday, Hiroto's preschoolers engaged in a rather messy activity using tempera paint. Later that day, the director called Hiroto into her office and said, "Please change these messy activities. The children will only produce scribbles, and parents expect art projects to look *real*." The director pulled a butterfly art pattern from a file in her office. She explained, "We usually copy art patterns like this one for the children to color and decorate."

Hiroto felt crushed that the director wanted him to use this "cookie cutter" art instead of the "real art" he had been organizing. He thought, *I've been taught so many ideas for helping children do creative art. Why can't the center embrace my ideas even if some of the art projects are messy?*

During the next week or so, Hiroto followed the director's instructions, although sending home "cookie cutter" art projects made him unhappy. Hiroto wondered, *Are my ideas about art for preschoolers wrong? How can I please the director while still giving my students the best education?*

Give It Some Thought

1. Whose ideas about art are most appropriate for preschoolers? How much of a difference does the type of art project make? Explain your answer.
2. Do you think Hiroto would be better off following the director's ideas or the ones he recently learned? Explain your answer.
3. Do you think parents really want "cookie cutter" art as the director indicated? Why or why not?

While studying this chapter, look for the online resources icon  to:

- **Practice** terms with e-flash cards and interactive games
- **Assess** what you learn by completing self-assessment quizzes
- **Expand** knowledge with interactive activities and graphic organizers

Companion G-W Learning

www.g-wlearning.com/childdevelopment

Study on the go

Use a mobile device to practice terms and review with self-assessment quizzes.

www.m.g-wlearning.com/0384

Lesson 20.1 The Importance of Play

Key Terms

active-physical play
imitative-imaginative play
language-logic play
manipulative-constructive play
play therapy

Academic Terms

graceful
strategize

Objectives

After studying this lesson, you will be able to

- describe the importance of play and play activities in children's lives.
- identify the stages of play with objects.
- explain how children's play with people changes during each stage of development.
- define *active-physical play* and explain its benefits for children.
- summarize the types of skills fostered by manipulative-constructive play.
- describe the benefits and identify the stages of imitative-imaginative play.
- list examples of language-logic play.
- identify two ways that adults can encourage play in children.

Reading and Writing Activity

Read the objectives for this lesson carefully and then write three paragraphs describing what you already know about these topics. Base your writing on personal experiences and observations of those around you. After reading this lesson, rewrite your three paragraphs to include relevant information you learned.

Graphic Organizer

Draw a comic strip and label it *Stages and Types of Play*. Then, as you are reading, take notes about how the stages and types of play change for children in each stage of development.

Children are active and curious learners who want to explore new objects, places, and people. They are also eager learners, asking countless questions as they strive for self-direction. For children, learning and expressing are closely related. The ways in which children express themselves—primarily through *play*—are reflective of what children have learned. In addition, children's expressions expand and refine their learning (**Figure 20.1**).

Research shows that the benefits of play are limitless and involve all domains of child development. Children play based on what they understand. If encouraged, they will go beyond their understanding to experiment and invent.

To encourage self-expression and to help children learn through play, adults must recognize the importance of play. Adults should also be familiar with the stages of play and types of play so they can encourage children to express and refine their learning through play at each stage of development.

Stages of Play

Play, often referred to as the *highest level of child development*, reflects changes that take place in children's physical, intellectual, and social-emotional development. As such, play proceeds through a series of stages as children grow and develop new skills.

Children's stages of play build on one another. Very young children will not begin to play in advanced stages until they have mastered early stages. Older children learn to play in advanced stages, but they can still play in earlier stages, too (**Figure 20.2**). New objects and people may cause a child to play at a less advanced stage until the child is accustomed to the change.

Child development experts describe the stages of play in several ways, depending on the aspects of play on which they focus. Piaget identified three

Figure 20.1 While playing with bubbles, a child can *express* what he or she knows while *learning* more about the nature of air and bubbles. *What was your favorite type of play as a child? How did that type of play allow you to express yourself while learning more?*

Figure 20.2 When older children play with younger children, the stage of play most often fits the ZPD for the younger child. However, older children may provide ideas that slightly "stretch" younger children's thinking. *Why do you think play most often fits the ZPD for the younger child?*

stages of play, which correspond with Piaget's first three stages of cognitive development. Other theorists have approached play from different perspectives. Stages of play involve children's play with objects and with people. **Figure 20.3** shows some of these stages of play with objects and with people although other child development experts may describe stages of play in different ways.

Investigate Special Topics

Theories of Play

Children's play has been a topic of discussion among child development experts for some time. Piaget, Vygotsky, and Erikson all studied the ways children play and how play affects children. Their findings illustrate the impact of play on intellectual and social-emotional development.

Play and Intellectual Development

Piaget's and Vygotsky's studies both highlight the importance of play. The theorists, however, reached slightly different conclusions about the role of play in learning.

According to Piaget, play is a way for children to practice concepts they already know, but play is *not* seen as a way for children to learn new concepts. For example, if a preschool child is lifting a block to represent an airplane, the child is showing his or her understanding that airplanes are objects that fly. During this activity, the preschool child will not learn, however, that an airplane's design is related to the lift needed for planes to fly. Recognizing the relationship between design and lift requires thinking more advanced than that of a preschooler.

In contrast to Piaget, Vygotsky believed that play *advances* a child's intellectual development. Children not only practice concepts they already know, but they also learn new concepts. Vygotsky believed that play works within a child's zone of proximal development (ZPD) and is similar to teaching a child a new concept.

Although Piaget's and Vygotsky's ideas about play may differ somewhat, both agree that play has intellectual benefits. Play aids children in learning and practicing intellectual concepts, such as physical knowledge concepts, logical thinking concepts, symbolic learning, language and literacy, and humor and creativity.

Play and Social-Emotional Development

Piaget, Vygotsky, and Erikson all studied the relationship between play and social-emotional development in children. According to Piaget, play interactions help children understand that other children may have perspectives different from their own, which is a key step in children's moral development. Vygotsky's studies illustrate that pretend play in children follows social rules (being true to the role one is playing and cooperating with others) and encourages the development of emotional self-regulation. Finally, Erikson saw play as a way for children to try new social skills and learn about cultural norms and gender roles. He also believed that through pretend play, children can dramatize child-adult conflicts safely—without rigid limits and strong consequences.

Speaking Activity

Choose one theorist discussed—Piaget, Vygotsky, or Erikson—and do further research into that theorist's ideas about play. Take notes of your findings and then write a persuasive speech about the importance of play from that theorist's point of view. Present your speech to the class.

Figure 20.3 **Stages of Play**

Play with Objects*	Play with People
Infancy and the Toddler Years	
Practice play. Children explore objects by picking them up or tracking them with their eyes. Play involves putting objects in mouth, moving body, listening to noises, exploring surroundings, and imitating others' actions. Play activities are repeated. (Also known as *sensory motor play*.)	***Solitary play.*** Infants ignore other children who are nearby. Sometimes infants treat others as objects to be pushed or walked on, to be poked in the eyes or nose, or to have hair pulled. ***Onlooker play.*** Toddlers watch others play, but do not join in their play. ***Parallel play.*** Children play near other children and often play with the same or similar toys. They note that others have interests and skills much like their own. There is no real interaction among children, however.
Preschool and the Early School-Age Years	
Symbolic play. Children engage in pretend play. They pretend they are someone else. Also, they project mental images on objects. For example, a stick can become a horse. Symbolic play becomes more complex as children age.	***Associative play.*** Two or more children play at a common activity. The children share ideas. The play is not well organized in terms of goals or roles, however. For example, one child may decide to run a food store and another may be a mother, but the mother never shops at the food store.
Late School-Age Years	
Rule play. Children make rules to govern their games or carefully follow the rules already established. Play becomes more logical and interactive.	***Cooperative play.*** Two or more children share common goals and play complementary roles, such as the chaser and the chased.

* The stages of play with objects were outlined by Piaget and follow Piaget's first three stages of cognitive development. *Practice play* corresponds to Piaget's sensorimotor stage; *symbolic play* to Piaget's preoperational stage; and *rule play* to Piaget's concrete operational stage.

Types of Play

Children play in many different ways depending on their interests, stages of development, and materials available. Different types of play encourage different skills and strengthen different areas of development. While play classifications may vary, some common types of play include *active-physical play*, *manipulative-constructive play*, *imitative-imaginative play*, and *language-logic play*. Knowing the types of play can help parents and other adults foster healthful and appropriate play in children.

Active-Physical Play

Active-physical play is a type of play in which children use their gross-motor skills. Gross-motor skills are used in activities, such as walking, running, hopping, jumping, twisting, bending, skipping, galloping, catching, throwing, balancing, pushing, pulling, and rocking. Through active-physical play, children test and improve various physical skills. They learn how strong they are by pushing, pulling, lifting, and carrying objects. Children learn how to spring up to lift their bodies, which is a skill they often need. They also learn how to catch themselves on impact, which protects the body from injury. Active-physical play also improves a child's reaction time and balance. Children need balance for almost every gross-motor movement. Active-physical play helps children become more **graceful** (able to move smoothly and elegantly). Grace improves as gross-motor skills develop and helps a person engage in many more fun activities.

Through active-physical play, children learn about spatial concepts. For example, they learn about the positions of objects and about the movements of their bodies in space. Names for movements and positions in space take on meaning. These names include *forward, backward, big, little, fast, slow, under, over, up, down, behind, in front of, through, beside,* and *between.* Children will also develop physical knowledge concepts through active-physical play. For example, they will become aware of the force of gravity on objects and on their bodies. They will experience going faster on a steep slide as compared to a slide with a gentle slope.

Figure 20.4 Manipulative-constructive play involves handling objects and may include art activities and fine-motor games. *What are some other examples of manipulative-constructive play?*

Manipulative-Constructive Play

Manipulative-constructive play is a type of play that involves the use of children's fine-motor skills. Children's fine-motor skills generally develop after basic gross-motor skills. For example, most children will not learn the fine-motor skill of writing until after they learn the gross-motor skill of walking. Even early in life, though, some fine-motor skills start to develop. Crawling infants can pick up small objects (such as gravel and paper) on a carpet. They can put objects in their mouths, ears, and noses. Manipulative-constructive play also benefits eye-hand coordination, which is crucial for children's writing and artwork (**Figure 20.4**).

Many toys and materials promote children's development of fine-motor skills. These include jigsaw puzzles, small blocks and other construction materials, beads for stringing, pegs and pegboards, art materials, woodworking tools, and cooking gadgets. Toys that promote fine-motor skills are made for little, unskilled hands as well as for more skilled hands.

In addition to promoting fine-motor skills, manipulative-constructive play helps children mentally picture objects. Furthermore, many visual and intellectual concepts, such as recognition of shapes and understandings of distance, math, sorting and classifying, and reversibility, are developed as children play with manipulative toys. Finally, manipulative-constructive play helps children create abstract models of what they see (such as by drawing their houses and yards).

Imitative-Imaginative Play

During **imitative-imaginative play**, children use words and actions to pretend to be objects or people other than themselves. Imitative-imaginative play has great value and involves creativity as children invent their own worlds. As children put themselves in different situations, they learn to plan, solve problems, and make decisions. Children choose props and actions in their play and can use imitative-imaginative play to test many roles. They can imagine or picture themselves as if they are other people and objects and can begin to understand others' real-life roles. Children can use pretend actions to depict holiday, work, family, and other rituals that begin to prepare them for adult life. In group play, leadership roles often emerge, too.

Imitative-imaginative play also helps improve children's memories because children must recall events in order to play. Children's language improves as they listen and speak during play. There is much freedom in expression as children try to bridge the gap between what they know and what they do not know. Children use their bodies to extend their language. For example, a child may say, "I'm a barber," while moving his or her fingers in a cutting motion.

Through imitative-imaginative play, children can also express fears, resentments, and even hostile feelings in ways that are socially acceptable. Role-playing has many healing qualities, which are utilized in activities like **play therapy** (the use of play between a child and a trained counselor to help the child resolve certain problems).

There are three stages of imitative-imaginative play. These stages are called *imitative play, dramatic play,* and *socio-dramatic play* (**Figure 20.5**). As children grow and progress through these stages, their roles and imaginations become more and more complex.

Language-Logic Play

Language-logic play is a form of intellectual play most often seen in school-age children. Language-logic play can include many different types of language and word games. In some language games, children compete by using vocabulary skills. Other language games include humor that is based on language, such as puns. Logic games, such as chess, object puzzles, word problems, and checkers, require much thought about one's actions. In these games, children must think ahead and **strategize** (plan strategies).

Encouraging Play in Children

Play is important for children's development and health, and it is important that adults (both parents and other adults who work with children)

Figure 20.5 Stages of Imitative-Imaginative Play

Stage	Characteristics	Example
Imitative play	• Begins at about two years of age, or just as children start to use symbolic thought. • Involves the child doing one imitative action to an object. • Occurs in short periods of time, but repeatedly over days, weeks, and even months.	For ten minutes every day, a child throws a stuffed animal into the air to pretend it is a spaceship.
Dramatic play	• Begins when the child is three or four years of age. • Involves role-playing with more than one child, but each child's role is independent of others' roles. • Often includes children engaging in collective monologue. • Involves several behaviors associated with a role.	Three children pretend to be space creatures by running around a room, but they are all playing different and sometimes contradictory roles.
Socio-dramatic play	• Is common in children between five and seven years of age. • Involves play associated with a theme. • Involves assigning special roles to each child.	Three children assign each other roles as explorers (a navigator, an astronaut, and a scientist) and pretend to look for new planets together.

encourage children to play. Children need support and need to know that adults recognize the importance of and approve of their play. Although how an adult specifically encourages a child's play will depend on the child and the type of play he or she enjoys, there are several principles adults can keep in mind when supporting play.

First, adults can allow freedom for children to explore and play. For the most part, children need time to explore on their own. While adults can observe play and, at times, model ideas or add materials, children need freedom to decide whether they will use these ideas. Rather than directing play, adults can add to play by playing along with children's pretend play in supportive roles and by explaining new concepts. As much as possible, children should take the lead in their own play. While some limits (such as rules for safety) are necessary, too many limits set by adults and sometimes children's peers may discourage a child.

In addition to letting children lead, adults can encourage play by displaying positive attitudes toward play. Adults' attitudes toward play influence how children view play. What adults do and say can promote or hamper children's creativity. To encourage children, adults can recognize the importance of play and then express that to children by providing plenty of playtime and by acknowledging children's learning, creativity, and fun.

Finally, adults can encourage play in children by providing toys that children will like. Children's preferences in toys change as children grow and develop. **Figure 20.6** lists toys that are attractive to children in different stages of development.

Figure 20.6 Attractive Toys for Children

Infancy and the Toddler Years
• Texture toys • Squeeze toys • Stuffed toys and dolls • Large balls • Toys that make sounds • Push-and-pull toys
Preschool Years
• Toys for gross-motor play (balls, pedal toys, and climbing toys) • Toys for fine-motor play (puzzles, beads, and pegs) • Floor blocks • Dress-up clothes and props • Toy cars, trucks, and planes • Toy animals • Puppets and toy people
School-Age Years
• Sports equipment • Bicycles • Board games • Digital games • Crafts and puzzles • Advanced construction sets • Collectibles

Lesson 20.1 Review and Assessment 

1. List the stages of play with objects and identify their corresponding stages of cognitive development.
2. Explain the difference between *associative play* and *cooperative play.*
3. Define *active-physical play* and identify the area of development it most affects.
4. _____ is a type of play that involves the use of children's fine-motor skills.
5. List three skills that imitative-imaginative play improves.
6. Give four examples of language-logic play.
7. Identify two ways adults can encourage play in children.
8. **Critical thinking.** Why is play important for children's learning and development? Write a short essay in response to this question and use examples from the text.

Play Activities for Children

Lesson 20.2

Objectives

After studying this lesson, you will be able to

- explain how block building strengthens children's visual literacy and intellectual development.
- identify the benefits of and explain how adults help children during sand play, water play, and cooking activities.
- identify the stages of art development and the benefits of visual arts activities for children.
- describe types of music and science activities for children.
- discuss the benefits of literature experiences and identify age-appropriate reading techniques for young children.

Key Terms

sand tables
unit blocks
visual arts
visual literacy
water tables

Academic Terms

tactile
tangible

Reading and Writing Activity

As you read this lesson, consider what each concept you learn might teach you about yourself. Keep a list of these ideas, placing a star beside any concepts that especially interest you. After reading the lesson, pick three of the ideas and write a few paragraphs reflecting on how these concepts helped or will help you understand yourself.

Graphic Organizer

Draw a three-column chart like the one shown and label the columns *Type of Play Activity*, *Benefits*, and *The Adult's Role*. As you read, organize your notes into these columns for each play activity.

Type of Play Activity	Benefits	The Adult's Role

Adults have a major role in children's play. Their abilities to recognize and implement various play activities impact children's play experiences. Quality play experiences should both entertain children and teach them. Because children learn through play, the potential benefits of planning quality play activities are enormous. Through play, children can become physically stronger and more coordinated, can practice new intellectual concepts, and can learn social skills that will strengthen their relationships.

Many play activities and games are available for children, but the best play activities tend to be open-ended and benefit all areas of development. Quality play activities that adults can plan for children include block building, sand play, water play, cooking experiences, art experiences, music experiences, science experiences, and literature experiences. By planning these activities and allowing children freedom to explore, adults foster children's development.

Block Building

Blocks are one of the most important play experiences and learning tools for children. Block building is a flexible, open-ended activity that extends to all areas of development, allowing for holistic learning. As children develop, they experience several stages of block building that correspond to their development of spatial concepts (**Figure 20.7**). Progress in block building also complements children's other understandings. For example, at three years of age, children can express symbolic understandings, such as saying a pile of blocks is a house. By four years of age, children express understandings about how environmental features are related, such as depicting houses by the side of a road. By seven years of age, children build more to scale, such as building a chair smaller than a house.

Unlike sand, water, and art materials, blocks are solid, constant shapes that create a stable environment, permit self-correction, and allow for endless repetitions. Block building has benefits in all areas of development. Through running, jumping, lifting, carrying, bending, reaching, grasping, and balancing, children develop gross- and fine-motor skills and eye-hand coordination. Block building enhances thinking skills and aids the beginning of logical thought by promoting **visual literacy** (the ability to draw meaning from observable and **tangible**—perceived by touch—objects). Concepts that children learn through visual literacy include spatial concepts, classification, seriation, and number and shape concepts. Block building may also promote physics concepts (such as gravity), social studies concepts (such as space planning), art concepts (through making designs), and language and literacy concepts (through using blocks in dramatic play). Finally, block building encourages social skills (such as taking turns and sharing), requires patience and persistence, and strengthens children's self-concepts.

To support children's block building, adults can provide blocks, space for block building, and time for children to build. Different types of blocks offer different learning opportunities for children. *Unit blocks* (commonly called *floor blocks*) are often considered the best set of blocks for preschool and school-age children. **Unit blocks** are naturally finished wooden blocks that are multiples or divisions of the basic unit size (1⅜" X 2¾" X 5½"). It is important that adults allow children freedom to play with blocks. Rather than taking the lead or attempting to teach concepts, adults can help children by giving occasional suggestions, such as "Do you think another block might fit?" Adults can also support block building through expressions of pride in their children's creations, such as by taking photos and encouraging children to talk about their structures.

Sand Play

Because sand is a natural substance, children have probably played in it throughout history (**Figure 20.8**). Children are attracted to natural substances, whether on beaches or in sandboxes or sand tables. Sand is a highly **tactile** (perceived by touch) and open-ended substance with properties that change depending on moisture, making it ideal for children's play.

Figure 20.7 Stages in Unit Block Building*

Toddlers and young preschoolers often begin block play by carrying blocks, looking at them, and manipulating them. Older children who have not played with blocks go through these same stages, but at a faster pace.

The earliest progression in block building is as follows:

1. Children make horizontal rows.

2. Children stack blocks.

3. Children make row-and-stack combinations.

4. Children build flat enclosures.

5. Children build standing enclosures (also called *bridging* and *arching*).

6. Children build combination enclosures.

After these stages, children begin to build structures and make decorative patterns.

*These stages were outlined by Harriett Johnson, who studied block building with unit blocks in 1928.

Figure 20.8 In the late 1800s, the sand gardens of Germany inspired the first children's playgrounds in the United States. Although playground equipment has replaced sandboxes in some areas, there is a movement toward natural play spaces for children, including sand, water, and gardens. *What natural play spaces exist in your community?*

Sand play, like block building, promotes holistic learning that extends to all areas of development. Children use gross-motor skills when digging, moving, or cleaning up sand. They use fine-motor skills for filling, pouring, smoothing, and sifting sand and for using sand tools, such as spades or tubing. Sand play enhances physical knowledge as children move sand buckets with pulleys. Children learn logical thinking concepts by discerning the weight of dry and wet sand and learn environmental concepts by observing sandy beaches and deserts. By writing letters and making patterns in the sand, children learn language and literacy concepts and creativity. As with block building, sand play refines children's social skills and emotional regulation when children work together.

The adult's role in sand play is one of support. Adults set the stage for sand play by providing equipment and accessories. Most sand play occurs in outdoor sandboxes or in **sand tables**, which are designed to hold sand and encourage experimental play (**Figure 20.9**). During play, adults can scaffold children's learning by asking questions, such as "What do you think would happen if you sprinkled more sand on top?" or "What shape are you making with that sand?" Finally, adults can show appreciation for children's sand play through photos, videos, drawings, and children's stories.

Water Play

Children can spend countless hours playing with water—pouring it back and forth between containers, making it spill over a container, or directing the flow by pushing water with their

Figure 20.9 Sandboxes, like the one shown, are ideal places for sand play and experimentation. Froebel, a German educator, created the first sandboxes for his kindergarten. *In what other places can children play with sand?*

Focus on Careers

Playground Designer

Playground designers are *landscape architects* who plan and design land and space for children. They design and create playgrounds, including playground equipment and areas for play activities (such as sand play and block building).

Playground designers analyze who will be using the space and for what purpose, the nature around the space, and how the environment will be impacted. They use sketches, models, and photographs to explain their ideas. Playground designers also work with building architects and engineers to complete a task.

Career cluster: Architecture and construction.

Education: Most playground designers have a bachelor's or master's degree in landscape architecture or a related subject. Most states require playground designers to be licensed.

Job outlook: Future employment opportunities for playground designers are expected to grow as fast as the average for all occupations.

To learn more about a career as a playground designer, visit the United States Department of Labor's *Occupational Outlook Handbook* website. You will also be able to compare the job responsibilities, educational requirements, job outlook, and average pay of playground designers with similar occupations.

hands or a paddle (**Figure 20.10**). Besides having fun, children can also learn new concepts through water play.

Water play is an open-ended activity that allows for children's explorations over many years. Because water, unlike other natural substances, can exist in three states (solid, liquid, and gas), water promotes even more lessons than many other activities. Children use gross-motor skills to run from sprinklers, wash toys, or water a garden. They use fine-motor skills and eye-hand coordination for filling, pouring, and emptying containers with water and for handling tubing and funnels. Although understanding the scientific concepts of water will take many years, water play can lay the foundations for these concepts. Children can learn physical knowledge concepts by watching water conform to the shape of its container. They can learn logical thinking concepts by practicing the conservation of continuous quantities and the conservation of volume. Through learning about the states of water, precipitation, weight, and volume, children can learn concepts in science and math. During water play, children can learn to work independently or cooperatively and can develop social skills through collaborating with peers.

As with block building and sand play, adults have the responsibility for supervising and supporting water play activities. Adults can provide equipment and materials for water play, such as **water tables**, which are designed to hold water

Mental Health Advisory

Children often feel freer and more in control of their play with sand than with many other toys and materials. This is because there are not right or wrong ways to explore sand. This feeling of freedom and control promotes learning and creativity and prevents the stress associated with closed-ended activities that have right and wrong ways of doing things.

Figure 20.10 Children can play with water in many places, including lakes, water tables, and pools. *What experiences did you have with water play as a child?*

and accessories for water play. As with other open-ended activities, adults can scaffold children's learning by planning activities in response to children's discoveries and questions. Adults should refrain from taking the lead during water play, overteaching, or expecting young children to understand concepts they cannot yet grasp (such as floating and sinking).

Cooking Experiences

Young children explore cooking in much the same way they do sand and water play. Children experiment with cooking tools and ingredients—making pretend foods—and then graduate to trying recipes.

Cooking experiences promote learning in all areas of development. Children use fine-motor skills as they stir, shake, pour, knead, and use many other cooking techniques and basic cooking tools. As children learn concepts about quality food (as opposed to "junk food") and the need for safety and health practices, they also begin to understand and practice good nutritional habits for physical growth. Almost every cooking and eating experience leads to intellectual learning. Children learn physical knowledge concepts as they observe changes in foods during freezing, thawing, or baking. They learn logical thinking concepts by using numerical measurements. Seeing math symbols and words in recipes helps teach children language concepts. Children learn to cooperate while cooking, and cooking aids self-concept as children learn to meet their basic needs for nourishment. Cooking also requires self-regulation, especially in the areas of inhibition (where children must carefully follow

Focus on

Health

Water Play Safety

Because of the risk for drowning, safety during water play is important. The most important factor in safe water play is adult supervision. Adults should never leave a child alone with standing water, even if the water is in a water table. For outdoor water play in pools, water parks, or natural bodies of water, adults should provide children with life jackets and watch to make sure children do not get into deep water if they cannot swim.

Sanitation is also a safety concern during water play. Outdoor bodies of water can contain harmful bacteria and poisonous plants. Children may consume or play with dangerous objects. Even the water in a water table may grow bacteria and become hazardous if the water is not changed daily. Adults can guard against these hazards by changing water regularly for indoor water play and by closely supervising children and removing dangerous objects during outdoor water play.

Focus on Reading

Learning Math Through Cooking

Because of the measurements involved in following a recipe, cooking experiences can be excellent opportunities for children to learn about math. Using the Internet, research articles about teachers who successfully used lessons in cooking to reinforce math concepts. What strategies did they use to help children understand measurement? What follow-up activities did they plan?

After reading the article, choose your favorite recipe and read it carefully. Take notes about ingredients and steps in the recipe that a teacher could use to reinforce math concepts. Working with a partner, follow the recipe and cook your favorite foods. Afterward, discuss how you would adapt the recipe to strengthen math concepts in an early childhood education classroom.

a recipe and use tools correctly) and the delay of gratification (when food preparation requires time before eating).

In *real* (as opposed to *pretend*) cooking activities, adults help children more directly than they do in block building, water play, and sand play. Cooking experiences generally require more adult guidance and supervision. Adults can support children's cooking experiences by

- purchasing or collecting appropriate equipment
- assigning a child developmentally appropriate cooking tasks
- supervising carefully
- demonstrating the use of equipment
- scaffolding learning with the child's safety in mind
- reinforcing cooking lessons by applying them to other areas, such as science, art, math, and language

Art Experiences

Art is important in children's lives. **Visual arts**, such as painting, molding, and photography, create products that appeal to children's sense of sight. Because a child's total development (including physical, intellectual, and social-emotional development) determines how he or she uses crayons, paints, clay, and other art materials, the child will progress through several stages of development in artistic expression (**Figure 20.11**).

Art experiences promote learning for children in all areas of development. As children learn to handle art tools, they develop the motor skills needed to draw, paint, or mold carefully and accurately. Art experiences improve general intellectual functioning, such as focused attention and motivation to improve. Sensory experiences help children expand their concepts of color, line, shape, form, texture, and size. Children also use spatial concepts when creating art. Young children illustrate what they know about their world. For example, a young child's drawing of a wagon will show all four wheels. Later in the school-age years, children will create perceptually correct representations, such as a wagon showing only two wheels if drawn from the front, one side, or back. Art also helps children develop socially and emotionally. Children make choices about what they want to do and how they want to do an art activity. As children play, they can use art to express feelings. (Some children who have experienced trauma or social-emotional disturbances receive *art therapy*, which encourages them to express fears or repressed emotions through creativity.) Finally, taking pride in art and knowing that others accept their products builds children's self-esteem.

Adults can support art experiences by introducing children to art tools and art activities suited to their stages of development. Once children understand how to use art tools, adults need to let children do their own work. Children's works should reflect their physical skills in handling art tools and their intellectual ways of seeing the world, not adults' physical skills and artistic stage of representation. If an adult corrects or redoes a child's artwork, the child may experience self-doubt and

Figure 20.11 Stages of Development in Visual Arts

Stage	Characteristics
Manipulative stage (birth–3½ years of age) 	• Children play with the art materials themselves instead of using them to create artwork. • Children under 2 years of age enjoy art for motor reasons. Around 2 to 2½ years of age, children begin *scribbling* (using hands and eyes together to draw dots, lines, and loops). • Around 2½ to 3½ years of age, children begin to draw basic shapes.
Transition between manipulative and representation stage (3½–5 years of age) 	• Children create their first symbols. • Around 2½ years of age, children begin to draw human figures. • Children draw no spatial relationships among objects.
Representation stage (5–6 years of age and older) 	• Children create symbols that represent objects, experiences, and feelings. • Children decide what a symbol is before creating it. • Children show spatial relationships among objects. • In the early part of the representation stage, children may draw *mixed perspectives*, *exaggerated images*, and *transparencies*. • Children draw more details and more accurate perspectives. • Around 9 to 10 years of age, children can draw objects from their perspectives *and* from the perspectives of others.

> **Mental Health Advisory**
>
> Because artwork reflects what children think about themselves and their worlds, mental health specialists sometimes use drawings as one tool for diagnosing mental health problems. Other adults, however, should be wary about reading too much into artwork.

lower self-esteem. Adults can also encourage children by showing interest in their artwork and joining children in art activities (**Figure 20.12**). They can display children's artwork to support self-esteem.

Music Experiences

Music surrounds people from birth. Children who have been exposed to a rich world of sound and movement will have good backgrounds for later learning and pleasure.

Music experiences promote growth in all areas of development. For young children, movement and music are viewed as one. Even toddlers move to music without being prompted by adults. During these movements, motor skills are enhanced. Preschool and school-age children who play instruments practice fine-motor skills and increase their dexterity, often in both hands. Some instruments, such as string instruments, require two different fine-motor movements at the same time. Intellectual skills are also enhanced through music. Young children who learn to play musical instruments tend to be high achievers in spatial concepts and math in later years. In addition, music provides chances for sensory and expressive experiences. Listening to the sounds of music can improve children's listening skills in general. As children become more attuned to the sounds around them, they learn to translate these sounds in musical ways. They may say that sounds have a high or low pitch or an even or uneven rhythm. Like pitch and rhythm, language is also involved in music. Singing involves adding words to pitch and rhythm (**Figure 20.13**). Singing and playing instruments seem to make children feel good and can be collaborative (such as in choirs, combos, bands, and orchestras), which fosters social learning. Finally, making music is fun for children.

To guide music experiences, adults can introduce children to music activities suited to their interests. These areas may include moving to music, listening, playing instruments, and singing. In addition to providing activities, including music lessons,

Figure 20.12 When children show adults their artwork, adults should always be supportive. Instead of asking "What is that?" adults can ask children to tell them about the artwork. ***Why is asking a child to talk about his or her artwork better than asking a direct question?***

Figure 20.13 Although young children do enjoy singing, they often cannot carry a tune. To sing with others, children must hear their own voices, the voices of other singers or instruments, and the unison sound. *Why do you think it is difficult for young children to match their pitches and thus produce a unison sound?*

adults can provide an environment that is rich in sound. They can model enthusiasm and enjoyment for various types of music (called *genres*, such as classical, modern, pop, folk, country, rock, and blues). Perhaps the adult's most difficult role is listening to a child's early attempts to play an instrument. However, parents need to encourage children's musical attempts if children are to practice enough to gain musical skills. Adults can encourage children by attending children's musical events, keeping music programs of these events, and even recording children's musical performances.

Science Experiences

Children are born scientists. They wonder and seek answers and test their answers repeatedly. To children, *science* is wondering about the world and everything in it, appreciating beauty, and caring for the world. Children experience science when they catch a cricket, put it in a jar, and watch it. They experience science when they watch water freeze and see snow melt. Children can learn about science when they ask, "Why do I need to eat my green beans?" or "How do clouds move?" Science can also be incorporated into many other activities, such as block building, sand play, water play, and cooking experiences.

Science activities foster growth in all areas of development. In exploring their worlds, children use their gross-motor skills for running, walking, jumping, and bending. They also practice fine-motor skills when they handle objects and creatures with care. During science experiences, intellectual development is also stimulated. Sensory experiences abound. For example, children explore *substances* (the physical matter of objects) and handle liquid, granular, and solid objects. Through many science experiences in which children observe and experiment, children learn cause-and-effect relationships and math skills. By using science resources, such as science magazines and websites, children practice and use their language and reading skills, too. Science aids social-emotional development. Through watching, listening to, and touching living things, when appropriate, children learn about and develop respect for the world around them. Children can also overcome some fears with science facts. For example, children may learn not to fear thunderstorms after learning how and why thunderstorms happen.

Adults can promote science experiences by encouraging children to appreciate the beauty of their world. For example, adults can call attention to the beauty of the environment, such as light coming through a prism, colors on butterflies' wings, the fragrance of roses, and the songs of birds. Along with appreciation, lessons on caring for nature can also begin early for children. Starting in the toddler years, adults can give children developmentally appropriate tasks in caring for living creatures and the environment. Adults can also read books about nature and science to children. They can visit zoos, gardens, and forests together (**Figure 20.14**). Adults should never present science as a magic show. Instead, adults can explain science so children can learn about their world.

Literature Experiences

Literature opens up a world of magic and new ideas for children, and literature experiences aid children in all areas of development. During literature experiences, children use fine-motor skills for turning pages and learn to move their eyes for reading. Literature activities arouse curiosity and spark imagination in children as children learn many new concepts and then expand these concepts by reading books that answer their endless questions. Literature experiences also help children enjoy learning and want to learn.

As would be expected, literature activities expand language skills. Literature activities aid children in developing vocabulary as well as sentence structure and grammar. Through quality stories and poems, children hear the rhythm of language, the rise and fall of the voice, and tongue-tickling phrases. Children build reading skills, such as reading direction (reading top to bottom and left to right) and print knowledge about letters, words, sentences, paragraphs, punctuation marks, and spacing. Children who are heavily exposed to literature often become good writers of stories, poems, and essays.

Literature expands children's understandings of themselves and others. Young children like to hear stories about others their age and about familiar people and objects. These young children better understand themselves by hearing stories that draw on their backgrounds. As older children read

Figure 20.14 Children experience science through their everyday lives, including their encounters with nature and new locations. *What science experiences do you best remember from your childhood?*

about people and places beyond their own immediate environment, they come to understand and respect diversity in their world. Finally, literature activities strengthen the adult-child relationship. Reading time is quality time. As adults, people often recall family reading experiences.

Adults have a primary responsibility in nurturing children's love of literature. Although most parents are not professional readers, children are an appreciative, uncritical audience. In fostering literature experiences, adults can begin to read aloud to children during the first few months of life and continue until the child learns to read well (**Figure 20.15**). Adults and children can read interesting stories to each other throughout the school-age and teen years, too. Adults can also extend children's understandings of what they read through story stretchers (additional activities in other areas that relate to the story, such as art, music, cooking, and dramatic play).

Lesson 20.2 Review and Assessment 

1. Name five intellectual concepts that block building can help children learn.
2. How can adults support children's learning during sand play?
3. How is the adult's role in cooking activities different from the adult's role in other types of play activities?
4. During which stage of visual arts development do children decide what a symbol is before creating it?
5. Describe two ways adults can support children's music activities.
6. Give an example of an activity into which science can be incorporated.
7. In what ways do literature experiences foster social-emotional development?
8. **Critical thinking.** Can water play teach young children scientific concepts about water before these children are capable of logical thought? Why or why not?

Figure 20.15 Age-Appropriate Reading

Stage of Development	Reading Methods
Infancy	• Point to, name, and talk about pictures. • Allow the infant to touch, grasp, and turn pages.
Toddler years	• Ask the toddler to point to or name pictures, make story-related sounds, and repeat repetitive phrases. • Substitute the toddler's name for the character's name to engage interest. • Compare story experiences to the toddler's experiences. • Use props.
Preschool years	• Look at the cover, read the title, and then read the author's and illustrator's names together. • Ask the preschooler to guess what the book is about. • Engage the preschooler by asking questions, such as "What might happen next?" or "Why did the character do this?" • Look closely at illustrations together. • Repeat interesting words and phrases. • Run fingers under the text while reading. • Talk about the story while reading it.
School-age years	• Set the stage before reading. • Relate the book to similar books (author, genre, content). • Ask questions about the story, such as "What would you do in a similar situation?"

Chapter 20

Review and Assessment

Summary

Play is a *holistic* way of learning that is fun and tends to reflect changes in children's developmental levels. As children grow, they experience several stages of play. While the stages of play are described differently by different child development experts, the stages of play can generally be classified as *play with objects* or *play with people*. The stages of play with objects correspond to Piaget's first three levels of cognitive development. The stages of play with people involve children's social skills and development. Many types of play exist. *Active-physical play* involves gross-motor skills, and *manipulative-constructive play* uses fine-motor skills. *Imitative-imaginative play* includes pretend play and involves several stages as children learn to use symbols. *Language-logic play* usually occurs in school-age children and involves logical thinking and strategy. Adults can encourage play experiences by allowing children freedom, displaying positive attitudes about play, and providing age-appropriate, attractive toys.

To encourage play and promote development, adults can plan a variety of play activities. Block building, sand play, and water play help children develop motor skills, intellectual understandings, and social skills. Cooking experiences, which enhance all areas of development, require more adult guidance than other enrichment activities. Arts activities promote fine-motor skills, perceptual learning, and social-emotional health. Music experiences also aid children's motor skills, intellectual development (including language concepts), and social-emotional development. Science experiences can be incorporated into many play activities and thus enhance all types of learning as well as respect for one's physical world. Literature experiences can stimulate creativity, take children to any real or imagined place, expose children to quality language, and reinforce the adult-child relationship.

College and Career Portfolio

Portfolio Presentation Research

Depending on the purpose of your portfolio, the way in which you present the portfolio may vary. For example, schools may expect you to submit your portfolio electronically. Employers may expect you to bring a physical copy of your portfolio to the interview and walk an interviewer through the portfolio's highlights.

- Talk to a college or career counselor or search online to find out how portfolios in your field are generally presented.
- Confirm the information you find with one or more sources and write a short summary about the presentation guidelines.

Vocabulary Activities

1. Working in small groups, locate a small image online that visually describes or explains each of the following terms. To create flashcards, write each term on a note card and paste the image that describes or explains the term on the opposite side.

Key Terms

active-physical play (20.1)	play therapy (20.1)
imitative-imaginative play (20.1)	sand tables (20.2)
language-logic play (20.1)	unit blocks (20.2)
manipulative-constructive play (20.1)	visual arts (20.2)
	visual literacy (20.2)
	water tables (20.2)

2. Write each of the following terms on a separate sheet of paper. For each term, quickly write a word you think relates to the term. In small groups, exchange papers. Have each person in the group explain a term on the list. Take turns until all terms have complete explanations.

Academic Terms

graceful (20.1)	tactile (20.2)
strategize (20.1)	tangible (20.2)

Critical Thinking

3. **Cause and effect.** The stages of play with objects were developed by Piaget to correspond to the first three stages of cognitive development. Working with a partner, review your notes about the sensorimotor, preoperational, and concrete operational stages of cognitive development. Then, analyze how the qualities of these stages connect to the stages of play with objects. Explain these cause-and-effect relationships to the class.
4. **Evaluate.** In small groups, create two active-physical play activities that you enjoy. Try these with children and then observe the children playing. What skills is the play activity helping children develop? Are children enjoying the activity? Evaluate your activity based on its value and fun.
5. **Compare and contrast.** Review the stages of imitative-imaginative play outlined in Figure 20.5. Read the examples for each stage carefully and then compare and contrast the key similarities and differences among the examples. Finally, write your own examples illustrating changes that occur among the stages of imitative-imaginative play.
6. **Identify.** Providing children with toys that they like encourages children to play. Use this text's list of attractive toys for children at each stage of development to identify current toys that would encourage play in children. Find toys in catalogs or visit a toy store and find three examples of attractive toys for infants, toddlers, preschoolers, and school-age children. Write a brief explanation about why each toy is attractive and appropriate in your opinion.
7. **Analyze.** Experiences in block building promote *visual literacy*, which is a key element influencing children's learning of intellectual concepts. Analyze how visual literacy influences concepts and give examples of other concepts children learn by developing this skill.
8. **Determine.** Obtain drawings by four- and six-year-olds and compare the drawings, keeping in mind the stages of visual arts development. What differences do you note among the drawings? Determine what developmental abilities or changes might account for these differences.
9. **Draw conclusions.** Art activities can be fun and useful ways for children to learn more about their worlds. Review the text's information about the benefits of art activities and then draw conclusions about other related benefits. Why are art activities important for children? Why is it important to allow a child freedom of expression?
10. **Make inferences.** In small groups, review the guidelines for age-appropriate reading during literature experiences (Figure 20.15). Then, organize a time for your group to visit a local library or bookstore. During your visit, explore books in the children's section. As a group, identify books that you think would provide the best literature experiences for infants, toddlers, preschoolers, and school-age children. Bring pictures of the books (or if possible, the books themselves) to class and deliver an oral presentation about how the books you chose would support quality literature experiences.

Core Skills

11. **Technology.** Children pass through five stages of "play with people." Review these stages of play (Figure 20.3) and then work in small groups to brainstorm real-life examples for each of

the five stages. After your discussion, create a visual representation of the stages of "play with people." Use digital or drawn artwork or videos to illustrate each stage. Also summarize how each stage of play reflects children's social worlds and development. Present your project to the class.

12. **Speaking.** In small groups, visit a beach, lake, water park, playground with a sandbox, or other location where sand play or water play could take place. Once at the location, plan water-play or sand-play activities that you think would be beneficial for all areas of children's development. Test these activities in your group and keep brainstorming activities until your group is confident you have devised the best and most helpful activity you can. Finally, present and explain your activity to the class.
13. **Reading and speaking.** Working with a partner, review this text's information about logical thinking concepts for preschoolers and school-age children. Take notes about what concepts children understand, when, and what types of activities support these lessons. Then, create one or two play activities to support or teach all of the logical thinking concepts children learn. Explain in detail how children will learn each concept and how adults can scaffold learning. Present your activities to the class and ask for feedback.
14. **Reading and science.** Visit a local library or search online to find magazines, articles, or books that outline science experiences for young children. Choose two resources and read them carefully, noting any activities you find especially interesting or fun. What concepts do your favorite activities teach? Are they stand-alone science activities or are they science experiences incorporated into other play activities? Choose one favorite activity and conduct it with your class. After the activity, explain the concepts taught and how easily the activity or experience could be incorporated into an early childhood education setting.
15. **Math and listening.** Math experiences can be incorporated into a wide range of play activities. Interview a preschool teacher about how he or she teaches math through other types of activities. What activities best lend themselves to math experiences? How does the teacher first introduce math concepts to children? What benefits do math experiences have on children's physical, intellectual, and social-emotional development?
16. **Research and writing.** Using reliable online or print resources, research the effects of music on social and emotional well-being. Read scientific studies about these effects and take notes, documenting your sources in a bibliography. Write a three- to four-page essay detailing your findings and explaining the importance of music for social-emotional development.
17. **Technology.** Electronic media can be a powerful tool for enhancing children's learning and play activities. Using reliable online or print resources, research ways in which technology and electronic media can be used in play activities. Share your findings with a partner. Then, work together with your partner to create a digital presentation illustrating how technology can be incorporated into two types of play activities. Be sure to include visuals in your presentation and explain how the use of technology reinforces and benefits the play experience.
18. **CTE Career Readiness Practice.** Imagine you are a recent graduate from a well-known early childhood education program. After being hired by a long-established child care center, you learn that the director of the center prioritizes academic learning and strict adherence to education standards more than he does children's play experiences. Concerned about the children in your care, you ask your director if you can meet with him. You know that you are relatively inexperienced, but you want to express why you think play is important. Write a short speech that respectfully and accurately describes the importance of play. Practice your speech with a partner and ask for feedback about whether you are approaching the issue tactfully.

Observations

19. Visit a local school or art fair and view children's artwork. As you view the artwork, take notes about each child's art skills and determine the child's stage of development in the visual arts. If the ages of the children are displayed, check your answers. If not, write short summaries explaining each identification.
20. As a class, visit a local child care center, preferably one with infants, toddlers, and preschoolers enrolled. Observe the children at the center playing and try to identify the children's stages of play. Back up your identifications with concrete examples and facts. Afterward, discuss as a class.

Chapter 21

Protecting Children's Physical Health and Safety

Essential Question

What can parents and other adults do to keep children healthy and safe, and how can parents treat children's illnesses and injuries when they do occur?

Case Study What Does It Take to Keep a Child Safe?

As a class, read the case study and discuss the questions that follow. After you finish studying the chapter, discuss this case study again. Have your opinions changed based on what you learned?

One cold, wintry morning, four-year-old Joaquin's mother took him with her to the grocery store. As she pulled into their driveway, Joaquin's father called to her, "Leave the car running. I just need to take this phone call and then I have to get to my meeting." She nodded, quickly got Joaquin into the house, left the door open, and then hurried back to the car to get the groceries.

Joaquin's father rushed through his call, impatient and already late for his meeting. Suddenly he was shocked to see the car, with Joaquin in it, rolling into the street. He rushed outside, but was too late to stop the car from being struck by a speeding minivan. Joaquin's parents frantically called 911. The paramedics took Joaquin to the hospital where he was admitted for a severe and potentially life-threatening blow to the head.

Phone records showed the father's call lasted less than one minute. Joaquin's parents did not know whether Joaquin returned to the car when his mother went to get her groceries or whether he slipped past his father during the phone call. They had thoroughly childproofed their home and yard. As parents, they modeled safety practices and taught Joaquin safety lessons, which he usually obeyed.

After weeks in the hospital, Joaquin's parents decided they wanted to do something to prevent other families from experiencing the terror they experienced. They wanted to tell their story and reach out to parents of preschoolers and school-age children about safety practices.

Give It Some Thought

1. How do children play their own role in injury protection? What role does the environment play? the caregivers' forethought and supervision? cultural norms?
2. What are some ways Joaquin's parents might reach out to other parents about safety?

While studying this chapter, look for the online resources icon  to:

- **Practice** terms with e-flash cards and interactive games
- **Assess** what you learn by completing self-assessment quizzes
- **Expand** knowledge with interactive activities and graphic organizers

Companion G-W Learning

www.g-wlearning.com/childdevelopment

Study on the go

Use a mobile device to practice terms and review with self-assessment quizzes.

www.m.g-wlearning.com/0384

Lesson 21.1 Maintaining Children's Health

Key Terms

allergen
allergy
asthma
communicable diseases
epilepsy
foodborne diseases
health screenings
immunization
noncommunicable diseases
preventive health care
vaccination
vaccines
well-child checkups

Academic Terms

anaphylaxis
immunity
unearth

Objectives

After studying this lesson, you will be able to

- describe aspects involved in basic health care for children, including meeting children's physical needs and providing children with preventive health care.
- give examples of two health screenings that are important for young children.
- differentiate among the terms *immunization*, *vaccine*, and *vaccination*.
- compare and contrast *communicable diseases* and *noncommunicable diseases*.
- identify five ways to prevent foodborne illness.
- explain what causes diabetes, epilepsy, allergies, and asthma.

Reading and Writing Activity

Read the list of terms at the beginning of this lesson and write what you think each term means. Then look up each term in this text's glossary and in a dictionary. Write the glossary and dictionary definitions and compare them. How are they similar? How are they different?

Graphic Organizer

Draw two columns for taking notes. As you read this lesson write main ideas in the left column and subtopics and detailed information in the right column. After reading, use your notes as a study guide. Cover the right column and use the left column to quiz yourself about the content in this lesson.

Main Topics	Subtopics and Detailed Information
Children need regular doctor and dental appointments to maintain good health	Checkups when a child is well are called well-child checkups

Today's advances in health and safety are greater than ever before. Growing up is still risky business, however. Each day infants and children face the risks of illness, injury, and even death. Sometimes adults can control these risks; at other times they cannot. Adults who care for children bear an enormous responsibility when it comes to keeping children healthy and safe.

Parents can promote their children's health and wellness by making sure they receive basic health care. Basic health care involves meeting children's physical needs for good nutrition, rest, physical activity, and cleanliness. Regular medical and dental appointments, health screenings, and immunizations are also necessary to support children's health and wellness. When children are in good health, they are better able to fight common childhood diseases.

Basic Health Care for Children

Children, like adults, need basic health care to ensure their bodies are developing properly and to treat infections and diseases. When health concerns are prevented, detected early, or treated properly, children have a better chance of leading a healthy and happy life. When disease or injury occurs, children who are otherwise healthy tend to recover quickly and completely. Neglecting health needs for long periods can cause health conditions with lasting effects. To promote children's health and safety, adults must meet children's physical needs and provide children with preventive health care.

Meeting Children's Physical Needs

Every person has basic physical needs. As you may recall, children's needs vary depending on a child's stage. Young children rely on adults to meet all their physical needs. As children grow older, they become capable of meeting some of their own needs. Adults, however, still pay careful attention to and meet many of children's needs.

Adults help meet children's physical needs by ensuring children eat healthfully, get plenty of rest, and are physically active. Maintaining cleanliness can protect children from certain illnesses, such as the flu or common cold. Adults can reduce children's risk of infection by

- encouraging proper handwashing (**Figure 21.1**)
- teaching children to cover their sneezes and coughs
- teaching children to not touch their eyes or mouth when around sick children
- modeling good health practices

Figure 21.1 Proper Handwashing Steps

- Wet hands with water and apply soap. (Children like colorful, foamy soap. Antibacterial products are not any more effective than other types of soap and may give rise to antibiotic-resistant bacteria.)
- Rub soap between hands, on backs of hands, between fingers, and under fingernails.
- Scrub lathered hands for at least 20 seconds. (Some sources say 30 seconds of scrubbing is needed. Sing the "Happy Birthday" song twice to time scrubbing.)
- Rinse hands thoroughly.
- Dry hands with a clean towel or air dry.

Providing Children with Preventive Health Care

Part of meeting children's basic health needs involves adults providing children with preventive health care. **Preventive health care** consists of measures taken to keep children well. Preventive health care includes regular doctor and dental appointments, health screenings, and immunizations.

Regular Doctor and Dental Appointments

Proper preventive health care for children involves regular **well-child checkups** (doctor's appointments while the child is not sick). During these visits, doctors monitor children's health and wellness and check their growth and development. They note children's eating, sleeping, and playing habits. Doctors also answer parents' questions about their child's development. Well-child checkups may **unearth** (reveal) possible health concerns before they become serious or cannot be repaired. These visits may even prevent certain health conditions altogether.

Because well-child checkups are so important, doctors suggest a schedule for regular visits. The schedule varies slightly among doctors, but the American Academy of Pediatrics (AAP) suggests children have 11 well-child checkups during the first three years of life (**Figure 21.2**). This does not include checkups made between birth and discharge from the hospital. Yearly examinations are recommended after three years of age. Infants of nursing mothers and premature infants may have extra checkups during their early weeks to ensure they are thriving. Children also need regular, preventive dental care from a pediatric or family dentist. Dental care usually begins by the first birthday with follow-up appointments every six months afterward.

Parents often have difficulty choosing health care for their children because there are so many health care providers available. In most regions, pediatricians and dentists abound, and parents are not always sure how to decide which health care services will best meet their children's needs.

Parents need to assess prospective medical personnel. To choose the best health care services for their children, parents need to consider several factors. Is the medical provider within the parents' insurance coverage network, and will the provider accept their insurance? Are office hours and location accessible? Is the medical professional open to parents' questions? Will he or she answer parents' questions clearly and calmly? Is he or she accepting of emergency calls?

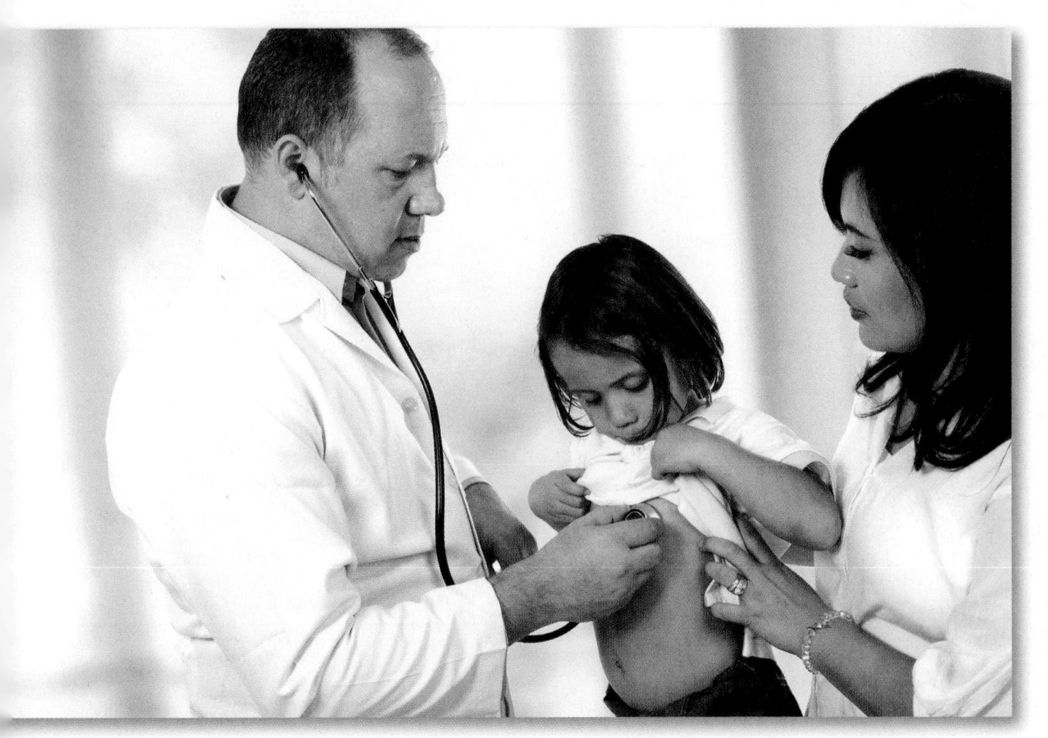

Figure 21.2 The AAP schedule recommends that children receive well-child checkups at 1, 2, 4, 6, 9, 12, 15, 18, 24, 30, and 36 months of age. Doctors may schedule additional or fewer visits depending on the child's health needs and parents' experience. *How do you think parents' experience impacts how often a child should receive well-child checkups?*

Focus on

Health

Supporting Children During an Exam

Some children may be nervous about the prospect of going to a doctor or receiving routine care. Children under two years of age often cry while being examined. Two- and three-year-olds may cry and hide from, kick, or push the doctor in an attempt to get rid of the person. Children often feel *situation stress* that is relieved within minutes after the examination.

The parents' role during a medical examination is to help the child feel more comfortable. To help the child during an examination, parents can try the following tips:

- Stay with the child and remain within the child's line of vision (unless the doctor or dentist prefers that parents stay in the waiting room).
- Use a soft, soothing voice. A child may stop crying to hear whispered words.
- Hold the child if the doctor asks.
- Do not tell the child a procedure will *not* hurt if, in fact, it will. Instead, tell the child "It will be all right" or "Soon it will be over." If the child cries, reassure him or her that crying is all right. Say, "I know this hurts, but it will stop hurting soon."
- Do not distract a baby or child by making noises, such as jingling keys. Such sounds interfere with a doctor's ability to hear internal sounds. Some babies and children cry louder when an adult tries to distract them.

While all licensed pediatric doctors and dentists are qualified to work with a child, parents often consider the older child's preference when choosing a medical professional. Choosing a doctor or dentist the child likes will make the child less anxious during examinations. Children generally like friendly medical personnel who greet them by name and smile. They also prefer colorful treatment rooms and pleasant waiting areas.

Health Screenings

Health screenings are standard tests that look for potential conditions or diseases that may affect children's health or development. These screenings aim to detect conditions often before symptoms appear, allowing for diagnostic confirmation and early treatment. The AAP recommends that children receive several health screenings at certain points in their development. Some of these screenings, including those for hearing and vision, should be given every year between 3 and 12 years of age and more often before 3 years of age. Hearing and vision screenings are especially important for young children to help prevent developmental lags and some medical conditions.

Health screenings also exist for certain special needs (such as autism) and for some infections and diseases (such as depression and sexually transmitted infections). The AAP website contains more information about health screenings recommended at each age. Some of these health screenings are conducted during well-child checkups.

Immunization

Providing children with preventive health care includes **immunization** (process to protect children, as well as adults, from certain serious diseases). Substances used to produce **immunity** (the body's ability to resist infection) from diseases are called **vaccines**. Vaccines can be administered through *injections* (shots), oral medications, or aerosol sprays. Some illnesses require a series

Focus on

Science

Types of Immunity

Children's health is partially dependent on their *immunity* (the body's defense against infection and disease). There are two types of immunity—*active immunity* and *passive immunity*. *Active immunity* results when a person's body produces *antibodies* (AN-ti-bah-deez), which are proteins in the blood that destroy toxins and disease-carrying organisms. Active immunity occurs through direct exposure to an illness or through vaccination, and takes several days or even weeks to become effective. Once developed, however, active immunity lasts several years or a lifetime.

Passive immunity results when antibodies are produced by one person's exposure to a disease and then passed to another person. This is what happens when mothers pass antibodies to their unborn babies across the placenta. People also receive transfusions of antibodies that are made by someone else's body (called *antiserums*). Unlike active immunity, passive immunity takes effect immediately, but lasts only a few weeks.

Immunity can be naturally or artificially acquired. *Naturally acquired immunity* (sometimes called *natural immunity*) is developed after direct contact with infection or by receiving antibodies from the mother during pregnancy or breast-feeding. *Artificially acquired immunity* (sometimes called *acquired immunity*) forms as a person's reaction to antibodies or an antigen received through medical care. *Antigens* (AN-ti-juhns) are substances made from bacteria, viruses, or toxins that prompt the body to produce antibodies that fight a disease. These substances are made in a laboratory and transferred to people in the form of vaccines.

of vaccines to produce immunity. The process of administering vaccines is known as **vaccination**.

From birth children are given vaccines to cause immunity. In the United States, all states require children to receive certain vaccinations for school admission. Although vaccination laws vary from state to state, some of the diseases children must be vaccinated against include diphtheria, *pertussis* (whooping cough), measles, *rubella* (German measles), mumps, tetanus, polio, and *varicella* (chicken pox). **Figure 21.3** outlines the *immunization schedule* often recommended for children from birth through 18 years of age. (Recommendations are reviewed and updated regularly.)

Doctors record children's vaccines on immunization records and then check these records before giving more vaccines. Parents should keep records, too, for their own information. Children's immunization records often need to be provided for entry into child care and education programs, schools, and camps. In rare cases, parents may submit a request for their children to be exempt from immunization due to religious or personal beliefs. If children who are not vaccinated become infected, however, these diseases can cause serious illness and even death. Unvaccinated children may also pose a greater disease-transmission risk to other children and adults who cannot be vaccinated due to age or medical conditions.

Childhood Diseases

Adults who care for children should be aware of diseases that are often contracted during childhood. These are called *childhood diseases*. If left untreated, children can suffer negative effects and even die from some childhood diseases. Serious effects usually occur when adults are unaware of the diseases and their symptoms and do not seek early treatment. Childhood diseases can be either *communicable diseases* or *noncommunicable diseases*.

Communicable Diseases

Communicable diseases are diseases that can be transmitted from an object to an individual or between individuals. *Influenza* (the flu) is just one example of a communicable disease. **Figure 21.4** shows other examples of communicable childhood diseases. Some of these diseases can be prevented with a vaccine.

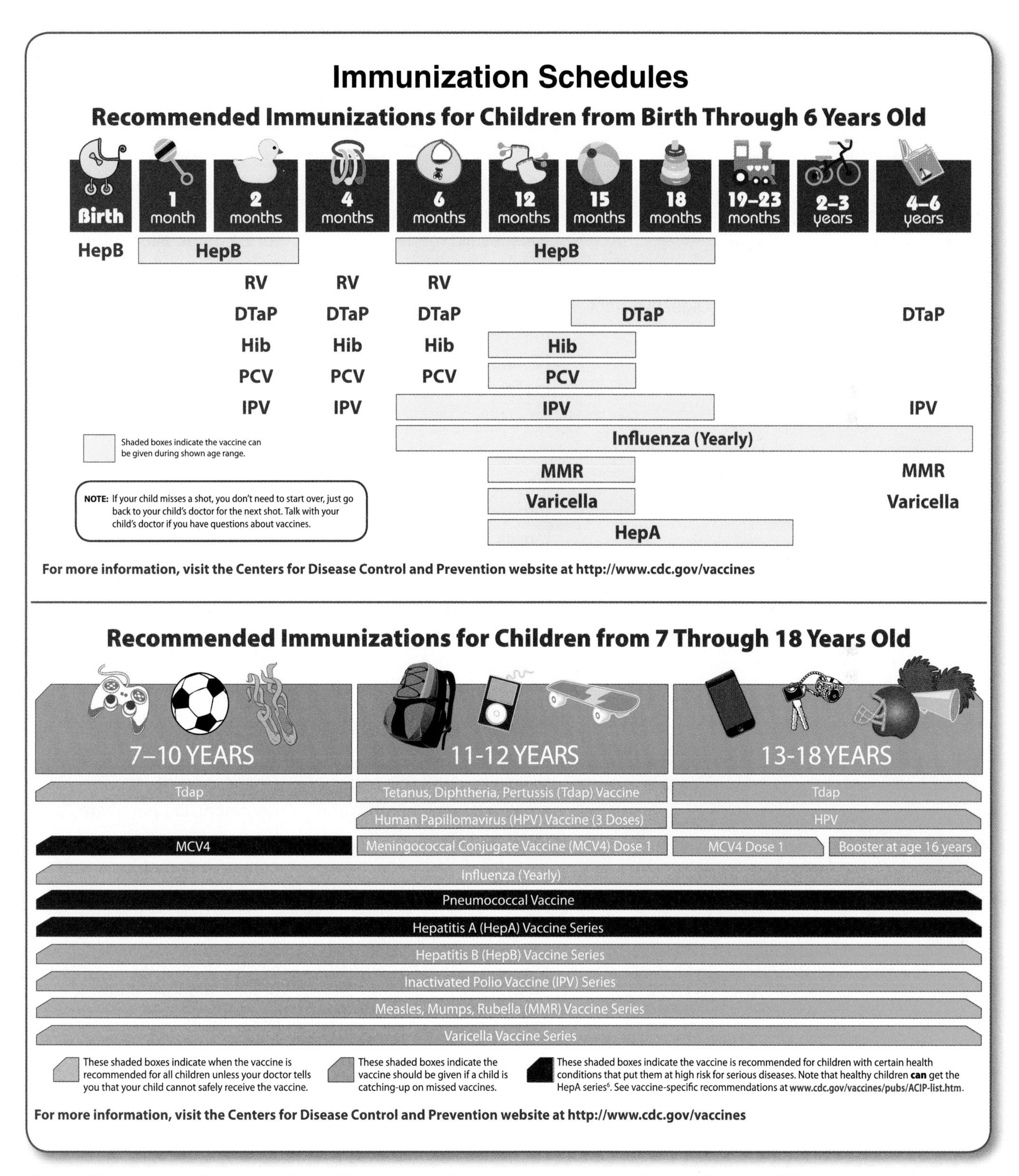

Figure 21.3 Immunization schedules outline when children should receive certain immunizations. *What memories do you have about receiving vaccines? How did your caregivers explain immunization to you?*

Figure 21.4 Communicable Childhood Diseases

Condition	Cause	Symptoms	Comments
***Chicken pox**, or *varicella*	Virus	Fever; runny nose; cough; rash (pimples, blisters, and scabs)	Seek medical treatment. Keep child away from others for six days after rash begins.
Cold	Virus	Runny nose; scratchy throat; coughing; sneezing; watery eyes	Seek medical treatment if child looks and acts very ill.
Conjunctivitis (kun-JUNK-ti-VY-tus), or *pink eye*	Virus and bacteria	Watery eyes; mucus in eyes; red or pink color in whites of eyes; eyelid redness	Seek medical treatment. Keep child away from others for 24 hours after starting treatment.
Coxsackie (kahk-SA-kee) **virus**	Digestive-tract virus	High fever; headaches; muscle aches; painful red blisters in the throat and mouth	Seek medical treatment if other symptoms surface. Keep child away from others; virus is spread through unwashed hands and surfaces.
***Diphtheria** (dif-THIR-ee-uh)	Bacteria	Headache; fever; severe sore throat with white fluid over tonsils and throat; cough	Seek medical treatment. Keep child away from others for two weeks after fever starts or when throat cultures are clear.
***Haemophilus** (hee-MAHF-uh-lus) **influenzae type b** (Hib)	Bacteria	Fever; lethargy; vomiting; poor appetite; earache; breathing and swallowing difficulties; cough; purple area on skin near eyes	Seek medical treatment. Keep child away from others until fever is gone or physician approves contact.
Head lice	Parasite	Visible lice and lice eggs; small red, itchy bumps on head and shoulders	Obtain medications for treatment. Do not share hats, combs, or other contaminated objects with others.
Hepatitis B	Virus	Fever; jaundice; loss of appetite; nausea; joint pain; rash	Seek medical treatment. Keep child away from others until fever is gone and skin rash is dry.
Impetigo (im-PUH-tee-go)	Bacteria	Red, cracking, oozing blister-like pimples often seen on the face	Seek medical treatment. Keep child away from others until 24 hours after starting treatment.

(Continued)

Figure 21.4 *(Continued)*

Condition	Cause	Symptoms	Comments
***Influenza**	Virus	Fever; headache; fatigue; cough; sore throat; body aches; vomiting	Seek medical treatment. Keep child away from others until 24 hours after fever is gone.
***Measles**	Virus	Fever; cough; runny nose; watery eyes; brownish red and blotchy rash	Seek medical treatment. Keep child away from others for six days after rash begins.
***Meningitis** (men-un-JYT-us)	Virus and bacteria	Fever; lethargy; poor appetite; vomiting; irritability; headache; stiff neck	Seek emergency medical help. Physician will determine if child can have contact with others.
***Mumps**	Virus	Fever; swelling of one or more salivary glands; earache; headache	Seek medical treatment. Keep child away from others for nine days after onset of swelling.
***Pertussis** (pur-TUS-us), or *whooping cough*	Bacteria	Runny nose; coughing spells; vomiting	Seek medical treatment. Keep child away from others for three weeks after onset of cough.
***Poliomyelitis** (PO-lee-oh-my-uh-LYT-us), or *polio*	Virus	Fever; vomiting; irritability; headache; stiff neck and back; paralysis in some cases	Seek medical treatment. Physician will determine when child may have contact with others.
Ringworm	Parasite	Scaly patches on the scalp	Treat for six weeks with medication. Can be spread through contact or contaminated objects.
Roseola (roh-zee-OH-luh) **infantum**	Virus	Fever followed by rash	Seek medical treatment. Keep child away from others until fever is gone.
***Rubella**, or *German measles*	Virus	Red rash; enlarged lymph nodes; joint pain	Seek medical treatment. Keep child away from others for six days after rash begins.
Scarlet fever, or *scarlatina*	Bacteria	Fever; rash that causes skin to peel	Seek medical treatment. Keep child away from others until 24 hours after starting treatment.
Strep throat	Bacteria	Sore throat; skin infections	Seek medical treatment. Keep child away from others until 24 hours after starting treatment.

* Vaccine may prevent disease.

Another type of communicable disease is spread through food. **Foodborne diseases** (also called *foodborne illnesses*) are caused by eating foods contaminated with harmful bacteria and other pathogens during food production or preparation. Examples of foodborne illnesses include *botulism*, *E. coli*, *listeria*, and *salmonella*. Young children are at high risk for foodborne illnesses and can suffer serious side effects.

To prevent foodborne illness, adults should pay careful attention to food safety, which involves

- keeping the food preparation area clean to avoid the spread of harmful bacteria
- washing utensils, dishes, and preparation supplies thoroughly with soap and water to prevent *cross-contamination* (the spread of bacteria from one food to another via an object)
- ensuring that all meats and egg dishes are cooked to the proper temperatures (**Figure 21.5**)
- storing foods safely before preparation and storing leftovers safely after preparation
- keeping foods at recommended temperatures (keep hot foods hot and cold foods cold)
- returning foods on recall and notifying your physician if these foods were eaten prior to knowledge of the recall

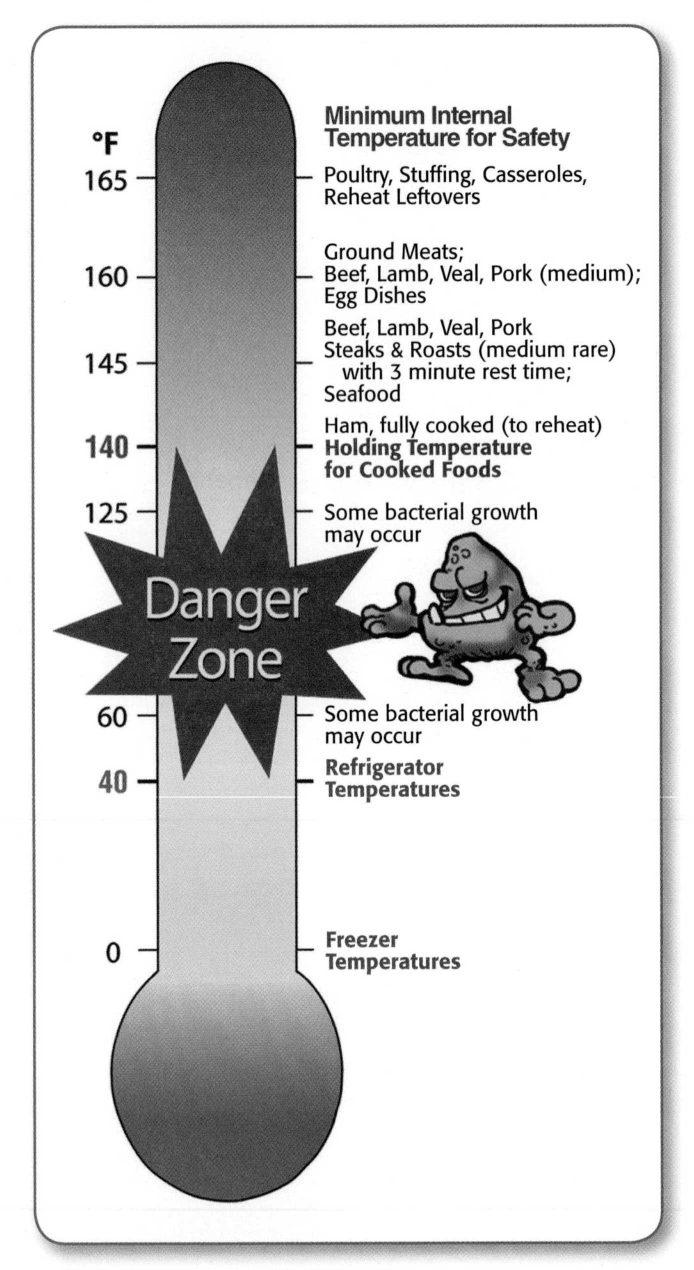

Figure 21.5 Adequate cooking kills the harmful bacteria that can reside in foods. *Is a casserole cooked to an internal temperature of 140°F safe to eat?*

Noncommunicable Diseases

Noncommunicable diseases are diseases that cannot be transmitted between an object and an individual or between individuals. Examples of noncommunicable childhood diseases include diabetes, epilepsy, allergies, and asthma.

Diabetes

Diabetes is a disease that occurs as a result of the body's inability to produce enough insulin, which causes too much sugar in the blood. Children may develop two types of diabetes: *type 1 diabetes* and *type 2 diabetes*. *Type 1 diabetes* is a condition in which the pancreas produces little or no insulin. This type of diabetes typically begins before the adult years. The cause is mainly genetic, but other unknown factors may contribute as well. *Type 2 diabetes* occurs when the body becomes resistant to the effects of insulin or when the pancreas does not produce enough insulin to maintain a normal blood sugar. The onset often occurs in the adult years, but school-age children are becoming more and more vulnerable. Causes of type 2 diabetes are genetic and lifestyle related. Genetic factors include a person's ethnicity and age. Lifestyle-related factors include poor diet and lack of physical activity.

The symptoms are similar for both type 1 and type 2 diabetes. Symptoms include increased thirst and urination, intense hunger, weight loss, fatigue, blurred vision, and slow-healing sores. If blood sugar drops too low, a person can go into a diabetic coma and die. Type 1 diabetes requires consistent care, blood sugar monitoring, and insulin delivery. Type 2 diabetes is treated by diet and physical activity to manage weight. If the condition worsens, oral medications or insulin treatments are needed.

Epilepsy

Epilepsy is a neurological disorder in which abnormal activity in brain cells causes seizures. *Seizures* are sudden attacks that vary in intensity from a blank stare for a few seconds (*petit mal*) to convulsions with loss of consciousness (*grand mal*). Although seizures vary in frequency and intensity, most people have repeated seizures. (Seizures may be infrequent or occur repeatedly throughout the day.) Epilepsy often begins in childhood and may be caused by defective genes or traced to accidents, diseases with high fevers, or medical trauma. Medications can help control epilepsy. Patients with severe seizures may wear helmets to prevent head trauma during a seizure. Knee pads and elbow pads may also be worn to help prevent injuries. Some children have service dogs that sense and warn them of upcoming seizures, allowing these children to get to a safe place quickly.

Allergies

Allergies are the greatest cause of chronic health conditions in young children, affecting over one-fourth of all children. An **allergy** is a negative reaction by the body's immune system to an allergen. An **allergen** (AL-lur-jun) is a substance that causes an allergic reaction. **Figure 21.6** shows types of allergens from which children may suffer. Symptoms of allergies may vary from cold-like symptoms or wheezing to **anaphylaxis** (AN-uh-fuh-LAK-sus)—life-threatening shock. Immediate treatment for severe allergic reactions requires epinephrine (EH-puh-NEH-frun) injections.

Figure 21.6 Types of Allergens

Agent	Symptoms
Foods (often cow's milk, tree nuts, chocolate, wheat, peanuts, eggs, soy, fish, and shellfish) and medicines taken by mouth*	• Tingling mouth • Swelling of tongue, face, or throat • Hives • *Anaphylaxis* (a potentially life-threatening allergic reaction)
Insect bites and stings, thorns, and medicines that are injected	• *Edema* (swelling) at the site of the injection • Cough, wheezing, or shortness of breath • Hives • Anaphylaxis
Latex and other touched substances	• Itchy skin • Flaking or peeling skin • Redness of skin
Airborne allergens	• Congestion • Itchy, runny nose • Itchy, watery eyes • Dark circles under eyes (called *allergic shiners*)

* Children with milk allergies are likely to be allergic to dustless chalk, which contains *casein* (a substance found in both chalk and milk).

Allergies may also be treated by

- removing or limiting contact with the substance (cleaning regularly to remove dust mites or staying inside as much as possible when the pollen count is high)
- using drugs that control allergic reactions (antihistamines, decongestants, and bronchodilators)
- receiving injections or other forms of administration of some allergens to desensitize the body (called *desensitization therapy*)

Asthma

Asthma, inflammation of the airways, is the most common chronic disease of childhood. Onset of asthma in children usually begins before five years of age. Eighty-five percent of asthma cases are triggered by allergens. Symptoms of asthma vary from coughing and wheezing to shortness of breath. Asthma can be aggravated by a virus, secondhand smoke, cold or dry air, and exercise. Asthma may lead to a number of other respiratory problems. Adults can take some measures to reduce children's risk of asthma (**Figure 21.7**). Oral, inhaled, and injected medications can be used to help prevent attacks and to treat ongoing ones.

Lesson 21.1 Review and Assessment 

1. Briefly describe proper handwashing procedure.
2. What is the purpose of preventive health care?
3. Identify two health screenings that are important for children.
4. Define the terms *immunization*, *vaccine*, and *vaccination*.
5. Explain the difference between *communicable* and *noncommunicable diseases*.
6. List five ways to prevent foodborne diseases.
7. Choose one of the noncommunicable diseases discussed in this lesson and briefly explain its causes.
8. **Critical thinking.** What factors might influence how parents choose health care services for their children besides considering the older child's preference of a medical professional?

Figure 21.7 Reducing the Risk of Asthma

- Breast-feed children for at least the first six months of life.
- Introduce solids after six months of age. Give only one tablespoon or less of a new food and wait five or more days between the introductions of new foods.
- Reduce children's exposure to some allergens, including dust mites, mold, air pollution, secondhand smoke, and cockroaches.
- Expose children to pets (cats or dogs) early in life. Children raised on farms are less likely than other children to develop allergies and asthma.

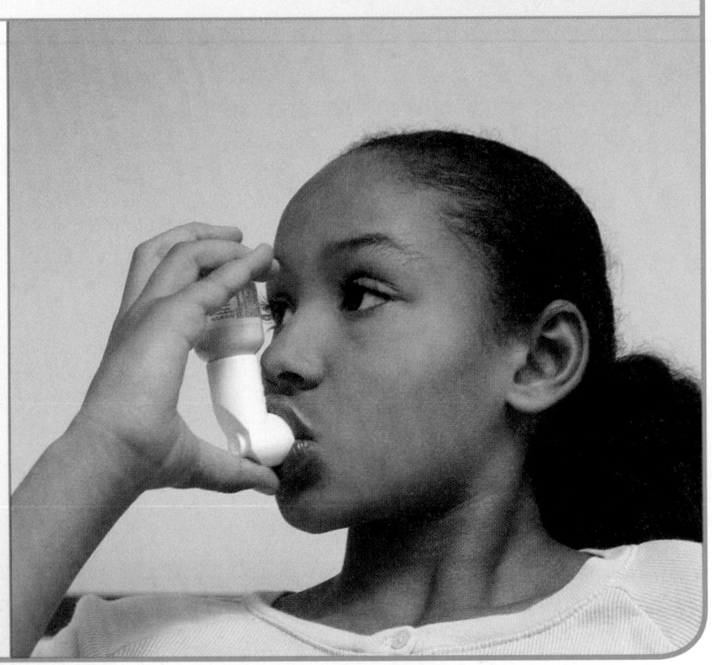

Ensuring Children's Safety

Lesson 21.2

Objectives

After studying this lesson, you will be able to

- explain why adequate supervision is essential throughout childhood.
- list examples of how safety measures should change with the growth and development of the child.
- define *childproofing* and identify three examples of indoor and outdoor hazards.
- identify safety standards for at least two types of child items.
- describe the importance of safety recalls in using safe child items and toys.
- list five safety standards for young children's toys.
- summarize three guidelines for teaching children safety lessons.

Key Terms

certified child safety seat
childproofing
safety recall

Academic Terms

cluttering
idle
neutralize
preoccupied
rigorous
ventilated

Reading and Writing Activity

Skim the main headings before reading this lesson. For each of the headings in the lesson, use online or print resources to find an image that represents your predictions about the section's content. Read the lesson and, after reading, select a second image that reflects what you have learned. Write a short paragraph comparing the images and explaining how they reflect what you predicted and what you now know.

Graphic Organizer

As you read this lesson, use a tree diagram like the one shown to organize information about children's safety. Write *Ensuring Children's Safety* in the top circle and write major categories and then specific activities and notes in the circles below.

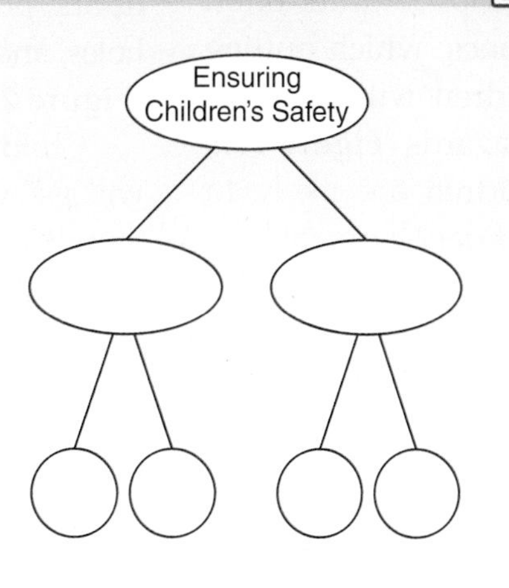

Accidents claim the lives of more children than any of the major childhood diseases. High accident rates among children are due to many factors, such as lack of supervision and unsafe equipment and toys. By the toddler years, children have the gross- and fine-motor skills to reach almost anything and get into potentially dangerous places. Children depend on adults to protect them by supervising them and creating a safe environment. Teaching safety lessons can make children aware of the need for safety.

Supervising Children

Parents and other adults worry about how to protect children from violence and strangers who may hurt them. Many adults do not think about the two major threats to children's safety—lack of constant and adequate supervision and home hazards. Children are much more likely to be injured in an accident at home than by a stranger's crime.

No safety device or lesson in the home can take the place of an adult's eyes and ears. Accidents happen more often when adults do not carefully supervise children. When adults are talking or texting on the phone, watching television, working on the computer, visiting a friend, feeling ill, or in any way **preoccupied** (focused on another task), accidents are more likely to occur. Accidents may also take place when supervision is unsuitable or lacking, such as when older children supervise younger children or when children (especially school-age children) are home alone for a brief time.

Part of supervising children is watching closely to anticipate the possible hazards a child may face as he or she grows and develops. Adults often refer to developmental milestones, which outline the *sequence of skills* their children will learn, to identify upcoming potential hazards. **Figure 21.8** shows common accidents children are likely to experience during each stage of development.

Creating a Safe Environment

After potential hazards are identified within a child's environment, adults can implement safety measures to **neutralize** (reduce the effect of) those hazards. For example, a child who can crawl up one step or onto any low object can soon climb an entire flight of steep stairs. To prevent the child from falling, an adult might install a child safety gate with locks for the stairs as soon as the child begins to crawl. As adults carefully supervise children's development and see growth occur, they can adjust and implement different safety measures accordingly. Adults can create a safe environment, both indoors and outdoors, through childproofing and selecting and using safe child items and toys.

Childproofing

Childproofing is the process in which adults note dangers in a child's environment and then make the area safe for the child. Childproofing an environment often takes place before the baby is even born. Parents can choose to childproof either through a professional childproofing service or on their own. A professional *childproofer* inspects the home so he or she can assess the need for safety devices. The service is expensive, but includes the costs of the advice, safety devices, and installation.

Indoor and outdoor environments in or around the home pose the greatest hazards to children. A home's structure, general furnishings, rooms, and household items kept in or near the residence all hold threats for young children. Each home is alike in some ways (containing doors, windows, electrical outlets) and different in others (stairs or no stairs, furnishings). The dangers adults look for will vary based on the layout of the home. There are, however, common indoor and outdoor hazards. These hazards may include unstable furniture, blinds and curtains, loose rugs, windows, firearms, hinged doors, poisonous plants, rocks, broken glass, ruts, holes, and old or homemade playground equipment (**Figure 21.9**).

Childproofing measures in or around the home will also vary based on the temperament of the child. Sometimes a child's personality (such as being especially curious or loving to climb) may call for additional childproofing measures. By taking measures to create a safe environment in and around the home, adults can help prevent, or at least minimize, various injuries that might befall children.

Figure 21.8 Common Accidents of Children

Infancy	• Bath scalding and burns from hot water faucets, open heaters, and floor furnaces • Falls from changing tables, carriers, stairs, or other high places • Injuries from swallowing small objects or putting them into eyes, ears, or nose • Drowning • Strangling on cords or smothering from items, such as dry-cleaning bags or balloons • Suffocation under blankets, pillows, or soft objects • Injuries from sharp or broken objects, such as glass, plastics, knives, or sharp-edged furniture • Injuries caused by pulling on cords of kitchen appliances, pulling or grasping containers filled with hot foods or beverages • Injuries from electrical outlets • Mishaps while using walkers, strollers, and riding toys
Toddler years	• Drowning in bathtubs, water features, or pools • Burns from cigarette lighters, matches, open flames, and stoves • Poisoning from medications and cleaning agents • Injuries from dangerous objects, such as knives, electrical outlets, breakable objects, toys with small parts, and sharp-edged objects • Injuries caused by getting into almost anything that is not locked or equipped with special devices • Injuries caused by falls from high places, jumps onto dangerous surfaces (such as concrete), falls off ride-on toys, swings, and slides • Injuries caused by playing in driveways and roads and darting across streets • Injuries caused by swallowing small objects or putting them into eyes, ears, and nose • Eye injuries due to dust and sand
Preschool years	• Poisoning from medications and household products • Injuries from being around or using home, shop, and garden tools • Injuries related to action games, bicycles, and rough play • Various injuries from hazards, such as old refrigerators, deep holes, trash heaps, and construction sites • Drowning • Burns from electrical outlets, appliances, and open flames • Traffic injuries • Injuries from vehicle doors, getting locked in car trunks, and putting the car in gear
School-age years	• Sports-related injuries • Drowning • Firearm and fireworks accidents • Traffic injuries

Figure 21.9 Indoor and Outdoor Safety

Indoor Hazards	Outdoor Hazards
• Glass doors may cause collision or pinched fingers. • Electrical outlets may cause electrocution. • Windows can be broken and cause cuts or falls. • Rugs may cause children to trip and fall. • Blind cords may cause strangulation. • Curtains may cause suffocation or strangulation.	• Landscaping around playground may cause falls. • If old, playground equipment may not adhere to most current safety standards. • Wood chips can get in children's eyes or cause scrapes. • If eaten, outdoor plants may be poisonous.
Childproofing Measures	**Childproofing Measures**
• Put colorful decals on doors at children's eye level; use doorstops and door holders to prevent pinched fingers. • Use electrical outlet covers or other safety devices; if safe, place heavy furniture in front of outlets. • Never put climbable furniture near windows; install window guards. • Use nonskid pads under rugs; tape loose edges of rugs to floor. • Cut or loop blind cords or place them on cleats; use cordless blinds if possible. • Keep young children away from curtains; use short curtains if possible.	• As much as possible, remove places where children can fall, such as landscaping and uneven surfaces. • Research most current safety standards and ensure equipment adheres to these standards. • Use rubber or another gentle material instead of wood chips. • Make sure all outdoor plants are nonharmful if eaten. Keep children away from poisonous plants.

Using Safe Child Items and Toys

Children require many *child items*, such as high chairs and cribs, and play with a variety of toys. Unfortunately, children's items and toys cause many injuries each year. These are injuries that could be avoided if adults knew which safety features to look for when selecting child items and toys. Properly storing and maintaining items and toys can also help in avoiding injuries. All items and toys need to be used under adult supervision, even if the items and toys are deemed safe.

Selecting Safe Child Items

Children's items do not just include items used in the home, such as a crib, changing table, high chair, or playyard. Items also include those used by children outside the home, such as a stroller or a *certified child safety seat*. A **certified child safety seat** (also called a *car seat*) is a restraint system for children under the age of 13, which is required when riding in a motor vehicle. Certified child safety seats, which are fitted to the child's size, have been tested and approved by federal agencies.

Over the years child items have evolved to meet more **rigorous** (demanding) safety standards. Some safety standards, such as no lead paint and 2⅜ inch-spaced slats on cribs and playyards, are now required by law. Items that are homemade or made prior to the enactments of these laws may not meet safety standards. **Figure 21.10** lists features that make a child item safe or unsafe.

All child items are sometimes subject to *safety recalls* issued by the manufacturers. In a **safety recall**, the manufacturer of a product issues a notice stating the product has been found to be unsafe. Consumers are asked to stop using the recalled, unsafe product unless the manufacturer can provide additional parts that will make the product safe.

When selecting safe child items, the use and installation of these items is as important as the initial selection. For example, unless certified child safety seats are installed and used properly, they offer little or no protection for a child in a crash. For this reason, it is important to read directions for all child items carefully.

Selecting Safe Toys

Most new toys that are unsafe for infants and toddlers carry warnings, such as "Not Intended for Children Under Three Years of Age." Other items, such as lawn darts, cannot be sold in toy departments or toy stores because they are dangerous for children to use. When selecting children's toys, adults need to carefully examine the toy for safety features, read all warning labels, and heed recommendations. Toys should be checked for durability and any unsafe small parts. Adults can also ensure children's safety by testing noisemakers for volume, avoiding toys that fly or shoot, and purchasing proper safety gear (such as helmets and pads) for ride-on toys.

Figure 21.10 Safety Standards for Child Items

Item	Safety Standards
Baby vehicle (carriage or stroller)	• Pretested for balance and weight distribution • Safety brake that can be set quickly • Protective bumpers should pad
Bassinet	• Sturdy bottom and wide, stable base • Smooth surfaces and secure leg locks • Firm mattress with snug fit
Bed (toddler)	• Detachable rails with openings no more than 3½ inches apart • Padding on floor next to bed in case child rolls out
Changing table	• Sturdy with safety strap • Guardrails are at least 2 inches high
Child safety seat	• *Rear-facing* if the child is younger than 2 years of age and weighs 22–40 pounds • *Convertible* if the child is younger than 8 years of age and weighs 40–80 pounds • *Three-in-one* if the child is younger than 12 years of age and weighs 80–120 pounds • *Booster* if the child is 8 through 12 years of age and is at least 4 feet 9 inches tall
Crib	• Slats must not be more than 2⅜ inches apart • Height of crib side from bottom of mattress to top of railing should be no less than 26 inches

(Continued)

Figure 21.10 *(Continued)*

Item	Safety Standards
Crib *(continued)*	• Child has outgrown crib when side rail is less than three-fourths of child's height • Children 35 inches and taller must be removed from portable cribs • Side rails must be fixed (not drop) and not adjustable • Paint should be lead free • Teething rails are preferred and should have a plastic covering • No horizontal bars inside crib because a baby can climb on them • Bumper pads should not be used • Corner posts should be flush with the headboard or should be 16 inches or higher for canopy beds • Placed away from windows, heaters, lamps, wall decorations, curtains, blinds, cords, and climbable furniture • Remove crib mobiles and hanging toys at five months; do not use stuffed animals or pillows until the toddler years • No cutout designs on head- or footboards • Crib hardware must have anti-loosening devices • All new cribs should have permanently fixed sides and come with a certificate of conformity—certificate indicates the crib has been rigorously tested and meets the Consumer Product Safety Commission (CPSC) standards
Crib mattress	• The top of the mattress support and the top of the rail should be no less than 9 inches for standard crib and 5 inches for portable crib • Mattress should be covered with durable plastic with air vents and then covered with a fitted sheet; torn mattress covers should be discarded • Mattress should be firm rather than soft and fit snugly in crib • Move mattress to the lowest point once child can pull self up to stand
Diaper pails and wastebaskets	• Keep out of reach of children • Choose models with child-resistant lids
High chair	• Wide-spread legs improve stability • Tray should lock in place • Crotch-snap and wrap-around seat straps are needed • Nonskid rubber mats placed on seat help prevent baby from sliding
Playyard	• Slats should be no more than 2⅜ inches apart • Any mesh netting weave should be smaller than tiny baby buttons • Floor should not collapse • Hinges on folding models should lock tightly • If a *rivet* (screwlike fastener) sticks out ¼ inch or more, stop using the playyard (May cause strangulation if clothing catches on rivet.) • Stop using playyard when child can crawl out of it
Miscellaneous	• Replace metal hangers with strong plastic hangers • Remove dry-cleaning bags or any dangerous product wrapping • Use finger-pinch guards for door hinges • Use products with the Underwriters Laboratories (UL) seal

Adults can select age-stage appropriate toys for their children by remembering that age is only a clue to stage. Toys need to be appropriate for the child's physical skills (ability to use the toy), intellectual abilities (understanding of how to use the toy), and interests. Age-stage safety features can make appropriate toys even safer (**Figure 21.11**). After purchasing a toy, it is important to discard toy packaging. Styrofoam®; plastic; small, plastic ties; and other packaging materials are safety hazards for young children. Keeping safety information about child items in a file folder can help adults check recall information or make a complaint, if necessary.

Storing and Maintaining Child Items and Toys

Child items and toys require appropriate space for storage. In some cases, the size of a toy during use and nonuse is about the same, such as a toy truck. In other cases, toys in use require much more space than they do when stored, such as building blocks. When storing toys, adults should consider the following: find indoor storage places near where each toy can be safely used; store outdoor toys where they can be secured when not in use; store all toys in spaces without **cluttering** (filling with many objects); and use special storage cabinets or shelves as needed.

Figure 21.11 Safety Features for Toys

For Infants and Toddlers

- ***Size should be larger than the child's two fists.*** Even large toys can break, exposing small parts. Laws ban small parts in new toys intended for children under three years of age. Older and handmade toys may still have small parts.
- ***Nonbreakable.*** Toys that break may expose small parts or break into small pieces. Toys made of glass or brittle plastic are the most unsafe.
- ***No sharp edges or points.*** Laws ban new toys with sharp edges or points intended for children under eight years of age. Broken toys often have sharp edges. Wires with sharp points are often inside stuffed toys.
- ***Nontoxic.*** Painted toys should be labeled *nontoxic*. Avoid all painted toys for children who put playthings in their mouth.
- ***No long cords or strings.*** Toys with long cords or strings should not be used with infants and young children because they may present a strangulation hazard.
- ***Nonflammable, flame retardant, or flame resistant.*** Dolls and stuffed toys should be made of materials not likely to ignite.
- ***Washable and hygienic materials.*** Dolls and stuffed toys must be clean when bought and must be easy to keep clean.
- ***No broken or uninflated balloons.*** These balloons are the most dangerous objects for suffocation. (Inflated balloons are not safe for children under five years of age.)
- ***No toys or games with marbles or balls smaller than 1¾ inches in diameter.*** These items are a choking hazard.
- ***No small parts.*** Laws ban small parts intended for children under three years of age. Older and handmade toys may still have small parts.
- ***No detachable clothing on dolls or stuffed animals.*** Fasteners used on clothing items for dolls or stuffed animals are very small and thus present a choking hazard.
- ***No toys with springs or hinges.*** Springs and hinges can pinch fingers.
- ***Sounds at acceptable levels.*** The law requires a label on toys that produce sounds above a certain level. The label warns, "Do not use within one foot of the ear. Do not use indoors." Toys making sounds that can result in hearing damage are banned.

(Continued)

Figure 21.11 *(Continued)*

For Older Children

- ***Safe electric toys.*** Electric toys must meet requirements for maximum surface temperatures, electrical wiring, and display of warning labels. Electrical toys that heat are intended for children over eight years of age.
- ***Items used for age intended.*** Chemistry sets, hobby sets, balloons, and games and toys with small parts are extremely dangerous if misused or left within the reach of younger children.
- ***Sturdy, safe, large outdoor equipment.*** Space between moving parts is wide enough to not pinch or crush fingers. Bolt ends should be covered with plastic end caps. Swing seats should be lightweight and have smooth, rolled edges. All swing sets, gyms, and other large equipment should be anchored firmly to the ground.
- ***Paints and crayons marked with designation ASTM D4236.*** The designation means the material has been examined and is either nontoxic or carries a warning.
- ***No toys that are projectiles.*** Projectiles cause many eye injuries.
- ***Safe tricycles and bicycles.*** Tricycles and bicycles need to be assembled properly and seats adjusted to the rider's height. (Size of tricycle or bicycle should be suitable for child's current size.) Pedals should have skid-resistant surfaces. Reflectors (at least two inches in diameter) should be used on bicycles. A proper fitting helmet should be worn at all times.

Toys and child items tend to be used often and sometimes roughly. Adults can take care to maintain these objects and should always check for the following:

- recalls issued by the manufacturer or the Consumer Product Safety Commission
- sharp points, jagged edges, and loose parts
- removable parts that are small enough to fit inside a child's mouth
- rust on outdoor equipment
- stuffed toys and dolls that must be repaired and cleaned (**Figure 21.12**)
- batteries not secured by a cover with a screw to prevent removal

Children can seriously injure themselves with broken toys. Adults should remove any broken toys from use, properly dispose of those that cannot be fixed, and repair any other broken items before they are put back into use.

Adults can also add safety devices to child items and toys. If a toy chest is not properly **ventilated** (accessible to air), an adult can drill a few air holes. If skates move too fast, adults can place a piece of adhesive tape around the wheel edge. To remind children not to hold the chains of a swing too low, adults can mark chains with tape at the proper holding height.

Teaching Safety Lessons

In addition to supervising children and using safe items and toys, adults can ensure children's safety by teaching their children *how* to be safe. Children often engage in unsafe behaviors because

Figure 21.12 Stuffed toys need to be cleaned and checked regularly. Otherwise, they may grow bacteria or have unsafe parts. *What types of hazards do unwashed stuffed toys pose for young children?*

Focus on Careers

Public Information Specialist

Public information specialists arrange and conduct programs to maintain contact between organization or business representatives and the public. They handle organizational functions, such as media, community, consumer, industry, and government relations. Public information specialists conduct research, prepare materials, maintain contacts, and respond to inquiries.

Career cluster: Marketing.

Education: Educational requirements include a bachelor's degree, preferably in public relations, journalism, communications, English, or business.

Job outlook: Future employment opportunities for public information specialists are expected to grow about as fast as the average for all occupations.

To learn more about a career as a public information specialist, visit the United States Department of Labor's *Occupational Outlook Handbook* website. You will also be able to compare the job responsibilities, educational requirements, job outlook, and average pay of public information specialists with similar occupations.

they are trying to achieve goals. While adults cannot always change children's goals, they can help children meet these goals safely. For example, when an infant wants to climb, a parent might let the infant climb up and down a single carpeted step. This environment is safe to explore, even if the infant takes small tumbles. Small risks teach children to cope with possible dangers. A steep staircase, however, poses too great a safety risk for such a young child.

Teaching safety is an ongoing process that begins almost at birth and continues for life. The first lessons occur in the home and yard. They expand to include the total environment, such as school, water, traffic, and job safety.

Adults can teach safety to young children in the following ways:

- ***Be a model for children.*** A child will absorb adults' approaches to everyday actions and safety measures, such as buckling seat belts and looking before crossing streets. Adults may even exaggerate behaviors to make safety measures clearer for the young child. They may stop, look, and say, "I don't see a car coming, so we can cross now," before walking across a street.
- ***Explain the boundaries of play.*** Show, as well as tell children, what they can and cannot do. Warnings are more helpful if they are stated in positive ways. An adult may say, "Grass is for playing, and streets are for cars and trucks." Warnings stated in negative ways may tempt children to act unsafely. Also, warnings that are repeated too often lose their meanings.
- ***Couple warnings with reasons.*** When communicating safety rules, adults can explain the reasons for these rules. For example, an adult may say, "I want you to put on your seat belt because it will protect you if we make a fast stop or get into a crash."
- ***Insist on obedience.*** To insist on obedience means taking action against wrongdoings, not simply making **idle** (inactive) threats of punishment. Taking action does not call for physical punishment, but rather discipline appropriate for the action. For example, an adult may say, "If you do not put on your life jacket, you will not be allowed to play in the water." The adult could then enforce that limit (**Figure 21.13**).

Focus on

Speech

Safety Around Strangers

As they grow older and meet more people, children will most likely encounter *strangers*, or adults whom they do not know. While adult supervision can reduce children's risks of being harmed by strangers or dangerous situations, children still need to be taught lessons about stranger safety. In learning about strangers, children first need to distinguish between *safe strangers*, such as police officers and firefighters, and *unsafe strangers*, such as unfamiliar adults who offer them rides home.

Using reliable online or print resources, research strategies for teaching children the difference between safe and unsafe strangers. Also research tips for teaching children stranger safety. After you research, deliver a short oral presentation summarizing what you learn.

- ***Practice safety measures with children.*** Adults can practice many safety measures with children, including safe walks to school or to other places, fire drills, and evacuation plans. To support safety lessons, adults can encourage to children talk about, act out, or illustrate safety actions.

Figure 21.13 Insisting on obedience involves setting and then enforcing limits. For example, a child may not be allowed to go into the water unless he or she is wearing a life jacket. *How did your caregivers insist on obedience?*

Lesson 21.2 Review and Assessment 

1. Identify two common accidents children are likely to experience during each stage of development from infancy through the school-age years.
2. ______ is the process in which adults note dangers in a child's environment and then make the area safe for the child.
3. List three examples of indoor and outdoor hazards.
4. Choose two types of child items and identify the safety standards for each.
5. What are *safety recalls* and why should adults pay attention to them?
6. Identify five safety standards for infant and toddler toys.
7. List three guidelines for teaching children safety lessons.
8. **Critical thinking.** What does it mean that children need *adequate* supervision? What makes supervision adequate?

Treating Children's Illnesses and Injuries

Lesson 21.3

Objectives

After studying this lesson, you will be able to

- identify symptoms that reveal a need for prompt medical attention.
- explain why accurate measuring devices are essential in giving medications.
- describe first aid for treating wounds; burns; fractures, bruises, and sprains; and splinters, bites, and stings.
- identify common household poisonings and describe what parents and other adults should do if a child has been poisoned.
- list steps to take for medical emergencies.

Key Terms

emergency situations
first aid
first-degree burns
fractures
second-degree burns
shock
splinters
sprains
third-degree burns
wounds

Academic Terms

abrasion
antiseptic
ingest

Reading and Writing Activity

As you read this lesson, put sticky notes next to sections that interest you or next to sections in which you have questions. Write your questions or comments on the sticky notes. After reading, find a partner and share your questions and comments. Ask your teacher any questions you and your partner cannot answer together.

Graphic Organizer

Divide a piece of paper into two columns, one labeled *Illnesses and Injuries* and the other labeled *Treatments*. As you read, write illnesses and injuries in the *Illnesses and Injuries* column and treatments under the *Treatments* column. Draw lines between items or notes in the two columns if you think an illness or injury and treatment are related.

Illnesses and Injuries	Treatments
Shallow cuts →	*Stop bleeding; use antiseptic; cover with bandage*

Even with preventive and basic health care, children still experience illness at times. Adults may be able to treat some minor illnesses children experience without medical help, but more serious illnesses may require immediate medical attention. To effectively care for children who are ill, adults must be able to recognize symptoms of illness and then make sure children receive the necessary treatment to get well. Sometimes treatment for an illness can be handled at home, and other times an illness may require immediate medical treatment from a doctor. If the illness is serious, children may need to stay in the hospital. Whether children are recovering from an illness at home or in the hospital, adults can help children by making them feel as comfortable as possible.

Similarly, even with proper safety measures in place, not all accidents can be prevented. Children will still experience many scrapes, bumps, and bruises as they learn what their bodies can and cannot do (**Figure 21.14**). Many injuries that occur during childhood are often minor, but some injuries can be serious, requiring immediate medical attention. Adults who work with children need to know basic first aid to treat children's injuries. They also need to know how to handle emergency situations.

Treating a Child's Illness

Most adults who work with children will eventually care for an ill child. To treat a child's illness, adults must recognize the need for medical intervention. In some cases, children need to be taken to a medical professional for treatment. In other cases, parents can care for children at home and treat them without assistance from medical professionals, often by giving medications and keeping children comfortable.

Recognizing the Need for Medical Intervention

Young children, especially those under seven or eight years of age, have many common illnesses, such as colds and digestive upsets. Minor illnesses such as these are typically taken care of at home without seeking professional medical attention. Other minor illnesses, which parents can often handle at home, include mild fevers (under 101°F), diarrhea, a runny nose, and short-term vomiting.

To safely treat children's illnesses, adults must first be able to recognize symptoms that require medical (sometimes immediate) intervention (**Figure 21.15**). For these illnesses, adults should take children to a doctor or seek urgent care if

Figure 21.14 As children grow and develop, their curiosity and energy motivate them to explore their worlds and test what they can do. ***How can adults encourage exploration while ensuring children's health and safety?***

Figure 21.15 Symptoms Requiring Medical Intervention

Areas of Concern	Symptoms	
Blood	• Large amount lost in bleeding • Bleeding that will not stop	
Body movement	• *Convulsions* (seizures) • Immobility in any part of the body	• Shaking • Stiffness of the body
Bones and muscles	• Swelling • Pain	• Difficulty in movement • *Bone fracture* (crack or break)
Brain	• Dizziness • Visual problems • Strange actions or appearance	• Unconsciousness • Headache
Breathing	• Difficulty breathing • Slow or rapid breathing • Continued coughing, sneezing, or wheezing	
Digestive system	• Sudden decrease in appetite • Nausea or forceful vomiting • Vomiting for several hours with inability to retain fluids • Abdominal pain or tenderness • Sudden increase or decrease in number of bowel movements • Stools or urine unusual in amount, color, odor, or consistency	
Eyes	• Irritation or redness • Sensitivity to light	• Blurred vision • Uneven pupils
Fever	• Rectal temperature of 101°F or higher • Mild fever that lasts several days	
General behavior	• Extremely ill appearance or demeanor that worsens quickly • Unusual quietness, irritability, confusion, or drowsiness • Strange behavior after a fall or other accident • If already ill, a rise in fever or new symptoms • Sharp screaming • Ear rubbing, head rolling, or drawing of legs toward abdomen	
Nose	• Nasal discharge (note color, amount, and consistency), congestion, or bleeding • Continuous clear drainage from the nose after a head injury	
Skin	• Dryness or hotness • Excessive perspiration • Rash or hives	• Severe cuts or *abrasions* (scrapes) • Deep bruising • Flushed or pale skin
Throat	• Soreness • Redness	• Choking or coughing

appropriate. For minor illnesses being handled at home, treatment usually involves taking children's temperatures, preparing specific foods, and sometimes giving children medications. Keeping children comfortable and ensuring they get plenty of rest are also important.

Giving Medications

For many illnesses, children need medication to get well. Medications for children include both *prescription medications* (medications prescribed by a doctor) and *over-the-counter medications* (medications that can be bought without a prescription). Parents and other adults should always read instructions for medications before giving them to children. Some over-the-counter medications, such as aspirin, should *never* be given to children. Any questions parents have about children's medications should be directed to the pharmacist or the child's doctor.

Medications are best given in accurate, medically defined measuring devices. Incorrect dosages may deliver too little medication and hinder infections from clearing up. Too much medication may poison the child. Medications work best when they are given in ways that are easy for children to consume. For example, infants may suck medication through a nursing nipple with a ring attached, and some children may take medication from a dropper or syringe (without a needle) inserted far back at the side of the mouth (**Figure 21.16**). A pharmacist can advise parents on how to give medications so children receive accurate dosages.

Medications are to be kept in *child-resistant containers* and disposed of properly (such as through a pharmacy, hospital, or trash service). Child-resistant caps need to be replaced carefully after use and medications kept in an out-of-reach place, such as a locked cabinet. Medication should never be given in the dark, referred to as "candy," or given in baby bottles or juice glasses. Lastly, adults can avoid taking medication (even vitamins) in front of young children and keep medication away from children's reach.

Making a Child Comfortable

When children are ill, they need extra attention. Infants and young children will need lots of holding and rocking. Older children may need their illness and the treatment explained to them. Most children who are ill also enjoy little surprises, such as a small gift of a new book or a stuffed animal. Above all, adults can appear cheerful and confident so they will not cause ill children to worry. If the child's attitude is positive, this can speed recovery.

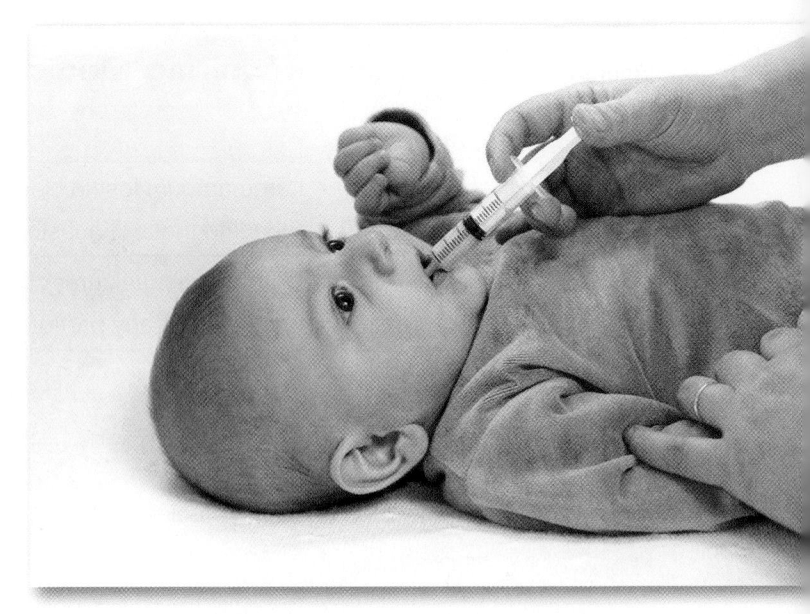

Figure 21.16 Many infants receive medication from a syringe inserted into the mouth. ***Why is this method of delivering medication developmentally appropriate for infants?***

As children begin to feel well, they often do not want to stay in bed. Keeping an active child in bed at this time can be quite challenging for adults. Quiet games, books, movies, music, and paper and crayons can help children pass time. Visits from adults and other children (if the illness is not contagious) also help.

Making a child comfortable can be especially important if the child is in a hospital. Adults can prepare children for hospital care by explaining hospital life, touring the hospital, and using play and other means to introduce hospital concepts. During the hospital stay, parents should stay with their children and, as much as possible, make the hospital feel like home.

Knowing Basic First Aid

In the case of a severe illness or injury, adults may be required to administer first aid. **First aid** is emergency treatment for an illness or injury that is given before professional medical help arrives. Training in first aid can be very helpful to caregivers and is required as part of teacher training. First-aid supplies, including a first-aid chart or book, should be kept current and nearby (**Figure 21.17**).

First aid includes guidelines for the treatment of wounds; burns; fractures, bruises, and sprains; splinters, bites, and stings; and poisonings. First aid also includes methods for dealing with emergency situations.

Wounds

Wounds are damage to the body's skin or tissue. Wounds may be caused by falls, punctures, collisions, and a variety of other accidents involving objects and other people. To properly treat wounds, adults should first identify the child's type of wound. Types of wounds include shallow cuts, abrasions, and deep cuts with heavy bleeding.

Figure 21.17 First-Aid Items

- Adhesive bandages (various sizes)
- Adhesive tape
- Antiseptic for cuts and scratches
- Calamine lotion (for insect bites)
- Gauze bandages and squares
- Scissors
- Activated charcoal (prevents poisons from entering the bloodstream)
- First-aid chart or book (for quick reference)

*Note: First-aid items need to be kept in both the home and in all vehicles in which a child is transported.

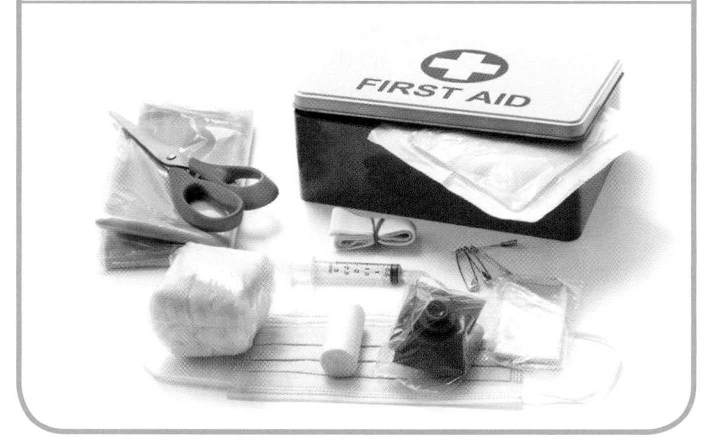

Shallow Cuts and Abrasions

Children can get shallow cuts from falling, handling an object incorrectly, or running into objects. These cuts may bleed a little, but usually only damage the first layer of skin. If a child has a shallow cut that bleeds, first stop the bleeding by applying pressure using sterile gauze. After the bleeding has stopped, wash the wound using soap and warm water and apply an **antiseptic** (substance that kills bacteria) to prevent infection. Cover the cut with an adhesive bandage or other dressing (**Figure 21.18**).

If a child has an **abrasion** (uh-BRAY-zhun)—a scrape—follow these same guidelines. Make sure to wash the affected area carefully so particles do not remain in the wound and infect it.

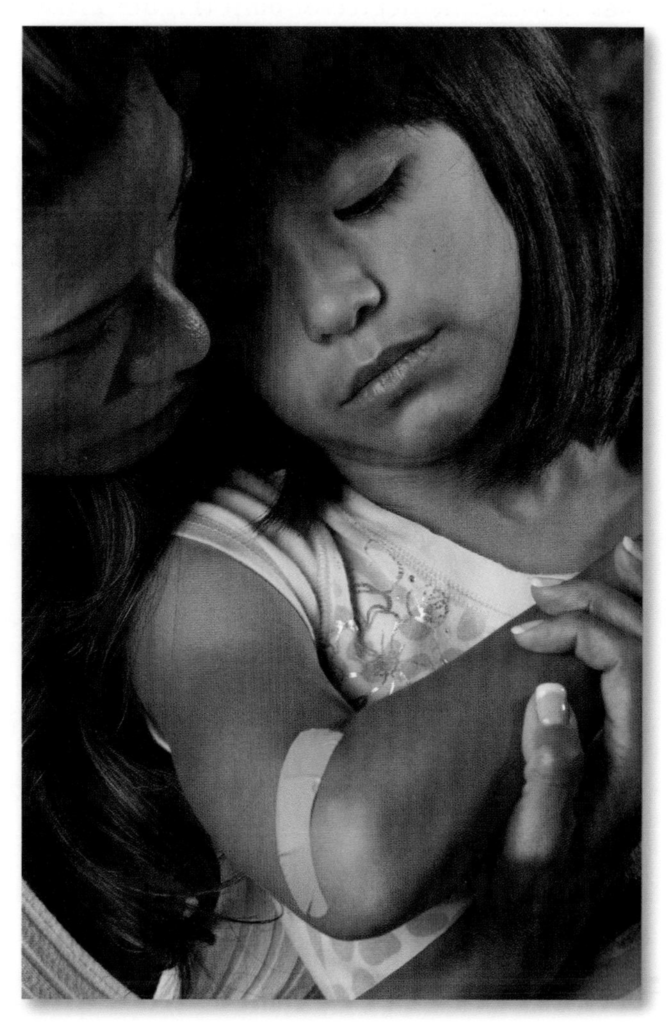

Figure 21.18 To prevent infection, shallow cuts should be covered with an adhesive bandage or other dressing. *How might an adult explain to a child the importance of wearing a bandage?*

Deep Cuts and Bleeding

If a child experiences a deep cut with much bleeding or bleeding that will not stop, seek medical attention immediately. While waiting for medical help, continue trying to stop the bleeding by applying pressure to the wound using a sterile dressing. Some children who experience much blood loss may go into **shock**, a condition in which the heartbeat and breathing slow. If a child goes into shock while awaiting medical help, lay the child on his or her back and elevate the child's legs. Keep the child warm until medical help arrives.

Burns

Children who experience burns are at risk for shock and infection. When treating a burn, first identify the degree of burn (**Figure 21.19**). **First-degree burns** occur when heat or radiation burns the top layer of skin. First-degree burns include mild sunburns, in which the skin turns pink but does not peel or blister. **Second-degree burns** affect layers of skin beneath the first layer. Symptoms include blistering, peeling, discoloration, swelling, or severe pain in the skin. Finally, **third-degree burns** affect the innermost layer of skin and sometimes the muscle and bone beneath. Symptoms include blackened or whitened skin. Following are methods for treating burns:

- ***First-degree burns.*** Run cold water over affected area 15 to 20 minutes. Dry area and keep it clean. Cover the burn with a clean dressing.
- ***Second-degree burns.*** Run cold water over affected area 15 to 20 minutes. Dry area and keep it clean. Cover the burn with a clean dressing. If the second-degree burn is deep or large, seek emergency medical attention immediately.
- ***Third-degree burns.*** Seek emergency medical attention immediately. Do *not* try to clean a severe burn. Observe the child for signs of shock and respond accordingly.

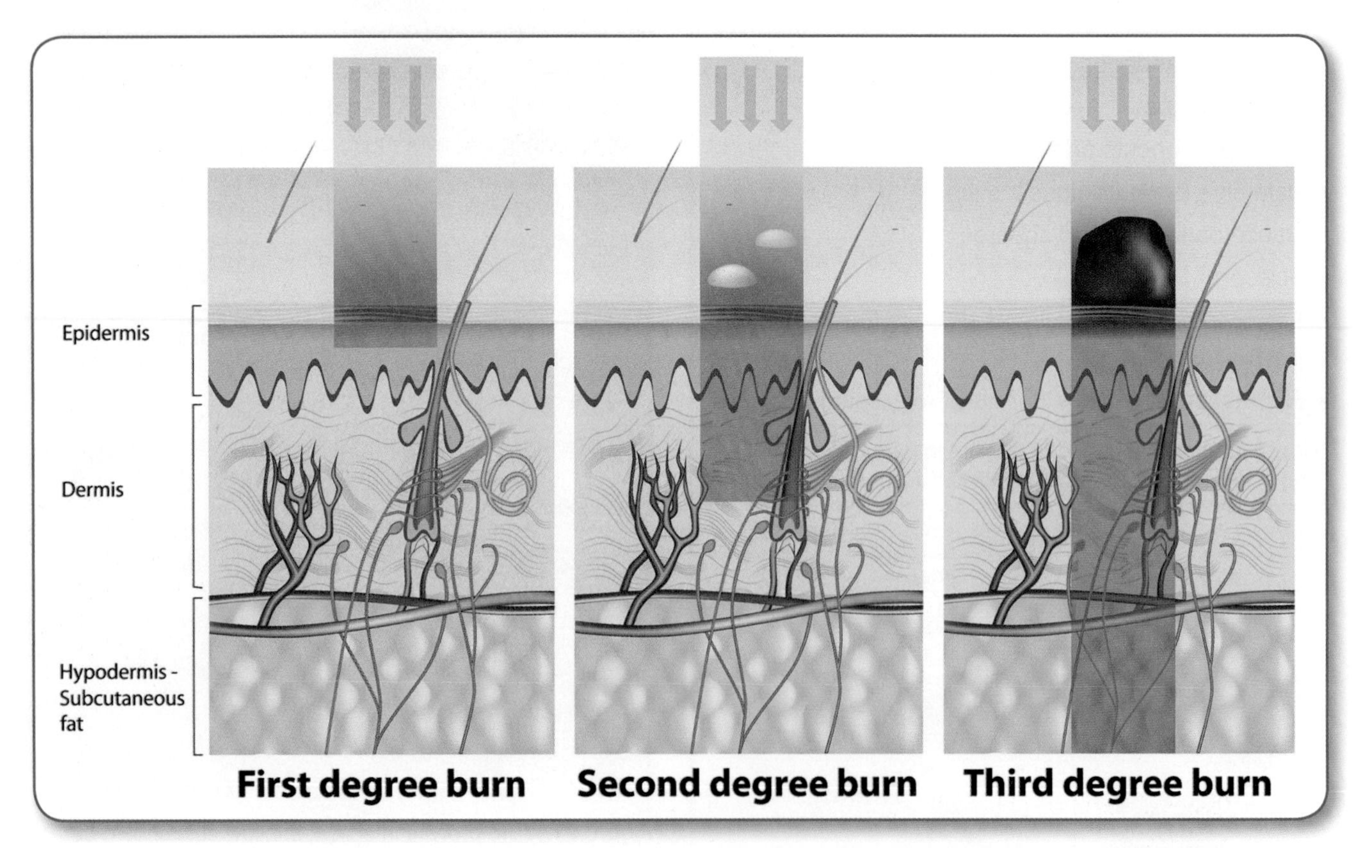

Figure 21.19 Burns that affect the innermost layer of skin (third-degree burns) are more serious than burns that affect the outermost layer of skin (first-degree burns). When treating a burn, it is not recommended that you use ointments or apply ice directly to the burn. *What is the most serious type of burn you have experienced?*

Fractures, Bruises, and Sprains

Falls or collisions can cause fractures or sprains in children. **Fractures** are cracks and breaks in bones, and **sprains** are injuries to joint ligaments. Symptoms for both fractures and sprains include swelling and pain around the site of the injury. If a child experiences a fracture or sprain, seek medical help immediately. There is no way of knowing the severity of the injury without examination by a medical professional. If the injury occurs in the neck or spinal region, do *not* try to move the child. Rather, call for emergency medical help.

Splinters, Bites, and Stings

Children who like to explore are prone to a number of injuries from their environment, including splinters, bites, and stings. **Splinters** are pieces of wood or plastic that become lodged in a child's skin. Shallow splinters can be removed with care using tweezers, but deep or large splinters should be removed by a medical professional. If a child is bitten or stung, check carefully for an allergic reaction. If the child is not allergic, wash the wound thoroughly to avoid infection. If a child is bitten by an animal, note the type of animal. Some animals

Investigate Special Topics: Emergency Preparedness

Emergency situations tend to be unexpected and stressful, especially when young children are involved. These situations, however, can be managed well if preparations are made ahead of time. *Emergency preparedness* usually refers to a collection of plans made in case of emergency situations. These plans might include evacuation plans, disaster plans, and preparations. For adults who work with young children, emergency preparedness can mean the difference between a serious accident and safety.

Establishing Emergency Plans

For most families and child care programs, emergency plans include preparations for fires, natural disasters (such as tornadoes), and other dangerous situations. Adults in these settings may plan evacuation routes, establish safe locations for children in case of emergency, and compile emergency preparedness kits. Typically, these plans must be taught to children. Evacuation routes must be practiced through fire drills, and children must be shown safe locations for natural disasters or dangerous events. If children know these routines well before an emergency, they will be more likely to remember them in the moment.

Guiding Children Through Emergency Plans

Children, especially children who are too young to understand an emergency, may feel upset and react strongly to emergency situations. Part of emergency preparedness is planning to help young children cope and guiding them through emergency plans. Young children cannot help their intense reactions to stressful events. Parents and other adults can keep in mind their children's developmental stages during emergency situations and can remain calm, reminding children of the plans that have been established and soothing fears as much as possible.

Research Activity

Working with a partner, search the Internet for reliable sources of information about emergency preparedness. These sources should be governmental websites or websites of authoritative organizations, such as the American Red Cross (ARC). During your research, take notes about tips for emergency preparedness. Afterward, create a short slideshow presentation of these tips. Present the slideshow to your class.

can carry dangerous diseases; if a child is bitten by one of these animals, seek medical help immediately. Also, certain insect and animal bites are poisonous, thus requiring emergency medical treatment.

Poisonings

The majority of childhood poisonings happen when children **ingest** (consume) dangerous substances found around the house. Implementing safety measures around the home can help lessen the chance of children being poisoned. Reading all product labels and warnings can help parents identify which products are dangerous (**Figure 21.20**). Storing household products high above floor level (rather than under sinks) and locking up household products may help keep them away from children. Potentially dangerous products should not be left unattended or within reach, even for a minute.

Poisonings can be deadly to children. If a child has ingested a poison, adults should take immediate action and call a hospital or poison control center. The person at the hospital or center will determine whether the child needs emergency medical attention. Symptoms of a poisoning might include fever, rash, choking or coughing, nausea, labored breathing, or irritation around the mouth or eyes.

Handling Emergency Situations

Sometimes, adults will face emergency situations with children. **Emergency situations** are dangerous, often unexpected or life-threatening events that require immediate action. Medical emergencies can arise from both illnesses and accidents. In a medical

Figure 21.20 Poisonous Household Products

Cleaning Products	Garage and Garden Products	Medications	Personal Products
Air fresheners	Antifreeze	Acetaminophen	Aftershave
Ammonia (used in many cleaning products)	Caustic lime	Amphetamines	Baby and bath oils
Bleach	Fertilizer	Analgesic creams	Cosmetics
Cleaners	Gasoline, kerosene, lighter fluid, oil, and other petroleum products	Antibiotics	Deodorant
Dishwasher and dishwashing products	Oils	Anticonvulsants	Hair coloring products
Disinfectant	Paint	Antidepressants	Hair removal products
Drain opener	Pesticides	Antidiarrheals	Hand sanitizers
Floor wax	Putty	Blood pressure drugs	Lotion
Furniture polish	Strychnine	Camphor	Mouthwash
Laundry products	Turpentine	Cold preparations	Nail polish and polish remover
Lye (sometimes found in soaps)	Varnish	Cough medications	Perfume
Metal polish	Weed killer	Diabetes drugs	Permanent wave solution
Oven cleaner	Windshield solution	Ear medications	Powder, talcum (baby and body powder)
Rust remover		Heart drugs	Water softener
Spot remover		Iron, vitamins with iron	Rubbing alcohol
Toilet bowl cleaner		Nasal sprays	Shampoo
Water softener		Oil of wintergreen	Soap
		Pain relievers	
		Sleeping pills	
		Topical anesthetics	
		Tranquilizers	
		Vitamins	

emergency, adults should always call for immediate medical help (**Figure 21.21**). When responding to emergency situations, adults need to know how to use choking maneuvers; *cardiopulmonary resuscitation* (CAR-dee-oh-PUL-muh-nar-ee ree-SUH-suh-TAY-shun), or *CPR*; and *automatic external defibrillators* (dee-FIH-bruh-lay-turs), or *AEDs*. Procedures for using these methods and devices are listed in **Figure 21.22**. Adults should continue first aid until professional help arrives and then not interfere with the assistance. The ARC and the American Heart Association (AHA) both offer first-aid and CPR training so adults can become certified to effectively and safely treat children's injuries.

Sometimes emergency situations occur due to fire, explosions, or weather situations. In these cases, adults or teachers should comfort children and follow the evacuation or safety plans that have been practiced. A caregiver or teacher could have a flashlight and first-aid kit next to the evacuation doors or in a safe area for easy access while helping children remain safe. The ARC's first-aid guides, available in both print and digital media formats, contain further pointers for preparing for emergencies.

Lesson 21.3 Review and Assessment 

1. List four symptoms that require medical (sometimes immediate) intervention.
2. Why are accurate measuring devices important in giving medications to children?
3. What is *shock*, and how can adults help a child who has gone into shock?
4. Choose one type of burn and explain how adults should treat it.
5. Why should adults seek medical help if a child experiences a fracture or sprain?
6. How should adults respond if a child has ingested poison?
7. List two organizations that offer first-aid and CPR training for adults.
8. **Critical thinking.** In small groups, create a short poem or saying to help you remember what types of symptoms require medical intervention.

Figure 21.21 The first step in handling any emergency situation is to call for emergency help. *Why should calling for emergency help be the first step?*

Figure 21.22 Handling Emergency Situations

Conscious Choking		
Adults trained to handle choking emergencies use the following steps if an infant, child, or adult is conscious and is choking. If the person is an infant or child, obtain parental consent, if possible.		
Steps	**Infants**	**Children and Adults**
Step 1: Give five back blows.	Give back blows with heel of hand between infant's shoulder blades.	Bend child or adult forward at waist and give back blows with heel of hand between shoulder blades.
Step 2: Give five thrusts.	Give five *chest thrusts* with two to three fingers at center of infant's chest just below nipple line. Compress breastbone about 1½ inches.	Give five *abdominal thrusts* with fist in middle of child's or adult's abdomen (thumb side against body; fist covered with other hand).
Step 3: Continue sets of five back blows and five thrusts until object is forced out, person can cough or breathe, or person becomes unconscious. If person becomes unconscious, call 911 and begin CPR.		

Cardiopulmonary Resuscitation (CPR)		
Adults trained in handling CPR use the following steps if an infant, child, or adult is unconscious and not breathing. If the person is an infant or child, obtain parental consent, if possible.		
Steps	**Infants**	**Children and Adults**
Step 1: Give 30 chest compressions in about 18 seconds.	Place two or three fingers in center of chest (on lower half of sternum, just below nipple line). Compress chest about 1½ inches.	Place two hands in center of chest (on lower half of sternum). Compress chest about 2 inches.
Step 2: Give two rescue breaths until the chest clearly rises (about one second per breath). **Step 3:** Continue cycle. Do not stop unless situation becomes unsafe, person shows sign of life, another person takes over, you are too exhausted to continue, or AED becomes available.		

Using an Automated External Defibrillator (AED)		
Adults trained in using an AED use the following steps if an infant, child, or adult is unconscious and not breathing. If the person is an infant or child, obtain parental consent, if possible.		
Steps	**Infants and Children Younger Than Eight Years of Age**	**Children Older Than Eight Years of Age and Adults**
Step 1: Turn on AED. **Step 2:** Wipe bare chest dry.		
Step 3: Attach pads.	Use *pediatric pads* if possible. Place one pad on the upper right side of the chest and the other pad on the left side of the chest. If the pads touch (because the infant or child is too small), place one pad in the middle of the chest and one pad in the middle of the back.	Place one pad on the upper right side of the chest and the other pad on the left side of the chest.
Step 4: If necessary, plug in connector. **Step 5:** Tell everyone to stand clear. **Step 6:** Deliver shock. **Step 7:** Perform about five cycles of CPR.		

Chapter 21 Review and Assessment

Summary

Protecting and maintaining children's physical health and safety is one of the major responsibilities of adults. Children need basic health care to grow and develop. Their physical needs must be met, and adults need to schedule regular doctor and dental appointments and well-child checkups. Health screenings are also an important part of children's health care; these screenings detect conditions often before they can become serious problems. Immunizations protect children from many serious diseases, and regular immunization schedules are recommended by doctors. Even with basic health care, however, children are at risk for communicable diseases (including foodborne diseases) and noncommunicable diseases (such as epilepsy, diabetes, allergies, and asthma).

In addition to health, adults are responsible for ensuring children's safety. The most important element of safety is supervision. *Supervision* involves anticipating and removing possible hazards for children. Children need a safe environment, which can be created through childproofing. Adults should take care to select safe child items and toys for children. They should also pay attention to safety recalls and store and maintain items well. As children grow older, adults can teach them safety lessons to help them take precautions to keep themselves safe.

Even with health care and adequate supervision, children may experience illnesses or injuries. In treating illness, adults need to recognize symptoms requiring medical intervention, know how to give medications, and make children comfortable. Knowing basic first aid and treatments for common injuries, such as cuts and burns, is also important when working with children. In emergency situations, adults can help by calling for help and knowing choking maneuvers, CPR, and how to use an AED.

College and Career Portfolio

Portfolio Review

Once you have selected, created, and compiled the elements of your portfolio, you can begin finalizing your work and preparing to present it. Now is a good time to have someone review your portfolio. The feedback you gain from a review can be extremely helpful.

- Select one adult (such as a teacher or counselor) to review your portfolio. Ask the adult for honest feedback.
- Listen to the adult's feedback and brainstorm how you can implement his or her advice at this stage.

Chapter 21 Review and Assessment

Vocabulary Activities

1. Review the following terms and identify any terms that can be divided into smaller parts, having *roots* and *suffixes* or *prefixes*. Write these terms on a sheet of paper. Beside each term, list the root word and prefix or suffix. Compare your list with those of your classmates. How is your list similar or different? As a class, discuss how root words, suffixes, and prefixes help you understand meaning.

Key Terms

allergen (21.1)
allergy (21.1)
asthma (21.1)
certified child safety seat (21.2)
childproofing (21.2)
communicable diseases (21.1)
emergency situations (21.3)
epilepsy (21.1)
first aid (21.3)
first-degree burns (21.3)
foodborne diseases (21.1)
fractures (21.3)
health screenings (21.1)
immunization (21.1)
noncommunicable diseases (21.1)
preventive health care (21.1)
safety recall (21.2)
second-degree burns (21.3)
shock (21.3)
splinters (21.3)
sprains (21.3)
third-degree burns (21.3)
vaccination (21.1)
vaccines (21.1)
well-child checkups (21.1)
wounds (21.3)

2. Draw a cartoon bubble for each of the following terms to express the meaning of each term as it relates to the chapter. Share your cartoons with the rest of the class.

Academic Terms

abrasion (21.3)
anaphylaxis (21.1)
antiseptic (21.3)
cluttering (21.2)
idle (21.2)
immunity (21.1)
ingest (21.3)
neutralize (21.2)
preoccupied (21.2)
rigorous (21.2)
unearth (21.1)
ventilated (21.2)

Critical Thinking

3. **Cause and effect.** Part of basic health care is meeting the physical needs of children. In small groups, review this text's chapters about meeting the physical needs of infants, toddlers, preschoolers, and school-age children. Then discuss how meeting these needs impacts the success of health care.
4. **Draw conclusions.** Write a short essay answering the question, *Why is supervision still important even in a thoroughly childproofed environment?* Draw conclusions about supervisory effects on physical, intellectual, and social-emotional development.
5. **Compare and contrast.** Safety precautions differ depending on the environment that must be childproofed. Working with a partner, compare and contrast the safety measures that might be taken in a house and in a child care center. How is childproofing similar in these two locations? How is it different?
6. **Evaluate.** Obtain a catalog or search online to review popular toys for children. As you view the toys, identify five toys as safe or unsafe. What safety features do the toys have? How, if at all, are the toys still hazardous? For what ages are the toys appropriate?
7. **Analyze.** It is not recommended that adults use old or antique child items or toys with their children. Why do experts make this recommendation? How would you explain to a parent the need for new or current child items and toys?
8. **Make inferences.** Choose one of the guidelines for teaching safety lessons discussed in this chapter. Then, working with a partner, discuss how the guideline is developmentally appropriate for young children.
9. **Identify.** Review the list of common household poisons in this chapter and then take an inventory of the items in your home's bathrooms and kitchen. What poisonous items does your family have? What childproofing measures would you take if a toddler or a preschooler were to stay in your home?
10. **Determine.** In small groups, write a short case study about a child who becomes injured. Then trade case studies with another group. Read the new case study in your group and determine the first-aid measures that should be taken to the treat the child.

Core Skills

11. **Listening and speaking.** In small groups, conduct research and visit local health care services for children. What features (such as colorful waiting rooms or books for reading) do they offer that appeal to children? Talk with someone who works at the health care service and ask what advice he or she might give families who are choosing health care services for their children. Finally, deliver your findings to the class in an oral presentation.
12. **Science.** Knowing the causes of common communicable and noncommunicable diseases can help adults prevent and treat these conditions. In small groups, choose one communicable and one noncommunicable disease. Research the causes and treatments of these diseases and create a public service announcement detailing your findings.
13. **Research and technology.** Food safety is a key component of ensuring children's health. To learn more about food safety, visit Foodsafety.gov and research the recommended temperatures, cooking times, and storage methods for various types of food. Then choose three meals that you prepare or eat on a regular basis. Create a slideshow presentation explaining how these meals are prepared and stored to ensure food safety.
14. **Listening and math.** Interview at least 10 families with school-age children about the childproofing measures they took when their children were younger. What childproofing devices did they install and when? How far ahead of their children's development did they try to childproof? After the interviews, compile your data and calculate, on average, how far ahead of their children's development parents childproofed.
15. **Research and reading.** Working with a partner, research the most current safety standards for child items. The most current safety standards should be outlined by the U.S. Consumer Product Safety Commission (U.S. CPSC). Then obtain three catalogs or other publications (one current, one from a few years ago, and one from more than a decade ago) with pictures of child items. Read these three publications and evaluate the child items by current safety standards. What items are safe? unsafe? What changes could be made to unsafe items to *make* them safe?
16. **Reading and writing.** Search the Internet to find examples of three recent safety recalls for child items or toys. For each recall, identify why the recall has been made and the manufacturer's recommended remediation. After reading these examples, choose one unsafe historical child item or toy. Write a recall for the product based on the examples you read. Share your recall with the class.
17. **Listening and writing.** Interview someone who works with children (such as a teacher, child care worker, or babysitter) and ask questions about how to recognize the need for medical intervention. Has the person ever called for emergency help while working with children? Has the person ever taken a child to the doctor? If so, how did the person decide that the child's condition required medical intervention? What advice does the person have about recognizing this need? After the interview, write a short summary about what you learned.
18. **CTE Career Readiness Practice.** Presume you are the director of a child care center and have planned a short training session to refresh your employees on the basics of performing choking maneuvers, administering CPR, and using AEDs. In preparation for the session, research the most current recommendations for these emergency procedures. Then create handouts to summarize each of the emergency procedures. Make your handouts professional and easy to follow. Use your handouts to remind or teach a partner about these techniques.

Observations

19. Search the Internet for videos of young children crawling or walking for the first time. During the video, pay attention to the environment around the children. What childproofing measures are evident in the environment? Does the environment seem safe or unsafe? What additional childproofing measures would you recommend?
20. As a class, visit a local child care center and observe a group of toddlers or preschoolers at play. As you observe, take notes about what developmental traits make the children prone to accidents. Give specific examples. (Refer to children's developmental milestones if need be.) How do adult actions or the environment of the center prevent or lessen potential accidents? After the observation, discuss your findings.

Chapter 22 Handling Family-Life Challenges

Essential Question

What types of challenges affect children, and how can parents and other adults protect children and help children develop resilience?

Lesson 22.1 **Helping Children Cope with Challenges**

Lesson 22.2 **Protecting Children from Neglect and Abuse**

Case Study: What Does It Mean to Be a Mandated Reporter?

As a class, read the case study and discuss the questions that follow. After you finish studying the chapter, discuss this case study again. Have your opinions changed based on what you learned?

Aleksandra has been a child care worker at a local preschool for six months and has enjoyed working with a diverse group of young children and their parents. About one month ago, a preschooler named Josh started attending the center. Since Josh joined the center, Aleksandra has had several meetings with Josh's family. From these meetings, Aleksandra surmises that Josh's father is suffering from severe depression after losing his job. She also thinks that Josh's mother is overwhelmed by the stress of caring for a new baby while working to support the family.

Lately, Josh has been coming to the center dressed in tattered clothes. He is always hungry and eats large amounts of food very quickly. One week ago, he contracted a rash while playing outside, and the rash has still not cleared up. When Aleksandra asked Josh's parents about the rash, they said they had not taken Josh to the doctor yet. For the past few days, Josh has been unusually tired and hesitant about engaging in physical activities. When helping Josh wash his hands, Aleksandra noticed several bruises on his arms.

Aleksandra knows that Josh's parents are in difficult emotional and financial straits, but she is worried about Josh and knows that by law she is a mandated reporter for neglect and abuse.

Give It Some Thought

1. What signs of neglect or abuse are present in Josh's behavior? Does Aleksandra have reason to be worried?
2. Aleksandra knows about the difficulties Josh's parents are facing. As such, should she try to talk with the parents? Why or why not?
3. What are Aleksandra's responsibilities as a mandated reporter of child neglect and abuse? What do those responsibilities mean concerning the action(s) she should take?

While studying this chapter, look for the online resources icon  to:

- **Practice** terms with e-flash cards and interactive games
- **Assess** what you learn by completing self-assessment quizzes
- **Expand** knowledge with interactive activities and graphic organizers

Companion G-W Learning

www.g-wlearning.com/childdevelopment

Study on the go

Use a mobile device to practice terms and review with self-assessment quizzes.

www.m.g-wlearning.com/0384

Lesson 22.1 Helping Children Cope with Challenges

Key Terms

buffers
custody plans
impoverished
resilient children
stages of grief
terminally ill

Academic Terms

adversity
feed
mourning
prognosis
severed
traumatized

Objectives

After studying this lesson, you will be able to

- identify how parents and other adults can help children cope with family moves.
- explain how financial strain affects children's development.
- name ways that parents and other adults can help children cope with family addiction.
- summarize how parents and other adults can help children who are exposed to violence and disasters.
- describe ways adults can help children handle divorce.
- summarize how adults can help children understand and cope with illness and death.
- explain *resilience* and how it can be fostered in children.
- identify resources for children in crises.

Reading and Writing Activity

Before reading this lesson, interview someone who works in a child-related career (such as a child care worker, pediatrician, or school counselor). Ask the person why it is important to know about the lesson topic and how this topic affects the person's job. Then, as you read the lesson, take notes about items you talked about that are discussed in the lesson.

Graphic Organizer

Challenges affect children in multiple and sometimes all areas of development. Before reading this lesson, draw three circles labeled *Physical Development*, *Intellectual Development*, and *Social-Emotional Development*. Then, as you are reading, write notes about how the challenges discussed affect each area of development.

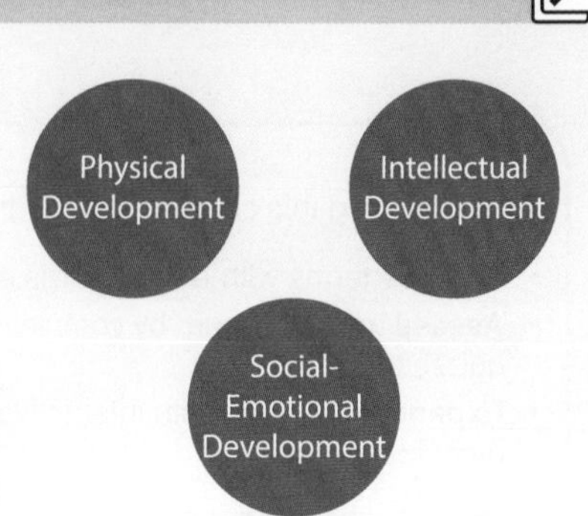

As children grow up, they will encounter challenges. Many of these challenges stem from within the family—the child's foundation for living and learning. Family life can be complex. Stressful events may occur that cause tensions and problems for many families. Family challenges, whether due to life circumstances or decisions, affect children. Family-life challenges that children may face include moving, financial strain, addiction, violence and disaster, divorce, and illness and death.

How a challenge affects a child depends on how the child learns to cope. It also depends on how parents and other adults (such as teachers) help the child in handling the challenge. Through learning to cope with challenges, many children will develop resilience. Resources for children in crisis situations are available.

Moving

Today, many societies are *mobile societies*, meaning that people move from place to place. Moving can be stressful for children, especially as children make friends and extend their social relations in a region. Family moves can lead to **severed** (ended) friendships, unfamiliar schools, and new dangers. During moves, children may experience loneliness, long for stability, and need some time to adjust.

To help children cope with moving, parents and other adults in children's lives need to work together to create stability. Parents can help their children by trying to plan moves so they fit well in children's lives. For example, a move that coincides with the death of a family member, divorce, or poor grades will be especially stressful. On the other hand, moving at the beginning or end of a school term may be less stressful. Parents can also help children by expressing why they are pleased about the move (better paying job, nearer relatives, safer neighborhood). Before the move, parents can involve children in the moving process and explain what will happen during the move. After the move, parents can encourage children to invest in new relationships and local activities (**Figure 22.1**).

Other adults who interact with children, such as teachers or other caregivers, can help children cope by providing as much stability as possible. This may mean allowing the preschool child to carry a favorite toy or photo or helping the child settle into new routines. Teachers and other adults can also help children cope by giving them opportunities to learn about moving. They may provide books or stories that talk about moving or may encourage a child to act out the move in play. For school-age children, teachers can help children catch up in new classes and encourage them to connect with new friends. This might involve providing workbooks or handouts that outline material already covered in class or referring children to tutoring resources or clubs.

Children adjust best to a move when parents and other adults work as a team to provide stability and

Mental Health Advisory

As they grow older, children tend to place more importance on social relationships, and especially on peer relationships. For this reason, older children may have a more difficult time adjusting to a move than younger children.

Figure 22.1 Becoming involved in activities and social groups can help children adjust after a family move. *Are peer relations more important for older children than for younger children? Why or why not?*

help the child. During or after a move, parents and teachers can collaborate by having parent-teacher conferences and by actively communicating about the child's needs.

Financial Strain

Lack of financial resources can cause significant stress for children. Families may lack financial resources for a number of reasons, including unemployment, underemployment, illness, unforeseen expenses (such as medical expenses), addiction, or lack of money-management skills. Some families experiencing financial strain may be **impoverished**, meaning they have inadequate funds to reasonably care for themselves and their children. No matter the reasons, financial strain can negatively impact children from before birth even into adulthood (**Figure 22.2**).

Children best cope with financial strain when their parents or caregivers and the other adults in their lives work together to support their development. Parents and caregivers can help children cope by accessing appropriate resources to support their children's development. Examples of these types of resources may include organizations that provide healthful lunches for children and not-for-profit child

Figure 22.2 Effects of Financial Strain on Children

Before Birth
• Low-quality prenatal care puts children at risk for complications and conditions. • Maternal stress and malnutrition may hinder children's development.
Infancy
• Family stress and lack of quality care may hinder infant attachments and social-emotional development. • Lack of nutritious foods may slow infants' physical development. • Lack of quality care and developmental experiences may affect infants' brain development and have adverse effects on intellectual development.
Toddler Years
• Lack of quality care and developmental experiences may cause missed windows of opportunity and stunt learning. • Family stress and lack of quality care may damage toddlers' relationships and cause social-emotional disturbances. • Lack of nutritious foods and physical activity may adversely affect children's health and development.
Preschool Years
• Lack of nutritious foods and physical activity may adversely affect children's health and development. • Family stress may harm familial relationships. Children learn to express emotions and stress by watching adults. • As children build peer relationships, rejection may cause sadness and a poor self-concept. • Lack of quality care and developmental experiences may cause missed windows of opportunity and slow learning.
School-Age Years
• Lack of quality care and experiences may cause poor habits. • Family stress may cause depression or aggression in children. • Children may suffer from poor grades due to lack of help at home, feelings of inadequacy, or depression. • Children may experience rejection from peers due to family circumstances.

> **Mental Health Advisory**
> Mental health problems of feeling anxious, depressed, or inferior are associated with being unemployed, homeless, or on public assistance.

care programs. Parents can also seek to address issues that cause financial strain and do everything in their power to provide for their children's needs. For older children, parents and caregivers may want to explain the financial strain, but not make children feel as though it is their problem to solve.

Teachers and other adults also play a key role in helping children cope with financial strain. Judgments passed by other adults and children's peers may hurt children's self-concepts. Teachers and other adults can help children cope in the following ways:

- ***Always model respect.*** Regardless of their opinions, teachers and other adults should always show respect for children and their families. This includes not making judgmental or insulting remarks. It also includes involving children in decisions and challenging them to excel.
- ***Encourage social interactions.*** Children whose families are experiencing financial strain may feel isolated or out of place among their peers. Teachers and other adults can help children cope by teaching younger children basic social skills and encouraging older children to form positive relationships with their peers. They can make children feel important by giving them responsibility and appreciating their contributions in class.
- ***Ensure that programs are inclusive.*** Programs or schools that require large donations, tuitions, or fees tend to exclude or place pressure on families experiencing financial strain. Teachers and other adults can help children cope by reducing the barriers to children participating in programs through scholarships and donations of school supplies and uniforms. They can be sure to thank children and families for their contributions (monetary or otherwise) to the program.
- ***Refer families to available resources.*** Teachers and other adults can help children cope with financial strain by referring children's families to appropriate resources. These resources may include programs that provide food, low-cost housing, and community- or government-subsidized child care programs (**Figure 22.3**).

Addiction

Family members' behaviors always affect children. *Addiction* (the dependency on a substance, such as alcohol or drugs, or action, such as gambling) causes a pattern of destructive behaviors that negatively affect children. People who are addicted to a substance or action feel they cannot continue to live without the substance or action in their life. As a result, people with addictions may hurt their families in order to **feed** (continue) their addiction. They may speak hurtful words, lie to their family members, and use family resources to

Figure 22.3 Government programs, such as the National School Lunch Program (NSLP), provide healthful lunches for children at little or no cost. *What are your state's regulations regarding which children are eligible for free or reduced-price lunches?*

Mental Health Advisory

Children's mental health problems stem from the following:

- trying to act as a surrogate "spouse" for the parent who is addicted
- developing elaborate systems of denial to protect themselves against the reality of the parents' addiction
- trying to compensate for a parent-deficiency if in a single-parent family
- dealing with a parent in about half of the families who is mentally ill in addition to being addicted

feed the addiction. They may also physically harm their family or be emotionally distant. People with addictions may also struggle to keep a job and contribute to their family.

Children are influenced by the behaviors and addictions of their family members. Children with parents or other family members who abuse substances are likely to abuse substances later in life. Children also suffer under the stress caused by addicted behaviors.

Parents and caregivers can help children cope by limiting children's contact with those who have addictions. They can assure children that the addiction is not their fault and can protect children from the hurtful words or actions of people who have addictions. Most importantly, parents and other caregivers can ensure that the person with the addiction is receiving help, either through a support group or other intervening organization.

Teachers and other adults can help children cope by being available to discuss children's stress. Children may confide in teachers, counselors, or therapists and may express their feelings about the addiction. Teachers and adults can work with parents to provide a stable environment for the child. If a child is in danger, teachers and adults may need to contact outside help. A *state department of child protective services* is a state agency that protects children's safety by intervening in potentially hazardous family situations.

Violence and Disasters

Even children who are loved and protected in the home may be exposed to violence and disaster in the world around them. Violence and disasters can occur unexpectedly and can happen to children, families, communities, and even countries. Children are affected by violence and disaster, whether it happens to them, to a person the child knows, or to a person or place the child has never encountered. Children's reactions to violence and disaster will vary depending on the child's age and development (**Figure 22.4**). News of violence and disaster can travel quickly by word of mouth and through the media.

Parents and caregivers can help children cope with violence and disaster by attempting to limit

Figure 22.4 Children's Reactions to Violence and Disaster

Age of Child	Typical Reactions
Infants and toddlers	• Being extremely afraid • Clinging to a caregiver • Screaming • Crying • Whimpering • Trembling • Moving violently • Not moving • Regressing in behaviors (such as returning to thumbsucking or bedwetting behaviors)
Preschoolers and school-age children	• Isolating self and not talking with others • Showing social-emotional disturbances, such as angry outbursts, depression, or feelings of numbness • Having trouble sleeping • Experiencing physical problems, such as digestive upsets • Losing interest in favored activities • Doing poorly in school or being unable to concentrate

Focus on

Speech

Media Depictions of Violence

Children do not have to be direct witnesses to be exposed to violence and disaster. Media depictions of violence—whether on the news, in films, or in video games—can upset children. These media depictions of violence are especially upsetting if children are experiencing other challenges or have witnessed other forms of trauma. Over the years, experts have conducted several studies about the effects of violence in the media on children.

Work with a partner to find and read one of the more recent studies. After reading, prepare a two-minute oral presentation for the class in which you and your partner summarize the study and discuss its relevance to child development.

children's exposure to these events. For example, if a robbery has occurred in the child's town, parents and caregivers might explain as needed, but then limit how much news coverage the child accesses. News and media coverage of violence and disaster can upset children and cause stress.

Unfortunately, limiting children's exposure to violence and disaster is not always possible. Parents and caregivers should be prepared to help their children process the event and related feelings. If a child has encountered violence or disaster, parents and caregivers can allow the child to express how he or she feels about the event. They should not dismiss or encourage children to stifle their emotions, but rather should give children opportunities to talk about their feelings. Parents and caregivers can be understanding of children's *regressive reactions* (such as bedwetting or thumbsucking), can engage children in standard routines, and can give children choices to reduce feelings of helplessness. If a child is **traumatized** (seriously disrupted socially or emotionally) by an event, parents and caregivers can help the child get appropriate treatment.

Teachers and other adults can help children cope by being understanding and not reacting harshly if children act out or express their emotions inappropriately. Instead of expecting children to overcome their emotions, adults can encourage emotional expression and listen carefully. As children heal, adults can reduce other stressors (such as school pressure and social tension) in the child's life and remind children that adults love them. Adults should pay attention to children as they recover from a traumatic event and note any especially severe or dangerous reactions. In these situations, adults may need to recommend help, such as therapy, for a child.

Mental Health Advisory

Acute responses to violence and threat often result in either *dissociation* (becoming detached or numb) or *hyper-arousal* (hyper-vigilant, anxious, extremely fearful, exhibiting panic). Years after exposure to violent and disastrous events, the person is at an increased risk for antisocial behaviors and mental health problems, such as stress and conduct disorders.

Divorce

In the United States, many couples divorce for a variety of reasons. Divorce affects both parents and children. Parents are challenged to overcome their negative feelings and adjust to a new lifestyle. Children are affected during the separation process and often for years following the divorce. Even children who were infants when their caregivers divorced still deal with these issues in their school-age years. Parents seeking to divorce may find professional counseling helpful. Counselors or members of support groups can discuss the effects of divorce on parents and their children. Both parents and children may need a support system for many years.

It is difficult to predict how divorce will affect a particular child. Age and gender tend to affect how children cope (**Figure 22.5**). Divorce usually confuses young children. They do not understand the divorce process, but they know that one parent is not living with the family. A child's personality will also affect how he or she will cope. Some children are more positive than others and have fewer coping problems.

Parents and caregivers can help preschoolers and older children cope by giving honest, but appropriate, answers to their questions. Parents should not discuss problems of the marriage or divorce with young children. Children cannot understand these complex issues, and because they cannot help solve the problems of marriage, they should not be burdened with them. Instead, both parents should explain and repeat the message that the divorce is not the child's fault and that both parents still love the child.

As much as possible, parents should support the child during the divorce. They can do this by keeping routines normal, helping the child stay in touch with other family members, listening to the child, and developing a positive new lifestyle for the child (**Figure 22.6**). Once **custody plans** (legal plans outlining who will care for the child and to what extent) are firm, parents should tell children about them if they are old enough to understand.

Mental Health Advisory

Parents should not expect children to handle divorce in an adult way. Children may feel stress if they are expected to act too maturely for their age. These children still need consistent, firm discipline.

Finally, parents can help children cope by alerting teachers and other adults in the child's life when the family structure changes.

Teachers and other adults can help children cope by offering support once they are aware of the situation. Children often need neutral adults who can help them express their sadness or anger in acceptable ways and cope with loneliness and a new lifestyle. Teachers and other adults can also serve as role models for expressing emotions and adjusting. Other ways that teachers and neutral adults can help children cope with divorce include

- keeping routines and discipline consistent
- supporting children's feelings of worth and confidence even when children struggle to concentrate or act out due to stress at home
- listening to children without judgment
- advocating for children, especially if parents are engaging in behaviors that harm them
- involving both parents in the children's care and education
- recommending therapy for children, if appropriate

Illness and Death

Illness and death are basic parts of life, and even young children need to come to terms with them. Some children may lose a parent before they finish elementary school. Many more witness the illness or death of a close friend, relative, or even a pet during childhood. In helping children cope, parents and other adults can help children understand illness and death and help children cope with grief.

Helping Children Understand Illness and Death

Children's understanding of illness and death develops gradually. Understandings of illness may focus on the effects of the illness (such as weakness or fatigue) rather than on the causes of or treatments for the illness. Death may be an even harder

Figure 22.5 **Reactions to Loss of a Parent Through Divorce or Death**

Age	Common Behaviors and Feelings
Toddlers	• Whining, crying, and clinging • Acting fretful • Having sleep and appetite problems • Experiencing possible regression (occurring most often at a time of day when the absent parent was usually with the child)
Preschoolers	• Whining and crying • Hitting or biting others • Feeling anxious • Seeming moody and restless • Acting aggressively • Wanting physical contact with others • Denying the loss and even pretending parents will be together again • Having problems in creative play • Feeling they caused the divorce or death
School-age children	• Daydreaming more and worrying more about the future • Denying the loss • Feeling angry and bitter (blaming the parent whom they think is responsible) • Feeling lonely, abandoned, and rejected by the absent parent • Showing antisocial behaviors, such as lying or stealing • Having more headaches and stomachaches than usual • Having school problems, such as not being able to pay attention • Showing premature detachment, rejecting the parent who is gone and the qualities shared with this absent parent • Becoming the *confidant* (close friend to whom secrets are entrusted) of the remaining parent and thus having too much adult-like pressure
Gender	**Common Behaviors and Feelings**
Boys	• Acting oblivious and inattentive • Having a drop in school achievement • Acting more aggressively • Having more problems during the divorce process and for the first two years after the divorce • Doing better if they have a positive relationship with the absent parent
Girls	• Feeling grief and frustration • Crying • Withdrawing • Blaming themselves • Being more troubled a year after the divorce than at the time of the divorce

Figure 22.6 After a divorce, creating a new, appealing space for children can help them positively embrace their new lifestyles. *Why do you think children respond positively to having their own space?*

concept for children to grasp. Around six or seven months of age, an infant will notice separations from caring adults. These separations, most of which are brief, are the earliest experiences of loss in a child's life. Early separation may set the stage for later responses to separation, loss, and even death. Until three or four years of age, children have little, if any, understanding of death. Preschool children may try to learn the physical facts of death, but will find many facts difficult to believe and thus question them. Even older preschoolers may find it difficult to understand their family's beliefs about death.

Usually, adults do not talk about illness or death with children unless a person or pet is sick or dies. These concepts, however, are important for children to grasp. In helping children understand illness, parents and caregivers need to answer children's questions about the illness honestly. These answers might include age-appropriate explanations of the illness, details about the effects of the illness, and treatments for the illness. If a family member or close friend is **terminally ill** (having an incurable disease that will result in death), adults can prepare the child for the upcoming death with simple, truthful statements. For example, a parent may say, "You know Grandma is very sick. The nurses and doctors are trying to help, but Grandma is getting sicker. She may soon die." Parents should not lie about a terminally ill person's **prognosis** (the predicted outcome of a disease or condition). In some cases, a child may be terminally ill. How a child perceives his or her condition greatly depends on the child's age. What and how much information a family tells a terminally ill child should depend on how much the sick child wants or needs to understand about his or her illness.

When death occurs, adults can explain at the child's level what has happened. They can answer questions honestly and say what they believe to be true about death. Children become worried if they feel adults are keeping facts from them or avoiding their questions. When explaining, adults can ensure that children do not expect the deceased person (or pet) to return. Instead of telling a child that the deceased person is sleeping, an adult may say, "Uncle Bill is dead. This means he does not move or breathe anymore." Adults can assure children that they did not cause the death. For a long time after the death, parents and other adults who work with children can be prepared to answer questions and

> **Mental Health Advisory**
>
> As children begin to understand death, they may become afraid that a parent or caregiver will die. Parents can reassure their children they will probably live a long time. They should never promise children they will not die. If a caregiver does die after such a promise, the child might feel betrayed and develop a lack of trust in others.

repeat facts. At first, for example, a child may seem to understand the death. A week later, however, the child may again ask about the death.

Special challenges occur when explaining suicide to children. Suicides are difficult for all survivors, including children, to understand. Older children will need some special guidance. In these situations, adults should give children clear facts about the suicide, but not overexplain. They can recall the good traits of the person, assure children the suicide was not their fault, and emphasize that everyone has choices.

Helping Children Cope with Grief

Once children understand and react to death, parents and other adults can help children cope. When it comes to death, children, like adults, experience *stages of grief*. The **stages of grief**, outlined in **Figure 22.7**, are feelings or mind-sets that most people experience when **mourning** (feeling sad about a loss). Although these grieving stages are universal, they do not always occur in order. Sometimes stages may be revisited or skipped entirely.

Parents can help children cope with grief by supporting children at home. Some ways they can help include

- watching for children's signs of grief (**Figure 22.8**)
- seeking close contact with loved ones
- using inappropriate reactions to grief as teaching opportunities for children

Figure 22.8 Signs of Grief in Children

Verbal responses	• Talking or not talking about the loss • Asking or not asking questions about the loss • Wanting or not wanting to hear about what happened • Having dreams about the person or pet who died • Trying to get attention from others • Wishing to see the person or pet again • Voicing worries about other people or pets becoming sick or injured
Emotional responses	• Crying • Overreacting to insignificant situations with tears or anger • Not focusing on tasks • Being irritable • Wanting to be near adults and close friends • Being noncompliant about "rules" and requests
Physical responses	• Experiencing changes in appetite • Experiencing changes in sleeping habits • Having urine and bowel accidents • Suffering from stomachaches or headaches • Regressing in behaviors • Feeling tired

Figure 22.7 Stages of Grief

Stage	Description
Shock and denial	This stage protects the child from immediately experiencing the entire intensity of the loss. It should never be confused with "not caring."
Anger	The child feels angry about the loss. This anger may extend to others who were involved with the person, such as doctors.
Bargaining	The child thinks about what "could have been done" to prevent the loss. Unless the child gets past the "if only" and lives in the present, he or she may always carry intense feelings of guilt.
Depression	The child now feels the entire intensity of the loss. Physical symptoms often appear.
Acceptance	The child comes to terms with the loss and integrates the loss into his or her other life experiences. The child recognizes the loss as the new reality.

- setting an example by not trying to mask sadness
- allowing children to talk about death and grieve in their own developmental ways, such as through pretend play or by carrying photos of a loved one

Children best cope with grief when parents and other adults (such as teachers) collaborate to help them. Parents should inform teachers and others who work with the child about the tragedy. Teachers and other adults can be understanding with the child. Teachers should maintain normal routines, but can also give the child room to grieve and express his or her feelings. They can also use inappropriate reactions to grief as opportunities to teach children about expressing emotions. Beliefs about death should be left for parents to explain. While teachers cannot share in the child's grief, they can demonstrate and encourage empathy and reduce other stressors in the child's life.

Resilience in Children

All children will cope with some challenges in their lives. How children react often depends on their *resilience* (their abilities to recover from stressful situations). **Resilient children** are children who adapt well, even when faced with **adversity** (risks and stress) in their lives. These children can adapt and survive even in difficult circumstances. Resilient children are autonomous, flexible, resourceful, and caring and can communicate their needs to others. Studies have shown that resilience at 10 years of age predicts how well people will adapt to life's circumstances by 40 years of age.

Resilience in children is a result of a child's inner qualities, as well as what **buffers** (protections or support systems), such as the child's family or community supports (**Figure 22.9**). For example, if family stress is toxic, a child might rely on a community buffer or on other relatives. If a child's community is violent, the child may be buffered by a protective family member.

Resilience is important for every child. Adults cannot correct or undo every mistake (such as replace a lost toy or ask a teacher for a retake of a test). They cannot shield children from all problems

Figure 22.9 Qualities of Resilient Children

Inner Qualities of Resilient Children

- Easy temperaments
- Affectionate and engaging personalities
- Vigorous
- Assertive
- Autonomous
- Healthy self-concept
- Able to distance themselves from their problems
- Believe they can beat the odds
- Communicate easily

Family or Community Buffers

- A trusting, secure, and ongoing relationship based on unconditional love from at least one person. (This person might be a parent, other relative, child care provider or teacher, or youth leader.)
- Resilience modeled by someone else.
- External supports given by teachers, youth leaders, or friends who validate and reinforce the inner qualities, competencies, and values of the child.
- Outside interests (extracurricular activities or youth groups) that relieve stress or remove the child from a stressful setting.

(such as financial problems or divorce). Adults also cannot remove all the obstacles children face (such as homework and social challenges). Adults can, however, help children develop resilience and protect children while encouraging them to cope with the stressors in their lives. Overprotecting or overparenting children does not aid resilience. To help children develop resilience, adults can ensure children

- develop secure attachments
- develop social skills needed to make friends
- see situations from different perspectives and deal with problems they can change
- be autonomous
- be confident in their abilities
- trust that adults will handle the "big problems" (finances, addiction, divorce) and will protect them

If children are not resilient, they may benefit from professional help. Professional help might be a counselor or therapist, a school counselor, or one of many other resources for children who struggle to cope with challenges.

Resources for Children in Crises

Many resources are available to help children in crises (**Figure 22.10**). Some of these resources directly assist children and their families. Others

Figure 22.10 Resources for Children in Crises

Resource	Description
Supplemental Nutritional Assistant Program (SNAP)	Provides financial support to help families purchase foods
Special Supplemental Program for Women, Infants, and Children (WIC)	Provides food assistance for infants, children four years of age or younger, and pregnant women
National School Lunch Program (NSLP)	Provides nutritious lunches to children in schools (at a reduced price or free for qualifying students)
Public Housing Program	Provides affordable housing for families experiencing financial strain
Child Protective Services	Handles reports of child neglect or abuse and investigates reports of unsafe environments
Early Intervention	Provides services for families with children under three years of age who have special needs
Medicaid and Children's Health Insurance Program (CHIP)	Provides health insurance coverage for children from families experiencing financial strain
Save the Children	In the event of a disaster, provides food, medical attention, and education to children
United Nations Children Fund (UNICEF)	Provides education, health care, safe environments, food, and emergency relief for children in crises
Child Crisis Centers and Crisis Nurseries	Provide shelter, food, and care for children in crisis situations
Crisis Mental Health Services	Provide help for children experiencing mental-health emergencies

provide information, registries, and referrals to local support groups or counselors.

Some resources that are available to help children in crises are departments and agencies of federal, state, or local governments. Other resources are national private agencies funded by membership dues and contributions. Still other resources are the work of religious groups, hospitals and medical associations, mental health centers, and crises intervention centers. Law enforcement agencies, legal associations, counseling services, schools, and civic or volunteer organizations are all resources as well (**Figure 22.11**).

Many resources for children in crises have online bookstores for purchasing books and other materials designed to aid children and families facing different challenges. When searching for items on a specific topic of interest, an online bookstore might also offer resources for parents, children, or families. Other books and materials can be located through online publishers and libraries. Conducting an Internet search and visiting the local library are other ways to find good resources for helping children in crises.

Lesson 22.1 Review and Assessment 

1. List two ways that teachers and other adults who work with children can help children cope with family moves.
2. Choose one stage of development and explain how familial financial strain can affect a child in that stage.
3. Name three ways that parents can help children cope with a family addiction.
4. Identify two ways teachers and other adults who work with children can help children cope with violence or disaster.
5. Why should parents not discuss the problems of the marriage or divorce with young children? What should parents do instead?
6. Identify the stages of grief.
7. Define *resilience* and list two inner qualities of resilient children.
8. **Critical thinking.** In small groups, identify five resources for children in crises that are available in your community.

Figure 22.11 There are many types of volunteer organizations that serve families in crises, such as organizations that provide food for families in need or child care centers that provide safe places for children in danger. ***What volunteer organizations serve families in crises in your community?***

Protecting Children from Neglect and Abuse

Lesson 22.2

Objectives

After studying this lesson, you will be able to

- identify the types of child neglect and abuse.
- explain the causes of child neglect and abuse.
- describe the effects of child neglect and abuse on children's physical, intellectual, and social-emotional development.
- describe sibling abuse.
- list the types of peer abuse.
- summarize how neglect and abuse are recognized and reported.
- explain how cases of neglect and abuse are treated.
- list strategies for preventing neglect and abuse.

Key Terms

bullying
child abuse
child neglect
child protection agencies
cyberbullying
educational neglect
emotional abuse
emotional neglect
home visitation
mandated reporters
medical neglect
moral neglect
peer abuse
physical abuse
physical neglect
sexual abuse
Shaken Baby Syndrome (SBS)
sibling abuse
six core strengths
social abuse
verbal abuse

Academic Terms

debase
perpetrated
rescinded
respite

Reading and Writing Activity

Write all of this lesson's key terms on a piece of paper, and before reading, record what you think each term means. As you read, update or correct definitions according to the lesson. Finally, highlight any definitions that changed significantly while reading. Make flashcards for these terms.

Graphic Organizer

Draw a mind map like the one shown and write *Neglect and Abuse* in the middle circle. Then, as you are reading, take notes about the types of neglect and abuse (including their causes and effects), guidelines for recognition, treatments, and methods of prevention.

Tragically, some children face the challenges of neglect and abuse. Neglect and abuse, whether inflicted by a parent or caregiver, other adult, or children's siblings or peers, have devastating physical, intellectual, and social-emotional effects on children. Neglect and abuse are not challenges children should expect or for which they should need to learn protective coping skills. Rather, neglect and abuse should be reported so children can be protected from all of these criminal behaviors. In facing these challenges, adults should know how to identify and report all cases of neglect and abuse. They should also take part in measures designed to prevent these happenings in society.

Figure 22.12 Children who have experienced neglect or abuse need comfort and protection from further neglect or abuse. *Why is it important that children's traumatic experiences not be repeated?*

Child Neglect and Abuse

Neglect and abuse are very serious problems that threaten children's health and welfare. **Child neglect** is the failure of an adult to provide for a child's basic needs. While states' legal definitions of neglect vary, neglect usually involves adults' failures to meet needs for food, clothing, shelter, hygiene, medical attention, or supervision. In contrast to neglect, **child abuse** refers to an intentional act committed by an adult that harms or threatens to harm a child's well-being.

Most cases of neglect and abuse occur in the home and are **perpetrated** (done) by a person the child knows and trusts. The vast majority of cases involve at least one parent, and about 1 case in 10 involves a relative other than parents. Very few cases involve adults working in child care education programs or in foster care settings and even fewer cases involve strangers.

About one-fourth of all children suffer more than one type of neglect or abuse. Many times, the reason abuse occurs is unknown although various factors (called *risk factors*) may contribute to incidences of neglect and abuse. The effects of neglect and abuse are harmful to children's physical, intellectual, and social-emotional development. People who work in **child protection agencies** (organizations that work to prevent and rescue children from neglect and abuse) try to protect children from further neglect or abuse (**Figure 22.12**).

Types of Child Neglect and Abuse

Child neglect and abuse can take many forms. Not all neglect and abuse are physical in nature. Children have many needs, including physical needs, intellectual needs, and social-emotional needs. The neglect of any of these needs can cause harm to a child.

Child neglect refers to harm or endangerment of a child caused by an adult's failure to do something legally expected of him or her. There are several types of neglect, which include the following:

- **Physical neglect** refers to endangering a child's health or safety by failing to provide basic needs (such as food, clothing, and shelter) and supervision. Physical neglect also refers to situations in which parents' troubled mental states (whether due to substance abuse or illness) make them unaware of their children's lack of basic necessities.
- **Educational neglect** is the failure to conform to state legal requirements regarding school attendance. In educational neglect, children do not experience sufficient learning. The standards for meeting children's educational needs are determined by the state and new standards are frequently implemented.

Domestic Violence

Abuse within the family, even if not directed at a child, can have serious negative effects on children's development. One type of abuse that may occur in families is *domestic violence* (also known as *partner abuse*). Domestic violence is *any* type of physical, sexual, emotional, or verbal abuse directed at a partner (such as a current or former spouse or non-married partner).

Domestic violence can take many forms. Some signs of domestic violence include

- physical injuries (such as bone fractures, cuts, or bruises) or the wearing of excessive clothing to hide injuries
- social-emotional disturbances, such as anxiety attacks and sleeping problems
- fear of a partner or overeagerness to please a partner
- lack of trust in others, resulting in poor relationships
- low self-esteem, as indicated by self-hate, self-blame, and sensitivity to rejection
- workplace problems, such as frequent absences, heated phone calls or e-mails, isolation, and crying
- limited access to social interactions, finances, and transportation

Domestic violence has serious consequences on children and on the family. Over three million children witness domestic violence each year, and 30 to 60 percent of children from violent homes experience child neglect and abuse. Children who witness domestic violence are more likely to become abusers, have academic problems, display anxiety and depression, and resort to substance abuse and other risky behaviors.

Speaking Activity

Domestic violence, like most abuse, is a complex cycle that is difficult to escape. In small groups, visit the website of The National Domestic Violence Hotline. Record the website's definition of *abuse* and research tips for recognizing signs of domestic violence and for escaping from an abusive situation. Afterward, arrange your findings into a short oral presentation for the class.

- **Medical neglect** is the harm or endangerment of a child caused by failure to seek treatment for health problems or accidents. Medical neglect can lead to serious health problems and even death.
- **Moral neglect** is the failure to teach a child right from wrong in terms of general social expectations. For example, a child who has been morally neglected might believe or have been taught that stealing is not wrong.
- **Emotional neglect** is the failure to meet a child's social-emotional needs at each stage of development. It may involve inadequate care and attention or violence and drug use in the home.

While neglect may be unintentional in nature, child abuse involves an intentional act that harms or threatens to harm a child. As with neglect, there are many types of child abuse. The types of child abuse include the following:

- **Physical abuse** is any intentional physical act that results in pain, injuries, or both, to a child. Physical abuse may involve violence or even physical punishment in the name of *discipline*.
- **Sexual abuse** is *any* act of a sexual nature that involves an adult and a child. Whether a child understands or does not resist a sexual act is irrelevant. Some states define *sexual abuse* as any act of a sexual nature between a child and someone who

Mental Health Advisory

Even partner abuse can result in mental health problems in children, such as anxiety, depression, addictions, and violence. These problems may last a lifetime.

is at least five years older than the child. **Figure 22.13** explains some of the myths and realities related to child sexual abuse.

- **Emotional abuse** is the abuse of power through devaluing, undermining, and coercing a child. This type of abuse tends to be indirect, but not unconscious. Emotional abuse harms a child's self-esteem.
- **Verbal abuse** is the use of words to control and **debase** (degrade) a child. It also harms a child's self-esteem.

Causes of Child Neglect and Abuse

There is no simple cause-and-effect explanation for why adults neglect or abuse a child. Very different reasons and causes can lead to the same results. For example, neglect may occur when parents cannot afford to meet a child's needs or when parents think only about their own needs. Sometimes neglect occurs when parents do not know how to provide proper care for children. In investigating instances of child neglect and abuse, experts have come across several principles that describe some of the causes.

- ***Neglectful and abusive parents come from all income, intelligence, and education levels.*** Generally, abusive parents do not exhibit obvious and observable signs of their problems. Abusive parents may seem nice, quiet, and kind when they are at work or with friends.
- ***Risk factors do exist for neglect and abuse.*** Experts who study neglect and abuse believe it is important to look at the entire family system for answers (**Figure 22.14**). Although experts cannot weigh the degree of risk for each factor, studies show that substance abuse is present in about two-fifths of reported neglect and abuse cases.
- ***Experts cannot always predict from the risk factors which form the abuse will take.*** Experts identify two exceptions

Figure 22.13 Myths and Realities About Child Sexual Abuse

Myth	Reality
Child sexual abuse is rare.	Child sexual abuse occurs often and can take many forms, such as pornography or incest.
The abuser is usually an unknown, dangerous person.	In the vast majority of cases, the abuser is a known person, such as a relative (including a sibling) or friend of the family.
The abuse occurs suddenly, such as when a non-abusing adult is momentarily out of the room.	The abuse is usually repeated over and over again and may continue for several years.
Child sexual abuse is usually a violent attack.	More often, child sexual abuse happens through subtle "force." The abuser may tell the child it is a "new game."
Children often make up stories of sexual abuse.	Children rarely make up stories about sexual abuse. In fact, they are often reluctant to talk about sexual abuse because they fear the abuser or feel guilty for being involved.
Children who recant stories of sexual abuse were lying about the first report.	Abusers may have pressured children to change their stories.

to this principle. First, a parent who physically abuses a spouse is likely to physically abuse a child. Second, a person who has a history of sexual abuse is more likely to sexually abuse others.

- ***Abuse is a complex, interactive process.*** Some parents may abuse only one child in the family or may abuse a child only during times of high parental stress. An unplanned pregnancy might lead to more financial stress, causing a mother not to

Figure 22.14 Risk Factors for Child Neglect and Abuse

Type of Risk Factor	Contributing Factors
Societal	• Poverty • Overcrowding • Illegal drug culture • High crime rates • High unemployment rates • Few social services • Unaffordable health care
Family	• Unwanted pregnancy • Single or teen parent • Physical, sexual, or emotional abuse as a child • Emotional neglect as a child • Use of violence to express anger • Lack of self-esteem • Emotional immaturity • Poor coping skills • Alcohol or illegal drug abuse • Marriage problems • Financial stress • Recent stressful events (divorce, recent move, death in family) • Illness (physical or mental health, especially depression) • Lack of parenting skills, including no preparation for the extreme stress of a new baby • Lack of knowledge of child development, leading to unrealistic expectations for the child • Heavy parenting responsibility (multiple births or single children less than 18 months apart in age) • Weak bonding or attachment to a child (often due to child's care in ICU after birth) • Use of physical punishment (also called *corporal punishment*) • Isolation (lack of family or friend support)
Child	• Under five years of age, especially under one year of age • Low birthweight or premature birth • Possession of the traits of a disliked relative • Irritability or frequent crying (sometimes due to colic or postnatal drug withdrawal) • Frequent disobedience or arguing

get prenatal care. Her baby may be born at a low birthweight and have feeding problems that cause the child to cry for hours at a time. The parent, who already has problems in coping, abuses the infant "to stop the crying." The fact that abuse is complex and interactive does *not* mean the child is to blame for the abuse. Abusers are *always* responsible for their own actions.

Effects of Child Neglect and Abuse

Most children who suffer neglect and abuse are left with deep and long-lasting scars. Neglect and abuse affect every aspect of a child's development. In many cases, the idea that "time heals all wounds" does not apply to those who have been neglected or abused as children. Child neglect and abuse can have serious physical, intellectual, and social-emotional effects.

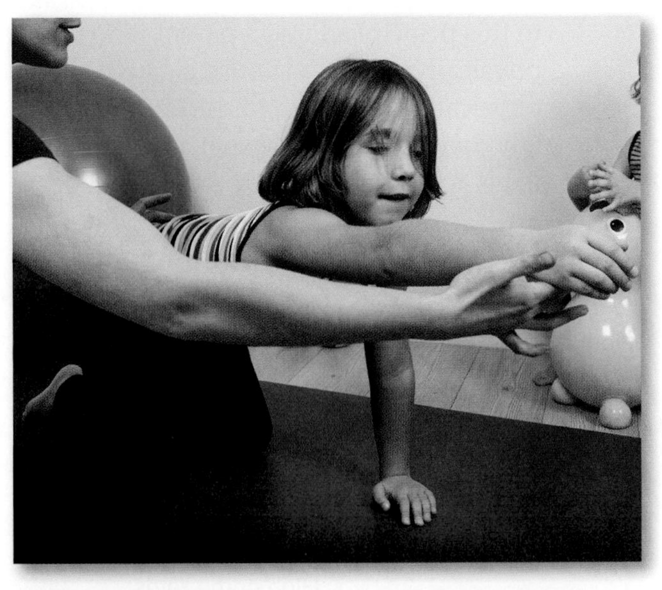

Figure 22.15 Children who have experienced neglect or abuse may need physical therapy to recover from their injuries. *What health care services in your community offer physical therapy for children?*

Effects on Physical Development

Many neglected children lack adequate food, clothing, or housing. Poor hygiene and other unsafe living conditions can hinder infants and young children from growing and thriving. Abused children may be beaten, bruised, burned, or cut. Their bones and teeth may be broken (**Figure 22.15**). Even without physical marks, they may suffer pain from slapping and other physical attacks. Children who are sexually abused suffer internal and external injuries, may contract STIs, and may become pregnant.

Statistics show that the youngest children are the most prone to die from physical neglect and abuse. For example, infants who are shaken in frustration may die as a result of *Shaken Baby Syndrome* (also called *traumatic brain injury abuse*). **Shaken Baby Syndrome (SBS)** is a condition in which the "whiplash" shaking motion causes an infant's brain to hit the skull repeatedly. These hits cause the eye retina to bleed and veins in the brain to break, filling the area around the brain with blood resulting in swelling. Swelling damages brain cells and puts pressure on the brain stem, which controls breathing and heartbeat. As a result, many shaken babies develop cerebral palsy, paralysis, brain seizures, blindness, deafness, and learning and behavioral problems. Between 15 and 30 percent of children with SBS will die from their injuries.

Mental Health Advisory

The majority of neglected and abused children do not trust others, have relationship difficulties, feel worthless or "damaged," and cannot emotionally self-regulate and thus may later abuse others, such as their spouse and even their own innocent children.

Effects on Intellectual Development

Child neglect and abuse can stunt and hinder children's intellectual development. Abuse may cause brain injuries, which make it harder for children to learn. Educational neglect and an inability to concentrate during learning tasks due to abuse may cause children to lag behind in learning and in school. Lack of brain stimulation during children's windows of opportunity can cause them not to learn vital skills. Studies indicate that about 30 percent of abused children have some type of language or learning problem. In addition, over half of all abused children have difficulty in school.

Effects on Social-Emotional Development

The social-emotional effects of child neglect and abuse are often referred to as *invisible*, but these effects can be clearly seen in children's behaviors. Child neglect and abuse can cause children to lack self-esteem; have feelings of anger, anxiety, shame, and guilt; and experience depression. Over half of neglected or abused children have social-emotional problems.

In one study, Dr. Bruce Perry, a pediatric psychiatrist at the Child Trauma Academy in Houston, Texas, found that children develop **six core strengths**, building blocks that make up children's foundation for future health, productivity, and happiness. These core strengths are attachment, self-regulation, affiliation, awareness (of how people are alike and different), tolerance, and respect. Children need nurturing and supportive parents to develop these core strengths (**Figure 22.16**). Neglected and abused children often need extensive treatment to overcome their past or ongoing traumas and develop these core strengths.

Sibling and Peer Abuse

In addition to abuse at the hands of adults, children can also experience abuse from siblings and peers. **Sibling abuse** is physical, verbal, emotional, or sexual abuse of one sibling by another. Sibling abuse happens to over one-third of all children, and the incidence is rising. It is more common than child abuse by adults. This form of abuse is much more than squabbles between siblings. The abuse takes several forms. Sibling abuse can range from pushing, shoving, and hitting to violent behavior, such as using weapons. Abuse often takes the form of stealing or breaking the victim's possessions. *Incest* (sexual acts between closely related individuals) is a common form of sibling abuse. Parents often do not see sibling abuse for what it is.

Peer abuse is some form of abuse (physical, verbal, social, or emotional) directed at a child or teen by someone in the same peer group. Based on self-reports, the majority of school-age children have been both perpetrators and victims of peer abuse. Peer abuse can have negative physical and social-emotional effects on children and can be deadly.

Bullying, the most common form of peer abuse, involves inflicting physical, verbal, and emotional abuse on another person. It also involves **social abuse**, which is restricting or intentionally harming a person's relationships with others. Bullying can include physical attacks, name-calling, harming a person's relationship in a peer group, and spreading rumors. Bullying may include **cyberbullying**, which involves bullying through a digital medium. Peer abuse may also include sexual abuse in the form of sexual acts or *sexting* (sending photographs

Figure 22.16 A nurturing, supportive environment helps children develop the six core strengths. *What might be the result if children do not develop the six core strengths?*

Mental Health Advisory

Children abused by siblings and peers often experience depression, anger, and anxiety and, as adults, may become violent.

of a sexual nature and explicit sexual messages through digital devices).

Some children may be exposed to peer abuse in the form of *gang violence*, which involves groups of bullies who use their power over others. Gang violence is more often seen in teen groups, but may be seen in the later school-age years. Gangs may target rival gang members and may also hurt and kill innocent bystanders.

Peer abuse often occurs in schools, where it may be known as *school violence* (violence that occurs on school property or at a school event). Often, school violence is done out of revenge, and many are hurt or killed who were not in any way connected with the perpetrator. Although school violence is a very high-profile form of peer abuse, less than two percent of all deaths among school-age children and teens are due to school violence. The number of incidences of school violence is increasing, however.

Recognizing and Reporting Neglect and Abuse

Untold numbers of children suffer neglect and abuse by parents, friends, relatives, child care and education teachers and other staff members, siblings, and peers. Statistics never tell the whole story. Many cases of neglect or abuse are never reported. Some reported cases are not investigated due to heavy caseloads of social workers. Still other cases are never confirmed or proven due to lack of evidence or legal definitions of neglect and abuse as given in a state's laws. Some experts believe these legal definitions should be expanded to include more cases.

To end neglect and abuse, people must recognize and report it. Knowing what behaviors are neglectful or abusive is the first step. Adults should be alert to signs that neglect and abuse may be occurring. Some common signs of child neglect and abuse are listed in **Figure 22.17**. Adults can look for signs of sibling or peer abuse by keeping the lines of communication open with their children and taking note of any physical injuries or disturbed behaviors.

When adults suspect and recognize signs of neglect or abuse, they should immediately report this to an agency or authority that can help. Some of these agencies include the local or state departments of human services. For child abuse, adults can also call hotlines to report suspected abuse. Some professionals who work with children are **mandated reporters**, meaning they are legally bound to report any known or suspected cases of neglect or abuse. Mandated reporters include health care workers, teachers, counselors, social service workers, and child care providers. In many states, mandated reporters can be charged with a criminal offense if they fail to report known or suspected cases of neglect or abuse. For cases of peer abuse, adults can report to a principal or school social worker, and in extreme cases, to the state justice system.

Cases of neglect and abuse are handled through the appropriate state agency within the state government. A social service caseworker is assigned a reported case. He or she investigates by making a visit to the home and talking to all family members and by interviewing others with whom the child has contact. A decision is made within the state agency on whether there is or is not enough evidence to pursue the case. If the case is confirmed, steps will be taken to handle the perpetrator and treat the child. In most cases, the name and information of the person initially reporting the case remains confidential. Even if the investigation does not conclude that neglect or abuse is occurring, the reporter is protected unless he or she willfully reported just to get another adult in trouble.

Treating Cases of Neglect and Abuse

Documented cases of neglect and abuse will be dealt with by the proper authorities. In child neglect or abuse, the case will be brought before the courts if there is enough evidence. In working with adults, courts and caseworkers will consider the severity of the neglect or abuse, the adult's relationship to the child, and any past history of neglectful or abusive behaviors. Several actions may be taken, including the following:

- Children may be returned to their parents with the requirement that the parents have therapy. This therapy could include treatment for mental illness or substance abuse, individual or group counseling, or attendance in classes for neglectful and abusive adults. The reason behind these treatments is to deter the adult from choosing further neglectful or abusive actions.
- Children may be put into the foster care system until the parents fulfill therapy and other requirements of the courts (**Figure 22.18**).
- Adults may be restricted from seeing the child or they may have their parental rights **rescinded** (ree-SIND-ed), taken away.
- Adults may be convicted of a crime or they may be ordered to receive therapy.

When a case of neglect or abuse is confirmed, children can begin to receive help and treatment. This is the first step toward being a neglect or abuse survivor rather than remaining a victim.

Figure 22.17 Signs of Child Neglect and Abuse

Child Neglect	
Type of Neglect	**Signs**
Physical and medical	• Is malnourished • Fails to receive needed health care (unless parent has objection, such as for religious reasons) • Fails to receive proper hygiene (is not washed or bathed; has poor oral hygiene; has skin, nails, and hair that are not groomed) • Has insufficient clothing or clothing that is dirty, tattered, or inappropriate for the weather • Lives in filthy conditions or inadequate shelter
Moral and educational	• Lacks moral training • Lacks constructive discipline • Does not receive positive examples from adults • Does not have adequate supervision • Is left alone for hours • Fails to attend school regularly because parents do not make certain their children attend school • Fails to receive parent stimulation toward learning or education suited to his or her ability • Is not allowed to take part in wholesome recreational activities
Emotional	• Experiences constant friction in the home • Is denied normal experiences that produce feelings of being wanted, loved, and protected • Is rejected through indifference • Is overly rejected, such as through abandonment

(Continued)

Figure 22.17 *(Continued)*

Child Abuse	
Type of Abuse	**Signs**
Physical	• Seems fearful or quiet around parents, but has no close feeling for them • Is wary of physical contact initiated by an adult • Has little or no reaction to pain and seems much less afraid than most children the same age • Has unexplained injuries or shows evidence of repeated injuries, such as having bruises in various stages of healing or repeated fractures • Is dressed inappropriately (such being dressed in pajamas after being injured on a "bicycle" or being dressed in a turtleneck in the summer to cover bruises) • Shows a history of past injuries to long bones • Has injuries not reported on previous health records • Has been taken by parents to many hospitals and doctors without appropriate explanation • Has parents who refuse further diagnostic studies of their child's injuries • Has parents who show detachment or see the child as bad or "different" during medical treatment • Has parents who give too many minute details about the cause of injury • Tries to protect parents when they are questioned about the child's injuries
Verbal and emotional	• Lacks self-esteem • Is either too quiet and polite or uses harsh and improper language when dealing with others, especially those who are smaller or younger • Expresses long-term feelings of damage and isolation
Sexual	• Has extreme and sudden changes in behavior, such as loss of appetite or sudden drop in grades • Has nightmares and other sleep problems • Regresses to previous behaviors, such as renewed thumb sucking • Has torn or stained underwear • Has infections (with symptoms like bleeding or other discharges and itching) or swollen genitals • Fears a person or shows an intense dislike of being left alone with that person • Has an STI or is pregnant • Has unusual interest in or knowledge of sexual matters for his or her age

Physical treatment for the neglected or abused child is the first priority. As a doctor examines and treats the child, he or she will take a history (from the child, an older sibling, or parents) and document the examination. Records will include the doctor's observations, lab reports, and photographs or drawings (**Figure 22.19**).

Caseworkers or advocates from a child abuse prevention agency may also be involved in helping the child. These professionals make decisions about the child's welfare and advocate on his or her behalf. As caseworkers make decisions about the child, they keep the following questions in mind:

Figure 22.18 Foster parents provide a temporary home and family life for children who need shelter after a case of neglect or abuse. *What qualities do you think foster parents need to have?*

- What is the relationship of the child to the abuser?
- What risks are present for further abuse?
- What role, if any, should the courts have in this case?
- Should the child remain with the family?
- What support services could help both the child and family?

The services recommended will depend on the particulars of the case and the age of the child. Foster care, residential treatment facilities, child advocacy centers, counseling, Head Start programs, group therapy, play therapy, family intervention therapy, and individual therapy are examples of support services that are often used.

In cases of peer abuse, the situation may be handled by a school counselor or principal, or in severe cases, by a court. Both victims and perpetrators of peer abuse will likely receive therapy, and the school may take measures to discipline perpetrators and protect victims.

Preventing Neglect and Abuse

Neglect and abuse have many causes. As such, these complex problems do not have a single, quick solution. Work must be done on many fronts to put an end to them. Preventing neglect and abuse will take the efforts of individuals, families, communities, and society at large. Each person's involvement counts in the fight against these crimes.

Promoting Public Awareness

The future of any society depends on the health and well-being of the next generation. Awareness of a problem is the first step in prevention. Neglect and abuse can be prevented by encouraging *public awareness*, which is people's knowledge about a problem and what constitutes it. Public awareness can help prevent neglect and abuse when people

- are made to understand what behaviors are neglectful or abusive
- learn more about how certain problems threaten children and affect families' lives
- are informed about how the public can help fight against these crimes
- are made aware of the legal consequences of neglect and abuse

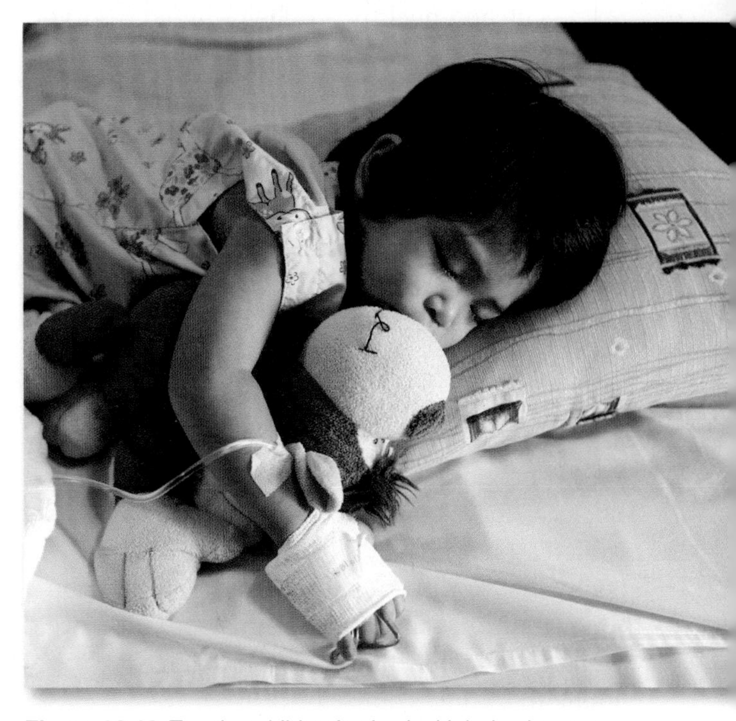

Figure 22.19 Treating children's physical injuries is a top priority after a case of neglect or abuse. *Why is physical health a top priority for children?*

Focus on

Careers

Recreational Therapist

Recreational therapists are mental health or physical therapists who use recreational activities (such as arts and crafts, play, drama, sports, games, or music) to improve people's physical or social-emotional well-being. They work with a variety of people, including people with mental health disorders, people with physical disabilities, and people recovering from traumatic events.

Career cluster: Human services.

Education: Educational requirements include a bachelor's degree in mental health or in a recreational area. Many employers expect recreational therapists to be state certified.

Job outlook: Future employment opportunities for recreational therapists are expected to grow as fast as the average for all occupations.

To learn more about a career as a recreational therapist, visit the United States Department of Labor's *Occupational Outlook Handbook* website. You will also be able to compare the job responsibilities, educational requirements, job outlook, and average pay of recreational therapists with similar occupations.

- understand that reporting suspected cases of neglect and abuse, although very important, is intervention, not prevention
- understand that prevention keeps children safe and healthy and helps avoid the over $100 billion spent each year on intervention services

Many organizations are leading the way to increased public awareness about neglect and abuse. These organizations provide a variety of information on prevention and support services. Some of these agencies host websites at which people can learn more about neglect and abuse.

Improving the Social Climate

Neglect and abuse are more likely to occur in a society where people feel undervalued, financial problems abound, and violence is condoned. To effectively prevent abuse, problems that contribute to a negative social climate must be addressed. Adults and organizations can help change the social climate that causes abuse by

- rejecting violence and aggression
- promoting better economic security for families
- reducing the numbers of mothers who do not receive adequate prenatal care
- educating parents and other caregivers about child development
- providing high-quality child care facilities, including crisis child care programs that provide **respite** (rest) for parents through child care
- collaborating with service providers who support families
- increasing the emphasis on respecting children, their needs, and their rights

Being active in groups that promote these changes can help prevent abuse. Making elected officials aware of needed changes is important, too. Instances of peer abuse can be reduced by school measures that clearly state the existence of peer abuse and how it is wrong. Schools and communities are establishing codes of behavior that prohibit peer abuse.

Providing Professional Support

Doctors and other professionals who come into contact with families need to be aware of risk factors that lead to neglect or abuse. They should note any risk factors they observe and connect high-risk families to the appropriate social programs.

Doctors can provide professional support by talking with parents and assessing a situation during a prenatal visit, well-child checkup, or medical visit. During a prenatal visit, a doctor might ask about how the pregnancy affects others in the family. If the family is facing problems, the doctor could make referrals for the family to seek other needed support services and social programs. During well-child checkups, doctors can talk with parents about child development. They can answer questions and offer advice about expected behaviors and issues, such as toilet learning, teething, crying, and sleep or eating problems. Understanding child development can help parents form more realistic expectations of their children. Appropriate expectations for children can reduce frustration and prevent some abusive outbursts. During each medical visit, doctors can assess a child's home life by asking simple questions, such as the following:

- What is it like for you taking care of your child?
- Do you get time for yourself?
- Do you get any help with your children from family or friends?
- How do you deal with your child's behavior problems?

It is not enough for professional support individuals and organizations just to assess, however. Support services must be available in the community. One type of support program is *home visitation*. In **home visitation**, a professional comes to the home to monitor the health of the mother and infant, to provide one-on-one parenting education, and to suggest other helpful community programs parents can access. Additionally, some hospitals and other agencies provide support services for new parents and respite child care for parents. Schools may also provide professional support by employing social workers who can talk with children and their families about any source of abuse.

Educating Adults

Adults can benefit from learning more about children and their care. This education may include life-skills training for children, teens, and young adults and education in child development and parenting. Learning more about healthy relationships, communication, stress and anger management, and coping skills will also help people prepare themselves to work with or care for children.

In addition, parents can also benefit from learning parenting techniques from parent-education programs, such as

- Parent Effectiveness Training (PET)
- Nurturing Parent Programs® (NPPs)
- Systematic Training for Effective Parenting (STEP)

In peer-abuse situations, adults should be educated about how to notice and follow up about instances in which children are being abused. **Figure 22.20** lists some principles adults should follow when dealing with these situations. Many schools are also developing programs to educate adults about lessening peer violence and its effects.

Stopping the Cycle of Neglect and Abuse

Stopping abusive cycles is a critical component of ending neglect and abuse. Children must not be allowed to go through life being neglected, abused, or both. Children need to receive help as soon as possible to end the harm and heal the wounds they have already experienced. Healing lessens children's chances of repeating these behaviors.

Another important piece of the puzzle lies within the abusers themselves. These abusive adults perhaps play the biggest role in stopping abuse. Abusive adults need to recognize that what they are doing is wrong and find help to stop. When abusers sincerely want to change their behaviors, the chances for success are much higher. If parents feel out of control and think they may abuse a child, they should call a national organization like *Parents Anonymous*®, which forms local chapters that provide support services any time. Parents can also call a crisis hotline to ask for help.

Figure 22.20 Preventing Children from Becoming Victims of Sibling or Peer Abuse

- Listen to the child and support his or her problem.
- Document ongoing abuse and seek adult help in the setting in which it occurs.
- Help the child learn the best strategies for dealing with abuse of other children. This does not include ignoring the abusers, walking away, or fighting. Teach the child self-assertive techniques and where to go for help.
- Help the child know how to make friends and be self-confident. Perpetrators often abuse other children with low self-confidence or those who irritate others. Although abuse by another is never right, every child needs to learn social skills that lessen the chance of abuse.
- Teach the child to think about everything he or she may want to post on the Internet. All writing, photos/drawings, and attachments can be forwarded.
- Teach the child to never hurt or embarrass anyone.
- Teach the child to share with a parent anything that makes him or her uncomfortable.
- Contact the appropriate authority to report incidences of bullying.
- Address the emotional bruises of violence inflicted by another child. Untreated victims often suffer from depression, anxiety, and other mental health issues even many years after the abuse.
- Teach the child how to avoid bullies.

In situations in which sibling or peer abuse is a risk, adults can help prevent their children from becoming perpetrators of sibling and peer abuse by

- modeling respectful relationships with colleagues, family, and friends. "Putting people down" teaches bullying.
- developing a close relationship with the child by keeping the lines of communication open.
- teaching the child respectful self-assertion. A child needs to use words, not aggression, to stick up for him- or herself.
- involving the child in community activities and home chores.
- including good role models in the child's life.
- monitoring violence in media content.
- involving the child in physical activities.
- taking even early, minor abuse seriously. Abuse that is not stopped always escalates.
- checking the child's use of social media. Explain the dangers of media use.

Lesson 22.2 Review and Assessment 

1. Explain the difference between *child neglect* and *child abuse.*
2. List and briefly define the types of child neglect and abuse.
3. Identify two principles that help explain the causes of child neglect and abuse.
4. List the six core strengths.
5. What is *bullying* and what types of abuse does it involve?
6. Some professionals who work with children are _____, meaning they are legally bound to report any known or suspected cases of neglect or abuse.
7. What four actions might be taken to treat a case of neglect or abuse?
8. **Critical thinking.** Choose one strategy for preventing neglect and abuse and give an example of how that strategy is at work in your community.

Chapter 22 Review and Assessment

Summary

Children and families face challenges. When families encounter challenges, it is important that parents and teachers work together to help children cope. When families move, parents and other adults working with children can strive to give children a sense of stability and can try to reduce other stressors. Financial strain in families also affects children, even before birth. Families facing financial strain can help children cope by providing as best they can and by seeking appropriate help to meet children's needs. The challenges of addiction and violence and disaster can be severe for children. Families with addictions need to ensure addicted family members receive help. Children who have experienced violence and disaster need support and comfort. Many children will face the challenge of divorce. To help children cope with divorce, parents can assure children they will always be loved. Illness and death are especially hard challenges for children, because children need help understanding these concepts and must experience grief. Many children who face challenges develop *resilience*, the ability to recover from stressful situations. By fostering resilience and seeking appropriate resources for children in crises, adults can help children cope well.

Neglect and abuse are major problems that threaten children's health and well-being. There are many types of neglect and abuse with many complex causes. All forms of neglect and abuse have serious effects on children's development. Besides abuse by adults, abuse of children by siblings and peers occurs. Sibling abuse takes the same forms as adult abuse. Peer abuse takes the forms of bullying, gang violence, and school violence. Sibling and peer abuse leaves much the same scars as abuse by adults. Recognition and reporting is an important step in stopping neglect and abuse, and some people are *mandated reporters*. When people report suspected cases of neglect and abuse, the children and adults involved can get the treatment they need. Many people are working to prevent and stop the cycle of neglect and abuse.

College and Career Portfolio

Portfolio Presentation Preparation

Presenting your portfolio well requires a great deal of preparation. At a job or school interview, you likely will not have time to present your entire portfolio. It is important, therefore, to highlight special achievements you want your audience to see.

Complete the following activities as part of your portfolio presentation preparation:

- Identify two or three components of your portfolio of which you are especially proud.
- Brainstorm ways to make these components the first and most important thing a potential employer or school would see.

Chapter 22 Review and Assessment

Vocabulary Activities

1. Work with a partner to write the definitions of the following terms based on your current understanding. Then pair up with another team to discuss your definitions and any discrepancies. Finally, discuss the definitions with the class and ask your instructor for necessary correction or clarification.

Key Terms

buffers (22.1)
bullying (22.2)
child abuse (22.2)
child neglect (22.2)
child protection agencies (22.2)
custody plans (22.1)
cyberbullying (22.2)
educational neglect (22.2)
emotional abuse (22.2)
emotional neglect (22.2)
home visitation (22.2)
impoverished (22.1)
mandated reporters (22.2)
medical neglect (22.2)
moral neglect (22.2)
peer abuse (22.2)
physical abuse (22.2)
physical neglect (22.2)
resilient children (22.1)
sexual abuse (22.2)
Shaken Baby Syndrome (SBS) (22.2)
sibling abuse (22.2)
six core strengths (22.2)
social abuse (22.2)
stages of grief (22.1)
terminally ill (22.1)
verbal abuse (22.2)

2. Work in pairs to write a *simile* for each of the following terms. Remember that a simile is a direct comparison of two items or factors that are *not* generally alike. When creating a simile, the comparisons are generally introduced by the words *like*, *as*, *seem*, or *appear*.

Academic Terms

adversity (22.1)
debase (22.2)
feed (22.1)
mourning (22.1)
perpetrated (22.2)
prognosis (22.1)
rescinded (22.2)
respite (22.2)
severed (22.1)
traumatized (22.1)

Critical Thinking

3. **Determine.** Interview three young children about their experiences moving. If you cannot find children to interview, read three different stories about children who have moved. How did the children feel about the move? How did their parents help them cope with the move? After the interviews, determine which factors most helped the children cope with their family moving and why.
4. **Draw conclusions.** Often, teachers and other adults who work with children are not aware of sensitive family issues, such as addiction in a child's family. Some signs, however, can alert adults to possible challenges in the child's family. In small groups, interview a social worker at a primary or middle school and ask about signs that indicate a child's family is struggling with addiction. Draw conclusions about why these signs might signify a problem.
5. **Analyze.** Using the Internet, research guidelines and instructions for parents helping their children cope with violence and disaster. Choose three suggestions given and analyze how the suggestions are or are not developmentally appropriate for young children.
6. **Make inferences.** When explaining illness and death to children, many adults are tempted to use *euphemisms* (such as *to pass away* instead of *to die*). Are euphemisms a good way to explain illness and death to children? Why or why not?
7. **Compare and contrast.** Working with a partner, research your state's definitions of *child neglect* and *child abuse*. According to your state, what is the primary difference between *neglect* and *abuse*? How do your state's definitions compare to the definitions in this text?
8. **Cause and effect.** In groups of three, assign each group member one area of development (physical, intellectual, social-emotional). Study the effects of *each type* of child neglect or abuse in your assigned area of development and create a spreadsheet documenting your thoughts. Finally, compare notes in your group and create a comprehensive spreadsheet detailing how each type of neglect or abuse affects all three areas of development.
9. **Identify.** Using reliable resources, find and read a scholarly study about the causes of child neglect and abuse. Identify which cause or causes are being researched and explain how the findings affect the likelihood of neglect or abuse.
10. **Evaluate.** Research school initiatives that seek to combat peer abuse. Choose one initiative and research its history, mission, and implementation. What services does the initiative offer? In your opinion, how effective is the initiative? Evaluate the initiative using examples from experience.

Core Skills

11. **Reading and speaking.** Search for articles written about families coping with financial strain. These articles should outline resources for families in these situations and should propose ways that parents and teachers can help children cope. Read two of the articles and summarize them in a short oral presentation. During the presentation, lead a class discussion analyzing whether you think the methods suggested in the articles would be helpful to children.
12. **Math.** Over the course of one day, tally every time that you are exposed to violence and disaster or reports of violence and disaster. This tally includes violence and disaster experienced, seen on the news, discussed at school, or read online. At the end of the day, calculate your total tally. As a class, average the individual tallies and discuss whether children are exposed to more or less violence and disaster.
13. **Writing and speaking.** Imagine you are a preschool teacher and one of your preschoolers, Raphael, is coping with his parents' divorce. Raphael has been acting out, crying, and refusing to participate. Working with a partner, write a short skit in which you help Raphael cope with his outbursts. Role-play your skit for the class and ask for feedback.
14. **Technology.** In small groups, review the information about illness and death in this chapter. Then, adapt the information into an interactive digital presentation and film about helping children cope. Include a sequential exploration of how children come to understand illness and death and select some practical videos that demonstrate effective techniques for helping children cope. Make your presentation visually appealing and easy to follow. Finally, present to the class.
15. **Research and technology.** Working with a partner, research resources for children in crises in your state. Resources might include federal or state agencies, crisis centers or nurseries, and hotlines for families in need. Create a five-panel pamphlet of these resources, including their names, contact information, and brief summaries of their services. Share your pamphlets with the class.
16. **Listening and technology.** Interview a school counselor about the most common types of peer abuse in school-age children. How has peer abuse changed over the past decade? Why do children abuse their peers? What can children do to protect themselves from abuse? Also ask about current measures that are being taken to reduce peer abuse. After the interview, create a digital poster highlighting your findings. Present your poster to the class.
17. **Research and speaking.** In groups of five, review the information on preventing neglect and abuse in this chapter. Assign each group member one method of prevention. Using the Internet, research examples of your method of prevention. Take notes about what made these examples successful or unsuccessful. Then, create your own movement, initiative, or club that uses your prevention method. Write a persuasive speech selling your movement, initiative, or club. Finally, practice in your group and deliver your persuasive speeches to the class.
18. **CTE Career Readiness Practice.** Imagine you are a child protective services caseworker who has been asked by a local child care center to deliver a presentation about recognizing abuse and mandated reporting requirements. In preparation for your presentation, research definitions of *neglect* and *abuse* in your state and tips for recognizing these problems. Also research the guidelines for mandated reporters and the legal penalties for failing to report neglect and abuse as a mandated reporter. Compile this information into a professional slideshow and oral presentation. Practice your presentation with the class. Ask for feedback about your professionalism and speaking skills (clarity and volume).

Observations

19. As a class, view a documentary about helping children recover from neglect or abuse. What behaviors or symptoms are typical of children who have been victims of neglect or abuse? What treatments do pediatricians and therapists administer to these children? How are caseworkers involved in children's treatment? After the documentary, discuss these questions in class.
20. In small groups, visit a local crisis child care center or disaster relief organization and interview someone about the effects of violence and disaster on children. How do children typically react to violence and disaster? How does the organization help these children obtain treatment? Write a brief report about your findings.

Chapter 23 Meeting Children's Special Needs

Essential Question

How do special needs impact children's development, and what help is available for meeting children's special needs?

Lesson 23.1 **Types of Special Needs**

Lesson 23.2 **Help for Children with Special Needs**

Case Study How Do Special Needs Affect Children and Families?

As a class, read the case study and discuss the questions that follow. After you finish studying the chapter, discuss this case study again. Have your opinions changed based on what you learned?

For the first three years of his life, Aram excelled at motor and physical activities. He was an active child who liked to run outside and kick the ball. As Aram entered the preschool years, his mother, Aida, noticed a change in Aram's physical development. Before, Aram had been growing stronger and testing his new skills eagerly. Now, Aram seemed tired and had trouble running across the backyard. At first, Aida thought her son just needed more sleep.

As Aram began his new preschool program, Aida hoped the new schedule would benefit him. Unfortunately, Aram only seemed to grow weaker. One day, Aram's preschool teacher met with Aida and expressed concerns that Aram had seemed stiff lately, was having trouble sitting down and standing up, and had started walking on his toes. The teacher recommended that Aram see his pediatrician.

Worried for her son, Aida acted promptly and told her son's pediatrician about the situation. The pediatrician examined Aram and referred him to a specialist for further testing. The tests revealed Aram has a condition known as *muscular dystrophy*. Aida felt overwhelmed, wondering: *How will I tell Aram? What will this mean for our son? What will it mean for our family? How will this change the way we live our lives?*

Give It Some Thought

1. What behaviors and signs caused Aida and the preschool teacher to worry about Aram? Why were these behaviors and signs alarming?
2. What does this new condition mean for Aida's family? How might this change the way Aida's family lives?
3. What advice would you give to Aida about how she should explain this condition to her son and how she should treat her son as they adjust?

While studying this chapter, look for the online resources icon  to:

- **Practice** terms with e-flash cards and interactive games
- **Assess** what you learn by completing self-assessment quizzes
- **Expand** knowledge with interactive activities and graphic organizers

www.g-wlearning.com/childdevelopment

Study on the go

Use a mobile device to practice terms and review with self-assessment quizzes.

www.m.g-wlearning.com/0384

Lesson 23.1 Types of Special Needs

Key Terms

anxiety disorder
attention-deficit hyperactivity disorder (ADHD)
autism spectrum disorder (ASD)
behavioral disorder
developmental dyscalculia
developmental dyslexia
intellectual disability
intelligence quotient (IQ) test
language disorder
learning disorder
oppositional defiant disorder (ODD)
physical disability
speech disorder
typical development

Academic Terms

causal
delusions
hallucinations
meningitis
misfires
paralysis
psychomotor ability

Objectives

After studying this lesson, you will be able to

- explain the principles behind developmental differences and special needs among children.
- describe physical special needs children may experience, including physical disabilities and speech disorders.
- summarize children's intellectual special needs, including intellectual disabilities, gifts and talents, learning disorders, and language disorders.
- explain the social-emotional special needs of children, including anxiety disorders, depression, childhood schizophrenia, and oppositional defiant disorder (ODD).
- identify special needs that affect multiple areas of children's development, including attention disorders and autism spectrum disorder (ASD).

Reading and Writing Activity

Arrange a study session to read the lesson aloud with a classmate. At the end of each section, stop and discuss any words you do not know. Refer to the dictionary or the text's glossary to learn the meanings of these words. Finally, take notes about words you would like to discuss in class.

Graphic Organizer

In a chart like the one shown, write the first- and second-level headings from this lesson. As you read, take notes and organize them by heading. Draw a star beside any words or concepts you do not yet understand.

Who Are Children with Special Needs?	
Children with Physical Special Needs	Children with Physical Disabilities
	Children with Speech Disorders

Many children develop in similar ways, achieving typical milestones in each stage of development. These children have basic needs that must be met. Sometimes, though, children's development differs from that which is expected. Children who experience developmental accelerations or delays have special needs, which need to be met in different ways.

There are many types of special needs, and not all of these types are fully understood. Children with physical special needs differ in their physical development. Intellectual special needs, such as intellectual disabilities and giftedness, both impact children's intellectual development. Learning disorders affect how children learn. A number of social-emotional special needs, including anxiety disorders, depression, childhood schizophrenia, and oppositional defiant disorder (ODD) can also set children apart. Sometimes children have special needs due to the complex interactions among multiple areas of development, as seen in attention disorders and autism spectrum disorder (ASD). Understanding these special needs is the first step in helping children who possess them.

Who Are Children with Special Needs?

Although each child is unique, children typically grow and develop in similar ways. Through research, child development experts have determined which developmental milestones (physical, intellectual, and social-emotional) children generally attain within each stage of development. A child whose development follows these patterns exhibits **typical development**. Some children, however, do not follow typical patterns of development. These children are known as *children with special needs. Special needs* are needs that go *beyond* the basic needs of all children (**Figure 23.1**).

Children with special needs may have abilities that differ from most other children. They may exhibit differences in motor skills, seeing, hearing, speech, intellectual abilities, learning, language, and social behaviors. In discussing children with special needs, it is important to consider several guidelines. These guidelines include the following:

- ***Special needs may occur in one or more areas of development.*** Children with special needs may differ from typical development in any area of development—physical,

Figure 23.1 Even though children with special needs have additional needs that must be met, they have much in common with children who do not have special needs. *What are examples of basic needs all children have in common?*

intellectual, or social-emotional. Just because a child has a special need in one developmental area does not mean he or she has special needs in another area. For example, one child may differ from typical development in language development alone. Another child may differ from typical development in both language development and social interactions.

- ***Special needs may develop due to acceleration or delay.*** Children who develop faster or achieve higher degrees of development than most other children are often described as *gifted* or *talented*. Children who experience *developmental delays* (the late achievement of a developmental milestone) may have *conditions*, *disabilities*, or *disorders*.
- ***Special needs are identified through observations and tests.*** To determine a child's type of special need, professionals (such as doctors or psychologists) make observations and perform tests. Some special needs are apparent at birth, but many special needs are not evident for several years or more.
- ***Special needs vary in intensity.*** Special needs exist on a spectrum of intensity, ranging from *borderline* to *profound* (**Figure 23.2**). The term *borderline* indicates that a talent or delay differs *very little* from typical development. The term *profound* indicates that a talent or delay differs *very much* from typical development.
- ***Special needs vary in duration and permanence.*** Types of special needs may be described as *correctable* or *chronic*. The term *correctable* indicates that a special need may be overcome or may subside with appropriate support and time. For example, many speech disorders are correctable through speech therapy. The term *chronic* indicates that a special need may exist for a long time, perhaps a lifetime. For example, Down syndrome presents a chronic, lifelong special need.

Children may possess different types of special needs, including needs that affect physical development (such as physical disabilities), needs that affect intellectual development (such as intellectual disabilities and gifts and talents), and needs that affect social-emotional development (such as anxiety disorders and other mental health disorders). Some types of special needs affect more than one area of development (such as attention disorders).

Children with Physical Special Needs

Physical special needs are needs that affect a child's physical development. Types of physical special needs include physical disabilities (such as gross-motor, vision, and hearing conditions) and speech disorders. Physicians and therapists often identify physical special needs by noting *physical developmental delays*. Developmental delays may occur during any stage of development, as shown in **Figure 23.3**.

Special Needs Spectrum

	Borderline	Mild	Moderate	Severe	Profound	
Least intense	differs *very little* from typical development	differs *little* from typical development	differs *somewhat* from typical development	differs *much* from typical development	differs *very much* from typical development	Most intense

Degree of Intensity

Figure 23.2 The spectrum of special needs reflects the varying intensities of children's needs. *Give an example of a special need at each point on the spectrum.*

Children with Physical Disabilities

A **physical disability** is a limitation of a person's body or its function. Physical disabilities indicate that a child is developing behind the typical physical development of most other children the same age. Children with physical disabilities differ from typical physical development for many reasons. Some of these reasons include

- genetic disorders
- congenital conditions
- serious illnesses, such as **meningitis** (MEH-nun-JY-tis), an inflammation of the thin membranes that cover the spinal cord and brain
- spinal cord, brain, or other bodily injuries

Children with Gross-Motor Conditions

One type of physical disability is a *gross-motor condition*. Gross-motor conditions may result from any of the following problems: bodily trauma; bone, joint, nerve, or muscle diseases; or damage

Figure 23.3 Physical Developmental Delays

Infancy	
3 months	• Does not reach for, grasp, or hold objects. • Does not support head well.
4 months	• Still exhibits *Moro* (startle) reflex. • Does not bring objects to mouth. • Does not push down with legs when feet are placed on a firm surface. • Cannot touch hands together in front of body.
6 months	• Does not roll over. • Head lags when infant is pulled into a sitting position. • Reaches for an object with only one hand while keeping the other hand tightly fisted.
7 months	• Has very stiff (tight) or floppy muscles. • Head flops when infant is pulled into a sitting position. • Cannot bring objects to mouth easily. • Does not bear weight on legs in a standing position.
8–12 months	• Cannot sit without support. • Drags one side of body while crawling. • Cannot stand when supported. • Does not creep.
Toddler Years	
18–24 months	• Cannot walk. • Walks on toes. • Cannot push a wheeled toy.
35 months	• Falls frequently. • Is unable to use stairs. • Cannot manipulate small objects. • Drools frequently.

(Continued)

Figure 23.3 *(Continued)*

Preschool Years	
3 years	• Falls and trips easily and frequently. • Seems to be clumsy. • Favors one side of body. • Cannot make marks on paper or cut snips with scissors. • Finds stacking 1-inch cube blocks almost impossible. • Shows great difficulty in putting pegs into holes or placing shapes over pegs.
4 years	• Cannot throw a ball overhead. • Cannot jump in place. • Cannot pedal a tricycle. • Uses the palm, rather than the thumb and finger, to hold crayons or markers. • Has trouble scribbling. • Cannot stack four 1-inch cube blocks.
5 years	• Cannot balance more than two seconds on each leg. • Shows poor overall coordination. • Cannot stack six to eight 1-inch cube blocks. • Has trouble taking off clothing. • Cannot brush teeth well. • Cannot wash and dry hands. • Has trouble using scissors.
School-Age Years	
6–12 years	• Walks abnormally. • Shows regression in gross-motor skills. • Seems uncoordinated and clumsy. • Has not established hand preference. • Cannot draw basic shapes; scribbles. • Cannot follow lines in cutting. • Cannot form manuscript letters and numerals. • Shows weak or stiff gross- or fine-motor movements.

to the brain or nervous system. Some gross-motor conditions include

- *muscular dystrophy*, a genetic disease that weakens the muscles
- *spina bifida*, a congenital disorder in which the spine does not completely cover the spinal cord, leading to physical complications and sometimes **paralysis** (the inability to move or feel parts of the body)
- *cerebral palsy*, a disorder resulting from damage to the brain that affects muscle coordination
- paralysis, which may be caused by a brain or spinal injury or disease
- amputated or missing limbs, which may lead to limited mobility

Any gross-motor condition may cause delays in gross-motor development. Children with gross-motor

Focus on

Developmental Delays

Developmental milestones measure children's progress at each stage of their physical, intellectual, and social-emotional development. Children who achieve a developmental milestone late, or do not achieve a milestone at all, are experiencing a *developmental delay*. Developmental delays can be difficult for caregivers and teachers to identify, and adults often have questions about how to identify a delay, when a delay is serious, and what to do about a delay. Questions that adults often have include the following:

- Do developmental milestones and their ages still apply to premature infants?
- If children regress in their skills, is this cause for concern?
- How absolute are the ages given for developmental milestones? When does the nonachievement of a milestone become a *developmental delay*?
- If children achieve milestones early, does that mean they have *gifts and talents*?

In small groups, search online or visit a local library and read reliable articles or books to answer these questions. Be sure to cite your sources in a short bibliography. Write your answers as a group and then compare answers with another group.

conditions may need special aids, such as artificial limbs, walkers, crutches, braces, or wheelchairs, to participate fully in daily life.

Children with Vision Conditions

Another type of physical disability is a *vision condition*, which causes children to experience challenges seeing. Signs of possible vision conditions include squinting, holding objects close to the face, and rubbing the eyes frequently. Poor depth perception may also signal that a child has a vision condition. Certain vision conditions may cause children to only see light, colors, shadow forms, or large pictures. Other conditions may cause children to be unable to see anything at all.

While some vision conditions are correctable as a result of wearing eyeglasses or having surgery, other vision conditions are chronic and cannot be corrected (**Figure 23.4**). One chronic vision condition is *legal blindness*, which occurs when a person's better eye has a corrected visual acuity of 20/200 and/or in which the visual field is 20 degrees or less.

Children with Hearing Conditions

A third type of physical disability is a *hearing condition*, which causes children to have difficulty hearing. This difficulty may include hearing loss

Figure 23.4 Vision conditions, such as nearsightedness or farsightedness, are correctable, usually through eyeglasses or contacts. *What other methods are used to help children with correctable vision conditions?*

ranging from borderline to profound. Profound hearing loss may result in *deafness*. Signs of a possible hearing condition include unresponsiveness to sounds, incorrect formation of speech sounds, or major delays in talking. Newborns are often tested for hearing conditions before they leave the hospital. Hearing conditions, however, can develop months or years after birth due to illnesses or exposure to loud sounds.

Children with hearing conditions may excel in some areas not affected by hearing loss. Many children with hearing conditions use their sense of touch far more than other children. They also watch other people's faces and mouths closely to understand messages that are being communicated.

Children with Speech Disorders

Some children with physical special needs have *speech disorders*. A **speech disorder** is a condition that causes a child to have difficulty speaking or being understood. For the most part, speech disorders involve children's physical development. Children with speech disorders typically face challenges in one or more of the following areas:

- ***Articulation.*** *Articulation* is the ability to pronounce words understandably. Children who face articulation challenges may substitute one sound for another, distort sounds, leave out sounds in words, or add sounds to words.
- ***Voice.*** Children who face voice challenges may speak with voices that are exceptionally high in pitch, low in pitch, loud, quiet, nasal, or husky. These qualities can hinder children's abilities to be understood by others.
- ***Rhythm.*** Everyone speaks at a certain rhythm. Children who face rhythm challenges may repeat sounds and words, have pauses between sounds, or use prolonged sounds (called *stuttering* or *stammering*). Other children may also speak especially fast, stumble on words or phrases, or double back to try to communicate meaning (called *cluttering*).

Speech disorders are often identified by doctors and teachers rather than by parents. Parents or caregivers may not hear differences in their children's speech because they are accustomed to these differences. Sometimes children even learn

Focus on Health

Continued Stuttering

Most cases of stuttering resolve over time and sometimes with therapy. Sometimes, however, stuttering does not resolve on its own. Some children may be at risk for *continued stuttering* (stuttering that continues over life). Children who are at risk for continued stuttering tend to

- have a family history of stuttering
- begin stuttering after 42 months of age and continue for more than 3 months
- show physical tension while speaking (such as jaw clenching or blinking eyes)
- have other speech problems
- be aware that they are stuttering
- be male
- have family members or friends who strongly react to the stuttering

Children with continued stuttering should receive professional help from speech and language therapists. Continued stuttering can hinder children's abilities to be understood and can lead to poor self-concept if children are criticized for their speech habits.

speech differences *from* their parents or caregivers. Children with suspected speech disorders need to be evaluated by a speech therapist (also called a *speech pathologist*). Speech therapists are also trained to treat speech disorders.

Children with Intellectual Special Needs

Children with intellectual special needs have needs that affect their intellectual development or their abilities to learn. Intellectual special needs may be indicated by *intellectual developmental delays*, such as those shown in **Figure 23.5**. They may also be indicated by accelerated intellectual development. Struggling to learn academic subjects or having difficulties understanding language may also be indicators that children have intellectual special needs. Types of intellectual special needs include intellectual disabilities, gifts and talents, learning disorders, and language disorders.

Children with Intellectual Disabilities

An **intellectual disability** is a condition in which a child's intellectual abilities are a year or more delayed when compared with other children the same age. Causes of intellectual disabilities include genetic disorders, congenital conditions, birth complications, and injuries to or infections of the brain after birth. A lack of basic experiences within the child's environment may also lead to intellectual delays.

Indications of intellectual disabilities vary widely, but most intellectual disabilities do share some

Figure 23.5 Intellectual Developmental Delays

Infancy	
2–3 months	• Does not notice hands. • Does not follow moving objects with eyes.
4–6 months	• Does not respond to loud noises. • Does not babble; or babbles some, but does not try to imitate sounds. • Cannot use eyes to follow objects that are close (one foot away) or objects that are far away (six feet away).
7–11 months	• Does not respond to sounds. • Does not use any single word. • Does not retrieve objects that are hidden while he or she watches. • Does not point to objects.
Toddler Years	
12 months	• Does not babble. • Does not attempt to say "mama" or "dada." • Does not use gestures, such as waving, shaking the head, or pointing. • Does not respond to "no" or "bye-bye."
15–18 months	• Does not say simple words. • Does not point to at least one body part. • Does not attempt to communicate needs. • Is not adding at least one new word per week to vocabulary.

(Continued)

Figure 23.5 *(Continued)*

Toddler Years *(Continued)*	
24 months	• Cannot speak 15 words. • Does not use two-word phrases. • Does not respond to simple directions. • Cannot point to or name pictures in a book. • Does not imitate actions. • Does not pretend at all. • Does not know functions of common objects.
25–35 months	• Cannot complete any familiar nursery rhymes. • Does not ask simple questions. • Cannot be understood by family members. • Does not maintain attention during an activity for at least 10 minutes.
Preschool Years	
3 years	• Does not understand simple, one-statement commands or directions. • Shows little interest in toys. • Does not explore the environment. • Cannot speak so that 75 percent of what is said is understood by parents and caregivers.
4 years	• Does not engage in pretend play. (Uses toys as objects only, not as symbols.) • Has no interest in interactive games. • Cannot speak so that anyone can understand.
5 years	• Is easily distracted. Cannot concentrate on an activity for more than five minutes. • Lacks interest in or curiosity about people or toys. • Uses phrases or gestures more than sentences to communicate. • Shows little interest in picture books. • Does not show any interest in print or numbers. • Cannot easily follow two- or three-part directions. • Is two or more years behind other children in comprehending logical thinking concepts.
School-Age Years	
6–12 years	• Does not know basic concepts (names of attributes, letters, numbers). • Cannot follow rules to simple games. • Cannot complete school assignments or do homework. • Cannot stay focused on tasks. • Lacks executive functions. • Is failing in school.

characteristics. Children with intellectual disabilities tend to

- experience delays in motor skills
- have small vocabularies and use short sentences
- grasp simple ideas, but not highly complex ideas
- avoid difficult tasks
- have short attention spans
- be especially fond of repetition
- have difficulty making choices

Intellectual disabilities can vary from borderline to profound. These disabilities are usually identified by doctors or other professionals through a combination of testing and assessment. Testing for intellectual disabilities may involve the administering of a specialized test called an *intelligence quotient (IQ) test*. An **intelligence quotient (IQ) test** measures how quickly a person can learn and how well a person can reason using words, numbers, and spatial concepts. Children with intellectual disabilities tend to score below 70 on IQ tests. IQ tests, however, do not totally define whether a child has an intellectual disability. True identification depends on assessment of children's functioning and overall ability, including multiple intelligences.

Children with Gifts and Talents

Although all children have strengths, *children with gifts and talents* are children who experience *accelerated intellectual development*, meaning they develop far ahead of most other children's intellectual development. Children with gifts and talents show high performance in one or more of the following areas:

- general intellectual ability (showing above-average intelligence)
- specific academic aptitude (excelling in one or more subject areas)
- creative or productive thinking (writing or inventing)
- leadership ability (planning or organizing)
- high skill in visual or performing arts (excelling in art, music, or dance)
- high **psychomotor ability**—the ability to coordinate muscle movements with mental processes (excelling in sports)

Just as all children are unique, so are children with gifts and talents. Some children with gifts and talents seem to be gifted or talented in almost all areas. Other children are talented in only one or two areas.

Children who are gifted and talented are not necessarily children who excel in school. Children who are gifted and talented may not excel in areas other than their area of giftedness. Just because a child is gifted or talented does not mean that child will not experience typical development or a developmental delay in another area. Giftedness and talent are not one in the same. **Figure 23.6** shows some traits that are characteristic of children with gifts and talents.

Children with Gifts

Children with gifts excel largely in intelligence, scoring significantly higher (130 or higher) on individual IQ tests than children who follow typical development. An IQ score between 140 and 160 indicates that a child is *highly gifted*, and a score of 160 or higher indicates that a child is *profoundly gifted*.

If a child is borderline gifted, parents may not recognize the child's giftedness. Often teachers see potential giftedness by noting high scores on *standardized* (not teacher-constructed) school achievement tests although many children achieve high scores without being truly gifted. Based on children's scores on these tests, children may be recommended by their teachers for further testing, such as being given an IQ test. To determine giftedness, children may also be given a college-admission aptitude test, such as the *Scholastic Aptitude Test (SAT)*, at a younger age than is typical. Giftedness in children is mostly *genetic* (inherited). These gifts must be nurtured, however, for children to reach their full potential.

Children with Talents

While children with gifts excel largely in intelligence, children with *talents* excel in other intellectual areas. For example, a preschooler who plays the violin more like a school-age child or teen is talented in music.

Figure 23.6 Traits of Children with Gifts and Talents

Children with Gifts

- Are inquisitive; try to determine the "hows and whys" behind everything.
- Want to explore, learn, and find out information.
- Tend to have widely *eclectic* (coming from many sources; hence, *diverse*) and focused interests.
- Have excellent and detailed memory skills.
- Learn very quickly and with little practice.
- Find repetition boring.
- Perceive similarities, differences, and inconsistencies.
- Mentally separate materials into components and systematically analyze materials.
- Can concentrate for long periods of time (long attention span).
- Are very organized.
- Are intrinsically motivated and use boundless energy to reach goals.
- Construct and handle abstractions early in development.
- Handle inferences without having to have them explained.
- Conceptualize and synthesize information.
- See cause-and-effect relationships early in development.
- Grasp underlying principles and correctly generalize.
- Read before school entrance without much adult assistance.
- Comprehend spoken and written language, including *nuances* (subtle differences in meaning or expression).
- Prefer reading materials written for children older than they are.
- Use many alternatives and approaches to problem solving.
- Have vivid dreams.
- Enjoy and use humor.
- Often have imaginary friends.
- Respond better to adults and older children than to peers.
- Are concerned about social issues.
- Are perfectionists.
- Remember emotions strongly.
- Feel an exceptional sense of responsibility for their own behaviors.

Children with Talents

- Develop specific interests early in development.
- Have intense interest in one or more specific areas.
- Show abilities in the area of a talent early in development.
- Enjoy sharing their skills, such as showing their visual art products and performing for others.
- Interact with others who have similar interests.

Children's talents are both genetic and environmental. While these traits do run in families, a supportive environment to meet these children's special needs is also required. Pediatricians, teachers, and other professionals may help parents identify talents their children might possess.

Many children with gifts are *also* children with talents. Because children with gifts have such high intelligence, they often perform well in many other areas (such as academics, music, art, leadership, or sports). Thus, these children are considered to have both gifts *and* talents.

Children with Learning Disorders

A **learning disorder** is a challenge in spoken or written language, math, or *spatial orientation* (the ability to see relationships among objects in space). Children with learning disorders have average or above-average intelligence. Nevertheless, the academic achievement of children with learning disorders is below what would be expected for their intelligence and grade level.

Studies show that learning disorders usually result from neural misfires in the brain. **Misfires** are electrical signals that either fail to cross neuron synapses or cross these synapses incorrectly. What causes these misfires is unknown. Some contributing factors, however, may include prenatal complications (such as lack of oxygen for the fetus), trauma during birth, accidents, high fevers, and breathing or nutritional problems after birth. The type of learning disorder depends on the part of the brain in which the misfiring repeatedly occurs. Children with learning disorders have a number of defining traits that set them apart from children who follow typical development (**Figure 23.7**).

Figure 23.7 Traits of Children with Learning Disorders*

Traits	Examples
Intelligence that is average or above average	• Score relatively well on IQ tests. • Are perceived to have average or high intelligence.
Academic achievement that is below what would be expected for a child of average intelligence	• Have school grades and performance that do not seem to reflect average intelligence. • Seem to struggle in school due to learning challenges, not due to motivation or stress at home.
Consistent difficulty in school, even when quality classroom instruction is provided	• Do not respond positively to quality instruction measures taken by teachers and other adults. • Do not seem to improve, even when special school measures are taken.
Brain messages that are jumbled even though the sense organs function normally	• Reverse letters when reading, writing, or speaking. For example, may read *on* as *no*, write *24* for *42*, or say *aminal* for *animal*. • Confuse related words, such as saying *breakfast* instead of *lunch*. • Stop frequently in midsentence and start expressing a new idea. • May have trouble identifying the question asked, such as confusing the questions, "How are you?" and "How old are you?"
Poor spatial orientation	• Have difficulty performing tasks that involve spatial concepts, such as *up*, *down*, *left*, *right*, *top*, *bottom*, *above*, and *below*. • Do not see items that are within the line of vision. • Have trouble judging distances. • Get lost often. • Have difficulty writing on a line. • Have difficulty putting together jigsaw puzzles.

(Continued)

Figure 23.7 *(Continued)*

Traits	Examples
Awkwardness or clumsiness	• Struggle with tying shoes or buttoning small buttons. • Do not perform well at sports. • Trip or lose balance because of misjudging distance. • Have difficulty judging timing (for example, timing needed for batting a ball). • Cannot coordinate several tasks at once.
Severe information processing deficits	• Have a very short attention span. Cannot listen to a story or finish a project. • Seem to struggle with forming and recalling long-term memories.
Overactivity	• Are always moving, to the point of distracting others. • Fidget constantly through quiet activities.
Disordered behavior	• Need more attention than most children of the same age and seek this attention by misbehaving. • May misbehave to convince others that they are "bad" and are not struggling with learning tasks.
Mental inflexibility	• Become upset when routines change. • Become anxious in new places or around new people. • Reject objects that are different (for example, refuses a cracker that is broken). • Demand that others cater to their needs, even when it is not possible.

*Some children who follow typical development may also experience these traits. While children who follow typical development are correcting some of these traits, however, children with learning disorders still struggle with them regularly.

Two common types of learning disorders identified in childhood are *developmental dyslexia* and *developmental dyscalculia*. **Developmental dyslexia** (dis-LEK-see-uh) affects a child's ability to read. Children with developmental dyslexia may also have problems writing and spelling. They may find it difficult to connect words with their written forms and may reverse words and letters when reading or writing. They may also confuse the order of letters in words or read words backward. Currently, dyslexia is more common in boys than girls. **Developmental dyscalculia** (DIS-kal-KYOO-lee-uh) affects a child's mathematical abilities. Children with dyscalculia may reverse numerals and may not develop a mental number line necessary for calculating. Unlike dyslexia, dyscalculia is equally common in boys and girls.

Children with Language Disorders

A **language disorder** involves a child's lack of ability to understand and use language. Language disorders tend to involve the brain and intellectual development, which makes them more serious and less correctable than speech disorders.

The most serious language disorder of childhood is *acquired childhood aphasia,* which is the partial or total loss of the ability to understand words and use language. The term *acquired* is used because this disorder occurs after children have developed some language skills. Acquired childhood aphasia develops due to a brain injury, which may be caused by head trauma, brain infection, a brain tumor, stroke, or other brain disorders. The possibility of recovery depends on the severity of the brain damage.

Children with Social-Emotional Special Needs

Children with special needs do not just experience these needs in their physical and intellectual lives. Children with special needs also include some children with social-emotional special needs. Social-emotional special needs are usually identified by serious changes in the ways children behave socially or regulate their emotions (**Figure 23.8**). These needs can also be signaled by lags or delays in children's achievement of social-emotional developmental milestones. The *social-emotional developmental delays* for infants, preschoolers, toddlers, and school-age children are outlined in **Figure 23.9**.

There are many types of social-emotional special needs. Many times, these needs take the form of

Figure 23.8 Behavioral Changes That May Indicate Social-Emotional Special Needs*

Toddlers
• Appears excessively fearful and cannot be easily soothed.
• Appears sad or withdrawn.
• Shows inappropriate impulsive or aggressive behaviors, especially toward family members and familiar children.
• Experiences many nightmares and night terrors.
• Has violent temper tantrums or frequent tantrums.
• Shows an unusual need for cleanliness and orderliness.
• Has inappropriate sexual behavior.
• Is extremely defiant.
Preschoolers
• Displays aggression directed at adults or is violently destructive toward an object, such as a toy.
• Intentionally injures self.
• Has five or more tantrums for several consecutive days. Tantrums last more than 25 minutes per tantrum.
• Shows a sudden, but long-term, change in personality, such as sunny to sullen or angry *or* outgoing to withdrawn.
• Has panic attacks.
• Has unusual sleep patterns with frequent night terrors.
• Cannot relax or is lethargic (unenergetic).
School-Age Children
• Shows severe mood changes (changes are prolonged or cause problems in family, school, and peer relationships).
• Has intense feelings (often accompanied by racing heart and fast breathing).
• Has fears and anxieties that interfere with daily tasks and enjoyment.
• Has behavioral changes (such as being withdrawn, threatening others, or fighting without any provocation).
• Has eating disorders or sleeping problems.
• Talks about or attempts self-injurious acts.
• Uses alcohol or other drugs to cope with feelings.
*New diagnostic criteria have been developed to identify social-emotional special needs and mental health disorders much earlier.

Figure 23.9 Social-Emotional Developmental Delays

Infancy	
3–6 months	• Does not smile. • Does not pay attention to new faces. • Is difficult to comfort at night. • Does not laugh.
7 months	• Refuses to cuddle. • Shows no affection for parents or regular caregivers. • Shows no enjoyment around people.
8–11 months	• Shows no interest in peek-a-boo. • Shows no back-and-forth sharing of sounds, smiles, or facial expressions. • Shows no back-and-forth gestures, such as waving, reaching, or pointing.
Toddler Years	
13–18 months	• Does not smile when looking at parent or caregiver. • Does not respond to name. • Does not express desires or feelings. • Does not engage in social games (such as patty-cake). • Shows excessive *or* no dependence on caregivers. • Does not show curiosity about people or toys and does not explore the environment.
19–24 months	• Only interacts with familiar adults *or* shows no caution interacting with strangers. • Does not enjoy play. • Does not imitate the actions or words of others.
25–35 months	• Does not express physical states, such as "I am hungry." • Uses language to meet needs exclusively; does not "visit." • Does not respond to people outside the family. • Has severe separation anxiety. • Does not want to play with other children.
Preschool Years	
3 years	• Shows little interest in other children. • Has poor eye contact. • Shows extreme separation anxiety.
4 years	• Displays no self-control emotionally. • Clings and cries when parents leave. • Has no desire to explore new places. • Responds only to family members. • Ignores other children. • Resists dressing, using the toilet, or sleeping. • Shows no executive functions.

(Continued)

Figure 23.9 *(Continued)*

	Preschool Years *(Continued)*
5 years	• Is fearful and timid; cannot be reassured. • Shows either aggression *or* passivity around other children. • Seems very unhappy. • Shows no interest in pretend play.
	School-Age Years
6–12 years	• Shows little or no interest in playing with others. • Does not share toys or equipment or take turns while playing. • Shows little to no self-regulation of emotions. • Has difficulty focusing on tasks or sitting still for even short periods of time. • Is "rigid" about routines; does not adapt to changes. • Does not want to try new activities others are doing. • Shows separation anxiety, extreme fears, and other anxieties.

mental health disorders. Some social-emotional special needs include anxiety disorders, depression, childhood schizophrenia, and oppositional defiant disorder (ODD).

Children with Anxiety Disorders

One type of social-emotional special need common in children is an *anxiety disorder*. *Anxiety* is a form of stress that all people feel from time to time, and some anxiety is healthy. An **anxiety disorder**, however, is a specific anxiety that interferes with a child's ability to achieve goals or enjoy life. Children with anxiety disorders are at increased risk for other conditions, such as eating disorders and sleep problems. All of these risks also have the potential to interfere with children's lives.

Several types of anxiety disorders occur in children, and each type of disorder has different symptoms (**Figure 23.10**). General symptoms of anxiety disorders include the following:

- excessive and prolonged worry
- trouble sleeping and fatigue during the day
- inability to focus on schoolwork and other goals
- irritability
- withdrawn behaviors after difficult social interactions
- resistance to change
- poor self-concept due to others' perceived judgments

Experts do not yet know exactly what causes anxiety disorders. Two people may have similar life experiences, and one person may develop an anxiety disorder while the other person may not. Several factors seem to contribute to anxiety disorders, such as genetics, brain chemistry, stressful life circumstances (such as neglect and abuse), and learned behaviors.

Children with Depression

Depression is the most common social-emotional special need in the United States. *Depression* is a serious mental health disorder characterized by a persistent sad mood and feeling of worthlessness. Children with depression can be as young as newborns. Children with depression may also experience *bipolar disorder*, a condition in which a child's mood alternates between depression and *high-energy mania* (irritability and an explosive temper). Depression can be caused by low levels of certain neurotransmitters in the brain, genetics, significant life events, and stress. Depression can be successfully treated in over 80 percent of children through medications and therapy.

Figure 23.10 Types and Symptoms of Anxiety Disorders

Type	Symptoms
Generalized anxiety disorder (GAD)	• Worrying excessively about many situations. • Thinking of the worst that can happen. • Striving for perfection. • Being hard on one's self. • Seeking constant approval. • Exhibiting physical symptoms, such as headaches and stomachaches.
Obsessive compulsive disorder (OCD)	• Having repeated and unwanted thoughts; also called *obsessions.* • Performing repetitive behaviors or mental acts (handwashing, counting, repeating words silently) in an attempt to reduce anxiety; also called *compulsions*. • Showing OCD symptoms by late childhood, but before the teen years.
Separation anxiety disorder	• Having separation anxiety continuing during the school-age years. • Believing something terrible will occur when a loved one is away. • Refusing to go to school, sleepovers with friends, and even to other relatives' homes if caregiver is not present. • Crying or hiding when caregivers are preparing to leave. • Following caregivers to prevent separation. • Sleeping only if caregiver is in the same room. • Having nightmares about separation. • Taking a long time to calm after being left by a caregiver. • Wanting to frequently check on caregiver's well-being, such as calling them, when separated.
Panic disorder	• Having *panic attacks* (increased heart rate, difficulty breathing, hot or cold flashes, dizziness, and tingling in legs or arms). • Displaying fears of panic attacks, dying, or losing one's mind. • Avoiding settings in which one experienced panic attacks. • Wanting someone to be nearby in case of an attack.
Specific phobia	• Becoming very fearful of something specific (storms, flying, dogs). • Attempting to avoid the feared object or situation. • Crying, clinging, trying to run away, or having sudden physical symptoms around feared object or situation.
Social anxiety disorder	• Having an intense fear of social or performance situations. • Believing one might be embarrassed in a social situation. • Appearing to be excessively shy. • Avoiding social situations with peers, talking with authority figures (teachers or group leaders), and speaking in public.

(Continued)

Figure 23.10 *(Continued)*

Type	Symptoms
Post-traumatic stress disorder (PTSD)	• Having directly witnessed a traumatic event or suffered because of it. (These events may be sudden, unexpected, or chronic, such as abuse.) • Showing intense fear and anxiety. • Becoming emotionally numb. • Withdrawing from people and activities. • Having flashbacks and nightmares. • Seeming tense (including sleep problems and being easy to startle).

Children with Childhood Schizophrenia

Childhood schizophrenia (also known as *pediatric schizophrenia, childhood-onset schizophrenia*, or *early-onset schizophrenia*) is one of the most serious social-emotional special needs children can experience. Although it is rare in children under seven years of age, it is usually more severe than adult-onset schizophrenia. Children with schizophrenia develop lags in motor and language skills and have poor school performance. Later, they have **hallucinations** (seeing, hearing, or smelling objects that seem real, but are not), **delusions** (beliefs that are not true), and deterioration of even basic self-care behaviors. They may also lack impulse control and thus become aggressive. Genetics and the environment both play a role in schizophrenia. Early identification and treatment by a psychiatrist improves the child's long-term outcome.

Children with Oppositional Defiant Disorder (ODD)

Some children with special needs have behavioral disorders. A **behavioral disorder** is a pattern of challenges that surfaces in a person's behavior. (Behavioral disorders are also called *conduct* or *disruptive disorders*.) Such disorders are often marked by extremes of behaviors. One such behavioral disorder is **oppositional defiant disorder (ODD)**, which involves *aggressive behaviors*, such as name-calling, fighting, and bullying without being provoked into such actions. These behaviors are common at times to most children, but for children with ODD, these behaviors gradually worsen rather than improve. ODD usually begins before eight years of age.

A professional identification is needed to recognize the difference between a child with sometimes difficult and challenging behavior and a child with ODD. Certain symptoms, such as those listed in **Figure 23.11**, are common identifiers. There is

Figure 23.11 Common Traits of Children with ODD

- Lose their temper, even over small situations.
- Argue with authority figures.
- Actively defy or refuse to comply with adults' requests or rules.
- Deliberately annoy others.
- Blame others for personal mistakes or misbehaviors.
- Are angry and resentful.
- Are aggressively spiteful.

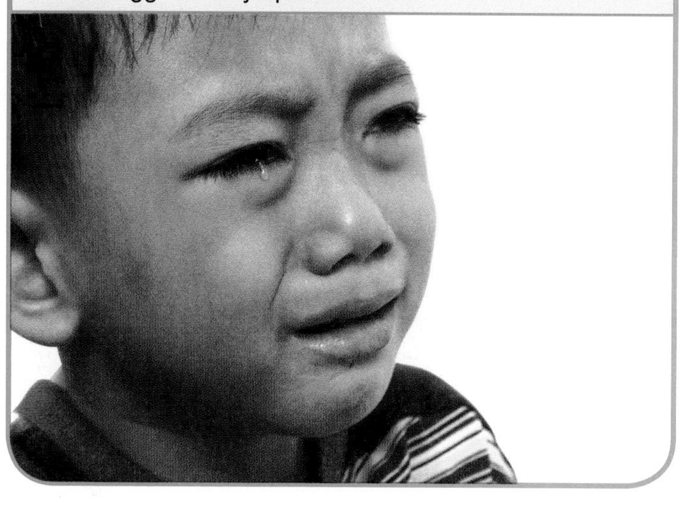

Mental Health Advisory

Children with mental health disorders may have difficulty leading fulfilling lives. Over half of untreated cases continue into the adult years. Early professional treatment helps prevent these problems from becoming more serious and difficult to treat effectively.

no known clear cause of ODD. ODD may have genetic components, such as gene mutations. Some environmental factors are also associated with ODD. These factors include

- abuse and neglect
- harsh or inconsistent discipline
- lack of positive parental involvement
- family instability
- depression and ADHD

Children with Other Types of Special Needs

While some special needs primarily affect one area of development, other special needs involve complex interactions between multiple areas of development. Special needs such as attention disorders and autism spectrum disorder (ASD) are some of the most difficult special needs to identify and treat.

Children with Attention Disorders

Children with attention disorders experience difficulty paying attention. People must use attention and memory to learn, retain information, and solve problems. To pay attention, a person has to focus one or more of the senses on a certain aspect of the environment and ignore irrelevant information. For example, to pay attention to music, a person must focus his or her senses on the music recording and ignore irrelevant sounds, such as humming fans.

Although all children can be distracted, some children are highly distractible. Until recently, attention disorders included *attention-deficit hyperactivity disorder (ADHD)* and *attention-deficit disorder (ADD)*. ADHD involved lack of attention, impulsivity, and *hyperactivity* (behavior that is extremely active beyond a child's normal energy level). ADD involved lack of attention, but did not include hyperactive behaviors. For this reason, ADD was sometimes called *hypoactivity disorder*.

Currently, experts identify only one attention disorder, **attention-deficit hyperactivity disorder (ADHD)**, which is classified into three types. These types are

- *inattentive type* (which was formerly known as *ADD*).
- *hyperactive/impulsive type* (formerly known as *ADHD*).
- *combined hyperactive/impulsive and inattentive type* (including characteristics of what was formerly known as ADD *and* what was formerly known as ADHD). This is the most common type of ADHD.

ADHD is difficult to identify. In children, identification is based on observation rather than on tests. ADHD has characteristics in common with childhood anxiety and depression, as well as some learning disorders. Common traits of children with ADHD are listed in **Figure 23.12**.

The causes of attention disorders are not yet clear. Brain studies show that children with attention disorders have brains with reduced regions for motor and some cognitive skills. Some experts think that attention disorders result from challenges in executive functions. Some environmental factors are associated with ADHD, including oxygen deprivation before birth and exposure to secondhand smoke and pesticides used on produce. Additional research is needed before more causes can be identified. Attention disorders are often identified in the school-age years by doctors and professionals.

Children with Autism Spectrum Disorder (ASD)

A number of children with special needs are children with *autism spectrum disorder (ASD)*. **Autism spectrum disorder (ASD)** is a general term used to describe complex communication, social,

Figure 23.12 Traits of Children with ADHD

Inattentive Type

- Seem to be inattentive; easily distracted; forgetful.
- Act disinterested ("tune-out") or daydream.
- Do not finish a task or play activity.
- Appear not to listen.
- Cannot organize work.

Hyperactive/Impulsive Type

- Seem to be inattentive; easily distracted; forgetful.
- Exhibit hyperactive behaviors.*
- Are fidgety; may constantly run, climb, or move in other ways; get out of their chairs or their places in group settings.
- Regularly change activities, often without completing them.
- Do incomplete and often disorganized work.
- Speak out of turn in class.
- Have difficulty waiting for their turns.
- Have frequent and intense emotional outbursts (fight, have self-imposed isolation, act defiant, respond strongly to criticism).
- Have difficulty coordinating movements and are prone to accidents.
- Have excessive REM activity in sleep.

Combined Hyperactive/Impulsive and Inattentive Type

- Have characteristics of both the inattentive and hyperactive/impulsive types.

*Hyperactivity is present in 75 percent of the cases involving attention disorders. Hyperactivity, however, is difficult to diagnose, especially in girls. For this reason, attention disorders seem to affect boys four to five times more often than girls.

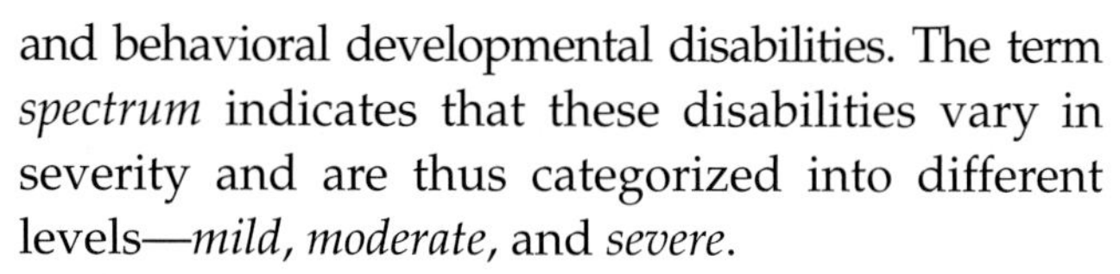

and behavioral developmental disabilities. The term *spectrum* indicates that these disabilities vary in severity and are thus categorized into different levels—*mild*, *moderate*, and *severe*.

Major indications of ASD include language, social, and behavioral challenges. Children with ASD often have other challenges associated with ASD, such as *sensory conditions* (inabilities to process and integrate sensory information), digestive conditions, sleep disturbances, seizures, and mental health disorders. At the same time, children with ASD often have exceptional strengths in some areas, such as in drawing, math, computers, music, or memory. There are no definitive medical tests that can be used to identify ASD. For the most part, a developmental pediatrician or a team of specialists identify ASD by the observation of signs and symptoms such as those listed in **Figure 23.13**.

Mental Health Advisory

According to the National Association of State Directors of Developmental Disabilities Services, one in three people with ASD are also diagnosed with a mental health disorder at some point in life.

Figure 23.13 Characteristics of Children with ASD

Social Interactions

- Do not respond to their names.
- Do not seem to hear others.
- Do not show interest in objects by 14 months.
- Do not play pretend games by 18 months.
- Appear disinterested in or unaware of others.
- Appear disinterested in activities around them.
- Do not know how to connect with adults or peers.
- Prefer not to be touched or cuddled.
- Do not play with toys creatively.
- Do not show interest in sharing with others.
- Cannot understand feelings of others.
- Want to be alone.

Verbal Communication

- Have unusual intonation patterns, such as a tone rise at the end of a statement.
- May repeat a question rather than answering it.
- Refer to self in third person.
- Find it difficult to communicate needs or wants; thus, may scream or grab.
- Repeat words and phrases over and over (called *echolalia*).
- Use incorrect words or grammar more frequently than children of the same age.
- Do not understand humor—take statements literally.
- Have delayed language development.
- Cannot initiate or sustain a conversation with others.
- Do not reflect feelings with tone of voice.

Nonverbal Communication

- Avoid eye contact.
- Do not understand others' body language.
- Use body language that does not correspond to what they are saying.
- Make few gestures or move stiffly.
- React inappropriately to sensory stimuli.
- May walk on tiptoes or in other unusual ways.

Mental Inflexibility

- Follow a rigid routine.
- Do not want change in their environment.
- Show attachments to strange objects, such as keys.
- Have narrow interests, such as reciting map facts or statistics.
- Obsessively arrange objects in a certain order even if the order is incorrect.
- Focus for a long time on moving objects, especially those with circular movements, such as a ceiling fan.
- Are upset by minor changes.
- Have preoccupations with parts of objects.

(Continued)

Figure 23.13 *(Continued)*

Self-Stimulating Behaviors*

- Rock body.
- Bang head.
- Spin in a circle.
- Tap ears.
- Stare at lights and turn light switches off and on.
- Spin objects.
- Open and close doors repeatedly without a typical purpose for the action.

*Self-stimulating behaviors are thought to be soothing to children with ASD.

The exact cause of ASD is not known. Research suggests that ASD may be caused by genetic factors as well as several environmental factors. ASD is associated with genetic mutations. However, many genes are involved in the development of ASD, making ASD very complex and difficult to analyze. Because so many genes are involved, researchers believe that there are many "autisms," not just one disorder.

Many environmental factors are associated with ASD, but these factors may or may not be **causal** (related to the cause). Some of these factors include close spacing between children, gestational diabetes, lack of folic acid supplements prior to pregnancy and during the first two stages of pregnancy, induced labor, and inflammation before birth. Recently, vaccines were ruled out as an environmental factor for ASD (**Figure 23.14**). Studies of potential environmental causes are just beginning.

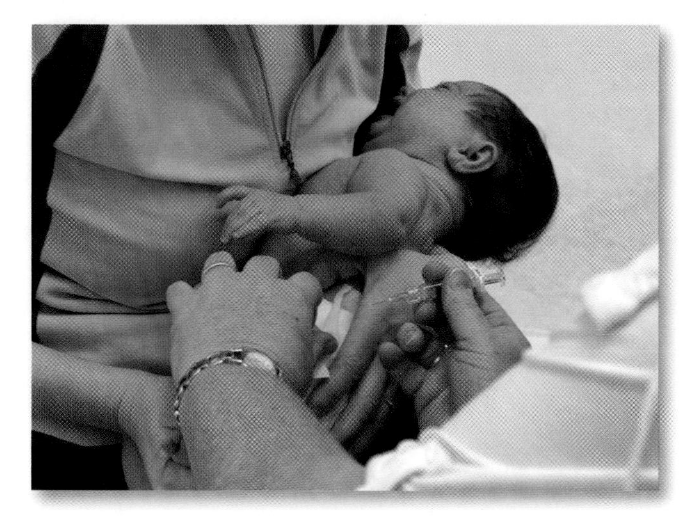

Figure 23.14 It was once thought that vaccines administered during early childhood were an environmental factor for children developing ASD. Recent research, however, has shown this not to be true. *Where could you go for reliable information about recent research concerning vaccines?*

Lesson 23.1 Review and Assessment 

1. List and explain in your own words two guidelines for discussing children with special needs.
2. What is a *physical disability* and what are four possible causes?
3. List three possible causes of intellectual disabilities.
4. Identify and define two common types of learning disorders.
5. What is an *anxiety disorder*?
6. Name three common identifiers for oppositional defiant disorder (ODD).
7. Autism spectrum disorder (ASD) is a general term used to describe complex ______ developmental disabilities.
8. **Critical thinking.** Choose one stage of development for children and review the physical, intellectual, and social-emotional developmental delays for that age range. Write your own case study in which a child experiences delays in at least one area of development.

Lesson 23.2 Help for Children with Special Needs

Key Terms

antidepressants
antipsychotics
Braille system
cognitive-behavioral therapy
Early Intervention Program for Infants and Toddlers with Disabilities
inclusion
Individualized Education Plan (IEP)
Individualized Family Service Plan (IFSP)
Individuals with Disabilities Education Act (IDEA)
mainstreaming
special education teachers

Academic Terms

baffle
curtailing
listlessness
psychosis

Objectives

After studying this lesson, you will be able to

- explain why children with and without special needs are more alike than different.
- summarize help for children with physical special needs, including children with physical disabilities and speech disorders.
- describe types of help available for children with intellectual disabilities, children with gifts and talents, and children with learning and language disorders.
- explain the types of help available for children with social-emotional special needs.
- identify help that is available for children with other types of special needs, including attention disorders and autism spectrum disorder (ASD).
- describe the three parts of the *Individuals with Disabilities Act (IDEA).*
- describe the role of support groups in helping families who have children with special needs.

Reading and Writing Activity

As you read the lesson, record any questions that come to mind. For each question, indicate where an answer might be found (such as in the text, in another book, on the Internet, or by asking a teacher). After reading, pursue the answers to your unanswered questions.

Graphic Organizer

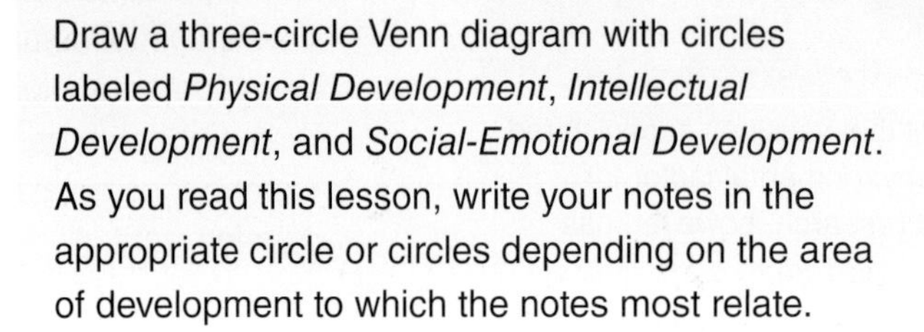

Draw a three-circle Venn diagram with circles labeled *Physical Development*, *Intellectual Development*, and *Social-Emotional Development*. As you read this lesson, write your notes in the appropriate circle or circles depending on the area of development to which the notes most relate.

An estimated 1 out of every 10 children has special needs. Some special needs are more common than others (**Figure 23.15**). Statistics are not exact because of variations in states' definitions of specific types of special needs. Also, many children have more than one special need.

Figure 23.15 Prevalence of Children with Special Needs

Type of Special Need	U.S. Prevalence Statistics
Children with Physical Disabilities	
Gross-Motor Conditions	
Cerebral Palsy	.23–.36%
Muscular Dystrophy	.01–.02%
Neural Tube Defect	.04%
Vision Conditions	.6–.7%
Hearing Conditions	.2–.3%
School-Age Children with Physical Disabilities and Health Concerns	.06%
Children with Speech and Language Disorders	24%
Children with Intellectual Disabilities	2–3%
Children with Gifts and Talents	3% with gifts; 13% with talents
Children with Learning Disorders	6–8%
Children with Anxiety Disorders	3%
Children with Depression	2.1%
Children with Childhood Schizophrenia	.0025%
Children with Oppositional Defiant Disorder (ODD)	2–16%
Children with Attention Disorders	9.5%
Children with Autism Spectrum Disorder (ASD)	1.5%

When considering the types of help that are needed for children with special needs, it is important to remember that *children are more alike than they are different*. All children have the same basic needs. They need physical care, intellectual stimulation, positive relationships with caregivers, and love. Help for children with special needs is based on the idea that, in addition to basic needs, children with special needs have additional needs that require different care. In addition to help for children's specific special needs, the government provides some services for the education and care of children with special needs. Lastly, help for children with special needs involves providing support for these children's families.

Help for Children with Physical Special Needs

Helping children with physical special needs involves providing resources for the child to function well among other children and teaching the child to use these resources. The types of resources provided depend on the type of physical special need. Different types of physical disabilities and speech disorders require different types of help.

Help for Children with Physical Disabilities

Help for children with physical disabilities varies depending on the child's type of disability. For example, *orthopedic surgeons* can perform surgery to correct conditions involving bone structure or muscles. *Physiotherapists* (therapists who treat injuries with exercises and other physical treatments) often coordinate therapy plans with orthopedic surgeons. They can also aid caregivers in learning how to safely assist a child (by lifting, positioning, and using special equipment).

Children with vision conditions can see *pediatric ophthalmologists*, doctors who specialize in eye treatment. Children with vision conditions can also use services and aids, such as special readers that magnify and light print to help them function daily. Children with legal blindness may be eligible to receive certain services. They might learn to use

Focus on

Speech

Early Identification

The first step in providing help for children with special needs is to *identify* the special needs of children. Children with special needs cannot get the help they need unless identification is made. Once a special need is identified, children with special needs should be given extra help or help that differs from that of most other children. According to brain development research, early identification and help make assistance more effective. Caregivers generally begin by seeking help from a pediatrician. Pediatricians can refer children for needed tests and can explain a child's condition to caregivers and discuss ways to help the child.

In small groups, research the importance of early identification for children with special needs. Also research the common challenges that pediatricians and parents face in identifying special needs. Then, as a group, write a speech to persuade classmates of this importance. Give a group presentation of your speech in class.

the **Braille system**, a system of raised dots enabling people with vision conditions to read by touch (**Figure 23.16**).

Audiologists, doctors who specialize in hearing, can provide help for children with hearing conditions. Children with hearing conditions might need a *cochlear implant* (electronic device that has an external part placed behind the ear and an implanted part under the skin) or hearing aids to help them hear and communicate. In cases in which the cochlear implant or hearing aids do not significantly help, children with hearing loss can use sign language to communicate with others.

Figure 23.16 The Braille system is a written system of raised dots that helps people with vision conditions read signs, papers, and books by touch. *Why do you think Braille is important for communities?*

Help for Children with Speech Disorders

Children with speech disorders need encouragement and sometimes therapy to communicate clearly. Some children need encouragement to speak more slowly. Children may also need to see speech therapists who will help them devise solutions to their communication challenges. In many cases, speech disorders resolve without assistance. For example, about 75 percent of children who stutter will stop on their own within one year.

Help for Children with Intellectual Special Needs

Helping children with intellectual special needs involves tailoring activities and tasks to the children's intellectual developmental level. This may include providing additional instruction, therapy, and modified activities.

Focus on

Careers

Special Education Teacher

Special education teachers work specifically with students who have special needs. They adapt school lessons to children's needs and teach a variety of subjects, such as writing and mathematics. They may also teach fundamental skills, such as communication skills and reading comprehension.

Career cluster: Education and training.

Education: Educational requirements include a relevant bachelor's degree and a state certification or license.

Job outlook: Future employment opportunities for special education teachers are expected to grow slower than the average for all occupations.

To learn more about a career as a special education teacher, visit the United States Department of Labor's *Occupational Outlook Handbook* website. You will also be able to compare the job responsibilities, educational requirements, job outlook, and average pay of special education teachers with similar occupations.

Help for Children with Intellectual Disabilities

The overall goal for helping children with intellectual disabilities is to develop their intellectual abilities to the fullest. As such, helping children with intellectual disabilities usually involves providing the children with additional, specialized instruction. Such help usually comes in the form of *special education teachers*. **Special education teachers** are teachers trained to work with children with special needs. In helping children with intellectual disabilities, they seek to teach and help these children grasp necessary information. They may also help assess children with intellectual disabilities. Special education teachers tend to work directly with parents and caregivers.

Help for Children with Gifts and Talents

Help for children with gifts and talents usually involves the placement of these children in groups of other children with gifts and talents. Children with gifts and talents who learn in typical classrooms may feel bored or distracted, act out, and not reach their full potential. As such, children with gifts and talents are helped by learning environments that include other children with gifts and talents and more rigorous standards in the child's area of accelerated intellectual development (**Figure 23.17**).

Some schools provide special curriculum programs for children with gifts and talents, and a few schools admit only children with gifts and talents. When schools do not have these programs, parents may often find extracurricular programs or private schools geared toward meeting these children's special needs.

Help for Children with Learning Disorders

Because learning disorders emerge as academic challenges, they are often identified in school settings. Identification of learning disorders is usually done by a psychologist, and early identification is most helpful. Once a learning disorder is identified, schools and teachers can take measures to meet children's special needs. Usually, these measures focus on helping the child build on his or her strengths and on developing ways to compensate for the child's areas of weakness. For example, if a child has dyslexia, he or she may have materials

Figure 23.17 Children with gifts and talents perform well in rigorous educational programs suited to their areas of giftedness or talent. *What schools for children with gifts and talents are in your community?*

read orally by someone else or be given spoken directions. Many experts on learning disorders believe these children can succeed if given a customized educational strategy.

Help for Children with Language Disorders

Children with language disorders may benefit from therapy to recover their use of language. Aphasia therapy works to restore language as much as possible. Therapy also aids children in using remaining language skills and learning other methods of communicating (drawings, gestures, writing, or technology) as a way "to talk." Treatment for aphasia usually begins with a *neurologist* (a doctor who treats brain conditions). Once the neurologist's work is completed, the child will work with a speech-language pathologist. Treatment usually continues for two or more years.

Help for Children with Social-Emotional Special Needs

Helping children with social-emotional needs usually involves some form of therapy. This therapy helps children sort through their social anxieties and emotions and develop ways to respond to social-emotional challenges. The type of help provided depends on the type of need.

Help for Children with Anxiety Disorders

Helping children with anxiety disorders who live in stressful life circumstances involves removing or shielding these children from these circumstances. Stressful life circumstances may include neglect, abuse, and a violent home or community.

For children with anxiety disorders who do not live in highly stressful environments, help involves regular appointments with a mental health specialist (**Figure 23.18**). Mental health specialists treat anxiety disorders using **cognitive-behavioral therapy**. This therapy teaches children to recognize their anxieties and develop coping strategies. Caregivers are included in the treatment and are taught how to reduce their children's anxieties and encourage them for their successes. Children with anxiety disorders benefit from having people who provide unconditional love and serve as "safety nets" (buffers). Help for many anxiety disorders is highly successful.

Help for Children with Depression

Children with depression can be helped by identification, therapy, and medications. Identification is perhaps the most important part of helping these children. Children with depression can go for years without their needs being identified due to fears of admitting their feelings of sadness and due to misconceptions about what depression is.

Once depression is identified, children can receive help in the form of therapy. Therapy will help children process their emotions and talk about

Figure 23.18 Children with anxiety disorders benefit from regular therapy with a mental health specialist. *Why is it important that therapy sessions be regular?*

possible roots of their feelings. Children with depression may be helped by **antidepressants**, which are medications used to correct the chemical imbalance in neurotransmitters, especially serotonin, in the brain and boost mood. While help will vary depending on the child, most psychologists recommend both therapy and medication for successfully helping children with depression.

Help for Children with Childhood Schizophrenia

Providing help for children with childhood schizophrenia will usually involve the intervention of a *psychiatrist* who will prescribe appropriate medications and organize a plan for therapy. Helping children with childhood schizophrenia usually involves administering **antipsychotics**, medications that reduce symptoms of psychosis (a serious mental state characterized by delusions). Helping these children also involves individual and family therapy, training for children in academic and social skills, and in severe cases, hospitalization (**Figure 23.19**).

Help for Children with ODD

Providing help for children with ODD usually involves both child and family therapy. During these therapy sessions, professionals teach children effective social skills. In addition, parents and caregivers are given strategies for more effective guidance. Therapy for children with ODD is usually long term.

Help for Children with Other Types of Special Needs

Special needs that affect multiple areas of development are some of the most difficult to identify. Providing help for these types of special needs can also be difficult. Helping children with special needs that affect multiple areas of development usually involves therapy and, at times, medications.

Help for Children with Attention Disorders

Children with attention disorders may need specific types of environmental and instructional changes to help them concentrate on tasks and stay

Figure 23.19 Hospitalization may be necessary to help a child with childhood schizophrenia. *How might hospitalization be helpful?*

Focus on

Science

Antidepressants and the Brain

Some studies show that depression in children and adults is linked to an imbalance in the levels of certain neurotransmitters in the brain. The brain is made up of many neurons, and as you may recall, neurotransmitters are chemicals that travel across neuron synapses. These neurotransmitters help transmit electrical signals. An imbalance of neurotransmitters possibly linked with depression includes *serotonin* (sir-uh-TOH-nun), *norepinephrine* (NOR-eh-puh-NEH-frun), and *dopamine* (DOH-puh-meen).

Antidepressants treat depression in several ways depending on the type of medication. The most common antidepressants prevent neurons from *reuptaking* (reabsorbing) neurotransmitters, especially serotonin. Preventing the uptake of serotonin changes its chemical balance, which seems to boost mood.

Antidepressants ease symptoms of moderate to severe depression in about 30 to 40 percent of people. Treatment-resistant depression, however, requires psychological therapy. Because brain chemistry is not fully understood, antidepressants are not considered the final answer to treating depression. For example, research is being conducted on the growth of new synapses and the generation and migration of new neurons as potentially causative of depression. Thus, before effective treatment of depression for all victims can occur, much more research will be needed.

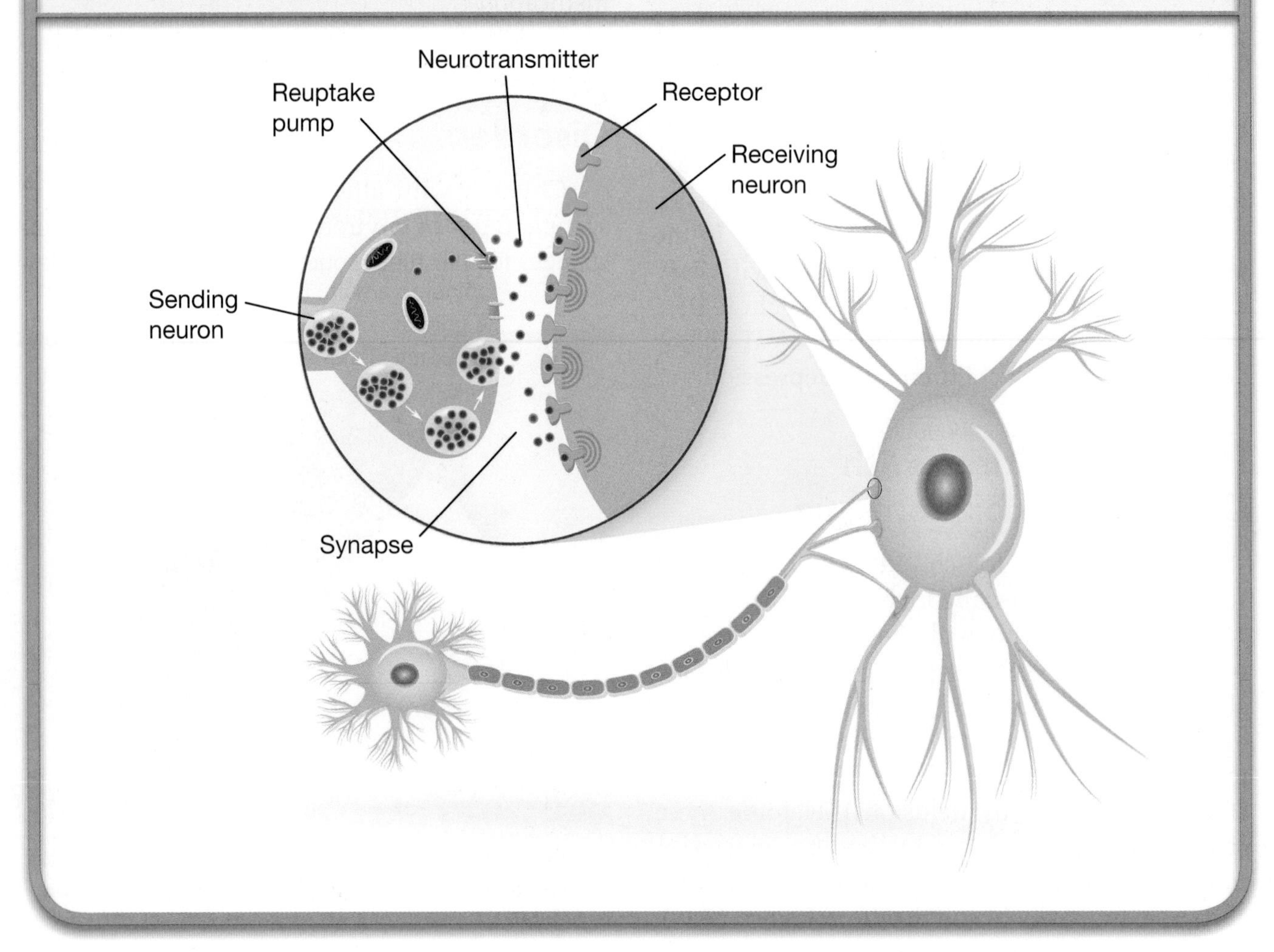

motivated. Some ways schools and teachers help these students include

- restricting stimuli (providing fewer items for children to see, hear, or touch) during times when children need to concentrate
- establishing and enforcing adherence to a routine
- giving short, clear instructions (**Figure 23.20**)
- using acknowledgement and rewards
- providing experiences that are challenging, but manageable
- offering physical activities while **curtailing** (reducing) overexcitement
- ensuring the child has a healthful diet

When carefully monitored by doctors, some children with attention disorders are helped by medications. Giving medication without careful observations has been criticized for several reasons, however. First, medications are often the first type of help offered. Second, these medications have side effects, such as slowing children's appetite and growth and causing sleeplessness, **listlessness** (low energy), and a stupor-like state. Third, frustrated adults may view these medications as a way to control high-energy children who do not have attention disorders.

Help for Children with ASD

Help for children with ASD is most successful when ASD is identified early and when children have a mild form of ASD. Children with ASD can be taught how to socially interact, recognize facial expressions for emotions, and use gestures. They can also learn how to regulate their emotions although learning these skills may require intensive behavioral therapy. With help, children with ASD can be fulfilled and manage their ASD throughout life.

Education and Services for Children with Special Needs

The United States government ensures that both education and appropriate services are available for children with special needs. To help meet children's special needs, the government has passed several acts and established a number of plans.

In 1990, the United States government passed the **Individuals with Disabilities Education Act (IDEA)**, a federal law governing the education of children with special needs. IDEA guarantees qualifying children with special needs the rights to receive free and appropriate public education (**Figure 23.21**).

Figure 23.20 Clear and concise instructions help children with attention disorders better grasp information. *What is an example of a clear and concise instruction?*

Figure 23.21 Under the provisions of IDEA, children with many types of special needs are guaranteed access to appropriate education. *What does it mean that IDEA guarantees* appropriate *education?*

Unless children with gifts and talents also have disabilities, disorders, or conditions, they do *not* qualify for help under IDEA. State and local funds are sometimes used to help these children develop their gifts and talents. On the whole, however, parents of children with gifts or talents are responsible for finding and financing services to meet their children's needs.

IDEA outlines ways for helping children with special needs and their families. IDEA includes three written documents that *outline* (specify; state clearly) required services for qualifying children with special needs.

Individualized Family Service Plan (IFSP)

The first document outlined by IDEA is the **Individualized Family Service Plan (IFSP)**. This plan guarantees that families can get the help they need for qualifying children with special needs from birth to three years of age. The IFSP focuses on the entire family's needs. The plan includes the formation of a team composed of parents or caregivers and experts from various agencies (such as from schools or social service agencies). One member of the team serves as a coordinator and ensures that the child and his or her parents receive all the services for which they are eligible under the IFSP. Usually, these services are administered near the family's home. An IFSP outlines the special caregiving skills parents and other caregivers need to perform to meet a child's special needs.

Individualized Education Plan (IEP)

The second document outlined by IDEA states that all qualifying children with special needs between 3 and 21 years of age are eligible to receive appropriate educational services. To receive these services, the child must be referred for testing, which requires parental consent (**Figure 23.22**). Based on testing results, an **Individualized Education Plan (IEP)**, which is tailored to the child's specific educational needs, is written. An IEP includes very specific goals for the child and a placement (typical class or special education class) agreement. The most common educational placement for children with special needs is **inclusion** (full-time placement in a regular classroom) rather than **mainstreaming** (a former term used for placing a child with special needs in a regular classroom for only part of the day). Together, parents, teachers, and school administrators design and implement the IEP. Parents also meet with their child's teachers on a regular basis. The child is retested routinely, and the plan is adjusted, as needed, to fit the child's changing educational needs and goals.

Figure 23.22 To be eligible for government services, children with special needs must undergo testing. This can sometimes be an obstacle for families because parents do not always want to give consent for this testing. *Why do you think some parents struggle with giving consent for their child to be tested?*

Early Childhood Education Programs for Children with Special Needs

As with schools and educational institutions, early childhood education programs are also evolving to practice inclusion for children with special needs. In early childhood education programs, *inclusion* involves placing children with special needs and other children in the same group while providing special help for the children who need it. In these programs, teachers and caregivers work in teams and collaborate with other adults who provide help for children with special needs.

Programs that enroll children with special needs do have some unique features. In inclusionary programs, rooms are arranged with children's special needs in mind. For example, some programs provide space for the easy movement of children with wheelchairs and walkers. Other programs may provide *adaptive equipment* (objects such as eating utensils or chairs that can be adjusted to accommodate children with special needs) or *assistive technology* (programs that help children with special needs use technology).

The staff in programs that enroll children with special needs use *teamwork* to plan activities. While all children work on many of the same concepts and skills, some activities must be adapted for children with special needs. For these activities, teachers enlist the help of adults who work with children with special needs. For example, while a child with a physical disability may not be able to do the same puzzle as some other children, the child could enjoy puzzle time with the other children by using a puzzle with fewer pieces or knobs attached to each piece. An adult who works with children with special needs might make this accommodation and suggest other appropriate accommodations.

Programs enrolling children with special needs also utilize many group activities. In group activities, many children can do all parts of an activity, and children with special needs can enjoy at least some parts. The nature of each child's needs determines specific tasks he or she can perform. For example, a child with a physical disability may not be able to squat or toss a beanbag, but he or she could learn a song. A child with a hearing condition could enjoy squatting and tossing the beanbag, even if he or she could not learn the song. By planning group activities, teachers can meet the needs of all children in the program.

Research Activity

Working with a partner, identify two early childhood education programs that enroll children with special needs. If possible, these programs should be local. Using reliable online resources, research the programs and take notes about types of accommodations the programs use to include children with special needs. If information is not available online, obtain needed information by visiting the program or interviewing the director or a teacher at the program site. Summarize your findings in a short essay.

Early Intervention Program for Infants and Toddlers with Disabilities

The third part outlined in IDEA, the **Early Intervention Program for Infants and Toddlers with Disabilities**, serves infants and toddlers (through two years of age) who have developmental delays or who have identified physical and intellectual conditions that will likely cause developmental delays. High-quality early intervention services prepare children to successfully transition to preschool and kindergarten.

Support Groups for Families of Children with Special Needs

Family members are often shocked when they first learn their child has special needs. Gifts or talents children possess may shock parents because the active minds or special talents of these children often **baffle** (confuse) adults. Children with disabilities may also baffle adults and cause them to feel stress. Caregivers may need some time to adjust and learn how to meet their child's special needs. Sometimes families face this adjustment when a child is born. Other times, a special need may not be identified until the school-age years. For still other parents, an accident or illness may cause a child to have a special need.

Members of families who have children with special needs often join support groups (**Figure 23.23**). At the national level, these groups provide family members with the latest information on children with special needs. National groups also seek money for research and assistance for families of children who need costly training or equipment. At the local level, groups support the goals of national groups. They also provide helpful contacts and services among those with similar needs.

Lesson 23.2 Review and Assessment 

1. What is the *Braille system* and how does it help children with vision conditions?
2. Identify the help needed for children with speech disorders.
3. What type of help is needed for children with gifts and talents?
4. Describe the help available for children with language disorders.
5. Explain the difference between *antidepressants* and *antipsychotics*.
6. List four ways schools and teachers can help children with attention disorders.
7. Identify and briefly define the three parts of the IDEA.
8. **Critical thinking.** What does it mean that *children are more alike than they are different*? How does this principle impact the ways adults help children with special needs?

Figure 23.23 Support groups provide relationships and education for families who have children with special needs. These groups might discuss common feelings or struggles and often refer families to helpful resources. ***What support groups for families of children with special needs are available in your community?***

Chapter 23 Review and Assessment

Summary

Children with special needs are children who differ from typical development in one or more ways. Special needs exist on a spectrum, and a child will be typical in all areas other than the area(s) of need. Some children have physical special needs, which are often identified by physical developmental delays. Types of physical special needs include physical disabilities (such as gross-motor conditions, hearing conditions, and vision conditions) and speech disorders. Children whose intellectual development differs from typical development have intellectual special needs. Intellectual special needs are often identified by intellectual developmental delays or accelerations. Types of intellectual special needs include intellectual disabilities, gifts and talents, learning disorders, and language disorders. Children who differ from typical development socially and emotionally have social-emotional special needs, which are identified by behavioral changes and by social-emotional developmental delays. These types of needs include anxiety disorders, depression, childhood schizophrenia, and ODD. Finally, some special needs affect many areas of development. These special needs include attention disorders and ASD.

Help for children with special needs hinges on the idea that children are more alike than they are different. Children with physical special needs may receive physical therapy and accommodations, such as adaptive equipment or correction devices. Intellectual special needs are met through additional services, such as special education teachers in classrooms, programs or schools for children with gifts and talents, and aid for children with learning disorders. Social-emotional special needs are met through therapy and some medications. Special needs involving multiple areas of development are some of the most difficult to meet, but help is available. Through a federal law, IDEA, the U.S. government funds and outlines three programs that provide for the identification of and services for children with special needs. Finally, support groups can help families struggling to meet children's special needs.

College and Career Portfolio

Portfolio Presentation Notes

As you prepare to present your portfolio, it is wise to prepare notes that you can quickly reference before or during the presentation. These notes will ensure that you do not forget anything important.

- Identify the highlights of your portfolio presentation. Verify these highlights with a teacher or college or career counselor.
- Create note cards or some other type of notes you can study or quickly reference in case you forget.

Chapter 23 Review and Assessment

Vocabulary Activities

1. Read the text passages that contain each of the following terms. Then write the definitions of each term in your own words. Double-check your definitions by rereading the text and using the text glossary.

Key Terms

antidepressants (23.2)
antipsychotics (23.2)
anxiety disorder (23.1)
attention-deficit hyperactivity disorder (ADHD) (23.1)
autism spectrum disorder (ASD) (23.1)
behavioral disorder (23.1)
Braille system (23.2)
cognitive-behavioral therapy (23.2)
developmental dyscalculia (23.1)
developmental dyslexia (23.1)
Early Intervention Program for Infants and Toddlers with Disabilities (23.2)
inclusion (23.2)
Individualized Education Plan (IEP) (23.2)
Individualized Family Service Plan (IFSP) (23.2)
Individuals with Disabilities Education Act (IDEA) (23.2)
intellectual disability (23.1)
intelligence quotient (IQ) test (23.1)
language disorder (23.1)
learning disorder (23.1)
mainstreaming (23.2)
oppositional defiant disorder (ODD) (23.1)
physical disability (23.1)
special education teachers (23.2)
speech disorder (23.1)
typical development (23.1)

2. Working in teams, create categories for the following terms and classify as many of the terms as possible. Then, share your team's ideas with the remainder of the class.

Academic Terms

baffle (23.2)
causal (23.1)
curtailing (23.2)
delusions (23.1)
hallucinations (23.1)
listlessness (23.2)
meningitis (23.1)
misfires (23.1)
paralysis (23.1)
psychomotor ability (23.1)
psychosis (23.2)

Critical Thinking

3. **Identify.** Draw the spectrum of special needs on a board or whiteboard and, as a class, brainstorm examples of specific types of special needs that fall in various places on the spectrum. Try to discuss an example of each special need covered in this chapter.
4. **Cause and effect.** While speech disorders and language disorders both affect children's communication abilities, the causes of these needs are different. Review this text's information about speech and language disorders and then read at least one reliable article about the causes of these disorders. Write a short essay comparing the causes of these needs.
5. **Draw conclusions.** Imagine a parent confides in you that her child is failing in school and she suspects the child may have an intellectual disability. You know the child is of average intelligence, so you doubt her assumption. To organize your thoughts, create a T-chart and list the characteristics of children with intellectual disabilities and children with learning disorders. Draw conclusions about how you would explain the difference to this parent.
6. **Compare and contrast.** In small groups, compare and contrast the traits of children with gifts and children with talents. Create two films in which you explain and demonstrate the characteristics of each special need. Also discuss traits of children with gifts *and* talents.
7. **Determine.** Working with a partner, discuss why depression and childhood schizophrenia are considered special needs. What qualities of special needs do they possess? If someone challenged the idea that these disorders were special needs, determine how you would explain your position.
8. **Analyze.** The way attention disorders are classified has changed since ADHD was first identified. In small groups, analyze why classifications for attention disorders changed as they did. What does the new classification achieve? How does the new classification affect the ways adults help children with attention disorders?
9. **Evaluate.** Imagine a local family with these three children: an infant who is legally blind, a preschooler who is gifted, and a school-age child who has ASD. Working with a partner, evaluate the

educational and other services that these three children and their parents are eligible to receive according to the programs under the federal law, IDEA. Research the next steps the family would need to take to obtain these services.

10. **Make inferences.** Learning that a child has special needs can be stressful for parents and caregivers, especially if parents did not foresee the need. Working with a partner, interview a parent whose child has a special need. How did the parent feel when his or her child's need was identified? What resources or support groups helped the parent?

Core Skills

11. **Technology.** In groups of four, review the physical, intellectual, and social-emotional developmental delays for infants, toddlers, preschoolers, and school-age children. Assign each group member one stage of development and study the developmental delays in detail. For each delay, write a real-life example and one way the delay could be identified. Then, as a group, combine your projects into a comprehensive digital presentation outlining examples and methods for identifying developmental delays. Deliver your presentation to the class and then lead a discussion about ways to optimize the development of children with these delays.
12. **Reading and speaking.** Visit a local library or search online to find articles or books describing types of physical disabilities. Choose one article or book and skim the material. Identify two types of physical disabilities not covered in this text and write a short summary of each, including the characteristics, causes, and treatments for each disability. Present the information orally to the class.
13. **Research and technology.** Techniques for identifying intellectual disabilities have changed over the years to rely less on IQ tests. Using reliable online or print resources, research the role of IQ tests in identifying intellectual disabilities and the most current methods for identification. Read at least three scholarly sources and compile them into a bibliography. Finally, present your findings in a slideshow presentation to the class.
14. **Reading and listening.** Visit the National Institute of Mental Health's website and read more about the causes, identification, and treatment for ASD. As you are reading, write questions you have about the material on the website. Then, arrange an interview with a special education teacher or other adult who works with children who have ASD. Ask questions and discuss your notes to increase your understanding of ASD.
15. **Research and writing.** Legislation and public policies for children with special needs have changed as new special needs and practices have developed. Using reliable online or print resources, research historical legislation, policies, or practices for educating and caring for children with special needs. Conduct research covering at least two historical periods and then write a three-page essay comparing historical practices to current policy.
16. **CTE Career Readiness Practice.** Imagine you are a crisis child care worker in a low-income area of the U.S. Many families in your area have children with special needs, but are not always aware of or able to access needed services. To help these families, research federal and state resources for low-income families who have children with special needs. How can families access government services? What other services are available for them? Create a professional-looking pamphlet including these services and their contact information. Working with a partner, practice walking a parent through the pamphlet.

Observations

17. In small groups, find and watch a documentary about the life of a person with a special need. During the documentary, take notes about the person's feelings toward the special need and how the person's needs were met. Afterward, discuss the documentary in your group.
18. As a class, visit an early childhood education program or classroom that has children with special needs. Observe how, if at all, the classroom or program accommodates children with special needs (such as: makes environmental changes; has special education teachers available; makes curriculum changes for those with differing needs). How are the children's needs being met?

Chapter 24 Providing Early Childhood Education in Group Settings

Essential Question

What are the types of early childhood education programs, and what are the indicators of high quality in these programs?

Lesson 24.1 **Early Childhood Education Programs**

Lesson 24.2 **Choosing an Early Childhood Education Program**

Case Study How Do Early Learning Standards Impact Preschool Programs?

As a class, read the case study and discuss the questions that follow. After you finish studying the chapter, discuss this case study again. Have your opinions changed based on what you learned?

When Martin's state announced the adoption of new early learning standards, Martin was worried about the effect on his career as a preschool teacher. At his preschool's first meeting about the standards, Martin noticed that other teachers were also concerned. No one wanted to lose their current preschool program and the developmentally appropriate practices (DAPs) they had worked so hard to implement.

As the meeting began, the preschool director distributed the new learning standards, listened to the teachers' comments, and explained that she understood their concerns. "The new learning standards should be viewed as an *outline* of possible learning content," she said. "It is up to us, as teachers, to *embed* the learning standards into quality learning experiences based on DAPs. Unlike standards that focus primarily on language arts, literacy, and mathematics, early learning standards focus on *all* domains of child development. Over the next few days, let us take one standard daily and talk about how our current learning activities are already meeting this standard."

Martin said, "Many parents do not seem to understand our use of DAPs. How can we help parents see the values of our approach?"

"That is a good question," the director said. "As we review these standards, let us consider how we might share our thinking with parents."

Give It Some Thought

1. Why are DAPs important when helping children meet standards in preschool programs?
2. What would happen if teachers taught content without adapting it to children's needs?

While studying this chapter, look for the online resources icon  to:

- **Practice** terms with e-flash cards and interactive games
- **Assess** what you learn by completing self-assessment quizzes
- **Expand** knowledge with interactive activities and graphic organizers

www.g-wlearning.com/childdevelopment

Study on the go

Use a mobile device to practice terms and review with self-assessment quizzes.

www.m.g-wlearning.com/0384

Lesson 24.1 Early Childhood Education Programs

Key Terms

center-based child care
child care programs
child care resources and referral (CCR&R) agencies
child development laboratories
early childhood education programs
family child care
fingerplays
for-profit programs
Head Start
in-home child care
kindergartens
Montessori schools
not-for-profit programs
preschool programs
preschools
private programs
public programs
school-age child care (SACC) programs
universal preschool programs
work-related child care programs

Academic Terms

franchises
national chains
parochial

Objectives

After studying this lesson, you will be able to

- compare the four types of child care programs.
- identify qualities unique to child development laboratories.
- explain the purposes of Head Start.
- describe characteristics of preschool programs.
- explain how Montessori schools differ from most other early childhood education programs.
- contrast early kindergartens with today's kindergartens.
- describe the importance of primary school programs.
- identify three trends in early childhood education programs.

Reading and Writing Activity

Read this lesson with a classmate. After you read each section independently, stop and tell each other the main points given in the section. Repeat this process for each section until you finish the lesson.

Graphic Organizer

For each type of early childhood education program discussed in this lesson, draw a picture that you think represents the type of program. As you read the lesson, take notes in and around the picture.

As children grow and develop, they will likely participate in an early childhood education program. **Early childhood education programs** are child care and education arrangements. These programs may be informal arrangements (such as in-home care and family care programs) or formal arrangements (such as center-based child care and preschools). Formal arrangements are more likely than informal arrangements to have a planned educational program in addition to care.

Many types of early childhood education programs exist, and types vary depending on the ages of the children participating, the children's developmental levels, and parents' preferences. Over the past few decades, the numbers of early childhood education programs have increased. The landscape of early childhood education programs continues to shift as new trends shape child care and education practices and programs.

Figure 24.1 Early childhood education programs vary from those that only care for basic needs to those that provide many special activities to enhance all areas of development. *Which local early childhood education programs are you familiar with?*

Types of Early Childhood Education Programs

There are many types of early childhood education programs, but all are either public or private in sponsorship. **Public programs** are early childhood education programs funded by local, state, or federal governments. **Private programs** are early childhood education programs owned by individuals and religious or other nongovernment groups. Whether public or private, types of early childhood education programs cater to families with varying needs. Some types of early childhood education programs include child care programs, child development laboratories, Head Start programs, preschool (prekindergarten) programs, Montessori schools, kindergartens, and primary school programs (**Figure 24.1**). These programs differ in several ways.

Child Care Programs

Child care programs refer to programs that provide care for children for extended hours, usually between 9 and 12 hours a day. The main purpose of child care programs is to provide *custodial care* (basic care) for children when parents or guardians are not available. Most child care programs also provide education for children from infancy through the preschool years. They may even serve school-age children at times when school is not in session.

There are four main types of child care programs—*in-home child care*, *family child care*, *center-based child care*, and *school-age child care*. Some caregivers use combinations of these arrangements, such as a center-based child care program for work hours and family child care for other hours. The type of care parents choose depends on many factors, including the number and ages of children, costs of care, family goals for children, locations of employment, work hours, and types of child care locally available. No one type of child care program is best for every family; each type has its advantages and disadvantages.

In-Home Child Care

In-home child care takes place in the child's own home. In these arrangements, parents can likely be assured that children receive all of a caregiver's attention. These children stay in a home atmosphere during care and can be cared for even if they are ill. While these child care programs provide limited education for children, they can be convenient and assuring for parents of young children.

In-home care can be provided by parents, relatives, or nonrelatives. Care by a parent may involve one parent staying home to care for the children. In families in which both parents work, parents may provide this type of care by working alternate schedules so one parent is always home or working from home. In-home care by a parent is more common for infants and toddlers than for preschoolers. *Homeschooling*, in which parents educate their children in the home, is also a type of in-home child care. Some homeschooling arrangements include several families.

Besides in-home care by a parent, in-home care by a relative is very common. For this type of care, parents may ask grandparents, aunts or uncles, cousins, or older siblings to care for children. This type of in-home child care is convenient for parents whose families live nearby or are available to care for children.

Only a small percentage of children have care provided by nonrelatives in the home. For the most part, nonrelative caregivers in the home are *housekeepers*, *au pairs* (oh PERS), or *nannies* (**Figure 24.2**).

Family Child Care

Family child care is care provided by a person for a small number of children in his or her own home. Some family child care homes are operated by people wanting a little business in their home. Other family child care homes are run by a parent of young children. The parent stays home with his or her own children and provides care for other children, too. Child care laws vary among the states, but most family child care homes serve a maximum of six or seven children, including the caregiver's own children. If any child is under two years of age, the maximum number of children served is often four or five.

The type of children's activities in family child care varies greatly. Some child care homes are run much like child care centers. For example, these homes might offer a structured schedule, meals and snacks, and activities. Many family child care homes follow less rigid schedules than child care centers. Children in family child care may do homelike activities, such as helping the caregiver do housekeeping tasks, visiting with friends who come to

Figure 24.2 In-Home Child Care by Nonrelatives

Nonrelative Caregivers	Characteristics
Housekeepers	• Often employed on an hourly basis • Take care of children as well as clean the house • Usually not hired specifically to care for children
Au pairs	• Provide child care for a host family as part of a cultural exchange program • Receive room, board, cultural experiences, and transportation from the host family for services • Often have limited child care knowledge and experience
Nannies	• Are professionals who contract with a family to provide in-home child care • Typically care for children from birth through 10 or 12 years of age • May live in a family's home or come to the home daily, but do not do housework beyond preparing meals for the children • Often have training beyond high school in early childhood education, health and safety, and nutrition • May be certified as *Certified Household Managers*, *Certified Professional Nannies*, or *Certified Professional Governesses* • Often earn more than housekeepers or au pairs

the home, and even going on shopping trips as well as playing with toys.

Many parents rely on family child care arrangements because they need more flexible hours than those often provided by other child care programs. Other families need family child care because other child care programs may not be available in their communities. Furthermore, many parents want family child care because they see this arrangement as similar to the type of care they would provide if not employed, but other parents see the program more like that of a small child care center. Other advantages of family child care programs are listed in **Figure 24.3**.

Family child care homes may be regulated or unregulated. *Regulated family child care homes* are homes that have reported their business to the state and have a state license or certification of registration to operate. In this type of home, parents can be assured of at least a minimum standard of quality. Due to the many advantages of family child care, the military and some large corporations are seeking ways to increase the number of regulated family child care homes for their employees' children.

Unregulated family child care homes are homes that do *not* report their business to the state. Therefore, they do not have a state license or certificate of registration to operate. If the state is unaware of a family child care home, it cannot regulate the care provided there. Some of these unregulated homes have too many children or do not provide safe care. Caregivers in these homes may not have had a criminal background check. Because parents cannot be certain of the quality of care provided in these homes, it is recommended that parents only enroll their children in regulated family child care homes.

Center-Based Child Care

Center-based child care is group child care provided in a center (not a home). For the most part, center-based child care serves parents who are full-time employees, but other at-home parents may also enroll their children for the benefits of

Figure 24.3 Advantages of Family Child Care

Type of Children	Advantages
Infants and toddlers	Using family child care for infants and toddlers is often much less expensive than using center-based child care. Also, infants and toddlers need much individual attention, which may be available in a family child care home.
Preschool children prone to aggression and tantrums	Using center-based child care seems to put preschool children with social-emotional challenges at an even higher risk. Family child care lowers this risk.
Children who are prone to mild illnesses, such as colds, sore throats, and ear infections	Pediatricians often advise parents of these children to limit the children's contact with large groups of children. Because family child care homes have fewer children, these may be a better choice than center-based child care.
Children who need part-time or flexible-schedule care	Part-time or flexible-schedule care is more often available in family child care homes than in center-based child care. Centers try to maximize their profits by filling as many placements as they can with children who need full-time care. Some centers charge the same rate for part- and full-time care, while many family child care providers charge a reduced rate for part-time care.
School-age children	Most center-based child care programs are designed for young children. These programs may not meet the needs of children who are school-age. Furthermore, many older children only need part-time care.
Children who live in rural areas	Many rural areas do not have much selection in center-based child care. In these areas, many more children attend family child care homes than centers.

the program. Sometimes, child care centers are called **preschools** because they serve preschool-age children. (The term *preschool program* refers to another type of program.)

Child care centers differ in the number of children they serve. Many centers serve 20 or fewer children who are cared for in a building with one or two large rooms. Others enroll several hundred children who are grouped by age and placed in classrooms with each group under the care of one teacher and an assistant teacher. Large centers are multiroom buildings resembling a school.

State licensing laws set the standards for all aspects of center-based child care programs (such as staff qualifications, numbers of children per teacher, building and outside requirements, food services, and basic program activities). Program activities can vary a great deal, but most programs have basic play areas, such as book, block building, dramatic play, art, science, and computer centers for play. Most groups have activities, too, such as story time, group games, music, and field trips. Due to the number of children and the emphasis on socialization of children, caregivers emphasize cooperative play and social living (**Figure 24.4**).

Figure 24.4 Center-based child care can have positive effects on children's social and collaboration skills. *What types of collaborative activities might take place in a child care center?*

There are many advantages to center-based child care. Large centers are often open long hours, which meet the needs of many working parents. They all have programs for preschool children, and some have programs for infants and toddlers,

Focus on

Health

Center-Based Child Care Reduces Risk of Child Neglect and Abuse

Center-based child care programs play a part in reducing risks of child neglect and abuse. These programs can be a service to at-risk families and can be a source of information for parents and caregivers who do not understand the development and needs of their children. Center-based child care programs reduce the risks of child neglect and abuse by

- providing caregivers with social connections to other caregivers (thus reducing feelings of isolation)
- providing knowledge about parenting, child development, and developmentally appropriate behaviors
- sharing guidance and discipline strategies with knowledge about the behaviors of children
- caring for children several hours a day and allowing parents or caregivers respite from full-time child care

too. Thus, children can stay in the same center for several years, and often siblings can be at the same center, too. Center-based child care programs must be licensed, ensuring the basic minimum quality of care. Many parents like the activities and equipment provided for children in these programs. Some programs also provide helpful special services, such as transportation for children and special classes, such as dance.

There are two basic types of center-based program ownership/sponsorship. These include the following:

- *for-profit programs.* Most center-based child care programs are **for-profit programs**, meaning they are set up to make money and run as businesses. These centers are owned either by individuals or corporations. Other for-profit center-based programs are *national chains* and *franchises*. **National chains** are a group of businesses owned by one company. **Franchises** are a group of businesses originally owned by a corporation and sold to different owners. These owners use the same name, building design and equipment, and often provide the same services. Franchise owners also receive business advice from the franchiser. Because child care is labor intensive and for-profit centers are businesses, these centers are often very expensive and thus not affordable for all families.
- *not-for-profit programs.* Other center-based programs are **not-for-profit programs** (also called *nonprofit programs*). A not-for-profit center's income only covers current costs and the surplus needed to keep the center operating on an ongoing basis or to expand services. Most not-for-profit programs are sponsored and partially funded by religious or service groups, businesses, hospitals, branches of the armed services, or colleges. Not-for-profit programs sponsored by businesses for their employees' children are called **work-related child care programs** and are an employee benefit. A few not-for-profit programs are *cooperatives* (co-ops) funded by families of enrolled children. In co-ops, parents offer their time and services to help keep costs low. Because fee income is not generated for making a profit and sponsors partially pay for the programs, not-for-profit programs are less expensive for parents than for-profit ones.

School-Age Child Care

School-age child care (SACC) programs, also known as *before- and after-school programs* or *out-of-school programs*, provide child care for children between 5 and 14 years of age. These programs provide care when school is not in session, including before and after school, on school holidays or vacations, and during the summer. The majority of households with school-age children have working parents, and a typical school day is shorter than the standard workday. Many families prefer to find part-time care for these times rather than leave their children in self-care. Because part-time care can be difficult to find, however, quality SACC programs are needed and important to communities (**Figure 24.5**).

Figure 24.5 SACC programs benefit children, families, and communities. If a SACC program or youth program is not available, parents can advocate for programs in their area. *What SACC programs are available in your community?*

Children in Self-Care

Many children in the United States do not attend early childhood education programs. Instead, they care for themselves while parents or other caregivers are not available. These children are known as *children in self-care*.

In many states, there are laws about the age at which children can legally be left in self-care. These laws vary, but the legal age is often around 12 years of age. In addition to the child's age, the success of self-care is dependent on several other factors. These include the child's maturity, the safety of the home and the neighborhood, and the child's feelings about self-care.

Successful self-care also depends on how well parents prepare their children. Children who are left in self-care need to learn effective self-care skills from their parents or other adults in their lives. To prepare children for self-care, parents and other caregivers can do the following:

- Make sure the child learns safety rules, such as those shown in the *Rules for Safe Self-Care* chart.
- Ensure that children communicate where they are, what they are doing, and whom they are with.
- Set rules for children about using appliances, digital media devices, power tools, and other equipment. Other rules may involve having friends over and leaving the house.
- Establish a routine for children to follow.
- Begin self-care gradually, if possible. Start with a short period when the child stays alone as the parent does a quick, nearby errand or visits briefly with a neighbor. As the child shows confidence, parents can gradually increase the time to cover the amount of time between school and the parents' arrival home.

Rules for Safe Self-Care

- Keep house keys with you at all times.
- If walking home from school, walk with friends; come straight home unless other plans are first approved by parent.
- Call parent upon arrival.
- Do not enter the house if a door is open or a window is broken.
- Tell parents if anything or anyone frightens you.
- Call 911 in case of emergency and know how to give address and directions to your house.
- Practice what to do while waiting for emergency responders. (For example, in the case of fire, evacuate house, call 911, and wait at a designated place for emergency responders.)
- Upon entering the house, use locks and set alarm system if you have one.
- Never open the door at home, but instead talk through the door.
- Answer phone calls because it may be a parent calling.
- Never tell people at the door or over the phone that you are home alone.
- Arrange an emergency evacuation plan.

Research Activity

In small groups, use reliable online or print resources to research the positive and negative effects of self-care on children, families, and communities. After researching, discuss your findings in your group. Share the highlights from your discussion with the class.

SACC programs have many advantages. These programs ensure the safety and health of children who might otherwise be in self-care. Programs often have a wide variety of activities from which children may choose. In some SACC programs called *clubs*, parents choose from a menu of activities for their children. Most SACC programs provide

- care (protection, shelter, food, and guidance)
- recreation (supervised play or specific skill development activities, such as dance, ball games, or swimming)
- diversion (crafts, drama, or field trips)
- education (such as help with homework or lessons in music or dance)

The majority of SACC programs are affiliated with schools or agencies that serve youth. In schools, SACC programs are often operated by nonschool sponsors, such as the YMCA. Other groups that operate SACC programs include religious groups, park and recreation facilities, housing authorities, military bases, family child care homes, child care centers, and companies.

As is true of all types of child care, parents may have trouble finding quality SACC programs and affording the costs for quality. For providers, the challenges of running an SACC program include finding suitable housing for a part-time program and planning details if space must be shared with other programs.

Child Development Laboratories

Child development laboratories, formerly called *nursery schools*, provide education and physical care for children who are under five years of age. Besides providing care services, these programs serve as child development research sites. They also offer training opportunities for adults in child-related careers. To enroll children in child development laboratories, parents must sign a release that allows the child to be part of all research studies being conducted and to be under the care and guidance of adults in child care and education training. Parents are guaranteed that observations and reports used for research or training purposes will follow ethical guidelines. Parents also get detailed oral and written reports about their child's development.

Child development laboratories first appeared in England in the early 1900s with the objective of

Focus on Careers

Child Development Professor

Child development professors are *postsecondary teachers*, meaning they teach at colleges, universities, and other professional schools. Many child development laboratories are run by these professors, who conduct research and teach classes to students. Child development professors are considered to be experts in their field.

Career cluster: Education and training.

Education: Educational requirements include a related master's degree or Ph.D. depending on the college or university.

Job outlook: Future employment opportunities for postsecondary teachers are expected to grow faster than the average for all occupations.

To learn more about a career as a child development professor, visit the United States Department of Labor's *Occupational Outlook Handbook* website. You will also be able to compare the job responsibilities, educational requirements, job outlook, and average pay of child development professors with similar occupations.

helping needy children. When child development laboratories first opened in the United States, child development was becoming a science. These child care programs opened as laboratory schools directed by staff members associated with research and teaching hospitals and colleges. Soon, the programs began to study children and train parents and teachers to care for and teach children.

Today, many child development laboratories are still part of research and teaching universities. These programs operate in some high schools, too. These high-quality programs employ university-associated child development professionals who oversee adults' research and teaching. The director and staff members of the children's program plan children's activities and establish a play setting that is rich with materials, equipment, other children, and teachers who are caring and well trained. Regrettably, due to the costs of these programs, several well-known programs have closed during recent years.

Figure 24.6 Children in Head Start programs may be in need of food and medical care and may need additional help in learning important concepts and language skills. *Why is meeting children's basic needs so important to learning?*

Head Start Programs

In the 1960s, Americans became concerned with the effects of poverty on young children. Studies had shown how important the early years were to a child's development. Americans wanted to help children living in poverty have quality experiences that were vital to their development. Therefore, in 1965, the federal government launched **Head Start**, a program for three- and four-year-old children from low-income families (**Figure 24.6**). As Head Start researchers realized that quality experiences for infants and toddlers were also critical for all later development, they launched the *Early Head Start program* in 1995 to serve children from birth through 35 months of age.

Today, the Office of Head Start provides grants to local public and private not-for-profit agencies to provide educational, health, nutritional, social, and other services to children and their low-income families. Parents and families play a key part in planning and operating local Head Start programs. Head Start often helps these parents progress toward their educational, literacy, and employment goals.

Head Start programs can have long-term benefits for children when the programs are of good quality and when families and schools follow through on children's basic goals. Overall, children from quality Head Start programs achieve greater school success and higher high school graduation rates than their peers from similar backgrounds. Head Start graduates also show better social behaviors as adults, including acting more responsibly in family, work, and community settings. Experience with Head Start has helped researchers learn more about how to meet the needs of children from low-income families. This research is being applied toward new Head Start goals, such as involving low-income fathers, and toward other early childhood education programs, such as preschool programs.

Preschool Programs

Preschool programs, also called *prekindergartens*, refer to state-financed programs for three- and four-year-olds from low-income families. The majority of preschool programs operate in public school settings, but some programs are affiliated with local Head Start programs. A few operate as research laboratories at universities. Some private center-based programs call their programs for three- and four-year-olds *preschools*, but often these are child care programs. A few states offer **universal preschool programs** (state-financed preschool programs for children from families of all income levels), and other states may soon follow as funding becomes available.

Because Head Start and state-funded preschool programs basically serve the same population of children and have many of the same program goals, many professionals believe that these two programs should be combined to form a national prekindergarten initiative. Unlike Head Start programs, however, preschool programs tend to offer fewer supportive services, such as medical and social services.

Research on the best curricula for children from low-income families has been an ongoing effort by professionals involved in laboratory-based and other select preschool programs. Three preschool curricula showing some of the best results are: High Scope®, Reggio Emilia, and Montessori. Most other preschool programs use their states' learning standards (as described in Lesson 24.2).

Figure 24.7 In Montessori classrooms, children learn through their own explorations of materials and ideas. ***How might the Montessori approach be beneficial to young children?***

Montessori Schools

Another type of early childhood education program is a Montessori school. These schools are based on the educational theory and practice of Maria Montessori, an Italian medical doctor. She began her work as an educator serving children with disabilities and later children from impoverished homes. Montessori's methods came to the United States in the 1950s. Today's Montessori early childhood classrooms include children beginning at 30 to 36 months of age through the preschool years. These children are not separated by age, grade, or level. Rather, they are free to move about the classroom, work with other children, and use any materials they understand (**Figure 24.7**). Montessori programs are also available for school-age children.

The primary principle of **Montessori schools** is that young children should learn independently through the use of highly specialized materials rather than through direct input from teachers. These materials, which are called *self-correcting materials* (such as puzzles that work only one way), aid children's independent work. Teachers trained in Montessori methods, called *directors* or *directresses*, guide (direct) children's use of materials, but they do *not* use direct teaching. In this way, Montessori schools strive to put each child more in charge of his or her own learning. Other Montessori education principles include an emphasis on work for work's sake. Therefore, play is not part of the Montessori program. For example, children prepare foods to eat rather than pretend-play food preparation and eating. Montessori programs operate on the belief that children absorb and learn from their world as they work at common tasks.

Montessori school curriculum begins with sensory learning involving specialized materials. Learning from these materials is the major focus of the early childhood Montessori curriculum. These materials work to refine the sensory perceptions for all senses beyond what is typical in other early childhood curricula. For example, children learn to recognize small differences in shades of colors rather than just the typical eight colors seen in crayon boxes. Materials are designed to teach math and literacy concepts, too. Thus, the curriculum moves the child from sensorimotor learning to some logical concept learning (math and literacy) during the early childhood program.

Another curricular goal is for children to develop self-help skills. Children work to learn grooming techniques (handwashing, handling clothes fasteners), household chores (pouring liquids, cutting foods, washing dishes, scrubbing tables, and cleaning the floor), and gardening. All of these activities are real, not play.

Kindergartens

Kindergartens are early childhood education programs for four- and five-year-old children. In the United States, kindergartens are part of each state's public education system although many private schools offer kindergarten, too.

Friedrich Froebel chose the name *kindergarten* (German for *children's garden*) because he thought children needed nurturing like plants. Froebel felt a school for young children should be different from the "harsh" academic (3R) schools typical for older children of his day.

Unlike Montessori, Froebel felt that play was the "highest level of child development." Children learned through an activity-oriented curriculum that was teacher-directed. The major emphasis of the curriculum was art and math activities. He developed many of the play activities that occur in today's kindergartens and other programs for young children. Examples include block building, stringing beads, drawing and paper folding, sand play, nature walks, gardening, animal care, stories, and music (**Figure 24.8**). Froebel also wrote **fingerplays** (poems and rhymes acted out with the hands) that taught moral lessons to children.

Due to today's academic focus, kindergartens are seen as an entrance to primary school education. While play is still used as the means for some kindergarten learning activities, current kindergarten programs tend to be more like first-grade classrooms with emphases on reading, writing, and arithmetic. Many professionals question the effectiveness and appropriateness of this "pushed-down" curriculum.

Figure 24.8 Froebel's emphasis on play set his activities apart from the drill methods used in other schools of Froebel's time. In fact, Froebel's statement that "play is the highest level of child development" was scorned by many of his contemporaries. ***Why do you think some parents still question the importance of play for young children?***

Primary School Programs

Because the early childhood years do not end until children are nine years of age, primary school programs are an important part of the education setting for young children. The United States has long mandated school attendance for primary school children. These children may attend private schools—which include **parochial** (puh-ROH-kee-ul), religious, schools—or public schools.

Educational standards used in primary school programs are relatively consistent throughout the nation. Children in all primary school programs continue to learn reading, writing, and arithmetic, as well as concepts in science and social studies. Many primary schools offer music, art, computer literacy, and physical education as parts of their programs, too.

Trends in Early Childhood Education Programs

Early childhood education programs have not always been common. For the last three decades, however, the numbers of these programs have been rapidly growing. This growth is partly due to the increasing numbers of parents in the workforce. It is also due to society's greater understanding about the benefits of early childhood education programs and the need for children's quality education.

As early childhood education programs grow and expand, new trends shape and will continue to shape the types of programs available. Current trends of early childhood education programs include the following:

- *Growth in infant and toddler programs.* The majority of working mothers return to their jobs within an infant's first year. Despite the growth in programs for infants and toddlers, these programs are still difficult to find and are often very expensive, making them unaffordable for many families.
- *Growth in school-age child care (SACC) programs.* Most SACC programs are in urban and suburban areas and serve children mainly in grades three and below. More programs are needed, especially programs with activities that interest older children.
- *Growth in work-related child care programs.* Some businesses, especially those employing many women and military personnel, provide work-related child care programs for their employees. Many other businesses promote the growth of child care programs within their communities and pay some child care costs.
- *Growth in child care resource and referral (CCR&R) agencies.* **Child care resources and referral (CCR&R) agencies** promote local early childhood education programs and help parents identify child care options (**Figure 24.9**). These agencies are funded by the state or by community business and civic groups. In CCR&R agencies, experts research the needs for and availability of local early childhood education programs. They then communicate information to providers about what types of care are most needed and about how to provide quality care. Although CCR&R staff members do not recommend specific programs to parents, they share listings of local providers, information about programs, and current openings. They also help parents learn how to select quality programs.

Figure 24.9 CCR&R agencies help parents choose quality early childhood education programs. *Why do you think some parents need help finding appropriate programs for their children?*

Lesson 24.1 Review and Assessment 

1. Name and briefly define the four types of child care programs.
2. How do child development laboratories differ from other early childhood education programs?
3. Explain one purpose of Head Start.
4. What are *preschool programs* and how are they different from *preschools*?
5. How do Montessori schools differ from most other early childhood education programs?
6. How are current kindergartens different from the kindergartens Friedrich Froebel envisioned?
7. Name three trends in early childhood education programs.
8. **Critical thinking.** In small groups, discuss why school attendance is mandatory for primary school children.

Lesson 24.2 Choosing an Early Childhood Education Program

Key Terms

accredited programs
activity plan
adult-child ratio
culture shock
developmentally appropriate practices (DAPs)
developmentally inappropriate practices (DIPs)
early learning standards
field trips
hidden added costs
hidden cost credits
lesson plan
regulations
staff turnover

Academic Terms

dismantle
homogeneous

Objectives

After studying this lesson, you will be able to

- differentiate between *licensing* and *accreditation* of early childhood education programs.
- explain why housing and equipment differ among the different types of early childhood education programs.
- summarize the three aspects of quality involved in staffing programs for young children.
- identify three signs that a program encourages parent communication and participation.
- contrast developmentally appropriate and inappropriate practices.
- list four indications of a culturally rich early childhood education program.
- describe ways to help children adjust to early childhood education programs.

Reading and Writing Activity

Before reading this lesson, skim each section and make two predictions describing the content covered in the section. Then read the lesson section by section. After reading each section, stop and write a three- to four-sentence summary of the section. Be sure to paraphrase.

Graphic Organizer

Create a fishbone map to organize your notes while reading this lesson. In the body of the map, write a short "topic sentence" that summarizes the main point of this lesson. In the surrounding scales, write your specific notes.

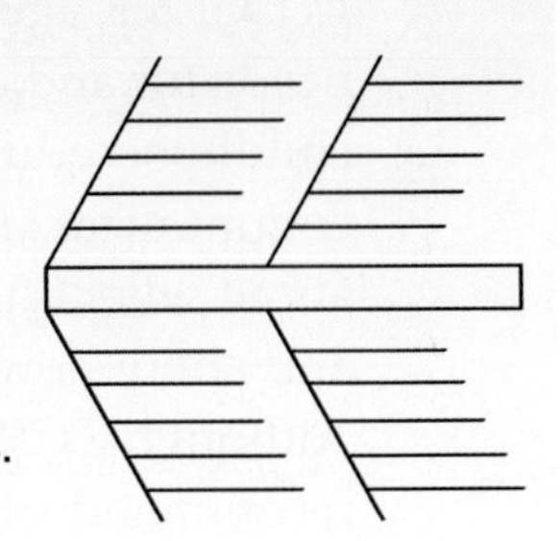

For many families, early childhood education programs are difficult to find, and it is even more difficult for families to find *quality* programs. When choosing programs, parents need to look for programs that meet the needs of their family and promote their beliefs and priorities. These needs differ depending on the family, and not all programs will meet each family's needs. To ensure a good fit in a quality early childhood education program, all families should consider a few basic factors.

Even in a quality program, children may have difficulty adjusting to new care. To make a child care arrangement work, parents can be prepared to help their children adjust and find new care if needed.

Factors to Consider When Choosing a Program

Choosing high-quality early childhood programs is vital to the successful care and education of children. Children are defenseless clients of the programs they attend. They cannot measure the quality of a program for themselves or take action if the quality is poor. Children depend on their parents to find quality programs for them.

Often, parents cannot judge a program by only meeting staff members, checking the indoor and outdoor areas, or seeing a posted certificate that states the program meets state standards. Rather, when assessing the quality of a program, parents should consider a number of factors and observe the program's day-to-day activities. Important factors to consider when choosing an early childhood education program include

- adherence to regulations
- housing and equipment
- quality and number of staff
- parent communication and participation
- use of early learning standards
- quality activities
- cultural diversity
- costs of child care
- special services

> **Mental Health Advisory**
>
> Low-quality early childhood education programs can have negative effects on children's mental health. In these programs, parents may not be allowed to visit without asking in advance. Staff members may not be trained and may lack interest in meeting children's needs. Finally, in low-quality programs, there is a tendency to push children to perform above their abilities, causing them stress.

Adherence to Regulations

All quality early childhood education programs are governed by regulations. **Regulations** are standards that govern how a program operates. Regulations applicable to various types of early childhood programs vary. Some regulations, such as fire safety, apply to all programs. Other regulations apply to either private programs or public programs or to either center-based or family child care programs. Almost all regulations are mandatory, but at least one is voluntary. The most common set of regulations for group programs is called a *license*. Licensing regulations address program housing, equipment, staff, children's services, and business operations. In all cases, certificates awarded to programs meeting regulations must be periodically renewed.

When choosing an early childhood education program, parents should ensure that these programs meet all appropriate regulations. Adherence to regulations, however, does not *guarantee* high quality. This is due to the following reasons:

- ***Most regulations are minimum standards.*** Programs may almost completely meet regulations, barely meet regulations, or fall somewhere in between these extremes. Licensing regulations vary because these regulations are not federal standards. Rather, licensing regulations are state-determined standards and thus vary from state to state; so quality, in like manner, varies with the regulations.

- ***Some regulations are easier to observe than others.*** Concrete regulations, such as having a fence around the outside play area, are easy to observe. More abstract regulations, such as the warmth and nurturance of staff, are much more difficult to observe.
- ***Regulations are not always enforced.*** Some regulations have little to no enforcement. For example, there are many regulations for family child care homes, but due to the number of homes and limited state funding for inspections, these programs are seldom checked. Regulations difficult to observe are not as likely to be enforced as those that are easy to observe.

To ensure quality beyond adherence to mandated regulations, adults may look for the *accreditation* of a program. **Accredited programs** are not only licensed, but have met even higher standards of quality set forth by a professional organization. Thus, accredited programs are like high achievers on tests. Accreditation attests to the fact that the program has voluntarily met standards of high quality.

Figure 24.10 Early childhood education programs must stay up-to-date on current safety standards. *Where can early childhood education workers go to research the most current safety standards?*

Housing and Equipment

The types of housing and equipment in an early childhood education program will vary with the program's goals. For example, a family child care home will have different housing than a kindergarten, and a kindergarten will provide different materials than a Montessori program. Furniture, equipment, and materials should always meet the needs of the children in the program.

Regardless of the type of housing and equipment that are provided, all housing and equipment must be safe, sanitary, and meet health standards (**Figure 24.10**). Equipment should be plentiful enough to prevent long waits and possible aggressive acts among children. Housing and equipment should also include adequate space for activities and comfort of both children and adults.

Quality and Number of Staff

A major factor in the quality of an early childhood education program is the quality and number of caregivers. Young children are dependent on caregivers and need plenty of adult help and supervision. Positive caregiver interactions can aid children's development, but negative caregiver interactions can have damaging effects. When choosing an early childhood education program, parents should consider the quality of the caregivers, the adult-child ratio, and staff turnover.

Quality of Caregivers

Caregivers for children should be in good physical and mental health. For a positive experience, children must feel secure, loved, and wanted, knowing they matter to others. Children need adults who hug, comfort, listen to them, talk with them, and say *no* and correct them when needed.

Quality caregivers provide guidance for children. They apply their knowledge of child development at each stage in a child's development. For example, quality caregivers of infants will cuddle them and accept their dependency. Quality caregivers of toddlers will encourage them to explore and learn, and quality caregivers of preschool children will welcome children's curiosity, questions, and energy.

Quality staff members must also be able to work well with coworkers as a team. They must also communicate effectively with parents, be sensitive to parents' concerns, and convey needed information.

Adult-Child Ratio and Group Size

State regulations identify the minimum required adult-child ratio and group sizes for various types of early childhood education programs. As is true

Focus on Careers

Child Care Center Director

Child care center directors supervise and lead the staff in a child care center. They oversee children's activities, plan schedules and budgets, keep staff up-to-speed on educational and safety standards, and advise staff in handling situations.

Career cluster: Human services.

Education: Educational requirements include a high school diploma and sometimes a college degree. Child care center directors must have experience in early childhood education, and in some states, must have a Child Development Associate (CDA) certification.

Job outlook: Future employment opportunities for child care center directors are expected to grow faster than the average for all occupations.

To learn more about a career as a child care center director, visit the United States Department of Labor's *Occupational Outlook Handbook* website. You will also be able to compare the job responsibilities, educational requirements, job outlook, and average pay of child care center directors with similar occupations.

of other licensing regulations, adult-child ratio and group-size requirements vary from state to state. All states, however, base their numbers on professional recommendations.

An **adult-child ratio** (read as *adult to child ratio*) is the number of adults per the number of children in a program. An adult-child ratio of 1:10 (read as *adult to child ratio of 1 to 10*) means 1 adult per 10 children. The way of presenting the ratio can be reversed by saying that the child-adult ratio is 10:1 (read as *child to adult ratio is 10 to 1*). This means exactly the same thing—there are 10 children for each adult. Support staff and regular volunteers, though vital to quality programs, are *not* counted when the adult-child ratio is calculated. Adult-child ratios tend to be highest for accredited programs and for programs enrolling very young children and children with special needs.

Group sizes refer to the number of children in one room who will interact with each other throughout the day. Accredited programs, programs for young children, and programs serving children with special needs tend to have the smallest group sizes. Because older children and those without disabilities tend to require less physical care compared with other children, they can be safely cared for and educated in rooms with a lower adult-child ratio and in groups that are somewhat larger.

When choosing early childhood education programs, parents can inquire about adult-child ratios and group size (**Figure 24.11**). After enrolling a child, they can also spot-check these numbers at different times throughout the day. (Some directors enroll the maximum number of children and then allow drop-in children to attend, which increases the number beyond licensing limits.)

Figure 24.11 Recommended Adult-Child Ratios and Group Size

Age of Children	Adult-Child Ratio*	Group Size*
Birth to one year	1:3	6
One to two years	1:4	8
Two to three years	1:6	12
Three to six years (excluding first grade)	1:9	18

*Numbers for children per adult and group size should be reduced if children with special needs are included.

Staff Turnover

Beyond parents, caregivers, and other family members, staff members are the most important people in children's lives. Infants and toddlers in child care can become deeply attached to these caregivers. They often spend more *waking hours* with their program caregivers than with their own parents. Despite this, most early childhood education programs experience some *staff turnover*. **Staff turnover** is a term used to describe caregivers who leave a program and are replaced (often statistically presented as a rate). Early childhood education programs with high staff turnover can be damaging to infants, toddlers, and children with special needs. Children need consistency, and it is recommended that they have the same caregivers for over a year.

In the United States, the annual staff turnover rate for early childhood education programs is about 40 percent. This is largely due to low pay, as caregivers leave programs to seek better-paying jobs. The median annual income for caregivers is about $21,000 annually. If wages were higher, staff turnover would decrease; however, higher wages would increase the cost of child care even more for parents, making programs even less affordable.

Mental Health Advisory

Attachments, critical for mental health, are broken with staff turnover. Programs with high staff turnover are detrimental to the mental health of young children and some children with special needs.

Parent Communication and Participation

In high-quality programs, staff members encourage parent involvement. Children benefit when all of their caregivers work together as a team. When choosing early childhood education programs, parents should look for programs that practice the following:

- ***Work with parents as a team.*** Quality programs employ teachers who know a great deal about child development and understand parents' specific goals for their children. These teachers respect parents' goals and work with parents to achieve them (**Figure 24.12**). An exception to this is when parents' wishes violate program policy or professional ethics.

Focus on Speech

Safety for Early Childhood Education Staff

Early childhood education staff members face unique challenges as they work with young children. Child care can expose caregivers to some illnesses and to risks associated with guiding children and regulating their behaviors. The *Occupational Safety and Health Administration (OSHA)* sets and enforces standards to protect employees in the workplace, including staff in early childhood education programs.

In small groups, research OSHA standards for health and safety. Take notes about standards that apply to early childhood education programs. After conducting your research, choose two standards and lead a class discussion about how these standards apply to programs. Also discuss ways in which directors and staff can ensure employee health and safety in a child care center.

Figure 24.12 An Example of Combining Parent and Teacher Goals

Goal area: Discipline

Teacher's goal and reason: Children should begin to learn self-control. Through learning self-control, children use problem-solving skills to resolve conflicts and gain self-esteem.

Parents' goal and reason: Children should respect authority. Children have to respect parents, just as adults have to respect the authority of their employers.

Using both goals: After discussing the teacher's and parents' goals, the teacher may suggest how both can be met. For example, children will be asked to resolve some of their conflicts with the teacher's help. They will also be expected to follow rules and show respect for other people and property. In some situations (such as safety issues), children will be expected to comply immediately with what the teacher says.

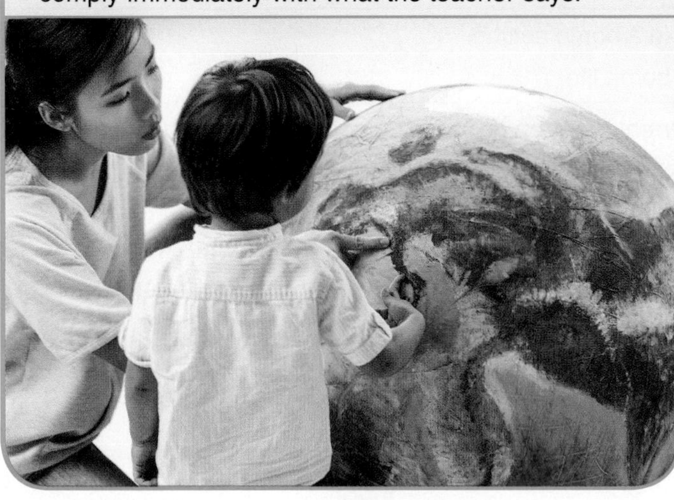

- ***Convey the importance of parent participation in the program.*** A quality program will communicate to parents that they play the most important role in their children's lives. These programs emphasize that staff members respect parents as children's first teachers and encourage parent participation. They acknowledge that the parent-child relationship influences a child's development more than any other aspect of a child's life.
- ***Know about each family they serve.*** Staff members at quality programs work to understand the cultures represented in the program and how these cultures affect families. They acknowledge that a family's culture might influence parenting practices and child development. They respect each culture and make efforts to get to know each child's family.
- ***Provide opportunities for parent communication and participation.*** Quality programs communicate frequently with parents and provide ample opportunities for parents who want to participate (**Figure 24.13**). Programs should respect parents' rights to refuse involvement, however.

Use of Early Learning Standards

All quality early childhood education programs are based on goals for children's development. Early childhood education program goals sometimes differ, however, making all programs unique. This is because various programs were founded at different periods in history and were based on the child development knowledge of that time.

Today, many preschool programs follow their states' **early learning standards** (also called *foundations* and *guidelines*), which are expectations for young children's development. Some learning standards include *benchmarks* under broader outcomes. All states have identified learning standards for preschool children. Besides preschool learning standards developed by each state, Head Start has defined outcomes for children enrolled in this federal program.

Early learning standards are used for deciding on program goals. They benefit program planners because they outline the rich potential for children's growth and development. How these standards are actually used by program planners and teachers depend on the early childhood education program.

Teachers in quality programs follow early learning standards, but plan how to meet them by using **developmentally appropriate practices (DAPs)**.

Figure 24.13 Opportunities for Parent Communication and Involvement

Area	Opportunities
Parent room or reception area	• Photos of and stories about program activities are displayed. • Materials, including videos and handouts on child development, are available for parents to read and view. • Informal networks often form among parents.
Group meetings and workshops	• Orientation meetings are helpful for parents and children. • Discussion groups on child development, program activities or policies, or community concerns can be planned as needed. • Make-and-take workshops are popular with parents. (Parents, who are provided materials and directions, make a take-home learning game for their children.)
Open house	• Parents see facilities and view displayed materials, such as children's drawings and stories. • Parents may participate in some of the children's activities. • Parents and other family members meet staff members and other families.
Individual conferences	• Teachers and parents set goals for children in the program. • Teachers and parents review children's goals and accomplishments.
Home visits	• Teachers see the child and family in a home setting. • Parents share some of the child's home life.
Newsletters	• Parents receive descriptions of current program activities, suggestions for home learning and fun activities, and information about new child-related books, websites, TV shows, or community events. • Parents receive newsletters weekly or monthly in a print or electronic format.
Informal notes to family members	• Parents learn about a child's activity or achievement. • Staff members recognize each family's special events (new baby, new job) and show concern for family challenges (illness, death).
Advisory board	• Parents help plan activities for program. • Parents can advise director or administration on desired program goals. • Parents can discuss general concerns.
Volunteering	• Parents can be regular volunteers either assisting in program activities or making learning materials for the children's use. • Parents can serve as occasional volunteers by helping teachers during children's outings or special activities in which extra adult help is needed.

DAPs are practices that are based on knowledge about

- child development
- the strengths, needs, and interests of each child within a group
- the social and cultural contexts in which children enrolled in a given program live

Developmentally inappropriate practices (DIPs) are the opposite of DAPs. DIPs are practices that do *not* take into account knowledge about child development, each child's strengths and needs, and the cultural context of the children's lives. A program that incorporates early learning standards using DIPs is not desirable for young children.

To determine whether a practice is developmentally appropriate or inappropriate, a person would consider not only the practice, but also the child and how the practice is conducted. For example, asking two-year-olds to sit still for a 15-minute story would likely be a DIP. This same activity, however, would likely be a DAP for five-year-olds, depending on their attention spans. Also, a well-presented story for a young audience makes the sit-still time seem less lengthy to children. In choosing a quality early childhood education program, caregivers can look for how these programs use DAPs to incorporate early learning standards (**Figure 24.14**).

Figure 24.14 Contrasting DAPs and DIPs

Area	DAPs	DIPs
Program goals	• Goals are planned for physical, intellectual, and social-emotional development. • Children are seen as *individuals* who differ developmentally and will grow and change at their own rates. • Children are seen as having their own unique styles of learning, interests, and cultural understandings.	• Goals are primarily planned for intellectual development. • Although children may differ developmentally at time of program entrance, they should achieve age norms by the end of the program. • Children's unique styles of learning, interests, and cultural understandings are *not* seen as important. • Children must conform to group instruction.
Housing and materials	• Ample space and materials are provided for the number of children in each group. • Room is arranged with several learning or activity centers (art, language, science, block building). • Materials are mainly for *play*. • Most materials have no right or wrong answers (dramatic play props, art materials, sand, water). • Many materials invite children to play together in small groups.	• Room is crowded, and materials are not plentiful, which causes stress and conflicts among children. • Room is often arranged in tables with an assigned place for each child facing the teacher's desk. • Materials are often workbooks or duplicated sheets for teaching beginning reading and arithmetic. • Drill software is often used on computers.
Curriculum content and teaching methods	• Children's activities help them develop gross- and fine-motor skills, literacy skills, social and scientific concepts, and creative abilities. (Technology literacy is integrated into activities, not taught for its own sake.) • Teachers permit children to work on their own or in small groups as much as possible. Through the teacher's constant observations, he or she decides when the children need a little help (called *scaffolding*) or when the housing arrangements or materials need changing.	• Children's learning is mainly focused on developing reading, arithmetic, and technology literacy skills. All other activities are not seen as important. • Teachers do a great deal of group "telling." Drill methods are often used for learning (such as for learning colors, letters, and numbers).

(Continued)

Figure 24.14 *(Continued)*

Area	DAPs	DIPs
Assessment	• Teachers assess children mainly through observations and note what they observe about each child in anecdotal records and check sheets. • Teachers often create a portfolio (much like a scrapbook), which includes the teacher's observations of a child and samples of the child's work. This portfolio is shared with the parents.	• Teachers assess children through tests and end-of-the-year standardized tests. • Teachers compare each child's test scores with the norms (how the typical child performs) and then share these results with the child's parents.
Guidance of children	• For a given child, teachers encourage self-control based on his or her stage of development. • Teachers help children achieve self-control through simple explanations, modeling the desired behavior, and redirecting. • Teachers use positive comments when children use self-control.	• Teachers expect all children to sit still and listen most of the day. • When children do not conform, they are often punished (such as by sitting in a time-out chair). • Treats are sometimes given as a way to keep children doing what teachers expect.

Quality Activities

Quality early childhood education programs provide appropriate and high-quality activities for children. Young children are holistic learners who learn best through play. Quality programs should acknowledge this importance and then *guide* play so it is goal-oriented, not random or chaotic.

Quality Activities for Infants and Toddlers

For infants and toddlers, quality activities mostly involve *primary care*. In primary care, one primary caregiver feeds, diapers, soothes, plays with, and reads to a given child. (Most primary caregivers are assigned three or four children.) Other caregivers who help the child are called *secondary*. Secondary caregivers provide care consistent with the primary caregiver. Because infants and young toddlers have their own learning agendas, caregivers plan quality activities by providing an interesting environment and following each child's lead.

Quality Activities for Preschoolers

During the preschool years, quality activities involving primary care are replaced by activities that promote learning in all domains, satisfy curiosity, and build confidence. Quality activities enable preschool children to develop feelings that they can handle tasks with just a little adult help.

Quality preschool programs use DAPs in their day-to-day routines and planned activities. For example, in these programs, eating serves a purpose beyond curbing hunger. Snacks and meals also offer time to learn about foods and styles of eating, practice table manners, and talk with others. During day-to-day routines, children also learn self-care, independence, and self-help skills.

In quality preschool programs with DAPs, all activities are planned to help children develop. These program activities often include

- ***language activities***, which improve language skills and involve talking, listening, reading (or looking at) books, and perhaps scribbling a grocery list in the housekeeping center or "signing" a drawing.
- ***math activities***, which improve math skills and involve counting, matching shapes in puzzles, measuring, and noting the use of math symbols in everyday life.

- *social activities*, which improve social interactions and involve children trying new roles, helping each other, recognizing emotions in others and showing empathy, and helping plan events (**Figure 24.15**).
- *science activities*, which teach children about their living and nonliving world. These activities involve pets, plants, foods, water, sand, weather and seasonal changes, and more.
- *creative activities*, which allow children to enjoy expressing themselves through art, dramatic play, music, and storytelling.
- *motor activities*, which help develop motor skills. Gross-motor skills develop through active play, especially outdoor play. Fine-motor skills become refined as children manipulate materials, such as art materials, writing tools, puzzles, and building materials.
- *multidevelopmental activities*, which aid multiple areas of development. For example, activities such as block building, sand and water play, cooking, visual arts, music, science, and literature impact many areas of development.

Figure 24.15 Many high-quality programs encourage social activities by inviting adults who are not on staff to share special skills or stories with children. *What are the benefits of volunteer participation for adults? for children?*

Quality activities might also include **field trips** (outings) to take children to new places. Field trips teach children about their communities and develop multicultural understandings. For example, a field trip to the fire station might help children learn about firefighters and experience firefighting in a new and exciting way.

Presenting worthwhile activities for children requires careful planning. In a quality program, teachers plan specific activities and materials to meet selected goals. Written plans are usually formatted as either *lesson plans* or *activity plans*. A **lesson plan** contains a specific goal objective (related to a standard), activities to help the child meet the objective, and assessment of the learning and is usually written for kindergarten or school-age children (**Figure 24.16**).

While a lesson plan contains one- or two-goal objectives, an **activity plan** incorporates several standards at the same time (for more holistic learning), potential activities to aid learning, and an informal assessment. Activity plans are mostly written for preschool children. In these plans, most activities are guided by a unifying *theme* (such as farms, weather, or families) that is carried through both large-group and individual learning activities (**Figure 24.17**). Activity plans tend to be more open-ended so preschool children can take the lead in their activities and teachers can scaffold children's learning. Unlike most lesson plans, activity plans usually last several days.

Cultural Diversity

High-quality early childhood education programs take steps to become culturally diverse. Cultural diversity provides opportunities for children's *multicultural education*, an important part of children's education in a global society.

Understanding of cultural diversity develops as a result of a positive approach by the parents and employees in an early childhood education program. In multicultural education, young children work to develop self-awareness and notice differences among themselves and others. In a carefully planned program, children will have the chance to establish their cultural identities, respect diversity,

Example of a Lesson Plan for Kindergarten Children

Content area	Measurement and Data
Standard	Classify objects and count the number of objects in each category.
Learning objective	Given 15 parquetry blocks in three colors and five shapes, the children will form a class and its complement and count the number of blocks in each. They will then do a second classification using different criteria and counting again.
Materials per child	15 parquetry blocks in various shapes and colors; two small, plastic trays
Procedure	1. Distribute materials. 2. Ask children how the materials are alike in some way (color or shape). 3. Ask children to choose *one* color or shape and put all other objects of the same color or shape on one tray. Have them name their color or shape and correct objects in the chosen class if necessary. Then count them. 4. Ask children to put all of the other objects on the other tray. Have them call these objects their *not group*, such as "not red" or "not square." Then count these objects. 5. Repeat steps 3 and 4 using a different group for the class and the complement.
Assessment	Using a check-and-comment evaluation form, check each child's ability to *classify objects* (form the class and complement), *name the class and complement*, and *count the number of objects* in the class and complement.

Figure 24.16 Lesson plans are usually written to address one early learning standard. These plans are for kindergarten and early school-age children. *What are the components of the lesson plan shown?*

and develop unbiased attitudes. In a culturally diverse program, staff and other adults do the following:

- ***Affirm children's identities.*** Staff learn how to pronounce children's names and say some words in each child's language. They help children learn to describe themselves and their activities. Affirming children's identities can help children who are experiencing **culture shock** (an uncomfortable response to an unfamiliar culture).
- ***Help children learn about people who are different from them.*** Staff aid children in noting differences, especially physical differences among people. Children are able to note these differences around 30 months of age and need experiences with people who are different from them. Programs with little diversity can find ways for children to explore differences outside of the classroom, such as through community resources.
- ***Encourage children to see people as individuals, not groups.*** Staff can affirm individual identities and **dismantle** (tear apart) cultural generalizations. They can provide multicultural books that point out the inaccuracies of sweeping generalizations. For example, children could read to learn that not all older people are inactive.
- ***Listen to and answer children's questions.*** Staff can use questions, even questions that reflect bias, as learning experiences. For example, if children mention skin color or eye shape, adults may say, "We are born with differences. These differences make all of us special." Instead of criticizing children for biased statements, staff can acknowledge statements with an explanation and show positive acceptance of differences. With older children, staff can explain that biased statements and behaviors hurt.

Example of an Activity Plan for Preschool Children

Theme	Farms
Learning standards	• Develop and use models to represent their ideas, observations, and explanations through approaches, such as drawing, building, or modeling with clay. • Use vocabulary that describes length, height, weight, capacity, and size. • With teacher assistance, discuss illustrations in books and make personal connections to the pictures and stories.
Originating idea	The children had been playing with model barns and farm animals in the dramatic play center. One child said, "My horses are running away; there is no fence." Another child put his arms around a barn and said, "I can be a fence!" It would be a good experience for the children to build fences for their barn animals in the block center.
Materials	• Model barns, farm animals, and unit blocks • Pictures and illustrated books • Paper for measuring • Field trip (to see fences and fencing materials)
Possible experiences to expand concepts and skills	1. Build enclosures and gates for their animals with blocks. Children could do the following: a. discuss the size of enclosures needed and use different block lengths to make the enclosures b. discuss why gates are needed and build these c. determine whether the enclosure is a *rectangle*, a *square*, or *another shape* 2. Find pictures of and talk about different types of animal enclosures—*backyard fence*; *cage*; *bird cage*; *stall*; *aquarium*; or *butterfly house*. 3. Discuss why some fences are taller than others; made of different materials; and have or do not have tops. 4. Read picture books about farms and fences: • H. Moser's *Snoopy the Sheep*, (Christian Light Publications, 2013). • A. Hunter. *On Grandpa's Farm*, (HMH Books, 1997). 5. Discuss purposes of fences—keep animals from getting away and protect them by keeping other animals out. 6. Take a community field trip to see various animal enclosures. 7. Discuss other uses of fences beyond animal protection, such as a fence around a swimming pool or around dangerous equipment. 8. Draw or make fences with art materials.
Assessment	Write notes or use check sheets that indicate children's knowledge, such as: William B. showed spatial orientation in block building by using both horizontal enclosures for pens and vertical enclosures for gates.
Possible follow-up ideas*	1. Children may need more experiences with other categories of animals, such as zoo animals, pets, insects, or fish. 2. Children could be introduced to other types of farms—*crop farms* or *fish farms*.

*These may lead to new originating ideas.

Figure 24.17 The format of a written plan sets the tone of the teacher's approach to children's learning (holistic or "bits and pieces") and determines the teacher's preparation (to allow children to take the lead or make the experience teacher-directed). *Why are activity plans most appropriate for preschool children?*

- ***Help children learn that almost all human activities can be done in different ways.*** Staff can affirm differences in the ways people speak, act out family roles and activities, appreciate art and music, and learn at home or school.
- ***Respect diversity by making the program culturally rich.*** Staff can work to include children representing many different cultures. They can include diverse materials, activities, and people in their programs (**Figure 24.18**).

Ensuring cultural diversity in early childhood education programs can be challenging for two reasons. First, many programs are fairly **homogeneous** (hoh-MUH-jee-nyus), more alike than different. This is because parents tend to choose programs similar to their family and religious backgrounds; cultures; and views on early education, guidance, and discipline. Second, multicultural education is not taught as directly as other types of learning. These understandings are not developed through specific curriculum activities, but rather through incorporation into many activities.

Costs of Child Care

Since 2000, the cost of child care has increased twice as fast as the median income of families. Today, child care costs almost equal college costs. Child care costs are more than rent costs, and in 20 states, child care for two children exceeds the cost of home mortgage payments.

While the quality of a program does not necessarily correlate to its cost, high-quality programs for young children do tend to be expensive. Costs of programs include costs of staff salaries, buildings, equipment, food, and supplies. These costs vary with the type of program, days and hours of care, age groups served, and location. For example, staffing costs for programs with infants, toddlers, and children with special needs may be higher than staffing costs for preschool programs. Before- and after-school programs serving only school-age children cost more per hour than most full-time child care programs. These costs increase with any added special services, such as transportation or special program activities (dance, gymnastics, and foreign languages).

Besides direct costs, early childhood education programs usually have both additional costs and cost credits, such as

- **hidden added costs** (costs that add to direct costs). Examples are costs of transportation, supplies, and disposable diapers (if cloth diapers would have otherwise been used). Services or items donated to an early childhood education program are hidden added costs, too.
- **hidden cost credits** (credits that lower direct costs of child care). These include money earned from a second income, money saved in the cost of utilities, food for in-home care, and child-care tax credits.

When choosing an early childhood education program, parents must assess program costs. While cost may sometimes indicate the high quality of a program, families will not benefit from paying for care they cannot afford.

Special Services

When choosing early childhood education programs, some families look for programs that offer *special services*. These services might include transportation to and from the program, child care for children with special needs, or extended-hour care. Programs with these services are not always conveniently located.

If several families need the same services, they may be able to persuade programs to add these services. Work-related child care programs are good examples of businesses that meet the special child care needs of their employees. For example, some hospital child care programs are open 24 hours a day to serve employees' children.

Helping Children Adjust to Care

Some children may experience difficulty or uneasiness transitioning from home care to an early childhood education program. These children may experience separation anxiety or may feel nervous for the first few days away from home.

Figure 24.18 Characteristics of a Culturally Rich Program

Materials

- Books about all types of children and families, books that show positive roles, and books that celebrate various cultural activities and customs
- Housekeeping centers filled with dolls of both genders and various cultural and ethnic groups; tools, play foods, and cooking utensils from various cultures
- Puzzles, pictures, and posters depicting families from various cultures
- Crayons, paints, and paper to represent all skin tones
- Musical instruments and recordings from various cultures
- Toys and games from around the world
- Photos and posters of multicultural activities shared in the program

Activities

- Reading stories, singing songs, learning poems, cooking foods, or playing games that have their origins in various cultures
- Learning words, phrases, songs, or rhymes in various languages
- Using art materials to depict oneself and others, various celebrations, and multicultural program activities
- Sharing an object from home or showing photos of a family activity
- Attending parades and festivals in the community
- Making a book of multicultural activities using photos, children's artwork, and child-dictated stories about these activities

People

- Welcoming volunteers of all cultural, ethnic, and generational groups
- Having parents from various cultures share activities involving favorite foods, songs, stories, and games
- Seeing people of various cultures and both genders engaged in their work roles

Once caregivers have chosen a quality program, they can help make the adjustment seem casual. Rather than talking often about the change and seeming anxious, caregivers can stay calm and confident about their children's ability to adjust (**Figure 24.19**). A parent may say, "I know there are many new boys and girls, but you will make new friends. Everyone is new for a while."

About a month before enrolling a child in an early childhood education program, a parent can explain to the child what the program is like. He or she may explain there will be other children, toys, and activities. The parent and child can also visit the program and get to know children who are enrolled.

If children do not adjust well to a program, even after a few weeks, parents should investigate the cause. Unannounced visits to the program might reveal problems. Parents can also ask teachers what problems they have noted and what efforts are being made to help the child adjust. Children can be encouraged to share with parents why the program makes them uncomfortable. Parents should take children's answers seriously.

If no care problems are found, parents can find other ways to help the child adjust. They might offer the child more chances to play with other children or ask their child's doctor for advice.

If parents do find problems with the care, they should immediately start to look for a new placement. With their children's safety and well-being as a primary concern, parents can monitor the situation closely until a new program can be found. They can also give the child extra love and support as they search for a more acceptable program. Once a new program is selected, parents may want to begin care gradually, if at all possible.

Figure 24.19 Being calm and confident about children's abilities can help these children believe they are capable of adjusting. *What was your most difficult adjustment as a young child?*

Lesson 24.2 Review and Assessment 

1. List three reasons adherence to regulations does not necessarily guarantee high quality.
2. What makes the housing and equipment in an early childhood education program effective or ineffective?
3. A(n) _____ is the number of adults per the number of children in a program.
4. Identify three signs that a program encourages parent communication and participation.
5. Explain the difference between *DAPs* and *DIPs*.
6. List four indications of a culturally rich program.
7. Explain the difference between *hidden added costs* and *hidden cost credits*.
8. **Critical thinking.** Why should parents always listen to children's answers about why a program is making them uncomfortable? What should a parent do if a child's answer does not seem to make sense?

Focus on Financial Literacy

Comparing Costs of Early Childhood Education Programs

When deciding on an early childhood education program, families often compare the costs of several programs. Costs of early childhood education programs vary depending on location, hours, quality of care, activities and special services provided, and the ages of the children.

In small groups, gather information on at least 10 early childhood education programs in your community. If possible, gather information about each of the types of programs discussed in this chapter. Try to include both for-profit and not-for-profit programs. During your research, determine the cost of care for one child for the operational hours of the program.

Make a spreadsheet tracking the quality of the programs you researched, their costs, and the hours of operation. Present your spreadsheet to the class. Compare the costs and discuss possible factors affecting the cost. Indicate which program you would choose for a child in each stage of development.

Chapter 24 Review and Assessment

Summary

Parents enroll their young children in early childhood education programs for many reasons, but mainly because they work outside the home. Parents have several options when it comes to early childhood education for their young children. Parents can choose child care programs, such as in-home child care, family child care, center-based child care, or school-age child care programs. Parents can also look for programs that provide more direct educational activities for their children. Some of these programs are child development laboratories, Head Start programs, preschool programs, Montessori schools, and kindergartens. Young school-age children attend primary schools. All of these have a history of meeting particular needs of children and families.

Because many children spend a great portion of their life in early childhood education programs, parents must choose these programs carefully. By learning about the key factors on which they should focus, parents can increase the chance they will find a quality program that is a good match for the child and the family. When choosing early childhood education programs, parents can consider a combination of factors, including adherence to regulations, housing and equipment, quality and number of staff, parent communication and participation, use of early learning standards, quality activities, cultural diversity, costs, and special services. Parents may need to help children adjust to group care. If children are not adjusting easily to group care, adults might try other programs.

College and Career Portfolio

Portfolio Presentation Practice

Before presenting your portfolio, you will want to practice. Practice can help you remain calm during a presentation and can help you choose the right words to communicate your skills and experiences.

- Practice presenting your portfolio. Time your presentation and pay attention to your body language and enunciation.
- Practice presenting your portfolio to a trusted adult or friend. Ask for feedback about how fast or loud you are talking. Practice until you feel comfortable with your presentation.

Chapter 24 Review and Assessment

Vocabulary Activities 

1. In teams, create categories for the following terms and classify as many of the terms as possible. Then, share your ideas with the remainder of the class.

Key Terms

accredited programs (24.2)
activity plan (24.2)
adult-child ratio (24.2)
center-based child care (24.1)
child care programs (24.1)
CCR&R agencies (24.1)
child development laboratories (24.1)
culture shock (24.2)
DAPs (24.2)
DIPs (24.2)
early childhood education programs (24.1)
early learning standards (24.2)
family child care (24.1)
field trips (24.2)
fingerplays (24.1)
for-profit programs (24.1)
Head Start (24.1)
hidden added costs (24.2)
hidden cost credits (24.2)
in-home child care (24.1)
kindergartens (24.1)
lesson plan (24.2)
Montessori schools (24.1)
not-for-profit programs (24.1)
preschool programs (24.1)
preschools (24.1)
private programs (24.1)
public programs (24.1)
regulations (24.2)
SACC programs (24.1)
staff turnover (24.2)
universal preschool programs (24.1)
work-related child care programs (24.1)

2. Write each of the following terms on a separate sheet of paper. For each term, quickly write a word you think relates to the term.

Academic Terms

dismantle (24.2)
franchises (24.1)
homogeneous (24.2)
national chains (24.1)
parochial (24.1)

Critical Thinking

3. **Determine.** In small groups, review the information about child care programs in this chapter. Create a poster identifying the types of child care programs, their advantages, and their disadvantages. Present your poster to the class and "sell" each type of program by explaining its benefits.
4. **Cause and effect.** Trends in early childhood education programs are often influenced by historical events and societal changes. Working with a partner, research one historical decade and discuss how events and changes in that decade affected the development and types of early childhood education programs.
5. **Identify.** Research current licensing regulations for preschools in your state. Make a list of these standards and research and explain any standards you do not understand. Rewrite the standards in your own words for understandability.
6. **Compare and contrast.** Research the NAEYC accreditation standards available from the Academy for Early Childhood Program Accreditation. Note similarities and differences between accreditation standards and your state's licensing regulations, which you researched in question #5. (Be sure that both sets of standards being considered are for the same ages of children.) Are accreditation standards more rigorous? Why or why not?
7. **Analyze.** Working with a partner, discuss important personal and professional characteristics of a quality caregiver. How should caregiving practices change as children grow older? Analyze what makes a quality caregiver for children at each stage of development. Do some characteristics of a quality caregiver remain the same for children at each stage of development?
8. **Draw conclusions.** In small groups, brainstorm ways that early childhood education programs can provide opportunities for parent communication and involvement. Choose one idea discussed in your group and then draw conclusions about how it could be implemented in an early childhood education program of your choice.
9. **Evaluate.** Research a local early childhood education program for a list of play activities that the program provides. What types of activities are offered? Evaluate any "holes" in the program's activity offerings. What types of activities would you suggest they add to their list?
10. **Make inferences.** Interview a parent of a young child about how his or her child adjusted to an early childhood education program. Was the transition difficult at first? Why or why not? What did the parent do to ease the child's transition? After the interview, discuss your findings with a partner. Discuss the differences and similarities between the parents you interviewed.

Core Skills

11. **Research and technology.** Choose one type of early childhood education program covered in this chapter. Then, use reliable online or print resources to research the program's history, principles and practices, prevalence, any standards that apply, and current considerations (such as current changes in the program or legislation that has affected the program's practices). After conducting your research, create a digital presentation outlining your findings.
12. **Research and speaking.** Using reliable online or print resources, research Head Start and other early childhood education programs for low-income families. What are the goals of these programs? What new initiatives or programs are they starting? How do staff members in these programs interact with children and families? Organize your findings and deliver an oral presentation to the class.
13. **Reading and writing.** Visit a local library or search online for scholarly articles about the effects of early childhood education programs on children. Read at least three articles and take notes about how group care affects children's physical, intellectual, and social-emotional development. After reading, write a three- to four-page essay discussing your research. Include a bibliography in APA format with your essay.
14. **Math.** Research the required adult-child ratio for one type of early childhood education program in your state. Then, calculate how many adults would be required if the program enrolled 5, 15, 25, and 50 children.
15. **Research and speaking.** Research current early learning standards in your state. Read the standards and take notes about the key areas they cover. What do you think are the goals of the standards? Are there any places in the standards where it would be difficult to incorporate DAPs? In small groups, discuss your answers. Share the highlights from your discussion with the class.
16. **Technology.** In small groups, identify three activities or tasks (such as math activities, science experiences, or diapering) that might occur in an early childhood education program. Then, make a list of DAPs and DIPs in each activity or task area. (Be sure to identify the ages of the children you are discussing. DAPs and DIPs will vary based on children's stages of development.) After your discussion, create a short film illustrating and explaining DAPs and DIPs for all three areas. In your film, explain why each practice is developmentally appropriate or inappropriate. Show your film to the class.
17. **Writing.** Review the information about lesson plans and activity plans in this chapter. Then, choose an activity that you think would be enjoyable and educational for young children. Using your state's early learning standards and your knowledge about child development, write a lesson plan and an activity plan incorporating your activity. Be sure to tailor the activity to the children's developmental stages. Finally, trade plans with a partner and peer review each other's work.
18. **CTE Career Readiness Practice.** Imagine you are a health and safety inspector and have been asked to visit a local child care center to ensure they meet state regulations. In preparation for your visit, you decide to refresh your memory about health and safety standards and create a checklist you can use during the inspection. Using reliable online or print resources, research current health and safety standards for child care centers in your state. Include standards about cleanliness, group size, adult-child ratio, and equipment safety. Then, create a checklist of the qualities you will assess during your visit. Compare checklists with a partner and ask for constructive criticism.

Observations

19. As a class, visit a local early childhood education program. Take notes about the multicultural materials available in the program. Which cultures are represented by materials? Do the cultures represented by the materials correspond with the cultures of the children enrolled in the program? How might the materials be used to present culturally diverse activities to the children enrolled in the program? After your visit, discuss what the staff members might do to make their program more culturally rich.
20. In small groups, search the Internet for early childhood education programs in your community. List as many programs as you can find and then review the programs' websites or visit the programs to determine each program by type using the classifications given in Lesson 25.1. Explain your reasoning for each identification.

Chapter
25

Preparing for a Child-Related Career

Essential Question

What types of child-related careers are available, and what qualities and next steps make for a successful career?

Lesson 25.1 **Making Career Decisions**
Lesson 25.2 **Learning About Careers That Involve Children**
Lesson 25.3 **Developing Skills for Career Success**
Lesson 25.4 **Finding, Succeeding in, and Leaving a Job**

Case Study Which Method of Instruction Is Best?

As a class, read the case study and discuss the questions that follow. After you finish studying the chapter, discuss this case study again. Have your opinions changed based on what you learned?

Janie, who graduated from high school two years ago, was speaking to the child development class in her high school about beginning a career in child development. She explained that she had just received CDA certification and was an associate teacher in a large child care and education program. Janie told the students about her plans to get a bachelor's degree in early childhood education because she loves working with children.

After Janie's presentation, one of the students raised his hand. He asked, "What is the most difficult aspect of your job?"

Janie replied: "I think it is being uncomfortable when you are not sure whether your decision is the correct one or even if there is a correct decision. I am not even sure experience teaches you *everything*. For example, some preschool teachers require children to sit in a certain way and not move during story time. Other teachers allow children to get comfortable and move during the reading of a story. All teachers can explain their reasons for these practices."

Reminded of some advice she had been given, Janie continued, "I talked about these differences with my director once. She told me educators must develop what Gwen Morgan called a *greater tolerance for ambivalence*, which means you have to learn to cope with different feelings or attitudes about the same topic. This is what I find most difficult in my career. Some things you know for sure, but other things are unclear."

Give It Some Thought

1. Why do you think teachers make different decisions about the same situation? How can people learn the same material, but arrive at different conclusions and ideas?
2. Do you agree with Janie's director that early childhood educators need to develop what Gwen Morgan called a *greater tolerance for ambivalence* in their profession? Why or why not?

While studying this chapter, look for the online resources icon  to:

- **Practice** terms with e-flash cards and interactive games
- **Assess** what you learn by completing self-assessment quizzes
- **Expand** knowledge with interactive activities and graphic organizers

www.g-wlearning.com/childdevelopment

Study on the go

Use a mobile device to practice terms and review with self-assessment quizzes.

www.m.g-wlearning.com/0384

Lesson 25.1

Making Career Decisions

Key Terms

abilities
aptitudes
career
career plan
job shadowing
occupation
occupational categories
personal plan of study
professional organization
self-assessment
values

Academic Terms

mentor
obsolete

Objectives

After studying this lesson, you will be able to

- explain the importance of self-assessment.
- differentiate between *aptitudes* and *abilities*.
- explain how to research careers using occupational categories, market analysis, education and training requirements, and inside views.
- list three types of work-based learning programs.
- describe how short- and long-term goals contribute to a career plan.
- summarize what is included in a personal plan of study.

Reading and Writing Activity

Before reading this lesson, skim the main headings. For each heading, write an *essential question* (a question that you think the section will answer). As you are reading, rewrite the question if necessary. After reading, write a short paragraph answering each essential question.

Graphic Organizer

Write *Making Career Decisions* in the middle circle of a chart like the one shown. Then, as you read this lesson, write the major steps in making a career decision in the surrounding boxes. After you have filled in the boxes, consider how far along you are in making career decisions. Mark which steps you have completed.

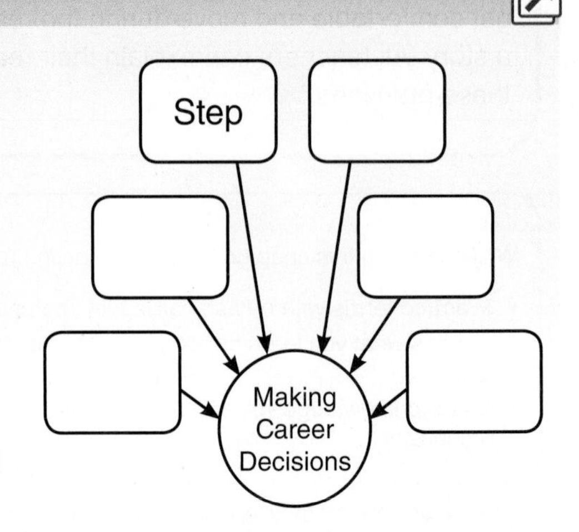

A career is more than just an **occupation** (a job). A **career** is a progression of related jobs that results in employment with opportunities for professional and personal growth.

Choosing a career will affect many factors in your lifestyle. Your career choices will likely influence where you live, what skills you develop, who your associates might be, what free time you have, and what your financial picture might look like.

Making career decisions involves learning about yourself and about different types of career paths, employment trends, and qualifications needed to reach a career outcome. Understanding your personal preferences, skill sets, and career options are important in making career choices and developing a career plan. As you make career decisions, you can begin assessing your interests, aptitudes, and abilities; and then continue by exploring careers and developing a career plan.

Assessing Your Interests, Aptitudes, and Abilities

One of the most difficult and important steps in career planning is **self-assessment** (identifying your interests, aptitudes, and abilities). Completing a self-assessment helps you learn more about who you are as a person and which types of jobs are likely a good fit. Self-assessment is worth the effort because it often leads to finding a career that is personally fulfilling. Without this step, some people might pursue a career that is unsatisfying.

Interests

Your *interests* include the objects or causes you care about, the achievements or qualities you are proud of, and the situations or activities that challenge you. Some of your deeper interests might be **values**, which are ideas, beliefs, and objects that are important and meaningful to you (**Figure 25.1**).

Figure 25.1 Your family, culture, experiences, and personality traits all help shape your values. *What are two of your values?*

Interests are a key part of your career decision, affecting what you feel motivated to do, what you feel satisfied doing, and what fulfills you. Many people seek and stay in careers that align with their interests and values. Showing interest in your work, however, is only one factor. Your abilities and aptitudes also play a role in your career decisions.

Aptitudes

Aptitudes are talents with which people are born; they are natural and a part of heredity. Some of your aptitudes may be quite obvious. These may be subjects or activities that come naturally to you. Other aptitudes may not be obvious to you. For example, if you have a natural talent for nurturing children, you may not realize this until you have an opportunity to interact with children.

Most people enjoy doing activities that come naturally, so aptitudes often align with interests. Sometimes, however, aptitudes and interests can differ. You might not have an *interest* in an area even if you have a *talent* in that area. For example, you might dislike math, but excel at setting up and solving problems. On the contrary, you might have interests in areas, such as music or performing arts, for which you have no natural talents.

Aptitudes influence career choices. To do well in a career, you must develop certain skills that enable you to perform the tasks of your chosen career. These career skills will come more quickly and easily if they align with your natural talents.

A guidance or career counselor can help you identify your aptitudes with an aptitude test. An *aptitude test* identifies areas in which you have aptitudes based on your responses to given questions and scenarios. The test may also reveal some career areas that might suit you well (**Figure 25.2**).

Abilities

Unlike aptitudes, people are not born with abilities. Instead, **abilities** are skills you learn or develop and acquire through effort and practice. For example, while you might have an *aptitude* for leading others, you will have to *develop* leadership abilities. Also, while you might not have an *aptitude* for teaching children, you can still develop *abilities* to interact well with them.

Focus on

Careers

Career Counselor

Career counselors focus on helping people with career decisions. They may assist college students entering the workforce, professionals advancing their careers, or people seeking to change fields. Career counselors explore and evaluate their clients' education, training, work history, interests, skills, and personality traits. They also work with clients to develop job-search skills and assist them in locating and applying for jobs. Career counselors provide support to people experiencing job loss, job stress, or other career transition issues.

Career cluster: Human services.

Education: Educational requirements include a master's degree. State requirements vary, but licensure and certification is typically required.

Job outlook: Future employment opportunities for career counselors are expected to grow as fast as the average for all occupations.

To learn more about a career as a career counselor, visit the United States Department of Labor's *Occupational Outlook Handbook* website. You will also be able to compare the job responsibilities, educational requirements, job outlook, and average pay of career counselors with similar occupations.

Figure 25.2 Aptitude tests may be taken in a formal setting (such as a college and career counselor's office) or online at a testing center. *Find and take an online aptitude test. What are your aptitudes?*

In careers, people need two types of abilities. First, they need *general abilities*—abilities that employers desire of all employees (such as communication skills). Second, they need *career-specific abilities*, which are abilities that employees must have for certain careers. For example, illustrating children's books requires general communication skills, but also certain career-specific abilities in drawing and graphic design. Developing abilities is a lifelong learning process. Many workplaces continue to teach new abilities to their employees.

Exploring Careers

As you learn about your interests, aptitudes, and abilities, you may begin to discover various types of careers and industries. You can use several sources of information to research career areas, opportunities, and realistic pictures of what it is like to work in a career field. As you examine career options, you can learn more by researching occupational categories, analyzing the market, researching the required education and training, and taking an inside view at the career field.

Research Occupational Categories

As you explore careers, you can begin by researching *occupational categories* (also known as *career clusters*). **Occupational categories** are industry areas that encompass a variety of different careers. There are 16 common occupational categories and industries, and each category contains groupings of similar or related careers (**Figure 25.3**). Most child-related careers fall into the *human services occupational category*, which also includes dietitians, psychologists, and cosmetologists. Learning about careers by category can help you discover a career path and multiple careers of interest.

Analyze the Market

An important step in learning about careers is analyzing the labor market for career opportunities. Learning about careers can help you identify career fields that are growing. Learning about an entire career field can also help you identify any specific careers that may be becoming **obsolete** (no longer useful; out of practice). When researching the outlook for a career, look for the following information:

- current and expected employment opportunities for specific occupations
- required education and training
- work conditions and environment
- typical work hours
- salaries for entry-level and experienced positions

Many career information sources are readily available online. You can also analyze the labor market by reading national and local newspapers, business magazines, and trade or professional journals published within a certain career field.

Figure 25.3 Common Occupational or Industry Categories

Category	Type of Job Emphasis
Agriculture, food, and natural resources	Agricultural products such as food, natural fibers, wood, plants, and animal products; the production, distribution, marketing, and financing of these products
Architecture and construction	Design, plan, or construct building structures; building management and maintenance
Arts, A/V technology, and communications	Visual and performing arts, journalism, and entertainment; designing, directing, exhibiting, writing, performing, and producing multimedia products
Business management and administration	Plan, organize, and evaluate business operations; sales, support services, and administration
Education and training	Teach in various learning environments; educational support services and administration
Finance	Investments, banking, insurance, financial planning, and financial management
Government and public administration	Local, state, and national government jobs
Health science	Health and medical services
Hospitality and tourism	Foodservice, lodging, travel, and tourism
Human services	Child and adult care services, counselors, therapists, home care assistants, and consumer services
Information technology	Relate information through communication systems, computers (including hardware, software, Internet), and other media
Law, public safety, corrections, and security	Public safety and security
Manufacturing	Production of goods; sourcing and distribution
Marketing	Sale of goods; advertising, marketing, forecasting, and planning
Science, technology, engineering, and mathematics	Scientific research, scientific services, and product development
Transportation, distribution, and logistics	Movement of people or goods through flight, rail, car, biking, trucking, walking, or by other means

Determine Needed Education and Training

All careers, including some training programs, have education and training requirements that a person must meet. If you know which career you would like to pursue, you can find out exactly what the requirements are and begin to work toward them while you are still in high school.

Once you know what education or training you need, you can search for the best place to acquire it. Some education and training options are listed in **Figure 25.4**. Most colleges and other training programs have information available online.

Figure 25.4 Education and Training Options

Type of Education or Training	Characteristics
Colleges and universities	• Students select *majors* (programs of study). • Upon completion of program of study, students receive an *associate's degree* (two-year), a *bachelor's degree* (four-year), or an advanced degree, such as a *master's degree* or a *Ph.D.*
Career and technical education	• Students receive occupational training in areas that require hands-on skills (such as health sciences, culinary arts, and automotive services). • Programs usually involve a combination of education through a classroom setting and hands-on training and experience. • Classes may begin in high school and continue after graduation. • Students may earn a *credential* (proof of having certain skills, such as a college degree, license, or certificate) after successfully completing all required training.
Military training	• Soldiers receive hands-on training in various occupational categories that are useful both while in the military as well as in a nonmilitary job. • Aptitude tests are used to determine placement. • Programs may offer scholarships and degrees for agreed-upon service.
Employer training (also called *inservice education*)	• Workers attend specialized courses or sessions that teach them about their job functions. • Programs may be short-term, involving only a few classes, or long-term, lasting one year or more.

As you search, you might wish to talk with a career counselor or meet with faculty at colleges or other training programs. After reviewing the requirements for your chosen career, you can move toward finalizing your educational and training plans.

Get an Inside View

Getting an inside view is the best way to learn about a particular career. An inside view allows you to witness the day-to-day functions of a certain career and compare your career expectations with your interests, aptitudes, and abilities. You can get an inside view of various careers by talking to people in the career field and by gaining related work experience.

When talking with people in a career field, get as many perspectives as possible. Ask each employer what qualities he or she desires in new employees. You can ask employees what they find to be most challenging about the job. You can also learn more about job duties and typical job demands through *job shadowing*. **Job shadowing** is following a competent worker through his or her workday. By job shadowing, you can experience the work environment, note the career skills in practice, and get a realistic feel for what a typical day on the job is like.

Another way to get an inside view is to join a **professional organization** (group of professionals who meet to discuss their career field). Professional organizations offer opportunities to meet people working in a particular career area and to become knowledgeable about industry-specific jargon, current events related to the field, and career opportunities.

Another way to get an inside look at careers is to work at a job related to your career of interest. For example, you might consider taking a babysitting class or volunteering at a children's program to

Reading

Career Narratives

Most workers are willing and even eager to share about their personal experiences on the job. There are many first-person accounts available describing how people in various occupational categories first chose and started their career paths. These career narratives often outline both the challenges and the rewards of a particular career and workplace. They may describe professionals' career paths and how they launched their careers as young adults. Some career narratives, such as *Learning To Listen* by T. Berry Brazelton, M.D., and *Being an Elementary School Teacher: Real-World Tips and Stories from Working Teachers* by L.J. Urbano, are books. Other narratives are articles published online or in trade or professional journals.

Search the Internet or visit the local library to find career narratives that might interest you. Select either one book or three articles to read. After you finish reading the career narrative(s), summarize what you have learned and then share this information with the class.

learn more about working with and providing care for young children. Even jobs not related to the career you are considering can help you develop general skills, and job experience during high school is considered positive for college applications.

Many high schools offer *work-based learning programs,* school programs that aid students in getting quality experiences in the world of work. In these programs, students take classes and are placed at a work site. A school program coordinator works with both the student and the work-site **mentor** (a person who counsels and advises) to make the student's learning meaningful. There are three different forms of work-based learning programs (**Figure 25.5**). In some cases, students may find entry-level positions with the employer who supervised their work-based learning.

Developing a Career Plan

After you have completed a self-assessment, investigated careers and occupational categories,

Figure 25.5 Types of Work-Based Learning Programs

Type	Description
Co-op programs	Students enroll in a cooperative education class to learn more about a career area and develop the general skills they need. Students receive paid, on-the-job training through part-time work.
Apprenticeships	Students take a specific career class, such as child care, and then apply what they learn in class by working under the supervision of a highly-skilled tradesperson.
Internships	Students work at a company for a specified amount of time and learn about professional organizations, career options, and the related industry. Interns are supervised and may be paid or unpaid. Some students may be able to earn academic credits for internships.

and chosen a possible career path, you are ready to develop a career plan. A **career plan** is a detailed list of steps a person works to complete to enter a chosen career path. A career plan will help you identify your *goals* (what you want to achieve or obtain), including short-term goals and long-term goals.

Short-term goals are achievements you desire in the near future. When planning for a career, short-term goals include the many steps you need to take as you work toward entry in your career field. Short-term goals help you break down long-term goals into manageable steps and focus on accomplishments you need to attain in the near future.

Long-term goals are the major achievements toward which you strive. Long-term goals take much more time to achieve than short-term goals. They help you focus on the abilities, experiences, and credentials you need for a career. Long-term goals also serve as a guide to planning short-term goals. For example, a long-term goal might be to obtain a bachelor's degree. To achieve this long-term goal, you will probably create many short-term goals along the way, such as applying for a scholarship or passing a rather difficult class.

Part of your career plan also involves developing a **personal plan of study**. This plan identifies the courses and other learning experiences you need to complete to meet your educational and career goals. Teachers and counselors can help you identify these courses. You may wish to design a plan that leads to several related occupations within an occupational group. You often have greater flexibility job hunting when your skills are broader. Because child development knowledge is used in all careers dealing with children, a course in child development is considered broader than a course in teaching music in the elementary school.

When developing a career plan, identify your *resources*, which are tools you can use in achieving your goals. Your goals and resources should be realistic and should challenge, but not overwhelm you. As you follow your career plan, keep a log of your achievements (**Figure 25.6**). This log will help you track your progress and motivate you to accomplish other goals. Reviewing your log and revising your goals when necessary can help you as you continue to make decisions about careers.

Figure 25.6 Tracking your achievements over time can help you remember the short- and long-term goals you have set. A record of your achievements can also help motivate you if you are feeling discouraged. *How do you keep track of your achievements?*

Lesson 25.1 Review and Assessment 

1. What is *self-assessment* and how does it help people make career decisions?
2. Describe the difference between *aptitudes* and *abilities*.
3. Most child-related careers fall into the _____ occupational category.
4. What are *professional organizations*, and how do they offer an inside view of a career?
5. List the three types of work-based learning programs.
6. Why are short-term goals important to a career plan?
7. What is a *personal plan of study*?
8. **Critical thinking.** In small groups, discuss the pros and cons of the various education and training options covered in this lesson.

Lesson 25.2 Learning About Careers That Involve Children

Key Terms

Association for Childhood Education International (ACEI)
career burnout
Child Development Associate (CDA)
direct intervention
entrepreneurship
health services
indirect intervention
leader
National Association for the Education of Young Children (NAEYC)
personal qualifications
professional qualifications
protective services

Academic Terms

benevolence
delinquency
genuine

Objectives

After studying this lesson, you will be able to

- explain the difference between child-related fields that involve *direct intervention* and those that involve *indirect intervention* with children.
- describe careers in the child-related fields of health and protective services; care and education; entertainment; design; advertising, marketing, and management; research, consulting, and advocacy; and entrepreneurship.
- identify the personal qualifications important for child-related careers, including concern for children, flexibility, and leadership.
- identify the professional qualifications important for child-related careers, including knowledge of child development, career specialization, education and certification, and lifelong learning.

Reading and Writing Activity

Arrange a study session to read the lesson aloud with a classmate. Take turns reading each section. As you read, stop at the end of each section to take notes about the main points and to discuss any questions you might have. Save any questions you cannot answer for a class discussion about this lesson.

Graphic Organizer

Create a KWL chart to organize what you already know (K), what you want to know (W), and what you learn (L) as you read this lesson.

K What you already **K**now	W What you **W**ant to know	L What you **L**earn

If you are interested in children and their development, then a career in a child-related field may be for you. Many opportunities exist for working in a career that involves children. Child-related careers are constantly growing, and the widespread effort to improve children's quality of life is one trend that makes child-related work a fulfilling career choice.

Learning more about the many types of careers that relate to children can help you decide whether this field is right for you. To be successful in child-related careers, workers will need certain personal and professional qualifications.

Types of Child-Related Careers

Child-related careers involve varying amounts of contact with children. In some careers, adults work and interact with children directly; this is called **direct intervention**. People in such careers include teachers and pediatricians. In other child-related careers, adults work on behalf of children, but not directly with children. Working indirectly with children is called **indirect intervention** (**Figure 25.7**). All adults in child-related careers, whether working directly or indirectly with children, must understand children and their needs to be successful on the job.

Careers in child-related fields can be grouped into seven areas. These areas include health and protective services; care and education; entertainment; design; advertising, marketing, and management; research, consulting, and advocacy; and entrepreneurship.

Health and Protective Services

Professionals in health and protective services attend to the health needs and protection of children. This career field encompasses two types of services: *health services* and *protective services*.

Workers in **health services** ensure that children receive adequate physical and mental health care. Adults in these services understand children's health needs and have the knowledge and skills needed to provide quality care. **Figure 25.8** lists examples of careers in children's health services.

Other workers in health services may not work *exclusively* with children, but still should know children's needs and how to meet them. Some of these health professionals include eye doctors, speech therapists, hearing specialists, sports medicine doctors, physical therapists, occupational therapists, play therapists, emergency room and hospital staff, and pharmacists. Some of these professionals, however, may specialize in pediatric work (pediatric eye doctors or pediatric dentists) or be employed in a setting that deals only with children (children's hospital).

Figure 25.7 Examples of child-related careers in direct intervention include child care workers and therapists. Examples of child-related careers in indirect intervention include child development professors, artists who design children's space, and manufacturers of children's products and toys. *Would you prefer to work in direct or indirect intervention with children? Why?*

Figure 25.8 Child-Related Careers in Health Services

Career	Description
Child psychiatrists	Physicians who specialize in the treatment of children's mental health issues.
Clinical child psychologists	Professionals who specialize in the social-emotional and mental health of children.
Clinical social workers	Social workers who offer diagnostic services, psychotherapy, and counseling in a variety of settings.
Counseling psychologists	Professionals who help families and children cope with life challenges.
Developmental psychologists	Professionals who research and assess children's developmental status and make recommendations.
Infant mental health specialists	Specialists trained to provide comprehensive and intensive mental health services to families with infants and toddlers. These specialists may help families in which parents have a history of substance abuse or mental illness. Specialists may also help parents who are young and inexperienced or who lack resources.
Neonatology nurses	Registered nurses who provide critical care to premature or sick newborns and offer support to parents of those infants.
Pediatric and school nurses	Nurses who specialize in the care of children.
Pediatric dentists	Dentists who specialize in the care of children.
Pediatricians	Doctors who specialize in the care of children.
Registered dietitians	Nutrition specialists who may plan the diets of healthy children and children with special food needs.
School foodservice personnel	People who plan school menus and prepare and serve food to meet children's needs.
School psychologists	Professionals who help school-age children and teens with educational decisions.

Adults with careers in **protective services** work to identify injustices to children and to correct or remove children from dangerous situations. Careers in protective services are growing as society becomes more concerned about the rights and needs of children. Some positions in protective services are listed in **Figure 25.9**.

Care and Education

Another area of child-related careers involves care and education. The career area of care and education includes parents, caregivers, teachers, and other caregiving or education professionals. Due to increased enrollments in early childhood education programs and to governmental commitments to children's education, these types of careers are always in demand. **Figure 25.10** lists some common careers in care and education.

Entertainment

In recent years, the business of children's entertainment has expanded greatly. Many new children's television programs, movies, and live programs have been produced. A wider variety of children's books and games (including video games, other interactive games, and apps) are available.

People in entertainment careers include producers, directors, actors, technicians, video game developers, writers, and performers.

Figure 25.9 Child-Related Careers in Protective Services

Career	Description
Child, family, and school social workers	Professionals who assist children and families in crisis, place foster children, arrange adoptions, and serve as a link between students' families and the schools.
Child protective services social workers	Professionals who investigate reports of neglect and abuse and intervene, if necessary. They can initiate legal action to remove children to a safe place until the case comes into the courts.
Juvenile officers and family court judges	Professionals who make legal decisions about children and their families' rights and responsibilities.
Licensing personnel	Professionals who check the quality of services for children, such as the quality of child care centers.
Medical and public health social workers	Professionals who help children and their families cope with chronic and terminal illnesses and help plan for the child's needs after hospital discharge.
Mental health and substance abuse social workers	Professionals who provide individual and group therapy, crisis intervention, and other supportive interventions.

Design

Due to their changing development, children need items especially designed to meet their physical, intellectual, and social-emotional needs. Items designed for children include clothing, personal care items, dishes and flatware, furniture, books, and toys.

People who work in design may include interior or playground designers, product developers, and illustrators or other artists involved in children's books or films. *Designers* plan indoor and outdoor spaces for children, such as playgrounds and child care centers. Other designers may also work in the entertainment industry, such as in set design or costuming for children's productions. *Product developers* may design toys or other items made especially for children. *Illustrators and other artists* bring print and electronic media to life with their developmentally appropriate and child-appealing artwork.

Advertising, Marketing, and Management

As children's products are produced, businesses need employees who are trained to advertise and market these products. Another growing career choice is managing the businesses that produce and sell children's products. Positions for advertising, marketing, and managing can be found in corporations, agencies, firms, and small businesses.

Research, Consulting, and Advocacy

Many career areas, such as health, education, entertainment, design, and business, conduct research on children and their needs. Research studies provide knowledge that allows people to serve children well. Because thousands of research studies on children and parents are published each year, a massive amount of child-related research and information is available. Workers in research, consulting, and advocacy are involved in both the research and application of this information. Examples of careers in this area include consultants and child advocates.

As the body of child development research grows, *consultants* will continue to be important in child-related career fields. Consultants work on behalf of children. They serve as a link between researchers and those in direct intervention, product development, and sales. Some consultants are child development experts who provide state and federal lawmakers with information. Others write informational papers or deliver oral presentations (**Figure 25.11**).

Figure 25.10 Child-Related Careers in Care and Education

Career	Description
Child and youth leaders	People who plan, organize, and work with children and their instructors in religious programs or youth organizations, such as scouting groups, recreational programs, and camps.
Child care providers	People who care for infants, toddlers, preschoolers, and school-age children (when school is not in session).
Children's librarians	Librarians trained to work in school libraries or in children's sections of other libraries.
Family life coordinators	People who connect and coordinate support, services, and resources for children and their families.
Family life educators	People who provide direct services to children and families or train professionals in providing services for children and families.
High school teachers and college professors	Teachers who instruct high school or college students in child-related courses, such as health, education, child or lifespan development, and parenting.
Leaders, managers, and administrators	Directors of child care and education programs as well as principals and supervisors of school programs.
Parent educators	People who teach parents about child development and parenting.
Recreational instructors	People who guide or teach children in areas, such as music, art, sports, and hobbies.
Special education teachers	Teachers who work with children who have special needs.
Teachers and teachers' assistants	People trained to teach or assist teachers in public and private school programs.

Child advocates are professionals who focus on research addressing mental health, education, and legal or medical issues that affect children. Most advocates specialize in one issue, such as child support, substance abuse, **delinquency** (misbehavior; illegal behavior), or housing. Advocates work in the judicial and legislative branches of government and through professional associations. They conduct and compile research on an issue, observe the issue, seek support for needed changes, and keep others informed on the issue's status.

Entrepreneurship

Many child-related careers offer chances for **entrepreneurship**, the creation of one's own business. Family child care homes are one of the most common child-related businesses started by entrepreneurs. Some entrepreneurs own and operate child care centers. Entrepreneurs can start many other types of businesses as well, such as: child photography; recreational instruction; private medical practice; children's retail, such as clothing, furniture, and toys; and writing for and about children. Entrepreneurship in a child-related field can be satisfying and rewarding. Creativity, knowledge, self-motivation, and hard work are keys to making a business profitable.

Personal Qualifications for a Child-Related Career

Success in a child-related career involves a number of **personal qualifications**, traits you possess

Figure 25.11 Consultants often share child development information through oral presentations that can be delivered to a variety of audiences. *In your opinion, what would be the benefits of a career as a consultant? What drawbacks would there be?*

that cannot be learned in career training. Personal qualifications are sometimes hard to define and measure, so they are less specific than professional qualifications. Personal qualifications for success in a child-related career include concern for children, flexibility, and leadership.

Concern for Children

For a person in a child-related career, the most important personal qualification is a **genuine** (JEN-yuh-wun), real, concern for children. Sometimes, in the effort to perform well, people lose sight of the most important concern of all—the children. If you work directly or indirectly with children, you must always make decisions based on what is best for them.

When working directly with children, concern is expressed as an authentic liking for children. Adults show they like children through their **benevolence** (well-meaning attitudes) toward children. **Figure 25.12** describes behaviors of adults who display a genuine concern for children.

Flexibility

In working with children, it is important to be *flexible* (to remain open to new ideas). Children can be unpredictable, and research has shown that the constant changes required in working with children can cause people to have *career burnout.* **Career burnout** is emotional exhaustion with a career. A person who is flexible will adapt more easily to change and will be less likely to have career burnout.

Focus on

Speech

Qualities of Entrepreneurs

Entrepreneurs need many skills other than those directly related to their specialties. For example, a person who owns and operates a child care center must know much more than how to teach and care for children. This entrepreneur must also be able to manage money, coordinate advertising, hire and supervise staff, oversee enrollment, know and follow laws and regulations, maintain the facilities, and communicate with parents. Many entrepreneurs want to have the freedom to run business in their own ways and like the variety of roles to be filled.

Search the Internet or visit a local library to research stories about entrepreneurs with successful businesses. What were the advantages of starting a business? What were the drawbacks? In the person's opinion, what key qualities make a good entrepreneur? Deliver an oral presentation to the class summarizing what you learn.

Figure 25.12 Behaviors of Adults Who Are Concerned for Children

- Respect the uniqueness of each child
- Show kindness and patience with children and families
- Tolerate noise and physical activity
- Enjoy the child's world—games, songs, stories, concepts, play, and humor
- Feel comfortable helping young children with physical needs—dressing, toileting, and caring for scrapes, bruises, and common childhood illnesses
- Accept physical closeness—the child's touching of hair, clothing, and jewelry; hugging; wet-cheek kisses; and clinging when hurt or distraught

Leadership

Being able to lead others is very important when working in a child-related career. Children see adults and teens as leaders, and those working in child-related careers should model positive forms of leadership. A **leader** is a person who inspires or motivates the thoughts, feelings, or actions of others. Effective leaders are self-confident, which helps children feel secure (**Figure 25.13**). They provide clear instructions for the group or individual and set firm limits with children when needed.

Leaders in child-related careers teach self-discipline and listen patiently to understand what a child is saying. Leadership skills are also needed in working with adults, such as other staff members or the children's parents.

Mental Health Advisory

Career burnout does not just affect workers in child-related careers. Career burnout can also occur when a person does not like his or her job or feels overwhelmed. When employees feel burned out, this harms work performance and may even lead to physical and mental health problems from stress. In fact, depression is high among child care workers.

Like other personal qualifications, leadership qualities are a part of your whole life, not just your working hours. For some people, leadership is an aptitude. These people seem to have more natural leadership talent than others. If leadership is not one of your aptitudes, you can improve your ability to lead through practice. Babysitting or providing child care could give you practice at making decisions and being responsible.

Professional Qualifications for a Child-Related Career

In addition to personal qualifications, workers need certain professional qualifications to succeed in child-related careers. **Professional qualifications** are the physical, intellectual, and social-emotional skills you need to perform well in a career. People most often learn these skills from education, training, or entry-level work experience. Training might include classes in high school or college as well as on-the-job training. Professional qualifications for child-related careers often include specialized knowledge and training, education and certification, and lifelong learning.

Knowledge of Child Development

Child development is the science of understanding children. If you want to have a career in a child-related field, you must have a thorough knowledge of child development and know how to use and apply child development concepts. Because

Figure 25.13 Qualities of Effective Leadership

- Have a positive outlook and motivate others; excite people about possibilities
- Handle responsibility by following through to complete tasks, accepting blame for mistakes, and keeping promises
- Are honest; are trusted because they do not take advantage of others
- Show acceptance of others; are flexible and open to others' ideas
- Are aware of differing points of view and work to resolve conflicts
- Share reasons and explain their positions
- Seek positive group interaction through open and ongoing communication
- Listen to get other people's perspectives and seek common ground
- Know how to set and articulate goals to help the team achieve its purpose
- Assign responsibilities to others
- Develop team support by getting all members to participate
- Make sound decisions and are confident in their choices

physical, intellectual, and social-emotional development are interrelated, workers in child-related careers must study *all* aspects of child development, even if professional training for a career only stresses one aspect. For example, although pediatricians primarily deal with children's physical aspects of development, they must also be aware of children's levels of comprehension (intellectual development) and fears (social-emotional development).

Career Specialization

In addition to learning about child development, workers in child-related careers must obtain specialized knowledge in their career areas. Specialized knowledge might include understanding

- how children learn
- what to teach and in what order to teach certain concepts and skills
- the best methods and materials for teaching
- how to assess children's knowledge

For some careers, people must learn specialties within a specialty. Specialties require in-depth learning. For example, a *pediatric ophthalmologist* (AWF-thuhl-mawl-oh-jist) is a children's eye doctor. These professionals first learn general medicine, then how to treat diseases of the eye, and finally how to care for children's eye problems. Because so few people have specialties within specialties, these professionals often serve as researchers or consultants. They may directly handle only the most difficult cases. As more professionals have specialties within specialties, these professionals are becoming more available to all children, especially those residing in urban areas.

Education and Certification

There are many levels of positions within child-related fields. Most child-related careers require a college degree. Teachers, especially those in public school programs, must have a bachelor's degree in education. Public school supervisors and directors generally have at least bachelor's degrees, and many have master's degrees in child development, early childhood education, or related areas. Most have had previous experience as teachers. Consultants for public school programs are usually employed by higher education institutions and are hired just for specific training purposes. They usually have more than one master's degree or a doctoral degree.

In addition to a college degree, most child-related careers also require a *specific certification* (state-required documentation that proves someone is qualified to perform a job). Examples of a specific certification include a teaching certificate for specific grade levels or subject matter areas, a school administrator certificate, or a counseling certificate. *Certification* is also called a *license* in some professions, such as health services. Earning a certification often includes

- passing a background check
- meeting certain education and experience requirements
- successfully completing a specific test
- obtaining the endorsement of the training institution

Investigate Special Topics: Setting Short- and Long-Term Goals in Child-Related Careers

Obtaining professional qualifications for and making progress toward a career choice can seem *daunting* (difficult), especially while you are still learning about career possibilities. Creating a career plan with short- and long-term goals, however, can help make your educational and professional steps clearer and more manageable.

As you read in Lesson 25.1, short- and long-term goals can help break down major career goals. For example, if your goal is to earn a CDA certification, you would need to hold a high school diploma or GED or be a junior or senior enrolled in a high school career and technical program in early childhood education and clock many hours of training and experience. CDA certification holders need to earn a high school diploma or be a junior or senior in an early education program, clock 120 hours of training, clock 480 hours of working with children, and take a test.

Because one professional qualification is to clock 120 hours of training, you might focus on dividing that long-term goal into smaller, short-term goals. First, you could focus on finding an organization that provides training. Finding one of these organizations may involve online searches or in-person visits to early education programs. Thus, one short-term goal may be to spend time each week researching early education programs. Another short-term goal may be to decide whether to take the training for college credit or no credit, which also affects where you might receive the training. Along with this decision, another short-term goal is to get a good estimate of the total cost of getting the CDA and develop a savings plan for this expenditure. These short-term goals will help you reach your long-term goal of achieving 120 hours of formal training.

Dividing your career plan into short- and long-term goals will make your career plans clearer and will keep you focused on the short-term goals you can achieve now. Achieving these goals will also give you a sense of satisfaction and success, which can strengthen your motivation to achieve your long-term goals.

Writing Activity

List one or more child-related careers that interest you. What are the professional requirements you would need to reach this career goal? Create a career plan sketch that identifies the major long-term goals (goals that can be achieved in five to ten years) for reaching a career. How could you meet those long-term goals with short-term goals (goals that can be achieved within a year or a few months)? After creating your sketch, write a short essay describing what you can do *now* to begin meeting your short- and long-term goals.

Certification requirements vary from state to state. Therefore, professionals who move to a different state must reapply for certification and meet any additional requirements. Certifications often expire within a couple years and must be renewed.

A common certification in child-related careers is the **Child Development Associate (CDA)** certification. The CDA is an entry-level position qualification for teaching in a child care and education program or working as a teacher's assistant in a preschool program. Earning a CDA requires students to

- select a specialization
- complete a certain number of hours of study and experience
- pass an exam

Generally, the amount of training a job requires depends on the level of responsibility it demands. Teachers have greater professional responsibilities than teachers' assistants. Some careers, such as a neonatologist nurse or an infant mental health specialist, require study in schools and colleges and supervised work in the career field. People may earn professional qualifications for other careers (such as entertainment) through on-the-job training rather than through schools and colleges. Many in these fields, however, also have degrees from colleges and other institutions.

Lifelong Learning

In addition to basic career training, adults in child-related careers are expected to keep up with the latest knowledge and practices in their field. Continuing to learn about a field of study even after earning a degree is called *lifelong learning*.

Keeping up in a child-related career may require more classroom study, seminar or webinar attendance, or on-the-job training. Independent study helps keep professionals informed. An example of independent study may include reading about current research and the application of research findings in journals and books. Lifelong learning may also involve exchanging knowledge and practices among those working in the many child-related careers. This type of exchange often occurs at professional meetings.

One way to foster lifelong learning in a career path is to join a professional organization. Two of the many professional organizations for those in child-related careers in care and education include the *National Association for the Education of Young Children (NAEYC)* and the *Association for Childhood Education International (ACEI).*

- The **National Association for the Education of Young Children (NAEYC)** is an organization that works on behalf of young children. Members receive educational materials, have access to child development research, and can attend conferences.
- The **Association for Childhood Education International (ACEI)** is an organization that focuses on the education and healthy development of children. Members receive educational resources, attend programs and conferences, and may qualify for scholarships, awards, or grants.

Lesson 25.2 Review and Assessment 

1. Explain the difference between child-related careers that involve *direct intervention* and *indirect intervention* with children.
2. List and briefly define three child-related careers in protective services.
3. Describe the purpose of child-related careers in design.
4. What are *personal qualifications*?
5. Why is leadership an important personal qualification for child-related careers?
6. The _____ is an entry-level position qualification for teaching in a child care and education program or working as a teacher's assistant in a preschool program.
7. Name two professional organizations for child-related careers.
8. **Critical thinking.** Working with a partner, discuss why genuine concern for children is the most important personal qualification for child-related careers.

Lesson 25.3 Developing Skills for Career Success

Key Terms

codes of professional ethics
collaboration skills
critical thinking skills
employability skills
interpersonal skills
mediation
negotiation
problem-solving skills
professionalism
role guilt
role strain
time management

Academic Terms

consensus
diplomatic
scarcest
suspension
termination

Objectives

After studying this lesson, you will be able to

- describe the type of employee whom employers seek today.
- identify interpersonal skills needed for career success, including positive attitude, strong work ethic, good manners, and excellent communication skills.
- list three behaviors of people with good collaboration skills.
- explain the importance of critical thinking, problem-solving, and conflict-resolution skills.
- describe professionalism skills, including codes of professional ethics.
- identify three behaviors of people with strong executive function skills.
- explain the importance of role-management skills for reducing role strain and role guilt.

Reading and Writing Activity

Read the lesson title and determine what you have experienced or already know about the topic. Write a paragraph describing what you would like to learn from reading this lesson. After you finish reading the lesson, write another paragraph describing what you learned.

Graphic Organizer

Write each of the objectives for this lesson on index cards and arrange these cards near you as you read. On each index card, take notes about the appropriate objective. Then, trade your index cards with a partner. Discuss how the content of your notes is similar or different from your partner's notes.

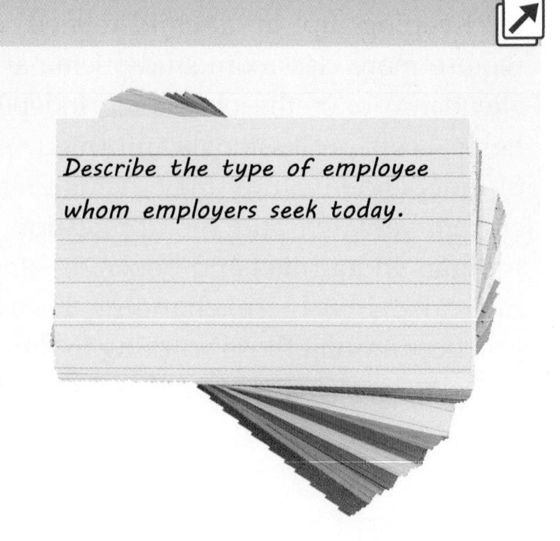

You live in a world of change where careers are becoming more knowledge-based as opposed to ones requiring *manual labor* (working with one's hands). In general, the information-age (also known as the *digital-age*) economy needs a new type of employee. This employee is one who

- adapts and copes with the stress of change
- learns quickly and is willing to learn new skills continuously
- possesses skills from more than one field that can be useful in a career
- is eager and able to learn about using new types of technology (**Figure 25.14**)

Career success today is defined more by the career skills gained and used than by keeping one job until retirement. Success also means finding work that is rewarding and fulfilling.

At this point in your life, you may not know exactly what type of career you want. You still have time to make this decision. You can start today, however, to develop **employability skills**, which are skills all employers seek in job candidates. Employability skills include interpersonal skills, collaboration skills, critical thinking and problem-solving skills, professionalism skills, strong executive function skills, and role-management skills. Chances are that you have already begun to develop some of these skills, but you can refine and enhance these skills throughout life. If you begin now, you will be much more prepared when it is time to enter the job market.

Figure 25.14 Most employees today are expected to be well-versed in technology and eager to learn and adapt to new types of work. *Why is knowledge about technology important for today's workplace?*

Interpersonal Skills

Interpersonal skills are skills you use to relate to and work with other people. These skills are perhaps the most important you will develop both professionally and personally. Interpersonal skills will often determine whether you will get a desired job, keep your job, or be promoted. Outside of the workplace, your interpersonal skills, or lack thereof, can strengthen or damage your relationships with family and friends. Interpersonal skills include a positive attitude, strong work ethic, good manners, and excellent communication skills.

Positive Attitude

Although a person's basic temperament is largely determined by genes, basic attitudes are influenced by the environment and begin to develop early in life. Attitude development is influenced by role models, such as family members, friends, and others, as well as by the media. Parents, teachers, and youth leaders often encourage children to develop positive attitudes. For example, they teach children to show respect and solve conflicts in a **diplomatic** (agreeable; polite) manner.

As adults, people are responsible for their own attitudes. To a great extent, work performance is linked to attitude. Employers need employees who have positive attitudes and who are friendly, cheerful, and considerate of others in the workplace. Employees with positive attitudes are generally liked and respected. Maintaining a positive attitude also involves respecting differences among people and getting along with coworkers, supervisors, and clients or customers (**Figure 25.15**).

Strong Work Ethic

In the workplace, *work ethic* refers to a standard of actions, behaviors, and values for job performance.

Figure 25.15 Having a positive attitude makes it easier to get along and work together with coworkers and clients. *Why is a positive attitude helpful for business relationships?*

A good employee is said to have a *strong work ethic*. This person understands what behaviors are appropriate for the workplace and is honest, hard-working, and dependable. A *dependable* employee shows up for work on time and works steadily through the workday except for normal breaks. He or she works independently and does more than that which is asked by the employer. An employee with a strong work ethic strives to get along with others, does the best work possible, and cares about his or her quality of work.

Good Manners

Manners are behaviors that make you comfortable around others and make others comfortable around you. Employers must trust you will not embarrass them in any situation. Furthermore, good manners help others take you seriously. The following are basic guidelines you can follow to practice good manners:

- avoid gossip
- be considerate of other people's feelings
- use manners in meetings and in verbal and written communications
- apologize if you must interrupt a meeting, conversation, or someone's concentration on a task
- keep any conflicts situation-related rather than personal
- keep your voice moderated in loudness and pitch
- talk to and visit with everyone
- be thoughtful of coworkers and clients

Excellent Communication Skills

Interpersonal communication skills involve the ability to read, write, speak, and listen well. In general, communication skills, especially writing skills, are listed as the **scarcest** (rarest) skills in the workforce.

Employees with good communication skills are expected to

- have good listening skills. *Active listening* involves devoting your full attention to the person communicating with you and then repeating what you have heard to ensure correct understanding.
- have excellent reading comprehension.
- use good *verbal communication skills* (communication involving words, such as speaking clearly and choosing words carefully).
- use good *nonverbal communication skills* (communication not involving words, such as appropriate body language and eye contact).
- communicate using standard English (grammar, mechanics, and spelling). For some careers, fluency in more than one language may be required.
- have needed computer and other technology skills.

In addition to these expectations, specific skill requirements vary with each career. Some of the communication skills that contribute to these expectations include those listed in **Figure 25.16**. Boosting these communication skills can greatly increase your chances of job success.

Collaboration Skills

The information-age economy has resulted in a more team-oriented workplace. Most workplaces require employees to have **collaboration skills** (the

Figure 25.16 Interpersonal Communication Skills

Skill	Examples
Listening skills	• Following directions • Grasping information • Clarifying information • Asking questions
Speaking skills	• Giving instructions • Responding to phone calls, voice mail, and personal conversations • Participating in meetings and conferences • Making presentations
Reading skills	• Understanding office signs and maps, such as evacuation plans • Comprehending office correspondence and manuals • Understanding career-specific jargon • Interpreting statistical data and understanding graphs and diagrams
Writing skills	• Writing messages and memos • Making records • Composing business letters • Drafting business reports
Nonverbal communication skills	• Appearing to be alert and interested • Focusing on the speaker • Smiling and greeting others with a friendly voice and firm handshake
Technology-based skills	• Organizing work tasks • Writing and responding to e-mail for business purposes • Using the Internet for gathering work-related information • Using word processing software and any company-specific software • Making spreadsheets and creating databases • Creating drawings and images (computer graphics) • Preparing multimedia presentations

skills needed to work well with others to combine knowledge, solve problems, reach common goals, and make decisions). Most careers, and especially child-related careers, involve team efforts.

Good teamwork involves getting along well with others. Team members work to develop problem-solving and decision-making skills. They learn to brainstorm, compromise, build **consensus** (group agreement) for ideas, and evaluate results of decisions. Good team players participate by listening and speaking. They also

- respect others' ideas
- take responsibility for assigned tasks
- accept accountability for the team as well as for themselves
- are adaptable and open to new ideas
- share roles with team members (**Figure 25.17**)
- deal with personality clashes and manage conflicts
- present an agenda
- keep the team focused on goals
- encourage every member to participate
- analyze ideas presented
- keep records of ideas and decisions

Figure 25.17 A person's willingness and ability to share roles with team members is a sign of excellent collaboration skills. *Why is collaboration important for the workplace?*

Developing collaboration skills takes time and usually begins in the early years of schooling. Working on group projects is the best way to learn teamwork. You can also build teamwork skills through participation in clubs, organizations, youth groups,and volunteer activities.

Collaboration skills also involve being an effective leader. Most effective leaders are also good team players. They have the skills to get along with others and work together. Leadership skills have their roots in the early years of life. As children, future leaders develop autonomy, responsibility, and self-confidence even in the face of risks. Young leaders-to-be often have leadership role models in their lives.

You can gain leadership skills through formal and informal leadership positions. A formal leadership position might be a position in a school organization. Career and technical student organizations (CTSOs), such as Family, Career and Community Leaders of America (FCCLA), also offer leadership opportunities. An informal leadership position might include taking charge during a group project.

Critical Thinking and Problem-Solving Skills

Critical thinking skills are the skills needed to analyze and evaluate situations to make reasonable judgments and decisions. Critical thinking skills are essential in every career and in everyday situations.

People use critical thinking to develop **problem-solving skills**, which are the skills used to analyze problems and formulate solutions. A key component of critical thinking and problem-solving skills is *conflict-resolution skills*, the skills required to resolve a situation in which a disagreement could lead to hostile behavior. **Figure 25.18** lists steps for resolving conflicts in a workplace setting.

Sometimes, formal methods such as negotiation or mediation are required to settle group conflicts. **Negotiation** occurs when individuals involved in a conflict come together to discuss a compromise. During negotiation, both parties are willing to give up something to meet the other party in the middle. For extreme conflicts, mediation may be needed. **Mediation** is the inclusion of a neutral person, called a *mediator*, to help the conflicting parties resolve their dispute and reach an agreement.

People can develop critical thinking and problem-solving skills by participating in school classes that encourage critical thinking. They can apply problem-solving skills to the challenges of everyday life and seek to resolve common conflicts they face.

Professionalism Skills

Many experts believe professionalism is missing or has declined in the workplace. **Professionalism** involves the skills, good judgment, and the attitudes

Figure 25.18 Conflict-Resolution Model

Step 1	Acknowledge the conflict and define the problem.
Step 2	Analyze and discuss the issue, list the facts, and get opinions on the issue. Divide into groups or brainstorm as a group for potential solutions.
Step 3	List all possible solutions.
Step 4	Evaluate each alternative.
Step 5	Reach a consensus to select a solution and implement the solution.
Step 6	Evaluate the results.

Focus on

Reading

Confidentiality in Child-Related Careers

Part of professionalism is following the ethical guidelines set by your employer. Child-related careers are especially concerned with ethical behaviors and with protecting children. Because of this, most child-related careers have established guidelines about confidentiality and information sharing. Guidelines about confidentiality affect how much information child care workers share with other parents about children's circumstances. They also affect how and to whom a pediatrician shares a child's health information.

Choose one child-related career and research typical guidelines about confidentiality in that career. Read two articles about these guidelines (or the guidelines themselves, if possible) and then write a short summary about typical guidelines in that career.

and behaviors expected from any person trained to do a job well. When professionalism is present, people who work together feel positive about each other and their work. There is also mutual respect present.

Professionalism requires the following:

- being skilled in your area of expertise and constantly searching for opportunities to grow in expertise
- being willing to go slightly above and beyond the minimum requirements or expectations
- being courteous and pleasant and maintaining a humble attitude in daily interactions
- having a strong sense of individual and group purpose
- taking personal responsibility, being accountable, and following through on your word
- being motivated to do your work and willing to share knowledge and information that help achieve group goals
- striving for excellence in each task
- bringing out strengths of others

Professionalism also involves following the ethical guidelines set down by an employer. Many professions have written standards of conduct for workers in a certain career field. These written standards are called **codes of professional ethics**. An employee is expected to follow any codes of professional ethics that apply to his or her profession (**Figure 25.19**). For example, the first principle within NAEYC's code of ethical conduct is never to harm a child physically, intellectually, or socially-emotionally.

In some careers, violating the code of professional ethics can result in **suspension** (temporary removal from a job) or **termination** (nontemporary removal from a job). People can develop professionalism skills by learning about career-specific ethics and professionalism requirements and by practicing good conduct before, as well as during, employment.

Strong Executive Function Skills

The executive functions (EFs) of working memory, cognitive flexibility, and inhibition allow people to self-regulate behavior. People with strong EF skills

Figure 25.19 It is important to read and carefully follow a workplace's code of professional ethics. Following these codes demonstrates professionalism and one's seriousness about a job. *What types of ethical standards are typical in child-related careers?*

exhibit a number of behaviors, including those shown in **Figure 25.20**.

One important EF skill is **time management**, the practice of organizing time and work assignments to increase personal efficiency. Time management involves prioritizing tasks by determining which ones should be completed before others. Time-management skills aid effectiveness when working independently or in a team and can be practiced in the daily management of a person's schedule and tasks. These skills are essential to success in the workplace, where an employee must regularly schedule time for and prioritize tasks.

Figure 25.20 Behaviors of People with Strong Executive Function Skills

- Focus on a stated goal
- Ask for help or get the information needed to achieve the goal
- Prioritize tasks and effectively manage time
- Organize workspace and thoughts
- Abandon ideas that are not working well and shift to alternative ways to reach a goal
- Outline major projects and create interim (in-between) deadlines
- Tackle one task at a time
- Tune out distractions
- Take regular breathers

Role-Management Skills

Most adults have more than one role, and each role comes with expectations. Many adults are simultaneously workers, spouses, family members, parents, consumers, and community members. Conflicts can occur among these many roles and their demands, and even the most satisfying roles can cause stress.

For social-emotional and physical health, a person must achieve a sense of balance between his or her roles. When a person's roles do not balance well, *role strain* can occur (**Figure 25.21**). **Role strain** is a feeling of having too many tasks to do at one time. Role strain can lead to **role guilt**, the feeling that one is not doing the best job at any role because of role strain. Role strain and role guilt can make people feel stressed, guilty, and unhappy.

People who want to be successful workers must have role-management skills. They need to learn to lead well-balanced lives using time management, prioritization, and healthful stress management skills. People can begin to practice these skills at any stage of life. You can practice role-management skills by managing the roles you have now, such as the roles of student, son or daughter, and friend.

Mental Health Advisory

Chronic role strain and role guilt can lead to mental health issues due to the stress involved in the person's life.

Figure 25.21 Signs of Role Strain

At Home	At Work
• Worrying about work while away from work • Being too tired to enjoy family life or to do household tasks • Not having time for leisure activities or not enjoying them • Bringing work home • Receiving complaints from family and friends about long work hours • Being irritable over little inconveniences • Not having time to relax • Feeling guilty about not having enough family time	• Being sleepy at work • Thinking about other things while at work • Feeling your employer expects too much of you • Being late for, or absent from, work • Spending time on the job dealing with family or other personal matters • Asking to leave early to deal with nonwork matters • Making lots of careless mistakes • Reacting in overly sensitive ways to others and hurting other people's feelings

Lesson 25.3 Review and Assessment 

1. What are *employability skills*?
2. List four interpersonal skills for career success.
3. Name three behaviors of people with good collaboration skills.
4. Describe the difference between *critical thinking* and *problem-solving skills*.
5. Many professions have ______, which are written standards of conduct for workers in a certain career field.
6. List three behaviors of people with strong EF skills.
7. Why are role-management skills important for career success?
8. **Critical thinking.** Which skills for career success are you best at practicing? Which skills do you need to practice more often for improvement?

Focus on

Social Studies

Children and Role Management

Decisions about how to handle multiple roles affect the entire family, including any children. In families in which parents experience role strain and role guilt, children may be affected by familial stress and lack of time with caregivers. To minimize the effects of role-management stress, adults can give themselves outlets for relieving stress and can help children cope.

Adults can cope with role-management stress by making time to relax. During the early evening hours, when adults and children are tired and hungry, children are most likely to express their feelings. Parents, however, may need to relax for a few minutes after long hours at work. To do this, parents or caregivers can take a brisk, short walk with their children or could set out a light snack and a board game for their children while they change into home clothes and take a few deep breaths before starting the evening routines.

To help children cope with role-management stress, adults can ensure that some of the time at home is *quality time* (time when caregivers are totally attentive to their children). Adults can also ensure that children's needs are met and can make time to attend school events or meet with children's teachers.

Lesson 25.4 Finding, Succeeding in, and Leaving a Job

Key Terms

cover message
job fair
networking
portfolio
references
résumé

Academic Terms

reiterate
vouch

Objectives

After studying this lesson, you will be able to

- identify resources for searching for jobs.
- explain the purpose of a résumé and identify its components.
- demonstrate how to write a cover message.
- list six items that could be included in a portfolio.
- identify questions one might be asking during an interview.
- describe guidelines for succeeding on the job.
- explain needed considerations for leaving a job.

Reading and Writing Activity

Before reading this lesson, find a partner and discuss what experiences you have with finding, succeeding in, and leaving a job. If you have had any jobs, how did you find them? What qualities made you successful or unsuccessful? How, if at all, did you leave the job? Write a short essay about your job experience.

Graphic Organizer

As you read this lesson, use a tree diagram like the one shown to organize your notes. Write *Finding, Succeeding in, and Leaving a Job* in the top circle and write major categories and then specific notes in the circles below.

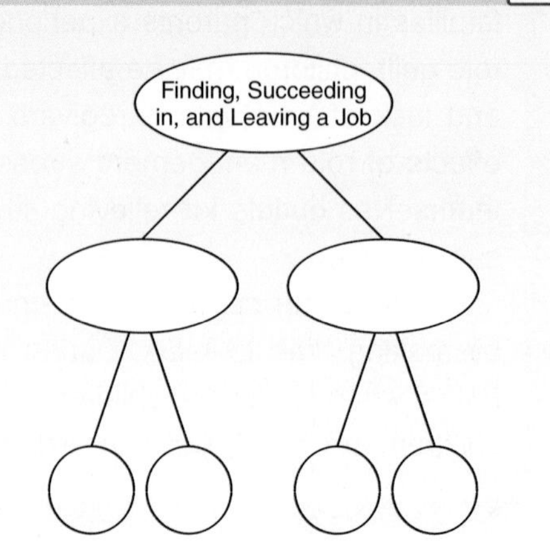

Once you have chosen a career, finding the job you want takes effort. Being qualified is only one part of gaining employment in a child-related career. Another part is looking for and securing a job in that career. There are many steps involved in the job-searching process. Knowing what to expect and how to handle yourself at each stage will increase your chances of job-search success. As you apply for jobs, you will need to write a résumé and cover message and prepare a portfolio. Applying for jobs most often involves an interview, which is a critical part of your search for a job. After a successful interview, it is important to know how to hone your skills, succeed on the job, and correctly leave a job if need be.

Searching for Jobs

Many resources are available to help you find employment opportunities. The most common method of job searching is using the Internet. On the Internet, you can visit credible websites dedicated to posting job opportunities in multiple industries. You can also visit specific company websites to view career opportunities available within a company.

You may also find job leads in your community. Jobs may be posted on bulletin boards located in shopping areas and recreational centers or at employment agencies or advertised in newspapers. Attending a **job fair**—a gathering of employers and job seekers to exchange information—can be helpful in finding job opportunities (**Figure 25.22**). You may also find job opportunities through **networking** (making professional contacts with family, friends, and others, especially professionals in your career area, for job information or referrals). Through networking, you can learn more about industry information, including potential job openings. Often, a combination of search methods is best used to find employment opportunities.

Applying for Jobs

Applying for jobs requires presenting your credentials and completing a job application. While seeking employment, it is wise to have your credentials ready before applying. To apply for a job, you should prepare a résumé and cover message, prepare a portfolio, and complete a job application.

Preparing a Résumé and Cover Message

To apply for jobs, you will need a résumé and a cover message. A **résumé** is a brief account of your career goals, education, work experience, and other employment qualifications. The purpose of the résumé is to acquire an opportunity for an interview. A **cover message** is a letter or e-mail message

Figure 25.22 Going to a job fair can be an excellent way to meet potential employers and other professionals. *What job fairs are usually held near your community?*

that accompanies a résumé. Its purpose is to invite potential employers to review your résumé.

Writing a Résumé

Prospective employers look at your résumé to understand more about your experiences. Your résumé helps them decide whether you are qualified for a job.

There are two types of résumés—functional résumés and chronological résumés. A *functional résumé* is best suited to applicants with much experience and emphasizes qualifications, skills, and achievements. A *chronological résumé* focuses on your experiences and how they make you an excellent candidate. An example of a chronological résumé is shown in **Figure 25.23**.

Mia Holtz
1603 Green Street
Southland Township, Wisconsin 66732
(262) 555-7472
miaholtz@provider.com
[name and personal information]

OBJECTIVE To become employed as a summer camp counselor. [career objective]

EDUCATION [education and degree type]

Southland High School 20XX to present
Southland Township, Wisconsin

- Focus on human services with an emphasis in child development courses
- Southland High Honor Roll, 20XX
- Graduating in June 20XX

EXPERIENCE [work experience]

Southland High School-Age Child Care Program 20XX to present
Volunteer

- Provide care for toddlers and preschoolers
- Develop lesson plans and activities
- Prepare nutritious snacks

Babysitter 20XX to present

- Provide quality child care for five families with children ages 10 months to 12 years

HONORS AND ACTIVITIES [honors, awards, achievements, memberships, and professional organizations]

- Southland High Ray Scholarship, 20XX
- Member, FCCLA, Southland High Chapter, 20XX to present
- Member, Southland High Writing Club, 20XX to present
- Team Captain, Southland High Volleyball Team, 20XX

SKILLS AND INTERESTS [skills and interests]

- Computer skills include Microsoft Office, Word, Excel, and Powerpoint; Word Processing; Adobe Photoshop
- Fluent in both English and Spanish

Figure 25.23 A résumé usually includes the components labeled in this figure. The order in which these components are presented depends on the résumé's intended purpose and audience. *How does order impact the effectiveness of a résumé?*

When preparing your résumé, keep it easy to review—use a bullet format, no full sentences, and clear, bold headings. Most employers and online job postings require the use of an *electronic résumé*, a text-only file without any special formatting. A text-only résumé allows potential employers to view your résumé regardless of the compatibility of computer programs.

It is important to carefully select educational and work history highlights when creating a personal résumé. The words you use in your résumé have never been more important. Many employers use applicant-tracking systems that perform *key word searches* based on the job description. These employers will view or not view your résumé depending on how many words it has in common with that description.

When writing a résumé, be sure to compile a list of references. **References** are people other than your family members who know you well enough to discuss your qualifications for a job, such as teachers, youth leaders, and former employers. Do not include references on your résumé, but always have a list available upon request.

Be sure that you carefully proofread your résumé and are as specific as possible. Customizing your résumé to the job description and using a professional sounding e-mail address can also increase your chances of getting an interview. For more information about résumé writing, you can attend a résumé writing workshop at your school or public library.

Writing a Cover Message

When applying for jobs, you may also need to submit a cover message with your résumé (**Figure 25.24**). In your cover message, you will introduce yourself and summarize the reason you are applying for the position without repeating your attached résumé. Remember, the purpose of a cover message is to highlight some of your job-related skills and qualifications and to capture the interest of the employer enough to arrange an interview with you. For online applications, a cover message is often transmitted in the body of an e-mail you send to a potential employer. Cover messages can make a lasting impression. A good message is brief, positive, customized to the job description, and follows specific instructions. Make sure your message is neat and follows standard business format. Be sure to check the spelling and punctuation. Many people seeking jobs have the qualifications that match the job description, but are not interviewed because of grammatical errors and misspellings in cover messages. Consider having several people proofread your message and offer advice on improvements.

Preparing a Portfolio

Many job seekers prepare a portfolio to show when interviewing with prospective employers. A **portfolio** is an organized collection of materials that supports your job qualifications and reflects your work, academic, and personal experiences.

Your portfolio may be a physical copy that you take with you to interviews or a digital copy (called an *electronic portfolio*). Electronic portfolios can be shared digitally or uploaded as websites. Whichever format you choose, make sure to update your portfolio on a regular basis to reflect new skills and qualifications.

Preparing a portfolio involves accumulating items for your portfolio over time and assembling them in an organized format. These portfolio items should be organized around an *objective*, or a purpose for your portfolio. For example, the objective of a portfolio might be to showcase your experience in child care to a hiring child care center. Some of the items you might want to include in a portfolio are

- your résumé and cover message
- transcripts from your education and standardized test scores
- samples of your best job- or school-related work, such as videos or writing samples
- letters of recommendation documenting work-related skills
- honors and awards
- proof of membership in student or professional organizations
- a personal statement describing your goals and how they came to be important to you
- summaries of volunteer work

1603 Green Street
Southland Township, Wisconsin 66732
April 15, 20XX

Ms. Anna Martinez
Program Director
Big Lake Day Camp
Rural Route 3
Southland Township, Wisconsin 66732

Dear Ms. Martinez:

I am interested in working as a counselor-in-training at Big Lake this summer. My guidance counselor at Southland High School, Mr. O'Brien, suggested I write you.

This job would be a good learning experience for me. I also have much to offer you as an employee. I have taken three child development classes in high school. Two of the classes included working eight hours per week in the school child care center. My duties involved planning a variety of activities for children, such as puppet shows, crafts, games, and snacks. I enjoy being with children and helping them learn. My long-term career goal is to open my own child care center when I graduate from college.

My résumé is attached. I would appreciate the opportunity to meet for an interview. I will call your office next week to see whether we can schedule an appointment. If you would like to speak with me sooner or have any questions, please contact me at (262) 555-7472 or at miaholtz@provider.com. Thank you for your time and consideration.

Sincerely,

Mia Holtz

Mia Holtz

Figure 25.24 A cover message should introduce you as a candidate and highlight the important parts of your education and experience. *What parts of your résumé would you highlight in a cover message?*

- certifications or licenses
- a list of references that can **vouch** (guarantee; verify) for your character and qualifications

If you are unsure what items to showcase in a portfolio, consider your career plan. If you are seeking an entry-level job upon graduation, showcase both the general and career-specific skills you need. For example, in child-related careers, experience working with children and families is most important. Your portfolio should reflect experience working with children and your understanding of child development. Your portfolio might include essays written for a child development course, lists of activities planned while working with children, or a summary of your experiences.

When using your portfolio to apply for college and scholarships, match your portfolio to admission and scholarship requirements. Student portfolios should contain samples of academic and extracurricular experiences.

Completing a Job Application

Prospective employers may ask you to complete a *job application*. The application asks for information such as your name, address, Social Security number, educational background, and work history. Information on your application and résumé should match. Job applications often ask for references, too. Employers may contact your references to find out more about you before making a hiring decision. Your references may include past employers, teachers, coaches, and other adults whom you know well (**Figure 25.25**).

Interviewing for a Job

After an employer has reviewed your job application or résumé and cover message, he or she may contact you for an interview. At the interview, you need to put your best foot forward by preparing before the interview, presenting yourself well during the interview, and following up well after the interview.

Before an Interview

The first step in preparing for a job interview is to learn as much as you can about the job and the employer. If the company has a website, thoroughly study the site. Use your network to find people who are familiar with the employer and learn as much information as you can from them.

Figure 25.25 Always ask your references before including them on a résumé, in a cover message, or in a job application. References need to be made aware that they might be contacted by an employer or college. *Why do references need to know that they may be contacted?*

As you prepare for the interview, consider some of the questions you might be asked and how you would answer them. It is also a good idea to prepare some questions for the interviewer. These questions should focus on information about the business, agency, or program seeking job applicants and on the work duties required for the job position. Asking these questions shows you are interested in the job and the employer. Avoid asking any questions about pay, vacation time, or other benefits until you receive a job offer.

Before the interview, ensure that your personal appearance is professional and neat. Clean, neat dress pants, dresses, or suits are appropriate (depending on the type of job you want). Be sure all of your digital devices are turned off before you approach the building site for the interview. Do not turn them on again until the interview is over and you have cleared the site.

During an Interview

When you arrive for the interview, introduce yourself and thank the interviewer for his or her time. Be sure to indicate your pleasure and enthusiasm for the interview opportunity. Offer a strong professional first impression by making direct eye contact and offering a firm handshake.

Let the interviewer lead the interview and ask you a variety of questions. Questions may be related to your educational background, work experience, goals, interests, and activities. Interviewers cannot, however, ask you certain questions. **Figure 25.26** lists common types of interview questions and questions interviewers cannot ask. If you are asked an illegal interview question, you can politely refuse to answer the question. Be sure to speak clearly and confidently and be yourself. Have a print copy of your résumé in your hands to consult if need be.

If you are given the opportunity, present your portfolio to the interviewer. If the interviewer asks you to explain one of your portfolio projects, be brief and to the point. Avoid talking while the interviewer examines your work. If the interviewer wants additional information, he or she will ask for it.

Figure 25.26 Interview Questions

Common Interview Questions
• Tell me about yourself.
• Why are you interested in this job?
• What are your strengths?
• What are your weaknesses?
• What are your favorite and least favorite classes or subjects?
• Tell me about your experience as a volunteer/babysitter/employee/member of an organization. What were your responsibilities?
• Have you had to assume a leadership role? What are some of your qualities as a leader?
• List one mistake you have made in the past. How did you correct this mistake, and how do you plan to prevent it from happening again?
• How do you keep yourself organized when working on more than one project at the same time?
• Where do you see yourself professionally in five years?
• Do you have any questions for me?
Questions Interviewers *Cannot* Ask
• Are you in a relationship?
• Are you married?
• Do you have children?
• When do you plan on having children?
• What ethnicity are you?
• What religion are you?
• Do you have a disability?

After the interview, you might be offered the job. Employers often have other applicants to interview, however, before making hiring decisions. If there are many applicants, you might be asked to interview a second or third time before the employer makes a decision. Potential employees may be called back to demonstrate their competencies, such as interacting with children in a center or using a specified computer application.

After an Interview

Immediately after the interview, send a *thank-you message* to the person who interviewed you. Thank the interviewer for taking the time to talk with you about the job and your career interests. Restate any important points that were made, and reinforce your strong interest in the job. A thank-you may be in the form of a printed letter sent through the mail or an e-mail. Keep the letter brief and to the point. Remind the interviewer of your name and **reiterate** (restate; emphasize) your enthusiasm, but do not be pushy.

Remember that employment decisions can take a long time. Some companies notify all applicants when a decision has been made, but some do not. If you have not heard anything for a week or two after the interview, it is appropriate to send a brief follow-up message. A *follow-up message* is a message you send to the employer to ask about the status of the job position. Be sure your tone is positive. Avoid sounding impatient or demanding. Simply restate your interest in the job and politely inquire whether a decision has been made.

A message or phone call accepting a job offer is fulfilling. When accepting an offer, remain professional and ensure your message is error free. Think of this as your first official act as a new

Focus on

Speech

Interviewing

You may want to rehearse for a job interview with a friend or family member before you go. This will help you prepare answers to some of the questions interviewers often ask. Consider the questions listed in Figure 25.26. Reflect how you might answer each question. What other questions might interviewers expect you to answer during an interview?

Conduct online research to view common interview questions. Select three questions to add to the list in Figure 25.26. Then work with a partner to conduct a mock interview. Take turns being the interviewer and the prospective employee. Offer each other *constructive criticism*, helpful advice and feedback that states how well your partner did and how he or she could strengthen interviewing skills.

employee. Let your natural enthusiasm show, be positive and thank the employer, and mention that you look forward to starting the job (**Figure 25.27**). You may also use this opportunity to confirm your understanding of the employment process going forward. If you decline the job or are not offered the position, it is still important to be polite and friendly. The employer may consider you for a future position and likely has colleagues who are employers in the same career areas.

Succeeding on the Job

Once you have been offered a job and accepted a position, put in your best effort to keep your position and succeed on the job. Continue to maintain your employability skills, such as interpersonal, communication, collaboration, and strong EF skills. Recall your work-ethic standards. Maintain a level of professionalism in interactions with coworkers, supervisors, and clients or customers. Show respect for your position by being reliable, dependable, and timely when you carry out job responsibilities.

Also make sure to follow safety practices in your workplace. The *Occupational Safety and Health Act* established a set of health and safety guidelines to follow in the workplace. These guidelines are regulated by the Occupational Safety and Health Administration (OSHA) of the U.S. Department of Labor. Under this act, the employer is responsible for providing a safe workplace. This includes ensuring employees use proper safety gear and the workplace is free of potential hazards. The employee is responsible for following established safety guidelines.

Figure 25.27 When accepting a job offer, express your enthusiasm and reiterate your interest in the job you have been offered. *Why is it important to let your excitement show when accepting a job offer?*

Leaving a Job

Few people stay in the same workplace for a career lifetime. People change jobs for many reasons. Sometimes people discover after working in a certain career that it is not a good match for them. Others outgrow their jobs for various reasons. Families are often mobile due to one spouse being transferred to another location and thus requiring the other spouse to seek new employment or due to reasons other than jobs. If you plan to voluntarily leave a job, it is best to secure employment elsewhere before leaving your current job. You should not use your work time at the current job to search for another job. You can look for another job, however, in your nonworking hours.

Even when leaving your current job, you have an obligation to treat your employer fairly. See **Figure 25.28** for guidelines to follow when you wish to leave a job. Regardless of why you are leaving, strive to end the job on a positive note. Leaving in this way helps others to remember you in a good light. In the future, you might need a reference or recommendation from your employer or coworkers.

Lesson 25.4 Review and Assessment 

1. What is *networking* and how does this process help people search for jobs?
2. Why is it important to include key words from the job description in your résumé?
3. What is the purpose of a cover message?
4. List six items that could be included in a portfolio.
5. Why should you prepare questions to ask during an interview?
6. The _____ established a set of health and safety guidelines to follow in the workplace.
7. Identify three considerations when leaving a job.
8. **Critical thinking.** Why do you think it is important to send a thank-you note after an interview? How is this step in the interviewing process an opportunity?

Figure 25.28 Guidelines When Leaving a Job

- Leave when the business is less busy, if possible. For example, a retailer might not want to lose employees during a busy holiday season.
- Avoid bragging about your new job.
- Show appreciation to your supervisor and coworkers for helping you to learn needed skills or for being positive role models.
- Consult the employee handbook or company policies to learn the correct procedure for *terminating* (ending) employment. Adhere to this procedure as you notify the employer you wish to leave the job.
- Provide ample notice so the employer can find a suitable replacement. The company policy may state the required time of termination notice. If it does not, you will need to decide how much notice to give the employer. An acceptable amount of notice depends on the level of skills required in the job. Employers often need more time to fill a high-skill job than an entry-level job. Two weeks' notice is generally the minimum for an entry-level job.
- Complete a letter of resignation and any other termination forms, if required by the employer. Address your notice to your direct supervisor. You may also have an exit interview. In this interview, employers may ask questions, such as "Why are you leaving?" or "What do you expect to find in another job?" Be honest, but remain professional and respectful.
- Try to complete all current tasks. Employers expect and are paying for your work through the final day. You may be expected to help train the employee who will take your place.

Chapter 25

Review and Assessment

Summary

Choosing a career is a crucial decision that affects your lifestyle. While you may not know what career you want, there are steps you can take now to help you determine. First, begin with self-assessment by assessing your interests, aptitudes, and abilities. Then you can begin researching careers. The information you gain researching careers will help you develop a career plan and personal plan of study.

Careers in child-related fields are diverse and growing. Child-related careers exist in the areas of health and protective services; care and education; entertainment; design; advertising, marketing, and management; research, consulting, and advocacy; and entrepreneurship. To work well with children, you will need personal qualifications (concern for children, flexibility, and leadership) and professional qualifications (knowledge of child development, career specialization, education and certification, and lifelong learning).

Some skills are crucial to career success. These involve interpersonal skills (including communication skills), collaboration skills, critical thinking and problem-solving skills, professionalism skills, strong executive function skills, and role-management skills.

Once you have made a career decision, you can begin to search for a job using several means. To apply for a job, you will need to write a résumé and cover message and you may need to compile a portfolio. Your performance during an interview will greatly affect your chances of getting a job. Once you have a job, it is important to do your best and be considerate of your present employer if leaving a job.

College and Career Portfolio

Portfolio Presentation

The portfolio you have been creating over the course of this text is now ready to present. Review your notes for your presentation, and in small groups of three, practice presenting your portfolios.

- Present your portfolio as if to a college admissions officer or employer.
- Ask your peers for feedback on your presentation. Also give feedback on your peers' presentations.

Chapter 25 Review and Assessment

Vocabulary Activities

1. For each of the following terms, draw a cartoon bubble to express the meaning of each term as it relates to the chapter.

Key Terms

abilities (25.1)
aptitudes (25.1)
ACEI (25.2)
career (25.1)
career burnout (25.2)
career plan (25.1)
CDA (25.2)
codes of professional ethics (25.3)
collaboration skills (25.3)
cover message (25.4)
critical thinking skills (25.3)
direct intervention (25.2)
employability skills (25.3)
entrepreneurship (25.2)
health services (25.2)
indirect intervention (25.2)
interpersonal skills (25.3)
job fair (25.4)
job shadowing (25.1)
leader (25.2)
mediation (25.3)
NAEYC (25.2)
negotiation (25.3)
networking (25.4)
occupation (25.1)
occupational categories (25.1)
personal plan of study (25.1)
personal qualifications (25.2)
portfolio (25.4)
problem-solving skills (25.3)
professionalism (25.3)
professional organization (25.1)
professional qualifications (25.2)
protective services (25.2)
references (25.4)
résumé (25.4)
role guilt (25.3)
role strain (25.3)
self-assessment (25.1)
time management (25.3)
values (25.1)

2. In teams, create categories for the following terms and classify as many of the terms as possible. Then, share your ideas with the remainder of the class.

Academic Terms

benevolence (25.2)
consensus (25.3)
delinquency (25.2)
diplomatic (25.3)
genuine (25.2)
mentor (25.1)
obsolete (25.1)
reiterate (25.4)
scarcest (25.3)
suspension (25.3)
termination (25.3)
vouch (25.4)

Critical Thinking

3. **Compare and contrast.** Working with a partner, brainstorm examples of short- and long-term goals in child-related careers. Then, compare and contrast these goals. How are short- and long-term goals different? How do both contribute toward your future career?
4. **Identify.** Choose one workplace with child-related careers and research the workplace's code of professional ethics. Identify ethical standards the workplace enforces. For each standard, list situations in which an employee would have to adhere to the standards.
5. **Analyze.** Collaboration skills are vital to success in the workplace. Using your knowledge and experiences, analyze why this is so. Why is teamwork so important? How can poor collaboration skills affect the work environment?
6. **Determine.** In small groups, discuss examples of critical thinking and problem-solving skills in practice. In what everyday situations do people use these skills? Then, determine practical ways you can practice these skills.
7. **Draw conclusions.** How do your time-management skills impact your life today? Are there ways you want to improve your time management? Write a short essay drawing conclusions about how time-management skills affect you now and will affect your future career.
8. **Evaluate.** The online job market is always changing as new websites emerge. Using the Internet, research current websites with job postings. You might also talk to a career counselor about which websites are most common. Identify five websites and evaluate how effectively they would aid your job search.

Core Skills

9. **Math and technology.** In small groups, research current statistics for how long the typical worker holds a job. What percentage of workers holds one job over an entire career? How long do workers typically stay at careers? Also discuss what cultural, economic, and field-related influences impact how long the typical worker holds a job. Use a digital device to create a graph illustrating your statistics.

10. **Research and technology.** In small groups, research child-related careers not discussed in this chapter. Each group member should choose one career to research in detail. For your chosen career, note typical job responsibilities, required education, average pay, and how much demand there is for the career. Use your findings to create a digital presentation for your class.
11. **Speaking.** Entrepreneurs need to know about many aspects of running a business to be successful. In small groups, research essential business knowledge and skills for entrepreneurs. Some of these essential skills might be setting tuition amounts, coordinating payroll deductions and insurance, or completing tax forms. Choose three essential skills and write a group speech explaining each skill and how entrepreneurs would apply it in an early childhood education business setting. Deliver your speech to the class and take notes about skills described by your classmates. Afterward, as a class, discuss the importance of business knowledge to child-related entrepreneurship.
12. **Research and technology.** Using reliable online or print resources, research current requirements for earning a CDA certification. How many hours of experience are required for the certification? What are the guidelines for basic eligibility? Use your findings to create a digital poster outlining the requirements. Compare posters with a partner.
13. **Listening and speaking.** Working with a partner, interview someone in a career of your interest about how he or she balances multiple roles. Has the person ever experienced role strain or role guilt? How did the person cope with these feelings? In the person's opinion, how are role-management skills important for career success? After the interview, present your findings in an oral presentation to the class
14. **Writing and listening.** Using an Internet job board, find a job posting for a child-related career of interest to you. Then, review your education and experiences to create a résumé. Tailor your résumé to the job description and make sure your résumé is as professional as possible. Then take your résumé to a writing center or college and career center and ask someone to review it. Take notes about their suggestions and implement them, if appropriate.
15. **Writing.** Reread the job description for which you wrote your résumé and then write a cover message as if you were applying for the job. In your cover message, explain why you are the ideal candidate. Be sure to check for grammar and spelling. Exchange cover messages with a partner for peer review.
16. **Reading.** Visit a local library to search online to find books or articles about interviewing techniques. Read two articles or chapters from a book and summarize the authors' main points. According to the authors, what questions are usually asked during interviews? What tips do they give for responding to interview questions?
17. **CTE Career Readiness Practice.** Imagine you are a human resources manager for a large chain of child care centers. You have been asked to deliver a presentation to middle-school students about the importance of interpersonal skills. Choose a presenting partner and develop three business situations in which someone would have to use interpersonal skills. With your partner, practice presenting these situations and guiding students in applying interpersonal skills to find a solution. While practicing, assess each other on professionalism and clarity. Deliver the presentation to your class.

Observations

18. As a class, arrange to visit a local workplace with child-related careers. Before the visit, research the workplace and write questions you have about the career and work environment. During the visit, ask your questions. Afterward, think about your visit and what you learned. Do you think the child-related career is one that might interest you? How well does the career align with your interests, aptitudes, and abilities?
19. In small groups, interview a worker in a child-related career who is a member of NAEYC. How did the person become a member of NAEYC? What privacy laws, professional practices and standards, and codes of professional ethics does NAEYC advocate? What are the benefits of participating in NAEYC? After the interview, discuss the benefits of professional organizations in your small group.

Photo Credits

Unit Openers

Unit 1 Opener bikeriderlondon/Shutterstock.com
Unit 2 Opener Vadym Zaitsev/Shutterstock.com
Unit 3 Opener Andy Lim/Shutterstock.com
Unit 4 Opener Kenishirotie/Shutterstock.com
Unit 5 Opener Carlos Horta/Shutterstock.com
Unit 6 Opener spotmatik/Shutterstock.com
Unit 7 Opener bikeriderlondon/Shutterstock.com

Recurring Images

Focus on Financial Literacy Noam Armonn/Shutterstock.com; Focus on Health wavebreakmedia/Shutterstock.com; Focus on Reading Andy-pix/Shutterstock.com; Focus on Science Otna Ydur/Shutterstock.com; Focus on Social Studies wavebreakmedia/Shutterstock.com; Focus on Speech naluwan/Shutterstock.com; Investigate Special Topics Tom Wang/Shutterstock.com

Chapter 1

Figure 1.0 Studio 1One/Shutterstock.com; Figure 1.1a Flashon Studio/Shutterstock.com; Figure 1.1b Aletia/Shutterstock.com; Figure 1.1c YanLev/Shutterstock.com; Figure 1.1d szefei/Shutterstock.com; Figure 1.2a wong sze yuen/Shutterstock.com; Figure 1.2b herjua/Shutterstock.com; Figure 1.2c Michel Borges/Shutterstock.com; Figure 1.2d Marlon Lopez MMG1 Design/Shutterstock.com; Figure 1.2e wong sze yuen/Shutterstock.com; Figure 1.2f Darrin Henry/Shutterstock.com; Figure 1.3 Carlush/Shutterstock.com; Figure 1.7 pavla/Shutterstock.com; Figure 1.8 Pavel L Photo and Video/Shutterstock.com; Figure 1.11 michaeljung/Shutterstock.com; Ch 01 Focus on Careers michaeljung/Shutterstock.com; Figure 1.12 Galushko Sergey/Shutterstock.com; Ch 01 Focus on Careers Kenishirotie/Shutterstock.com; Figure 1.13 Pressmaster/Shutterstock.com; Figure 1.14 Samuel Borges Photography/Shutterstock.com

Chapter 2

Figure 2.0 Poznyakov/Shutterstock.com; Figure 2.1 Allison Herreid/Shutterstock.com; Figure 2.3 ducu59us/Shutterstock.com; Figure 2.4 Body Scientific International, LLC; Figure 2.5 Body Scientific International, LLC; Figure 2.6 Body Scientific International, LLC; Figure 2.9 Dmitry Melnikov/Shutterstock.com; Figure 2.10 Robert Kneschke/Shutterstock.com; Ch 02 Focus on Careers Monkey Business Images/Shutterstock.com; Figure 2.11 CroMary/Shutterstock.com; Figure 2.12 Monkey Business Images/Shutterstock.com; Figure 2.13 Chepko Danil Vitalevich/Shutterstock.com; Figure 2.16 titov dmitriy/Shutterstock.com

Chapter 3

Figure 3.0 Kenishirotie/Shutterstock.com; Figure 3.1 Edyta Pawlowska/Shutterstock.com; Figure 3.2 Dragon Images/Shutterstock.com; Figure 3.4a Ivan Galashchuk/Shutterstock.com; Figure 3.4b Andy Dean Photography/Shutterstock.com; Figure 3.4c Monkey Business Images/Shutterstock.com; Figure 3.4d XiXinXing/Shutterstock.com; Figure 3.4e bikeriderlondon/Shutterstock.com; Figure 3.4f KPG_Payless/Shutterstock.com; Ch 03 Focus on Careers wavebreakmedia/Shutterstock.com; Figure 3.6a Blend Images/Shutterstock.com; Figure 3.6b Monkey Business Images/Shutterstock.com; Figure 3.8 XiXinXing/Shutterstock.com; Figure 3.9a Monkey Business Images/Shutterstock.com; Figure 3.9b Sergey Nivens/Shutterstock.com; Figure 3.10 Blend Images/Shutterstock.com; Figure 3.11 Marina Dyakonova/Shutterstock.com; Ch 03 Focus on Careers Varina and Jay Patel/Shutterstock.com; Figure 3.14 Ana Blazic Pavlovic/Shutterstock.com

Chapter 4

Figure 4.0 wavebreakmedia/Shutterstock.com; Figure 4.1 StockLite/Shutterstock.com; Figure 4.2 iofoto/Shutterstock.com; Figure 4.7 Blend Images/Shutterstock.com; Ch 04 Focus on Careers Monkey Business Images/Shutterstock.com; Figure 4.9 Syda Productions/Shutterstock.com; Figure 4.10 bikeriderlondon/Shutterstock.com; Figure 4.11 lightwavemedia/Shutterstock.com

Chapter 5

Figure 5.0 hartphotography/Shutterstock.com; Figure 5.1 Lukiyanova Natalia/frenta/Shutterstock.com; Figure 5.2 Body Scientific International, LLC; Figure 5.3 Body Scientific International, LLC; Figure 5.4 Body Scientific International, LLC; Figure 5.5 Monkey Business Images/Shutterstock.com; Figure 5.6 Body Scientific International, LLC; Figure 5.7 Sashkin/Shutterstock.com; Figure 5.8 Biamb/Shutterstock.com; Ch 05 Focus on Careers Monkey Business Images/Shutterstock.com; Figure 5.12 JPC-PROD/Shutterstock.com; Figure 5.17 wavebreakmedia/Shutterstock.com; Ch 05 Focus on Careers Monkey Business Images/Shutterstock.com; Figure 5.22 Ken Hurst/Shutterstock.com

Chapter 6

Figure 6.0 Galina Barskaya/Shutterstock.com; Figure 6.2 Michael Zysman/Shutterstock.com; Figure 6.7 sf2301420max/Shutterstock.com; Figure 6.8 Shestakoff/Shutterstock.com; Figure 6.13 Monkey Business Images/Shutterstock.com; Figure 6.15 Photodisc/Photodisc/Thinkstock; Figure 6.16 NotarYES/Shutterstock.com; Figure 6.17 travis manley/Shutterstock.com; Ch 06 Focus on Careers Monkey Business Images/Shutterstock.com

Chapter 7

Figure 7.0 XiXinXing/Shutterstock.com; Lesson 7.1 Graphic Organizer George Dolgikh/Shutterstock.com; Figure 7.1 StockLite/Shutterstock.com; Figure 7.2 Shanta Giddens/Shutterstock.com; Ch 07 Focus on Careers Monkey Business Images/Shutterstock.com; Figure 7.6 Alila Medical Media/Shutterstock.com; Figure 7.7 Body Scientific International, LLC; Figure 7.8 Dave Clark Digital Photo/Shutterstock.com; Figure 7.11 USGirl/iStock/Thinkstock; Figure 7.13 Paul Hakimata Photography/Shutterstock.com; Figure 7.14 Alila Medical Media/Shutterstock.com; Ch 07 Focus on Careers Steve Lovegrove/Shutterstock.com; Figure 7.15 Taylor Architectural Photography; Figure 7.18 Genotar/Shutterstock.com; Figure 7.19 Jo Tunney/Shutterstock.com; Figure 7.20 Joe Belanger/Shutterstock.com; Figure 7.21 Monkey Business Images/Shutterstock.com

Chapter 8

Figure 8.0 aslysun/Shutterstock.com; Lesson 8.1 Graphic Organizer Carolyn Franks/Shutterstock.com; Figure 8.1a John and Stacy Richardson; Figure 8.1b John and Stacy Richardson; Figure 8.1c John and Stacy Richardson; Figure 8.3a postolit/Shutterstock.com; Figure 8.3b Hans Kim/Shutterstock.com; Figure 8.4 Deviant/Shutterstock.com; Figure 8.5 Body Scientific International, LLC; Figure 8.6a Vladimir Prusakov/Shutterstock.com; Figure 8.6b Tatiana Makotra/Shutterstock.com; Figure 8.6c YUVIS Studio/Shutterstock.com; Figure 8.6d Denniro/Shutterstock.com; Figure 8.6e Kiselev Andrey Valerevich/Shutterstock.com; Figure 8.7 GTeam/Shutterstock.com; Figure 8.8a Alena Ozerova/Shutterstock.com; Figure 8.8b AnikaNes/Shutterstock.com; Figure 8.10a eurobanks/Shutterstock.com; Figure 8.10b Mark and Jaye Warwick; Figure 8.10c Flashon Studio/Shutterstock.com; Figure 8.10d Mastering_Microstock/Shutterstock.com; Figure 8.10e Monkey Business Images/Shutterstock.com;

Figure 8.13 Shanta Giddens/Shutterstock.com; Figure 8.15 Monkey Business Images/Shutterstock.com; Figure 8.16 John and Stacy Richardson; Ch 08 Focus on Careers Blend Images/Shutterstock.com; Figure 8.17 Kletr/Shutterstock.com; Figure 8.18 Rayes/Digital Vision/ Thinkstock; Figure 8.20 leungchopan/Shutterstock.com; Figure 8.21 Johnathan Shoff

Chapter 9

Figure 9.0 Samuel Borges Photography/Shutterstock.com; Lesson 9.1 Graphic Organizer Body Scientific International, LLC; Figure 9.1 Monkik/Shutterstock.com; Figure 9.2 Body Scientific International, LLC; Ch 09 Focus on Careers Monkey Business Images/ Shutterstock.com; Figure 9.6 Velazquez77/Shutterstock.com; Figure 9.7 Jack.Q/Shutterstock.com; Figure 9.8 Rohappy/ Shutterstock.com; Figure 9.9 mimagephotography/Shutterstock.com; Figure 9.11 wong sze yuen/Shutterstock.com; Figure 9.13a vita khorzhevska/Shutterstock.com; Figure 9.13b Chin Kit Sen/ Shutterstock.com; Figure 9.13c Fuse/Thinkstock; Figure 9.13d durganand/ iStock/Thinkstock; Figure 9.14 John and Stacy Richardson; Figure 9.15a Cheryl E. Davis/Shutterstock.com; Figure 9.15b sattva78/ Shutterstock.com; Figure 9.15c Elena Schweitzer/Shutterstock.com; Figure 9.15d monticello/Shutterstock.com; Figure 9.16 bokan/ Shutterstock.com; Figure 9.17 Svetlana Larina/Shutterstock.com

Chapter 10

Figure 10.0 John and Stacy Richardson; Figure 10.1 FamVeid/ Shutterstock.com; Figure 10.2 Tony Wear/Shutterstock.com; Figure 10.3 Monkey Business Images/Shutterstock.com; Figure 10.6 leungchopan/Shutterstock.com; Figure 10.7 MitarArt/ Shutterstock.com; Figure 10.8 Jaochainoi/Shutterstock.com; Figure 10.9a Mark and Jaye Warwick; Figure 10.9b John and Stacy Richardson; Figure 10.9c Flashon Studio/Shutterstock.com; Figure 10.9d Mark and Jaye Warwick; Figure 10.11 Anneka/ Shutterstock.com; Figure 10.12 stockphoto mania/Shutterstock.com; Figure 10.13 Rehan Qureshi/Shutterstock.com; Figure 10.14 siamionau pavel/Shutterstock.com; Ch 10 Focus on Careers wavebreakmedia/ Shutterstock.com

Chapter 11

Figure 11.0 rSnapshotPhotos/Shutterstock.com; Figure 11.1 Anetta/ Shutterstock.com; Figure 11.2 snapgalleria/Shutterstock.com; Figure 11.4 Monkey Business Images/Shutterstock.com; Figure 11.5 John and Stacy Richardson; Figure 11.6 Eran Yardeni/ Shutterstock.com; Figure 11.7a John and Stacy Richardson; Figure 11.7b leungchopan/Shutterstock.com; Figure 11.8a Mark and Jaye Warwick; Figure 11.8b John and Stacy Richardson; Figure 11.8c Julie Pigors; Figure 11.10 Dream79/Shutterstock.com; Figure 11.11 Ami Parikh/ Shutterstock.com; Ch 11 Focus on Careers Keith Weller/ARS–USDA; Figure 11.13 Kamira/Shutterstock.com; Figure 11.15 Olinchuk/ Shutterstock.com; Figure 11.16 Flashon Studio/Shutterstock.com

Chapter 12

Figure 12.0 Elena Stepanova/Shutterstock.com; Figure 12.1 Aniriana/ Shutterstock.com; Figure 12.3 Dragon Images/Shutterstock.com; Figure 12.4 Olga Bogatyrenko/Shutterstock.com; Figure 12.5 Jupiterimages/Stockbyte/Thinkstock; Figure 12.6 pavla/ Shutterstock.com; Figure 12.7 Blend Images/Shutterstock.com; Ch 12 Focus on Careers Monkey Business Images/Shutterstock.com; Figure 12.9 AntonioDiaz/Shutterstock.com; Figure 12.10 Jenkedco/ Shutterstock.com; Figure 12.11 John and Stacy Richardson; Figure 12.12a Jupiterimages/Stockbyte/Thinkstock; Figure 12.12b James Tutor/iStock/Thinkstock; Figure 12.12c DragonImages/iStock/Thinkstock; Figure 12.13a pavla/Shutterstock.com; Figure 12.13b Dan Howell/ Shutterstock.com; Figure 12.15 judwick/iStock/Thinkstock; Figure 12.17 Becky Lane

Chapter 13

Figure 13.0 Dan Howell/Shutterstock.com; Lesson 13.1 Graphic Organizer Agata Dorobek/Shutterstock.com; Figure 13.1 Pressmaster/ Shutterstock.com; Ch 13 Focus on Careers Andresr/Shutterstock.com; Figure 13.2 Laikwunfai/iStock/Thinkstock; Figure 13.3 rSnapshotPhotos/ Shutterstock.com; Figure 13.5 Mark and Jaye Warwick; Figure 13.6 Monkey Business Images/Monkey Business/Thinkstock; Figure 13.7a zhu difeng/Shutterstock.com; Figure 13.7b Alesya Novikova/Shutterstock.com; Figure 13.7c Janell Johnson; Figure 13.9 Aslanov/Shutterstock.com; Figure 13.10 BananaStock/ BananaStock/Thinkstock; Figure 13.11 tratong/Shutterstock.com; Figure 13.12 BananaStock/BananaStock/Thinkstock; Figure 13.14 John and Stacy Richardson; Figure 13.15 Juriah Mosin/Hemera/Thinkstock;

Chapter 14

Figure 14.0 d13/Shutterstock.com; Ch 14 Focus on Science Body Scientific International, LLC; Figure 14.2 Medioimages/Photodisc/Valueline/Thinkstock; Figure 14.3 Body Scientific International, LLC; Figure 14.4 Feverpitched/iStock/Thinkstock; Figure 14.5 Andresr/ Shutterstock.com; Figure 14.6a Sergey Novikov/iStock/Thinkstock; Figure 14.6b Fuse/Thinkstock; Figure 14.6c MIXA next/Thinkstock; Figure 14.9 Comstock/Stockbyte/Thinkstock; Figure 14.10 Julie Pigors; Figure 14.11 Azurita/iStock/Thinkstock; Lesson 14.3 Graphic Organizer tomertu/Shutterstock.com; Figure 14.12 Seiya Kawamoto/Photodisc/ Thinkstock; Figure 14.13 Vstock LLC/VStock/Thinkstock; Figure 14.14 anocha98/iStock/Thinkstock; Ch 14 Focus on Careers Karin Dreyer/Blend Images/Thinkstock; Figure 14.15a betoon/iStock/ Thinkstock; Figure 14.15b Sokolova Maryna/Shutterstock.com

Chapter 15

Figure 15.0 Phase4Studios/Shutterstock.com; Figure 15.1 Blend Images/Shutterstock.com; Figure 15.2 Pavel Lysenko/Shutterstock.com; Figure 15.3 Photographs in the Carol M. Highsmith Archive, Library of Congress, Prints and Photographs Division; Figure 15.5 Photodisc/ Photodisc/Thinkstock; Ch 15 Focus on Science Anna Marynenko/ Shutterstock.com; Figure 15.9 wong sze yuen/Shutterstock.com; Lesson 15.2 Graphic Organizer Carolyn Franks/Shutterstock.com; Figure 15.11 Blend Images/Shutterstock.com; Figure 15.12 ChameleonsEye/Shutterstock.com; Figure 15.13 Shapiro Svetlana/Shutterstock.com; Figure 15.14 MAKI STUDIO/Shutterstock.com; Figure 15.18 kiep/Shutterstock.com; Figure 15.19 Fuse/Thinkstock; Figure 15.22 Robert Kneschke/Shutterstock.com; Figure 15.23a Milica Nistoran/Shutterstock.com; Figure 15.23b David Sacks/Digital Vision/ Thinkstock; Figure 15.23c Max Topchii/Shutterstock.com; Figure 15.24 Blend Images/Shutterstock.com; Figure 15.25 MIXA next/ Thinkstock; Figure 15.27 shipfactory/Shutterstock.com; Figure 15.28 MIXA next/Thinkstock; Figure 15.29 Olesya Feketa/Shutterstock.com; Figure 15.30 Rob Hainer/Shutterstock.com; Figure 15.32 Jupiterimages/ Photos.com/Thinkstock; Ch 15 Focus on Careers amana productions, inc./ Thinkstock

Chapter 16

Figure 16.0 YanLev/Shutterstock.com; Figure 16.1 Mike Watson Images/ moodboard/Thinkstock; Figure 16.4 Blend Images/Shutterstock.com; Figure 16.6 Andersen Ross/Blend Images/Thinkstock; Figure 16.7 vesmil/iStock/Thinkstock; Figure 16.8a Mark and Jaye Warwick; Figure 16.8b Dragon Images/Shutterstock.com; Figure 16.8c Monkey Business Images/Shutterstock.com; Figure 16.9 Ellen Endres; Figure 16.10 Fuse/Thinkstock; Figure 16.11 Steve Mason/Digital Vision/Thinkstock; Figure 16.12 Riley Dahlman; Figure 16.13 YanLev/Shutterstock.com; Figure 16.14 Kenishirotie/Shutterstock.com; Figure 16.15 Fuse/ Thinkstock; Figure 16.17 michaeljung/Shutterstock.com; Ch 16 Focus on Careers wavebreakmedia/Shutterstock.com; Figure 16.18 Mark and Jaye Warwick

Chapter 17

Figure 17.0 spotmatik/Shutterstock.com; Ch 17 Focus on Science okili77/ Shutterstock.com; Figure 17.3a Chase and Hayden Volkmar; Figure 17.3b Chase and Hayden Volkmar; Figure 17.3c Chase and Hayden Volkmar; Figure 17.4 Body Scientific International, LLC; Figure 17.6a KPG_Payless/Shutterstock.com; Figure 17.6b Sveta Orlova/Shutterstock.com; Figure 17.7a Monkey Business Images/ Shutterstock.com; Figure 17.7b Ingram Publishing/Thinkstock; Figure 17.7c Barry Austin/Photodisc/Thinkstock; Lesson 17.2 Graphic Organizer XiXinXing/Shutterstock.com; Figure 17.8 Monkey Business Images/Shutterstock.com; Figure 17.10 John S. Quinn/Shutterstock.com;

Figure 17.11a HandmadePictures/Shutterstock.com; Figure 17.11b Hannahmariah/Shutterstock.com; Figure 17.13 Anton_Ivanov/Shutterstock.com; Figure 17.14 hl-studios/Thinkstock; Figure 17.15 Blend Images/Shutterstock.com; Ch 17 Focus on Careers Creatas Images/Creatas/Thinkstock

Chapter 18

Figure 18.0 Pressmaster/Shutterstock.com; Figure 18.1 Vector Monkey/iStock/Thinkstock; Figure 18.2 Wavebreakmedia Ltd/Wavebreak Media/Thinkstock; Figure 18.3 Diego Cervo/Shutterstock.com; Figure 18.6 Fuse/Thinkstock; Figure 18.9 anekoho/Shutterstock.com; Figure 18.10 tmcphotos/Shutterstock.com; Figure 18.11 Poznukhov Yuriy/Shutterstock.com; Figure 18.12 michaeljung/Shutterstock.com; Figure 18.13 Monkey Business Images/Shutterstock.com; Figure 18.14a Ariel Skelley/Blend Images/Thinkstock; Figure 18.14b Ronnie Chua/Shutterstock.com; Figure 18.14c Samuel Borges Photography/Shutterstock.com; Figure 18.15 allensima/Shutterstock.com; Figure 18.18 AVAVA/Shutterstock.com; Ch 18 Focus on Careers Creatas/Creatas/Thinkstock; Figure 18.21 Jose Gil/Shutterstock.com; Figure 18.22 CREATISTA/Shutterstock.com

Chapter 19

Figure 19.0 Andresr/Shutterstock.com; Figure 19.1 Blend Images/Shutterstock.com; Figure 19.2 Alinute Silzeviciute/Shutterstock.com; Figure 19.6 Lucian Coman/Shutterstock.com; Figure 19.8 Olesya Feketa/Shutterstock.com; Figure 19.9 ©iStock.com/JBryson; Figure 19.11a Monkey Business Images/Shutterstock.com; Figure 19.11b Monkey Business Images/Shutterstock.com; Figure 19.11c CREATISTA/Shutterstock.com; Figure 19.12 Blend Images/Shutterstock.com; Figure 19.13 Carlos Horta/Shutterstock.com; Figure 19.14 Monkey Business Images/Shutterstock.com; Ch 19 Focus on Careers Zurijeta/Shutterstock.com; Figure 19.16 wavebreakmedia/Shutterstock.com; Figure 19.17 oliveromg/Shutterstock.com

Chapter 20

Figure 20.0 Samuel Borges Photography/Shutterstock.com; Figure 20.1 fuyu liu/Shutterstock.com; Figure 20.2 ©iStock.com/acfrank; Figure 20.4 Ellen Endres; Figure 20.7a Nenov Brothers Images/Shutterstock.com; Figure 20.7b Nenov Brothers Images/Shutterstock.com; Figure 20.7c Nenov Brothers Images/Shutterstock.com; Figure 20.7d Nenov Brothers Images/Shutterstock.com; Figure 20.7e Tomas Hilger/Shutterstock.com; Figure 20.7f Vladimir Prusakov/Shutterstock.com; Figure 20.8 Irina Fischer/Shutterstock.com; Figure 20.9 Ami Parikh/Shutterstock.com; Ch 20 Focus on Careers Solis Images/Shutterstock.com; Figure 20.10 John and Stacy Richardson; Figure 20.11a AnRo brook/Shutterstock.com; Figure 20.11b AnRo brook/Shutterstock.com; Figure 20.11c s_oleg/Shutterstock.com; Figure 20.12 wavebreakmedia/Shutterstock.com; Figure 20.13 KPG Payless2/Shutterstock.com; Figure 20.14 John and Stacy Richardson

Chapter 21

Figure 21.0 Evgeny Bakharev/Shutterstock.com; Figure 21.1 Dejan Ristovski/Shutterstock.com; Figure 21.2 Odua Images/Shutterstock.com; Figure 21.3 Centers for Disease Control and Prevention; Figure 21.5 USDA/FSIS; Figure 21.7 bikeriderlondon/Shutterstock.com; Figure 21.9a Iriana Shiyan/Shutterstock.com; Figure 21.9b Iriana Shiyan/Shutterstock.com; Figure 21.12 ©iStock.com/dmbaker; Ch 21 Focus on Careers Spotmatik Ltd/Shutterstock.com; Figure 21.13 ©iStock.com/XiXinXing; Figure 21.14 Blend Images/Shutterstock.com; Figure 21.16 Marius Pirvu/Shutterstock.com; Figure 21.17 omphoto/Shutterstock.com; Figure 21.18 zulufoto/Shutterstock.com; Figure 21.19 Alila Medical Media/Shutterstock.com; Figure 21.21 ©iStock.com/katifcam

Chapter 22

Figure 22.0 VP Photo Studio/Shutterstock.com; Figure 22.1 Rawpixel/Shutterstock.com; Figure 22.3 Monkey Business Images/Shutterstock.com; Figure 22.6 Monkey Business Images/Shutterstock.com; Figure 22.9 Blend Images/Shutterstock.com; Figure 22.11a ©iStock.com/monkeybusinessimages; Figure 22.11b ©iStock.com/diego_cervo; Figure 22.12 dr322/Shutterstock.com; Figure 22.15 purplequeue/Shutterstock.com; Figure 22.16 Monkey Business Images/Shutterstock.com; Figure 22.18 Ruslan Guzov/Shutterstock.com; Figure 22.19 Roylee_photosunday/Shutterstock.com; Ch 22 Focus on Careers wavebreakmedia/Shutterstock.com

Chapter 23

Figure 23.0 Denis Kuvaev/Shutterstock.com; Figure 23.1 Jaren Jai Wicklund/Shutterstock.com; Figure 23.4 Blend Images/Shutterstock.com; Figure 23.6a Monkey Business Images/Shutterstock.com; Figure 23.6b Daisy Daisy/Shutterstock.com; Figure 23.11 ©iStock.com/paulaphoto; Figure 23.12 Blend Images/Shutterstock.com; Figure 23.14 ChameleonsEye/Shutterstock.com; Figure 23.16 Alsu/Shutterstock.com; Ch 23 Focus on Careers Olesia Bilkei/Shutterstock.com; Figure 23.17 ©iStock.com/JackQ; Figure 23.18 Image Point Fr/Shutterstock.com; Figure 23.19 wavebreakmedia/Shutterstock.com; Ch 23 Focus on Science Designua/Shutterstock.com; Figure 23.20 michaeljung/Shutterstock.com; Figure 23.21 wavebreakmedia/Shutterstock.com; Figure 23.22 Tyler Olson/Shutterstock.com; Figure 23.23 Monkey Business Images/Shutterstock.com

Chapter 24

Figure 24.0 michaeljung/Shutterstock.com; Lesson 24.1 Graphic Organizer Artex67/Shutterstock.com; Figure 24.1 Singkham/Shutterstock.com; Figure 24.4 Robert Kneschke/Shutterstock.com; Figure 24.5 ©iStock.com/diane555; Ch 24 Focus on Careers bikeriderlondon/Shutterstock.com; Figure 24.6 ©iStock.com/AndreyStratilatov; Figure 24.7 Monkey Business Images/Shutterstock.com; Figure 24.8 Blend Images/Shutterstock.com; Figure 24.9 Dragon Images/Shutterstock.com; Figure 24.10 ©iStock.com/real444; Ch 24 Focus on Careers mangostock/Shutterstock.com; Figure 24.12 luminaimages/Shutterstock.com; Figure 24.15 ©iStock.com/monkeybusinessimages; Figure 24.18 ©iStock.com/Squaredpixels; Figure 24.19 ©iStock.com/XiXinXing

Chapter 25

Figure 25.0 michaeljung/Shutterstock.com; Figure 25.1 XiXinXing/Shutterstock.com; Ch 25 Focus on Careers Monkey Business Images/Shutterstock.com; Figure 25.2 Goodluz/Shutterstock.com; Figure 25.6 Lorelyn Medina/Shutterstock.com; Figure 25.7a Dave Clark Digital Photo/Shutterstock.com; Figure 25.7b bikeriderlondon/Shutterstock.com; Figure 25.11 l i g h t p o e t/Shutterstock.com; Figure 25.12 XiXinXing/Shutterstock.com; Lesson 25.3 Graphic Organizer Carolyn Franks/Shutterstock.com; Figure 25.14 michaeljung/Shutterstock.com; Figure 25.15 Rawpixel/Shutterstock.com; Figure 25.17 Monkey Business Images/Shutterstock.com; Figure 25.19 Dean Drobot/Shutterstock.com; Figure 25.22 Rawpixel/Shutterstock.com; Figure 25.25 Gromovataya/Shutterstock.com; Figure 25.27 michaeljung/Shutterstock.com

Glossary

A

abilities. Skills people learn or develop and acquire through effort and practice. (25.1)

abnormalities. Flaws or irregularities. (5.2)

abrasion (uh-BRAY-zhun). Scrape. (21.3)

abrupt. Sudden; unanticipated. (8.2)

abstinence. Refusal to engage in a sexual relationship. (6.2)

abundance. Large amount. (2.1)

accredited programs. Early childhood education programs that are not only licensed, but have met even higher standards of quality set forth by a professional organization. (24.2)

acrid. Bitter and unpleasant. (14.2)

active listening. Communication technique in which the receiver of a message provides feedback to the speaker, indicating that the message is understood. (3.1)

active-physical play. Type of play in which children use their gross-motor skills. (20.1)

active vocabulary. Words a person uses in talking or writing. (9.2)

activity plan. Teacher plan that outlines activities around a theme; usually written for preschool children. (24.2)

actuality. Reality; fact. (12.1)

adoption. Process by which a child of one pair of parents legally becomes the child of other parents (or parent). (3.2)

adoption agency. State-funded or private agency licensed by the state to handle adoptions. (3.2)

adult-child ratio. Number of adults per the number of children in an early childhood education program. (24.2)

adverse. Harmful. (8.2)

adversely. Unfavorably. (6.2)

adversity. Risks and stress. (22.1)

advocates. People who actively support a cause. (1.3)

after-school programs. Programs that supervise, care for, and teach children after school until parents or caregivers finish the workday. (18.3)

age-appropriate behaviors. Proper or expected ways to express emotions at certain ages. (10.1)

age norm. Typical time when a developmental milestone, such as walking or talking, occurs; an age norm can be expressed as an average age or an age range. (1.2)

age of viability. Time from when a baby can survive if born early; possibly as early as 23 weeks, but 24–28 weeks improves chances. (5.1)

agile. Able to move quickly and easily. (14.3)

AIDS. Acquired immunodeficiency syndrome; disease caused by the human immunodeficiency virus (HIV), which attacks the body's immune system. (5.2)

allergen (AL-lur-jun). Substance that causes an allergic reaction. (21.1)

allergy. Negative reaction by the body's immune system to an allergen. (21.1)

alleviates. Relieves. (8.2)

alphabetize. Put in alphabetical order. (18.2)

altruism (ALL-troo-ih-zuhm). Desire to help others without seeking a reward. (16.2)

altruistic behaviors. Actions that show concern for others, but without an expectation for a reward. (16.2)

ambidextrous (am-bih-DECK-struhs). Ability to use the right or left hand, as the preferred hand, almost equally well for many tasks. (14.1)

ambiguous (am-BIH-gyuh-wuhs). Less-defined. (16.2)

amenable (uh-MEH-nuh-buhl). Receptive to. (16.2)

amniocentesis (AM-nee-oh-sen-TEE-sis). Prenatal test in which a needle is inserted through the woman's abdomen into the amniotic sac and a sample of the fluid is removed for cell study. (5.3)

amnion. Fluid-filled sac that surrounds the baby in the uterus. (5.1)

ample. A generous amount. (4.1)

anaphylaxis (AN-uh-fuh-LAK-sus). Life-threatening shock. (21.1)

anemia. Condition that occurs when the level of healthy red blood cells, which carry oxygen to all parts of the body, becomes too low. (7.3)

animism (AN-ih-mism). Attribution of living qualities to inanimate objects. (15.2)

antidepressants. Medications that treat depression by working to correct the chemical imbalance in neurotransmitters, especially serotonin, in the brain and boost mood. (23.2)

antiperspirants. Substances that dry up sweat. (17.3)

antipsychotics. Medications that reduce symptoms of psychosis and help children with schizophrenia. (23.2)

antiseptic. Substance that kills bacteria. (21.3)

anxiety. Fear of a possible future event. (10.1)

anxiety disorder. Specific anxiety that interferes with a child's ability to achieve goals or enjoy life. (23.1)

Apgar test. Test that measures the newborn's chance of survival by checking the baby's pulse, breathing, muscle tone, responsiveness, and skin color. (7.3)

apt. Likely. (3.2)

aptitudes. Talents with which people are born; they are natural and a part of heredity. (25.1)

articulate. Clearly vocalize. (9.2)

articulation. Person's ability to pronounce words that can be understood by others. (12.2)

artificial insemination. Assisted reproductive technology (ART) procedure that involves introducing sperm into the vagina or uterus by a medical procedure rather than by intercourse; also called *intrauterine insemination*. (6.1)

aspects. Parts of something. (4.2)

assertive. Able to speak out, stand up for one's rights, and defend one's self. (16.2)

assimilate. Fully understand and use knowledge of. (13.1)

assisted reproductive technologies (ARTs). Methods infertile couples can use to help them conceive. (6.1)

Association for Childhood Education International (ACEI). Professional organization that focuses on the education and healthy development of children by providing educational resources, programs and conferences, scholarships, awards, and grants. (25.2)

asthma. Chronic inflammation of the airways. (21.1)

attachment. Closeness between people that remains over time. (10.1)

attachment behaviors. Actions one person demonstrates to another person to show closeness to that person. (10.1)

attention-deficit hyperactivity disorder (ADHD). Disorder that involves lack of attention and extremely active behavior that exceeds a typical high energy level. (23.1)

attributes. Properties. (12.2)

auditory. Relating to hearing. (9.2)

authoritarian. Parenting style in which the main objective is to make children completely obedient. (4.2)

authoritative. Parenting style in which parents set some rules, but allow children some freedom; also called *assertive-democratic*. (4.2)

autism spectrum disorder (ASD). General term used to describe complex communication, social, and behavioral developmental disabilities. (23.1)

autonomy. Form of self-governance in which a toddler seeks to do his or her will. (13.1)

autonomy versus shame and doubt. Conflict toddlers must resolve according to the second stage of Erikson's psychosocial theory. (13.1)

axons. Long, thick cables that transmit all the signals from a neuron to other neurons. (2.1)

B

babbling. Infant speech using the tongue and the front of the mouth to make a consonant-vowel sound, such as *ba*. (9.2)

baby agenda. Term that describes how all infants, regardless of culture, are born with the internal drive to learn certain concepts and skills in holistic ways and at approximately the same age. (9.3)

baby blues. Mild postpartum mood disorder that goes away on its own. (7.4)

baffle. Confuse. (23.2)

bassinet. Basketlike bed newborns may use during the first few weeks after birth. (8.3)

behavioral disorder. Pattern of challenges that surfaces in a person's behavior. (23.1)

belabor. Drag out for too long. (18.3)

benevolence. Well-meaning attitudes. (25.2)

bewilders. Confuses. (13.2)

bias. Favoring; unequal treatment. (3.1)

bilingual. Being fluent in two languages. (12.2)

binge. Overeat. (17.2)

binocular vision. Vision achieved when using both eyes in unison, equally, and accurately to fuse in the brain the two images into one image. (9.1)

biochemistry. The chemistry of living organisms. (2.1)

birth control methods. Measures couples use to help prevent pregnancy. (4.1)

body language. Type of nonverbal communication that involves sending and receiving messages through body movements, such as facial expressions, eye contact, gestures, and posture. (3.1)

body proportions. Relative size of body parts. (8.1)

body rotation. Using the axis of the spine for rotation, the hips (pelvis) and then the shoulders turn toward the back while the throwing arm comes forward. (14.1)

bolster. Lend support to. (19.2)

bonding. Developing a feeling of affection. (7.2)

botanist. Person who studies plant life. (5.2)

Braille system. System of raised dots enabling people with vision conditions to read by touch. (23.2)

Brazelton scale. Test doctors use to determine whether a baby has problems interacting with the environment, handling motor processes, controlling his or her physical state, or responding to stress. (7.3)

breech birth position. Common abnormal birth position in which a baby enters the birth canal feet-, legs-, or buttocks-first. (7.2)

budget. Financial plan for spending and saving money. (3.1)

buffers. Protections or support systems. (22.1)

bullying. Most common form of peer abuse; involves inflicting physical, verbal, and emotional abuse on another person. (22.2)

C

career. Progression of related jobs that results in employment with opportunities for professional and personal growth. (25.1)

career burnout. State in which a person becomes emotionally exhausted with a career. (25.2)

career plan. Detailed list of steps a person works to complete to enter a chosen career path. (25.1)

cartilage. Firm, but flexible connective tissue found in parts of the body. (8.1)

categorization. Grouping similar objects or events into a group. (9.2)

causal. Related to the cause of something. (23.1)

cavities. Areas of decay in teeth. (14.3)

cell. Smallest unit of life that is able to reproduce itself. (5.1)

center-based child care. Group child care that is provided in a center rather than in a home. (24.1)

centration (sen-TRAY-shun). Focusing on only one part of an object or event instead of seeing all parts at the same time. (15.1)

cephalocaudal (sef-uh-lo-KAW-dahl) development. Progression of development beginning with the head and moving down to the feet; also called *head-to-foot development*. (8.1)

certified child safety seat. Restraint system for children under the age of 13, which is required when riding in a motor vehicle; also called a *car seat*. (21.2)

certified nurse-midwife (CNM). Nurse who has special training in delivering babies during low-risk pregnancies. (7.1)

cervix (SER-viks). Lower, narrow portion of the uterus that connects the uterus to the vagina, or *birth canal*. (5.1)

cesarean (sih-ZARE-ee-uhn) section. Delivery method in which the mother's abdomen and uterus are surgically opened and the baby is removed; also called *C-section*. (7.2)

character. Principles and beliefs that guide a person's conduct and define his or her personality and behavior. (4.2)

child abuse. Intentional act committed by an adult that harms or threatens to harm a child's well-being. (22.2)

child care programs. Early childhood education programs that provide care for children for extended hours, usually between 9 and 12 hours a day. (24.1)

child care resources and referral (CCR&R) agencies. Agencies that promote local early childhood education programs and help parents identify child care options. (24.1)

child-centered society. Society that sees children as important, cares about their well-being, and works to meet their needs. (1.3)

child development. Scientific study of children from conception to adolescence. (1.1)

Child Development Associate (CDA). Entry-level position qualification for teaching in a child care and education program or working as a teacher's assistant in a preschool program. (25.2)

child development laboratories. Early childhood education programs for children under five years of age that also serve as child development research sites and offer training programs for adults in child-related careers; formerly called *nursery schools*. (24.1)

child neglect. Failure of an adult to provide for a child's basic needs. (22.2)

child protection agencies. Organizations that work to prevent and rescue children from neglect and abuse. (22.2)

child support order. Judgment of the court that states how much the noncustodial parent must pay toward the children's expenses. (3.2)

childproofing. Process in which adults note dangers in a child's environment and then make the area safe for the child. (21.2)

chorion (CORE-ee-ahn). Outermost membrane that surrounds the baby in the uterus. (5.1)

chorionic villus sampling (CVS). Prenatal procedure for finding abnormalities in the fetus by testing a small sample of the chorion. (5.3)

chromosomal disorders. Defects in the chromosomes that usually occur due to an error in cell division. (5.2)

chromosomes (KRO-muh-zomes). Threadlike structures that carry genes in living cells. (5.2)

circumference. Linear distance around the edge of a closed curved or circular object. (8.1)

circumstances. Situations or conditions. (3.2)

classifying. Choosing an attribute and grouping all the objects from a set (either physically or mentally) that possess that attribute. (15.2)

closed adoption. Adoption in which the identity of the birthparents and adopting family are not revealed; also called *confidential adoption*. (3.2)

closed-ended questions. Questions that only require a one- or two-word response. (12.3)

cluttering. Filling a space with many objects. (21.2)

codes of professional ethics. Sets of standards created by various professions to govern the conduct of employees in these careers. (25.3)

code-switch. Changing grammar and vocabulary usage when communicating with different cultural and age groups. (18.2)

codified. Arranged in an orderly way. (1.2)

cognition. Act or process of knowing or understanding. (9.1)

cognitive-behavioral therapy. Therapy that teaches children to recognize their anxieties and develop coping strategies. (23.2)

cognitive flexibility. Being able to adjust to changing demands. (2.2)

cognizant. Aware. (13.1)

coherently. Clearly and understandably. (15.2)

coincides. Happens together. (7.4)

colic. Condition in which a baby has intense abdominal pain and cries inconsolably. (8.2)

collaboration skills. Skills needed to work well with others to combine knowledge, solve problems, reach common goals, and make decisions. (25.3)

collective monologue. Talking to another person, but not listening to what the other person has said. (15.2)

collective symbolism. Second level of pretense in which the toddler uses one set of objects to represent another set of objects and pretends to do something that involves other people (parents) or objects (stuffed animals). (12.1)

communicable diseases. Diseases that can be transmitted from an object to an individual or between individuals. (21.1)

communication. Exchange of messages and information between at least two people. (3.1)

competence. Confidence a person has in his or her own abilities. (13.1)

competent. Knowledgeable. (7.4)

complementary foods. Solid foods that provide the nutrients infants and toddlers need in addition to their breast milk, formula, or whole cow's milk. (11.2)

comprise. Make up. (3.1)

concept. Idea formed by combining what is known about a person, object, place, quality, or event. (9.2)

conception. Joining of the ovum and sperm cells. (5.1)

conceptualize. Form a concept of. (15.1)

concrete operational stage. Piaget's third stage of intellectual development in which children begin to think logically, but base their logic on past experiences. (18.1)

conduct. Person's actions and manners. (4.2)

confirm. Prove accurate. (1.2)

congenital condition. Physical or biochemical problem that is present at birth and may be caused by genetic or environmental factors. (5.3)

consensus. Group agreement. (25.3)

consenting. Giving permission. (3.2)

conservation. Concept that changing an object's shape, direction, or position does not alter the quantity of the object. (18.1)

consolidate. Combine together. (9.3)

constancy. Quality of being unchanging. (1.2)

constitute. Make up. (16.1)

constrict. Become smaller; more closed. (11.1)

contraction. Tightening or shortening of a muscle. (7.2)

contrariness. Tendency to oppose almost everything others do or say. (13.2)

control. Influence over one's environment of people, things, and events. (13.1)

conversely. Versus; on the other hand. (9.2)

coo. Light, happy, vowel-like sound babies use to communicate between six and eight weeks after birth. (9.2)

cooperation. Action of helping or working with someone. (16.2)

coordination. Working together of muscles to form movements. (9.3)

cope. Handle challenges in a healthy manner. (3.2)

co-regulation. Soothing the baby to aid him or her to calm down. (10.2)

cover message. Letter or e-mail message that accompanies a résumé to invite potential employers to review the résumé. (25.4)

crawl. Moving by pulling with the arms, but not lifting the abdomen from the floor. (8.1)

creep. Moving by using the hands and knees or the hands and feet with the abdomen off the floor. (8.1)

critical periods. Times when some part of the body is very vulnerable to lack of stimulation or to negative experiences. (2.1)

critical thinking skills. Skills needed to analyze and evaluate situations in order to make reasonable judgments and decisions. (25.3)

cruising. Walking by holding onto something for support. (8.1)

crystallized (KRIS-tuh-lyzd). Clear and fully formed in the mind. (15.1)

cultural diversity. Having more than one culture represented. (3.1)

culture. Way of life within a group of people that includes language, beliefs, attitudes, values, rituals, and skills. (3.1)

culture shock. Uncomfortable response to an unfamiliar culture. (24.2)

culture-specific knowledge. Culturally relevant knowledge that one learns by being told or shown. (18.2)

cumulative (KYOO-muh-luh-tihv). Composed of accumulated parts. (16.1)

cursory. Nonthorough. (17.3)

curtailing. Reducing. (23.2)

custodial parent. Parent who heads the household and has legal responsibility for caregiving. (3.2)

custody plans. Legal plans outlining who will care for the child and to what extent. (22.1)

cyberbullying. Bullying through a digital medium. (22.2)

D

debase. Degrade. (22.2)

deciduous (deh-SID-joo-uhs) teeth. First set of teeth, which will later be replaced by permanent teeth; also called *nonpermanent teeth* or *baby teeth*. (8.1)

deductive reasoning. Reasoning from the general to the specific. (18.1)

deemed. Considered to be. (19.1)
defective. Flawed; imperfect. (6.1)
deferred. Delayed or postponed. (12.1)
deferred imitation. Ability to recall and later imitate someone's behavior. (12.1)
deflected. Changing direction. (5.3)
deformation. Abnormal or unusual formation. (11.1)
dehydration. Condition in which the body is lacking fluids. (14.1)
delay gratification. Wait until later to get what is wanted. (13.2)
delinquency. Misbehavior; illegal behavior. (25.2)
delusions. Beliefs that are not true. (23.1)
dendrites (DEHN-drights). Short, bushy cables that allow each neuron to receive signals sent by other neurons. (2.1)
deodorants. Substances that hide body odor. (17.3)
depleted. Used up the supply of something. (4.1)
depth perception. Ability to tell how far away something is. (9.2)
derived. Sourced from. (16.1)
development. Gradual process of change through many stages, such as before birth, infancy, childhood, adolescence, and adulthood. (1.1)
developmental acceleration. When a child performs like an older child. (1.2)
developmental delay. When a child performs like a younger child. (1.2)
developmental dyscalculia (DIS-kal-KYOO-lee-uh). Learning disorder that affects a child's mathematical abilities. (23.1)
developmental dyslexia (dis-LEK-see-uh). Learning disorder that affects a child's ability to read, write, and spell. (23.1)
developmentally appropriate practices (DAPs). Child care and education practices that use knowledge about child development and consider each child's strengths, needs, interests, and culture. (24.2)
developmentally inappropriate practices (DIPs). Child care and education practices that do *not* take into account knowledge about child development, each child's strengths and needs, and the cultural context of the child's life. (24.2)
developmental milestones. Physical, intellectual, and social-emotional tasks most children learn to accomplish by a certain age. (8.1)
developmental tasks. Skills that should be mastered at a certain stage in life. (2.2)
deviate. Depart; stray. (19.1)
dexterity. Fine-motor movements that are smooth and rather effortless. (11.1)
diabetes. Disorder caused by the body's inability to use sugar properly. (5.2)
dilate. Become larger; more open. (11.1)
dilation. First stage of labor during which the cervix opens. (7.2)
diligent. Hardworking. (19.2)
dilute. Mix with liquid to reduce strength. (8.2)
diplomatic. Agreeable; polite. (25.3)
direct costs. Expenses related to raising a child, such as clothing, food, housing, child care and education, transportation, and toys and activities. (4.1)
direct intervention. Term used to describe a child-related career in which a person works in close contact with children. (25.2)
direct observation. Watching children in their natural environments. (1.3)
discipline. Use of methods and techniques to teach children self-control. (4.2)
discontentment. Unhappiness. (3.1)
dislodged. Forcefully removed. (7.2)
dismantle. Tear apart. (24.2)
disposition. General mood of a person. (10.1)
disprove. Show to be wrong or false. (1.2)
domains. Areas. (1.1)
domains of self-definition. Categories (physical, intelligence, social skills, and self-regulation of emotions) in which children can describe themselves. (19.1)
dominant traits. Traits that are always expressed in a person even if only one gene of the pair is inherited for that trait. (5.2)
Down syndrome. Chromosomal condition that occurs when each body cell has three copies of chromosome 21 instead of two copies. (5.2)
drastically. Greatly. (19.1)
dynamic balance. Balance maintained while moving. (14.1)

E

early childhood education programs. Child care and education arrangements; may be informal or formal. (24.1)

Early Intervention Program for Infants and Toddlers with Disabilities. Program that provides intervention services for infants and toddlers (through two years of age) with developmental delays or who have been diagnosed with physical and intellectual conditions that will likely cause developmental delays. (23.2)

early learning standards. Expectations for young children's development; also called *foundations* and *guidelines*. (24.2)

eating disorder. Illness characterized by distorted behaviors and emotions about food and weight. (17.2)

eco-friendly. Not harmful to the environment. (8.3)

educational neglect. Failure to conform to state legal requirements regarding school attendance. (22.2)

egalitarian. Belief that all people are equal. (16.2)

egocentric speech. Way in which preschoolers talk as though the listener will understand what they are trying to communicate in the same way as they do. (15.2)

egocentrism (ee-goh-SEN-trism). Child's belief that everyone thinks in the same way and has the same ideas as he or she does. (15.1)

elastic. Stretchable. (7.2)

elicits. Calls forth. (16.2)

elongates. Lengthens. (14.1)

embed. Attach. (5.1)

embryo. Medical term used to describe the unborn baby in the embryonic stage of development—weeks three through eight of the pregnancy. (5.1)

embryonic stage. Second stage of prenatal development, lasting six weeks. (5.1)

emergency situations. Dangerous, often unexpected or life-threatening events that require immediate action. (21.3)

emergent literacy. Conceived as all aspects of literacy, including reading and writing, are developmental and acquired in interactive ways, beginning in infancy as children learn to understand spoken words. (15.3)

emotional abuse. Abuse of power through devaluing, undermining, and coercing a child. (22.2)

emotional dependency. Act of seeking attention, approval, comfort, and contact. (16.1)

emotional neglect. Failure to meet a child's social-emotional needs at each stage of development. (22.2)

emotions. Thoughts that lead to feelings and cause changes in the body. (10.1)

empathize. Understand and relate to others. (1.3)

empathy. Ability to recognize and identify with the emotions of others. (13.2)

employability skills. Skills all employers seek in job candidates; includes interpersonal skills, collaboration skills, critical thinking and problem-solving skills, professionalism skills, strong executive function skills, and role-management skills. (25.3)

empty calories. Contained in foods supplying the body with energy, but having few or no nutrients, such as fats and sugars. (14.2)

endeavors. Attempts to achieve plans and goals. (6.1)

endorse. To support. (4.2)

enriched environment. Setting that offers a person many chances to learn. (9.3)

enrichment activities. Any activities beyond academic subjects that help children develop intellectually. (18.3)

entitlement. Having a right to particular privileges or benefits. (4.2)

entrepreneurship. Creation of one's own business. (25.2)

enuresis (en-yoo-REE-sis). *Involuntary* (by accident) urination two or more times a week for at least three months by a child over three years of age. (14.3)

environment. Sum of all the conditions and situations that surround and affect a child's growth and development. (1.1)

environmental factors. Factors caused by a person's surroundings. (5.2)

epigenome (eh-pih-JEE-nohm). Chemicals that can turn genes on and off. (1.1)

epilepsy. Neurological disorder in which abnormal activity in brain cells causes seizures. (21.1)

episiotomy (ih-pea-zee-AW-tuh-mee). Incision made to widen the birth canal and prevent tearing. (7.2)

episodic memory. Memory of personal experiences and events, including the emotion and context of the event. (15.1)

erratic. Unusual; inconsistent. (11.2)

essential life skills. Intellectual, social, and emotional skills that prepare children for the pressures of modern life, according to Galinsky. (2.2)
exclusively. Not shared; the only one. (7.1)
executive functions (EFs). Intellectual functions people use to manage themselves and their resources (knowledge, time) to achieve goals. (2.2)
exert. Forcibly place. (5.2)
expenditures. Expenses. (4.1)
explicit. Clearly described. (2.2)
explicit memory. Involves a person's conscious, intentional recalling of experiences and facts. (9.1)
exponentially. Rapidly. (5.2)
expulsion. Forcing out. (6.1)
extended family. Family that extends past the parent or parents and their children to include other adult relatives who interact within the same household. (3.2)
extraneous (ek-STRAY-nee-us). Nonessential. (18.2)
eye-hand coordination. Ability to coordinate sight with movement of the hands. (11.1)

F

failure to thrive. Condition in which a child fails to grow at a healthy rate. (8.1)
fallopian tubes. Two hollow tubes that extend from the right and left sides of the uterus and have fingerlike projections that reach toward each ovary. (5.1)
Family and Medical Leave Act (FMLA). Law that protects the rights of qualified employees to take unpaid leave for various family-related reasons, such as maternity or paternity leave. (7.1)
family child care. Child care provided by a person for a small number of children in his or her own home. (24.1)
family life cycle. Series of six stages that many families go through over the years. (3.1)
family planning. Decisions couples make about whether or not they want to have children and when to have them. (4.1)
fear-conditioning. Associating a fearful stimulus with a neutral stimulus. (16.1)
feats. Accomplishments. (13.1)
feed. Continue. (22.1)
fertility counseling. Medical evaluation that seeks to determine the reasons for fertility problems and explore available treatment options. (6.1)
fetal alcohol spectrum disorders (FASDs). Group of symptoms that occurs in infants whose mothers drank during pregnancy. (5.2)
fetal stage. Third stage of prenatal development, lasting from nine weeks after conception until birth. (5.1)
fetus. Medical term used to describe the unborn baby in the fetal stage of development—week nine until the end of pregnancy. (5.1)
field trips. Outings to take children to new places. (24.2)
filtering program. Application designed to prevent children from accessing inappropriate content when using electronic media. (18.3)
fine-motor skills. Being able to use and control the small muscles, especially those in the fingers and hands. (8.1)
fingerplays. Poems and rhymes acted out with the hands. (24.1)
firing. Process by which a neurotransmitter leaves the axon of one neuron and jumps the synapse to travel to the dendrite of another neuron. (2.1)
first aid. Emergency treatment for an illness or injury that is given before professional medical help arrives. (21.3)
first-degree burns. Damage to body tissue when heat or radiation burns the top layer of skin. (21.3)
flame-resistant. Resist burning. (8.3)
flexibility. Ability to move, bend, and stretch easily. (17.1)
flipped classroom. Mode of teaching in which children learn concepts and facts by reading their textbooks and watching videos at home, and then do homework-type assignments while at school. (18.3)
folic acid. B-vitamin that reduces the baby's risk for neural tube defects. (5.3)
food allergy. Abnormal response to a food triggered by the body's immune system. (11.2)
foodborne diseases. Diseases caused by eating foods contaminated with harmful bacteria and other pathogens during food production or preparation; also called *foodborne illnesses*. (21.1)

food-insecure households. Households that are regularly unable to supply healthful meals. (17.2)

forceps. Curved instrument that fits around the sides of a baby's head and is used to help the doctor ease the baby down the birth canal during a contraction. (7.2)

foregone income. Potential income given up by a parent who leaves the workforce and stays home to raise a child. (4.1)

formal operational stage. Piaget's final stage of intellectual development in which a person can reason abstractly. (18.1)

formative. Shaping. (5.1)

for-profit programs. Early childhood education programs set up to make money and run as businesses by individuals or corporations. (24.1)

foster family. Family in which an adult provides a temporary home for a child who cannot live with his or her birthparents. (3.2)

fractures. Cracks and breaks in bones. (21.3)

franchises. Group of businesses originally owned by a corporation and sold to different owners who use the same name, building design and equipment, and often provide the same services; also receive business advice from the franchiser. (24.1)

fraternal births. Term used to describe children from multiple pregnancies who develop from two or more fertilized ova and differ in genetic makeup; also called *dizygotic* (DYE-zye-GAW-tik) *births*. (6.1)

friction. Conflict; tension. (6.2)

functional specialization. Development of special abilities in different regions (areas) of the brain. (14.1)

G

gamete intrafallopian transfer (GIFT). Assisted reproductive technology (ART) procedure in which a mixture of sperm and eggs is placed in the woman's fallopian tubes, where fertilization can occur. (6.1)

gender constancy. Understanding that clothing, hairstyles, and actions do not change a person's gender. (16.1)

gender identity. Ability to label self and others as male or female (also called *gender labeling*). (13.1)

gender-role learning. Knowing what behaviors are expected of males and females within one's society. (16.1)

gender schools. Same-sex peer groups that teach members what it means to be masculine or feminine. (19.1)

gender stability. Understanding that a person who is born either male or female will remain so throughout life. (16.1)

General Educational Development (GED) test. Opportunity for people who do not graduate from high school to earn a state-issued certificate of high school equivalency. (6.2)

genes. Sections of the DNA molecule found in a person's cells that determine his or her individual traits. (1.1)

genetic disorder. Defect caused by one or more abnormalities in the genome. (5.2)

genetic factors. Person's inherited traits passed to him or her through the parents' genes at conception. (5.2)

genetics (juh-NET-iks). Study of the factors involved in the passing of traits in living beings from one generation to the next. (1.1)

genuine (JEN-yuh-wun). Real. (25.2)

germinal stage. First stage of prenatal development, lasting two weeks after conception. (5.1)

glial cells. Brain cells that support neurons. (2.1)

goal-corrected partnership. Relationship in which both parties are willing to compromise to reach a common goal. (19.1)

graceful. Able to move smoothly and elegantly. (20.1)

grammar. Study of word usage and order in a given language. (12.2)

grapple. Struggle. (18.3)

gross-motor skills. Being able to use the large muscles to roll over, sit, crawl, stand, and walk. (8.1)

growth. Change in size, such as height, or in quantity, such as vocabulary. (1.1)

growth pains. Muscle aches caused by muscles growing rapidly to catch up with increasing skeletal size during the school-age years. (17.1)

growth spurt. Period of rapid growth that heralds pubescence. (17.1)

guardian. Person who is legally appointed by the court to take responsibility for a child in the event of the birthparents' death or extended absence. (3.2)

guidance. Words and actions parents use to influence their children's behavior. (4.2)

guilt. Feeling of remorse that comes from the inner voice of conscience when a person has behaved unacceptably; is based in empathy and remorse for the misdeed. (19.1)

H

habituated. Familiarized. (9.2)

hallucinations. Seeing, hearing, or smelling objects that seem real, but are not. (23.1)

hamper. Interfere with. (6.1)

hand preference. Tendency to use one hand more skillfully than the other hand for most tasks; also called *handiness* and *hand dominance.* (14.1)

havoc. Chaos. (12.1)

Head Start. Federal program for three- and four-year-old children from low-income families. (24.1)

health screenings. Standard tests that look for potential conditions or diseases that may affect children's health or development. (21.1)

health services. Career area in which workers ensure children receive adequate physical and mental health care. (25.2)

heavily processed foods. Foods containing hidden sources of solid fats, sodium, and added sugars. (17.2)

hectic. Very busy. (7.1)

heralds. Signals the beginning of something. (17.1)

heredity. Sum of all the traits that are passed to a child from blood relatives. (1.1)

hidden added costs. Costs of child care that add to the direct costs. (24.2)

hidden cost credits. Credits that lower the direct costs of child care. (24.2)

hierarchical (HY-uh-RAHR-kuh-kul) classification. Type of classification in which select classes may contain subclasses. (18.2)

hierarchy. Rank order. (1.3)

high-reactive infants. Infants who react to anything new with caution and can easily become physically agitated and distressed; formerly called *difficult infants.* (10.1)

HIV. Human immunodeficiency virus; STI that causes the disease AIDS. (5.2)

holistic. Whole; complete. (9.3)

home visitation. Type of support in which a professional comes to the home to monitor the health of the mother and infant, to provide one-on-one parenting education, and to suggest other helpful community programs parents can access. (22.2)

homogeneous (hoh-MUH-jee-nyus). More alike than different. (24.2)

hysterectomy (HIS-ter-ECK-toh-mee). Surgical removal of a woman's uterus. (7.2)

I

identical births. Term used to describe children from multiple pregnancies who develop from one fertilized ovum and have the same genetic makeup; also called *monozygotic* (MAWN-oh-zye-GAWT-ik) *births.* (6.1)

idle. Inactive. (21.2)

illegal market adoption. Adoption in which a child is bought or sold, which is against the law in all states. (3.2)

imitating. Copying another person's actions. (9.1)

imitative-imaginative play. Type of play in which children use words and actions to pretend to be objects or people other than themselves. (20.1)

immerse. Cover in liquid. (8.3)

immunity. Body's ability to resist infection. (21.1)

immunization. Process to protect children, as well as adults, from certain serious diseases. (21.1)

impart. Give or share. (4.2)

implicit. Implied or understood without describing in detail. (2.2)

implicit memory. Involves a person's unconscious awareness of past experiences to perform tasks. (9.1)

impoverished. Having inadequate funds to reasonably care for one's family. (22.1)

inadvertently. Unintentionally. (10.2)

incessantly. Constantly; without break. (4.2)

incision. Cut. (7.2)

inclusion. Full-time placement of a child with special needs in a regular classroom. (23.2)

inclusive. Accessible to a variety of people. (15.3)

income. Money received for working. (3.1)

inconsolable. Unable to be soothed. (6.2)

independent adoption. Adoption in which a person, such as a lawyer or physician, works out the details between the birthparents and adoptive parents. (3.2)

indirect costs. Resources used to meet child-related expenses that could have been used to meet other goals. (4.1)

indirect intervention. Term used to describe a child-related career in which a person works on behalf of, but not directly with, children. (25.2)

indirect observation. Observation done by methods other than watching children, including asking other people questions about the children and observing the products children make. (1.3)

Individualized Education Plan (IEP). Educational plan tailored to the specific educational needs of a child who has special needs and who is between 3 and 21 years of age. (23.2)

Individualized Family Service Plan (IFSP). Plan that guarantees families can get the help they need for qualifying children with special needs from birth to three years of age. (23.2)

individual life cycle. Description of the stages of change people experience throughout life. (1.1)

Individuals with Disabilities Education Act (IDEA). Federal law governing the education of children with special needs. (23.2)

indomitable. Incapable of being subdued; stubborn-like. (11.3)

induction. Technique in which parents discipline their children by reasoning and explaining to them why they should or should not use certain behaviors. (4.2)

inductive reasoning. Reasoning from specific facts to general conclusions; also called *scientific reasoning*. (18.1)

Industrial Revolution. Time in history in which society began to focus on industry and manufacturing. (3.1)

industry. Desire to join others in striving to become a competent member of society. (19.1)

industry versus inferiority. Erikson's fourth stage of personality development in which children strive to be industrious, but may feel inferior if criticized. (19.1)

infancy. Stage of development during the first year of life. (8.1)

inferiority. Feeling of incompetence and low value as a member of society. (19.1)

infertile. Term used to refer to a person who is unable to conceive after a year of trying. (6.1)

inflections. Changes of pitch. (9.2)

infringe. Restrict. (19.1)

ingest. Consume. (21.3)

inherent. Basic. (3.1)

inhibition. Filtering thoughts and feelings so as not to act impulsively. (2.2)

in-home child care. Child care that takes place in the child's own home. (24.1)

initiate. Start. (6.2)

initiative. Ability to think or act without being urged. (16.1)

initiative versus guilt. Erikson's third stage of personality development in which children want to take initiative, but may be hindered by guilt. (16.1)

innate. Inborn; natural. (8.1)

innocuous. Not harmful. (17.3)

instilling. Gradually establishing. (19.1)

intellectual development. Development that concerns how people learn, what people learn, and how people express what they know through language. (1.1)

intellectual disability. Condition in which a child's intellectual abilities are a year or more delayed when compared with other children the same age. (23.1)

intelligence quotient (IQ) test. Test that measures how quickly a person can learn and how well a person can reason using words, numbers, and spatial concepts. (23.1)

interactive media. Media systems, such as computers, that respond to the user's actions. (15.3)

internal organs. Collections of tissues that independently carry out special functions and are located inside the body, such as heart, lungs, and liver. (14.1)

interpersonal skills. Skills a person uses to relate to and work with other people. (25.3)

interpretive stage. Galinsky's parenting stage during which parents are tasked with modeling their values and attitudes about almost all aspects of life. (19.2)

interrelated. Connect to and interact with one another. (1.2)

intervals. Periods of time in between events. (7.2)

intolerance. Negative physical reaction that eating a certain food can cause. (8.2)

intonation. Rise and fall of a person's voice while speaking. (12.3)

intricate. Complex. (9.2)

intrinsic. Naturally occurring trait. (12.2)

intrusive. Controlling. (10.1)

intuition. Natural ability to know something without evidence. (15.1)

intuitive substage. Substage of the preoperational stage during which children rely on their mental imagery rather than logical reasoning to grasp a problem's solution. (15.1)

in vitro fertilization (IVF). Assisted reproductive technology (ART) procedure in which some of the mother's eggs are surgically removed, fertilized with sperm in a laboratory dish, and then implanted in the mother's uterus. (6.1)

involuntary. Not by choice. (7.2)

irreducible. Impossible to make smaller or simpler. (1.3)

irregular. Occurring at different times; unusual. (7.2)

J

jaundice. Liver condition that can make the skin, tissues, and body fluids look yellow. (7.3)

job fair. Gathering of employers and job seekers to exchange information. (25.4)

job shadowing. Following a competent worker through his or her workday. (25.1)

joint custody. Shared legal right of parents who are not married to provide care for and make decisions about their children's lives. (3.2)

junk foods. Foods that are high in calories and low in nutrition. (17.2)

K

kindergartens. Early childhood education programs for four- and five-year-old children; serve as an entrance to primary school education. (24.1)

L

labor. Process that moves the baby out of the mother's body. (7.1)

lactation consultant. Breast-feeding expert. (8.2)

Lamaze method. Delivery method in which the pregnant woman is trained to use breathing patterns to keep her mind off the pain. (7.1)

language disorder. Condition involving a child's lack of ability to understand and use language. (23.1)

language-logic play. Form of intellectual play common in school-age children that involves words and logical concepts. (20.1)

large-muscle development. Development of the trunk and arm and leg muscles. (11.1)

leader. Person who inspires or motivates the thoughts, feelings, or actions of others. (25.2)

learning disorder. Challenge in spoken or written language, math, or spatial orientation. (23.1)

lenient. Easy-going; not strict. (11.3)

lesson plan. Teacher plan that contains a specific goal objective (related to a standard), activities to help the child meet the objective, and assessment of the learning; usually written for kindergarten and school-age children. (24.2)

lifelong learning. The ongoing pursuit of learning throughout life. (2.2)

lightening. Change in the baby's position in which the uterus settles downward and forward, and the baby descends lower into the pelvis. (7.2)

listlessness. Low energy. (23.2)

logical thinking concepts. Concepts that are not directly experienced through the senses, but are developed through thought, such as noting similarities and differences in objects and coordinating simple relationships (classifying, ordering by attribute, counting). (15.2)

love withdrawal. Discipline technique in which parents threaten children with being unloved or suggest some form of parent/child separation. (4.2)

low-birthweight. Weight under 5.5 pounds at birth for a single birth and under 3.3 pounds per baby in a multiple birth. (6.1)

low-reactive infants. Infants who tend to be sociable and bold (trying new challenges); formerly called *easy infants*. (10.1)

M

mainstreaming. Former term used for placing a child with special needs in a regular classroom for only part of the day. (23.2)

malnutrition. Condition in which one's diet supplies an excess, shortage, or imbalance of calories or one or more nutrients. (17.2)

mandated reporters. Professionals who are legally bound to report any known or suspected cases of neglect or abuse. (22.2)

manipulate. Using the hands to work with objects. (14.1)

manipulating. Moving or changing. (2.2)

manipulative-constructive play. Type of play that involves the use of children's fine-motor skills. (20.1)

marriage. Legal contract and, ideally, an emotional and social union between two partners. (3.1)

maternity leave. Time a woman takes off from work for the birth or adoption of a child. (7.1)

maturational theory of child development. Based on the premise that children mature on a genetic timetable (upon which the environment has little impact) and that skills and concepts should only be taught when children are biologically ready to learn them. (15.3)

maturity. Having the intellectual and emotional capacity of a healthy, responsible adult. (4.1)

mediation. Inclusion of a neutral person, called a *mediator*, to help the conflicting parties resolve their dispute and reach an agreement. (25.3)

medical neglect. Harm or endangerment of a child caused by failure to seek treatment for health problems or accidents. (22.2)

memory capacity. What a person does with his or her memory (not how *much* is remembered). (15.1)

menarche (men-AR-kee). First menstrual cycle in girls. (17.1)

meningitis (MEH-nun-JY-tis). Inflammation of the thin membranes that cover the spinal cord and brain. (23.1)

mental imagery. Seeing in the "mind's eye" or hearing in the "mind's ear" in the absence of a stimulus. (12.1)

mental images. Symbols of objects and past experiences that are stored in the mind. (15.1)

mental maps. Remembered mental constructions (seen in the "mind's eye") that organize spatial relationships from an individual's perspective. (15.2)

mentor. Person who counsels and advises. (25.1)

merits. Deserves; warrants. (11.2)

metabolize. Break down in the digestive system. (7.3)

metacognition. Awareness of one's own knowledge and thinking. (18.1)

middle school. School including children in the fifth or sixth through eighth or ninth grades. (18.3)

miscarriage. Expulsion of a baby from the mother's body before week 20 of pregnancy. (6.1)

misfires. Electrical signals that either fail to cross neuron synapses or cross synapses incorrectly. (23.1)

mitigate. Lessen. (18.3)

mixed-type births. Term used to describe children from higher multiple pregnancies (three or more children) some of whom are identical and one or more fraternal. (6.1)

monolingual. Person who speaks only one language. (12.2)

monologue. Talking to oneself as though thinking aloud. (15.2)

monotone. Single pitch without variation. (9.2)

Montessori schools. Early childhood education programs that encourage children to learn independently through the use of highly specialized materials rather than through direct input from teachers. (24.1)

moral character. Acting in accordance with what is perceived as morally right. (16.1)

moral development. Process by which children develop proper attitudes toward others (based on sociocultural, familial, school, peer, religious, and societal expectations). (16.1)

moral emotions. Person's reactions to acceptable and unacceptable behaviors. (16.1)

moral judgment and reasoning. Ability to perceive an action as right or wrong. (16.1)

moral neglect. Failure to teach a child right from wrong in terms of general social expectations. (22.2)

mortality rate. Rate of death. (6.2)

motivation. Desire to achieve. (1.2)

motor development. Use and control of muscles that direct body movements. (8.1)

mourning. Feeling sad about a loss. (22.1)

multicultural family. Family with members from two or more cultural groups. (3.1)

multiple intelligences. Intellectual abilities that contribute to overall intelligence. (18.1)

multiple pregnancy. Pregnancy in which two or more babies develop. (6.1)

muscle development. Lengthening and thickening of muscles. (11.1)

myelin. Fatty substance formed by glial cells that wraps around longer axons and cushions the cell bodies of neurons. (2.1)

MyPlate. Food guidance system developed by the U.S. Department of Agriculture to help people two years of age and older make nutritious food choices. (5.3)

N

National Association for the Education of Young Children (NAEYC). Professional organization that works on behalf of young children by providing educational materials, child development research, and conferences. (25.2)

national chains. Group of businesses owned by one company. (24.1)

natural childbirth. Delivery method in which the pregnant woman learns about the birth process and uses breathing and relaxation techniques to reduce fear and pain during labor. (7.1)

negotiation. Process of individuals involved in a conflict coming together to discuss a compromise. (25.3)

neonatal intensive care unit (NICU). Part of a hospital where premature, low-birthweight, or other high-risk babies can receive immediate, specialized, round-the-clock care and treatment; also called *intensive care nursery*. (7.3)

neonate. Medical term used to describe the baby from birth to one month of age. (7.3)

neonatology (NEE-oh-nay-TAW-lo-gee). Branch of medicine concerned with the care, development, and diseases of newborns. (7.3)

networking. Term used for making professional contacts with family, friends, and others, especially professionals in your career area, for job information or referrals. (25.4)

neurons. Brain cells that send and receive chemical and electrical impulses amongst each other to direct the various tasks of the brain. (2.1)

neuroscience. Study of the brain. (2.2)

neutralize. Reduce the effect of. (21.2)

noncommunicable diseases. Diseases that cannot be transmitted between an object and an individual or between individuals. (21.1)

noncustodial parent. Parent who lives separately from his or her children. (3.2)

nonessential. Not vital. (6.2)

noninteractive media. Media systems, such as television programs, over which the user has only a limited amount of control; also called *passive media*. (15.3)

noninvasive. Not requiring insertion or cutting. (5.3)

norm. Normal, socially acceptable pattern. (3.1)

not-for-profit programs. Early childhood education programs for which income only covers current costs and the surplus needed to keep the center operating on an ongoing basis or to expand services; also called *nonprofit programs*. (24.1)

nuclear family. Family consisting of a father, a mother, and their biological child or children who live together. (3.2)

***nucleus accumbens* (NOO-klee-us uh-KUM-buhnz).** Pleasure and reward system of the brain. (18.1)

numerosity (noo-mer-AHS-ih-tee). Numerousness. (15.2)

nurturance. Providing all aspects of care for a child, which includes meeting physical, intellectual, and social-emotional needs. (4.2)

nutrient-dense foods. Foods that are high in lean protein, complex carbohydrates, healthy fats, vitamins, and minerals and contain relatively few calories. (14.2)

nutrients. Substances that give the body what it needs to grow and function. (5.3)

O

obedience. Acting within the limits set by others. (13.2)

object concept. Ability to understand that objects, people, and events are separate from a person's interactions with them. (9.2)

object constancy. Ability to understand that objects remain the same even if they appear different. (9.2)

object identity. Ability to understand that an object stays the same from one time to the next. (9.2)

object permanence. Ability to understand that people, objects, and places still exist even when they are no longer seen, felt, or heard. (9.2)

obsolete. No longer useful; out of practice. (25.1)

obstetricians. Doctors who specialize in pregnancy and birth. (5.3)

occupation. Job. (25.1)

occupational categories. Sixteen industry areas that encompass a variety of different careers. (25.1)

oils. Fats that are liquid at room temperature. (11.2)

onomatopoeic (ahn-uh-mat-uh-PEE-ik). Words that imitate sounds, such as *pop*, *fizz*, and *buzz*. (12.3)

onset. Beginning. (8.1)

open adoption. Adoption that involves some degree of communication between the birthparent(s) and adoptive family. (3.2)

open-ended questions. Questions that require a descriptive response for an answer. (12.3)

oppositional defiant disorder (ODD). Behavioral disorder involving aggressive behaviors that are not provoked and worsen over time. (23.1)

optimum. Best. (5.3)

orthopedic problems. Problems relating to the bones and muscles. (17.3)

ossification (AWS-sih-fih-CAY-shun). Hardening of bones caused by the depositing of the minerals *calcium* and *phosphorus*. (8.1)

ovaries. Female reproductive glands. (5.1)

overgeneralization. Assumption that because something is true for one event or object, it is true for all similar events or objects. (15.1)

overindulgent. Providing everything a child wants. (4.2)

overnutrition. Condition in which the body's ongoing intake of calories is more than is needed for good health. (17.2)

overparenting. Parenting style in which parents desire to provide for and protect their children beyond what is in the best interest of children. (4.2)

overtures. Cues for positive relationship building. (10.2)

ovum. Female sex cell; also called *the egg*. (5.1)

P

paralysis. Inability to move or feel parts of the body. (23.1)

parentese. Infant-directed, sing-song, high-pitched style in which parents and other adults speak to babies (9.2)

parochial (puh-ROH-kee-ul). Religious. (24.1)

passive vocabulary. Words a person understands, but does not say or write. (9.2)

paternal postpartum depression (PPPD). Mood disorders in men that may occur after the birth of a child. (7.4)

paternity leave. Time a man takes off from work (usually without pay) for a set period after a child's birth or adoption. (7.1)

pediatrician. Doctor who cares for infants, children, and teens until adulthood when physical growth is complete. (7.3)

peer abuse. Some form of abuse (physical, verbal, social, or emotional) directed at a child or teen by someone in the same peer group. (22.2)

peer pressure. Desire to be like one's peers. (17.3)

penetrate. Enter. (9.2)

perception. Organizing information that comes through the senses. (9.1)

perceptual learning. Process of making sense out of sensory stimuli. (9.1)

perinatal (per-ih-NAY-tuhl) depression. Mood disorder that can occur during pregnancy or during the postpartum period or even afterward. (7.4)

period of gestation. Time between conception and birth; also called *pregnancy*. (5.1)

permanent teeth. Teeth that are intended to last a lifetime; are harder and less sharp than deciduous teeth. (17.1)

permissive. Parenting style in which parents give children almost no guidelines or rules. (4.2)

perpetrated. Done. (22.2)

personal plan of study. Plan that identifies the core courses and other learning experiences a person needs to complete to meet his or her educational and career goals. (25.1)

personal qualifications. Traits a person has that cannot be learned in career training. (25.2)

pheromones (FER-uh-mohns). Substances that are produced and secreted through sweat; cause body odor through contact with bacteria on skin and clothing. (17.3)

phonics. Sounds of letters and syllables. (12.2)

physical abuse. Any intentional physical act that results in pain, injuries, or both to a child. (22.2)

physical attributes. Concrete qualities of objects that can be sensed. (15.2)

physical development. Growth of the body and development of the large and small motor skills. (1.1)

physical disability. Limitation of a person's body or its function. (23.1)

physical knowledge. Knowledge acquired through observations of the physical world, such as attributes of objects (color, shape) and observable phenomenon (how gravity works and the comparative speed of balls rolled on flat surfaces and inclines). (15.2)

physical neglect. Endangering a child's health or safety by failing to provide basic needs (food, clothing, and shelter) and supervision. (22.2)

pique. Stir up interest in. (15.3)

pivotal. Crucial or key. (17.2)

placate. Calm; soothe. (16.2)

placenta (pluh-SENT-uh). Organ filled with blood vessels that nourish the baby in the uterus. (5.1)

plaque. Sticky, mineral deposit coating the teeth while it colonizes bacteria on food particles left in the mouth causing cavities and leading to gum disease. (14.3)

plasticity. Ability of the brain to be shaped and reshaped, which is greatest early in life. (2.1)

play therapy. Use of play between a child and a trained counselor to help the child resolve certain problems. (20.1)

playyard. Enclosed play space for babies; formerly called a *playpen*. (8.3)

portfolio. Organized collection of materials that supports a person's job qualifications and reflects work, academic, and personal experiences. (25.4)

postpartum care. Care the mother receives during the six to eight weeks following the birth of her baby; also called *postnatal care*. (7.4)

postpartum depression (PPD). Less frequent than "baby blues," but a serious form of depression that may occur after giving birth. (7.4)

postpartum mood disorder (PPMD). Mental health condition, characterized by feelings of sadness, guilt, or depression, that men and women may experience after the birth of their baby. (7.4)

postpartum psychosis (PPP). Rare and extremely severe mental illness that may result after giving birth. (7.4)

potential. Greatest amount or level possible. (1.1)

power assertion. Discipline technique in which parents use or threaten to use some form of physical punishment or deny privileges. (4.2)

practical. Usable; applicable. (6.2)

precedes. Comes before something. (10.1)

precision. Ability to perform motor skills accurately. (17.1)

preconceptual substage. Substage of the preoperational stage in which children two to four years of age begin to develop and understand some concepts; also known as the *symbolic substage*. (15.1)

predictor. Something that is useful in making a prediction. (10.2)

prefrontal cortex. Section near the front of the brain that is involved in logical thinking, forming judgments, memory, weighing consequences, decision making, and controlling impulses and emotions. (18.1)

Pregnancy Discrimination Act (PDA). Law that protects the rights of pregnant women who work. (7.1)

pregnancy-induced hypertension (PIH). High blood pressure caused by pregnancy. (5.2)

pregnancy leave. Leave from work taken by mothers-to-be who cannot work for part or all of the pregnancy due to health reasons. (7.1)

premarital counseling. Type of therapy for couples who are preparing for marriage. (3.1)

premature birth. Born too soon. (5.3)

premoral. Not self-guided by internal values. (13.2)

prenatal development. Development that takes place between conception and birth. (5.1)

prenatal vitamin. Supplement containing extra folic acid, iron, calcium, and other important vitamins and minerals that pregnant women take during pregnancy. (5.3)

preoccupied. Focused on another task. (21.2)

preoperational stage. Second of Piaget's stages of cognitive development in which children begin to think through problems rather than solve all their problems through physical actions. (15.1)

preschool programs. State-financed early childhood education programs for three- and four-year-olds from low-income families; also called *prekindergartens*. (24.1)

preschools. Child care centers that serve preschool-age children. (24.1)

pretense. Symbolic actions seen in play that mimic real situations. (12.1)

preterm birth. Delivery that occurs before 39 weeks of pregnancy. (6.1)

preventive health care. Measures taken to keep children well, including regular doctor and dental appointments, health screenings, and immunization. (21.1)

primary school. School including the elementary grades first through fifth or sixth and sometimes the kindergarten; also called *elementary school*. (18.3)

principles of growth and development. Statements of the general patterns in which growth and development take place in people. (1.2)

private programs. Early childhood education programs owned by individuals and religious or other nongovernment groups. (24.1)

problem-solving skills. Skills used to analyze problems and formulate solutions. (25.3)

procreation. The producing of children. (4.1)

prodigious (pruh-DIH-jus). Tremendous. (19.1)

professionalism. Involves the skills, good judgment, and the attitudes and behaviors expected from any person trained to do a job well. (25.3)

professional organization. Group of professionals who meet to discuss their career field. (25.1)

professional qualifications. Physical, intellectual, and social-emotional skills a person needs to perform well in a career. (25.2)

proficiency. Mastery of a skill. (9.2)

prognosis. Predicted outcome of a disease or condition. (22.1)

prompt. Immediate. (5.3)

prone. Likely. (4.2)

prosocial. Refers to social behaviors that are positive, such as kind and helpful behaviors. (16.2)

protective services. Career area in which workers identify injustices to children and correct or remove children from dangerous situations. (25.2)

protrudes. Sticks out. (8.1)

proximity. Nearness. (10.2)

proximodistal (prahk-sum-oh-DIS-tahl) development. Direction of development from the center of the body to the extremities; also called *center-to-extremities development*. (8.1)

pruning. Process of weeding out underused or weak pathways between neurons. (2.1)

psychological security. Feeling that someone cares and will help when needed. (19.1)

psychomotor ability. Ability to coordinate muscle movements with mental processes. (23.1)

psychosis. Serious mental state characterized by delusions. (23.2)

psychosocial. Relating to psychological and social aspects. (10.2)

puberty. Process by which the body becomes capable of reproduction. (17.1)

pubescent. Being in puberty. (17.1)

public programs. Early childhood education programs funded by local, state, or federal government. (24.1)

Q

quickening. Movements of the fetus that can be felt by the mother. (5.1)

R

reaction time. Time required to respond to a sight, sound, or other stimuli. (14.1)

reading readiness. Belief that children should be formally taught reading and writing when developmentally ready for instruction; also refers to pre-reading programs taught through direct instruction. (15.3)

reassure. Encourage; remove doubts and fears. (7.1)

recession. Economic period with minimal or no growth. (3.2)

recessive traits. Traits that are not typically expressed in a person unless both genes for the trait are inherited. (5.2)

references. People other than family members who know a person well enough to discuss his or her qualifications for a job. (25.4)

refined. Sophisticated; fine-tuned. (12.2)

reflexes. Automatic, unlearned movements in response to stimuli. (8.1)

regression. Going back to an earlier stage of development. (11.3)

regulations. Standards that govern how an early childhood education program operates. (24.2)
reinforcement. Rewards. (2.2)
reiterate. Restate; emphasize. (25.4)
repertoire (reh-pur-TWAHR). Skill set. (12.1)
repressed jealousy. Jealousy that is not directly expressed and may even be denied. (16.1)
rescinded (ree-SIND-ed). Taken away. (22.2)
resilient children. When faced with adversity in their lives, children who adapt well. (22.1)
respite. Rest. (22.2)
résumé. Brief account of a person's career goals, education, work experience, and other employment qualifications. (25.4)
resuscitate. Bring to an active state; revitalize. (7.3)
Rh factor. Protein substance found in the red blood cells of about 85 percent of the population. (5.2)
rigid. Stiff; restricted. (11.1)
rigorous. Demanding. (21.2)
role guilt. Feeling that one is not doing the best job at any role because of role strain. (25.3)
role strain. Feeling of having too many tasks to do at one time. (25.3)
rote memorization. Learning by repetition. (15.2)
rubella. Virus that can cross the placenta and affect the baby during the first three months of pregnancy. (5.2)

S

safety recall. Notice issued by a product manufacturer stating a product has been found to be unsafe. (21.2)
sand tables. Large, wooden or plastic containers on legs that are designed to hold sand and sand accessories for play. (20.2)
satiety. Being full. (8.2)
scaffolding. Varying levels of instructional support given to help children learn a new concept or skill. (9.1)
scapegoating. Blaming others for one's own mistakes. (19.1)
scarcest. Rarest. (25.3)
school-age child care (SACC) programs. Child care programs that provide child care for children between 5 and 14 years of age when school is not in session; also called *before- and after-school programs* or *out-of-school programs.* (24.1)
second-degree burns. Damage to body tissue when heat or radiation burns the middle layer of skin. (21.3)
sedentary. Characterized by little physical activity. (11.3)
seldom. Rarely. (2.1)
self-actualization. To grow and feel fulfilled as a person. (1.3)
self-assertion. Doing as one chooses rather than what others want. (13.2)
self-assessment. Step in career planning that involves a person identifying his or her interests, aptitudes, and abilities. (25.1)
self-awareness. Understanding someone has of him- or herself as a person. (10.2)
self-concept. Picture a person has of him- or herself. (16.1)
self-esteem. Confidence a person has in his or her own worth (feelings of being valued by others), competence (confidence in one's abilities to achieve goals), and control (sense one can affect outcomes and events in his or her life). (13.1)
self-restraint. Ability to control oneself. (13.2)
self-reward. Person's good feelings about his or her actions. (16.2)
sensitive periods. Times when the brain is best able to wire specific skills for all children. (2.1)
sensorimotor stage. First of Piaget's stages of cognitive (intellectual) development in which children use their senses and motor skills to learn and communicate. (9.1)
sensory stimulation. Using the senses to learn about the environment. (9.3)
separation anxiety. Anxiety common in infants caused by the fear that loved ones who leave them in the care of others will not return. (10.1)
sequenced steps. Steps in growth and development that follow one another in a set order. (1.2)
sequential. Following in an order. (7.2)
seriation (seer-ee-AY-shun). Arranging objects in order by the increasing or decreasing magnitude of one of the object's attributes, such as length, shade of a color, texture, or pitch. (15.2)
sever. End or cut off. (3.2)
severed. Ended. (22.1)
severity. Seriousness. (5.3)
sex typing. Process by which a person adopts the attitudes and behaviors considered culturally appropriate for his or her gender. (16.1)

sexual abuse. Any act of a sexual nature that involves an adult and a child. (22.2)

sexually transmitted infections (STIs). Infectious illnesses contracted primarily through sexual intercourse. (5.2)

sexual stereotyping. Stating or even hinting that men and women always behave in certain ways or should always do particular tasks, but not other tasks. (16.1)

shaken baby syndrome (SBS). Condition in which the "whiplash" shaking motion causes an infant's brain to hit the skull repeatedly. These hits cause the eye retina to bleed and veins in the brain to break, filling the area around the brain with blood resulting in swelling; also called *traumatic brain injury abuse.* (22.2)

shame. Self-focused feeling that involves a loss or threat of a loss to a child's basic security. (16.2)

shock. Condition in which the heartbeat and breathing slow. (21.3)

shortcomings. Areas in which a person wants or needs to improve. (19.1)

sibling abuse. Physical, verbal, emotional, or sexual abuse of one sibling by another. (22.2)

siblings. Brothers and sisters. (10.1)

simultaneously. At the same time. (18.1)

single-parent family. Family headed by one adult. (3.2)

six core strengths. Building blocks developed by Perry that make up children's foundation for future health, productivity, and happiness; includes attachment, self-regulation, affiliation, awareness (of how people are alike and different), tolerance, and respect. (22.2)

six-year molars. Large teeth near the back of the jaw that come in around six years of age and are used for grinding food (17.1)

skeletal system. Framework of the body that consists of cartilage, bones, and teeth. (8.1)

sleep-deprived. Having less than the recommended amount of sleep. (17.3)

small-muscle development. Development of muscles, especially those in the hands and fingers. (11.1)

social abuse. Restricting or intentionally harming a person's relationships with others. (22.2)

social-emotional development. Development that involves interactions with people and social groups, disposition, and emotions. (1.1)

socialize. To train a child to live as part of a group, such as the family, culture, or society. (4.2)

social referencing. Evaluating how to respond to a situation by getting a social cue from a more experienced person. (13.2)

society of children. Peer groups that prepare children for independence. (19.2)

sociocultural. Relating to social and cultural factors. (9.1)

socioeconomic. Social and economic factors. (4.1)

solidarity. Sense of belonging. (19.2)

solid fats. Found mainly in animal-based foods, such as butter and beef fat. (14.2)

solids. Semiliquid and mushy foods fed to an infant by spoon. (8.2)

solitary symbolic play. First level of pretense in which the toddler uses real objects or realistic toys and pretends to do something that has to do with him- or herself. (12.1)

spatial. Pertaining to space. (9.2)

special education teachers. Teachers trained to work with children with special needs. (23.2)

special lessons and activities. Classes or clubs where children can discover their own interests and talents. (18.3)

speech disorder. Condition that causes a child to have difficulty speaking or being understood. (23.1)

sperm. Male sex cell. (5.1)

spermarche (SPERM-ar-kee). First ejaculation in boys. (17.1)

splinters. Pieces of wood or plastic that become lodged in the skin. (21.3)

sponge bath. Using a washcloth to wash the baby's body instead of immersing the baby in water. (8.3)

sprains. Injuries to joint ligaments. (21.3)

staff turnover. Term used to describe caregivers who leave a program and are replaced; often statistically presented as a rate. (24.2)

stages of grief. Feelings or mind-sets that most people experience when mourning; includes shock and denial, anger, bargaining, depression, and acceptance. (22.1)

stamina. Ability to continually do something. (8.1)

static balance. Balance maintained while being still. (14.1)

stature. A person's height. (11.1)

stepfamily. Family that forms when a single parent marries another person. (3.2)
sterile. Condition of being permanently unable to conceive or carry fully biological children. (6.1)
stifle. To suppress. (4.1)
stillbirth. Loss of a fetus after 20 weeks of pregnancy. (6.1)
stimuli. Changes in the environment, such as light, sound, heat, or texture, that affect the sensory organs causing the person to react. (9.1)
stipulation. Specified condition. (15.3)
strategize. Plan strategies. (20.1)
stressors. Situations that cause worry and anxiety. (1.1)
subdivided. Divided into smaller parts. (18.2)
subsequent. Following. (5.1)
subside. Lessen in severity. (7.4)
subtle. Not obvious. (9.1)
sudden infant death syndrome (SIDS). Condition in which a sleeping baby dies without warning and for medically unexplained reasons. (8.3)
sufficient. Adequate. (17.3)
surpass. Do better than. (17.1)
surrogate mother. Woman who bears (sometimes both conceives and bears) a child for a couple. (6.1)
susceptible. Prone. (14.2)
suspension. Temporary removal from a job. (25.3)
symbolic thought. Ability to use symbols to represent objects, actions, or events from a person's world of experiences. (15.1)
synapse. Tiny gap between a dendrite of one neuron and the axon of another across which electrical impulses can be transmitted. (2.1)
syntax. Sentence structure. (18.2)
synthetic. Not natural. (5.3)

T

table foods. Foods prepared for the entire family. (11.2)
tactile. Perceived by touch. (20.2)
tag questions. Making a statement and then adding *yes* or *no* to ask a question. (15.2)
tangible. Perceived by touch; *tactile.* (20.2)
tattling behaviors. Behaviors that seek to get another child in trouble by telling adults or other children about something a child has done. (16.2)
teachable moment. Optimal time when a person can learn a new task. (1.2)
temperament. Inherited tendency to react in a certain way to events. (10.1)
temper tantrum. Sudden emotional outburst of anger commonly displayed by a toddler. (13.1)
tentative. Not permanent; may change. (2.1)
terminally ill. Having an incurable disease that will result in death. (22.1)
termination. Nontemporary removal from a job. (25.3)
tertiary. Third in a sequence. (12.1)
testes. Male reproductive glands. (5.1)
theory. Set of statements offered as a possible explanation for a phenomenon, such as child growth and development. (1.2)
third-degree burns. Damage to body tissue when heat or radiation burns the innermost layer of skin or the muscle and bone beneath. (21.3)
time management. Practice of organizing time and work assignments to increase personal efficiency. (25.3)
timid. Shy. (11.1)
toilet learning. Process by which adults help children control their excretory systems, namely bowel movements and urination. (11.3)
training pants. Special underpants or pants made of disposable diaper material that help lessen the mess of accidents during toilet learning. (11.3)
trajectories. Paths objects take. (12.2)
transductive (trans-DUCT-ihv) reasoning. Mentally linking events without using logic. (15.1)
transformations. Sequences of changes. (15.1)
transposition. Changing of the order of something. (15.1)
traumatized. Seriously disrupted socially or emotionally. (22.1)
trimester. Period of three months. (5.1)
trust versus mistrust. Conflict infants must resolve according to the first stage of Erikson's psychosocial theory. (10.2)
typical development. Development that follows typical patterns of achieving developmental milestones. (23.1)

U

ubiquitous (yoo-BIH-kwuh-tuhs). Found everywhere. (15.3)
ultrasound. Prenatal test in which sound waves bounce off the fetus to produce an image of the fetus inside the womb. (5.3)
umbilical cord. Contains three blood vessels that connect the baby to the placenta. (5.1)
unconditional love. Deep affection without limitations. (10.2)
undernutrition. Condition in which food is being eaten, but is continuously lacking one or more nutrients required to meet the body's needs. (17.2)
underutilized. Underused. (18.3)
unearth. Reveal. (21.1)
uniform. Items that look the same. (14.2)
unit blocks. Naturally finished wooden blocks that are multiples or divisions of the basic unit size (1⅜" X 2¾" X 5½"); also called *floor blocks*. (20.2)
universal preschool programs. State-financed early childhood education programs for preschool children from families of all income levels. (24.1)
upheaval. Potentially upsetting change. (18.3)
uterus. Organ in which the baby develops and is protected until birth. (5.1)

V

vaccination. Process of administering vaccines. (21.1)
vaccines. Substances used to produce immunity from diseases. (21.1)
vacuum extraction. Technique that uses suction to help the doctor move the baby down the birth canal as the mother pushes. (7.2)
values. Ideas, beliefs, or objects that are important and meaningful to a person. (25.1)
ventilated. Accessible to air. (21.2)
verbal abuse. Use of words to control and debase a child. (22.2)
vicarious. Experienced through another person or object. (12.3)
vigor. Strength and energy. (3.2)
visual arts. Two- and three-dimensional art forms appealing to the sense of sight. (20.2)
visual literacy. Ability to draw meaning from observable and tangible objects and images. (20.2)
voluntary grasping. The intentional grasping of objects. (8.1)
vouch. Guarantee; verify. (25.4)
vulnerable. Easily affected; sensitive. (5.2)

W

wane. Diminish. (9.1)
water tables. Large, plastic containers (tub-like and on legs) that are designed to hold water and accessories for play. (20.2)
weaning. Gradual process of taking infants off the breast or bottle. (8.2)
weight shift. Shifting the hips (pelvis) forward to transfer body weight onto the forward leg in order to offset equal weight on both legs. (14.1)
well-baby checkup. Routine medical visit in which the doctor examines a baby for signs of good health and proper growth. (7.3)
well-child checkups. Doctor's appointments while the child is not sick. (21.1)
window of opportunity. Prime period in a child's life for developing a particular skill if given the opportunity. (2.1)
wiring. Network of fibers that carry brain signals between neurons. (2.1)
work ethic. Person's sense of responsibility and diligence toward work tasks. (19.1)
working memory. Storing, organizing, and manipulating information while working on a task. (2.1)
work-related child care programs. Not-for-profit programs sponsored by businesses for their employees' children. (24.1)
worth. Usefulness; importance. (13.1)
wounds. Damage to the body's skin or tissue. (21.3)

Z

zone of proximal development (ZPD). Level in which a child can learn with help. (9.1)
zygote (ZIGH-goht). Single cell formed at conception; also called a *fertilized egg*. (5.1)

Index

A

B

C

D

E

F

G

H

I

J

K

L

M

N

O

P

Q

R

S

T

U

V

W

Z